OZ CLARKE'S WINE BUYING GUIDE 2001

SEVENTEENTH EDITION

'WEBSTER'S'

THE COMPLETE WINE BUYER'S HANDBOOK

TED SMART

The information and prices contained in the Guide were correct to the best of our knowledge when we went to press, and the impression of relative price and relative value is almost certainly still accurate, even if a particular price has changed.

Although every care has been taken in the preparation of the guide, neither the publishers nor the editors can accept any liability for any consequences arising from the use of information contained herein.

Oz Clarke's Wine Buying Guide *is an annual publication. We welcome any suggestions you might have for the next edition.*

Editors Bill Evans, Maggie Ramsay
Wine Editor Margaret Rand
Database Managing Editor Lorna Bateson
Price Guides Editor Julie Ross
Editorial Assistants Sarah Cooke, Claire Hodgson, Jo Turner, Andrew Walker, Athina Ypsilanti
DTP Consultant Keith Bambury
Indexer Naomi Good
Database Consultants Cognitive Applications, Brighton
Production Kâren Smith
Publishing Director Claire Harcup
Art Director Nigel O'Gorman
Photography for 2001 – A Taste Odyssey Stephen Bartholomew

Corporate Sales

Companies, institutions and other organizations wishing to make bulk purchases of this or any other Oz Clarke title published by Little, Brown should contact the Special Sales Department on +44(0)20-7911 8089.

Advertising Sales

Logie Bradshaw Media Limited,
Strathallan House, Fernville Lane,
Midland Road, Hemel Hempstead,
Herts HP2 4LS
tel 0144 2233331, fax 0144 2231131

A LITTLE, BROWN/WEBSTERS BOOK

This edition first published in 2000 by
Little, Brown and Company (UK)
Brettenham House
Lancaster Place
LONDON WC2E 7EN

This edition produced for The Book People Ltd,
Hall Wood Avenue, Haydock, St Helens WA11 9UL
by Websters International Publishers Limited,
Axe and Bottle Court
70 Newcomen Street
London SE1 1YT
www.websters.co.uk
www.ozclarke.com

A CIP catalogue for this book is available from the British Library.

ISBN 0-316-85396-8

Printed and bound in the UK by
Clays Ltd, St Ives plc

CONTENTS

INTRODUCTION

Yum. This sounds nice: 'Delightful dry white with gentle floral perfume and a lively lime zest acidity.' My mouth's watering already, and it sounds like a fiver's worth of pleasure. Or what about this: 'Lovely mellow red made from little known grapes like Negrette and Tannat that combines gentle strawberry and plum fruit with a flicker of leafy bite.' That sounds like a fiver's worth of fun too. Or this: 'Fistfuls of ripe fruit, bay leaf perfume and cherry cake.' Sounds good? Sure it does. Do you think you'd like to drink a red containing 'sweet plum fruit, a whiff of kitchen spice and just a dusting of pepper'? I would. And I'd probably expect to pay a fiver for it.

Well, you don't have to. All of these wines are on our shelves right now for the princely sum of £2.99. Yes, just £2.99 a bottle. Turn to page 26 and you'll find these and almost a dozen more, own-label supermarket wines from Asda, Budgens, the Co-op, Marks & Spencer, Safeway, Sainsbury's, Tesco and Waitrose. And those wine descriptions are taken directly from my tasting notes.

I got a real kick out of that. It made me realize that there has never been less excuse for wine snobbery than there is today. There has never been less validity in choosing a wine solely because it has a famous name, a smart label and an inflated price tag. And there has never been a time when the producers cared more about the consumer than they do today.

A MATTER OF TASTE

One of the more damning attitudes that the wine snob has towards cheap wine is that it all tastes the same. Well, that first wine description was of a Hungarian white that expertly married the zip and the perfume typical of Hungary's native grape varieties. The second wine, the red, showed the classic softness of the Negrette grape from South-West France along with the more aggressive attack of the Tannat. It tasted of the grapes, and it tasted of the place. There were Hungarian reds in the tasting that had the unmistakable crunchy pepper and celery bite allied with ripe plum fruit that shouts of the Danube. South African reds with the characteristic trail of lava dust in the wine, Corbières with its powerful scent of bay leaf and wild mountain passes. Chianti, for goodness' sake, Côtes du Rhône – both recognizable and different – at £2.99.

All of this says a lot about our British wine world. If we went into a French supermarket and bought their cheap Côtes du Rhône, Beaujolais, Bordeaux or whatever, it wouldn't taste any good. Believe me. I've tried. I've been over to Calais and bought these bottles from the big hypermarkets there and they're unspeakably poor. You wouldn't get these flavours in a German supermarket, or an Italian one. And that's because when it comes to wine there's a fundamental difference between British supermarkets and their mainland European counterparts. There, cheap wine is generally regarded as a commodity bought and sold at the lowest possible price regardless of flavour. Here, wine is seen as a sweetener, a way to get people into your store who are likely to be interested in more aspirational things than simply the cheapest loaf of bread and largest packet of washing powder. Here, with more wine criticism and media discussion of the subject than in any other nation on earth, the supermarket buyers realize that we, the consumers, have an opinion, and we make that opinion heard by buying wine with flavours that we like.

Does that sound like I'm stating the obvious? I'm not. In any given supermarket or high street chain store there could be as many as 500 different wines on sale, maybe more. Some of these will try to attract our attention with ritzy labels or cute names. Some will be heavily advertised and promoted brands like Gallo or Jacob's Creek. But most will be relying on just one thing for us to make a repeat purchase: we have to like the taste. And that puts us, the consumers, into the driving seat.

Which is exactly how I like it. There are too many areas of modern life where the individual is losing control. Wine is one area where we are gaining control. Now it's a case of having the confidence to enjoy exercising that control.

RULE 1: THERE ARE NO RULES

In which case, we should re-state one or two basic principles. And the most basic wine principle of all is: if you don't feel like drinking wine, don't. There's absolutely no social requirement to do so. If you prefer sparkling water stick with that.

Secondly, drink the flavours you like. Whether they're sweet or dry, fruity or austere, perfumed or restrained, it's you who is doing the drinking and you should drink precisely what you want. And if that means Lambrusco with your roast leg of lamb, well, go ahead, do it. Just so long as it makes you happy, because although wine buffs spend hour upon hour laying down rules about what we should like, when we should drink it, and with what foods we must or must not drink it, there's only one real rule – this. If wine isn't about pleasure, if wine isn't about having fun and feeling good, there's no point to it.

And that leads on to a third principle. Only pay a price that you're happy with. As our tastings have shown, there's excellent wine to be had for £2.99. There's masses more at £3.99 and oceans more again at £4.99. If you like a £3.99 wine's flavour, don't presume that you'll like a £9.99 wine from an overrated region any better. And don't listen to any wine snob who tells you that you should. There's no should. You like what you like and it's entirely up to you if you want to trade up.

But if you do, we're here to help you. We've tasted wines that sell for up to £25, from old-established merchants, modern retailers, internet and mail-order only outlets, high street chains – as well as the supermarkets. I've picked out my favourites, all of which thrilled my taste buds, grabbed my imagination and struck me as excellent value, whatever their price.

With our recommendations and in our regional chapters, we're here to try to nudge you in the right direction, giving advice on what grape varieties are hot and what are not. If you want to stick to your old favourites – Cabernet and Shiraz, Chardonnay and Sauvignon – we'll give you hundreds of suggestions as to new ones to try. If you're tiring of those flavours and want a change, we've made some mouthwateringly good discoveries. Juicy young reds? How about Malbec or Bonarda from Argentina? Great deep superripe mouthfuls of red? Primitivo from southern Italy, Zinfandel from California, perhaps Grenache from Spain or Australia.

And talking of countries, do you want to stick to Australia and France? What about Hungary? Or Portugal, Chile, Argentina, Uruguay, Canada or Georgia? Whether the countries produce hundreds of different wines or just a handful, whether they charge an arm and a leg or merely a fistful of loose change, we're here to offer guidance, advice and opinion in about equal measures to help you get the best from what is the best wine market place in the world – ours!

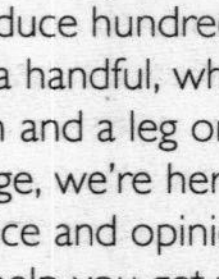

HOW TO USE THIS BOOK

If you are looking for specific wines, turn straight to the **Price Guides**. These are the pages on which we have collated the current retail prices of the thousands of wines we hold on our computer database. **The letters in brackets are abbreviations for the names of the stockists for each of the wines listed.** The key to these abbreviations is on the facing page and full details of these and other merchants appear in the **Merchant Directory** on pages 456–92.

If you want to find local suppliers, merchants are listed by region on page 493; if you want to find a specialist in a particular country's wines, these are listed at the beginning of each country's Price Guides.

Please remember that the Price Guides are not meant to replace up-to-date merchants' lists. What they *do*, however, is give you a unique opportunity to compare prices; to develop a sense of what you can expect to pay for any given wine; to spot a bargain – *and to find it.*

Buying wine can feel like a lucky dip when you are faced with shelves or lists full of unfamiliar names: the chapters on the **wine-producing countries** of the world provide a quick introduction to the grapes, wine styles, regions and producer names. In most of these chapters you'll also find specific recommendations in the form of an **Instant Cellar:** a selection of wines to help you acquaint yourself with the region.

★–★★★★★ ratings in the **Producers Who's Who** sections apply to the quality of wine being made, ranging from good to world class. A star in brackets (★) indicates that the producer can attain that quality but does not always do so.

We aim to improve this *Guide* every year. Please let us know what you think by returning the cut-out **questionnaire** at the back of the book; that way we can produce an even better guide next year – and you could win a case of wine in our prize draw.

USING THE PRICE GUIDES

When using the **Price Guides** you should be aware of the following:

- All prices listed are *per bottle inclusive of VAT*, unless otherwise stated. The prices are those which applied in the early summer of 2000. When comparing prices remember that some wine merchants sell only by the case. In this instance, we have arrived at a bottle price by dividing by 12 the VAT-inclusive price of a single case. Where merchants who sell by the case will sell cases of mixed bottles, we have used the bottle price that would apply in a mixed case.
- When clubs have both member and non-member prices we have used the *non-member* prices.
- Wines are listed in price bands, and in alphabetical order within each band. If more than one vintage of the same wine appears within one price band, these run from the most recent to the oldest.
- All stockists for a particular wine are listed in ascending order of price. The wines are placed in bands according to the lowest price for which each is available. This means that the highest prices may overstep the upper limit of the price band in which the wine is featured. Variations in price are the result of a combination of factors: wine warehouses, for example, often come out much cheaper than individual merchants because they sell only by the case, they do not deliver, they do not have smart high street premises to maintain, and so on.
- The **Red Bordeaux Price Guides** are a special case. The châteaux are listed alphabetically, then in order of vintage. There are some dramatic price variations here; for a full explanation, see page 134.
- **NV** denotes non-vintage wines in the **Champagne Price Guides.**
- A ★ in the Price Guides indicates a wine recommended by Oz Clarke in the **Best Buys** section which begins on page 10.

MERCHANT NAME CODES

These are the merchants whose prices are featured in the Price Guides. The abbreviations are shown in brackets after the price of each of the listed wines they stock.

AD	Adnams
AME	Amey's Wines
AS	Ashley Scott
ASD	ASDA
AUS	Australian Wine Club
AV	Averys of Bristol
BAL	Ballantynes of Cowbridge
BALL	Balls Brothers
BAN	H & H Bancroft
BEN	Bennetts
BER	Berry Bros. & Rudd
BIB	Bibendum
BOT	Bottoms Up
BO	Booths
BOD	Bordeaux Direct
BU	Butlers Wine Cellar
BUD	Budgens
BY	Anthony Byrne
CAP	Cape Province Wines
CAV	Cave Cru Classé
CB	Corney & Barrow
CHA	Châteaux Wines
CO	CWS (Co-op)
COC	Cockburns of Leith
CON	Connolly's
CRO	Croque-en-Bouche
DI	Direct Wine Shipments
DOM	Domaine Direct
ELL	Ben Ellis Wines
FA	Farr Vintners
FLE	Le Fleming Wines
FORT	Fortnum & Mason
FRI	Friarwood
GAU	Gauntleys
GN	Great Northern Wine Co
GOE	Goedhuis & Co
GW	Great Western Wine
HA	John Harvey & Sons
HAH	Haynes Hanson & Clark
HAW	Roger Harris Wines
HED	Hedley Wright
HIG	High Breck Vintners
JER	Jeroboams
JON	S H Jones
JU	Justerini & Brooks
LAY	Lay & Wheeler
LEA	Lea & Sandeman
LIB	Liberty Wines
LLO	Lloyd Taylor Wines
MAJ	Majestic
MAR	Marks & Spencer plc
MI	Millésima
MON	Montrachet
MOR	Moreno Wines
MV	Morris & Verdin
NA	Nadder Wines Ltd
NEZ	Le Nez Rouge
NI	James Nicholson
NO	The Nobody Inn
NZW	New Zealand Wines Direct
OD	Oddbins
PEN	Penistone Court Wine Cellars
PHI	Philglas & Swiggot
PIP	Christopher Piper Wines
PLA	Terry Platt
PLAY	Playford Ros
POR	Portland Wine Co
RAE	Raeburn Fine Wines
REI	Reid Wines (1992) Ltd
RES	La Réserve
RIP	Howard Ripley
ROB	Roberson
RSJ	RSJ Wine Company
SAF	Safeway
SAI	Sainsbury's
SAV	Savage Selection
SO	Somerfield
SOM	Sommelier Wine Co
STA	Frank Stainton Wines
STE	Stevens Garnier Wine Merchants
SUN	Sunday Times Wine Club
TAN	Tanners
TES	Tesco
THR	Thresher
TW	T & W Wines
UB	The Ubiquitous Chip
UN	Unwins
VA	Valvona & Crolla
VIC	Victoria Wine
VIN	Vintage Wines Ltd
WAI	Waitrose
WAT	Waterloo Wine Co
WR	Wine Rack
WRI	Wright Wine Co
WS	Wine Society
WT	Wine Treasury
WY	Peter Wylie Fine Wines
YAP	Yapp Brothers
YOU	Noel Young Wines

BUYING WINE ON THE WEB

You can't ignore the internet. It's a hot topic in every newspaper and magazine. Every second advert on the billboards seems to be for something or other www.com. 'E-tailing' is supposed to be revolutionizing the way we shop. But when it comes to wine buying, do we need it? Well, no, we don't. Not really. We can get by quite happily popping down to the shops or using mail order just like we have done for years.

So, now we've got the opportunity to buy wine on the web, what advantages can it offer us? Greater choice, lower prices, the convenience of ordering from your desk when you ought to be working – those are all potential advantages. And what about consumer power? There are definite possibilities here. The internet provides opportunities for customer feedback at a level never seen before. The ever-expanding Virgin organization, and Aussie-owned WinePlanet, have plans to build wine evaluation systems around customer responses not just expert assessments. Will they evolve into reliable guides to what you want to drink? I don't see why not.

WHAT'S ON THE WEBSITE?

When looking at a website, hold on to your critical faculties. Consider the following. Is this company offering the sort of wines you want? Will it deliver the wines swiftly and at your convenience? Are the prices (including delivery) competitive? What will happen if you are dissatisfied with the wine? And, ultimately, do you trust these people? Merchants with an established trading base are unlikely to let you down, and any serious online retailer will have invested in effective credit card security systems.

Because websites are constructed around huge computer databases, they are able to

PICK OF THE SITES

EveryWine (www.everywine.co.uk) sets out to offer every single wine available in the UK. Other megasites are **Virgin Wines** (www.virginwines.com) and **MadAboutWine** (www.madaboutwine.com). They don't hold all of the wines in stock, but they have deals set up to supply the wines.

Berry Brothers & Rudd (www.bbr.com) A complete wine experience, with news, courses and advice.

Great Western Wine (www.greatwesternwine.co.uk) Here you can read reviews and order wine that has been recommended in the national press.

Valvona & Crolla (www.valvonacrolla.com) Wine, plus food and recipes with an Italian slant.

WinePlanet (www.wineplanet.co.uk) is about to launch in the UK as we go to press (.com.au gives you the idea).

Seckford Wines (www.seckfordwines.co.uk) claims to update its list of 1000 fine wines every two hours.

Bordeaux Direct (www.bordeauxdirect.co.uk), the **Sunday Times Wine Club** (www.sundaytimeswineclub.co.uk) and **ChateauOnline** (www.chateauonline.co.uk) are all helpful and varied sites.

AmiVin (www.amivin.com) for anniversary vintages.

Pure Wine Co (www.purewine.co.uk) and **Vintage Roots** (www. vintageroots.co.uk) for organic wines.

offer facilities for searching for wines in all sorts of ways. Generally you will be able to select a region that interests you, or set a price range or pick on a style, or specify all three. Once you have entered your search criteria, you should be presented with a range of wines that meet them. If you're lucky you will also find some tasting notes.

So here you are, wandering around the virtual shop, merrily filling your virtual shopping trolley with booze. What's missing from this picture? The ability to handle bottles and to chat away to the wine merchant as you do. Much the same as the traditional mail-order scenario, in fact.

But, oddly enough, the internet offers excellent access to well-informed personal service. Most sites already carry a fair amount of wine information and the best offer a question-and-answer service, which operates by email. You will have access to advice from experts with a far greater level of knowledge than you will encounter in most shop staff.

Before I go any further, I had better declare my own interests here: I too have gone online. After an early leap into cyber-space with my www.ozclarke.com site, I head the European tasting panel of WineToday (www.winetoday.com), to which I also contribute monthly features. You will also find wine advice based on Oz Clarke's Wine Guide CD-ROM in the 'Ask Oz' section of WinePlanet (www.wineplanet.co.uk), which combines wine e-tailing with independent comment. Okay, so there you have it – I'm a global presence.

Many of the merchants featured in this guide have set up websites, but only a few have invested in making their online presence a significant addition to their existing business: you'll find some of these in the box (left).

When you're on the trail of a specific bottle, perhaps something special for an anniversary gift, then the internet comes into its own and so do the megasites: it won't take long to search them all for availability and to compare prices. Any fine wine specialist with a website is also worth investigating.

SAFE NET SHOPPING

- Find out who you are dealing with: well-known companies are more likely to have secure sites. UK-based companies are covered by UK laws.
- Look for the 'small print' telling you about the company, its guarantees, delivery systems and refund or returns policy. Beware of PO Box addresses, but look for a telephone number.
- Check that the company uses SSL (secure sockets layer) technology, which makes your details unavailable to other web users.
- Before you enter your credit card details a box should appear to tell you you are entering a secure connection, which scrambles the details in transit.
- Save all the information relating to your purchase, so you have proof if anything goes wrong.
- Check your credit card statement for unauthorized purchases.
- Look for a firm that abides by a code of practice; participating retailers will display the relevant logo. These include: Which? Web Trader Scheme (www.which.net/webtrader/index.html); Interactive Media in Retail Group (www.imrg.org); Consumer Assistance Bureau (www.isitsafe.com).

Equally, if you have just enjoyed a fabulous bottle of wine in a restaurant, megasites may well be the best place to look to find a supply for yourself. And as the internet and mobile phones become more intimately acquainted you should even be able to do this from the restaurant, while the bottle is in front of you. This facility is already envisaged by Virgin. Restaurants with high mark-ups beware.

The internet can give us access to a greater range of wines than ever. Conventional wine retailing is not about to join the dinosaurs, but you know what? Buying online can be fun – and that's what wine is all about.

BEST BUYS

Britain's wine merchants – from specialists to supermarkets – have once again risen to the challenge of our annual tasting, sending in an inspired selection of wines with memorable personalities and a host of exciting flavours

Each year I worry about the gradual consolidation of companies that make, ship and sell wine. This year has seen a number of shippers sink or amalgamate under the widening umbrellas of brewery groups and venture capitalists; we've also seen some high street specialists lose their independence. And this means that, once again, I worry we're going to see originality and personality disappear from our annual tastings, that we won't any longer find wines that thrill and shock or seduce, that the big brand hordes will drag our lively wine world downmarket into a morass of lowest common denominator swill.

But it doesn't happen. At least, not with the merchants, both big and small, who respond to our call to send in wines that make our hearts flutter and our taste buds snap into overdrive. This year we've tasted so much exciting stuff that we've added an extra 'unoaked' category to scoop up some delightful wines that might otherwise have got lost in the millrace. And as for bargains, the £4.99 and £3.99 price points have never been better served.

Please bear in mind that wines are not made in infinite quantities – some of these may well sell out, but the following year's vintage should then become available

---

MY 2001 TOP DOZEN

What a mouthwatering bevy of beauties we've found this year – and look at the prices. Only two of these fantastic wines pass the dreaded £20 mark and half are under a tenner. Out with the folding ones. Rush to the stores

❶ 1997 Ribera del Duero Tinto Roble, Briego, £8.99, Raeburn (red, Spain)
Just once in a while you come across a wine that makes you look suspiciously at your tasting notes and say, no, it can't have been that gorgeous, that incomparable, that irresistible. Then you taste it again – and it's even better than you thought. An astonishing combination of gravadlax dill, coriander, oyster sauce and a cinnamon stick, all thrown into a celestial stew that's already bursting over the cauldron's edge with blackcurrant, raspberry, grilled pork, sun-dried tomatoes, butter and rosemary.

❷ 1998 Shiraz, Tim Adams, Clare Valley, £8.99, Australian Wine Club/Tesco (red, Australia)
This is Tim Adams' greatest Shiraz yet, with a wonderful scent that's as sticky and sinus-scouring as crunched eucalyptus gum leaves. Add this to perfumed blueberry and blackberry fruit, the richness of melting Harrogate toffee and the softness of pie crust going soggy next to the fruit and you've got an Aussie classic.

❸ 1998 Shiraz, Hewitson, Barossa Valley, £12.95, Waterloo Wine Co (red, Australia)
Tim Adams may have a challenger here; this guy's a newcomer but he clearly understands the Barossa, because this is everything Barossa Shiraz should be: gorgeously rich, throbbing with the dark, sweet juice of blackberries and morello cherries, made even more succulent by melting treacle toffee but just kept semi-serious by the black, brooding chewiness of a liquorice stick.

4 1997 Geyserville, Ridge, California, £20.95, Adnams (red, United States)
I don't think Ridge has ever let me down. This is a fabulous, indulgent fandango of headstrong flavours: rum fudge and date and crystallized plums from the Christmas tree, burnished with newly shined leather and taunted by the dust from the bottom of a pepper grinder.

5 1998 Côtes du Rhône-Villages Rasteau, Domaine Gourt de Mautens, £17.95, Raeburn (red, Rhône)
This is startling stuff. Its only problem is that it's a bit too tannic, but the violet scent, the sandalwood perfume, the cherries and plums and raspberry sauce are so exciting – well, slap a big juicy steak down next to it and even those tannins will disappear.

6 1998 Merlot, Steenburg, Constantia, £9.99, Waitrose (red, South Africa)
Find me a more harmonious red wine than this. A heavenly scent of eucalyptus and spearmint leaves, the mouthwatering pungency of roasting coffee beans, and a sweet, succulent flavour of superripe blackcurrants boiled into rich dark jam.

7 1997 Triple C, Santa Rita, Maipo Valley, £10.99, Majestic (red, Chile)
Powerful, muscle-rippling red, dark and brooding but laced with wonderfully sweet blackcurrant and morello cherry fruit, minty perfume and bonfire-scented oak.

8 1996 Shiraz, Chateau Reynella, McLaren Vale, £11.99, Waitrose (red, Australia)
You may wonder, is this going to be just too much of a mouthful for me? That disturbing smell of engine oil and mouthwash, do I want it in my mouth? Hell, yes. And you'll see why: there *is* a curiously attractive slick of petrol running through it, but it seems perfectly at ease with the stewed plums and cream, the liquorice, the chocolate and the bouquet garni of Mediterranean herbs.

9 1999 Riesling, Tim Adams, Clare Valley, £7.99, Australian Wine Club/£7.50, Tesco (white, Australia)
This delightful white has a scent of apple blossom and lime and Darjeeling tea leaf and a marvellous tingling taste of piercing lime acid wrapped in the flesh of sweet apples and ripe white peaches.

10 1996 Côte-Rôtie, Louis Drevon, £21.12, Christopher Piper (red, Rhône)
Austere, almost haughty, but Côte-Rôtie is such a wonderful wine that it can't keep a smile off its face for long. This soon breaks through its carapace of tar and pebble dryness to reveal delicious blackberry fruit, then a strange, starchy creaminess of freshly sliced raw potato and the bitter-sweet richness of liquorice toffee.

11 1998 Graves, Clos Floridène, £12.97, Anthony Byrne (white, Bordeaux)
I can never work out why people won't buy top white Bordeaux. I mean, where else would you find a sultry temptress like this, with custard, coffee creams, nectarines and grapefruit pith splashed with ground hazelnuts and fresh excited sweat?

12 1997 St-Joseph, Domaine du Chêne, £8.95, The Wine Society (red, Rhône)
St-Joseph is supposed to be the softest, most scented red of the northern Rhône and, made like this one, it is. A languid, sensuous, violet perfume floats over ripe loganberry and blackberry fruit and crème fraîche richness lightly sprinkled with rockface dust.

1998 Chardonnay, Allandale, Hunter Valley, £8.50, Australian Wine Club (white, Australia)
This startling Aussie Chardie was our top wine last year. We loved it then, we love it now, but there's not enough left to give it the crown again. Even so, I think you're barmy not to have bought it all last year.

THE RUNNERS UP

Don't think of these as second best. They're a bunch of superb wines packed with character and excitement – and at every price level

❶ 1998 Minervois, Château d'Oupia, £5.26, Christopher Piper Wines (red, southern France)
Value for money doesn't come much better than this. A thrilling punchbowl of deep dark flavours, stewed cherries and damsons, black chocolate and freshly ground pepper all whirl about like dervishes, while a dainty perfume of lilac and bay leaves pirouettes on the surface.

❷ 1999 Riesling, Allan Scott, Marlborough, £7.10, Lay & Wheeler (white, New Zealand)
If the flower of the lemon tree is sweet it must smell like this Riesling, whose lemon-flower perfume soars into the sky, while the flavour is a cascade of lime and lemon, grapes, greengages and honeysuckle.

❸ 1998 Cabernet Sauvignon, Tim Adams, Clare Valley, £8.99, Australian Wine Club (red, Australia)
I'm not sure Tim Adams has ever made a better Cabernet than this marvellously intense wine: it has enough attack to invigorate your palate at the same time as the eucalyptus and mint leaf scent and the dark, sweet, stewed plum and morello cherry fruit lull your senses with their bitter-sweet beauty.

❹ 1999 Malbec, Finca Il Retiro, Pacífico Tittarelli, Mendoza, £5.99, Liberty Wines/Valvona & Crolla (red, Argentina)
Superbly arrogant damson fruit, ginger and nutmeg spice and violet scent are still wrapped around with an inky wood bark power that will soften irresistibly over the next year or so.

❺ 1997 The Society's Exhibition Shiraz, Mount Langi Ghiran, Victoria, £9.95, The Wine Society (red, Australia)
Beautiful, succulent Aussie Shiraz: a sweet perfume of mint and eucalyptus, rich black plum and cherry fruit, just turning to chocolate – deep, ripe, delicious.

❻ 1999 Sauvignon Blanc, Nepenthe, South Australia, £8.99, Waitrose (white)
An absorbing mouthful of flavours that surely won't marry – but they do. Nettles and passionfruit, melons and lime argue the toss with wax and coffee bean and sandalwood.

❼ 1998 Crozes-Hermitage Cuvée Alberic Bouvet, Domaine Gilles Robin, £9.99, Great Western Wine/£10.95, Lea & Sandeman (red, Rhône)
Utterly delightful Rhône red. Its texture is absurdly soft for such a supposedly beefy wine style, but who cares? Just grab a mouthful of this lovely stuff, scented like polished leather and lilac, tasting of the deep liquid red fruit of loganberries and sloes, fattened by chocolate and creamed potatoes, and yet still hinting darkly at a medicinal core.

❽ 1997 Shiraz, Chapel Hill, McLaren Vale, £9.99, Australian Wine Club/First Quench (red, Australia)
Rich, dark wine that coats your palate with its thick, unctuous personality. It's almost treacly, like Harrogate toffee, but the gorgeous black cherry and black plum keep it fresh, and there's liquorice bitterness, too.

❾ 1998 Ram Paddock Red, Waipara West, Waipara, £8.59, Waterloo Wine (red, New Zealand)
The epitome of cool-climate red, restrained but beautifully ripe. This has a lovely, mouthwatering, blackcurrant and stewed plums depth, drizzled with melted toffee then scattered with mint and blackcurrant leaves, as the smoke from the barbecue drifts idly by.

⑩ 1998 Mâcon-Viré Quintaine, Domaine Emilian Gillet, £13.95, Lea & Sandeman (white, Burgundy)
Viré is one of the top villages in the Mâconnais, but that means nothing if the vigneron doesn't care. Well, this guy cares and this is a high-quality Burgundy, laced with honeysuckle, greengage and angelica fruit and streaked with lime zest acid.

⑪ 1999 Sauvignon Blanc, Kim Crawford, Marlborough, £7.99, Liberty Wines (white, New Zealand)
Aggressive lip-smacker, piled up with grapefruit, lime, green apple and nettles.

⑫ 1997 Pouilly-Fuissé, Domaine Manciat-Poncet, £11.90, Roger Harris Wines (white, Burgundy)
This marvellously old-fashioned white – its heart crammed with oatmeal, cream and hazelnuts just flecked with the spicy perfume of a hot cross bun straight from the oven – shows how good Pouilly-Fuissé can be in the right hands.

⑬ 1998 Sancerre, Lucien Crochet, £8.50, Justerini & Brooks (white, Loire)
Sancerre has probably been the Loire Valley's most abused wine name over the years, but this mouthwatering broth of gooseberries, watercress and fresh pork sausage (honest! uncooked, with herbs), shows you why Sancerre became so popular in the first place.

⑭ 1999 Sauvignon Blanc, Clifford Bay, Marlborough, £7.49, Friarwood (white, New Zealand)
Excellent, aggressive lime and lemon and Bramley apple acidity scything through a fully ripe white perfumed with fresh mint.

⑮ 1997 Merlot, Viña Casablanca, Casablanca, £6.49, Lloyd Taylor Wines (red, Chile)
This is why we buy Chilean reds: a gorgeous surge of superripe freshness swamping our thirsty palates. This succulent stew is oozing blackcurrant and blackberry fruit, with a surprisingly tasty smear of smoky tarpaulin.

⑯ 1997 Semillon, Tim Adams, Clare Valley, £7.99, Australian Wine Club/Tesco (white, Australia)
A classic Semillon, built for the long haul. It's still a little hard-edged, tasting almost salty, but scented with peach and pear and lemon peel it'll end up tasting of custard and honey and lime marmalade in about 3–5 years, and will still be good in 2020.

⑰ 1998 Bergerac Sec Cuvée des Conti, Château Tour des Gendres, £6.50, Lea & Sandeman (white, southern France)
Gentle white, smelling of Ogen melon and nectarine and wrapping them round the palate with honeycomb and flowers and the skin of sun-soaked golden peaches.

⑱ 1997 Chardonnay/Semillon, Bodega Infinitus, Patagonia, £7.65, Raeburn Fine Wines (white, Argentina)
More Ogen melon and golden peach in this lovely soft-centred Chardonnay. It starts out smelling a little grassy, but shoves such flavours aside in favour of melon, peach, and pineapples scented with honeysuckle.

⑲ 1998 Pinot Noir Reserve, Viña Carmen, Maipo Valley, £7.45, Nadder Wines (red, Chile)
Chile is producing some impressive Pinot Noirs, and this one is quite intense, perfumed with wild strawberries, packed with strawberry and cherry fruit, wrapped round with an almost nutty syrup richness.

⑳ 1999 Beaujolais Villages, Jean-Charles Pivot, £5.86, Domaine Direct (red, Burgundy)
Oh, what blissful memories of summer picnics as the cool red liquid gurgled past the laughter down our throats. And in the hands of M. Pivot you can still enjoy this almost forgotten strawberry and peaches red wine style.

BEST BUYS UNDER £5

This is what I like to see. France, fighting back against the New World at under a fiver. Argentina is left in sole defence against the Old World

1 1998 Vin de Pays des Côtes de Gascogne Sauvignon, Domaine du Tariquet, £4.99, First Quench (white, southern France)
A wine that's as teeth-chattering as a midnight dip on New Year's Eve. Piles of blackcurrant leaf, gooseberry, nettles and coffee beans, all beautifully balanced.

2 1998 Vin de Pays d'Oc Sauvignon, Domaine de Barthes, J & F Lurton, £4.79, S H Jones (white, southern France)
Brimming with bright apple and passionfruit freshness, streaked with lime and just lightly brushed with aniseed.

3 1999 Vin de Pays des Côtes de Gascogne Blanc de Blancs Selection Cazaux, Domaine La Rieste, £4.99, Bordeaux Direct (white, southern France)
Snappy but full-flavoured white, seething with the sharpness of Bramley apples and lime and the swish of nettle.

4 1998 Pedras do Monte, Castelão, Terras do Sado, £4.99, Unwins (red, Portugal)
A most unusual mix of strawberry syrup and apple that quickly gets swamped by brown sugar, sultanas and a welcome wad of tobacco leaf. Can you handle that?

5 1999 Vin de Pays d'Oc Viognier, Domaine de la Ferrandière, £4.95, Waterloo Wine Co (white, southern France)
Lovely, round, glyceriny texture, a perfume of mayblossom and tea rose and the soft orchard ripeness of peaches and pears.

6 1999 Syrah Finca Norte, Villa Atuel, Mendoza, £4.99, Liberty Wines (red, Argentina)
Ripe juicy red, bulging with sun-soaked fruit, this is brawny, gutsy stuff, a casserole of dates and damsons and floral perfume.

7 1999 Vin de Pays d'Oc Roussane, Domaine du Bosc, £4.75, H & H Bancroft (white, southern France)
Really interesting white – dry, quite acid, even slightly hard-edged and dusty, but with a strangely beguiling blend of sandalwood, Bramley apple and violet.

8 1998 Jaen, Bela Fonte, Vinho Regional de Beiras, £4.99, Unwins (red, Portugal)
A really original Portuguese red from a single grape variety (Jaen). It starts out tasting of apple and cranberry, rapidly slithers into sloes and red cherries cloaked in clove spice before collapsing contentedly into a mush of raisins and black chocolate.

9 1999 Negroamaro, Promessa, Puglia, £4.99, Liberty Wines (red, Italy)
Quite aggressive stuff, smelling of apple and banana toffees, and tasting of sandalwood, cranberries and subtly perfumed cherries.

10 1999 Dry English Table Wine, Three Choirs Vineyard/Nobody Inn, £4.99, The Nobody Inn (white)
Excellent tangy white, spilling over with elderflower and grapefruit scent, and tasting like a really snappy Sauvignon with the addition of tea leaves and a hop or two.

11 1999 Vin de Pays d'Oc Sauvignon Blanc, Domaine de Coussergues, £4.79, Lloyd Taylor Wines (white, southern France)
Tongue-tingling Sauvignon: lime zest, apple purée and kiwi fruit fattened up with gooseberries stewed in sugar.

12 1998 Costières de Nîmes Plan Macassan, Penval, £4.49, Oddbins (red, southern France)
Splendid deep, plummy red with a touch of herb perfume and some strawberry that you sometimes find in southern French red with an Aussie touch.

BEST BUYS UNDER £4

You can still find them. Really enjoyable wines at under £4. And our selection covers six different countries

❶ 1999 Corbières Grande Réserve, Domaine Madelon, £3.69, Majestic (red, southern France)
Powerful stuff, packed with plum and cranberry fruit, perfumed with violets and bay leaf. Just what Corbières should be.

❷ 1999 Riesling, Rawson's Retreat Bin 202, Penfolds, South Australia, £3.99, First Quench (white)
Full-flavoured Aussie Riesling, with a honeyed softness roughened by dry desert dust, shot through with lime, and rubbed down with leather.

❸ 1997 Best Cellar Reserve Selection Red, Hilltop Neszmély, £3.49, Great Northern Wine Company (Hungary)
Fantastic value for a truly original red – the softness of strawberry fruit gums, the fire of peppercorns and the crunchiness of celery stalks. Utterly unusual. Utterly enjoyable.

❹ 1999 Vin de Pays des Côtes de Gascogne, Vivian Ducourneau, £3.99, Majestic (white, southern France)
Knock-your-socks-off aggressive dry white, with powerful grapefruit and lemon peel acidity – but not raw. In fact it's surprisingly ripe, but would still kick start a pterodactyl.

❺ 1998 Barbera Elsa, San Rafael, £3.99, CWS (red, Argentina)
If you're used to Italian Barbera this may come as a shock, but it's a good shock because of the price and the come-hither clove spice and rounded red plum fruit.

❻ 1999 The Society's South African Chenin Blanc, Stellenbosch, £3.75, The Wine Society (white)
Much South African Chenin Blanc is instantly forgettable. but this one's nice, with fresh melon fruit and a rounded, honeyed, biscuity softness.

❼ 1999 Shiraz Rosé, Balbi, Mendoza, £3.99, CWS (Argentina)
This is pretty good rosé, with lots of bright strawberry and apple jelly fruit and a tingling acidity.

❽ 1998 Vin de Pays des Côtes de Gascogne Gros Manseng/Sauvignon, Alain Brumont, £3.98, Anthony Byrne (white, southern France)
Alain Brumont is one of South-West France's best red wine makers, but he can clearly cut it with whites as well, as this interesting mix of digestive biscuit softness and lemony acid shows.

❾ 1998 Côtes de Duras Sémillon, Honoré de Berticot, £3.88, John Harvey & Sons (white, southern France)
South-West France again – they really do make very good whites down there – this time not completely dry, but a very attractive marriage of honey and angelica with a darting apple peel and lemon sherbet acidity.

❿ 1998 Best Cellar Reserve Selection White, Hilltop Neszmély, £3.49, Great Northern Wine Company (Hungary)
Mild, easy-going white smelling of rose petals and tasting of lychee laced with lemon peel.

⓫ 1998 Pinot Gris Classic, £3.89, Budgens (white, Romania)
Rather good grapy white that is kept refreshing by a bright elderflower scent and the smack of lemon zest.

⓬ 1998 Torrontés/Chardonnay, Navarro Correas, Tupungato, £3.99, First Quench (white, Argentina)
Soft dry white with just enough lychee and rose petal jam scent to render it reasonably exotic.

THE GREAT UNOAKED

We have introduced this section because we have tasted so many wines with marvellous, pinging, vivid fruit not seasoned by oak – just divinely drinkable – that we couldn't bear to miss them out

❶ 1999 Sauvignon Blanc, Churton, Marlborough, £6.90, Tanners (white, New Zealand)
Aggressive, inspired, and shimmering with nettle and passionfruit and fragrant coffee beans, yet beautifully ripe at the same time.

❷ 1999 Unwooded Chardonnay, Madfish Bay, Western Australia, £8.25, H & H Bancroft (white)
If the fruit is this good, Chardonnay doesn't need oak. This fascinating, refreshing white balances a mouthwatering lemony acidity with goldengage and melon fruit that drips ripeness down your chin, and a lingering perfume of honeysuckle and lemon flower.

❸ 1999 Sauvignon Blanc, Palliser Estate, Martinborough, £7.52, Anthony Byrne (white, New Zealand)
All the grapefruit zest aggression your palate can cope with, but here it is blended with elderflower perfume and a green streaked richness like passionfruit and baked apple soused with syrup.

❹ 1999 Beaujolais, Blaise Carron, £6.45, Roger Harris Wines (red, Burgundy)
What sheer delight! Beaujolais as it once was. Beaujolais that tumbles down your throat, leaving a trail across the palate of bananas, pears, juicy raspberry and stones warmed in the summer sun.

❺ 1998 Pouilly-Fumé Villa Paulus, Domaine Masson-Blondelet, £9.95, Christopher Piper Wines (white, Loire)
Long, long before they invented New Zealand Sauvignon, the guys at Pouilly in the Loire Valley were doing the business with the Sauvignon grape. This lovely ripe but mouthwatering white shows how: a splash of gooseberry and nettle, a touch of lime zest, a handful of chalk and a sweet memory of honeysuckle carried on the evening breeze.

❻ 1998 Riesling, St Hallett, Eden Valley, £8.99, Australian Wine Club (white, Australia)
South Australia's Eden Valley has gained a reputation for invigorating, perfumed Rieslings. This one is so full of lime zest acid, lime flower perfume and apple purée mixed with lime marmalade that you begin to wonder what fruit they actually grow up there in the Valley.

❼ 1999 Sauvignon Blanc Life from a Stone, Springfield Estate, Robertson, £6.65, Bibendum (white, South Africa)
Aggressive enough to have your eyeballs juddering in their sockets. But if that turns you on, this is an excellent stone-dry assault force of grapefruit, lime zest and nettles.

❽ 1999 Riesling, Clifford Bay, Marlborough, £6.99, Friarwood (white, New Zealand)
The way New Zealand Rieslings should be: a beguiling blend of mouthwatering lime acid and a soothing fragrance of rose petals.

❾ 1998 Mâcon Milly-Lamartine, Cave de Prissé-Sologny-Verzé, £7.05, Roger Harris Wines (white, Burgundy)
Bright, fresh, melon scented wine, as crunchy as a Cox's Orange Pippin that has been brushed with lime and rolled in new season's Darjeeling tea leaves.

❿ 1998 Riesling Kabinett, Carl Aug. Immich-Batterieberg, Mosel-Saar-Ruwer, £7.95, Adnams (white, Germany)
Perfumed, wonderfully gentle on the tongue, yet just streaked with enough ripe acidity of aniseed and lime to temper the honeyed fruit.

SWEETIES

Rather than choose a whole slew of reasonable, sweetish, vaguely gooey wines, we've plumped for half a dozen absolute crackers

❶ 1998 Ruster Ausbruch Gelber Muskateller, Heidi Schröck, Neusiedlersee Hügelland, £16.60/50cl, Savage Selection (Austria)
One day everyone's going to catch on to the idea that Austria makes many of the world's greatest stickies. If you want proof, snatch a mouthful of this absurdly delicious nectar – thick with honey, crammed with grape and pineapple and blood orange fruit, yet fresh as a springtime flower garden.

❷ 1996 Coteaux du Layon Chaume, Château Pierre-Bise, £11.95, Lea & Sandeman (Loire)
Loire sweeties are some of the unsung glories of France. This delectable example has a sweet core of quince and cling peach ripeness swathed with glycerine and honey.

❸ 1997 Late Harvest Riesling, Chateau des Charmes, Niagara Peninsula, £8.45/half bottle, Nadder Wines (Canada)
The snow may already have blanketed the vineyards when the grapes are picked, and the result is a thrilling pas de deux between acidity and sugar. Here the acidity is like that of a crunchy green apple and the sweetness – with the richness of honey and the scent of a ripe Cox's Orange Pippin – barely dominates the final flavour.

❹ 1997 Coteaux du Layon, Domaine des Forges, £6.95, Adnams (Loire)
Another delightful Loire sweetie, not massively rich, and sprinkled lightly with earth, but rounded out with honey and the faded beauty of loft apples at Christmastime.

❺ 1962 Late Harvest Pinot Gris, SCV Murfatlar, £10.95, Wright Wine (Romania)
A forgotten treasure from Romania. This is nearly 40 years old but it still feels as though it could age more, with its mellow, semi-sweet quince and peach fruit lightly dipped in honey then brushed by the smoke of a Havana cigar.

❻ Moscatel de Valencia, £3.79, Somerfield (Spain)
The old standby sticky. Whenever you need a bargain bottle of something rich and satisfying, this soup of crunchy Muscatel, honey and orange can't be beat.

FORTIFIEDS

We weren't all that taken with a lot of the commercial port and sherry offerings this year, so we have just put together an elite handful of wines that are a little bit special and a little bit different

❶ Joseph 'The Fronti' III, Primo Estate, £16.99/half bottle, Australian Wine Club (Australia)
If you want original off-the-wall flavours, Joe Grilli, sweating away in the heat of the Adelaide Plains, is your man. This is a riproaring shotgun wedding between tawny port and a Mediterranean Muscatel, so rich and powerfully sweet that the dark date and sultana fruit rumbles across your palate and down your throat leaving a gorgeous sticky swathe of Muscat, muscovado sugar and treacle glistening in its wake.

❷ 1996 Dulce Monastrell, Olivares, £14.99, Oddbins (red, Spain)
And another fantastic, inspired creation, this time from Spain. Unbelievably thick and rich, with an intensity of raspberry and blackberry essence that threatens to block

off your air supply until its gross embrace is forced apart by the bitter power of Fowler's Black Treacle and the kick-start perfume of freshly ground black peppercorns.

3 Fino Puerto, Emilio Lustau, £9.20, Morris & Verdin (Spain)
Well at least Morris & Verdin keep their sherry spanking fresh; several other samples should have been similarly appetizing, but weren't. This is the classic appetite tickler: bone dry, marvellously fresh, with a strange, creamy-sour quality like bread yeast, and the scrape of cold, old wood.

4 Palo Cortado Sherry, Harveys, £8.69, John Harvey & Sons (Spain)
Rare but beautiful sherry style. It smells sweet – the sweetness of hazelnuts and dates and brown Manila envelopes. You taste it – it's rich, with buttered brazils and popcorn, but it's dry. Totally, magically dry.

5 Fine White Port, Càlem, £6.99, Unwins (Portugal)
I don't usually much like white port, but this is far more drinkable than most – sweet, slightly spirity, but perfumed with herbs. Trouble is, I can almost feel the headache I'd have after a bottle of this.

FIZZ

I'm not sure I didn't have enough fizz in 2000 to keep me gently foaming at the mouth for several years yet. And maybe our merchants are suffering from Millennium reaction as well, because our sparklers were not particularly brilliant. Still, here's a clutch of bubblies that should hit the spot

1 1994 Marlborough Cuvée Blanc de Blancs, Deutz, £11.99, Oddbins (New Zealand)
This is what Champagnes should taste like, yet this is made 13,000 miles away. Still, it does use the Champagne grapes, the Champagne method and Champagne expertise from Deutz, so I suppose we should expect nothing less than this lovely, foaming oatmeal and crème fraîche flavoured beauty.

2 Champagne Blanc de Blancs Premier Cru Brut, Pierre Gimonnet, £14.99, Oddbins
Good, yeasty Champagne, even if it doesn't seem totally dry, and it really needs a couple more years aging.

3 The Vixen Sparkling Shiraz/Cabernet Franc, Fox Creek, McLaren Vale, £10.99, Noel Young (red, Australia)
When those dread November nights begin to wrap their gloomy arms around you, reach for this ruddy-cheeked bucolic beauty from the Southern Seas. This is a tongue-staining riot of liquorice and black chocolate, squashy plums and herbs. Real red wine with bubbles? Barmy bliss.

4 Champagne Cuvée Chardonnay, Le Brun de Neuville, £14.15, Waterloo Wine
Fresh apple fruit and some yeasty softness that will turn to hazelnuts and brioche with a little more time.

5 Crémant de Loire, Domaine de Nerleux, £7.25, RSJ
In a blind tasting I'd have said this was Champagne. Good fresh crisp apple fruit, but also oatmeal and puffed wheat softness and a titillating twist of pepper.

6 The Wine Society's Private Cuvée Champagne Brut, Alfred Gratien, £17, The Wine Society
Made by Alfred Gratien, one of my fave producers, but this really does need one or two years more age to develop its yeasty, nutty depth. At present it's good but appley and it fizzes pretty fiercely. Just give it time: it'll get there.

MAGNIFICENT MISFITS

We absolutely love some wines and yet when the marks are totted up they just seem to miss out to the brasher crowd-pleasers. Well, here are the not-quite-mainstream mouthfuls that we liked a lot

1 1999 Notios, Gaia Estate, Peloponnese, £5.99, Oddbins (red, Greece)
Gorgeously irresistible red with wonderfully fresh, sweet red cherry fruit and violet and cinnamon scent.

2 1999 Primitivo, A Mano, Puglia, £6.49, Hedley Wright/£5.99 Liberty Wines (red, Italy)
If you want two mouthfuls for the price of one, look no further than this stonker from the heel of Italy; it's a sultry, steaming cauldron of dates and damson skins, marzipan, cloves and briar.

3 1997 Grenache Samuel's Bay, Adam Wynn, South Australia, £6.49, First Quench (red)
Aussie Shiraz is now so well known it's easy to forget that the other great Rhône grape, the Grenache, also does well Down Under. Once you get this boisterous bruiser on your tongue you won't forget its blast of strawberry and ink in a hurry – nor the bite of pepper fresh from the grinder laying into your taste buds.

4 1999 Pinotage, Clos Malverne, Stellenbosch, £6.99, Waitrose (red, South Africa)
Love it or loathe it stuff. This splendid bulldozer of a wine is a turbulent broth of damson fruit and marshmallows burnt on the bonfire and smothered with the brutal kiss of tarpaulin.

5 1997 Chinon les Graves, Gasnier £8.33, Playford Ros (red, Loire)
One of my very favourite styles of red. After creeping to ripeness beneath the cool Loire Valley sun, you can taste the pebbles of the vineyard jostling with the tea bag perfume and the raw blackcurrant and raspberry fruit.

6 1998 Fleurie, Clos de la Roilette, £8.97, Savage Selection (red, Rhône)
Is it possible there is a revival going on among the cloud-capped towers of the real Beaujolais? We've tasted several beauts this year, and here's another, thirst-quenching banana, pear and strawberry fruit lightly wrapped with the more serious aromas of pepper and grilled meat.

7 1996 Valpolicella Superiore Ripassa, Zenato, £7.49, First Quench (red, Italy)
If you've been cruising down the four-lane highway of wine for too long, turn off into this flavour-choked layby and experience this dark primal stew of bitter black chocolate, bitter-sweet morello cherries boiled to within an inch of their life, and the bitter rasp of rosemary and thyme.

8 1998 Soave Classico Superiore Monte Alto, Ca' Rugate Amadeo e Giovanni Tessari, £8.99, Valvona & Crolla (white, Italy)
An unlikely but delicious mishmash of brioche and baked apple cake, leather thongs steeped in lanolin and the haughty aroma of sage and tea rose.

9 1998 Corbières, Domaine de Courtilles, Bernard Schurr, £8.99, Waitrose (red, southern France)
Marvellous, powerful southern French mountain red from a top estate. Muscular, clean-limbed black plum fruit flexed with liquorice, pepper and the furious scented rasp of bay leaf.

10 1996 Costers del Segre, Gotim Bru, Castell del Remei, £5.99, Moreno Wines (red, Spain)
Superripe red, its lovely juice fruit laced with the sweetness of butterscotch and teased with gingerbread spice.

SUPERMARKET SELECTION

What pleased me most about this year was that I was able to lower price ceilings on the wines and still end up with a better range of high street goodies than ever before

Talk of rationalization of retailers, mergers, take-overs by both friendly and hostile groups, disappearance of well-known names abound, and I'm as nervous as the next bloke about loss of choice, homogenization and a creeping escalation of price. But it isn't happening yet.

In fact, the supermarkets seem to be applying their considerable muscle in imaginative and consumer-friendly ways – in the world of wine, at least. As is shown in the wide and enjoyable range of wines at £2.99. As is shown in the excellent cluster of reds and whites at £3.99. As is shown in the exceptional quality of our Superstars, and the consistently enjoyable reserve team of High Street Heroes.

If there's a hero at the lower price levels, it has to be from South America, with Argentina romping to the fore in the budget red stakes. At the top level, the champions of the Old and the New Worlds are slugging it out. France achieved eight places in the top two categories, just beating Australia with seven. But the Superstars? Well five are Aussies, and three more come from South America. The Old World is fighting back, but it'll have one helluva job wresting the consumer crown from the New.

Please bear in mind that wines are not made in infinite quantities – some of these may well sell out, but the following year's vintage should then become available.

SUPERMARKET SUPERSTARS

The supermarkets are becoming more and more dominant in our wine world. But it doesn't seem to be diminishing their ability to buy super wines at the top end of the market. This stellar dozen is full of real crackers

1 1998 Saint-Chinian Cuvée des Fées, Château Cazal-Viel, £6.49, Somerfield (red, southern France)
You want a faceful of gooey plum syrup and loganberries and the sticky richness of dates? Here it is. You want the scratch of tree bark, the fragrance of bay leaf and the wild smell of Languedoc hillsides? It's all here in this fabulous dry red. Just get yourself down to Somerfield and buy it.

2 1996 Sotelo Cabernet Sauvignon, Navarra, £6.99, Marks & Spencer (red, Spain)
Oh yes! More like this one, PLEASE!!! This is a walloping great splurge of blackcurrant and buttermilk, mint and a grainy dusty depth as dark as coal. Well done M&S for catching hold of one of Spain's greatest winemakers and squeezing his juicy genius into the bottle.

3 1998 Sierra Los Andes Reserve Merlot/Cabernet, Curicó £6.99, Marks & Spencer (red, Chile)
And again! Alvaro Espinoza Duran is one of Chile's most thrillingly talented young tyros and he's made a magnificent monster here – bulging with muscular plum and pepper power, brooding tannin and sweet, syrupy oak. It's almost as though someone had made a Bordeaux Classed Growth in the foothills of the Andes, except it's £6.99 not £26.99.

4 1996 Merlot/Cabernet Franc/Cabernet Sauvignon, Rymill, Coonawarra, £7.99, ASDA (red, Australia)
Lovely mature Coonawarra Cab. Beautifully restrained for an Aussie, almost austere. But you can't keep the lid on Aussie fruit for long, and out it bounces: crunchy raw blackcurrant, a leaf or two of mint and the polished elegance of sandalwood.

5 1998 Vin de Pays d'Oc Grand Cuvée Chardonnay, Laroche, £5.49, Budgens (white, southern France)
Made by one of the maestros of Chablis, Michel Laroche, down in the south of France: he's clearly revelling in having some really ripe fruit to play with for once, and he's produced a really classy white, dripping with lovely fresh fruit and excellent, toasty, spicy oak.

6 1996 Ribera del Duero Crianza, Bodegas Fuentespina, £7.49, ASDA (red, Spain)
Some of Europe's most distinctive reds are coming from Ribera del Duero in northern Spain. They're not cheap, but they really do deliver. This one mixes a brilliantly savoury quality, like grilled hazelnuts soused in melted butter, with an incredibly mouthwatering dry blackcurrant fruit and mint leaf perfume.

7 1997 Pinot Noir Relativo, Viña Gracia, Bió-Bió Valley, £7.99, CWS (red, Chile)
Delightful scented Pinot Noir is rare enough in Burgundy, its birthplace, but to find it at £7.99 from Chile is exciting. A lovely gentle soothing texture and a perfume of wild strawberries make for a seriously sophisticated mouthful.

8 1998 Grenache, McLaren Vale, £5.99, Tesco (red, Australia)
This is the kind of rip-roaring stuff that gives wine-drinking a good name – although I can't vouch for all wine drinkers' behaviour if they lay in to this one too enthusiastically. This beautiful bruiser is a great wodge of strawberry syrup, sprinkled with pulverized rock and summer dust, and you can't get it near your mouth without realizing it is full of alcoholic power.

9 1999 Chardonnay, Tatachilla, Padthaway, £6.49, Safeway (white, Australia)
It's the texture of this that gets me going. Padthaway is an Australian region that always produces wines with a syrupy, waxy, mouthfilling quality, and if you ally that to some soft pineapple and white peach fruit – saved from blowsiness by a fine film of summer dust – you've got a beaut of a Chardie.

10 1999 Chardonnay, Lindemans, South Eastern Australia, £4.99, Marks & Spencer (white, Australia)
This is altogether a lighter, less in-yer-face style, but it is exactly what most people want when they think of Aussie Chardonnay: soft, round pear and banana fruit, gentle clove spice and just a hint of bacon smoke from the oak.

11 1999 Chardonnay Reserve, Bright Brothers, San Juan, £5.49, CWS (white, Argentina)
And another interpretation of Chardonnay, this time by an Aussie based in Portugal but working in Argentina. This is fairly full, but not heavy, the fruit is melon and apple and pear, and the oak swims in a toasty, grilled nuts swirl that reminds me more than a little of Burgundy.

12 1999 Mighty Murray Cabernet Sauvignon/Merlot, Andrew Peace Wines, Victoria, £4.49, ASDA (red, Australia)
Good, characterful, power-packed red. The fruit is exactly that mouthwatering blackcurrant that Australia does so well, but this time there's the added pleasure of eucalyptus leaves and mint and a snappy lime zest acidity.

HIGH-STREET HEROES

Another lovely medley of fruit and oak and I-feel-good flavours here – and over half of them are less than a fiver a bottle

❶ 1999 Sierra Alta Tempranillo, La Mancha, £4.29, Somerfield (red, Spain)
Portuguese-based Aussie Peter Bright makes wine just about anywhere you can fly a plane to, but this time he has just hopped over the border to Spain and produced a light red, finely balanced between being sweet and being savoury, but eventually dominated by the fruit: sour cherry, banana cream and pink, perfumy apple jelly.

❷ 1998 Beaumes de Venise, £5.49. Somerfield (red, Rhône)
This Rhône village is best known for making lovely perfumed sweet whites, but most of its wine is beefy red; this powerful, dusty, herb-strewn mouth-stainer is a good example of Beaumes-de-Venise's more masculine side.

❸ 1999 Tasmanian Chardonnay, £6.99, Tesco (white, Australia)
Really interesting Chardie from Pipers Brook, one of Tasmania's best producers. Although it is Australian it doesn't taste like it. Why? Well, Tasmania is way off south towards Antarctica, where the winds battle with the sunshine to keep a chill in the air. The result is fruit which is fully ripe, but instead of tropical fruits, the ripeness is almost like peach stones and pear skins washed with honeysuckle.

❹ 1999 Alsace Gewurztraminer, £5.99, Somerfield (white, Alsace)
Delightful white made by the generally reliable Turckheim co-op. It's scented with orange blossom and rose petals and the perfumed soap in a country house hotel bathroom. It doesn't taste like the soap, I promise – it just smells like it – and it's a lovely scented white well worth trying to pronounce!

❺ 1999 Vin de Pays d'Oc Viognier Reserve, Tramontane, £4.99, ASDA (white, southern France)
This should be equally scented, but in fact it smells a bit flat. But it tastes good, like a soft lemon and apricot jelly baby – if there is such a thing – and there's a peck of pepper too.

❻ 1999 Far Flung Cabernet Sauvignon/Merlot, £4.99, ASDA (red, Argentina)
The only thing wrong with this gutsy red is a touch too much bitter tannin. But pour yourself a mugful as you pull a big, juicy steak off the barbie and you'll discover a good wodge of savoury plum and spicy pudding fruit – and you won't even notice the tannin.

❼ 1998 Sierra los Andes Merlot/Cabernet £4.99, Marks & Spencer (red, Chile)
Here's Alvaro Espinoza Duran again, with the lighter version of wine number 3 in the Superstars. This is just what you want a Chilean red to be – full of blackcurrant and dark plum fruit, softened by a slice or two of buttered-toast oak and kept serious by the rough kiss of tannin.

❽ 1997 Australian Shiraz, £4.99, Sainsbury's (red)
This is just absurdly easy to enjoy. With its irresistible flavour of fudge and chocolate brownies, prune juice and spice you'd be forgiven for thinking it was sweet.

❾ 1998 Negroamaro/Cabernet Sauvignon, Roman Vines, Bright Brothers, £4.49, Somerfield (red, Italy)
Globetrotting Peter Bright has produced a powerful southern Italian red, pulsating with dark, sweet fruit that's verging on the

overripeness of dates and sultanas, and yet it never loses a fresh streak of acid and the uplifting summer scent of hot earth.

⑩ 1998 Dâo, Dom Ferraz, £4.99, Budgens (red, Portugal)
Trust good old Portugal to come up with something different – a big, serious red full of the bone-dry flavours of cracked black pepper, blackberry, celery and finely polished leather.

⑪ 1998 Vin de Pays d'Oc Oak Aged Chardonnay, Domaine Sainte Agathe, £5.29, Somerfield (white, southern France)
A fairly rich style of Chardonnay. The makers have clearly used quite a bit of oak, because there's a fatness like cream and the flesh of a brazil nut, but the fruit's nice, too, and there's even a suggestion of floral perfume.

⑫ 1997 Terrace View Cabernet Sauvignon/Merlot, £4.79, CWS (red, New Zealand)
New Zealand reds aren't everyone's cup of tea, but if you don't mind a streak of leafy greenness, a vaguely nettly sting and a sharpness like a blade of grass cutting your finger, this full flavoured, blackcurranty red is a pretty good drink.

⑬ 1998 Château Saint Robert, Graves, £6.99, Somerfield (red, Bordeaux)
Somerfield have persisted with this wine for quite a while, keeping the price constant and the quality consistent. At a time when few red Bordeaux get anywhere near the winning line-up in our tastings, this red – with dark blackcurranty fruit, slightly buttery oak, but above all a pebbly dryness – is worth a try.

⑭ 1999 Cabernet Sauvignon/Shiraz, Adiseño, £4.99, CWS (red, Argentina)
If I were a steak and a bottle of this were open, I'd be nervous. It's a deep, brawny red that's a bit tannic, so it's better with food than without, but it has a hedonistic heart of rich, stewed black plums and toffee.

⑮ 1999 Viognier, Cono Sur, £4.99, Somerfield (white, Chile)
Ideally with Viognier you get a perfumed smell and taste. Well, you can't win 'em all – this doesn't smell of much, but it does have a nice succulent apricot flavour dusted down with talc.

⑯ 1998 Corbières Côte 125, Courtilles, £5.49, Somerfield (red, southern France)
Big, assertive dry red, its ripe cherry fruit swished and whipped with bay leaf and the scent of hillside herbs.

⑰ 1998 Sauvignon Blanc, Oyster Bay, Marlborough, £6.99, Safeway (white, New Zealand)
I've had better Kiwi Sauvignons from the 1999 vintage, but there's nice melon fruit and a fair rasp of lime zest and nettles, so it'll do.

⑱ 1998 Atlantic Vines Baga, Bright Brothers, £4.49, Somerfield (red, Portugal)
You want wild? This is wild – grilled meat, bilberry syrup, toffee, tomatoes and smoke. It's coarse, it's crude and it's in a shop near you.

⑲ 1999 Campo Ran Garnacha, £3.99, Marks & Spencer (red, Spain)
A smashing, tub-thumping red made by Telmo Rodriguez, one of Europe's most imaginative winemakers. Hold on to your hats for a barnstorming mouthful of apples and dates, strawberries, bay leaf and plum.

⑳ 1999 Emerald Sauvignon Blanc, £3.99, Tesco (white, Hungary)
No one makes good cheap Sauvignon Blanc as well as the Hungarians. This is an aggressive, barbed-wire bundle of nettles and lime zest and Bramley apples to spring-clean your tonsils.

THE ECONOMY CLASS

We've never been presented with so many delicious wines at the £3.99 level. King of the hill here is without question South America

❶ 1998 Riverview Kékfrankos, £3.99, Safeway (red, Hungary)
Hungarian reds have a unique range of flavours, so, if you're up to it, take a blast of this gorgeous, shocking marriage of celery and white pepper, sweetened up with strawberry fruit gums.

❷ 1998 Argentinian Bonarda, £3.79, ASDA (red, Argentina)
The face of the future for lush, juicy, basic red wines to hoover down by the jugful. 1998, 1999 or 2000, the vintage hardly matters, though I'd prefer it younger rather than older. It's the Turkish delight and soft red-cherry fruit, roughened up by a whiff of tomato and tobacco, that I go for.

❸ 1999 Vin de Pays d'Oc Chardonnay, La Cité, £3.99, Waitrose (white, southern France)
Why can't more French Chardonnay be like this, combining New World cleanness and freshness with Old World subtlety? Ah well, at least enjoy this delightful perfumed dry white with its bright melon and apple fruit and creamy soft texture.

❹ 1999 Argentine Sangiovese, £3.99, Somerfield (red)
Splendid, powerful stuff. Sangiovese is the main grape of Chianti in Italy, but I wonder if I'd ever really tasted it ripe until I discovered the Argentine examples: ruddy red, puffed up with cherry fruit and rosehip syrup, but also roughened by a nice rasp of tannin.

❺ 1999 Argentine Tempranillo, £3.99, Somerfield (red)
Well, if the Argentines can do it for the Italian Sangiovese grape, they can do it for the Spanish Tempranillo, too. This is a big, juicy wine full of squashy banana and strawberry fruit, butterfat and herbs. It would dance a mean tango partnered with a sirloin steak, seared on the outside, pink on the inside.

❻ 1999 Long Slim Red Cabernet/Merlot, £3.79, CWS (red, Chile)
Over the Andes to Chile for a different kind of red, one that hums with blackcurrant throat pastille fruit and a grainy, meaty texture. Spot-on Chilean red – and cheap!

❼ Chilean Sauvignon Blanc, £3.99, Sainsbury's (white)
And here's a sparkling fresh white from Chile. Really tangy nettle, passion fruit and lime aggression, but there's a soothing sweetness to the fruit that shows you the grapes were properly ripe.

❽ Cabernet Sauvignon/Malbec, Mendoza, £3.99, Sainsbury's (red, Argentina)
Well, this is turning into the South America show now. Another really tasty number from Argentina – black plums and a swipe of herbs in a full, beefy wine. Bordeaux weight meets Argentine ripeness.

❾ Australian Chardonnay, £3.99, Sainsbury's (white)
It's about time another country got in on the act, and, typically, it's Australia. But less typically, we haven't seen much decent £3.99 Aussie Chardie for a while. This is gentle-textured stuff with mild peach and banana fruit scented with cinnamon and honey.

❿ 1999 Torrontés, Caballo de Plata, £3.99, Safeway (white, Argentina)
Well, what a surprise! Back to South

America. But another surprise is the delightful mega-perfumed Torrontés grape that gives a full-bodied wine with nice fresh acidity and a basketful of melon and white peach fruit, with ginger and nutmeg spice.

11 1999 Cape Ruby Cabernet, £3.99, CWS (red, South Africa)
Ruby Cabernet is not a cabaret artiste. In fact the flavour of Ruby is anything but slinky and sexy, having a serious Bordeaux-like earthiness that is here happily matched by grassy acidity and dry red plum fruit.

12 1999 Chenin Blanc, Ryland's Grove, £3.99, Tesco (white, South Africa)
Chenin is an overlooked grape, but South Africa has oodles of it, and when looked after properly it comes up with a mellow wine with goldengage fruit, apple freshness and a little dusty honey richness.

13 1999 Shiraz/Ruby Cabernet, South Eastern Australia, £3.99, Safeway (red)
Attractive Aussie red with stewed plums, prunes, toffee fudge and spice. No hard edges, just a lovely soft centre.

14 1999 Rio Santos Bonarda/Barbera, £3.99, Marks & Spencer (red, Argentina)
A couple of Italian grapes, made more succulent and approachable under the blazing Argentine sun. Perfumed fruit, plum and date richness and perhaps just a little too much oak.

15 1999 Old Vines Carignan, £3.99, CWS (red, Chile)
For an old bruiser like Carignan, this is positively well mannered – not subtle, but good dry wine with a certain toffee softness and a whiff of spice.

16 Chilean Merlot, Central Valley, £3.99, Tesco (red)
Good, typical Chilean Merlot – dead straight blackcurrant and coffee bean scent with some leafy freshness tempering a deep inky ripeness.

17 1998 Portada, £3.99, Somerfield (red, Portugal)
Interesting, original flavours that only Portugal produces. Dusty spices, sweet-sour damson and cranberry fruit and a smudgy richness rather like cherry cake.

18 1999 Argentinian Cabernet Sauvignon, £3.99, Safeway (red)
Fairly powerful mouthful for £3.99: no great complexity but a splash of deep plum fruit and toasty oak.

19 1999 Reggiano Rosso Single Estate, £3.99, Marks & Spencer (red, Italy)
Fascinating sort of semi-wine. This is the still version of what used to be Lambrusco and it's well worth a try for its bright, rosy-cheeked personality and banana split and pear juice taste.

20 1999 Chilean Cabernet Sauvignon, £3.99, Safeway (red, Chile)
Not top-notch Chilean Cab – it doesn't have the crystal clarity of the best examples – but it has got some nice plum and blackcurrant fruit, a green grass streak and a suggestion of mint.

21 Alteza 640 Oaked Viura, £3.99, Sainsbury's (white, Spain)
Rather good wine from a slightly dull Spanish grape. Pale fruit, soft spice and a touch of the perfume of violet cachou icing on party biscuits.

22 Chardonnay, Tupungato Region, £3.99, Sainsbury's (white, Argentina)
Nice, bright New World style – not memorable, but pleasant apple and nut fruit smeared with runny honey.

23 1999 Rio Santos Torrontés, £3.99, Marks & Spencer (white, Argentina)
That fascinating Torrontés grape, this time managing to conjure up flavours of white peach, pear and lime zest and mix them up with Bay Rum hair oil. And if you can remember that, you *are* showing your age.

BARGAIN BASEMENT

Last year we upped our price ceiling to £3.49. This year there were so many good bottles at £2.99 that we moved it back down again. Two things stood out: the Old World, in particular France, Italy and Hungary, dominates this section; and over half the wines had artificial closures rather than traditional corks and were fresher and fruitier because of them

1 1999 Matra Springs, £2.99, Waitrose (white, Hungary)
Delightful dry white with gentle floral perfume and a lively lime zest acidity from Hungary – Europe's best supplier of good, cheap whites.

2 1999 Vin de Pays du Comté Tolosan House Red, £2.99, Marks & Spencer (southern France)
Lovely mellow red made from little-known grapes like Negrette and Tannat in a blend with Gamay that combines gentle strawberry and plum fruit with a flicker of leafy bite. [Plastic cork]

3 Hungarian Red, £2.99, CWS
It's not just whites that Hungary can do. This is a bright, light red bursting with character and managing to mix together an unlikely gypsy soup of apples and red plums with the crunch of celery and the smack of white pepper.

4 South African Red, £2.99, Tesco
Excellent basic red that nonetheless has a strong South African personality of red fruit, lava dust and slightly burnt marshmallows. [Plastic cork]

5 1999 Karalta Australian Dry Red, £2.99, ASDA
Really nice easy-drinking stuff: light and mild but not short of character, showing a sweet plum fruit, a whiff of kitchen spice and just a dusting of pepper. [Plastic cork]

6 1999 Corbières, £2.99, Safeway (red, southern France)
Good, sturdy, chewy red. It's a bit tannic – but it's Corbières, so it's meant to be! Anyway, the fistfuls of ripe fruit, bay leaf perfume and cherry cake finish cope easily with all that tough stuff.

7 1999 Vin de Pays du Gers, £2.99, Marks & Spencer (white, southern France)
Fierce, no-prisoners-taken, tongue-tingling dry white, full of grapefruit and green Bramley apples and enough acidity to make your eyeballs shiver. [Plastic cork]

8 1998 Chianti, £2.99, Tesco (red, Italy)
Decent Chianti at £2.99? Impossible? Well, no, actually. This isn't raw, this isn't tannic, but it is obviously Tuscan, with a nice, direct, dry cherrystone style.

9 1999 Woodcutters White, £2.99, Safeway (white, Hungary)
The grape variety is unpronounceable, so they call it Woodcutters White. But it's not as rugged as the name suggests: in fact it's a very easy-going, breezy, bright glugger.

10 1999 Karalta Australian Dry White, £2.99, ASDA
Nice, attractive, slightly sherbety Aussie white. I'd prefer a little more fruit, but it is only £2.99. [Plastic cork]

11 Provincia di Verona Rosso, £2.99, Sainsbury's (red, Italy)
Great picnic red in a screwtop bottle. Forget the corkscrew and get going on this refreshing, not completely dry mouthful of strawberry, ripe tomato and leafy acidity. [Screwtop]

12 Soave, £2.49, Tesco (white, Italy)
And if you want picnic white at a giveaway price, this is bright, simple and appley as a

fresh dry cider with a tiny prickle on the tongue. [Screwtop]

⓭ Claret, £2.99, Budgens (red, Bordeaux)
Most cheap claret is frightful, but this is a fair mix of butter and earth and a flicker of bone-dry fruit.

⓮ Sicilia White, £2.99, Sainsbury's (Italy)
Dry, bright, soft, clean, with a hint of spice: a totally easy white glugger.

⓯ Côtes du Rhône, £2.99, Tesco (red)
Pleasant light Rhône red, soft red fruit and a touch of herbs from the sun-soaked hillsides. [Plastic cork]

SUPERMARKET FIZZ

There seems to be a bit of a lull on the fizz front at the moment, which is not really surprising in the wake of last year's excesses. Some of our erstwhile favourites were tasting a bit green and raw, but here's a handful that won't have you reaching for the Alka Seltzer

❶ Cava Rosé Brut, £4.99, Somerfield (Spain)
Smashing stuff, with a come-hither pink hue, lots of strawberry and apple fruit, a bit of toffee softness and a perfume like fresh dried peppercorns.

❷ 1999 South African Sparkling Sauvignon Blanc, £4.99, Tesco
I wish more people would use Sauvignon for fizz, because the bubbles marry brilliantly with the coffee bean, pear and blackcurrant leaf flavours of the wine.

❸ Saumur Brut, £6.49, CWS (Loire)
This is much less raw and harsh than most sparkling Saumur. It has a soft, foaming fizz and a slightly toasty mellow taste.

❹ 1995 Australian Chardonnay Brut, £6.99, Somerfield
Pretty mature for a supermarket fizz, with a leather and nuts flavour, but it's not at all tired. Fine for if you're in reflective mood.

❺ Cava, £4.99, Tesco (Spain)
Nice, bright, easy fizz – fresh, simple and fun, flecked with the springtime perfume of apple blossom.

❻ Vin Mousseux Merlot-Gamay Brut, Le Baron de Monceny, £4.99, Safeway (red, France)
This is pretty mad stuff. It's red and will stain your carpet if you open it carelessly. But the risk is worth it because it's bubbling over with plum and blackberry fruit.

SUPERMARKET CHAMPAGNE

Don't believe anyone who tells you there's a shortage of Champagne at the moment. There isn't. The warehouses are packed full of the stuff the shops bought for Millennium night but didn't sell. A lot of it is pretty mean stuff, but here are a few that still do the business.

❶ NV Brut, £14.99, Waitrose
This really is classy stuff – at a truly excellent price. A very attractive gentle foaming style of Champagne with a lovely deep, smooth flavour of biscuit and brioche.

❷ NV Prince William Premier Cru Brut, £13.99, Somerfield
Somerfield's own-label fizz is always good, and this year is no exception – soft and foaming, with that classic flavour of nuts and Sugar Puffs just peeking out.

3 1990 Brut, £17.99, Waitrose
This particular vintage Champagne is still quite young, with strong acidity, but the biscuit and the brioche flavours are starting to show and this well-made little number will continue to improve for several years.

4 NV Prince William Rosé, £14.99, Somerfield
Attractive salmon-pink fizz. It's got quite a mature strawberry flavour and some pleasing syrupy softness. That's a good thing here: you don't want a pink fizz that stings.

5 NV Prince William Blanc de Noirs Brut, £11.99, Somerfield
Blanc de Noirs is a dry style of Champagne, but has a rich feeling to it because it's made of black grapes, despite being white in colour. The flavour? Peach and bruised apple fruit and a crumb or two of biscuit.

6 1993 Special Cuvée, Albert Etienne, £16.99, Safeway
A perennially reliable supermarket own-label. This comes from the unexciting 1993 vintage, but they've made a good job of it and the wine is ready to drink with some loft-apple fruit and nutty softness.

SUPERMARKET SWEETIES

Lots of good stuff here, ranging from Mr. Reliable, Moscatel de Valencia, up to some really impressive and keenly priced special stickies. And do try the fizzy Moscatos. They're ace

1 1996 Botrytis Semillon, Cranswick Estate, Riverina, £4.99/half bottle, ASDA (Australia)
Wow! This is the business! Pineapple and barleysugar richness, the smooth caress of lanolin, a hint of tobacco and some eye-opening acidity – a magnificent mouthful of Aussie goo.

2 1997 Muscat de Rivesaltes, Domaine Brial, £4.49/half bottle, Safeway (southern France)
Delightful, eager-to-please sweetie. Gooey hothouse Muscatel grapes, crunchy comb honey as well as a hint of orange blossom and a sprinkling of rather good talc.

3 1997 Monbazillac, Domaine du Haut-Rauly, £3.99/half bottle, CWS (southern France)
Monbazillac is almost a neighbour of the far more famous Sauternes, yet manages to make excellent rich wine for a fraction of the price. This isn't particularly fragrant, but has a lovely waxy consistency and a richness of butterscotch and pineapple.

4 1996 Saussignac, Domaine Léonce Cuisset, £9.99, Sainsbury's (southern France)
Another Sauternes neighbour making seriously classy stuff. This is full, fat and succulent, overflowing with honey, peach syrup and the perfume of cloves.

5 1998 Kirchheimer Schwarzerde Beerenauslese, Zimmerman-Graeff, £3.99/half bottle, CWS (Germany)
This is always one of the best sweet wines on the market – real, genuinely rich German wine, not sugar water, with a lusciousness of barleysugar and pineapple syrup that fairly swamps the throat.

6 Moscato d'Asti, Villa Jolanda, £3.49, Tesco (sparkling, Italy)
Many people look down their noses at sweet sparkling Moscato. More fool them: this is such a refreshing and adaptable dessert wine, bubbling over with grape and honeysuckle and candyfloss sweetness, freshened up with white peach and blood orange and scented with tobacco.

7 Moscatel de Valencia, £3.99, Sainsbury's (Spain)
Moscatel de Valencia is the most reliable of all budget stickies. You can tell the style by the colour in the bottle. This is quite dark, so you get a full, fat wine tasting of breakfast marmalade and honey.

8 1999 Moscatel de Valencia, £3.99, Safeway (Spain)
This is also quite full in colour and even slightly spirity in the mouth, but there's loads of grape and orange and crunchy honey sweetness, so it gets away with it.

9 1999 Moscatel de Valencia, £3.99, Marks & Spencer (Spain)
This is the lightest and brightest of the three Moscatels: it's rich and honeyed with pleasant peach syrup and orange sweetness.

10 Moscato Spumante, £3.99, CWS (sparkling, Italy)
Go on, give it a try! Lovely breezy elderflower, pear and hothouse grape sweetness – all this, and bubbles too!

SUPERMARKET FORTIFIEDS

We were pretty unimpressed with the majority of the fortifieds we tasted this year. Tawny ports that weren't remotely tawny and dry sherries that had lost both dryness and freshness were the main problem. Dumbing down? Cost cutting? A bit of both, I fear. Still, these ones make the grade

1 Warre's 1987 Quinta da Cavadinha Vintage Port, £20.49, Somerfield
Expensive in supermarket terms, but by far the best port in our tasting, so well done to Somerfield for snapping it up. Really good deep, rich blackberry and Harrogate toffee, pepper and herbs all flailing about together. Splendid, sexy, satisfying.

2 Solera Reserva Dry Oloroso Sherry £5.59, Waitrose
Thank goodness for this. A classic sherry style – packed with hazelnuts, treacle, toffee and herbs, lovely, rich coffee bean flavours, and yet it's dry. Smashing.

3 Fino Sherry, £4.85, Waitrose
Made by Caballero, the best producer of own-label sherries, but this year we found only the Waitrose version was on song. This is what I'm looking for in a fino sherry: it's tangy but soft; bone dry but with an attractive bread and apple freshness.

4 1994 LBV Port, Smith Woodhouse, £7.59, Safeway
Made by Smith Woodhouse, who are the best own-label port producers and do an excellent Unfiltered LBV of their own. This is not up to that standard, but it is a big rich mouthful of mulberry, prune and pepper – black-hearted and good.

5 10-Year-Old Tawny Port, Smith Woodhouse, £10.69, Safeway
Smith Woodhouse doing the goods with a russet amber-coloured tawny showing the beginnings of a classic sweetness that hovers between hazelnuts, raisins and a new manila envelope.

6 Fine Tawny Port, Smith Woodhouse, £5.89, Safeway
Third of a successful trio from Smith Woodhouse. This is the cheaper tawny and it's not very tawny in style, being a bit rich and powerful, but there is some hazelnut softness to go with the strawberry fruit and peppery rasp.

IDEAL CELLARS

With budgets of £100, £500 and £1000 we asked our contributors to fill their fantasy cellars with wines for everyday pleasure and wines to dream about for years to come. If you think that sounds like fun, a swift calculation will tell you that even £1000 is not a huge sum for a year's drinking, and our guest writers have worked hard to recommend a varied selection that emphasizes exciting, original flavours. They've found wines to thrill you tonight and, occasionally, ten years from now. All except David Gleave have chosen wines exclusively from their own lists. Me – well, what did you expect? I've flown, Puck-like, around the world, picking a miraculous mouthful here, an unmissable flavour sensation there.

LUCY FAULKNER
MORRIS & VERDIN

£100

The beautiful span of France that extends from the southern Rhône to the western Languedoc is an area bursting with wines of real character at very reasonable prices – perfect for everyday drinking. These three wines put a selection of the Rhône Valley's many grape varieties to good use.

1999 Vin de Pays d'Oc Marsanne/Viognier, Domaine de la Cessane (white, southern France)
A cunning blend of crisp, lemony Marsanne and richer, apricot-infused Viognier.
£31.80 for 6

1999 Vin de Pays des Coteaux de Murviel Rosé, Domaine de Limbardie (southern France)
One of the most moreish rosés in the universe and perfect on hot days. Light, refreshing and delicious strawberry fruit.
£31.80 for 6

1998 Côtes du Rhône, Domaine Chaume-Arnaud (red, Rhône)
A surprisingly soft and delicate Côtes du Rhône with juicy cherry and raspberry fruit.
£38.40 for 6

Total cost: £102

£500

Now we can touch on some 'classic' regions while also including some surprises.

Fino Puerto, Emilio Lustau (sherry, Spain)
A classic fino sherry, delicious as an apéritif with almonds and olives. Chill well to make the most of its fresh, salty tang.
£49.68 for 6

1998 Grüner Veltliner Alte Reben, Oberfeld, Dr Unger (white, Austria)
A spicy superstar – medium-bodied, richly textured but dry. An unusually scented varietal: grapefruit and bay leaf with an unmistakable pepperiness.
£101.52 for 12

1998 Mâcon-La Roche Vineuse Blanc, Jeunes Vignes, Domaine du Vieux St-Sorlin (white, Burgundy)
Superbly balanced Mâcon, lightly creamy, with ripe apple fruit and crisp acidity.
£90.72 for 12

1998 Côtes du Roussillon-Villages, 'Les Terrasses', Domaine des Schistes (red, southern France)
The rich, dark chocolaty texture and unmistakable elderberry nose belie this

wine's Roussillon heritage. Full-bodied, with a classic tannic structure fit for short-term aging if you would rather wait.

£88.55 for 12

1998 Big House Red, Bonny Doon (California)
Typically eccentric and eclectic blend from Bonny Doon including Syrah, Mourvèdre, Refosco and Pinot Noir to name but a few. Spicy, cherry-scented, with very soft tannins.

£50.40 for 6

1998 Mercurey, Les Veleys, Domaine François Raquillet (red, Burgundy)
Raquillet produces succulent, sweet-fruited reds. A herbal overlay adds complexity.

£124.20 for 12

Total cost: £505.07

£1000

I have chosen wines that you can either drink now or watch develop in the coming years.

NV Champagne Carte Blanche, André Jacquart
A delicate, creamy Champagne that will benefit from further aging, taking on a lovely toasty richness.

£99 for 6

1998 Zeltinger Sonnenuhr Riesling Spätlese, Selbach-Oster (white, Germany)
A wine of incredible minerality, scented with blossom and acacia. Off-dry in style, it is a fabulous match for food, and will continue to develop over the next ten years.

£75 for 6

1999 Riesling Klaus Smaragd, Weingut Prager (white, Austria)
What a difference between Rieslings from the Mosel in Germany and the Wachau in Austria. The one connection is the sheer minerality of both. This Riesling is full-bodied, warm in alcohol and bone dry, with white peach fruit. Probably best to wait at least a year before drinking.

£121 for 6

1998 Chardonnay, Isabel Estate (white, New Zealand)
A Burgundy lookalike, with quince fruit and an elegant but rich toastiness.

£66 for 6

1999 Jurançon Sec, Domaine Cauhapé (white, southern France)
Unusual and intriguing fruit – grapefruit, lime, apricot – with a zesty acidity that is brilliant at cutting through creamy sauces.

£54 for 6

1998 Monthelie, Domaine Fichet (red, Burgundy)
One of the stars of the awkward 1998 vintage in Burgundy. Attractive red cherry and strawberry fruit and good structure. Drink over the next five years.

£87 for 6

1997 Pinot Noir 'La Détente', Au Bon Climat (red, California)
A Pinot packed tight with impressive dense fruit, lovely vanilla oak and the capacity to go on and on.

£119.40 for 6

1998 Cornas, Domaine de Fauterie (red, Rhône)
A fabulous Cornas from one of the greatest vintages in the area this century. Dark purple colour, forward, spicy, peppery nose and ripe blackberry fruit.

£87 for 6

1996 Alión, Bodegas Alión (red, Spain)
Full-bodied, herb-infused Tempranillo with delicious fruit so ripe it is almost sweet.

£114 for 6

1990 Vouvray Moelleux Trie, Bourillon Dorléans (white, Loire)
A stunning, botrytis-infused, rich, sweet Chenin Blanc with its balancing acidity that prevents any cloying stickiness and gives the wine an almost indefinite shelf-life.

£174 for 6

Total: £996.40

BILL ROLFE
UNWINS

£100

Easy-drinking wines from four countries: two New World and two Old World.

1999 Semillon, Canepa, Cachapoal (white, Chile)
Clean, fresh, citrus aromas underline the tropical lime fruit of the Semillon grape.
£21.55 for 6

1999 Chardonnay, Banrock Station, South Eastern Australia (white, Australia)
Gold medal-winning wine which shows what Australia is capable of even at these modest prices. **£21.55 for 6**

1997 Montepulciano d'Abruzzo, Miglianico (red, Italy)
Soft, approachable red with stewed plum and strawberry fruit flavours. **£21.55 for 6**

1994 Viña Albali Reserva, Valdepeñas (red, Spain)
American oak underlines a clean palate full of ripe red fruit balanced by savoury notes.
£26.95 for 6

Total cost: £91.60

£500

These wines all display some of the best characteristics of their provenance and, of course, the grape varietal.

1998 Cabernet Sauvignon, Wakefield, Clare Valley (red, Australia)
A beautifully made wine which is not totally fruit driven and seems to fall between New World and Old World styles.
£75.50 for 12

1998 Cabernet Sauvignon/Merlot, Leef Op Hoop, Stellenbosch (red, South Africa)
We all 'live in hope' that the next bottle of wine will be delicious, just like this blackcurrant-fruited blend.
£75.50 for 12

1997 Zinfandel, De Loach, California (red, United States)
Spicy, zingy fruit which is vibrant and overlaid with vanilla oak. It reminds me of rhubarb and custard! **£91.70 for 12**

1997 Hautes-Côtes de Nuits Tastevinage, Yves Chaley (red, Burgundy)
A good example of pure Pinot fruit from the lesser known Hautes-Côtes de Nuits which lies behind the Côte d'Or proper.
£102.50 for 12

1999 Sauvignon Blanc, Oyster Bay, Marlborough (white, New Zealand)
A modern classic from the new home of Sauvignon: Marlborough. Crisp, highly pitched gooseberry fruit flavours. A perfect match for fish dishes. **£70.10 for 12**

1998 Chardonnay, Raimat, Costers del Segre (white, Spain)
Classic stuff from an area that was once almost desert and is now an oasis of vineyards. **£80.90 for 12**

Total cost: £496.20

£1000

Some old favourites such as Chateau Musar sprinkled with some modern classics such as the Finca Valpiedra from Martínez Bujanda. All these wines will develop and improve with some bottle aging.

1994 Chateau Musar (red, Lebanon)
A great wine that is consistently good vintage after vintage. It will last for years.
£121.94 for 12

1994 Rioja Reserva, Finca Valpiedra, Martínez Bujanda (red, Spain)
This wine will become a collector's item no doubt. From one of the most highly rated Rioja bodegas, Martínez Bujanda.
£205.10 for 12

1998 Côtes du Rhône-Villages Valréas, Domaine de la Grande Bellane (red, Rhône)
Organically produced wine redolent of black fruit and spice. **£73.34 for 12**

1997 Trincadeira, Esporão, Alentejo (red, Portugal)
Australian winemaker David Baverstock surpasses himself with this fantastic berry fruit expression of the Trincadeira grape.
£86.30 for 12 50cl bottles

1996 San Martino, Villa Cafaggio (red, Italy)
Super-Tuscan red from a highly rated estate. It needs time – another two or three years – to develop.
£161.90 for 12

1998 Alsace Tokay-Pinot Gris Cuvée Tradition, Kuentz-Bas (white)
One of the more characterful white wines, this will improve with some bottle aging.
£97.10 for 12

1998 Condrieu, Guigal (white, Rhône)
Made from the exquisite Viognier grape, offering wild peach and apricot notes and fleeting hints of elderflower.
£234.26 for 12

Total cost: £979.94

DAVID GLEAVE
LIBERTY WINES

£100

I like to drink a wide range of styles of wine from many different regions. The recurring theme is top quality fruit expertly transformed into wines of character, balance and length.

1999 Riesling Mount Barker, Plantagenet, Lower Great Southern (white, Australia)
A minerally, dry, steely and intense yet restrained Riesling that has the potential to age wonderfully.
£26.97 for 3, Liberty Wines

1998 Brauneberger Juffer-Sonnenuhr Riesling Spätlese, Fritz Haag (white, Germany)
Haag is one of the world's great white wine makers. His Rieslings from the Mosel have a purity and balance that is remarkable. If you've given up on German wine, buy some of this: it will change your mind.
£15.95, Lay & Wheeler

1999 Valpolicella Classico, Allegrini (red, Italy)
Young, exuberant and eminently quaffable, from one of Italy's great estates.
£6.99, Valvona & Crolla

1999 Tempranillo Finca El Retiro, Mendoza (red, Argentina)
This wine shows the potential that exists in Argentina. It has an intensity of fruit that few other countries can match.
£5.49, Waitrose

1998 Chianti Rufina, Selvapiana (red, Italy)
Archetypal Chianti: rich yet austere with a tingling acid bite on the finish.
£8.99, Liberty Wines

1998 Coteaux du Languedoc Pic St-Loup Cuvée Les Escarboucles, Château l'Euzière (red, southern France)
Few southern French wines can match the richness and oak balance displayed by this fine example.
£16.98 for 2, Unwins

1998 Pinot Noir Mount Barker/ Pemberton, Plantagenet, Lower Great Southern (red, Australia)
A Pinot Noir with remarkable balance and length.
£23.90 for 2, Liberty Wines

Total cost: £105.27

£500

21 bottles for £500 means quality over quantity.

1990 Jacquesson Grand Vin Signature Champagne
Stunning Champagne, dry yet rich, with remarkable acid balance.
£60 a bottle, Mayfair Cellars

1999 Riesling Watervale, Mount Horrocks, Clare Valley (white, Australia)
Perfumed and delicate yet intense and balanced. And if you forget a few bottles, they will age wonderfully.
£68.94 for 6, Liberty Wines

1998 Langhe Bianco, Aldo Vajra (white, Italy)
A rarity – a Riesling from the land of Barolo. And a pretty convincing one at that.
£19.95, Liberty Wines

1998 Condrieu Coteau de Chéry, André Perret (white, Rhône)
One of the greatest white wines produced.
£53.90 for 2, Bennett's

1995 Côte-Rôtie, Domaine Clusel-Roch (red, Rhône)
Few wines have such innate balance as this one. Not a blockbuster, but stunning.
£56.85 for 3, Lea & Sandeman

1998 Langi Shiraz, Mount Langi Ghiran, Victoria (red, Australia)
Aussie Shiraz at its best: concentrated and big, with pepper and spice fruit dominating the oak. **£59.85 for 3, Liberty Wines**

1996 La Poja, Allegrini, Veneto (red, Italy)
Intense, persistent and complete.
£83.85 for 3, Liberty Wines

1996 Barolo Vigna Cicala, Aldo Conterno (red, Italy)
Aldo Conterno is a great winemaker, Cicala one of the best vineyards in the Langhe and 1996 one of the best recent vintages.
£95.90 for 2, Liberty Wines

Total cost: £499.24

£1000

Another meagre crop: 28 bottles for £1,000. But all are wines that magnificently repudiate the UK market's obsession with price points and compromised quality.

1997 Bâtard-Montrachet, Blain-Gagnard (white, Burgundy)
Top white Burgundy. Its combination of intensity and elegance sets it apart.
£124.22 for 3, Haynes Hanson & Clark

1998 Friuli Isonzo Chardonnay 'Vie di Romans', Vie di Romans (white, Italy)
Gianfranco Gallo produces some of Italy's best white wines, and this Burgundy ringer is probably the country's top Chardonnay.
£53.85 for 3, Liberty Wines

1996 Clos des Lambrays, Domaine des Lambrays (red, Burgundy)
Young but great red Burgundy.
£110 for 3, Haynes Hanson & Clark

1997 Sassicaia, Tuscany (red, Italy)
The original super-Tuscan – and still unsurpassed. 1997 promises to be one of the fabled vintages like 1990, and the 1998 to follow will be even better.
£165 for 3, Liberty Wines

1998 Solengo, Argiano, Tuscany (red, Italy)
This is only the fourth vintage of Argiano's flagship wine, but it is already a Tuscan classic. **£120 for 3, Liberty Wines**

1997 Flaccianello della Pieve, Fontodi, Tuscany (red, Italy)
Sangiovese seldom achieves such quality, probably because it is seldom planted in such sites as Fontodi's.
£86.85 for 3, Liberty Wines

1998 Cepparello, Isole e Olena, Tuscany (red, Italy)
Another great Sangiovese in a series of classics from one of Italy's greatest devotees of the vineyard.
£105 for 3, Liberty Wines

1995 Barolo Gran Bussia, Aldo Conterno (red, Italy)
The most complete Barolo of them all. The first vintage released since 1990, so eagerly anticipated by addicts like myself.
£100 a bottle, Liberty Wines

1997 Passito della Rocca, Pieropan, Veneto (sweet, Italy)
Pieropan's sweet wines age slowly and wonderfully, and this is one of the best, with flavours of apricots mingling with the honeyed fruit.
£67.47 for 3 (50cl) bottles, Liberty Wines

1999 Botrytis Riesling Reka, Kim Crawford, Marlborough (sweet, New Zealand)
A stunning sweet wine – all botrytis and honey, yet with superb balance.
£56.85 for 3 (50 cl) bottles, Liberty Wines

Total cost: £989.24

MARK SAVAGE M.W.

SAVAGE SELECTION

£100

At this level I am looking for wines that are without faults but not dull. Everyday wines should be refreshing, attractive and not too assertive. You must be able to drink them on a regular basis without getting tired of them.

1999 Vin de Pays des Cotes de Gascogne, Domaine de Bergerayre (white, southern France)
Crisp, refreshing white from the Armagnac country in south-western France.
£52.80 for 12

1998 Vin de Pays du Gard, Mas Montel (red, southern France)
This blend of Merlot with a little Syrah and Grenache is the perfect compromise for lovers of Bordeaux and Rhône wines. It tastes as if it should cost over £7 a bottle instead of less than £5.
£52.80 for 12

Total cost: £105.60

£500

With £500 to spend you can explore the enormous potential for variety that is available to the wine enthusiast today. Here you can find wines for most moods, meals and occasions, wines that transcend the facile flavours of everyday single-varietal wines such as Chardonnay and Cabernet and venture into more interesting pastures.

1999 Bergerac Blanc Sec, Château les Miaudoux (white, southern France)
Succulent dry white wine from Sauvignon and Sémillon grapes. Like a Sancerre but with a twist of honey to balance the gooseberries and redcurrants. **£23.52 for 4**

1998 Beaujolais Blanc Chardonnay 'En Fût', Jean-Paul Brun (white, Burgundy)
A producer who knows how to make both red and white Beaujolais with elegance and finesse. This is affordable white Burgundy with the style and class of a Meursault.
£34.48 for 4

1990 Rioja, Viña Gravonia, Lopez de Heredia (white, Spain)
Classic traditional white Rioja like this has become a rarity, outflanked in the modern marketplace by the overstandardized international fruit- and/or oak-driven styles of so much Chardonnay and Sauvignon Blanc.
£37.60 for 4

1999 Pinot Gris, Margrain Vineyards, Martinborough (white, New Zealand)
The potential for Pinot Gris was the revelation of my last trip to NZ. This is from a new estate in the particularly desirable district of Martinborough at the south end of the North Island. Much more intriguing than the ubiquitous NZ Sauvignon Blanc.
£55.60 for 4

1993 Chardonnay, Vickers Vineyard, Idaho (white, United States)
Kirby Vickers grows nothing but Chardonnay on his plot near the Snake River. The climate has proved itself perfect for wines with ripeness and natural acidity. This is not just another international-style Chardonnay: it has as much class, originality and sense of place as a Chablis Grand Cru. Drink it now or watch it evolve very slowly over the next 20 years. **£50.12 for 4**

1998 Ruster Ausbruch, Heidi Schröck, Burgenland (white, Austria)
With their ideal combination of sweetness and natural acidity, Austrian wines from small growers like Heidi Schröck are in my book equal at least to the finest dessert wines in the world. **£50 for 4 half bottles**

1999 Fleurie, Clos de la Roilette (red, Burgundy)
This will come as a shock to most drinkers of modern Beaujolais. It's a dark, spicy wine, closer to old-fashioned Burgundy or good Châteauneuf-du-Pape and needs a few years to reach its real peak. **£35.20 for 4**

1998 Minervois, L'Amourier (red, southern France)
Earthy red wine that could only be French, with underlying structure and a proper sense of place. It is restrained and intriguing, with a Burgundian elegance. **£30 for 4**

1996 Bordeaux, Domaine de Cambes (red, Bordeaux)
Classic claret at a sensible price. Drink now or keep for 20 years. **£62 for 4**

1999 Pinot Noir, The Eyrie Vineyards, Oregon (United States)
David Lett pioneered Pinot in the Pacific Northwest and consistently produces delicately delicious wine. **£56.40 for 4**

1997 Pinotage, Vriesenhof, Stellenbosch (red, South Africa)
Really elegant Pinotage. **£35.52 for 4**

1998 Douro Quinta do Crasto (red, Portugal)
An exciting single-vineyard red wine from the Upper Douro. **£27.84 for 4**

Total cost: £498.28

£1000

These five wines are representative of the finest quality in their respective regions, with great potential for longer term aging if so desired.

1995 Champagne Cramant Grand Cru, Larmandier Père & Fils
Cramant is considered one of the greatest of the Champagne villages: this grower's wine shows why. **£253.80 for 6 magnums**

1996 Côtes de Bourg, Château Roc de Cambes, (red, Bordeaux)
The outstanding wine in the Côtes de Bourg, made by François Mitjavile on similar soils to those at his famous Château Tertre Rôteboeuf in St-Émilion. **£258.48 for 12**

1998 Mâcon-Clessé, Domaine de la Bongran (white, Burgundy)
Who needs expensive Meursault and Puligny when they can buy wines of often greater class and concentration from the maestro of the Mâconnais, Jean Thévenet? **£89.28 for 6**

1999 Côte-Rôtie, Montsalier, Château de St-Cosme (red, Rhône)
Owner and winemaker Louis Barruol is surely right to consider that 1999 will go down as a famous vintage for Côte-Rôtie. **£129.24 for 6**

1999 Cabernet Sauvignon, Monte Bello, Ridge (red, United States)
A wine of balance, structure and breathtaking intensity, and power without aggression, that fully deserves to rank alongside the first growths of Bordeaux. Ridge has a track record for class, originality and longevity. **£300 for 6**

Total cost: £1030.80

OZ CLARKE

It's fantasy time. Me and my thirst and the publisher's money. Well, his 'virtual' money. My thirst isn't virtual. I knew there must be a catch

£100

Eastern Europe has got loads of goodies at bargain basement prices. Party time starts on the Danube, with two tongue-tingling whites:
Sauvignon Blanc, Deer Leap, £23.94 for 6, Waitrose (Hungary) *and*
Sauvignon/Feteasca, Willow Ridge, £20.94 for 6, Waitrose (Romania)

Now for some reds. From Austria, a brilliant, crunchy red that veers between cranberry juice and celery sticks but is always sprinkled with white pepper. If that's too 'original', there's a pleasant, simple – and cheap – Bulgarian, full of bright red fruit, and a very attractive, powerful, plummy red from Georgia:
Blauer Zweigelt, Lenz Moser, £23.94 for 6, Tesco (Austria); Domaine Boyar Sapphire Cove, £16.74 for 6, Safeway (Bulgaria); 1998 Matrassa, Caucasus Valley, £11.97 for 3, Safeway (Georgia)

Which means a bottle of lovely, juicy, foamy **Moscato d'Asti, Villa Jolanda, £3.49, Tesco (Italy)** *will push the total up to* **£101.02**.

£500

Here we get serious. Well, not too serious. I fancy some pink, and all I ask is a lovely come-hither hue and a fresh fruity flavour. Here's a pair that fit the bill:
Malbec rosé, Valdivieso, £26.94 for 6, Tesco (Chile) *and* **Cabernet Sauvignon rosé, Valley of the Roses, £20.94 for 6, Safeway (Bulgaria)**

Argentina has some beauties at under 4 quid. For pure, unbridled floral perfume and just a little nip of grapefruit, I'll have this white:
Torrontés, Caballo de Plata, £23.94 for 6, Safeway (Argentina)

But it's the reds that make me salivate with excitement. First, two juicy, perfumed, head-spinning bargains:
Argentinian Bonarda, La Agrícola, Mendoza, £22.74 for 6 *and* **Far Flung Malbec, £26.82 for 6, ASDA; Tesco** *sell the same wines under the* **Picajuan Peak** *label.*

A Kiwi is the winemaker at Orfila and he does a smashing Shiraz and a magnificent Malbec Reserva:
1999 Shiraz Bodegas Rosca, Orfila, £34.14 for 6, Oddbins (red) *and* **1999 Adiseno Malbec Reserva, Orfila, £35.94 for 6, Safeway (red)**

Over the Andes, then, to Chile, where I've picked up a melony unoaked Chardonnay and snappy, pear-juice-streaked Sauvignon:
1999 Chardonnay, La Palmería, £26.94 for 6, First Quench (white) *and* **1999 Sauvignon, Casa Silva, £32.52 for 6, John Harvey (white)**

And both 1999 and 2000 have produced lush, rich reds that overflow with spicy fruit:
1999 Merlot, Concha y Toro, £29.70 for 6, Tanners *and* **1999 Carmenère, Casa Silva, available early 2001, c.£35 for 6, John Harvey**

Back in Europe, first stop is southern France for a couple of organic reds: lovely, herb-strewn Corbières and soft, plummy Merlot:
1998 Corbières, Château Pech-Latt, £29.94 for 6, Waitrose *and* **1999 Vin de Pays d'Oc Merlot, Emilien d'Albret, £28.50 for 6, Vintage Roots**

The sexy white from the Mediterranean just now is Viognier, so here are two, bursting with apricot fruit and a mayblossom scent:
1999 Vin de Pays d'Oc Viognier, Domaine de la Ferrandière, £29.70 for 6, Waterloo Wine Co; 1999 Viognier Limited Release, Oxford Landing, £35.94 for 6, Unwins

Sorry? Oxford Landing's in Australia. Well, I knew it was somewhere hot. Back to the Med. Spain is making some utterly gluggable reds – so long as you avoid areas like Rioja. Don't worry, I shall. I'm going to the vinous wilderness to pluck out two gems: a Garnacha bubbling with juicy strawberry fruit and celery crunchiness, and a Tempranillo full of soft cherry and damson fruit:
1999 Calatayud Garnacha, Viña Fuerte, £23.94 for 6, Waitrose *and* **1999 Cigales**

Tempranillo, Marisa, £29.94 for 6, Marks & Spencer

Fizz for a fiver? Sure – good, clean, foaming fun from **Chardonnay/Pinot Noir, Chapel Hill, £4.99, Waitrose.** *I make that* **£498.57**.

£1000

Right. Now I get serious. But not too serious. There are some brilliant winemakers at work in Spain, producing some of Europe's most irresistible flavours:

1996 Can Feixes Negre Seleccio, Huguet, Penedès, £36 for 4, John Armit (red); 1996 Ribera del Duero, Arzuaga Navarro, £54.64 for 4, OW Loeb (red); 1998 Toro Dehesa Gago, £26 for 4, Adnams (red)

And now I will get really serious. 1998 was New Zealand's best ever vintage for reds and here are a beautifully crunchy European-style Syrah and a Cabernet/Merlot blend that Bordeaux would be proud of:

1998 Syrah La Strada, Fromm, £124.50 for 6, Lay & Wheeler *and* **1998 Unison Selection, Hawke's Bay, £95.70 for 6, Waitrose**

Italy has some serious stuff too, and an exciting new brood of winemakers. So I'll go for two Tuscan classics and then a couple of whacky originals. The Aleatico is sweet and perfumed, the Amarone is dark, strange and disturbing. And expensive.

1996 Chianti Rufina Riserva Bucerchiale, Selvapiana, £47.85 for 3, Liberty Wines (red); 1996 Rosso di Montalcino, Ciacci Piccolomini d'Aragona, £58.74 for 6, Savage Selection (red); 1995 Amarone della Valpolicella Classico, Allegrini, £74.85 for 3, Liberty Wines (red); 1989 Aleatico di Puglia, Candido, £8.99, Swig (red)

From Italy it's a short hop to southern France, so I'll stop off there for a delicious red from the tantalizingly good 1998 vintage:

1998 Coteaux du Languedoc, Mas de la Seranne, £47.40 for 6, Laytons (southern France)

If you love the dusty scent of herb-strewn hills in high summer, hurled into a broth of rich, sweet, strawberry fruit, the southern Rhône has the wines for you:

1998 Vacqueyras, Montirius, £59.94 for 6, Tesco (red); 1997 Côtes du Rhône les Garrigues, Domaine de la Janasse, £89.94 for 6, Swig (red); 1998 Côtes du Rhône Vieilles Vignes, Domaine de la Vieille Julienne, £40.56 for 6, OW Loeb (red)

I've not forgotten the northern Rhône – not when they're on such a hot streak too:

1998 Crozes-Hermitage, Domaine du Murinais, £49.38 for 6, OW Loeb (red) *and* **1998 Crozes-Hermitage, Domaine Combier, £65.94 for 6, Swig (red)**

While I'm in the northern Rhône I can't resist a couple of blossom-scented, pulse-quickening Condrieu. Nectar. Ecstasy.

1997 Condrieu les Chaillets Vieilles Vignes, Domaine Cuilleron, £32.99, Swig *and* **1998 Condrieu 'Puyvert', Ch de St-Cosme, £22, Savage Selection**

And there's some fantastic white Burgundy being made in the most unlikely spots.

1996 Mâcon-Clessé, Dom. René Michel, £7.95, Raeburn; 1998 Maranges en Borgy, Jean Rijckaert, £11.75, Laytons

More whites? Yes. I've picked a lovely honeyed Pinot Blanc, a delicious Chardonnay – from Greece – and some thrilling stuff from Down Under:

1998 Pinot Blanc Vieilles Vignes, Meyer-Fonné, £6.85, Lay & Wheeler (Alsace); 1998 Chardonnay Château Julia, Dom. Constantin Lazaridi, Drama, £7.99, Oddbins (white); 1999 Chardonnay, Craggy Range, £10.99, Waitrose (white, New Zealand): 1998 Louis Semillon, Henschke, £12.60, Lay & Wheeler (white, Australia)

Whoops. That doesn't really leave me enough for this inspired fizz from Tasmania:

1995 Pirie, Pipers Brook, £15.20, Sommelier Wine Co

Well, I never got to Bordeaux and all that long-faced stuff. But I have got a cellar full of happy juice, full of serious wine characteristics, for a total of **£1008.75**

Swig, tel: 020-7431 4412
Vintage Roots, freephone: 0800 980 4992
OW Loeb, tel: 020-7928 7750

ARGENTINA

A source of terrific wine is taking shape before our eyes. Blink and you may miss something

The thing that strikes me about Argentina is that it could make pretty well any style of wine it wanted. Not just because it has umpteen different grape varieties planted – varieties from France, from Italy, from Spain – but because if you have the foothills of the Andes at your disposal you can pick your climate. It's a bit like picking wallpaper out of a sample book (and just as expensive if you get it wrong).

But I also think that Argentina is still flipping through the patterns, trying to decide what would suit it best. Because in wine terms this is still a very young country. Yes, it's been making the stuff for centuries, but only in the last couple of decades has it begun to address the question of making the sort of wine that foreigners want to drink. So its achievements are remarkable: all that lush Malbec, all that rich fruit.

We're going to see more and more of it, because they're busy planting more and more red vines. And they're getting better and better at the sort of techniques that produce good, rich, inexpensive flavours: techniques like using oak chips or oak staves instead of pricier new oak barrels. They're modernizing fast, and experimenting as they go. Winewise, it's one of the most exciting countries in the world.

GRAPE VARIETIES

BARBERA (red) Mendoza and San Juan are the main regions for this Italian import. It doesn't bear much resemblance to the tannic, acidic reds of north-west Italy; it's juicier and softer. But it can be aged, if you're so inclined.

BONARDA (red) A middling quality grape that is planted in enormous quantities. It probably isn't the same variety as the Bonarda found in north-western Italy, but since the flavour can be pretty good that's really neither here nor there. Expect ripe wines with good concentration and sweet fruit. Most is blended with other varieties, however.

CABERNET SAUVIGNON (red) Of course Argentina makes Cabernet: who doesn't? It can be made as a varietal or blended, often with Merlot. Flavours are rich, ripe, and sometimes a bit jammy.

CHARDONNAY (white) Good but not great, but getting better: that's my verdict on Argentinian Chardonnay. There's still not much planted, and it remains to be seen how much plantings will increase now that the world is demanding more and more red wine.

MALBEC (red) Argentina's main red variety reaches heights here that it achieves nowhere else. Elsewhere (which mostly means France) Malbec produces rather plain, rustic wine; but in Mendoza the wines are concentrated, balanced and lush, and almost gamy in flavour: think of red Bordeaux crossed with Australian Shiraz. It can age surprisingly well, too.

MERLOT (red) There's quite a lot of the world's most fashionable red grape in Argentina – nearly as much as there is Cabernet Sauvignon, though both play second fiddle (both in quantity and in quality) to Malbec. At the moment a lot gets blended in with Cabernet Sauvignon, but varietal Merlot is flavour of the year everywhere, so look out for them here.

SANGIOVESE (red) Don't expect Argentinian Sangiovese to taste like Chianti: it doesn't. Instead it's chunkier, with sweeter fruit and an altogether lusher style. It doesn't have that austere bite that Tuscan examples have, nor the elegance. Drink it on its own terms.

SYRAH (red) There's more and more of this planted every year, though overall quantities are still small. It seems thoroughly at home, and makes perfumed, lush wines.

TEMPRANILLA (red) Never heard of it? That's because this is the local name for the Spanish Tempranillo. It doesn't make particularly good quality in Argentina, since it is mostly light-coloured and dilute, and comes from over-irrigated vineyards. It's losing ground to other varieties.

TORRONTÉS (white) A wildly aromatic grape that knocks spots off most of the Viogniers from the south of France that are supposed to be aromatic but often don't quite manage it. It succeeds in having good crisp acidity as well.

OTHER VARIETIES These include Sauvignon Blanc, which has yet really to succeed here, Riesling and Semillon. Individual examples can be good. Red varieties that are sometimes seen include Nebbiolo and Pinot Noir; the former probably has more potential here, but neither is particularly easy to grow.

WINE REGIONS

The most promising wine regions are those that hug the Andes, and nearly all the vineyards are in the western part of the country. Most are semi-desert: if it wasn't for all that melted snow pouring from the mountains there would be no wine made here at all.

MENDOZA This is where the majority of the wine industry is situated, and where most of the wine we see over here comes from. It's also the region that supplies the domestic market with cheap bulk production. Malbec rules among the better grapes, though there's quite a bit of Tempranillo, too, and some Italian varieties. There are lots of sub-regions, of which the best are Luján de Cuyo (especially for Malbec), Agrelo, Maipú and Tupungato (some promising Chardonnay). Good producers include: *Altos de Temporada, Anubis, Arizu (Luigi Bosca label), Bodegas Balbi, Bodegas Bianchi, Catena, Etchart, Fabre Montmayou, Finca Flichman, La Agrícola, La Rural, Bodegas J & F Lurton, Nieto & Senetiner, Norton, Pascual Toso, Peñaflor, Bodegas Santa Ana, Tittarelli (Finca el Retiro), Trapiche, Villa Atuel, Bodegas Weinert.*

SAN JUAN It gets far hotter here than it does in Mendoza, and the idea of making high quality wine is relatively new. Watch this space.

SALTA This relatively small region is where some of the most exciting wines are being made. The sub-region of Cafayate is the home of Torrontés, and the wines are ripe, quite weighty, dry or a fraction off-dry, and with a wonderful, seductive Muscat perfume. Cabernet Sauvignon also does well here. The vineyards are at terrifically high altitude – the Calchaquies Valley is at around 1500 metres – which gives elegance to the wines in spite of the hot, dry climate of this region. Look for wines from *Etchart* and *Norton*.

RíO NEGRO Cool and well to the south, this is mostly a fruit-growing region, but is showing considerable promise for wines; Torrontés, Sauvignon Blanc and Semillon look good so far. Good names to look for include *Infinitus* (Chardonnay/Semillon, Cabernet/Merlot and Malbec/Syrah) and *Bodegas Humberto Canale*, which is even trying some Pinot Noir down here.

PRODUCERS WHO'S WHO

ANUBIS ★★★ Impressive Malbec and Syrah/Bonarda. The same winemaking team produces the wines of Villa Atuel.

LEONCIO ARIZU ★★★ The varietal Syrah and Malbec under the Luigi Bosca label are the best here: concentrated fruit and good aromas.

HUMBERTO CANALE ★★ Assertive Sauvignon Blanc and ripe Semillon from Río Negro. Prices are not high.

NICOLAS CATENA ★★★★ The Alta range is tops at the Esmeralda winery: Cabernet Sauvignon is dense, chocolaty and will age; Malbec is all blackberries and liquorice. Alamos Ridge wines, especially the Cabernet Sauvignon, Malbec and Chardonnay, are also well worth a look.

INSTANT CELLAR: ARGENTINA'S BEST

- **1995 Syrah, Luigi Bosca, Leoncio Arizu, £6.90, Croque-en-Bouche** Rich and well structured: superripe Syrah with lots of spice.
- **1999 Syrah, Finca Norte, Villa Atuel, £5.25, Bennetts** Good structure and dark, spicy fruit.
- **1997 Malbec, Catena Alta, £20.83, Bibendum** One of the best wines in South America: concentrated, complex and finely balanced. Chile had better watch out.
- **1999 Chardonnay, Valle de Vistalba, Nieto y Senetiner, £5.99, Amey's Wines** Ripe and toasty but not over-tropical.
- **1999 Viognier, la Chamiza, Viña Patagonia, £5.50, Wine Society** The exotic perfume of Viognier from Mendoza.
- **1995 Cabernet Sauvignon, Weinert, £11.99, Hedley Wright** Terrific flavours of blackcurrants and eucalyptus, utterly seductive.
- **1997 Malbec, Elsa's Vineyard, Valentin Bianchi, £5.40, Great Western Wine** Vibrant, delicious Malbec from Mendoza.

ETCHART ★★★ Top of the range Arnaldo B is a blend of Malbec and Cabernet Sauvignon. Check out the varietal lines like Malbec and Bonarda. Torrontés is wonderfully grapy; Cabernet Sauvignon from Cafayate is real cassis.

FINCA FLICHMAN ★★★ Terrifically spicy Caballero de la Cepa Syrah; the leathery Malbec is also excellent. The basic Flichman range has appealing Sangiovese, but Syrah here is more interesting.

LA AGRíCOLA ★★★★ Great export success; labels include Santa Julia and Picajuan Peak. Reds are always good. Look for the Bonarda/Sangiovese.

LA RURAL ★★★ Look for the Rutini Reserve Chardonnay, Malbec and Merlot wines. Those under the La Rural label itself are more basic.

NORTON ★★ Norton Privada is the top wine: a Cabernet Sauvignon/Malbec/Merlot blend full of blackberry and cloves. Reds generally are better than whites. Barbera and Sangiovese are worth a look.

TRAPICHE ★★ Chardonnay is improving here, as are Merlot and Cabernet Sauvignon, especially the top Medalla range.

DOMAINE VISTALBA ★★★★ A French-owned group that includes Fabre Montmayou, Altos de Temporada and Infinitus. Look for Fabre Montmayou Grand Vin, a complex blend of Malbec and Cabernet Sauvignon. Altos de Temporada has promising Merlot, Malbec and Cabernet. Infinitus has some good blends.

BODEGAS WEINERT ★★★ Very, very good peppery, fleshy Malbec, and good chocolaty Cabernet. Cavas de Weinert (Cabernet, Merlot and Malbec) is intense and complex.

ARGENTINA PRICES

RED

Under £4.00

★ Barbera Elsa, San Raphael **1999** £3.99 (CO)
Malbec/Sangiovese La Rural Libertad **1999** £3.79 (WR)
Mission Peak Red **Non-vintage** £3.29 (BO) £3.65 (BUD)
Sangiovese Viña Patagonia Trivento **1999** £3.99 (WAI)
Tempranillo La Bamba **1999** £3.99 (WAI)
Tempranillo/Malbec Etchart Rio de Plata **1998** £3.99 (BUD)

£4.00 → £4.99

Barbera Vistalba **1998** £4.79 (BO) £5.25 (CON)
Bonarda Bodegas Lurton **1997** £4.99 (POR)
Cabernet Sauvignon Balbi **1998** £4.95 (HA)
Cabernet Sauvignon Etchart Rio de Plata **1997** £4.49 (ASD)
Cabernet Sauvignon Finca El Retiro **1998** £4.85 (SOM) £5.95 (POR)
Cabernet Sauvignon Norton **1997** £4.95 (WS) £4.99 (OD) £4.99 (UN) £5.80 (TAN)
Cabernet Sauvignon Norton **1996** £4.99 (NEZ)
Cabernet Sauvignon Trapiche **1996** £4.99 (DI)
Cabernet Sauvignon Viniterra Omnium **1997** £4.95 (STE)
Malbec Balbi **1998** £4.49 (OD) £4.68 (HA)
Malbec Bodegas Esmeralda Catena Argento **1999** £4.99 (VIC) £4.99 (THR) £4.99 (WR) £4.99 (BOT)
Malbec Finca El Retiro **1998** £4.85 (SOM) £5.79 (BO) £5.95 (POR)
Malbec La Rural 1885 **1998** £4.59 (BO)
Malbec Norton **1998** £4.99 (TES) £4.99 (OD)
Malbec Norton **1996** £4.99 (NI) £4.99 (UN)
Malbec Trapiche **1997** £4.99 (DI)
Malbec Viniterra Omnium **1997** £4.95 (STE)
Malbec/Cabernet Sauvignon La Agricola Magdalena River **1997** £4.99 (UN)
Malbec/Cabernet Sauvignon La Agricola Santa Julia **1998** £4.49 (WAI)
Malbec/Sangiovese Trapiche Parral **1999** £4.45 (STE)
Malbec/Syrah Balbi **1998** £4.70 (HA)
Merlot La Rural 1885 **1998** £4.28 (PIP)
Merlot Norton **1996** £4.99 (OD)
Sangiovese/Bonarda La Agricola Magdalena River **1998** £4.99 (UN)
Shiraz Balbi **1997** £4.99 (UN)
Syrah Nieto y Senetiner Valle de Vistalba **1998** £4.95 (SOM)
★ Syrah Finca Norte Villa Atuel **1999** £4.95 (WS) £5.25 (BU) £5.50 (VA)£4.99 (LIB)
Tempranillo Finca El Retiro **1999** £4.50 (SOM) £5.49 (LIB) £5.49 (WAI) £5.75 (BU) £5.99 (VA) £6.17 (REI) £6.79 (PHI)
Tempranillo La Agricola Santa Julia Oak-Aged **1997** £4.49 (TES)

£5.00 → £5.99

Barbera Simonassi Lyon **1998** £5.49 (SAF)
Bonarda Medrano **1999** £5.04 (PLA)
Cabernet Sauvignon Bodegas Esmeralda Alamos Ridge **1997** £5.97 (BIB)
Cabernet Sauvignon Bodegas Esmeralda Alamos Ridge **1996** £5.95 (WS)
Cabernet Sauvignon Finca El Retiro **1999** £5.99 (LIB) £5.99 (VA) £6.15 (BU)
Cabernet Sauvignon Medrano **1999** £5.04 (PLA)
Cabernet Sauvignon Navarro Correas Correas **1997** £5.49 (MOR)
Cabernet Sauvignon Trapiche Oak Cask **1995** £5.99 (DI)
Cabernet Sauvignon Vistalba **1996** £5.99 (CON)
Cabernet Sauvignon/Syrah Viniterra Terra **1996** £5.25 (STE)

MERCHANTS SPECIALIZING IN ARGENTINA

see Merchant Directory (page 456) for details

No merchant actually specialises in Argentian wines, though some have better lists than others. Most only stock a few wines at best. Try Adnams, (AD),Bennetts (BEN) John Harvey (HA), Hedley Wright (HED), Lloyd Taylor (LLO), Moreno Wines (MOR), Sommelier Wine Co (SOM), The Wine Society (WS), Wine Treasury (WT)

Malbec Alta Vista **1997** £5.95 (JU)
Malbec Valentin Bianchi Elsa's Vineyard **1997** £5.40 (GW)
Malbec Bodegas Esmeralda Alamos Ridge **1997** £5.99 (TES) £6.23 (PIP)
Malbec Bodegas Esmeralda Alamos Ridge **1996** £5.95 (WS)
★ Malbec Finca El Retiro **1999** £5.49 (WAI) £5.79 (BO) £5.99 (LIB) £5.99 (VA) £6.60 (PIP) £6.79 (PHI)
Malbec La Agricola Santa Julia Oak Reserve **1996** £5.99 (UN)
Malbec Bodegas Lurton **1998** £5.49 (POR) £5.69 (JON) £5.70 (TAN)
Malbec Bodegas Lurton **1997** £5.95 (JER)
Malbec Medrano **1999** £5.04 (PLA)
Malbec/Syrah Leoncio Arizu Finca La Linda **1996** £5.25 (AD)
Merlot Norton **1995** £5.99 (NEZ)
Pedro del Castillo Weinert **1998** £5.45 (STE)
Sangiovese Norton **1997** £5.55 (NI)
Syrah Navarro Correas **1996** £5.70 (GW)
Syrah Viña Patagonia Isla Negra **1997** £5.50 (WS)
Syrah Vistalba **1996** £5.99 (CON)
Tempranillo Anubis **1999** £5.99 (LIB) £7.99 (VA)
Tempranillo Finca El Retiro **1998** £5.79 (BAL) £5.95 (POR)
Tempranillo La Agricola Santa Julia Oak Reserve **1997** £5.99 (UN)

£6.00 → £6.99

Cabernet Sauvignon Domaine Vistalba Altos de Temporada **1996** £6.50 (WS)
Cabernet Sauvignon Domaine Vistalba Fabre Montmayou **1996** £6.99 (OD)
Cabernet Sauvignon Etchart Cafayate **1996** £6.29 (JON)
Cabernet Sauvignon Nieto y Senetiner Valle de Vistalba **1996** £6.17 (REI)
Cabernet Sauvignon Norton Reserve **1997** £6.99 (NEZ)
Cabernet Sauvignon/Merlot Domaine Vistalba Infinitus **1996** £6.95 (WS)
Malbec Humberto Canale **1997** £6.50 (HED)
Malbec Domaine Vistalba Altos de Temporada **1996** £6.50 (WS)
Malbec Domaine Vistalba Fabre Montmayou **1996** £6.99 (OD)
Malbec Bodegas Lurton Reserva **1998** £6.46 (CB)
Malbec Norton Reserve **1997** £6.99 (NEZ)
Malbec Trapiche Oak Cask **1995** £6.99 (DI)
Malbec/Syrah Domaine Vistalba Infinitus **1996** £6.79 (BO)
Merlot Domaine Vistalba Altos de Temporada **1996** £6.50 (WS)
Merlot Domaine Vistalba Fabre Montmayou **1996** £6.99 (OD)
Merlot La Rural Rutini **1996** £6.76 (BIB)
Pinot Noir Humberto Canale **1998** £6.95 (ELL) £6.95 (HED)
Syrah Leoncio Arizu Luigi Bosca **1995** £6.90 (CRO)
Syrah/Bonarda Anubis **1999** £6.95 (LIB) £7.99 (VA)
Tempranillo La Agricola Santa Julia Oak Reserve **1999** £6.99 (ASD)

£7.00 → £8.99

Cabernet Sauvignon Leoncio Arizu Luigi Bosca **1996** £7.75 (AD)
Cabernet Sauvignon Bodegas Esmeralda Catena Agrelo **1996** £8.95 (WS)
Cabernet Sauvignon Bodegas Lurton Gran Lurton **1997** £7.99 (UN)
Carrascal Weinert **1997** £7.61 (PIP)
Carrascal Weinert **1996** £7.90 (TAN)
Carrascal Weinert **1995** £7.49 (JON) £7.69 (CON) £9.95 (JER)
Carrascal Weinert **1994** £7.50 (BAL)
Malbec Leoncio Arizu Luigi Bosca **1997** £7.99 (PHI)
Malbec Bodegas Esmeralda Catena Agrelo **1997** £8.81 (BIB)
Malbec Trapiche **1995** £8.88 (HA)
Malbec Trapiche **1994** £7.65 (UB)
Malbec Viniterra **1997** £7.95 (STE)
Malbec Weinert **1994** £8.25 (WS) £9.59 (PIP) £9.85 (CON) £9.95 (BAL) £11.05 (NO)
Merlot Weinert **1996** £8.45 (STE) £10.81 (CB) £11.42 (PLAY)
Miscelánea Weinert **1997** £7.95 (STE)
Privada Norton **1996** £7.99 (NEZ) £8.99 (NI)
Syrah Leoncio Arizu Luigi Bosca **1996** £7.75 (AD)
Syrah Navarro Correas **1995** £8.98 (HA)
Syrah Navarro Correas **1993** £8.99 (MOR)
Syrah Viniterra **1997** £7.95 (STE)
Tempranillo La Agricola Familia Zuccardi 'Q' **1998** £7.99 (TES)

Stars (★) indicate wines selected by Oz Clarke in the Best Buys section which begins on page 10.

£9.00 → £9.99

Barbaro Balbi **1997** £9.99 (SAF) £10.06 (HA)
Cabernet Sauvignon La Agricola Familia Zuccardi 'Q' **1998** £9.99 (TES)
Cabernet Sauvignon Bodegas Lurton Gran Lurton **1996** £9.99 (POR)
Cabernet Sauvignon Weinert **1995** £9.75 (STE) £11.50 (BAL) £11.60 (JER)
Caves de Weinert Weinert **1994** £9.95 (STE) £10.25 (NO) £11.50 (CON)
Caves de Weinert Weinert **1993** £9.95 (WS)
Malbec Weinert **1992** £9.95 (JER)

Over £10.00

Cabernet Sauvignon Bodegas Esmeralda Catena Alta **1995** £21.95 (YOU)
Cabernet Sauvignon Weinert **1994** £11.25 (CON) £11.45 (JON) £13.20 (PLAY)

WHITE

Under £4.00

Chardonnay Etchart Rio de Plata **1998** £3.99 (ASD)
Country White Peñaflor Bright Bros Mendoza **Non-vintage** £2.99 (UN)
Pinot Gris Bodegas Lurton **1999** £3.95 (WS)
Pinot Gris Bodegas Lurton **1998** £3.99 (UN) £4.95 (TAN) £4.99 (POR) £5.09 (JON)
Torrontés/Chardonnay Etchart Rio de Plata **1998** £3.49 (BUD)
★ Torrontés/Chardonnay Navarro Correas Correas **1998** £3.99 (VIC) £3.99 (THR) £3.99 (BOT) £3.99 (WR) £4.80 (GW) £4.99 (MOR)

£4.00 → £4.99

Chardonnay Balbi **1999** £4.45 (HA)
Chardonnay Bodegas Esmeralda Alamos Ridge **1997** £4.99 (UN) £5.95 (WS) £5.97 (BIB)
Chardonnay La Agricola Magdalena River **1997** £4.99 (UN)
Chardonnay La Rural Libertad **1999** £4.50 (BIB)
Chardonnay Trapiche **1998** £4.99 (DI)
Chardonnay Viniterra Omnium **1999** £4.95 (STE) £5.33 (NO)
Torrontés Norton **1998** £4.49 (NEZ) £4.49 (VIC) £4.49 (THR) £4.49 (OD) £4.49 (BOT)
Torrontés Norton **1997** £4.99 (NI)

£5.00 → £5.99

Chardonnay La Agricola Santa Julia Oak Reserve **1997** £5.99 (UN)
Chardonnay Vistalba **1998** £5.95 (CON)
Chenin Blanc Bodegas Lurton **1997** £5.95 (JER)
Sauvignon Blanc Norton **1997** £5.50 (NEZ)
Torrontés Etchart Rio de Plata **1997** £5.19 (JON) £5.35 (UB)

£6.00 → £6.99

Carrascal Weinert White **1998** £6.45 (STE)
Chardonnay Bodegas Esmeralda Alamos Ridge **1996** £6.23 (PIP)
Chardonnay Bodegas Lurton **1998** £6.58 (CB)
Chardonnay Norton Reserve **1997** £6.99 (NEZ)
Chardonnay Trapiche Andean **1998** £6.78 (PLAY)
Chardonnay Trapiche Oak Cask **1997** £6.99 (DI) £7.49 (JON)
Riesling Leoncio Arizu Luigi Bosca **1997** £6.90 (CRO)

£7.00 → £10.99

Chardonnay Leoncio Arizu Luigi Bosca **1997** £7.75 (AD)
Chardonnay Bodegas Esmeralda Catena Agrelo **1997** £7.99 (UN) £8.81 (BIB)
★ Chardonnay/Semillon Bodegas Infinitus **1997** £7.65 (RAE)
Chardonnay Bodegas Lurton **1995** £7.90 (CRO)
Chardonnay Viniterra **1997** £10.52 (NO)
Chardonnay Viniterra **2000** £7.95 (STE)
Riesling Leoncio Arizu Luigi Bosca **1998** £7.40 (AD)

ROSÉ

Under £5.00

Malbec Santa Ana **1999** £3.99 (SAF)
★ Syrah Balbi **1999** £3.99 (CO) £4.49 (SAF)

SPARKLING

Under £10.00

Chandon Argentina **Non-vintage** £8.75 (STE)
Viniterra Sparkling **Non-vintage** £9.75 (STE)

AUSTRALIA

Australians usually have their finger firmly on the pulse when it comes to knowing what we want to drink. And they think we've got enough Chardonnay

Australians have pretty well stopped planting Chardonnay. Should you be interested in this? Well, yes, because if they're not planting any more (except for a few tip-top sites) then it means that they think the world has enough already.

It's true that Australian Chardonnay is the easiest wine to buy that has ever existed. You know what it's going to taste like, and you know it's going to be fair value for money. And that's not changing. They're not uprooting the stuff, for Heaven's sake. Just not planting any more.

They think that we're ready to move on to other flavours. And if fashions in Australia are anything to go by, they're right.

Of course, everybody's drinking red wine. Everybody's drinking red wine the world over. In Australia right now that means Shiraz. Yes, Cabernet Sauvignon is still there, no worries. But Shiraz is the flavour of the moment, all leather and wild berries and smoke. A really good Barossa Shiraz can make Cabernet Sauvignon look tame and polite. There's going to be a lot more Shiraz coming out of Australia in the future, which means lots more red goodies to explore. Look out for Grenache, too, which has the same fashionably luscious fruit and spice and rich, rich tannins.

But Aussies haven't deserted white wines, and nor have we. What they're making is lots more whites with lovely rich lime-and-lemon flavours, perhaps with a touch of spicy oak, perhaps not. Semillon, that great Australian speciality, is popping up all over the place, and there's more Verdelho than there used to be, too. Both have lovely lime cordial flavours, with a touch of greengage, a touch of lemon peel. They go brilliantly with all sorts of food, particularly veggie dishes and anything involving lemons. Lemon chicken? Pasta with lemon? Perfect. The Shirazes I'll keep for sausages and casseroles, steak and roast beef and game. Sounds all right to me.

GRAPE VARIETIES

CABERNET SAUVIGNON (red) This can be rich and chocolaty in the Barossa, austere and minty in Victoria's Pyrenees, full of moss, tobacco and cedar flavours in the Eden Valley, and dense, phenolic and black in the Hunter. Sometimes it can be all of these, sometimes it can taste of nothing more than simple blackcurrant jelly. It's an Aussie staple these days, and even cheaper ones generally have clear fruit, without the muddiness that can mar cheap claret. And when it's good, it's breathtaking. It's also often blended with other grapes, particularly Shiraz or the Bordeaux varieties Cabernet Franc and/or Merlot. Best: *Clancy's Shiraz/Cabernet, Greenock Creek, Peter Lehmann, Rockford, St Hallett Cabernet/Merlot, Seppelt's Dorrien, Yalumba The Menzies* and *The Signature* (Barossa); *Grosset, Knappstein Cabernet/Merlot* (also a good Cabernet Franc), *Leasingham Cabernet/Malbec* and *Classic, Wendouree* (Clare); *Bowen Estate, Hollick's Ravenswood, Katnook Odyssey, Leconfield, Lindemans Pyrus, Lindemans Limestone Ridge* and *Lindemans St George, Orlando, Parker, Penley Estate, Petaluma, Wynns Coonawarra* and *John Riddoch, Yalumba* (Coonawarra); *Heggies, Henschke Cyril Henschke, Hill-Smith Estate, Mountadam The Red, Seppelt's Partalunga* (Eden Valley); *Chateau Tahbilk* (Goulburn Valley); *Mount Langi Ghiran* (Grampians); *Frankland Estate,*

Goundrey, Howard Park, Plantagenet (Great Southern); *Brokenwood, Lake's Folly, Rothbury Shiraz/Cabernet* (Hunter); *Cape Mentelle, Capel Vale, Chateau Xanadu, Cullen, Devil's Lair, Leeuwin Estate, Lenton Brae, Moss Wood, Sandstone, Vasse Felix The Heytesbury* (Margaret River); *Chapel Hill The Vicar, Chateau Reynella, Coriole Shiraz/Cabernet, d'Arenberg Coppermine Road, Mount Hurtle, Chateau Reynella Basket Press, Shottesbrooke, Simon Hackett Foggo Road, Wirra Wirra* (McLaren Vale); *Dromana Estate* (Mornington Peninsula); *Taltarni* (Pyrenees); *Domaine A, Freycinet* (Tasmania); *Seppelt's Drumborg, Tisdall Mt Helen* (Victoria); *Coldstream Hills, Mount Mary, Seville Estate, St Huberts, Yarra Yering* (Yarra); *Geoff Merrill, Penfolds* (various).

CHARDONNAY (white) Australia has done more than most to give this grape mass appeal with its rich, fruity wines. Most are now far more restrained than they were, but the fruit is still there. The best have kept their original appeal and gained complexity. Best: *Ashton Hills, Bridgewater Mill, Penfolds, Petaluma, Shaw & Smith Reserve* (Adelaide Hills); *Andrew Garrett, Basedow, St Hallett, Greenock Creek, Peter Lehmann* (Barossa); *Giaconda* (Beechworth); *Grosset* (Clare); *Katnook* (Coonawarra); *Richmond Grove* (Cowra); *Henschke, Hill-Smith Estate, Mountadam, Seppelt's Partalunga* (Eden Valley); *Bannockburn* (Geelong); *Michelton Preece* (Goulburn); *Frankland Estate, Howard Park, Plantagenet, Wignalls* (Great Southern); *Allandale, Allanmere, Brokenwood, Glenguin, McWilliams' Mount Pleasant, Rosemount, Scarborough* (Hunter); *Knappstein, Stafford Ridge* (Lenswood); *Chateau Reynella, Geoff Merrill, Wirra Wirra* (McLaren Vale); *Cape Mentelle, Chateau Xanadu, Cullen, Evans & Tate, Leeuwin Estate, Lenton Brae, Moss Wood, Pierro* (Margaret River); *Dromana Estate* (Mornington Peninsula); *Goundry* (Mount Barker); *Hardy Eileen Hardy, Lindemans* (Padthaway); *Pipers Brook* (Tasmania); *Tisdall Mt Helen* (Victoria); *Coldstream Hills* (Yarra); *Koonunga Hill* (various).

CHENIN BLANC (white) The Australian incarnation of this grape ripens to a much fuller, fruitier and blander style than its steely Loire counterpart. *Moondah Brook* (Swan District) does a good example; *Sandalford* (Western Australia) blends it with the Madeira grape Verdelho.

FORTIFIEDS Shiraz and other Rhône-type grapes are often used to make port styles. Vintage is wonderful. Best: *Chateau Reynella, Lindemans, Montara, Penfolds, Saltram, Seppelt, Stanton & Killeen, Yalumba.*

GEWÜRZTRAMINER (white) Decent, faintly spicy examples smelling of lychees and honeydew melon are made by *Brown Brothers, Delatite* and *Lillydale* (Victoria), and *Knappstein* (Clare). *Orlando Flaxman's* (Eden Valley) and *Tolleys* (Barossa) are always good. *Rymill's* botrytis version (Coonawarra) is intense.

GRENACHE (red) The Southern Vales around Adelaide are the heartland of this Mediterranean variety, and the rediscovery of old vines sitting there squeezing out more and more concentrated grapes has resulted in a range of wonderful wines; the *Turkey Flat* vines have been in constant production since 1847. Best: *Peter Lehmann, Charles Melton, RBJ, Rockford, St Hallett Gamekeeper's Reserve, Turkey Flat, Whitmore Old Vineyard, Yaldara Reserve, Yalumba Bush Vine Grenache* and *The Reserve* (Barossa); *Tim Adams The Fergus* (Clare); *James Halliday Shiraz/Grenache, Mitchelton III* (Goulburn); *d'Arenberg Ironstone Pressings, Tim Gramp* (McLaren Vale).

MARSANNE (white) In Central Victoria, both *Chateau Tahbilk* and *Mitchelton* have made big, broad, ripe Marsanne.

MUSCAT (white) There are two types of Muscat in Australia: first, the bag-in-box Fruity Gordo or Muscat of Alexandria – fruity, sweetish, swigging wine, from a heavy-cropping lowish-quality grape grown along

ON THE CASE

It's become harder and harder to find Cabernet Sauvignon/Shiraz blends – both are made as varietals these days. But don't ignore any you see: it's a classic Aussie red blend

the Murray River; second, liqueur Muscat, made from the Brown Muscat, a strain of the top quality Muscat à Petits Grains, grown in Victoria. It is a sensation: dark, treacly even, with a perfume of strawberry and honeyed raisins. Best producers: *All Saints, Baileys, Bullers, Campbells, Chambers, Morris, Stanton & Killeen* and *Yalumba*.

PINOT NOIR (red) It looks increasingly as if New Zealand is Pinot Noir's Southern Hemisphere heartland. But Australia makes a few decent ones. Best: *Ashton Hills, Hillstowe, Pibbin* (Adelaide Hills); *Giaconda* (Beechworth); *Mountadam* (Eden Valley); *Bannockburn* (Geelong); *Wignall's* (Great Southern); *Tyrrell Vat 6* (Hunter); *Ashton Hills, Henschke, Lenswood Vineyards* (Lenswood); *Moss Wood* (Margaret River); *Freycinet, Spring Vale, Pipers Brook, Tasmania Wine Co* (Tasmania); *Coldstream Hills, Mount Mary, St Huberts, Tarrawarra, Yarra Yering* (Yarra).

RIESLING (white) Australia makes highly individual Rieslings, all sharing a lime aroma: some are clean and crisp (*Ashton Hills, Pewsey Vale, Leeuwin Estate*), some softer and more rounded (*Heritage, Skillogalee*), and others beg to be aged (*Orlando Steingarten, Mount Langhi Ghiran*). It's a wonderful apéritif and the perfect partner for Thaï and Pacific Rim cooking: not many white wines could stand up to those flavours, but Australian Riesling sails through them. Other good ones: *Rockford* (Barossa); *Tim Adams, Jim Barry, Grosset, Hewitson, Knappstein, Mitchell, Petaluma, Pikes* (Clare); *Heggies, Hill-Smith Estate, Lindemans, Leo Buring, Orlando St Helga, St Hallett, Seppelt's Partalunga* (Eden Valley); *Frankland Estate, Howard Park* (Great Southern); *Henschke* (Lenswood or Eden Valley); *Pipers Brook* (Tasmania); *Delatite* (Victoria), *Tim Gramp* (McLaren Vale). Botrytis-affected wines: *Mount Horrocks, Petaluma* and *St Huberts*.

SAUVIGNON BLANC (white) Here too New Zealand is leading the field in the southern hemisphere, though cool Adelaide Hills is proving its worth, with *Lenswood, Nepenthe, Shaw & Smith* and *Stafford Ridge*, while Margaret River's richer styles are like southern hemisphere Graves (*Cullen, Evans & Tate*). Best: *Jim Barry, Pikes* (Clare); *Katnook, Riddoch* (Coonawarra); *Hill-Smith Estate* (Eden Valley); *Bannockburn, Scotchmans Hill* (Geelong); *Frankland Estate, Wignalls* (Great Southern); *Amberley Estate, Ribbon Vale* (Margaret River); *Mount Hurtle, Wirra Wirra* (McLaren Vale); *Hardy, Lindemans* (Padthaway); *Yarra Valley Hills* (Yarra); *Brown Brothers, Mitchelton Preece* (Victoria); *Bridgewater Mill* (various).

SEMILLON (white) Unoaked Aussie Semillon is rare and great; lean and grassy when young, and needing years for its flavours of toast and honey to emerge. That makes it hopelessly uncommercial: you can hardly blame the producers for opting for oak and a quick sale. *Glenguin, McWilliams Elizabeth* and *Tyrrell's Vat 1* are the unoaked versions to look for. But oaked Semillon is delicious as well, waxy and toasty, and the best will age. Try: *Heritage, Peter Lehmann, Rockford, Grant Burge* (Barossa); *Grosset, Mitchell, Mount Horrocks* (Clare); *Henschke, Hill-Smith Estate* (Eden Valley); *Cassegrain* (Hastings Valley); *Brokenwood, Lindemans, Petersen, Rothbury* (Hunter); *Knappstein* (Lenswood); *Evans & Tate, Moss Wood, Sandstone* (Margaret River); *Simon Hackett* (McLaren Vale); *Brown Bros* (King Valley). Best blends with Sauvignon: *St Hallett* (Barossa); *Brokenwood* (Hunter); *Cape Mentelle, Pierro, Xanadu Secession, Cullen* (Margaret River); *Wirra Wirra* (McLaren Vale). *Geoff Merrill* blends with Chardonnay.

Best sweet wines: *Peter Lehmann, Tim Adams, de Bortoli, Fern Hill, Cranswick.*

SHIRAZ (red) The most widely planted red vine in Oz, but look for wine from old vines for greatest depth of flavour. There's the dense, black iron intensity of Clare, the chocolate, earth and moss of the Barossa, the black pepper of the cooler bits of Victoria and Western Australia, or the simple red berry sweetness of the hot Murray Valley. Try: *Basedow, Grant Burge Meshach, Hewitson, Greenock Creek, Peter Lehmann, Charles Melton, Rockford, St Hallett Old Block, Yalumba Octavius* (Barossa); *McWilliams* (Barwang); *Jasper Hill, Passing Clouds* (Bendigo); *Tim Adams, Jim Barry The Armagh, Mitchell, Pikes, Wendouree* (Clare); *Bowen, Majella, Wynns, Zema* (Coonawarra); *Craneford, Henschke, David Wynn Patriarch* (Eden); *Bannockburn* (Geelong); *Ch. Tahbilk* (Goulburn); *Mount Langi Ghiran* (Grampians); *Plantagenet* (Great Southern); *Allandale Matthew, Brokenwood, McWilliams Old Paddock* and *Old Hill, Rothbury, Tulloch Hector, Tyrrell's Vat 9* (Hunter); *Craiglee* (Macedon); *Cape Mentelle* (Margaret River); *Chapel Hill, Chateau Reynella, d'Arenberg Old Vine* and *Dead Arm, Hardy* (McLaren Vale); *Goundrey* (Mt Barker); *Dalwhinnie, Taltarni* (Pyrenees); *Baileys* (Rutherglen); *Baileys 1920s Block* (Victoria); *Yarra Yering* (Yarra Valley); *Hardy, Penfolds, Yaldara Reserve* (various).

SPARKLING WINES In the lead for quality are *Croser, Green Point, Pipers Brook Pirie, Yalumba D, Salinger* and *Jansz*. Cheaper ones include: *Seaview, Angas Brut, Orlando Carrington*. Upmarket: *Seppelt's Blanc de Blancs* and *Pinot Noir/Chardonnay*. And try *Yalumba's Cabernet* and *Seppelt's Shiraz* (sparkling red).

OTHER GRAPES *Heggies* is increasing plantings of Viognier, and very good it is too. Verdelho makes rich, lime-flavoured wines (*Chapel Hill, Richmond Grove, Pendarves Estate, Rothbury Estate, Broke Fordwich Wine Co, Moondah Brook, Hill of Hope*). Look too for Rhône grapes like Mourvèdre and Grenache, and blends of these from *St Hallett, d'Arenberg, Basedow, Grant Burge* and *Tim Gramp*.

WINE REGIONS

The Australian Geographical Indication system aims to identify areas that produce wines with their own distinct character. But it also has to accommodate the widespread system of inter-regional blending: that is, trucking grapes from several different regions, possibly in different states, to a central winery for blending together. Some of Australia's most famous wines (*Grange*, for example) are blended like this.

The most general designation is Produce of Australia. The next most general is South-Eastern Australia, which is much seen; it covers most of the wine-producing area. Then there is the more specific State of Origin, and then there are zones, regions and sub-regions. In all there will be about 400 Geographical Indications and progress is now well advanced.

ADELAIDE HILLS (South Australia) Cool area pioneered by *Petaluma*, now joined by *Shaw & Smith, Stafford Ridge, Henschke* and *Lenswood*, making classically pure Sauvignon Blanc, Chardonnays with great length and classy Pinot Noir. *Penfolds* is making a bid for white wine fame here.

BAROSSA VALLEY (South Australia) This is the heart of the Australian wine industry, planted originally by immigrants from Silesia. Most of Australia's wine passes through the Barossa Valley, if only for bottling or aging. It's also a source of wonderful old-vine Grenache and Shiraz. Best: *Penfolds, Orlando, Peter Lehmann, Mildara-Blass, Rockford, Greenock Creek, Charles Melton, Grant Burge, St Hallett, Hewitson, Basedow.*

INSTANT CELLAR:
RIESLING REVOLUTION

• **1999 Henschke, Green's Hill, Eden Valley, £11.99, Philglas & Swiggot** Intense dried limes and great acidity. Drink it now or keep it for a decade, if you can.
• **1999 Chateau Leamon, Bendigo, £10.58, Noel Young Wines** Intensely ripe, weighty and concentrated, but finely balanced.
• **1998 Capel Vale, Western Australia, £8.79, Lloyd Taylor** Good honeyed lemony fruit, and a touch of diesel.
• **1998 Tim Adams, Clare Valley, £7.99, Australian Wine Club** Lovely limy Riesling, elegant and concentrated.
• **1998 St Hallett, Eden Valley, £8.99, Australian Wine Club** A touch austere; just beginning to open up in bottle.
• **1997 Hell's Window, Delatite, Mansfield, £8.75, John Armit** Pure fruit and a mineral edge.
• **1998 Winstead, Tasmania, £9.25, Wine Society** Bone dry, with lots of bouquet and a very long finish.
• **1997 Tim Knappstein, Clare Valley, £8.49, Nobody Inn** The list describes this as light, 'with the slight Riesling flysprayness'.

BENDIGO (Victoria) This 19th-century region, destroyed by phylloxera, has been replanted with excellent Cabernet, good Shiraz and some Pinot Noir. *Balgownie* is the leader, with *Chateau Leamon, Craiglee, Harcourt Valley, Heathcote, Mount Ida, Passing Clouds* and *Yellowglen* important.

CANBERRA DISTRICT (ACT) Some modest wineries producing wines to match.

CLARE VALLEY (South Australia) An upland complex of four valleys (Skillogalee, Clare, Watervale and Polish River), Clare is all things to many grapes: cool and dry for steely, limy Riesling (*Adams, Jim Barry, Leo Buring, Grosset, Knappstein, Pikes*) and soft, light Chardonnay (*Penfolds*), but warm enough for rounded Semillon (*Mitchell*) and long-living reds (*Adams, Knappstein, Leasingham, Skillogalee, Watervale, Wendouree*).

COONAWARRA (South Australia) A big, flat, wide open landscape with the famous cigar-shaped strip of *terra rossa* soil at its heart. It is Australia's most profitable red wine vineyard, and its incredibly expensive land is jam-packed with great names. Coonawarra is best at Cabernet and unirrigated Shiraz. Try: *Bowen, Brand's, BRL Hardy, Hollick, Katnook, Lindemans, Majella, Mildara, Orlando, Penfolds, Penley, Petaluma, Rouge Homme, Rosemount, Rymill, Wynns* and *Zema*. Other similar limestone ridges nearby are currently being planted, with promising results.

EDEN VALLEY (South Australia) Home to some of Australia's oldest vineyards, like *Henschke*'s 120-year-old Hill of Grace, and some of the newest and most high-tech (*Mountadam* and *Seppelt's Partalunga*). Most of the major Barossa companies take fruit from these rolling uplands. *Yalumba* is here, with *Heggies* and *Hill-Smith Estate* vineyards.

GEELONG (Victoria) Best are intense Cabernets from vineyards like *Idyll* and *Bannockburn*, Pinot Noir from *Prince Albert* and *Bannockburn*, and whites from *Idyll*.

GOULBURN VALLEY (Victoria) This houses *Mitchelton*, a medium-sized modern winery, and *Chateau Tahbilk*, one of the nation's oldest, still making traditional intense reds and long-lived Marsanne.

GRAMPIANS (Victoria) The new name for Great Western; still the source of base wine for *Seppelt*'s *Great Western* fizz, but more exciting for its reds. Shiraz is full of chocolate, coconut and cream at *Cathcart Ridge*, or licorice and pepper at *Mount Langi Ghiran*. *Best's, Montara* and *Seppelt* are other top names. Excellent Chardonnay from *Best's* and *Seppelt*, Cabernet from *Mount Langi Ghiran*, fortified from *Montara*.

GRANITE BELT (Queensland) The vines are planted high up in what is otherwise a banana and mango belt. Most wines serve the local market and some (*Ballandean, Kominos Wines, Rumbalara, Robinsons Family* and *Stone Ridge*) are good. *Ironbark Ridge* is one to watch.

GREAT SOUTHERN (Western Australia) One of Australia's most promising wine areas, good for Riesling, limy Chardonnay, peppery Shiraz and magnificent Cabernet. Try *Goundrey, Alkoomi, Plantagenet, Frankland Estate* and *Howard Park*, home of *Madfish* blends.

HILLTOPS (New South Wales) Excellent-value Shiraz and Cabernet. Restraint and elegance are the watchwords.

HUNTER VALLEY (New South Wales) Old-established region, home to wonderful individual Semillons that last for decades, and great leathery Shiraz. Best producers include: *McWilliams Mount Pleasant, Tyrrell's, Rosemount* and its *Roxburgh* vineyard, *Reynolds, Rothbury, Allandale* and *Glenguin*.

KING VALLEY (Victoria) Cool, high-altitude region with fine Riesling, Shiraz and fizz, plus exciting Italian varietals.

MACEDON RANGES (Victoria) Region dominated by small family wineries, with good Pinot Noir, Chardonnay and Riesling. The cool climate can be just a bit *too* cool.

MARGARET RIVER (Western Australia) A source of increasingly poised wines that reek of a sense of place, combining richness of fruit with elegance of structure. *Moss Wood, Cape Mentelle, Cullen, Pierro, Vasse Felix* and *Leeuwin Estate* are the names to watch, and while Semillon and Sauvignon, Cabernet and Chardonnay are the most common wines, there is a scattering of other grapes like Zinfandel, Malbec, Sangiovese and Nebbiolo.

MCLAREN VALE (South Australia) Some wonderful old Shiraz vineyards are now under tarmac, thanks to the spread of Adelaide suburbia. Building has been slowed by a revival of interest in the quality of the area's fruit: the boldness of the black pepper Shiraz and the sweet concentration of Grenache and Chardonnay Recommended are *Chapel Hill Chardonnay, Four Sisters, Chateau Reynella Basket Pressed Shiraz, Coriole Redstone Shiraz/Cabernet, d'Arenberg (Ironstone Pressings, Twentyeight Road, Custodian* and *Coppermine Road), Geoff Merrill, Mount Hurtle.*

MORNINGTON PENINSULA (Victoria) One of the coolest Aussie wine zones, this is a weekend playground for the Melbourne rich. Good for light Chardonnay, sparkling wine and sometimes Pinot Noir. Among the best wineries are *Dromana, Stonier's* and *Moorooduc Estate*.

MUDGEE (New South Wales) Though Mudgee was established on Shiraz (*Montrose* is outstanding), the best reds have been tarry, plummy Cabernets. But Chardonnay is even better, usually rich, soft and full of fruit-salad flavours. *Rosemount* is leading a surge in quality. Best: *Craigmoor, Huntington, Miramar, Montrose, Rosemount.*

ORANGE (New South Wales) A new cool-climate region already making intense Loire-style Sauvignon Blanc (*Highland Heritage*) and cashew nut Chardonnay *(Rosemount)*, while the reds, notably Shiraz Cabernet and Merlot (from *Bloodwood, Reynolds* and *Rosemount)* are outstanding.

OVENS VALLEY (Victoria) Former tobacco region now making steely Riesling and Chardonnay, but also intense Merlot, Cabernet and Shiraz.

PADTHAWAY (South Australia) High quality whites, notably Chardonnay, Riesling and Sauvignon Blanc. Grapes for sparkling wine are grown here, and there is some excellent sweet Riesling. Best: *Hardy, Lindemans, Seppelt*; major names like *Orlando* and *Penfolds* also use the grapes.

PEMBERTON (Western Australia) Promising region for cool-climate Pinot Noir, Chardonnay and Sauvignon Blanc.

PYRENEES (Victoria) Very dry Shiraz and Cabernet reds, and mostly Sauvignon whites. Tops: *Dalwhinnie, Mount Avoca, Redbank, Taltarni, Warrenmang*, and for fizz, *Chateau Remy* (also stylish Cabernet and Chardonnay) and *Taltarni.*

RIVERINA (New South Wales) The vast irrigated Riverina (which used to be called Murrumbidgee Irrigation Area) provides ten to 15 per cent of the total Australian crop. Most is bulk wine, but *McWilliams* makes some attractive wines, as does *de Bortoli*, including a Sauternes-style Semillon and marmalady Rare Dry Botrytis Semillon.

RIVERLAND (South Australia) A vast irrigation project on the Murray River, providing a large chunk of the national crop. Dominated by the huge *Angove's* winery, and the even bigger *Berri-Renmano-Loxton* group (part of BRL Hardy), it makes huge amounts of bag-in-box wines of consistently good quality. But it also yields fresh, fruity Riesling, Chardonnay, Chenin, Sauvignon, Colombard, Cabernet and Shiraz. *Deakin Estate* and *Kingston Estate* stand out for good, fresh, fruity flavours.

RUTHERGLEN (Victoria) Here and Glenrowan to the south make up the centre of the fortified wine tradition. The white table wines are generally dull, except for the reliably fine *St Leonards*. The reds are rich and robust. The fortifieds, either as solera-method 'sherries', as 'vintage ports', or as intense, brown sugar-sweet Tokays, are all memorable. The true heights are achieved by sweet Muscats, unbearably rich but irresistible with it. Best: *Bullers, Campbells, Chambers, Morris, Stanton & Killeen* (Rutherglen); *Baileys* (Glenrowan).

SWAN DISTRICT (Western Australia) This hot region made its reputation on big, rich reds and whites, but even the famous *Houghton Supreme* is now much lighter and fresher. Good names: *Bassendean, Evans & Tate, Houghton, Moondah Brook, Sandalford.*

TASMANIA Only tiny amounts, but there is some remarkable Chardonnay from *Pipers Brook* and *Tasmanian Wine Co.*, and Cabernet from *Freycinet* and *Domaine A.* Pinot Noir can be terrific.

YARRA VALLEY (Victoria) Victoria's superstar. It suits the Champagne grapes, Pinot Noir and Chardonnay, for fizz, plus Cabernet and Pinot for superb reds. Best producers include: *Coldstream Hills, de Bortoli, Diamond Valley, Lillydale, Mount Mary, St Huberts, Seville, Tarrawarra, Yarra Burn, Yarra Ridge, Yarra Yering* and *Yeringberg*. Lots of big names are moving in, so expect more Yarra wines on the shelves.

MATURITY CHART

1994 Old Vines Shiraz, Barossa

Often approachable early

These wines can last and last

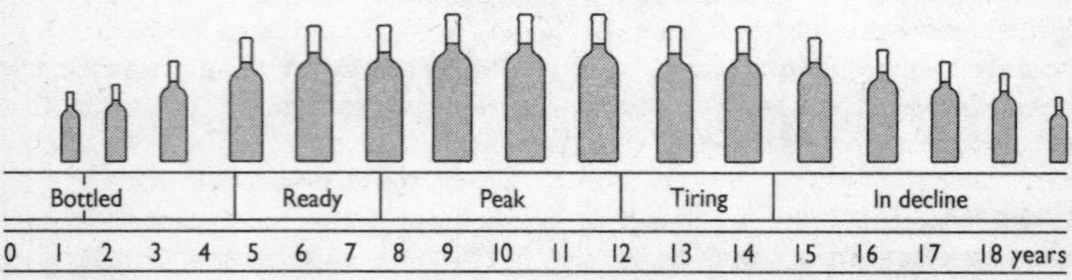

PRODUCERS WHO'S WHO

TIM ADAMS ★★★★(★) (South Australia) Spellbinding Semillon, wild Grenache and dense, full-flavoured Shiraz.

ALLANDALE ★★★(★) (New South Wales) One of the best Hunter Semillons; also complex, slightly honeyed Chardonnay and the excellent Matthew Shiraz.

BAILEYS OF GLENROWAN ★★★(★) (Victoria) Traditional winery famous for stunning sweet Muscats and Tokays, which are reassuringly rich. Red table wines are full and correct, though lacking the sense of history.

BANNOCKBURN ★★★★ (Victoria) Some of cool-climate Geelong's best wines: a rich Pinot Noir, full-bodied Chardonnay and Shiraz.

BAROSSA VALLEY ESTATES ★★(★) (South Australia) BRL Hardy-owned, this specializes in good quality, cheap wine.

JIM BARRY ★★★★ (South Australia) Clare Valley winery; outstanding unwooded Chardonnay, Rhine Riesling, Sauvignon Blanc and a splendidly rich Shiraz, The Armagh.

BASEDOW ★★★★ (South Australia) Barossa winery with big, toasty, oaky Chardonnay and Semillon, fine Watervale Riesling, chocolaty Shiraz and Cabernet. Old fashioned in the best way.

WOLF BLASS ★★★(★) (South Australia) The wines are decent at this Mildara-owned winery – modern, well plumped out with fruit and oak – but rarely match the silky, come-hither brilliance of the old days. Voluptuous Chardonnay, good Riesling and five styles of red which have, in rising price order, red, yellow, grey, brown and black labels.

BOWEN ESTATE ★★★★ (South Australia) The best value in Coonawarra: elegant Cabernet/Merlot and razor-fine Shiraz renowned for consistency and quality. Very good Riesling and Chardonnay.

BRL HARDY★★★★ (South Australia) Huge company making both high-standard, cheap own-labels and Hardy's impressive range from Nottage Hill to Chateau Reynella and Eileen Hardy. Look out, too, for Hardy's rich, sweet Botrytized Riesling.

BROKENWOOD ★★★★(★) (New South Wales) Small, high-class Hunter Valley winery noted for eclectic blends such as Hunter/Coonawarra Cabernet and latterly Hunter/McLaren Vale Semillon/Sauvignon Blanc. Low-yielding Graveyard vineyard produces one of Australia's best Shirazes: concentrated, profound and long-living.

BROWN BROTHERS ★★★ (Victoria) A huge range of good wine. The best vineyards are the cool Koombahla and even cooler Whitlands; look for Muscat, Semillon, Chardonnay, Koombahla Cabernet, Whitlands Gewürz and Riesling, the last in every style up to sweet and botrytized.

CAPE MENTELLE ★★★★(★) (Western Australia) Excellent Cabernet and variations on the Semillon/Sauvignon theme as well as Shiraz – and Zinfandel.

CHAPEL HILL ★★★★ (South Australia) Impressive wines with restraint and style include toasty Eden Valley Riesling, unwooded Chardonnay and chocolaty, blackberry-flavoured The Vicar, a blend of Cabernet and Shiraz.

CHATEAU TAHBILK ★★★★ (Victoria) Historic Goulburn Valley winery with great traditional Shiraz and Cabernet Sauvignon, and excellent Marsanne.

COLDSTREAM HILLS ★★★★ (Victoria) World-class Pinot Noir, exciting Chardonnay and Cabernet-Merlot blend, Briarston. Now owned by giant Southcorp, which seems to want to maintain quality.

CULLEN ★★★★(★) (Western Australia) Cullen has made consistently intense wines from the word go, and gets better with each vintage. Releases include a benchmark Sauvignon Blanc, a richly elegant Cabernet/Merlot and good Pinot Noir.

D'ARENBERG ★★★★ (South Australia) Firmly traditional winemaking produces powerfully rich Shiraz capable of almost infinite aging, sweetly fruity Custodian Grenache and densely structured Ironstone Pressings Grenache/Shiraz. Dead Arm is Cabernet and Shiraz; The Other Side is Chardonnay; Twentyeight Road is Mourvèdre; and Nostalgia is 12-year-old fortified.

DE BORTOLI ★★★(★) (New South Wales) Rich sweet Noble One Botrytis Semillon, plus a string of well-priced basics. Rare Dry Botrytis Semillon has bags of marmalade flavour but little subtlety. De Bortoli's Yarra Valley property makes good Chardonnay, Cabernet and Shiraz.

DELATITE ★★★★ (Victoria) Wines with individuality of style plus superb wine-making which puts them in the top class. Dry Riesling is delicious, the sweet version superb, while Pinot Noir, Gewürztraminer, Cabernet and Shiraz are brilliant.

DROMANA ★★★(★) (Victoria) Excellent Chardonnay, promising Pinot Noir and Cabernet/Merlot in the Mornington Peninsula, as well as a fascinating new range of Italian varietals.

EVANS & TATE ★★★(★) (Western Australia) Beautifully crafted, stylish wines; in particular weighty Semillon (straight and blended with Sauvignon), Merlot and Shiraz.

GOUNDREY ★★★(★) (Western Australia) Wines of real concentration, including Windy Hill Chardonnay and Cabernet, and the soft, coffee bean aromas of Shiraz from Mount Barker.

GREEN POINT ★★★★ (Victoria) Moët & Chandon's Australian outpost, making possibly Australia's best sparklers from Champagne grape varieties. The standard fizz is now called Chandon Australia.

HENSCHKE ★★★★★ (South Australia) Old red vines, some of them 100 years old, that yield deep, dark, curranty wines of top class. Cyril Henschke Cabernet Sauvignon is terrifically rich. Whites are equally stunning – Riesling, Semillon and Chardonnay.

HERITAGE ★★★(★) (South Australia) Among Barossa's boisterous winemakers, Heritage is a hidden gem, quietly producing classic wines from a wide range of varieties – limy Riesling, softly honeyed Semillon and an elegant Cabernet Franc.

HILL-SMITH/YALUMBA ★★★★ (South Australia) A large Barossa company producing good wines under the Yalumba and Hill-Smith labels, and exceptional ones under the Heggies and Pewsey Vale labels, where dry and sweet Rieslings are some of the finest in Australia. Yalumba D is very good fizz; Yalumba Signature is an outstanding blend of Cabernet Sauvignon and Shiraz. Also look out for Yalumba's Octavius Shiraz and Antipodean Red – a blend of Shiraz and other Rhône grapes.

HOLLICK ★★★ (South Australia) Some of Coonawarra's suavest reds; rich Wilgha Shiraz and an outstanding Bordeaux blend, Ravenswood. There is also fine Chardonnay and the district's most successful Riesling.

HOWARD PARK ★★★(★) (Western Australia) Expensive but superb, long-living wines. Intense, structured Chardonnay and rich Cabernet/Merlot. Both need cellaring.

KNAPPSTEIN ★★★ (South Australia) Ageworthy Riesling, spicy, restrained Traminer, nutty, long Chardonnay and ripe, grassy Cabernet Franc.

LAKE'S FOLLY ★★★★ (New South Wales) Tiny Hunter Valley winery making highly idiosyncratic Chardonnay and Cabernet Sauvignon that can become very exciting with age.

LEEUWIN ESTATE ★★★★ (Western Australia) Ultra-high profile, ultra-high prices for exciting Chardonnay and Pinot Noir, blackcurrant-and-leather Cabernet Sauvignon, good Riesling and Sauvignon.

LINDEMANS ★★★★ (Victoria) Exceptionally good basic varietals, while Coonawarras, Padthaways and Hunters are among Australia's finest. Coonawarra reds Limestone Ridge and St George are tip-top, as is the Bordeaux blend, Pyrus. New is smoky, leafy Bin 70: Semillon, Verdelho, Sauvignon and Chardonnay. Bin 65 Chardonnay is consistently good value.

MCWILLIAMS ★★(★) (New South Wales) Blends like the Hillside Colombard/ Chardonnay show what can be done with fairly basic fruit. Unoaked Elizabeth Semillon repays aging.

CHARLES MELTON ★★★★ (South Australia) A small Barossa winery with Grenache-based Nine Popes and a Shiraz of exceptional concentration and character.

GEOFF MERRILL ★★★(★) (South Australia) Wines here include worthy Cabernet, full Chardonnay, crisp Sauvignon/ Semillon and thirst-quenching Grenache rosé at Mount Hurtle.

MILDARA-BLASS ★★★ (South Australia) Own labels include Jamieson's Run and Robertson's Well and the Coonawarra reds are beginning to live up to their potential. Chardonnay is also improving, but Sauvignon and Pinot Noir need a bit of work yet. Umpteen subsidiaries: see also entries for Baileys of Glenrowan, Wolf Blass and Rothbury and St Huberts.

MITCHELTON ★★★(★) (Victoria) Wide range of styles, notably fine, full-flavoured Rieslings, good Chardonnay under the Preece label and the speciality of the house, Marsanne. Also interesting Rhône blends: Mitchelton III white is Marsanne, Roussanne and Viognier; Mitchelton III red is Shiraz, Grenache and Mourvèdre.

MOORILLA ESTATE ★★(★) (Tasmania) A polished range of crisp, cool-climate wines. Pinot Noir is a speciality; aromatic Riesling, Chardonnay and Gewürztraminer are also good.

MATURITY CHART

1997 Top Oaked Semillon

The best improve with up to eight years' bottle age

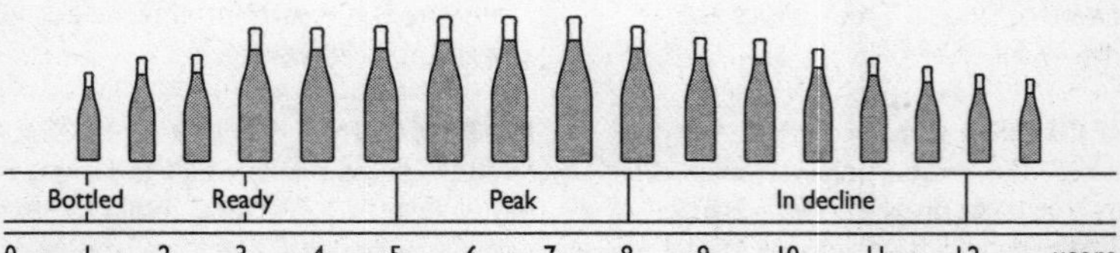

MORRIS ★★★★(★) (Victoria) The leading producer of sweet liqueur Muscat and Tokay which give a new meaning to the words 'intense' and 'concentrated'.

MOSS WOOD ★★★★ (Western Australia) Superbly original wines. Semillon, with and without wood-aging, is some of the best in Australia. Pinot Noir is daring and delicious, Chardonnay less daring but just as delicious, Cabernet rich and structured. All have lots of polished fruit.

MOUNTADAM ★★★★(★) (South Australia) French-trained Adam Wynn makes complex, Burgundian Chardonnay, substantial Pinot Noir, idiosyncratic Riesling and lean Cabernet. David Wynn Patriarch is a rich, fruit-laden Shiraz. The Red is a Cabernet/Merlot blend, and there's good rosé fizz, too.

MOUNT LANGI GHIRAN ★★★★ (Victoria) Grampians winery making richly flavoured, dry, intense Shiraz, long-lived Cabernet Sauvignon and properly spicy Pinot Grigio.

MOUNT MARY ★★★★ (Victoria) Finely structured Cabernet-based Bordeaux blend and a Pinot Noir improving with age. Tiny production, much sought-after.

ORLANDO ★★★ (South Australia) Barossa winery with fine quality at every level. Its boxed wine is outstanding, its RF Cabernet, Riesling and Chardonnay are usually the best in the price bracket, and St Helga Riesling, St Hilary Chardonnay and St Hugo Cabernet are among the best. Excellent Jacaranda Ridge Cabernet from Coonawarra. Jacob's Creek basics are deservedly successful.

PENFOLDS ★★★★★ (South Australia) Great red wine producer, and now good in whites too, particularly Old Vine Barossa Valley Semillon. Its basics are clean and tasty, its varietals packed with flavour, and its special selection reds, culminating in the deservedly legendary Grange, are superlative wines of world class. Overpriced Yattarna Chardonnay from Adelaide Hills is supposed to be the 'white Grange'.

PENLEY ESTATE ★★★★ (South Australia) There's rich, concentrated Shiraz/Cabernet from here as well as ageworthy Cabernet Sauvignon, supple Phoenix Cabernet and elegant Chardonnay.

PETALUMA ★★★★(★) (South Australia) Brian Croser's fizz is always correct, and his tip-top Chardonnay deserves aging. Riesling is limy and elegant. Coonawarra red is good, but the whites are even better.

PIPERS BROOK ★★★★ (Tasmania) Steely aromatic Riesling, classically reserved Chardonnay, serious Gewürztraminer and Pinot Gris are joined by excellent traditional-method fizz, Pirie.

PLANTAGENET ★★★(★) (Western Australia) Noted for peppery Shiraz, melony/nutty Chardonnay, fine limy Riesling and elegant Cabernet Sauvignon. Sparkling wine is good too, as is Pinot Noir.

REYNOLDS ★★★★ (New South Wales) This recently established Upper Hunter estate has already built a reputation with its chocolaty Cabernet, powerful Shiraz and well-structured Semillon.

ROCKFORD ★★★★(★) (South Australia) The individuality of Rocky O'Callaghan's wines, especially his Basket Press Shiraz, has made him a Barossa cult. Grenache and Riesling are marvellous, too, and all improve with aging.

ROSEMOUNT ★★★(★) (New South Wales) The company which did more than any to help Australia take Britain by storm with Chardonnay, Fumé Blanc and Cabernet. The last two are no longer so good, though Chardonnay is on the way back and the single-vineyard Roxburgh and Show Reserve Chardonnays are impressive. Exciting new Mountain Blue and Hill of Gold wines from Mudgee, surprising Pinot Noir and excellent Semillon and Shiraz.

ROTHBURY ★★★★ (New South Wales) Idiosyncratic but successful when it was under Len Evans' obsessive control; now owned by Mildara-Blass. Can produce the Hunter's greatest Semillon and juicy, fat crowd-pleasing Chardonnays. Some great Shiraz and Pinot Noir on occasion, too.

ST HALLETT ★★★★ (South Australia) Full, oaky Semillon and Chardonnay and a rich Shiraz, Old Block, from old vines. Gamekeeper's Reserve is Shiraz, Grenache, Mourvèdre and Touriga Nacional, brambly and spicy. One of the leading names in the Barossa revival.

ST HUBERTS ★★★(★) (Victoria) At best produces superb Chardonnays, exciting Cabernets and Pinots plus the odd thrilling sweetie, but has never settled into a totally reliable groove and some vintages fail to convince.

SEPPELT ★★★ (Victoria) Leading makers of quality fizz from Champagne grapes, peaking with Salinger. Also fruity, easy-drinking styles, and blackberryish sparkling red Shiraz.

SHAW & SMITH ★★★★ (South Australia) Fine Sauvignon Blanc and Chardonnay – including an unoaked version.

STAFFORD RIDGE ★★★★(★) (South Australia) Adelaide Hills winery with crisply intense and pure Sauvignon Blanc and delicate but long Chardonnay.

STONIER'S ★★★ (Victoria) Good cool-climate Chardonnay and Cabernet from this Mornington Peninsula winery.

TALTARNI ★★★ (Victoria) Remarkable bone-dry, grassy-sharp Fumé Blanc; fine Cabernet and Shiraz which soften (after about a decade) into classy, if austere reds.

TISDALL ★★★ (Victoria) Winery with excellent grape sources, but which has never quite lived up to its exceptional potential. If less oak were used the fruit would sing through. That said, there's good Chardonnay here and Mount Ida Reserve Shiraz is a cracker.

TYRRELL'S ★★★(★) (New South Wales) Eccentrically brilliant Hunter winery which sells 'port' and 'blackberry nip' to tourists through the front door while making some classic wines out the back. Vat 1 Semillon is excellent, as is the 'plonk' – Long Flat Red and White, named after the vineyard. Vat 9 is supple, leathery Shiraz.

VASSE FELIX ★★★★ (Western Australia) One of the original Margaret River wineries, producing a classic regional style of rich, leafy, curranty Cabernet and spicy, fleshy Shiraz. Classic Dry White is a blend of Chardonnay, Semillon and Sauvignon Blanc.

WIRRA WIRRA★★★★ (South Australia) Fine, concentrated reds, whites and sparkling wine, and exceptional Angelus Cabernet.

WYNNS ★★★★ (South Australia) Big, oaky Chardonnay, refined Cabernet and Shiraz from this Coonawarra company. Top-line John Riddoch Cabernet is expensive but worth every penny.

YARRA YERING ★★★★★ (Victoria) Wonderful Yarra Valley winery, where Bailey Carrodus labels his Cabernet-based wine Dry Red No.1 and his Shiraz-based wine Dry Red No. 2: exceptional, powerful and concentrated yet fragrant reds. Fine Pinot Noir and Chardonnay as well, in a very personal style.

AUSTRALIA PRICES

RED

Under £4.00

Dry Red Dalwood **Non-vintage** £3.60 (SOM)
Dry Red Lindemans Cawarra **1999** £3.99 (BUD) £3.99 (WAI)
Malbec/Ruby Cabernet Angove's Nanya Estate **1998** £3.99 (THR) £3.99 (BOT)
Shiraz/Cabernet Dalwood **1997** £3.95 (SOM)
Shiraz/Mataro Hardys Banrock **1999** £3.99 (UN) £3.99 (SAF)
Shiraz/Merlot Barramundi **Non-vintage** £3.99 (ASD) £3.99 (TES)

£4.00 → £4.99

Dry Red Rolleston Vale **Non-vintage** £4.00 (GW) £4.25 (CON)
Grenache Kingston Estate **1996** £4.50 (UB)
Grenache Peter Lehmann **1998** £4.99 (ASD)
Grenache Peter Lehmann Vine Vale **1998** £4.69 (UN)
Grenache/Shiraz Orlando Jacob's Creek **1999** £4.99 (BUD) £4.99 (WAI)
Long Flat Red Tyrrell's **1998** £4.95 (COC) £5.99 (JON)
Merlot Lindemans Cawarra **1999** £4.99 (SAF)
Rawson's Retreat Bin 35 Penfolds **1999** £4.99 (BUD) £5.49 (WAI)
Rawson's Retreat Bin 35 Penfolds **1998** £4.80 (SOM) £5.49 (BO) £5.49 (TES) £5.49 (VIC) £5.49 (THR) £5.49 (WR) £5.49 (BOT) £5.49 (SAF) £5.50 (WS) £5.59 (JON)
Red Ochre d'Arenberg **1997** £4.95 (WS)
Shiraz Lindemans Bin 50 **1998** £4.69 (TES) £4.95 (WS) £4.99 (ASD) £4.99 (MAJ)
Shiraz/Cabernet Sauvignon Aldridge Estate **1998** £4.99 (CON)
Shiraz/Cabernet Sauvignon De Bortoli Sacred Hill **1998** £4.95 (LEA) £4.95 (STE)
Shiraz/Cabernet Sauvignon Hardys Stamp **1999** £4.99 (TES) £4.99 (SAF) £4.99 (WAI)
Shiraz/Cabernet Sauvignon Hardys Stamp **1998** £4.99 (SO) £4.99 (VIC) £4.99 (THR) £4.99 (UN) £4.99 (WR) £4.99 (BOT)
Shiraz/Cabernet Sauvignon Lindemans Cawarra **1998** £4.69 (ASD) £4.99 (MAJ) £4.99 (UN)
Shiraz/Cabernet Sauvignon Miranda Opal Ridge **1998** £4.99 (CON)
Shiraz/Cabernet Sauvignon Orlando Jacob's Creek **1998** £4.79 (TES) £5.49 (VIC) £5.49 (THR) £5.49 (WR) £5.49 (BOT) £5.49 (SAF) £5.49 (BUD)
Shiraz/Cabernet Sauvignon Penfolds Rowlands Brook **1998** £4.79 (JON) £4.95 (POR)
Shiraz/Cabernet Sauvignon Rolleston Vale **1998** £4.49 (CON) £4.49 (GW)
Shiraz/Cabernet Sauvignon Tatachilla Wattle Park **1998** £4.95 (BAN)

£5.00 → £5.99

Cabernet Sauvignon Hardys Nottage Hill **1997** £5.49 (ASD)
Cabernet Sauvignon Lindemans Bin 45 **1998** £5.99 (MAJ) £5.99 (UN)
Cabernet Sauvignon McWilliams Hanwood **1997** £5.95 (COC)
Cabernet Sauvignon Sunnycliff **1998** £5.40 (HAH) £5.49 (POR) £5.49 (JON) £5.60 (TAN)
Cabernet Sauvignon David Wynn **1997** £5.70 (SOM)
Cabernet Sauvignon/Merlot Cockatoo Ridge **1997** £5.95 (RES)

MERCHANTS SPECIALIZING IN AUSTRALIA

see Merchant Directory (page 456) for details

Virtually every merchant will be able to sell you some Australian wines. But for more than the usual, try: Adnams (AD), Australian Wine Club (AUS), Averys of Bristol (AV), Ballantynes (BAL), Bennetts (BEN), Bibendum (BIB), Anthony Byrne (BY), Direct Wine Shipments (DI), Domaine Direct (DOM), First Quench Group (BOT, THR, VIC, WR), Lay & Wheeler (LAY), James Nicholson (NI), The Nobody Inn (NO), Oddbins (OD), Terry Platt (PLA), Philglas & Swiggot (PHI), Raeburn Fine Wines (RAE), Roberson (ROB), Sainsbury's (SAI), Safeway (SAF), Sommelier Wine Co (SOM), Tanners (TAN), The Ubiquitous Chip (UB), Wine Society (WS), Wine Treasury (WT), Noel Young (YOU).

Cabernet Sauvignon/Mourvèdre Grant Burge Oakland **1997** £5.49 (UN)
Cabernet Sauvignon/Mourvèdre Grant Burge Oakland **1996** £5.99 (CON)
Cabernet Sauvignon/Shiraz Hardys Nottage Hill **1999** £5.79 (WAI) £5.79 (SAF)
Cabernet Sauvignon/Shiraz Hardys Nottage Hill **1998** £5.49 (SAI) £5.49 (VIC) £5.49 (THR) £5.49 (UN) £5.49 (WR) £5.49 (BOT) £5.79 (TES) £5.79 (BUD)
Cabernet Sauvignon/Shiraz Penfolds Koonunga Hill **1996** £5.99 (SOM) £6.95 (COC)
Cabernet Sauvignon/Shiraz Rosemount **1998** £5.49 (ASD)
Cabernet Sauvignon/Shiraz Yalumba Oxford Landing **1999** £5.49 (WAI) £5.69 (BUD) £6.25 (STE)
Cabernet Sauvignon/Shiraz Yalumba Oxford Landing **1998** £5.49 (TES) £5.49 (WR) £5.49 (SAF) £5.99 (NI) £5.99 (VIC) £5.99 (THR) £5.99 (JON)
Cabernet Sauvignon/Shiraz/Merlot Woolshed **1998** £5.99 (SAF)
Grenache Basedow Bush Vine **1998** £5.99 (SAF)
Grenache Peter Lehmann **1996** £5.35 (UB)
Jacob's Creek Red Orlando **1998** £5.49 (SO)
Long Flat Red Tyrrell's **1999** £5.62 (PIP)
Merlot Deakin Estate **1998** £5.49 (DI)
Pinot Noir David Wynn **1997** £5.70 (SOM)
Rawson's Retreat Bin 35 Penfolds **Non-vintage** £5.49 (UN)
Rawson's Retreat Bin 35 Penfolds **1997** £5.39 (POR)
Shiraz Aldridge Estate **1998** £5.99 (CON)
Shiraz Deakin Estate **1999** £5.49 (DI) £5.49 (OD)
Shiraz Hardys Banrock **1998** £5.49 (ASD)
Shiraz Peter Lehmann Vine Vale **1997** £5.25 (BO)
Shiraz McWilliams Hanwood **1998** £5.95 (COC)
Shiraz David Wynn **1998** £5.70 (SOM) £6.74 (FLE) £7.25 (STE) £7.75 (AD)
Shiraz Yaldara Reserve **1997** £5.65 (SOM)
Shiraz/Cabernet Sauvignon Orlando Jacob's Creek **Non-vintage** £5.49 (ASD)

Stars (★) indicate wines selected by Oz Clarke in the Best Buys section which begins on page 10.

Shiraz/Cabernet Sauvignon Orlando Jacob's Creek **1999** £5.49 (WAI)
Shiraz/Cabernet Sauvignon Penfolds Koonunga Hill **1997** £5.99 (SOM) £6.95 (WS) £6.99 (VIC) £6.99 (THR) £6.99 (UN)
Shiraz/Cabernet Sauvignon Rouge Homme **1996** £5.99 (POR)
Shiraz/Cabernet Sauvignon Yalumba Oxford Landing **1998** £5.79 (UN)
Shiraz/Grenache Ironstone **1996** £5.99 (CON)
Shiraz/Mourvèdre Penfolds Bin 2 **1998** £5.95 (WS) £6.49 (TES) £6.49 (THR)
Shiraz/Mourvèdre Penfolds Bin 2 **1997** £5.60 (SOM) £6.49 (WR) £6.75 (POR)
Tarrango Brown Brothers **1999** £5.56 (PIP) £5.95 (STE) £5.99 (DI) £5.99 (TES) £5.99 (WAI) £6.50 (AD)
Tarrango Brown Brothers **1998** £5.29 (JON) £5.49 (BO) £5.75 (PLA) £5.75 (CON) £5.95 (POR) £5.99 (GW)

£6.00 → £6.99

Barbera Brown Bros **1997** £6.99 (WAI) £7.45 (STE) £7.48 (GW) £7.75 (STA)
Cabernet Sauvignon Best's Victoria **1994** £6.50 (CRO)
Cabernet Sauvignon Lindemans Bin 45 **1997** £6.19 (JON)
Cabernet Sauvignon Mitchelton Preece **1996** £6.74 (NO)
Cabernet Sauvignon Wakefield **1997** £6.75 (BO) £6.99 (UN)
Cabernet Sauvignon Wyndham Estate Bin 444 **1996** £6.99 (COC)
Cabernet Sauvignon David Wynn **1998** £6.74 (FLE) £7.25 (STE) £7.75 (AD) £7.99 (GW) £8.00 (MV)
Cabernet Sauvignon/Cabernet Franc/Merlot St Hallett **1997** £6.99 (SOM)
Cabernet Sauvignon/Merlot Rosemount **1999** £6.99 (SAF)
Cabernet Sauvignon/Merlot St Hallett **1997** £6.99 (TES) £7.99 (AUS)
Cabernet Sauvignon/Merlot Tyrrell's Old Winery **1998** £6.99 (SAI) £7.64 (PLAY)
Cabernet Sauvignon/Merlot Tyrrell's Old Winery **1997** £6.99 (UN)
Cabernet Sauvignon/Merlot Yaldara Reserve **1995** £6.70 (FLE)
Cabernet Sauvignon/Shiraz Penfolds Koonunga Hill **1998** £6.99 (OD)
Cabernet Sauvignon/Shiraz Penfolds Koonunga Hill **1997** £6.89 (POR)
Durif De Bortoli Vat 1 **1998** £6.45 (STE)

Gamekeeper's Reserve St Hallett **1997** £6.49 (POR)
Grenache Bethany **1998** £6.49 (MAJ) £8.67 (NO)
Grenache Simon Hackett McLaren Vale Old Vine **1998** £6.92 (FLE) £7.49 (CON) £8.50 (BER)
★ Grenache Adam Wynn Samuel's Bay **1997** £6.49 (VIC) £6.49 (THR) £6.49 (WR) £6.49 (BOT)
Grenache/Shiraz Rosemount **1999** £6.49 (TES) £6.49 (VIC) £6.49 (THR) £6.49 (WR) £6.49 (BOT) £6.49 (SAF) £6.99 (WAI)
Pinot Noir Fox River **1998** £6.99 (ASD)
Pinot Noir Tyrrell's **1997** £6.20 (COC)
Pinot Noir Tyrrell's Old Winery **1997** £6.99 (UN)
Pinot Noir/Shiraz Montara 'M' **1997** £6.15 (SOM) £6.90 (CRO)
Shiraz Best's Victoria **1998** £6.99 (UN) £7.46 (PLA) £7.95 (NI)
Shiraz Best's Victoria **1997** £6.99 (GW)
Shiraz d'Arenberg Old Vine **1997** £6.99 (OD)
Shiraz Simon Hackett Anthony's Reserve **1997** £6.92 (FLE) £9.49 (CON)
Shiraz Hardys Bankside **1998** £6.99 (SAI) £6.99 (UN) £6.99 (SAF)
Shiraz Haselgrove Sovereign **1998** £6.50 (BU)
Shiraz Houghton Wildflower Ridge **1997** £6.99 (ASD) £7.49 (CON)
Shiraz Lindemans Bin 50 **1997** £6.66 (BY)
Shiraz Lindemans Limestone Coast **1998** £6.75 (STE)
Shiraz McGuigan Bros Bin 2000 Millennium **1999** £6.22 (PLA)
Shiraz Rosemount **1998** £6.90 (CRO) £7.49 (SO) £7.49 (TES) £7.49 (WR) £7.49 (SAF)
Shiraz Rothbury Mudgee **1997** £6.90 (CRO)
Shiraz Trentham Willandra **1998** £6.49 (HED)
Shiraz Wakefield **1998** £6.99 (UN) £7.49 (BAL) £9.97 (VIN)
Shiraz Wyndham Estate Bin 555 **1996** £6.99 (COC)
Shiraz Wynns Coonawarra Estate **1997** £6.95 (POR) £6.99 (MAJ)
Shiraz Yaldara Reserve **1998** £6.99 (GW) £7.04 (PLA) £8.19 (PLAY)
Shiraz Yalumba Oxford Landing **1998** £6.95 (STE)
Shiraz/Cabernet Sauvignon Penfolds Koonunga Hill **1998** £6.99 (SO) £6.99 (TES) £6.99 (WR) £6.99 (BOT) £6.99 (BUD)
Shiraz/Cabernet Sauvignon Rosemount **1999** £6.45 (TES) £6.49 (SAI) £6.49 (VIC) £6.49 (THR) £6.49 (WR) £6.49 (BOT) £6.49 (SAF) £6.79 (UN)
Shiraz/Cabernet Sauvignon Rouge Homme **1995** £6.49 (AME)
Shiraz/Cabernet Sauvignon Saltram Stonyfell Metala **1997** £6.99 (SAF) £7.49 (BO) £7.99 (AME)
Shiraz/Cabernet Sauvignon Seppelt Moyston **1998** £6.85 (VIN)
Shiraz/Cabernet Sauvignon Wolf Blass Red Label **1996** £6.49 (TES)
Shiraz/Grenache d'Arenberg d'Arry's Original **1997** £6.99 (BO)
Shiraz/Grenache Ironstone **1998** £6.49 (BO) £6.99 (UN) £7.25 (STE) £7.65 (AD)
Shiraz/Grenache Ironstone **1997** £6.95 (NI)
Shiraz/Mourvèdré Penfolds Bin 2 **1999** £6.49 (BOT) £7.75 (FORT)

£7.00 → £7.99

Antipodean Red Yalumba **1996** £7.95 (UB)
Barbera Brown Bros **1996** £7.45 (STE) £7.95 (DI) £8.65 (UB)
Cabernet Sauvignon Best's Victoria **1996** £7.50 (FLE)
Cabernet Sauvignon Brown Bros **1997** £7.95 (DI) £7.99 (PIP) £8.50 (TAN)
Cabernet Sauvignon Richard Hamilton Hut Block **1996** £7.95 (SOM) £10.99 (BOD) £10.99 (SUN)
Cabernet Sauvignon Heatherfield Ridge Endeavour **1998** £7.99 (SAF)
Cabernet Sauvignon Maglieri **1997** £7.99 (TES)
Cabernet Sauvignon Montara Estate **1997** £7.75 (SOM) £9.95 (AD)
Cabernet Sauvignon Rosemount **1999** £7.49 (WAI)
Cabernet Sauvignon Rosemount **1998** £7.49 (VIC) £7.49 (SO) £7.49 (SAI) £7.49 (BO) £7.49 (TES) £7.49 (THR) £7.49 (WR) £7.49 (BOT) £7.59 (BUD)
Cabernet Sauvignon David Traeger **1996** £7.99 (AUS)
Cabernet Sauvignon Wakefield **1998** £7.49 (BAL) £7.63 (PLA)
Cabernet Sauvignon Wolf Blass Yellow Label **1998** £7.29 (BUD) £7.49 (PHI) £7.49 (SAI) £7.49 (MAJ) £7.49 (SAF) £8.72 (BY)
Cabernet Sauvignon Wolf Blass Yellow Label **1997** £7.49 (ASD) £7.49 (VIC) £7.49 (THR) £7.49 (UN) £7.49 (BOT) £8.95 (JER)

Cabernet Sauvignon Wolf Blass Yellow Label **1995** £7.50 (CRO)
Cabernet Sauvignon/Merlot Bethany **1996** £7.75 (SOM)
Cabernet Sauvignon/Merlot Goundrey **1995** £7.55 (SOM)
Cabernet Sauvignon/Merlot Koppamurra **1996** £7.99 (AUS) £9.34 (REI)
Cabernet Sauvignon/Merlot Maxwell **1997** £7.65 (SOM)
Cabernet Sauvignon/Merlot Neil Paulett **1997** £7.90 (JU)
Cabernet Sauvignon/Shiraz Riddoch **1997** £7.99 (SAF)
Cabernet Sauvignon/Shiraz/Merlot Wynns Coonawarra Estate **1996** £7.99 (TES) £8.29 (JON)
Clancy's Red Peter Lehmann **1998** £7.99 (SAI) £7.99 (OD) £7.99 (UN) £7.99 (SAF)
Grenache Yalumba Barossa Growers Bush Vine **1997** £7.99 (VIC) £7.99 (THR) £8.99 (BEN) £8.99 (NI) £8.99 (WR) £8.99 (BOT)
Grenache Yalumba Barossa Growers Bush Vine **1996** £7.75 (SOM) £9.25 (UB)
Merlot Brown Bros **1996** £7.95 (DI) £8.35 (AD) £8.45 (STE)
Merlot Miranda High Country **1997** £7.41 (COC) £7.65 (CON)
Merlot Rosemount **1998** £7.99 (TES) £7.99 (UN) £7.99 (SAF)
Merlot/Cabernet Sauvignon Rymill **1996** £7.99 (ASD)
Pinot Noir Ninth Island **1998** £7.95 (SOM) £7.99 (TES) £8.49 (CON) £8.99 (REI)
Pinot Noir Rouge Homme **1996** £7.49 (AME)
Pinot Noir Tyrrell's Old Winery **1998** £7.95 (WS)
Pinot Noir David Wynn **1998** £7.25 (STE) £7.59 (NI) £7.75 (AD) £8.00 (MV)
Pinot Noir/Shiraz Montara 'M' **1998** £7.95 (AD) £8.45 (PHI)
Shiraz Baileys **1996** £7.49 (AME)
Shiraz Brown Bros **1997** £7.95 (DI) £7.99 (TES) £7.99 (PIP) £8.45 (STE) £8.50 (GW)
Shiraz Campbells Bobbie Burns **1994** £7.78 (NO)
Shiraz Capel Vale CV **1998** £7.99 (SAF)
Shiraz D'Arenberg The Footbolt Old Vine **1998** £7.99 (BIB)
Shiraz Leasingham **1995** £7.99 (UN)
Shiraz McWilliams JJ McWilliam **1998** £7.25 (COC)
Shiraz Normans Old Vine **1997** £7.99 (SAF)
Shiraz Neil Paulett **1997** £7.90 (JU)
Shiraz Penfolds Kalimna Bin 28 **1996** £7.80 (SOM) £8.75 (POR) £8.99 (ASD) £8.99 (SO) £8.99 (TES) £8.99 (UN) £9.18 (PIP) £9.29 (JON) £9.49 (BO) £9.68 (BY) £16.67 (MI)
Shiraz Plantagenet Omrah **1997** £7.95 (POR) £8.75 (STE)
Shiraz Rothbury Hunter Valley **1996** £7.99 (DI)
Shiraz St Hallett **1998** £7.99 (BOT)
Shiraz St Hallett **1997** £7.99 (VIC) £7.99 (THR) £7.99 (WR) £8.52 (REI) £8.99 (AUS)
Shiraz Taltarni **1994** £7.58 (REI)
Shiraz Wolf Blass **1996** £7.95 (JER)
Shiraz/Cabernet Sauvignon Penfolds Koonunga Hill **1996** £7.19 (JON)
Shiraz/Grenache d'Arenberg d'Arry's Original **1998** £7.99 (OD)

£8.00 → £8.99

Cabernet Franc Knappstein **1997** £8.49 (BO) £9.50 (PIP)
★ Cabernet Sauvignon Tim Adams **1997** £8.99 (AUS)
Cabernet Sauvignon Jim Barry **1997** £8.95 (TAN) £9.99 (DI)
Cabernet Sauvignon Bremerton **1994** £8.92 (NO)
Cabernet Sauvignon Brown Bros **1996** £8.25 (CON) £8.95 (POR)
Cabernet Sauvignon Brown Bros Milawa **1996** £8.39 (JON)
Cabernet Sauvignon Grant Burge **1998** £8.99 (UN) £10.85 (AS)
Cabernet Sauvignon Cape Mentelle **1995** £8.84 (NO) £14.98 (PLA) £16.50 (PHI) £16.74 (REI)
Cabernet Sauvignon Maglieri **1996** £8.99 (UN)
Cabernet Sauvignon Mitchell **1997** £8.99 (JON)
Cabernet Sauvignon Mitchell **1996** £8.60 (AD) £8.70 (TAN) £8.95 (POR)
Cabernet Sauvignon Pewsey Vale **1996** £8.99 (TES)
Cabernet Sauvignon Rouge Homme **1994** £8.99 (AME) £13.89 (VIN)
Cabernet Sauvignon Stonier's **1997** £8.99 (DI)
Cabernet Sauvignon Water Wheel **1998** £8.80 (PLA)
Cabernet Sauvignon/Malbec Galah **1995** £8.99 (AUS)
Cabernet Sauvignon/Merlot Cape Mentelle **1997** £8.30 (NO) £8.95 (STA) £9.75 (PHI) £9.95 (AD) £9.95 (NI)

Cabernet Sauvignon/Merlot Cape Mentelle **1996** £8.75 (CON) £8.99 (RAE) £8.99 (REI) £9.78 (PLAY)
Cabernet Sauvignon/Merlot Hollick Coonawarra **1996** £8.95 (NI) £9.49 (HED)
Cabernet Sauvignon/Merlot Hollick Coonawarra **1993** £8.20 (SOM)
Cabernet Sauvignon/Merlot Yalumba **1996** £8.99 (NI)
Cabernet Sauvignon/Shiraz Ironstone **1995** £8.50 (CRO)
Cabernet Sauvignon/Shiraz Riddoch **1998** £8.91 (BIB) £8.99 (DI)
Cabernet Sauvignon/Shiraz Wirra Wirra Church Block **1997** £8.95 (WS) £8.99 (PHI) £8.99 (OD) £9.49 (WAI)
Grenache Tim Gramp **1997** £8.95 (RES)
Grenache Rockford Dry Country **1997** £8.13 (FLE) £8.36 (PIP) £9.10 (TAN)
Grenache/Shiraz Wirra Wirra Original Blend **1998** £8.99 (OD)
Merlot Brown Bros **1997** £8.49 (CON)
Pinot Noir Hollick Coonawarra **1997** £8.99 (HED) £8.99 (NI)
Richardsons Red Block Rouge Homme **1995** £8.49 (AME) £8.95 (POR)
Sangiovese Coriole **1994** £8.90 (CRO)
Sharefarmer's Red Petaluma **1996** £8.50 (STE)
★ Shiraz Tim Adams **1998** £8.95 (WS) £8.99 (TES) £8.99 (AUS)
Shiraz Alkoomi **1996** £8.45 (JER)
Shiraz Brown Bros **1996** £8.25 (CON) £8.75 (POR)
Shiraz Campbells Bobbie Burns **1997** £8.95 (UB) £9.61 (PIP)
★ Shiraz Chapel Hill McLaren Vale **1997** £8.99 (TES) £9.99 (AUS) £9.99 (WR) £9.99 (VIC) £9.99 (THR) £9.99 (BOT)
Shiraz Coriole **1997** £8.95 (TAN)
Shiraz Goundrey **1992** £8.50 (CRO)
Shiraz Madfish Bay **1998** £8.99 (GW) £10.95 (BAL) £10.99 (NI)
Shiraz Madfish Bay **1997** £8.45 (SOM)
Shiraz Maglieri **1997** £8.99 (TES)
Shiraz Mitchell Peppertree **1998** £8.45 (TAN) £8.95 (AD) £8.95 (POR) £8.99 (JON)

- *All prices for each wine are listed together in ascending order.*
- *Price bands refer to the lowest price for which the wine is available.*

Shiraz Mitchelton **1995** £8.99 (AME)
Shiraz Montara Estate **1997** £8.99 (FLE) £8.99 (PHI) £9.95 (AD)
Shiraz Penfolds Coonawarra Bin 128 **1996** £8.20 (SOM) £8.75 (POR) £9.49 (BO) £9.49 (TES) £9.49 (UN) £9.49 (SAF) £10.21 (BY)
Shiraz Penfolds Kalimna Bin 28 **1997** £8.99 (VIC) £8.99 (THR) £8.99 (WR) £8.99 (BOT)
Shiraz Taltarni **1997** £8.95 (BER)
Shiraz David Traeger **1996** £8.99 (AUS)
Shiraz Trentham **1997** £8.99 (AME)
Shiraz Water Wheel **1998** £8.80 (PLA)
Shiraz/Grenache Veritas Christa-Rolf **1999** £8.65 (LAY)
Shiraz/Grenache/Mourvèdre Penfolds Old Vine **1995** £8.65 (SOM)

£9.00 → £9.99

Cabernet Franc Knappstein **1994** £9.00 (CRO)
Cabernet Sauvignon Alkoomi **1995** £9.50 (JER)
Cabernet Sauvignon Jim Barry **1998** £9.40 (BEN)
Cabernet Sauvignon Best's Great Western **1993** £9.50 (CRO)
Cabernet Sauvignon Grant Burge **1997** £9.65 (CON) £9.95 (RES)
Cabernet Sauvignon Eden Ridge **1997** £9.50 (AD)
Cabernet Sauvignon Hardys Coonawarra **1996** £9.99 (SAF)
Cabernet Sauvignon Penfolds Bin 407 **1996** £9.50 (SOM) £10.99 (BO) £10.99 (TES) £18.33 (MI)
Cabernet Sauvignon Pikes **1997** £9.95 (LEA)
Cabernet Sauvignon Rymill **1994** £9.95 (RAE)
Cabernet Sauvignon Saltram Mamre Brook **1997** £9.99 (SAF)
Cabernet Sauvignon Taltarni **1996** £9.95 (STA)
Cabernet Sauvignon Wynns **1996** £9.95 (POR)
Cabernet Sauvignon Wynns Coonawarra Estate **1996** £9.99 (BOD) £9.99 (SUN)
Cabernet Sauvignon Wynns Coonawarra Estate **1995** £9.99 (MAJ) £9.99 (AME)
Cabernet Sauvignon/Malbec Galah **1996** £9.50 (AUS)
Cabernet Sauvignon/Malbec Leasingham Bin 56 **1996** £9.99 (VIC) £9.99 (THR) £9.99 (WR) £9.99 (BOT)
Cabernet Sauvignon/Merlot Dromana Estate **1998** £9.99 (FLE)

THE HANGING GARDENS OF AUSTRALIA
Australia's Vineyards are its gardens. Its grape varieties, perennials spread across the wine growing regions, from Western Australia to New South Wales, from the garden state of South Australia to Tasmania.
The complex interaction of soil, climate, variety, and viticultural practice give the grapes individuality and so the wines. It is hardly surprising that such a vast continent as Australia with widely differing environments produces so many diverse wine styles.
Explore the hanging gardens of Australia.
WINE OF AUSTRALIA

Cabernet Sauvignon/Merlot Yaldara Reserve **1998** £9.55 (VIN)
Cabernet Sauvignon/Shiraz Wirra Wirra Church Block **1998** £9.75 (AD)
Durif Morris **1994** £9.65 (SOM)
The Fergus Tim Adams **1998** £9.99 (AUS)
The Fergus Tim Adams **1997** £9.49 (WR) £9.49 (BOT) £9.99 (REI)
Fifth Leg Devil's Lair **1997** £9.69 (GW)
Merlot/Cabernet Sauvignon Hillstowe Buxton **1997** £9.38 (NO)
Pinot Noir Dromana Estate **1998** £9.99 (FLE)
Pinot Noir Montara **1997** £9.50 (AD)
Shiraz Baileys 1920s Block **1996** £9.95 (AME)
Shiraz Grant Burge Old Vine **1997** £9.99 (UN) £11.95 (LEA)
Shiraz Cape Mentelle **1997** £9.99 (REI) £10.16 (PLA) £10.49 (AME) £10.99 (PHI) £10.99 (VA)
Shiraz Cape Mentelle **1995** £9.99 (RAE)
Shiraz Coriole **1994** £9.42 (NO) £18.00 (CRO)
Shiraz Fern Hill **1995** £9.99 (FRI)
Shiraz Frankland Estate Isolation Ridge **1996** £9.50 (BAN) £10.99 (YOU)
Shiraz Leasingham **1996** £9.99 (ASD)
Shiraz McWilliams Mount Pleasant **1994** £9.69 (HA) £9.95 (COC)
Shiraz Mitchell Peppertree **1997** £9.99 (PHI)
Shiraz Mitchelton Goulburn Valley **1996** £9.95 (WS)
Shiraz Penfolds Coonawarra Bin 128 **1998** £9.99 (SO)
Shiraz Penfolds Coonawarra Bin 128 **1995** £9.45 (COC)
Shiraz Penley Estate Hyland **1997** £9.65 (LAY)
Shiraz Pikes Polish Hill River **1997** £9.95 (LEA)
Shiraz Rothbury Reserve **1995** £9.95 (DI)
Shiraz Saltram Mamre Brook **1997** £9.99 (BOD) £9.99 (SUN)
Shiraz Taltarni **1996** £9.30 (AV) £9.95 (STA)
Shiraz The Willows Vineyard **1996** £9.99 (AUS)
Shiraz/Cabernet Sauvignon Henschke Keyneton Estate **1995** £9.22 (REI) £12.20 (SOM) £15.00 (FLE) £21.15 (JER) £25.85 (FA)
★ The Society's Exhibition Shiraz Mount Langi Ghiran **1997** £9.95 (WS)
Tamar Cabernets Ninth Island **1997** £9.25 (CON)

£10.00 → £10.99

Barbera Dromana Estate Gary Crittenden 'I' **1998** £10.99 (WAI)
Cabernet Sauvignon Best's Great Western **1996** £10.99 (UN) £11.99 (GW)
Cabernet Sauvignon Bowen Estate **1997** £10.99 (AUS) £11.46 (REI)
Cabernet Sauvignon Grant Burge Cameron Vale **1998** £10.85 (AS)
Cabernet Sauvignon Katnook **1997** £10.99 (YOU) £11.75 (BIB) £11.99 (DI)
Cabernet Sauvignon Marienberg **1994** £10.15 (JER)
Cabernet Sauvignon Maxwell Lime Cave **1997** £10.99 (YOU)
Cabernet Sauvignon Penley Estate Phoenix **1997** £10.82 (WT)
Cabernet Sauvignon Plantagenet **1995** £10.75 (STE)
Cabernet Sauvignon Taltarni **1992** £10.49 (CON)
Cabernet Sauvignon Vasse Felix **1997** £10.75 (SOM) £13.95 (RES)
Cabernet Sauvignon Yalumba Menzies **1995** £10.85 (SOM) £12.95 (NI)
Cabernet Sauvignon/Merlot Mount Helen **1997** £10.83 (BOD)
Cabernet Sauvignon/Shiraz Penfolds Bin 389 **1995** £10.40 (SOM) £12.95 (COC)
Grenache Simon Hackett McLaren Vale Old Vine **1997** £10.79 (VIN)
Merlot Katnook **1997** £10.99 (AME) £11.99 (DI)
Merlot Tatachilla Clarendon Vineyard **1997** £10.99 (YOU)
Pinot Noir Cullen **1994** £10.49 (AME)
Pinot Noir Old Kent River **1997** £10.75 (JER)
Pinot Noir Stonier's **1998** £10.99 (DI) £11.49 (YOU)
Pinot Noir Tarrawarra Tunnel Hill **1998** £10.25 (AS) £10.95 (RES)
Shiraz Balgownie **1986** £10.50 (CRO)
Shiraz Grant Burge 60-year-old vines **1997** £10.75 (CON)

- *Wines are listed in A–Z order within each price band.*
- *For each wine, vintages are listed in descending order.*
- *Each vintage of any wine appears only once.*

Shiraz Clarendon Hills Astralis **1997** £10.18 (FA) £85.00 (JU)
Shiraz Fern Hill **1996** £10.50 (AS)
Shiraz Tim Gramp **1996** £10.75 (SOM)
Shiraz Mount Ida **1996** £10.99 (PHI)
Shiraz Penley Estate Hyland **1996** £10.21 (WT)
Shiraz Plantagenet **1996** £10.75 (STE) £13.95 (RES)
Shiraz David Wynn Patriarch **1996** £10.50 (SOM) £14.35 (NI) £14.50 (WRI)
Shiraz/Malbec/Cabernet Sauvignon Hollick Wilgha **1997** £10.81 (TW)

£11.00 → £11.99

Cabernet Sauvignon Bowen Estate **1996** £11.46 (REI)
Cabernet Sauvignon Simon Hackett Foggo Road **1996** £11.25 (WRI)
Cabernet Sauvignon Leconfield **1997** £11.95 (JU)
Cabernet Sauvignon Penfolds Bin 407 **1995** £11.23 (NO)
Cabernet Sauvignon Plantagenet **1996** £11.99 (LIB) £12.20 (HAH) £12.95 (VA)
Cabernet Sauvignon Stonier's Reserve **1994** £11.99 (WAT)
Cabernet Sauvignon Wolf Blass President's Selection **1996** £11.40 (COC)
Cabernet Sauvignon/Merlot Amberley Estate **1997** £11.50 (ELL)
Cabernet Sauvignon/Merlot Amberley Estate **1996** £11.60 (AD)
Cabernet Sauvignon/Merlot Hollick Coonawarra **1995** £11.69 (TW)
Cabernet Sauvignon/Merlot Voyager Estate **1995** £11.50 (JU)
Cabernet Sauvignon/Shiraz Penfolds Bin 389 **1996** £11.40 (SOM) £12.95 (POR) £12.99 (YOU) £12.99 (BO) £12.99 (TES) £12.99 (WR) £12.99 (SAF) £13.50 (TAN)
Cabernet Sauvignon/Shiraz Penfolds Koonunga Hill **1990** £11.00 (CRO)
Grenache/Mourvèdre/Shiraz Penfolds Barossa Valley Old Vine **1996** £11.29 (JON)
Grenache/Shiraz Richard Hamilton Marions Vineyard **1997** £11.20 (SOM)
Obliqua Ashton Hills **1996** £11.99 (AUS)
Opimian Pipers Brook **1997** £11.99 (SOM)
Pinot Noir Coldstream Hills **1998** £11.29 (YOU) £14.35 (UB)
Pinot Noir De Bortoli **1997** £11.95 (BAL)
Pinot Noir De Bortoli Yarra Valley **1997** £11.60 (HA) £11.95 (LEA) £12.99 (PHI)
Pinot Noir Pipers Brook Pellion **1998** £11.25 (SOM) £13.69 (AME) £13.79 (CON)
Pinot Noir Plantagenet Mount Barker Pemberton **1997** £11.95 (VA)
Pinot Noir Scotchman's Hill **1997** £11.90 (JU)
Shiraz Balgownie **1997** £11.49 (AME)
Shiraz Jim Barry McCrae Wood **1995** £11.75 (SOM) £13.64 (NO)
Shiraz Bowen Estate **1997** £11.50 (AUS)
Shiraz Grant Burge Filsell Vineyard Old Vine **1998** £11.50 (HIG)
Shiraz Grant Burge Filsell Vineyard Old Vine **1997** £11.95 (RES)
Shiraz Grant Burge Old Vine **1998** £11.45 (AS) £11.75 (BU)
★ Shiraz Chateau Reynella **1997** £11.99 (WAI)
Shiraz Chateau Reynella **1996** £11.99 (YOU)
Shiraz De Bortoli Yarra Valley **1996** £11.95 (STE) £12.99 (PHI)
Shiraz Maxwell Ellen Street **1997** £11.99 (YOU)
Shiraz Miranda Family Reserve Old Vine **1996** £11.75 (AV)
Shiraz Penfolds Magill Estate **1996** £11.75 (SOM)
Shiraz St Hallett Blackwell **1996** £11.99 (AUS) £12.49 (THR) £12.49 (WR) £12.49 (BOT) £12.75 (REI) £12.99 (POR)
Shiraz St Hallett Old Block **1995** £11.99 (SOM) £13.99 (WR) £14.99 (AUS) £14.99 (TES) £15.00 (FORT)
Shiraz Wolf Blass President's Selection **1996** £11.55 (PHI)
Shiraz/Cabernet Sauvignon Penley Estate **1995** £11.28 (WT)

£12.00 → £12.99

Cabernet Sauvignon Balgownie **1998** £12.95 (BEN)
Cabernet Sauvignon Cape Mentelle **1993** £12.99 (RAE) £16.74 (REI)
Cabernet Sauvignon Chateau Xanadu **1996** £12.99 (DI)
Cabernet Sauvignon Simon Hackett Foggo Road **1997** £12.08 (PIP) £13.65 (CON)
Cabernet Sauvignon Vasse Felix **1996** £12.99 (YOU) £13.50 (BAL)

Cabernet Sauvignon Yalumba Menzies **1996** £12.49 (YOU) £13.50 (WRI) £13.50 (FORT) £13.95 (RES) £13.99 (BOD)
Cabernet Sauvignon/Shiraz Penfolds Bin 389 **1997** £12.99 (OD)
Limestone Ridge Lindemans **1996** £12.99 (TES) £14.99 (YOU)
Limestone Ridge Lindemans **1994** £12.05 (SOM) £13.99 (UN)
Olmo's Reward Frankland Estate **1995** £12.35 (BAN) £13.49 (YOU) £16.95 (RES)
Pinot Noir Cullen **1998** £12.24 (SAV) £12.49 (YOU) £13.99 (PHI)
Pinot Noir Lenswood **1997** £12.80 (NEZ) £15.99 (YOU) £16.70 (HAH)
Pinot Noir Nepenthe **1998** £12.99 (GW) £12.99 (YOU)
Pinot Noir Pipers Brook Pellion **1997** £12.50 (POR) £13.50 (STA)
St George Lindemans **1995** £12.99 (TES)
Shiraz Balgownie **1998** £12.95 (BEN)
Shiraz Best's Great Western **1995** £12.99 (JON)
Shiraz Best's Victoria **1994** £12.99 (PHI)
Shiraz Brokenwood **1997** £12.95 (RES)
★ Shiraz Hewitson Barossa Valley **1998** £12.95 (WAT)
Shiraz St Hallett Blackwell **1997** £12.49 (WR)
Shiraz Vasse Felix **1997** £12.45 (SOM) £14.99 (YOU) £15.50 (PHI) £16.50 (RES)
Shiraz Woodstock 'The Stocks' **1996** £12.99 (MAJ)
Shiraz David Wynn Patriarch **1997** £12.35 (SOM) £13.58 (FLE) £14.99 (YOU)
Zinfandel Cape Mentelle **1992** £12.50 (CRO)

£13.00 → £13.99

Angelus Wirra Wirra **1996** £13.99 (PHI)
Cabernet Sauvignon Chain of Ponds Amadeus **1994** £13.40 (SOM)
Cabernet Sauvignon Chateau Xanadu **1997** £13.95 (DI)
Cabernet Sauvignon De Bortoli **1993** £13.95 (BAL)
Cabernet Sauvignon Devil's Lair **1995** £13.75 (SOM)
Cabernet Sauvignon Kangaroo Island **1994** £13.99 (YOU)
Cabernet Sauvignon Stonier's Reserve **1995** £13.99 (DI)
Cabernet Sauvignon Taltarni **1995** £13.22 (TW)
Cabernet Sauvignon Vasse Felix **1998** £13.55 (BEN) £15.99 (PHI)
Cabernet Sauvignon/Merlot Leeuwin Estate Prelude **1996** £13.20 (SOM)
Long Flat Red Tyrrell's **1982** £13.80 (CRO)
'Mary Kathleen' Coriole **1997** £13.79 (YOU)
Olmo's Reward Frankland Estate **1994** £13.00 (FORT)
Pinot Noir Mountadam **1997** £13.29 (FLE) £14.29 (YOU) £14.79 (NI) £14.95 (STE) £14.99 (BOT) £15.95 (RES) £15.99 (VA)
Pyrus Lindemans **1996** £13.99 (SAI) £14.39 (JON) £14.99 (YOU) £14.99 (OD)
Shiraz Bannockburn **1996** £13.45 (SOM) £16.20 (TAN) £22.20 (JER)
Shiraz Jim Barry McCrae Wood **1996** £13.64 (NO) £14.99 (YOU) £14.99 (OD) £14.99 (BOD) £14.99 (SUN) £15.00 (TAN)
Shiraz De Bortoli Yarra Valley **1995** £13.50 (BAL) £13.50 (STA)
Shiraz Hillstowe Mary's Hundred **1997** £13.57 (NO) £14.50 (FLE)
Shiraz Charles Melton **1996** £13.60 (SOM)
Shiraz Plantagenet **1997** £13.95 (LIB)
Shiraz St Hallett Old Block **1996** £13.50 (FLE) £13.99 (POR) £13.99 (WR) £13.99 (BOT) £14.98 (DOM) £14.99 (TES)
Shiraz Wirra Wirra R.S.W. **1996** £13.99 (PHI)

£14.00 → £15.99

Angelus Wirra Wirra **1997** £14.45 (WAI)
Cabernet Sauvignon Brown Bros Family Reserve **1990** £15.92 (PLA) £16.37 (PIP)
Cabernet Sauvignon Cape Mentelle **1994** £14.20 (TAN) £14.99 (NI) £16.50 (RAE) £16.74 (REI) £18.35 (PLAY)
Cabernet Sauvignon d'Arenberg The Coppermine Road **1995** £15.99 (YOU)
Cabernet Sauvignon Devil's Lair **1996** £15.50 (PHI)
Cabernet Sauvignon Mountadam **1994** £14.99 (YOU)
Cabernet Sauvignon Rosemount Show Reserve **1996** £14.99 (SAF)
Cabernet Sauvignon Seppelt Drumborg **1994** £15.49 (AME)
Cabernet Sauvignon/Merlot Chateau Reynella Basket Pressed **1994** £14.77 (HA)
Cabernet Sauvignon/Merlot Nepenthe Fugue **1997** £14.79 (YOU)
Cabernet Sauvignon/Shiraz Passing Clouds Angel Blends **1996** £14.99 (AUS)
Cabernet Sauvignon/Shiraz Penfolds Bin 389 **1994** £14.95 (FORT)
Coonawarra Petaluma **1996** £14.70 (BEN)

Diva Coriole **1997** £14.79 (YOU)
Diva Coriole **1996** £14.25 (FLE)
GSM Rosemount **1997** £14.95 (WS) £14.99 (WR) £14.99 (BOD) £14.99 (SUN)
GSM Rosemount **1995** £15.90 (CRO)
Nine Popes Charles Melton **1998** £15.50 (FLE) £16.99 (NI) £17.95 (BEN) £19.95 (LIB) £20.73 (PIP) £21.95 (VA)
Nine Popes Charles Melton **1997** £15.99 (SOM) £18.95 (NO) £18.95 (RES)
Pinot Noir De Bortoli Yarra Valley **1998** £15.45 (STE)
Pinot Noir Henschke Giles **1994** £14.26 (NO) £23.00 (CRO)
Pinot Noir Lenswood **1996** £14.95 (PHI) £16.00 (CRO)
Pinot Noir Moss Wood **1997** £15.95 (JER)
Pinot Noir Moss Wood **1994** £14.95 (BAL)
Pinot Noir Mountadam **1996** £15.25 (FORT) £15.95 (AD) £15.98 (GW)
Pinot Noir Stonier's Reserve **1995** £15.75 (DI)
Pinot Noir Tarrawarra **1997** £15.50 (WS) £16.75 (PHI) £17.95 (RES)
Pyrus Lindemans **1991** £14.09 (NO)
St George Lindemans **1996** £14.99 (YOU) £14.99 (OD) £15.25 (FORT)
Shiraz Amberley Estate Margaret River **1997** £14.50 (ELL)
Shiraz Bannockburn **1997** £15.99 (YOU) £17.95 (RES) £18.99 (PHI)
Shiraz Jim Barry McCrae Wood **1997** £15.50 (BEN)
Shiraz Jim Barry McCrae Wood **1994** £14.34 (PIP)
Shiraz Coriole **1996** £14.00 (CRO)
Shiraz Tim Gramp **1997** £14.75 (AD)
Shiraz Lengs & Cooter Clare Valley Old Vine **1995** £15.15 (NO)
Shiraz Lengs & Cooter Clare Valley Old Vine **1994** £15.25 (CON)
Shiraz Charles Melton **1998** £14.99 (FLE) £16.99 (NI) £21.95 (VA)
Shiraz Mount Langi Ghiran **1997** £15.99 (SOM) £18.99 (YOU) £18.99 (BO) £19.75 (CON) £19.75 (WRI) £19.95 (BAL) £19.99 (PHI) £21.95 (RES)
Shiraz Mount Langi Ghiran **1996** £14.43 (NO) £15.50 (BAL) £20.15 (HAH)
Shiraz Penfolds Coonawarra Bin 128 **1992** £14.69 (REI)
Shiraz Rockford Basket Press **1998** £15.95 (PHI)
Shiraz Rockford Basket Press **1996** £14.99 (JON) £15.35 (WRI)
Shiraz St Hallett Old Block **1994** £15.50 (CRO)
Shiraz Saltram No 1 **1997** £15.99 (YOU)
Shiraz Saltram No 1 **1995** £15.49 (AME)
Shiraz Taltarni **1988** £14.00 (CRO)
Shiraz Tatachilla Foundation **1997** £14.95 (WAI)
Shiraz Vasse Felix **1998** £14.87 (PIP) £15.45 (BEN)
Shiraz Wolf Blass President's Selection **1993** £15.00 (CRO)
Shiraz/Cabernet Sauvignon Yalumba The Signature **1995** £15.99 (YOU)
Zinfandel Cape Mentelle **1993** £14.50 (CRO)

£16.00 → £19.99

Cabernet Sauvignon Chain of Ponds Amadeus **1997** £17.99 (PHI)
Cabernet Sauvignon Chateau Tahbilk **1985** £17.00 (CRO)
Cabernet Sauvignon Dalwhinnie **1997** £17.00 (JU)
Cabernet Sauvignon d'Arenberg The Coppermine Road **1997** £16.99 (YOU)
Cabernet Sauvignon Haselgrove H Series **1997** £18.99 (YOU)
Cabernet Sauvignon Hollick Ravenswood **1994** £18.99 (AME) £22.95 (RES)
Cabernet Sauvignon Howard Park **1996** £19.02 (GW) £23.99 (PHI)
Cabernet Sauvignon Leasingham Classic Clare **1996** £19.99 (YOU)
Cabernet Sauvignon Leeuwin Estate Art Series **1995** £19.35 (SOM)
Cabernet Sauvignon Mountadam **1996** £16.55 (NI)
Cabernet Sauvignon Mountadam **1995** £19.95 (AD)
Cabernet Sauvignon Penley Estate **1994** £18.08 (WT) £18.50 (RES)
Cabernet Sauvignon Rosemount Show Reserve **1988** £18.00 (CRO)
Cabernet Sauvignon Seppelt Black Label **1983** £18.00 (CRO)
Cabernet Sauvignon Yarra Yering Dry Red No.1 **1997** £18.75 (SOM) £22.95 (BEN)
Cabernet Sauvignon Yarra Yering Dry Red No.1 **1996** £19.99 (CON) £22.99 (NI)£28.41 (PLAY)
Cabernet Sauvignon Yeringberg **1997** £19.29 (YOU)
Cabernet Sauvignon/Merlot Coldstream Hills Briarston **1994** £16.15 (UB)

Cabernet Sauvignon/Merlot Cullen **1997** £18.00 (FLE) £19.95 (DI) £19.99 (YOU) £22.75 (AD) £23.99 (VA)
Cabernet Sauvignon/Merlot Henschke Abbott's Prayer **1995** £19.95 (SOM)
Cabernet Sauvignon/Merlot Howard Park **1995** £17.10 (SOM) £19.99 (YOU)
Cabernet Sauvignon/Shiraz Yalumba The Signature **1995** £17.75 (NI) £17.95 (RES) £17.99 (BAL)
Coonawarra Petaluma **1995** £16.16 (PLAY)
Gaia Grosset **1997** £17.04 (DOM)
Grenache Clarendon Hills Clarendon Vineyard Old Vines **1997** £19.00 (JU) £19.99 (YOU)
Grenache Clarendon Hills Kangarilla Vineyard Old Vines **1997** £17.53 (FA) £19.00 (JU) £19.99 (YOU)
Grenache/Shiraz d'Arenberg Ironstone Pressings **1997** £17.95 (FORT) £18.99 (PHI)
Merlot Mountadam **1996** £18.99 (YOU) £19.95 (AD)
Merlot Taltarni **1992** £18.00 (CRO)
Nine Popes Charles Melton **1996** £18.99 (PHI)
Nine Popes Charles Melton **1991** £19.00 (CRO)
Pinot Meunier Best's Great Western Old Vine **1994** £17.00 (CRO)
Pinot Meunier Best's Great Western Old Vine **1993** £16.70 (NI)
Pinot Noir Bannockburn **1997** £18.00 (TAN) £18.95 (BEN) £18.95 (RES)
Pinot Noir Bannockburn **1996** £17.95 (BAL) £22.20 (JER) £32.95 (UB)
Pinot Noir Coldstream Hills Reserve **1997** £16.99 (YOU) £16.99 (OD)
Pinot Noir Giaconda **1997** £18.90 (SOM)
Pinot Noir Henschke Giles **1998** £18.79 (YOU)
Pinot Noir Henschke Giles **1995** £17.50 (NI)
Pinot Noir Moss Wood **1996** £17.60 (PLAY)
Pinot Noir Scotchman's Hill **1996** £16.15 (UB)
Pinot Noir Stonier's Reserve **1997** £16.99 (DI)
The Red Mountadam **1996** £19.95 (AD) £20.95 (STE)
The Red Mountadam **1994** £18.50 (FLE) £18.99 (YOU)
Shiraz Bannockburn **1995** £17.95 (BAL)
Shiraz Jim Barry McCrae Wood **1992** £19.50 (CRO)
Shiraz Brokenwood Rayners Vineyard **1996** £17.44 (NO) £22.95 (RES)
Shiraz Dalwhinnie **1997** £17.00 (JU) £17.95 (YOU)
Shiraz d'Arenberg Dead Arm **1996** £17.95 (FORT)
Shiraz Henschke Mount Edelstone **1995** £19.95 (SOM) £22.00 (FLE) £25.61 (NO) £25.95 (NI) £32.80 (JER) £35.00 (CRO)
Shiraz Leasingham Classic Clare **1996** £19.99 (YOU)
Shiraz Peter Lehmann Stonewell **1994** £19.95 (WAI) £19.99 (OD)
Shiraz Maglieri Steve Maglieri **1993** £19.00 (CRO)
Shiraz McWilliams Maurice O'Shea **1994** £17.70 (COC)
Shiraz Charles Melton **1997** £18.50 (AD) £18.99 (PHI)
Shiraz Mount Langi Ghiran **1998** £19.95 (LIB)
Shiraz Neil Paulett Andreas **1996** £16.50 (JU) £16.99 (YOU)
Shiraz Penfolds Kalimna Bin 28 **1991** £16.00 (CRO)
Shiraz St Hallett Old Block **1992** £19.50 (PHI)
Shiraz Saltram No 1 **1996** £16.66 (SUN)
Shiraz Veritas Heysen Vineyard **1992** £17.04 (REI)
Shiraz Yarra Yering Dry Red No.2 **1996** £19.99 (CON) £21.99 (NI)
Shiraz Yarra Yering Underhill **1997** £18.75 (SOM) £22.95 (BEN)
Shiraz Yarra Yering Underhill **1996** £19.99 (CON) £22.99 (NI)
Shiraz/Cabernet Sauvignon Henschke Keyneton Estate **1997** £17.49 (YOU)
Shiraz/Cabernet Sauvignon Henschke Keyneton Estate **1996** £16.25 (FORT) £16.68 (NO) £28.00 (CRO)
Shiraz/Cabernet Sauvignon Yalumba The Signature **1993** £19.50 (FORT)
Shiraz/Mourvèdre Grant Burge The Holy Trinity **1996** £19.50 (HIG) £19.75 (BU)
Shiraz/Mourvèdre Leconfield **1997** £18.00 (JU) £18.99 (YOU)

£20.00 → £29.99

Cabernet Sauvignon Chateau Reynella Basket Pressed **1984** £28.00 (CRO)
Cabernet Sauvignon Chateau Tahbilk **1982** £25.00 (CRO)
Cabernet Sauvignon Cullen Reserve **1997** £22.95 (PHI)

Cabernet Sauvignon Henschke Cyril Henschke **1995** £28.55 (JER) £35.49 (NO) £35.50 (PHI) £45.43 (FA)
Cabernet Sauvignon Hollick Ravenswood **1993** £22.95 (NI)
Cabernet Sauvignon Howard Park **1995** £22.95 (BAL) £25.00 (WS)
Cabernet Sauvignon Lake's Folly **1987** £25.00 (CRO)
Cabernet Sauvignon Moss Wood **1994** £24.75 (PLAY)
Cabernet Sauvignon Moss Wood **1989** £27.00 (CRO)
Cabernet Sauvignon Parker Coonawarra Estate Terra Rossa **1996** £23.97 (CB)
Cabernet Sauvignon Penfolds Bin 707 **1996** £29.95 (SOM) £34.99 (YOU) £34.99 (UN)
Cabernet Sauvignon Penfolds Coonawarra **1989** £29.00 (CRO)
Cabernet Sauvignon Rosemount Show Reserve **1985** £23.00 (CRO)
Cabernet Sauvignon Rouge Homme **1985** £25.00 (BU)
Cabernet Sauvignon Wolf Blass Black Label **1992** £26.00 (CRO)
Cabernet Sauvignon Wolf Blass President's Selection **1990** £22.00 (CRO)
Cabernet Sauvignon Wynns Coonawarra Estate **1990** £26.44 (REI)
Cabernet Sauvignon Wynns John Riddoch **1994** £28.45 (SOM) £32.95 (POR) £36.11 (NO) £59.00 (CRO)

Cabernet Sauvignon Yarra Yering Dry Red No.1 **1984** £27.61 (REI)
Cabernet Sauvignon/Merlot Cullen **1986** £21.00 (CRO)
Cabernet Sauvignon/Merlot Henschke Abbott's Prayer **1997** £27.49 (YOU)
Cabernet Sauvignon/Merlot Howard Park **1996** £21.49 (BAN) £22.95 (FORT) £25.00 (WS)
Cabernet Sauvignon/Merlot/Shiraz Blue Pyrenees Estate **1982** £24.00 (CRO)
Cabernet Sauvignon/Shiraz Penfolds Bin 389 **1992** £22.00 (CRO)
Cabernet Sauvignon/Shiraz Yalumba The Reserve **1992** £24.75 (SOM) £29.95 (YOU) £29.95 (NI)
E&E Black Pepper Shiraz **1995** £29.50 (WRI)
E&E Black Pepper Shiraz **1993** £29.00 (CRO)
Grenache Clarendon Hills Kangarilla Vineyard Old Vines **1998** £25.99 (YOU)
Limestone Ridge Lindemans **1988** £29.00 (CRO)
Merlot Clarendon Hills **1997** £26.00 (JU)
Merlot Clarendon Hills **1996** £25.99 (YOU)
Meshach Grant Burge **1992** £24.50 (WRI)
Octavius Yalumba **1995** £26.12 (FLE) £29.95 (NI) £29.99 (YOU) £33.00 (BAL)
Pinot Noir Coldstream Hills Reserve **1993** £20.00 (CRO)
Pinot Noir Yarra Yering **1997** £25.99 (YOU) £28.50 (BEN)
Pinot Noir Yarra Yering **1990** £21.75 (SOM)
Pyrus Lindemans **1993** £21.00 (CRO)
St George Lindemans **1988** £28.00 (CRO)
Shadrach Grant Burge **1996** £28.50 (BU) £29.95 (LEA) £29.99 (UN)
Shiraz Jim Barry The Armagh **1996** £27.75 (SOM) £32.90 (TAN) £33.00 (PHI) £34.99 (OD) £35.99 (JON) £37.00 (BAL) £38.78 (NO) £39.95 (DI) £44.00 (CRO)
Shiraz Brokenwood Graveyard Vineyard **1998** £26.50 (BAN)
Shiraz Brokenwood Graveyard Vineyard **1996** £28.86 (NO)
Shiraz Brokenwood Rayners Vineyard **1997** £22.95 (RES)
Shiraz Clarendon Hills **1996** £21.00 (JU) £22.91 (FA)
Shiraz Elderton Command **1994** £27.91 (NO)
Shiraz Henschke Mount Edelstone **1997** £28.49 (YOU) £29.20 (LAY)
Shiraz Henschke Mount Edelstone **1996** £26.50 (FORT) £27.06 (NO) £27.75 (PHI) £36.00 (CRO)
Shiraz Jasper Hill Georgia's Paddock **1998** £27.32 (YAP)
Shiraz Mitchelton Print Label **1996** £25.75 (STE)
Shiraz Rockford Basket Press **1995** £24.00 (CRO)
Shiraz St Hallett Old Block **1993** £21.00 (CRO)
Shiraz Taltarni **1982** £26.00 (CRO)
Shiraz Tyrrell's Vat 9 Winemakers Selection **1990** £25.00 (CRO)
Shiraz Veritas Heysen Vineyard **1990** £20.56 (REI)

Shiraz Wynns Michael **1994** £28.45 (SOM) £32.99 (POR) £45.43 (FA)
Shiraz Yarra Yering Dry Red No.2 **1995** £22.00 (FORT)
Shiraz/Mourvèdre Grant Burge The Holy Trinity **1997** £20.95 (LEA)

£30.00 → £39.99

Cabernet Sauvignon Henschke Cyril Henschke **1996** £36.99 (YOU)
Cabernet Sauvignon Henschke Cyril Henschke **1992** £38.00 (CRO)
Cabernet Sauvignon Moss Wood **1996** £30.00 (WS) £32.25 (JER)
Cabernet Sauvignon Penfolds Bin 707 **1994** £32.95 (POR) £51.23 (NO)
Cabernet Sauvignon Rouge Homme **1982** £35.00 (CRO)
Cabernet Sauvignon Taltarni **1980** £30.00 (CRO)
Cabernet Sauvignon Wolf Blass Black Label **1994** £36.00 (PHI)
Cabernet Sauvignon Wynns John Riddoch **1996** £34.99 (YOU)
Cabernet Sauvignon/Merlot Henschke Abbott's Prayer **1996** £33.00 (NO)
Cabernet Sauvignon/Merlot Henschke Abbott's Prayer **1991** £30.00 (CRO)
Cabernet Sauvignon/Shiraz Petaluma **1988** £33.00 (CRO)
Limestone Ridge Lindemans **1984** £35.00 (CRO)
Meshach Grant Burge **1995** £38.49 (PLAY) £38.50 (BU) £39.95 (LEA) £39.99 (UN)
Meshach Grant Burge **1994** £32.50 (CON) £34.95 (STA)
St George Lindemans **1985** £33.00 (CRO)
Shiraz Jim Barry The Armagh **1997** £34.00 (YOU) £34.95 (BEN)
Shiraz Jim Barry The Armagh **1995** £36.40 (JER) £38.78 (NO) £47.00 (CRO)
Shiraz Jasper Hill Georgia's Paddock **1996** £30.00 (FORT)
Shiraz Penfolds Kalimna Bin 28 **1978** £35.00 (CRO)
Shiraz Wynns Michael **1991** £31.67 (REI) £49.00 (CRO)
Shiraz Yarra Yering Dry Red No.2 **1989** £30.00 (CRO)
Shiraz/Cabernet Sauvignon Peter Lehmann **1989** £32.31 (REI)
Shiraz/Cabernet Sauvignon Rouge Homme **1976** £32.00 (CRO)
Syrah Rosemount Balmoral **1997** £34.99 (BOD) £34.99 (SUN)

£40.00 → £59.99

Cabernet Sauvignon Henschke Cyril Henschke **1994** £40.89 (NO)
Cabernet Sauvignon Moss Wood **1991** £41.13 (REI)
Cabernet Sauvignon Parker Coonawarra Estate Terra Rossa **1988** £40.00 (CRO)
Cabernet Sauvignon Penfolds Bin 707 **1992** £41.13 (REI) £55.00 (CRO)
Cabernet Sauvignon Penley Estate **1989** £45.00 (CRO)
Cabernet Sauvignon Wynns John Riddoch **1991** £47.00 (REI) £69.00 (CRO)
Cabernet Sauvignon/Shiraz Petaluma **1985** £44.00 (CRO)
Cabernets Mount Mary Quintet **1997** £52.88 (REI) £65.00 (BAL)
Cabernets Mount Mary Quintet **1996** £46.95 (BER)
Limestone Ridge Lindemans **1978** £44.00 (CRO)
Octavius Yalumba **1994** £52.00 (CRO)
Shiraz Elderton Command **1992** £58.26 (CAV)
Shiraz Henschke Mount Edelstone **1993** £41.00 (CRO)
Shiraz Yarra Yering Dry Red No.2 **1982** £52.88 (REI)

£60.00 → £99.99

Cabernet Sauvignon Henschke Cyril Henschke **1985** £76.00 (CRO)
Cabernet Sauvignon Penfolds Bin 707 **1989** £60.00 (CRO)
Grange Penfolds **1994** £89.99 (UN)
Grange Penfolds **1993** £80.66 (BY) £99.50 (BEN) £109.00 (CRO)
Pinot Noir Mount Mary **1997** £65.00 (BAL)
Shiraz Clarendon Hills Astralis **1998** £79.99 (YOU) £99.29 (FA)
Shiraz Henschke Mount Edelstone **1989** £70.50 (FA)

£100.00 → £199.99

Cabernet Sauvignon Wynns John Riddoch **1986** £110.00 (CRO)
Cabernet Sauvignon Wynns John Riddoch **1982** £116.00 (UB)
Grange Penfolds **1992** £102.00 (CRO) £130.00 (BEN) £158.63 (REI)
Grange Penfolds **1989** £148.25 (FA) £229.13 (CAV)
Grange Penfolds **1986** £199.00 (BEN) £212.87 (FA)

Grange Penfolds **1979** £170.38 (REI) £193.88 (FA) £282.00 (CAV)
Shiraz Clarendon Hills Astralis **1995** £120.83 (FA)
Shiraz Henschke Hill of Grace **1991** £105.75 (NO) £146.88 (REI) £160.00 (CRO)
Shiraz Lindemans Hunter Valley **1965** £140.00 (CRO)

Over £200.00

Grange Penfolds **1990** £221.68 (FA) £275.00 (BEN) £323.13 (REI)
Grange Penfolds **1988** £230.10 (CAV)
Grange Penfolds **1971** £353.87 (FA)

WHITE

Under £4.00

Chardonnay Hardys Banrock **1999** £3.99 (UN)
Colombard Deakin Estate **1996** £3.99 (DI)
Colombard/Chardonnay Hardys Banrock **1999** £3.79 (TES) £3.79 (SAF) £3.99 (UN)
Colombard/Chardonnay Lindemans Cawarra **1998** £3.60 (SOM)
Dry White Dalwood **1999** £3.60 (SOM)
Medium Dry White Dalwood **1999** £3.60 (SOM)
Rawson's Retreat Bin 21 Penfolds **1997** £3.98 (SOM)
Riesling Peter Lehmann Vine Vale **1999** £3.99 (SAF)
Riesling Lindemans Cawarra Dry **1998** £3.99 (BUD)
★ Riesling Penfolds Bin 202 Rawson's Retreat **1999** £3.99 (VIC) £3.99 (THR) £3.99 (BOT) £3.99 (WR)£4.49 (WAI) £4.49 (SAF) £4.49 (BUD)
Sauvignon Blanc Deakin Estate **1997** £3.99 (DI)
Semillon/Chardonnay Barramundi **Non-vintage** £3.99 (ASD) £3.99 (TES)
Semillon/Chardonnay Orlando Jacob's Creek **1999** £3.79 (TES) £4.59 (SAF)

£4.00 → £4.99

Chardonnay Cockatoo Ridge **1998** £4.50 (SOM) £4.95 (RES)
Chardonnay Dalwood **1999** £4.64 (BY)
Chardonnay Dalwood **1998** £4.95 (RES)
Chardonnay Deakin Estate **1999** £4.99 (BIB)
Chardonnay Deakin Estate **1998** £4.99 (BO)
Chardonnay Deakin Estate Alfred Barrel-Fermented **1998** £4.99 (OD)
Chardonnay Hardys Nottage Hill **1999** £4.99 (SO) £4.99 (TES) £4.99 (WAI) £4.99 (SAF)
Chardonnay Hardys Nottage Hill **1998** £4.99 (ASD) £4.99 (UN)
Chardonnay Lindemans Bin 65 **1999** £4.35 (SOM) £4.49 (TES) £4.95 (WS) £4.99 (SO) £4.99 (SAI) £4.99 (MAJ) £4.99 (POR) £4.99 (VIC) £4.99 (THR) £4.99 (WR) £4.99 (BOT) £4.99 (SAF) £4.99 (BUD) £5.50 (BY)
Chardonnay Lindemans Bin 65 **1998** £4.99 (ASD) £4.99 (OD) £4.99 (WAI)
Chardonnay Lindemans Cawarra Unoaked **1999** £4.49 (TES) £4.49 (VIC) £4.49 (THR) £4.49 (SAF)
Chardonnay Lindemans Cawarra Unoaked **1998** £4.49 (ASD) £4.49 (MAJ)
Chardonnay Orlando Jacob's Creek **1999** £4.99 (TES) £4.99 (BOT) £4.99 (BUD)
Chardonnay Orlando Jacob's Creek **1998** £4.99 (VIC) £4.99 (THR) £4.99 (UN)
Chardonnay Penfolds Koonunga Hill **1999** £4.80 (SOM) £5.49 (SO) £5.49 (TES) £5.50 (WS) £5.59 (JON) £5.80 (TAN) £6.03 (BY)
Chardonnay Penfolds Koonunga Hill **1998** £4.64 (BY) £5.45 (COC) £5.49 (POR) £5.49 (VIC) £5.49 (THR) £5.49 (UN) £5.49 (WR) £5.49 (BOT) £5.49 (WAI) £5.59 (BUD) £6.45 (FORT)
Chardonnay Penfolds Rowlands Brook **1998** £4.99 (POR) £4.99 (JON)
Chardonnay Rolleston Vale **1999** £4.70 (GW)
Chardonnay Rolleston Vale **1998** £4.95 (CON)
Chardonnay Yalumba Oxford Landing **1999** £4.99 (SAF) £4.99 (BUD) £5.50 (NI) £5.75 (STE)
Chardonnay Yalumba Oxford Landing **1998** £4.99 (VIC) £4.99 (THR) £4.99 (WR)
Chardonnay/Semillon Hardys Stamp **1999** £4.49 (VIC) £4.49 (THR) £4.49 (WAI) £4.49 (SAF) £5.99 (ASD)
Chenin Blanc Peter Lehmann **1998** £4.69 (UN)
Chenin Blanc/Semillon/Sauvignon Blanc Tatachilla Growers **1998** £4.40 (BAN)

Please remember that
Oz Clarke's Wine Buying Guide
*is a price **guide** and not a price **list**. It is not meant to replace up-to-date merchants' lists.*

Colombard/Chardonnay Lonsdale Ridge **1999** £4.79 (BIB)

Colombard/Chardonnay Sunnycliff **1999** £4.95 (POR)

Colombard/Chardonnay Sunnycliff **1998** £4.49 (JON)

Dry White Rolleston Vale **Non-vintage** £4.00 (GW) £4.25 (CON)

HWB Houghton **1997** £4.95 (SOM)

Jacob's Creek White Orlando **1999** £4.99 (SO)

Poachers Blend St Hallett **1998** £4.99 (TES)

Riesling Penfolds Rawson's Retreat Bin 202 **1998** £4.49 (POR)

Rawson's Retreat Bin 21 Penfolds **1999** £4.49 (ASD) £4.49 (BO) £4.49 (VIC) £4.49 (THR) £4.49 (BOT) £4.50 (WS) £4.69 (BUD)

Rawson's Retreat Bin 21 Penfolds **1998** £4.49 (COC) £4.50 (POR) £4.69 (UN)

Riesling Orlando Jacob's Creek Dry **1999** £4.59 (TES) £4.99 (SAF) £4.99 (BUD)

Riesling Orlando Jacob's Creek Dry **1998** £4.59 (VIC) £4.59 (THR) £4.59 (WR) £4.59 (BOT)

Riesling Pewsey Vale **1999** £4.99 (OD) £5.99 (TES) £5.99 (BEN) £6.25 (FORT)

Riesling David Wynn **1998** £4.99 (MAJ) £6.95 (AD) £8.00 (MV)

Riesling/Gewürztraminer Hardys Stamp **1999** £4.49 (VIC) £4.49 (THR) £4.49 (UN)

Sauvignon Blanc Deakin Estate **1998** £4.99 (BO) £5.49 (DI)

Sauvignon Blanc Sunnycliff **1998** £4.95 (TAN) £4.99 (JON) £5.29 (POR)

Sauvignon Blanc Yalumba Oxford Landing **1999** £4.99 (TES) £4.99 (THR) £4.99 (WR) £4.99 (SAF) £5.50 (NI) £5.75 (STE)

Sauvignon Blanc Yalumba Oxford Landing **1998** £4.99 (VIC) £4.99 (THR) £4.99 (UN) £4.99 (WR) £4.99 (BOT)

Semillon/Chardonnay Aldridge Estate **1998** £4.99 (CON)

Semillon/Chardonnay Dalwood **1999** £4.39 (BY)

Semillon/Chardonnay De Bortoli Sacred Hill **1999** £4.95 (STE)

Semillon/Chardonnay Hardys Stamp **1999** £4.49 (SO) £4.49 (TES) £4.49 (BUD)

Semillon/Chardonnay Hardys Stamp **1998** £4.49 (ASD) £4.49 (UN)

Semillon/Chardonnay Orlando Jacob's Creek **Non-vintage** £4.49 (ASD)

Semillon/Chardonnay Orlando Jacob's Creek **1998** £4.59 (VIC) £4.59 (THR) £4.59 (UN)

Semillon/Chardonnay Orlando Jacob's Creek **1997** £4.59 (BOT)

Semillon/Chardonnay Penfolds Rowlands Brook **1998** £4.49 (POR) £4.90 (HAH)

Semillon/Chardonnay Penfolds Rowlands Brook **1996** £4.59 (JON)

Semillon/Chardonnay Rosemount **1998** £4.49 (ASD) £5.99 (BO) £5.99 (BOT) £5.99 (BUD)

Semillon/Chardonnay Tatachilla Wattle Park **1997** £4.95 (BAN)

White Ochre d'Arenberg **1997** £4.95 (WS)

£5.00 → £5.99

Chardonnay Aldridge Estate **1998** £5.95 (CON)

Chardonnay Jim Barry Clare Valley **1998** £5.95 (TAN) £6.45 (STE)

Chardonnay Grant Burge Barossa Vines **1998** £5.99 (CON) £6.50 (LEA) £6.50 (RES)

Chardonnay Cockatoo Ridge **1997** £5.20 (BAL)

Chardonnay Krondorf **1998** £5.99 (DI)

Chardonnay Lindemans Limestone Coast **1998** £5.99 (UN)

Chardonnay Miranda **1998** £5.29 (CON)

Chardonnay Penfolds Private Bin **1999** £5.75 (BY) £5.95 (STE)

Chardonnay Penfolds The Valleys **1997** £5.99 (SOM)

Chardonnay Rosemount **1998** £5.49 (ASD) £5.90 (CRO) £6.99 (BO) £6.99 (VIC) £6.99 (THR) £6.99 (WR) £6.99 (BOT)

Chardonnay Rothbury Cowra **1998** £5.99 (DI)

Chardonnay Sunnycliff **1998** £5.45 (HAH) £5.49 (POR) £5.49 (JON) £5.80 (TAN)

Chardonnay Trentham Willandra **1998** £5.99 (HED)

Chardonnay Woolshed **1998** £5.99 (SAF)

Chardonnay David Wynn **1998** £5.70 (SOM) £6.95 (AD) £6.99 (UN) £7.25 (STE)

Chardonnay David Wynn **1997** £5.70 (SOM) £7.48 (GW) £13.75 (ELL)

Chenin Blanc Brown Bros **1999** £5.95 (AD)

Chenin Blanc Brown Bros **1998** £5.45 (STE) £5.49 (POR) £5.75 (DI)

Chenin Blanc Brown Bros **1997** £5.52 (GW) £5.65 (UB)

Colombard Deakin Estate **1998** £5.49 (DI)

GTR Rosemount **1999** £5.99 (BUD)

HWB Houghton **1999** £5.99 (WAI)

Long Flat White Tyrrell's **1998** £5.15 (PIP)

Long Flat White Tyrrell's **1997** £5.65 (UB) £5.99 (JON)

Marsanne Chateau Tahbilk **1997** £5.99 (BO) £6.50 (WS)
Marsanne Mitchelton Unoaked **1998** £5.49 (OD)
Muscat Brown Bros Dry **1999** £5.14 (PIP) £5.65 (WRI) £5.65 (STA) £5.95 (AD) £6.10 (TAN)
Muscat Brown Bros Dry **1998** £5.49 (POR) £5.49 (TES) £5.49 (JON) £5.69 (GW) £5.75 (DI)
Muscat Brown Bros Dry **1997** £5.63 (COC)
Muscat Grant Burge Dry Late-Picked **1999** £5.95 (BU)
Muscat Grant Burge Dry Late-Picked **1998** £5.99 (CON)
Poachers Blend St Hallett **1999** £5.79 (POR)
Poachers Blend St Hallett **1997** £5.40 (SOM) £5.99 (AUS) £6.17 (REI)
Riesling Pewsey Vale **1997** £5.99 (VIC) £5.99 (THR) £5.99 (WR) £5.99 (BOT)
Riesling Wakefield **1997** £5.99 (BAL)
Riesling Wynns Coonawarra Estate **1998** £5.09 (JON)
Sauvignon Blanc Deakin Estate **1999** £5.49 (DI)
Sauvignon Blanc Rosemount **1999** £5.99 (TES) £5.99 (WAI)
Semillon Basedow **1998** £5.99 (SAF)
Semillon Peter Lehmann **1999** £5.49 (SAF)
Semillon Peter Lehmann **1997** £5.49 (ASD)
Semillon/Chardonnay Ironstone **1998** £5.99 (BO) £6.49 (UN) £6.49 (JON) £6.69 (PHI) £6.75 (STE) £6.95 (AD) £6.95 (NI)
Semillon/Chardonnay Ironstone **1997** £5.73 (NO) £8.49 (VA)
Semillon/Chardonnay Penfolds Barossa Valley **1998** £5.49 (ASD) £5.95 (POR) £5.99 (THR) £5.99 (WR) £5.99 (BOT)
Semillon/Chardonnay Rosemount **1999** £5.99 (VIC) £5.99 (THR) £5.99 (SAF)
Semillon/Sauvignon Blanc Rosemount **1999** £5.99 (TES) £5.99 (UN)
Viognier Yalumba Oxford Landing **1998** £5.99 (UN) £6.29 (BAL)
Viognier/Roussanne Mitchelton **1996** £5.31 (HA)
White Clare Wakefield **1995** £5.99 (UN)

£6.00 → £6.99

Chardonnay Jim Barry Clare Valley **1999** £6.45 (STE)
Chardonnay Jim Barry Clare Valley **1997** £6.49 (JON) £9.40 (BEN)
Chardonnay Grant Burge Barossa Vines **1999** £6.40 (AS) £7.00 (HIG)
Chardonnay Chapel Hill Unwooded **1998** £6.99 (TES) £7.99 (AUS) £8.81 (REI)
Chardonnay d'Arenberg Olive Grove **1999** £6.51 (BIB)
Chardonnay d'Arenberg Olive Grove **1998** £6.49 (OD)
Chardonnay Simon Hackett Barossa Valley **1997** £6.86 (NO)
Chardonnay Houghton Wildflower Ridge **1998** £6.50 (CON)
Chardonnay Leasingham **1997** £6.99 (WAI)
Chardonnay Lindemans Limestone Coast **1997** £6.29 (JON)
Chardonnay McWilliams JJ McWilliam **1997** £6.95 (COC)
Chardonnay Penfolds The Valleys **1999** £6.95 (SO) £6.99 (SAI)
Chardonnay Penfolds The Valleys **1998** £6.99 (VIC) £6.99 (THR) £7.49 (POR)
Chardonnay Plantagenet Omrah Unoaked **1999** £6.99 (LIB)
Chardonnay Plantagenet Omrah Unoaked **1998** £6.95 (POR)
Chardonnay Riddoch **1998** £6.99 (SAF)
Chardonnay Rosemount **1999** £6.99 (TES) £6.99 (SAF) £6.99 (BUD)
Chardonnay Rosemount Diamond **1998** £6.99 (UN)
Chardonnay Saltram Mamre Brook **1998** £6.99 (SAF)
Chardonnay Saltram Mamre Brook **1997** £6.99 (MAJ)
Chardonnay Tatachilla Padthaway **1999** £6.49 (SAF)
Chardonnay Wakefield **1997** £6.99 (UN)
Chardonnay Wirra Wirra Unwooded **1997** £6.99 (BAL)
Chardonnay Wolf Blass **1998** £6.99 (WR) £7.72 (BY) £7.95 (JER)
Chardonnay David Wynn **1999** £6.35 (FLE)
Chardonnay Yaldara Reserve **1998** £6.64 (PLAY) £9.55 (VIN)
Chenin Blanc Houghton Wildflower Ridge **1998** £6.25 (CON)
Colombard Primo La Biondina **1999** £6.99 (AUS) £7.34 (REI)
Marsanne Chateau Tahbilk **1998** £6.95 (AD) £6.99 (WAI)
Marsanne Chateau Tahbilk **1996** £6.99 (UB)

Stars (★) indicate wines selected by Oz Clarke in the Best Buys section which begins on page 10.

Riesling Jim Barry Watervale **1998** £6.25 (ELL) £6.25 (BEN) £6.29 (PHI) £6.50 (TAN) £6.99 (DI)
Riesling Best's Victoria **1996** £6.19 (GW)
Riesling Brown Bros King Valley **1997** £6.40 (STA) £6.45 (STE) £6.50 (WRI)
Riesling Hollick Coonawarra **1999** £6.98 (NO)
Riesling Knappstein **1996** £6.50 (CRO)
Riesling Mitchell Watervale **1999** £6.75 (TAN) £6.85 (HAH) £6.95 (POR) £7.35 (AD)
Riesling Mitchell Watervale **1998** £6.99 (JON)
Riesling Wakefield **1992** £6.50 (WRI)
Riesling Wolf Blass **1999** £6.99 (PHI)
Riesling David Wynn **1997** £6.35 (FLE)
Sauvignon Blanc Dromana Estate Schinus **1999** £6.82 (FLE)
Sauvignon Blanc Plantagenet Omrah **1998** £6.95 (POR)
Sauvignon Blanc Rymill **1998** £6.99 (ASD)
Sauvignon Blanc David Wynn **1999** £6.35 (FLE)
Sauvignon Blanc David Wynn **1998** £6.95 (AD) £7.25 (STE) £7.59 (NI) £8.00 (MV)
Semillon Bethany **1997** £6.15 (NO)
Semillon Penfolds Barossa Valley Old Vine **1996** £6.90 (SOM)
Semillon/Chardonnay Ironstone **1999** £6.75 (STE)
Semillon/Chardonnay Penfolds Barossa Valley **1996** £6.15 (WAT)
Semillon/Chardonnay Tatachilla Wattle Park **1998** £6.99 (VIC) £6.99 (THR)
Semillon/Sauvignon Blanc Mitchell The Growers **1998** £6.95 (POR) £7.10 (TAN)
Verdelho Rothbury Hunter Valley **1999** £6.99 (DI) £6.99 (SAF)
White Clare Wakefield **1997** £6.29 (BAL)

£7.00 → £7.99

Chardonnay Capel Vale CV Unwooded **1999** £7.99 (SAF)
Chardonnay Capel Vale CV Unwooded **1997** £7.99 (UN)
Chardonnay Coriole **1997** £7.65 (TAN)
Chardonnay De Bortoli Windy Peak **1998** £7.25 (STE)
Chardonnay Simon Hackett Barossa Valley **1998** £7.35 (CON) £7.50 (FLE)
Chardonnay Hardys Padthaway **1999** £7.99 (SO)
Chardonnay Leconfield **1998** £7.90 (JU)
Chardonnay Lindemans Padthaway **1998** £7.99 (SO) £8.49 (WR) £8.49 (BOT)
Chardonnay Madfish Bay Unwooded **1998** £7.30 (SOM) £8.99 (BAL)
Chardonnay Maxwell **1997** £7.20 (SOM)
Chardonnay Ninth Island **1998** £7.25 (SOM) £7.99 (POR) £7.99 (BO) £7.99 (TES) £8.49 (CON) £8.75 (PHI) £8.75 (STA) £9.40 (MV)
Chardonnay Neil Paulett **1997** £7.90 (JU)
Chardonnay Penfolds Barrel-Fermented **1998** £7.55 (PIP)
Chardonnay Plantagenet Omrah Unoaked **1997** £7.75 (STE)
Chardonnay Tyrrell's Old Winery **1997** £7.20 (PIP)
Chardonnay Water Wheel **1999** £7.98 (PLA)
Chardonnay Wynns Coonawarra Estate **1997** £7.77 (BY)
Chardonnay Yalumba Antipodean **1998** £7.80 (NI)
Chardonnay/Verdelho Brokenwood Harlequin **1998** £7.50 (BAN)
Chenin Blanc Richard Hamilton **1998** £7.10 (SOM)
Fifth Leg Devil's Lair **1998** £7.95 (SOM) £9.92 (GW)
Gewürztraminer Knappstein **1997** £7.95 (FORT)
Marsanne Mitchelton **1997** £7.99 (AME)
★ Riesling Tim Adams **1999** £7.50 (TES) £7.99 (AUS)
Riesling Brown Bros **1995** £7.99 (VIN)
Riesling Tim Gramp Watervale **1997** £7.99 (UN)
Riesling Heggies Vineyard **1991** £7.99 (BAL)
Riesling Howard Park **1998** £7.50 (BAN)
Riesling Leconfield **1997** £7.20 (JU)
Riesling Mount Langi Ghiran **1996** £7.99 (VA) £10.55 (NI)
Riesling Orlando St Helga **1998** £7.99 (WR)
Riesling Neil Paulett **1998** £7.50 (JU)
Riesling Pikes Polish Hill River **1997** £7.50 (LEA)
Sauvignon Blanc Brown Bros **1998** £7.10 (PIP) £7.45 (STE)
Sauvignon Blanc Brown Bros **1997** £7.25 (CON)
Sauvignon Blanc Mitchelton Preece **1997** £7.30 (UB)
Sauvignon Blanc Neil Paulett **1998** £7.95 (JU)
Sauvignon Blanc Riddoch **1999** £7.75 (DI)
Sauvignon Blanc/Chardonnay/Semillon Vasse Felix **1998** £7.35 (SOM) £8.95 (TAN)
Sauvignon Blanc/Semillon Hollick Coonawarra **1998** £7.95 (NI) £7.99 (HED)

★ Semillon Tim Adams **1997** £7.99 (TES) £7.99 (AUS) £8.99 (VIC) £8.99 (THR) £8.99 (BOT) £9.69 (REI)

Semillon Brown Bros **1997** £7.10 (PIP) £7.75 (STA)

Semillon Brown Bros **1996** £7.49 (DI) £7.75 (WRI) £7.88 (GW)

Semillon Grant Burge Old Vine **1998** £7.75 (WRI) £7.95 (BU) £9.18 (PLAY)

Semillon Grant Burge Old Vine **1997** £7.99 (UN) £8.50 (RES)

Semillon Grant Burge Old Vine **1995** £7.95 (CON)

Semillon McWilliams Mount Pleasant Elizabeth **1994** £7.99 (TES)

Semillon/Sauvignon Blanc Cape Mentelle **1996** £7.94 (NO)

Semillon/Sauvignon Blanc St Hallett **1994** £7.34 (REI)

Verdelho Bremerton **1999** £7.52 (FLE)

Verdelho Brown Bros **1999** £7.25 (PIP)

Verdelho Capel Vale **1998** £7.99 (MAJ) £7.99 (SAF) £8.99 (AME)

Verdelho Chapel Hill **1998** £7.49 (WR) £7.49 (BOT) £7.49 (WAI) £7.99 (AUS)

Verdelho Pendarves Estate **1998** £7.95 (STA)

Verdelho David Traeger **1998** £7.99 (AUS) £8.49 (VIC) £8.49 (BOT) £8.50 (ELL)

£8.00 → £8.99

Chardonnay Allandale **1998** £8.99 (AUS)

Chardonnay Brown Bros **1997** £8.40 (PIP) £8.49 (DI) £8.70 (TAN)

Chardonnay Brown Bros King Valley **1998** £8.45 (STE) £11.22 (TW)

Chardonnay Brown Bros King Valley **1997** £8.39 (JON) £8.45 (STE) £8.50 (CON) £8.60 (STA) £8.95 (POR)

Chardonnay Campbells Bobbie Burns **1997** £8.95 (UB)

Chardonnay Green Point **1993** £8.99 (RAE) £12.50 (CRO)

Chardonnay Hollick Coonawarra **1996** £8.99 (HED) £9.49 (AME) £9.64 (NO) £11.57 (TW)

- *Wines are listed in A–Z order within each price band.*
- *For each wine, vintages are listed in descending order.*
- *Each vintage of any wine appears only once.*

★ Chardonnay Madfish Bay Unwooded **1999** £8.25 (BAN) £9.99 (VA)

Chardonnay Mitchelton **1997** £8.99 (WR)

Chardonnay Mitchelton **1996** £8.99 (AME)

Chardonnay Mitchelton Preece **1998** £8.37 (PLAY)

Chardonnay Nepenthe Unwooded **1997** £8.99 (GW)

Chardonnay Rothbury Hunter Valley **1997** £8.39 (JON)

Chardonnay St Hallett **1998** £8.21 (DOM) £8.52 (REI) £8.99 (AUS)

Chardonnay Shaw & Smith Unoaked **1998** £8.99 (LIB) £8.99 (TES) £9.35 (CON) £9.50 (WRI) £9.95 (RES) £10.70 (TAN)

Chardonnay Stonier's **1998** £8.99 (DI)

Chardonnay Tatachilla Adelaide Hills **1998** £8.99 (SAF)

Chardonnay Water Wheel **1998** £8.99 (AUS)

Chardonnay Yarra Valley Hills **1998** £8.99 (OD)

De Bortoli Rare Dry Botrytis Semillon **1996** £8.95 (AD)

Gewürztraminer Pipers Brook **1999** £8.55 (SOM)

Marsanne Mitchelton Victoria Reserve **1994** £8.51 (PIP) £8.90 (TAN)

Marsanne Mitchelton Victoria Reserve **1993** £8.99 (BEN)

Marsanne Mitchelton Wood-Matured **1994** £8.95 (WRI)

Pinot Gris Pipers Brook **1998** £8.55 (SOM) £10.75 (CON)

Riesling Tim Adams **1997** £8.20 (SOM)

Riesling Alkoomi **1997** £8.95 (JER)

Riesling Brown Bros Family Reserve **1995** £8.99 (DI)

Riesling Tim Gramp Watervale **1998** £8.50 (AD)

Riesling Heggies Vineyard **1987** £8.99 (BAL)

Riesling Henschke Julius Eden Valley **1997** £8.70 (SOM)

Riesling Knappstein **1997** £8.49 (NO)

Riesling Leeuwin Estate Art Series **1998** £8.81 (DOM) £9.95 (SOM)

Riesling Pikes Polish Hill River **1998** £8.95 (LEA)

Riesling Pipers Brook **1998** £8.55 (SOM)

★ Riesling St Hallett Eden Valley **1998** £8.99 (AUS)

★ Sauvignon Blanc Nepenthe **1999** £8.99 (WAI) £9.99 (GW)

Sauvignon Blanc Ninth Island **1998** £8.49 (SAF) £8.99 (REI)

Sauvignon Blanc Shaw & Smith **1998** £8.99 (BO) £8.99 (TES) £9.35 (CON) £9.50 (WRI) £9.90 (FLE) £9.95 (RES) £10.70 (TAN) £11.75 (FORT)
Sauvignon Blanc/Chardonnay/Semillon Vasse Felix **1999** £8.95 (STE)
Sauvignon Blanc/Semillon Henschke Eden Valley **1998** £8.55 (SOM) £12.70 (JER)
Sauvignon Blanc/Semillon/Riesling Marienberg **1996** £8.00 (JER)
Scrubby Rise Wirra Wirra **1999** £8.75 (WS)
Semillon Basedow **1994** £8.38 (NO)
Semillon Grant Burge Zerk Vineyard Old Vine **1998** £8.50 (LEA)
Semillon Coriole Lalla Rookh **1998** £8.95 (TAN)
Semillon Henschke **1997** £8.20 (SOM)
Semillon St Hallett Select **1998** £8.52 (REI) £8.99 (AUS)
Semillon Voyager Estate **1997** £8.90 (JU)
Semillon Willows Vineyard **1996** £8.49 (VIC) £8.49 (THR) £8.49 (WR) £8.49 (BOT) £8.50 (AUS)
Semillon/Sauvignon Blanc Cape Mentelle **1999** £8.54 (NO) £8.95 (TAN) £8.95 (STA) £9.04 (PLA) £9.41 (HAH) £9.45 (PHI)
Semillon/Sauvignon Blanc Cape Mentelle **1998** £8.99 (CON) £9.49 (AME) £9.50 (RAE) £9.99 (NI) £10.90 (UB)
Semillon/Sauvignon Blanc Cape Mentelle **1997** £8.99 (JON)
Sharefarmer's White Petaluma **1997** £8.75 (STE)
Verdelho Chapel Hill **1996** £8.52 (REI)
Viognier Yalumba Barossa Growers **1997** £8.99 (BAL)

£9.00 → £9.99

Chardonnay Bethany **1997** £9.45 (NO)
Chardonnay Coriole **1996** £9.10 (TAN)
Chardonnay Fern Hill **1997** £9.25 (FRI)
Chardonnay Green Point **1996** £9.60 (TAN)
Chardonnay Heggies Vineyard **1997** £9.95 (WS) £10.00 (FORT)
Chardonnay Heggies Vineyard **1996** £9.95 (RES) £12.70 (JER)
Chardonnay Madfish Bay Wooded **1997** £9.39 (BAN) £10.45 (NI)

- *All prices for each wine are listed together in ascending order.*
- *Price bands refer to the lowest price for which the wine is available.*

Chardonnay Marienberg Reserve **1996** £9.40 (JER)
Chardonnay McWilliams Mount Pleasant **1996** £9.39 (HA) £9.45 (COC)
Chardonnay Montara Estate **1997** £9.50 (AD)
Chardonnay Mount Helen **1997** £9.66 (SUN)
Chardonnay Nepenthe Unwooded **1995** £9.50 (CRO)
Chardonnay Penley Estate **1998** £9.95 (LAY)
Chardonnay Pikes **1999** £9.95 (LEA)
Chardonnay Pipers Brook **1996** £9.85 (SOM) £13.50 (STA)
Chardonnay Plantagenet Mount Barker **1998** £9.95 (BU) £11.95 (LIB)
Chardonnay Rosemount Show Reserve **1998** £9.99 (UN) £9.99 (WAI) £9.99 (SAF)
Chardonnay Rosemount Show Reserve **1997** £9.99 (VIC) £9.99 (THR) £9.99 (WR) £9.99 (BOT)
Chardonnay Wirra Wirra **1998** £9.99 (OD)
Chardonnay Wolf Blass President's Selection **1999** £9.60 (CRO)
Fifth Leg Devil's Lair **1997** £9.80 (BAN)
Riesling Howard Park **1999** £9.06 (GW)
Riesling Mount Langi Ghiran **1998** £9.21 (FLE) £10.50 (RES)
Riesling Penfolds Eden Valley Reserve **1999** £9.99 (SAF)
Riesling Petaluma **1998** £9.60 (TAN) £10.50 (FORT)
Riesling Petaluma **1997** £9.53 (PIP) £9.95 (BEN)
Riesling Petaluma **1996** £9.99 (PHI)
Sauvignon Blanc Alkoomi **1997** £9.70 (JER)
Sauvignon Blanc Amberley Estate **1998** £9.95 (AD)
Sauvignon Blanc Amberley Estate Margaret River **1999** £9.75 (ELL)
Sauvignon Blanc Eden Ridge **1998** £9.50 (AD)
Sauvignon Blanc Katnook **1999** £9.99 (BIB)
Sauvignon Blanc Lenswood **1998** £9.20 (SOM) £9.30 (NEZ)
Sauvignon Blanc Scotchman's Hill **1996** £9.90 (JU)
Semillon Amberley Estate Margaret River **1998** £9.62 (PIP)£9.95 (AD) £9.99 (MAJ)
Semillon Amberley Estate Margaret River **1997** £9.99 (VIC) £9.99 (THR)
Semillon Brokenwood **1997** £9.16 (NO)

Semillon Henschke **1998** £9.69 (REI)
Semillon Henschke **1996** £9.75 (FORT)
Semillon McWilliams Mount Pleasant Elizabeth **1993** £9.45 (COC)
Semillon Tyrrell's Lost Block **1997** £9.99 (JON)
Semillon/Chardonnay Henschke Tilly's Vineyard Eden Valley **1998** £9.95 (LAY)
Semillon/Chardonnay Henschke Tilly's Vineyard Eden Valley **1996** £9.99 (JON)
Semillon/Sauvignon Blanc Pierro LTC **1999** £9.99 (PHI)
Viognier Heggies Vineyard **1998** £9.60 (SOM) £11.79 (YOU) £11.99 (PHI) £12.25 (FORT) £12.95 (RES)

£10.00 → £10.99

Chardonnay Alkoomi **1996** £10.75 (JER)
Chardonnay Ashton Hills **1996** £10.99 (AUS)
Chardonnay Best's Victoria **1997** £10.64 (FLE)
Chardonnay Best's Victoria **1996** £10.69 (GW)
Chardonnay Blue Pyrenees Estate **1997** £10.79 (TES)
Chardonnay Cape Mentelle **1997** £10.26 (NO) £10.50 (CRO) £11.95 (NI) £11.99 (VA) £12.50 (FORT)
Chardonnay Cape Mentelle **1996** £10.99 (PHI)
Chardonnay Chain of Ponds **1997** £10.95 (BAN) £16.99 (PHI)
Chardonnay Chapel Hill Reserve **1996** £10.87 (REI)
Chardonnay De Bortoli Yarra Valley **1996** £10.67 (HA)
Chardonnay De Bortoli Yarra Valley **1995** £10.95 (BAL) £10.95 (WRI)
Chardonnay Goundrey Reserve **1998** £10.75 (PLAY) £10.99 (SAF)
Chardonnay Hillstowe Udy's Mill **1995** £10.86 (NO)
Chardonnay Lenswood **1997** £10.40 (SOM)
Chardonnay Mountadam **1994** £10.50 (SOM) £14.00 (CRO)
Chardonnay Old Kent River **1997** £10.35 (JER)
Chardonnay Penfolds Adelaide Hills **1996** £10.35 (SOM) £11.43 (NO) £11.95 (POR) £12.99 (JON)
Chardonnay Penley Estate **1996** £10.71 (WT)
Chardonnay Tarrawarra Tunnel Hill **1999** £10.25 (AS)
Chardonnay Voyager Estate **1996** £10.95 (JU)
Marsanne Chateau Tahbilk **1990** £10.46 (NO)
Riesling Brown Bros Family Reserve **1991** £10.50 (NO)
Riesling Grosset Polish Hill **1999** £10.99 (PHI) £12.50 (WS) £13.99 (BEN)
Riesling Heggies Vineyard **1996** £10.35 (JER)
Riesling Henschke Green's Hill **1997** £10.65 (FLE)
Riesling Howard Park **1996** £10.15 (BAN) £11.35 (NI)
Riesling Pipers Brook **1997** £10.75 (CON) £10.95 (PHI)
Sauvignon Blanc Shaw & Smith **1997** £10.99 (PHI)
Sauvignon Blanc Geoff Weaver **1999** £10.99 (BAL)
Sauvignon Blanc/Semillon Cullen **1998** £10.97 (SAV) £10.99 (DI) £12.75 (AD) £12.99 (PHI) £12.99 (VA)
Semillon Brokenwood **1999** £10.95 (RES)
Semillon Henschke Louis **1997** £10.77 (NO)
Semillon Moss Wood **1997** £10.55 (JER)
Terra White Hollick **1993** £10.52 (TW)

£11.00 → £12.99

Chardonnay Brown Bros Family Reserve **1994** £11.60 (DI)
Chardonnay Cape Mentelle **1998** £11.49 (AME) £11.50 (PLA) £11.75 (REI) £11.95 (HAH) £12.83 (PLAY)
Chardonnay Chateau Xanadu **1996** £12.95 (DI)
Chardonnay Cullen **1995** £11.30 (FLE)
Chardonnay De Bortoli Yarra Valley **1997** £11.95 (STA)
Chardonnay Devil's Lair **1996** £11.70 (SOM)
Chardonnay Grosset Piccadilly **1998** £12.50 (WS)
Chardonnay Howard Park **1997** £12.25 (SOM) £13.99 (GW) £14.20 (BAN) £14.99 (YOU) £15.95 (FORT)
Chardonnay Katnook **1996** £11.75 (BO)
Chardonnay Leeuwin Estate Prelude **1998** £11.46 (DOM)
Chardonnay Lenswood **1995** £12.90 (HAH)
Chardonnay Long Gully **1997** £11.95 (JER)
Chardonnay Miranda Family Reserve **1998** £11.75 (AV)
Chardonnay Mountadam **1997** £12.99 (VIC) £12.99 (THR) £12.99 (WR) £12.99 (BOT) £13.50 (WRI) £13.69 (GW) £13.75 (STE) £13.95 (AD) £14.55 (NI) £14.99 (VA)

Chardonnay Mountadam **1996** £12.99 (YOU) £14.25 (FORT) £15.75 (PHI)
Chardonnay Mountadam **1993** £11.99 (AME) £12.84 (NO)
Chardonnay Nepenthe **1997** £11.98 (GW)
Chardonnay Pipers Brook **1998** £12.50 (POR) £13.69 (AME) £13.79 (CON)
Chardonnay Pipers Brook **1993** £12.50 (CRO)
Chardonnay Rosemount Giants Creek **1997** £12.95 (WS)
Chardonnay Rosemount Show Reserve **1995** £11.50 (CRO)
Chardonnay Scotchman's Hill **1997** £11.50 (JU)
Chardonnay Shaw & Smith Reserve **1998** £12.99 (YOU)
Chardonnay Voyager Estate **1997** £11.99 (YOU)
Pinot Gris T'Gallant Mornington Peninsula **1998** £12.99 (PHI)
Riesling Grosset Polish Hill **1997** £11.50 (FORT)
Riesling Henschke Green's Hill **1996** £11.99 (NI)
Riesling Henschke Julius Eden Valley **1999** £12.99 (YOU)
Riesling Henschke Julius Eden Valley **1998** £11.09 (NO)
Riesling Jasper Hill **1998** £12.63 (YAP)
Riesling David Wynn **1995** £11.85 (UB)
Sauvignon Blanc Cullen **1996** £12.55 (NO)
Sauvignon Blanc Lenswood **1997** £11.50 (PHI)
Sauvignon Blanc Paracombe **1997** £12.50 (PHI)
Sauvignon Blanc/Semillon Chain of Ponds **1997** £11.95 (BAL)
Semillon Henschke Louis **1998** £11.09 (NO)
Semillon Henschke Louis **1995** £12.70 (JER)
Semillon Tyrrell's Vat 1 **1992** £12.61 (NO) £16.95 (STA) £17.50 (BAL)
Viognier Heggies Vineyard **1997** £11.95 (WRI) £11.95 (NI) £14.21 (PLAY) £16.90 (JER)

£13.00 → £15.99

Chardonnay Bannockburn **1997** £15.95 (TAN) £16.95 (BEN) £17.95 (RES)
Chardonnay Capel Vale Reserve Frederick **1995** £15.50 (WRI)
Chardonnay Coldstream Hills Reserve **1996** £14.99 (YOU)
Chardonnay Dalwhinnie **1997** £14.00 (JU)
Chardonnay Devil's Lair **1997** £14.99 (YOU)
Chardonnay Grosset Piccadilly **1997** £14.99 (PHI)
Chardonnay Grosset Piccadilly **1996** £14.25 (FORT)
Chardonnay Henschke Croft **1997** £15.99 (PHI) £17.50 (NI)
Chardonnay Howard Park **1996** £14.99 (YOU) £15.99 (PHI) £15.99 (NI)
Chardonnay Moss Wood **1994** £15.00 (CRO)
Chardonnay Petaluma **1997** £13.95 (TAN) £13.99 (YOU) £14.70 (BEN) £14.95 (STE) £14.99 (PHI) £15.50 (FORT) £16.13 (PLAY)
Chardonnay Shaw & Smith Reserve **1996** £13.35 (CON)
Chardonnay Tarrawarra **1997** £14.95 (WS) £14.99 (YOU)
Chardonnay Vasse Felix Heytesbury **1998** £14.99 (YOU) £16.50 (RES)
Marsanne/Roussanne Yeringberg **1998** £15.99 (YOU)
Semillon Moss Wood Wooded **1991** £13.50 (CRO)
The Virgilius Yalumba **1998** £13.75 (SOM) £16.49 (YOU)

£16.00 → £19.99

Chardonnay Bannockburn **1996** £19.65 (JER) £32.95 (UB)
Chardonnay Brokenwood Graveyard **1998** £17.50 (BAN)
Chardonnay Brokenwood Graveyard **1997** £18.95 (RES)
Chardonnay Chain of Ponds **1996** £16.99 (VA)
Chardonnay Cullen **1998** £16.95 (DI) £17.99 (YOU) £19.95 (AD) £20.00 (FORT)
Chardonnay Henschke Eden Valley **1997** £16.35 (NI)
Chardonnay Henschke Eden Valley **1991** £16.00 (CRO)
Chardonnay Moss Wood **1993** £18.00 (CRO)
Chardonnay Petersons **1991** £19.39 (REI)
Chardonnay Scotchman's Hill **1995** £16.70 (UB)
Chardonnay Tarrawarra **1995** £16.75 (PHI)
Chardonnay Tyrrell's Vat 47 **1997** £16.85 (WRI)
Chardonnay Yarra Yering **1990** £18.88 (NO)
Semillon Clarendon Hills **1997** £19.00 (JU)
Semillon Tyrrell's Vat 1 **1993** £16.99 (YOU) £17.05 (NO) £17.50 (FORT)
Semillon Tyrrell's Vat 1 **1990** £16.75 (RAE)

£20.00 → £24.99

Chardonnay Clarendon Hills Kangarilla Vineyard **1997** £23.00 (JU)
Chardonnay Giaconda **1997** £24.75 (SOM) £29.79 (YOU) £33.00 (BAL)
Chardonnay Leeuwin Estate **1995** £23.40 (SOM)
Chardonnay Moss Wood **1998** £22.56 (PLAY)
Chardonnay Petaluma **1991** £21.00 (CRO)
Chardonnay Vasse Felix Heytesbury **1997** £22.99 (YOU)

Over £25.00

Chardonnay Lake's Folly **1986** £28.00 (CRO)
Chardonnay Leeuwin Estate Art Series **1998** £34.00 (RES)
Chardonnay Leeuwin Estate Art Series **1996** £27.25 (SOM)
Chardonnay Leeuwin Estate Art Series **1995** £35.00 (FORT)
Chardonnay Leeuwin Estate **1996** £29.95 (PHI)
Chardonnay Rosemount Roxburgh **1998** £34.99 (UN)
Chardonnay Rosemount Roxburgh **1992** £33.00 (CRO)
Chardonnay Yarra Yering **1997** £28.50 (FORT)
Yattarna Penfolds **1996** £29.95 (SOM)
Yattarna Penfolds **1995** £53.97 (NO)

ROSÉ

Under £10.00

Grenache/Shiraz Hardys Stamp **1999** £4.49 (TES) £4.79 (WAI) £4.79 (SAF)
Rose of Virginia Charles Melton **1999** £9.75 (LIB)
Rose of Virginia Charles Melton **1998** £8.10 (SOM)

SPARKLING

Under £5.00

Angas Brut **Non-vintage** £4.75 (SOM) £5.99 (TES) £5.99 (VIC) £5.99 (THR) £5.99 (OD) £5.99 (UN) £5.99 (WR) £5.99 (BOT)
Angas Brut Rosé **Non-vintage** £4.75 (SOM) £5.99 (TES) £5.99 (VIC) £5.99 (THR) £5.99 (OD) £5.99 (UN) £5.99 (BOT)
Killawarra Brut **Non-vintage** £4.50 (SOM) £5.69 (GW) £5.82 (BY)
Seppelt Great Western Brut Rosé **Non-vintage** £4.99 (WR) £4.99 (BOT) £5.45 (CON) £5.80 (TAN) £5.99 (VIC) £5.99 (THR)

£5.00 → £5.99

Barramundi Brut **Non-vintage** £5.29 (ASD)
Carrington Extra Brut **Non-vintage** £5.99 (JON) £6.60 (UB)
Carrington Vintage Brut **1996** £5.99 (UN)
Killawarra Rosé **Non-vintage** £5.99 (POR)
Penfolds Rowlands Brook **Non-vintage** £5.89 (JON) £6.49 (POR)
Rolleston Vale Brut **Non-vintage** £5.45 (CON)
Seppelt Great Western Brut **Non-vintage** £5.99 (THR) £6.85 (VIN)

£6.00 → £7.99

Aldridge Estate Brut **Non-vintage** £6.95 (CON)
Carrington Brut Rosé **Non-vintage** £6.60 (UB)
Deakin Estate Brut **1999** £6.99 (DI)
Deakin Estate Brut **1998** £6.07 (BIB)
Jacob's Creek Sparkling Chardonnay/Pinot Noir **Non-vintage** £6.99 (SAI) £6.99 (TES)
Nottage Hill Chardonnay Brut Hardys **Non-vintage** £6.99 (SAI)
Nottage Hill Chardonnay Brut Hardys **1998** £6.99 (SAF)
Redbank Cuvée Emily **Non-vintage** £6.95 (ROB)
Seaview Brut **Non-vintage** £6.49 (MAJ) £6.49 (POR) £6.49 (BO) £6.49 (TES) £6.49 (VIC) £6.49 (THR) £6.49 (UN) £6.49 (WR) £6.49 (BOT) £6.50 (WS) £6.99 (ASD)
Seaview Brut Rosé **Non-vintage** £6.49 (UN) £6.49 (WAI) £6.59 (BUD) £6.99 (SAF)
Seaview Pinot Noir/Chardonnay **1995** £7.10 (SOM) £8.79 (POR) £8.99 (JON)
Tatachilla Brut Non-Vintage **Non-vintage** £6.55 (BAN)
Yalumba Pinot Noir/Chardonnay Cuvée One Prestige **Non-vintage** £6.50 (SOM)

£8.00 → £9.99

Brown Bros Sparkling Pinot Noir/Chardonnay **Non-vintage** £9.95 (AD) £9.99 (DI) £10.45 (STE)
Chandon Australia **Non-vintage** £9.99 (COC) £9.99 (JON)
Green Point Brut **Non-vintage** £9.95 (JER) £12.50 (CRO) £13.45 (STE)

Jansz Pipers River Brut **1995** £9.45 (SOM)
Seaview Pinot Noir/Chardonnay **1996** £8.99 (SAF)
Seaview Pinot Noir/Chardonnay **1994** £8.99 (UN)
Seppelt Salinger Brut **1993** £8.99 (OD)
Seppelt Show Sparkling Shiraz **1995** £8.99 (OD)
Seppelt Show Sparkling Shiraz **1994** £8.99 (BO)
Seppelt Sparkling Shiraz **1996** £8.99 (VIC) £8.99 (THR) £8.99 (WR)
Seppelt Sparkling Shiraz **1994** £8.99 (UN) £12.10 (TAN)
Taltarni Brut Taché **Non-vintage** £8.50 (TAN) £8.80 (AV) £8.95 (STA) £8.99 (CON) £8.99 (POR) £8.99 (AME) £9.30 (COC) £10.99 (PHI) £11.69 (TW)
Yalumba Pinot Noir/Chardonnay **Non-vintage** £8.49 (WR) £9.75 (NI)
Yellowglen Brut **1997** £9.99 (OD)

£10.00 → £11.99

Grant Burge Méthode Traditionelle **Non-vintage** £10.45 (CON) £10.95 (LEA)
★ Fox Creek The Vixen Sparkling Shiraz/Cabernet Franc **Non-vintage** £10.99 (YOU)
Green Point Blanc de Blancs **1994** £11.99 (OD) £12.99 (WR)
Green Point Brut **1996** £11.49 (TES) £11.49 (BOT) £11.49 (SAF) £11.74 (PLA) £11.75 (DI) £11.99 (PHI) £11.99 (OD) £11.99 (WAI) £12.09 (BIB) £13.95 (JU)
Green Point Brut **1995** £10.40 (SOM) £11.49 (VIC) £11.49 (THR) £11.49 (UN) £11.49 (WR) £11.99 (MAJ) £11.99 (POR) £11.99 (JON) £12.65 (HAH) £12.95 (ROB)
Green Point Brut **1994** £10.99 (COC)
Green Point Brut Rosé **1996** £11.99 (DI)
Green Point Brut Rosé **1995** £11.25 (SOM)
Miranda Family Reserve Sparkling Shiraz **Non-vintage** £11.75 (CON)
Miranda Family Reserve Sparkling Shiraz **1994** £11.40 (AV) £12.95 (POR)
Padthaway Estate Eliza Brut **1996** £10.49 (AME)

£12.00 → £15.99

Clover Hill **1996** £13.10 (AV)
Clover Hill **1995** £12.99 (AME) £14.50 (STA)
Croser **1995** £13.95 (FORT)
Croser **1993** £13.90 (BEN)
Green Point Blanc de Blancs **1993** £12.99 (WR)
Green Point Brut Rosé **Non-vintage** £12.99 (JON)
Mitchell Sparkling Shiraz **Non-vintage** £13.99 (YOU)
Pipers Brook Pirie **1995** £15.20 (SOM) £17.99 (AME)

£16.00 → £19.99

Croser **1994** £18.00 (CRO)
Mountadam Chardonnay/Pinot Noir **1992** £19.95 (AD) £19.99 (YOU)
Mountadam Chardonnay/Pinot Noir **1991** £16.75 (FLE) £17.59 (CON)
Seppelt Show Sparkling Shiraz **1987** £18.99 (PHI)
Seppelt Sparkling Shiraz **1987** £17.04 (REI)

Over £20.00

Charles Melton Sparkling Red **Non-vintage** £25.95 (LIB)
Yarra Yering Sparkling **1992** £25.99 (YOU)

SWEET & FORTIFIED

Under £5.00

Morris Liqueur Muscat **Non-vintage** £4.99 (TES)
Penfolds Magill Tawny ½ bottle **Non-vintage** £4.99 (UN) £4.99 (JON) £5.65 (SOM) £5.99 (BO)

£5.00 → £5.99

Brown Bros Muscat Late-Harvest **1999** £5.94 (PIP) £5.99 (TES) £6.35 (STA) £6.50 (DI) £6.70 (TAN) £6.75 (AD)
Brown Bros Orange Muscat & Flora ½ bottle **Non-vintage** £5.99 (SAI)
Brown Bros Orange Muscat & Flora ½ bottle **1999** £5.93 (PIP) £5.99 (TES) £5.99 (WAI) £6.20 (GW) £6.25 (STE) £6.30 (TAN) £6.35 (STA) £6.75 (AD) £8.10 (PLAY)
Brown Bros Orange Muscat & Flora ½ bottle **1998** £5.99 (VIC) £5.99 (POR) £5.99 (DI) £5.99 (BO) £5.99 (THR) £5.99 (UN) £5.99 (WR) £5.99 (JON) £5.99 (BOT) £6.35 (WRI) £7.45 (UB) £8.17 (TW)
Brown Bros Orange Muscat & Flora ½ bottle **1997** £5.99 (OD) £6.99 (VIN)
Brown Bros Orange Muscat & Flora ½ bottle **1995** £5.99 (COC)
Lindemans Coonawarra Botrytis Riesling ½ bottle **1996** £5.90 (SOM) £5.99 (JON)
Morris Liqueur Muscat ½ bottle **Non-vintage** £5.30 (SOM) £7.00 (UB)

Stanton & Killeen Rutherglen Liqueur Muscat ½ bottle **Non-vintage** £5.99 (AME) £6.25 (WS) £6.45 (WAT) £6.49 (BAL) £6.49 (UN) £6.50 (PHI) £6.69 (CON) £7.19 (NO)

Stanton & Killeen Rutherglen Liqueur Tokay (Muscadelle) ½ bottle **Non-vintage** £5.99 (AME) £6.45 (WAT)

£6.00 → £6.99

Brown Bros Muscat Late-Harvest **1998** £6.19 (JON) £6.45 (WRI)

Brown Bros Noble Riesling ½ bottle **1982** £6.80 (UB)

Brown Bros Orange Muscat & Flora ½ bottle **1996** £6.25 (CON) £6.45 (JU)

Campbells Liqueur Muscat ½ bottle **Non-vintage** £6.65 (PIP)

Campbells Rutherglen Liqueur Muscat **Non-vintage** £6.95 (AD) £13.41 (NO)

Chambers Rosewood Liqueur Muscat ½ bottle **Non-vintage** £6.83 (NO)

Chambers Rutherglen Liqueur Muscat ½ bottle **Non-vintage** £6.75 (PHI) £6.95 (FORT)

Peter Lehmann Botrytis Semillon ½ bottle **1997** £6.99 (OD)

Seppelt Show Fino DP117 ½ bottle **Non-vintage** £6.42 (NO) £6.99 (PHI)

£7.00 → £9.99

Brown Bros Muscat Reserve **Non-vintage** £8.99 (DI) £9.49 (JON)

Brown Bros Noble Riesling ½ bottle **1996** £7.99 (DI) £9.05 (PIP)

Cranswick Estate Botrytis Semillon ½ bottle **1996** £9.99 (OD) £10.93 (CB)

d'Arenberg Noble Riesling ½ bottle **1996** £7.99 (OD)

Primo Joseph La Magia Botrytis Riesling ½ bottle **1996** £7.34 (REI) £9.99 (AUS)

Seppelt Show Reserve DP63 ½ bottle **Non-vintage** £7.49 (OD)

Vasse Felix Noble Riesling ½ bottle **1996** £7.25 (SOM) £8.95 (BEN) £9.62 (PLAY) £9.99 (PHI)

Yalumba Museum Release Rutherglen Muscat **Non-vintage** £7.99 (OD)

Oz Clarke's Wine Buying Guide
is an annual publication.
We welcome your suggestions for next year's edition.

£10.00 → £11.99

Chambers Rutherglen Liqueur Muscat **Non-vintage** £10.47 (NO) £14.00 (CRO)

Cranswick Estate Botrytis Semillon ½ bottle **Non-vintage** £11.29 (BO)

De Bortoli Noble One Botrytis Semillon ½ bottle **1993** £10.85 (SOM) £13.25 (WRI)

Primo Joseph La Magia Botrytis Riesling ½ bottle **1990** £11.57 (REI)

£12.00 → £13.99

Brown Bros Liqueur Muscat **Non-vintage** £12.75 (DI) £12.81 (PIP) £13.52 (GW) £13.95 (WRI) £13.99 (JON) £14.22 (NO)

Chambers Rutherglen Old Vine ½ bottle **Non-vintage** £13.07 (NO) £13.99 (YOU)

Chambers Special Liqueur Muscat **Non-vintage** £13.79 (NO)

Cranswick Estate Botrytis Semillon ½ bottle **1995** £12.00 (WRI) £12.75 (NO)

De Bortoli Black Noble ½ bottle **Non-vintage** £12.99 (BAL) £12.99 (OD) £13.25 (WRI) £13.50 (LEA) £14.50 (PHI) £14.95 (STE)

De Bortoli Noble One Botrytis Semillon ½ bottle **1996** £13.75 (STE)

De Bortoli Noble One Botrytis Semillon ½ bottle **1995** £12.37 (NO) £12.50 (STA) £12.51 (REI) £12.99 (BAL) £14.50 (PHI) £14.95 (LEA) £14.95 (JER)

De Bortoli Noble One Botrytis Semillon ½ bottle **1994** £12.95 (BEN) £13.30 (NO)

Seppelt Old Trafford **Non-vintage** £12.85 (NO)

£14.00 → £19.99

Campbells Old Rutherglen Liqueur Muscat **Non-vintage** £15.62 (NO)

★ Primo Estate Joseph 'The Fronti' III ½ bottle **Non-vintage** £16.99 (AUS)

Seppelt Para Port **Non-vintage** £15.99 (AME)

Seppelt Para Port **1976** £19.51 (NO)

Over £20.00

Brown Bros Noble Riesling **1982** £20.00 (CRO)

Campbells Merchant Prince Liqueur Muscat **Non-vintage** £37.99 (NO)

Chambers Old Liqueur Muscat ½ bottle **Non-vintage** £39.64 (NO)

De Bortoli Noble One Botrytis Semillon **1995** £28.50 (BEN)

CHILE

It's not often that a whole new grape variety is launched on the world. Chile is going one better, with a brand new old grape variety

The world has a new grape variety – yippee. It's called Carmenère, and Chile is full of it. Absolutely stuffed with it.

Well, actually, it's not a new grape variety at all. It's a very old grape variety indeed, and it grew all over Bordeaux until the vine pest called *Phylloxera vastatrix* came and wiped it out, along with all the other vines in Bordeaux, at the end of the 19th century.

But what nobody realized until a few years ago was that when cuttings of French vines had been taken to Chile from Bordeaux before phylloxera hit, a lot of those cuttings were Carmenère. Everybody thought they were Merlot, you see: the two vines look practically identical. You have to have them side by side and know what the differences are before you can tell one from the other.

So an awful lot of what we know as Chilean Merlot is, in fact, Carmenère. Most Chilean bottles labelled as Merlot contain a fair proportion of Carmenère: could be a third, could be two-thirds. It's not a con-job. In fact, only in the last couple of years has it become legal to put the word 'Carmenère' on the label. Now we're starting see Carmenère bottled on its own – and very good it is too. If you fancy a mouthful of soft, rich spice, look out for it.

GRAPE VARIETIES

CABERNET SAUVIGNON (red) Characterized by relatively soft, well-rounded tannins; unusually, Chilean Cab often doesn't need Merlot to fill it out. Unoaked versions are best within two years of the vintage. Best unoaked Cabernets: *Montes La Finca, La Rosa, Andes Peak.* Best premium: *Concha y Toro Don Melchor, Canepa Magnificum.*

CARMENÈRE (red) Marvellously spicy wines, sometimes under its alias of Grande Vidure. Try *Carmen, Montes.*

CHARDONNAY (white) Generally light and melony, with or without oak, but some properly complex wines are emerging. Unoaked: *La Rosa, Luis Felipe Edwards, Casa Porta, Santa Monica.* Wild-yeast wines: *Viña Casablanca, Errázuriz, Montes.* As with Cabernet, subtler oaking is increasingly the norm. Cool-climate Casablanca tends to produce a crisper, more citrus-fresh Chardonnay than its Central Valley counterparts.

GEWÜRZTRAMINER (white) The lychee and rose petal packed *Viña Casablanca* version of this grape is still the best. Others seem to lack heart.

MERLOT (red) Ever more fashionable, and bursting with colour and vibrant, plummy fruit. Try *La Rosa, Santa Monica, Carta Vieja, La Fortuna, Canepa* (all for drinking young); *Errázuriz Reserve, Casa Lapostolle, Carmen, Viña Porta, Mont Gras, Montes, Concha y Toro* and *Segú Ollé* (all with aging potential).

PINOT NOIR (red) Chile is a prime source of inexpensive Pinot Noir, but there's still not that much. Try *Concha y Toro Explorer, Villard, Cono Sur.*

RIESLING (white) Only minimal amounts of the great German grape are grown in Chile, and it's not being pursued with any great zeal. Nor are the results terribly exciting. *Miguel Torres* makes a good Gewürztraminer/Riesling blend in the

Curicó Valley, however; try also *Santa Monica* and *Santa Rita*.

SAUVIGNON BLANC (white) The Casablanca region leads and is the only region with a distinct style (ripe gooseberry and asparagus fruit, and firm acidity). *Viña Casablanca's Santa Isabel Estate, Villard, Concha y Toro* and *Caliterra* are the labels to watch. Outside Casablanca, the Curicó Valley is producing some goodies (*Viña Casablanca White Label, Montes, San Pedro*).

SEMILLON (white) Widely planted but rarely used for the domestic market. For exports, *Carmen*'s Alvaro Espinoza uses it in a good Chardonnay blend and a rich, oily Late Harvest. *Viña San Carlos* is decent.

WINE REGIONS

Although grapes are grown in the far north and pretty far south, quality wine is only produced in a 400km stretch of this long, narrow country. Frost and rain limit development further south, searing heat and desert are the problems to the north.

Recent appellation legislation splits the main wine-growing area into Aconcagua (incorporating the sub-region of Casablanca), the Central Valley (including Maipo, Rapel, Curicó and Maule) and the Southern Region (including the valleys of Itata and Bío-Bío).

ACONCAGUA VALLEY Dominated by one producer (*Errázuriz*) in Panquehue. The main vine is Cabernet Sauvignon (*Errázuriz' Don Maximiano* is one of the top Cabernets in Chile) and new plantings of Sangiovese, Nebbiolo and Zinfandel add to the red bias.

CASABLANCA VALLEY Chile's premier white wine region, and the only one with an identifiable style (though look out for Limari Valley in years to come). Chardonnay dominates, with Sauvignon Blanc and Gewürztraminer, and small amounts of Cabernet Sauvignon, Merlot and Pinot Noir. Chardonnay tends to be green and citrus-flavoured, often with figgy aromas, and Sauvignons are grassy and crisp with firm acidity. Best: *Caliterra, Concha y Toro, Veramonte, Villard, Viña Casablanca*.

CURICÓ Mainly known for its Chardonnay (*Valdivieso, Montes, San Pedro, Caliterra*). Valdivieso has emerged as the leading producer, also making beautiful Pinot Noir, Merlot and Cabernet.

MAIPO VALLEY Birthplace of the Chilean wine industry and home to some of the biggest and most traditional players (*Santa Rita, Concha y Toro, Santa Carolina*). Alto Maipo (*Aquitania, Cousiño Macul, William Fèvre*) has colder nights, so the grapes keep their acidity better. Cabernet Sauvignon made the valley's name and is still the main grape, although excellent Chardonnay is made here, too. The spread of Santiago's suburbs and smog is creating pressure on some producers. Best: *Canepa, Carmen, Concha y Toro, Tarapacá*.

MAULE A handful of producers (*Carta Vieja, Domaine Oriental, Segú Ollé, Terra Noble*) are achieving variable results, with reds (particularly Merlot) so far beating whites hands down on quality.

RAPEL A seedbed of new winery activity with two zones: Cachapoal Valley and Colchagua Valley to the south, where *Mont Gras, Luis Felipe Edwards* and *Casa Lapostolle* are producing good Chardonnay and Cabernet. Top Pinot Noir comes from *Cono Sur*, and Merlot from *La Rosa* and *Concha y Toro. Viña Porta* and *Santa Monica* make top-class Cabernet and Merlot.

SOUTHERN REGION *Concha y Toro* has produced a top-class Gewürztraminer from Mulchen.

PRODUCERS WHO'S WHO

FRANCISCO DE AGUIRRE ★★★ Clean, fresh Chardonnay and Cabernet under the Palo Alto label.

AQUITANIA ★★★ Made by Bordelais duo Bruno Prats of Ch. Cos d'Estournel and Paul Pontallier of Ch. Margaux. It's questionable whether the Domaine Paul Bruno is worth its hefty price tag.

CANEPA ★★★★ The company behind many of the best own-labels here, Canepa also makes the good Montenuevo and Rowan Brook. Merlot, Zinfandel and Magnificum Cabernet are its top reds.

CARMEN ★★★★ State-of-the-art sister operation to Santa Rita. Reds are best; beautiful Merlot Reserve, Grande Vidure/Cabernet and Petite Sirah.

INSTANT CELLAR: BEST CHILEANS

- **1997 Cabernet Sauvignon, Montes Alpha, £9.99, Hedley Wright** Lush blackcurrant and plums and vanilla fruit.
- **1998 Cabernet Sauvignon, Miraflores Estate, Viña Casablanca, £5.50, Wine Society** Refined and serious, with good depth.
- **1998 Carmenère Reserva, Mont Gras, Colchagua Valley, £5.99, Waitrose** Lush chocolaty fruit and a touch of spice, soft flavours and low acidity.
- **1997 Grande Vidure/Cabernet Reserve, Carmen, Maipo Valley, £7.95, Berry Bros & Rudd** Carmenère under its other name of Grande Vidure, blended with Cabernet. Rich and blackberryish.
- **Caballo Loco No 3, Valdivieso, £14.45, Christopher Piper Wines** The grapes in this red blend vary and the price seems to rise every year: but it's worth it. It's beautifully supple, rich and spicy.
- **1999 Gewurztraminer, Santa Isabel Estate, Viña Casablanca, £6.99, Hedley Wright** Fresh, perfumed and delicate.

CARTA VIEJA ★★★ Old Maule Valley winery delivering good value, inexpensive wine. Reds are best. Very good Merlot.

CASA LAPOSTOLLE ★★★(★) No-expense-spared winery making grassy Sauvignon, rich, buttery Chardonnay and spectacular oak-aged Merlot.

CONCHA Y TORO ★★★★ Chile's biggest winery has resources to reach both good value and premium ends. Trio red and white are superb, as is Amelia Chardonnay, a new Syrah, and constantly improving Don Melchor Cabernet. Latest is a joint venture with Ch. Mouton-Rothschild in Bordeaux.

CONO SUR ★★★★ Superb Pinot Noir and Isla Negra red are both excellent value.

COUSIÑO MACUL ★★ Traditionalist making old-style reds under the Santiago smog. A new location and a new wine-making philosophy would help.

ECHEVERRÍA ★★★ Leading boutique winery with vineyards in Curicó Valley. Good Reserve Chardonnay and Cabernet.

LUIS FELIPE EDWARDS ★★★(★) Large specialist in Chardonnay and Cabernet.

ERRÁZURIZ ★★★★ Chardonnay and Reserve Merlot have improved; there is also a wild yeast Chardonnay. A joint venture with Robert Mondavi of California has produced Seña, an extremely expensive, lush Cabernet/Merlot/Carmenère blend.

LA FORTUNA ★★★ Malbec is best here, but Merlot and Cabernet are both good. Decent whites.

LA ROSA ★★★★ Top unwooded Chardonnay and Merlot. Look out for La Palmería Cabernet and Merlot.

ON THE CASE
There's some interesting Syrah emerging from Chile at the moment. It's good in blends, too, so check the back labels

LOS ROBLES ★★★ Upfront flying winemaker-style Cabernet and Merlot.

LOS VASCOS ★★★ Château Lafite-Rothschild of Bordeaux's joint venture in Chile. So far, the Cabernet has not lived up to its potential.

MONT GRAS ★★★ Go for the reds here: Cabernet and Merlot are both good. Whites are less impressive so far.

MONTES ★★★ Slightly erratic, but currently on form with intense Malbec, good Merlot and juicy unoaked La Finca and premium Montes Alpha Cabernets.

SAN PEDRO ★★★ Good Chardonnay and Cabernet Sauvignon under the Castillo de Molina label.

SANTA CAROLINA ★★★ Reliable reds, particularly Merlot from San Fernando in the Colchagua Valley, Rapel. Whites are dull compared with the vibrant wines of its sister company Viña Casablanca.

SANTA INÉS ★★★ Small company making good quality wines.

SANTA MONICA ★★★ Family-run winery with excellent Riesling and Merlot.

SANTA RITA ★★★ The 120 range is reliable, and the latest release of premium Casa Real shows welcome restraint with the new oak. New Triple C is a fine Chilean response to the classic Bordeaux blend.

SEGÚ OLLÉ ★★★ Merlot is the star turn here, but the Cabernet Sauvignon is also good and worth a punt.

TARAPACÁ ★★★★ Rapidly improving winery with stylish red blend Milenium (the Spanish spelling) and Gran Reserva Merlot.

TERRA NOBLE ★★★★ Winery based at Talca in the Maule Valley, where Touraine wizard Henri Marionnet makes very good Sauvignon Blanc and Merlot.

TORRÉON DE PAREDES ★★★(★) Large winery based in Rapel. Good range, particularly an award-winning Merlot.

TORRES ★★★ A piece of foreign investment that has been slow to deliver the goods. Whites are above average but not spectacular.

UNDURRAGA ★★★ One of the old camp that needs an injection of inspiration. Merlot and Cabernet are good.

VALDIVIESO ★★★★ Traditional sparkling wine producer, now top of the premium still wine league. Excellent oaked Pinot Noir, Merlot, and red blend (grapes vary from year to year) Caballo Loco.

VILLARD ★★★★ Good Sauvignon and Chardonnay from Casablanca, and fruity Merlot from Maipo.

VIÑA CASABLANCA ★★★★ White label wines come from outside the Casablanca area (El Bosque Cabernet is from Maipo). From the valley itself, Santa Isabel Estate Sauvignon, Chardonnay and Gewürztraminer are all excellent, as are the Merlot and Cabernet Sauvignon.

VIÑA PORTA ★★★★ Boutique winery delivering consistently good oak-aged Chardonnay and Cabernet. A good Merlot here, too.

VIU MANENT ★★★ The 19th-century San Carlos winery makes ripe Semillon, intense Malbec Reserve and Cabernet/ Malbec blend that's worth trying.

CHILE PRICES

RED

Under £4.00

Merlot Carta Vieja **1998** £3.99 (SAF)
Merlot Las Colinas **1999** £3.99 (VIC) £3.99 (THR) £4.49 (WR) £4.49 (BOT)

£4.00 → £4.49

Cabernet Sauvignon Casa Leona **1998** £4.49 (MAR)
Cabernet Sauvignon Concha y Toro **1999** £4.49 (POR)
Cabernet Sauvignon Luis Felipe Edwards Pupilla **1999** £4.49 (OD)
Cabernet Sauvignon Gracia **1998** £4.49 (BUD)
Cabernet Sauvignon San Pedro Sur 35 **1998** £4.49 (ASD) £4.49 (SAF)
Cabernet Sauvignon Santiago **1998** £4.49 (BAL)
Cabernet Sauvignon Santiago **1997** £4.49 (MOR)
Cabernet Sauvignon Vistamar Vistasur **1999** £4.49 (MAJ)
Cabernet Sauvignon/Merlot Concha y Toro **1997** £4.35 (UB)
Cabernet Sauvignon/Merlot La Rosa La Palmeria **1998** £4.49 (BOT)
Cabernet Sauvignon/Merlot Norte Chico **1998** £4.25 (CON)
Campero Chilean Red **Non-vintage** £4.25 (CON)
Dry Red Santa Carolina **1997** £4.10 (UB)
Merlot Concha y Toro **1999** £4.39 (WAI) £4.49 (POR) £4.95 (TAN) £5.39 (PLA)
Merlot Cono Sur **1999** £4.49 (ASD)
Merlot La Rosa La Palmeria **1999** £4.49 (WAI) £4.69 (OD)
Merlot MontGras **1998** £4.49 (TES) £4.95 (SOM) £5.46 (FLE) £5.99 (VA)
Merlot Santa Emiliana Acacias Estate **1997** £4.45 (SOM)

£4.50 → £4.99

Cabernet Sauvignon Caliterra **1998** £4.99 (VIC) £4.99 (THR) £4.99 (WR) £4.99 (BOT)
Cabernet Sauvignon Carmen **1998** £4.96 (FLE)
Cabernet Sauvignon Carmen **1996** £4.99 (UN)
Cabernet Sauvignon Concha y Toro **1998** £4.99 (CON) £5.30 (TAN) £5.39 (PLA)
Cabernet Sauvignon Concha y Toro Casillero del Diablo **1998** £4.99 (VIC) £4.99 (THR) £4.99 (BOT) £4.99 (SAF)
Cabernet Sauvignon Cono Sur **1999** £4.99 (WAI) £4.99 (SAF)
Cabernet Sauvignon Cono Sur **1998** £4.99 (BO)
Cabernet Sauvignon Cono Sur Isla Negra **1999** £4.99 (WAI)
Cabernet Sauvignon Cono Sur Isla Negra **1998** £4.99 (TES) £4.99 (OD) £5.49 (BOT)
Cabernet Sauvignon Domaine Oriental **1998** £4.99 (UN)
Cabernet Sauvignon Linderos **1998** £4.99 (BO) £5.45 (STE)
Cabernet Sauvignon Santa Emiliana Andes Peaks **1997** £4.75 (CON)
Cabernet Sauvignon Santa Emiliana Palmeras Estate **1998** £4.69 (BO)
Cabernet Sauvignon Santa Rita **1997** £4.99 (NEZ)
Cabernet Sauvignon Santa Rita 120 **1998** £4.99 (WAI) £5.29 (DI)
Cabernet Sauvignon Tarapacá **1998** £4.79 (BUD)
Cabernet Sauvignon Valdivieso **1999** £4.79 (SAI) £4.99 (BIB)
Cabernet Sauvignon Valdivieso **1998** £4.99 (VIC) £4.99 (THR) £4.99 (BOT)
Cabernet Sauvignon Viña Porta Reserve **1996** £4.99 (UN)
Cabernet Sauvignon/Merlot Concha y Toro **1999** £4.75 (STA)

MERCHANTS SPECIALIZING IN CHILE

see Merchant Directory (page 456) for details

Not many merchants stock a long list, but the following have a good choice: First Quench Group (BOT, THR, VIC, WR), Hedley Wright (HED), Lay & Wheeler (LAY), Oddbins (OD) – few independent merchants have as much variety, Safeway (SAF), Sommelier (SOM), Tanners (TAN), The Ubiquitous Chip (UB), Noel Young (YOU).

Merlot Carmen **1998** £4.95 (WS) £5.26 (FLE) £5.49 (BO)
Merlot Concha y Toro **1998** £4.99 (CON)
Merlot Concha y Toro **1997** £4.90 (UB)
Merlot Domaine Oriental **1998** £4.99 (UN)
Merlot La Rosa La Palmeria **1998** £4.99 (UN)
Merlot Millaman **1998** £4.75 (CON)
Merlot Santa Emiliana Andes Peaks **1998** £4.75 (CON) £5.30 (MV)
Merlot Santa Inés **1998** £4.99 (WR)
Merlot Santa Rita **1997** £4.99 (NEZ)
Merlot Valdivieso **1999** £4.99 (BIB) £4.99 (SAI)
Merlot Valdivieso **1998** £4.99 (BO) £4.99 (VIC) £4.99 (THR) £4.99 (UN) £4.99 (WR) £4.99 (BOT)
Pinot Noir Concha y Toro **1997** £4.75 (UB) £5.49 (UN) £5.99 (CON)
Pinot Noir Cono Sur **1999** £4.95 (WS) £4.99 (ASD) £4.99 (TES)
Pinot Noir Undurraga **1999** £4.99 (TES) £6.99 (PLAY)
Zinfandel Canepa **1998** £4.99 (UN)

£5.00 → £5.99

Cabernet Franc Francisco de Aguirre Palo Alto **1998** £5.30 (AV)
Cabernet Sauvignon Concha y Toro **1997** £5.10 (UB)
Cabernet Sauvignon Concha y Toro Trio **1998** £5.99 (VIC) £5.99 (THR) £5.99 (WR)
Cabernet Sauvignon Concha y Toro Trio **1997** £5.99 (BOT)
Cabernet Sauvignon Cono Sur Reserve **1998** £5.99 (ASD)
Cabernet Sauvignon Cousiño Macul **1994** £5.65 (UB)
Cabernet Sauvignon Domaine Oriental Clos Centenaire **1997** £5.99 (UN) £6.21 (COC)
Cabernet Sauvignon Errázuriz **1998** £5.49 (VIC) £5.49 (THR) £5.49 (WR) £5.49 (SAF) £5.99 (BO)
Cabernet Sauvignon Errázuriz **1997** £5.49 (UN)
Cabernet Sauvignon Francisco de Aguirre Palo Alto **1996** £5.99 (CON)

Stars (★) indicate wines selected by Oz Clarke in the Best Buys section which begins on page 10.

Cabernet Sauvignon Los Vascos **1998** £5.90 (CRO) £6.95 (HAH) £6.99 (BEN) £7.63 (PLAY)
Cabernet Sauvignon Millaman **1998** £5.25 (CON)
Cabernet Sauvignon Montes **1999** £5.08 (PIP) £5.50 (HED)
Cabernet Sauvignon Montes **1998** £5.85 (PLAY) £6.50 (JU)
Cabernet Sauvignon Montes **1996** £5.99 (POR)
Cabernet Sauvignon Montes Oak-Aged Reserve **1997** £5.80 (PIP) £6.20 (UB) £6.29 (AME)
Cabernet Sauvignon MontGras **1998** £5.99 (SAI)
Cabernet Sauvignon MontGras **1997** £5.75 (NI) £5.99 (VA)
Cabernet Sauvignon Palomar Estate **1999** £5.90 (JU)
Cabernet Sauvignon Portal del Alto **1998** £5.50 (HAH)
Cabernet Sauvignon Santa Emiliana Palmeras Estate **1997** £5.35 (CON)
Cabernet Sauvignon Santa Rita Reserva **1997** £5.99 (SAF) £5.99 (NEZ) £6.49 (MAJ)
Cabernet Sauvignon Torres **1997** £5.95 (POR)
Cabernet Sauvignon Torres Santa Digna **1998** £5.99 (DI)
Cabernet Sauvignon Torres Santa Digna **1997** £5.99 (DI)
Cabernet Sauvignon Veramonte Central Valley **1997** £5.99 (SOM)
Cabernet Sauvignon Villa Montes **1998** £5.49 (SAI)
Cabernet Sauvignon Villard Estate **1997** £5.99 (SAF) £6.90 (TAN)
Cabernet Sauvignon Villard Estate **1996** £5.95 (WS)
Cabernet Sauvignon Viña Casablanca Miraflores **1998** £5.50 (WS) £5.95 (NI)
Cabernet Sauvignon Viña Casablanca Miraflores **1997** £5.99 (POR)
Cabernet Sauvignon Viña Casablanca White Label **1998** £5.99 (MOR)
Malbec Santa Carolina **1999** £5.95 (AD)
Malbec Villa Montes **1998** £5.99 (POR) £6.50 (FORT) £7.70 (TW)
Malbec Viña Casablanca White Label **1999** £5.99 (MOR)
Merlot Antu Mapu Reserva **1998** £5.39 (BUD)
Merlot Casa del Bosque **1999** £5.99 (ASD)

Merlot Château Los Boldos Tradition **1998** £5.50 (STA)
Merlot Cono Sur Isla Negra **1999** £5.49 (TES)
Merlot Cono Sur Isla Negra **1998** £5.49 (SAF)
Merlot Domaine Oriental Clos Centenaire **1998** £5.99 (UN)
Merlot Errázuriz **1999** £5.99 (TES) £5.99 (UN)
Merlot La Rosa Cornellana **1999** £5.20 (AD)
Merlot La Rosa Cornellana **1998** £5.00 (AS)
Merlot MontGras **1997** £5.75 (NI) £5.99 (PHI)
Merlot Santa Rita 120 **1998** £5.29 (DI)
Merlot Santa Rita Reserva **1997** £5.99 (NEZ) £6.99 (DI)
Merlot Torreón de Paredes **1999** £5.99 (AME)
Merlot Veramonte **1997** £5.99 (SOM)
Merlot/Cabernet Sauvignon La Rosa La Palmeria Reserve **1998** £5.49 (UN)
Merlot/Syrah Morandé **1998** £5.99 (UN)
Pinot Noir Concha y Toro Explorer **Non-vintage** £5.99 (JON)
Quatro MontGras **1998** £5.99 (TES)
Syrah Concha y Toro Explorer **1997** £5.99 (JON)
Zinfandel Peteroa **1997** £5.39 (CON)

£6.00 → £6.99

Cabernet Sauvignon Caliterra Reserve **1997** £6.99 (VIC) £6.99 (THR) £6.99 (WR) £6.99 (BOT)
Cabernet Sauvignon Carmen **1997** £6.35 (JER)
Cabernet Sauvignon Carmen Reserve **1997** £6.95 (STE) £8.95 (JER)
Cabernet Sauvignon Carmen Reserve **1996** £6.50 (WS) £6.89 (FLE)
Cabernet Sauvignon Casa Lapostolle **1998** £6.99 (MAJ)
Cabernet Sauvignon Casa Lapostolle **1997** £6.49 (VIC) £6.49 (THR) £6.49 (WR) £6.49 (BOT) £6.99 (POR) £7.34 (GOE) £8.23 (PLA) £8.99 (PHI)
Cabernet Sauvignon Cousiño Macul **1996** £6.25 (NI)
Cabernet Sauvignon Cousiño Macul Antiguas Reservas **1997** £6.95 (POR)
Cabernet Sauvignon Cousiño Macul Antiguas Reservas **1996** £6.95 (POR) £7.15 (WRI) £7.27 (PLA) £7.30 (TAN) £7.45 (STA) £8.20 (MV)
Cabernet Sauvignon Cousiño Macul Antiguas Reservas **1992** £6.70 (UB) £7.59 (NI)
Cabernet Sauvignon Echeverria Reserva **1997** £6.99 (COC)
Cabernet Sauvignon Luis Felipe Edwards Reserva **1997** £6.49 (MAJ)
Cabernet Sauvignon Gracia Reserve **1997** £6.99 (WAI)
Cabernet Sauvignon Los Vascos **1997** £6.10 (COC) £6.79 (BAL) £6.99 (PHI) £7.46 (REI)
Cabernet Sauvignon Montes **1997** £6.46 (REI) £7.70 (TW)
Cabernet Sauvignon Montes Oak-Aged Reserve **1996** £6.30 (AS) £6.89 (PLAY)
Cabernet Sauvignon MontGras Reserva **1996** £6.25 (SOM)
Cabernet Sauvignon Santa Carolina Gran Reserva **1996** £6.99 (UN)
Cabernet Sauvignon Santa Rita Reserva **1998** £6.99 (DI)
Cabernet Sauvignon Santa Rita Reserva **1996** £6.49 (DI)
Cabernet Sauvignon Torres Curico **1998** £6.19 (AME)
Cabernet Sauvignon Valdivieso Reserve **1998** £6.99 (WR)
Cabernet Sauvignon Valdivieso Reserve **1997** £6.99 (BOT)
Cabernet Sauvignon Veramonte Central Valley **1998** £6.99 (OD)
Cabernet Sauvignon Viña Alamosa Reserve **1998** £6.50 (GW)
Cabernet Sauvignon Viña Casablanca Santa Isabel **1998** £6.60 (SAV) £8.99 (OD)
Carmenère William Fèvre La Mission **1998** £6.95 (STA)
Grande Vidure/Cabernet Sauvignon Carmen **1998** £6.95 (STE)
Merlot Carmen **1997** £6.95 (JER)
Merlot Carmen Reserve **1997** £6.95 (WS) £7.50 (FLE) £8.50 (ELL) £9.10 (JER)
Merlot Casa Lapostolle **1998** £6.99 (WR) £7.83 (GOE) £7.95 (POR) £8.46 (PLA) £8.95 (PHI) £8.95 (FORT)
Merlot Casa Lapostolle **1997** £6.50 (WS) £6.99 (BOT) £8.50 (HAH) £10.74 (NO)
Merlot Cono Sur Reserve **1998** £6.49 (SAF)
Merlot Cousiño Macul **1996** £6.25 (NI)
Merlot Domaine Oriental Clos Centenaire **1996** £6.21 (COC)
Merlot Echeverria Reserva **1997** £6.99 (COC)

Merlot Errázuriz **1998** £6.80 (HAH)
Merlot Errázuriz **1997** £6.80 (CRO)
Merlot Montes **1998** £6.30 (AS) £6.95 (JU)
Merlot MontGras Reserva **1997** £6.25 (SOM) £7.95 (NI) £7.99 (VA)
Merlot Santa Rita Reserva **1998** £6.99 (DI)
Merlot Veramonte **1998** £6.99 (WR) £6.99 (BOT)
Merlot Viña Casablanca White Label **1998** £6.99 (BAL) £6.99 (MOR)
Merlot Viña Casablanca White Label **1997** £6.99 (MOR) £7.95 (POR)
★ Merlot Viña Casablanca **1997** £6.49 (LLO)
Pinot Noir Cono Sur Reserve **1999** £6.99 (UN)
Pinot Noir Cono Sur Reserve **1997** £6.50 (WS) £6.99 (OD)
Pinot Noir Cono Sur Reserve **1996** £6.99 (TES)
Pinot Noir Valdivieso Reserve **1997** £6.99 (WAI) £7.99 (WR)
Pinot Noir Villard Estate **1997** £6.90 (SOM)

£7.00 → £7.99

Cabernet Franc Valdivieso Single Vineyard Reserve **1996** £7.99 (UN)
Cabernet Sauvignon Cousiño Macul Antiguas Reservas **1998** £7.50 (AD)
Cabernet Sauvignon Cousiño Macul Antiguas Reservas **1995** £7.25 (CON)
Cabernet Sauvignon Gracia Reserve **1996** £7.95 (POR)
Cabernet Sauvignon Jacques Lurton Estate-Bottled **1996** £7.15 (JER)
Cabernet Sauvignon Marqués de Casa Concha **1996** £7.50 (TAN)
Cabernet Sauvignon MontGras Reserva **1997** £7.95 (NI)
Cabernet Sauvignon Santa Rita Medalla Real **1996** £7.99 (NEZ)
Cabernet Sauvignon Viña Casablanca El Bosque **1998** £7.99 (POR)
Cabernet Sauvignon Viña Casablanca El Bosque **1997** £7.99 (MOR) £8.95 (WS)
Grande Vidure/Cabernet Sauvignon Carmen **1997** £7.50 (FLE) £7.50 (WRI) £8.20 (NO)
Grande Vidure/Cabernet Sauvignon Carmen **1996** £7.49 (BO)
Merlot Carmen Reserve **1998** £7.45 (STE)
Merlot Cousiño Macul **1997** £7.45 (STA)
Merlot De Martino Prima Oaked **1999** £7.40 (AS)
Merlot MontGras Reserva **1998** £7.32 (FLE)
Merlot Valdivieso Reserve **1998** £7.99 (SAF)
★ Pinot Noir Carmen Reserve **1999** £7.45 (NA)
Pinot Noir Valdivieso Reserve **1996** £7.99 (BOT)

Pinot Noir Villard Estate **1998** £7.99 (OD) £8.49 (AME) £8.99 (PHI)

£8.00 → £9.99

Cabernet Franc Valdivieso Single Vineyard Reserve **1997** £8.95 (WS) £8.99 (SAF)
Cabernet Sauvignon Carmen Nativa Organic **1998** £8.95 (STE)
Cabernet Sauvignon Casa Lapostolle Cuvée Alexandre **1996** £8.95 (WS) £12.50 (CRO)
Cabernet Sauvignon Montes Alpha **1997** £9.93 (PLA) £9.99 (HED) £11.30 (PLAY)
Cabernet Sauvignon Montes Alpha **1996** £9.49 (POR) £9.95 (WRI) £9.95 (AME) £11.50 (JU)
Cabernet Sauvignon MontGras Ninquen **1997** £9.99 (FLE)
Cabernet Sauvignon MontGras Ninquen **1996** £8.90 (SOM)
Cabernet Sauvignon Santa Rita Medalla Real **1998** £8.64 (DI)
Cabernet Sauvignon Viña Alamosa Reserve Prestige **1997** £8.70 (GW)
Cabernet Sauvignon Viña Casablanca Santa Isabel **1999** £8.99 (MOR)
Cabernet Sauvignon Viña Casablanca Santa Isabel **1997** £8.99 (MOR)
Cordillera Torres **1998** £9.99 (DI)
Malbec Valdivieso Single Vineyard Reserve **1996** £9.99 (SAF)
Merlot Casa Lapostolle Cuvée Alexandre **1997** £9.99 (WR) £10.99 (BOT) £11.90 (CRO) £11.99 (POR) £12.50 (MI) £12.95 (JER) £13.75 (FORT) £13.92 (REI)
Merlot Errázuriz Reserva **1997** £9.99 (SAF)
Merlot Montes Alpha **1997** £9.95 (AS) £9.95 (HED) £10.65 (AD) £11.30 (PLAY)

Merlot Montes Alpha **1996** £9.49 (POR)
Merlot MontGras Ninquen **1996** £8.90 (SOM) £10.90 (NO)
Merlot Valdivieso Single Vineyard Reserve **1998** £8.99 (MAJ)
Merlot Viña Casablanca Santa Isabel **1998** £8.99 (MOR)
Merlot Viña Casablanca Santa Isabel **1997** £8.95 (WS) £8.99 (MOR) £9.99 (POR) £10.95 (UB)
Merlot Viña Casablanca Santa Isabel **1996** £9.85 (NI)
Primus Veramonte **1997** £8.25 (SOM)
Syrah Errázuriz Reserve **1998** £9.99 (SAF) £10.95 (POR)

£10.00 → £12.99

Caballo Loco Valdivieso **Non-vintage** £11.99 (WR) £14.45 (PIP) £14.99 (BIB) £14.99 (UN)
Cabernet Sauvignon Casa Lapostolle Cuvée Alexandre **1997** £10.99 (UN) £12.53 (GOE) £12.95 (JER)
Cabernet Sauvignon Echeverria Family Reserve **1996** £11.40 (AV) £11.95 (COC)
Cabernet Sauvignon Montes Alpha **1998** £10.65 (AD) £10.99 (OD)
Cabernet Sauvignon Torres Manso de Velasco **1996** £12.95 (DI)
Cabernet Sauvignon Torres Manso de Velasco **1995** £12.95 (DI) £13.95 (POR)
Cabernet Sauvignon Torres Manso de Velasco **1993** £10.95 (DI)
Merlot Casa Lapostolle Cuvée Alexandre **1998** £12.99 (MAJ) £13.61 (GOE) £13.99 (SAF) £14.17 (MI)
Merlot Cono Sur 20 Barrels **1998** £10.95 (WS)
Pinot Noir Cono Sur **1997** £10.99 (WR)
Syrah Errázuriz Reserve **1997** £10.65 (FLE)
★ Triple C Santa Rita **1997** £10.99 (MAJ)

Over £13.00

Alpha 'M' Montes **1997** £29.95 (POR) £30.00 (HED) £34.18 (PLAY)
Alpha 'M' Montes **1996** £30.62 (NO)
Cabernet Sauvignon Carmen Gold Reserve **1997** £18.95 (STE) £19.50 (WRI)
Cabernet Sauvignon Casa Lapostolle Cuvée Alexandre **1998** £13.33 (MI)
Cabernet Sauvignon Concha y Toro Don Melchor **1996** £14.95 (STA) £15.15 (TAN)
Cabernet Sauvignon Concha y Toro Don Melchor **1995** £14.55 (UB)
Cabernet Sauvignon Errázuriz Don Maximiano Founders Reserve **1997** £17.95 (POR) £17.99 (WR)
Casa Real Santa Rita **1997** £17.99 (DI)
Casa Real Santa Rita **1996** £15.90 (NEZ) £16.50 (DI)
Donoso Domaine Oriental **1997** £16.95 (COC)
Finis Terrae Cousiño Macul **1996** £15.85 (WRI)
Seña Caliterra **1996** £29.96 (PLA)

WHITE

Under £4.00

Sauvignon Blanc Canepa **1999** £3.99 (UN)
Semillon Canepa **1999** £3.99 (WAI)
Semillon Canepa **1998** £3.99 (UN)

£4.00 → £4.99

Chardonnay Caliterra **1999** £4.99 (VIC) £4.99 (THR) £4.99 (WR)
Chardonnay Caliterra **1998** £4.75 (WAI) £4.99 (BOT)
Chardonnay Concha y Toro **1999** £4.49 (POR) £5.39 (PLA)
Chardonnay Concha y Toro **1998** £4.89 (JON) £4.99 (CON) £5.40 (TAN)
Chardonnay Concha y Toro **1996** £4.99 (UB)
Chardonnay Concha y Toro Casillero del Diablo **1998** £4.99 (OD) £4.99 (UN) £4.99 (BOT)
Chardonnay Cono Sur **1999** £4.49 (ASD) £4.99 (SAF)
Chardonnay Cono Sur Isla Negra **1998** £4.99 (BO) £5.49 (VIC) £5.49 (THR) £5.49 (UN) £5.49 (BOT)
Chardonnay Domaine Oriental **1998** £4.99 (UN)
Chardonnay Luis Felipe Edwards **1999** £4.99 (MAJ)
Chardonnay Gracia **1998** £4.49 (BUD)
Chardonnay La Rosa La Palmeria **1998** £4.49 (VIC) £4.49 (THR) £4.49 (BOT) £4.99 (UN)

Please remember that ***Oz Clarke's Wine Buying Guide*** *is a price **guide** and not a price **list**. It is not meant to replace up-to-date merchants' lists.*

Chardonnay Millaman **1997** £4.75 (CON)
Chardonnay MontGras **1998** £4.95 (SOM)
Chardonnay San Pedro Sur 35 **1998** £4.49 (SAF)
Chardonnay Santa Emiliana Andes Peaks **1997** £4.75 (CON)
Chardonnay Santa Emiliana Cordillera Estate **1998** £4.99 (BO)
Chardonnay Tarapacá **1999** £4.79 (BUD)
Chardonnay Valdivieso **1999** £4.99 (BIB)
Chardonnay Valdivieso **1998** £4.99 (UN)
Chardonnay Valdivieso Reserva **1997** £4.99 (UN)
Chardonnay Viña Casablanca **1999** £4.99 (POR) £5.19 (BAL) £5.75 (NI)
Chardonnay Viña Casablanca **1998** £4.99 (BO) £6.60 (SAV)
Chardonnay Viña Casablanca White Label **1998** £4.95 (WS) £5.49 (MOR) £5.49 (UN)
Chardonnay Viña Porta Casa Porta **1999** £4.99 (OD)
Chardonnay Vistamar Vistasur **1999** £4.49 (MAJ)
Chardonnay/Sauvignon Blanc Norte Chico **1998** £4.25 (CON)
Chardonnay/Semillon Santiago **1999** £4.49 (BAL) £4.49 (MOR)
Chardonnay/Semillon Santiago **1998** £4.49 (MOR)
Chenin Blanc Santa Carolina **1996** £4.93 (HA)
Gewürztraminer Concha y Toro **1999** £4.49 (UN) £5.39 (PLA) £5.49 (JON) £5.60 (STA)
Gewürztraminer Concha y Toro **1997** £4.99 (CON)
Gewürztraminer Cono Sur **1999** £4.99 (TES) £4.99 (WR)
Gewürztraminer Cono Sur **1998** £4.95 (WS) £4.99 (VIC) £4.99 (THR) £4.99 (WR) £4.99 (BOT)
Sauvignon Blanc Antu Mapu Reserva **1998** £4.89 (BUD)
Sauvignon Blanc Carmen **1998** £4.74 (FLE) £6.35 (JER)
Sauvignon Blanc Concha y Toro **1999** £4.39 (WAI) £4.49 (POR) £4.95 (TAN) £5.39 (PLA)
Sauvignon Blanc Concha y Toro **1998** £4.99 (OD)
Sauvignon Blanc Francisco de Aguirre Tierra Arena **1998** £4.49 (CON) £4.65 (COC)
Sauvignon Blanc Millaman **1998** £4.75 (CON)
Sauvignon Blanc Montes **1996** £4.40 (UB)
Sauvignon Blanc San Pedro Sur 35 **1999** £4.49 (WAI) £4.49 (SAF)
Sauvignon Blanc San Pedro Sur 35 **1998** £4.49 (ASD)
Sauvignon Blanc Santa Emiliana Andes Peaks **1998** £4.75 (CON) £5.30 (MV)
Sauvignon Blanc Santa Rita 120 **1999** £4.99 (DI)
Sauvignon Blanc Santa Rita 120 **1998** £4.99 (DI)
Sauvignon Blanc Santa Rita Reserva **1998** £4.99 (DI) £5.49 (NEZ)
Sauvignon Blanc Santiago **1999** £4.49 (BAL) £4.49 (MOR)
Sauvignon Blanc Santiago **1998** £4.49 (MOR)
Sauvignon Blanc Valdivieso **1999** £4.99 (BIB)
Sauvignon Blanc Villard Estate Casablanca **1997** £4.75 (SOM)
Sauvignon Blanc Viña Casablanca White Label **1999** £4.99 (POR) £5.49 (MOR)
Sauvignon Blanc Viña Casablanca White Label **1998** £4.95 (WS) £5.49 (MOR)
Semillon Viña Alamosa **1999** £4.80 (GW)

£5.00 → £5.99

Chardonnay Carmen **1999** £5.49 (OD)
Chardonnay Château Los Boldos Tradition **1999** £5.50 (STA)
Chardonnay Concha y Toro Trio **1998** £5.99 (VIC) £5.99 (THR) £5.99 (WR) £5.99 (BOT)
Chardonnay Cono Sur Reserve **1998** £5.99 (ASD) £5.99 (MAJ)
Chardonnay Cousiño Macul **1998** £5.79 (POR) £5.90 (TAN) £5.99 (JON) £6.20 (NI) £6.50 (STA)
Chardonnay Domaine Oriental **1997** £5.00 (COC)
Chardonnay Errázuriz **1999** £5.49 (TES)
Chardonnay Errázuriz **1998** £5.49 (VIC) £5.49 (THR) £5.49 (OD) £5.49 (BOT) £5.95 (HAH)
Chardonnay Errázuriz **1997** £5.49 (SAF)
Chardonnay La Rosa Cornellana **1999** £5.20 (AD)
Chardonnay MontGras Reserva **1998** £5.99 (SAI) £7.99 (VA)
Chardonnay Palomar Estate **1998** £5.90 (JU)
Chardonnay Santa Emiliana Palmeras Estate **1997** £5.25 (BU)
Chardonnay Santa Rita Reserva **1997** £5.99 (NEZ) £5.99 (SAF)

Chardonnay Torres Santa Digna **1998** £5.99 (DI)
Chardonnay Veramonte **1998** £5.99 (SOM) £6.99 (OD) £6.99 (WR) £6.99 (BOT)
Chardonnay Villard Estate **1997** £5.95 (WS)
Chardonnay Villard Estate **1996** £5.20 (SOM)
Chardonnay Viña Casa Silva **1999** £5.42 (HA)
Chardonnay Viña Casablanca White Label **1999** £5.49 (SAI) £5.49 (MOR)
Chenin Blanc Santa Carolina **1999** £5.95 (AD)
Fumé Blanc Montes **1999** £5.95 (FORT)
Fumé Blanc Montes **1998** £5.51 (PLA)
Riesling/Gewürztraminer Torres Don Miguel **1999** £5.90 (PIP)
Sauvignon Blanc Caliterra **1998** £5.40 (PLA)
Sauvignon Blanc Carmen **1999** £5.79 (JON)
Sauvignon Blanc Casa Lapostolle **1999** £5.49 (WR) £5.78 (GOE)
Sauvignon Blanc Casa Lapostolle **1998** £5.49 (VIC) £5.49 (THR) £5.49 (WR) £5.49 (BOT) £5.95 (POR) £6.52 (PLA)
Sauvignon Blanc Concha y Toro **1997** £5.15 (UB)
Sauvignon Blanc Concha y Toro Explorer **1998** £5.60 (WRI)
Sauvignon Blanc Concha y Toro Explorer **1997** £5.75 (CON)
Sauvignon Blanc Domaine Oriental **1997** £5.00 (COC)
Sauvignon Blanc Errázuriz **1999** £5.49 (WR)
Sauvignon Blanc Errázuriz **1998** £5.49 (VIC) £5.49 (THR) £5.49 (BOT) £5.80 (CRO) £5.95 (HAH)
Sauvignon Blanc William Fèvre La Mission **1999** £5.95 (STA)
Sauvignon Blanc Montes **2000** £5.50 (HED)
Sauvignon Blanc Montes **1999** £5.08 (PIP) £5.35 (ELL) £5.46 (REI) £6.40 (TW) £6.52 (PLAY)
Sauvignon Blanc Montes **1998** £5.90 (JU)
Sauvignon Blanc Santa Rita Reserva **1999** £5.99 (MAJ) £5.99 (DI)
Sauvignon Blanc TerraMater Select Cuvée Casablanca **1999** £5.99 (SAF)
Sauvignon Blanc Torreón de Paredes **1997** £5.70 (UB)
Sauvignon Blanc Torres **1999** £5.25 (STA)
Sauvignon Blanc Torres **1998** £5.49 (POR)
Sauvignon Blanc Torres Santa Digna **1999** £5.99 (DI)
Sauvignon Blanc Villard Estate Casablanca **1998** £5.49 (POR) £5.60 (TAN) £5.75 (BU)
Sauvignon Blanc Viña Casablanca **1999** £5.19 (BAL) £5.75 (NI)
Sauvignon Blanc Viña Casablanca Santa Isabel **1999** £5.99 (PHI)
Sauvignon Blanc Viña Casablanca Santa Isabel **1998** £5.99 (TES) £5.99 (OD) £6.99 (MOR) £7.25 (NI)
Semillon Peteroa **1997** £5.39 (CON)

£6.00 → £6.99

Chardonnay Caliterra Reserve **1998** £6.99 (WR)
Chardonnay Caliterra Reserve **1997** £6.99 (VIC) £6.99 (THR) £6.99 (BOT)
Chardonnay Carmen **1998** £6.35 (JER)
Chardonnay Carmen Reserve **1998** £6.25 (STE)
Chardonnay Carmen Reserve **1997** £6.25 (STE) £6.50 (WRI) £8.75 (JER)
Chardonnay Carta Vieja Antigua **1996** £6.99 (JON)
Chardonnay Casa Lapostolle **1999** £6.99 (UN)
Chardonnay Casa Lapostolle **1998** £6.99 (POR) £7.34 (GOE) £8.20 (WRI) £8.25 (FORT) £8.45 (PHI)
Chardonnay Cousiño Macul Antiguas Reserva **1997** £6.95 (POR) £7.15 (WRI)
Chardonnay Domaine Oriental Clos Centenaire **1998** £6.21 (COC)
Chardonnay Gracia Reserve **1997** £6.99 (WAI)
Chardonnay Los Vascos **1998** £6.99 (PHI)
Chardonnay Montes **1998** £6.45 (BER) £6.90 (PLAY)
Chardonnay Montes Barrel-Fermented **1999** £6.25 (HED)
Chardonnay Santa Rita Medalla Real **1997** £6.99 (NEZ) £7.75 (DI)

- *Wines are listed in A–Z order within each price band.*
- *For each wine, vintages are listed in descending order.*
- *Each vintage of any wine appears only once.*

Chardonnay Santa Rita Reserva **1999** £6.18 (DI)
Chardonnay Torres Miguel **1998** £6.99 (POR)
Chardonnay Torres Santa Digna **1997** £6.79 (JON)
Chardonnay Valdivieso Reserva **1998** £6.99 (BIB)
Chardonnay Villa Montes **1998** £6.05 (PLA)
Chardonnay Viña Casa Silva Reserva **1997** £6.65 (HA)
Chardonnay Viña Casablanca Barrel-Fermented **1998** £6.99 (OD)
Chardonnay Viña Casablanca Santa Isabel **1998** £6.95 (WS) £7.99 (MOR)
Gewürztraminer Viña Casablanca Santa Isabel **1999** £6.99 (POR) £6.99 (MOR)
Gewürztraminer Viña Casablanca Santa Isabel **1998** £6.49 (OD) £6.99 (NI) £6.99 (MOR)
Gewürztraminer Viña Casablanca Santa Isabel **1997** £6.99 (BAL)
Merlot Francisco de Aguirre Palo Alto Reserva **1998** £6.00 (AV)
Sauvignon Blanc Carmen Reserve **1999** £6.25 (STE)
Sauvignon Blanc Echeverria **1998** £6.35 (JER)
Sauvignon Blanc Santa Rita Medalla Real **1998** £6.99 (NEZ)
Sauvignon Blanc Viña Casablanca **1998** £6.60 (SAV) £6.90 (UB)
Sauvignon Blanc Viña Casablanca Santa Isabel **1997** £6.99 (PHI)

£7.00 → £8.99

Chardonnay Carmen Nativa Organic **1999** £7.95 (WRI)
Chardonnay Carmen Nativa Organic **1998** £7.95 (STE) £8.18 (NO)
Chardonnay Cousiño Macul Antiguas Reserva **1996** £7.25 (CON)
Chardonnay Errázuriz Reserve **1997** £7.99 (TES)
Chardonnay Errázuriz Reserve **1995** £7.90 (CRO)
Chardonnay Errázuriz Wild Ferment **1998** £8.99 (OD) £9.95 (BER)
Chardonnay Gracia Reserve **1998** £7.49 (UN)
Chardonnay La Rosa La Palmeria Gran Reserva **1998** £7.99 (OD)
Chardonnay Los Vascos **1999** £7.63 (PLAY)
Chardonnay Marqués de Casa Concha **1997** £7.49 (JON)
Chardonnay Montes Barrel-Fermented **1998** £7.70 (TW)
Chardonnay Villard Estate Reserve **1998** £8.95 (TAN)
Chardonnay Villard Estate Reserve **1997** £7.40 (SOM)
Chardonnay Viña Casablanca Santa Isabel Barrel-Fermented **1998** £7.95 (WS)
Sauvignon Blanc Jacques Lurton Estate-Bottled **1998** £7.15 (JER)

Over £9.00

Chardonnay Carmen Winemakers Reserve **1998** £10.45 (STE)
Chardonnay Carmen Winemakers Reserve **1997** £10.45 (STE)
Chardonnay Casa Lapostolle **1997** £10.58 (NO)
Chardonnay Casa Lapostolle Cuvée Alexandre **1998** £12.50 (FORT)
Chardonnay Casa Lapostolle Cuvée Alexandre **1997** £9.99 (UN) £9.99 (SAF) £11.26 (GOE) £11.45 (WRI) £11.67 (MI) £12.90 (JER)
Chardonnay Casa Lapostolle Cuvée Alexandre **1996** £10.28 (GOE)
Chardonnay Concha y Toro Amelia **1997** £11.40 (UB) £11.95 (STA)
Chardonnay Montes Alpha **1997** £9.49 (POR)
Chardonnay MontGras Ninquen **1997** £10.99 (VA)
Chardonnay Viña Casablanca Santa Isabel Barrel-Fermented **1997** £9.99 (MOR)

ROSÉ

Under £5.00

Cabernet Sauvignon Torres Santa Digna Rosado **1998** £4.99 (POR)

c. £5.50

Cabernet Sauvignon Torres Santa Digna Rosado **1999** £5.19 (JON) £5.20 (GW) £5.49 (DI)

SPARKLING

c. £6.50

Valdivieso Brut Reserve Methode Traditionelle **1997** £6.26 (BIB)

EASTERN EUROPE

It would be easier to recommend Eastern European wines if one could be sure of their quality. But they're too variable, too patchy

Yes, things are changing in Eastern Europe. We're seeing younger, fresher styles of wine, sometimes from familiar international grape varieties like Chardonnay and Cabernet, and sometimes from indigenous and barely-pronounceable grapes like Kékfrankos. When they're good they're very, very good, and very, very good value, too. The trouble is that when they're bad – yes, you've guessed it – they're horrid. And knowing in advance which are going to be very, very good and which are not requires a talent for clairvoyance.

Unreliability is still the besetting fault of these countries. Some of the individual wineries are far less unreliable than they were, and those where the investment is from the West and the winemaking from Down Under are likely to be the best bet. Wines like this might have great difficulty in standing out in even quite a small, dull sort of crowd, but if you want an inexpensive bottle for Monday night supper they fit the bill. But you need both those elements: investment and good winemaking. Investment on its own is no good, since a bad winemaker can wreak havoc with even the best equipment. And good winemakers get fed up if there's no investment to back up what they're doing.

Is investment going into Eastern Europe? Well, yes and no. The smarter money is often going elsewhere – to South America, for example. Prices for Eastern European wines stay stubbornly low because on the whole we're not prepared to pay more. And why aren't we? Because we can't be certain of the quality, that's why. And I'm not giving a blanket recommendation to a region in those circumstances.

GRAPE VARIETIES

ALIGOTÉ (white; Romania, Bulgaria, Moldova) Used for sparkling wine and some passable neutral dry white. Often blended with Chardonnay.

BURGUND MARE (red; Romania) Probably the Blauburgunder (Pinot Noir) grape by another name. Produces a light shadow of Pinot Noir style.

CABERNET FRANC (red; Hungary, Moldova, Bulgaria) Lovely velvety, fruity young reds in Hungary.

CABERNET SAUVIGNON (red; Bulgaria, Croatia, Romania, Macedonia, Moldova, SW Hungary) Capable of producing ripe, long-lived wines in Romania, Moldova and Bulgaria.

CHARDONNAY (white; Bulgaria, Hungary, Moldova, Romania) Good dry whites, usually fresh nowadays. Sometimes barrel fermented, sometimes overoaked.

DIMIAT (white; Bulgaria) Often bulk produced, blended with Muscat and Rhine Riesling. Best are gentle and summer-fruited.

FETEASCĂ ALBĂ/LEANYKA/MÄDCHENTRAUBE (white; Romania, Hungary) Rich, floral, short-lived, flabby.

FETEASCĂ NEAGRĂ (red; Romania) At best, slightly vegetal with sooty tannins.

FURMINT (white; Hungary) The top Tokaji grape; good acidity, concentration, long life, very good quality.

GAMZA (red; Bulgaria) Soft, light, and early maturing.

GEWÜRZTRAMINER (white; everywhere) Usually known as Traminer, and has typical spicy style. Amazing dessert wines in Moldova.

GRÜNER VELTLINER (white; CZ, Slovakia) Intense greengage fruit at best; hard acidity if not ripened properly.

HÁRSLEVELÜ (white; Hungary) Earthy, big, peachy, long-lived.

IRSAI OLIVÉR (white; CZ, Slovakia, Hungary) A Muscat cross, very perfumed.

KADARKA (red; Hungary) Seldom allowed to produce the weight that made its reputation. Usually tough, green wines.

KÉKFRANKOS/FRANKOVKA/ BLAUFRANKISCH (red; Hungary, CZ, Slovakia) Mostly vegetal young reds.

KÉKOPORTO/BLAUER PORTUGIESER (red; Hungary) Light, ordinary, short-lived reds.

MATRASSA (red; Georgia) Plummy reds.

MAVRUD (red; Bulgaria) Hefty dark reds; best examples have plummy fruit.

MELNIK (red; Bulgaria) Firm, spicy reds.

MERLOT (red; everywhere except CZ and Slovakia) Very successful in Romania, good in southern Bulgaria.

MISKET (white; Bulgaria) Lightly perfumed, tending to blow over quickly.

MÜLLER-THURGAU (white; Hungary; CZ, Slovakia) Floral, early-drinking type.

MUSCAT OTTONEL (white; everywhere) Perfumed but short-lived.

PAMID (red; Romania, Bulgaria) Short-lived, empty, can blend well with Merlot.

PINOT BLANC (white; Hungary, CZ, Slovakia) At its best similar to dry Alsace.

PINOT GRIS (white; Hungary, CZ, Slovakia, Romania, Moldova) Can make outstanding dry and off-dry wines with wonderful spicy aroma.

PINOT NOIR (red; Romania, Hungary, Moldova, Slovakia) Can be true to type and elegant, but often too poorly handled.

PLAVAC MALI (red; Croatia) Good, tannic red with potential to age.

RHINE RIESLING (white; everywhere) Can be lemony and true to type; rarely as intense as good German versions.

ST LAURENT/BLAUER LIMBERGER/SVATOVAVRINECKE (red; CZ, Slovakia) Delicious soft reds with black cherry flavours when allowed to ripen.

SAPERAVI (red; Moldova) Very good spicy wine; lots of potential.

SAUVIGNON BLANC (white; everywhere) Needs good technology; grassy and vegetal otherwise. Hungary is producing high-quality wines.

TĂMÎIOASĂ ROMANEASCĂ/ TAMIANKA (white; Romania, Bulgaria) Classic noble rot grape. Very sweet, raisiny flavours, long-lived.

VRANAC (red; Macedonia, Montenegro) Good solid performer. Takes well to oak.

WELSCHRIESLING/LASKI RIZLING/ VLASSKY RIZLING/ OLASZ RIZLING/ RIZLING ITALICO (white; everywhere) Nothing to do with Rhine Riesling. Earthy, lowish-acid, but can be good; ages well occasionally.

WINE REGIONS AND PRODUCERS

ASSENOVGRAD (Bulgaria) Quite good rustic reds.

BALATON (Hungary) Region centred on Lake Balaton. Well structured wines.

BALATONBOGLÁR (Hungary) Go-ahead winery south of Lake Balaton, source of predominantly clean, fragrant whites made by flying winemaker Kym Milne. Sold under Chapel Hill label in the UK.

BOHEMIA (Czech Republic) Region making light whites from Riesling, Traminer and others. Quality is fair.

COTNARI (Romania) Region producing excellent, ageworthy botrytized wines from Tămîioasă, Grasa and Fetească Albă grapes.

DEALUL MARE (Romania) Rich, slightly jammy reds come from this region; also some whites. Tămîioasă can be good.

DISZNÓKÖ (Hungary) Western-owned company in Tokaj. Tremendous dry Furmint of exceptional quality.

DOMAINE BOYAR (Bulgaria) Owns a number of modern wineries, concentrating on Cabernet Sauvignon and Merlot.

DRAVA VALLEY (Slovenia) Region also known as Podravski. Good, well-structured, aromatic whites.

GEORGIA Known for primitive, tannic whites; Western influence is now appearing, for example in plummy Matrassa reds.

GYÖNGYÖS (Hungary) An estate, and also a region. The estate was the source of Hugh Ryman's pioneering Chardonnay and Sauvignon Blanc.

HASKOVO (Bulgaria) Stick to the young Merlot.

HICKORY RIDGE (Moldova) Wines made by Hugh Ryman. The name goes down well in the US, apparently. Nice smoky, nutty Chardonnay and characterful Merlot.

HUNGAROVIN (Hungary) This used to be the name (in small print) on every bottle of Hungarian wine exported. Now it's German owned. It's still exporting, but these are not Hungary's finest.

IAMBOL (Bulgaria) Source of decent fruity reds, in particular a nice young Merlot.

LITTORAL (Slovenia) Region making northern Italian-style reds, especially Refosco, Barbera, Cabernet and Merlot. Known as Primorski in Slovenia.

LJUTOMER-ORMOZ (Slovenia) Leading white region capable of producing excellent Laski Rizling, the best of which seems to stay *in situ* while the poor stuff comes here.

MASSANDRA (Ukraine) The Tsar's old cellars made fortified wines in every conceivable style, aping port, sherry, Madeira and a few other things besides. They're still making them, too.

EASTERN EUROPEAN CLASSIFICATIONS

Quality wine, equivalent to France's Appellation Contrôlée, is Minöségi bor in Hungary, Controliran in Bulgaria, and in Slovenia Vrhunsko Vino or, below this, Kakovostno Vino. Romania's system is too complicated to give in full, but the best are VSOC, which can be late harvest up to nobly rotten; VSO from specific grapes and regions; VS for quality wine.

ON THE CASE
Be glad of good value from Eastern Europe, but don't always expect consistency. Buy young wines, and drink them fast

MÓR (Hungary) Good quality region, especially for whites.

MORAVIA (Czech Republic) Region with similar grapes (though not always as good quality) to neighbouring Austria.

MURFATLAR (Romania) Black Sea region producing erratic quality. Botrytized Chardonnay is a speciality, but can lack acidity.

PRESLAV (Bulgaria) Winery making decent whites. To catch them at their best, make sure they're young.

ROUSSE (Bulgaria) Currently one of the best in Bulgaria: good tasty reds and whites. Rocky Valley wines are especially good; Yantra Valley reds are oak-aged.

ROYAL TOKAJI WINE COMPANY (Hungary) Excellent quality new-style Tokaji from this joint venture between British, Danish and Hungarian investors.

SAVA VALLEY (Slovenia) Region with promising whites from Sauvignon Blanc and Laski Rizling, and light reds.

SHUMEN (Bulgaria) Winery producing good fresh whites, but avoid the Premium Oak range unless you really want wine that tastes of little else. Save trees: drink unoaked Chardonnay.

SLIVEN (Bulgaria) Quite attractive reds and whites. The Chardonnay-Misket blend is nicely aromatic.

SLOVAKIA Most of the former Czechoslovakia's vineyards ended up here: there's even a chunk of Hungary's Tokaj. Good, spicy whites; fair reds.

SOPRON (Hungary) Region just south of Austria's Neuseidlersee, producing mostly red wines.

STARA ZAGORA (Bulgaria) A glamorous name for a mere wine region; but the Cabernets and Merlots are decent.

SUHINDOL (Bulgaria) Fair quality, but not as good as it once was.

SVISHTOV (Bulgaria) Quality seems to be sliding here. Light, tired reds.

TÎRNAVE (Romania) Cool region making promising whites, especially Fetească. Best winery: *Jidvei*.

TOKAJ (Hungary) Tokaj is the region, Tokaji the luscious sweet white wine it produces. We've all adopted the Hungarian spelling now; the English used to spell it Tokay. The style has also changed: from being oxidized and tasting like cheap sherry, it is now (as a result of Western investment) fresher and infinitely more delicious. The grapes are Furmint, Muscat Lunel and Hárslevelü. It's made from botrytized grapes (known as *aszú*) which are added to dry base wine in measures known as *puttonyos*. A three-puttonyos Tokaji will be sweet, a four-puttonyos one sweeter, and a five or six-puttonyos one very concentrated and rich. Aszú Eszencia is sweeter again, and Eszencia on its own means juice too sweet to ferment to more than a few per cent alcohol; it's used for blending in tiny quantities into lesser wines to pep them up or (according to legend) for reviving dying monarchs. Tokajis of three to six puttonyos are a more practical buy: they have a smokiness to their fruit which sets them apart from all other dessert wines, and they age superbly. Best: *Royal Tokaji Wine Company, Disznókö.*

EASTERN EUROPE PRICES

BULGARIA RED

Under £4.50

Bulgarian Reserve Merlot **1996** £3.99 (SAI)
Domaine Boyar Cabernet Sauvignon Reserve **Non-vintage** £3.99 (UN)
Iambol Reserve Cabernet Sauvignon **1995** £3.79 (BOT)
Oriahovitza Cabernet Sauvignon **1995** £3.49 (ASD)
Oriahovitza Cabernet Sauvignon Reserve **1998** £4.39 (SO)
Sliven Merlot/Pinot Noir **Non-vintage** £2.99 (UN)
Stambolovo Merlot Reserve **1994** £4.09 (SO)

HUNGARY WHITE

Under £4.00

Chapel Hill Chardonnay **1998** £3.69 (BO)
Chapel Hill Irsai Oliver **1998** £3.29 (WAI) £3.35 (UN) £3.79 (OD)
★ Hilltop Neszmély Best Cellar Reserve Selection **1998** £3.49 (GN)
Lakeside Oak Chardonnay **1998** £3.49 (WAI)
Nagyréde Dry Muscat **1998** £3.79 (OD)

£4.00 → £9.99

Tokaji Fordítás Dessewffy **1988** £7.50 (CRO)
Tokaji Szamorodni Sweet ½ litre, Oremus **1989** £5.99 (DI)

£10.00 → £19.99

Tokaji Aszú 4 Putts ½ litre, Château Pajzos **1991** £18.00 (JU)
Tokaji Aszú 5 Putts ½ litre, Disznókö **1992** £15.99 (OD)
Tokaji Aszú 5 Putts ½ litre, Royal Tokaji Wine Co. **1995** £19.92 (REI) £21.15 (CB)
Tokaji Aszú 5 Putts ½ litre, Royal Tokaji Wine Co. **1993** £17.50 (HED) £20.45 (HAH) £20.59 (GW)
Tokaji Aszú 5 Putts ½ litre, Tokaji Kereskedöhóz **1990** £11.60 (STA)

£20.00 → £49.99

Tokaji Aszú 5 Putts ½ litre Birsalmàs, Royal Tokaji Wine Co. **1993** £23.80 (TAN) £29.95 (LEA) £35.00 (FORT)
Tokaji Aszú 6 Putts ½ litre Szt Tamas, Royal Tokaji Wine Co. **1993** £35.00 (JU)

Over £50.00

Tokaji Aszú Essencia ½ litre, J Monyok **1957** £210.00 (UB)
Tokaji Aszú Essencia ½ litre, Royal Tokaji Wine Co. **1993** £86.36 (REI) £89.50 (LEA)

HUNGARY RED

Under £8.00

Eger Bull's Blood **1997** £3.99 (UN)
★ Hilltop Neszmély Best Cellar Reserve Selection **1997** £3.49 (GN)
Tiffans Cuvée Cabernet Sauvignon/Kekfrankos **1994** £7.93 (REI)

ROMANIA

Under £4.00

Classic Dealul Mare Merlot **1995** £3.25 (UB)
Classic Murfatlar Chardonnay **1996** £3.25 (UB)
★ Classic Pinot Gris **1998** £3.89 (BUD)
Classic Tarnave Sauvignon Blanc **1997** £3.25 (UB)

c. £11.00

★ SCV Murfatlar Pinot Gris Late-Harvest **1962** £10.95 (WRI)

MERCHANTS SPECIALIZING IN EASTERN EUROPE

see Merchant Directory (page 456) for details

If you want to look beyond bargain Cabernet Sauvignon, try the following merchants: Butlers Wine Cellar (BU) – good for curiosities, First Quench Group (BOT, THR, VIC, WR), Morris & Verdin (MV), Sainsbury's (SAI), Safeway (SAF), T&W Wines (TW) – good for old Tokaji, Wines of Westhorpe.

FRANCE

Some of the newest ideas, embraced by some of France's best producers, make one wonder about the difference between tradition and modernity

How forward-thinking is France these days, winewise? How traditional? Is it keen to embrace new ideas, or does it refuse to admit that new ideas exist?

The answer to each of these questions is 'Extremely so'. That is, there are elements of French vinous life that are extremely forward-thinking, and elements that are also very traditional. And France has the knack of embracing new ideas while appearing to look the other way.

Take bio-dynamism, for example. Now, this mixture of good sense and magic has not spread everywhere in France; by its nature it will always be a minority interest. But leading growers in Burgundy, the Rhône, Alsace and elsewhere (not Bordeaux, interestingly) are busy burying cows' horns full of manure over the winter, in order to dig them up in the spring, add the manure to water and 'dynamize' the mix by stirring it in a particular pattern, by hand, for an hour, and then sprinkling it on to the vineyards at times dictated by the movements of the planets and the time of day. It's all to do with the etheric and astral forces with which the horns were in touch when they were on the cow. And, since you ask, 'bonkers' is not a word I would use lightly in the company of producers like Lalou Bize-Leroy of Burgundy or Chapoutier of the Rhône. Not twice, anyway.

These producers find that these methods give them better wines than ever. Why? Are they forward-looking or ultra-traditional? Search me if I know.

WINE CLASSIFICATIONS

The French have the most far-reaching system of wine control of any nation, even though its adequacy as a form of quality control is now in question. The key factors are the 'origin' of the wine, its historic method of production and the use of the correct grape types. The three defined levels are: AC, VDQS, and vin de pays.

APPELLATION D'ORIGINE CONTROLÉE (AC, AOC) To qualify for AC a wine must meet specific requirements on seven fronts:
Land: Suitable vineyard land is minutely defined. **Grape**: Only those grapes traditionally regarded as suitable can be used. **Degree of alcohol**: Wines must reach a minimum (or maximum) degree of natural alcohol. **Yield**: A basic permitted yield is set for each AC, but the figure may be increased or decreased year by year after consultation between the growers of each AC region and the Institut National des Appellations d'Origine (INAO).
Vineyard practice: AC wines must follow rules about pruning methods and density of planting. **Winemaking practice**: Each AC wine has its own regulations as to what is allowed. Typically, chaptalization – adding sugar during fermentation to increase alcoholic strength – is accepted in the North, but not in the South. **Tasting and analysis**: Since 1979 wines must pass a tasting panel.

VIN DÉLIMITÉ DE QUALITÉ SUPÉRIEURE (VDQS) This second group is, in general, slightly less reliable in quality. It is in the process of being phased out. No more vins de pays are being upgraded to VDQS but there is still no news on when any of the existing ones will be upgraded to AC status (or downgraded to vin de pays).

VIN DE PAYS The third category gives a regional definition to France's basic blending wines. The rules are similar to AC, but allow a good deal more flexibility and some wonderful cheap wines can be found which may well surprise. Quality can be stunning, and expect fruit, value and competent winemaking. There are also one or two high-priced superstars in this category.

VIN DE TABLE 'Table wine' is the title for the rest. No quality control except as far as basic public health regulations demand. Vins de pays are always available for approximately the same price, and offer a far more interesting drink. Many vins de table here are dull and poorly made, and the branded, heavily advertised ones are seldom good value.

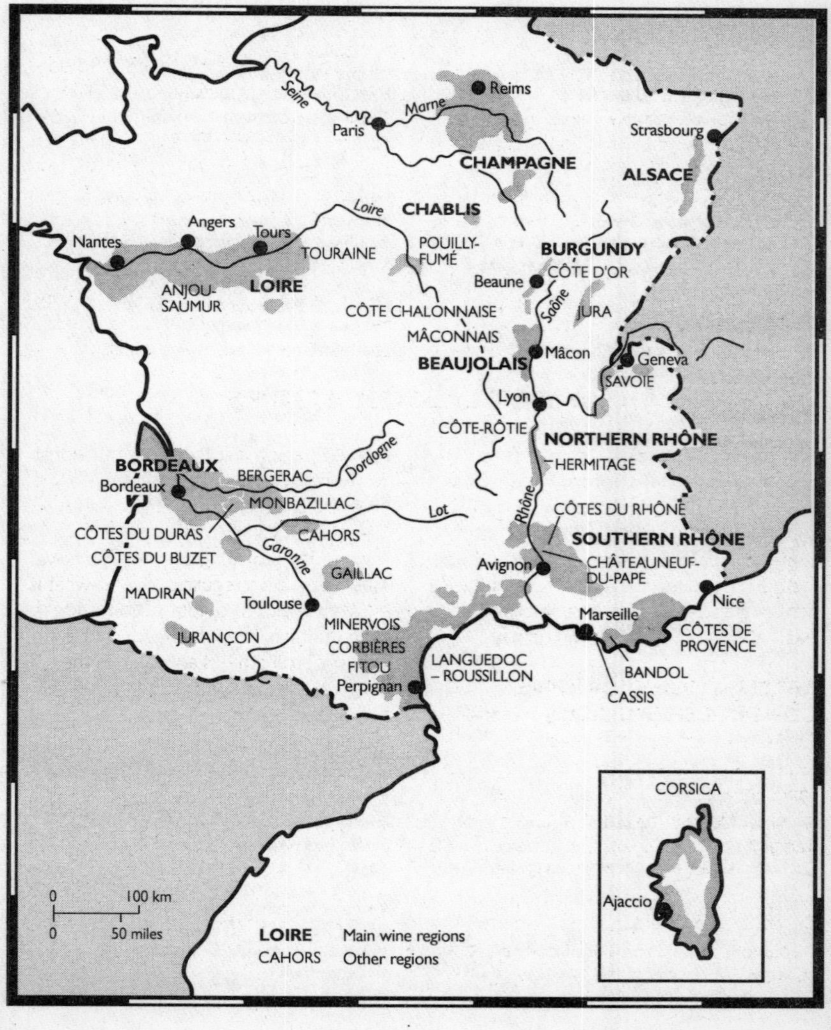

WINE-FINDER: FRANCE

France is packed with famous wine names, but if you don't know whereabouts in the country a wine comes from, life can get confusing. In the following 209 pages we have divided the huge number of appellations in France into eight clearly defined regions: Alsace, Bordeaux, Burgundy, Champagne, Jura & Savoie, Loire, Rhône and Southern France. In Burgundy, we have separated Basic Burgundy and the subregions Beaujolais, Chablis, Côte Chalonnaise, Côte d'Or and Mâconnais. So, if you know the name but are wondering which section to look in, this quick guide to some of the best-known wine names will help.

Aloxe-Corton – *Burgundy, Côte d'Or*
Auxey-Duresses – *Burgundy, Côte d'Or*
Bandol – *Southern France*
Barsac – *Bordeaux (sweet white)*
Beaune – *Burgundy, Côte d'Or*
Blagny – *Burgundy, Côte d'Or*
Bourgueil – *Loire (red)*
Brouilly – *Burgundy, Beaujolais*
Cadillac – *Bordeaux*
Cahors – *Southern France*
Cérons – *Bordeaux*
Chablis – *Burgundy, Chablis*
Chambolle-Musigny – *Burgundy, Côte d'Or*
Chassagne-Montrachet – *Burgundy, Côte d'Or*
Châteauneuf-du-Pape – *Rhône*
Chénas – *Burgundy, Beaujolais*
Chinon – *Loire (red)*
Chiroubles – *Burgundy, Beaujolais*
Chorey-lès-Beaune – *Burgundy, Côte d'Or*
Clairette de Die – *Rhône (sparkling)*
Condrieu – *Rhône (white)*
Corbières – *Southern France*
Cornas – *Rhône (red)*
Coteaux du Tricastin – *Rhône*
Côte-Rôtie – *Rhône* (red)
Côtes de Beaune – *Burgundy, Côte d'Or*
Côtes de Bourg – *Bordeaux*
Côtes de Nuits – *Burgundy, Côte d'Or*
Côtes du Ventoux – *Rhône*
Crozes-Hermitage – *Rhône*
Entre-deux-Mers – *Bordeaux*
Fitou – *Southern France*
Fixin – *Burgundy, Côte d'Or*
Fleurie – *Burgundy, Beaujolais*
Fronsac – *Bordeaux*
Gevrey-Chambertin – *Burgundy, Côte d'Or*
Gigondas – *Rhône (red)*
Givry – *Burgundy, Côte Chalonnaise*
Graves – *Bordeaux (dry white)*
Hautes-Côtes de Beaune – *Burgundy, Côte d'Or*
Hautes-Côtes de Nuit – *Burgundy, Côte d'Or*
Haut-Médoc – *Bordeaux*
Hermitage – *Rhône*
Juliénas – *Burgundy, Beaujolais*
Languedoc-Roussillon – *Southern France*
Listrac – *Bordeaux*
Loupiac – *Bordeaux*
Mâcon – *Burgundy, Mâconnais*
Margaux – *Bordeaux*
Marsannay – *Burgundy, Côte d'Or*
Médoc – *Bordeaux*
Mercurey – *Burgundy, Côte Chalonnaise*
Meursault – *Burgundy, Côte d'Or*
Minervois – *Southern France*
Montagny – *Burgundy, Côte Chalonnaise*
Monthelie – *Burgundy, Côte d'Or*
Morey-St-Denis – *Burgundy, Côte d'Or*
Morgon – *Burgundy, Beaujolais*
Moulin-à-Vent – *Burgundy, Beaujolais*
Moulis – *Bordeaux*
Muscadet – *Loire (dry white)*
Muscat de Beaumes-de-Venise – *Rhône (fortified white)*
Nuits-St-Georges – *Burgundy, Côte d'Or*
Pauillac – *Bordeaux*
Pernand-Vergelesses – *Burgundy, Côte d'Or*
Pessac-Léognan – *Bordeaux*
Pomerol – *Bordeaux*
Pommard – *Burgundy, Côte d'Or*
Pouilly-Fuissé – *Burgundy, Mâconnais*
Pouilly-Fumé – *Loire (dry white)*
Provence – *Southern France*
Puligny-Montrachet – *Burgundy, Côte d'Or*
Régnié – *Burgundy, Beaujolais*
Rully – *Burgundy, Côte Chalonnaise*
St-Amour – *Burgundy, Beaujolais*
Ste-Croix-du-Mont – *Bordeaux*
St-Émilion – *Bordeaux*
St-Estèphe – *Bordeaux*
St-Joseph – *Rhône (red)*
St-Julien – *Bordeaux*
St-Véran – *Burgundy, Mâconnais*
Sancerre – *Loire*
Saumur-Champigny – *Loire (red)*
Sauternes – *Bordeaux (sweet white)*
Sauvignon de St-Bris – *Burgundy, Basic*
Savigny-lès-Beaune – *Burgundy, Côte d'Or*
Tavel – *Rhône* (rosé)
Vins de pays – *various*
Volnay – *Burgundy, Côte d'Or*
Vosne-Romanée – *Burgundy, Côte d'Or*
Vougeot – *Burgundy, Côte d'Or*
Vouvray – *Loire*

ALSACE

Dry wines are dry and sweet wines are sweet, right? Well, no. Not exactly. This is Alsace, and anything can happen

Now, I've said it before and I'll say it again: I love Alsace wines. But like so many things one loves, they have great power to irritate.

What's my current irritation? Not knowing how sweet they're going to be, that's what. It seems to me, as a mere consumer buying his bottle to accompany his poor supper – just a bowl of gruel, you understand, nothing fancy – that wines should be dry unless stated otherwise. Most of the time – nearly all the time, in fact – one wants dry wines. When I get on to dessert (chocolate-flavoured gruel, since you ask), that's different. Then I want sweet wine. But with chicken-flavoured gruel, monkfish-flavoured gruel or Thai green curry-flavoured gruel, I want dry wines. And when I buy a bottle of Alsace, I never quite know if it's going to be dry or not.

I'm not talking about the confessedly sweet wines, the Vendange Tardives and Sélection de Grains Nobles. I'm talking about the fact that some producers even make standard wines that are semi-sweet and Vendange Tardives that are dry. Now, are they nuts or am I?

Their reasoning is that the Vendange Tardives are to go with food. In which case what are the others for, pray?

All I can say is: Don't do this to me, guys. I'm your friend. Give me a break.

GRAPE VARIETIES

In Alsace wines are generally labelled according to their grape variety. Cheap blends of two or more varieties are sold as Edelzwicker; go instead for upmarket ones.

AUXERROIS Fatter and more buttery than Pinot Blanc, with a touch of spice and musk. Generally inexpensive, and often blended. Best: *André Kientzler, Marc Kreydenweiss, Josmeyer, Landmann-Ostholt, Rolly Gassmann, Bruno Sorg.*

CHASSELAS Rare now in Alsace, Chasselas has never been complex, but the few true examples can be vibrantly fruity and must be drunk young. Best: *André Kientzler, Josmeyer, Schoffit.*

CLASSIC BLENDS These can be superb, and their producers avoid the Edelzwicker designation like the plague. Best: *Hugel Gentil, Marc Kreydenweiss Clos du Val d'Eléon, Co-op de Ribeauvillé Clos du Zahnacker, Schlumberger Réserve, Jean Sipp Clos du Schlossberg, Louis Sipp Côtes de Ribeauvillé, Willm Gentil Clos Gaensbrœnnel.* They will almost all be best in riper years.

EDELZWICKER Seldom exciting, but *Schlumberger Cristal-Maree* is quite good.

GEWÜRZTRAMINER The least dry of all Alsace, though *Beyer Cuvée des Comtes d'Eguisheim* and *Trimbach Cuvée des Seigneurs de Ribeaupierre* are bone dry. Gewürztraminer is the most voluptuous, upfront and fat of all Alsace wines, overflowing with exotic aromas. In hot years it can lack acidity and turn flabby. Best: *Blanck, Deiss, Hugel, Koehly, Kreydenweiss, Kuentz-Bas, Muré, Ostertag, Rolly Gassmann, Schoffit, Trimbach, Turckheim* co-op, *Weinbach, Willm Clos Gaensbrœnnel, Zind-Humbrecht.*

MUSCAT Light, fragrant, wonderfully grapy. Imagine crushing a fistful of green grapes and gulping the juice. That's how fresh and grapy a good Muscat should be.

> **ON THE CASE**
> ***The more expensive Alsace wines generally need some aging, so check the vintage before you buy. Simpler ones can be drunk immediately***

Hotter years give heavy wines that are far from ideal. Seldom made sweet in Alsace. Look for *Becker, Ernest Burn, Joseph Cattin, Dirler, Charles Koehly, Marc Kreydenweiss, Kuentz-Bas, Rolly Gassmann, Pfaffenheim co-op, Schlumberger, Bruno Sorg, Weinbach, Zind-Humbrecht.*

PINOT BLANC At its best, this is plump, rich and ripe, with apple or floral overtones and a long creamy finish. May also be called Klevner. Best: *J B Adam, Camille Braun, Théo Cattin, Co-opérative de Cléebourg, Marcel Deiss, Dopff au Moulin, Hugel, Charles Koehly, Kreydenweiss, Albert Mann, Muré, Ostertag, Rolly Gassmann, Schlumberger, Schoffit, Martin Spielmann, Turckheim co-op, Weinbach, Zind-Humbrecht.*

PINOT NOIR The Burgundy grape makes light reds, perfumed and strawberryish, but lacking in complexity. Most are overpriced for the quality. Best include *J B Adam, Jean Becker, Marcel Deiss, René Fleith, Albert Hertz, Hugel, Jacques Iltis, Albert Mann, Co-opérative de Pfaffenheim, Turckheim co-op, Wolfberger.*

RIESLING Powerful, structured, steely wines that grow 'petrolly' with age. It's with Riesling that the subtleties of *grand cru* soils are most evident. Can be long-lived. Best producers: *Becker, Beyer, Paul Blanck, Deiss, Dirler, Dopff au Moulin, Pierre Freudenreich, Pierre Frick, Kreydenweiss, Mader, Frédéric Mallo, Frédéric Mochel, Ostertag, Rolly Gassmann, Edgar Schaller, Schlumberger, Schoffit, Sick-Dreyer, Jean Sipp, Louis Sipp, Bruno Sorg, Trimbach, Weinbach, Wunsch & Mann, Zind-Humbrecht.*

SYLVANER Light, tart, slightly earthy. With age it tastes of tomatoes, for some reason. Best: *Christian Dolder, J Hauller, Ostertag* (especially the *Vieilles Vignes*), *Rolly Gassmann, Martin Schaetzel, Schoffit, Albert Seltz, Zind-Humbrecht.*

TOKAY-PINOT GRIS Rich, musky and honeyed, though can run to flab if badly made. Even the lighter ones are luscious behind their dry fruit. The best can age well. Best: *Lucien Albrecht, Barmès-Buecher, Léon Beyer, Ernest Burn, Claude Dietrich, Robert Dietrich, Pierre Frick, Marc Kreydenweiss, Kuentz-Bas, Frédéric Mallo, Schlumberger, Schoffit, Bruno Sorg, Turckheim co-op, Weinbach, Zind-Humbrecht.*

WINE CLASSIFICATIONS

VIN D'ALSACE, AC The simple generic appellation covers the whole Alsace region. It is normally used in conjunction with a grape name, so a wine might be called 'Riesling – Appellation Alsace Contrôlée'.

CRÉMANT, AC White, Champagne-method fizz, made mainly from Pinot Blanc. Usually crisp and decent quality. Look for wines from *Paul Blanck, Robert Dietrich, Dopff & Irion, Dopff au Moulin, Laugel, Co-opérative de Pfaffenheim, Co-opérative de Turckheim, Wolfberger.*

GRAND CRU A decree of 1992 brought the number of *grand cru* vineyards to 50. They can only be planted with Riesling, Tokay-Pinot Gris, Gewürztraminer or Muscat, and notably lower (but still high) yields apply. They can be recognized from the words 'Appellation Alsace Grand Cru Contrôlée' on the label. Grand cru wines should reflect the great variety of soils to be found in Alsace – limestone, schist, granite, clay, sandstone – offering a superb palate of flavours and nuances. The best do when yields are modest.

ON THE CASE
Everyday wines from the Alsace co-ops are a good buy; you can experiment with flavours for about a fiver

SÉLECTION DE GRAINS NOBLES (SGN) The higher of two 'super-ripe' legal descriptions, applying to very sweet wines made from botrytized grapes. It applies only to Riesling, Tokay-Pinot Gris, Muscat (very rare) and Gewürztraminer; the wines are not dissimilar to Sauternes in style, though the flavour is different. Acidity levels can be lower, especially from Pinot Gris or from Gewürztraminer. All benefit from aging, for ten years or more. For some of Alsace's top tastes, try producers such as *Beyer, Paul Blanck, Bott-Geyl, Hugel, Kuentz-Bas, Meyer, Muré, Ostertag, Schlumberger, Schoffit, Trimbach, Weinbach, Zind-Humbrecht.*

VENDANGE TARDIVE The lesser of the 'super-ripe' categories, made from late-picked grapes, as opposed to the botrytized ones used for *sélection de grains nobles*. Only applies to Riesling, Tokay-Pinot Gris, Muscat (rare) and Gewürztraminer. They are very full, fairly alcoholic and vary in sweetness from richly dry to dessert-sweet. They, too, can be aged, particularly if from *grand cru* vineyards. Up to ten years is a good rule of thumb.

ALSACE VINTAGES

1999 There'll be a lot of dilute wines this year. Choose top names only.

1998 A very good year for sweet wines – but don't open them for a while.

1997 Potentially great: beautifully ripe wines of good body and weight.

1996 A mostly good, ripe vintage with nice acidity levels. Small quantities of *vendange tardive* and even *sélection de grains nobles* were made.

1995 Similar to 1994, but possibly with lower acidity. Stick to good names.

1994 Mixed: some wines are too light; but conversely other producers made phenomenally rich late-harvest wines.

1993 Good to average, but there is excellent Riesling.

1992 The wines are sound, and range from dilute to excellent. Choose wines from good producers, who have a reputation to maintain.

1991 Fresh, clean wines, but it is not a late-harvest year. Not one to keep, either.

1990 With healthy grapes and no noble rot, 1990 was a *vendange tardive* year. Rieslings are powerful and will age well.

1989 Very good but not top quality. The wines have lively fruit, though some are low in acidity. Abundant and superb late-harvest wines.

1988 Pleasant, but hardly inspiring wine. Tokay-Pinot Gris and Riesling are best.

1987 Not great, but better than first thought. Good single-vineyard wines.

1986 The best are at their peak. Good *vendange tardive* and even some SGN.

1985 An absolute corker – wonderful wines to drink now but they will keep.

ALSACE PRICES

WHITE

Under £5.00

Pinot Blanc Blanck Frères **1998** £4.95 (WAI)
Pinot Blanc Fuchs **1996** £4.34 (NO)
Pinot Blanc Horstein, Cave Vinicole de Pfaffenheim **1998** £4.99 (POR) £5.55 (HAH) £5.59 (JON)
Pinot Blanc Tradition, Cave Vinicole de Turckheim **1998** £4.95 (WS) £5.39 (AME)
Pinot Blanc Cave Vinicole de Turckheim **1998** £4.49 (BO) £4.99 (OD)
Riesling Rolly Gassmann ½ bottle **1992** £4.99 (RAE)

£5.00 → £5.99

Chevalier d'Alsace, Hügel et Fils **1995** £5.95 (JU)
Gentil Hugel **1998** £5.99 (DI)
Gewürztraminer Cave Vinicole de Turckheim **1999** £5.95 (SO)
Gewürztraminer Cave Vinicole de Turckheim **1998** £5.69 (BO) £5.95 (WS) £6.49 (AME)
Muscat Réserve, Cave Vinicole de Turckheim **1998** £5.99 (OD)
Pinot Blanc Cuvée Reservée, Schaetzel **1998** £5.99 (GW)
Pinot Blanc Baron de Hoen **1997** £5.99 (WAI)
Pinot Blanc Réserve, Seltz **1998** £5.39 (WAT)
Pinot Blanc Cave du Roi Dagobert **1998** £5.75 (FRI)
Pinot Blanc Cave Vinicole de Turckheim **1997** £5.29 (UN)
Pinot Blanc Cave Vinicole de Turckheim **1995** £5.79 (NI)
Sylvaner Hugel **1998** £5.60 (WS)
Tokay-Pinot Gris Cave de Beblenheim **1998** £5.75 (WAI)
Tokay-Pinot Gris Tradition, Vinicole de Turckheim **1998** £5.60 (WS) £6.19 (AME)
Tokay-Pinot Gris Cave Vinicole de Turckheim **1998** £5.99 (OD) £6.29 (UN)

£6.00 → £6.99

Fleur d'Alsace, Hugel **1998** £6.25 (CON) £6.45 (STA) £6.99 (PLA)
Fleur d'Alsace, Hugel **1996** £6.65 (VIN)
Fruits de Mer, Wiederhirn **1997** £6.00 (HIG)
Gewürztraminer Hornstein, Cave Vinicole de Pfaffenheim **1998** £6.39 (JON) £6.40 (HAH) £6.49 (POR) £6.60 (TAN)
Gewürztraminer Steingrubler, Albert Mann **1997** £6.99 (SOM)
Pinot Auxerrois Vieilles Vignes, Albert Mann **1998** £6.25 (OD)
Pinot Blanc Béblenheim, Bott-Geyl **1996** £6.99 (BAL)
Pinot Blanc Cattin **1996** £6.99 (CB)
Pinot Blanc Hugel **1997** £6.87 (REI)
Pinot Blanc Muré **1997** £6.55 (NEZ)
Pinot Blanc Rolly Gassmann **1991** £6.99 (RAE)
Pinot Blanc les Vignards, Hugel **1997** £6.50 (WS)
Riesling Brandluft, Seltz **1986** £6.10 (WAT)
Riesling Tradition, Kuentz-Bas **1998** £6.95 (WS)
Riesling Cave Vinicole de Turckheim **1997** £6.29 (UN)
Sylvaner Deiss **1994** £6.99 (BAL)
Sylvaner Schleret **1996** £6.75 (YAP)

£7.00 → £7.99

Chasselas Cuvée Caroline, Schoffit **1998** £7.50 (GAU) £8.75 (AD)
Chasselas Vieilles Vignes, Schoffit **1997** £7.95 (FLE)
Gewürztraminer Réserve Prestige, Cave Vinicole de Turckheim **1998** £7.59 (NI)

MERCHANTS SPECIALIZING IN ALSACE

see Merchant Directory (page 456) for details

Adnams (AD), Ballantynes (BAL), Bennetts (BEN), Berry Bros (BER), Butlers (BU), A Byrne (BY), Croque-en-B (CRO), Direct Wine (DI), Cockburns (COC), First Quench (BOT, THR, VIC, WR), Lay & Wheeler (LAY), Mayfair, Morris & Verdin (MV), Oddbins (OD), Reid (REI), T&W (TW), Ubiquitous Chip (UB), Wine Soc (WS), Noel Young (YOU).

Gewürztraminer Wiederhirn **1997** £7.20 (HIG)
Muscat Albert Mann **1998** £7.99 (OD)
Pinot Blanc Deiss **1995** £7.99 (BAL)
Pinot Blanc Hugel **1998** £7.50 (STA) £7.59 (DI)
Pinot Blanc Hugel **1996** £7.34 (PLA)
Pinot Blanc Cave du Roi Dagobert **1997** £7.56 (VIN)
Pinot Blanc Schlumberger **1998** £7.85 (WRI) £7.98 (PLA)
Pinot Blanc Schlumberger **1997** £7.99 (POR) £8.19 (JON) £8.25 (FORT)
Pinot Blanc Tradition, Kuentz-Bas **1998** £7.13 (COC)
Pinot Blanc Trimbach **1996** £7.20 (COC)
Pinot Blanc Vieilles Vignes, Meyer-Fonné **1998** £7.50 (LAY)
Riesling Brandluft, Boeckel **1998** £7.49 (CHA)
Riesling Cuvée Reservée, Schaetzel **1998** £7.48 (GW)
Riesling Hugel **1998** £7.95 (WS)
Riesling Kuentz-Bas **1997** £7.62 (COC)
Riesling Schleret **1996** £7.95 (YAP)
Sylvaner Deiss **1998** £7.95 (LEA)
Sylvaner Vieilles Vignes, Domaine Ostertag **1998** £7.75 (WRI) £8.00 (MV)
Tokay-Pinot Gris Hornstein, Cave Vinicole de Pfaffenheim **1998** £7.30 (TAN)
Tokay-Pinot Gris Hornstein, Cave Vinicole de Pfaffenheim **1997** £7.39 (JON)
Tokay-Pinot Gris Wiederhirn **1997** £7.20 (HIG)

£8.00 → £8.99

Chasselas Vieilles Vignes, Schoffit **1998** £8.85 (BER)
Gewürztraminer Blanck **1999** £8.95 (AD)
Gewürztraminer Cuvée Caroline Harth, Schoffit **1999** £8.95 (AD)
Gewürztraminer Cuvée Reservée, Schaetzel **1998** £8.70 (GW)
Gewürztraminer Dopff au Moulin **1997** £8.90 (CRO)
Gewürztraminer Hugel **1998** £8.95 (STA) £8.99 (OD) £9.85 (CON) £9.99 (DI)

Please remember that ***Oz Clarke's Wine Buying Guide*** *is a price* ***guide*** *and not a price* ***list****. It is not meant to replace up-to-date merchants' lists.*

Gewürztraminer Cave du Roi Dagobert **1998** £8.49 (FRI) £8.49 (FRI)
Gewürztraminer Zotzenberg, Seltz **1998** £8.25 (WAT)
Muscat Koehly **1997** £8.85 (HAH)
Muscat Réserve, Trimbach **1998** £8.35 (WS)
Muscat Tradition, Hugel **1997** £8.99 (DI) £12.95 (FORT)
Muscat Tradition, Hugel **1996** £8.81 (REI) £8.95 (STA) £11.16 (TW)
Muscat Trimbach **1993** £8.90 (CRO)
Pinot Blanc Blanck Frères **1996** £8.00 (FLE)
Pinot Blanc Rolly Gassmann **1997** £8.18 (BIB)
Pinot Blanc Rosenbourg, Blanck **1999** £8.95 (AD)
Pinot Blanc Schleret **1998** £8.25 (YAP)
Riesling Beyer **1998** £8.45 (AV)
Riesling les Faitières, Cave d'Orschwiller-Kintzheim **1997** £8.01 (CHA)
Riesling Hugel **1996** £8.49 (OD) £8.95 (STA) £8.99 (CON)
Riesling Hugel **1989** £8.99 (CON)
Riesling Meyer-Fonné **1998** £8.95 (FORT)
Riesling Trimbach **1997** £8.50 (WS)
Riesling Trimbach **1996** £8.40 (COC)
Sylvaner Reserve Fut 1, Domaine Weinbach **1996** £8.95 (JU)
Tokay-Pinot Gris Réserve Personnelle, Seltz **1997** £8.09 (WAT)
Tokay-Pinot Gris Cave du Roi Dagobert **1996** £8.28 (VIN)
Tokay-Pinot Gris Tradition, Kuentz-Bas **1998** £8.99 (UN)

£9.00 → £10.49

Auxerrois Rolly Gassmann **1993** £9.30 (RAE) £9.90 (GAU)
Auxerrois Seefel, Rolly Gassmann **1993** £9.50 (JU)
Gewürztraminer Beyer **1998** £9.60 (AV)
Gewürztraminer Bollenberg, Cattin **1998** £9.99 (CB)
Gewürztraminer Cuvée des Evêques, Hügel et Fils **1995** £9.50 (JU)
Gewürztraminer Hugel **1996** £9.19 (BOD)
Gewürztraminer Hugel **1995** £10.28 (REI)
Gewürztraminer Kuentz-Bas **1997** £9.45 (COC)
Gewürztraminer Albert Mann **1998** £9.15 (WRI)
Gewürztraminer Réserve Personnelle, Kuentz-Bas **1996** £9.05 (COC)

Gewürztraminer Réserve Personnelle, Kuentz-Bas **1995** £10.49 (UN)
Gewürztraminer Réserve Personnelle, Wiederhirn **1998** £9.50 (HIG)
Gewürztraminer Rolly Gassmann **1992** £9.95 (RAE)
Gewürztraminer Trimbach **1998** £9.95 (WS) £11.46 (REI)
Gewürztraminer Trimbach **1997** £9.85 (COC) £12.18 (PLAY)
Muscat Deiss **1991** £9.49 (BAL)
Muscat Moenchreben, Rolly Gassmann **1987** £9.65 (RAE)
Muscat Réserve, Trimbach **1994** £10.49 (JON)
Muscat Schleret **1996** £9.75 (YAP)
Pinot Blanc Burn **1997** £9.50 (BEN)
Pinot Blanc Réserve, Domaine Weinbach **1996** £9.95 (JU)
Riesling Bennwihr, Deiss **1996** £9.49 (BAL)

Riesling les Princes Abbés, Schlumberger **1996** £9.46 (PLA)
Riesling Rolly Gassmann **1997** £9.49 (BIB)
Riesling Wintzenheim, Zind-Humbrecht **1997** £9.99 (WR) £9.99 (BOT)
Sylvaner Réserve, Domaine Weinbach **1995** £9.45 (JU)
Tokay-Pinot Gris Barriques, Domaine Ostertag **1995** £10.35 (SOM)
Tokay-Pinot Gris Cuvée Caroline, Schoffit **1997** £9.95 (GAU)
Tokay-Pinot Gris Grand Cru Brand, Cave Vinicole de Turckheim **1997** £9.95 (AME)
Tokay-Pinot Gris Réserve Personnelle, Wiederhirn **1994** £9.50 (HIG)
Tokay-Pinot Gris Tradition, Kuentz-Bas **1996** £9.05 (COC)

£10.50 → £12.99

Auxerrois 'H' Vieilles Vignes, Josmeyer **1997** £11.75 (GAU)
Auxerrois 'H' Vieilles Vignes, Josmeyer **1996** £12.30 (HAH)
Gewürztraminer Clos Gaensbroennel, A Willm **1998** £11.95 (AS)
Gewürztraminer les Princes Abbés, Schlumberger **1996** £10.99 (JON)
Gewürztraminer les Princes Abbés, Schlumberger **1995** £10.95 (FORT)
Gewürztraminer les Princes Abbés, Schlumberger **1994** £11.55 (PHI)
Gewürztraminer Réserve Personnelle, Kuentz-Bas **1991** £11.59 (COC)
Gewürztraminer Rolly Gassmann **1995** £12.43 (BIB)
Gewürztraminer St-Hippolyte, Deiss **1995** £11.50 (BAL)
Gewürztraminer Schléret **1998** £10.50 (YAP)
Gewürztraminer Tradition, Hugel **1997** £11.00 (WS) £11.95 (STA)
Gewürztraminer Tradition, Hugel **1996** £10.99 (OD) £15.25 (FORT)
Muscat Clos St-Imer, Burn **1997** £11.29 (YOU)
Muscat Deiss **1998** £10.95 (LEA)
Pinot Blanc Réserve, Domaine Weinbach **1995** £11.50 (JU)
Pinot Blanc Domaine Weinbach **1998** £10.95 (TAN)
Pinot Blanc Zind-Humbrecht **1997** £12.50 (CRO) £13.99 (NI)
Pinot Blanc Zind-Humbrecht **1995** £10.61 (FLE) £13.99 (NI) £20.00 (CRO)
Riesling Altenberg de Bergheim, Koehly **1993** £11.95 (HAH)
Riesling Clos St-Imer, Burn **1997** £11.50 (BEN)
Riesling Cuvée Caroline Harth, Schoffit **1998** £11.65 (AD)
Riesling Frédéric Émile, Trimbach **1995** £12.00 (WS) £17.50 (GAU) £19.39 (REI) £19.99 (YOU) £19.99 (BOD) £20.00 (MI)
Riesling Herrenweg, Zind-Humbrecht **1990** £10.93 (BY)
Riesling Réserve, Trimbach **1995** £11.60 (GAU)
Riesling Rosenbourg, Blanck **1996** £10.99 (FLE)
Riesling Schoenenbourg, Dopff au Moulin **1995** £12.45 (COC)
Riesling Schoenenbourg, Wiederhirn **1995** £11.00 (HIG)
Riesling Tradition, Hugel **1996** £10.99 (OD)
Riesling Tradition, Hugel **1995** £11.00 (WS)
Riesling Trimbach **1995** £11.69 (TW)
Riesling Wineck-Schlossberg, Meyer-Fonné **1997** £12.95 (LAY)
Tokay-Pinot Gris Barriques, Domaine Ostertag **1996** £12.50 (MV)

Tokay-Pinot Gris Beblenheim, Deiss **1995** £11.95 (BAL)
Tokay-Pinot Gris Bergheim, Deiss **1998** £10.50 (LEA)
Tokay-Pinot Gris Cuvée Caroline, Schoffit **1998** £10.95 (BER) £11.40 (AD)
Tokay-Pinot Gris Hatschbourg, Cattin **1997** £11.41 (CB)
Tokay-Pinot Gris Hugel **1997** £11.95 (DI)
Tokay-Pinot Gris Domaine Ostertag **1996** £12.99 (PHI)
Tokay-Pinot Gris les Princes Abbés, Schlumberger **1997** £10.99 (POR)
Tokay-Pinot Gris Réserve, Trimbach **1997** £12.75 (PLAY)
Tokay-Pinot Gris Réserve, Trimbach **1995** £11.40 (GAU)
Tokay-Pinot Gris Schleret **1996** £11.95 (YAP)
Tokay-Pinot Gris Schlumberger **1997** £11.75 (PLA)
Tokay-Pinot Gris Tradition, Hugel **1997** £11.50 (WS) £11.75 (STA)
Tokay-Pinot Gris Tradition, Hugel **1995** £10.99 (CON)
Tokay-Pinot Gris Trimbach **1997** £11.00 (WS)

£13.00 → £14.99

Gewürztraminer Herrenweg, Zind-Humbrecht **1986** £13.48 (BY)
Gewürztraminer Jubilee, Hugel **1997** £14.55 (AD)
Gewürztraminer Kappelweg, Rolly Gassmann **1993** £14.95 (RAE)
Gewürztraminer Réserve, Trimbach **1997** £13.33 (MI)
Gewürztraminer Réserve, Trimbach **1990** £14.00 (WS)
Gewürztraminer Rolly Gassmann **1991** £13.99 (RAE)
Gewürztraminer St-Hippolyte, Deiss **1998** £13.95 (LEA)
Muscat les Amandiers, Dopff & Irion **1994** £13.50 (UB)
Muscat les Amandiers, Dopff & Irion **1983** £14.50 (CRO)
Muscat Goldert, Zind-Humbrecht **1991** £13.68 (BY)
Muscat Herrenweg de Turckheim, Zind-Humbrecht **1996** £14.00 (CRO)
Muscat Moenchreben, Rolly Gassmann **1996** £14.78 (BIB)
Muscat Réserve No 6, Domaine Weinbach **1996** £14.50 (JU)
Pinot Blanc Zind-Humbrecht **1996** £13.50 (CRO) £13.99 (NI)
Riesling Clos Haüserer, Zind-Humbrecht **1997** £14.49 (WR) £14.49 (BOT)
Riesling Cuvée Théo, Domaine Weinbach **1995** £14.95 (JU)
Riesling Heissenberg **1996** £13.00 (MV)
Riesling Herrenweg, Zind-Humbrecht **1997** £13.68 (BY)
Riesling Kappelweg, Rolly Gassmann **1993** £14.50 (JU)
Riesling Schlossberg, Albert Mann **1997** £13.79 (YOU)
Tokay-Pinot Gris Furstentum, Albert Mann **1996** £14.25 (LAY)
Tokay-Pinot Gris Réserve Millésime, Rolly Gassman **1994** £14.95 (RAE) £18.90 (JU)
Tokay-Pinot Gris Tradition, Hugel **1996** £14.68 (TW)

£15.00 → £19.99

Gewürztraminer Cuvée Laurence, Domaine Weinbach **1996** £19.99 (YOU)
Gewürztraminer Cuvée Laurence, Domaine Weinbach **1995** £19.50 (JU)
Gewürztraminer Cuvée Théo, Domaine Weinbach **1995** £16.50 (JU)
Gewürztraminer Hengst, Zind-Humbrecht **1993** £19.95 (PHI)
Gewürztraminer Hengst, Zind-Humbrecht **1987** £17.50 (WAI)
Gewürztraminer Herrenweg, Zind-Humbrecht **1997** £19.20 (NI)
Gewürztraminer Jubilee, Hugel **1996** £15.15 (PLA) £17.95 (DI)
Gewürztraminer Jubilee, Hugel **1988** £15.49 (CON)
Gewürztraminer Jubilee, Hugel **1985** £15.86 (REI)
Gewürztraminer Kitterlé, Schlumberger **1994** £17.39 (NI)
Gewürztraminer Réserve, Trimbach **1994** £15.00 (MI)
Gewürztraminer Seigneurs de Ribeaupierre, Trimbach **1993** £17.99 (GAU)
Gewürztraminer Seigneurs de Ribeaupierre, Trimbach **1988** £17.29 (YOU) £17.45 (PLA) £18.33 (MI)
Gewürztraminer les Sorcières, Dopff & Irion **1996** £15.30 (UB)
Muscat Goldert, Zind-Humbrecht **1997** £16.00 (WS)
Muscat, Domaine Weinbach **1995** £17.95 (JU)

Riesling Brand, Zind-Humbrecht **1991** £17.46 (BY) £25.00 (CRO)
Riesling Clos Haüserer, Zind-Humbrecht **1996** £15.90 (GAU)
Riesling Clos Haüserer, Zind-Humbrecht **1992** £18.00 (CRO)
Riesling Clos St-Imer Cuvée Chapelle, Burn **1998** £15.10 (GAU)
Riesling Clos St-Imer Cuvée Chapelle, Burn **1997** £15.99 (YOU) £17.95 (BEN)
Riesling Cuvée Ste-Catherine II, Domaine Weinbach **1994** £18.90 (JU)
Riesling Frédéric Émile, Trimbach **1993** £18.99 (PHI) £19.85 (PLA) £19.95 (BAL) £26.42 (TW)
Riesling Frédéric Émile, Trimbach **1992** £16.90 (GAU) £20.96 (PLAY) £22.91 (TW)
Riesling Furstentum, Albert Mann **1996** £16.49 (YOU)
Riesling Herrenweg, Zind-Humbrecht **1996** £15.55 (NI)
Riesling Jubilee, Hugel **1997** £16.65 (CON)
Riesling Jubilee, Hugel **1995** £17.95 (DI)
Riesling Jubilee Réserve Personnelle, Hugel **1996** £17.50 (STA)
Riesling Muenchberg, Domaine Ostertag **1997** £18.00 (MV)
Riesling Muenchberg, Domaine Ostertag **1996** £17.99 (YOU) £18.00 (MV)
Riesling les Pierrets, Josmeyer **1995** £17.50 (GAU)
Riesling Réserve Particulière, Faller **1987** £19.39 (REI)
Riesling Réserve, Trimbach **1989** £19.85 (TW)
Riesling Schlossberg, Blanck **1996** £15.25 (AD)
Riesling Schlossberg II, Domaine Weinbach **1996** £18.00 (JU)
Riesling Turckheim, Zind-Humbrecht **1997** £15.35 (NI)
Tokay-Pinot Gris Bergheim, Deiss **1995** £17.20 (GAU)
Tokay-Pinot Gris Clos St-Imer Cuvée Chapelle, Burn **1997** £15.50 (GAU) £15.99 (YOU) £17.95 (BEN)
Tokay-Pinot Gris Clos St-Imer Cuvée Chapelle, Burn **1996** £16.95 (BEN)
Tokay-Pinot Gris Jubilee, Hugel **1996** £17.33 (PLA)

A key to name abbreviations is available on page 7.

Tokay-Pinot Gris Jubilee, Hugel **1994** £16.00 (WS)
Tokay-Pinot Gris Millesime, Rolly Gassmann **1992** £19.50 (UB)
Tokay-Pinot Gris Réserve Personnelle Sigillé de Qualité, Kuentz-Bas **1990** £15.00 (JU)
Tokay-Pinot Gris Réserve Personnelle, Trimbach **1996** £18.33 (MI) £19.20 (GAU)
Tokay-Pinot Gris Réserve, Rolly Gassmann **1989** £18.99 (RAE)
Tokay-Pinot Gris Vendange Tardive, Deiss **1994** £18.95 (BAL)
Tokay-Pinot Gris Zind-Humbrecht **1996** £17.00 (CRO)

£20.00 → £24.99

Gewürztraminer Altenbourg Cuvée Laurence, Domaine Weinbach **1996** £24.00 (JU)
Gewürztraminer Clos Windsbuhl, Zind-Humbrecht **1992** £20.25 (NI)
Gewürztraminer Clos Windsbuhl, Zind-Humbrecht **1991** £22.90 (GAU)
Gewürztraminer Goldert, Zind-Humbrecht **Non-vintage** £22.49 (WR)
Gewürztraminer Réserve Particulière, Faller **1986** £21.74 (REI)
Gewürztraminer Cave du Roi Dagobert **1989** £23.13 (VIN)
Gewürztraminer Seigneurs de Ribeaupierre, Trimbach **1986** £21.74 (REI)
Gewürztraminer Seigneurs de Ribeaupierre, Trimbach **1983** £24.17 (MI) £35.00 (CRO)
Gewürztraminer Vendange Tardive, Wiederhirn **1990** £22.50 (HIG)
Riesling Brand, Zind-Humbrecht **1996** £22.43 (BY)
Riesling Clos Haüserer, Zind-Humbrecht **1994** £23.00 (CRO)
Riesling Clos St-Théobald Rangen de Thann, Schoffit **1997** £22.50 (GAU)
Riesling Cuvée Ste-Catherine, Domaine Weinbach **1995** £22.50 (JU)
Riesling Frédéric Émile, Trimbach **1983** £22.00 (CRO) £29.20 (GAU) £29.96 (TW) £65.00 (YOU)
Riesling Jubilee, Hugel **1990** £20.00 (WS)
Riesling Schoenenbourg Vendange Tardive, Dopff au Moulin **1981** £22.00 (CRO)
Tokay-Pinot Gris Cuvée Ste-Catherine II, Domaine Weinbach **1996** £23.50 (JU) £23.99 (YOU)
Tokay-Pinot Gris Cuvée Ste-Cathérine, Domaine Weinbach **1996** £21.49 (YOU)

Tokay-Pinot Gris Heimbourg, Zind-Humbrecht **1997** £24.17 (MI)
Tokay-Pinot Gris Réserve, Faller **1986** £21.74 (REI)
Tokay-Pinot Gris Réserve Personnelle, Hugel **1983** £20.56 (REI)
Tokay-Pinot Gris Réserve, Rolly Gassmann **1983** £22.95 (RAE)
Tokay-Pinot Gris Vendange Tardive, Deiss **1989** £24.50 (BAL)
Tokay-Pinot Gris Zind-Humbrecht **1995** £22.00 (CRO)

£25.00 → £29.99

Gewürztraminer Cuvée Christine, Schlumberger **1989** £29.88 (NO)
Gewürztraminer Furstentum Cuvée Laurence, Domaine Weinbach **1995** £29.00 (JU)
Gewürztraminer Hengst, Zind-Humbrecht **1997** £29.17 (MI)
Muscat les Amandiers, Dopff & Irion **1976** £29.00 (CRO)
Riesling Clos Ste-Hune, Trimbach **1992** £28.20 (GAU) £29.96 (REI) £47.00 (TW)
Riesling Frédéric Émile, Trimbach **1986** £27.00 (CRO)
Riesling Réserve Personnelle, Hugel **1983** £29.00 (CRO)
Riesling Réserve Personnelle, Hugel **1969** £26.44 (REI)
Riesling Schlossberg Cuvée Ste-Catherine, Domaine Weinbach **1998** £28.50 (TAN)
Riesling Schoenenbourg Vendange Tardive, Dopff au Moulin **1983** £29.00 (CRO)
Riesling Vendange Tardive, Hugel **1989** £28.95 (AD) £34.17 (MI)
Tokay-Pinot Gris Altenbourg, Domaine Weinbach **1996** £29.00 (JU)
Tokay-Pinot Gris Clos St-Imer Vendange Tardive, Burn **1995** £29.95 (BEN)
Tokay-Pinot Gris Cuvée Ste-Catherine III, Domaine Weinbach **1995** £29.00 (JU)
Tokay-Pinot Gris Heimbourg, Zind-Humbrecht **1996** £25.00 (MI) £27.50 (FORT)
Tokay-Pinot Gris Vendange Tardive, Hugel **1990** £28.95 (WAI) £32.50 (MI)

£30.00 → £39.99

Gewürztraminer Altenbourg Cuvée Laurence, Domaine Weinbach **1998** £33.90 (TAN)
Gewürztraminer Herrenweg, Zind-Humbrecht **1989** £38.19 (REI)
Gewürztraminer Vendange Tardive, Beyer **1990** £33.50 (AV)
Gewürztraminer Vendange Tardive, Hugel **1994** £33.33 (MI)
Gewürztraminer Vendange Tardive, Hugel **1985** £34.60 (DI) £42.89 (TW)
Gewürztraminer Vendange Tardive, Trimbach **1996** £32.50 (MI)
Riesling Altenberg Sélection des Grains Nobles, Deiss **1989** £37.30 (GAU) £39.50 (LEA)
Riesling Brand, Zind-Humbrecht **1997** £33.30 (NI)
Riesling Brand, Zind-Humbrecht **1990** £32.00 (CRO)
Riesling Clos Ste-Hune, Trimbach **1993** £39.99 (YOU) £47.00 (TW)
Riesling Clos Ste-Hune, Trimbach **1986** £33.00 (BAL) £33.00 (GAU) £38.00 (CRO)
Riesling Frédéric Émile, Trimbach **1985** £31.14 (REI) £38.00 (CRO)
Riesling Frédéric Émile, Trimbach **1981** £33.48 (TW)
Riesling Frédéric Émile Vendange Tardive, Trimbach **1990** £35.83 (MI) £36.99 (YOU)
Riesling Frédéric Émile Vendange Tardive, Trimbach **1983** £35.83 (MI) £52.88 (REI) £88.12 (TW)
Riesling Herrenweg, Zind-Humbrecht **1989** £38.00 (CRO)
Riesling Vendange Tardive, Dopff & Irion **1976** £33.00 (CRO)
Riesling Vendange Tardive, Hugel **1983** £38.19 (REI) £39.95 (DI) £45.00 (BEN)
Riesling Vendange Tardive, Wiederhirn **1983** £31.00 (CRO)
Tokay-Pinot Gris Réserve, Heydt **1983** £32.31 (REI)
Tokay-Pinot Gris Vendange Tardive, Domaine Weinbach **1995** £31.50 (JU) £34.30 (TAN)
Tokay-Pinot Gris Zind-Humbrecht **1990** £37.00 (CRO)

£40.00 → £49.99

Gewürztraminer Cuvée Anne, Schlumberger **1989** £42.00 (BAL) £55.06 (NO) £57.80 (BEN)
Gewürztraminer Herrenweg Vendange Tardive, Zind-Humbrecht **1989** £45.00 (YOU)
Gewürztraminer Herrenweg, Zind-Humbrecht **1990** £40.00 (CRO)
Gewürztraminer Vendange Tardive, Hugel **1983** £41.71 (REI)

Gewürztraminer Vendange Tardive, Trimbach **1989** £46.44 (PLAY)

Riesling Clos Ste-Hune, Trimbach **1995** £49.94 (REI)

Riesling Frédéric Émile, Trimbach **1979** £41.12 (TW)

Riesling Vendange Tardive, Hugel **1990** £44.06 (REI)

Tokay-Pinot Gris Cuvée Clarisse, Schlumberger **1989** £43.90 (BAL) £58.00 (CRO)

Tokay-Pinot Gris Réserve Personnelle, Hugel **1976** £41.13 (REI)

Tokay-Pinot Gris Vendange Tardive, Faller **1983** £46.00 (CRO)

£50.00 → £59.99

Gewürztraminer Cuvée Anne, Schlumberger **1988** £57.50 (FORT)

Gewürztraminer Cuvée Christine, Schlumberger **1985** £56.00 (CRO)

Gewürztraminer Seigneurs de Ribeaupierre, Trimbach **1976** £54.00 (CRO)

Gewürztraminer Sélection de Grains Nobles, Hugel **1989** £57.50 (MI)

Gewürztraminer Sélection de Grains Nobles, Hugel **1986** £57.00 (WS) £75.00 (DI)

Gewürztraminer Sélection de Grains Nobles, Fuchs **1989** £59.18 (NO)

Riesling Clos Ste-Hune, Trimbach **1989** £50.00 (FORT) £52.88 (REI)

Riesling Vendange Tardive, Hugel **1976** £59.00 (CRO) £88.13 (TW)

Riesling Vendange Tardive, Domaine Weinbach **1990** £54.00 (JU)

Tokay-Pinot Gris Clos St-Imer Sélection de Grains Nobles, Burn **1994** £59.50 (BEN)

£60.00 → £74.99

Gewürztraminer Clos St-Imer Sélection de Grains Nobles, Burn **1994** £66.00 (BEN)

Gewürztraminer Cuvée Anne Vendange Tardive, Rolly Gassmann **1985** £68.00 (UB)

Gewürztraminer Furstentum Selection des Grains Nobles, Domaine Weinbach **1994** £62.00 (JU)

Gewürztraminer Sélection de Grains Nobles, Hugel **1988** £67.84 (VIN)

Riesling Clos Haüserer, Zind-Humbrecht **1989** £65.00 (YOU)

Riesling Clos Ste-Hune, Trimbach **1981** £64.62 (TW)

Riesling Frédéric Émile, Trimbach **1976** £65.00 (CRO)

Riesling Sélection de Grains Nobles, Fuchs **1989** £62.07 (NO)

£75.00 → £99.99

Gewürztraminer Cuvée Christine, Schlumberger **1976** £92.00 (CRO)

Gewürztraminer Sélection de Grains Nobles, Hugel **1981** £76.96 (REI)

Gewürztraminer Sélection de Grains Nobles, Hugel **1976** £80.00 (CRO)

Riesling Frédéric Émile Vendange Tardive, Trimbach **1989** £84.60 (TW)

Riesling Vendange Tardive, Hugel **1971** £76.38 (REI)

Tokay-Pinot Gris Sélection de Grains Nobles, Hugel **1976** £92.00 (CRO)

Over £100.00

Gewürztraminer Cuvée Anne, Schlumberger **1976** £120.00 (CRO)

Gewürztraminer Cuvée d'Or Quintessence Selection des Grains Nobles, Domaine Weinbach **1994** £138.00 (JU)

RED

Under £10.00

Pinot Noir Beyer **1997** £9.60 (AV)

Pinot Noir Hugel **1997** £9.95 (STA)

Pinot Noir Hugel **1995** £9.95 (DI)

Pinot Noir Rolly Gassmann **1992** £9.70 (RAE)

£10.00 → £20.00

Pinot Noir Burlenberg, Deiss **1996** £13.95 (LEA)

Pinot Noir Herrenweg, Zind-Humbrecht **1991** £12.14 (BY)

Pinot Noir Réserve, Rolly Gassmann **1990** £19.99 (RAE) £22.69 (BIB)

Pinot Noir Schleret **1997** £10.50 (YAP)

SPARKLING

Under £8.00

Crémant d'Alsace Cuvée Julien, Dopff au Moulin **Non-vintage** £7.95 (WS) £9.44 (COC)

BORDEAUX

The more I look at Bordeaux pricing, the more I think it's all a trick done with mirrors. Certainly the link between price and quality is remarkably weak here

There's a basic logic about wine prices, isn't there? It states that better wines are more expensive than less good wines, and older wines are more expensive than younger wines. That's how we all automatically think of it, surely. Older is rarer and more mature, therefore more expensive. Older whisky is pricier than younger; older Cognac costs far more than five-year-old firewater. Therefore wine should be the same.

Well, there's wine, and there's Bordeaux. A quick glance at the price guides that follow will show that older vintages can be far, far cheaper than newer ones. And as for lesser years being cheaper than great years, forget it.

The reason that some older Bordeaux seems cheap is simply that newer vintages can be so amazingly expensive. (Although once you get into the old and great years, like 1961 or 1959, nothing is cheap.) Bordeaux has the extraordinary knack of charging what the market will bear, regardless of the quality of the year's wine. Take the 1997s, for example. It was a reasonable vintage; not bad, not outstanding. (Sauternes, being excellent, was the exception.) It was not as good as the 1996 vintage, and the producers knew this and admitted it openly. Nevertheless, when it came to offering the vintage to the market, they charged an average of 30 to 40% more than for the 1996s. And they sold them. The brokers and merchants who form the middlemen in Bordeaux took the wines at the asking prices.

The fact that they couldn't sell them on, that we weren't buying the 1997s because they were too expensive and not good enough, didn't matter to the château proprietors. The proprietors had washed their hands of them. The merchants and brokers, at the time of writing, were still holding on to the 1997s, waiting until a moment when they can get rid of them. They were wines that should have been cheaper than the 1996s – 30 to 40% cheaper, perhaps. Cheaper, certainly, than the very good 1995s. But that is how Bordeaux works; and that is why price, in Bordeaux, is no indication of quality.

GRAPE VARIETIES

Fine claret has the most tantalizing and unlikely combination of flavours of any red wine. There's the blast of pure, fragrant blackcurrant fruit, and then the exotic, dry perfumes of lead pencil shavings, fresh-wrapped cigars and cedar to weave an endlessly fascinating balance of sweet and dry tastes with, increasingly, the buttery overlay of new oak barrels.

Bordeaux's vineyards are so poised on the knife-edge of ripening their grapes or failing to do so that every vintage is fascinatingly different. If the year gets too hot, the flavour can be rich, strong and burnt, more like the Californian or Italian attempts at claret. If the summer rains and autumn gales roll in off the Bay of Biscay and the grapes can't ripen, then the taste may be thin and green, resembling the Cabernets of the Loire Valley. But in the years of balance, like 1988, '89, '90 and '95, those astonishing sweet and dry, fruity and tannic flavours mix to produce the glory that is claret.

As for the whites – well, for years the sweet, botrytized wines of Sauternes and Barsac were the only ones that could compete in quality with the reds, and not

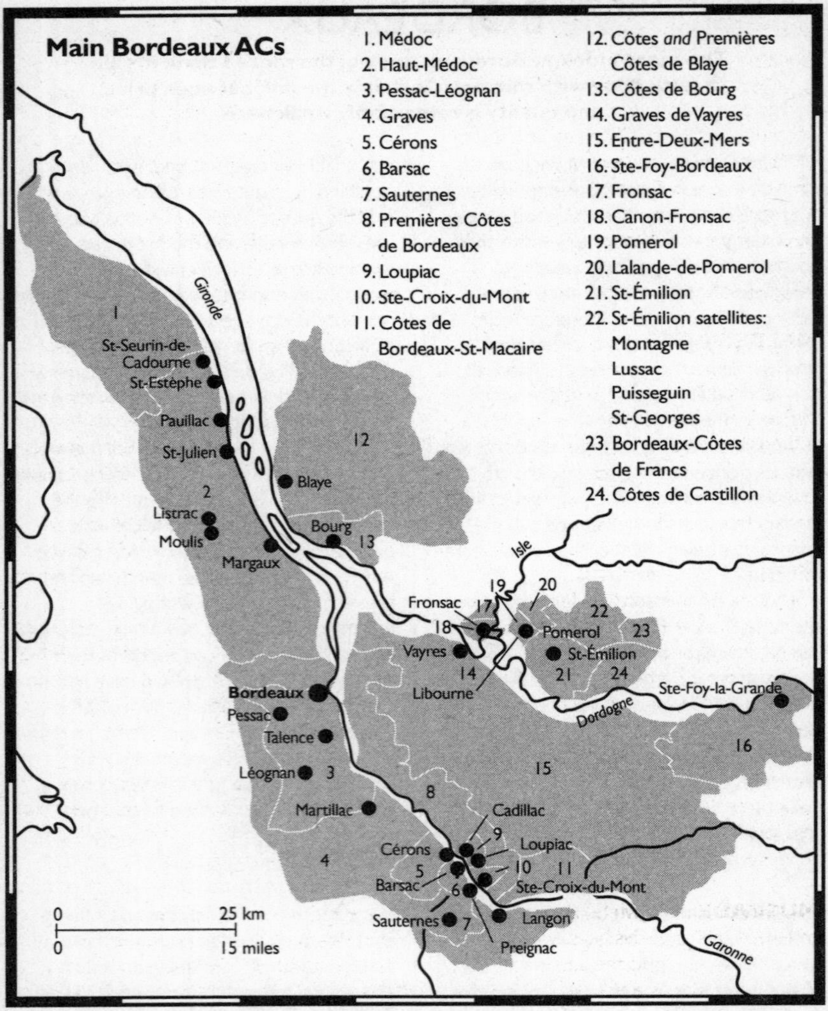

always successfully. But recent years have seen a revolution. The sweet whites have improved beyond measure, helped by massive investment and a run of excellent vintages in the 1980s, but so have the dry ones. Inexpensive Bordeaux Blanc, based on Sauvignon, is usually crisp and grassy these days, while fine oak-aged white Graves has taken its place among the greats.

CABERNET FRANC (red) The lesser of the two Cabernets, giving lighter-coloured, softer wines than Cabernet Sauvignon, often slightly earthy but with good, blackcurranty fruit. It's always blended in Bordeaux. In St-Émilion and Pomerol it can give fine flavours and is widely planted. Château Cheval-Blanc in St-Émilion is two-thirds Cabernet Franc.

CABERNET SAUVIGNON (red) This world-famous Bordeaux grape surprisingly covers only a fifth of the vineyard area. Crucially, a wine built to age needs tannin and acidity, and the fruit and extract to keep up with them. Cabernet Sauvignon has all these in abundance. It gives dark, tannic wine with a strong initial acid attack, and stark blackcurrant fruit. When aged in new oak, it can be stunning. It's the main grape of the Haut-Médoc, but other varieties soften it and add complexity.

MALBEC (red) A rather bloated, juicy grape, little seen nowadays in Bordeaux, though it appears in some blends, especially in Bourg and Blaye. In Bordeaux it tastes rather like a feeble version of Merlot, soft and low in acidity. Upriver in Cahors it has real style, which probably explains why there's lots of it there and little in Bordeaux.

MERLOT (red) Bordeaux has more Merlot than Cabernet Sauvignon. It covers almost a third of the vineyard, and is the main grape in St-Émilion and Pomerol, whereas in the Médoc and Graves it's used to soften and enrich the Cabernet. It ripens early and gives a gorgeous, succulent, minty, blackcurranty or plummy wine, which explains why Pomerols and St-Émilions are easier to enjoy than Médocs. It also makes less long-lived wine than Cabernet, and tends to peak and fade sooner.

MUSCADELLE (white) A very little (up to five per cent) of this headily perfumed grape often goes into the Sauternes blend. In dry white blends a few per cent can add a very welcome honeyed softness. It is now being produced in small quantities as a varietal: dry, lean, but perfumed.

PETIT VERDOT (red) A dark, tough grape with a liquorice-and-plums taste, and a violet perfume, used for colour. It adds quality in a late, ripe year.

SAUVIGNON BLANC (white) There has been a rush to plant more of this fashionable grape in Bordeaux in recent years, but with a couple of exceptions – such as *Couhins-Lurton, Malartic-Lagravière* and *Smith-Haut-Lafitte* – Sauvignon by itself here often gives rather muddy, tough wine. The best are almost always blended with Sémillon. Even so, many of the cheaper dry white Bordeaux are entirely Sauvignon, and these can be fresh and flowery if from careful winemakers like *Coste, Dourthe, Ginestet* and *Mau*. A little Sauvignon adds acidity to Sauternes and other sweet whites.

SÉMILLON (white) The most important grape of Sauternes, and vital to the best dry wines, too. With modern techniques one can hardly tell a good dry Sémillon from a Sauvignon, except that it's a little fuller. But ideally they should be blended, with Sémillon the main variety. It gives a big, round dry wine, slightly creamy but with an aroma of fresh apples and a lanolin smoothness in the mouth. The result is a wonderful, soft, nutty dry white, often going honeyed and smoky as it ages for seven to 15 years. Like this it produces one of France's great whites, and is an antidote to anyone getting just a little tired of varietals.

WINE REGIONS

BARSAC, AC (sweet white) The only one of the five Sauternes villages with the right to use its own name as an official appellation (it may also call itself Sauternes – or Sauternes-Barsac). The wines tend to be lighter, and the best combine marvellous richness with a certain delicacy of texture.

BORDEAUX BLANC, AC (dry white) This AC is the catch-all name for all white Bordeaux. Château wines are usually the best and should generally be drunk as young as possible. Recommended names include: *Birot, Grand-Mouëys, du Juge, Lamothe, Reynon*. Good blends are likely from the following merchants: *Coste, Dourthe, Dubroca, Ginestet, Joanne, Lurton, Mau, Sichel* and *Univitis*.

Some classy properties in red areas make good, dry white which is allowed only this AC. *Château Margaux*'s white, for instance, is a simple AC Bordeaux Blanc. Many great Sauternes châteaux make a dry wine from the grapes deemed unsuitable for Sauternes. These also take the Bordeaux Blanc AC and are often named after the initial letter of the château's name – as in 'G' of *Guiraud*, 'R' of *Rieussec* and 'Y' of *Yquem*. They're expensive but complex and unusual. 'Y' can really be spectacular.

BORDEAUX BLANC SUPÉRIEUR, AC (dry white) Rarely used, but requires higher basic strength and lower vineyard yield than Bordeaux Blanc AC.

BORDEAUX ROUGE, AC (red) Unless qualified by one of the other ACs below, this is the everyday red wine of Bordeaux, from co-ops, from properties in undistinguished localities, or wine disqualified from one of the better ACs. It is a delicious, appetizing meal-time red when good – and a palate-puckering disappointment when bad. Too many are muddy, coarse and lacking in style.

BORDEAUX SUPÉRIEUR, AC (red) Similar to Bordeaux Rouge but with more alcohol and produced from a slightly lower yield. The same comments on quality apply. Best results are often from properties producing white Entre-Deux-Mers and from the Premières Côtes. Best châteaux: *Brethous, Cayla, Domaine de Terrefort, Fayau, la Gabory, le Gay, Grand-Moüeys, Gromel Bel-Air, Jalousie-Beaulieu, Jonqueyres, du Juge, Lacombe, Méaume, Peyrat, Pierredon, Reynon, la Roche, Tanesse, Thieuley, de Toutigeac, de la Vieille Tour.*

CADILLAC, AC (sweet white) This small region can produce attractive sweet whites, but many properties produce more commercial dry whites and reds – which do *not* qualify for the AC Cadillac. The AC is so involved that few growers bother with it.

CÉRONS, AC (sweet white) Good, fairly sweet whites, but many growers now prefer to produce dry whites instead, which can be sold as Graves. *Château Archambeau* is typical, producing tiny amounts of very good Cérons and larger amounts of good, fresh dry Graves. *Château Cérons* makes splendidly complex sweet whites worthy of the AC of Barsac. Other good names to look out for: *Grand Enclos du Château Cérons, Haura*.

CÔTES DE BLAYE, AC (dry white) and **PREMIÈRES CÔTES DE BLAYE, AC** (red, dry white) The reds are sometimes a little 'cooked' in taste, but they're improving. The whites are getting better, too. Good names: *Bas Vallon, Bourdieu, Charron, Crusquet-Sabourin, l'Escadre, Fontblanche, Grand Barail, Haut-Bertinerie, Haut-Sociondo, Jonqueyres, Peybonhomme.*

CÔTES DE BOURG, AC (red) The rather full, savoury style of these reds is backed up by sweet Merlot fruit and occasionally a touch of new oak. As Médoc and St-Émilion prices spiral, Bourg wines are coming into their own. Best châteaux: *de Barbe, du Bousquet, Brûlesécaille, la Croix, Dupeyrat, Falfas, Grolet, Haut-Guiraud, Haut-Rousset, de Millorit, Roc de Cambes, Tayac* and wines from the co-op at *Tauriac*.

CÔTES DE CASTILLON, AC (red) and **BORDEAUX-CÔTES DE FRANCS, AC** (red) Two small regions which are turning out an increasing number of exciting wines. They can be a little too earthy, but at their best they combine a grassy Cabernet Franc freshness with a gorgeous, juicy, minty Merlot sweetness. Several leading Bordeaux proprietors have bought properties here and are leading the way. Best châteaux in the Côtes de Castillon: *Arthus, Beau-Séjour, Belcier, Brisson,*

Canon-Monségur, La Clarière-Laithwaite, Ferrasses, Fonds Rondes, Grand Taillac, les Hauts-de-Grange, Lessacques, Moulin-Rouge, Parenchère, Peyrou, Pitray, Poupille, Rocher-Bellevue, Vernon. The Côtes de Francs is increasingly producing fruity, light, delicious wines to drink early, using a lot of Cabernet Franc. Best châteaux here are *la Claverie, de Francs, Lauriol, Marsau, du Moulin-la-Pitié, la Prade, Puygueraud.*

ENTRE-DEUX-MERS, AC (dry white) Every vintage produces more good, fresh, grassy wines here. Many properties make red, which take the AC of Bordeaux or Bordeaux Supérieur. Best: *Bonnet, Ducla, de Florin, Fondarzac, Moulin-de-Launay, Tertre du Moulin, Thieuley, Union des Producteurs de Rauzan.*

FRONSAC, AC (red) with the (in theory) superior **CANON-FRONSAC, AC** (red) Lesser St-Émilion lookalikes, sometimes a bit grassy and tannic, but often supple, balanced clarets of some elegance – even in bad years like 1992. Best: *Barrabaque, Canon-de-Brem, Canon-Moueix, Cassagne Haut-Canon, Dalem, de la Dauphine, Fonteuil, Mayne-Vieil, Mazeris, Moulin Haut-Laroque, Moulin Pey-Labrie, Plain Point, la Rivière, la Truffière, Toumalin, la Valade, La Vieille Cure.*

GRAVES, AC (red, dry white) Red Graves run the gamut of claret flavours, and are less easy to sum up than others. Though the Cabernet Sauvignon is the dominant grape in the North, as in the Médoc, there's more stress on Merlot, so the wines are slightly softer. They tend to have some of the blackcurrant and cedar of the Médoc, but without the sheer size of, say, Pauillac; they have some of the full, plummy richness of St-Émilion, yet it never dominates; and there is a slightly gravelly quality in many of them, too. The less well-known châteaux are good value.

Modern white Graves, even at the level of commercial blends, can be sharply fruity and full in style, although too many are overoaked. Best châteaux: *Archambeau, Bouscaut, Cabannieux, Carbonnieux, Domaine de Chevalier, Couhins-Lurton, de Cruzeau, Domaine la Grave, de Fieuzal, la Garance, la Garde, Haut-Brion, Landiras, Latour-Martillac, Laville-Haut-Brion, la Louvière, Malartic-Lagravière, Montalivet, Rahoul, Respide, Rochemorin, Roquetaillade-la-Grange, Smith-Haut-Lafitte.* (Note that in 1987 the top properties in the North were grouped into a separate AC, Pessac-Léognan.)

GRAVES SUPÉRIEURES, AC (sweet or dry white) Graves with a minimum natural alcohol of 12 degrees. Often made sweet. Best property: *Clos St-Georges.*

HAUT-MÉDOC, AC (red) Geographically, the prestigious southern part of the Médoc, nearest Bordeaux. The AC, however, covers the less exciting vineyards because the really juicy business gets done at Margaux, St-Julien, Pauillac, St-Estèphe, Listrac and Moulis, which have their own ACs. Even so, the AC Haut-Médoc has five Classed Growths including two superb ones – *Cantemerle* and *la Lagune* – and an increasing number of fine bourgeois properties like *Beaumont, de Castillon, Cissac, Hanteillan, Lamarque, Lanessan, Liversan, Pichon, Sociando-Mallet* and *la Tour-du-Haut-Moulin* – plus lots of lesser properties, such as châteaux *Bernadotte, Cambon-la-Pelouse, Coufran, le Fournas, Grandis, du Junca, Larose-Trintaudon, Malescasse, Maucamps, Moulin de Labarde, Quimper, Sénéjac* and *Verdignan.*

LALANDE-DE-POMEROL, AC (red) Pomerol's equally tiny northern neighbour is often accused of being overpriced, but since it can produce rich, plummy wines with a distinct resemblance to those of Pomerol at a distinctly less painful price, this criticism is not entirely justified. Best: *Annereaux, Bel-Air, Belles-Graves, Bertineau-St-Vincent, Clos des Moines, Clos des Templiers, la Croix Bellevue, la Fleur St-Georges, Garraud, Grand*

> **ON THE CASE**
> *If you crave the traditional cedary, tobaccoey flavours that are harder to find in red Bordeaux nowadays, try Graves*

Ormeau, Haut-Ballet, Haut-Chaigneau, les Hauts-Tuileries, Lavaud-la-Maréchaude, Siaurac, les Templiers, Tournefeuille, de Viaud.

LISTRAC, AC (red) One of the less prestigious communes of the Haut-Médoc. The wines contain a higher proportion of Merlot than elsewhere, but nevertheless are rather tough and charmless, only lightly perfumed wines. But some properties rise above this, such as *la Bécade, Cap-Léon-Veyrin, Clarke, Fonréaud* (since 1988), *Fourcas-Dupré, Fourcas-Hosten, Fourcaud, Lestage* and the *Grand Listrac* co-op.

LOUPIAC, AC (sweet white) These wines are not as sweet as Sauternes, and most are light, lemony, honeyed Barsac styles. The general improvement in Bordeaux's sweet wines has filtered down here, as well. Best: *Domaine du Noble, Loupiac-Gaudiet, Ricaud.*

MARGAUX, AC (red) Rather sludgy, solid wines at one extreme, and the most fragrant, perfumed red wines France has yet dreamed up at the other. The best include: *d'Angludet, la Gurgue, d'Issan, Labégorce-Zédé, Margaux, Monbrison, Palmer, Prieuré-Lichine, Rauzan-Ségla, du Tertre*. Among the next best are *Durfort-Vivens, Giscours, Lascombes, Marquis d'Alesme-Becker, Marquis de Terme, Siran* and *la Tour-de-Mons.*

MÉDOC, AC (red) This name covers the long tongue of land north of Bordeaux town, between the Gironde river and the sea, including the Haut-Médoc and all its famous communes. As an AC it refers to the less-regarded but important northern part of the area. Médoc reds, with a high proportion of Merlot grapes, are drinkable more quickly than Haut-Médocs and the best have a refreshing, grassy, juicy fruit, and just enough tannin and acidity. Easily the best property is *Potensac*. Other good wines are *le Bernadot, Cardonne, Cassan d'Estevil, David, d'Escot, la Gorce, Greysac, Grivière, Haut-Canteloup, Lacombe-Noaillac, Noaillac, Ormes-Sorbet, Patache d'Aux, la Tour-de-By, la Tour-St-Bonnet, Loudenne, Vieux-Château-Landon*. Most of the co-ops – especially *Bégadan, Ordomac, St-Yzans* – make good fruity stuff in the best years.

MOULIS, AC (red) Another lesser commune of the Haut-Médoc next door to, and similar to, Listrac, but with more potentially outstanding properties and a softer, more perfumed style in the best which can equal Classed Growths. Best are *Bel-Air-Lagrave, Brillette, Chasse-Spleen, Duplessis-Fabre, Dutruch-Grand-Poujeaux, Grand-Poujeaux, Gressier-Grand-Poujeaux, Maucaillou, Moulin-à-Vent, Poujeaux.*

PAUILLAC, AC (red) The most famous of the Haut-Médoc communes, Pauillac has three of the world's greatest red wines sitting inside its boundaries: *Latour, Lafite* and *Mouton-Rothschild*. This is where the blackcurrant really comes into its own. The best wines are almost painfully intense, a celestial mixture of blackcurrant and lead pencil sharpenings that sends well-heeled cognoscenti leaping for their cheque books. Best: *d'Armailhac* (formerly known as *Mouton-Baronne-Philippe), Grand-Puy-Lacoste, Haut-Bages-Avérous, Haut-Bages-Libéral, Lafite-Rothschild, Latour, Lynch-Bages, Mouton-Rothschild, Pichon-Baron, Pichon-Lalande*. Next best: *Batailley, Clerc-Milon-Rothschild, Duhart-Milon, Grand-Puy-Ducasse, Haut-Bages-Monpelou.*

PESSAC-LÉOGNAN, AC (red, dry white) Traditionally the Graves' best area, containing all the *crus classés*. The whites at their best offer a depth surpassed only by the best Burgundies. They start out with a blast of apricot, peach and cream ripeness and slowly mature to a superb nutty richness with a dry savoury finish. The reds have a biscuity, bricky warmth. Best reds: *Carbonnieux, Carmes-Haut-Brion, Cruzeau, Domaine de Chevalier, Domaine de Gaillat, Domaine la Grave, Ferrande, de Fieuzal, Haut-Bailly, Haut-Brion, Haut-Portets, Latour-Martillac, la Louvière, Malartic-Lagravière, la Mission-Haut-Brion, Pape-Clément* (since 1985), *Rahoul, Rochemorin, de St-Pierre, Smith-Haut-Lafitte* (since 1988), *Roquetaillade-la-Grange, Tourteau-Chollet.* Best whites: *Bouscaut, Carbonnieux* (from 1988), *Couhins-Lurton, Domaine de Chevalier, de Fieuzal, Haut-Brion, Latour-Martillac, la Louvière, Malartic-Lagravière, Rochemorin, Smith-Haut-Lafitte.*

POMEROL, AC (red) The Merlot grape is even more dominant in Pomerol than in St-Émilion, and most Pomerols have a deeper, rounder flavour, the plummy fruit going as dark as prunes in great years, but with the mineral backbone of toughness preserving it for a very long time. Pomerol harbours the *Château Pétrus*, and what is often the world's most expensive red wine, *Le Pin*. Other top names: *Beauregard, le Bon Pasteur, Bourgneuf-Vayron, Certan-de-May, Certan-Giraud, Clinet, Clos René, Clos du Clocher, Clos l'Église, la Conseillante, la Croix-de-Gay, l'Église Clinet, l'Évangile, le Gay, la Grave-Trigant-de-Boisset, Lafleur, la Fleur-de-Gay, Lafleur-Gazin, la Fleur-Pétrus, Lagrange-à-Pomerol, Latour-à-Pomerol, Petit-Village, Trotanoy, Vieux-Château-Certan.*

PREMIÈRES CÔTES DE BORDEAUX, AC (red, white) Some very attractive reds and excellent dry whites in the bang-up-to-date, fruit-all-the-way style, plus some reasonable sweetish wines. Best châteaux: *de Berbec, Brethous, Cayla, Fayau, Grands-Moüeys, du Juge, Lamothe, de Lucat, Peyrat, la Roche, Reynon, Tanesse.*

ST-ÉMILION, AC (red) Soft, round and rather generous wines, because the main grape is the Merlot, aided by Cabernet Franc and Malbec, and only slightly by Cabernet Sauvignon. St-Émilions don't always have Pomerol's minerally backbone, and the sweetness is usually less plummy and more buttery, toffeed or raisiny. Top wines add to this a blackcurranty, minty depth. Basic St-Émilions are seldom exciting, and quality is extremely variable. It's a well-known name, yet with few famous châteaux: the top ones are *Cheval-Blanc* and *Ausone*. Some satellite areas also annex the name, like St-Georges-St-Émilion or Puisseguin-St-Émilion. They're okay, but would be better value if they didn't trade greedily on the St-Émilion handle. Best in satellites: *Montaiguillon, St-Georges, Tour du Pas St-Georges* (St-Georges-St-Émilion); *Haut-Gillet, de Maison Neuve* (Montagne-St-Émilion); *Bel Air, la Croix-de-Berny* (Puisseguin-St-Émilion); *Lyonnat* (Lussac-St-Émilion). Best St-Émilion: *Angélus, l'Arrosée, Ausone, Balestard-la-Tonnelle, Beauséjour-Duffau-Lagarosse, Canon, Canon-la-Gaffelière, Cheval-Blanc, Clos des Jacobins, la Dominique, Figeac, Fonroque, Larmande, Magdelaine, Pavie, Pavie-Decesse, Soutard, Tertre-Rôteboeuf, Troplong-Mondot.* Next best: *Belair, Cadet-Piola, Berliquet, Cap-de-Mourlin, Cardinal Villemaurine, Carteau, Clos Fourtet, Corbin-Michotte, Côtes Daugay, Couvent des Jacobins, Destieux, de Ferrand, Fombrauge, Franc-Mayne, la Gaffelière, Grand-Mayne, Gravet, Magnan-la-Gaffelière, Mauvezin, Monbousquet, Pavie-Macquin, Rolland-Maillet, Tour-des-Combes, la-Tour-du-Pin-Figeac, Trappaud, Trottevieille, Villemaurine.* There's a trend towards producing *micro-vins*: take perhaps a single hectare of vines, make a wine of great concentration and oak, then charge a fortune for it. *Valandraud* and *La Mondotte* are leading players; also *Le Dôme.*

ST-ESTÈPHE, AC (red) The northernmost of the great Haut-Médoc communes is a more everyday performer. There are few famous names, and most are relatively cheap. Best: *Calon-Ségur, Chambert-Marbuzet, Cos d'Estournel, Haut-Marbuzet, Lafon-Rochet, Marbuzet, Meyney, Montrose,* *les Ormes-de-Pez, de Pez, Phélan-Ségur*. Next best: *Andron-Blanquet, Beausite, du Boscq, Cos Labory, le Crock, Lavillotte.*

ST-JULIEN, AC (red) There are two main styles here. One is almost honeyed: gentle, round, wonderfully easy-to-love. The other has glorious cedar-cigar-box fragrance and just enough fruit to make it satisfying as well as exciting. Best: *Beychevelle, Ducru-Beaucaillou, Gruaud-Larose, Lagrange, Lalande-Borie, Langoa-Barton, Léoville-Barton, Léoville-Las-Cases, St-Pierre, Talbot.* Next: *Branaire-Ducru, Gloria, Hortevie, Léoville-Poyferré* and *Terrey-Gros-Caillou.*

STE-CROIX-DU-MONT, AC (sweet white) Very attractive when properly made. *Château Loubens* is the best-known wine, but *la Grave, Lousteau-Vieil, la Rame, Domaine du Tich, des Tours* and the minuscule *de Tastes* are also good.

SAUTERNES, AC (sweet white) The overall appellation for a group of five villages: Sauternes, Bommes, Fargues, Preignac and Barsac. (Barsac wines may use their own village name, if they wish.) Concentrated by noble rot, the Sémillon, along with Sauvignon and Muscadelle, produces at its best a brilliantly rich and glyceriny wine, combining honey and cream, pineapple and nuts when young; becoming oily and penetrating with age. The sweetness has an intensity of volatile flavours, like a peach, bruised and browned in the sun, then steeped in syrup. These are the fine wines; but the average wines have soared in quality recently, as indeed they ought given their prices. Best include: *Bastor-Lamontagne, Climens, Doisy-Daëne, Doisy-Védrines, de Fargues, Gilette, Guiraud, Lafaurie-Peyraguey, Lamothe-Guignard, Rabaud-Promis, Raymond-Lafon, Rayne-Vigneau, Rieussec, St-Amand, Suduiraut, la Tour Blanche, d'Yquem.*

PRODUCERS WHO'S WHO

ANGÉLUS *1er cru classé St-Émilion* ★★★★★ Wonderful: gutsy, rich and soft. New management has brought it to new heights, and it excelled even in the difficult years of the early 1990s. 1996 is superb, '95 even better, '97 and '98 excellent.

D'ANGLUDET *cru bourgeois Margaux* ★★★ **£** Tremendous value *bourgeois* red easily attaining Classed Growth standards. Much of the perfume of good Margaux without ever going through the traditional lean period. 1983 and '90 are the finest ever, '95 and '96 are worthy of their vintages.

D'ARCHE *2ème cru Sauternes* ★★★(★) A little-known property now increasingly highly thought of. 1983, '86, '88, '89 and '90 are good but a little over-alcoholic, perhaps.

> **£** *This symbol denotes producers who offer particularly good value – that's not the same as saying that they're cheap.*

D'ARMAILHAC *5ème cru classé Pauillac* ★★★ (formerly Mouton-Baronne-Philippe) A red of very good balance, with the cedar perfume particularly marked. 1983 and '86 are especially good, as are '96 and (even better) '95.

AUSONE *1er grand cru classé St-Émilion* ★★★★(★) Between 1976 and 1994 the wines were made in a very fine, understated style. A new winemaker was appointed for the 1995, and it's altogether gutsier. The 1985, '86, '89 and above all the '90, are especially good, as are the '96 and '97.

BASTOR-LAMONTAGNE *cru bourgeois Sauternes* ★★★ Marvellous, widely available sweet whites. Pricy, but as rich as many Classed Growths. 1983, '86, '88, '89 and '90 epitomize quality Sauternes. Nice but not thrilling since then.

THE 1855 CLASSIFICATION

This is the most famous and enduring wine classification in the world – but it was intended merely as an impromptu guide to the Bordeaux wines entered for the Great Paris Exhibition of 1855, based on the prices the wines had obtained over the previous century.

Since this classification applies only to the Médoc and one château, Haut-Brion, in the Graves, all the wines are red. The Graves has its own classification, for reds and whites, and Sauternes and St-Émilion are also classified. Pomerol steers clear of any official hierarchy. The only change so far has been the promotion of Mouton-Rothschild to First Growth in 1973.

In general, classified properties do deserve their status, but that's never yet stopped anyone from arguing about it.

CLARET CLASSIFICATIONS

First Growths (1ers crus)
Margaux – *Margaux*; Lafite-Rothschild, Latour, Mouton-Rothschild (promoted in 1973) – *Pauillac;* Haut-Brion – *Pessac-Léognan* (formerly *Graves*).

Second Growths (2èmes crus)
Brane-Cantenac – *Cantenac-Margaux*; Durfort-Vivens, Lascombes, Rauzan-Gassies, Rauzan-Ségla – *Margaux*; Pichon-Longueville, Pichon-Longueville-Lalande (formerly Pichon-Lalande) – *Pauillac*; Cos d'Estournel, Montrose – *St-Estèphe*; Ducru-Beaucaillou, Gruaud-Larose, Léoville-Barton, Léoville-Las-Cases, Léoville-Poyferré – *St-Julien*.

Third Growths (3èmes crus)
Boyd-Cantenac, Cantenac-Brown, d'Issan, Kirwan, Palmer – *Cantenac-Margaux*; Giscours – *Labarde-Margaux*; la Lagune – *Ludon-Haut-Médoc*; Desmirail, Ferrière, Malescot-St-Exupéry, Marquis d'Alesme-Becker – *Margaux*; Calon-Ségur – *St-Estèphe;* Lagrange, Langoa-Barton – *St-Julien*.

Fourth Growths (4èmes crus)
Pouget, Prieuré-Lichine – *Cantenac-Margaux*; Marquis-de-Terme – *Margaux*; Duhart-Milon-Rothschild – *Pauillac*; Lafon-Rochet – *St-Estèphe*; Beychevelle, Branaire (formerly Branaire-Ducru), St-Pierre, Talbot – *St-Julien*; la Tour-Carnet – *St-Laurent-Haut-Médoc*.

Fifth Growths (5èmes crus)
du Tertre – *Arsac-Margaux*; Dauzac – *Labarde-Margaux*; Cantemerle – *Macau-Haut-Médoc;* d'Armailhac (formerly Mouton-Baronne-Philippe), Batailley, Clerc-Milon-Rothschild, Croizet-Bages, Grand-Puy-Ducasse, Grand-Puy-Lacoste, Haut-Bages-Libéral, Haut-Batailley, Lynch-Bages, Lynch-Moussas, Pédesclaux, Pontet-Canet – *Pauillac*; Cos Labory – *St-Estèphe*; Belgrave, de Camensac – *St-Laurent-Haut-Médoc*.

SAUTERNES CLASSIFICATIONS

Grand 1er cru d'Yquem – *Sauternes*.

1er crus Climens, Coutet – *Barsac*; Haut-Peyraguey, Lafaurie-Peyraguey, Rabaud-Promis, Rayne-Vigneau, Sigalas-Rabaud, la Tour-Blanche – *Bommes*; Rieussec – *Fargues*; Suduiraut – *Preignac*; Guiraud – *Sauternes*.

2èmes crus Broustet, Caillou, Doisy-Daëne, Doisy-Dubroca, Doisy-Védrines, Nairac, de Myrat, Suau – *Barsac*; Romer-du-Hayot – *Fargues*; de Malle – *Preignac*; d'Arche, Filhot, Lamothe, Lamothe-Guignard – *Sauternes*.

BATAILLEY *5ème cru classé Pauillac* ★★★ £ The wines have been getting a lot better. Drinkable young, they age well too. 1990 is excellent, and relatively affordable. Look out for the 1995, too, but '97 and '98 were less successful.

BELAIR *1er cru classé St-Émilion* ★★★★ Biodynamic since 1994, Belair steadfastly ignores the fashion for ever more richness and focuses instead on seriousness and finesse. The 1996 has lovely structure.

BEYCHEVELLE *4ème cru classé St-Julien* ★★★ The most expensive Fourth Growth; only the best vintages merit the high price. It takes time to mature to a beautifully balanced, scented, blackcurranty red. 1989 and '90 are sublime, but there is still sometimes a tendency to overproduce. '95 and '96 are both worthy of the property.

BRANAIRE *4ème cru classé St-Julien* ★★★★ (formerly Branaire-Ducru) Soft, smooth red with plums and chocolate flavours, achieving a classic, cedary St-Julien perfume in maturity. The 1980s were erratic, but 1989 and '90 saw a return to form. Recent vintages are excellent.

BRANE-CANTENAC *2ème cru classé Margaux* ★★ A famous property which was underachieving when most of the other Second Growths were shooting ahead. Late-'90s vintages look far more positive.

BROUSTET *2ème cru classé Barsac* ★★★ A reliable, fairly rich sweet white not often seen, but worth trying: the 1988 and '90 are especially good. Dry white is disappointing.

CALON-SÉGUR *3ème cru classé St-Estèphe* ★★★(★) Intensely traditional claret that needs time. 1982 is wonderful, if you can find it; '95, '96 and '98 are all impressive.

CANON *1er grand cru classé St-Émilion* ★★★★(★) Mature Canon reeks of the soft, buttery Merlot grape as only a top St-Émilion can. It's marvellously rich stuff, though 1998 was the first really good vintage of the '90s.

CANON-LA-GAFFELIÈRE *1er grand cru classé St-Émilion* ★★★★(★) German owners have invested a fortune here, and everything is of the most modern, including the wine: rich, seductive, luscious. Very good 1990, '93 and '97.

CANTEMERLE *5ème cru classé Haut-Médoc* ★★★(★) Often up to Second Growth standards. Sometimes a little light, as in 1995, but it's always attractive.

CARBONNIEUX *cru classé Pessac-Léognan* ★★★(★) Balanced reds and oaky whites. 1996 may have the edge over '95, but both are good.

CHASSE-SPLEEN *cru bourgeois Moulis* ★★★(★) A tremendously consistent wine, at the top of the *bourgeois* tree. It sells above the price of many Classed Growths, but it's worth it. Look for the superb 1995 and the very good 1996.

CHEVAL-BLANC *1er grand cru classé St-Émilion* ★★★★★ There's some sturdy richness here, but wonderful spice and fruit too, perhaps due to the very high proportion of Cabernet Franc. Good years are succulent. 1995 is as good as claret gets.

DOMAINE DE CHEVALIER *cru classé Pessac-Léognan* ★★★★(★) The red has a superb balance of fruit and oak, and the white is simply one of France's greatest. Very successful in 1995, '96 and '98. Look also for the refined red and sweetly oaky white second wines, Esprit de Chevalier.

CISSAC *cru grand bourgeois Haut-Médoc* ★★★ £ Well-structured wine made in traditional, slow-maturing style, and one of the best-known *bourgeois* reds. It is best in richly ripe years like 1982 and '85. 1996 is spicy, '95 full of cassis, '97 very good.

CLIMENS *1er cru Barsac* ★★★★★ Undoubtedly the best property in Barsac, making some of the most consistently fine sweet wines in France. 1990 was the best recent year, though '91 is good, too. The delicious second wine, les Cyprès, is well worth seeking out in off vintages.

COS D'ESTOURNEL *2ème cru classé St-Estèphe* ★★★★★ **£** The undoubted leader of St-Estèphe. The wines are dark, tannic and oaky: classically made for long aging. Fairly priced, too. 1995 and '96 are both lovely, and '97 looks as good.

COUHINS-LURTON *cru classé Pessac-Léognan* ★★★★ 100 per cent Sauvignon dry white fermented in new oak barrels, producing a blend of grassy fruit and oaky spice. Recent vintages have been excellent.

COUTET *1er cru Barsac* ★★(★) A great sweet wine property but never a match for neighbouring Climens; also a dry white.

DOISY-DAËNE *2ème cru Barsac* ★★★(★) Very good, consistent, relatively light, but extremely attractive sweet wine, plus a particularly good dry white.

DOISY-VÉDRINES *2ème cru Barsac* ★★★★ **£** A rich, concentrated sweet white which is usually good value. 1989 and '90 are very good, and '95 is good.

DUCRU-BEAUCAILLOU *2ème cru classé St-Julien* ★★★★(★) Great depth and warmth, and lovely balance. Back on form again after a few problematic years in the late '80s: '95, '96 and '97 are excellent.

L'ÉVANGILE *Pomerol* ★★★(★) Top-line Pomerol, lacking the sheer intensity of its neighbour Pétrus, but irresistibly perfumed and rich. In huge demand, so it's expensive. 1993 was very good; '97 also looks terrific.

DE FARGUES *cru bourgeois Sauternes* ★★★★(★) Stunning, rich wines in the best years. Sells at exactly half the price of Yquem, so it ain't cheap.

DE FIEUZAL *cru classé Pessac-Léognan* ★★★★(★) One of the stars of Pessac-Léognan, the white only just behind Domaine de Chevalier. The red starts plum-rich and buttery, but develops earthiness and cedar scent allied to lovely fruit. The 1995 and 1996 are equally good. The unclassified white is scented, complex, deep and exciting. Even the '92 is good.

FIGEAC *1er grand cru classé St-Émilion* ★★★★ Figeac shares many of the qualities of Cheval Blanc but it's always ranked as the ever-reliable star of the second team. A pity, as its beauty and blackcurranty, minty scent are rare in St-Émilion. Seductive '89 and '90, tremendous '95, excellent '96 and good '98.

FILHOT *2ème cru Sauternes* ★★(★) The wines are fairly light, and not particularly complex, although Crème de Tête, made in the best years like 1990, is a winner.

LA FLEUR-PÉTRUS *Pomerol* ★★★★ This red is in the top flight, having some of the mineral roughness of much Pomerol, but also tremendous perfume and length. The 1989 is excellent, as is the 1996, and the 1995 is not far behind.

FOURCAS-DUPRÉ *cru bourgeois Listrac* ★★(★) A top performer in this generally underperforming AC: tough and closed when young, but opening up beautifully into rich fruit and spice. Look for the 1995.

FOURCAS-HOSTEN *cru bourgeois Listrac* ★★(★) Slightly better than its very good neighbour, Fourcas-Dupré, and making wines in a similarly long-lived style. All the '90s vintages have been good.

GAZIN *Pomerol* ★★★★ Lovely perfume and sweetness. 1989 and '90 are really very fine. 1995 is first rate, even better than the very good 1996. Also a great '98.

GILETTE *cru bourgeois Sauternes* ★★★★ This property ages its sweet whites in concrete tanks for 20 to 30 years before releasing them. Usually delicious, with a dry richness unique in Sauternes thanks to the long maturation and absence of wood.

GISCOURS *3ème cru classé Margaux* ★★★ Exceedingly nice wines in '91, '92 and '93, and considerable stylishness in 1995 and '96. But the 1980s were difficult here and a scandal over switched vats in 1998 has raised doubts again.

GLORIA *cru bourgeois St-Julien* ★★★ The quality of this quick-maturing red has not always lived up to its hype. But 1995 is super, '96 is very good and '94 is good for the vintage. Gloria is never cheap, though.

GRAND-PUY-DUCASSE *5ème cru classé Pauillac* ★★★ **£** Nice, but lagging far behind Grand-Puy-Lacoste in quality.

GRAND-PUY-LACOSTE *5ème cru classé Pauillac* ★★★★ **£** Perfume, power and consistency: Pauillac at its brilliant best. Blackcurrant and cigar-box perfumes are rarely in better harmony than here. Consistent even in the poor years of the early '90s. 1989 is gorgeously perfumed with robust fruit; '90, '95 and '96 are super.

GRUAUD-LAROSE *2ème cru classé St-Julien* ★★★★(★) Often starts rich, chunky and sweetish but will achieve its full cedary glory in time, while still retaining a lovely sweet centre. The early nineties were all good, '90 was almost unnervingly juicy and ripe and '95, '96, '97 and '98 are all on form.

GUIRAUD *1er cru Sauternes* ★★★★(★) The wines are difficult to taste when young but are very special, and the 1983, '86, '88, '89 and '90 are outstanding.

HAUT-BAILLY *cru classé Pessac-Léognan* ★★★★ Haut-Bailly red (there is no white) tastes sweet, rich and perfumed from its youth. But the wines do age well. 1993 was outstanding for the year, and '95 and '96 are both terrific.

HAUT-BATAILLEY *5ème cru classé Pauillac* ★★★ Stylish, relatively light wine, although 1989 is marvellously concentrated. 1986 and '88 are the best of earlier wines; '95 and '96 look very promising.

HAUT-BRION *1er cru classé Pessac-Léognan* ★★★★★ The wines are not big, but are almost creamy in their gorgeous ripe taste, slightly resembling the great Médocs. Although 1982 is insubstantial, the next four vintages are all very fine, and '88 and '89 are outstanding, while '90 could not quite compete. 1996 is outstanding, '95 even better. 1997 is very good. Also makes a little fine, long-lived white (appealing when young, too). '85 and '94 is spectacular.

D'ISSAN *3ème cru classé Margaux* ★★(★) Traditionally one of the truest Margaux wines, austere when young, but perfumed and deep after ten to 12 years. Fabulous in 1983, '88 and '90, first rate in '85, '86 and '89, with a good '87 too; but d'Issan underperformed in the '90s.

KIRWAN *3ème cru classé Margaux* ★★★★ Hugely improved, thanks largely to the efforts of oenologist Michel Rolland. Riper, richer – you name it.

LAFAURIE-PEYRAGUEY *1er cru Sauternes* ★★★★(★) Fine sweet wine property back on form. Good in difficult years, and stunning in '83, '86, '88 and '90; 1997 also looks very good.

LAFITE-ROTHSCHILD *1er cru classé Pauillac* ★★★★★ Most difficult of all the great Médocs to get to know. It doesn't stand for power like Latour, or perfume like Mouton, but for the elegant, restrained balance that is the perfection of great claret. 1986, '88, '89, '90, '95 and '96 are the best recent vintages, followed by '82.

LAFLEUR *Pomerol* ★★★★★ The only Pomerol with the potential to be as great as Pétrus. They couldn't be further apart in style, and Lafleur has an astonishing austere concentration of dark fruit and tobacco spice perfume. The 1982 almost knocks you sideways with its naked power, and the '83 and '85 are also remarkable. 1989 is superb, as is '95, and '96 is almost as good.

LAFON-ROCHET *4ème cru classé St-Estèphe* ★★★(★) Much improved, with as much body and a little more perfume than most. 1982, '83 and '85 are all good, though not stunning, while '86, '87, '88, '89 and '90 show real class and a welcome consistency of style. 1995, '96 and '97 are good.

LAGRANGE *3ème cru classé St-Julien* ★★★(★) Impressive, but not quite great: the vineyard is not one of St-Julien's best, but there is masses of technical expertise. Look particularly for the 1995 and 1996.

LA LAGUNE *3ème cru classé Haut-Médoc* ★★★★ Making Second Growth-standard red, with a rich, soft intensity. The wine was consistently good, until the disappointing 1994. The 1982 is rich and juicy, with '85 and '88 not far behind, and '83 on their tails. 1986 is burly but brilliant stuff, as is '89. 1987 is more delicate but good. 1995 and '96 are back on form.

LAMOTHE-GUIGNARD *2ème cru Sauternes* ★★★ Recent years have seen dramatic improvements here. 1983, '86, '88, '89 and '90 show how good it can be.

LANESSAN *cru bourgeois Haut-Médoc* ★★★ Ever correct, consistently attractive. 1982, '83 and '88 are exhibiting classic claret flavours now, and '90 is a wine of balance and depth. Very promising 1995 and 1996.

LANGOA-BARTON *3ème cru classé St-Julien* ★★★★ **£** Very good, in the dry, cedary style, and sometimes regarded as a lesser version of Léoville-Barton. 1982 and '85 are exciting, '86 and '87 typical, but the '88 may be the best for 30 years. The '89 and '96 almost matched Léoville-Barton for elegance and '90 and '95 were its equal. 1997 looks good.

INSTANT CELLAR:
UNSUNG HEROES

- **1999 Château Haut-Rian, £5.99, Bennetts** White Bordeaux made from Sauvignon and Sémillon, with considerable depth.
- **1996 Château de Musset, Montagne-St-Émilion, £11.55, Philglas & Swiggot** A St-Émilion satellite area, and a château that is, as they say, under new management. Good rich fruit, and good value.
- **1996 Château la Patache, Pomerol, £15.86, Savage Selection** A tiny property making wine of real finesse at an excellent price.
- **1998 Château la Fleur Beauséjour, Côtes de Castillon, £4.45, Corney & Barrow** That's the in-bond price, without duty and VAT, but 1998 is a very good year, and this has lots of depth and perfume.
- **1995 Château Robin, Côtes de Castillon, £9.90, Justerini & Brooks** The best recent vintage, and a good producer.
- **1996 Château la Prade, Côtes de Francs, £7.50, The Wine Society** A largely Merlot wine from a very good year; it combines juicy fruit with plenty of character.

LARRIVET-HAUT-BRION *Pessac-Léognan* ★★★★ The red 1996 here is superb wine with lots of finesse, but '98 wasn't so hot. Lovely white.

LASCOMBES *2ème cru classé Margaux* ★★★ Good vintages are attractive, but too many are flat and unenjoyable. 1986 is the most serious effort for a long time. '89, '90 and '95 keep up the good work; '96 doesn't seem quite so good, but '97 is better.

LATOUR *1er cru classé Pauillac* ★★★★★ The easiest of all the First Growths to comprehend. It's a huge, dark, hard brute when young, eventually spreading out to a superb, blackcurrant and cedar flavour. It used to take ages to come round, but some

> **ON THE CASE**
> *Think before you buy red Bordeaux: could you get the same quality more cheaply from the New World? Often you could*

recent vintages have seemed a little softer and lighter, whilst retaining their tremendous core of fruit. Let's hope they age as well as the previous ones, because although the '82 is a classic, both '81 and '83 are definitely not. '86 and '88 seem to be back on course, and '89 and '90 look splendidly powerful. '91, '92, and the superb '96 are the best wines of their years. The second wine, les Forts-de-Latour, is getting better and better. A third wine, Pauillac de Latour, is made in most years.

LAVILLE-HAUT-BRION *cru classé Pessac-Léognan* ★★★★ This should be one of the greatest of all white Pessac-Léognan, since it is owned by Haut-Brion, but despite some great successes, the general effect is patchy. But 1992 and 1993 are wonderful.

LÉOVILLE-BARTON *2ème cru classé St-Julien* ★★★★★ **£** Traditionalist's dream. Anthony Barton ignores fashion and simply goes on making superlative, old-fashioned wine for long aging. All the vintages of the 1980s have been attractive, and '95, '96, '97 and '98 are tremendous. 1991, '92 and '93 are also among the best of their vintages. All the wines are *wonderfully* fairly priced.

LÉOVILLE-LAS-CASES *2ème cru classé St-Julien* ★★★★★ The most brilliant of the St-Juliens, combining all that sweet, honeyed ripeness with strong, dry, cedary perfume. The 1982 is more exciting every time a bottle is broached, and all the vintages of the 1980s are top examples of their year. The 1995 is wonderful, the '96 nearly as good, and prices are startlingly high. But perhaps these recent vintages are just a bit *too* deep and concentrated.

LÉOVILLE-POYFERRÉ *2ème cru classé St-Julien* ★★★★ Things have been looking up here for some while, and 1995 is wonderful. The 1994 is remarkably good and 1996, too, is extremely attractive.

LILIAN-LADOUYS *cru bourgeois St-Estèphe* ★★(★) A newish property, its wines are certainly promising, with a good 1989 and '90. 1995 is good, 1996 seems a bit muddy but '97 is good again.

LOUDENNE *cru bourgeois Médoc* ★(★) Both red and white are fruity and agreeable, and best drunk young.

LA LOUVIÈRE *cru bourgeois Pessac-Léognan* ★★★★ Lovely, modern, oak-aged whites. Reds are also very good, and quite earthy. Quality seems to be on a roll.

LYNCH-BAGES *5ème cru classé Pauillac* ★★★★★ Astonishingly soft and drinkable when very young, yet it ages brilliantly, and has one of the most beautiful scents of minty blackcurrant in all Bordeaux. Most likely to show that character are '83, '86 and '87, but for sheer starry-eyed brilliance '85, '88 and particularly '82, '95 and '96 are the ones. The '89 is unusually big and powerful; the '90 marginally more restrained.

MAGDELAINE *1er grand cru classé St-Émilion* ★★★★ Combines the soft richness of Merlot with the sturdiness needed to age. Expensive, but one of the best. 1982, '85 and '95 are classics, '88, '89 and '96 tremendously good.

MALARTIC-LAGRAVIÈRE *cru classé Pessac-Léognan* ★★★ Improving under its new ownership, but still a tough, traditional style. 1997 and '98 continue the good work.

MALESCOT-ST-EXUPÉRY *3ème cru classé Margaux* ★★★ Seemed to have lost its way in the '80s: the wines were becoming too light. Improved in '88, '89 and '90, and continued with a very good 1995.

DE MALLE *2ème cru Sauternes* ★★★ Good, relatively light sweet white. It went through a bad patch in the 1980s, but since '88 the wines have been back on course.

MARGAUX *1er cru classé Margaux* ★★★★★ Refinement and sheer, ravishing perfume: weightier and more consistent than in the past, yet with all its beauty intact. 1982, '83 and '86 are about as brilliant as claret can be, while the '88 may well be the wine of the vintage. The deep, concentrated '89 doesn't seem to match up to the '88, but the '90 is as fragrant and powerful as the '86 – which is saying a lot. In the difficult '91 and '92 vintages the wines were better than most First Growths, and the '95 is stunning.

MEYNEY *cru bourgeois St-Estèphe* ★★★(★) **£** This epitomizes St-Estèphe reliability, yet is better than that. It is big, meaty and strong, but never harsh. Recent wines are increasingly impressive, and although it is difficult to taste young, the '82, '83, '85, '86, '88 and '89 are all remarkable, and the '84, '87 and '90 are good. The 1995 is lovely, 1996 seems a touch disappointing.

LA MISSION-HAUT-BRION *cru classé Pessac-Léognan* ★★★★★ La Mission likes to put itself in a class apart, between Haut-Brion and the rest. Yet one often feels this red relies more on weight and massive, dark fruit and oak flavours than on any great subtleties. Even so it has considerable richness, and 1982, '85, '86, '89, '90, '91 and '95 are the best recent vintages, with great consistency and fragrance.

MONTROSE *2ème cru classé St-Estèphe* ★★★★ Famous for its dark, tannic character, and its slow, ponderous march to maturity. 1989 and '90, and even '91 and '92, saw a return to form after some lightish years. 1995, 1996 and 1997 are excellent.

MOUTON-ROTHSCHILD *1er cru classé Pauillac* ★★★★★ An astonishing flavour, piling intense cigar-box and lead-pencil perfume on to the rich blackcurrant fruit. The 1982 is already a legend, '86 and '89 are likely to join it, and '83, '84 and '85 are well worth the asking price. 1988 and '90 are below par, but the '95 is fabulous.

NENIN *Pomerol* ★★ A thoroughly old-fashioned red, rather chunky and solid with quite a tough core for a Pomerol, which doesn't always attain mellow fruitfulness. The 1985 and '86 aren't bad, but the '82, the '83 and the '88 were pretty feeble here. Recent vintages have improved, though, with a much better 1995 and 1996.

PALMER *3ème cru classé Margaux* ★★★★ Palmer can occasionally out-perform some First Growths in tastings. The 1980s weren't so good, and the '83 lacks some of its neighbours' class. But 1990 was better than most of them. 1996 is very good.

PAPE-CLÉMENT *cru classé Pessac-Léognan* ★★★★(★) Capable of mixing considerable sweetness from ripe fruit and new oak with a good deal of tough structure. Outstanding since 1985, with the 1990 and 1995 both examples of Pessac-Léognan at its best.

PAVIE *1er grand cru St-Émilion* ★★★(★) Generally good but not wonderful, stylish but not grand. But it has the gentle flavours of true St-Émilion. The best recent releases show a deeper, more passionate style which puts it into the top flight, but others lack guts. 1985, '86, '87, '88, '89, '90, '95 and '96 are good examples.

PETIT-VILLAGE *Pomerol* ★★★★ Not usually one of the softest, most plummy Pomerols. The wine is worth laying down, but the price is always high. 1983, '85 and the juicy '82 are all very good, but the '88, '89, '90 and '95 look likely to be the best yet.

PÉTRUS *Pomerol* ★★★★★ One of the world's most expensive reds, and often one of the greatest, its fame has been acquired since 1945. Christian Moueix says his intention is to ensure no bottle of Pétrus ever disappoints. 1982, '89, '90 and '95 were stupendous; 1985 and '96 aren't far off.

DE PEZ *cru bourgeois St-Estèphe* ★★★ Almost always of Classed Growth standard: big, rather plummy and not too harsh. 1982 and '83 and the excellent '86 are the sort of thing. 1995 and 1996 are both successful.

PHÉLAN-SÉGUR *cru bourgeois St-Estèphe* ★★★ £ Classed Growth quality at a *bourgeois* price. Good rich fruit, and it ages well. 1995 and '96 are well worth a punt.

PICHON-LONGUEVILLE *2ème cru classé Pauillac* ★★★★(★) Often described as more masculine than its 'sister', Pichon-Longueville-Lalande, this very correct Pauillac (formerly Pichon-Longueville-Baron) turned out a tremendous 1995, a very good 1996 and '97 and a good 1994. The '87 was very good, the '88 superb, the '89 even better, broodingly intense, while the '90 is one of the Médoc's greatest.

PICHON-LONGUEVILLE-LALANDE *2ème cru classé Pauillac* ★★★★★ Rich, concentrated red of great quality. Its price has risen inexorably and it wishes to be seen as equal to St-Julien's leading pair, Léoville-Las-Cases and Ducru-Beaucaillou. 1982, '83, '85 and '86 all brim with exciting flavours. '87 and '88 are good, but both '89 and '90 are below par, and outclassed by its neighbour Pichon-Longueville. But since then Lalande has been right back on form, and seems to have the edge on Longueville in '95 and '96.

LE PIN *Pomerol* ★★★★★ This is it: the most expensive red wine in the world. Is it the best? Well, it's very, very good, and utterly seductive. It's tiny – less than two hectares carved out in the late 1970s – and it reached cult status only in the late '80s. If you didn't buy it then you probably can't afford it now. 1997 is lovely, though.

PONTET-CANET *5ème cru classé Pauillac* ★★★ Famous but unpredictable, and still trying to regain its traditionally reliable form. The 1985 and '86 are hopeful, '87 and '88 less so, '90 hopeful again, and '95 and '97 very good.

POTENSAC *cru bourgeois Médoc* ★★★★ £ Delicious blackcurrant fruit, greatly improved by a strong taste of oak. Not expensive for the quality. Beats many *crus classés* every year for sheer flavour. Both the 1995 and '96 look good buys.

POUJEAUX *cru bourgeois Moulis* ★★★★ Good, spicy, rich wine with plenty of concentration; made to last. 1990, '93, '94, '95 and '97 are all excellent.

PRIEURÉ-LICHINE *4ème cru classé Margaux* ★★★ £ Reliable, fairly priced and, though not that perfumed, good and sound. 1983, '86, '88 and '89 are good, but '90 was the first real excitement for some time. Further improved in '91 and '92; now on top form with good '94, better '95 and '96.

RABAUD-PROMIS *1er cru Sauternes* ★★★(★) At last! The 1986, '88, '89 and '90 are excellent and show a long-awaited return to First Growth sweet wine quality.

RAHOUL *cru bourgeois Graves* ★★(★) A leader of the modern oak-aged white style, and generally good red. 1988, '89 and '90 were not as special as previous years, but still good. The mid-'90s were better.

RAUZAN-GASSIES *2ème cru classé Margaux* ★★(★) For years below most Third Growths in quality, but the 1995 and '96 suggest that attitudes could be changing.

RAUZAN-SÉGLA *2ème cru classé Margaux* ★★★★(★) 1983, '85 and '86 were triumphs. 1987 was declassified as Château Lamouroux but is still delicious. The '88, '89, '90, '93 and '94 are all very good. 1996 wasn't quite as good as it

CLARETS OUT OF THEIR CLASS

One of the great excitements in wine is to catch a château at the beginning of a revival in its fortunes. While reputations are being built or re-built, quality keeps ahead of the price for a while – though some wines have maintained high quality at fair prices year after year. For good value, look out for the names below.

Médoc *Minor châteaux performing like top bourgeois:* Tour-de-By, Tour Haut-Caussan, Tour du Haut-Moulin, Tour-St-Bonnet.

Top bourgeois performing like Classed Growths: d'Angludet, Chasse-Spleen, Citran, Fourcas-Dupré, Fourcas-Hosten, Haut-Marbuzet, Labégorce-Zédé, Lanessan, Meyney, Monbrison, Ormes-de-Pez, Phélan-Ségur, Pibran, Potensac, Poujeaux, Siran, Sociando-Mallet, Tour-de-Mons.

Classed Growths performing above their station: Clerc-Milon, Cos d'Estournel, Ducru-Beaucaillou, Grand-Puy-Lacoste, la Lagune, Léoville-Barton, Léoville-Las-Cases, Lynch-Bages, Montrose, Pichon-Longueville, Pichon-Lalande, Pontet-Canet, Rauzan-Ségla.

Graves and Pessac-Léognan
Outperformers: White: de Fieuzal, Montalivet, Olivier, Smith-Haut-Lafitte. *Red:* de Fieuzal, Haut-Bailly, Larrivet-Haut-Brion, la Tour-Martillac, Pape-Clément, Roquetaillade la Grange.

Pomerol
Outperformers: Beauregard, Bon-Pasteur, Certan-de-May, Clinet, l'Église-Clinet, l'Évangile, Gazin, Vieux Château 132 .

St-Émilion
Outperformers: l'Arrosée, Beau-Séjour-Bécot, Bellefont-Belcier, la Dominique, Grand-Mayne, Larmande, Pavie-Macquin, Tertre Rôteboeuf, Troplong-Mondot.

Sauternes
Outperformers: Bastor-Lamontagne, Chartreuse, Climens, Doisy-Daëne, de Fargues, Gilette, Liot, de Malle, Nairac, Roumieu Lacoste, St-Amand.

Satellites
Outperformers: Canon de Brem, Canon Moueix, Charlemagne, Cassagne-Haut-Canon – *Canon-Fronsac*; Lyonnat – *Lussac-St-Émilion*; Tour-du-Pas-St-Georges – *St-Georges-St-Émilion*; la Prade, de Francs – *Côte de Francs*; des Annereaux, Bertineau-St-Vincent – *Lalande-de-Pomerol*.

should have been, but '95 was excellent and '98 back on top form.

RAYMOND LAFON *cru bourgeois Sauternes* ★★★★ Owned by the former manager of neighbouring d'Yquem, this is fine wine but overpriced.

RIEUSSEC *1er cru Sauternes* ★★★★★ One of the richest, most exotic Sauternes; particularly good during the 1980s. The 1982 is good, the '83, '86 and '88 really special, the '89 and '90 wonderful. 1996, '97 and '98 confirm Rieussec's status.

ST-AMAND *cru bourgeois Sauternes* ★★★(★) £ Splendid property making truly rich wines that age well, and are affordable. Also seen as Château de la Chartreuse.

ST-PIERRE *4ème cru classé Médoc* ★★★★ Small St-Julien property producing

ON THE CASE
Prices of good white Graves currently look quite appealing compared to cult whites from other regions – and they age sensationally well

superb, slow-maturing, old-fashioned red. Produced wonderful wines in the 1980s, and judging by 1995 and 1996 is still well on form.

DE SALES *Pomerol* ★★★ £ A really enormous estate producing a wine which, though it is good round claret, doesn't often excite. 1995 and '96 are, well, respectable.

SÉNÉJAC *cru bourgeois Haut-Médoc* ★★(★) Finesse rather than concentration. It made an excellent 1995 and has in fact been good pretty well every year. The white, made entirely from Sémillon, will age.

SIRAN *cru bourgeois Margaux* ★★★ All vintages have been good lately, and 1995 and 1996 look well worth buying.

SMITH-HAUT-LAFITTE *cru classé Pessac-Léognan* ★★★★ Increasingly concentrated reds and whites that are benefiting from huge investment. All 1990s vintages have been terrific.

SUDUIRAUT *1er cru Sauternes* ★★★(★) Rich, exciting Sauternes, frequently deeper and more intense than any except d'Yquem. A remarkable 1982 was followed by a fine '83, a very good '85, but disappointing '86 and '88. 1989 and '90 were a leap up again and '95 looks good.

TALBOT *4ème cru classé St-Julien* ★★★ Has seemed in recent years to be lagging behind in quality. The mid- to late 1980s vintages haven't shaped up as well as they should have done, with the 1988 in particular showing poorly (though the '82, '83 and '84 were very good). The '90 seems to lack concentration, and the early '90s are disappointing. 1995 and '96 look better.

DU TERTRE *5ème cru classé Margaux* ★★★(★) Slightly uneven of late. At best it has a lot of body for a Margaux, and the flavour is direct and pure. 1985 is rich and dense but keeps its perfume intact, while '82, '83 and '86 are rich and blackcurranty – already good and sure to improve for ten years more. 1988 was not quite so good, but '89 was back to normal. 1995 was a disappointing effort, '96 an improvement.

LA TOUR-DE-BY *cru bourgeois Médoc* ★★★ Well-made: plenty of juicy fruit, good structure and a touch of rusticity. Increasingly reliable: look for '95, '96, '97.

TROTANOY *Pomerol* ★★★★ If you didn't know Pétrus existed, you'd say this had to be the perfect Pomerol – rich, plummy, chocolaty fruit, some mineral hardness, and tremendous fat perfume. The 1982 is brilliant, and although the '85 is also wonderfully good, the mid- and late 1980s weren't quite as thrilling. 1992 and '93 were good in difficult years; '95 is glorious.

VALANDRAUD *St-Émilion* ★★★★ Super-rich wine for the super-rich. The idea at this micro-property is to do everything with extreme care. How the wines will age is unproven, since the first vintage was '91.

VIEUX CHÂTEAU CERTAN *Pomerol* ★★★★(★) Practically as good as Pétrus, but more austere in style. 1995 is terrific, 1996 very good, 1997 lovely.

D'YQUEM *grand 1er cru classé Sauternes* ★★★★★ The pinnacle of achievement in great sweet wines. Almost every vintage of d'Yquem is a masterpiece and its outlandish price is almost justified, since d'Yquem at its best is undoubtedly the greatest sweet wine in the world. And it lasts – well, forever, really. There's also a dry white made here, called Ygrec, which can be remarkable.

BORDEAUX VINTAGES

Generic wines like Bordeaux Rouge rarely need any aging. A *petit château* wine from a good vintage might need five years to be at its best, a good *bourgeois* might need ten, and a *premier cru* might need 20. Pomerols and St-Émilions come round faster than Médocs.

1999 An erratic vintage, spoiled by last-minute rain. Dry whites should be good, reds supple and ripe. Sauternes suffered from rot of the wrong sort.

1998 A Merlot year rather than a Cabernet one; Pomerol and St-Émilion look very good. There'll be some good Sauternes, too.

1997 A mixed vintage of mostly soft, ripe wines, attractive for relatively early drinking: a good year, but not as good as 1996, which isn't as good as 1995. Being overhyped.

1996 The 1994s were hyped, the 1995s were hyped, and the 1996s too. Increasingly they look good but not great, and they're certainly expensive. Sauternes are good in parts.

1995 Red wines of charm and structure, with a handful of really great wines at the top. Not much noble rot in Sauternes, though the dry whites of the Graves look good.

1994 Most successful in Pomerol, though most regions produced reds with good concentration, but often not much more.

1993 A dilute year, in which the good wines are drinking nicely now. St-Émilion and Pomerol are probably best. Decent dry whites but little of quality in Sauternes.

1992 An unripe vintage: stick to reliable names and drink early.

1991 Wildly variable for reds, and few thrills in Sauternes. Dry whites were good. Most should have been drunk by now.

1990 Excellent quality; the third of a great trio of vintages. Reds are immensely rich, as are Sauternes; lesser regions like Loupiac also came up trumps. It was a bit too hot for the dry whites, though.

1989 A wonderful Médoc year, although Pomerol and St-Émilion also did well. Graves and Pessac-Léognan were uneven, as was Sauternes. Dry whites were rather overripe.

1988 Classically balanced reds and very fine Sauternes.

1987 These have proved to be soft, wonderfully drinkable reds – but drink them now: they won't keep. Dry whites were better than sweet; again, they need drinking.

1986 Superb Sauternes, dripping with noble rot, and drinking beautifully now. Reds are good, sometimes very good, but not quite as good as 1988.

1985 Pretty well all the reds are delicious now. Sauternes are pleasant but light.

1984 A fruitless, joyless year in which the Merlot failed.

1983 Classics, especially in Margaux, and delicious now. Superb, rich, exciting Sauternes.

1982 Fabulous fat, ripe, juicy wines. The best still need a year or two; some of the lesser wines are lovely now and shouldn't be kept much longer. Sauternes was mixed in quality.

EARLIER BORDEAUX VINTAGES

1981 Good but not spectacular. Quite light wines, which need drinking. A slightly graceless year in Sauternes.

1980 Nice light, grassy claret, which should have been drunk by now. The best Sauternes are still drinking well.

1979 All but the very best should be drunk up. There was attractive, mid-weight Sauternes.

1978 All but the top wines are starting to dry out now. Graves and St-Émilion are lovely, and won't improve.

1976 Rather soft and sweet; not inspiring, drink up. Best Sauternes are still fat and rich.

1975 Very tannic wines; frequently they went stale and brown before they had time to soften. The best may yet bloom; I'm not sure when. Nice, well-balanced Sauternes.

1966 All the wines are ready, and some are tipping over the edge.

1961 One of the classic vintages of the century, but now beginning to fade a little. Well, they had an amazing innings.

Most other vintages of the 1960s will now be risky; '64s can still be good, rather solid wines and '62, one of the most gorgeous, fragrant vintages since the war, is showing its age. If your godfather's treating you, and offers '59, '55 or '53, accept with enthusiasm. If he offers you '49, '47 or '45, get it in writing before he can change his mind.

MATURITY CHART

1990 Cru Classé Sauternes

May turn out to be one of the greatest vintages of the century

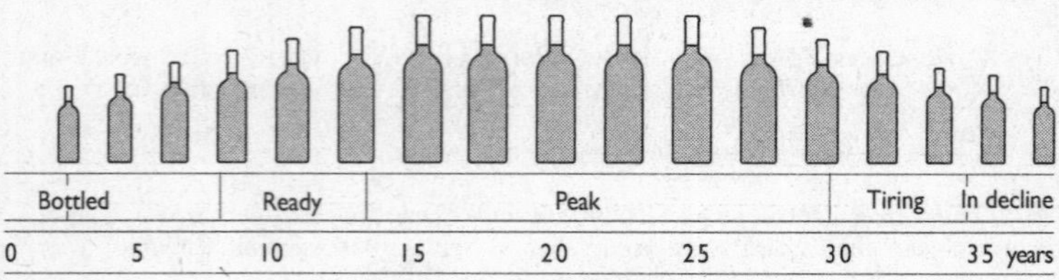

1995 Cru Classé White Pessac-Léognan

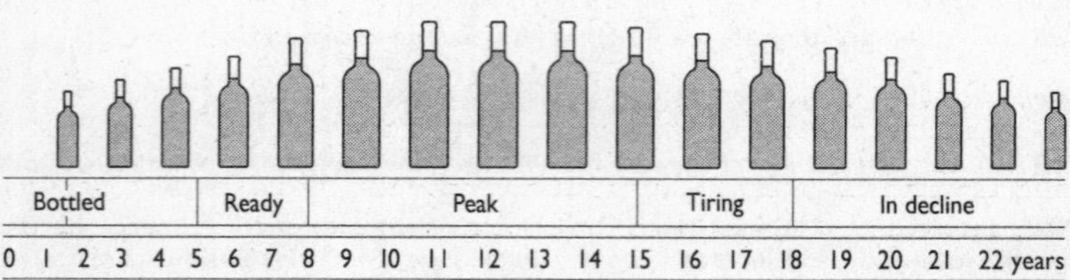

MATURITY CHART

1995 Cru Classé Médoc

A vintage for the medium to long term

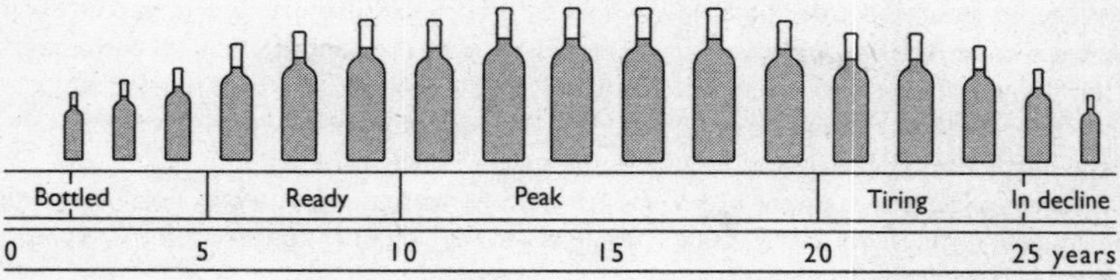

1995 Good Cru Bourgeois Médoc

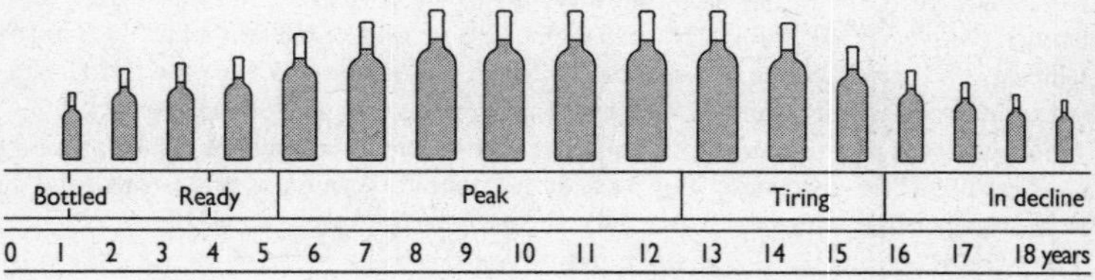

1996 Cru Classé Médoc

A good year, but less long-lived than 95

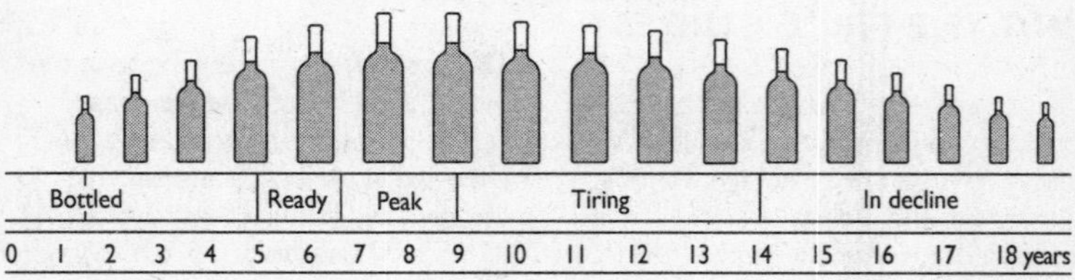

1996 Good Cru Bourgeois Médoc

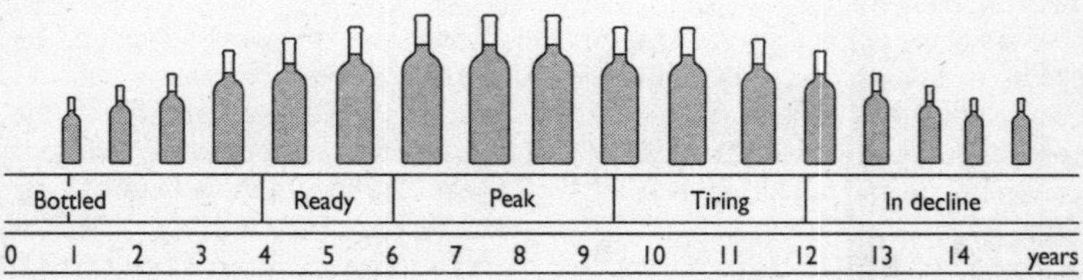

BUYING CLARET EN PRIMEUR

In the spring after the vintage the Bordeaux châteaux make their opening offers. This means that their capital is not tied up in very expensive stock for the next year or two, until the wines are bottled and ready to ship. In theory this also means that you can buy the wine at a preferential price – but do not forget that the cost of shipping, duties and other taxes will appear on your final bill. Traditionally merchants would buy for stock while offering their customers the chance to take advantage of the opening prices as well. In the heady days of the 1980s, however, the market really took off.

There is a lot to be said for buying en primeur. For one thing, you may be able to find the finest and rarest wines far more cheaply than they will ever appear again. This was especially true of the 1990 vintage.

But you should be aware of the risks: as they say in the investment world, prices can go down as well as up. They may easily not increase significantly in the few years after the campaign (witness prices for 1985s and 1989s). The second risk is that a tasting assessment is difficult at an early date. However, consideration can be given to both the producer's reputation for consistency and to the general vintage assessment for the region.

Another risk is that the merchant you bought the wine from may not still be around to deliver it to you two years later. Buy from a merchant you can trust, one with a solid trading base in other wines.

Once the wines are shipped you may want your merchant to store the wine for you. If so, you should insist that (1) you receive a stock certificate; (2) your wines are stored separately from the merchant's own stocks; and (3) your cases are identifiable as your property and are labelled accordingly. All good merchants will offer these safeguards as a minimum service. Of course, in an ideal world your house is equipped with its own temperature-controlled cellar, because the best solution is certainly to take possession of your cases yourself.

USING THE PRICE GUIDES

In the Red Bordeaux Price Guides the châteaux are listed alphabetically regardless of appellation or class, with prices for each château given in order of vintage from the most recent to the oldest.

In the Médoc, there is a middle level of châteaux – *cru bourgeois* – below the *crus classés*. The *bourgeois* properties adhere to fairly strict rules governing winemaking, and are often excellent value.

There are some dramatic price variations here. Note that while most of the prices are per bottle, inclusive of all duty and VAT charges, others are per case, with extra to pay on top before you can have the wine delivered.

A wine quoted **EC** (ex-cellars) is offered on an *en primeur* basis (i.e. as a young wine) in Bordeaux or at the château in the summer following the vintage; one quoted **IB** (in bond) is offered in bond in the UK. All EC and IB prices are **per case**.

The EC price simply includes the price of the wine in the bottle and excludes shipping, duties and taxes such as VAT. The IB price includes shipping, but still excludes duties and taxes.

The EC price is usually payable when the wine is offered *en primeur*. Other costs (including VAT on both invoices) become payable when the wine is shipped. The *crus classés* and better *bourgeois* are shipped two years after the wine is offered, the *petits châteaux* and the lesser *bourgeois* after a year. You should check beforehand the exact terms of sale with your merchant who will give you a projection of the final 'duty paid delivered' price at current rates of shipping, duty and VAT.

RED BORDEAUX PRICES

d'Aiguilhe *Côtes de Castillon*
1998 IB £65.00 (FA)
1998 EC £75.00 (CAV)
1997 £7.99 (WAI)
1996 £8.71 (BIB)
1995 £8.49 (WR) £8.49 (THR) £8.49 (VIC) £8.49 (BOT)

Amiral-de-Beychevelle *St-Julien*
1995 £18.55 (GN)

Andron-Blanquet *cru grand bourgeois exceptionnel St-Estèphe*
1995 £13.10 (GN) £13.92 (PIP) £13.99 (AME) £14.95 (HED)

Angélus *1er grand cru classé St-Émilion*
1998 £63.65 (GOE)
1998 IB £580.00 (FA) £650.00 (WY) £680.00 (FRI)
1997 £63.00 (JU)
1997 IB £420.00 (FA) £594.00 (RAE)
1996 £52.39 (GOE) £69.50 (FRI)
1996 IB £480.00 (FA) £495.00 (BIB) £850.00 (CAV)
1995 £94.00 (WY)
1995 IB £750.00 (FA) £895.00 (CAV)
1994 £65.00 (BAL)
1994 IB £460.00 (FA) £650.00 (CAV)
1993 £53.85 (HA)
1990 £165.68 (WY)
1990 IB £1,200.00 (CAV) £1,250.00 (FA)
1989 IB £925.00 (FA) £1,200.00 (CAV)
1988 IB £620.00 (FA)
1985 £110.00 (UB)
1983 IB £280.00 (FA)
1970 IB £250.00 (FA)
1959 £179.48 (WY)

d'Angludet *cru bourgeois supérieur exceptionnel Margaux*
1998 EC £110.00 (ELL) £120.00 (JON) £126.00 (TAN)
1997 £10.77 (HA) £11.99 (BO) £12.45 (BER) £14.30 (AD) £119.00 (TAN)
1996 £22.10 (TAN) £22.50 (CON)
1995 £19.95 (CON) £20.00 (FLE) £24.70 (AME) £29.50 (WR)
1994 £16.25 (HIG) £18.49 (BOD) £18.49 (SUN) £19.39 (REI)
1993 £18.50 (FLE) £19.39 (REI)
1988 £30.55 (GW)
1986 £31.00 (CRO) £45.00 (FORT)
1983 £27.50 (BU) £31.00 (HIG) £44.95 (ROB)
1982 £35.00 (BU)
1981 £24.85 (WY)
1978 £42.00 (CRO)

des Annereaux *Lalande-de-Pomerol*
1997 £12.44 (PLAY)
1996 £8.95 (GN) £9.99 (POR) £10.99 (AME)
1995 £9.25 (CON)

Anthonic *cru bourgeois supérieur Moulis*
1998 IB £99.00 (CB)
1997 £9.99 (CB) £13.97 (PLA)

d'Armailhac (was Mouton-Baronne-Philippe) *5ème cru classé Pauillac*
1998 EC £195.00 (CAV)
1997 £15.01 (HA) £16.67 (MI) £17.00 (HIG)
1996 £18.50 (SOM) £18.99 (BOD) £18.99 (SUN) £19.50 (HIG) £20.83 (MI) £31.49 (VIN)
1995 £19.99 (UN)
1995 IB £185.00 (FA)
1994 £27.67 (PLAY)

MERCHANTS SPECIALIZING IN BORDEAUX

see Merchant Directory (page 456) for details

Adnams (AD), Averys (AV), Ballantynes (BAL), Bennetts (BEN), Berry Bros. & Rudd (BER), Bibendum (BIB), Bordeaux Index, Butlers (BU), Anthony Byrne (BY), Cave Cru Classé (CAV), Châteaux Wines (CHA), Corney & Barrow (CB), Croque-en-Bouche (CRO), Direct Wine (DI), Farr Vintners (FA), First Quench Group (BOT, THR, VIC, WR), Fortnum & Mason (FORT), Friarwood (FRI), Goedhuis & Co (GOE), Great Western (GW), John Harvey (HA), High Breck (HIG), Justerini & Brooks (JU), Lay & Wheeler (LAY), Millésima (MI), Montrachet (MON), Oddbins (OD), Christopher Piper (PIP), Raeburn Fine Wines (RAE), Reid (REI), T&W Wines (TW), Tanners (TAN), Turville Valley, Ubiquitous Chip (UB), Wine Society (WS), Peter Wylie (WY), Noel Young (YOU).

1993 £19.95 (CON) £24.45 (TAN)
1992 £30.50 (ROB)
1990 £27.00 (FLE)
1989 £59.00 (UB)
1982 IB £380.00 (FA)
1966 IB £265.00 (FA)
1961 £165.68 (WY)
1947 £146.88 (REI)
1945 £586.77 (WY)
1941 £332.74 (WY)
1914 £448.71 (WY)
1908 £269.23 (WY)

Arnauld *Haut-Médoc*
1997 £7.34 (GOE)
1996 £11.09 (WAT) £11.82 (HA)
1995 £11.95 (ROB) £14.07 (HA)

l'Arrosée *grand cru classé St-Émilion*
1998 £28.89 (GOE)
1997 £31.67 (MI)
1996 £30.00 (MI) £35.00 (WS) £38.00 (JU)
1995 £28.40 (GOE)
1994 IB £192.00 (RAE) £200.00 (BIB)
1989 £32.50 (MI)
1988 £34.00 (CRO)
1985 £79.50 (BAL) £129.78 (WY)
1982 £82.00 (BAL)
1961 IB £2,000.00 (FA)

Ausone *1er grand cru classé St-Émilion*
1998 IB £1,250.00 (FA) £1,320.00 (WY) £1,400.00 (FRI)
1998 magnum IB £1,260.00 (FA)
1996 £177.50 (MI)
1995 £220.00 (JU)
1994 £139.17 (MI)
1994 IB £680.00 (FA) £740.00 (BIB)
1993 £90.22 (BY)
1990 £241.67 (MI)
1989 IB £980.00 (FA)
1988 £95.00 (CON)
1985 £95.00 (YOU) £110.00 (FRI) £149.99 (PLAY)
1983 £88.00 (CRO) £195.00 (UB)
1983 IB £960.00 (FA)
1982 £223.25 (CAV)

EC *(ex-cellar) price per dozen, excluding shipping, duty and VAT.*
IB *(in bond) price per dozen, excluding duty and VAT.*
All other prices, per bottle incl VAT.

1981 IB £700.00 (FA)
1981 magnum IB £700.00 (FA)
1979 £120.00 (ROB)
1959 IB £2,280.00 (FA)
1955 magnum £528.75 (REI)
1950 £264.38 (FA)
1934 £230.00 (JU)
1928 £380.00 (JU)

Bahans-Haut-Brion *Graves*
1998 £23.50 (GOE)
1998 IB £290.00 (WY)
1997 £21.05 (GOE) £26.00 (JU)
1996 IB £300.00 (BIB)
1995 £25.46 (GOE) £32.90 (WY) £35.00 (JU)
1995 IB £300.00 (BIB)
1995 ½ bottle £16.45 (WY)
1986 £56.95 (ROB)

Balestard-la-Tonnelle *grand cru classé St-Émilion*
1995 £36.00 (STA)

Baret *Pessac-Léognan*
1996 £11.75 (HIG)

Barreyres *cru bourgeois Haut-Médoc*
1997 £7.49 (SAI)
1995 £7.52 (CB)

Batailley *5ème cru classé Pauillac*
1997 £16.99 (HA) £17.50 (HIG) £19.95 (DI) £21.95 (AV)
1996 £17.50 (HIG) £19.50 (ELL) £19.95 (BER)
1995 £19.58 (HIG) £19.99 (UN) £22.50 (ELL) £23.50 (GOE) £29.96 (REI)
1989 £30.85 (WRI)
1986 £34.99 (SUN)
1985 £21.00 (WRI) £33.29 (GOE) £86.00 (UB)
1982 £45.24 (REI)
1970 £31.00 (CRO)
1966 £52.00 (YOU)
1960 £25.26 (REI)
1945 £229.13 (REI)

Beau-Séjour-Bécot *1er grand cru classé St-Émilion*
1998 EC £285.00 (CAV) £356.00 (TAN)
1997 £35.70 (TAN)
1997 IB £338.40 (CB)
1996 £32.99 (OD) £35.95 (LEA) £49.75 (BER)
1995 IB £285.00 (FA)
1994 £20.60 (TAN) £25.75 (STE) £27.95 (LEA)
1990 IB £380.00 (FA)
1989 IB £275.00 (FA)

Beau-Site *cru grand bourgeois exceptionnel St-Estèphe*
1997 £15.50 (AV)
1995 £13.75 (WS) £14.45 (HAH) £14.75 (BER)
1970 £25.00 (BU)

Beau-Site-Haut-Vignoble *cru bourgeois St-Estèphe*
1986 £17.50 (MI)

Beaumont *cru grand bourgeois Haut-Médoc*
1996 £11.99 (CON)
1995 £10.30 (NO) £10.83 (MI) £12.95 (WS) £15.18 (GOE) £15.65 (JER) £17.99 (SAI)
1994 £9.50 (WS) £11.63 (HA)
1990 £29.45 (AV) £45.50 (UB)
1989 £29.95 (CON)

Beausejour *Côtes de Castillon*
1998 IB £53.40 (CB)
1998 magnum IB £56.40 (CB)
1953 £88.13 (REI)
1924 £117.50 (REI)

Beauséjour-Duffau-Lagarrosse *1er grand cru classé St-Émilion*
1997 £36.00 (JU)
1996 £50.00 (JU)
1990 £225.00 (CAV) £265.00 (BAL)

Bel-Air *Pomerol*
1997 IB £192.00 (CB)

Bel-Air *Puisseguin-St-Émilion*
1997 £8.85 (HAH)

Bel-Air-Marquis d'Aligre *cru bourgeois supérieur exceptionnel Margaux*
1986 £24.17 (MI)

Belair *1er grand cru classé St-Émilion*
1983 £39.50 (BU)
1961 £85.00 (BU)

de Belcier *Côtes de Castillon*
1994 £7.29 (GN) £8.99 (AME)
1993 £6.99 (CON)

Belgrave *5ème cru classé Haut-Médoc*
1997 £15.00 (MI)
1996 £14.89 (YOU) £17.50 (MI) £19.50 (HED)
1995 £23.50 (PEN)
1988 £25.00 (BU)
1985 IB £160.00 (FA)

Belles-Graves *Lalande-de-Pomerol*
1996 £18.11 (GOE)

Bellevue *grand cru classé St-Émilion*
1995 £16.45 (NI)

Bertin *Montagne-St-Émilion*
1998 IB £69.00 (CB)
1997 IB £77.40 (CB)
1996 £7.64 (CB)
1995 £8.17 (CB)

Bertineau-St-Vincent *Lalande-de-Pomerol*
1995 £9.99 (WAI)

Beychevelle *4ème cru classé St-Julien*
1997 £22.50 (MI)
1996 £28.33 (MI) £30.49 (FRI) £30.53 (PLAY)
1996 double magnum £94.00 (WY)
1995 £26.67 (MI) £29.00 (HIG) £29.38 (GW) £29.50 (UN) £29.95 (CON) £32.90 (WY)
1995 double magnum £152.75 (WY)
1994 £24.50 (UN) £25.00 (MI) £27.50 (BAL) £30.80 (HA) £35.50 (STA)
1992 £22.50 (MI) £28.19 (WY)
1990 magnum IB £400.00 (FA)
1989 £44.06 (GOE) £80.13 (PLAY) £110.00 (UB)
1989 IB £420.00 (FA)
1988 £45.00 (FRI) £47.00 (YOU) £51.36 (BY)
1987 IB £195.00 (FA)
1986 £54.00 (FRI) £59.16 (PIP) £60.95 (ROB)
1986 IB £425.00 (FA)
1985 £55.23 (WY)
1984 £26.99 (FRI)
1983 £48.95 (ROB) £59.37 (WY)
1983 IB £330.00 (FA)
1983 magnum £120.00 (FRI)
1982 £63.00 (YOU) £90.00 (FRI) £98.72 (PLAY)
1982 IB £620.00 (FA)
1975 £41.13 (PLA)
1966 £60.00 (YOU)
1966 ½ bottle £34.52 (WY)
1961 £151.87 (WY)
1961 IB £1200.00 (BIB)
1959 £146.88 (REI) £172.58 (WY)
1959 IB £1600.00 (FA)
1945 £676.51 (WY)
1937 £96.64 (WY)
1928 IB £3,600.00 (FA)
1922 ½ bottle £31.76 (WY)

le Bon-Pasteur *Pomerol*
1998 £79.00 (POR)
1997 £28.33 (MI)
1996 £32.25 (CB)
1995 £38.00 (TAN) £49.75 (STA)
1995 IB £295.00 (CAV)
1994 £27.50 (MI)
1993 £27.50 (BU)
1982 IB £1,650.00 (FA)

Bonnet *Bordeaux Supérieur*
1997 £7.49 (WR) £7.49 (BOT)
1996 £7.45 (NI) £7.49 (THR) £7.49 (VIC)

le Boscq *cru bourgeois supérieur St-Estèphe*
1997 £13.00 (JU) £14.45 (TAN) £15.00 (MI) £15.99 (UN)
1996 £14.00 (JU) £17.50 (MI)
1995 £16.67 (MI)

de Bourgueneuf *Pomerol*
1995 £32.00 (WS)
1994 £18.50 (WS)

Bouscaut *cru classé Pessac-Léognan*
1959 £88.13 (REI)

Boyd-Cantenac *3ème cru classé Margaux*
1989 IB £250.00 (FA)
1985 £33.49 (REI)
1960 £35.00 (BU)

Branaire *4ème cru classé St-Julien*
1998 EC £150.00 (CAV)
1997 £22.50 (MI) £26.90 (TAN)
1996 £24.95 (LEA) £27.26 (CB) £27.90 (TAN) £28.33 (MI) £28.50 (NI)
1996 IB £190.00 (FA) £210.00 (RAE)
1995 £25.00 (FLE) £33.50 (LEA)
1995 IB £220.00 (FA)
1990 £44.17 (MI) £48.00 (AME)
1989 £59.50 (BU)
1989 IB £395.00 (FA)
1988 £49.60 (UB)
1986 £44.00 (GW)
1986 IB £320.00 (FA)
1985 IB £320.00 (FA)
1982 £52.90 (TAN)
1982 IB £420.00 (FA)
1981 IB £240.00 (FA)
1970 £48.00 (CRO)
1959 IB £950.00 (FA)
1929 £250.00 (CRO)

Brane-Cantenac *2ème cru classé Margaux*
1997 £22.50 (MI)
1996 £26.79 (CB)
1995 £35.00 (UN)
1994 £24.75 (UN)
1985 IB £360.00 (FA)
1985 magnum IB £360.00 (FA)
1984 £12.95 (BU)
1984 IB £130.00 (FA)
1983 £48.50 (ROB)
1982 £34.66 (REI)
1982 IB £380.00 (FA)
1979 magnum £75.00 (BU)
1978 £16.57 (WY) £36.85 (NI)
1970 £27.50 (BU) £33.49 (REI)
1967 £19.39 (REI) £26.99 (RAE)
1961 £76.38 (REI) £103.55 (WY)
1957 £64.63 (REI)
1928 £290.00 (JU)
1928 IB £3,000.00 (FA)
1920 £200.00 (CRO)

du Breuil *cru bourgeois supérieur Haut-Médoc*
1996 £9.95 (DI)
1994 £9.70 (TAN)

Cabannieux *Graves*
1995 £7.75 (CON)
1994 £9.93 (CB)

Calon-Ségur *3ème cru classé St-Estèphe*
1998 £17.14 (GOE)
1998 IB £170.00 (FA)
1997 £15.18 (GOE) £17.48 (HA) £18.50 (JU) £20.40 (TAN) £22.50 (MI)
1997 IB £189.60 (CB)
1996 £31.95 (DI) £35.25 (WY) £35.99 (FRI) £36.67 (MI) £39.99 (CON)
1996 IB £265.00 (FA)
1995 £34.27 (GOE) £47.75 (TAN) £50.67 (FRI) £52.88 (WY) £70.82 (BY)
1995 IB £350.00 (FA) £450.00 (CAV)
1994 £23.50 (UN) £24.99 (POR) £34.00 (TAN)
1990 IB £450.00 (FA)
1989 £51.77 (WY)
1989 IB £385.00 (FA)

All châteaux are listed alphabetically regardless of class.

1988 £43.50 (WRI)
1985 £47.75 (WY) £55.95 (ROB)
1983 £46.94 (WY)
1982 IB £600.00 (FA)
1981 £27.50 (BU) £31.76 (WY)
1970 £52.46 (WY)
1966 £50.00 (BU)
1961 £85.00 (BU)
1959 £99.88 (REI) £179.48 (WY)
1947 £290.00 (CRO)

de Camensac *5ème cru classé Haut-Médoc*
1990 £29.50 (BU)
1982 £18.50 (BAL)
1978 £25.00 (BU)
1975 £17.04 (REI)

Cana *Côtes de Bourg*
1996 £6.59 (FRI)
1995 £6.59 (FRI)

Canon *1er grand cru classé St-Émilion*
1997 £12.50 (HAH) £23.50 (GOE) £25.88 (HA)
1997 IB £316.00 (CB)
1996 £23.01 (GOE) £34.37 (CB)
1995 £25.00 (CON) £31.99 (FRI) £33.33 (MI) £33.49 (REI) £37.50 (UN)
1995 IB £205.00 (FA)
1994 £27.50 (MI) £35.99 (JON)
1993 £28.33 (MI) £28.79 (REI)
1990 £58.95 (ROB)
1989 IB £420.00 (FA)
1988 £45.00 (FRI)
1986 £54.00 (FRI) £70.37 (PLAY)
1986 IB £400.00 (FA)
1985 £52.86 (REI)
1983 IB £400.00 (FA)
1982 £90.00 (JU) £112.50 (BEN)
1982 IB £850.00 (FA)
1981 £34.50 (BEN) £38.19 (REI)
1979 £34.95 (BEN)
1979 IB £320.00 (FA)
1975 IB £240.00 (FA)
1964 IB £900.00 (FA)
1955 £186.39 (WY)

Canon-de-Brem *Canon-Fronsac*
1997 IB £127.80 (CB)
1996 £12.46 (CB)
1995 £14.40 (CB)
1994 £9.85 (WAI) £11.99 (CB)
1993 £11.75 (WS)
1990 IB £180.00 (FA)

Canon-la-Gaffelière *grand cru classé St-Émilion*
1998 IB £345.00 (LEA)
1997 £37.50 (MI) £39.95 (TAN) £40.24 (CB) £42.00 (LEA)
1996 £32.80 (GOE) £35.00 (CON) £38.48 (CB) £39.17 (MI)
1996 IB £260.00 (FA) £295.00 (CAV)
1995 £29.95 (CON) £34.96 (GOE) £37.01 (REI)
1994 £28.00 (JU)
1990 IB £450.00 (FA)
1989 £75.94 (WY)

Canon-Moueix *Canon-Fronsac*
1997 £12.63 (CB)
1995 £14.10 (AD) £14.51 (CB)
1992 £11.75 (GOE)
1989 £20.56 (REI)

Cantemerle *5ème cru classé Haut-Médoc*
1998 £6.22 (BIB) £11.75 (GOE)
1997 £15.83 (MI) £18.95 (LEA)
1996 £18.35 (SOM) £19.17 (MI) £22.50 (CON) £24.00 (WRI) £29.99 (SAI)
1996 IB £150.00 (FA)
1995 £17.50 (MI) £20.56 (GOE) £22.25 (STE) £22.50 (UN) £23.99 (POR)
1993 £18.99 (BOT) £19.95 (WAI)
1990 £29.75 (WRI) £30.00 (HIG)
1989 £53.60 (TAN)
1989 IB £395.00 (FA)
1988 £29.50 (BU)
1983 £84.00 (UB)
1979 £29.50 (BU)
1970 £28.79 (REI)
1952 £117.50 (REI)
1947 £205.62 (REI)

Cantenac-Brown *3ème cru classé Margaux*
1997 £17.36 (HA) £18.33 (MI)
1995 £18.33 (MI) £21.99 (UN) £22.50 (BU)
1995 IB £150.00 (FA)
1994 £21.50 (UN)
1989 £55.00 (UB)
1926 £146.88 (REI)

Please remember that
Oz Clarke's Wine Buying Guide
*is a price **guide** and not a price **list**. It is not meant to replace up-to-date merchants' lists.*

Cap-de-Faugères *Côtes de Castillon*
1996 £7.97 (BIB)
1996 ½ bottle £4.47 (BIB)
1995 £7.85 (HAH)
1994 £7.05 (GOE)

Carbonnieux *cru classé Pessac-Léognan*
1998 £14.10 (GOE)
1998 magnum £28.20 (GOE)
1997 £16.67 (MI)
1996 £19.17 (MI) £21.44 (CB)
1996 magnum £44.06 (CB)
1995 £18.33 (MI)
1985 £26.44 (REI)
1959 £138.06 (WY)
1955 £52.88 (FA)
1928 IB £1,250.00 (FA)

de Cardaillan *Graves*
1993 £9.95 (COC)

la Cardonne *cru grand bourgeois Médoc*
1996 £9.99 (OD) £9.99 (POR)
1995 £9.99 (SAI) £10.74 (PIP) £10.95 (STA) £11.75 (PEN) £14.50 (CRO)

les Carmes-Haut-Brion *Pessac-Léognan*
1997 £25.03 (CB)
1997 IB £185.00 (BIB)
1995 £18.80 (WY)

Caronne-Ste-Gemme *cru grand bourgeois exceptionnel Haut-Médoc*
1996 IB £92.00 (FA)
1995 £11.40 (NO) £11.95 (SOM) £13.95 (ROB)
1995 IB £85.00 (FA)
1994 £11.99 (BUD) £13.40 (TAN) £14.99 (POR)
1993 £10.95 (CON)

Carruades de Lafite (Moulin des Carruades until 1987) *Pauillac*
1998 £170.00 (HIG)
1998 IB £188.00 (LEA)
1997 £21.00 (HIG) £21.00 (JU) £39.99 (PHI)
1997 IB £189.00 (RAE)
1996 £24.48 (GOE) £25.00 (JU) £27.03 (WY) £30.00 (MI)
1995 £28.33 (MI)
1995 IB £215.00 (FA)
1990 IB £410.00 (BIB)
1985 £33.95 (ROB)
1983 £39.95 (ROB)
1934 £234.71 (WY)

Carsin *Ières Côtes de Bordeaux*
1996 £6.99 (SAI)

Carteau-Côtes-Daugay *grand cru St-Émilion*
1996 £10.50 (WS)

Cazebonne *Graves*
1996 £8.85 (JER)

Certan-Giraud *Pomerol*
1997 IB £316.20 (CB)
1995 IB £376.20 (CB)
1990 £28.79 (REI)

Certan-de-May *Pomerol*
1998 IB £620.00 (FA) £620.00 (BIB)
1997 £46.00 (JU) £55.23 (CB)
1996 £45.80 (LAY) £54.34 (CB) £70.00 (JU)
1994 £28.99 (YOU) £35.25 (CB) £65.00 (JU)
1993 £28.99 (YOU) £33.49 (REI)
1991 £33.49 (REI)
1990 IB £620.00 (FA)
1989 IB £480.00 (FA)
1988 £80.00 (FORT)
1988 IB £550.00 (FA)
1986 IB £500.00 (FA) £650.00 (CAV)
1982 IB £1,900.00 (FA)

la Chapelle de la Mission *Pessac-Léognan*
1996 IB £180.00 (FA)
1995 IB £240.00 (BIB)

Charmail *cru bourgeois Haut-Médoc*
1997 £13.95 (LEA)
1995 £11.99 (UN)
1994 £8.99 (UN)

Charron *Ières Côtes de Blaye*
1996 £7.90 (TAN)
1992 £9.99 (TW)

Chasse-Spleen *cru grand bourgeois exceptionnel Moulis*
1998 EC £152.00 (TAN)
1997 £16.67 (MI) £18.55 (TAN) £18.95 (FORT)
1996 £16.47 (HA) £19.50 (ELL) £20.00 (JU) £20.83 (MI) £21.15 (CB) £21.95 (ROB) £23.65 (FRI) £30.20 (BY)
1996 IB £150.00 (FA)
1995 £17.95 (CON) £22.50 (UN) £24.99 (FRI)
1995 IB £170.00 (FA)
1995 magnum £49.50 (LEA)

1994 £18.33 (MI) £21.80 (PIP) £30.00 (FORT)
1993 £16.67 (MI) £17.14 (GOE)
1990 £37.50 (ROB)
1989 £34.35 (NO) £46.60 (TAN)
1989 IB £290.00 (FA)
1987 magnum £56.00 (RES)
1986 £36.00 (CRO) £49.50 (ROB)
1985 £42.00 (CRO)
1983 £25.00 (BU) £30.00 (CRO) £35.95 (TAN)
1983 IB £220.00 (FA) £340.00 (BIB)
1982 £44.60 (TAN) £50.52 (GW)
1971 IB £200.00 (FA)
1967 IB £155.00 (FA)

Chauvin *grand cru classé St-Émilion*
1995 £25.00 (JU)
1989 £21.50 (WS)
1982 £18.50 (BU)

Cheval-Blanc *1er grand cru classé St-Émilion*
1998 IB £1,600.00 (FA)
1997 £77.84 (GOE) £93.33 (MI) £99.00 (JU)
1997 IB £110.45 (CB) £765.00 (BIB)
1997 EC £995.85 (HAH)
1996 £105.00 (TAN) £111.21 (CB) £135.00 (FRI) £160.00 (JU) £173.33 (MI)
1996 IB £950.00 (FA) £1,050.00 (BIB)
1995 £141.98 (GOE) £155.00 (ELL) £165.00 (FRI) £173.33 (MI)
1995 IB £1,180.00 (FA) £1,250.00 (BIB)
1994 £64.63 (GOE) £68.88 (HA) £77.08 (WY) £98.00 (JU) £110.00 (ROB) £121.67 (MI) £146.88 (PEN)
1994 magnum £139.04 (GOE)
1993 £47.62 (FLE) £79.17 (MI)
1993 IB £700.00 (FA) £750.00 (BIB)
1993 magnum IB £640.00 (FA)
1990 £410.00 (ROB)
1990 IB £2,750.00 (FA)
1989 £130.00 (BEN)
1989 IB £1,180.00 (FA)
1989 magnum IB £1,180.00 (FA)
1988 £99.50 (BEN)
1988 magnum IB £1,000.00 (FA)
1986 £125.00 (CON) £138.06 (WY) £146.88 (REI) £175.00 (FORT) £210.56 (BY)
1986 IB £1,180.00 (FA)
1986 magnum £296.84 (WY)
1985 £150.00 (YOU) £200.20 (WY) £225.00 (ROB) £296.00 (UB)
1985 IB £1,420.00 (FA)
1983 £193.29 (WY)
1982 £414.19 (WY) £525.00 (FORT) £665.00 (ROB)
1982 IB £3,400.00 (BIB) £3,500.00 (FA) £3,700.00 (CAV)
1981 £123.49 (BY) £130.00 (ROB)
1981 IB £880.00 (FA)
1979 IB £820.00 (FA)
1978 £130.00 (JU)
1978 IB £920.00 (FA)
1976 £56.40 (FA) £105.43 (BY)
1975 £185.00 (ROB)
1974 £50.00 (BU)
1970 £193.29 (WY) £195.00 (ROB)
1970 ½ bottle £82.84 (WY)
1970 magnum IB £1,200.00 (FA)
1966 £200.20 (WY)
1966 IB £1,800.00 (FA)
1964 £320.00 (BEN) £352.50 (FA)
1959 £207.09 (WY)
1958 magnum £317.54 (WY)
1953 £379.68 (WY)
1953 IB £5,000.00 (FA)
1953 ½ bottle £158.78 (WY)
1949 ½ bottle £317.54 (WY)
1947 £1,903.50 (FA) £3,658.66 (WY)
1947 ½ bottle £989.35 (REI)
1945 £1,366.82 (WY)

Cheval-Noir *St-Émilion*
1995 £9.75 (WS)

Chicane *Graves*
1997 £9.60 (TAN)

Cissac *cru grand bourgeois exceptionnel Haut-Médoc*
1998 EC £98.00 (TAN)
1997 £10.14 (HA) £12.50 (TAN)
1996 £10.70 (HA) £14.00 (JU) £14.95 (DI) £17.95 (CON)
1996 magnum £38.99 (UN)
1995 £13.95 (CON) £15.95 (DI) £15.99 (JON)
1995 magnum £37.99 (UN)
1994 IB £135.00 (BIB)
1994 magnum £34.99 (UN)
1992 £14.95 (CON) £16.50 (ROB) £16.70 (AV)
1990 £25.00 (TAN) £29.20 (JER)
1989 £24.68 (GW) £26.20 (TAN)
1989 IB £150.00 (FA)
1988 £19.50 (BU) £27.60 (TAN)
1985 £22.50 (BU)
1981 £20.56 (REI)
1978 £31.95 (ROB)
1978 magnum £59.95 (ROB)
1975 magnum £55.95 (ROB)

Citran *cru grand bourgeois exceptionnel Haut-Médoc*
1997 £14.50 (FORT)
1996 £14.17 (MI) £16.49 (BOD) £16.49 (SUN)
1995 £19.39 (DOM)
1994 £11.95 (WAI) £15.99 (SAI)
1993 £13.71 (GOE) £15.86 (DOM)

la Clare *cru bourgeois Médoc*
1996 £8.87 (PLA)

Clarke *cru bourgeois Listrac*
1995 £13.95 (ROB)

la Claverie *Côtes de Francs*
1988 £9.50 (CRO)

Clerc-Milon *5ème cru classé Pauillac*
1997 £20.83 (MI) £29.95 (DI)
1996 £24.95 (DI) £26.41 (CB) £33.33 (MI)
1996 IB £220.00 (FA)
1995 £21.50 (DI) £29.50 (UN) £37.01 (REI) £41.13 (WY)
1995 IB £295.00 (FA)
1994 £24.50 (UN)
1993 £17.50 (WS)
1992 £34.95 (ROB)
1989 £56.30 (UB)
1988 £28.79 (REI)
1986 £41.13 (PLA)
1985 £59.37 (WY)

Clinet *Pomerol*
1998 IB £590.00 (FA) £690.00 (WY)
1997 £48.00 (JU)
1997 IB £420.00 (FA)
1996 £64.62 (WY)
1995 IB £820.00 (FA) £1,050.00 (CAV)
1994 £63.51 (WY)
1993 IB £330.00 (FA)
1992 £52.46 (WY) £55.23 (WY)
1992 IB £511.13 (WY)
1990 £158.78 (WY)
1990 IB £900.00 (FA)
1989 IB £2400.00 (CAV)
1982 £117.36 (WY)

Clos Beauregard *Pomerol*
1995 £15.50 (FLE)

Clos du Clocher *Pomerol*
1997 £15.50 (JU)
1995 £20.00 (JU)
1995 IB £145.00 (FA)

Clos de l'Eglise *Lalande-de-Pomerol*
1998 IB £750.00 (FRI)
1997 £52.00 (JU)
1996 IB £159.00 (RAE)
1993 £18.30 (HAH)
1983 IB £180.00 (FA)
1982 £48.50 (NI)

Clos Fourtet *1er grand cru classé St-Émilion*
1998 IB £300.00 (FRI)
1997 £29.17 (MI)
1996 £29.37 (GOE) £30.00 (MI) £32.31 (REI) £48.00 (STA)
1996 IB £240.00 (FA) £295.00 (CAV)
1995 £29.99 (FRI)
1995 IB £290.00 (BIB)
1994 £23.33 (MI) £23.99 (GOE)
1989 IB £220.00 (FA)
1988 IB £195.00 (FA)
1960 £35.00 (BU)
1949 £331.35 (WY)

Clos des Jacobins *grand cru classé St-Émilion*
1995 £23.95 (BER)
1989 IB £240.00 (FA)
1988 IB £200.00 (FA)
1979 £22.50 (BU)

Clos Magne-Figeac *grand cru St-Émilion*
1994 £9.99 (SAI)

Clos du Marquis *St-Julien*
1998 £16.16 (GOE)
1998 IB £165.00 (BIB) £174.00 (LEA) £185.00 (WY) £195.00 (LAY) £214.80 (CB)
1997 £19.58 (GOE) £25.00 (JU) £25.83 (MI) £26.13 (CB) £28.95 (LEA)
1997 EC £249.00 (JON)
1996 £25.99 (OD) £27.35 (SOM) £27.50 (MI) £30.60 (NI) £31.43 (CB)
1996 IB £220.00 (FA)
1995 £26.67 (MI) £30.00 (JU)
1995 IB £210.00 (FA) £220.00 (BIB)
1993 £23.33 (MI) £31.14 (REI)

1992 £18.33 (MI) £24.95 (LEA)
1989 IB £320.00 (FA)
1986 £32.31 (REI)
1986 IB £350.00 (FA)
1985 £33.49 (REI)
1985 IB £320.00 (FA)
1983 £18.50 (BU) £29.96 (REI)
1982 IB £400.00 (FA)

Clos René *Pomerol*
1998 IB £150.00 (FRI)
1997 £14.21 (HA) £15.00 (MI) £21.95 (DI)
1996 £15.18 (GOE) £15.83 (MI)
1995 £17.49 (BOD) £17.49 (SUN) £19.45 (BER) £24.99 (POR)
1994 £21.99 (TES) £24.99 (SAI)
1985 £46.70 (UB)
1978 £48.00 (CRO)
1961 £200.20 (WY)

du Clos Renon *Bordeaux*
1995 £7.39 (FRI)

Clos des Templiers *Lalande-de-Pomerol*
1996 £9.26 (HA)

Connétable Talbot *St-Julien*
1996 £16.67 (MI)
1996 IB £105.00 (FA) £120.00 (BIB)
1995 £15.00 (MI)
1994 £13.33 (MI) £20.95 (ROB)
1992 £9.99 (UN)

la Conseillante *Pomerol*
1998 IB £650.00 (FRI) £840.00 (CB)
1998 EC £650.00 (ELL)
1997 IB £440.00 (BIB)
1996 £51.67 (MI) £56.70 (LAY) £60.00 (JU) £68.15 (CB)
1996 IB £360.00 (FA) £450.00 (BIB) £495.00 (CAV)
1995 £48.47 (GOE) £56.50 (FRI) £59.67 (NO) £61.10 (WY) £62.79 (FLE) £70.00 (JU)
1995 IB £395.00 (FA)
1994 £32.80 (GOE) £40.83 (MI) £58.75 (PEN)
1993 £39.95 (BAL) £40.83 (MI)
1993 IB £300.00 (FA)
1990 £147.50 (MI)
1990 IB £1,300.00 (FA)
1989 IB £1,150.00 (FA)
1988 IB £420.00 (FA)
1985 £110.00 (CRO)
1982 £146.88 (REI) £158.63 (GW)
1982 IB £1,150.00 (FA)

1979 £41.13 (REI)
1975 IB £520.00 (FA)
1962 £88.13 (REI)
1953 £155.00 (CRO)
1947 £323.13 (REI)
1945 £324.45 (WY)

Corbin *grand cru classé St-Émilion*
1995 £17.99 (MAJ)
1994 £15.99 (AME)

Corbin-Michotte *grand cru classé St-Émilion*
1995 £34.99 (SAI)

Cos d'Estournel *2ème cru classé St-Estèphe*
1998 £33.78 (GOE)
1998 IB £350.00 (FRI) £365.00 (WY) £379.00 (LEA)
1998 EC £395.00 (CAV)
1998 double magnum £164.50 (GOE)
1998 jeroboam £264.38 (GOE)
1997 £38.68 (GOE) £51.00 (JU) £51.67 (MI) £53.30 (TAN) £55.00 (LEA) £55.52 (CB)
1997 IB £492.00 (RAE)
1997 jeroboam £293.75 (GOE)
1997 imperial £346.63 (GOE)
1996 £54.83 (WY) £59.57 (CB) £65.00 (ELL) £65.00 (MI) £67.50 (FRI) £75.00 (ROB)
1996 IB £520.00 (FA)
1996 magnum £117.50 (WY)
1996 magnum IB £520.00 (FA)
1996 double magnum £258.50 (WY)
1996 imperial £552.25 (WY)
1995 £50.00 (FORT) £50.92 (GOE) £58.50 (YOU) £60.14 (HA) £66.49 (FRI)
1994 £34.27 (GOE)
1994 IB £360.00 (FA)
1994 magnum IB £360.00 (FA)
1993 £31.33 (GOE) £35.00 (WS) £54.46 (BY) £59.50 (LEA)
1993 IB £280.00 (FA) £320.00 (BIB)
1990 £89.00 (BAL) £110.00 (PHI)
1990 magnum IB £720.00 (FA)
1989 £58.75 (GOE) £67.50 (FRI) £73.50 (LAY) £79.95 (TAN) £89.00 (BAL) £94.49 (PLAY)
1989 IB £600.00 (FA)
1988 £47.50 (CON)
1988 IB £480.00 (FA)
1987 £16.50 (BU) £31.14 (REI)
1986 £72.50 (CON) £75.00 (BU) £88.13 (REI) £90.00 (JU) £94.89 (BY)
1986 IB £720.00 (FA)

1985 £81.03 (PLA) £97.50 (BEN) £98.00 (BAL)
1985 IB £730.00 (FA)
1983 £45.00 (BU) £49.94 (REI)
1983 magnum IB £420.00 (FA)
1982 £120.00 (BEN)
1982 IB £1,020.00 (FA)
1982 magnum IB £1,250.00 (CAV)
1982 double magnum £946.50 (BIB)
1981 £33.49 (REI)
1981 IB £360.00 (FA)
1979 £49.94 (REI)
1978 £52.00 (YOU)
1978 IB £400.00 (FA)
1975 £37.01 (REI) £49.00 (YOU) £82.25 (PEN)
1970 £72.95 (ROB) £75.00 (BU) £89.75 (WY)
1970 IB £850.00 (CAV)
1955 £227.81 (WY)
1949 £400.38 (WY)
1928 IB £3,800.00 (FA)

Cos Labory *5ème cru classé St-Estèphe*
1995 £20.81 (PIP)
1993 £19.95 (ROB)
1990 £37.60 (GW) £41.13 (REI)
1989 £26.44 (REI)
1989 IB £250.00 (BIB)
1988 £27.50 (BU)
1986 £22.50 (BU) £54.00 (UB)

Coufran *cru bourgeois Haut-Médoc*
1996 £12.99 (SAI)
1994 £13.71 (GOE)
1973 £9.95 (BU)

la Couspaude *grand cru St-Émilion*
1998 £25.95 (GOE)
1998 IB £260.00 (FA)
1996 £33.95 (DI)
1996 IB £190.00 (FA)
1995 £25.83 (MI)
1995 IB £220.00 (FA)

Couvent-des-Jacobins *grand cru classé St-Émilion*
1996 £26.00 (WS)

EC (ex-cellar) price per dozen, excluding shipping, duty and VAT.
***IB** (in bond) price per dozen, excluding duty and VAT.*
All other prices, per bottle incl VAT.

le Crock *cru grand bourgeois exceptionnel St-Estèphe*
1996 IB £111.00 (RAE)
1995 £16.50 (ROB) £19.99 (POR)
1993 £16.10 (BIB)
1990 £24.68 (COC) £49.00 (UB)

la Croix *Pomerol*
1993 £22.43 (NO)
1989 £39.60 (NO)
1959 £50.00 (BU)

la Croix-du-Casse *Pomerol*
1998 EC £195.00 (CAV)
1997 £22.00 (JU) £24.95 (BER)
1996 £23.00 (JU)
1996 IB £150.00 (FA) £150.00 (BIB)
1994 £21.50 (BAL) £22.95 (STE) £23.00 (JU) £23.50 (STA)
1990 £26.44 (REI)

la Croix-de-Gay *Pomerol*
1998 IB £180.00 (FRI)
1995 £26.99 (FRI) £28.36 (PIP)
1995 IB £190.00 (BIB)
1993 IB £140.00 (FA)
1989 IB £265.00 (FA)
1988 IB £320.00 (BIB)

la Croix-des-Moines *Lalande-de-Pomerol*
1997 £10.86 (BIB)
1996 £10.86 (BIB) £11.75 (GOE)
1995 £8.50 (WS) £12.99 (JON)
1994 £10.99 (RAE)

Croizet-Bages *5ème cru classé Pauillac*
1995 £18.45 (HA) £22.50 (UN)
1994 £19.50 (UN)
1983 IB £180.00 (FA)
1945 £146.88 (REI)

Croque-Michotte *grand cru classé St-Émilion*
1995 £18.59 (FRI) £22.10 (PIP)
1979 £20.00 (BU)
1979 IB £165.00 (FA)
1970 £40.54 (REI)

Curé-Bon-la-Madeleine *grand cru classé St-Émilion*
1992 £25.73 (TW)

Dalem *Fronsac*
1997 £14.95 (DI)
1988 IB £100.00 (FA)

la Dame de Montrose *St-Estèphe*
1996 £20.83 (MI) £21.95 (LAY)
1995 £19.17 (MI) £25.00 (FORT)
1995 IB £150.00 (BIB)
1994 £17.50 (MI) £19.80 (REI)
1993 £16.67 (MI)
1992 £15.00 (MI)

Dassault *grand cru classé St-Émilion*
1997 £20.00 (FORT)
1995 £19.39 (REI)
1994 £23.95 (LEA)

de la Dauphine *Fronsac*
1997 £12.63 (CB)
1996 £10.69 (CB)
1995 £9.75 (WAI) £13.00 (JU)

Dauzac *5ème cru classé Margaux*
1996 £24.79 (FRI)
1995 £20.95 (BAL) £28.00 (FRI)

Deyrem-Valentin *cru bourgeois Margaux*
1998 £16.75 (STA)
1995 £13.25 (SOM)

Domaine de Chevalier *cru classé Pessac-Léognan*
1998 £230.00 (HIG)
1998 IB £240.00 (FRI)
1998 EC £245.00 (ELL) £250.00 (CAV)
1997 £27.50 (MI)
1997 IB £228.00 (RAE)
1996 £22.11 (HA) £25.95 (LEA) £28.15 (FRI) £30.00 (FORT) £30.83 (MI)
1996 IB £190.00 (FA) £228.00 (RAE)
1995 £22.50 (MI) £27.95 (AD) £31.45 (NI) £32.50 (FORT) £35.00 (JU)
1995 IB £195.00 (FA) £228.00 (RAE)
1994 £22.50 (MI)
1994 IB £150.00 (FA) £150.00 (BIB) £216.00 (RAE)
1993 £18.95 (RAE) £19.09 (GOE) £21.67 (MI) £26.44 (REI)
1993 ½ bottle £9.99 (RAE) £14.69 (REI)
1990 £56.50 (ROB) £57.50 (MI)
1989 £43.08 (GOE) £57.50 (MI) £75.94 (WY)
1989 ½ bottle £20.99 (RAE)
1988 £46.67 (MI)
1988 IB £360.00 (FA)
1988 ½ bottle £19.50 (CRO)
1986 £53.33 (MI)
1986 IB £390.00 (FA)
1985 IB £400.00 (FA)
1983 £49.00 (CRO)
1982 £38.19 (REI) £49.17 (MI)
1978 ½ bottle £29.50 (CRO)
1971 £37.01 (REI)
1966 £62.00 (CRO)
1934 £129.25 (REI)

Domaine de l'Eglise *Pomerol*
1998 £155.00 (HIG)
1996 £18.95 (DI) £19.50 (HIG)
1995 £17.99 (UN) £22.75 (BER)
1994 £18.95 (DI)
1992 £12.99 (UN)

Domaine de Gaillat *Graves*
1995 £8.50 (HAH) £9.85 (UB)
1993 magnum £16.95 (CON)

Domaine la Grave *Graves*
1995 £8.49 (HED)

Domaine de la Solitude *Pessac-Léognan*
1997 £10.00 (MI)
1996 £12.50 (MI)
1995 £9.99 (WAT) £11.67 (MI)
1993 £10.83 (MI)

la Dominique *grand cru classé St-Émilion*
1998 IB £369.00 (CB)
1997 £29.95 (BAL) £30.00 (MI) £33.55 (CB)
1996 £30.00 (MI) £35.00 (AD) £35.00 (CON) £35.99 (FRI) £38.00 (JU) £41.13 (CB)
1995 £29.95 (CON) £31.99 (FRI) £33.78 (CB) £35.25 (WY) £40.00 (JU)
1995 IB £225.00 (FA) £250.00 (BIB)
1994 £34.00 (JON) £34.50 (BAL)
1993 IB £170.00 (FA)
1990 IB £440.00 (FA)
1988 IB £240.00 (FA)
1982 £49.50 (BEN)

Ducru-Beaucaillou *2ème cru classé St-Julien*
1998 IB £350.00 (FRI) £350.00 (FA) £379.00 (LEA) £385.00 (WY)
1998 EC £460.00 (TAN)
1997 £38.68 (GOE) £42.95 (LAY) £44.17 (MI) £49.00 (JU) £49.79 (CB) £50.85 (TAN)
1997 IB £337.00 (BIB) £450.00 (RAE)
1997 EC £475.00 (FRI)
1997 ½ bottle £20.07 (GOE) £23.95 (LEA)
1997 magnum £77.35 (GOE) £100.00 (FORT)
1997 jeroboam £293.75 (GOE)
1997 imperial £346.63 (GOE)

1996 £62.18 (WY) £65.00 (MI) £71.45 (HA) £73.25 (FRI) £82.25 (GW) £82.50 (ELL)
1996 IB £575.00 (FA)
1996 double magnum £289.83 (WY)
1996 imperial £587.50 (WY)
1995 £74.91 (GOE) £75.00 (MI) £90.00 (FRI) £91.65 (WY)
1995 ½ bottle IB £750.00 (FA)
1995 magnum IB £750.00 (FA)
1995 jeroboam £634.50 (WY)
1995 imperial £775.50 (WY)
1994 £45.00 (BAL)
1994 IB £350.00 (FA)
1993 £35.83 (MI)
1992 £33.27 (WY)
1991 £32.00 (WS)
1990 £55.00 (RAE) £60.83 (MI) £66.27 (WY) £85.00 (ROB)
1990 IB £450.00 (FA) £480.00 (BIB)
1989 £57.18 (BY) £57.50 (MI) £59.40 (GW) £62.13 (WY)
1989 IB £450.00 (FA)
1988 £39.95 (BU) £46.67 (MI) £78.00 (UB)
1988 IB £400.00 (FA)
1986 £47.50 (CON) £61.67 (MI) £69.03 (WY) £69.20 (BY) £75.00 (FORT) £85.00 (PHI)
1986 magnum £99.88 (REI)
1985 £59.57 (NO) £59.95 (YOU)
1985 IB £600.00 (FA)
1983 £55.48 (PIP) £59.00 (GW) £60.75 (WY) £68.50 (ROB)
1983 IB £420.00 (FA)
1983 double magnum £298.00 (LEA)
1982 £88.13 (REI) £94.50 (BEN) £100.82 (NO) £110.45 (WY) £112.94 (BY)
1982 IB £900.00 (FA) £1,100.00 (CAV)
1981 £49.94 (REI)
1981 IB £380.00 (FA)
1981 magnum £99.88 (REI)
1979 IB £350.00 (FA)
1979 double magnum £170.38 (FA)
1978 £62.86 (REI) £79.95 (LEA)
1978 IB £480.00 (FA)
1975 £41.13 (REI)
1975 jeroboam £315.00 (DI)
1971 £27.50 (BU)
1970 £88.13 (REI) £109.00 (CRO) £125.00 (ROB)
1970 IB £880.00 (FA)
1966 IB £660.00 (FA)
1964 £45.00 (BU)
1961 £170.38 (REI) £240.00 (CRO) £331.35 (WY)
1959 £217.38 (REI)
1924 £324.45 (WY)

Duhart-Milon-Rothschild *4ème cru classé Pauillac*
1998 IB £150.00 (FRI) £169.95 (LEA)
1997 £19.17 (MI) £20.42 (CB) £24.95 (PHI)

1996 £21.95 (DI) £22.50 (LEA) £24.50 (HIG) £25.32 (CB) £38.58 (NI)
1995 £25.00 (UN) £26.67 (MI)
1994 £21.50 (UN)
1991 £21.29 (WY)
1990 £34.52 (WY) £52.00 (UB)
1988 £41.95 (ROB) £42.79 (FRI) £45.00 (PIP)
1985 £42.50 (FRI)
1985 IB £260.00 (FA)
1981 IB £200.00 (FA)
1970 £38.19 (REI)
1952 £80.49 (REI)
1950 £88.13 (REI)

Durand-Laplagne *Puisseguin-St-Émilion*
1997 £7.50 (AD)
1996 £7.60 (TAN)

Durfort-Vivens *2ème cru classé Margaux*
1998 £13.22 (GOE)
1997 £18.75 (BER)
1997 IB £174.00 (RAE)
1996 IB £159.00 (RAE)
1995 £20.95 (ROB) £21.54 (GOE) £25.99 (FRI)
1995 IB £159.00 (RAE)
1994 £27.00 (STA)

Dutruch-Grand-Poujeaux *cru grand bourgeois exceptionnel Moulis*
1997 £9.99 (CB)

l'Église-Clinet *Pomerol*
1997 £72.00 (BAL)
1997 IB £700.00 (FA)
1996 £105.00 (JU)
1996 IB £780.00 (FA)
1995 £160.00 (JU)
1995 IB £1,200.00 (FA) £1,250.00 (CAV)
1994 £47.00 (BAL)

1993 IB £380.00 (FA) £385.00 (BIB)
1990 IB £1,100.00 (FA)
1989 IB £780.00 (FA)
1988 IB £520.00 (FA)
1985 £135.00 (BEN)
1982 £76.38 (REI)
1979 IB £480.00 (FA)

l'Enclos *Pomerol*
1998 IB £135.00 (FA) £150.00 (FRI)
1997 £21.95 (DI)
1996 £19.68 (HA)
1995 £21.15 (WY) £21.50 (STE) £23.50 (POR)
1994 £18.60 (PIP) £20.75 (STA) £22.00 (JU)
1990 £23.00 (CRO)

l'Ermitage de Chasse-Spleen *Haut-Médoc*
1997 £10.83 (MI)
1996 £11.67 (MI) £13.95 (CON)
1995 £10.83 (MI) £11.16 (REI)
1994 £10.95 (WRI)

l'Évangile *Pomerol*
1998 IB £775.00 (LEA) £1,080.00 (WY)
1998 EC £895.00 (ELL)
1997 £58.75 (GOE) £68.33 (MI) £72.00 (JU) £75.00 (LEA) £82.43 (CB) £85.00 (RES)
1996 £79.17 (MI) £85.00 (JU) £88.36 (CB)
1996 IB £460.00 (BIB)
1995 £97.92 (GOE) £180.00 (JU)
1995 IB £780.00 (FA)
1993 £43.33 (MI) £47.35 (TAN)
1993 IB £340.00 (BIB) £350.00 (FA)
1990 £200.00 (ROB)
1990 IB £1300.00 (FA) £1420.00 (BIB)
1988 IB £420.00 (FA)
1985 IB £950.00 (FA)
1982 IB £1,550.00 (FA)
1976 IB £470.00 (BIB)
1975 IB £1,950.00 (FA) £3,000.00 (CAV)
1971 IB £720.00 (FA)
1970 £165.68 (WY)
1952 £146.88 (REI)

Falfas *Côtes de Bourg*
1997 £7.99 (WAI) £8.95 (AD) £8.99 (GW)

Fayau *1ères Côtes de Bordeaux*
1997 £5.94 (MV)

Ferrande *Graves*
1990 £16.50 (HED)
1989 £14.95 (HED)

Ferrière *3ème cru classé Margaux*
1994 £44.00 (FORT)

Feytit-Clinet *Pomerol*
1997 £14.45 (TAN) £16.98 (CB)
1996 £17.63 (CB)
1995 £27.00 (WS)
1989 £46.00 (UB)

les Fiefs-de-Lagrange *St-Julien*
1998 IB £110.00 (WY)
1997 £13.33 (MI)
1996 £16.67 (MI) £18.95 (LEA) £18.99 (PHI)
1995 £17.63 (DOM) £23.50 (ROB)
1994 £13.99 (UN)
1993 £20.95 (ROB)
1989 £22.91 (REI)

de Fieuzal *cru classé Pessac-Léognan*
1998 EC £185.00 (CAV)
1997 EC £240.00 (ELL)
1996 £22.50 (MI)
1995 £22.85 (SOM) £22.99 (UN) £22.99 (UN) £24.99 (NI) £27.50 (HED)
1994 £18.50 (TAN) £21.59 (YOU) £21.95 (BER) £22.95 (ROB)
1990 IB £280.00 (BIB)
1989 £42.30 (NO)
1989 IB £330.00 (BIB)
1988 £35.24 (PIP) £55.00 (UB)
1988 ½ bottle £14.98 (REI)
1986 £47.00 (PEN)
1985 £28.79 (REI)

Figeac *1er grand cru classé St-Émilion*
1998 IB £425.00 (FRI) £460.00 (FA)
1998 EC £415.00 (CAV) £450.00 (ELL)
1997 £36.67 (MI)
1997 EC £415.20 (JON)
1996 £46.67 (MI) £65.51 (PLAY)
1995 £45.00 (MI) £47.50 (FRI) £49.35 (WY)
1994 £32.50 (MI) £36.50 (UN)
1989 IB £500.00 (FA)
1988 £92.00 (UB)
1985 £80.08 (WY)
1983 IB £550.00 (FA)
1983 magnum IB £550.00 (FA)
1982 £124.26 (WY)
1982 IB £850.00 (FA)
1982 magnum IB £850.00 (FA)
1981 £44.06 (REI) £79.99 (POR)
1979 £41.48 (FLE)
1979 IB £420.00 (FA)
1975 £103.55 (WY)
1961 IB £1,900.00 (FA)

Fleur Cardinale *grand cru St-Émilion*
1997 EC £95.40 (JON)
1993 £17.50 (ROB)

la Fleur-Pétrus *Pomerol*
1998 EC £408.00 (JON)
1997 £32.00 (JU) £42.95 (CB)
1996 £34.66 (CB)
1994 £31.73 (CB)
1988 £53.00 (CRO)
1982 IB £1,050.00 (FA)
1976 £41.13 (REI)
1970 IB £1,150.00 (CAV)

Fombrauge *grand cru St-Émilion*
1993 £11.75 (GOE) £15.65 (JER)
1989 IB £266.50 (BIB)
1975 magnum £41.13 (REI)

Fonpiqueyre *cru bourgeois Haut-Médoc*
1978 £18.50 (CRO)

Fonréaud *cru bourgeois Listrac*
1996 £9.95 (TAN) £10.83 (MI)
1995 £10.83 (MI)

Fonroque *grand cru classé St-Émilion*
1997 £14.83 (CB)
1996 £15.22 (CB)
1994 £15.50 (WS)
1986 IB £130.00 (FA)
1983 £19.00 (YOU)

les Forts-de-Latour *Pauillac*
1998 EC £230.00 (CAV) £245.00 (ELL)
1997 £27.50 (MI) £30.00 (JU) £30.95 (LAY) £31.20 (CB) £33.50 (LEA)
1996 £38.33 (MI)
1996 IB £330.00 (FA)
1995 £33.00 (FLE) £37.60 (WY)
1994 £29.50 (BAL)
1994 IB £300.00 (BIB) £358.38 (WY)
1993 £25.00 (BU)
1990 £76.38 (REI)
1990 IB £650.00 (FA)
1989 £39.50 (BU)
1989 IB £420.00 (FA) £475.00 (BIB)
1979 £51.70 (PEN)
1970 £68.74 (REI)

All châteaux are listed alphabetically regardless of class.

Fourcas-Dupré *cru grand bourgeois exceptionnnel Listrac*
1996 £8.54 (HA) £12.50 (WS) £13.75 (PIP)
1994 £13.99 (PHI)
1983 £18.00 (CRO)

Fourcas-Hosten *cru grand bourgeois exceptionnnel Listrac*
1997 £10.50 (HIG)
1996 £9.99 (HIG) £10.95 (STA) £10.99 (POR) £10.99 (SAI) £12.95 (BER) £13.80 (TAN)
1995 £9.99 (HIG)
1994 £10.50 (HIG)

Franc-Mayne *grand cru classé St-Émilion*
1997 £17.50 (MI)
1995 £29.99 (UN)

de Francs *Côtes de Francs*
1996 £7.99 (WR) £7.99 (THR) £7.99 (VIC) £7.99 (BOT)
1995 £7.99 (BOT)

la Gaffelière *1er grand cru classé St-Émilion*
1998 IB £250.00 (FRI)
1997 £28.33 (MI)
1996 £30.00 (MI)
1996 IB £240.00 (BIB)
1995 £25.25 (HA) £30.00 (MI) £31.99 (FRI)
1995 IB £280.00 (BIB)
1994 £23.33 (MI) £29.50 (UN)
1994 IB £186.00 (RAE)
1989 £65.50 (UB)
1988 IB £300.00 (BIB)
1985 £30.39 (REI)
1983 £33.33 (MI)
1979 IB £180.00 (FA)
1970 £34.52 (WY)

la Garde *Pessac-Léognan*
1996 £6.99 (SAI)
1996 IB £100.00 (CAV)
1994 £8.75 (WAI)

le Gardera *1ères Côtes de Bordeaux*
1989 £11.75 (BU)
1988 £10.75 (BU)

le Gay *Pomerol*
1996 £21.50 (WS)
1990 £46.00 (BAL)
1990 IB £420.00 (FA)
1986 £47.00 (REI)

Gazin *Pomerol*
1998 IB £500.00 (FA)
1998 EC £385.00 (ELL)
1997 £38.00 (JU) £38.00 (JU) £45.00 (TAN) £45.38 (CB)
1996 £32.00 (JU) £41.13 (REI) £43.80 (TAN)
1996 IB £320.00 (FA) £350.00 (BIB)
1995 £37.99 (UN)
1990 £83.00 (UB)
1989 £49.17 (MI)
1985 IB £275.00 (FA)
1982 £52.25 (TAN)
1966 £32.31 (REI)

Giscours *3ème cru classé Margaux*
1997 £18.33 (MI) £26.95 (DI)
1996 £21.67 (MI) £22.50 (FRI) £22.95 (NI)
1995 £20.00 (MI) £24.99 (FRI) £27.50 (UN) £31.00 (YOU)
1995 magnum £54.50 (FRI)
1990 £44.17 (MI)
1989 £35.00 (BU) £40.83 (MI)
1982 IB £420.00 (FA)
1970 £65.00 (YOU) £94.00 (REI) £95.00 (BEN)
1966 £49.50 (BEN) £61.69 (REI) £62.13 (WY)
1961 £151.87 (WY)

du Glana *cru grand bourgeois exceptionnel St-Julien*
1996 £15.00 (MV)

Gloria *cru bourgeois St-Julien*
1998 EC £154.30 (HAH)
1997 £19.17 (MI)
1996 £20.83 (MI) £21.39 (FRI)
1995 £19.17 (MI) £21.95 (BER) £23.99 (BOD) £23.99 (SUN) £25.99 (FRI)
1994 £17.50 (MI) £21.49 (PIP)
1993 £16.67 (MI) £19.99 (PHI) £19.99 (POR)
1993 magnum £52.50 (ROB)
1990 £29.38 (COC)
1988 £41.85 (NI)

la Gorce *cru bourgeois Médoc*
1996 £8.15 (PIP)

Grand-Corbin *grand cru classé St-Émilion*
1996 £25.19 (PLAY)
1993 £12.60 (NI)

Grand-Lartigue *St-Émilion*
1997 £10.57 (BIB)
1995 £9.99 (RAE)
1994 £9.99 (RAE)

Grand-Mayne *grand cru classé St-Émilion*
1997 EC £315.00 (ELL)
1996 £28.65 (LAY)
1996 IB £205.00 (FA) £210.00 (CAV)
1995 £26.50 (BAL) £37.00 (JU)
1994 £21.50 (BAL)

Grand Ormeau *Lalande-de-Pomerol*
1997 £14.49 (SAV)

Grand-Pontet *grand cru classé St-Émilion*
1998 £16.16 (GOE)
1998 IB £150.00 (BIB)
1998 EC £155.00 (CAV)
1996 £16.65 (GOE) £25.00 (JU)
1995 £19.99 (BOD) £19.99 (SUN) £30.00 (JU)

Grand-Puy-Ducasse *5ème cru classé Pauillac*
1998 IB £130.00 (FRI)
1997 £16.67 (MI) £22.95 (DI)
1996 £18.99 (NI) £22.50 (MI)
1990 IB £250.00 (FA)
1989 £33.00 (COC)
1982 £35.00 (YOU)
1982 IB £265.00 (FA)
1961 £89.75 (WY) £97.00 (CRO)
1957 £76.38 (REI)
1948 £189.39 (WY)

Grand-Puy-Lacoste *5ème cru classé Pauillac*
1998 IB £240.00 (FRI) £309.00 (CB)
1998 EC £250.00 (CAV) £289.00 (TAN)
1997 £22.03 (GOE) £28.00 (JU) £29.17 (MI) £29.95 (LEA) £30.55 (CB) £30.80 (TAN)
1997 IB £195.00 (BIB)
1997 magnum £44.06 (GOE)
1996 £22.03 (WY) £47.50 (MI) £52.88 (REI) £56.39 (FRI)
1996 IB £380.00 (FA)
1996 magnum £91.06 (WY)
1995 £36.67 (MI) £47.00 (WY) £52.39 (FRI)
1994 £25.00 (MI) £29.20 (LAY) £33.95 (PHI) £38.50 (POR) £38.60 (JER) £42.50 (WR) £45.00 (TAN)
1994 IB £220.00 (BIB)
1993 £21.20 (TAN) £25.00 (MI)
1993 IB £210.00 (FA)
1989 £39.95 (BU)
1989 IB £450.00 (FA)
1986 IB £440.00 (FA) £495.00 (BIB)
1985 £42.00 (CRO)
1983 £43.00 (COC)
1983 IB £300.00 (FA)

1982 £72.00 (FLE) £73.44 (GOE) £89.00 (POR)
1982 IB £780.00 (FA)
1979 £38.00 (CRO)
1975 £35.00 (BU) £77.55 (PEN)
1970 £48.35 (BY)
1961 £140.00 (CRO)

Grandes-Murailles *grand cru classé St-Émilion*
1998 EC £195.00 (CAV)
1997 IB £270.00 (CB)

Grangeneuve de Figeac *grand cru St-Émilion*
1994 IB £130.00 (BIB)
1993 £15.00 (MI)

de la Grave *Côtes de Bourg*
1997 £5.50 (WS)
1995 £6.95 (WS)

la Grave-Figeac *grand cru St-Émilion*
1995 £19.95 (ELL)

la Grave-Trigant-de-Boisset *Pomerol*
1986 £25.26 (REI)

Gressier-Grand-Poujeaux *cru bourgeois supérieur Moulis*
1996 £16.50 (WS)
1995 £17.50 (ROB)
1993 £11.49 (CON)

Greysac *cru grand bourgeois Médoc*
1995 £11.50 (ROB)

Grivière *Médoc*
1995 £10.37 (BIB)
1994 £9.94 (BIB)
1992 £8.99 (RAE)

Gros-Moulin *Côtes de Bourg*
1970 £10.75 (BU)

Gruaud-Larose *2ème cru classé St-Julien*
1998 IB £270.00 (FRI)
1998 EC £275.00 (CAV) £275.00 (ELL)
1997 £37.50 (MI)
1996 £37.50 (LEA) £38.33 (MI) £38.85 (HAH) £38.99 (WS) £40.00 (FORT) £40.50 (ELL) £40.59 (FRI) £43.50 (TAN) £44.18 (PLAY) £45.00 (JU)
1996 IB £275.00 (FA)
1996 magnum £80.00 (FORT)
1996 double magnum £117.50 (FA)
1995 £29.99 (UN) £36.67 (MI) £40.95 (ROB) £47.50 (FRI)
1995 IB £280.00 (FA) £300.00 (BIB)
1994 £27.50 (MI) £28.50 (UN) £31.95 (WR) £31.95 (BOT)
1994 IB £230.00 (FA)
1993 £24.99 (BOT)
1992 £21.67 (MI) £35.95 (ROB) £36.95 (STE)
1990 £49.99 (OD) £53.33 (MI)
1990 IB £500.00 (FA)
1989 £45.99 (JON) £46.94 (PLA) £49.69 (VIN) £78.00 (WS)
1989 IB £440.00 (FA)

1988 £78.00 (UB)
1986 £75.00 (BU) £80.08 (WY)
1986 IB £620.00 (FA) £750.00 (CAV)
1986 magnum IB £850.00 (CAV)
1986 double magnum £246.75 (FA)
1985 £54.00 (CRO) £66.27 (WY) £70.00 (FORT)
1985 IB £500.00 (FA)
1985 ½ bottle £28.00 (CRO) £35.90 (WY)
1985 magnum IB £500.00 (FA)
1985 double magnum IB £600.00 (BIB)
1983 £45.24 (REI) £59.37 (WY)
1983 IB £480.00 (FA) £480.00 (BIB)
1983 ½ bottle £35.90 (WY)
1983 magnum £89.89 (REI)
1982 £87.50 (MI) £87.64 (GOE) £89.50 (BEN) £103.50 (STA) £117.36 (WY) £125.00 (FORT)
1982 IB £830.00 (BIB) £880.00 (FA) £1,050.00 (CAV)
1982 jeroboam £998.75 (GOE)
1981 £38.66 (WY)
1978 £32.50 (BU) £78.00 (WAI)
1978 jeroboam £258.50 (FA)
1976 double magnum £197.40 (REI)
1973 magnum £39.50 (BU)
1971 magnum £70.50 (REI)
1970 £69.03 (WY) £89.50 (POR)
1970 IB £420.00 (FA)
1970 magnum £138.06 (WY)
1966 £91.12 (WY)

1961 £235.00 (FA) £331.35 (WY)
1945 £293.75 (REI)
1934 £227.81 (WY)
1928 £411.25 (FA) £455.61 (WY)
1922 £146.88 (FA)
1918 IB £2,000.00 (FA)

Guillot *Pomerol*
1998 £16.16 (GOE)
1997 £16.67 (MI)
1996 £16.99 (BOD) £16.99 (SUN) £18.33 (MI)
1995 £18.33 (MI) £26.00 (JU)

Guionne *Côtes de Bourg*
1997 £5.95 (COC)

la Gurgue *cru bourgeois supérieur Margaux*
1997 £14.45 (TAN) £15.00 (FORT)
1989 £22.00 (CRO)

Haut-Bages-Avérous *cru bourgeois Pauillac*
1997 £16.67 (MI)
1996 £18.33 (MI) £21.95 (LEA)
1995 £30.88 (BY)
1995 IB £140.00 (FA)
1994 £26.79 (BY)
1993 £17.25 (WRI)
1993 IB £110.00 (FA)
1985 £30.00 (BU)

Haut-Bages-Libéral *5ème cru classé Pauillac*
1998 EC £154.00 (TAN)
1997 £15.83 (MI) £18.80 (TAN) £20.00 (FORT)
1997 magnum £42.50 (FORT)
1996 £20.83 (MI)
1996 magnum £47.00 (STE)
1995 £19.17 (MI) £21.25 (BER) £21.50 (STE) £26.99 (PHI)
1993 £25.26 (REI)
1989 £23.50 (WS) £48.00 (UB)
1986 £26.44 (REI)

Haut-Bailly *cru classé Pessac-Léognan*
1997 £21.54 (GOE) £24.17 (MI)
1997 EC £258.00 (JON)
1996 £29.17 (MI) £29.21 (HA) £40.00 (JU)
1996 IB £310.00 (BIB)
1995 £24.48 (GOE) £29.50 (ELL) £29.95 (LEA) £39.95 (AD)
1995 IB £192.00 (RAE) £250.00 (FA)
1994 £22.91 (REI) £22.95 (ROB) £24.50 (STA) £24.50 (BAL)
1993 £19.50 (RAE) £19.59 (YOU) £21.50 (BAL) £21.74 (REI)
1990 IB £340.00 (FA)
1985 IB £280.00 (FA)
1978 £31.14 (REI) £33.49 (REI)
1978 magnum £77.21 (PLAY)

Haut-Batailley *5ème cru classé Pauillac*
1998 IB £145.00 (WY)
1997 £15.18 (GOE) £19.00 (JU) £19.50 (LAY) £19.62 (CB) £20.00 (MI) £22.95 (TAN)
1996 £22.50 (MI) £23.99 (WY)
1996 IB £200.00 (FA)
1995 £20.83 (MI) £21.54 (GOE) £21.99 (BOD) £21.99 (SUN) £24.00 (UN) £28.20 (WY) £37.50 (FORT)
1994 £18.95 (HED) £19.17 (MI) £27.25 (STA)
1994 IB £160.00 (FA)
1993 £19.39 (REI)
1991 £22.44 (WY)
1989 £19.50 (WS) £36.24 (WY)
1983 £29.50 (BU)
1983 IB £240.00 (FA)
1981 IB £220.00 (FA)
1971 £31.00 (YOU)

Haut-Bergey *Pessac-Léognan*
1996 £13.50 (GN) £16.50 (NO)
1995 £14.00 (JU)

Haut-Brion *1er cru classé Pessac-Léognan*
1998 IB £1,250.00 (FA) £1,350.00 (WY)
1998 EC £995.00 (ELL)
1998 magnum IB £1,250.00 (FA)
1997 £93.20 (LAY) £93.33 (MI) £98.85 (TAN) £99.00 (JU) £109.28 (CB)
1997 IB £882.00 (RAE) £950.00 (BIB)
1997 EC £995.00 (ELL)
1996 £105.75 (WY) £107.51 (CB) £135.00 (FRI) £173.33 (MI)
1996 IB £1,000.00 (FA)
1996 magnum £355.00 (BEN)
1996 magnum IB £1,000.00 (FA)
1996 imperial £1,045.75 (WY)
1995 £155.00 (FRI) £173.33 (MI) £230.57 (BY)
1995 IB £1,050.00 (FA) £1,150.00 (BIB)
1994 £67.50 (UN) £72.00 (BAL) £76.38 (REI) £78.18 (HA) £89.00 (POR) £95.00 (WAI) £121.67 (MI)
1994 IB £690.00 (FA) £750.00 (BIB)
1994 magnum £145.00 (UN)
1994 double magnum £282.00 (FA)

1993 £76.00 (YOU) £79.17 (MI) £117.11 (BY)
1992 £89.50 (WR) £89.50 (BOT) £94.46 (BY)
1992 IB £600.00 (FA)
1991 £118.23 (BY)
1991 IB £620.00 (FA)
1990 IB £1,550.00 (FA)
1990 magnum IB £1,550.00 (FA)
1989 £331.35 (WY) £495.00 (CON)
1988 £73.85 (TAN) £99.88 (REI) £199.54 (BY)
1988 IB £900.00 (BIB) £950.00 (FA)
1987 £49.50 (BU) £95.08 (BY)
1987 IB £600.00 (FA)
1986 £85.00 (CON) £119.99 (OD) £131.17 (WY) £150.00 (FORT)
1986 IB £1,200.00 (FA) £1,200.00 (BIB)
1986 magnum IB £1,200.00 (FA)
1985 £137.62 (BY) £175.00 (ROB)
1985 IB £1,250.00 (FA) £1,250.00 (BIB)
1985 magnum IB £1,200.00 (FA)
1984 £67.95 (ROB)
1984 IB £550.00 (FA)
1983 £75.00 (BU) £75.71 (BY) £110.45 (WY) £117.50 (MI) £125.00 (FORT)
1983 IB £850.00 (BIB) £920.00 (FA)
1983 magnum IB £920.00 (FA)
1982 £180.00 (JU) £195.00 (BEN) £220.90 (WY) £250.00 (BAL) £258.33 (MI)
1982 IB £1,900.00 (BIB)
1981 £105.61 (WY)
1981 IB £750.00 (FA)
1981 magnum IB £750.00 (FA)
1980 IB £500.00 (FA)
1980 double magnum £217.38 (FA)
1979 £115.00 (ROB)
1978 £94.00 (YOU) £117.44 (BY)
1978 IB £900.00 (FA) £900.00 (BIB)
1976 £75.00 (BU)
1975 IB £995.00 (CAV)
1970 £114.73 (BY) £120.00 (BEN) £131.17 (WY)
1970 IB £950.00 (FA) £1,100.00 (CAV)
1970 magnum £310.65 (WY)
1970 magnum IB £950.00 (FA)
1966 £179.48 (WY)
1966 IB £1,350.00 (FA)
1964 £142.97 (BY)
1961 £600.00 (CAV)

Please remember that
Oz Clarke's Wine Buying Guide
is a price ***guide*** *and not a price* ***list****. It is not meant to replace up-to-date merchants' lists.*

1960 £289.93 (WY)
1959 £587.50 (FA) £795.00 (CAV) £855.99 (WY)
1955 £176.50 (BEN)
1953 IB £4,500.00 (CAV)
1952 £179.48 (WY)
1949 £862.90 (WY)
1947 £524.64 (WY)
1945 magnum £3,106.41 (WY)
1940 £175.00 (BU)
1929 £1,014.77 (WY)
1928 £495.00 (ROB) £980.24 (WY)
1926 £531.55 (WY)
1920 magnum £1,028.13 (REI)

Haut-Gardère *Pessac-Léognan*
1996 £11.00 (ELL)
1993 £8.79 (WAT)

Haut-Guiraud *Côtes de Bourg*
1997 £7.60 (JER)

Haut-Marbuzet *cru grand bourgeois exceptionnel St-Estèphe*
1998 EC £195.00 (CAV)
1997 £23.00 (JU) £24.17 (MI) £25.99 (AME)
1996 £24.31 (NO) £25.00 (MI) £29.00 (JU)
1996 IB £190.00 (FA) £190.00 (BIB)
1995 £25.00 (ELL)
1995 IB £215.00 (FA)
1994 £21.50 (BAL)
1986 £33.49 (REI)
1962 £25.00 (BU)

Haut-Mazeris *Canon-Fronsac*
1996 £8.11 (PEN)

Haut-Pontet *grand cru St-Émilion*
1996 £15.50 (WS) £17.50 (MI)
1996 IB £125.00 (CAV)
1995 £15.00 (MI)

Haut-Sarpe *grand cru classé St-Émilion*
1959 £50.00 (BU)
1953 £85.00 (BU)
1947 £95.00 (BU)

de Haut-Sociondo *1ères Côtes de Blaye*
1997 EC £30.00 (JON)
1994 £10.35 (STA)

l'Hermitage *grand cru St-Émilion*
1998 £44.06 (GOE)
1998 IB £380.00 (FA)
1997 £55.00 (MI)

Hortevie *cru bourgeois St-Julien*
1997 £11.45 (BER)
1996 £12.99 (HED) £13.15 (GN)
1995 £12.95 (BAL)
1994 £12.49 (HED) £13.50 (BAL)
1993 £13.50 (LEA)
1993 IB £120.00 (BIB)

d'Issan *3ème cru classé Margaux*
1997 £16.64 (HA) £17.50 (MI)
1996 £21.00 (HIG) £21.67 (MI)
1995 £20.00 (MI) £25.00 (FLE) £28.00 (FRI)
1994 £18.33 (MI) £23.69 (HA)
1989 £25.26 (REI) £41.50 (ROB)
1988 £36.63 (PIP)
1986 £28.00 (CRO)
1985 £25.26 (REI)

les Jonqueyres *1ères Côtes de Blaye*
1996 £7.49 (BAL)
1995 £7.49 (BAL)

Jonqueyres *Bordeaux Supérieur*
1997 £6.95 (RES) £8.00 (JU)
1996 £8.50 (JU)
1995 £8.50 (JU) £9.61 (WT)

Kirwan *3ème cru classé Margaux*
1997 £18.57 (CB) £19.95 (TAN) £21.00 (JU)
1997 magnum £37.72 (CB)
1996 magnum £51.90 (WY)
1995 £24.50 (UN) £35.00 (WRI) £329.00 (WY)
1994 £34.52 (WY)
1989 £44.99 (POR)
1988 £55.40 (AV)
1982 £28.79 (REI)
1981 £41.50 (WRI)

Labégorce *cru bourgeois supérieur Margaux*
1996 £18.15 (HAH) £18.39 (CB)
1989 £29.38 (COC)

Labégorce-Zédé *cru bourgeois supérieur Margaux*
1998 £11.75 (GOE)
1997 £14.50 (JU)
1997 IB £133.80 (RAE)
1997 EC £141.00 (JON)
1996 £17.14 (GOE) £18.50 (JU)
1995 £21.45 (NI)
1995 IB £132.00 (RAE)
1990 £46.00 (UB)
1985 £28.79 (REI)

Lacaussade-St-Martin *1ères Côtes de Blaye*
1997 £8.21 (PLA) £10.02 (WT)

Lacoste-Borie *Pauillac*
1996 £15.50 (WAI) £15.95 (WS) £18.33 (MI)
1996 IB £120.00 (FA)
1995 £15.83 (MI) £19.00 (CRO) £23.50 (RES)
1995 IB £135.00 (FA)
1994 £14.17 (MI) £20.64 (BY)
1992 IB £120.00 (BIB)
1986 £20.97 (REI)
1982 £33.49 (REI)

Lafite-Rothschild *1er cru classé Pauillac*
1998 IB £790.00 (WY) £820.00 (FA) £980.00 (FRI) £1,089.00 (CB)
1998 EC £795.00 (ELL) £895.00 (TAN)
1997 £77.84 (GOE) £93.04 (HA) £93.33 (MI) £98.85 (TAN) £99.00 (JU)
1996 £131.30 (TAN) £158.00 (PHI) £158.63 (GW) £200.00 (FRI) £207.50 (MI)
1996 IB £1,620.00 (FA) £1,685.00 (BIB)
1996 imperial £1,410.00 (FA)
1995 £141.98 (GOE) £173.33 (MI) £180.00 (FRI) £258.22 (BY)
1995 IB £1,220.00 (FA) £1,250.00 (BIB) £1,650.00 (ELL)
1995 magnum IB £1,200.00 (FA)
1995 double magnum £558.13 (WY)
1994 £67.50 (UN) £100.00 (JU) £104.58 (PEN) £121.67 (MI) £125.00 (ROB)
1994 magnum IB £720.00 (FA)
1993 £79.17 (MI) £86.45 (LAY) £117.11 (BY)
1993 IB £750.00 (FA)
1992 £49.95 (BU) £101.97 (BY)
1992 ½ bottle £52.50 (ROB)
1991 £82.84 (WY)
1991 IB £700.00 (FA)
1990 £114.07 (GOE) £210.00 (FRI) £215.83 (MI) £235.00 (ROB)
1990 IB £1,500.00 (FA) £1,900.00 (CAV)
1990 magnum IB £1,500.00 (FA)
1990 imperial £1,175.00 (FA)
1989 £140.00 (SUN) £155.00 (FRI) £169.17 (MI) £175.00 (FORT)
1989 IB £1,300.00 (FA) £1,350.00 (CAV)
1989 imperial £1,034.00 (FA)
1988 £120.46 (BY) £125.50 (BEN) £140.00 (FRI) £151.87 (WY)
1988 magnum IB £1,180.00 (FA)
1988 double magnum £810.00 (FRI)
1988 imperial £940.00 (FA)

1987 £95.00 (FRI)
1987 IB £660.00 (FA)
1987 magnum IB £620.00 (FA)
1986 £175.00 (BU) £200.00 (FRI) £214.00 (WY) £220.00 (MI) £250.00 (FORT)
1986 IB £1,700.00 (FA) £1,700.00 (BIB)

1985 £100.00 (BU) £139.17 (MI) £165.68 (WY) £175.00 (JU)
1985 IB £1,306.50 (BIB) £1,320.00 (FA)
1985 ½ bottle £125.00 (UB)
1985 magnum IB £1,320.00 (FA)
1985 imperial £1,034.00 (FA)
1983 £135.00 (POR) £150.00 (FORT) £160.00 (STA)
1983 magnum £350.00 (FORT)
1982 £309.00 (FRI) £310.00 (CRO) £350.00 (BU) £352.07 (WY) £400.00 (FORT) £412.50 (MI)
1982 magnum IB £2,900.00 (FA) £3,642.50 (WY)
1979 IB £875.00 (FA)
1979 magnum IB £800.00 (FA)
1979 double magnum £586.77 (WY)
1978 £178.99 (VIN)
1978 magnum IB £1,000.00 (FA)
1978 imperial £810.75 (FA)
1976 IB £1,280.00 (FA)
1976 magnum IB £1,280.00 (FA)
1975 £117.50 (CAV) £145.00 (BEN) £179.48 (WY)
1975 magnum IB £1,250.00 (FA)
1974 £74.55 (WY)
1970 £96.64 (WY) £175.00 (ROB)
1970 IB £1,000.00 (FA)
1970 double magnum £676.51 (WY)
1970 double magnum IB £1,171.50 (BIB)
1966 £129.25 (REI) £186.39 (WY)
1966 imperial £940.00 (FA)
1962 £111.63 (REI)
1961 £558.13 (REI) £648.89 (WY)
1961 ½ bottle £186.39 (WY)
1961 magnum £1,063.08 (WY)
1961 double magnum £1,551.00 (FA)
1961 imperial £3,466.25 (FA)
1959 £763.75 (FA)
1958 £138.06 (WY)
1956 £57.50 (BU)
1955 £400.38 (WY)
1953 £350.00 (BU) £538.44 (WY)
1953 ½ bottle £264.38 (REI)
1953 magnum £1,173.53 (WY)
1949 £650.00 (CAV) £945.73 (WY)
1949 magnum £2,968.34 (WY)
1948 £475.00 (CRO) £538.44 (WY)
1948 ½ bottle £124.26 (WY)
1945 £1,449.66 (WY)
1934 £441.80 (WY)
1929 £510.83 (WY)
1929 magnum £3,244.47 (WY)
1928 £918.12 (WY)
1923 £517.74 (WY)
1918 £579.86 (WY)
1908 £646.25 (REI)
1900 £3,675.00 (ROB)

Lafleur *Pomerol*
1998 IB £1,575.00 (WY) £1,750.00 (FA)
1997 IB £1,250.00 (FA)
1996 IB £1,350.00 (FA)
1995 £250.00 (YOU)
1995 IB £2,000.00 (FA) £2,065.00 (BIB)
1994 IB £840.00 (BIB) £900.00 (FA) £1,700.00 (CAV)
1992 £70.50 (REI) £96.64 (WY)
1990 £487.63 (REI)
1990 IB £3,200.00 (FA)
1989 IB £2,400.00 (FA) £2,850.00 (BIB)
1986 IB £1,800.00 (FA) £2,500.00 (CAV)
1983 £235.00 (CAV)
1983 IB £2,600.00 (FA)
1978 £352.50 (CAV)
1964 IB £320.00 (FA)

Lafleur-Gazin *Pomerol*
1998 EC £155.00 (CAV)
1997 £13.50 (JU)
1996 £16.50 (JU)

Lafon-Rochet *4ème cru classé St-Estèphe*
1998 £155.00 (HIG)
1998 EC £150.00 (CAV)
1997 £15.18 (GOE) £17.50 (MI) £19.62 (CB) £20.70 (TAN)
1996 £22.50 (FRI) £23.01 (WY) £23.74 (CB) £25.26 (REI)
1996 IB £180.00 (FA)
1995 £23.50 (GOE) £26.67 (MI) £29.28 (FRI) £30.33 (HA)
1994 £29.75 (STA)
1982 £48.33 (WY)

Lagrange *Pomerol*
1998 IB £165.00 (CB)
1997 £18.36 (CB) £22.95 (LAY)
1995 £27.50 (WS)
1990 IB £240.00 (FA)
1979 £19.33 (WY)

Lagrange *3ème cru classé St-Julien*
1998 IB £195.00 (LEA) £195.00 (WY)
1997 £22.50 (MI) £24.32 (CB) £27.95 (LEA)
1997 IB £160.00 (BIB)
1996 £26.93 (WY) £28.95 (DI) £30.49 (FRI) £31.00 (CON) £49.95 (VIN)
1996 IB £230.00 (FA)
1995 £25.50 (UN) £31.73 (WY)
1994 £25.00 (MI)
1993 £24.99 (UN) £31.91 (BY) £34.50 (ROB)
1992 £26.00 (HA) £29.00 (WY)
1990 £56.00 (ROB) £69.03 (WY)
1990 IB £425.00 (FA)
1989 £49.00 (ROB) £71.79 (WY)
1988 IB £320.00 (FA)
1986 IB £380.00 (FA)
1983 £40.95 (ROB)
1983 IB £240.00 (FA)

la Lagune *3ème cru classé Haut-Médoc*
1998 IB £150.00 (FRI)
1997 £19.17 (MI)
1997 EC £147.15 (HAH)
1996 £20.50 (HIG) £21.39 (FRI) £23.50 (WY) £25.00 (MI) £26.95 (CON)
1996 IB £162.00 (RAE)
1996 imperial £193.88 (WY)
1995 £19.50 (ELL) £24.75 (STE) £25.00 (MI) £25.85 (WY) £25.99 (POR) £26.99 (FRI) £29.50 (UN) £29.95 (PHI)
1995 IB £185.00 (FA)
1995 ½ bottle £14.99 (FRI)
1995 magnum £58.99 (FRI)
1995 double magnum £105.75 (WY)
1995 imperial £211.50 (WY)
1994 £21.50 (UN) £23.33 (MI)
1993 £16.50 (WS) £22.91 (REI) £23.33 (MI)
1992 £26.95 (ROB)
1991 £24.95 (ROB)
1991 IB £150.00 (FA)

Oz Clarke's Wine Buying Guide
is an annual publication.
We welcome your suggestions for next year's edition.

1990 £45.00 (CRO)
1990 magnum IB £375.00 (FA)
1989 £39.99 (SUN) £55.25 (BEN) £57.99 (WY)
1988 £37.85 (BY) £44.50 (BEN)
1988 IB £340.00 (FA)
1988 magnum IB £340.00 (FA)
1986 £39.50 (BU) £45.00 (CON)
1986 IB £375.00 (FA)
1985 £55.00 (ROB)
1983 £42.00 (CRO) £51.09 (WY)
1983 IB £360.00 (FA)
1982 £62.00 (CRO) £64.60 (TAN) £64.63 (REI) £75.50 (BEN)
1982 IB £600.00 (FA)
1981 £29.96 (REI)
1981 magnum IB £250.00 (FA)
1981 double magnum £105.75 (FA)
1979 £36.08 (BY)
1979 IB £260.00 (FA)
1979 magnum £75.00 (BU)
1978 £39.00 (CRO) £45.00 (ROB)
1977 imperial £105.75 (FA)
1975 £21.15 (FA)
1975 magnum £76.38 (REI)
1975 magnum IB £240.00 (FA)
1973 £23.50 (REI)
1973 magnum £47.00 (REI)
1970 £44.00 (CRO)
1968 £55.23 (WY)

Lalande-Borie *cru bourgeois supérieur St-Julien*
1995 £17.50 (MI) £17.50 (WS)
1995 IB £130.00 (FA)
1994 £14.20 (GOE) £14.50 (WS) £15.00 (MI)
1993 £14.17 (MI) £17.95 (RES)
1990 £25.00 (MI)
1982 £33.49 (REI)

de Lamarque *cru grand bourgeois Haut-Médoc*
1998 IB £108.00 (CB)
1997 £13.51 (CB)
1996 £13.81 (CB)
1995 £13.51 (CB)

Lamothe *1ères Côtes de Bordeaux*
1998 £6.95 (STE)
1997 £6.95 (STE)

Lamothe-Bergeron *cru bourgeois Haut-Médoc*
1997 £6.79 (HA)
1995 £11.95 (COC)

Lamothe-Cissac *Haut-Médoc*
1997 £8.49 (DI)

Lanessan *cru bourgeois supérieur Haut-Médoc*
1998 £15.80 (CHA)
1997 £11.67 (MI) £15.95 (DI)
1996 £14.17 (MI)
1995 £12.50 (MI) £17.95 (NI) £21.50 (FORT) £22.50 (WR)
1995 IB £110.00 (FA)
1993 £13.95 (TAN)
1990 IB £200.00 (FA)

Langoa-Barton *3ème cru classé St-Julien*
1998 £19.09 (GOE)
1998 IB £199.00 (LEA)
1998 EC £222.00 (JON) £240.00 (TAN)
1997 £17.14 (GOE) £20.23 (HA) £21.95 (BER) £22.00 (JU) £25.40 (TAN) £25.60 (AD) £25.95 (LEA)
1997 EC £219.60 (JON)
1996 £29.95 (DI) £30.60 (TAN)
1995 £22.00 (TAN) £24.36 (HA) £24.48 (GOE) £29.95 (DI) £29.99 (POR)
1994 £22.25 (STE) £23.99 (GOE) £24.74 (WY) £28.95 (WR) £28.99 (JON) £35.64 (BY)
1993 £27.75 (BO)
1992 £20.42 (BIB) £26.20 (NI) £26.38 (BY)
1990 £45.69 (JON)
1989 £35.00 (BU) £35.00 (WS) £46.94 (WY)
1986 £26.44 (REI) £30.88 (BY)
1985 £37.33 (PIP)
1984 magnum IB £120.00 (FA)
1979 £29.50 (BU)
1978 £31.14 (REI)
1967 £20.56 (REI)

Larmande *grand cru classé St-Émilion*
1998 £17.62 (GOE)
1998 EC £170.00 (CAV)
1997 £20.83 (MI) £25.40 (TAN)
1996 £21.67 (MI) £25.95 (DI)
1996 IB £170.00 (FA) £200.00 (CAV)
1995 IB £186.50 (BIB) £195.00 (FA)
1994 £18.60 (GOE) £19.99 (BOD)
1983 £35.00 (WS)

Laroque *grand cru St-Émilion*
1996 £14.25 (WAI)

Larose-Trintaudon *cru grand bourgeois Haut-Médoc*
1996 £13.59 (FRI)

Larrivet-Haut-Brion *Pessac-Léognan*
1997 £18.95 (TAN)
1994 £20.27 (WT)
1978 £22.50 (BU)
1970 £27.50 (BU)

Lascombes *2ème cru classé Margaux*
1997 £23.33 (MI)
1996 £24.79 (FRI) £25.00 (MI)
1995 £23.95 (NI) £25.95 (WY) £25.99 (BOD) £25.99 (SUN) £28.00 (FRI) £40.00 (UN)
1994 £25.95 (JER) £28.50 (UN)
1990 £39.00 (COC)
1989 £26.44 (REI)
1989 IB £275.00 (FA)
1988 IB £300.00 (BIB)
1982 £38.18 (REI)
1982 IB £400.00 (FA)
1975 £76.38 (PEN)
1961 £117.36 (WY)

Latour *1er cru classé Pauillac*
1998 IB £855.00 (BIB) £980.00 (FRI)
1998 EC £795.00 (ELL)
1997 £77.84 (GOE) £89.00 (LEA) £92.84 (HA) £93.33 (MI) £98.85 (TAN) £99.00 (JU) £100.00 (FORT) £109.28 (CB)
1997 IB £765.00 (BIB) £886.20 (RAE)
1997 EC £995.00 (ELL)
1996 £125.00 (BU) £145.90 (WY) £173.33 (MI) £175.00 (FRI)
1996 IB £1,400.00 (FA)
1996 double magnum £646.25 (WY)
1995 £141.98 (GOE) £158.63 (GW) £180.00 (FRI) £410.59 (BY)
1995 IB £1,400.00 (FA) £1,500.00 (BIB)
1995 magnum £381.88 (REI)
1995 magnum IB £1,450.00 (FA)
1994 £69.95 (BU) £145.00 (ROB)
1994 IB £800.00 (FA) £850.00 (BIB)
1994 magnum £300.00 (ROB)
1994 double magnum £352.50 (FA)
1993 £67.50 (BU) £76.38 (REI) £79.17 (MI) £83.50 (YOU) £90.22 (BY)
1993 IB £750.00 (FA) £800.00 (BIB)
1993 magnum IB £750.00 (FA)
1992 £57.50 (BU) £125.04 (BY)
1991 £128.11 (BY)
1991 IB £600.00 (FA)
1990 £225.00 (BU) £279.06 (GOE) £296.83 (WY) £400.00 (FORT) £495.00 (ROB)
1990 IB £2,650.00 (FA) £2,690.00 (BIB) £3,200.00 (CAV)
1990 magnum IB £2,650.00 (FA)

1989 £125.00 (BU) £137.99 (SUN) £146.95 (LAY) £155.00 (FRI) £169.17 (MI) £170.00 (ROB) £175.00 (FORT) £183.10 (PLAY)
1989 IB £1,250.00 (FA)
1989 magnum IB £1,250.00 (FA)
1988 £113.33 (MI) £150.00 (FORT)
1988 IB £1,030.00 (FA)
1988 magnum £300.00 (FORT)
1987 £57.50 (BU)
1987 IB £650.00 (FA)
1986 £120.00 (CON) £139.17 (MI) £169.00 (NI)
1986 IB £1,150.00 (FA) £1,200.00 (BIB)
1986 magnum IB £1,150.00 (FA)
1985 £140.00 (TAN) £169.00 (NI)
1985 IB £1,180.00 (FA)
1985 magnum IB £1,100.00 (FA)
1984 £57.50 (BU) £78.95 (ROB)
1984 IB £540.00 (FA)
1983 £75.00 (BU) £117.50 (MI) £131.17 (WY) £145.00 (FORT)
1983 magnum IB £980.00 (FA)
1982 £332.92 (GOE) £393.48 (WY) £412.50 (MI) £450.00 (FORT) £540.00 (ROB)
1981 £90.15 (BY) £105.16 (PLA)
1981 magnum IB £820.00 (FA)
1980 £62.00 (ROB)
1980 IB £500.00 (FA)
1979 £140.00 (FORT)
1979 IB £950.00 (FA)
1979 magnum IB £950.00 (FA)
1978 £100.00 (BU) £150.00 (FORT) £190.00 (ROB)
1978 double magnum £470.00 (FA)
1976 IB £600.00 (FA)
1975 £320.00 (UB)
1975 double magnum £470.00 (FA)
1971 magnum £150.00 (BEN)
1970 £275.00 (BEN) £425.00 (FORT)
1967 £64.63 (FA)
1966 £193.88 (WY) £195.00 (BU) £229.13 (REI) £280.00 (CRO) £293.75 (CAV) £395.00 (TAN) £400.00 (FORT)
1964 £195.00 (BAL) £205.63 (CAV) £255.42 (WY) £287.88 (REI)
1964 IB £2,150.00 (FA)
1964 magnum £464.13 (CAV)

> ***EC*** *(ex-cellar) price per dozen, excluding shipping, duty and VAT.*
> ***IB*** *(in bond) price per dozen, excluding duty and VAT.*
> *All other prices, per bottle incl VAT.*

1962 £296.84 (WY) £350.00 (ROB)
1961 £998.75 (REI) £1,152.83 (WY)
1961 IB £10,000.00 (FA)
1961 magnum £3,382.53 (WY)
1960 £45.00 (BU) £393.48 (WY)
1959 £855.99 (WY)
1958 £165.68 (WY)
1958 magnum £400.38 (WY)
1955 £445.00 (CRO)
1953 £386.58 (WY)
1953 magnum £994.05 (WY)
1952 £338.26 (WY)
1950 £483.22 (WY)
1949 £1,014.77 (WY)
1945 £1,960.49 (WY)
1940 £211.50 (FA) £434.90 (WY)
1937 £258.50 (REI) £264.38 (CAV) £289.93 (WY)
1934 £441.80 (WY)
1924 £635.09 (WY)
1916 £441.80 (WY)
1909 £1,090.69 (WY)

Latour-à-Pomerol *Pomerol*
1998 IB £400.00 (FA)
1997 £34.84 (CB)
1996 £33.49 (CB)
1995 IB £320.00 (FA)
1994 £26.85 (CB) £39.09 (HA)
1994 IB £250.00 (FA)
1983 IB £360.00 (FA)
1982 £158.78 (WY)
1982 IB £1,200.00 (FA)
1981 £55.23 (WY)
1971 IB £600.00 (FA)

Lavillotte *cru bourgeois Médoc*
1996 £12.50 (FORT)

Léoville-Barton *2ème cru classé St-Julien*
1998 IB £260.00 (FRI) £280.00 (WY) £285.00 (FA)
1998 EC £295.00 (ELL) £305.00 (TAN)
1997 £14.95 (AD) £23.50 (GOE) £29.95 (LEA) £30.83 (MI) £31.00 (JU) £31.75 (TAN) £35.00 (FORT) £35.13 (CB) £39.95 (DI)
1997 IB £264.00 (RAE)
1997 EC £291.00 (JON) £305.00 (ELL)
1997 magnum £47.00 (GOE)
1996 £33.78 (GOE) £35.00 (BU) £37.70 (WY) £40.83 (MI) £43.99 (FRI) £45.00 (FORT) £49.95 (DI) £59.56 (BY)
1996 double magnum £152.75 (FA) £172.33 (WY)

1995 £34.27 (GOE) £39.95 (BU) £42.30 (WY) £43.95 (LAY) £44.99 (FRI) £50.35 (GW) £78.20 (BY)
1995 IB £340.00 (FA)
1995 magnum £83.23 (WY)
1995 double magnum £217.38 (WY)

1994 £24.50 (DI) £24.95 (BU) £25.95 (GOE) £28.50 (UN) £31.00 (HIG) £33.49 (BOD) £33.49 (SUN) £35.79 (JON) £38.66 (WY) £44.45 (JER)
1994 IB £250.00 (FA)
1994 magnum £82.84 (WY)
1993 £28.02 (PLAY) £29.95 (BU)
1992 £29.95 (BU) £33.75 (WR) £33.75 (BOT)
1991 £20.00 (BU) £29.34 (WY)
1990 £59.50 (BU) £65.00 (TAN)
1990 IB £550.00 (FA)
1989 £46.41 (REI) £62.90 (LAY) £63.51 (WY) £64.60 (TAN)
1988 £39.95 (BU) £40.21 (PIP) £48.18 (GW) £51.17 (BY) £58.70 (LAY)
1988 IB £380.00 (FA)
1986 £45.00 (CON) £49.50 (BEN) £64.35 (GW) £64.90 (TAN) £70.00 (FORT) £80.00 (ROB)
1986 IB £500.00 (FA) £551.50 (BIB)
1986 magnum £144.97 (WY)
1985 £41.13 (REI) £59.57 (NO) £75.00 (FORT)
1985 IB £500.00 (FA)
1983 £36.00 (YOU) £55.23 (WY)
1982 £82.25 (CAV)
1982 IB £650.00 (FA) £740.00 (CAV)
1975 £37.01 (REI)
1970 £59.50 (BU) £82.84 (WY)
1970 magnum £179.48 (WY)
1966 £69.50 (BU)
1961 £165.00 (CRO) £193.29 (WY)

Léoville-Las-Cases *2ème cru classé St-Julien*
1998 £58.26 (GOE)
1998 IB £600.00 (FRI) £659.00 (LEA) £798.00 (CB)
1998 EC £595.00 (CAV) £675.00 (ELL)
1997 £63.65 (GOE) £79.00 (JU) £79.00 (JU) £83.33 (MI) £89.00 (LEA) £89.89 (CB) £98.85 (TAN)
1997 IB £600.00 (BIB)
1997 EC £795.00 (ELL)
1996 £109.67 (WY) £113.33 (MI) £124.00 (FRI)
1996 imperial £881.25 (FA) £1,086.88 (WY)
1995 £70.50 (GOE) £85.00 (YOU) £87.50 (MI) £90.00 (FRI) £109.50 (WR)
1995 IB £710.00 (BIB) £720.00 (FA)
1995 magnum IB £720.00 (FA)
1994 £38.68 (GOE) £49.50 (BAL) £53.50 (YOU) £59.95 (WAI) £62.50 (MI)
1994 IB £420.00 (FA)
1994 magnum IB £420.00 (FA)
1994 double magnum £193.88 (FA)
1993 £54.95 (LEA) £58.33 (MI) £59.95 (DI)
1990 £110.00 (YOU) £125.00 (POR) £125.95 (TAN)
1990 IB £950.00 (FA)
1990 ½ bottle IB £950.00 (FA)
1989 £94.00 (REI) £96.64 (WY) £97.50 (BEN) £98.00 (BAL) £101.67 (MI)
1989 IB £750.00 (FA)
1988 £55.00 (HA) £64.63 (REI) £75.20 (BY) £78.50 (BEN) £93.00 (BER)
1988 IB £550.00 (FA)
1988 imperial £423.00 (FA)
1986 £149.00 (BAL) £151.58 (REI)
1986 IB £950.00 (FA) £950.00 (BIB)
1986 imperial £735.38 (FA)
1985 £89.50 (BEN)
1985 IB £750.00 (FA) £850.00 (CAV)
1985 imperial £799.00 (FA)
1983 £48.47 (GOE) £66.27 (WY) £90.00 (JU)
1983 magnum IB £500.00 (FA)
1982 £175.00 (POR) £193.29 (WY) £195.00 (BEN) £250.00 (FORT)
1982 IB £1,550.00 (FA) £1,600.00 (BIB) £1,795.00 (CAV)
1982 magnum £323.13 (CAV)
1981 £54.05 (REI)
1981 magnum IB £420.00 (FA)
1980 double magnum £99.88 (FA)
1980 imperial £193.88 (FA)
1979 £39.95 (BU) £41.13 (REI) £53.50 (BEN)
1979 IB £450.00 (FA)
1979 double magnum £164.50 (FA)
1978 £78.50 (BEN) £82.20 (TAN) £82.91 (BY)
1978 IB £650.00 (CAV)
1978 magnum IB £695.00 (CAV)
1977 imperial £193.88 (FA)

1975 £47.00 (YOU) £75.00 (BAL)
1975 IB £500.00 (FA)
1970 £52.00 (HIG) £52.88 (REI)
1970 IB £420.00 (FA)
1970 double magnum £448.71 (WY)
1964 IB £550.00 (FA)
1962 £99.88 (REI) £105.00 (YOU)
1961 £205.63 (REI) £234.71 (WY)
1955 £95.00 (CRO)
1945 £579.86 (WY)
1937 £75.00 (BU)

Léoville-Poyferré *2ème cru classé St-Julien*
1998 IB £210.00 (FRI) £220.00 (LEA)
1998 EC £295.00 (CAV)
1997 £22.03 (GOE) £27.50 (MI) £30.53 (CB) £35.70 (TAN)
1997 IB £198.00 (BIB) £200.00 (FA) £270.00 (RAE)
1996 £32.00 (AD) £32.90 (LAY) £37.13 (CB) £40.59 (FRI)
1996 IB £270.00 (FA) £270.00 (RAE) £280.00 (BIB)
1996 magnum £74.85 (CB)
1995 £33.50 (FRI) £35.25 (WY)
1995 IB £275.00 (FA) £320.00 (CAV)
1995 magnum IB £275.00 (FA)
1994 £22.50 (UN) £29.50 (LEA)
1994 magnum £47.98 (GOE)
1993 £27.61 (BY)
1992 £15.99 (RAE)
1990 IB £560.00 (FA) £850.00 (CAV)
1990 magnum IB £560.00 (FA) £795.00 (CAV)
1986 £41.95 (NI)
1986 IB £375.00 (FA)
1986 imperial £311.38 (FA)
1985 £27.60 (FLE) £46.02 (GOE)
1985 IB £350.00 (FA)
1983 £56.95 (TAN)
1983 IB £400.00 (FA)
1983 imperial £387.75 (FA)
1982 £75.00 (BU)
1970 £37.28 (WY)
1961 £131.17 (WY)
1961 IB £1,180.00 (FA)
1959 IB £1,050.00 (FA)
1947 £346.63 (CAV)
1924 £103.55 (WY)

Lestage *cru bourgeois supérieur Listrac*
1993 £7.99 (WAT)
1961 £35.00 (BU)
1936 £64.63 (REI)

Liversan *cru grand bourgeois Haut-Médoc*
1997 £9.99 (SAF)
1985 £24.00 (CRO)
1982 £19.00 (CRO)

Loudenne *cru grand bourgeois Médoc*
1997 £11.67 (MI)
1996 £14.17 (MI)
1995 £12.50 (MI) £13.00 (JU)
1994 £10.49 (CON)
1990 IB £140.00 (BIB)

la Louvière *Pessac-Léognan*
1995 £16.95 (DI) £22.95 (LEA) £23.45 (NI)

Lynch-Bages *5ème cru classé Pauillac*
1998 £250.00 (FRI)
1998 EC £250.00 (ELL) £295.00 (CAV)
1998 magnum £270.00 (FRI)
1997 £37.50 (MI) £40.10 (CB) £40.60 (TAN)
1997 EC £365.00 (ELL)
1996 £35.25 (WY) £39.17 (MI) £39.50 (FRI) £42.50 (TAN) £43.50 (CON) £50.00 (FORT)
1996 IB £295.00 (CAV) £300.00 (FA)
1996 magnum £83.50 (FRI)
1996 jeroboam £235.00 (FA)
1995 £36.50 (UN) £36.67 (MI) £41.50 (FRI) £42.30 (WY) £47.95 (LEA) £74.31 (BY)
1995 magnum £86.50 (FRI)
1995 magnum IB £340.00 (FA)
1995 jeroboam £334.88 (WY)
1994 £29.17 (MI) £29.99 (BOD) £29.99 (SUN) £31.50 (UN) £31.55 (JER) £32.79 (WY)
1994 IB £260.00 (FA)
1993 £29.17 (MI) £41.13 (REI)
1993 IB £260.00 (FA)
1992 £32.21 (WY) £40.50 (STE)
1990 £72.66 (NO) £84.50 (FRI) £98.45 (PIP)
1990 IB £720.00 (FA)
1990 magnum £175.00 (FRI)
1989 £100.00 (WAI) £110.45 (WY)
1989 IB £850.00 (FA)
1988 £69.03 (WY) £80.00 (FORT)
1988 IB £550.00 (FA)
1988 magnum IB £550.00 (FA)
1986 £85.00 (FORT)
1986 IB £625.00 (FA)
1986 magnum IB £625.00 (FA)
1985 £85.00 (BU) £88.13 (GOE) £107.69 (WY) £115.00 (BEN) £115.00 (ROB) £120.00 (FORT)
1985 IB £850.00 (FA)
1983 £49.50 (BU) £75.94 (WY)

1982 £124.26 (WY) £245.00 (UB)
1982 IB £1,020.00 (FA)
1982 jeroboam £1,350.00 (FRI)
1978 £56.99 (REI) £69.03 (WY)
1975 £52.88 (REI)
1975 IB £360.00 (FA)
1970 £150.00 (FORT) £151.87 (WY)
1970 IB £1,050.00 (FA)
1966 magnum £220.90 (WY)
1964 magnum £88.13 (REI)
1961 £205.63 (REI) £310.65 (WY)
1961 IB £2,200.00 (FA)
1957 £64.63 (REI)
1945 £129.25 (REI) £738.64 (WY)
1937 £111.63 (REI)

Lynch-Moussas *5ème cru classé Pauillac*
1997 £15.83 (MI)
1997 IB £108.00 (BIB)
1996 £14.99 (OD) £17.50 (MI) £18.95 (LEA) £23.95 (PHI)
1995 £17.50 (MI)
1983 £28.79 (REI)
1982 IB £215.00 (FA)

du Lyonnat *Lussac-St-Émilion*
1997 £11.37 (PLAY)
1996 £9.50 (ROB) £9.99 (JON) £9.99 (POR)
1995 £9.95 (ROB)

Macquin-St-Georges *St-Georges-St-Émilion*
1998 IB £78.00 (CB)
1997 £7.99 (POR) £8.08 (CB) £8.10 (HAH)
1997 magnum £16.74 (CB)
1996 £8.34 (CB) £8.50 (TAN)

Magdelaine *1er grand cru classé St-Émilion*
1998 IB £339.00 (CB) £360.00 (FA)
1997 £32.61 (CB)
1996 £27.44 (CB) £29.50 (WS)
1996 IB £250.00 (BIB)
1994 £54.05 (CB)
1987 IB £150.00 (FA)
1981 £22.09 (WY)
1978 IB £340.00 (FA)
1964 IB £500.00 (FA)

Malartic-Lagravière *cru classé Pessac-Léognan*
1997 £17.50 (MI)
1996 £21.99 (UN) £21.99 (UN)
1988 £22.91 (REI)
1985 £26.44 (REI)

Malescasse *cru bourgeois Haut-Médoc*
1996 £12.99 (NI) £14.95 (CON)
1995 £13.22 (GOE) £13.25 (HIG) £14.95 (STE)
1988 £18.50 (FLE)
1985 £18.00 (CRO)

Malescot-St-Exupéry *3ème cru classé Margaux*
1997 £22.50 (BAL) £29.99 (POR)
1996 £24.00 (JU) £29.99 (POR)
1995 £21.99 (UN) £32.50 (AME)
1995 IB £320.00 (BIB)
1986 £22.50 (BU) £33.49 (REI)
1985 £38.19 (REI)
1983 £26.44 (REI) £27.50 (BU)
1982 £33.49 (REI)
1970 £26.44 (REI)

de Malleret *cru grand bourgeois Haut-Médoc*
1996 £11.10 (HAH)
1985 IB £80.00 (FA)

de Marbuzet *cru grand bourgeois exceptionnel St-Estèphe*
1997 £16.50 (JU)
1996 £21.00 (JU)
1990 £23.99 (GOE)
1989 IB £200.00 (FA)
1985 £37.50 (BU)

Margaux *1er cru classé Margaux*
1998 IB £980.00 (FRI)
1998 EC £795.00 (ELL) £850.00 (CAV) £895.00 (TAN)
1997 £80.78 (GOE) £93.33 (MI) £98.85 (TAN) £99.00 (JU) £102.07 (HA) £110.45 (CB)
1997 EC £995.00 (ELL)
1996 £160.00 (DI) £172.82 (GOE) £200.00 (FRI) £207.50 (MI) £245.00 (CON)
1996 IB £1,700.00 (FA) £1,780.00 (BIB)
1995 £245.00 (FRI)
1994 £128.08 (PEN) £139.17 (MI)
1994 IB £900.00 (FA) £940.00 (BIB)
1994 magnum IB £850.00 (FA)
1993 £99.88 (PEN) £108.43 (BY) £150.00 (FLE)
1993 IB £900.00 (FA) £940.00 (BIB)
1993 magnum IB £850.00 (FA)
1990 £318.12 (WY) £320.00 (BEN) £440.00 (ROB)
1989 IB £1,500.00 (FA)
1988 £130.50 (BEN)

1988 magnum IB £1,200.00 (FA)
1987 £207.02 (BY)
1986 £164.01 (GOE) £235.00 (TAN) £250.00 (FORT) £250.00 (ROB) £275.00 (BAL)
1986 IB £1,600.00 (FA)
1986 magnum IB £1,600.00 (FA)
1985 £129.25 (GOE) £180.00 (BAL) £225.00 (ROB)
1985 IB £1,550.00 (FA)
1985 magnum £329.00 (REI)
1985 magnum IB £1,550.00 (FA)
1984 IB £600.00 (FA)
1983 £170.00 (YOU) £170.38 (REI) £200.00 (BEN) £235.00 (FORT) £300.00 (ROB)
1983 IB £1,600.00 (FA) £1,650.00 (BIB)
1982 £336.53 (WY) £350.00 (ROB) £450.00 (FORT)
1982 IB £3,000.00 (BIB) £3,100.00 (FA)
1982 magnum £611.00 (CAV)
1981 £132.00 (NI) £135.00 (ROB) £135.13 (REI)
1981 IB £1,100.00 (FA)
1981 magnum IB £1,100.00 (FA)
1979 £180.00 (ROB)
1979 magnum £415.00 (UB)
1978 £225.00 (ROB)
1978 IB £1,300.00 (FA)
1971 £41.13 (FA)
1970 £58.75 (FA)
1970 magnum £205.63 (REI)
1967 IB £360.00 (FA)
1966 £103.55 (WY) £176.25 (REI)
1966 IB £1,426.50 (BIB)
1962 £95.00 (BU) £164.50 (REI)
1961 £581.63 (REI) £699.13 (CAV) £850.00 (FORT)
1961 IB £5,750.00 (FA)
1960 £75.00 (BU)
1959 £510.83 (WY)
1959 IB £4,000.00 (FA)
1959 magnum IB £4,000.00 (FA)
1953 £493.50 (CAV)
1953 magnum £1,311.59 (WY)
1952 £146.88 (REI)
1949 £731.73 (WY)
1945 £800.00 (CAV) £1,000.00 (DI) £1,353.01 (WY)
1929 £1,090.69 (WY)
1926 £323.13 (REI) £724.83 (WY)
1924 £441.80 (WY)
1921 £517.74 (WY)
1917 £131.17 (WY)
1908 £883.60 (WY)

Marquis d'Alesme-Becker *3ème cru classé Margaux*
1989 IB £265.00 (BIB)
1982 £44.18 (WY)

Marquis-de-Terme *4ème cru classé Margaux*
1996 £19.00 (JU) £21.50 (WS) £25.95 (CON)
1993 ½ bottle £9.69 (REI)
1989 IB £200.00 (FA)
1924 £193.29 (WY)
1920 £89.75 (WY)

Marsau *Côtes de Francs*
1997 £5.99 (SAI)
1997 IB £60.00 (FA)
1996 £10.00 (MV)

de Martouret *Bordeaux*
1997 £5.99 (AME)

Maucaillou *cru bourgeois Moulis*
1997 £17.95 (DI)
1996 £14.60 (HIG) £14.95 (BER) £14.99 (JON)
1995 £13.05 (HA) £17.95 (STE) £19.99 (TES)
1994 £12.45 (STE)
1990 £29.45 (TAN)
1989 £52.00 (UB)
1988 IB £190.00 (FA)

Mayne-Vieil *Fronsac*
1996 £6.54 (NO) £6.85 (BO)

Mazeris *Canon-Fronsac*
1998 IB £99.00 (CB)
1996 £10.99 (CB) £11.00 (JU)
1995 £12.98 (CB) £15.00 (JU)
1985 £23.50 (BAL) £24.68 (REI)

Méaume *Bordeaux Supérieur*
1997 £5.20 (HA) £5.99 (MAJ)
1996 £5.20 (HA) £6.90 (JU)
1995 £7.90 (JU)

le Menaudat *1ères Côtes de Blaye*
1996 £6.45 (AV)

Meyney *cru grand bourgeois exceptionnel St-Estèphe*
1996 £18.00 (JU) £18.00 (ELL) £23.35 (NO)
1996 IB £120.00 (BIB) £125.00 (FA)
1995 £16.49 (UN) £18.50 (ROB) £21.19 (HA)
1995 IB £150.00 (FA)
1994 £21.00 (STA)

1993 £15.95 (COC) £19.85 (HA)
1990 £27.50 (BU) £28.89 (GOE) £34.95 (DI)
1989 £44.00 (UB)
1988 IB £225.00 (FA)
1987 £14.50 (BU)
1986 IB £260.00 (FA)
1982 IB £360.00 (FA)
1976 magnum £50.00 (BU)
1953 £65.00 (BU)

Millet *Graves*
1996 £10.99 (FRI)
1995 £10.99 (FRI) £11.25 (SOM) £14.32 (PLAY)

la Mission-Haut-Brion *cru classé Pessac-Léognan*
1998 IB £680.00 (FA) £680.00 (BIB) £800.00 (WY)
1997 £65.00 (JU) £65.00 (BAL) £65.00 (MI) £68.15 (CB)
1997 IB £618.00 (RAE)
1996 £51.41 (WY) £66.67 (MI) £75.00 (CON) £90.00 (JU)
1996 IB £500.00 (FA)
1995 £70.50 (CON) £90.00 (JU)
1995 IB £500.00 (FA)
1994 £49.00 (POR) £49.50 (BAL) £70.00 (JU)
1994 IB £395.00 (FA)
1993 £45.00 (FLE)
1993 IB £380.00 (BIB)
1993 magnum IB £350.00 (FA)
1992 £54.65 (WY)
1992 IB £380.00 (BIB)
1991 £41.42 (WY)
1990 £110.00 (YOU) £113.33 (MI)
1990 IB £1,000.00 (FA)
1988 £47.50 (CON) £64.00 (CRO) £79.31 (REI)
1988 IB £550.00 (FA)
1988 magnum IB £550.00 (FA)
1986 £72.50 (CON) £75.00 (CRO) £86.99 (WY)
1986 magnum £146.88 (REI)
1985 £70.50 (GOE)
1985 IB £750.00 (FA)
1982 £173.00 (NI) £214.00 (WY) £225.00 (FORT)
1976 £50.00 (YOU)
1976 magnum £117.36 (WY)
1975 £323.13 (CAV) £325.00 (YOU)
1975 IB £3,000.00 (FA)
1971 £88.13 (REI)
1970 £146.88 (REI)
1970 IB £1,000.00 (FA) £1,650.00 (CAV)
1966 IB £1,900.00 (FA)
1966 magnum £364.25 (REI)
1962 IB £1,250.00 (FA)
1959 £646.25 (FA) £763.75 (REI) £800.00 (CAV)
1955 £611.00 (FA) £646.25 (CAV)
1995 double magnum £244.79 (WY)
1953 £334.88 (FA) £528.75 (CAV)
1949 £759.34 (WY)
1945 £1,449.66 (WY)
1920 £869.79 (WY)

Monbousquet *grand cru St-Émilion*
1998 IB £285.00 (FA)
1998 EC £275.00 (CAV)
1997 IB £220.00 (BIB)
1996 £32.31 (REI) £33.35 (TAN) £46.13 (PLAY)
1996 IB £240.00 (FA)
1995 IB £300.00 (FA)

Monbrison *cru bourgeois Margaux*
1998 EC £152.60 (HAH)
1997 £13.71 (GOE)
1996 £15.67 (HA) £21.00 (JU)
1989 IB £300.00 (BIB)

Monlot-Capet *St-Émilion*
1996 £12.50 (CON) £12.90 (HAH)

Montaiguillon *Montagne-St-Émilion*
1996 £8.90 (TAN) £9.95 (LEA)
1995 £8.50 (LEA) £8.65 (NEZ) £8.95 (TAN)

Montbrun *cru bourgeois Margaux*
1945 £179.48 (WY)

Montrose *2ème cru classé St-Estèphe*
1998 IB £310.00 (FRI) £336.00 (LEA)
1998 EC £295.00 (CAV)
1997 £34.27 (GOE) £39.17 (MI) £42.00 (JU) £45.95 (LEA) £48.85 (CB) £48.90 (TAN)
1997 ½ bottle £17.63 (GOE)
1996 £46.67 (MI) £56.50 (FRI) £58.75 (GW) £58.95 (BER) £59.95 (TAN)
1996 imperial £329.00 (FA)
1995 £29.96 (REI) £36.67 (MI) £38.68 (GOE) £40.00 (YOU) £43.95 (LEA) £50.67 (FRI)
1995 IB £340.00 (FA) £350.00 (BIB)
1995 ½ bottle £26.50 (FRI)
1994 £34.85 (JER)
1993 £25.56 (PIP) £29.99 (POR) £30.00 (MI) £42.50 (WRI) £48.60 (BY)
1993 IB £195.00 (FA)
1992 £24.95 (TAN)

1992 IB £175.00 (FA) £300.00 (BIB)
1991 £36.24 (WY)
1991 IB £360.00 (BIB)
1990 £170.38 (REI) £172.58 (WY) £180.00 (BAL) £250.00 (ROB)

1990 IB £1,300.00 (FA) £1,600.00 (CAV)
1989 £63.65 (GOE) £73.00 (FRI) £85.60 (WY)
1989 ½ bottle £38.50 (FRI)
1988 £36.00 (SOM) £45.00 (FRI)
1988 IB £380.00 (FA)
1986 £54.00 (FRI) £57.50 (MI) £57.95 (BAL) £80.08 (WY)
1986 IB £500.00 (FA) £560.00 (BIB)
1985 £51.00 (FRI) £55.95 (ROB) £69.94 (PLAY)
1984 IB £150.00 (FA)
1983 £49.30 (AV) £75.00 (UB)
1983 IB £340.00 (FA)
1982 £69.00 (POR) £82.84 (WY) £84.50 (FRI)
1982 IB £680.00 (CAV)
1982 jeroboam £810.00 (FRI)
1982 imperial £1,080.00 (FRI)
1981 £74.85 (VIN)
1981 double magnum £123.38 (FA)
1981 imperial £275.00 (BEN)
1979 imperial £264.38 (FA)
1978 £55.23 (WY)
1975 £150.00 (BU)
1974 £14.99 (BU)
1970 £84.21 (BY) £117.36 (WY) £117.50 (TAN)
1970 IB £880.00 (FA) £995.00 (CAV)
1966 £50.00 (YOU)
1966 IB £600.00 (FA)
1961 £155.00 (CRO) £219.00 (NI) £229.13 (REI) £270.00 (ROB)
1959 £205.63 (REI)
1955 IB £1,600.00 (FA)
1945 £579.86 (WY)
1934 £88.13 (FA)
1928 £287.88 (REI) £434.90 (WY)
1912 £146.88 (REI)

Moulin-du-Cadet *grand cru classé St-Émilion*
1996 £15.57 (CB)
1995 £18.45 (CB)

Moulin Haut-Villars *Fronsac*
1997 £7.25 (WS) £10.15 (JER)

Moulin Pey-Labrie *Canon-Fronsac*
1994 £13.85 (CB)

Moulin-à-Vent *cru grand bourgeois Moulis*
1996 £10.99 (SAF)

Moulinet *Pomerol*
1996 £16.49 (BOT)
1989 £22.50 (BU)
1979 £20.00 (BU)

Mouton-Rothschild *1er cru classé Pauillac*
1998 IB £800.00 (WY) £820.00 (FA) £980.00 (FRI)
1997 £77.84 (GOE) £93.33 (MI) £94.90 (LAY) £98.85 (TAN) £99.00 (JU) £99.00 (BAL) £109.28 (CB) £144.00 (DI)
1997 IB £765.00 (BIB)
1997 EC £995.00 (ELL)
1997 magnum £155.69 (GOE)
1997 imperial £743.78 (GOE)
1996 £50.00 (UN) £119.95 (WY) £120.00 (HIG) £152.00 (FRI) £173.33 (MI)
1996 IB £1,150.00 (FA) £1,250.00 (BIB)
1996 ½ bottle IB £1,190.00 (FA)
1996 magnum IB £640.00 (BIB) £1,250.00 (FA)
1996 imperial £1,104.50 (WY)
1995 £141.98 (GOE) £145.00 (SUN) £200.00 (FRI) £282.80 (BY)
1995 IB £1,250.00 (FA)
1994 £68.50 (UN) £75.00 (DI) £85.00 (BAL) £95.00 (WAI) £106.93 (PEN) £121.67 (MI)
1994 magnum IB £720.00 (FA)
1993 £79.17 (MI) £90.00 (UN) £95.00 (ROB) £138.00 (BY)
1993 IB £720.00 (FA)
1993 magnum IB £720.00 (FA)
1992 £96.64 (WY) £111.63 (PLA) £141.48 (BY)
1992 IB £650.00 (FA) £760.00 (BIB)
1992 magnum IB £650.00 (FA)
1991 £87.95 (ROB) £96.64 (WY) £135.64 (BY)
1991 IB £660.00 (FA)
1991 magnum IB £660.00 (FA)

1990 £114.07 (GOE) £139.00 (FRI) £139.95 (DI) £147.50 (MI) £151.87 (WY) £180.95 (PEN) £235.00 (ROB)
1990 IB £1,150.00 (FA)
1990 magnum IB £1,150.00 (FA)
1989 £145.00 (BEN) £165.00 (FRI) £186.39 (WY)
1989 magnum IB £1,400.00 (FA)
1989 double magnum £564.00 (FA)
1989 imperial £1,104.50 (FA)
1988 £125.00 (BU) £130.50 (BEN) £175.00 (FORT)
1988 IB £1,050.00 (FA)
1988 magnum IB £1,050.00 (FA)
1988 jeroboam £681.50 (FA)
1987 £96.64 (WY)
1987 IB £720.00 (FA)
1987 magnum IB £710.00 (FA)
1986 £235.00 (GOE) £289.93 (WY) £350.00 (FORT) £350.00 (ROB)
1986 IB £2,200.00 (FA) £2,850.00 (CAV)
1986 double magnum £1,169.13 (REI)
1985 £122.40 (GOE) £135.00 (BU) £146.88 (REI) £158.00 (BEN) £200.00 (FORT) £220.00 (ROB) £222.04 (PLAY) £235.00 (VIN)
1985 IB £1,320.00 (FA) £1,350.00 (BIB)
1985 magnum IB £1,320.00 (FA)
1985 double magnum £96.94 (REI)
1985 jeroboam £846.00 (FA)
1984 £88.00 (ROB)
1983 £107.71 (GOE) £110.00 (BEN) £135.30 (WY) £145.00 (ROB)
1983 IB £1,000.00 (FA)
1983 magnum IB £950.00 (FA)
1982 £337.81 (GOE) £360.00 (JU) £395.00 (TAN) £407.29 (WY) £500.00 (FORT)
1982 IB £3,400.00 (FA) £3,500.00 (CAV)
1982 jeroboam £2,820.00 (FA)
1981 £88.13 (REI) £110.00 (ROB) £110.45 (WY)
1981 IB £780.00 (FA)
1981 ½ bottle IB £780.00 (FA)
1980 IB £620.00 (FA)
1980 jeroboam £393.63 (FA)
1979 £76.38 (FA) £82.25 (REI) £115.00 (ROB)
1979 jeroboam £493.50 (FA)

Oz Clarke's Wine Buying Guide
is an annual publication.
We welcome your suggestions for next year's edition.

1978 £88.13 (REI) £90.00 (ROB)
1978 IB £890.00 (FA)
1978 jeroboam £564.00 (FA)
1976 £95.00 (BU) £110.45 (WY)
1976 magnum £234.71 (WY) £390.00 (UB)
1976 imperial IB £626.00 (BIB)
1975 £91.65 (FA) £115.00 (BEN) £144.97 (WY)
1975 double magnum £55.22 (WY)
1974 £151.87 (WY)
1973 £158.78 (WY)
1972 magnum £205.62 (REI)
1971 £172.58 (WY) £225.00 (VIN)
1971 magnum £289.93 (WY)
1970 £150.00 (BEN) £158.63 (REI) £179.48 (WY) £185.00 (ROB)
1970 IB £1,400.00 (FA)
1970 magnum £364.25 (REI)
1970 magnum IB £1,400.00 (FA)
1966 £258.50 (REI) £324.45 (WY) £395.00 (VIN)
1965 £386.58 (WY)
1964 £220.90 (WY)
1962 £146.88 (REI) £345.16 (WY)
1962 magnum £564.00 (FA)
1961 £763.75 (FA) £822.50 (CAV) £881.25 (REI)
1961 jeroboam £7,637.50 (FA)
1958 £381.88 (REI) £531.55 (WY)
1957 £129.25 (REI) £566.06 (WY)
1953 £1,035.47 (WY)
1950 £323.13 (REI)
1947 £2,347.06 (WY)
1947 magnum £2,526.25 (REI)
1945 £3,231.25 (REI) £5,798.63 (WY)
1944 £642.00 (WY)
1934 £400.38 (WY)
1934 ½ bottle £165.68 (WY)
1933 £205.62 (REI)
1929 £2,485.13 (WY)
1926 £1,366.82 (WY)
1926 magnum £3,348.75 (REI)
1920 £731.73 (WY)
1914 £566.06 (WY)
1909 ½ bottle £324.45 (WY)

Nenin *Pomerol*
1998 £43.08 (GOE)
1998 IB £440.00 (FRI)
1998 EC £475.00 (ELL)
1997 £36.72 (GOE)
1996 £7.49 (HED) £7.64 (GOE)
1995 £29.50 (UN) £29.99 (FRI)
1990 £48.33 (WY)
1983 IB £220.00 (FA)

les Ormes-de-Pez *cru grand bourgeois St-Estèphe*
1998 EC £144.50 (HAH)
1997 £15.83 (MI) £19.95 (LEA)
1996 £19.17 (MI) £19.20 (FRI) £21.00 (STA) £21.74 (CB) £21.95 (BER)
1995 £18.33 (MI) £22.50 (BU) £24.99 (FRI)
1994 £15.50 (WS) £16.65 (GOE) £17.50 (MI) £19.50 (BU) £20.81 (PIP)
1993 £17.50 (MI)
1990 £40.95 (ROB)
1986 £29.50 (BU) £46.00 (UB)
1985 £25.26 (REI)

Palmer *3ème cru classé Margaux*
1998 IB £440.00 (FRI)
1998 EC £495.00 (ELL)
1997 £44.65 (HA) £49.95 (TAN) £55.00 (MI)
1997 EC £475.00 (ELL)
1996 £43.00 (FLE) £65.00 (CON) £66.67 (MI)
1995 £43.00 (FLE) £49.50 (CON) £56.40 (WY) £56.85 (TAN) £66.67 (MI)
1995 IB £420.00 (FA)
1994 £33.50 (UN) £43.33 (MI) £47.29 (HA)
1994 IB £320.00 (FA)
1993 £43.33 (MI)
1990 £75.00 (CON) £80.00 (WAI) £85.00 (FORT) £85.60 (WY)
1990 IB £650.00 (FA)
1989 £94.00 (YOU) £95.00 (CON) £100.00 (FRI) £113.33 (MI) £114.60 (WY) £115.00 (ROB) £125.00 (FORT) £150.17 (PLAY)
1988 £52.88 (REI) £75.00 (CON)
1986 £63.65 (GOE) £68.00 (SOM) £69.00 (NI) £75.00 (CON) £80.08 (WY) £90.00 (FORT)
1986 IB £580.00 (FA)
1985 £63.65 (GOE) £75.00 (CON) £82.84 (WY) £90.00 (FORT) £105.00 (FRI)
1983 £120.00 (CRO) £142.00 (STA) £146.90 (TAN) £175.00 (FORT) £195.00 (ROB)
1983 IB £1,200.00 (FA) £1,200.00 (BIB)
1983 magnum £303.74 (WY) £330.00 (FORT)
1982 £75.00 (SOM) £77.84 (GOE)
1982 IB £790.00 (FA)
1982 magnum £193.29 (WY)
1981 £56.99 (REI)
1981 IB £280.00 (FA)
1981 magnum £112.21 (REI)
1979 IB £480.00 (BIB)
1978 £155.00 (UB)
1976 IB £300.00 (FA)
1975 £56.99 (REI) £95.00 (ROB) £96.64 (WY)
1975 IB £720.00 (FA)
1970 £140.00 (BU) £140.00 (YOU) £165.00 (NI) £165.68 (WY)
1970 IB £1,250.00 (FA) £1,500.00 (CAV)
1966 £325.00 (FORT)
1966 IB £2,200.00 (FA)
1961 £738.64 (WY) £875.38 (REI)
1961 IB £8,800.00 (FA)
1959 £293.75 (FA)

Pape-Clément *cru classé Pessac-Léognan*
1998 IB £260.00 (FA)
1998 EC £340.00 (TAN)
1997 £31.00 (JU) £33.33 (MI)
1997 IB £291.00 (RAE)
1996 £37.00 (JU) £45.00 (MI)
1996 IB £280.00 (FA)
1995 £49.17 (MI)
1995 IB £320.00 (FA)
1994 £32.50 (MI) £35.00 (JU)
1990 IB £440.00 (FA)
1989 £44.95 (BEN)
1989 IB £330.00 (FA)
1988 £72.00 (UB)
1988 IB £380.00 (FA)
1986 £59.50 (TAN)
1986 IB £440.00 (FA)
1985 IB £420.00 (FA)
1982 £98.00 (ROB)
1970 £41.13 (REI)
1970 IB £390.00 (CAV)
1961 IB £1,200.00 (FA)

Patache d'Aux *cru grand bourgeois Médoc*
1997 £6.79 (HA) £8.05 (TAN)
1997 EC £58.56 (JON)
1996 £9.99 (POR)
1995 £8.35 (GN) £9.80 (TAN) £10.99 (JON)
1994 £8.90 (TAN) £9.75 (COC) £9.95 (ROB)
1993 £9.00 (CRO) £9.99 (JON)
1978 £18.51 (REI)

Paveil-de-Luze *cru bourgeois Margaux*
1970 £18.50 (BU)

***EC** (ex-cellar) price per dozen, excluding shipping, duty and VAT.*
***IB** (in bond) price per dozen, excluding duty and VAT.*
All other prices, per bottle incl VAT.

Pavie *1er grand cru classé St-Émilion*
1998 EC £495.00 (CAV)
1997 £29.99 (BOD) £29.99 (SUN)
1996 £28.18 (HA) £31.50 (FRI)
1996 IB £230.00 (BIB) £264.00 (RAE)
1995 £29.95 (BAL) £31.99 (FRI)
1994 £32.50 (UN) £35.00 (POR)
1994 IB £195.00 (RAE)
1993 IB £150.00 (FA)
1990 IB £450.00 (FA)
1989 £50.35 (GW)
1988 £38.19 (REI) £50.00 (FRI)
1988 IB £340.00 (FA)
1987 £31.49 (FRI)
1986 £54.00 (FRI) £72.27 (PLAY)
1985 IB £330.00 (FA)
1983 magnum £245.00 (UB)
1982 £50.00 (YOU) £145.00 (UB)
1975 £40.54 (REI)
1924 £165.68 (WY)

Pavie-Decesse *grand cru classé St-Émilion*
1998 IB £400.00 (BIB)
1998 EC £450.00 (CAV)
1997 £45.83 (MI)
1996 £26.95 (LEA)
1995 £25.00 (UN) £26.99 (FRI)
1994 £17.14 (GOE)
1993 £22.95 (ROB)
1993 IB £160.00 (FA)
1983 IB £320.00 (BIB)

Pavie-Macquin *grand cru classé St-Émilion*
1997 £35.00 (JU) £48.33 (MI)
1997 IB £350.00 (FA)
1996 £30.00 (JU) £32.50 (MI) £35.00 (WAI)
1996 IB £230.00 (FA)
1995 £24.97 (GOE) £32.50 (MI) £37.00 (JU)

Pavillon-Rouge-du-Château Margaux *Margaux*
1998 IB £250.00 (WY)
1997 £21.05 (GOE) £25.00 (JU) £26.67 (MI) £27.50 (LEA)
1997 IB £180.00 (BIB)
1996 £30.84 (WY) £31.82 (GOE) £32.50 (MI) £34.35 (LAY) £36.23 (CB)
1996 IB £265.00 (FA) £320.00 (CAV)
1995 £37.60 (WY)
1990 £57.50 (BU)
1990 IB £480.00 (FA)
1986 £32.00 (CRO) £66.27 (WY)
1985 IB £400.00 (FA)
1983 £35.00 (BU) £96.64 (WY)
1982 IB £500.00 (FA)

Pédesclaux *5ème cru classé Pauillac*
1996 £19.17 (MI) £27.99 (SAI)
1995 £16.67 (MI)

Petit-Village *Pomerol*
1998 IB £320.00 (FRI) £325.00 (BIB)
1997 £30.00 (MI)
1996 £31.49 (FRI) £40.00 (FORT)
1995 £36.50 (FRI) £49.50 (CON)
1994 £26.93 (GOE) £27.50 (MI)
1990 IB £500.00 (FA)
1989 IB £360.00 (FA)
1982 IB £560.00 (FA)
1934 £220.00 (CRO)

la Petite Eglise *Pomerol*
1998 IB £150.00 (FA)
1998 EC £150.00 (CAV)
1997 £15.50 (JU)
1997 IB £130.00 (FA)
1996 IB £165.00 (FA)
1988 IB £240.00 (FA)

les Petits Arnauds
1994 £6.20 (COC)

Pétrus *Pomerol*
1998 £587.50 (REI)
1997 IB £3,500.00 (FA)
1995 IB £5,200.00 (FA) £5,365.00 (BIB)
1995 magnum IB £5,500.00 (FA)
1994 £300.00 (CAV) £311.38 (REI)
1994 IB £1,500.00 (BIB) £2,850.00 (FA)
1993 magnum IB £2,850.00 (BIB)
1993 magnum IB £2,400.00 (FA)
1990 £855.99 (WY)
1990 IB £7,200.00 (FA)
1990 magnum IB £7,200.00 (FA)
1989 IB £7,200.00 (FA)
1988 £500.00 (FORT)
1988 IB £3,300.00 (FA)
1985 £462.52 (WY) £550.00 (JU)
1983 £365.87 (WY) £400.00 (JU)
1983 IB £2,750.00 (FA)
1983 magnum IB £2,600.00 (FA)
1982 £1,242.56 (WY) £1,500.00 (FORT)
1982 IB £9,950.00 (FA)

Please remember that
Oz Clarke's Wine Buying Guide
*is a price **guide** and not a price **list**. It is not meant to replace up-to-date merchants' lists.*

1981 **magnum IB** £2,500.00 (FA)
1979 £430.00 (ROB)
1979 IB £2,500.00 (FA)
1979 magnum £705.00 (REI)
1979 magnum IB £2,500.00 (FA)
1975 £740.00 (ROB)
1975 IB £5,500.00 (CAV)
1971 IB £5,500.00 (FA)
1970 £800.76 (WY) £969.38 (REI) £1,000.00 (FORT)
1970 IB £7,200.00 (FA) £7,200.00 (BIB)
1964 £728.50 (FA) £1,100.00 (ROB)
1961 £3,285.89 (WY)
1959 £1,175.00 (FA)
1955 £699.13 (CAV) £705.00 (FA) £881.25 (REI) £1,200.00 (JU)
1952 £646.25 (FA)
1947 £863.63 (REI)
1928 £2,500.00 (JU)

Peybonhomme-les-Tours *1ères Côtes de Blaye*
1998 £9.99 (NI)
1997 £6.29 (ASD) £7.95 (STE)

Peyrabon *cru grand bourgeois Haut-Médoc*
1997 £10.83 (MI)
1996 £13.33 (MI)

du Peyrat *1ères Côtes de Bordeaux*
1997 IB £76.20 (CB)

de Pez *cru bourgeois supérieur St-Estèphe*
1995 £15.40 (NO) £19.95 (BOT) £20.56 (PEN)
1994 £13.00 (UN)
1988 £29.00 (BU)
1986 £35.00 (BU)
1985 £40.95 (ROB)
1983 £26.44 (REI)
1980 £17.04 (REI)
1970 £49.50 (ROB)
1962 £64.63 (REI)
1949 £129.25 (REI)

Phélan-Ségur *cru grand bourgeois exceptionnel St-Estèphe*
1997 £18.75 (TAN) £19.68 (CB)
1996 £19.95 (DI) £19.95 (BER) £22.56 (CB) £23.00 (JU)
1995 £19.75 (HA) £20.50 (UN) £22.69 (JON) £29.15 (PLAY)
1990 £49.50 (ROB)
1983 £35.00 (BU)
1982 £99.00 (UB)

Pibran *cru bourgeois Pauillac*
1997 £15.00 (MI) £17.95 (LEA)
1996 £18.50 (FORT) £19.17 (MI) £19.50 (LEA)
1995 £17.50 (MI)
1994 £22.50 (LEA)
1989 £29.95 (ROB)

Picard *cru bourgeois St-Estèphe*
1997 £10.64 (HA)
1996 £13.95 (WS)

Pichon-Longueville (called Pichon-Baron until 1988) *2ème cru classé Pauillac*
1998 IB £280.00 (FRI) £349.20 (CB)
1998 magnum IB £300.00 (FRI)
1997 £32.31 (GOE) £37.50 (LEA) £37.50 (MI) £38.00 (JU) £40.10 (CB) £45.00 (RES)
1997 IB £280.00 (BIB)
1997 EC £380.95 (HAH)
1996 £33.29 (GOE) £38.50 (LEA) £39.17 (MI) £39.40 (FRI) £39.99 (UN) £43.50 (CON) £45.00 (JU) £51.50 (ELL)
1996 IB £265.00 (FA) £450.00 (CAV)
1996 magnum £72.46 (WY)
1995 £29.95 (CON) £31.82 (GOE) £35.25 (WY) £38.47 (GW) £41.50 (FRI) £45.00 (AD) £49.00 (JU)
1994 £23.99 (GOE) £27.50 (MI) £30.50 (UN)
1993 £27.50 (MI)
1992 IB £295.00 (BIB)
1990 £84.50 (FRI) £99.50 (ROB) £110.00 (FORT)
1990 IB £840.00 (FA)
1989 £131.17 (WY)
1988 £53.85 (GOE)
1988 IB £500.00 (FA)
1986 £57.50 (MI) £68.00 (WS)
1983 £85.00 (CRO)
1982 £59.73 (GOE)
1982 IB £560.00 (FA)
1981 IB £396.50 (BIB)
1978 £38.68 (GOE)
1970 £55.23 (WY)
1966 IB £511.50 (BIB)
1962 £49.94 (REI)
1961 £76.38 (FA)
1950 £158.78 (WY)
1928 £330.00 (JU)

All châteaux are listed alphabetically regardless of class.

Pichon-Longueville-Lalande (called Pichon-Lalande until 1993) *2ème cru classé Pauillac*
1998 IB £410.00 (FRI) £412.00 (LEA)
1998 EC £395.00 (CAV) £498.00 (TAN)
1997 £38.68 (GOE) £43.80 (HA) £45.55 (LAY) £48.90 (TAN) £49.00 (JU) £49.95 (LEA) £50.29 (CB)
1997 IB £337.00 (BIB) £360.00 (FA) £459.00 (RAE)
1997 EC £475.00 (ELL)
1997 magnum £77.35 (GOE)
1997 imperial £376.00 (GOE)
1996 £67.56 (WY) £80.49 (REI) £89.99 (FRI) £95.00 (HED)
1996 IB £625.00 (FA) £725.00 (CAV)
1996 imperial £658.00 (WY)
1995 £70.50 (GOE) £86.45 (LAY) £91.75 (FRI)
1995 IB £720.00 (FA)
1995 jeroboam £616.88 (WY)
1994 £29.50 (BAL) £43.18 (HA) £55.00 (BER) £55.00 (WAI)
1994 IB £375.00 (FA)
1994 magnum IB £380.00 (FA)
1993 £31.00 (JU)
1993 IB £320.00 (FA)
1992 IB £250.00 (FA)
1990 £64.63 (REI) £84.50 (FRI) £98.00 (ROB)
1990 IB £650.00 (FA) £822.50 (WY)
1990 magnum £175.00 (FRI)
1989 £64.63 (REI) £75.00 (CON) £78.73 (CAV) £84.50 (FRI) £89.40 (LAY) £95.00 (FORT) £96.64 (WY) £105.00 (ROB)
1989 IB £750.00 (FA) £795.00 (CAV)
1989 imperial £564.00 (FA)
1988 £57.77 (GOE) £73.00 (FRI) £82.84 (WY) £85.00 (FORT)
1988 IB £625.00 (FA)
1988 imperial £493.50 (FA)
1987 £47.99 (FRI)
1987 IB £240.00 (FA)
1986 £88.50 (BEN) £93.02 (GOE) £107.69 (WY) £110.00 (FRI) £110.00 (JU) £125.00 (BAL) £145.00 (WR)
1986 IB £820.00 (FA)
1985 £88.00 (WS) £89.50 (BEN) £96.64 (WY) £100.00 (FORT) £120.00 (ROB)
1985 IB £750.00 (FA)
1984 £21.74 (REI) £29.50 (BAL) £39.50 (FRI)
1983 £54.17 (FLE) £79.00 (BAL) £84.50 (FRI) £102.00 (STA) £110.45 (WY) £115.00 (FORT)
1983 IB £780.00 (FA)
1983 magnum IB £780.00 (FA)
1982 £170.00 (BEN) £200.00 (FRI) £207.09 (WY) £230.00 (ROB) £250.00 (FORT)
1982 IB £1,650.00 (BIB) £1,700.00 (FA)
1982 jeroboam £1,890.00 (FRI)
1982 imperial £2,700.00 (FRI)
1982 magnum IB £1,700.00 (FA)
1981 IB £500.00 (FA)
1981 magnum IB £740.25 (WY)
1980 jeroboam £164.50 (FA)
1979 IB £560.00 (FA)
1978 £77.00 (CRO)
1978 magnum IB £690.00 (FA)
1970 £89.00 (CRO) £110.45 (WY) £125.00 (BER)
1966 £151.87 (WY)
1964 IB £550.00 (FA)
1959 £129.25 (REI) £338.26 (WY)
1952 £111.63 (REI)
1948 £146.88 (REI)
1947 £229.13 (REI)
1940 £241.62 (WY)
1928 £276.13 (REI)
1914 £276.13 (WY)

le Pin *Pomerol*
1998 IB £4,600.00 (FA)
1998 magnum IB £4,700.00 (FA)
1997 £220.31 (GOE)
1997 IB £2,400.00 (FA)
1996 IB £3,600.00 (FA)
1995 £386.77 (GOE)
1995 IB £3,600.00 (FA) £5,000.00 (CAV)
1994 IB £3,900.00 (CAV)
1993 IB £2,500.00 (FA)
1992 IB £2,250.00 (FA) £2,330.00 (BIB)
1992 magnum IB £2,250.00 (FA)
1990 IB £6,500.00 (FA)
1989 £549.80 (GOE) £650.00 (BAL) £875.38 (REI)
1988 £569.88 (REI) £775.00 (FORT)
1988 IB £3,250.00 (FA)
1987 IB £2,400.00 (FA)
1986 £600.00 (FORT)
1986 magnum £763.75 (FA)
1985 £700.00 (FORT)
1981 IB £3,000.00 (FA)

Pipeau *grand cru St-Émilion*
1993 £11.40 (TAN)

Pique-Caillou *Pessac-Léognan*
1997 £11.67 (MI)
1996 £13.33 (MI) £13.49 (GW)
1995 £13.33 (MI)
1994 £12.50 (MI)

Pitray *Bordeaux Supérieur Côtes de Castillon*
1997 EC £33.48 (JON)
1996 £6.49 (HED) £7.50 (JU)
1995 £7.25 (HED) £7.25 (WS) £8.00 (JU) £8.81 (REI)
1994 £8.90 (PIP)

Plagnac *cru bourgeois Médoc*
1995 £10.99 (UN)
1994 £8.99 (UN)

Plaisance *Montagne-St-Émilion*
1998 £8.90 (BIB)
1997 £7.49 (SO) £8.90 (BIB)
1995 £10.15 (JER)

Plince *Pomerol*
1997 £11.60 (HA)
1994 £21.95 (PHI)
1990 £52.00 (UB)

la Pointe *Pomerol*
1998 IB £180.00 (FRI) £180.00 (WY) £241.20 (CB)
1997 £16.67 (MI)
1997 EC £162.00 (JON)
1996 £19.39 (GW) £19.98 (CB)
1995 £20.83 (MI)
1995 IB £155.00 (FA)
1994 £17.50 (MI) £22.67 (JON) £27.61 (WY)
1990 £39.50 (BEN)

Pontet-Canet *5ème cru classé Pauillac*
1998 £15.67 (GOE)
1998 EC £188.85 (HAH) £195.00 (CAV)
1997 £19.09 (GOE) £22.00 (JU) £23.33 (MI) £26.03 (CB) £26.40 (TAN)
1997 IB £157.00 (BIB) £216.00 (RAE)
1997 magnum £38.19 (GOE)
1996 £26.93 (GOE) £28.79 (CB) £28.95 (DI) £31.00 (JU) £32.50 (MI)
1996 IB £245.00 (FA) £275.00 (CAV)
1995 £24.97 (GOE) £30.00 (JU) £32.50 (MI) £49.50 (AV)
1994 £25.00 (MI) £29.20 (HA) £29.99 (POR)
1994 magnum £59.50 (POR)
1993 £19.99 (BOD) £19.99 (SUN) £22.50 (MI) £29.95 (BO)
1989 £42.50 (MI) £45.49 (SUN)
1983 IB £195.00 (FA)
1982 £50.35 (GW)
1982 IB £330.00 (FA)
1928 £111.63 (REI)
1914 £234.71 (WY)

Potensac *cru grand bourgeois Médoc*
1998 £17.20 (CHA)
1998 IB £150.00 (CB)
1997 £12.73 (GOE) £16.67 (MI) £17.92 (CB)
1997 EC £137.50 (ELL) £146.40 (JON)
1996 £16.25 (SOM) £17.00 (JU) £17.50 (MI) £17.95 (ELL) £19.95 (CON) £20.29 (FRI)
1996 IB £125.00 (FA) £132.00 (RAE)
1995 £17.50 (MI) £18.11 (GOE) £18.40 (TAN)
1994 £16.67 (MI) £19.99 (POR) £33.00 (FORT)
1993 £15.83 (MI) £15.95 (DI)
1990 £27.00 (CRO) £44.60 (UB)
1989 £25.50 (STA) £27.50 (TAN) £33.15 (BY)
1989 IB £300.00 (BIB)
1986 IB £160.00 (FA)
1985 £21.74 (REI)
1983 £18.50 (BU)

Pouget *4ème cru classé Margaux*
1988 £28.79 (REI)

Poujeaux *cru grand bourgeois exceptionnel Moulis*
1998 EC £159.00 (JON)
1997 £16.67 (MI) £16.98 (CB) £19.35 (TAN)
1996 £15.67 (GOE) £17.49 (OD) £19.95 (CON) £20.00 (JU) £21.95 (ROB) £25.26 (REI)
1995 £19.09 (GOE) £19.17 (MI) £19.50 (WS) £19.99 (BOD) £19.99 (SUN) £27.50 (FORT)
1994 £17.50 (MI) £22.95 (CON)
1990 £37.50 (BU)
1988 £30.00 (BU)

la Prade *Côtes de Francs*
1994 £8.30 (TAN)

Prieuré-Lichine *4ème cru classé Margaux*
1997 £22.38 (CB)
1996 £28.30 (CB)
1995 £21.50 (HIG) £21.54 (HIG) £23.50 (GW) £34.40 (JER)
1990 £40.00 (ROB)
1988 IB £240.00 (FA)
1985 £39.00 (COC)
1970 £49.00 (CRO)

Puy-Castéra *cru bourgeois Haut-Médoc*
1997 £8.61 (SAV)
1996 £11.75 (SAV)
1995 £23.50 (SAV)
1993 £7.75 (CON)

Puylazat *Côtes de Castillon*
1995 £5.95 (WS)

Rahoul *Graves*
1982 £18.50 (BU)

Ramage-la-Bâtisse *cru bourgeois Haut-Médoc*
1996 £11.99 (POR)
1995 £10.95 (WR) £10.95 (THR) £10.95 (VIC) £10.95 (BOT)
1994 £10.99 (BO) £11.45 (CON) £11.49 (AME) £11.99 (POR)

Rauzan-Gassies *2ème cru classé Margaux*
1996 £34.99 (SAI)
1995 £35.00 (UN)
1985 £26.44 (REI)
1983 £26.44 (REI)
1982 £98.00 (UB)
1970 £25.00 (BU)
1959 £136.69 (WY)
1945 £200.20 (WY)
1928 £303.74 (WY)
1918 £151.87 (WY)

Rauzan-Ségla *2ème cru classé Margaux*
1997 £24.48 (GOE) £28.56 (HA) £29.17 (MI) £29.95 (BAL) £30.00 (JU) £32.17 (CB)
1997 magnum £48.96 (GOE)
1996 £32.80 (WY) £38.48 (CB) £40.83 (MI) £42.25 (FRI)
1996 IB £285.00 (FA)
1995 IB £351.50 (BIB)
1994 £30.35 (GOE)
1993 £27.91 (GOE) £28.33 (MI) £30.49 (REI) £32.00 (TAN) £37.01 (HA)
1993 IB £180.00 (FA)
1992 £32.79 (WY)
1990 £40.00 (FLE) £66.65 (TAN) £70.50 (PEN)
1990 IB £495.00 (FA)
1989 IB £400.00 (FA)
1988 IB £420.00 (FA)
1986 IB £600.00 (FA) £600.00 (BIB)
1986 magnum IB £600.00 (FA)
1985 £29.75 (WRI)
1985 IB £400.00 (FA)
1985 magnum IB £400.00 (FA)
1983 IB £360.00 (FA)
1982 IB £420.00 (FA)
1981 £25.00 (BU)
1961 £100.00 (BU)
1948 £65.00 (BU)

Réserve de la Comtesse *Pauillac*
1997 £20.80 (LAY)
1997 IB £145.00 (FA)
1996 IB £180.00 (BIB)
1995 £26.00 (WS) £26.40 (TAN)
1994 £16.50 (WS) £22.03 (GOE) £27.50 (TAN) £27.99 (RAE)
1988 £33.49 (REI)
1985 IB £320.00 (FA)

la Réserve du Général *Margaux*
1995 £24.19 (JON)

Respide-Médeville *Graves*
1995 £18.45 (TW)

Reynier *Bordeaux Supérieur*
1998 £6.45 (STE)

Reysson *cru bourgeois Haut-Médoc*
1996 £9.95 (LEA)

la Rivière *Fronsac*
1995 £12.49 (AME) £12.95 (PHI)
1983 £16.50 (BU)

Roc-de-Cambes *Côtes de Bourg*
1998 EC £220.00 (SAV) £225.00 (CAV)
1997 £21.54 (SAV)
1996 £16.50 (FORT) £21.54 (SAV)
1995 £21.54 (SAV)
1994 £15.97 (SAV)
1988 IB £180.00 (FA)

Rollan-de-By *cru bourgeois Médoc*
1991 £14.80 (WT)

Roquevieille *Côtes de Castillon*
1996 £6.95 (STA)
1995 £7.49 (HED)

Rouet *Fronsac*
1994 £9.00 (BER)

Rouget *Pomerol*
1998 EC £195.00 (CAV)
1996 IB £135.00 (FA)

Rozier *grand cru St-Émilion*
1996 £8.94 (HA) £10.50 (SOM) £11.70 (MV) £11.99 (SAF)

Ruat-Petit-Poujeaux *cru bourgeois Moulis*
1994 £8.75 (CON)

St-Georges *St-Georges-St-Émilion*
1996 £15.99 (FRI)
1995 £15.99 (FRI) £23.12 (PLAY)
1995 IB £135.00 (FA)

St-Pierre *Lussac-St-Émilion*
1989 £31.14 (REI)

St-Pierre *4ème cru classé St-Julien*
1997 £22.50 (MI)
1996 £28.33 (MI)
1995 £26.67 (MI)
1994 £25.00 (FORT) £25.00 (MI)
1983 £21.00 (CRO)

St-Saturnin *cru bourgeois Médoc*
1988 £14.50 (BU) £15.35 (UB)

de Sales *Pomerol*
1997 £15.00 (MI)
1996 £18.33 (MI) £21.99 (MAJ)
1995 £18.33 (MI) £31.00 (STA)
1993 £15.83 (MI)
1978 £50.00 (BU)

Sarget de Gruaud-Larose *St-Julien*
1997 £15.00 (MI)
1996 £16.67 (MI)
1994 £17.49 (WR) £17.49 (BOT) £22.00 (STA)
1993 £16.99 (NI) £22.49 (BO) £23.49 (GW)

Segonzac *1ères Côtes de Blaye*
1997 £5.95 (WAI)
1996 £7.99 (SAI)
1995 £5.75 (DI)

Sénéjac *cru bourgeois supérieur Haut-Médoc*
1997 £9.95 (BU)
1996 £10.50 (ELL)
1989 £25.26 (REI)

la Serre *grand cru classé St-Émilion*
1998 EC £171.00 (JON)
1997 EC £168.60 (JON)
1994 £19.25 (ROB) £20.49 (JON)

Siaurac *Lalande-de-Pomerol*
1998 EC £73.00 (TAN) £85.00 (CAV)

Siran *cru bourgeois supérieur Margaux*
1996 £18.25 (BER) £19.55 (GN)
1995 £21.50 (STA) £26.33 (PIP)
1993 £14.15 (COC)
1988 £41.25 (PIP)

Sirius *Bordeaux*
1997 £5.99 (SO) £6.99 (WR) £6.99 (THR) £6.99 (VIC) £6.99 (BOT)
1996 £7.25 (CON)

Smith-Haut-Lafitte *cru classé Pessac-Léognan*
1998 EC £225.00 (CAV)
1997 £29.02 (CB)
1996 £27.50 (MI) £33.00 (CON) £36.13 (CB)
1996 IB £220.00 (FA) £230.00 (CAV)
1995 IB £240.00 (FA)
1994 £25.26 (REI)
1994 IB £215.00 (FA) £225.00 (BIB)
1993 £18.95 (NI)
1993 IB £150.00 (FA)
1985 £16.95 (WRI) £26.44 (REI)
1924 £124.26 (WY)

Sociando-Mallet *cru grand bourgeois Haut-Médoc*
1998 EC £192.60 (HAH) £195.00 (CAV)
1997 £22.00 (JU) £23.33 (MI) £24.95 (BAL) £26.00 (RES) £31.95 (DI)
1997 IB £198.00 (RAE)
1996 £19.68 (HA) £24.00 (JU) £29.89 (JON) £32.50 (MI) £33.00 (CON)
1996 IB £230.00 (FA) £235.00 (CAV) £235.00 (BIB)
1995 £27.95 (CON)
1994 £22.50 (MI)
1993 £21.67 (MI) £28.95 (ROB)
1992 £16.50 (NI)
1990 IB £475.00 (FA)
1989 IB £320.00 (BIB)
1988 IB £230.00 (FA)
1985 £44.65 (TAN)

de Sours *Bordeaux Supérieur*
1997 £7.74 (GOE)
1997 IB £76.50 (CB)
1996 £7.74 (GOE)

Soutard *grand cru classé St-Émilion*
1997 £16.67 (MI) £19.95 (BAL)
1996 £18.33 (MI) £19.99 (UN)
1994 £16.67 (MI)
1990 £30.83 (MI)
1989 £29.95 (BU)
1982 IB £520.00 (FA)

de Tabuteau *Lussac-St-Émilion*
1997 £9.14 (NO)
1996 £9.95 (VIN)

du Tailhas *Pomerol*
1995 £21.00 (RES)

Taillefer *Pomerol*
1988 IB £165.00 (FA)

Talbot *4ème cru classé St-Julien*
1998 IB £170.00 (FRI)
1998 EC £175.00 (CAV)
1997 £19.09 (GOE) £20.05 (HA) £22.50 (MI) £25.32 (CB) £26.50 (FORT) £27.95 (LEA)
1997 EC £235.00 (ELL)
1997 ½ bottle £14.95 (LEA)
1996 £14.99 (BOD) £14.99 (SUN) £24.99 (BOD) £24.99 (SUN) £28.33 (MI) £28.95 (CON) £30.00 (JU) £30.49 (FRI)
1996 double magnum £125.33 (WY)
1995 £24.48 (GOE) £25.00 (UN) £26.67 (MI) £28.20 (WY) £28.49 (FRI) £37.94 (PLAY)
1995 IB £230.00 (FA)
1995 ½ bottle £16.45 (WY)
1995 double magnum £125.33 (WY)
1994 £23.50 (PEN) £25.00 (MI) £31.15 (HA) £32.50 (STA)
1993 £25.00 (MI)
1990 £39.00 (COC) £44.06 (GOE) £44.17 (MI) £59.00 (PHI) £85.00 (UB)
1989 £46.67 (MI) £53.00 (ROB) £60.75 (WY) £64.45 (VIN) £70.50 (NO)
1989 IB £400.00 (FA)
1988 £55.00 (ROB)
1988 IB £365.00 (FA)
1988 ½ bottle IB £365.00 (FA)
1986 £47.50 (HIG) £69.95 (DI) £80.08 (WY)
1986 IB £560.00 (FA)
1985 £41.13 (REI)
1985 IB £460.00 (FA)
1985 magnum £92.24 (REI)
1985 magnum IB £460.00 (FA)
1983 £49.00 (CRO) £69.03 (WY) £75.00 (ROB)
1983 IB £450.00 (FA)
1982 £45.00 (BU) £66.58 (GOE)
1981 £40.54 (REI)
1981 IB £280.00 (FA)
1981 magnum £70.50 (REI)

> ***EC** (ex-cellar) price per dozen, excluding shipping, duty and VAT.*
> ***IB** (in bond) price per dozen, excluding duty and VAT.*
> *All other prices, per bottle incl VAT.*

1978 £59.50 (LEA)
1978 ½ bottle £29.95 (LEA)
1975 magnum £82.84 (WY)
1970 £66.67 (MI)
1966 £70.50 (REI)
1961 £94.00 (REI)
1959 IB £1,000.00 (FA)
1958 £124.26 (WY)
1955 £214.00 (WY)
1949 £150.00 (YOU)
1937 £99.88 (REI)

Tayac *Côtes de Bourg*
1990 IB £139.50 (BIB)

Terre Rouge *Médoc*
1997 £6.35 (HA)
1997 EC £56.40 (JON)
1995 £8.59 (JON)

Terrey-Gros-Cailloux *cru bourgeois St-Julien*
1988 IB £236.50 (BIB)
1975 £14.50 (BU)

du Tertre *5ème cru classé Margaux*
1990 £38.95 (ROB)
1989 £31.99 (SUN)
1985 £49.00 (UB)
1983 IB £150.00 (FA)

Tertre-Daugay *grand cru classé St-Émilion*
1993 £21.67 (MI)
1990 £30.83 (MI)
1988 IB £180.00 (FA)
1924 £179.48 (WY)
1900 £688.94 (WY) £735.00 (ROB)

Tertre Rôteboeuf *St-Émilion*
1998 IB £570.00 (CB) £750.00 (FA)
1998 EC £660.00 (SAV)
1997 £55.81 (SAV) £64.63 (CB)
1996 £64.63 (SAV) £79.90 (CB)
1996 IB £495.00 (FA)
1995 IB £780.00 (FA) £900.00 (CAV)
1994 IB £450.00 (FA) £550.00 (CAV)
1992 IB £265.00 (FA) £320.00 (CAV)
1989 IB £1,350.00 (FA) £1,695.00 (CAV)
1988 £120.00 (CRO)
1986 £67.50 (BU) £80.00 (CRO)
1986 IB £820.00 (CAV)
1985 £95.50 (BEN)
1985 IB £900.00 (FA)
1982 £121.50 (WY)

Teyssier *grand cru St-Émilion*
1998 £8.81 (GOE)
1998 EC £85.00 (ELL)
1997 £9.30 (GOE) £9.50 (JU) £10.68 (NO) £12.50 (AD) £12.99 (DI)
1996 £10.68 (NO) £12.99 (POR) £13.99 (JON)

Timberlay *Bordeaux Supérieur*
1998 £6.65 (DI)

la Tonnelle *St-Émilion*
1996 £4.95 (WS)

Toumalin *Canon-Fronsac*
1997 EC £44.40 (JON)
1995 £8.79 (JON)

la Tour-de-By *cru grand bourgeois Médoc*
1999 £11.90 (COC)
1998 EC £75.00 (JON) £79.00 (TAN)
1997 £8.24 (HA) £11.98 (PIP)
1996 £8.94 (HA) £10.49 (HED) £10.99 (POR) £11.55 (TAN)
1995 £9.95 (HED) £11.90 (UN)
1994 £9.75 (WS) £9.90 (BER)
1993 £15.60 (TAN)
1990 £19.99 (SUN)
1985 £23.32 (REI)
1982 £28.50 (TAN)

la Tour-Carnet *4ème cru classé Haut-Médoc*
1995 £17.45 (HA)
1992 £16.58 (BY)

la Tour-Figeac *grand cru classé St-Émilion*
1997 IB £264.60 (CB)
1995 IB £155.00 (FA)

la Tour-Haut-Brion *cru classé Pessac-Léognan*
1998 IB £230.00 (FA)
1997 £29.17 (MI)
1996 IB £265.00 (BIB)
1995 IB £280.00 (FA)

Tour-Haut-Caussan *cru bourgeois Médoc*
1997 £12.92 (BIB)
1997 EC £85.80 (JON)
1996 £11.95 (ELL) £12.04 (GOE) £12.92 (BIB) £12.95 (BAL)
1996 IB £96.00 (RAE)
1994 £10.99 (RAE) £13.45 (MV)

la Tour-Martillac *cru classé Pessac-Léognan*
1997 £15.00 (MI)
1996 £18.33 (MI)
1995 £17.50 (MI)
1994 £16.67 (MI)
1993 £15.83 (MI)
1990 £27.50 (MI)

Tour-du-Mirail *cru bourgeois Haut-Médoc*
1997 £15.99 (UN)

la Tour-de-Mons *cru bourgeois supérieur Margaux*
1997 £14.17 (MI)
1996 £15.83 (MI) £17.00 (JU) £17.99 (TES)
1995 £15.00 (MI)
1990 £23.33 (MI)
1989 £23.33 (MI)
1985£20.56 (REI)
1924 £125.00 (CRO)
1920 £150.00 (CRO)

Tour-du-Pas-St-Georges *St-Georges-St-Émilion*
1997 £8.42 (BIB) £9.45 (MV)
1996 £8.50 (WS)
1994 £9.30 (BIB)

la Tour-du-Pin-Figeac *grand cru classé St-Émilion*
1998 IB £150.00 (FRI)

la Tour-St-Bonnet *cru bourgeois Médoc*
1996 £9.00 (MV) £9.49 (HED) £10.00 (JU)
1996 IB £75.00 (BIB)
1995 £10.28 (REI) £10.95 (HED) £10.99 (JON) £11.50 (FLE) £12.45 (JER)
1990 IB £226.50 (BIB)

les Tourelles de Longueville *Pauillac*
1997 £16.67 (MI)
1996 £18.33 (MI) £18.50 (FORT) £18.95 (LEA) £21.68 (CB)
1996 IB £156.00 (RAE)

Tourteau-Chollet *Graves*
1996 £7.33 (HA)

Tronquoy-Lalande *cru grand bourgeois St-Estèphe*
1997 £14.17 (MI)
1996 £12.50 (WS) £16.67 (MI) £33.49 (REI)
1995 £12.00 (JU) £15.00 (MI)

Troplong-Mondot *grand cru classé St-Émilion*
1998 IB £320.00 (FA) £325.00 (LEA)
1998 EC £295.00 (CAV)
1997 £37.31 (CB) £37.50 (MI)
1997 IB £75.00 (BIB)
1996 £30.90 (LAY) £39.17 (MI) £39.19 (CB)
1996 IB £250.00 (FA)
1995 £38.60 (TAN)
1995 IB £340.00 (FA)
1993 £28.33 (MI)
1993 IB £250.00 (FA)
1989 £87.64 (GOE) £99.50 (TAN)
1989 IB £900.00 (FA)
1986 £55.00 (UB)
1986 IB £395.00 (FA)

Trotanoy *Pomerol*
1997 £56.17 (CB)
1996 £48.18 (CB)
1994 IB £350.00 (FA)
1993 £45.00 (ROB)
1992 IB £380.00 (BIB)
1990 IB £720.00 (FA)
1989 £65.00 (CRO)
1986 £49.50 (BU)
1985 IB £520.00 (FA)
1983 IB £480.00 (FA)
1982 £315.00 (ROB)
1982 IB £1,800.00 (FA)
1981 £41.13 (REI) £89.75 (WY)
1981 IB £420.00 (FA)
1978 £82.25 (REI) £100.00 (BU)
1976 £95.00 (UB)
1971 £241.62 (WY)

Trottevieille *1er grand cru classé St-Émilion*
1997 £31.45 (AV)
1996 £24.00 (HIG) £26.95 (DI)
1994 £22.00 (HIG)

de Valandraud *grand cru St-Émilion*
1998 £26.93 (GOE)
1998 IB £240.00 (FA)
1998 EC £1,900.00 (CAV)
1997 £200.00 (JU)
1996 IB £2,100.00 (FA)
1995 IB £2,200.00 (FA)
1994 IB £1,900.00 (FA) £2,002.50 (BIB)

Verdignan *cru grand bourgeois Haut-Médoc*
1996 £12.99 (SO) £13.99 (SAI)
1995 £14.69 (GOE)

Vieux-Château-Certan *Pomerol*
1998 IB £1,200.00 (FA)
1997 £42.00 (BAL) £43.33 (MI) £45.00 (JU) £45.65 (LAY) £51.94 (CB) £53.80 (TAN)
1997 IB £340.00 (BIB) £420.00 (RAE)
1996 £44.55 (GOE) £49.17 (MI) £52.99 (FRI) £57.50 (ELL) £60.00 (JU) £60.81 (CB)
1996 IB £420.00 (FA) £420.00 (BIB) £495.00 (CAV) £495.00 (RAE)
1995 £70.00 (JU)
1995 IB £400.00 (BIB)
1994 £36.50 (RAE) £36.72 (GOE) £65.00 (JU)
1994 IB £380.00 (BIB)
1994 magnum £73.44 (GOE)
1993 £22.95 (RAE) £30.00 (FLE) £38.33 (MI)
1992 £18.95 (RAE) £20.00 (BU) £23.33 (MI)
1990 IB £580.00 (FA)
1989 £41.13 (REI) £96.64 (WY)
1988 £80.00 (FORT)
1988 IB £420.00 (FA)
1986 £165.00 (UB)
1982 IB £780.00 (FA)
1982 jeroboam £810.00 (FRI)
1981 £55.00 (FORT)
1975 £47.00 (YOU)
1966 £64.63 (REI)
1970 magnum IB £450.00 (FA)
1962 £99.88 (REI)
1961 IB £1,950.00 (FA)

Vieux-Château-Landon *cru bourgeois Médoc*
1996 £9.99 (SAI)

Vieux-Château-St-André *Montagne-St-Émilion*
1996 £8.95 (WS)

Villegeorge *cru bourgeois supérieur exceptionnel Médoc*
1994 £11.95 (RAE)
1983 £45.50 (UB)

Villemaurine *grand cru classé St-Émilion*
1996 £20.30 (AV)

Villeneuve de Cantemerle *Haut-Médoc*
1994 £12.95 (BOT)

Yon Figeac *grand cru classé St-Émilion*
1997 £21.03 (NO)
1996 £15.99 (BOT) £21.03 (NO) £22.27 (PLA)
1995 £14.26 (NO) £17.95 (DI)
1994 £15.99 (WR) £19.99 (DI)

WHITE BORDEAUX PRICES

DRY

Under £5.00

Bel Air **1995** £4.49 (CON)
Moulin de Launay **1997** £4.99 (POR) £4.99 (JON)
la Perrière **1998** £4.60 (WS)
Thieuley **1998** £4.95 (SOM) £6.52 (GW) £6.60 (AD) £6.99 (JON)
Trois Mouline Sauvignon **1999** £4.10 (JU)

£5.00 → £6.99

Antonins **1996** £5.99 (RAE)
Archambeau **1996** £6.50 (HIG)
Bel Air **1999** £5.95 (TAN)
Bel Air **1998** £5.50 (WS)
Bonnet **1998** £5.99 (WR) £5.99 (BOT)
Bonnet **1996** £6.39 (NI)
le Chec **1997** £6.95 (AD)
la Clyde **1998** £5.20 (UB)
Coucheroy **1997** £6.99 (THR) £6.99 (WR)
Ducla **1998** £5.99 (UN)
l'Étoile **1997** £5.70 (REI) £6.20 (TAN) £6.35 (AD) £6.49 (JON)
Haut-Bertinerie **1998** £5.95 (BER)
Haut-Rian **1999** £5.30 (PIP) £5.50 (ELL)
Haut-Rian **1998** £5.50 (COC)
Haut-Rian **1997** £6.50 (FORT)
Lacroix **1998** £5.78 (GOE) £5.79 (NO) £6.50 (AD) £6.50 (JU) £6.65 (DI)
Maître d'Estournel **1996** £5.99 (OD)
Montalivet **1998** £6.45 (SOM)
Moulin de Launay **1998** £5.10 (TAN)
Mouton-Cadet **1998** £5.99 (SAI) £5.99 (VIC) £5.99 (THR) £5.99 (UN) £5.99 (WR) £5.99 (BOT) £5.99 (BUD)
Pierrail **1998** £5.80 (CHA)
Reynon **1998** £6.72 (BY)
Roquefort **1998** £6.45 (HAH)
Sirius **1995** £6.39 (CON)
Thieuley **1999** £5.95 (WS)
Tour de Mirambeau **1998** £5.99 (NI)

£7.00 → £8.99

Baret **1998** £7.50 (HIG)
Baret **1997** £8.00 (AV)
Cabannieux **1995** £7.64 (CB)
Civrac Lagrange **1997** £7.55 (JER)
Ferrande **1998** £7.80 (AD)
Loudenne **1998** £8.50 (JU)
de Sours **1998** £7.49 (CB)

£9.00 → £11.99

Bouscaut **1988** £10.95 (RAE)
de Castelneau **1993** £9.85 (RAE) £12.15 (UB)
Doisy-Daëne Grand Vin Sec **1992** £10.60 (TAN)
Domaine de la Solitude **1997** £10.83 (MI)
Haut-Lagrange **1996** £9.69 (JON)
Hostens-Picant **1996** £9.95 (ROB)
de Seuil **1998** £9.50 (JU)
de Seuil **1997** £9.50 (JU) £9.95 (STA) £10.25 (ELL) £10.95 (DI)
Thieuley Cuvée Francis Courselle **1998** £10.40 (CB)
Thieuley Cuvée Francis Courselle **1996** £10.02 (GW)
Tour de Mirambeau Cuvée Passion **1997** £9.80 (NI)

£12.00 → £14.99

Bouscaut **1989** £12.95 (RAE)
★ Clos Floridène **1998** £12.97 (BY)
Couhins-Lurton **1994** £13.80 (TAN) £14.39 (REI) £14.50 (STA) £15.75 (ROB)
Couhins-Lurton **1993** £13.99 (RAE)
Domaine de la Solitude **1995** £14.17 (MI)
la Garde **1970** £14.69 (REI)
de Landiras **1994** £12.95 (HED)

£15.00 → £19.99

Carbonnieux **1996** £19.17 (MI)
Carbonnieux **1995** £15.95 (JU) £18.33 (MI)
Carbonnieux **1983** £17.04 (REI)
Couhins-Lurton **1995** £15.10 (REI) £16.35 (AD) £19.90 (NI)
Couhins-Lurton **1981** £16.95 (RAE)
Domaine de la Solitude **1996** £15.00 (MI)
l'Esprit de Chevalier **1995** £16.06 (FA) £19.17 (MI)
l'Esprit de Chevalier **1994** £19.17 (MI)
l'Esprit de Chevalier **1993** £17.50 (RAE)
l'Esprit de Chevalier **1992** £16.95 (RAE)

- *Wines are listed in A–Z order within each price band.*
- *For each wine, vintages are listed in descending order.*
- *Each vintage of any wine appears only once.*

Larrivet-Haut-Brion **1996** £16.00 (JU)
Latour-Martillac **1997** £16.67 (MI)
Latour-Martillac **1995** £18.33 (MI)
Latour-Martillac **1994** £17.50 (MI)
la Louvière **1996** £17.90 (HAH) £18.00 (JU)

£20.00 → £29.99

Bouscaut **1967** £29.95 (RAE)
Carbonnieux **1982** £20.86 (REI)
Domaine de Chevalier **1993** £26.83 (FA) £33.40 (RAE) £37.50 (MI)
l'Esprit de Chevalier **1996** £20.83 (MI)
de Fieuzal **1998** £22.91 (FA)
de Fieuzal **1996** £28.33 (MI) £33.00 (JU) £34.42 (PIP)
de Fieuzal **1988** £28.79 (REI)
de Fieuzal **1986** £28.79 (REI)
Latour-Martillac **1996** £20.00 (MI)
Latour-Martillac **1990** £26.67 (MI)
Malartic-Lagravière **1997** £21.67 (MI)
Pavillon Blanc du Château Margaux **1998** £20.95 (FA) £22.81 (RAE)
Pavillon Blanc du Château Margaux **1997** £26.67 (MI) £34.08 (CB)
Pavillon Blanc du Château Margaux **1996** £28.33 (MI) £33.49 (CB) £35.20 (HAH)
Pavillon Blanc du Château Margaux **1987** £20.56 (REI)
Smith-Haut-Lafitte **1996** £25.83 (MI) £33.49 (CB) £36.50 (JER)
Smith-Haut-Lafitte **1995** £20.95 (FA) £24.17 (MI) £35.00 (FORT)
Smith-Haut-Lafitte **1994** £27.50 (MI)
Smith-Haut-Lafitte **1993** £22.50 (MI)
Talbot Caillou Blanc **1996** £20.60 (JER)

£30.00 → £39.99

Doisy-Daëne Grand Vin Sec **1998** £31.00 (YOU)
Domaine de Chevalier **1997** £37.21 (RAE) £39.17 (MI)
Domaine de Chevalier **1996** £36.62 (FA) £42.75 (BEN) £45.00 (MI)
Domaine de Chevalier **1995** £30.75 (FA) £43.33 (MI) £43.67 (RAE) £45.00 (JU)
Domaine de Chevalier **1992** £36.62 (FA) £36.67 (MI) £55.00 (FORT)
de Fieuzal **1995** £39.00 (BER)
de Fieuzal **1993** £39.40 (TAN)
de Fieuzal **1985** £38.19 (REI)
Laville-Haut-Brion **1990** £38.58 (FA) £47.50 (MI)
Laville-Haut-Brion **1988** £35.64 (FA) £49.50 (BEN) £50.00 (ROB)
Smith-Haut-Lafitte **1997** £30.00 (FORT)

£40.00 → £49.99

Domaine de Chevalier **1994** £46.67 (MI)
Domaine de Chevalier **1990** £43.37 (RAE) £51.67 (MI) £58.16 (FA)
Domaine de Chevalier **1989** £46.41 (FA)
de Fieuzal **1989** £41.13 (REI)
Haut-Brion Blanc **1988** £49.50 (RAE) £64.63 (REI) £125.00 (FORT)
Laville-Haut-Brion **1996** £47.50 (MI)
Laville-Haut-Brion **1992** £40.05 (FA)
Laville-Haut-Brion **1982** £48.37 (FA)

£50.00 → £69.99

Carbonnieux **1954** £56.99 (REI)
Domaine de Chevalier **1988** £69.03 (WY)
Domaine de Chevalier **1981** £56.99 (REI)
Haut-Brion Blanc **1992** £62.08 (FA)
Haut-Brion Blanc **1982** £60.12 (FA)
Laville-Haut-Brion **1983** £56.50 (ROB)
'Y' d'Yquem **1988** £68.00 (UB)
'Y' d'Yquem **1985** £60.12 (FA) £70.50 (REI)
'Y' d'Yquem **1980** £64.63 (REI)
'Y' d'Yquem **1968** £52.88 (FA)

£70.00 → £99.99

Haut-Brion Blanc **1994** £98.00 (JU)
Haut-Brion Blanc **1981** £89.75 (WY)
Laville-Haut-Brion **1967** £82.84 (WY)
'Y' d'Yquem **1978** £96.64 (WY)

Over £100.00

Haut-Brion Blanc **1997** £105.00 (MI) £120.00 (JU)
Haut-Brion Blanc **1996** £115.00 (JU)
Haut-Brion Blanc **1989** £200.00 (FORT)
Olivier **1947** £151.87 (WY)
Pavillon Blanc du Château Margaux **1926** £103.55 (WY)
Pavillon Blanc du Château Margaux **1924** £124.26 (WY)
'Y' d'Yquem **1964** £131.17 (WY)

SWEET

Under £7.00

Domaine du Noble ½ bottle **1994** £4.99 (RAE)
Filhot ½ bottle **1985** £6.07 (FA)
Marquis de Beausoleil Ste-Croix-du-Mont **1994** £6.99 (UN)
Tour Balot **1995** £6.70 (AS)

£7.00 → £8.99

des Arroucats **1997** £8.46 (CB)
des Arroucats **1995** £7.85 (CON)
la Caussade **1997** £7.75 (WAI)
Domaine du Noble **1993** £8.99 (RAE)
Fayau **1995** £8.10 (MV)
Filhot ½ bottle **1996** £8.27 (FA) £9.99 (MAJ)
de Ménota **1996** £8.25 (JER)
des Tours **1995** £8.95 (AD) £9.49 (JON) £9.60 (LAY)

£9.00 → £11.99

d'Arricaud **1975** £9.95 (RAE)
Broustet ½ bottle **1996** £10.49 (FRI)
Broustet ½ bottle **1986** £11.57 (REI)
la Chartreuse ½ bottle **1996** £9.99 (SAI)
la Chartreuse ½ bottle **1995** £9.75 (HAH)
Clos Labère ½ bottle **1997** £10.03 (PIP)
Filhot ½ bottle **1988** £9.50 (FA) £15.10 (REI) £22.03 (NO)
Filhot ½ bottle **1986** £9.50 (FA) £21.74 (REI)
Liot ½ bottle **1997** £9.75 (WAI)
Liot ½ bottle **1996** £9.99 (SAI)
Liot ½ bottle **1995** £9.99 (POR)
Liot ½ bottle **1994** £11.37 (WT)
Lousteau-Vieil **1995** £9.40 (COC)
Myrat ½ bottle **1996** £11.95 (BU)
Nairac ½ bottle **1996** £9.01 (FA)
la Rame **1997** £10.95 (AD)
la Rame **1996** £9.99 (MAJ)
la Rame **1995** £10.35 (NI)
Rayne-Vigneau ½ bottle **1995** £10.95 (TAN)
Peter A Sichel **1996** £11.99 (WR) £11.99 (BOT)
Peter A Sichel **1994** £9.75 (CON)

£12.00 → £14.99

Bastor-Lamontagne ½ bottle **1988** £14.69 (REI)
Broustet ½ bottle **1989** £12.75 (REI)
Climens ½ bottle **1995** £14.95 (LEA)
Climens ½ bottle **1982** £14.50 (RAE)
Clos d'Yvigne **1994** £13.50 (JU)
Cyprès de Climens **1992** £12.95 (RAE)
Doisy-Daëne ½ bottle **1997** £12.34 (LEA)
Doisy-Daëne ½ bottle **1996** £12.95 (RES) £14.95 (DI)
Doisy-Védrines ½ bottle **1996** £12.95 (LEA)
Filhot **1996** £14.59 (FA) £17.43 (HA) £21.39 (CB)
Filhot **1983** £14.50 (BU) £27.61 (REI)
Haut-Caplane **1992** £13.95 (ROB)
Lafaurie-Peyraguey ½ bottle **1996** £12.87 (LEA)
Lafaurie-Peyraguey ½ bottle **1995** £14.95 (RES)
Nairac ½ bottle **1997** £14.69 (LEA)
Nairac ½ bottle **1987** £13.50 (ROB)
la Rame Reserve du Château **1995** £12.99 (OD) £14.95 (NI)
Rayne-Vigneau ½ bottle **1997** £12.93 (LEA) £14.50 (RES)
Rieussec **1987** £13.12 (FA)
Rieussec ½ bottle **1996** £14.95 (LEA) £16.35 (FRI) £16.95 (WAI)
Suduiraut ½ bottle **1983** £14.15 (FA) £19.39 (REI)
la Tour Blanche ½ bottle **1990** £14.95 (BU)

£15.00 → £19.99

Accabailles de Barréjats **1995** £18.00 (JU)
Bastor-Lamontagne **1997** £16.51 (CB)
Bastor-Lamontagne **1994** £17.90 (JU)
Broustet **1996** £18.50 (FRI) £22.35 (PIP)
Caillou **1996** £16.67 (MI)
la Chartreuse **1996** £17.95 (AD)
la Chartreuse **1995** £18.40 (HAH) £18.95 (CON)
Climens ½ bottle **1996** £19.95 (LEA) £19.99 (WAI)
Climens ½ bottle **1991** £18.95 (RES)
Climens ½ bottle **1989** £19.00 (RAE)
Coutet ½ bottle **1997** £16.95 (RES)
Coutet ½ bottle **1996** £16.95 (WAI) £21.05 (WY)
Coutet ½ bottle **1994** £16.39 (PLAY)
Coutet ½ bottle **1979** £16.57 (WY)
Doisy-Daëne **1970** £19.00 (FA)
Doisy-Daëne ½ bottle **1988** £16.95 (ROB)
Doisy-Védrines ½ bottle **1983** £19.39 (REI)
Filhot **1998** £18.75 (HIG)
Filhot ½ bottle **1990** £19.95 (RES)
Filhot ½ bottle **1989** £15.10 (REI)
Guiraud **1995** £19.95 (TAN) £26.92 (GOE)
Guiraud ½ bottle **1997** £15.22 (LEA)
Guiraud ½ bottle **1996** £16.95 (WAI)
Haura **1976** £15.99 (RAE)
les Justices ½ bottle **1996** £19.38 (TW)
Lafaurie-Peyraguey **1985** £18.02 (FA)
Lafaurie-Peyraguey **1977** £19.95 (BU)
Lafaurie-Peyraguey ½ bottle **1997** £16.95 (RES)
Lafaurie-Peyraguey ½ bottle **1985** £18.00 (COC)
Lamothe-Guignard **1989** £19.49 (FA)
Liot **1996** £15.49 (BOD) £15.49 (SUN)
Liot **1995** £16.45 (BER) £16.75 (ELL) £18.75 (STE)

Liot **1990** £18.21 (REI) £21.00 (YOU)
Liot **1989** £18.33 (MI) £18.99 (JON)
Loubens **1995** £16.70 (LAY)
Myrat **1996** £18.00 (JU) £18.33 (MI) £18.95 (DI)
Nairac **1990** £18.51 (FA) £24.95 (TAN)
Nairac ½ bottle **1990** £15.95 (LEA)
Nairac ½ bottle **1983** £15.00 (CRO)
Rabaud-Promis **1997** £18.76 (RAE) £23.33 (MI)
Rabaud-Promis **1996** £17.82 (RAE) £23.00 (JU)
Rabaud-Promis **1995** £18.11 (GOE)
Rabaud-Promis **1988** £19.50 (RAE) £47.95 (ROB)
Rabaud-Promis ½ bottle **1986** £17.63 (REI)
Rabaud-Promis ½ bottle **1985** £18.95 (RES)
la Rame Reserve du Château **1990** £18.57 (NO)
Rayne-Vigneau **1995** £19.17 (MI) £23.40 (HAH)
Rayne-Vigneau **1986** £19.00 (FA) £25.75 (TAN) £43.00 (CRO)
Rayne-Vigneau ½ bottle **1986** £17.63 (REI) £24.00 (CRO)
de Ricaud **1994** £16.95 (PHI)
Rieussec ½ bottle **1997** £18.50 (RES)
Rieussec ½ bottle **1995** £16.99 (FRI)
Rieussec ½ bottle **1990** £18.31 (FA) £22.50 (WS) £22.91 (REI)
Rieussec ½ bottle **1989** £18.00 (WS) £18.56 (FA) £32.00 (STA)
St-Amand **1983** £19.50 (BU)
Suduiraut **1996** £19.00 (FA) £24.17 (MI) £30.49 (FRI) £31.50 (TAN) £33.14 (CB)
Suduiraut ½ bottle **1997** £15.22 (LEA)
Suduiraut ½ bottle **1996** £16.70 (HAH)
Suduiraut ½ bottle **1989** £17.29 (BO) £24.85 (WY)
la Tour Blanche ½ bottle **1983** £15.95 (RES)

£20.00 → £29.99

d'Arche **1989** £22.62 (REI) £29.32 (PLA)
d'Arche **1988** £24.31 (PIP)
Bastor-Lamontagne **1988** £26.44 (REI)
Bastor-Lamontagne **1983** £29.96 (REI) £36.95 (RES)
Broustet **1989** £21.67 (MI) £27.50 (ROB)
Broustet **1988** £21.50 (FRI) £24.42 (PIP)
Climens **1995** £27.50 (HA) £29.00 (JU) £29.95 (LEA)
Climens **1994** £21.50 (WR)
Climens **1991** £25.95 (RAE) £28.79 (PLA)
Climens **1981** £29.96 (REI) £34.25 (TAN)
Climens **1974** £27.95 (RAE) £31.50 (AD)
Climens **1970** £28.30 (FA)
Climens ½ bottle **1988** £24.19 (FA)
Climens ½ bottle **1983** £27.50 (BEN)
Coutet **1997** £28.98 (RAE) £32.00 (JU) £32.17 (CB) £35.95 (TAN) £39.95 (DI)
Coutet **1996** £26.67 (MI) £29.95 (LAY) £30.00 (JU) £31.50 (TAN) £32.74 (CB)
Coutet **1995** £25.46 (HA) £28.00 (JU) £29.25 (HAH) £39.50 (UN) £39.68 (PLAY)
Coutet **1989** £29.50 (WS) £32.00 (CRO)
Coutet **1987** £22.95 (ROB)
Coutet ½ bottle **1989** £21.95 (ROB)
Coutet ½ bottle **1988** £22.95 (BEN)
Doisy-Daëne **1997** £23.44 (LEA) £25.64 (CB) £25.95 (LAY) £28.00 (JU)
Doisy-Daëne **1996** £25.00 (JU) £25.20 (TAN) £25.25 (HIG) £25.79 (CB) £25.95 (DI)
Doisy-Daëne **1989** £26.50 (BER) £32.39 (JON)
Doisy-Daëne ½ bottle **1976** £22.09 (WY)
Doisy-Daëne ½ bottle **1971** £28.79 (REI)
Doisy-Védrines **1997** £25.32 (CB) £27.50 (MI)
Doisy-Védrines **1996** £21.99 (OD) £22.50 (MI) £22.95 (LAY)
Doisy-Védrines **1995** £22.99 (OD)

Doisy-Védrines **1990** £26.67 (MI)
Doisy-Védrines **1989** £27.50 (WS) £28.33 (MI)
Doisy-Védrines ½ bottle **1986** £20.50 (ROB)
de Fargues **1982** £29.17 (MI)
de Fargues **1979** £28.79 (FA)
Filhot **1997** £23.85 (CB)
Filhot **1990** £20.46 (FA) £22.99 (OD) £25.95 (VIC) £25.95 (THR) £25.95 (WR) £26.95 (BOT) £27.95 (ROB) £28.00 (JU) £31.35 (NI) £32.00 (RES)
Filhot **1989** £25.00 (WAI)
Filhot **1975** £28.79 (REI) £110.45 (WY)
Guiraud **1997** £25.32 (HA) £30.83 (MI) £32.67 (CB) £34.00 (JU)
Guiraud **1996** £22.52 (GOE) £25.00 (MI) £28.50 (LAY) £29.00 (JU) £31.86 (CB)
Guiraud **1971** £28.30 (FA)
Guiraud ½ bottle **1988** £21.95 (BEN) £34.99 (NO)

Lafaurie-Peyraguey **1996** £26.50 (LEA) £30.00 (JU) £32.74 (CB)
Lafaurie-Peyraguey **1995** £29.50 (BER)
Lafaurie-Peyraguey **1994** £24.95 (STE)
Lafaurie-Peyraguey **1981** £26.44 (REI)
Lafaurie-Peyraguey **1966** £27.50 (BU)
Lamothe-Guignard **1997** £21.40 (AV)
de Malle **1997** £23.33 (MI) £24.70 (LAY) £27.00 (JU)
de Malle **1996** £21.67 (MI) £22.45 (BER)
de Malle **1995** £27.85 (CB)
Myrat **1997** £20.83 (MI)
Nairac **1997** £23.47 (HA) £32.80 (TAN)
Nairac **1996** £26.00 (FORT) £28.00 (HIG)
Nairac **1995** £20.56 (HIG) £27.90 (JER) £31.73 (CB)
Nairac **1988** £22.95 (LEA)
Nairac ½ bottle **1975** £24.00 (CRO)
Rabaud-Promis **1990** £21.00 (HIG) £24.87 (FA)
Rabaud-Promis **1989** £24.95 (RAE)
Rabaud-Promis ½ bottle **1989** £21.00 (RES)
Rayne-Vigneau **1997** £25.95 (LAY)
Rayne-Vigneau **1996** £21.67 (MI) £25.79 (CB)
Rayne-Vigneau **1988** £25.00 (BU) £27.32 (FA) £30.39 (PIP)
Rayne-Vigneau **1976** £29.50 (BU)
Rayne-Vigneau ½ bottle **1988** £20.72 (WY) £23.95 (ROB)
Rieussec **1998** £22.91 (WY) £25.50 (HIG)
Rieussec **1996** £29.95 (LEA) £30.49 (FRI) £32.00 (JU) £33.14 (CB) £34.20 (HAH) £35.20 (LAY)
Rieussec ½ bottle **1988** £23.65 (FRI) £24.95 (BEN) £31.76 (WY) £33.32 (NO)
Romer du Hayot **1971** £24.87 (FA)
Suduiraut **1995** £29.50 (FRI)
Suduiraut **1988** £25.85 (FA) £32.50 (MI) £37.95 (TAN) £42.95 (ROB) £49.00 (BER)
Suduiraut **1983** £26.83 (FA) £37.95 (PIP) £38.95 (ROB) £39.00 (RES) £41.42 (WY)
Suduiraut **1982** £25.85 (FA) £33.50 (FRI) £92.60 (UB)
Suduiraut **1975** £28.79 (FA) £41.75 (BEN)
Suduiraut ½ bottle **1990** £26.00 (CRO) £26.00 (RES) £27.50 (ROB)
la Tour Blanche **1996** £29.00 (JU)

- *All prices for each wine are listed together in ascending order.*
- *Price bands refer to the lowest price for which the wine is available.*

la Tour Blanche **1995** £27.11 (HA) £29.50 (FRI)
la Tour Blanche **1989** £28.30 (FA) £32.50 (FRI) £33.00 (JU)
la Tour Blanche **1983** £27.99 (JON)
la Tour Blanche **1978** £27.50 (BU)
la Tour Blanche ½ bottle **1996** £25.00 (NO)

£30.00 → £39.99

Climens **1997** £35.45 (RAE) £47.00 (REI) £48.00 (JU) £49.17 (MI)
Climens **1996** £33.40 (RAE) £45.00 (JU)
Climens **1989** £36.00 (RAE) £48.95 (BEN) £60.00 (FORT)
Climens **1983** £39.00 (VA) £75.94 (WY)
Coutet **1990** £31.00 (COC) £31.14 (PLA)
Coutet **1988** £32.50 (SOM) £43.75 (ROB)
Coutet **1986** £31.99 (JON)
Coutet **1983** £31.70 (TAN) £35.95 (RES) £39.95 (ROB)
Coutet **1975** £32.70 (FA)
Coutet **1964** £31.14 (REI)
Cru Barréjats **1992** £38.00 (JU)
Doisy-Daëne **1978** £30.37 (WY)
Doisy-Dubroca **1975** £31.50 (ROB)
de Fargues **1985** £37.50 (MI)
de Fargues **1965** £35.25 (REI)
Filhot **1988** £31.50 (ROB)
Guiraud **1990** £35.00 (CRO)
Guiraud **1983** £30.00 (MI) £34.50 (LEA)
Lafaurie-Peyraguey **1997** £32.67 (CB) £36.00 (JU)
Lafaurie-Peyraguey **1989** £35.00 (HIG) £37.00 (JU) £38.00 (BER) £39.95 (ROB) £42.75 (STE)
Lafaurie-Peyraguey **1988** £31.91 (NO) £36.62 (FA) £41.13 (REI) £47.50 (FORT)
Lafaurie-Peyraguey ½ bottle **1986** £38.50 (RES)
de Malle **1990** £35.00 (SOM)
de Malle **1988** £30.50 (ROB) £34.99 (NO)
de Malle **1986** £39.98 (COC)
Nairac **1983** £37.95 (ROB)
Rabaud-Promis **1971** £39.50 (BU)
Raymond-Lafon **1986** £36.62 (FA)
Rayne-Vigneau **1971** £33.49 (REI)
Rieussec **1997** £32.67 (CB) £36.00 (JU)
Rieussec **1995** £30.50 (FRI)
Rieussec **1990** £34.66 (FA) £46.45 (TAN) £48.01 (NO) £56.99 (REI)
Rieussec **1989** £35.00 (RAE) £37.00 (TAN) £37.11 (FA) £48.01 (NO) £51.11 (REI)
Rieussec **1988** £33.32 (NO) £37.11 (FA) £44.00 (FRI) £45.24 (REI) £49.99 (POR) £51.50 (STE) £61.00 (STA)

Rieussec **1981** £38.19 (REI)
Rieussec ½ bottle **1983** £33.00 (RES) £37.50 (ROB) £44.80 (UB)
Sigalas-Rabaud **1997** £30.00 (JU)
Sigalas-Rabaud **1989** £32.50 (BEN) £34.95 (ROB) £46.50 (BER)
Sigalas-Rabaud **1988** £30.14 (PIP)
Suduiraut **1997** £30.83 (MI) £31.95 (TAN) £32.67 (CB) £39.95 (DI)
Suduiraut **1989** £34.59 (BO) £35.95 (BEN) £35.95 (DI) £49.99 (POR)
Suduiraut **1986** £38.80 (TAN)
Suduiraut ½ bottle **1988** £34.99 (NO)
la Tour Blanche **1997** £36.00 (JU)

£40.00 → £59.99

de Cérons **1942** £57.99 (WY)
Climens **1990** £49.17 (MI) £55.00 (FORT)
Climens **1988** £45.43 (FA) £60.00 (FORT)
Climens **1979** £40.00 (HED)
Climens ½ bottle **1967** £59.00 (RES)
Coutet **1967** £47.00 (FA) £80.08 (WY)
Coutet **1961** £46.41 (REI) £103.55 (WY)
Coutet ½ bottle **1990** £42.00 (UB)
de Fargues **1998** £57.50 (TAN)
de Fargues **1990** £48.33 (MI) £55.00 (JU) £65.00 (RES) £80.00 (FORT)
de Fargues **1988** £40.00 (MI) £42.99 (FA)
Gilette **1962** £58.00 (CRO) £129.25 (TW)
les Justices **1983** £47.00 (TW)
Lafaurie-Peyraguey **1998** £45.00 (YOU)
Lafaurie-Peyraguey **1990** £44.47 (REI) £45.00 (NO)
Lafaurie-Peyraguey **1983** £41.13 (REI)
Lafaurie-Peyraguey **1938** £52.46 (WY)
Nairac **1964** £48.33 (WY)
Raymond-Lafon **1988** £47.00 (JU)
Rieussec **1986** £49.00 (WR) £49.00 (BOT) £50.00 (FORT) £62.13 (WY)
Rieussec **1985** £41.13 (REI)
Rieussec **1983** £43.47 (FA) £50.24 (TAN) £62.00 (RES) £62.13 (WY)
Rieussec **1975** £48.37 (FA) £54.00 (CRO) £56.69 (JON)
Romer du Hayot **1967** £51.09 (WY)
Suduiraut **1971** £55.23 (WY)
la Tour Blanche **1990** £45.00 (BER)
d'Yquem ½ bottle **1994** £56.30 (CAV)

£60.00 → £99.99

Climens **1976** £89.75 (WY)
Climens **1967** £69.00 (RAE) £82.84 (WY) £95.00 (SOM)
Climens **1966** £68.74 (REI) £103.55 (WY)
Climens **1955** £88.13 (REI)
Climens ½ bottle **1949** £69.50 (BU) £111.63 (REI)
Coutet **1971** £64.63 (REI) £70.00 (CRO)
Coutet **1959** £99.88 (FA) £193.88 (REI)
Doisy-Daëne **1953** £99.88 (REI)
Filhot **1955** £68.74 (REI)
Gilette **1955** £99.88 (REI)
Gilette Crème de Tête **1953** £72.00 (CRO)
Guiraud **1961** £89.50 (FA)
Guiraud ½ bottle **1924** £75.94 (WY)
Lafaurie-Peyraguey **1949** £75.00 (BU)
Lafaurie-Peyraguey **1926** £69.03 (WY)
Rayne-Vigneau **1953** £99.88 (REI)
Rieussec **1967** £88.13 (REI)
Rieussec **1962** £73.44 (REI)
Romer du Hayot **1955** £60.12 (FA)
Sigalas-Rabaud **1962** £64.63 (REI)
Sigalas-Rabaud **1959** £96.35 (FA)
Suduiraut **1966** £64.63 (REI)
Suduiraut **1958** £88.13 (REI)
Suduiraut **1957** £82.84 (WY)
la Tour Blanche **1962** £66.00 (CRO) £75.94 (WY)
la Tour Blanche **1923** £86.99 (WY)
d'Yquem **1994** £99.29 (FA) £116.20 (LAY) £125.83 (MI) £127.00 (TAN)
d'Yquem **1991** £97.33 (FA) £110.00 (WS) £115.00 (MI) £116.20 (LAY) £150.00 (BER)
d'Yquem **1987** £87.54 (FA) £117.36 (WY)
d'Yquem **1984** £83.62 (FA)
d'Yquem **1981** £94.00 (CAV) £126.70 (FA) £179.48 (WY)
d'Yquem ½ bottle **1990** £76.57 (FA) £79.99 (OD) £90.00 (WS) £99.30 (TAN) £135.00 (RES)
d'Yquem ½ bottle **1989** £74.99 (OD) £76.57 (FA) £95.99 (FRI) £107.69 (WY) £115.00 (LEA) £115.00 (ROB)
d'Yquem ½ bottle **1988** £79.02 (FA) £105.00 (RES) £106.99 (FRI) £115.00 (FORT)
d'Yquem ½ bottle **1986** £95.00 (FORT)

£100.00 → £149.99

Climens **1962** £116.50 (BEN)
Climens **1953** £148.25 (FA) £180.00 (BEN)
Climens **1952** £112.21 (REI)
Coutet **1934** £124.26 (WY)
Doisy-Daëne **1961** £117.36 (WY)
Doisy-Daëne **1947** £111.63 (REI)
Doisy-Védrines **1959** £111.63 (REI)
Gilette **1947** £146.88 (REI)
Guiraud **1953** £118.87 (FA)
Lafaurie-Peyraguey **1953** £141.00 (CAV)
Rayne-Vigneau **1926** £110.45 (WY)
Rayne-Vigneau **1908** £148.25 (FA)

Suduiraut 1962 £131.17 (WY)
d'Yquem 1993 £116.20 (LAY)
d'Yquem 1990 £138.45 (FA) £149.99 (OD) £150.00 (HIG) £155.00 (TAN) £155.00 (WS) £155.83 (MI) £170.00 (WAI) £180.00 (JU) £185.00 (RES) £186.39 (WY) £199.80 (HAH)
d'Yquem 1989 £144.99 (OD) £147.50 (MI) £160.00 (JU) £185.00 (FORT) £193.29 (WY) £195.00 (BEN) £198.00 (ROB) £210.33 (TW)
d'Yquem 1988 £146.29 (FA) £155.83 (MI) £160.00 (JU) £172.58 (WY) £195.00 (FORT) £208.31 (FRI)
d'Yquem 1986 £148.25 (FA) £170.00 (JU) £177.50 (MI) £179.48 (WY) £184.57 (CAV) £200.00 (FORT) £205.00 (BER) £223.25 (TW)
d'Yquem 1963 £135.13 (REI) £395.00 (VA)

£150.00 → £199.99

d'Arche 1949 £165.68 (WY)
Caillou 1943 £160.00 (CRO)
Coutet 1948 £165.68 (WY)
Filhot 1948 £179.48 (WY)
Gilette 1952 £182.13 (TW)
Lafaurie-Peyraguey 1947 £164.50 (REI)
Rabaud-Promis 1918 £165.68 (WY)
Rayne-Vigneau 1948 £193.29 (WY)
Rieussec 1961 £151.87 (WY)
Rieussec 1959 £176.25 (REI)
Suduiraut 1967 £150.00 (FORT)
Suduiraut 1959 £176.25 (REI)
Suduiraut 1923 £170.36 (REI)
la Tour Blanche 1948 £156.28 (REI)
la Tour Blanche 1935 £151.87 (WY)
d'Yquem 1985 £160.00 (DI)
d'Yquem 1983 £175.76 (CAV) £177.62 (FA) £234.71 (WY) £235.00 (FORT) £235.00 (VA) £275.00 (ROB)
d'Yquem 1982 £175.00 (BER)
d'Yquem 1970 £182.52 (FA) £293.75 (CAV)
d'Yquem ½ bottle 1982 £150.00 (UB)

£200.00 → £299.99

Climens 1950 £258.50 (REI)
Coutet 1950 £205.63 (REI)
Filhot 1934 £227.81 (WY)
Gilette 1950 £241.62 (WY)
Gilette 1934 £293.75 (TW)
Lafaurie-Peyraguey 1959 £205.63 (REI)
Rayne-Vigneau 1939 £269.23 (WY)
Rayne-Vigneau 1937 £217.38 (REI)
Sigalas-Rabaud 1919 £262.32 (WY)
Suduiraut 1945 £293.75 (CAV)
la Tour Blanche 1920 £200.20 (WY)
d'Yquem 1976 £221.68 (FA) £324.45 (WY) £345.00 (FORT) £370.00 (ROB)
d'Yquem 1975 £258.50 (REI) £260.85 (FA) £336.05 (TW)
d'Yquem 1966 £289.93 (WY)
d'Yquem 1956 £258.50 (REI) £282.00 (FA) £331.35 (WY) £435.00 (VA)
d'Yquem 1954 £287.88 (REI) £455.61 (WY)
d'Yquem 1950 £282.00 (FA) £411.25 (REI) £470.00 (TW) £483.22 (WY)

£300.00 → £399.99

Climens 1928 £365.43 (WY)
Coutet 1921 £330.00 (CRO)
d'Yquem 1967 £350.00 (DI) £440.63 (FA) £495.00 (BEN) £670.00 (FRI) £750.00 (FORT)
d'Yquem 1948 £311.38 (FA)
d'Yquem 1944 £323.13 (FA) £621.28 (WY)

£400.00 → £499.99

d'Yquem 1955 £417.52 (FA) £495.00 (BEN) £685.00 (ROB)
d'Yquem 1953 £425.00 (BEN) £440.63 (REI) £451.79 (FA) £700.00 (VA)
d'Yquem 1945 £470.00 (FA) £687.38 (REI)
d'Yquem 1918 £469.41 (WY) £646.25 (REI)
d'Yquem 1908 £470.00 (FA)

Over £500.00

d'Yquem 1980 £550.00 (VA)
d'Yquem 1959 £500.00 (NO) £745.54 (WY)
d'Yquem 1947 £822.50 (FA) £855.99 (WY)
d'Yquem 1934 £940.00 (VA)
d'Yquem 1933 £731.73 (WY)
d'Yquem 1932 £587.50 (FA) £690.31 (WY)
d'Yquem 1928 £938.83 (WY)
d'Yquem 1926 £593.38 (REI) £975.00 (VA)
d'Yquem 1925 £900.00 (VA)
d'Yquem 1919 £531.55 (WY)
d'Yquem 1900 £2,937.50 (WY) £2,937.50 (FA)

ROSÉ

Under £7.00

Bel Air 1998 £5.25 (WS)
Lacroix 1998 £5.78 (NO) £6.65 (DI)
de Sours Rosé 1999 £6.99 (MAJ) £6.99 (GOE)
de Sours Rosé 1998 £6.85 (GOE) £8.23 (CB) £9.22 (PLAY)
Thieuley Clairet 1998 £4.95 (SOM)

BURGUNDY

There is no such thing as very good, very cheap white Burgundy. If you want lesser white Burgundy it's only worth buying from a very good grower – and then it's unlikely to be all that cheap

I don't know about lesser white Burgundy. I really don't.

In theory it should be easy. Chardonnay from the Côte d'Or costs an arm and a leg, but there's lots of it a bit further south, in the Côte Chalonaise and Mâconnais. Masses of it. And hell, it's white and it's from Burgundy. Therefore it should have, as its back labels tend to claim, the style of great white Burgundy at a fraction of the price.

Well, some do. A few do. But most, you know, don't. Most taste like simple, rather melony-appley Chardonnay. Perfectly nice, but not hugely distinguishable from melony-appley Chardonnay from anywhere else in the world, except that it may be a smidgen more expensive.

The famous style of white Burgundy is found more in the breach than the observance in these parts. And for a very simple reason: to reproduce it you need not only the time-consuming attention to detail that the top Côte d'Or growers give their wines, but also the growing conditions on the Côte d'Or.

How much of the style of great white Burgundy comes from the winemaking, and how much from the vineyard, is open to debate. What is clear is that some of it is reproduceable in lesser wines, but that it takes a very good producer to do it. And very good producers tend to charge a bit more for their wines.

So if you want the authentic style of the Côte d'Or at a non-Côte d'Or price, don't be disappointed if you still have to shell out quite a lot. There's a limit to how low it's worth going.

GRAPE VARIETIES

ALIGOTÉ (white) Not planted in the best sites – though there are a few vines in Corton-Charlemagne. Aligoté from old vines can produce a lovely, refreshing wine, scented like buttermilk soap yet as sharp and palate-cleansing as a squeeze of lemon juice. *Dujac* and a few others barrique-ferment it with surprising success. *Aubert de Villaine*'s Aligoté de Bouzeron is tops.

CHARDONNAY (white) Burgundy makes the most famous Chardonnay of all. Even in the decidedly dicky Burgundian climate, it produces good to excellent wine almost every year. Chardonnays made without the use of oak barrels for aging will taste very different from barrel-aged wines. A Mâcon produced in stainless steel will have appley fruit; Côte Chalonnaise Chardonnay is generally rather taut and chalky-dry, but given some oak, it can become delicately nutty. In the north of the Beaujolais region Chardonnay has a stony dryness; in the south it is nearer to the fatter, softer, wines of southern Burgundy. Chablis generally produces lean wine, but in riper years and with some oak aging it can get much rounder. The Côte d'Or is the peak of achievement and top wines from the Côte de Beaune are luscious, creamy and honeyed yet totally dry, the rich, ripe fruit entwined with the scents of oak in a surprisingly powerful wine – from the right producer, the world's greatest dry white.

GAMAY (red) The Gamay has no pretensions: in Beaujolais it can simply make one of the juiciest, most gulpable, gurgling wines the world has to offer. *Can*, I stress: not all Beaujolais is like this. Ideally it is simple, cherry-sharp, with candy-like fruit, sometimes with hints of raspberry or strawberry. The wines from the *crus* go further, but in the main their similarity from the grape is greater than the differences in the places they come from. All but the wines of the top villages should be drunk as young as you can find them.

PINOT BEUROT (white) Known elsewhere as Pinot Gris. Very rare in Burgundy, but it produces rich, buttery wine usually used to soften Chardonnay. There is a little blended Pinot Beurot in the Hautes-Côtes and Aloxe-Corton.

PINOT BLANC (white) There is a little of this in the Côte d'Or – in Aloxe-Corton, for instance, where it makes a soft, quick-maturing wine. Rully in the Côte Chalonnaise has some and it ripens well in the Hautes-Côtes. There is also an odd white mutation of Pinot Noir – found in Nuits-St-Georges where the *premier cru* vineyard la Perrière makes a savoury white, and in the Monts Luisants vineyard in Morey-St-Denis.

PINOT NOIR (red) The sulkiest, trickiest fine-wine grape in the world is the exclusive grape in almost all red Burgundies. It needs a more delicate balance of spring, summer and autumn climate than any other variety to achieve greatness. It used to be true to say that no other part of the world could produce a Pinot Noir to match those of Burgundy, but isolated growers in Oregon, California, New Zealand, Australia and South Africa are now making very fine examples. Even so, Burgundy is still the only place on earth where fine Pinot Noirs are made in any great quantity. The problem is, there are still some awful ones, too: heavy, chewy and sweet-fruited or thin and pallid. But quality is far higher than it used to be. From a good producer it should be light, elegant, intense, and perfumed with raspberry or strawberry fruit and a hint of violets. Oak will add spicier, complex notes. Except for wine from the very top vineyards, Burgundy can be drunk young with pleasure. But a great *cru* from a great vintage really benefits from a decade or more in bottle.

WINE REGIONS

ALOXE-CORTON, AC (Côte de Beaune; red, white) Overwhelmingly a red-wine village, and it has the only red *grand cru* in the Côte de Beaune, le Corton, also sold under various subdivisions like Corton-Bressandes and Corton Clos du Roi and more widely available than the other *grands crus* of Burgundy. If we're talking about village wines, then the reds of Savigny are at least as good, and you're not paying a premium there for the hyphenated Corton. Go for *Chandon de Briailles, Drouhin, Jadot, Jaffelin, Leroy, Daniel Senard* and *Tollot-Beaut.* Also good: *Bouzereau-Gruère, Dubreuil-Fontaine, Faiveley, Juillot, Michel Voarick.*

The village also has one of the Côte's most famous white *grands crus*, Corton-Charlemagne. This can be a magnificent, blasting wall of flavour, not big on nuance, but strong, buttery and ripe, traditionally supposed to require long aging to show its full potential. See Corton-Charlemagne for producers, if you think you can afford it.

AUXEY-DURESSES, AC (Côte de Beaune; red, white) A village with a deservedly high reputation for full, but fairly gentle, nicely fruity reds. Look for *Ampeau, Diconne, Duc de Magenta, Alain Gras, Leroy, Pascal Prunier, Roy, Thévenin.*

The best whites here can be excellent, from producers like *Ampeau, Diconne, Duc de Magenta, Jadot, Leroy* and *Pascal Prunier. Leroy's* are probably the best of all, but prices at that domaine are astronomical.

BÂTARD-MONTRACHET, AC (Côte de Beaune; white) *Grand cru* of Chassagne and Puligny lying just below le Montrachet and, from a good producer, displaying a good deal of its dramatic flavour, almost thick in the mouth, all roast nuts, butter,

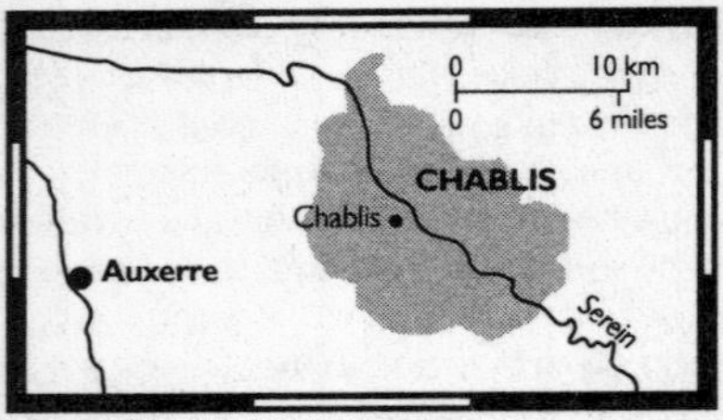

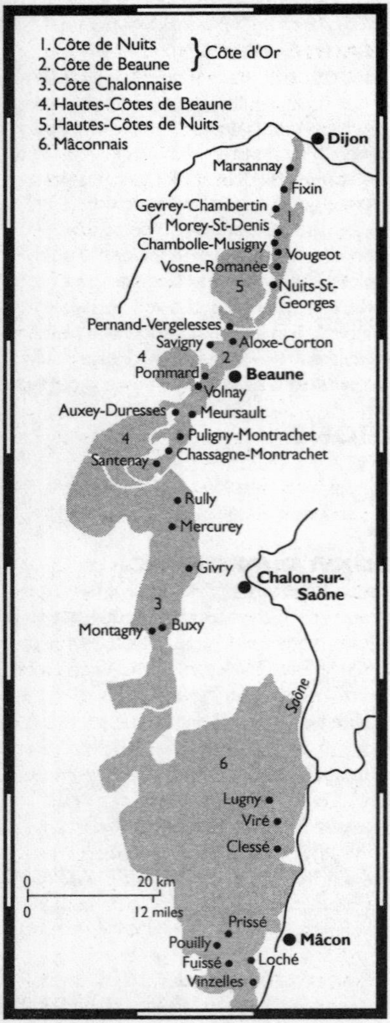

CLASSIFICATIONS

Burgundy has five different levels of classification:

Non-specific regional appellations with no geographical definition, e.g. Bourgogne, which may come from inferior land or young vines.

Specific regional appellations, e.g. Côte de Beaune-Villages, generally a blend from one or more villages. Côte de Nuits-Villages is usually better.

Village commune wines Each village has its vineyards legally defined. Vineyards with no special reputation are usually blended together under the village name. But there is a growing move towards even relatively unknown vineyards appearing on the label. These unclassified vineyards are called *lieux-dits* or 'stated places'. They can only appear on the label in letters half the size of the village name.

Premier cru It's typical of Burgundy that *premier cru* or 'First Growth' actually means 'Second Growth', because these are the second-best vineyard sites. Even so, they contain some of Burgundy's finest wines. They are classified by both village and vineyard names, e.g. Gevrey-Chambertin, Combe-aux-Moines. The vineyard name must follow the village name on the label, and it may be in the same size print. Confusingly, some growers use smaller print, but the appellation should make it clear whether it is a *premier cru* or a *lieu-dit*.

Grand cru These are the real top growths. Not every village has one. The reds are mostly in the Côte de Nuits, the whites in the Côte de Beaune. A *grand cru* vineyard name can stand alone on the label without the village – for example, Chambertin from the village of Gevrey-Chambertin. (Note that by tradition, a Burgundy village is allowed to tack on the name of its *grand cru* vineyard, and use the compound name for wines that have nothing to do with the *grand cru*, for instance Puligny-Montrachet.)

toast and honey. Should be wonderfully exciting, if expensive. Good names: *Blain-Gagnard, Carillon, Jean-Noël Gagnard, Leflaive, Bernard Morey, Pierre Morey, Michel Niellon, Pernot, Poirier, Ramonet* and *Sauzet*.

BEAUJOLAIS, AC (red) This covers all the basic wines, the produce of the flatter, southern part of Beaujolais. Much of the best is now sold as Nouveau. Run-of-the-mill Beaujolais, apart from Nouveau, can be good, fruity stuff but generally costs too much for the quality. Best: *Blaise, Carron, Charmet, Ch. de la Plume,* the co-op at *Bully, Duboeuf Bouteille Cristal, Garlon, Labruyère, Loron, Paul Sapin, Domaine des Vissoux.*

BEAUJOLAIS BLANC, AC (white) Usually quite expensive, and seldom has much character. At best it should be light and minerally.

BEAUJOLAIS NOUVEAU (or PRIMEUR) (red) The new vintage wine of Beaujolais, released in the November after the harvest. It will normally improve for several months in bottle, and even longer in good Nouveau vintages – a couple of years, maybe. There's seldom much difference in quality between Beaujolais-Villages Nouveau and simple Beaujolais Nouveau.

BEAUJOLAIS ROSÉ, AC (rosé) Usually an apology for a wine, although a good one can be very good indeed. But it's usually too expensive.

BEAUJOLAIS SUPÉRIEUR, AC (red) *Supérieur* means that the basic alcoholic content is higher. It doesn't ensure a better wine, and is rarely seen on the label.

BEAUJOLAIS-VILLAGES, AC (red) Thirty-nine villages can use this title. The wines are certainly better than basic Beaujolais, a little fuller and deeper, and the cherry-sharp fruit of the Gamay is usually more marked. However, always look for a wine bottled in the region, and preferably one from a single vineyard. *Noël Aucoeur, Château Gaillard, Château des Loges, Château des Vergers, Jacques Dépagneux, Domaine de la Brasse, Domaine de la Chapelle de Vatre (Sarrau), de Flammerécourt, Gutty Père et Fils, André Large, Jean-Charles Pivot, Jean-Luc Tissier* and *Trichard* are good and local, but most domaines are bottled by one of the region's merchants. Labelling by domaine is on the increase.

BEAUNE, AC (Côte de Beaune; red, white) One of the few reliable commune wines, usually quite light, with a soft, 'red fruits' sweetness and a flicker of something minerally to smarten it up nicely. The wines are nearly all red. Beaune has the largest acreage of vines of any Côte d'Or commune, and they are mostly owned by merchants. It has no *grands crus* but many excellent *premiers crus*, for example Grèves, Marconnets, Teurons, Boucherottes, Vignes Franches and Cent Vignes. Prices tend to be reasonable, as Beaune is less fashionable than many. The best producers here are *Morot, Drouhin, Jadot, Lafarge* and *Tollot-Beaut,* but reliable wines are also made by *Besancenot-Mathouillet, Bouley, Germain, Jaffelin* and *Morey. Drouhin*'s Clos des Mouches is a cut above the rest.

BIENVENUES-BÂTARD-MONTRACHET, AC (Côte de Beaune; white) A tiny *grand cru* situated in Puligny below le Montrachet, and within the larger Bâtard-Montrachet AC, whose wines are similar. The Bienvenues wines are often lighter and more elegant, although they may lack a tiny bit of Bâtard's drive. Best: *Carillon, Clerc, J-N Gagnard, Leflaive, Pernot, Ramonet.*

BLAGNY, AC (Côte de Beaune; red) The red wines are usually a bit fierce, but then this is the white wine heartland of Burgundy, so I'm a bit surprised they grow any red at all. Best: *Leflaive, Matrot.*

BONNES-MARES, AC (Côte de Nuits; red) Usually one of the most – or should I say one of the very few – reliable *grands crus*, which ages extremely well over ten to 20 years to a lovely smoky, chocolate-and-prunes richness. Best names: *Domaine des Varoilles, Drouhin, Dujac, Groffier, Jadot, Roumier, de Vogüé*.

BOURGOGNE ALIGOTÉ, AC (white) Usually rather sharp and green except where old vines make exciting wine, but the locals add crème de cassis to it to make kir – which tells you quite a lot about it. Best: *Coche-Dury, Confuron, Devevey, Diconne, Jobard, Rion, Rollin*.

BOURGOGNE ALIGOTÉ DE BOUZERON, AC (Côte Chalonnaise; white) The white wine pride of the Côte Chalonnaise. The vines are frequently old – this seems to be more crucial for Aligoté than for most other wines – and the buttermilk-soap nose is followed by a very dry, slightly lemony, pepper-sharp wine, too good to mix with cassis. The best Aligoté of all, rich and oaky, comes from *de Villaine*. *Chanzy* and *Bouchard Père et Fils* are also good. Top ones can age for five years or so.

BOURGOGNE BLANC, AC (white) Anything from a basic Burgundy grown in the less good spots anywhere between Chablis and the Mâconnais to a carefully matured wine from a serious producer, either from young vines or from vineyards that just miss a superior AC, especially on the borders of Meursault. Best: *Boisson-Vadot, Michel Bouzereau, Boyer-Martenot, Boisson-Morey, Coche-Dury, J Deverey, Dussort, Jadot, Javillier, Jobard, Labouré-Roi, Lafon, René Manuel, Millot-Battault* and the *Buxy* co-op (look for *Clos de Chenoves*).

BOURGOGNE GRAND ORDINAIRE, AC (red) Très ordinaire. Pas très grand. The bottom of the Burgundy barrel, rarely seen outside Burgundy. It may be made from Pinot Noir and Gamay, and even a couple of obscure grapes, the Tressot and César, as well.

BOURGOGNE PASSE-TOUT-GRAINS, AC (red) Often decent, lightish wine made usually in the Côte d'Or or the Côte Chalonnaise from Gamay blended with a minimum of one-third Pinot Noir. In some years it may be mostly Pinot. *Chanson* and *Rodet* make it well; *Chaley, Cornu, Léni-Volpato, Rion* and *Thomas* are also good. But even at its absolute best, true Burgundy it ain't.

BOURGOGNE ROUGE, AC (red) The basic red AC, stretching from Chablis in the north to the Beaujolais *crus* in the south. Unknown Bourgogne Rouge is best avoided – much of it is very basic indeed. Domaine-bottled Bourgogne Rouge from good growers – and a handful of merchants – can be excellent value. The best wines come from vineyards just outside the village appellations. Look for *Bourgeon, Coche-Dury, Germain, d'Heuilly-Huberdeau, Juillot, Lafarge, Mortet, Parent, Pousse d'Or, Rion* and *Rossignol*. Good merchants include *Drouhin, Faiveley, Jadot, Jaffelin, Labouré-Roi, Latour, Olivier Leflaive, Leroy, Rodet, Vallet*. The co-ops at *Buxy* and *Igé* are also good as is the *Caves des Hautes-Côtes*. Most wines should be drunk quite young.

BROUILLY, AC (Beaujolais; red) Brouilly usually makes one of the lightest *cru* wines, and in general rarely improves much with keeping. In fact, it makes a very good Nouveau. A few properties make a bigger wine to age – but even then, nine months to a year is quite enough. Good names include *Château de la Chaize, Château de Fouilloux, Château de Nevers, Château de Pierreux, Domaine Crêt des Garanches, Domaine de Combillaty (Duboeuf), Domaine de Garanches, Hospices de Belleville* and *André Large. Château des Tours*, although lovely young, can age longer.

CHABLIS, AC (white) Simple Chablis, mostly soft, sometimes acidic, covers the widest area of the appellation. So it covers a multitude of sins, with a lot of wine going under négociants' labels, and a lot being sold by the local co-op, *la Chablisienne* – they make most of the négociants' stuff too. Some of the co-op's best *cuvées* are outstandingly good, but many are too bland and soft. New oak, which is lavishly used by growers such as Fèvre and Droin, often smothers the steely and minerally qualities that make top Chablis so exciting. Best: *Adhémar-Boudin, Christian Adine, Pascal Bouchard, Jean-Marc Brocard, la Chablisienne co-op, Jean Collet, René Dauvissat, Defaix, Jean-Paul Droin, Joseph Drouhin, William Fèvre, Alain Geoffroy, Jean-Pierre Grossot, Michel Laroche, Bernard Légland, Long Depaquit, Louis Michel, Dom. des Milandes, Moreau, Guy Mothe, Raveneau, Regnard, Savary, Simmonet-Fèbvre, Robert Vocoret.*

CHABLIS GRAND CRU, AC (white) The seven *grands crus* (Blanchots, Preuses, Bougros, Grenouilles, Valmur, Vaudésir and les Clos) can be outstanding, though they seldom rival the *grands crus* of the Côte de Beaune. To get the best out of them, you need to age them, preferably after oaking, although *Louis Michel*'s oak-free wines age superbly. Recent vintages have seen a growing use of oak, sometimes giving deeper, richer wines which will benefit from bottle-aging, but some wines are marred by clumsy or excessive use of new oak.

CHABLIS PREMIER CRU, AC (white) There are some 30 vineyard names in this category, but they have been rationalized into 12 main plots. Expansion mania has meant that many hardly suitable pieces of vineyard are now accorded *premier cru* status, so the difference in quality between basic Chablis and *premier cru* isn't always all that it should be. However, in recent years there has been a definite move towards quality by the better growers and *la Chablisienne* co-op.

CHAMBERTIN, AC (Côte de Nuits; red) Most famous of the eight *grands crus* of Gevrey-Chambertin, this vineyard should

CHABLIS VINEYARDS

Grands Crus

Blanchots, Bougros, les Clos, Grenouilles, Preuses, Valmur, Vaudésir. La Moutonne, considered a *grand cru*, is from a parcel in Preuses and Vaudésir.

Premiers Crus

Fourchaume (including Fourchaume, Vaupulent, Côte de Fontenay, Vaulorent, l'Homme Mort); Montée de Tonnerre (including Montée de Tonnerre, Chapelot, Pied d'Aloup); Monts de Milieu; Vaucoupin; les Fourneaux (including les Fourneaux, Morein, Côte des Prés-Girots); Beauroy (including Beauroy, Troesmes); Côte de Léchet; Vaillons (including Vaillons, Châtains, Séché, Beugnons, les Lys); Mélinots (including Mélinots, Roncières, les Epinottes); Montmains (including Montmains, Forêts, Butteaux); Vosgros (including Vosgros and Vaugiraut); Vaudevey.

and can make wines that are big, strong and intense in their youth, mellowing to a complex, perfumed, plummy richness with age – good ones need ten to 15 years. Best: *Drouhin, Faiveley, Leroy, Denis Mortet, Ponsot, Rebourseau, Rousseau, Tortochot.*

CHAMBERTIN CLOS-DE-BÈZE, AC (Côte de Nuits; red) *Grand cru* in the village of Gevrey-Chambertin next to Chambertin both geographically and in quality. It needs seven to ten years in bottle. May be sold as Chambertin. Best: *Drouhin, Bruno Clair, Faiveley, Gelin, Mugneret-Gibourg, Rousseau, Thomas-Moillard* and *Damoy* since 1992.

CHAMBOLLE-MUSIGNY, AC (Côte de Nuits; red) This village can make light, cherry-sweet, intensely perfumed Burgundy. Best is *Georges Roumier*, with wonderful wines in every vintage from 1985. The best *premier cru* is les Amoureuses: it deserves to be *grand cru* and is priced accordingly. Top producers: *Barthod-Noëllat, Château de Chambolle-Musigny, Drouhin, Dujac, Groffier, Hudelot-Noëllat, Rion, Serveau, de Vogüé.*

CHAPELLE-CHAMBERTIN, AC (Côte de Nuits; red) The wines of this *grand cru* are typically lighter and more delicate than the other *grands crus*. But over-lightness – resulting from over-production – is their curse. The best producers are *Damoy* (since 1993), *Louis Jadot* and *Rossignol-Trapet*.

CHARMES-CHAMBERTIN, AC (Côte de Nuits; red) This is the biggest of the *grands crus* of Gevrey-Chambertin. It can be fine, strong, sensuous wine, but as with all of them, it can also be disgracefully light. Best producers: *Bachelet, Charlopin-Parisot, Drouhin, Dugat, Dugat-Py, Dujac, Rebourseau, Roty, Rousseau, Tortochot*.

CHASSAGNE-MONTRACHET, AC (Côte de Beaune; red, white) Its fame lies in its large share of the white *grand cru* vineyard of le Montrachet. The reds are a puzzle. At their best they're good value, if a bit heavy, plummy and earthy. The best names for red are *Amiot, Carillon, Colin, Duc de Magenta, Jean-Noël Gagnard, Gagnard-Delagrange, René Lamy, Albert Morey, Moreau, Jean Pillot, Ramonet*. Of the whites, the *grands crus* are excellent, but the *premiers crus* rarely dazzle quite like those of nearby Puligny-Montrachet. Best: *Blain-Gagnard, Carillon, Colin, Duc de Magenta, Fontaine-Gagnard, Jean-Noël Gagnard, Gagnard-Delagrange, Lamy-Pillot, Laguiche, Château de la Maltroye, Moreau, Albert Morey, Bernard Morey, Niellon, Fernand Pillot* and *Ramonet*. *Jaffelin* is the top merchant.

CHÉNAS, AC (Beaujolais; red) This is the second-smallest Beaujolais *cru*, making strong, dark wines, sometimes a bit tough, that can be drunk a year after the harvest, or aged to take on a Pinot Noir-like flavour. Ultra-fashionable in France at the moment. Look out for *Louis Champagnon, Charvet, Château de Chénas, Domaines des Brureaux, Domaine Chassignon, Domaine de la Combe Remont (Duboeuf), Pierre Perrachon* and *Émile Robin*.

CHEVALIER-MONTRACHET, AC (Côte de Beaune; white) A *grand cru* vineyard of the village of Puligny, giving a leaner wine than le Montrachet itself, but one with a deep flavour as rich and satisfying as a dry white wine can get. Good ones will last 20 years. Best: *Bouchard Père et Fils, Clerc, Jadot, Latour, Leflaive, Niellon*.

CHIROUBLES, AC (Beaujolais; red) A *cru* for early drinking: naturally light, similar to Beaujolais-Villages in weight, but with a cherry scent that makes it France's favourite Beaujolais *cru*. Look for *Georges Boulon, René Brouillard, Cheysson, Château Javernand, Château de Raousset, Jean-Pierre Desvignes, Duboeuf, Méziat* and *Georges Passot*.

CHOREY-LÈS-BEAUNE, AC (Côte de Beaune; red) Good value, soft, fruity reds. The village isn't overhyped, so makes some of the few affordable Burgundies. *Drouhin, Germain* and *Tollot-Beaut* are best.

CLOS DES LAMBRAYS, AC (Côte de Nuits; red) This single-owner *grand cru* in Morey-St-Denis changed hands recently. The estate had become run down and the wines were not only very rare but also not very tasty. Let's hope things change now.

CLOS DE LA ROCHE, AC (Côte de Nuits; red) Largest and finest *grand cru* of Morey-St-Denis. If not too light, it can be splendid, redcurrant-and-strawberry rich when young, like pretty good Chambertin after ten years. Best: *Amiot, Dujac, Leroy, Hubert* and *Georges Lignier, Ponsot, Rousseau*.

CLOS ST-DENIS, AC (Côte de Nuits; red) Has rarely achieved great heights and is probably least famous of all the *grands crus*. Best known is *Dujac*'s; look for *Charlopin-Parisot, Georges* or *Hubert Lignier, Ponsot*.

CLOS DE TART, AC (Côte de Nuits; red) *Grand cru* of Morey-St-Denis owned by Beaujolais merchants *Mommessin*. At best it is light but intense wine which lasts.

CLOS DE VOUGEOT, AC (Côte de Nuits; red) Over 80 growers share this *grand cru* and, while the land at the top of the slope is very fine, the land by the road is not. That rare thing, a good bottle of Clos de Vougeot, is fat, rich, strong and thick with the sweetness of perfumed plums and honey, unsubtle but exciting. It is only found in top vintages, and then only from the best producers. Best: *Arnoux, Ch. de la Tour, Jacky Confuron, Drouhin-Laroze, Engel, Grivot, Gros, Hudelot-Noëllat, Jadot, Lamarche, Leroy, Meo-Camuzet, Mugneret, Raphet.*

CORTON, AC (Côte de Beaune; red, white) The only red *grand cru* vineyard in the Côte de Beaune. Ideally, red Corton should have something of the richness and strength of Clos de Vougeot, but it tends to be four-square and unrewarding until it is mature, and then only the top wines are good. Best producers include: *Chandon de Briailles, Dubreuil-Fontaine, Faiveley, Gaunoux, Laleur-Piot, Maldant, Prince de Mérode, Rapet, Daniel Senard, Tollot-Beaut.* The finest white is the *Hospices de Beaune*'s Corton-Vergennes, and *Chandon de Briailles* makes Corton-Bressandes that is half Pinot Blanc.

CORTON-CHARLEMAGNE, AC (Côte de Beaune; white) *Grand cru* of Aloxe-Corton and Pernand-Vergelesses that occupies the upper half of the hill of Corton. It is planted almost entirely with Chardonnay, but a little Pinot Blanc or Pinot Beurot can add intriguing fatness to the wine. Look for: *Bitouzet, Bonneau du Martray, Chandon de Briailles, Chapuis, Coche-Dury, Dubreuil-Fontaine, M Juillot, Hospices de Beaune, Jadot, Laleure-Piot, Latour, Rapet, Rollin.*

CÔTE CHALONNAISE, AC (red, white) Light, usually clean-tasting Chardonnay predominates among the whites – although at long last the idea of oak-aging is catching on. But the Côte Chalonnaise has one star that cannot be overshadowed by the famous Côte d'Or: the village of Bouzeron makes the finest and the most famous Aligoté in all France. The top three villages of Rully, Mercurey and Givry all produce good reds, too, with a lovely, simple strawberry-and-cherry fruit.

INSTANT CELLAR: GREAT GROWERS

- **1999 Chablis Premier Cru, Côte de Léchet, Dom. Daniel Dampt, £11.60, Haynes Hanson & Clark** Terrifically stylish wine, with good grip and intensity.
- **1998 Mâcon-Villages, Tête de Cuvée, Verget, £9.95, Lay & Wheeler** A Mâcon of great breeding and elegance.
- **1997 Beaune Premier Cru, Les Epenottes, Domaine Parent, £13.99, Safeway** A very good price for a wine of this status from a good grower.
- **1995 Morey St Denis, en la rue de Vergy, Henri Perrot-Minot, £14.95, Waterloo Wine Co** A good concentrated year.
- **1995 Beaune les Mariages, Rossignol-Trapet, £15.75, Wright Wine Co** Lovely, round, silky seduction.
- **1997 Bourgogne Rouge Pressonnier, Roty, £11.16, Corney & Barrow** Surprisingly intense stuff from a controversial but brilliant producer.
- **1997 Savigny-lès-Beaune, Lucien Camus-Bruchon, £14.50, Raeburn** Good Savigny is utterly seductive, all incense and strawberries. Drink it, don't keep it.

CÔTE DE BEAUNE (red, white) Wine from the commune of Beaune that doesn't quite rate village status. Not much found.

CÔTE DE BEAUNE-VILLAGES, AC (red) Catch-all red wine appellation for 16 villages on the Côte de Beaune. Only Aloxe-Corton, Beaune, Volnay and Pommard cannot use the appellation. Rarely seen nowadays, and rarely exciting. Still, it *is* worth checking out the wines of *Bachelet, Jaffelin* and *Lequin-Roussot.*

CÔTE DE BROUILLY, AC (Beaujolais; red) The Mont de Brouilly, a pyramid-shaped hill in the middle of the *cru* of Brouilly, makes quite different wine to

Brouilly itself. The soil is of volcanic origin, and the slopes lap up the sun. Best: *Château Thivin, Conroy, Domaine de la Pierre Bleue, Jean Sanvers, Lucien Verger, Chanrion.*

CÔTE DE NUITS (red, white) The northern part of the Côte d'Or, in theory producing the biggest wines. It is almost entirely devoted to Pinot Noir. Standards have risen in recent years. This doesn't mean you won't ever be disappointed, because unpredictability is built into red Burgundy. But your chances are an awful lot better than they used to be.

CÔTE DE NUITS-VILLAGES, AC (red) Covers the three southernmost villages of Prissey, Comblanchien and Corgoloin, plus Fixin and Brochon in the north. Usually fairly light and dry, it can have good cherry fruit and the delicious vegetal decay taste of good Côte de Nuits red. Often good value. Best producers: *Durand, Rion, Rossignol* and *Tollot-Voarick*, and especially *Chopin-Groffier* and *Domaine de l'Arlot.*

CÔTE D'OR (red, white) The source of Burgundy's fame – a thin sliver of land worth its weight in gold. It has two halves, the Côte de Nuits in the north and the Côte de Beaune in the south, with a fine crop of illustrious wines.

CRÉMANT DE BOURGOGNE, AC (white, rosé) Good, quite broad, eminently affordable sparkling wine, made by the Champagne method, from Chardonnay and Pinot Noir. Try *Caves de Lugny* for white and *Caves de Bailly* for lovely fresh, strawberryish pink.

CRIOTS-BÂTARD-MONTRACHET, AC (Côte de Beaune; white) Tiny *grand cru* in Chassagne-Montrachet nuzzled up against Bâtard-Montrachet. The wines resemble Bâtard's power and concentration but are leaner, more minerally – and rarely seen. Best: *Blain-Gagnard, Fontaine-Gagnard.*

CRU The ten Beaujolais *crus* or growths (Fleurie, Moulin-à-Vent, Brouilly, Chénas, Côte de Brouilly, Chiroubles, Juliénas, St-Amour, Morgon, Régnié) are the top villages in the steeply hilly, northern part of Beaujolais. All *should* have definable characteristics, but the produce of different vineyards and growers is all too often blended to a mean by merchants elsewhere. There's also a distressing tendency now to age the wines in new oak, which destroys their point. Any old red can taste of new oak; only good Beaujolais has the juiciness of Gamay. Always buy either a single-estate wine, or one from a good local merchant like *Chanut Frères, la Chevalière, Duboeuf, Dépagneux, Ferraud, Loron, Sarrau, Louis Tête,* and *Trenel*. Elsewhere in Burgundy the best vineyards are labelled *grand cru*, and the second-best *premier cru*.

ÉCHÉZEAUX, AC (Côte de Nuits; red) Large, slightly second-line *grand cru* vineyard in Vosne-Romanée. Best: *Domaine de la Romanée-Conti, Engel, Faiveley, Forey, Louis Gouroux, Grivot, Mongeard-Mugneret, Mugneret-Gibourg, Rouget.*

EPINEUIL, AC (red) Tiny region in the north of Burgundy, producing light but fragrant styles of Pinot Noir.

FIXIN, AC (Côte de Nuits; red) A suburb of Dijon, Fixin can make some of Burgundy's sturdiest reds: deep, strong, tough but plummy when young; capable of mellowing with age. Such wines are slowly reappearing. If you want to feel you're drinking Gevrey-Chambertin without shouldering the cost, Fixin from the following producers could fit the bill: *Bordet, Charlopin-Parizot, Bruno Clair, Fougeray, Roger Fournier, Gelin, Guyard, Joliet, Jadot, Moillard, Philippe Rossignol.*

FLAGEY-ÉCHÉZEAUX, AC (Côte de Nuits; red) A commune that sells its basic wines as Vosne-Romanée but, in Échézeaux and Grands-Échézeaux, has two *grands crus.*

FLEURIE, AC (Beaujolais; red) Often the most delicious of the *crus*, gentle and round, its sweet cherry-and-chocolate fruit just held firm by a touch of tannin and acid. Its deserved popularity in Britain and the US has led to high prices. Look out for: *Château de Fleurie (Loron), Chauvet, Chignard, Colonge, Domaine de la Grand, Grand Pré (Sarrau), Domaine de la Presle, Domaine des Quatre Vents, Duboeuf's la Madone, Bernard Paul, Verpoix*, the *Fleurie* co-op's *cuvées, Cuvée Présidente Marguerite* and *Cuvée Cardinale*.

GEVREY-CHAMBERTIN, AC (Côte de Nuits; red) This village has eight *grands crus*, and two of them, Chambertin and Chambertin Clos-de-Bèze can be some of the world's greatest wines. They should have rough, plumskins and damson strength, fierce when young, but assuming a brilliant, wafting perfume and intense, plummy richness when mature. *Bachelet, Boillot, Burguet, Dugat, Michel Esmonin, Philippe Leclerc, Mortet, Naddef* and *Rossignol-Trapet* are the names to look out for among younger producers. Of the old estates, *Rousseau* is best but *Domaine des Varoilles* is also good. Also look for *Frédéric Esmonin, René Leclerc, Maume* and *Roty*, and for the merchants' bottlings from *Drouhin, Faiveley, Jadot* and *Jaffelin*. Be aware that there are still some overpriced horrors bearing the sacred name.

GIVRY, AC (Côte Chalonnaise; red) Small but important red wine village. At their best, the wines are deliciously warm and cherry-chewy with a slightly smoky fragrance to them, but too many are mediocre, especially from négociants. *Baron Thénard* is best, but *Chofflet, Clos Salomon, Joblot, Laborbe, Lespinasse, Mouton* and *Ragot* are also worth investigating.

LA GRANDE RUE, AC (Côte de Nuits; red) This vineyard is wholly owned by the Lamarche family. Elevated to *grand cru* status in 1990, more because of its potential than because of recent wines.

ON THE CASE

Some Burgundy growers are now aiming for greater colour and substance in their wines: if you want more delicate, silky wines, ask to taste before you buy

GRANDS-ÉCHÉZEAUX, AC (Côte de Nuits; red) A *grand cru* capable of delicately scented, plum-and-woodsmoke wine which goes rich and chocolaty with age. Best names: *Domaine de la Romanée-Conti, Drouhin, Engel, Mongeard-Mugneret*.

GRIOTTE-CHAMBERTIN, AC (Côte de Nuits; red) One of the smallest *grands crus* of Gevrey-Chambertin. Best: *Drouhin, Claude Dugat, F Esmonin, Ponsot, Roty*.

HAUTES-CÔTES DE BEAUNE and HAUTES-CÔTES DE NUITS (red, white) A hilly backwater consisting of 28 villages which make fairly good, light, strawberry-like Pinot and a lot of reasonably good, light, dry Chardonnay at a decent price. The red grapes do not always ripen fully every year. Look out for the red Hautes-Côtes de Nuits wines of *Cornu, Domaine des Mouchottes, Jayer-Gilles, Thévenet* and *Verdet* and the red Hautes-Côtes de Beaunes of *Bouley, Capron Manieux, Chalet, Guillemard, Joliot, Mazilly* and *Plait*. The *Caves des Hautes-Côtes* is beginning to produce some of the best-value wines in the whole of Burgundy. Good whites come from *Chaley, Cornu, Devevey, Goubard, Jayer-Gilles, Thévenot-le-Brun, Alain Verdet* (organic).

IRANCY, AC (red) Mostly Pinot Noir from vineyards just to the south-west of Chablis, sometimes with a little of the darker, tougher local grape, César. Rarely deep in colour, but always perfumed, slightly plummy and attractive. Cool years can provide disappointingly thin wines. Best drunk while young and fresh. It must legally be labelled 'Bourgogne Irancy'. Good producers: *Léon & Serge Bienvenu, Bernard Cantin, André & Roger Delaloge, Gabriel Delaloge, Jean Renaud, Simmonet-Fèbvre.*

JULIÉNAS, AC (Beaujolais; red) This *can* be big, with tannin and acidity, but many of the best more closely resemble the mixture of fresh red fruit and soft, chocolaty warmth that makes for good Fleurie. Good: *Château du Bois de la Salle, Château des Capitans, Château de Juliénas, Domaine des Bucherats, Domaine de la Dîme, Domaine de la Vieille Église, Duboeuf, René Monnet, Pelletier.*

LADOIX-SERRIGNY, AC (Côte de Beaune; red) Overshadowed by the more famous Aloxe-Corton next door. But it's worth a look: *Capitain-Gagnerot, Chevalier, Cornu, Prince de Mérode* and *Ravaut* all make decent, crisp wines at fair prices.

LATRICIÈRES-CHAMBERTIN, AC (Côte de Nuits; red) Small *grand cru* vineyard in Gevrey-Chambertin and very similar in style to Chambertin though without all the power. Best producers: *Leroy, Ponsot, Rossignol-Trapet.*

MÂCON BLANC, AC (Mâconnais; white) This should be good-value, light Chardonnay, but too often it's not. Most Mâcon simply cannot compete with the best-value New World wines.

MÂCON ROUGE, AC (Mâconnais; red) There's a lot of red wine made in the Mâconnais but it's usually fairly lean, earthy Gamay without the spark of Beaujolais' fruit. If it appeals, try wines from Igé and Mancey, or *Lafarge*'s wine from Bray. *Lassarat* is improving things by using new oak.

MÂCON-VILLAGES, AC (Mâconnais; white) One step up from basic Mâcon Blanc, this must come from the 43 Mâcon communes with the best land. The rare good ones show the signs of honey and fresh apples and some of the nutty, yeasty depth associated with fine Chardonnay. These come from those villages that add their own village names (Mâcon-Chaintry, etc). Wines from four of the best villages have now been renamed Viré-Clessé. There is a handful of growers making serious, oak-aged wine from low-yielding vines. *Guffens Heynen, Merlin, Rijckaert* and *Jean Thévenet* are names to look for. Others include: *Bicheron, Bonhomme, Danauchet, Goyard, Guillemot-Michel, Josserand, Lassarat, Manciat-Poncet, Signoret, Talmard* and *Thévenet-Wicart.*

MARANGES, AC (Côte de Beaune; red) The sturdy, rustic reds from this AC created in 1989 are now coming into their own. *Drouhin*'s is good and so are *Bachelet, Charlot, Girardin* and *Rijckaert.*

MARSANNAY, AC (Côte de Nuits; red, rosé) Used to produce mostly rosé under the name Bourgogne Rosé de Marsannay, but the introduction of an appellation for reds in 1987 has encouraged growers to switch. The first results of this new seriousness are most encouraging and some lovely wines are already emerging, usually quite dry and cherry-perfumed, sometimes more full-blown and exciting. One to watch. Best: *Bouvier, Charlopin-Parizot, Bruno Clair, Collotte, Fougeray, Fournier, Geantet-Pansiot, Huguenot, Jadot, Naddef, Roty.*

MAZIS-CHAMBERTIN, AC (Côte de Nuits; red) This *grand cru* in Gevrey-Chambertin can have a superb deep blackberry-pip, damson-skin and black-currant fruit which gets more exciting after six to 12 years. Best: *Faiveley, Gelin, Hospices de Beaune, Maume, Rebourseau, Roty, Rousseau, Tortochot.*

MAZOYÈRES-CHAMBERTIN, AC (Côte de Nuits; red) *Grand cru* of Gevrey-Chambertin, rarely seen since producers generally take up the option of using the *grand cru* Charmes-Chambertin instead. *Perrot-Minot* produces a fine example.

MERCUREY, AC (Côte Chalonnaise; red, white) The biggest Chalonnais village, producing half the region's wines. Indeed many call the Côte Chalonnaise the 'Région de Mercurey'. It's mostly red wine, often fairly full, with attractive strawberry fruit and a little smoky fragrance. *Faiveley* and *Juillot* make a fine range of red Mercureys, but look out also for *Chandesais, Chanzy, Ch. de Chamirey, Domaine la Marche, Dufouleur, Jacqueson, de Launay, Meix-Foulot, Monette, Saier* and *de Suremain*. Whites have been improving, as rising prices have spurred producers to greater efforts. Good examples come from *Château de Chamirey, Faiveley, M Juillot, Protheau, Rodet.*

MEURSAULT, AC (Côte de Beaune; white) It has by far the largest white production of any commune in the Côte d'Or, and this is one of several reasons why its traditionally high overall standard is gradually being eroded. The wines should be big and nutty and have a delicious, vegetal lusciousness, and sometimes even peachy, honeyed flavours. Try *Ampeau, Pierre Boillot, Boisson-Vadot, Boyer-Martenot, Michel Bouzereau, Buisson-Battault, Coche-Debord, Coche-Dury, Comtes Lafon, Fichet, Gauffroy, Henry Germain, Jean Germain, Grivault, Patrick Javillier, François Jobard, René Manuel, Matrot, Michelot-Buisson, Millot-Battault, Pierre Morey, Prieur, Roulot.*

MONTAGNY, AC (Côte Chalonnaise; white) Quite nice round, ripe wines. Best: *Arnoux*, the co-op at *Buxy, Latour, Olivier Leflaive, B Michel, de Montorge, Rodet, Alain Roy* and *Vache.*

MONTHELIE, AC (Côte de Beaune; red) These wines deserve recognition: they're full, dry, rather herby or piney, but with a satisfying rough fruit. Often a good buy but stick to growers, not négociants. Best: *Boussey, Caves des Hautes-Côtes, Château de Monthelie, Deschamps, Doreau, Garaudet, Monthelie-Douhairet, Potinet-Ampeau, de Suremain, Thévenin-Monthelie.*

LE MONTRACHET, AC (Côte de Beaune; white) This is white Burgundy at its absolute greatest, the finest of fine white *grands crus* in the villages of Puligny and Chassagne. Does it mean most enjoyable, most happy-making? Not really. In fact the flavours can be so intense it's difficult sometimes to know if you're having fun drinking it or merely giving your wine vocabulary an end-of-term examination. So be brave if someone opens a bottle and let the incredible blend of spice and smoke, honey and ripeness flow over you. Best: *Amiot, Comtes Lafon, Domaine de la Romanée-Conti, Drouhin*'s *Laguiche, Jadot, Pierre Morey, Prieur, Thénard* and, since 1991, *Leflaive.*

MOREY-ST-DENIS, AC (Côte de Nuits; red) Expensive, and can suffer from overproduction. At their best they blend the perfume of Chambolle-Musigny with the body of Gevrey-Chambertin, and exhibit a slight savouriness that mellows into a rich chocolaty mouthful. You'll find exciting bottles from *Pierre Amiot, Bryczek, Charloppin, Dujac, Georges* and *Hubert Lignier, Marchand, Perrot-Minot, Ponsot, Serveau* and *Vadey-Castagnier.*

MORGON, AC (Beaujolais; red) The wines of this *cru* can be glorious. They can start thick and dark, and age to a chocolaty, plummy depth with an amazing cherries smell. A sort of reserve category called Morgon Age has to be kept for at least 18 months before release. *Jacky Janodet's* Morgon is intense. Look also for *Aucoeur, Château de Pizay, Château de Raousset, Descombes, Desvignes, Domaine de la Chanaise, Domaine Roche-St-Jean, Domaine de Ruyère, Drouhin, Gobet, Lapierre, Félix Longepierre* and *Georges Vincent.*

MOULIN-À-VENT, AC (Beaujolais; red) Enter the heavy brigade. These *cru* wines should be solid, and should age for three to five years and more from good years. The best of them have a big, plummy, Burgundian style, and their toughness doesn't give you much option but to wait for them to mellow. This is one of the few Beaujolais *crus* that can respond well to discreet oak aging. *Louis Champagnon*'s is good, as is *Brugne, Charvet, Château des Jacques, Château du Moulin-à-Vent, Château Portier, Domaine de la Tour de Bief, Duboeuf, Jacky Janodet, Raymond Siffert* and *Héritiers Maillard* (formerly *Héritiers Tagent*).

MUSIGNY, AC (Côte de Nuits; red, white) Extremely fine *grand cru* which gave its name to Chambolle-Musigny. All but a third of a hectare is planted with Pinot Noir, capable of producing Burgundy's most heavenly scented wine. Look for *Château de Chambolle-Musigny, Jadot, Leroy, Jacques Prieur, Georges Roumier, de Vogüé* (white, too).

NUITS-ST-GEORGES, AC (Côte de Nuits; red) When it's good, this has an enthralling decayed – rotting even – brown richness of chocolate and prunes rising out of a fairly light, plum-sweet fruit – gorgeous, whatever it sounds like. It is expensive but increasingly reliable. *Labouré-Roi* is the most consistent merchant for Nuits, although *Jadot, Jaffelin* and *Moillard* are increasingly good particularly at *premier cru* level. The most famous growers are *Robert Chevillon, Gouges, Michelot* and *Daniel Rion,* but excellent wines are also made by *Ambroise, Jean Chauvenet, Chicotot, Jean-Jacques Confuron, Domaine de l'Arlot,* and then there's the amazingly deep (and amazingly expensive) *Leroy.*

PERNAND-VERGELESSES, AC (Côte de Beaune; red, white) The village whites are generally fairly lean and need time to soften, but can be gently nutty and very enjoyable from a good producer. They can also be quite good value. Best names in white: *Dubreuil-Fontaine, Germain, Laleure-Piot, Pavelot, Rapet, Rollin.* Some quite attractive, softly earthy reds are made. Look for the *premier cru* Île de Vergelesses. Best reds: *Besancenot-Mathouillet, Caves des Hautes-Côtes, Chandon des Briailles, Delarche, Dubreuil-Fontaine, Laleure-Piot, Pavelot, Rapet* and *Rollin.*

PETIT CHABLIS, AC (Chablis; white) There used to be lots of this grown on the least-good slopes. But the growers objected that it made it sound as though their wine was a lesser form of Chablis. Nowadays, pretty well the whole lot is called 'Chablis' – so *we* can't tell what's what, *they're* all richer, they're happy, we're not… I give up.

POMMARD, AC (Côte de Beaune; red) From good producers, Pommard can have a strong, meaty sturdiness, backed by slightly jammy but attractively plummy fruit. Not subtle, but many people's idea of what red Burgundy should be. They need ten years to show their class. The most consistently fine wines are made by *Comte Armand, de Courcel* and *de Montille,* but also look out for the wines of *Boillot, Château de Pommard, Girardin, Lahaye, Lejeune, Jean Monnier, Parent, Pothier* and *Pousse d'Or.*

MATURITY CHART

1996 Red Côte de Nuits Premier Cru

Silky, forward wines

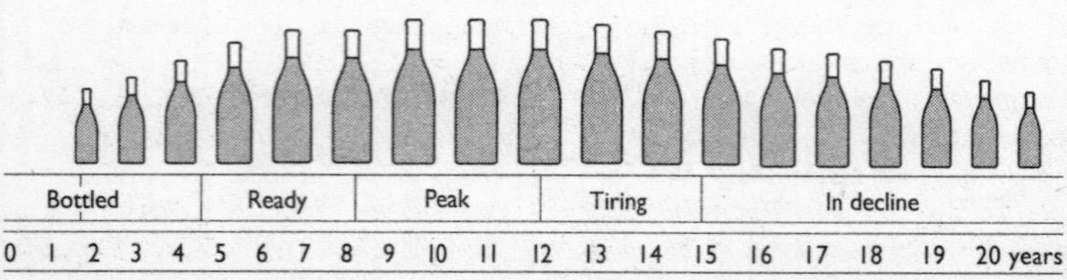

POUILLY-FUISSÉ, AC (Mâconnais; white) Prices here yo-yo according to supply and demand. It is sometimes best in years which are not too rich. Best: *Barraud, Béranger, Cordier, Corsin, Duboeuf*'s top selections, *Ferret, M Forest, Guffens-Heynen, Leger-Plumet, Loron*'s *les Vieux Murs, Manciat-Poncet, Noblet, Roger Saumaize, Valette, Vincent* at *Château Fuissé*. Adjoining villages Pouilly-Loché, AC and Pouilly-Vinzelles, AC are similar at half the price.

PULIGNY-MONTRACHET, AC (Côte de Beaune; white) The peak of great white pleasure is to be found in the various Montrachet *grands crus*. Le Montrachet is peerless, showing how humble words like honey, nuts, cream, smoke, perfume and all the rest do no honest service to a wine that seems to combine every memory of ripe fruit and scent with a dry, penetrating savouriness. Several other *grands crus* are less intense, but offer the same unrivalled mix. There are *premiers crus* as well. Standards here have risen, and there are many serious producers. Look for *Amiot-Bonfils, Jean-Marc Boillot, Boyer-Devèze, Carillon, Gérard Chavy, Drouhin, Jadot, Labouré-Roi, Laguiche*, both *Domaine Leflaive* and *Olivier Leflaive, Pernot, Ramonet-Prudhon, Antonin Rodet, Sauzet, Thénard*.

RÉGNIÉ, AC (Beaujolais; red) Beaujolais' tenth *cru*. Quite similar to Brouilly in ripe years but a bit weedy when the sun doesn't shine. *Duboeuf Bouteille Cristal* is best.

RICHEBOURG, AC (Côte de Nuits; red) Exceptional *grand cru* of Vosne-Romanée. It's a wonderful name for a wine – Richebourg – and, at its best, it manages to be fleshy yet filled with spice and perfume and the clinging richness of chocolate and figs. Best producers: *Domaine de la Romanée-Conti, Grivot, Anne Gros, A-F Gros, Leroy, Méo-Camuzet*.

LA ROMANÉE, AC (Côte de Nuits; red) This *grand cru* is the smallest AC in France, solely owned by the Liger-Belair family and sold by *Bouchard Père et Fils*. Now that Bouchard is under new and more rigorous ownership, we may see whether Romanée, solid but never sensational hitherto, deserves its status.

LA ROMANÉE-CONTI, AC (Côte de Nuits; red) This tiny *grand cru* is capable of a more startling brilliance than any other Burgundy. The 7,000 or so bottles it produces per year are instantly seized on by the super-rich before we mortals can even get our tasting sheets out. Wholly owned by the *Domaine de la Romanée-Conti*.

LA ROMANÉE-ST-VIVANT, AC (Côte de Nuits; red) *Grand cru* in the village of Vosne-Romanée. It is far less easy to taste young than its neighbouring *grands crus* and needs a good 12 years to show what can be a delicious, savoury yet sweet personality. Best names: *Arnoux, Domaine de la Romanée-Conti, Latour, Leroy*.

MATURITY CHART
1995 Chablis Premier Cru
An excellent vintage for laying down

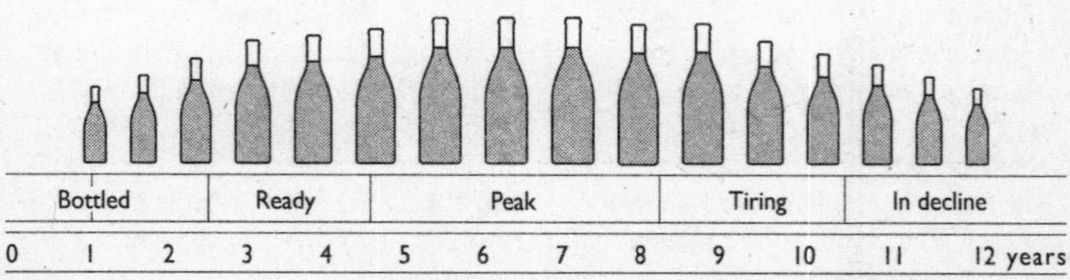

RUCHOTTES-CHAMBERTIN, AC (Côte de Nuits; red) This is the smallest Gevrey-Chambertin *grand cru*, with wines of deeper colour and longer-lasting perfumed richness than most of the village's other *grands crus*. Best producers: *F Esmonin, Georges Mugneret, Roumier, Rousseau.*

RULLY, AC (Côte Chalonnaise; red white) This village gets my vote for the most improved white AC in Burgundy. The use of new oak to ferment and age the wine is producing wonderfully soft, spicy Burgundies of good quality – and still at relatively low prices. Relative to the rest of Burgundy, that is. Best whites: *Bêtes, Chanzy, Cogny, Delorme, Domaine de la Folie, Drouhin, Dury, Duvernay, Jacqueson, Jaffelin, Olivier Leflaive, Rodet*. Best for red: *Chanzy, Ch. de Rully, Delorme, Domaine de la Folie, Duvernay, Faiveley, Jacqueson, Jaffelin.*

ST-AMOUR, AC (Beaujolais; red) Among the most perfect Beaujolais, this pink-red wine usually has freshness and peachy perfume and good, ripe fruit all at once. It isn't that common here (though the French love it), and yet it is frequently the most reliable and most enjoyable *cru*. Look for *Buis, Château de St-Amour, Domaine des Billards (Loron), Domaine des Ducs, Domaine du Paradis, Patissier, André Poitevin, Francis Saillant, Paul Spay.*

ST-AUBIN, AC (Côte de Beaune; red, white) Some of Burgundy's best-value wines, though the reds are a touch earthy. They are reliable, and can give real pleasure after a few years of aging. Best: *Bachelet, Clergy, Lamy, Prudhon, Gérard Thomas* and *Roux*, but wines from négociants *Jadot* and *Olivier Leflaive* are their equal. Good whites come from *Bachelet, Clerget, Lamy, Olivier Leflaive, Prudhon, Thomas* and *Roux*.

ST-ROMAIN, AC (Côte de Beaune; red, white) Full, rather broad-flavoured, cherry-stone dry reds, that perform best in very warm years. On the whole they are sold cheaper than they deserve. Look for *Bazenet, Buisson, Gras, Thévenin* and *Thévenin-Monthelie*. The flinty, dry whites are often of decent quality and pretty good value. Beware cooler vintages, when the grapes sometimes don't ripen properly. Best are: *Bazenet, Buisson, Germain, Gras, Thévenin, Thévenin-Monthelie.*

ST-VÉRAN, AC (Mâconnais; white) Pouilly-Fuissé's understudy, capable of simple, soft, quick-maturing but attractive, rather honeyed white Burgundy. Best: *Corsin, Dépardon, Dom. des Deux Roches, Duboeuf, Grégoire, Lassarat, de Montferrand, Saumaize, Thibert, Vincent* – and, above all, *Drouhin.*

SANTENAY, AC (Côte de Beaune; red) Rough and ready red. At its best it has a strong, savoury flavour and good strawberry fruit, though nowadays is frequently rather lean and mean. Best: *Belland, Drouhin, Girardin, Lequin-Roussot, Morey, Pousse d'Or, Prieur-Bonnet, Roux*. Even these are variable.

SAVIGNY-LÈS-BEAUNE, AC (Côte de Beaune; red) Gaining in reputation at the expense of Beaune. Light, attractive earthiness and strawberry fruit. Try *Bize, Camus-Bruchon, Capron-Manieux, Chandon de Briailles, Écard-Guyot, Girard-Vollot, Guillemot, Pavelot, Tollot-Beaut.*

SAUVIGNON DE ST-BRIS, VDQS (white) Wine of AC quality grown south-west of Chablis that languishes as a VDQS because Sauvignon Blanc is not an AC grape in the area. Can be one of the most nettly, most greeny-gooseberryish of all French Sauvignons, but these days it seems less exciting than it used to be. It has not really faced up to the competition from New Zealand – and Bordeaux. Best: *Louis Bersan, Jean-Marc Brocard, Robert & Philippe Defrance, Michel Esclavy, Goisot, André Sorin.*

LA TÂCHE, AC (Côte de Nuits; red) Another *grand cru* monopoly of the *Domaine de la Romanée-Conti*. The wine is heavenly, so rich and heady that the perfumes are sometimes closer to age-old brandy than table wine and the flavour loaded with spice, dark fruits and the acrid richness of really good black chocolate.

VOLNAY, AC (Côte de Beaune; red) One of the most perfumed red Burgundies, with a memorable cherry-and-strawberry spice, but also, in its *premiers crus*, able to turn on a big, meaty style without losing the perfume. The best are *Lafon, Lafarge, Marquis d'Angerville, de Montille* and *Pousse d'Or*, Other good names: *Ampeau, Blain-Gagnard, Boillot, Bouley, Clerget, Delagrange, Vaudoisey-Mutin, Voillot.*

VOSNE-ROMANÉE, AC (Côte de Nuits; red) The greatest Côte de Nuits village. Its *grands crus* cost more than any red on earth, and, remarkably for Burgundy, they are dominated by a single estate, *Domaine de la Romanée Conti*. These vineyards make wines capable of more startling brilliance than any other, with flavours as disparate yet as intense as the overpowering, creamy savouriness of fresh *foie gras* and the deep, sweet scent of ripe plums and prunes in brandy. There are also fine *premiers crus*, and the village wines can reflect their leaders. The Domaine de la Romanée Conti is by far the most famous estate here, but *Leroy*, owned by a former director of the DRC, is making wines that rival it in both quality and price. Others making terrific wine: *Arnoux, Sylvain Cathiard, Confuron-Cotétidot, Engel, Grivot, Jean Gros, Hudelot-Noëllat, Georges Jayer, Henri Lamarche, Méo-Camuzet, Mongeard-Mugneret, Georges Mugneret, Pernin-Rossin, Rouget, Daniel Rion* and *Jean Tardy*.

VOUGEOT, AC (Côte de Nuits; red) A village famous only because of its *grand cru*, Clos de Vougeot, which at its best is plummy and broad. However, there are some decent wines made outside the Clos – most notably from *Bertagna* and *Clerget.*

BURGUNDY AND BEAUJOLAIS VINTAGES

Red Burgundy is more subject to vintage fluctuation than white; with the latter, most years can produce a fair amount of pretty good wine. The rule for Beaujolais: drink as young as possible. Only top wines from the best villages will benefit much from aging, although Nouveau may improve with a month or two's rest.

1999 Quite good to very good, in spite of tricky weather. Whites may lack some acidity, and some reds and whites will be a bit insubstantial. The best reds have good colour and structure, but there was rain at the end of September, which affected the Côte de Nuits more than the Côte de Beaune – the former was largely picked by then. It was a big vintage, which might discourage some producers from yet more price hikes; but on the other hand, worldwide demand shows no sign of easing.

1998 A mixed year. Reds are often big, substantial and tannic with lots of acidity – and all that is fine if they have the fruit to go with it. Some do, some don't. A lot of the reds lack silkiness, which is surely the main reason for spending all that money on them. Whites can be superb, but at the lower end lack acidity. Taste before you buy.

1997 Soft, approachable reds and whites of middling to good quality which should be ready before the 1996s. Not a vintage to buy without tasting first, but there are some very attractive wines.

1996 Excellent, concentrated, classic Chablis; the Côte d'Or whites and reds are also ripe, with good acidity, and should age well. Whites are not as concentrated as in 1995.

1995 A year of low yields, ripe tannins and good concentration in the reds, and good quality but not greatness in the whites. For once, there is little to choose in quality between the Côte de Beaune and the Côte de Nuits. In Chablis quality is first-rate.

1994 Light wines with attractive, reasonable colours and lowish acidity. The best whites show a raciness and vigour. Now a vintage to drink up rather than keep.

1993 The reds from the best producers have good depth of colour, power of fruit and well-constructed tannins, and most are drinking very nicely now. The whites turned out far better than at first seemed likely. They plumped up nicely and had plenty of fruit, but it's time to drink them up now.

1992 Acidity is low among the reds, but it's a good year to choose in restaurants, as the wines are fast developers. The whites were far better, with masses of exuberant fruit and seemingly better acidity than their 1991 counterparts. All are drinking now.

1991 There were some very good concentrated reds made, but it's a very patchy vintage. Don't keep them any longer. The whites also should be drunk.

1990 The 1990 reds are brilliantly fruity, naturally high in sugars. Most producers now consider this the best of the great trio of 1988, 1989 and 1990. Almost all are drinking beautifully now; the best are sumptuously rich. The whites are proving to be inferior to the reds. A good rather than a great vintage for white Burgundy. Again, they're at their peak, and lesser wines from the Mâconnais and Chalonnais are on the downward slope.

1989 A lot of good reds, but only a few exceptional ones. They are softer than the 1988s, though some are superbly concentrated, particularly in the Côte de Beaune. It was an outstanding year for white Burgundy, at least in the hands of competent winemakers. Almost all the best growers' wines are beautifully balanced, despite their richness, though some are aging fast. Lesser wines should have been drunk; others are good now.

1988 Many growers produced firm, concentrated reds, now at their best. Some superb wines, but quite a few dour ones, too. Among the whites, Mâconnais wines had a bright, fresh fruit not seen down that way for a few years, but should have been drunk by now. Beaujolais was exceptional, with marvellous, luscious, clear, ripe fruit, but even the best should be finished up now.

1987 The best 1987 reds are very good indeed, Côte de Beaune having the edge over Côte de Nuits. The lesser wines aren't as good as those of 1985, but are better than those of 1986. Drink now, especially the whites.

1986 The reds are showing good perfume but need drinking soon, as do most whites. Chablis *grands crus* are drinking well.

1985 The reds turned out unevenly, and only the very best are still good. Chablis started out with a lesser reputation, but top *grand cru* wines from good producers can still be good.

1983 Impressive reds, although Vosne-Romanée, Chambolle-Musigny and Morey-St-Denis didn't have such a good year. The whites were frequently heavy, rather unrefreshing, soggy-flavoured wines (made, all too often, from overripe, rot-affected grapes) which rapidly lost their fruit. Nothing will improve further, and almost all should have been drunk by now.

BASIC BURGUNDY PRICES

RED

Under £8.00

Bourgogne Coteaux de St-Bris, Brocard **1997** £7.75 (AD)
Bourgogne Lucien Denizot **1996** £7.50 (JU)
Bourgogne Passe-Tout-Grains, Michel Lafarge **1996** £7.95 (CON)
Bourgogne Passe-Tout-Grains, Michel Lafarge **1995** £7.99 (RAE)
Bourgogne Rouge, Jean-Claude Boisset **1998** £5.99 (WAI)
Bourgogne Rouge, Cave de Buxy **1998** £7.99 (MAR)
Bourgogne Rouge, Faiveley **1996** £7.95 (CON)
Bourgogne Rouge, Roger et Joël Remy **1998** £7.50 (LEA)

£8.00 → £9.99

Bourgogne Rouge, Domaine Boillot **1997** £8.32 (MON)
Bourgogne Rouge, Chevillon **1997** £9.25 (FORT)
Bourgogne Rouge, Faiveley **1997** £8.49 (DI) £9.75 (STE)
Bourgogne Rouge, Faiveley **1995** £9.95 (WS)
Bourgogne Rouge, Jadot **1998** £8.49 (VIC) £8.49 (THR)
Bourgogne Rouge, Machard de Gramont **1997** £8.81 (CB)
Bourgogne Rouge, Parent **1994** £8.00 (NEZ)
Bourgogne Rouge, Domaine de la Pousse d'Or **1997** £9.20 (TAN) £9.95 (CON)
Bourgogne Rouge, Prudhon **1996** £8.50 (JU)
Bourgogne Rouge, Rion **1997** £8.25 (WS)

£10.00 → £12.99

Bourgogne Rouge, Burguet **1996** £10.90 (JU)
Bourgogne Rouge, Chevillon **1996** £10.90 (JU)
Bourgogne Rouge, Dugat-Py **1997** £12.60 (NI) £13.50 (LEA)
Bourgogne Rouge, Georges Roumier **1997** £11.80 (TAN)
Bourgogne Rouge, Leroy **1996** £10.18 (FA)
Bourgogne Rouge, Michel Lafarge **1997** £10.28 (GOE) £10.80 (GAU)
Bourgogne Rouge, Denis Mortet **1997** £11.16 (DOM) £11.75 (BER)
Bourgogne Rouge, Thierry Mortet **1998** £10.95 (LEA)
Bourgogne Rouge, Mugneret-Gibourg **1998** £11.95 (LEA)
Bourgogne Rouge, Mugneret-Gibourg **1997** £11.95 (LEA)
Bourgogne Rouge, Domaine de la Pousse d'Or **1995** £10.49 (CON)

Over £13.00

Bourgogne Rouge, Dugat-Py **1998** £13.95 (LEA)
Bourgogne Rouge, Leroy **1997** £14.00 (JU)
Bourgogne Rouge, Leroy **1995** £13.50 (BAL)
Bourgogne Rouge, Méo-Camuzet **1998** £13.12 (RAE)
Bourgogne Rouge, Méo-Camuzet **1997** £14.00 (JU)
Bourgogne Rouge, Michel Lafarge **1995** £14.69 (TW)

MERCHANTS SPECIALIZING IN BURGUNDY

see Merchant Directory (page 456) for details

Adnams (AD), Averys (AV), Ballantynes (BAL), Bancroft (BAN), Bennetts (BEN), Berry Bros (BER), Bibendum (BIB), Bordeaux Index, Butlers (BU), A Byrne (BY), Cave Cru Classé (CAV), Châteaux Wines (CHA), Corney & Barrow (CB), Direct Wine (DI), Domaine Direct (DOM), Farr Vintners (FA), Fortnums (FORT), Goedhuis (GOE), Roger Harris (HAW) – for Beaujolais, John Harvey (HA), Haynes Hanson (HAH), Justerini & Brooks (JU), Lay & Wheeler (LAY), Lea & Sandeman (LEA), Montrachet (MON), Morris & Verdin (MV), Le Nez Rouge (NEZ), J Nicholson (NI), Oddbins (OD), Christopher Piper (PIP), Raeburn (RAE), Reid (REI), La Reserve (RES) Howard Ripley (RIP), T&W (TW), Tanners (TAN), Turville, Wine Soc (WS), Wine Treasury (WT), Peter Wylie (WY), Noel Young (YOU).

WHITE

Under £6.00

Bourgogne Aligoté, Brocard **1998** £5.99 (POR) £7.39 (JON)
Bourgogne Blanc, A Bichot **1998** £5.99 (UN)
Bourgogne Blanc, Jean-Claude Boisset **1998** £5.99 (WAI)

£6.00 → £7.99

Bourgogne Aligoté, Larousse **1998** £7.30 (JER)
Bourgogne Aligoté, Mouton **1998** £6.95 (TAN)
Bourgogne Aligoté, Rollin **1998** £6.72 (RAE)
Bourgogne Aligoté, Rollin **1997** £7.55 (JU)
Bourgogne Blanc, Brocard **1998** £7.39 (JON)
Bourgogne Blanc, Cave de Buxy **1997** £7.99 (VA)
Bourgogne Blanc, Cuvée Icarus **1997** £6.50 (BU)
Bourgogne Blanc, Matrot **1998** £6.99 (BO)
Bourgogne Blanc, Verget **1997** £7.25 (FA) £8.99 (BOD) £8.99 (SUN) £9.95 (LEA)

£8.00 → £9.99

Bourgogne Aligoté de Bouzeron, Villaine **1997** £8.95 (AD) £9.69 (CB)
Bourgogne Aligoté, Jayer-Gilles **1998** £9.25 (AD)
Bourgogne Aligoté, Jayer-Gilles **1997** £9.00 (JU)
Bourgogne Aligoté, Olivier Leflaive **1996** £8.37 (PLAY)
Bourgogne Blanc, Guy Amiot **1998** £8.95 (BAN)
Bourgogne Blanc, Faiveley **1997** £8.79 (DI)
Bourgogne Blanc, Latour-Giraud **1999** £8.86 (BIB)
Bourgogne Blanc les Setilles, Olivier Leflaive **1998** £9.69 (CB) £9.80 (LAY)
Bourgogne Blanc, Matrot **1997** £8.45 (CON)
Bourgogne Blanc, Sauzet **1997** £9.95 (TAN) £12.50 (JU) £13.51 (DOM) £14.40 (HAH)
Bourgogne Blanc, Verget **1998** £9.95 (LAY)

£10.00 → £14.99

Bourgogne Blanc, Guy Amiot **1997** £10.25 (SOM)
Bourgogne Blanc, Boyer-Martenot **1997** £10.28 (MON)
Bourgogne Blanc, Charles et Remi Jobard **1997** £10.95 (LEA)
Bourgogne Blanc, Clerc **1995** £10.95 (VIN)
Bourgogne Blanc, Clos du Château de Meursault **1995** £12.99 (POR)
Bourgogne Blanc Cuvée des Forgets, Patrick Javillier **1997** £11.70 (LAY)
Bourgogne Blanc Cuvée des Forgets, Patrick Javillier **1996** £14.60 (ROB)
Bourgogne Blanc Cuvée des Forgets, Patrick Javillier **1995** £10.25 (SOM)
Bourgogne Blanc, Domaine Jobard **1996** £12.95 (HAH) £14.00 (JU)
Bourgogne Blanc, Domaine Jobard **1992** £13.99 (RAE)
Bourgogne Blanc, Leroy **1996** £11.65 (FA)
Bourgogne Blanc, Leroy **1992** £10.50 (WS)
Bourgogne Blanc les Setilles, Olivier Leflaive **1996** £10.90 (CRO)
Bourgogne Blanc les Setilles, Olivier Leflaive **1993** £12.45 (TW)
Bourgogne Blanc, Michelot **1997** £11.19 (JON) £12.95 (RES)
Bourgogne Blanc Oligocene, Javillier **1997** £11.75 (BAN) £17.50 (PHI)
Bourgogne Blanc Oligocene, Javillier **1995** £12.90 (LAY)
Bourgogne Blanc, Sauzet **1998** £10.65 (TAN) £11.95 (RES)

Over £15.00

Bourgogne Blanc, Clos du Château de Meursault **1994** £19.99 (VIN)
Bourgogne Blanc, Coche-Dury **1997** £19.00 (FA) £19.95 (VA)
Bourgogne Blanc, Domaine Leflaive **1998** £17.14 (GOE)
Bourgogne Blanc, Domaine Leflaive **1997** £17.04 (FA) £19.00 (JU) £19.95 (BAL)
Bourgogne Blanc Seigneurie de Posanges, Remoissenet **1992** £21.00 (CRO)

ROSÉ

c. £7.00

Bourgogne Rosé de Marsannay, Bruno Clair **1998** £6.75 (SOM)

SPARKLING

Under £8.00

Crémant de Bourgogne Cave de Lugny **Non-vintage** £5.70 (SOM) £8.54 (PIP) £8.60 (HAH)
Crémant de Bourgogne Rosé Cave de Lugny **Non-vintage** £7.49 (WAI)

BEAUJOLAIS PRICES

RED

Under £5.00

Beaujolais Ravier **1998** £4.89 (OD)
Beaujolais Cave de Sain Bel ½ bottle **1999** £3.30 (HAW)
Beaujolais-Villages Duboeuf **1998** £4.99 (MAJ) £5.49 (VIC) £5.49 (THR) £5.49 (UN) £5.49 (BOT)
Régnié Paul Sapin **1998** £4.99 (MAJ)

£5.00 → £5.99

Beaujolais Cuvée Tradition, Brun **1997** £5.75 (JU)
Beaujolais Loron **1998** £5.75 (TAN) £5.95 (DI)
Beaujolais Château de Pizay **1998** £5.75 (CON)
Beaujolais Cave de Sain Bel **1999** £5.90 (HAW)
Beaujolais Paul Sapin **1999** £5.50 (MAR)
Beaujolais-Villages Château du Basty **1998** £5.69 (OD)
Beaujolais-Villages les Champs Bouthier, Sapin **1998** £5.95 (STA)
Beaujolais-Villages Jadot **1998** £5.99 (TES) £5.99 (WAI)
Beaujolais-Villages Château de Lacarelle **1998** £5.50 (WS)
★ Beaujolais-Villages Pivot **1999** £5.86 (DOM) £6.26 (PIP) £6.65 (HAW)
Beaujolais-Villages Château des Vierres, Duboeuf **1997** £5.99 (NI)
Coteaux du Lyonnais, Cave de Sain Bel **1999** £5.75 (HAW)

£6.00 → £6.99

★ Beaujolais Blaise Carron **1999** £6.45 (HAW)
Beaujolais Pierre Jomard **1999** £6.25 (HAW)
Beaujolais Lantignié, Domaine Joubert **1999** £6.55 (AD)
Beaujolais Domaine de Milhomme **1999** £6.40 (HAW)
Beaujolais Vieilles Vignes, Garlon **1999** £6.50 (HAW)
Beaujolais Vieilles Vignes, Cave de St-Vérand **1999** £6.40 (HAW)
Beaujolais-Villages Domaine Aucoeur **1999** £6.35 (RSJ) £7.00 (HAW)
Beaujolais-Villages Colonge **1999** £6.35 (ELL)
Beaujolais-Villages Colonge **1998** £6.49 (AME) £6.75 (STA)
Beaujolais-Villages Dumas **1998** £6.95 (LEA)
Beaujolais-Villages Domaine de Franc-Pierre, Cave Co-op Fleurie **1999** £6.25 (HAW)
Beaujolais-Villages Lacondemine **1998** £6.95 (JU)
Beaujolais-Villages Domaine de la Pavé **1999** £6.80 (HAW)
Beaujolais-Villages le Perréon, Bererd **1998** £6.85 (HAW)
Beaujolais-Villages Roux **1999** £6.65 (HAW)
Beaujolais-Villages Domaine St Cyr **1999** £6.10 (HAW)
Chiroubles Loron **1998** £6.85 (SOM) £7.65 (BER) £7.70 (TAN)
Côte de Brouilly Domaine de la Pierre Bleue, Ravier **1999** £6.99 (OD)
Juliénas Loron **1997** £6.99 (UN)
Morgon Duboeuf **1998** £6.99 (TES)
Morgon Jambon **1997** £6.49 (ASD)
Morgon Château de Pizay **1997** £6.49 (CON)
Régnié Château Chassantour, Perroud **1998** £6.95 (TAN)
Régnié Duboeuf **1997** £6.49 (UN)

£7.00 → £7.99

Beaujolais-Villages les Larmoises Vieilles Vignes, Lacondemine **1998** £7.90 (JU)
Beaujolais-Villages Château des Vergers **1996** £7.70 (UB)
Brouilly Domaine de Combillaty, Duboeuf **1998** £7.55 (NEZ)
Brouilly Duboeuf **1996** £7.99 (POR)
Brouilly Domaine du Griffon **1999** £7.85 (HAW)
Brouilly Large **1999** £7.58 (CHA)
Brouilly Château Thivin **1999** £7.49 (GW) £7.95 (AD) £8.10 (HAW)
Chénas Benon **1998** £7.65 (HAW)
Chénas Château Bonnet **1999** £7.90 (AV)
Chénas Domaine Louis Champagnon **1998** £7.55 (PIP)
Chénas Domaine Louis Champagnon **1996** £7.81 (NO)
Chénas Château de Chénas **1999** £7.05 (HAW)
Chénas Léspinasse **1998** £7.50 (HAW)
Chiroubles Domaine de la Grosse Pierre **1997** £7.29 (CON)

Chiroubles Loron **1996** £7.50 (BU)
Chiroubles Méziat **1997** £7.99 (GW)
Côte de Brouilly Domaine du Griffon **1999** £7.85 (HAW)
Côte de Brouilly Loron **1998** £7.20 (TAN)
Côte de Brouilly Château Thivin **1999** £7.49 (GW) £8.40 (HAW)
Côte de Brouilly Domaine de la Voûte des Crozes, Chanrion **1999** £7.95 (ELL)
Côte de Brouilly Domaine de la Voûte des Crozes, Chanrion **1998** £7.30 (RSJ)
Fleurie Denojean **1998** £7.50 (WS)
Fleurie Duboeuf **1998** £7.99 (TES) £8.49 (VIC) £8.49 (THR) £8.49 (BOT)
Fleurie Château de Fleurie, Loron **1998** £7.95 (TAN) £8.30 (WRI)
Fleurie Sapin **1999** £7.99 (MAR)
Juliénas Domaine de Beauvernay, Piat **1998** £7.20 (COC) £8.75 (BU)
Juliénas Côte de Bessay **1998** £7.49 (CON)
Juliénas les Envaux, Pelletier **1998** £7.80 (CHA)
Juliénas Domaine Joubert **1999** £7.50 (AD)
Juliénas Domaine Joubert **1998** £7.30 (TAN)
Juliénas Domaine Joubert **1997** £7.69 (JON) £7.99 (POR)
Juliénas Léspinasse **1999** £7.50 (HAW)
Juliénas Domaine de la Seigneurie **1998** £7.50 (NEZ)
Juliénas Domaine de la Vieille Église, Loron **1998** £7.99 (DI)
Morgon Aucoeur **1999** £7.30 (RSJ) £8.25 (HAW)
Morgon Domaine de la Chanaise **1998** £7.95 (FORT) £9.21 (PLAY)
Morgon Descombes, Duboeuf **1998** £7.49 (MAJ)
Morgon Domaine Jean Descombes, Duboeuf **1998** £7.60 (NEZ) £8.30 (NI)
Morgon Château Gaillard **1997** £7.20 (COC)
Morgon les Versauds, Jacques Perrachon **1999** £7.35 (PIP)
Moulin-à-Vent Cave du Château de Chénas **1998** £7.75 (HAW)
Moulin-à-Vent Duboeuf **1996** £7.65 (NI) £7.79 (UN)
Moulin-à-Vent Fessy **1998** £7.99 (OD)
Moulin-à-Vent Domaine les Fine Graves, Janodet **1998** £7.50 (WS) £8.75 (STA) £9.50 (FORT)
Moulin-à-Vent Domaine les Fine Graves, Janodet **1997** £7.25 (SOM) £8.50 (BER)
Moulin-à-Vent Domaine Gay-Coperet **1998** £7.95 (LEA)
Moulin-à-Vent Domaine de la Tour du Bief, Duboeuf **1997** £7.99 (VIC) £7.99 (THR) £8.75 (BU) £9.99 (NI)
Régnié Desplace **1999** £7.30 (HAW)
Régnié Roux **1997** £7.61 (FLE)
St-Amour Domaine des Pins, Echallier **1998** £7.99 (AME)

£8.00 → £8.99

Brouilly Domaine Crêts des Garanches, Bernard Dufaitre **1996** £8.99 (PHI)
Brouilly Michaud **1998** £8.95 (WRI)
Brouilly Château Thivin **1998** £8.59 (JON)
Brouilly Château des Tours **1999** £8.25 (PIP)
Brouilly Château des Tours **1998** £8.95 (STA) £9.11 (NO)
Chénas Domaine de Mongrin, Gaec des Ducs **1996** £8.23 (REI)
Chénas Trenel **1999** £8.99 (BEN)
Chénas Domaine des Vieilles Caves, Charvet **1997** £8.95 (ROB)
Chiroubles Loron **1997** £8.95 (ROB)
Chiroubles Méziat **1999** £8.10 (HAW)
Chiroubles Passot **1999** £8.40 (HAW)
Chiroubles Château de Raousset **1998** £8.10 (PIP) £8.45 (JU)
Chiroubles la Maison des Vignerons **1999** £8.20 (HAW)
Côte de Brouilly Château Thivin **1998** £8.99 (DI)
Fleurie Domaine Paul Bernard **1996** £8.49 (OD)
Fleurie Berrod **1998** £8.85 (CON)
Fleurie Clos de la Chapelle des Bois, Verpoix **1999** £8.28 (PIP)
★ Fleurie Clos de la Roilette **1999** £8.97 (SAV)
Fleurie Colonge **1998** £8.75 (BER) £8.95 (STA) £8.99 (AME) £9.20 (TAN) £9.69 (REI)
Fleurie Cave Co-op de Fleurie **1999** £8.15 (HAW)
Fleurie les Garans, Latour **1997** £8.70 (COC)
Fleurie Domaine de la Grand' Cour **1999** £8.99 (AME)
Fleurie Grille Midi **1998** £8.85 (CON)
Fleurie Château de Labourons **1998** £8.65 (HAW)
Fleurie la Madone, Duboeuf **1998** £8.50 (NEZ)
Fleurie la Madone, Louis Tête **1997** £8.95 (COC)
Fleurie Domaine des Quatre Vents, Duboeuf **1998** £8.40 (NEZ) £9.39 (NI)
Fleurie Château de Raousset **1998** £8.95 (JU)

Fleurie Sélection Éventail, Domaine de Montgénas **1998** £8.44 (CHA)
Juliénas Aujas **1997** £8.90 (HAW)
Juliénas Condemine **1998** £8.55 (HAW)
Morgon Cuvée de Py, Château de Pizay **1997** £8.25 (CON)
Morgon Fontcraine, Loron **1996** £8.45 (UB)
Morgon Château de Raousset **1998** £8.45 (JU)
Moulin-à-Vent Château Bonnet **1998** £8.85 (AV)
Moulin-à-Vent Brugne **1998** £8.28 (CHA)
Moulin-à-Vent Grille Midi **1997** £8.29 (CON)
Moulin-à-Vent Janin **1998** £8.69 (PIP)
Moulin-à-Vent Janin **1997** £8.52 (DOM)
Moulin-à-Vent Domaine Lemonon, Loron **1997** £8.25 (WRI)
Moulin-à-Vent Le Vieux Domaine **1996** £8.99 (GW)
Régnié Domaine des Pillets **1998** £8.13 (BIB)
St-Amour Poitevin **1999** £8.90 (HAW)

£9.00 → £10.99

Beaujolais Château de Fleurie, Loron **1999** £9.50 (DI)
Brouilly Fessy **1997** £10.35 (UB)
Brouilly Michaud **1999** £9.20 (MV)
Brouilly Château des Tours **1997** £10.75 (ROB)
Côte de Brouilly Domaine de la Pierre Bleue, Ravier **1997** £10.10 (TW)
Fleurie Drouhin **1997** £9.39 (NI)
Fleurie Dumas **1998** £9.50 (LEA)
Fleurie Cave Co-op de Fleurie **1998** £9.25 (FRI)
Fleurie Château de Fleurie, Loron **1994** £9.75 (BU)
Fleurie Loron **1997** £9.70 (UB)
Fleurie Domaine des Quatre Vents, Duboeuf **1994** £9.80 (CRO)
Morgon Charmes Château Fuissé, Vincent **1998** £9.55 (AD)
Morgon Charmes, Domaine Prince Lieven **1993** £10.45 (JER)
Morgon Marcel Lapierre **1999** £10.28 (BIB)
Moulin-à-Vent Domaine Berrod **1998** £9.95 (AD)

Oz Clarke's Wine Buying Guide
is an annual publication.
We welcome your suggestions for next year's edition.

Moulin-à-Vent Cuvée Exceptionnelle, Château du Moulin-à-Vent **1996** £10.45 (HAW)
Moulin-à-Vent Domaine les Fine Graves, Janodet **1993** £9.75 (BU)
Moulin-à-Vent les Hospices, Collin & Bourisset **1995** £10.95 (ROB)
Moulin-à-Vent Château du Moulin-à-Vent **1998** £9.10 (HAW)
Régnié Domaine de la Plaigne **1997** £9.25 (ROB)
St-Amour Domaine des Billards, Loron **1996** £9.15 (UB)
St-Amour Domaine des Duc **1999** £9.00 (HAW)

Over £11.00

Chiroubles Domaine du Moulin **1989** £85.00 (JU)
Fleurie Michel Chignard **1998** £12.25 (FORT)
Fleurie les Garans, Latour **1998** £11.05 (WY)
Juliénas Domaine du Clos du Fief, Michel Tête **1998** £11.70 (UB)
Moulin-à-Vent Lafond **1988** £15.00 (CRO)
Moulin-à-Vent Domaine Lemonon, Loron **1996** £12.50 (UB)

WHITE

Under £7.00

Beaujolais Blanc Château de Chanzé **1999** £6.55 (HAW)
Beaujolais Blanc Château de Pizay **1998** £6.69 (CON)
Beaujolais Blanc Domaine des Terres Dorées **1998** £6.76 (SAV) £7.20 (AD)
Coteaux du Lyonnais, Cave de Sain Bel **1999** £5.90 (HAW)

Over £7.00

Beaujolais Blanc Pierre Carron **1999** £7.30 (HAW)
Beaujolais Blanc Jean-Jacques Martin **1999** £8.55 (HAW)
Beaujolais Blanc Domaine des Terres Dorées **1997** £7.50 (JU)

ROSÉ

c. £7.00

Beaujolais Rosé Cave Beaujolais du Bois d'Oingt **1999** £6.55 (HAW)

CHABLIS PRICES

WHITE

Under £6.00

Chablis Domaine de la Conciergerie, Adine ½ bottle **1997** £5.55 (JER)
Chablis Domaine de Vauroux ½ bottle **1997** £4.39 (CON)
Sauvignon de St-Bris, Brocard **1998** £4.99 (WAI)
Sauvignon de St-Bris, Goisot **1998** £4.95 (SOM) £6.46 (DOM)

£6.00 → £7.99

Chablis 1er Cru Grand Cuvée, la Chablisienne **1998** £7.95 (STE)
Chablis Alain Geoffroy **1998** £7.69 (OD) £8.49 (CON)
Chablis Brocard **1998** £7.99 (OD)
Chablis la Chablisienne **1997** £7.25 (SOM) £7.99 (MAR) £8.57 (FLE)
Chablis Durup **1999** £7.99 (BO)
Chablis Domaine des Iles, Tremblay **1997** £7.95 (COC)
Chablis Domaine des Manants, Brocard **1998** £7.99 (POR)
Chablis Séguinot **1997** £7.92 (HA)
Chablis Domaine Servin **1998** £7.99 (MAJ) £9.64 (CB)
Chablis Vocoret **1998** £7.99 (MAJ) £11.99 (VIN)
Petit Chablis Brocard **1998** £6.99 (POR)
Petit Chablis Château de Maligny **1997** £7.49 (VIC) £7.49 (THR) £7.49 (BOT) £7.85 (BY)
Petit Chablis Simonnet-Febvre **1997** £7.82 (CHA)
Sauvignon de St-Bris, Defrance **1994** £7.50 (RAE)
Sauvignon de St-Bris, Domaine des Remparts **1998** £6.50 (HIG)
Sauvignon de St-Bris, Sorin-Defrance **1998** £7.00 (WRI)

£8.00 → £9.99

Chablis les Ardilles, Vernion **1997** £8.11 (BY)
Chablis Domaine de Biéville, J Moreau **1997** £8.99 (VIC) £8.99 (THR)
Chablis Brocard **1992** £9.95 (BU)
Chablis Cuvée Reserve, Pautré **1998** £9.80 (HIG) £13.95 (VIN)
Chablis Droin **1998** £8.81 (GOE)
Chablis Drouhin **1995** £9.60 (NI)
Chablis Durup **1997** £8.33 (DOM)
Chablis Domaine de l'Églantière **1998** £8.99 (AME)
Chablis Fèvre **1998** £9.69 (REI) £10.95 (FORT)
Chablis Fourchaume, Château de Maligny **1995** £9.89 (BY)
Chablis Grossot **1997** £9.25 (LAY)
Chablis Laroche **1999** £8.99 (DI)
Chablis Légland **1998** £9.02 (GW)
Chablis Long-Depaquit **1998** £9.95 (BAL)
Chablis Château de Maligny, Durup **1998** £8.99 (VIC) £8.99 (THR) £8.99 (WR) £8.99 (BOT)
Chablis Château de Maligny, Durup **1997** £9.07 (BY)
Chablis Domaine des Manants, Brocard **1997** £8.59 (JON)
Chablis Montmains, Domaine de Vauroux **1996** £9.95 (CON)
Chablis Pautré **1998** £9.00 (HIG)
Chablis Picq **1998** £9.90 (MV)
Chablis Pinson **1998** £9.22 (PIP)
Chablis Tremblay **1997** £8.95 (ROB)
Chablis Domaine du Valéry, Durup **1997** £8.90 (TAN)
Chablis Domaine de Vauroux **1995** £8.99 (NI)
Chablis Vieilles Vignes, Château de Maligny **1997** £9.48 (BY)
Petit Chablis Pautré **1998** £8.00 (HIG)

£10.00 → £11.99

Chablis Adhémar Boudin, Domaine de Chantemerle **1998** £10.95 (LEA)
Chablis Chevallier **1996** £10.25 (BEN)
Chablis Daniel Defaix **1996** £10.99 (VIC) £10.99 (THR) £10.99 (WR) £10.99 (BOT)
Chablis Fourchaume, Château de Maligny **1996** £11.22 (BY) £13.99 (WR) £13.99 (BOT)
Chablis Laroche **1998** £10.90 (DI)
Chablis Montée de Tonnerre, Durup **1997** £11.52 (DOM)
Chablis Montmains, Brocard **1996** £10.50 (WS) £12.99 (JON) £14.00 (JU)
Chablis Montmains, Légland **1998** £11.02 (GW)
Chablis Tremblay **1996** £11.30 (VIN)
Chablis Tribut **1998** £10.95 (LEA)

Chablis Vaillons, Collet **1997** £11.95 (RES)
Chablis Vau-Ligneau, Alain Geoffroy **1998** £10.99 (OD) £11.99 (CON)
Chablis Vau-Ligneau, Hamelin **1997** £10.50 (NEZ) £12.95 (BEN)
Chablis Vaudevey Domaine des Valéry, Durup **1997** £11.90 (TAN)
Chablis Vieilles Vignes, Brocard **1998** £10.99 (OD) £11.95 (POR)
Chablis Vieilles Vignes, Daniel Defaix **1996** £10.48 (GOE) £10.95 (CON) £11.99 (JON) £14.80 (TW)
Petit Chablis Dauvissat-Camus **1995** £10.90 (JU)

£12.00 → £13.99

Chablis 1er Cru, Drouhin **1995** £12.30 (NI)
Chablis 1er Cru Grand Cuvée, la Chablisienne **1995** £12.99 (MAR)
Chablis Beauroy, la Chablisienne **1998** £12.95 (STE)
Chablis Côte de Léchet, Tribut **1998** £13.95 (LEA)
Chablis la Forêt, Pinson **1997** £12.56 (PIP)
Chablis Fourchaume, Louis Michel **1997** £12.75 (REI)
Chablis Fourchaume, Château de Maligny **1997** £12.46 (BY)
Chablis Mont de Milieu, Moreau **1997** £12.62 (COC)
Chablis Montée de Tonnerre, Château de Maligny **1997** £12.46 (BY)
Chablis Montée de Tonnerre, Louis Michel **1997** £13.85 (HAH)
Chablis Montée de Tonnerre, Domaine Servin **1997** £12.75 (BOD)
Chablis Montmains, Domaine Adine **1997** £12.70 (JER)
Chablis Montmains, Brocard **1997** £13.25 (AD)
Chablis Montmains, Droin **1998** £13.22 (GOE)
Chablis Montmains, Laroche **1995** £13.95 (DI)
Chablis Montmains, Race **1998** £12.00 (MV)
Chablis Montmains, Race **1997** £12.50 (BU)
Chablis Montmains, Simonnet-Febvre **1998** £13.79 (CHA)
Chablis Vaillons, Collet **1994** £13.95 (RES) £14.15 (JER)
Chablis Vaillons, Fèvre **1997** £13.92 (REI)
Chablis Vaillons, J Moreau **1998** £12.49 (WR) £12.49 (BOT)
Chablis Vaillons, Simonnet-Febvre **1998** £13.79 (CHA)
Chablis Vaudevey, Laroche **1998** £12.90 (CRO) £15.99 (DI)
Chablis Vieilles Vignes, Brocard **1996** £12.50 (JU)
Chablis Vieilles Vignes, Daniel Defaix **1995** £12.95 (ROB)

£14.00 → £16.99

Chablis 1er Cru, Domaine Vocoret **1997** £14.99 (VIN)
Chablis Beauroy, Tribut **1997** £14.10 (DOM) £14.50 (JU)
Chablis Côte de Léchet, Daniel et Etienne Defaix **1995** £15.18 (GOE) £17.20 (TAN) £18.85 (BER) £18.99 (JON)
Chablis Côte de Léchet, Daniel et Etienne Defaix **1994** £15.95 (CON) £16.50 (ROB)

Chablis Côte de Léchet, Tribut **1997** £14.10 (DOM) £14.50 (JU)
Chablis la Forest, René et Vincent Dauvissat **1998** £16.95 (LEA)
Chablis la Forest, René et Vincent Dauvissat **1997** £14.69 (DOM) £17.53 (FA)
Chablis la Forêt, Domaine Dauvissat-Camus **1997** £14.20 (TAN) £17.00 (JU)
Chablis Fourchaume, Brocard **1996** £15.00 (JU)
Chablis Latour **1995** £16.57 (WY)
Chablis les Lys, Daniel Defaix **1994** £15.95 (CON) £16.10 (TAN)
Chablis Montée de Tonnerre, Simonnet-Febvre **1998** £14.36 (CHA)
Chablis Montmains, Louis Michel **1994** £14.69 (REI)
Chablis Séchet, René et Vincent Dauvissat **1997** £14.69 (DOM) £17.53 (FA) £21.25 (FORT)
Chablis Vaillons, Daniel Defaix **1995** £15.18 (GOE) £17.99 (JON)
Chablis Vaillons, Daniel Defaix **1994** £15.95 (CON)
Chablis Vaillons, Droin **1997** £14.10 (DOM)
Chablis Vaillons, Laroche **1995** £14.95 (DI)
Chablis Vosgros, Droin **1997** £14.69 (DOM)

£17.00 → £19.99

Chablis Bougros, Domaine de Vauroux **1997** £19.95 (CON)
Chablis les Clos, Droin **1991** £18.80 (CAV)
Chablis les Clos, Servin **1997** £19.49 (BOD) £19.49 (SUN)
Chablis Côte de Léchet, Daniel et Etienne Defaix **1997** £17.99 (WR) £17.99 (BOT)
Chablis Fourchaume, Laroche **1997** £18.99 (DI)
Chablis Château de Grenouille, la Chablisienne **1995** £17.99 (SAF) £23.00 (JU) £32.69 (FRI) £353.87 (FA)
Chablis Grenouilles, Domaine de Château Grenouille **1993** £19.99 (MAR) £23.50 (RIP)
Chablis Montée de Tonnerre, Verget **1994** £19.00 (FA)
Chablis Vaillons, Drouhin **1997** £17.00 (JU)
Chablis Vaudésir, J Moreau **1993** £18.35 (COC)

£20.00 → £24.99

Chablis Beauroy, Tribut **1996** £20.95 (FORT)
Chablis les Clos, Bouchard Père **1997** £21.85 (WAT)
Chablis les Clos, Brocard **1997** £20.99 (YOU) £22.00 (AD)
Chablis les Clos, Brocard **1994** £22.87 (FLE)
Chablis les Clos, Droin **1998** £23.50 (DOM)
Chablis les Clos, J Moreau **1996** £21.20 (COC)
Chablis les Clos, Pinson **1997** £20.07 (PIP)
Chablis les Clos, Pinson **1995** £22.10 (NO)
Chablis Côte de Léchet, Daniel et Etienne Defaix **1993** £21.03 (TW)
Chablis la Forest, René et Vincent Dauvissat **1995** £20.95 (FA)
Chablis Montée de Tonnerre, Verget **1995** £20.95 (FA)
Chablis la Moutonne, Long-Depaquit **1995** £22.99 (UN)
Chablis les Preuses, la Chablisienne **1998** £24.25 (STE)
Chablis les Preuses, la Chablisienne **1995** £21.00 (JU)
Chablis Séchet, René et Vincent Dauvissat **1995** £20.95 (FA)
Chablis Vaillons, René et Vincent Dauvissat **1996** £22.42 (FA)
Chablis Vaillons, Daniel Defaix **1992** £22.91 (TW)
Chablis Valmur, Droin **1995** £24.50 (ELL)
Chablis Valmur, Droin **1994** £23.00 (RAE)
Chablis Vaudésir, Drouhin **1995** £22.29 (NI)
Chablis Vaudésir, Louis Michel **1997** £21.45 (BER) £25.26 (REI)

£25.00 → £29.99

Chablis Butteaux, Raveneau **1994** £29.77 (FA)
Chablis les Clos, Domaine Dauvissat-Camus **1997** £26.00 (JU)
Chablis les Clos, René et Vincent Dauvissat **1998** £29.50 (LEA)
Chablis les Clos, René et Vincent Dauvissat **1997** £27.99 (YOU) £30.75 (FA)
Chablis les Clos, Droin **1996** £26.49 (JON)
Chablis Château de Grenouille, la Chablisienne **1997** £29.50 (STE)
Chablis Grenouilles, Droin **1997** £26.45 (BER)
Chablis la Moutonne, Long-Depaquit **1998** £29.50 (BAL)
Chablis les Preuses, Domaine Dauvissat-Camus **1997** £25.00 (JU)
Chablis les Preuses, René et Vincent Dauvissat **1997** £25.85 (DOM) £29.50 (LEA) £30.75 (FA) £37.50 (FORT)
Chablis Vaillons, Daniel Defaix **1990** £26.44 (TW)
Chablis Valmur, Droin **1996** £26.49 (JON)
Chablis Vaudésir, Drouhin **1997** £26.00 (JU) £26.95 (BEN)
Chablis Vaudésir, Reynier **1996** £25.00 (RES)

Over £30.00

Chablis Blanchots, Daniel Defaix **1993** £32.50 (ROB)
Chablis Butteaux, Raveneau **1996** £38.09 (FA) £39.75 (WAI)
Chablis les Clos, René et Vincent Dauvissat **1993** £33.49 (REI)
Chablis Château de Grenouille, la Chablisienne **1996** £33.99 (FRI)
Chablis Montée de Tonnerre, Raveneau **1996** £42.50 (FA)
Chablis les Preuses, René et Vincent Dauvissat **1995** £32.70 (FA)
Chablis Vaillons, Raveneau **1997** £30.75 (FA)
Chablis Valmur, Raveneau **1997** £48.37 (FA)
Chablis Vaudésir, Louis Michel **1988** £37.00 (CRO)
Chablis Vaudésir, Reynier **1983** £42.00 (CRO)
Chablis Vaulorent, Fèvre **1983** £31.00 (CRO)

CÔTE CHALONNAISE PRICES

RED

Under £9.00

Bourgogne du Chapitre, Jaffelin **1992** £7.75 (BU)
Bourgogne Clos du Liron, Sarrazin **1996** £8.65 (WT)
Givry Latour **1998** £7.99 (MAJ)
Rully Varot Domaine de la Renarde, Delorme **1997** £8.69 (WAT)

£9.00 → £10.99

Givry Boischevaux, Thenard **1996** £10.95 (JER)
Givry Clos Jus, Mouton **1997** £10.50 (SOM) £11.40 (TAN)
Givry le Pied de Clou, Lumpp **1998** £10.95 (LEA)
Givry le Pied de Clou, Lumpp **1997** £10.95 (LEA)
Givry le Pied de Clou, Lumpp **1996** £10.95 (LEA)
Mercurey Château de Chamilly **1993** £10.95 (CON) £12.99 (JON)
Mercurey Maréchal **1996** £10.87 (PIP)
Mercurey les Mauvarennes, Faiveley **1997** £10.99 (DI)
Rully Dureuil-Janthial **1998** £9.54 (RAE)

£11.00 → £14.99

Givry 1er Cru Clos Salomon, du Gardin **1996** £11.80 (TAN)
Givry Clos Jus, Lumpp **1998** £12.95 (LEA)
Givry Clos Jus, Lumpp **1997** £12.95 (LEA)
Givry Clos Jus, Lumpp **1996** £11.95 (LEA)
Givry Clos Jus, Mouton **1994** £12.95 (ROB)
Givry Clos de la Servoisine, Jean Marc Joblot **1998** £14.55 (AV) £14.69 (GOE)
Givry la Grande Berge, Ragot **1996** £13.95 (BEN)
Givry Gérard Mouton **1996** £12.60 (STA)
Givry Remmoissenet **1995** £14.25 (AV)
Mercurey Carillon **1997** £11.75 (MON)
Mercurey Domaine Louis Carillon **1997** £12.75 (STE)
Mercurey Domaine Louis Carillon **1996** £12.75 (STE)
Mercurey Château de Chamirey **1997** £13.50 (WS) £15.18 (PLAY)
Mercurey les Combins, Juillot **1998** £12.50 (LEA)
Mercurey les Combins, Juillot **1997** £12.95 (LEA)
Mercurey les Combins, Juillot **1996** £12.50 (LEA)
Mercurey Domaine de la Croix Jacquelet, Faiveley **1998** £13.51 (PLA)
Mercurey Domaine de la Croix Jacquelet, Faiveley **1997** £12.29 (CON)
Mercurey Domaine de la Croix Jacquelet, Faiveley **1996** £12.50 (WRI)
Mercurey la Framboisière, Faiveley **1997** £13.99 (BEN)

Mercurey Juillot **1996** £11.69 (DOM)
Mercurey Juillot **1995** £12.87 (DOM) £16.95 (FORT)
Mercurey Domaine du Meix-Foulot **1995** £13.95 (ROB)
Rully 1er Cru les Clouds, Jacqueson **1996** £13.85 (NI)
Rully les Chaponnières, Jacqueson **1997** £11.20 (TAN)
Rully Dureuil-Janthial **1997** £11.95 (RES) £12.14 (PIP)
Rully Dureuil-Janthial **1996** £11.73 (PIP)
Rully Faiveley **1997** £11.80 (BEN)
Rully Domaine de l'Hermitage, Chanzy **1997** £11.10 (PLA)
Rully Préaux, Eric de Suremain **1997** £13.90 (JU)
Rully Château de Rully, Rodet **1992** £12.99 (UN)

£15.00 → £17.99

Givry Clos de la Servoisine, Jean Marc Joblot **1997** £15.27 (GOE) £15.76 (RES) £15.99 (DI) £16.00 (JU)
Givry Clos de la Servoisine, Jean Marc Joblot **1996** £16.50 (JU)

Mercurey Clos des Barraults, Juillot **1996** £17.04 (DOM)
Rully Préaux, Eric de Suremain **1996** £16.00 (JU)
Rully Préaux, Eric de Suremain **1995** £16.00 (JU)

Over £18.00

Mercurey les Combins, Juillot **1992** £23.26 (TW)
Mercurey Juillot **1988** £23.38 (TW)
Mercurey Sazenay, Suremain **1985** £18.95 (LEA)

WHITE

Under £8.00

Montagny 1er Cru, Cave de Buxy **1998** £7.99 (MAR) £9.49 (FRI)

£8.00 → £8.99

Mercurey Émile Voarick **1996** £8.57 (HA)
Montagny 1er Cru les Loges, Cave de Buxy **1998** £8.95 (AD) £9.20 (TAN)
Rully Jaffelin **1996** £8.99 (MAJ)

£9.00 → £10.99

Givry Clos des Vignes Rondes, Lumpp **1998** £10.95 (LEA)
Givry Clos des Vignes Rondes, Lumpp **1996** £10.95 (LEA)
Mercurey Chartron et Trébuchet **1997** £9.75 (BAN)
Mercurey Domaine du Meix-Foulot **1998** £9.95 (SOM)
Montagny 1er Cru, Olivier Leflaive **1997** £10.95 (LAY)
Montagny Latour **1997** £9.95 (POR) £9.95 (STA) £10.83 (PLAY)
Montagny 1er Cru Domaine des Moirots, Denizot **1998** £9.31 (CHA)
Montagny Roy **1998** £10.85 (WRI)
Rully 1er Cru Meix Cadot, Dury **1995** £9.95 (RAE)
Rully Bouchard Père **1997** £9.80 (COC)
Rully Chanson **1996** £9.69 (HA)
Rully la Chaume, Dury **1997** £9.99 (JON)
Rully Faiveley **1996** £10.99 (DI)
Rully Domaine de l'Hermitage, Chanzy **1995** £10.92 (PLA)
Rully Olivier Leflaive **1997** £10.40 (LAY) £10.99 (PHI) £11.67 (MI)
Rully Château de Rully, Rodet **1997** £10.99 (SAI)

£11.00 → £12.99

Mercurey Clos Rochette, Faiveley **1995** £11.16 (REI) £13.55 (HAH)
Mercurey Juillot **1997** £12.87 (DOM)
Mercurey Juillot **1996** £12.93 (DOM)
Montagny 1er Cru, Bertrand et Juillot **1994** £12.45 (TW)
Montagny 1er Cru, Olivier Leflaive **1998** £11.75 (CB)
Montagny 1er Cru, Olivier Leflaive **1995** £12.45 (ROB)
Rully la Chaume, Chartron et Trébuchet **1997** £11.82 (BAN) £13.20 (JER)
Rully les Clous, Olivier Leflaive **1997** £11.95 (LAY)
Rully les Clous, Olivier Leflaive **1996** £11.95 (LAY) £14.31 (PLAY)
Rully Grésigny, Jacqueson **1997** £11.06 (RES) £11.95 (TAN) £13.95 (RES)
Rully Olivier Leflaive **1998** £11.75 (HAH)
Rully Marissou, Dury **1990** £11.95 (RAE)
Rully la Pucelle, Domaine Jacqueson **1997** £12.95 (LEA)
Rully la Pucelle, Domaine Jacqueson **1996** £12.95 (NEZ) £14.25 (STA)
Rully Château de Rully, Rodet **1995** £11.00 (WS)
Rully Château de Rully, Rodet **1994** £11.16 (REI)
Rully les St-Jacques, Villaine **1998** £12.63 (CB)

£13.00 → £14.99

Mercurey Château de Chamirey, Rodet **1997** £13.99 (YOU)
Mercurey Clos Rochette, Faiveley **1996** £14.70 (WRI)
Montagny 1er Cru, Bertrand et Juillot **1992** £14.98 (TW)
Rully 1er Cru, de Suremain **1996** £14.50 (JU)
Rully Mont Palais, Olivier Leflaive **1995** £13.75 (UB)

Over £15.00

Mercurey Clos Rochette, Faiveley **1997** £15.80 (PLA)
Mercurey Juillot **1995** £18.95 (FORT)
Montagny Latour **1990** £20.72 (WY)

A key to name abbreviations is available on page 7.

CÔTE D'OR PRICES

RED

Under £8.00

Hautes-Côtes de Beaune, Caves des Hautes-Côtes **1997** £6.75 (AS) £6.99 (TES)
Hautes-Côtes de Beaune Tête de Cuvée, Caves des Hautes-Côtes **1997** £7.49 (WAI)
Hautes-Côtes de Nuits Tête de Cuvée, Caves des Hautes-Côtes **1997** £7.60 (AS)

£8.00 → £9.99

Chassagne-Montrachet Louis Carillon **1997** £9.65 (SOM) £12.24 (MON)
Chorey-lès-Beaune Roger et Joël Remy **1998** £9.95 (LEA)
Côte de Beaune-Villages Chanson **1996** £8.95 (POR)
Côte de Nuits-Villages Domaine Boillot **1998** £9.99 (MON)
Fixin Gelin **1996** £8.95 (SOM) £13.98 (PLA)
Hautes-Côtes de Beaune, Hubert Lamy **1996** £8.00 (BAN)
Hautes-Côtes de Beaune Rollin **1996** £9.90 (JU)
Hautes-Côtes de Nuits Bouchard Père **1996** £8.42 (BY) £8.68 (HA)
Hautes-Côtes de Nuits, Michel Gros **1997** £9.75 (TAN) £10.40 (REI)
Hautes-Côtes de Nuits, Caves des Hautes-Côtes **1997** £8.75 (BU)
Monthélie Bouchard Père **1994** £8.97 (BY)
Morey-St-Denis Georges Lignier **1993** £9.99 (RAE)
St-Aubin Prudhon **1997** £9.25 (WS) £9.90 (JU)
Santenay les Gravières, Roger Belland **1995** £9.99 (WAT)
Savigny-lès-Beaune Latour **1997** £9.95 (TAN) £11.46 (PLA) £12.56 (PLAY)

£10.00 → £11.99

Auxey-Duresses Bouchard Père **1995** £10.14 (BY)
Beaune Épenottes, Mussy **1996** £11.25 (SOM)
Chassagne-Montrachet Blain-Gagnard **1996** £11.85 (HAH)
Chassagne-Montrachet Louis Carillon **1998** £11.75 (MON)
Chassagne-Montrachet les Chaumes, Amiot **1996** £11.95 (SOM) £14.95 (LEA)
Chassagne-Montrachet Lamy **1997** £10.73 (BY)
Chassagne-Montrachet Ramonet **1993** £11.75 (CAV)
Chassagne-Montrachet Villamont **1993** £11.50 (ROB)
Chorey-lès-Beaune Tollot-Beaut **1997** £11.65 (TAN) £12.34 (DOM) £12.99 (DI) £13.00 (JU)
Chorey-lès-Beaune Tollot-Beaut **1996** £11.99 (BOT) £12.34 (DOM) £12.99 (JON)
Chorey-lès-Beaune Tollot-Beaut **1995** £11.49 (THR) £11.49 (VIC)
Côte de Beaune-Villages Chanson **1997** £11.16 (HA)
Côte de Nuits-Villages Clos du Chapeau, Domaine de l'Arlot **1997** £10.77 (GOE) £13.48 (BY)
Côte de Nuits-Villages René Durand **1996** £10.48 (PIP)
Gevrey-Chambertin Claude Dugat **1992** £11.75 (CAV)
Hautes-Côtes de Beaune, Caves des Hautes-Côtes **1996** £10.99 (VA) £11.95 (BU)
Hautes-Côtes de Beaune Rollin **1995** £11.50 (JU)
Marsannay Bruno Clair **1995** £11.50 (JU)
Marsannay les Longeroies, Bruno Clair **1996** £11.95 (SOM) £14.00 (JU)
Marsannay les Vaudenelles, Bruno Clair **1996** £10.50 (SOM) £13.00 (JU)
Monthélie Garaudet **1993** £11.35 (NEZ)
Monthélie Château de Monthélie, Suremain **1995** £10.45 (SOM) £19.00 (JU)
St-Aubin les Frionnes, Prudhon **1997** £10.95 (TAN) £11.50 (JU)
St-Aubin les Frionnes, Prudhon **1996** £10.99 (RAE) £12.99 (YOU) £13.99 (JON)
St-Aubin Pitangerets, Domaine Louis Carillon **1998** £11.95 (AD)
St-Aubin Prudhon **1996** £11.50 (JU)
St-Aubin Sentier du Clou, Prudhon **1997** £10.75 (WS)
St-Romain Buisson **1997** £11.16 (DOM)
St-Romain Gras **1997** £11.95 (TAN)
Santenay Bouchard Père **1997** £11.95 (WAI)
Santenay Latour **1996** £11.34 (PLAY)
Savigny-lès-Beaune Girard-Vollot **1997** £10.77 (MON)

£12.00 → £13.99

Aloxe-Corton Roger et Joël Remy **1998** £13.95 (LEA)
Auxey-Duresses Michel Prunier **1997** £12.50 (TAN)
Auxey-Duresses Michel Prunier **1996** £13.48 (NO)
Beaune Clos du Dessus des Marconnets, Pernot **1994** £12.65 (NEZ)
Beaune Épenottes, Parent **1997** £13.99 (SAF)
Chassagne-Montrachet les Chaumes, Amiot **1998** £13.95 (LEA)
Chassagne-Montrachet Henri Germain **1997** £13.35 (TAN) £13.65 (AD) £14.95 (LEA)
Chassagne-Montrachet Latour **1996** £12.40 (PLA)
Chassagne-Montrachet Vieilles Vignes, Bernard Morey **1997** £13.71 (MON)
Chorey-lès-Beaune Maillard **1995** £13.00 (CRO)
Chorey-lès-Beaune Tollot-Beaut **1998** £12.15 (AD)
Chorey-lès-Beaune Château de Chorey-lès-Beaune, Jacques Germain **1997** £12.87 (DOM) £14.50 (AS)
Côte de Beaune-Villages Carillon **1997** £12.75 (STE)
Côte de Beaune-Villages Drouhin **1997** £12.70 (NI)
Côte de Nuits-Villages Chopin-Groffier **1997** £12.95 (PHI) £12.95 (FORT)
Côte de Nuits-Villages Clos du Chapeau, Domaine de l'Arlot **1998** £12.24 (GOE)
Côte de Nuits-Villages Faiveley **1996** £13.25 (CON)
Marsannay Grasse-Tête, Bruno Clair **1997** £12.00 (JU)
Marsannay les Longeroies, Bruno Clair **1997** £13.50 (JU)
Marsannay Monchenevoy, Charlopin-Parizot **1997** £13.95 (LEA)
Marsannay les Vaudenelles, Bruno Clair **1995** £12.50 (JU)
Monthélie Bouchard Père **1996** £12.37 (HA)
Monthélie Clos Gauthey, Garaudet **1995** £13.24 (PIP)
Nuits-St-Georges Gouges **1997** £13.25 (SOM)
Pernand-Vergelesses Rollin **1997** £12.90 (TAN)
Pernand-Vergelesses Rollin **1993** £12.50 (RAE)
Pernand-Vergelesses Sous le Bois de Noël et Belles Filles, Rollin **1997** £12.50 (JU)
Pernand-Vergelesses Sous le Bois de Noël et Belles Filles, Rollin **1994** £13.00 (JU)
Pommard les Cras, Belland **1995** £13.95 (WAT)
St-Aubin les Castets, Lamy **1997** £13.50 (LAY) £13.95 (LEA)
St-Aubin Pitangerets, Domaine Louis Carillon **1997** £12.73 (MON)
Santenay Bouchard Père **1995** £13.30 (JER)
Santenay Drouhin **1996** £13.81 (WY)

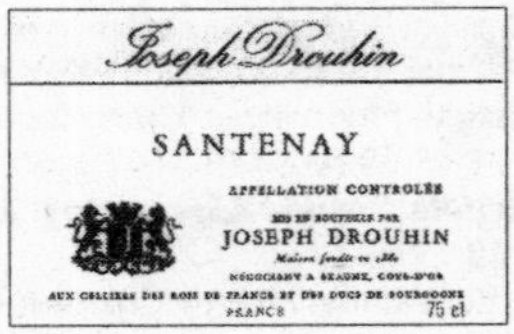

Santeney les Gravières, Girardin **1997** £12.45 (SOM) £16.90 (JU) £16.95 (AD) £18.50 (ELL) £19.65 (NI)
Savigny-lès-Beaune les Bourgeots, Bize **1996** £13.79 (JON)
Savigny-lès-Beaune aux Grands Liards, Bize **1996** £12.45 (SOM)
Savigny-lès-Beaune les Lavières, Camus-Bruchon **1998** £13.83 (RAE)
Savigny-lès-Beaune Pavelot **1996** £12.34 (DOM) £17.50 (FORT)
Savigny-lès-Beaune les Serpentières, Drouhin **1994** £13.81 (WY)

£14.00 → £15.99

Aloxe-Corton Latour **1996** £14.50 (TAN)
Aloxe-Corton Rollin **1996** £15.47 (RAE) £19.90 (JU)
Auxey-Duresses les Ecusseaux, Ampeau **1992** £14.69 (REI)
Beaune 1er Cru, Bouchard Père **1995** £15.52 (BY)
Beaune Bressandes, Henri Germain **1990** £14.95 (BAL)
Beaune Cent Vignes, Bouchard Père **1997** £15.95 (WAI)
Beaune Cent Vignes, Roger et Joël Remy **1998** £14.95 (LEA)
Beaune Cent Vignes, Roger et Joël Remy **1995** £15.95 (LEA)
Beaune Clos des Avaux, Guillemard-Pothiers **1992** £15.95 (CON)

Beaune Clos du Roi, Camus-Bruchon **1994** £15.99 (RAE)
Beaune Marconnets, Remoissenet **1988** £14.95 (BAL)
Beaune les Mariages, Rossignol-Trapet **1996** £15.75 (WRI)
Beaune les Mariages, Rossignol-Trapet **1995** £15.86 (HA) £18.21 (TW)
Beaune Teurons, Bouchard Père **1995** £15.95 (COC)
Chassagne-Montrachet Blain-Gagnard **1995** £14.60 (JER)
Chassagne-Montrachet les Chaumes, Amiot **1997** £14.95 (LEA)
Chassagne-Montrachet Clos St-Jean, J-N Gagnard **1997** £15.00 (JU)
Chassagne-Montrachet Vieilles Vignes, Amiot **1995** £14.95 (LEA)
Chassagne-Montrachet Vieilles Vignes, Bernard Morey **1996** £14.69 (DOM) £17.50 (STA)
Côte de Beaune Drouhin **1996** £14.75 (UB)
Côte de Nuits-Villages Clos du Chapeau, Domaine de l'Arlot **1996** £14.30 (BY) £16.99 (WR)
Fixin la Croix Blanche, André Geoffroy **1996** £15.00 (JU)
Gevrey-Chambertin Domaine Boillot **1998** £15.66 (MON)
Gevrey-Chambertin Rossignol-Trapet **1997** £14.99 (SAF) £21.50 (CON)
Gevrey-Chambertin Rossignol-Trapet **1996** £15.73 (BY) £16.74 (CB) £19.39 (TW)
Gevrey-Chambertin Vieilles Vignes, Trapet **1995** £15.85 (NI)
Hautes-Côtes de Nuits, Jayer-Gilles **1998** £15.00 (AD)
Hautes-Côtes de Nuits, Jayer-Gilles **1994** £15.00 (WS) £17.00 (JU)
Maranges Clos des Loyères Vieilles Vignes, Girardin **1996** £15.50 (ROB)
Marsannay Clos du Roy, Regis Bouvier **1997** £14.04 (DOM)
Marsannay Grasse-Tête, Bruno Clair **1996** £14.00 (WS)
Marsannay les Longeroies, Bruno Clair **1995** £14.00 (JU)
Marsannay Longeroies, Denis Mortet **1997** £14.69 (DOM)
Marsannay Monchenevoy, Charlopin-Parizot **1994** £14.00 (MV)
Meursault Coche Debord **1982** £15.00 (CRO)
Monthélie Château de Monthélie, Suremain **1993** £15.00 (JU)
Monthélie Parent **1996** £15.89 (JON)
Morey-St-Denis Bouchard Père **1990** £15.50 (BY)
Morey-St-Denis Cuvée des Grives, Ponsot **1996** £14.69 (FA)
Morey-St-Denis en la Rue de Vergy, Bruno Clair **1996** £15.75 (SOM) £20.00 (JU)
Morey-St-Denis en la Rue de Vergy, Domaine Henri Perrot-Minot **1995** £14.95 (WAT) £16.50 (BAL)
Nuits-St-Georges Domaine de l'Arlot **1997** £14.69 (GOE) £16.96 (BY)
Nuits-St-Georges Jean Chauvenet **1998** £14.59 (RAE) £15.67 (GOE)
Nuits-St-Georges Jean Chauvenet **1997** £15.67 (GOE) £22.35 (HA)
Nuits-St-Georges les Damodes, Jean Chauvenet **1998** £15.76 (RAE)
Nuits-St-Georges les Fleurières, Jean-Jacques Confuron **1995** £15.95 (BAL)
Nuits-St-Georges Labouré-Roi **1996** £14.99 (SAF)
Pernand-Vergelesses Île de Vergelesses, Rollin **1996** £15.47 (RAE) £21.00 (JU)
Pernand-Vergelesses Sous le Bois de Noël et Belles Filles, Rollin **1996** £14.00 (JU)
Pernand-Vergelesses les Vergelesses, Pavelot **1996** £14.69 (DOM)
Pommard Bouchard Père **1995** £14.40 (COC)
St-Aubin les Frionnes, Prudhon **1995** £15.00 (JU)
Santenay Clos Tavannes, Domaine de la Pousse d'Or **1994** £15.95 (DI)
Santenay la Maladière, Girardin **1998** £14.99 (OD)
Santenay la Maladière, Girardin **1995** £14.60 (NEZ)
Santeney les Gravières, Girardin **1998** £14.68 (MON) £16.50 (AD)
Savigny-lès-Beaune Bouchard Père **1995** £15.20 (JER)
Savigny-lès-Beaune Champs-Chevrey, Tollot-Beaut **1998** £14.06 (RAE)

Please remember that **Oz Clarke's Wine Buying Guide** *is a price* **guide** *and not a price* **list**. *It is not meant to replace up-to-date merchants' lists.*

Savigny-lès-Beaune les Fourneaux, Bize **1997** £14.25 (SOM)
Savigny-lès-Beaune les Guettes, Pavelot **1995** £14.69 (DOM)
Savigny-lès-Beaune Domaine Guyon **1996** £15.75 (FRI)
Savigny-lès-Beaune Latour **1993** £15.19 (WY)
Savigny-lès-Beaune les Lavières, Bouchard Père **1996** £15.53 (COC)
Savigny-lès-Beaune les Lavières, Camus-Bruchon **1995** £14.50 (RAE)
Savigny-lès-Beaune les Lavières, Chandon de Briailles **1995** £15.50 (HAH) £16.60 (SAV)
Savigny-lès-Beaune Narbantons, Camus-Bruchon **1995** £14.99 (JON)
Volnay Bouchard Père **1993** £14.95 (COC)
Volnay Edouard Delaunay **1995** £14.16 (CHA)

£16.00 → £17.99

Aloxe-Corton Latour **1997** £17.49 (POR)
Aloxe-Corton Rollin **1997** £17.00 (JU)
Aloxe-Corton Rollin **1993** £17.50 (RAE)
Beaune Bressandes, Henri Germain **1997** £16.60 (TAN) £16.95 (AD) £18.95 (LEA)
Beaune Cent Vignes, Monnier **1995** £17.99 (NI)
Beaune Clos des Avaux, Guillemard-Pothiers **1985** £17.95 (LEA)
Beaune Clos du Roi, Camus-Bruchon **1998** £16.94 (RAE)
Beaune Clos des Ursules, Jadot **1994** £17.14 (CAV) £24.09 (REI)
Beaune Teurons, Bouchard Père **1997** £17.65 (COC)
Beaune Teurons, Rossignol-Trapet **1995** £16.67 (PIP)
Beaune Vignes Franches, Latour **1996** £17.15 (PLA) £17.26 (WY) £17.50 (STA) £17.58 (PLAY)
Chambolle-Musigny Ghislaine Barthod-Noëllat **1998** £17.82 (GOE) £18.41 (RAE)
Chambolle-Musigny Ghislaine Barthod-Noëllat **1997** £17.53 (GOE) £20.00 (JU)
Chambolle-Musigny les Charmes, Ghislaine Barthod-Noëllat **1987** £17.99 (RAE)
Chambolle-Musigny Confuron **1996** £16.95 (BAL)
Chambolle-Musigny Domaine Roumier **1997** £17.99 (GW) £21.20 (TAN) £21.95 (RES) £22.91 (FA)
Chassagne-Montrachet Champs-Gains, Jean Marc Morey **1996** £17.99 (PIP)
Chassagne-Montrachet Clos St-Jean, J-N Gagnard **1996** £17.00 (JU)
Gevrey-Chambertin Chanson **1995** £17.59 (JON) £17.99 (POR) £19.85 (HA)
Gevrey Chambertin Estournelles-St-Jacques, Frédéric Esmonin **1997** £17.50 (BAN)
Gevrey-Chambertin Thierry Mortet **1998** £17.95 (LEA)
Gevrey-Chambertin Perrot-Minot **1996** £16.99 (BOD) £16.99 (SUN) £17.50 (CON) £18.50 (BAL)
Gevrey-Chambertin Perrot-Minot **1995** £16.29 (CON) £16.60 (NEZ)
Gevrey-Chambertin Rebourseau **1997** £17.85 (SOM)
Gevrey-Chambertin Rossignol-Trapet **1995** £16.22 (CB)
Gevrey-Chambertin Vieilles Vignes, Trapet **1996** £17.04 (FA)
Hautes-Côtes de Nuits, Jayer-Gilles **1997** £16.00 (JU) £16.30 (AD)
Marsannay Longeroies, Denis Mortet **1994** £16.00 (WS)

Monthélie les Duresses, Coche-Bizouard **1993** £16.95 (ROB)

Monthélie Château de Monthélie, Suremain **1997** £16.00 (JU)

Nuits-St-Georges Jean Chauvenet **1995** £16.99 (RAE)

Nuits-St-Georges Robert Chevillon **1997** £16.50 (FORT) £16.90 (JU) £18.85 (WT)

Nuits-St-Georges Faiveley **1992** £16.75 (CON)

Nuits-St-Georges les Fleurières, Jean-Jacques Confuron **1994** £16.95 (BAL)

Nuits-St-Georges Michelot **1995** £17.25 (NEZ)

Pernand-Vergelesses Île de Vergelesses, Chandon de Briailles **1996** £17.50 (LEA)

Pommard Jean-Marc Boillot **1996** £17.53 (RAE) £19.09 (GOE)

Pommard Clos Blanc, Albert Grivault **1993** £17.00 (JU)

Pommard Clos du Pavillon, Bouchard Père **1995** £17.49 (UN)

Pommard Coste-Caumartin **1997** £16.00 (JU)

Pommard les Vignots, Coste-Caumartin **1997** £16.99 (GW) £17.00 (JU)

Santenay Clos Tavannes, Gagnard **1997** £16.00 (JU)

Santenay Clos Tavannes, Domaine de la Pousse d'Or **1996** £17.14 (GOE)

Santenay Grand Clos Rousseau, Bernard Morey **1996** £17.63 (DOM)

Santenay la Maladière, Girardin **1997** £17.00 (WS)

Santeney les Gravières, Girardin **1996** £16.50 (TAN) £21.95 (PHI)

Savigny-lès-Beaune la Dominode, Bruno Clair **1997** £17.60 (SOM) £22.00 (JU)

Savigny-lès-Beaune la Dominode, Pavelot **1997** £17.63 (DOM)

Savigny-lès-Beaune aux Grands Liards, Javillier **1997** £16.60 (LAY)

Savigny-lès-Beaune les Lavières, Ampeau **1987** £16.74 (REI)

Savigny-lès-Beaune les Lavières, Chandon de Briailles **1996** £16.95 (LEA)

Oz Clarke's Wine Buying Guide
is an annual publication.
We welcome your suggestions for next year's edition.

Savigny-lès-Beaune les Lavières, Tollot-Beaut **1997** £16.00 (JU) £16.99 (DI)

Savigny-lès-Beaune les Lavières, Tollot-Beaut **1996** £16.45 (DOM)

Savigny-lès-Beaune les Peuillets, Pavelot **1995** £16.45 (DOM)

Volnay Champans, Monthélie-Douhairet **1995** £16.90 (SOM)

Volnay Domaine de la Pousse d'Or **1997** £17.35 (CON)

Volnay Santenots Latour **1995** £17.05 (STA) £20.13 (WY)

Vosne-Romanée Engel **1996** £17.95 (CON) £18.65 (SOM) £20.00 (WAI) £25.00 (FORT) £25.26 (TW)

Vosne-Romanée Gros Frère et Soeur **1995** £16.06 (FA)

£18.00 → £19.99

Aloxe-Corton les Chaillots, Latour **1996** £18.95 (STA) £19.56 (WY)

Aloxe-Corton Tollot-Beaut **1996** £19.00 (JU)

Aloxe-Corton Tollot-Beaut **1995** £19.49 (JON)

Auxey-Duresses les Ecusseaux, Ampeau **1983** £18.21 (REI)

Beaune Bressandes, Henri Germain **1996** £19.95 (LEA)

Beaune Clos du Roi, Tollot-Beaut **1997** £19.58 (GOE)

Beaune Clos des Ursules, Jadot **1997** £19.00 (FA) £22.03 (CAV) £24.38 (REI)

Beaune Grèves, Tollot-Beaut **1996** £19.00 (RAE) £21.95 (DI) £25.85 (FA)

Beaune les Montrevenots, Jean-Marc Boillot **1997** £19.39 (DOM) £21.50 (LEA)

Beaune les Sizies, Michel Prunier **1997** £18.50 (JU)

Beaune Teurons, Jadot **1993** £19.99 (POR)

Beaune Teurons, Rossignol-Trapet **1996** £18.62 (CB) £21.03 (TW)

Blagny, Olivier Leflaive **1993** £19.09 (CAV)

Chambolle-Musigny Ghislaine Barthod-Noëllat **1994** £18.50 (RAE)

Chambolle-Musigny les Charmes, Hudelot-Noëllat **1995** £18.40 (SOM)

Chambolle-Musigny Hudelot-Noëllat **1995** £18.25 (STE) £23.50 (ROB)

Chambolle-Musigny les Véroilles, Bruno Clair **1997** £18.00 (JU)

Chassagne-Montrachet la Maltroie, Amiot **1993** £19.09 (CAV)

Chassagne-Montrachet Morgeot, Jean Pillot **1997** £19.95 (RES)
Clos de la Roche Ponsot **1990** £19.00 (FA)
Corton les Renardes, Delarche **1997** £19.25 (SOM)
Côte de Nuits-Villages Jayer-Gilles **1997** £19.50 (JU) £19.75 (AD)
Gevrey-Chambertin Domaine Boillot **1997** £18.00 (WS)
Gevrey-Chambertin Bouchard Père **1996** £19.62 (COC)
Gevrey-Chambertin Cuvée de l'Abeille, Ponsot **1995** £19.95 (BAL)
Gevrey-Chambertin Latour **1996** £19.50 (STA)
Gevrey-Chambertin Hubert Lignier **1997** £19.97 (FA)
Gevrey-Chambertin Denis Mortet **1997** £19.92 (DOM) £21.99 (YOU) £22.00 (JU) £23.75 (TAN) £28.89 (CAV)
Gevrey-Chambertin Thierry Mortet **1997** £19.39 (SAV) £19.95 (LEA)
Gevrey-Chambertin Armand Rousseau **1997** £19.00 (FA) £21.95 (TAN) £26.44 (REI) £27.50 (FORT)
Gevry-Chambertin Vieilles Vignes, Geantet-Pansiot **1996** £19.98 (DOM)
Monthélie Château de Monthélie, Suremain **1996** £18.00 (JU)
Monthélie Château de Monthélie, Suremain **1990** £18.99 (RAE)
Monthélie sur la Velle, Château de Monthélie **1997** £18.50 (JU)
Morey-St-Denis Georges Lignier **1996** £19.71 (HA)
Morey-St-Denis Hubert Lignier **1997** £19.97 (FA)
Morey-St-Denis Monts Luisants, Pernin-Rossin **1996** £19.95 (BAN)
Morey-St-Denis en la Rue de Vergy, Bruno Clair **1997** £19.00 (JU)
Morey-St-Denis en la Rue de Vergy, Domaine Henri Perrot-Minot **1996** £18.50 (CON) £19.95 (BAL) £19.95 (BAL)
Nuits-St-Georges Domaine de l'Arlot **1996** £18.19 (BY) £23.99 (YOU)
Nuits-St-Georges Domaine de l'Arlot **1994** £19.92 (TW)
Nuits-St-Georges Bouchard Père **1996** £19.99 (BOT)
Nuits-St-Georges Robert Chevillon **1996** £18.50 (JU) £20.11 (WT)
Nuits-St-Georges Clos des Forêts St-Georges, Domaine de l'Arlot **1994** £19.78 (GOE) £23.10 (BY)
Nuits-St-Georges Clos de la Maréchale, Faiveley **1994** £19.25 (TAN) £21.00 (WRI)
Nuits-St-Georges les Damodes, Lescure **1996** £19.60 (PIP)
Nuits-St-Georges Faiveley **1995** £19.75 (DI)
Nuits-St-Georges les Fleurières, Jean-Jacques Confuron **1997** £19.50 (BAL) £22.33 (CAV)
Nuits-St-Georges les Hauts-Pruliers, Machard de Gramont **1997** £18.62 (CB)
Nuits-St-Georges les Pruliers, Gouges **1997** £18.40 (SOM) £25.30 (AV) £26.20 (TAN)
Nuits-St-Georges les Pruliers, Grivot **1995** £18.95 (SOM) £23.40 (RAE) £26.00 (BAL)
Pernand-Vergelesses Île de Vergelesses, Rollin **1995** £18.50 (RAE) £24.00 (JU)
Pommard Jean-Marc Boillot **1998** £19.29 (RAE)
Pommard Jean-Marc Boillot **1997** £19.09 (GOE)
Pommard Clos Blanc, Albert Grivault **1997** £18.00 (JU)
Pommard Clos des Épeneaux, Armand ½ bottle **1995** £19.39 (TW)
Pommard Coste-Caumartin **1993** £19.00 (JU)
Pommard les Épenots, Domaine Mussy **1994** £18.60 (SOM)
Pommard les Fremiers, Coste-Caumartin **1997** £18.50 (JU)
Pommard Parent **1992** £19.00 (CRO)
Pommard les Vignots, Coste-Caumartin **1996** £19.00 (JU)
Santenay Clos Tavannes, Gagnard **1995** £19.00 (JU)
Santenay les Passetemps, Faiveley **1988** £19.50 (JU)
Savigny-lès-Beaune Champs-Chevrey, Tollot-Beaut **1996** £19.97 (FA)
Savigny-lès-Beaune les Lavières, Ampeau **1988** £18.95 (LEA) £21.74 (REI)
Volnay Marquis d'Angerville **1996** £19.68 (CB) £21.00 (JU)
Volnay Jean-Marc Boillot **1997** £19.39 (DOM) £21.50 (LEA)
Volnay Carelle sous la Chapelle, Boillot **1994** £19.99 (RAE)
Volnay Clos d'Audignac, Domaine de la Pousse d'Or **1996** £19.97 (FA)
Volnay Michel Lafarge **1997** £19.25 (GAU)
Volnay Santenots Roger Belland **1997** £18.00 (WAT)

Volnay Taillepieds, Bouchard Père **1993** £19.25 (COC)
Vosne-Romanée les Brulées, Engel **1994** £19.95 (ROB)
Vosne-Romanée Champs Perdrix, Bruno Clair **1993** £19.90 (JU)
Vosne-Romanée Engel **1997** £18.11 (GOE) £19.20 (GAU) £21.50 (CON) £24.95 (RES) £25.00 (FORT)
Vosne-Romanée la Montagne, Clavelier **1997** £19.00 (SAV)
Vosne-Romanée Domaine Mugneret-Gibourg **1996** £18.80 (SAV) £19.95 (HAH) £19.95 (LEA)
Vosne-Romanée Rion **1996** £19.75 (SOM)

£20.00 → £22.49

Aloxe-Corton les Chaillots, Latour **1995** £20.03 (PLAY)
Aloxe-Corton les Fournières, Tollot-Beaut **1997** £20.56 (DOM) £23.00 (JU)
Auxey-Duresses les Ecusseaux, Ampeau **1985** £22.03 (REI)
Auxey-Duresses Roulot **1990** £20.56 (REI)
Beaune Bressandes, Henri Germain **1995** £21.95 (LEA)
Beaune Cent Vignes, Lois Dufouleur **1996** £20.70 (JER)
Beaune Clos du Roi, Ampeau **1984** £21.74 (REI) £22.50 (LEA)
Beaune Clos du Roi, Tollot-Beaut **1998** £20.56 (GOE)
Beaune Clos du Roi, Tollot-Beaut **1996** £22.27 (DOM)
Beaune Clos des Ursules, Jadot **1996** £22.08 (CAV)
Beaune Grèves, Tollot-Beaut **1997** £20.56 (DOM) £22.00 (JU) £22.95 (DI)
Beaune Grèves, Tollot-Beaut **1992** £21.19 (JON)
Beaune les Montrevenots, Jean-Marc Boillot **1998** £20.50 (LEA)
Beaune les Sizies, Michel Prunier **1996** £21.00 (JU)
Beaune Teurons, Jacques Germain **1997** £22.33 (DOM)
Beaune Teurons, Thévenin **1976** £21.74 (REI)
Blagny la Pièce sous le Bois, Matrot **1993** £20.86 (CB)
Chambolle-Musigny Beaux Bruns, Ghislaine Barthod-Noëllat **1996** £21.93 (RAE)
Chambolle-Musigny les Charmes, Hudelot-Noëllat **1997** £20.65 (SOM)
Chambolle-Musigny Confuron **1997** £20.95 (BAL)
Chambolle-Musigny Latour **1995** £20.71 (WY)
Chambolle-Musigny Domaine Roumier **1987** £21.95 (ROB)
Chambolle-Musigny les Véroilles, Bruno Clair **1996** £20.00 (JU)
Chambolle-Musigny Vieilles Vignes, Geantet-Pansiot **1996** £21.15 (DOM)
Chassagne-Montrachet Fontaine-Gagnard **1997** £20.65 (SOM)
Chassagne-Montrachet Morgeot, Jean Pillot **1996** £21.95 (NI)
Chassagne-Montrachet Morgeot, Ramonet **1996** £20.95 (RES)
Corton Latour **1992** £20.60 (TAN) £24.95 (POR)
Côte de Nuits-Villages Jayer-Gilles **1996** £22.00 (JU)
Gevrey-Chambertin Clos de la Justice, Pascal **1993** £21.75 (VIN)
Gevrey-Chambertin les Corbeaux, Domaine Boillot **1997** £21.54 (MON)
Gevrey-Chambertin Cuvée de l'Abeille, Ponsot **1993** £20.56 (CAV)
Gevrey-Chambertin Cuvée de la Fauvette, Ponsot **1994** £21.54 (GOE)
Gevrey-Chambertin Drouhin-Laroze **1996** £21.20 (HAH)
Gevrey-Chambertin Fourrier **1997** £20.95 (BAL)
Gevrey-Chambertin Hubert Lignier **1995** £21.93 (FA)
Gevrey-Chambertin Denis Mortet **1998** £21.35 (RAE)
Gevrey-Chambertin Vieilles Vignes, Alain Burguet **1996** £22.00 (JU)
Gevrey-Chambertin Vieilles Vignes, Alain Burguet **1995** £21.74 (REI)
Gevrey-Chambertin Vieilles Vignes, Marchand-Grillot **1996** £20.95 (LAY)
Gevry-Chambertin les Jeunes Rois, Geantet-Pansiot **1996** £21.15 (DOM)
Gevry-Chambertin Vieilles Vignes, Bachelet **1995** £21.74 (REI)
Hautes-Côtes de Nuits, Jayer-Gilles **1995** £20.00 (JU)
Monthélie sur la Velle, Château de Monthélie **1994** £21.00 (JU)

A key to name abbreviations is available on page 7.

Morey-St-Denis Clos des Lambrays, Domaine des Lambrays **1997** £20.35 (HAH) £36.75 (LEA)
Morey-St-Denis Hubert Lignier **1994** £20.95 (FA)
Morey-St-Denis en la Rue de Vergy, Bruno Clair **1995** £22.00 (JU)
Nuits-St-Georges Domaine de l'Arlot **1991** £21.00 (FLE)
Nuits-St-Georges Bouchard Père **1995** £20.95 (JER)
Nuits-St-Georges les Chaignots, Robert Chevillon **1997** £22.00 (JU) £26.02 (WT)
Nuits-St-Georges les Chaignots, Chopin-Groffier **1993** £21.74 (REI)
Nuits-St-Georges Robert Chevillon **1995** £21.00 (JU)
Nuits-St-Georges Clos de l'Arlot, Domaine de l'Arlot **1998** £22.03 (GOE)
Nuits-St-Georges Clos des Forêts St-Georges, Domaine de l'Arlot **1992** £20.56 (GOE) £31.50 (ROB)
Nuits-St-Georges Clos de la Maréchale, Faiveley **1992** £21.50 (CON)
Nuits-St-Georges Clos les Porets St-Georges, Gouges **1998** £22.03 (MON)
Nuits-St-Georges les Porets, Michelot **1995** £22.33 (DOM)
Nuits-St-Georges les Pruliers, Grivot **1996** £21.50 (SOM) £21.93 (RAE) £27.50 (BAL)
Nuits-St-Georges Richemone, Pernin-Rossin **1996** £21.50 (BAN)
Nuits-St-Georges les Roncières, Robert Chevillon **1997** £22.00 (JU) £26.02 (WT)
Nuits-St-Georges les St-Georges, Gouges **1997** £22.35 (SOM)
Nuits-St-Georges les Vaucrains, Jean Chauvenet **1994** £22.03 (GOE)
Nuits-St-Georges les Vaucrains, Gouges **1997** £22.35 (SOM) £28.40 (MON)
Pernand-Vergelesses Île de Vergelesses, Chandon de Briailles **1992** £20.00 (CRO) £22.91 (TW)
Pommard Ampeau **1992** £21.74 (REI) £23.95 (LEA)
Pommard les Bertins, Lescure **1995** £20.50 (PIP)
Pommard Clos des Boucherottes, Coste-Caumartin **1997** £20.50 (GW) £21.00 (JU)
Pommard Coste-Caumartin **1990** £22.00 (JU)
Pommard les Fremiers, Coste-Caumartin **1996** £21.00 (JU)
Pommard Pezerolles, Domaine de Montille **1992** £21.85 (HAH)
Pommard les Saucilles, Jean-Marc Boillot **1993** £21.50 (RAE)
Pommard les Vignots, Coste-Caumartin **1994** £21.00 (JU)
Santenay Clos Tavannes, Domaine de la Pousse d'Or **1992** £20.56 (TW)
Savigny-lès-Beaune les Vergelesses, Bize **1995** £20.60 (AD) £28.79 (TW)
Volnay Marquis d'Angerville **1997** £20.00 (JU)
Volnay Jean-Marc Boillot **1996** £20.95 (LEA)
Volnay les Caillerets, Domaine de la Pousse d'Or **1992** £20.95 (CON) £22.95 (DI) £26.95 (RES)
Volnay Carelle sous la Chapelle, Boillot **1996** £21.64 (RAE)
Volnay Darviot Perrin **1995** £21.74 (TW)
Volnay Frémiets, Marquis d'Angerville **1996** £21.62 (CB) £27.32 (FA)
Volnay Michel Lafarge **1995** £20.07 (GOE) £28.40 (RAE)
Volnay Santenots Pierre Boillot **1993** £22.03 (SAV)
Volnay Santenots Matrot **1993** £21.50 (ELL)
Volnay Vendange Selectionée, Lafarge **1995** £21.74 (REI) £23.50 (HAH) £33.49 (TW)
Vosne-Romanée les Brulées, Engel **1997** £21.05 (GOE) £24.95 (CON) £26.50 (YOU)
Vosne-Romanée les Brulées, Engel **1996** £21.75 (CON) £28.79 (TW) £28.79 (REI)
Vosne-Romanée Champs Perdrix, Bruno Clair **1997** £22.00 (JU)
Vosne-Romanée Michel Gros **1997** £20.95 (TAN)
Vosne-Romanée Domaine Mugneret-Gibourg **1998** £20.95 (LEA)
Vosne-Romanée Rion **1997** £20.00 (WS)
Vosne-Romanée les Suchots, Hudelot-Noëllat **1997** £20.65 (SOM)
Vosne-Romanée les Violettes, Georges Clerget **1996** £22.03 (PLA)

£22.50 → £24.99

Beaune Champs Pimonts, Lois Dufouleur **1996** £24.95 (VIN)
Beaune Clos du Roi, Ampeau **1987** £22.91 (REI)
Beaune Clos des Ursules, Jadot **1995** £23.99 (CAV) £25.26 (REI)
Beaune Épenottes, Domaine Boillot **1998** £23.25 (LEA)
Beaune Vignes Franches, François Germain **1996** £24.68 (DOM)

Blagny la Pièce sous le Bois, Matrot **1996** £24.26 (CB)
Chambolle-Musigny Beaux Bruns, Ghislaine Barthod-Noëllat **1997** £23.99 (GOE)
Chambolle-Musigny Beaux Bruns, Ghislaine Barthod-Noëllat **1994** £22.91 (GOE) £23.60 (RAE)
Chambolle-Musigny les Charmes, Hudelot-Noëllat **1990** £24.25 (SOM)
Chambolle-Musigny Clos du Village Domaine Guyon **1993** £23.65 (FRI)
Chambolle-Musigny les Cras, Ghislaine Barthod-Noellat **1994** £23.60 (RAE)
Chambolle-Musigny Ponnelle **1997** £23.00 (AV)
Chambolle-Musigny les Veroilles, Ghislaine Barthod-Noëllat **1994** £22.91 (GOE) £27.00 (JU)
Chassagne-Montrachet Latour **1993** £24.85 (WY)
Chassagne-Montrachet la Maltroie, Amiot **1997** £22.75 (LEA)
Chassagne-Montrachet Morgeot, Ramonet **1997** £22.95 (RES)
Corton Pougets, Jadot **1995** £23.40 (FA) £28.89 (GOE)
Côte de Nuits-Villages Jayer-Gilles **1995** £23.00 (JU)
Échézeaux Engel **1997** £24.67 (GOE) £31.50 (CON)
Gevrey-Chambertin Clos Prieur, Rossignol-Trapet **1993** £23.94 (PIP) £33.84 (TW)
Gevrey-Chambertin Lavaux-St-Jacques, Maume **1998** £24.87 (RAE)
Gevrey-Chambertin Hubert Lignier **1996** £22.91 (FA)
Gevrey-Chambertin Armand Rousseau **1996** £24.00 (JU) £29.75 (WAI)

Gevrey-Chambertin au Vellé, Denis Mortet **1993** £22.95 (RAE)
Gevrey-Chambertin Vieilles Vignes, Charlopin-Parizot **1997** £24.50 (LEA)
Gevrey-Chambertin Vieilles Vignes, Dugat-Py **1995** £24.50 (ROB)
Mazis-Chambertin Frédéric Esmonin **1997** £23.00 (BAN) £25.99 (SOM)
Monthélie sur la Velle, Château de Monthélie **1995** £24.00 (JU)
Morey-St-Denis Clos de la Bussière, Domaine Roumier **1997** £23.40 (TAN) £25.85 (FA)
Morey-St-Denis Clos des Ormes, Georges Lignier **1992** £23.25 (PLA)
Morey-St-Denis Hubert Lignier **1996** £22.91 (FA)
Morey-St-Denis en la Rue de Vergy, Domaine Henri Perrot-Minot **1997** £22.65 (CON)
Nuits-St-Georges Domaine de l'Arlot **1993** £22.50 (CRO)
Nuits-St-Georges les Boudots, Grivot **1996** £23.25 (SOM) £23.40 (RAE) £34.66 (FA)
Nuits-St-Georges les Boudots, Grivot **1995** £23.40 (RAE)
Nuits-St-Georges Aux Bousselots, Jean Chauvenet **1995** £24.48 (GOE)
Nuits-St-Georges les Chaignots, Robert Chevillon **1995** £24.87 (FA) £27.00 (JU)
Nuits-St-Georges les Chaignots, Faiveley **1993** £23.00 (DI) £27.00 (WS) £28.40 (HAH)
Nuits-St-Georges les Chaignots, Mugneret-Gibourg **1996** £24.48 (SAV)
Nuits-St-Georges Clos des Forêts St-Georges, Domaine de l'Arlot **1998** £23.99 (GOE)
Nuits-St-Georges Clos des Forêts St-Georges, Domaine de l'Arlot **1988** £23.50 (GOE) £28.32 (BY)
Nuits-St-Georges les Damodes, Jean Chauvenet **1997** £23.50 (GOE)
Nuits-St-Georges les Damodes, Jean Chauvenet **1996** £22.82 (RAE)
Nuits-St-Georges les Damodes, Jean Chauvenet **1993** £24.95 (RAE)
Nuits-St-Georges Drouhin **1996** £24.85 (WY)
Nuits-St-Georges Jadot **1992** £22.99 (YOU)
Nuits-St-Georges les Perrières, Jean Chauvenet **1998** £24.28 (RAE)
Nuits-St-Georges les Perrières, Jean Chauvenet **1993** £24.95 (RAE)
Nuits-St-Georges les Perrières, Robert Chevillon **1997** £23.00 (JU) £26.02 (WT) £28.79 (REI)
Nuits-St-Georges les Perrières, Robert Chevillon **1992** £24.99 (YOU) £47.20 (UB)

Nuits-St-Georges les Porets, Michelot **1996** £22.91 (DOM)
Nuits-St-Georges les Porets St-Georges, Faiveley **1992** £22.99 (POR)
Nuits-St-Georges les Pruliers, Lucien Boillot **1997** £22.52 (MON)
Nuits-St-Georges les Pruliers, Grivot **1997** £24.50 (SOM) £29.95 (BAL)
Nuits-St-Georges les Roncières, Robert Chevillon **1995** £23.40 (FA) £27.00 (JU)
Nuits-St-Georges les Roncières, Robert Chevillon **1994** £23.00 (JU) £28.79 (TW)
Nuits-St-Georges les St-Georges, Gouges **1996** £22.85 (SOM)
Pommard Jean-Marc Boillot **1993** £23.95 (ROB)
Pommard Clos des Boucherottes, Coste-Caumartin **1996** £24.00 (JU)
Pommard les Jarollières, Jean-Marc Boillot **1996** £24.48 (GOE) £32.31 (DOM)
Pommard les Jarollières, Jean-Marc Boillot **1991** £23.95 (RAE)
Pommard les Vignots, Coste-Caumartin **1995** £23.00 (JU)
Ruchottes-Chambertin Frédéric Esmonin **1997** £23.00 (BAN)
Savigny-lès-Beaune la Dominode, Bruno Clair **1994** £23.00 (JU) £29.00 (CRO)
Savigny-lès-Beaune aux Grands Liards, Bize **1995** £22.91 (TW)
Savigny-lès-Beaune les Vergelesses, Bize **1994** £23.26 (TW)
Volnay Marquis d'Angerville **1994** £23.95 (ROB)
Volnay les Caillerets, Henri Boillot **1997** £23.99 (CAV)
Volnay les Caillerets Cuvée Carnot, Bouchard Père **1996** £23.56 (COC)
Volnay les Caillerets, Domaine de la Pousse d'Or **1995** £22.50 (GAU) £25.50 (CON) £25.95 (GOE)
Volnay les Caillerets, Domaine de la Pousse d'Or **1993** £23.93 (CON) £44.00 (PHI)
Volnay Carelle sous la Chapelle, Boillot **1998** £23.70 (RAE)
Volnay Champans, Marquis d'Angerville **1987** £23.32 (REI) £32.95 (RES)

Please remember that
Oz Clarke's Wine Buying Guide
*is a price **guide** and not a price **list**. It is not meant to replace up-to-date merchants' lists.*

Volnay Clos d'Audignac, Domaine de la Pousse d'Or **1995** £23.95 (CON)
Volnay Clos des Chênes, Domaine Guyon **1993** £24.99 (FRI)
Volnay Darviot Perrin **1996** £22.91 (TW)
Volnay Santenots Matrot **1996** £24.26 (CB)
Volnay Vendange Selectionée, Lafarge **1996** £22.50 (CON) £23.95 (HAH)
Vosne-Romanée les Brulées, Engel **1998** £24.97 (GOE)
Vosne-Romanée les Brulées, Engel **1993** £24.87 (FA)
Vosne-Romanée Champs Perdrix, Bruno Clair **1996** £24.00 (JU)
Vosne-Romanée Confuron-Cotétidot **1998** £22.50 (LEA)
Vosne-Romanée Rion **1995** £23.32 (REI) £30.75 (FA)

£25.00 → £27.49

Auxey-Duresses les Ecusseaux, Ampeau **1990** £26.40 (CHA)
Beaune Clos du Roi, Ampeau **1990** £26.40 (CHA)
Beaune Clos du Roi, Tollot-Beaut **1993** £25.00 (WS)
Beaune Épenottes, Domaine Boillot **1997** £25.50 (LEA)
Beaune Épenottes, Parent **1985** £25.26 (REI)
Chambolle-Musigny Beaux Bruns, Ghislaine Barthod-Noëllat **1998** £25.75 (RAE)
Chambolle-Musigny les Charmes, Ghislaine Barthod-Noëllat **1994** £27.00 (RAE)
Chambolle-Musigny Clos du Village Domaine Guyon **1996** £25.99 (FRI)
Chambolle-Musigny la Combe d'Orveaux, Clavelier **1997** £25.95 (SAV)
Chambolle-Musigny la Combe d'Orveaux, Grivot **1996** £25.95 (LAY)
Chambolle-Musigny les Cras, Ghislaine Barthod-Noellat **1998** £26.93 (RAE)
Chambolle-Musigny les Feusselottes, Georges Mugneret **1996** £26.93 (SAV)
Chambolle-Musigny les Feusselottes, Georges Mugneret **1994** £25.95 (LEA)
Chambolle-Musigny Domaine Roumier **1998** £26.44 (REI)
Chambolle-Musigny les Veroilles, Ghislaine Barthod-Noëllat **1997** £27.00 (JU) £34.66 (REI)
Charmes-Chambertin Armand Rousseau **1994** £26.93 (GOE) £59.00 (UB)
Corton-Bressandes Dubreuil-Fontaine **1992** £26.95 (RES)

Corton Clos de la Vigne au Saint, Latour **1993** £25.94 (HA) £27.61 (WY) £28.00 (WRI)
Corton Grancey, Latour **1995** £26.99 (MAJ) £32.99 (WY) £34.50 (STA) £35.00 (FORT)
Corton Maréchaudes, Chandon de Briailles **1996** £26.40 (HAH) £28.79 (REI) £30.75 (FA)
Corton Pougets, Jadot **1996** £27.32 (FA) £32.31 (REI)
Corton Tollot-Beaut **1996** £26.34 (RAE) £34.27 (GOE)
Gevrey-Chambertin Champeaux, Denis Mortet **1992** £25.50 (RAE)
Gevrey-Chambertin Clos de Fonteny, Bruno Clair **1996** £27.00 (JU)
Gevrey-Chambertin Denis Mortet **1995** £26.00 (JU) £29.38 (CAV)
Gevrey-Chambertin au Vellé, Denis Mortet **1997** £25.00 (JU) £25.85 (DOM) £27.00 (TAN) £33.29 (CAV)
Gevrey-Chambertin Vieilles Vignes, Charlopin-Parizot **1996** £25.50 (LEA)
Griotte-Chambertin Ponsot **1994** £25.85 (FA) £44.06 (CAV) £45.00 (BAL)
Morey-St-Denis Clos de la Bussière, Domaine Roumier **1995** £26.50 (ROB) £29.77 (FA)
Morey-St-Denis Dujac **1995** £25.00 (FORT) £29.75 (STA) £35.99 (UB)
Nuits-St-Georges les Boudots, Grivot **1994** £25.50 (RAE)
Nuits-St-Georges les Cailles, Robert Chevillon **1994** £27.00 (JU)
Nuits-St-Georges les Chaignots, Mugneret-Gibourg **1998** £26.95 (LEA)
Nuits-St-Georges Clos des Forêts St-Georges, Domaine de l'Arlot **1996** £26.93 (GOE) £30.07 (BY)
Nuits-St-Georges Clos des Forêts St-Georges, Domaine de l'Arlot **1995** £25.00 (FLE) £25.56 (BY) £32.50 (LAY)
Nuits-St-Georges Clos des Porets, Gouges **1997** £26.00 (WS)
Nuits-St-Georges aux Cras, Clavelier **1997** £27.22 (SAV)
Nuits-St-Georges les Perrières, Robert Chevillon **1996** £26.00 (JU)
Nuits-St-Georges les Pruliers, Grivot **1998** £25.75 (RAE) £27.42 (GOE)
Nuits-St-Georges les Vaucrains, Jean Chauvenet **1993** £26.95 (RAE)
Pommard Ampeau **1988** £26.44 (REI)
Pommard Clos des Boucherottes, Coste-Caumartin **1994** £27.00 (JU)
Pommard Clos des Épeneaux, Armand **1994** £25.95 (LEA) £29.00 (MV) £35.01 (TW)
Pommard les Fremiers, Coste-Caumartin **1993** £25.00 (JU)
Pommard les Jarollières, Domaine de la Pousse d'Or **1995** £26.90 (GAU) £32.95 (ROB) £38.19 (TW)
Pommard les Jarollières, Domaine de la Pousse d'Or **1994** £26.95 (DI)
Pommard Pezerolles, Domaine de Montille **1994** £25.20 (HAH)
Savigny-lès-Beaune Ampeau **1990** £26.40 (CHA)
Savigny-lès-Beaune la Dominode, Pavelot **1995** £26.25 (FORT)
Savigny-lès-Beaune les Serpentières, Drouhin **1985** £26.44 (REI)
Volnay 1er Cru, Michel Lafarge **1995** £25.73 (TW) £26.95 (CON) £28.40 (RAE)
Volnay les Caillerets, Clos des 60 Ouvrées, Domaine de la Pousse d'Or **1996** £25.50 (CON) £26.83 (FA) £30.50 (ROB) £32.00 (WAI) £37.07 (TW)
Volnay les Caillerets, Domaine de la Pousse d'Or **1994** £26.50 (BER)
Volnay les Caillerets, Domaine de la Pousse d'Or **1983** £26.44 (REI)
Volnay Champans, Marquis d'Angerville **1997** £25.56 (CB) £27.00 (JU) £28.30 (FA)
Volnay Champans, Marquis d'Angerville **1996** £25.56 (CB) £30.75 (FA)
Volnay Clos des Chênes, Domaine Guyon **1996** £26.99 (FRI)
Volnay Clos des Ducs, Marquis d'Angerville **1994** £27.00 (JU) £29.95 (ROB)
Volnay Cuvée Général Muteau, Hospices de Beaune **1996** £25.46 (RAE)
Volnay Frémiets, Marquis d'Angerville **1993** £27.00 (JU)
Volnay la Gigotte, Darviot-Perrin **1996** £25.26 (TW)
Volnay Santenots Ampeau **1990** £26.40 (CHA)
Volnay Santenots Lafon **1994** £27.03 (FLE)
Volnay Taillepieds, Marquis d'Angerville **1994** £25.00 (JU)
Vosne-Romanée les Beaux Monts, Clavelier **1997** £27.22 (SAV)
Vosne-Romanée les Beaux Monts, Domaine Jean Grivot **1997** £26.35 (SOM)
Vosne-Romanée les Brulées, Clavelier **1997** £25.95 (SAV)
Vosne-Romanée Cacheux **1996** £25.95 (PHI)

Vosne-Romanée Champs Perdrix, Bruno Clair **1995** £27.00 (JU)
Vosne-Romanée Remoissenet **1997** £26.75 (AV)
Vosne-Romanée les Suchots, Domaine de l'Arlot **1998** £26.93 (GOE)

£27.50 → £29.99

Aloxe-Corton Tollot-Beaut **1991** £27.61 (REI)
Beaune Clos des Mouches, Chanson **1992** £29.95 (DI)
Beaune Clos des Mouches, Drouhin **1996** £27.85 (NI) £37.50 (UB)
Beaune Clos des Ursules, Jadot **1970** £28.50 (YOU)
Beaune Hospices de Beaune, Rolin **1996** £28.89 (CAV)
Blagny la Pièce sous le Bois, Matrot **1991** £29.38 (TW)
Chambolle-Musigny les Cras, Ghislaine Barthod-Noellat **1990** £28.79 (FA)
Chambolle-Musigny les Feusselottes, Georges Mugneret **1998** £28.95 (LEA)
Chambolle-Musigny Jadot **1984** £28.79 (REI)
Chambolle-Musigny Georges Lignier **1983** £28.00 (CRO)
Chambolle-Musigny de Vogüé **1996** £29.95 (DI) £34.27 (CAV) £36.62 (FA)
Charmes-Chambertin Perrot-Minot **1995** £27.95 (CON) £29.15 (WAT)
Clos de Vougeot Grivot **1991** £28.95 (SOM)
Clos de Vougeot Mongeard-Mugneret **1991** £29.38 (CAV)
Clos de Vougeot Roumier **1992** £28.99 (GW)
Corton-Bressandes Chandon de Briailles **1996** £28.70 (TAN) £33.49 (REI)
Corton-Bressandes Comte Senard **1992** £27.95 (ROB)
Corton Clos des Meix, Comte Senard **1988** £28.50 (ROB)
Corton Clos du Roi, Dubreuil-Fontaine **1993** £27.81 (BY)
Corton Grancey, Latour **1993** £27.90 (TAN) £31.06 (WY) £33.50 (PLAY) £34.95 (ROB)
Corton Grancey, Latour **1992** £29.50 (ROB) £30.39 (JON)
Corton le Rognet, Chevalier **1993** £27.97 (GW)
Corton Tollot-Beaut **1998** £27.81 (RAE) £30.84 (GOE)
Échézeaux Engel **1996** £29.50 (CON) £29.95 (SOM) £39.36 (TW)
Échézeaux Lamarche **1997** £27.75 (SOM) £30.45 (GOE)
Gevrey-Chambertin Champeaux, Denis Mortet **1994** £27.95 (RAE)
Gevrey-Chambertin Clos St-Jacques, Fourrier **1995** £29.50 (BAL)
Gevrey-Chambertin Vieilles Vignes, Alain Burguet **1993** £29.00 (JU)
Gevrey-Chambertin Vieilles Vignes, Dugat-Py **1998** £27.50 (LEA)
Mazis-Chambertin Maume **1991** £29.95 (RAE)
Nuits-St-Georges les Argillières, Dubois **1996** £27.75 (VIN)
Nuits-St-Georges Domaine de l'Arlot **1988** £28.89 (CAV)
Nuits-St-Georges les Boudots, Grivot **1998** £27.81 (RAE)
Nuits-St-Georges Aux Bousselots, Jean Chauvenet **1993** £28.20 (GOE)
Nuits-St-Georges les Cailles, Robert Chevillon **1997** £29.95 (PHI)
Nuits-St-Georges les Chaignots, Michelot **1993** £28.00 (CRO)
Nuits-St-Georges Clos des Forêts St-Georges, Domaine de l'Arlot **1993** £27.81 (BY) £30.90 (RIP) £41.13 (TW)
Nuits-St-Georges Clos les Porets St-Georges, Gouges **1986** £28.79 (REI)
Nuits-St-Georges Méo-Camuzet **1994** £27.50 (BER)
Nuits-St-Georges les Porets St-Georges, Faiveley **1996** £29.10 (HAH)
Nuits-St-Georges les Vaucrains, Robert Chevillon **1997** £27.50 (FORT) £29.95 (WT)
Nuits-St-Georges les Vaucrains, Robert Chevillon **1994** £28.00 (JU)
Pommard Boigelot **1990** £29.95 (ROB)
Pommard Clos des Boucherottes, Coste-Caumartin **1995** £28.00 (JU)
Pommard Clos des Épeneaux, Armand **1995** £29.95 (LEA) £30.00 (CON) £37.01 (TW)
Pommard Grand Clos des Épenots, Domaine de Courcel **1998** £29.95 (LEA)
Pommard Grand Clos des Épenots, Domaine de Courcel **1996** £28.95 (RES)
Pommard les Jarollières, Domaine de la Pousse d'Or **1996** £28.79 (FA) £28.89 (GOE) £33.95 (ROB) £40.89 (TW)
Pommard les Jarollières, Domaine de la Pousse d'Or **1993** £29.00 (WS)
Pommard les Saucilles, Jean-Marc Boillot **1996** £28.79 (DOM)

Savigny-lès-Beaune Marconnets, Bize **1992** £28.79 (TW)
Volnay 1er Cru, Michel Lafarge **1997** £28.95 (GAU)
Volnay les Caillerets, Marquis d'Angerville **1995** £28.00 (JU)
Volnay les Caillerets, Clos des 60 Ouvrées, Domaine de la Pousse d'Or **1995** £27.95 (CON) £29.77 (FA)
Volnay les Caillerets, Clos des 60 Ouvrées, Domaine de la Pousse d'Or **1983** £28.79 (REI)
Volnay Champans, Marquis d'Angerville **1993** £29.00 (JU)
Volnay Clos de la Bousse d'Or, Domaine de la Pousse d'Or **1996** £28.95 (CON) £32.70 (FA) £41.77 (TW)
Volnay la Gigotte, Darviot-Perrin **1992** £29.20 (HA)
Volnay Vendange Selectionée, Lafarge **1994** £28.79 (TW)
Vosne-Romanée Bertrand de la Bussière **1978** £27.50 (BU)
Vosne-Romanée Clos de la Fontaine, Michel Gros **1993** £28.00 (JU)
Vosne-Romanée Gros Frère et Soeur **1988** £29.50 (BAL)
Vosne-Romanée les Malconsorts, Lamarche **1998** £28.10 (RAE) £28.89 (GOE)
Vosne-Romanée les Malconsorts, Lamarche **1996** £27.80 (RAE)
Vosne-Romanée Méo-Camuzet **1994** £27.75 (BER)

£30.00 → £34.99

Beaune Clos des Mouches, Drouhin **1997** £30.00 (WS) £32.95 (BEN)
Beaune Clos des Ursules, Jadot **1993** £31.95 (ROB)
Beaune Cuvée Maurice Drouhin, Hospices de Beaune **1996** £31.50 (BEN)
Beaune Grèves, Michel Lafarge **1996** £33.78 (GOE)
Beaune Grèves, Michel Lafarge **1993** £32.31 (REI) £33.78 (GOE) £37.50 (RAE)
Beaune Grèves, Michel Lafarge **1992** £34.50 (RAE) £39.89 (TW)

- *All prices for each wine are listed together in ascending order.*
- *Price bands refer to the lowest price for which the wine is available.*

Beaune Grèves Vigne de l'Enfant Jesus, Bouchard Père **1996** £34.00 (BAL)
Beaune Grèves Vigne de l'Enfant Jesus, Bouchard Père **1971** £32.70 (FA)
Beaune Teurons, Leroy **1980** £32.00 (JU)
Bonnes-Mares Roumier **1994** £34.52 (GW)
Bonnes-Mares de Vogüé **1987** £32.70 (FA) £38.19 (REI)
Chambertin Trapet **1983** £33.49 (REI)
Chambolle-Musigny les Cras, Roumier **1995** £34.15 (HAH)
Chambolle-Musigny les Fuées, Ghislaine Barthod-Noëllat **1994** £32.00 (JU)
Chambolle-Musigny de Vogüé **1997** £30.75 (FA) £35.00 (DI) £36.23 (GOE) £38.68 (CAV) £55.81 (CAV) £56.00 (DI)
Charmes-Chambertin Perrot-Minot **1996** £30.85 (WAT) £33.50 (CON)
Charmes-Chambertin Domaine Henri Rebourseau **1997** £32.75 (SOM)
Charmes-Chambertin Domaine des Varoilles **1972** £34.66 (REI)
Clos St-Denis Georges Lignier **1988** £33.68 (FA)
Clos de Vougeot Grivot **1997** £31.40 (SOM) £36.62 (FA) £42.00 (BAL)
Clos de Vougeot Grivot **1996** £30.75 (SOM) £42.50 (FA) £53.85 (GOE)
Clos de Vougeot Hudelot-Noëllat **1996** £34.50 (SOM)
Clos de Vougeot Musigni, Gros Frère et Soeur **1995** £34.66 (FA)
Clos de Vougeot Roumier **1997** £33.50 (GW)
Corton Bouchard Père **1995** £30.00 (COC)
Corton Bouchard Père **1971** £34.66 (FA)
Corton-Bressandes Chandon de Briailles **1997** £30.50 (TAN) £32.20 (HAH) £32.50 (LEA)
Corton-Bressandes Chandon de Briailles **1993** £33.49 (REI)
Corton-Bressandes Tollot-Beaut **1996** £33.89 (JON) £34.27 (GOE)
Corton Clos des Cortons, Faiveley **1991** £30.70 (FLE)
Corton Clos du Roi, Chandon de Briailles **1998** £33.95 (LEA)
Corton Clos de la Vigne au Saint, Latour **1989** £33.14 (WY)
Corton Grancey, Latour **1996** £32.79 (WY)
Corton Perrières, Juillot **1996** £30.55 (DOM)
Corton Tollot-Beaut **1997** £30.35 (GOE)

Corton Tollot-Beaut **1995** £32.31 (DOM)
Échézeaux Lamarche **1998** £32.51 (RAE)
Échézeaux Mongeard-Mugneret **1993** £34.95 (ROB)
Gevrey-Chambertin Cazetiers, Bruno Clair **1994** £32.00 (JU)
Gevrey-Chambertin Cazetiers, Armand Rousseau **1997** £32.31 (REI) £40.00 (FORT)
Gevrey-Chambertin Cazetiers, Armand Rousseau **1994** £30.00 (WS) £41.13 (REI)
Gevrey-Chambertin Champeaux, Denis Mortet **1998** £34.56 (RAE)
Gevrey-Chambertin Clos de Fonteny, Bruno Clair **1997** £30.00 (JU)
Gevrey-Chambertin Coeur du Roy, Dugat-Py **1997** £30.60 (NI)
Gevrey-Chambertin les Corbeaux, Bachelet **1996** £32.95 (ROB)
Gevrey-Chambertin Lavaux-St-Jacques, Maume **1997** £32.00 (BAL)
Gevrey-Chambertin Denis Mortet **1996** £30.25 (CAV)
Gevrey-Chambertin au Vellé, Denis Mortet **1995** £31.00 (JU)
Gevrey-Chambertin Vieilles Vignes, Alain Burguet **1992** £30.32 (TW)
Grands-Échézeaux Thénard **1987** £33.49 (REI)
Mazis-Chambertin Maume **1996** £33.68 (RAE) £43.00 (BAL)
Morey-St-Denis 1er Cru, Faiveley **1990** £34.66 (REI)
Morey-St-Denis 1er Cru, Ponsot **1995** £31.95 (ROB)
Morey-St-Denis Dujac **1996** £31.95 (ROB)
Morey-St-Denis Dujac **1990** £30.75 (FA)
Nuits-St-Georges Bouchard Père **1962** £31.50 (YOU)
Nuits-St-Georges Clos de l'Arlot, Domaine de l'Arlot **1991** £33.78 (TW)
Nuits-St-Georges Gouges **1988** £30.00 (RES)
Nuits-St-Georges les Perrières, Robert Chevillon **1993** £32.95 (ROB)
Nuits-St-Georges les Porets St-Georges, Faiveley **1990** £34.66 (REI)

- *Wines are listed in A–Z order within each price band.*
- *For each wine, vintages are listed in descending order.*
- *Each vintage of any wine appears only once.*

Nuits-St-Georges les St-Georges, Robert Chevillon **1997** £30.64 (WT)
Nuits-St-Georges les St-Georges, Gouges **1998** £31.33 (MON)
Nuits-St-Georges Vignes Rondes, Rion **1996** £33.95 (ROB)
Nuits-St-Georges Vignes Rondes, Rion **1995** £33.00 (MV)
Nuits-St-Georges Georges & Henri Jayer **1997** £33.00 (JU)
Pommard Clos des Épeneaux, Armand **1998** £32.95 (LEA)
Pommard Clos des Épeneaux, Armand **1996** £32.50 (CON) £36.50 (WRI) £39.83 (TW)
Pommard les Épenots, Armand **1998** £32.95 (GAU)
Pommard les Épenots, Armand **1995** £32.70 (FA)
Pommard les Jarollières, Jean-Marc Boillot **1998** £30.26 (GOE) £30.75 (RAE)
Pommard Rugiens, Domaine de Courcel **1997** £30.95 (LEA) £39.95 (RES)
Ruchottes-Chambertin Domaine Mugneret **1997** £34.50 (BAN)
Savigny-lès-Beaune les Lavières, Ampeau **1978** £32.31 (REI)
La Tâche Domaine de la Romanée-Conti **1966** £31.33 (FA)
Volnay 1er Cru, Michel Lafarge **1996** £30.00 (CON)
Volnay les Caillerets, Marquis d'Angerville **1996** £32.00 (JU)
Volnay les Caillerets, Clos des 60 Ouvrées, Domaine de la Pousse d'Or **1989** £33.19 (FA)
Volnay les Caillerets, Domaine de la Pousse d'Or **1991** £34.66 (TW)
Volnay les Caillerets, Domaine de la Pousse d'Or **1990** £34.66 (FA)
Volnay Champans, Marquis d'Angerville **1995** £30.75 (FA)
Volnay Clos de la Bousse d'Or, Domaine de la Pousse d'Or **1995** £30.75 (FA) £33.78 (GOE) £35.50 (ROB) £40.54 (TW)
Volnay Clos du Château des Ducs, Lafarge **1995** £34.66 (REI)
Volnay Clos des Chênes, Michel Lafarge **1994** £34.95 (RAE) £42.18 (TW)
Volnay Clos des Chênes, Michel Lafarge **1991** £34.95 (RAE) £41.40 (RIP)
Volnay Clos des Santenots, Prieur **1997** £34.99 (YOU)
Volnay Frémiets, Marquis d'Angerville **1995** £30.26 (FA)

Volnay Santenots Lafon **1996** £30.55 (DOM) £34.66 (FA) £36.00 (YOU)
Volnay Taillepieds, Marquis d'Angerville **1998** £30.35 (MON)
Volnay Taillepieds, Marquis d'Angerville **1997** £31.72 (FA)
Volnay Vendange Selectionée, Lafarge **1992** £31.14 (TW)
Vosne-Romanée les Beaux Monts, Clavelier **1995** £31.29 (NI)
Vosne-Romanée les Beaux Monts, Domaine Rion **1995** £31.28 (FLE)
Vosne-Romanée Cacheux **1990** £31.00 (CRO)
Vosne-Romanée les Chaumes, Arnoux **1997** £33.78 (MON)
Vosne-Romanée les Chaumes, Jean Tardy **1992** £34.95 (RES)
Vosne-Romanée Méo-Camuzet **1997** £32.00 (TAN)
Vosne-Romanée Rion **1993** £30.26 (FA)
Vosne-Romanée Rouget **1998** £31.14 (GOE) £33.68 (RAE)
Vosne-Romanée les Suchots, Hudelot-Noëllat **1995** £31.50 (ROB)

£35.00 → £39.99

Beaune Clos des Mouches, Drouhin **1995** £38.00 (CRO)
Beaune Clos des Mouches, Drouhin **1972** £38.19 (REI)
Beaune Grèves, Michel Lafarge **1990** £39.99 (RAE)
Bonnes-Mares de Vogüé **1992** £36.62 (FA) £59.00 (DI) £72.65 (RAE)
Chambolle-Musigny les Cras, Roumier **1996** £35.64 (FA)
Chambolle-Musigny les Veroilles, Ghislaine Barthod-Noëllat **1995** £35.00 (JU)
Chambolle-Musigny de Vogüé **1995** £38.58 (FA) £39.50 (BAL) £80.00 (ROB)
Chambolle-Musigny les Charmes, Christian Clerget **1997** £38.19 (PLAY)
Charmes-Chambertin Armand Rousseau **1997** £35.64 (FA) £38.35 (TAN) £41.13 (REI)
Charmes-Chambertin Armand Rousseau **1982** £36.62 (FA)
Clos de la Roche Armand Rousseau **1997** £35.64 (FA) £41.25 (TAN) £44.06 (REI) £55.00 (FORT)
Clos de la Roche Armand Rousseau **1996** £39.56 (FA) £49.75 (WAI) £51.11 (REI) £55.50 (BEN)
Clos de Tart Mommessin **1993** £39.75 (WAI)
Clos de Vougeot Drouhin **1985** £36.50 (ROB)
Clos de Vougeot Engel **1997** £38.68 (GOE) £46.50 (CON) £47.50 (FORT)
Clos de Vougeot Méo-Camuzet **1994** £36.72 (GOE) £42.00 (RAE)
Clos de Vougeot Denis Mortet **1994** £39.95 (RAE)
Clos de Vougeot Musigni, Gros Frère et Soeur **1993** £38.58 (FA)
Corton Bonneau du Martray **1997** £39.00 (JU)
Corton Bouchard Père **1996** £37.50 (BAL)
Corton-Bressandes Chandon de Briailles **1995** £35.25 (SAV)
Corton-Bressandes Tollot-Beaut **1997** £35.64 (FA) £39.00 (JU)
Corton Grancey, Latour **1988** £37.00 (YOU)
Corton Maréchaudes, Chandon de Briailles **1997** £35.95 (RES)
Corton Pougets, Jadot **1997** £38.19 (REI)
Échézeaux Engel **1998** £37.01 (REI)
Échézeaux Mugneret **1998** £39.95 (LEA)
Gevrey-Chambertin Cazetiers, Bruno Clair **1997** £38.80 (TAN)
Gevrey-Chambertin Clos de Fonteny, Bruno Clair **1995** £35.00 (JU)
Gevrey-Chambertin Clos St-Jacques, Bruno Clair **1993** £39.00 (JU)
Gevrey-Chambertin la Combe aux Moines, Faiveley **1995** £35.00 (POR)
Gevrey-Chambertin Lavaux-St-Jacques, Dugat-Py **1997** £39.60 (NI)
Gevrey-Chambertin au Vellé, Denis Mortet **1994** £35.00 (RES)
Latricières-Chambertin Faiveley **1995** £38.95 (DI)
Latricières-Chambertin Faiveley **1992** £39.00 (WRI)
Latricières-Chambertin Ponsot **1992** £38.19 (REI) £48.47 (GOE)
Latricières-Chambertin Trapet **1995** £39.80 (HA) £40.54 (FA)
Mazis-Chambertin Armand Rousseau **1997** £38.35 (TAN)
Morey-St-Denis Clos des Lambrays, Domaine des Lambrays **1996** £39.50 (LEA) £40.70 (HAH)
Nuits-St-Georges les Boudots, Méo-Camuzet **1994** £35.64 (FA)
Nuits-St-Georges Clos des Argillières, Rion **1995** £39.50 (ROB)

Nuits-St-Georges Haut-Poiret, Jayer-Gilles **1997** £35.00 (JU)
Nuits-St-Georges les Murgers, Méo-Camuzet **1994** £35.64 (FA) £47.85 (BER)
Pommard Clos des Épeneaux, Armand **1997** £35.50 (LEA)
Richebourg Domaine de la Romanée-Conti **1975** £35.25 (FA)
Ruchottes-Chambertin Clos des Ruchottes, Armand Rousseau **1994** £39.95 (STE)
Ruchottes-Chambertin Armand Rousseau **1997** £36.62 (FA) £36.72 (GOE) £47.00 (REI)
Volnay 1er Cru, Michel Lafarge **1992** £35.07 (TW)
Volnay les Caillerets, Marquis d'Angerville **1993** £35.00 (JU)
Volnay les Caillerets, Marquis d'Angerville **1991** £38.19 (REI)
Volnay Clos de la Bousse d'Or, Domaine de la Pousse d'Or **1988** £37.50 (CON)
Volnay Clos du Château des Ducs, Lafarge **1996** £38.95 (CON)
Volnay Clos des Chênes, Michel Lafarge **1998** £36.62 (RAE)
Volnay Clos des Ducs, Marquis d'Angerville **1997** £35.00 (JU) £38.58 (FA)
Volnay Clos des Ducs, Marquis d'Angerville **1993** £35.25 (CAV)
Volnay Santenots Ampeau **1979** £38.19 (REI)
Volnay Santenots Lafon **1997** £37.11 (FA)
Volnay Santenots Matrot **1989** £38.19 (TW)
Volnay Santenots-du-Milieu, Lafon **1994** £35.00 (JU)
Vosne-Romanée Rion **1990** £37.00 (CRO)

£40.00 → £49.99

Beaune Clos des Mouches, Drouhin **1985** £41.13 (REI)
Beaune Grèves, Michel Lafarge **1994** £40.54 (TW)
Beaune Pertuisots, Leroy **1982** £45.00 (ROB)
Bonnes-Mares Drouhin **1970** £49.00 (UB)
Bonnes-Mares Jadot **1994** £44.06 (CAV)
Bonnes-Mares de Vogüé **1994** £44.45 (FA) £49.00 (DI) £70.00 (FORT) £75.00 (ROB)
Chambertin Clos-de-Bèze, Bruno Clair **1996** £46.50 (SOM)
Chambertin Clos-de-Bèze, Bruno Clair **1994** £48.00 (JU)
Chambertin Clos-de-Bèze, Drouhin **1995** £49.84 (FA) £65.50 (BEN)
Chambertin Clos-de-Bèze, Faiveley **1994** £44.00 (WS) £49.00 (POR)
Chambertin Clos-de-Bèze, Armand Rousseau **1994** £43.08 (GOE) £48.37 (FA) £60.00 (JU)
Chambertin Trapet **1993** £42.26 (PIP) £50.33 (FA)
Chambolle-Musigny les Amoureuses, de Vogüé **1994** £49.00 (DI) £58.80 (TAN)
Chambolle-Musigny les Amoureuses, de Vogüé **1992** £47.00 (CAV) £55.00 (RES)
Chambolle-Musigny les Gruenchers, Dujac **1994** £46.88 (TW)
Chambolle-Musigny de Vogüé **1993** £47.00 (YOU)
Chapelle-Chambertin Jadot **1993** £41.13 (REI)
Chapelle-Chambertin Trapet **1997** £45.43 (FA) £58.26 (CAV)
Charmes-Chambertin Bachelet **1990** £42.50 (FA)
Charmes-Chambertin Dujac **1994** £45.24 (REI)
Charmes-Chambertin Faiveley **1988** £43.87 (NO)
Charmes-Chambertin Jean Raphet **1997** £49.50 (BEN)
Clos de la Roche Jean Raphet **1996** £49.50 (BEN)
Clos de la Roche Armand Rousseau **1995** £42.50 (FA)
Clos de Tart Mommessin **1996** £47.50 (WAI) £55.00 (JU)
Clos de Tart Mommessin **1994** £40.00 (WS) £50.22 (PLAY)
Clos de Vougeot Arnoux **1996** £49.94 (MON)
Clos de Vougeot Confuron **1997** £47.00 (BAL)
Clos de Vougeot Confuron-Cotétidot **1998** £40.95 (LEA)
Clos de Vougeot Engel **1996** £45.00 (CON)
Clos de Vougeot Grand Cru, Prieur **1997** £46.99 (YOU)
Clos de Vougeot Denis Mortet **1998** £49.84 (RAE)
Clos de Vougeot Georges Mugneret **1998** £49.50 (LEA)
Clos de Vougeot Rebourseau **1997** £44.20 (SOM)
Clos de Vougeot Roumier **1994** £40.40 (TAN)
Clos de Vougeot Roumier **1993** £48.37 (FA)
Corton Bonneau du Martray **1996** £41.35 (HAH)

Corton-Bressandes Tollot-Beaut **1989** £42.50 (FA)
Corton Clos des Cortons, Faiveley **1995** £48.25 (HAH)
Corton les Renardes, Leroy **1994** £48.37 (FA)
Corton Tollot-Beaut **1991** £45.00 (RAE)
Échézeaux Drouhin **1995** £49.50 (BEN)
Échézeaux Dujac **1994** £45.00 (BER) £50.23 (TW)
Échézeaux Engel **1995** £49.94 (TW)
Échézeaux Henri Jayer **1992** £42.00 (RAE)
Gevrey-Chambertin Clos St-Jacques, Bruno Clair **1995** £43.00 (JU)
Gevrey-Chambertin Clos St-Jacques, Armand Rousseau **1997** £44.06 (GOE) £50.33 (FA) £55.81 (REI)
Gevrey-Chambertin Clos St-Jacques, Armand Rousseau **1992** £44.06 (GOE)
Gevrey-Chambertin Clos des Varoilles, Domaine des Varoilles **1978** £44.00 (CRO)
Gevrey-Chambertin Combettes, Dujac **1996** £45.00 (JU)
La Grande Rue François Lamarche **1997** £48.45 (SOM) £57.18 (GOE)
Grands-Échézeaux Engel **1997** £41.12 (GOE) £49.50 (CON)
Grands-Échézeaux Gros Frère et Soeur **1993** £48.37 (FA)
Griotte-Chambertin Domaine des Chezeaux **1996** £45.43 (FA)
Latricières-Chambertin Faiveley **1993** £48.94 (REI)
Latricières-Chambertin Leroy **1993** £44.06 (FA)
Latricières-Chambertin Trapet **1997** £45.43 (FA) £58.26 (CAV)
Latricières-Chambertin Trapet **1992** £49.35 (TW)
Mazis-Chambertin Faiveley **1992** £42.30 (HAH)
Mazis-Chambertin Maume **1997** £45.00 (BAL)
Mazis-Chambertin Roty **1994** £42.30 (CB)
Mazis-Chambertin Armand Rousseau **1996** £47.00 (REI)
Morey-St-Denis Clos des Ormes, Faiveley **1976** £46.41 (TW)
Musigny Vieilles Vignes, de Vogüé **1987** £44.45 (FA) £67.01 (RAE)
Nuits-St-Georges aux Allots, Leroy **1988** £48.37 (FA)
Nuits-St-Georges les Boudots, Méo-Camuzet **1998** £43.57 (GOE)
Nuits-St-Georges Clos des Forêts St-Georges, Domaine de l'Arlot **1989** £41.13 (TW)
Nuits-St-Georges les Damodes, Jayer-Gilles **1997** £42.00 (JU)
Nuits-St-Georges Haut-Poiret, Jayer-Gilles **1995** £45.00 (JU)
Nuits-St-Georges les Murgers, Méo-Camuzet **1998** £43.96 (RAE)
Nuits-St-Georges Georges & Henri Jayer **1995** £40.00 (JU)
Pommard Ampeau **1978** £48.76 (REI)
Pommard Clos des Épeneaux, Armand **1993** £40.00 (FORT)
Pommard Clos des Épeneaux, Armand **1990** £48.37 (FA)
Pommard Pezerolles, Domaine de Montille **1989** £43.95 (ROB)
Pommard Rugiens, Domaine de Courcel **1993** £41.25 (ROB)
Richebourg Gros Frère et Soeur **1994** £45.43 (FA)
Ruchottes-Chambertin Clos des Ruchottes, Armand Rousseau **1992** £40.00 (JU)
Ruchottes-Chambertin Domaine Mugneret **1998** £49.50 (LEA)
Volnay 1er Cru, Michel Lafarge **1990** £47.45 (HAH)
Volnay Clos de la Bousse d'Or, Domaine de la Pousse d'Or **1990** £42.50 (FA)
Volnay Clos du Château des Ducs, Lafarge **1994** £42.18 (TW)
Volnay Clos des Ducs, Marquis d'Angerville **1990** £41.13 (FA)
Volnay Santenots Ampeau **1978** £46.41 (REI) £49.95 (LEA)
Volnay Santenots Lafon **1993** £45.00 (CRO)
Volnay Santenots-du-Milieu, Lafon **1996** £42.00 (JU)
Vosne-Romanée les Brulées, Méo-Camuzet **1994** £48.47 (GOE) £62.00 (JU)
Vosne-Romanée les Chaumes, Méo-Camuzet **1998** £41.12 (GOE)
Vosne-Romanée les Chaumes, Méo-Camuzet **1997** £45.00 (JU)
Vosne-Romanée les Chaumes, Méo-Camuzet **1996** £45.43 (FA)

- *All prices for each wine are listed together in ascending order.*
- *Price bands refer to the lowest price for which the wine is available.*

£50.00 → £59.99

Beaune Marconnets, Bouchard Père **1962** £56.99 (REI)
Bonnes-Mares Jadot **1997** £58.75 (REI) £65.02 (FA) £77.84 (CAV)
Chambertin Armand Rousseau **1994** £59.95 (ROB) £70.00 (FORT)
Chambertin Clos-de-Bèze, Bruno Clair **1997** £55.00 (JU) £66.00 (FA)
Chambertin Clos-de-Bèze, Bruno Clair **1993** £52.92 (WY)
Chambertin Leroy **1993** £53.85 (FA)
Chambolle-Musigny les Baudes, Hubert Lignier **1996** £50.33 (FA)
Chambolle-Musigny les Gruenchers, Dujac **1995** £58.75 (TW)
Chambolle-Musigny Latour **1971** £55.23 (WY)
Chapelle-Chambertin Jadot **1996** £53.49 (YOU)
Clos de la Roche Dujac **1996** £55.00 (JU)
Clos de la Roche Leroy **1993** £53.85 (FA)
Clos de la Roche Vieilles Vignes, Ponsot **1992** £52.88 (REI)
Clos St-Denis Dujac **1994** £52.64 (TW)
Clos de Vougeot Drouhin **1997** £50.00 (WS)
Clos de Vougeot Grivot **1993** £54.00 (CRO)
Clos de Vougeot Méo-Camuzet **1998** £57.18 (RAE)
Clos de Vougeot Méo-Camuzet **1997** £58.16 (FA) £60.00 (JU) £67.50 (TAN)
Corton Clos des Cortons, Faiveley **1993** £52.90 (HAH)
Corton Méo-Camuzet **1997** £58.16 (FA)
Échézeaux Faiveley **1993** £52.00 (WS)
Échézeaux Georges & Henri Jayer **1994** £54.00 (JU)
Échézeaux Emmanuel Rouget **1994** £54.00 (JU)
Gevrey-Chambertin Combettes, Dujac **1995** £53.46 (TW)
Gevrey-Chambertin Combettes, Dujac **1992** £50.95 (RES)
La Grande Rue François Lamarche **1998** £58.36 (RAE) £59.73 (GOE)
La Grande Rue François Lamarche **1976** £52.88 (REI)
Grands-Échézeaux Drouhin **1993** £56.99 (REI)
Grands-Échézeaux Domaine de la Romanée-Conti **1965** £58.75 (FA)
Griotte-Chambertin Domaine des Chezeaux **1995** £55.22 (FA)
Griotte-Chambertin Ponsot **1998** £58.26 (GOE) £82.25 (REI)
Mazis-Chambertin Faiveley **1995** £50.33 (FA) £54.00 (BER)
Musigny Jadot **1994** £58.26 (CAV)
Musigny Vieilles Vignes, de Vogüé **1983** £55.89 (NO)
Musigny de Vogüé **1987** £54.64 (REI)
Nuits-St-Georges aux Boudots, Leroy **1994** £55.22 (FA)
Nuits-St-Georges les Boudots, Méo-Camuzet **1997** £54.50 (TAN) £58.16 (FA)
Nuits-St-Georges aux Lavières, Leroy **1988** £59.00 (ROB)
Nuits-St-Georges les Murgers, Méo-Camuzet **1997** £56.00 (TAN) £58.16 (FA)
Pommard Pezerolles, Domaine de Montille **1991** £51.70 (UB)
Pommard les Vignots, Leroy **1995** £54.25 (FA)
Richebourg Leroy **1993** £53.85 (FA) £528.75 (CAV)
Ruchottes-Chambertin Clos des Ruchottes, Armand Rousseau **1997** £52.20 (TAN)
Ruchottes-Chambertin Armand Rousseau **1996** £53.46 (REI)
Volnay Champans, Marquis d'Angerville **1988** £58.00 (UB)
Vosne-Romanée les Brulées, Méo-Camuzet **1993** £57.00 (CRO)
Vosne-Romanée Cros Parantoux Emmanuel Rouget **1994** £58.00 (JU)

£60.00 → £79.99

Bonnes-Mares Groffier **1991** £67.70 (JER)
Bonnes-Mares Roumier **1997** £65.02 (FA)
Bonnes-Mares de Vogüé **1996** £72.00 (DI) £90.87 (RAE) £99.29 (FA) £115.00 (ROB) £117.01 (CAV) £128.86 (WY) £135.13 (REI)
Bonnes-Mares de Vogüé **1989** £62.00 (CRO)
Chambertin Clos-de-Bèze, Damoy **1993** £64.63 (TW)
Chambertin Clos-de-Bèze, Drouhin **1993** £60.12 (FA)
Chambertin Clos-de-Bèze, Faiveley **1993** £77.60 (HAH)
Chambertin Clos-de-Bèze, Jadot **1995** £70.05 (FA)
Chambertin Clos-de-Bèze, Armand Rousseau **1992** £60.00 (JU) £60.00 (FORT)
Chambertin Armand Rousseau **1983** £79.70 (FA)
Chambertin Trapet **1997** £74.81 (FA) £77.84 (CAV)

Chambolle-Musigny les Amoureuses, de Vogüé **1996** £72.00 (DI) £90.87 (RAE) £99.29 (FA)
Chapelle-Chambertin Ponsot **1998** £79.31 (REI)
Chapelle-Chambertin Ponsot **1996** £60.71 (GOE) £68.95 (LAY)
Charmes-Chambertin Dugat-Py **1998** £79.00 (LEA)
Charmes-Chambertin Dujac **1991** £68.74 (TW)
Clos de la Roche Dujac **1988** £62.08 (FA)
Clos de la Roche Vieilles Vignes, Ponsot **1996** £70.50 (GOE) £97.43 (CAV)
Clos St-Denis Dujac **1996** £70.00 (ROB)
Clos St-Denis Georges Lignier **1985** £60.00 (CRO)
Clos de Vougeot Engel **1991** £62.28 (TW)
Clos de Vougeot Grand Cru, Prieur **1959** £65.00 (BU)
Clos de Vougeot Leroy **1994** £60.12 (FA) £85.95 (LAY)
Clos de Vougeot le Prieuré, Ponnelle **1993** £70.50 (TW)
Clos de Vougeot Château de la Tour **1995** £61.28 (HA)
Corton Chandon de Briailles **1992** £64.63 (TW)
Corton Clos des Cortons, Faiveley **1992** £75.00 (POR)
Corton Grancey, Latour **1971** £60.00 (YOU)
Corton Méo-Camuzet **1996** £67.95 (FA)
Échézeaux Drouhin **1990** £76.38 (REI)
Échézeaux Georges & Henri Jayer **1998** £66.00 (RAE)
Échézeaux Domaine de la Romanée-Conti **1976** £76.38 (REI)
Échézeaux Emmanuel Rouget **1998** £68.93 (RAE)
Gevrey-Chambertin Clos St-Jacques, Armand Rousseau **1996** £65.21 (REI) £66.00 (FA)
Gevrey-Chambertin Latour **1971** £62.13 (WY)
La Grande Rue François Lamarche **1995** £73.55 (JER)
Grands Echézeaux Gros Frère et Soeur **1996** £65.01 (FA)
Grands-Échézeaux Domaine de la Romanée-Conti **1994** £69.03 (WY)
Griotte-Chambertin Ponsot **1996** £65.60 (GOE) £71.87 (FA)
Latricières-Chambertin Faiveley **1990** £60.00 (WS)
Latricières-Chambertin Ponsot **1993** £77.75 (FA)
Musigny Vieilles Vignes, de Vogüé **1994** £73.60 (TAN) £80.00 (ROB) £88.13 (REI)
Musigny Vieilles Vignes, de Vogüé **1992** £78.29 (RAE)
Nuits-St-Georges aux Allots, Leroy **1995** £71.87 (FA)
Nuits-St-Georges aux Boudots, Leroy **1992** £62.08 (FA)
Nuits-St-Georges les Murgers, Méo-Camuzet **1996** £67.95 (FA)
Nuits-St-Georges les Murgers, Méo-Camuzet **1993** £60.00 (ROB)
Nuits-St-Georges Richemone, Pernin-Rossin **1985** £65.00 (CRO)
Pommard Clos de la Commaraine, Jaboulet-Vercherre **1955** £75.00 (ROB)
Pommard Clos Micault, Parent **1978** £75.00 (CRO)
Pommard Pezerolles, Domaine de Montille **1978** £76.38 (REI)
Richebourg Gros Frère et Soeur **1993** £69.91 (FA)
Richebourg Hudelot-Noëllat **1997** £77.50 (SOM)
Richebourg Mongeard-Mugneret **1991** £70.50 (CAV)
Romanée-St-Vivant Domaine de l'Arlot **1992** £68.15 (TW)
Romanée-St-Vivant Hudelot-Noëllat **1997** £77.50 (SOM)
Romanée-St-Vivant les Quatres Journaux, Latour **1989** £75.94 (WY)
Volnay Santenots Lafon **1983** £60.00 (CRO)
Vosne-Romanée les Beaux Monts, Leroy **1992** £66.00 (FA)
Vosne-Romanée les Brulées, Méo-Camuzet **1998** £66.00 (RAE)
Vosne-Romanée Cros Parantoux, Méo-Camuzet **1998** £66.00 (RAE)
Vosne-Romanée Cros Parantoux Emmanuel Rouget **1998** £74.81 (RAE)
Vougeot Clos de la Perrière, Bertagna **1978** £65.00 (CRO)

£80.00 → £99.99

Bonnes-Mares Dujac **1996** £84.60 (LAY)
Bonnes-Mares de Vogüé **1997** £87.00 (DI) £94.39 (FA) £102.81 (GOE) £117.01 (CAV)
Bonnes-Mares de Vogüé **1993** £89.50 (FA)
Chambertin Clos-de-Bèze, Drouhin **1976** £89.75 (WY)
Chambertin Clos-de-Bèze, Armand Rousseau **1997** £89.50 (FA)

Chambertin Clos-de-Bèze, Armand Rousseau **1988** £99.29 (FA)

Chambolle-Musigny les Amoureuses, de Vogüé **1997** £87.00 (DI) £94.39 (FA) £117.01 (CAV)

Chambolle-Musigny les Amoureuses, de Vogüé **1995** £99.29 (FA)

Chambolle-Musigny de Vogüé **1990** £88.13 (REI)

Clos de la Roche Ponsot **1997** £99.29 (FA) £111.63 (REI)

Clos de Vougeot Faiveley **1978** £82.00 (CRO)

Corton Clos des Cortons, Faiveley **1978** £88.00 (CRO)

Échézeaux Domaine de la Romanée-Conti **1996** £94.39 (FA) £116.85 (LAY)

Griotte-Chambertin Ponsot **1995** £83.62 (FA)

Musigny Prieur **1997** £82.99 (YOU)

Musigny Vieilles Vignes, de Vogüé **1988** £83.82 (RAE) £94.00 (TW)

Nuits-St-Georges aux Vignerondes, Leroy **1988** £90.00 (JU)

Richebourg Grand Cru, Grivot **1991** £91.45 (FA)

Richebourg Gros Frère et Soeur **1995** £94.39 (FA)

Richebourg Michel Gros **1993** £95.00 (JU)

Richebourg Mongeard-Mugneret **1992** £85.00 (ROB)

Richebourg Domaine de la Romanée-Conti **1974** £88.13 (REI)

La Romanée Domaines du Château de Vosne-Romanée, Bouchard Père **1982** £99.88 (REI)

Vosne-Romanée Cros Parantoux, Méo-Camuzet **1997** £97.33 (FA)

Please remember that
Oz Clarke's Wine Buying Guide
*is a price **guide** and not a price **list**. It is not meant to replace up-to-date merchants' lists.*

£100.00 → £149.99

Bonnes-Mares de Vogüé **1995** £105.75 (FA)

Chambertin Clos-de-Bèze, Jadot **1990** £109.08 (FA)

Chambertin Clos-de-Bèze, Armand Rousseau **1996** £113.97 (FA) £122.40 (GOE)

Chambertin Clos-de-Bèze, Armand Rousseau **1995** £104.18 (FA) £111.63 (REI)

Chambertin Ponsot **1996** £118.87 (FA)

Chambertin Armand Rousseau **1995** £111.04 (FA) £111.63 (REI)

Chambolle-Musigny les Charmes, Leroy **1995** £117.50 (FA)

Clos de la Roche Leroy **1994** £143.35 (FA)

Clos de la Roche Ponsot **1988** £130.62 (FA)

Clos de la Roche Vieilles Vignes, Ponsot **1995** £111.63 (CAV)

Clos de Tart Mommessin **1945** £105.00 (ROB)

Clos de Vougeot Drouhin **1959** £111.63 (REI)

Clos de Vougeot Leroy **1992** £125.00 (RES) £150.00 (JU) £232.65 (TW)

Échézeaux Henri Jayer **1984** £111.63 (REI)

Échézeaux Domaine de la Romanée-Conti **1993** £128.86 (WY)

Échézeaux Domaine de la Romanée-Conti **1989** £129.25 (FA)

Gevrey-Chambertin Combottes, Leroy **1995** £118.87 (FA)

Grands-Échézeaux Domaine de la Romanée-Conti **1988** £148.25 (FA)

Latricières-Chambertin Ponsot **1990** £148.25 (FA)

Musigny Vieilles Vignes, de Vogüé **1997** £101.00 (DI) £126.70 (FA)

Musigny Vieilles Vignes, de Vogüé **1996** £105.55 (RAE) £141.00 (CAV) £158.63 (TW)

Richebourg Grand Cru, Grivot **1997** £109.08 (FA)

Richebourg Domaine Anne Gros **1989** £113.21 (VIN)

Richebourg Gros Frère et Soeur **1990** £118.87 (FA)

Richebourg Leroy **1994** £148.25 (FA)

Richebourg Méo-Camuzet **1998** £143.74 (RAE)

Richebourg Méo-Camuzet **1994** £118.87 (FA) £150.00 (FORT)

La Romanée Domaines du Château de Vosne-Romanée, Bouchard Père **1989** £125.00 (COC)

Romanée-Conti Domaine de la Romanée-Conti **1993** £117.50 (FA) £1,478.42 (WY)
Romanée-St-Vivant Leroy **1994** £148.25 (FA)
Romanée-St-Vivant Noëllat **1959** £129.25 (REI)
Romanée-St-Vivant Domaine de la Romanée-Conti **1994** £135.00 (FORT) £174.88 (WY)
Romanée-St-Vivant Domaine de la Romanée-Conti **1993** £126.70 (FA) £150.00 (BEN) £176.03 (WY)
La Tâche Domaine de la Romanée-Conti **1975** £146.88 (REI)
Vosne-Romanée les Beaux Monts, Leroy **1988** £146.88 (TW)
Vosne-Romanée les Brulées, Méo-Camuzet **1995** £105.75 (FA)
Vosne-Romanée Cros Parantoux Emmanuel Rouget **1997** £136.59 (CAV)

£150.00 → £199.99

Chambertin Leroy **1994** £162.93 (FA)
Clos de Vougeot Leroy **1997** £176.00 (JU)
Clos de Vougeot Leroy **1996** £197.20 (FA) £239.90 (CAV) £253.11 (WY)
Clos de Vougeot Leroy **1995** £195.25 (FA)
Corton les Renardes, Leroy **1993** £197.20 (FA)
Échézeaux Henri Jayer **1981** £158.63 (REI)
Échézeaux Domaine de la Romanée-Conti **1966** £150.00 (BU)
Grands-Échézeaux Domaine de la Romanée-Conti **1993** £172.58 (WY)
Musigny Leroy **1994** £182.51 (FA)
Nuits-St-Georges aux Boudots, Leroy **1996** £177.62 (FA)
Richebourg Méo-Camuzet **1997** £165.00 (TAN) £182.52 (FA)
Richebourg Domaine de la Romanée-Conti **1994** £179.48 (WY) £185.00 (FORT)
Richebourg Domaine de la Romanée-Conti **1993** £195.00 (BEN) £225.00 (FORT) £237.01 (WY)
Richebourg Domaine de la Romanée-Conti **1988** £197.20 (FA) £226.83 (NO)
Romanée-St-Vivant Domaine de la Romanée-Conti **1996** £162.93 (FA)
Romanée-St-Vivant Domaine de la Romanée-Conti **1995** £186.04 (CAV) £186.38 (WY)
La Tâche Domaine de la Romanée-Conti **1970** £176.25 (FA)
Vosne-Romanée les Beaux Monts, Leroy **1996** £177.62 (FA)

£200.00 → £299.99

Clos de Vougeot Leroy **1961** £229.13 (REI)
Échézeaux Henri Jayer **1979** £270.25 (FA)
Grands-Échézeaux Domaine de la Romanée-Conti **1971** £235.00 (FA)
Nuits-St-Georges aux Boudots, Leroy **1993** £246.16 (FA)
Richebourg Méo-Camuzet **1996** £226.58 (FA)
Richebourg Domaine de la Romanée-Conti **1996** £216.79 (FA)
Richebourg Domaine de la Romanée-Conti **1979** £258.50 (REI)
Romanée-St-Vivant Domaine de la Romanée-Conti **1990** £290.00 (ROB)
La Tâche Domaine de la Romanée-Conti **1996** £270.64 (FA)
La Tâche Domaine de la Romanée-Conti **1994** £205.00 (BER) £217.45 (WY)
La Tâche Domaine de la Romanée-Conti **1991** £221.68 (FA)
La Tâche Domaine de la Romanée-Conti **1983** £272.66 (VIN)

£300.00 → £499.99

Clos de la Roche Leroy **1995** £353.87 (FA)
Clos de Vougeot Leroy **1993** £428.88 (FA) £441.80 (WY)
Latricières-Chambertin Leroy **1996** £353.87 (FA)
Musigny Leroy **1995** £352.50 (FA)
Richebourg Leroy **1996** £376.00 (FA) £528.75 (CAV)
Richebourg Domaine de la Romanée-Conti **1990** £334.87 (FA) £350.00 (BEN)
Romanée-St-Vivant Leroy **1990** £471.37 (FA)
La Tâche Domaine de la Romanée-Conti **1995** £304.89 (WY) £395.00 (BAL)
La Tâche Domaine de la Romanée-Conti **1993** £325.00 (FORT) £333.65 (WY) £375.95 (BEN)
Vosne-Romanée Cros Parantoux, Henri Jayer **1991** £352.50 (CAV)

Over £500.00

Chambertin Leroy **1996** £581.63 (CAV)
Romanée-Conti Domaine de la Romanée-Conti **1985** £2,643.75 (FA) £2,937.50 (CAV)
Romanée-Conti Domaine de la Romanée-Conti **1978** £2,937.50 (CAV)
Romanée-Conti Domaine de la Romanée-Conti **1971** £1,650.00 (BEN)

WHITE

Under £10.00

Hautes-Côtes de Nuits Chaley **1998** £7.75 (STE)
Hautes-Côtes de Nuits Clos du Vignon, Domaine Thévenot-le-Brun **1996** £9.98 (RES)
Puligny-Montrachet les Combettes, Sauzet **1976** £5.87 (CAV)

£10.00 → £11.99

Marsannay Bruno Clair **1996** £11.50 (JU)
Meursault Domaine Jobard ½ bottle **1992** £11.99 (RAE)
Pernand-Vergelesses Pavelot **1997** £11.95 (RES)
St-Aubin 1er Cru, Bachelet **1993** £11.95 (RAE) £18.40 (UB)
St-Aubin Prudhon **1997** £10.95 (JU)
St-Aubin Gerard Thomas **1996** £11.99 (BO)
St-Romain Buisson **1998** £11.16 (DOM)
St-Romain Chartron et Trebuchet **1989** £11.95 (DI)
St-Romain sous le Château, Coste-Caumartin **1997** £10.50 (JU) £11.02 (GW)
Santenay Clos des Champs des Carafe, Olivier Père et Fils **1996** £10.00 (HIG)

£12.00 → £13.99

Auxey-Duresses Coche-Bizouard **1996** £12.65 (RAE)
Auxey-Duresses Olivier Leflaive **1997** £13.95 (LAY)
Auxey-Duresses Michel Prunier **1996** £13.50 (TAN)
Bienvenues-Bâtard-Montrachet Domaine Ramonet **1989** £13.02 (FA)
Chevalier-Montrachet Domaine Leflaive **1997** £12.14 (FA) £133.95 (CB) £141.98 (CAV)
Hautes-Côtes de Beaune Jayer-Gilles **1994** £12.50 (JU)
Marsannay Bruno Clair **1997** £12.00 (JU)
Marsannay Jadot **1995** £12.99 (VIC) £12.99 (THR) £12.99 (BOT)
Meursault Domaine Jobard ½ bottle **1986** £13.99 (RAE)
Monthélie le Champ Fulliot, Garaudet **1996** £13.49 (PIP)
Pernand-Vergelesses Jacques Germain **1997** £12.93 (DOM) £14.50 (AS)
Pernand-Vergelesses Olivier Leflaive **1998** £12.34 (CB)
Pernand-Vergelesses Pavelot **1996** £12.95 (RES)
Pernand-Vergelesses Rollin **1996** £13.12 (RAE) £14.90 (JU)
St-Aubin 1er Cru, Bachelet **1992** £13.29 (YOU)
St-Aubin la Chatenière, Gerard Thomas **1996** £12.98 (PIP)
St-Aubin Frionnes, Lamy **1997** £13.50 (LEA)
St-Aubin Jadot **1995** £12.49 (UN)
St-Aubin les Murgers des Dents de Chien, Henri Prudhon **1997** £13.90 (JU)
St-Aubin Prudhon **1996** £12.99 (JON)
St-Aubin la Pucelle, Lamy-Pillot **1998** £13.89 (BY) £15.99 (WR)
St-Aubin en Remilly, Hubert Lamy **1997** £13.95 (LAY)
St-Romain Chartron et Trebuchet **1997** £13.75 (JER)
St-Romain sous le Château, Coste-Caumartin **1995** £13.00 (JU)
Santenay le Biévaux, Olivier Père et Fils **1996** £12.50 (HIG)
Savigny-lès-Beaune Camus-Bruchon **1997** £12.00 (WS)
Savigny-lès-Beaune Camus-Bruchon **1995** £13.65 (RAE) £13.99 (JON)

£14.00 → £15.99

Auxey-Duresses Chartron et Trebuchet **1997** £14.80 (JER)
Auxey-Duresses Olivier Leflaive **1995** £14.00 (CRO)
Chassagne-Montrachet Jadot **1994** £15.75 (UN)
Chassagne-Montrachet Morey-Coffinet **1996** £15.06 (RAE)
Hautes-Côtes de Beaune Jayer-Gilles **1996** £15.00 (JU)
Marsannay Jadot **1997** £14.69 (REI)
Pernand-Vergelesses les Caradeux, Chanson **1997** £15.54 (HA)
Pernand-Vergelesses Dubreuil-Fontaine **1997** £14.95 (RES)
Pernand-Vergelesses Rollin **1997** £14.95 (JU)
Pernand-Vergelesses Rollin **1994** £15.50 (RAE)

A key to name abbreviations is available on page 7.

Puligny-Montrachet Carillon **1997** £15.75 (SOM) £20.07 (MON) £20.99 (YOU) £21.54 (GOE)
Puligny-Montrachet Carillon **1996** £14.75 (SOM) £21.25 (FLE)
Puligny-Montrachet Jean Germain **1988** £15.00 (CRO)
St-Aubin la Chatenière, Gerard Thomas **1995** £14.50 (ROB)
St-Aubin Frionnes, Lamy **1998** £14.95 (LEA)
St-Aubin les Murgers des Dents de Chien, Henri Prudhon **1996** £14.50 (JU)
St-Aubin la Pucelle, Lamy-Pillot **1996** £14.82 (BY)
Santenay Blanc le St-Jean, Girardin **1997** £14.95 (TAN) £15.99 (UN) £16.65 (NI)
Savigny-lès-Beaune Pavelot **1997** £14.69 (DOM)

£16.00 → £17.99

Chassagne-Montrachet Bachelet **1992** £17.99 (RAE)
Chassagne-Montrachet la Boudriotte, Domaine Ramonet **1993** £17.14 (CAV)
Chassagne-Montrachet Colin-Deleger **1996** £17.55 (NEZ)
Chassagne-Montrachet Marc Colin **1997** £17.53 (FA)
Chassagne-Montrachet Pillot **1997** £16.95 (LEA) £18.11 (MON)
Chassagne-Montrachet Pillot **1996** £16.25 (SAV)
Hautes-Côtes de Beaune Jayer-Gilles **1997** £16.00 (JU)
Hautes-Côtes de Nuits Jayer-Gilles **1996** £16.00 (JU)
Marsannay Bruno Clair **1993** £17.00 (CRO)
Meursault-Blagny, Domaine Jobard **1989** £17.99 (RAE)
Meursault Clos du Cromin, Javillier **1998** £17.35 (BAN)
Meursault Clos du Cromin, Monnier **1997** £17.78 (BY)
Meursault Clos du Cromin, Monnier **1995** £17.75 (SUN)
Meursault Clos St-Felix, Domaine Michelot **1997** £16.00 (HA)
Meursault Coche-Bizouard **1998** £17.82 (RAE)
Meursault Jadot **1996** £16.55 (FA)
Meursault Matrot **1997** £17.14 (GOE) £21.95 (GAU) £22.50 (CON)
Meursault l'Ormeau, Coche-Debord **1990** £16.99 (RAE)
Meursault les Tillets, Javillier **1998** £17.35 (BAN)
Pernand-Vergelesses Rapet **1996** £17.95 (RES)
Puligny-Montrachet les Charmes, Chavy **1996** £16.99 (SAF) £19.10 (FLE)
Puligny-Montrachet Domaine Gérard Chavy **1997** £16.94 (PIP) £17.78 (BY)
Puligny-Montrachet Clerc **1997** £16.95 (BAN)
Puligny-Montrachet Drouhin **1994** £17.80 (CRO)
St-Aubin la Chatenière, Roux Père et Fils **1996** £17.27 (TW)
St-Aubin Combe, Pierre Morey **1996** £16.50 (TAN) £17.00 (JU)
St-Aubin Drouhin **1997** £16.00 (JU) £16.95 (LEA)
St-Aubin Olivier Leflaive **1995** £17.50 (MI)
Savigny-lès-Beaune Montchenevoy, Javillier **1996** £17.25 (LAY)

£18.00 → £19.99

Chassagne-Montrachet Domaine Guy Amiot **1996** £19.95 (BAL)
Chassagne-Montrachet les Macherelles, Amiot **1998** £19.95 (BAN)
Chassagne-Montrachet Morgeot, Gagnard-Delagrange **1997** £19.50 (BAN) £23.99 (MON)
Chassagne-Montrachet en Pimont, Château de Chassagne-Montrachet **1995** £19.79 (FRI)
Chassagne-Montrachet Verget **1997** £19.00 (FA) £22.99 (YOU)
Marsannay Bruno Clair **1995** £19.50 (CRO)
Meursault-Blagny, Domaine Jobard **1990** £19.55 (RAE)
Meursault-Blagny, Latour **1996** £18.51 (FA) £24.50 (FORT) £26.50 (STA)
Meursault-Blagny Thomas **1996** £19.95 (ROB)
Meursault Clos de la Barre, Monnier **1997** £18.19 (BY)
Meursault Clos du Cromin, Monnier **1998** £18.19 (BY)
Meursault les Clous, Javillier **1998** £18.75 (BAN)
Meursault Henri Germain **1997** £19.95 (LEA)
Meursault les Grands Charrons, Domaine Michelot **1995** £18.80 (FLE)
Meursault Henri de Villamont **1995** £19.95 (ROB)

Meursault Domaine Jobard **1997** £18.80 (SAV)
Meursault Domaine Jobard **1996** £19.00 (FA) £23.50 (HAH)
Meursault Latour **1995** £18.30 (COC)
Meursault Matrot **1996** £18.11 (GOE)
Meursault Matrot **1993** £19.99 (CON) £20.95 (GAU)
Meursault les Narvaux, Girardin **1998** £18.95 (AD)
Meursault les Tillets, Javillier **1997** £18.80 (SOM) £26.50 (ELL)
Nuits St-Georges Robert Chevillon **1997** £19.00 (JU)
Puligny-Montrachet les Charmes, Chavy **1998** £19.50 (BU) £19.50 (MV)
Puligny-Montrachet les Enseignères, Prudhon **1994** £18.50 (RAE)
Puligny-Montrachet les Folatières, Chavy **1996** £18.95 (SOM)
Puligny-Montrachet Latour **1995** £18.00 (COC)
Puligny-Montrachet sous les Puits, Bachelet **1996** £19.88 (RAE)
St-Aubin le Charmois, Jean-Marc Morey **1997** £18.95 (RES)
St-Aubin Combe, Pierre Morey **1997** £18.90 (JU)

£20.00 → £24.99

Chassagne-Montrachet Domaine Guy Amiot **1998** £24.50 (LEA)
Chassagne-Montrachet la Boudriotte, Blain-Gagnard **1996** £21.65 (HAH)
Chassagne-Montrachet la Boudriotte, Gagnard-Delagrange **1998** £23.50 (MON)
Chassagne-Montrachet la Boudriotte, Gagnard-Delagrange **1997** £24.30 (BAN) £24.45 (HAH) £25.99 (PHI)
Chassagne-Montrachet les Caillerets, Morey-Coffinet **1998** £23.50 (GOE) £23.70 (RAE)
Chassagne-Montrachet les Caillerets, Morey-Coffinet **1996** £21.36 (RAE)
Chassagne-Montrachet les Caillerets, Jean-Marc Morey **1988** £24.87 (FA)
Chassagne-Montrachet les Chenevottes, Colin-Deleger **1994** £21.15 (CAV)

Oz Clarke's Wine Buying Guide
is an annual publication.
We welcome your suggestions for next year's edition.

Chassagne-Montrachet les Houillères, Olivier Leflaive **1997** £21.95 (LAY)
Chassagne-Montrachet Jadot **1996** £24.99 (BOT)
Chassagne-Montrachet Latour **1996** £23.50 (FORT) £25.79 (PLAY)
Chassagne-Montrachet les Macherelles, Amiot **1997** £23.45 (SOM) £24.50 (LEA) £24.95 (BAL) £25.95 (DI)
Chassagne-Montrachet Morey-Coffinet **1997** £21.00 (BER)
Chassagne-Montrachet Morgeot, Gagnard-Delagrange **1996** £24.10 (HAH)
Chassagne-Montrachet Morgeot, Domaine Ramonet **1997** £22.91 (FA)
Chassagne-Montrachet en Pimont, Château de Chassagne-Montrachet **1993** £21.95 (ROB)
Chassagne-Montrachet Roux **1996** £23.50 (TW)
Chassagne-Montrachet Sauzet **1996** £23.89 (FA)
Chassagne-Montrachet les Vergers, Colin-Deléger **1997** £24.97 (CAV) £30.79 (JON)
Chassagne-Montrachet les Vergers, J-M Pillot **1996** £24.50 (ROB)
Chassagne-Montrachet Vide-Bourse, Pillot **1997** £21.49 (YOU)
Meursault en la Barre, Domaine Jobard **1997** £23.00 (JU)
Meursault-Blagny, Domaine Jobard **1996** £24.87 (FA) £29.69 (RAE)
Meursault-Blagny, Matrot **1997** £23.50 (GOE) £26.50 (GAU)
Meursault-Blagny Thomas **1997** £21.95 (CON)
Meursault Bouchard Père **1996** £21.60 (COC)

Meursault Charmes, Matrot **1997** £24.48 (GOE) £30.90 (GAU)
Meursault Charmes, Monnier **1996** £20.25 (SOM)
Meursault Charmes, Pierre Boillot **1996** £22.03 (SAV)

Meursault Chevalières, Charles et Remi Jobard **1998** £24.50 (LEA)
Meursault Clos du Château, Château de Meursault **1995** £22.99 (POR)
Meursault Darviot-Perrin **1994** £22.26 (TW)
Meursault Goutte d'Or, Coche-Bizouard **1998** £23.99 (RAE)
Meursault Albert Grivault **1997** £24.00 (JU)
Meursault Domaine Jobard **1990** £23.95 (RAE)
Meursault Lafarge **1998** £20.00 (GAU)
Meursault Limozin, Domaine Henri Germain **1997** £22.95 (LEA)
Meursault les Luchets, Roulot **1997** £23.50 (DOM)
Meursault Matrot **1998** £21.95 (GAU)
Meursault les Meix Chavaux, Roulot **1997** £23.50 (DOM)
Meursault Michelot **1997** £21.95 (STE)
Meursault Millot-Battault **1990** £20.56 (REI)
Meursault Monatine, Rougeot **1998** £20.15 (BAN)
Meursault Monatine, Rougeot **1996** £23.50 (ROB)
Meursault les Narvaux, Girardin **1997** £21.00 (JU) £21.74 (REI) £22.00 (WS) £22.95 (RES) £24.50 (NI)
Meursault Perrières, Gaunoux **1997** £22.45 (SOM)
Meursault Rougeots, Verget **1997** £22.91 (FA) £27.99 (YOU)
Meursault sous la Velle, Charles et Remi Jobard **1997** £22.50 (LEA)
Meursault Verget **1996** £24.87 (FA)
Meursault les Vireuils, Dupont-Fahn **1997** £23.99 (NI)
Morey St-Denis Bruno Clair **1997** £23.00 (JU)
Morey-St-Denis Clos de Monts Luisants, Ponsot **1995** £23.99 (GOE) £28.50 (BAL)
Nuits St-Georges Robert Chevillon **1995** £22.00 (JU)
Puligny-Montrachet Jean-Marc Boillot **1998** £24.97 (GOE) £26.50 (LEA)
Puligny-Montrachet Bouchard Père **1996** £23.95 (COC)
Puligny-Montrachet Carillon **1998** £21.54 (GOE) £25.25 (STE)
Puligny-Montrachet les Chalumeaux, Matrot **1992** £24.50 (GAU)
Puligny-Montrachet Champ Canet, Carillon **1997** £22.45 (SOM)
Puligny-Montrachet Champ Canet, Latour-Giraud **1998** £23.99 (BIB)
Puligny-Montrachet les Charmes, Chavy **1992** £22.00 (CRO)
Puligny-Montrachet Clerc **1996** £21.95 (ROB) £23.70 (AV) £29.28 (FRI)
Puligny-Montrachet Clos de la Mouchère, Henri Boillot **1997** £24.68 (CAV) £27.50 (FORT)
Puligny-Montrachet les Enseignères, Prudhon **1996** £20.39 (JON)
Puligny-Montrachet les Folatières, Chavy **1998** £23.20 (PIP) £24.00 (MV)
Puligny-Montrachet les Folatières, Clerc **1996** £23.75 (BAN) £31.00 (FRI)
Puligny-Montrachet la Garenne, Thomas **1997** £21.95 (CON)
Puligny-Montrachet Jadot **1997** £24.99 (POR) £25.26 (REI)
Puligny-Montrachet Jadot **1996** £20.99 (UN)
Puligny-Montrachet Domaine Leflaive **1991** £20.95 (FA)
Puligny-Montrachet Monnier **1997** £20.23 (BY)
Puligny-Montrachet les Perrières, Carillon **1996** £21.75 (SOM) £31.33 (GOE) £33.68 (FA) £34.95 (BER)
Puligny-Montrachet les Pucelles, Marc Morey **1987** £23.50 (CAV)
Puligny-Montrachet Sauzet **1998** £22.03 (CAV) £27.10 (AD)
Puligny-Montrachet Sauzet **1997** £23.50 (CAV) £28.00 (JU) £31.95 (RES)
Puligny-Montrachet Sauzet **1996** £22.91 (FA) £26.93 (CAV) £26.99 (JON)
St-Aubin la Chatenière, Chartron et Trébuchet **1998** £20.95 (DI)
St-Aubin Olivier Leflaive **1996** £20.83 (MI)

£25.00 → £29.99

Bâtard-Montrachet Sauzet **1991** £29.33 (CAV)
Chassagne-Montrachet les Baudines, Bernard Morey **1996** £27.03 (DOM)
Chassagne-Montrachet les Caillerets, Amiot **1998** £25.00 (BAN) £31.00 (LEA)

- *Wines are listed in A–Z order within each price band.*
- *For each wine, vintages are listed in descending order.*
- *Each vintage of any wine appears only once.*

Chassagne-Montrachet les Caillerets, Amiot **1997** £28.75 (SOM) £31.00 (LEA)
Chassagne-Montrachet les Caillerets, Marc Morey **1996** £26.83 (FA)
Chassagne-Montrachet les Champs Gains, Amiot **1998** £27.95 (LEA)
Chassagne-Montrachet Chaumées, Colin-Deleger **1997** £26.44 (GOE) £27.03 (CAV)
Chassagne-Montrachet Clos St-Jean, Amiot **1997** £27.00 (SOM)
Chassagne-Montrachet Marc Colin **1996** £27.50 (ROB)
Chassagne-Montrachet Drouhin **1997** £26.00 (JU)
Chassagne-Montrachet Drouhin **1988** £28.79 (REI)
Chassagne-Montrachet les Embrazées, Albert Morey **1996** £29.49 (JON)
Chassagne-Montrachet Grandes, Pillot **1998** £27.95 (LEA)
Chassagne-Montrachet Latour **1995** £25.89 (WY)
Chassagne-Montrachet les Macherelles, Amiot **1996** £25.50 (LEA)
Chassagne-Montrachet les Maltroie, Colin-Deléger **1996** £25.85 (FA)
Chassagne-Montrachet Morgeot, Henri Germain **1997** £29.95 (LEA)
Chassagne-Montrachet Morgeot, Jadot **1996** £26.93 (GOE)
Chassagne-Montrachet Morgeot Vieilles Vignes, Verget **1997** £28.79 (FA)
Chassagne-Montrachet Niellon **1995** £29.38 (CAV)
Chassagne-Montrachet Ramonet **1989** £25.85 (FA)
Chassagne-Montrachet Sauzet **1998** £25.20 (AD)
Chassagne-Montrachet les Vergers, Colin-Deléger **1998** £25.75 (RAE)
Chevalier-Montrachet Sauzet **1994** £26.40 (CRO) £80.49 (REI)
Corton-Charlemagne Bruno Clair **1994** £27.75 (SOM)
Hautes-Côtes de Nuits Caves des Hautes-Côtes **1996** £28.79 (REI)
Meursault Ampeau **1992** £28.68 (CHA)
Meursault en la Barre, Domaine Jobard **1996** £25.00 (JU)
Meursault-Blagny, Jadot **1995** £28.95 (POR) £34.99 (VIC) £34.99 (THR) £34.99 (BOT)
Meursault-Blagny, Domaine Jobard **1993** £29.95 (RAE)
Meursault-Blagny, Latour **1997** £26.25 (JER) £28.95 (POR)
Meursault les Casse-Tête, Javillier **1990** £25.36 (FA)
Meursault Charmes, Ampeau **1992** £28.68 (CHA)
Meursault Charmes, Henri Germain **1996** £26.40 (TAN) £29.95 (LEA)
Meursault Charmes, Matrot **1996** £26.50 (CON) £28.10 (GOE) £29.95 (ROB)
Meursault Charmes, Rougeot **1998** £26.50 (BAN)
Meursault Charmes, Rougeot **1996** £28.50 (PHI)
Meursault les Clous, Javillier **1997** £25.65 (LAY)
Meursault Darviot-Perrin **1996** £26.14 (TW)
Meursault Drouhin **1997** £25.00 (JU)
Meursault Drouhin **1996** £25.00 (FORT)
Meursault Genevrières, Domaine Jobard **1996** £29.69 (RAE) £38.58 (FA)
Meursault Goutte d'Or, Latour **1996** £28.99 (JON)
Meursault Lafarge **1995** £25.26 (TW)
Meursault Latour **1997** £25.79 (PLAY)
Meursault Olivier Leflaive **1994** £25.26 (TW)
Meursault Limozin, Domaine Henri Germain **1996** £25.95 (LEA)
Meursault Pierre Morey **1997** £26.00 (RES) £27.00 (JU)
Meursault les Narvaux, Pierre Morey **1993** £28.00 (CRO)
Meursault Perrières, Gaunoux **1996** £26.93 (GOE)
Meursault Perrières, Albert Grivault **1996** £29.00 (JU)
Meursault Perrières, Michelot **1997** £28.98 (HA) £39.95 (RES)
Meursault la Pièce sous le Bois, Ampeau **1992** £28.20 (CHA)
Meursault Poruzots, Domaine Jobard **1997** £26.93 (SAV) £34.00 (JU)
Meursault Poruzots, Domaine Jobard **1994** £29.95 (RAE) £33.00 (JU)
Meursault Poruzots, Roux Père et Fils **1997** £27.50 (BEN)
Meursault les Tillets, Javillier **1996** £27.95 (ROB)
Meursault les Vireuils, Roulot **1996** £28.79 (DOM)
Morey-St-Denis Clos de Monts Luisants, Ponsot **1996** £28.50 (BAL)
Nuits-St-Georges Clos de l'Arlot, Domaine de l'Arlot **1994** £29.71 (FLE)
Puligny-Montrachet Jean-Marc Boillot **1996** £28.95 (LEA) £33.95 (TW)

Puligny-Montrachet Bouchard Père **1997** £27.79 (BY)
Puligny-Montrachet les Chalumeaux, Matrot **1996** £26.50 (CON) £28.50 (GAU) £29.95 (ROB)
Puligny-Montrachet Champ Canet, Carillon **1994** £29.28 (FA)
Puligny-Montrachet Champ Canet, Sauzet **1994** £29.38 (CAV) £42.00 (WS)
Puligny-Montrachet les Champs Gains, Michel Bouzereau **1994** £28.20 (FLE)
Puligny-Montrachet Chartron et Trébuchet **1997** £27.50 (JER)
Puligny-Montrachet Clavoillon, Domaine Leflaive **1991** £29.38 (CAV)
Puligny-Montrachet Drouhin **1997** £27.00 (JU)
Puligny-Montrachet les Enseignères, Olivier Leflaive **1996** £27.95 (PHI)
Puligny-Montrachet les Folatières, Chartron **1997** £28.95 (BAN)
Puligny-Montrachet les Folatières, Drouhin **1997** £29.86 (GOE) £29.95 (ROB) £36.00 (WS) £38.00 (JU)
Puligny-Montrachet la Garenne, Sauzet **1991** £29.00 (CRO)
Puligny-Montrachet Domaine Leflaive **1997** £25.95 (GOE) £27.00 (JU) £28.79 (FA)
Puligny-Montrachet Domaine Leflaive **1996** £29.28 (FA) £52.35 (JER)
Puligny-Montrachet Domaine Leflaive **1995** £26.74 (FLE) £27.32 (FA)
Puligny-Montrachet sous le Puits, Verget **1997** £26.83 (FA) £35.99 (YOU)
Puligny-Montrachet sous les Puits, Bachelet **1997** £29.50 (BAL)
Puligny-Montrachet les Truffières, Colin-Deleger **1994** £25.85 (CAV)

£30.00 → £39.99

Bâtard-Montrachet Gagnard **1987** £38.68 (CAV)
Beaune Clos des Mouches, Drouhin **1997** £33.29 (GOE) £33.50 (ROB) £34.00 (JU) £40.35 (NI) £45.00 (LEA)
Beaune Clos des Mouches, Drouhin **1996** £36.72 (GOE) £41.95 (BER) £44.50 (BAL)
Chassagne-Montrachet Blanchots Dessus, Darviot-Perrin **1994** £35.25 (TW)
Chassagne-Montrachet la Boudriotte, Blain-Gagnard **1990** £38.00 (CRO)
Chassagne-Montrachet la Boudriotte, Domaine Ramonet **1996** £30.75 (FA) £41.13 (REI)
Chassagne-Montrachet les Caillerets, Amiot **1996** £31.00 (BAL) £33.50 (LEA)
Chassagne-Montrachet les Caillerets, Jean Noël Gagnard **1997** £30.26 (FA) £35.00 (JU) £42.89 (REI)
Chassagne-Montrachet les Caillerets, Domaine Ramonet **1993** £35.25 (CAV)
Chassagne-Montrachet Marc Colin **1983** £37.01 (REI)
Chassagne-Montrachet Marquis de Laguiche, Drouhin **1997** £30.84 (GOE) £38.00 (JU) £38.00 (WS) £42.00 (LEA)
Chassagne-Montrachet Marquis de Laguiche, Drouhin **1996** £36.50 (BEN) £38.50 (BAL) £42.00 (LEA)
Chassagne-Montrachet Morgeot, Jean Noël Gagnard **1997** £32.00 (JU)
Chassagne-Montrachet Morgeot, Domaine Ramonet **1994** £34.95 (ROB) £39.50 (BAL)
Chassagne-Montrachet Morgeot, Domaine Ramonet **1993** £31.99 (YOU)
Chassagne-Montrachet Morgeot, Verget **1997** £30.99 (NI)
Chassagne-Montrachet Morgeot Vieilles Vignes, Verget **1996** £33.68 (FA)
Chassagne-Montrachet Remilly, Verget **1997** £30.75 (FA) £45.00 (LEA)
Chassagne-Montrachet la Romanée, Olivier Leflaive **1997** £32.90 (CB)
Chassagne-Montrachet les Ruchottes, Domaine Ramonet **1997** £39.56 (FA)
Chassagne-Montrachet Sauzet **1995** £33.00 (CRO)
Chassagne-Montrachet les Vergers, Olivier Leflaive **1995** £32.25 (TW) £34.17 (MI)
Chassagne-Montrachet les Vergers, J-M Pillot **1997** £33.00 (RES)
Chassagne-Montrachet les Vergers, Domaine Ramonet **1991** £33.49 (REI)
Chevalier-Montrachet Sauzet **1995** £32.50 (CRO)
Corton Domaine Chandon de Briailles **1998** £37.95 (LEA)
Corton-Charlemagne Bouchard Père **1996** £38.58 (FA) £48.00 (COC)

- *All prices for each wine are listed together in ascending order.*
- *Price bands refer to the lowest price for which the wine is available.*

Corton-Charlemagne Bouchard Père **1994** £37.12 (BY)
Corton-Charlemagne Bruno Clair **1997** £36.45 (SOM) £46.00 (JU)
Corton-Charlemagne Latour **1997** £35.64 (FA) £37.70 (CAV) £39.99 (MAJ)
Corton-Charlemagne Latour **1995** £36.50 (COC) £48.37 (FA) £50.30 (PLAY) £77.32 (WY)
Corton-Charlemagne Rollin **1996** £36.62 (RAE) £60.00 (JU)
Meursault-Blagny, Domaine Jobard **1998** £32.80 (RAE)
Meursault Charmes, Jadot **1997** £34.27 (CAV)
Meursault Charmes, Charles et Remi Jobard **1998** £35.00 (LEA)
Meursault Charmes, Matrot **1998** £30.90 (GAU)
Meursault Charmes, Monnier **1998** £30.99 (WR)
Meursault Charmes, Pierre Morey **1996** £35.90 (TAN) £39.00 (RES)
Meursault Genevrières, Henri Boillot **1997** £30.00 (FORT)
Meursault Genevrières, Domaine Jobard **1994** £32.50 (RAE) £33.00 (JU)
Meursault Genevrières, Charles et Remi Jobard **1998** £33.50 (LEA)
Meursault Limozin, Domaine Henri Germain **1992** £35.00 (CRO)
Meursault les Narvaux, Pierre Morey **1996** £31.00 (RES)
Meursault Perrières, Ampeau **1979** £38.19 (REI) £45.00 (LEA)
Meursault Perrières, Albert Grivault **1997** £35.00 (JU)
Meursault les Perrières, Pierre Morey **1996** £35.64 (FA)
Meursault la Pièce sous le Bois, Ampeau **1985** £39.50 (LEA)
Meursault le Poruzot Dessus, Charles et Remi Jobard **1998** £31.00 (LEA)
Meursault Poruzots, Domaine Jobard **1998** £32.80 (RAE)
Meursault Poruzots, Domaine Jobard **1996** £32.70 (FA) £35.00 (JU)
Meursault les Tessons Clos de Mon Plaisir, Roulot **1997** £32.31 (DOM)
Meursault les Tessons, Pierre Morey **1997** £33.00 (JU) £38.95 (RES)
le Montrachet Château des Herbeux **1983** £35.64 (FA)
Morey-St-Denis Clos de Monts Luisants, Ponsot **1994** £32.50 (BAL)
Morey-St-Denis Clos de Monts Luisants, Ponsot **1985** £35.25 (CAV) £38.19 (REI)
Puligny-Montrachet Champ Canet, Carillon **1998** £33.29 (MON) £36.50 (STE)
Puligny-Montrachet Champ Canet, Sauzet **1997** £36.62 (FA) £38.68 (CAV)
Puligny-Montrachet les Champs Gains, Michel Bouzereau **1995** £38.50 (ROB)
Puligny-Montrachet Clavoillon, Domaine Leflaive **1997** £35.00 (JU) £36.62 (FA) £38.89 (CB) £48.50 (BAL) £50.62 (WY)
Puligny-Montrachet Clavoillon, Domaine Leflaive **1996** £37.11 (FA) £42.99 (JON) £45.00 (FORT) £45.00 (WAI)
Puligny-Montrachet Clavoillon, Domaine Leflaive **1994** £30.70 (TAN) £77.00 (UB)
Puligny-Montrachet les Combettes, Ampeau **1992** £32.67 (CHA)
Puligny-Montrachet les Combettes, Prieur **1996** £37.50 (HED)
Puligny-Montrachet les Combettes, Sauzet **1997** £38.58 (FA) £48.47 (CAV) £54.40 (HAH) £64.00 (RES)
Puligny-Montrachet les Demoiselles, Amiot **1993** £36.72 (CAV)
Puligny-Montrachet les Folatières, Jadot **1997** £34.27 (CAV)
Puligny-Montrachet les Folatières, Domaine Leflaive **1991** £38.58 (FA)
Puligny-Montrachet les Folatières, Sauzet **1997** £36.62 (FA) £41.61 (CAV)
Puligny-Montrachet la Garenne, Sauzet **1997** £30.75 (FA) £38.68 (CAV) £39.00 (JU) £41.13 (DOM)
Puligny-Montrachet la Garenne, Sauzet **1996** £32.70 (FA) £37.60 (CAV) £40.00 (JU)
Puligny-Montrachet Domaine Leflaive **1994** £36.38 (PLAY)
Puligny-Montrachet Mouchère, Boillot **1997** £35.95 (LEA)
Puligny-Montrachet les Perrières, Carillon **1998** £33.29 (GOE) £36.95 (STE)
Puligny-Montrachet les Perrières, Sauzet **1997** £39.00 (JU)
Puligny-Montrachet les Perrières, Sauzet **1993** £30.75 (FA)
Puligny-Montrachet les Pucelles, Domaine Leflaive **1993** £36.62 (FA)
Puligny-Montrachet les Referts, Carillon **1998** £34.27 (GOE)
Puligny-Montrachet les Referts, Sauzet **1997** £30.75 (FA) £38.68 (CAV) £39.00 (JU) £39.86 (BY) £42.20 (TAN)

Puligny-Montrachet les Referts, Sauzet **1996** £35.64 (FA) £41.13 (DOM)
Puligny-Montrachet les Referts, Sauzet **1995** £39.50 (FRI)
Puligny-Montrachet les Referts, Sauzet **1991** £34.00 (CRO)
Puligny-Montrachet sous le Puits, Verget **1998** £33.50 (LEA)
Puligny-Montrachet les Truffières, Colin-Deleger **1997** £38.68 (CAV)

£40.00 → £49.99

Bâtard-Montrachet Drouhin **1981** £41.13 (REI)
Bâtard-Montrachet Fontaine-Gagnard **1996** £46.50 (SOM)
Bâtard-Montrachet Gagnard-Delagrange **1997** £44.00 (BAN) £58.26 (MON)
Bienvenues-Bâtard-Montrachet Bachelet **1996** £40.44 (RAE)
Bienvenues-Bâtard-Montrachet Clerc **1994** £46.00 (UN)
Chassagne-Montrachet Drouhin **1961** £44.06 (REI)
Chassagne-Montrachet Marquis de Laguiche, Drouhin **1988** £48.33 (WY)
Chassagne-Montrachet les Ruchottes, Domaine Ramonet **1993** £41.52 (FA)
Chevalier-Montrachet Bouchard Père **1983** £47.00 (REI)
Corton Domaine Chandon de Briailles **1996** £49.00 (LEA)
Corton-Charlemagne Bonneau du Martray **1998** £40.44 (RAE) £49.50 (LEA)
Corton-Charlemagne Bonneau du Martray **1997** £44.45 (FA) £49.00 (JU) £49.50 (LEA)
Corton-Charlemagne Bonneau du Martray **1995** £48.37 (RAE) £48.37 (FA) £69.50 (ROB)
Corton-Charlemagne Bouchard Père **1995** £48.00 (COC)
Corton-Charlemagne Domaine Chandon de Briailles **1997** £49.50 (LEA)
Corton-Charlemagne Chapuis **1997** £41.75 (STE)
Corton-Charlemagne Bruno Clair **1995** £45.00 (JU)
Corton-Charlemagne Delarche **1992** £45.50 (ROB)
Corton-Charlemagne Drouhin **1997** £40.64 (GOE)
Corton-Charlemagne Drouhin **1996** £49.50 (BEN)
Corton-Charlemagne Jadot **1994** £41.13 (CAV)
Corton-Charlemagne Juillot **1997** £45.83 (DOM)
Corton-Charlemagne Latour **1996** £48.37 (FA) £51.00 (STA) £52.88 (CAV) £75.94 (WY)
Corton-Charlemagne Olivier Leflaive **1997** £41.89 (CB) £45.00 (MI)
Corton-Charlemagne Rapet **1997** £42.95 (RES)
Corton-Charlemagne Rollin **1997** £46.25 (TAN) £48.00 (JU)
Corton-Charlemagne Rollin **1994** £41.50 (RAE)
Corton-Charlemagne Georges Roumier **1994** £48.37 (FA)
Meursault Charmes, Pierre Morey **1997** £42.00 (JU) £45.95 (RES)
Meursault Clos des Perrières, Albert Grivault **1997** £45.00 (JU)
Meursault Genevrières, Pierre Morey **1997** £42.00 (JU)
Meursault Lafon **1997** £48.95 (BEN) £52.29 (FA)
Meursault Perrières, Prieur **1997** £48.99 (YOU)
Puligny-Montrachet Champ Canet, Sauzet **1998** £41.61 (CAV)
Puligny-Montrachet Champ Canet, Sauzet **1996** £41.13 (DOM) £41.99 (BY) £42.50 (FA)
Puligny-Montrachet Champ Canet, Sauzet **1988** £45.43 (FA)
Puligny-Montrachet Clavoillon, Domaine Leflaive **1995** £47.00 (CAV)
Puligny-Montrachet Clavoillon, Domaine Leflaive **1993** £49.00 (CRO)
Puligny-Montrachet les Combettes, Ampeau **1979** £49.00 (LEA)
Puligny-Montrachet les Combettes, Domaine Leflaive **1993** £42.50 (FA)
Puligny-Montrachet les Combettes, Domaine Leflaive **1989** £48.37 (FA)
Puligny-Montrachet les Combettes, Sauzet **1998** £48.47 (CAV)
Puligny-Montrachet les Combettes, Sauzet **1987** £44.06 (REI)
Puligny-Montrachet les Demoiselles, Amiot **1997** £42.00 (LEA)
Puligny-Montrachet les Folatières, Drouhin **1988** £49.70 (WY)
Puligny-Montrachet les Folatières, Jadot **1992** £49.50 (ROB)
Puligny-Montrachet les Folatières, Domaine Leflaive **1994** £40.54 (FA) £49.99 (FRI)

Puligny-Montrachet les Folatières, Sauzet **1998** £41.61 (CAV)
Puligny-Montrachet les Folatières, Sauzet **1995** £41.13 (DOM) £55.95 (ROB)
Puligny-Montrachet Clos de la Garenne, Drouhin **1992** £41.42 (WY)
Puligny-Montrachet Clos de la Garenne, Drouhin **1988** £49.70 (WY)
Puligny-Montrachet Domaine Leflaive **1993** £42.99 (FRI)
Puligny-Montrachet les Perrières, Carillon **1995** £42.50 (ELL)
Puligny-Montrachet les Pucelles, Domaine Leflaive **1994** £42.50 (FA) £64.67 (CB) £67.50 (ROB) £74.87 (PLAY)
Puligny-Montrachet Sauzet **1986** £45.24 (REI)

£50.00 → £69.99

Bâtard-Montrachet Blain-Gagnard **1996** £51.00 (HAH)
Bâtard-Montrachet Jean-Marc Boillot **1994** £63.00 (RAE)
Bâtard-Montrachet Jean-Marc Boillot **1991** £52.88 (GOE)
Bâtard-Montrachet Gagnard **1997** £69.91 (FA)
Bâtard-Montrachet Gagnard **1994** £65.00 (JU)
Bâtard-Montrachet Latour **1996** £58.26 (GOE) £79.96 (WY)
Bâtard-Montrachet Domaine Leflaive **1994** £62.08 (FA) £70.00 (JU) £78.99 (FRI) £95.00 (ROB)
Bâtard-Montrachet Remoissenet **1989** £58.75 (FA)
Bâtard-Montrachet Sauzet **1994** £64.63 (CAV)
Beaune Clos des Mouches, Drouhin **1989** £52.88 (REI)
Bienvenues-Bâtard-Montrachet Bachelet **1997** £57.00 (BAL)
Bienvenues-Bâtard-Montrachet Bachelet-Ramonet **1995** £65.50 (FRI)
Bienvenues-Bâtard-Montrachet Domaine Leflaive **1991** £52.29 (FA) £80.00 (ROB)
Chassagne-Montrachet Marquis de Laguiche, Drouhin **1989** £60.75 (WY)
Chassagne-Montrachet les Ruchottes, Domaine Ramonet **1989** £51.00 (YOU)
Chevalier-Montrachet les Desmoiselles, Latour **1988** £64.63 (FA)
Corton-Charlemagne Bonneau du Martray **1996** £68.50 (BEN) £70.00 (JU)
Corton-Charlemagne Bonneau du Martray **1994** £63.39 (PLA) £67.50 (FORT)
Corton-Charlemagne Bonneau du Martray **1993** £69.03 (WY)
Corton-Charlemagne Bruno Clair **1996** £55.00 (JU)
Corton-Charlemagne Jadot **1997** £53.85 (CAV)
Corton-Charlemagne Jadot **1991** £58.16 (REI)
Corton-Charlemagne Latour **1981** £62.13 (WY)
Corton-Charlemagne Olivier Leflaive **1989** £50.00 (CRO)
Corton-Charlemagne Rollin **1995** £55.00 (JU)
Corton-Charlemagne, Verget **1997** £69.00 (LEA) £77.75 (FA)
Côte de Beaune Villamont **1964** £55.00 (ROB)
Meursault Clos de la Barre, Lafon **1997** £50.00 (YOU) £71.87 (FA)
Meursault Lafon **1996** £52.29 (FA)
le Montrachet Thénard **1997** £67.95 (FA)
Puligny-Montrachet Champ Canet, Sauzet **1995** £55.00 (ROB)
Puligny-Montrachet les Combettes, Ampeau **1983** £59.00 (LEA)
Puligny-Montrachet les Combettes, Domaine Leflaive **1997** £55.22 (FA) £58.16 (CB) £62.18 (CAV)
Puligny-Montrachet les Folatières, Drouhin **1983** £55.23 (WY)
Puligny-Montrachet les Folatières, Domaine Leflaive **1997** £52.29 (FA) £56.40 (CB) £63.16 (CAV)
Puligny-Montrachet les Pucelles, Domaine Leflaive **1998** £64.14 (GOE)
Puligny-Montrachet les Pucelles, Domaine Leflaive **1997** £56.20 (FA) £68.05 (CAV)
Puligny-Montrachet les Pucelles, Domaine Leflaive **1991** £51.95 (ROB)
Puligny-Montrachet les Pucelles, Domaine Leflaive **1989** £62.08 (FA)

£70.00 → £99.99

Bâtard-Montrachet Clerc **1998** £88.99 (FRI)
Bâtard-Montrachet Drouhin **1997** £89.59 (GOE) £129.00 (LEA)
Bâtard-Montrachet Gagnard **1996** £80.00 (JU)
Bâtard-Montrachet Latour **1995** £78.00 (STA) £79.39 (WY)
Bâtard-Montrachet Latour **1988** £95.00 (VIN)

Bâtard-Montrachet Domaine Leflaive **1997** £94.39 (FA) £105.16 (CB) £122.40 (CAV)
Bâtard-Montrachet Pierre Morey **1997** £93.50 (TAN) £98.00 (RES)
Bâtard-Montrachet Domaine Ramonet **1997** £89.50 (FA)
Bâtard-Montrachet Sauzet **1997** £79.70 (FA) £97.43 (CAV)
Bienvenues-Bâtard-Montrachet Louis Carillon **1995** £85.00 (FORT)
Bienvenues-Bâtard-Montrachet Clerc **1998** £87.99 (FRI)
Bienvenues-Bâtard-Montrachet Domaine Leflaive **1997** £83.72 (GOE) £91.45 (FA) £105.75 (CAV)
Bienvenues-Bâtard-Montrachet Domaine Leflaive **1996** £80.00 (JU) £94.39 (FA)
Bienvenues-Bâtard-Montrachet Domaine Ramonet **1996** £94.39 (FA)
Bienvenues-Bâtard-Montrachet Sauzet **1997** £77.75 (FA) £99.88 (CAV)
Chassagne-Montrachet Marquis de Laguiche, Drouhin **1984** £99.88 (REI)
Chevalier-Montrachet Bouchard Père **1996** £71.87 (FA)
Chevalier-Montrachet Bouchard Père **1995** £79.00 (COC)
Chevalier-Montrachet Colin-Deleger **1997** £70.01 (GOE)
Chevalier-Montrachet Colin-Deleger **1996** £89.50 (FA)
Chevalier-Montrachet les Desmoiselles, Latour **1995** £83.62 (FA) £96.64 (WY)
Chevalier-Montrachet les Desmoiselles, Latour **1994** £85.00 (ROB)
Chevalier-Montrachet les Desmoiselles, Latour **1982** £88.13 (FA)
Chevalier-Montrachet Domaine Leflaive **1993** £74.81 (FA) £94.00 (CRO)
Chevalier-Montrachet Olivier Leflaive **1995** £96.64 (WY)
Chevalier-Montrachet Olivier Leflaive **1992** £76.38 (TW)
Chevalier-Montrachet Niellon **1991** £94.00 (FA)
Chevalier-Montrachet Sauzet **1993** £78.00 (JU)
Corton-Charlemagne Bonneau du Martray **1990** £80.00 (ROB)
Corton-Charlemagne Bouchard Père **1971** £76.38 (REI)
Corton-Charlemagne Drouhin **1985** £96.64 (WY)
Corton-Charlemagne Jadot **1992** £70.00 (ROB)
Corton-Charlemagne Jadot **1989** £89.50 (FA)
Corton-Charlemagne Latour **1988** £71.79 (WY)
Corton-Charlemagne Olivier Leflaive **1986** £86.99 (WY)
Corton-Charlemagne Georges Roumier **1988** £99.00 (YOU)
Corton-Charlemagne, Verget **1996** £89.50 (FA)
Corton-Charlemagne Michel Voarick **1992** £74.55 (WY)
Criots-Bâtard-Montrachet Olivier Leflaive **1998** £78.43 (CB)
Criots-Bâtard-Montrachet Olivier Leflaive **1995** £89.75 (WY)
Meursault Charmes, Lafon **1997** £75.00 (YOU) £99.29 (FA)
Meursault Charmes, Lafon **1993** £77.75 (FA)
Meursault Clos de la Barre, Lafon **1989** £91.45 (FA)
Meursault Genevrières, Lafon **1994** £89.50 (FA)
Meursault Perrières, Lafon **1997** £80.00 (YOU) £113.97 (FA)
Meursault Perrières, Lafon **1994** £89.50 (FA) £105.75 (CAV)
Meursault Rougeots, Coche-Dury **1997** £84.60 (FA) £87.64 (CAV)
le Montrachet Jadot **1988** £99.88 (FA)
le Montrachet Marquis de Laguiche, Drouhin **1991** £82.70 (NI)
le Montrachet Thénard **1991** £74.00 (CRO)
Puligny-Montrachet Domaine Leflaive **1983** £96.64 (WY)
Puligny-Montrachet les Pucelles, Domaine Leflaive **1996** £88.02 (WY)
Puligny-Montrachet les Pucelles, Domaine Leflaive **1992** £99.35 (NO)
Puligny-Montrachet les Pucelles, Domaine Leflaive **1986** £71.87 (FA)

£100.00 → £199.99

Bâtard-Montrachet Latour **1986** £118.73 (WY)
Bâtard-Montrachet Domaine Leflaive **1996** £120.95 (LAY) £123.38 (CAV) £172.58 (WY)
Bâtard-Montrachet Domaine Leflaive **1995** £100.00 (FORT)
Bâtard-Montrachet Domaine Leflaive **1986** £108.10 (FA)
Bâtard-Montrachet Domaine Leflaive **1982** £141.00 (CAV)

Bâtard-Montrachet Domaine Ramonet **1989** £165.87 (FA)
Bâtard-Montrachet Sauzet **1990** £118.87 (FA)
Bienvenues-Bâtard-Montrachet Domaine Ramonet **1990** £128.66 (FA)
Bienvenues-Bâtard-Montrachet Sauzet **1992** £105.75 (CAV)
Chevalier-Montrachet les Desmoiselles, Latour **1996** £100.10 (WY)
Chevalier-Montrachet Domaine Leflaive **1983** £164.50 (FA)
Chevalier-Montrachet Sauzet **1997** £104.18 (FA) £129.25 (CAV)
Corton-Charlemagne Drouhin **1989** £103.55 (WY)
Corton-Charlemagne Latour **1978** £124.26 (WY)
Meursault Charmes, Lafon **1990** £138.45 (FA)
Meursault Genevrières, Lafon **1996** £138.45 (FA)
Meursault Perrières, Lafon **1992** £138.45 (FA)
le Montrachet Amiot **1991** £148.25 (FA)
le Montrachet Bouchard Père **1995** £141.00 (CAV) £157.00 (COC)
le Montrachet Bouchard Père **1993** £100.00 (CRO)
le Montrachet Gagnard-Delagrange **1997** £128.80 (HAH)
le Montrachet Jadot **1997** £146.87 (CAV)
le Montrachet Jadot **1986** £110.67 (NO)
le Montrachet Marquis de Laguiche, Drouhin **1997** £185.00 (FORT)
le Montrachet Marquis de Laguiche, Drouhin **1996** £124.75 (RAE) £143.35 (FA) £170.00 (BEN)
le Montrachet Marquis de Laguiche, Drouhin **1993** £198.00 (ROB)
le Montrachet Marquis de Laguiche, Drouhin **1988** £117.50 (FA)
le Montrachet Marquis de Laguiche, Drouhin **1987** £188.00 (TW)
le Montrachet Marquis de Laguiche, Drouhin **1986** £195.00 (ROB)
le Montrachet Latour **1997** £109.08 (FA)
le Montrachet Latour **1995** £179.48 (WY)
le Montrachet Prieur **1997** £190.00 (YOU)
le Montrachet Sauzet **1997** £158.04 (FA)
le Montrachet Sauzet **1996** £197.20 (FA)
le Montrachet Sauzet **1995** £177.62 (FA) £229.13 (DOM)
le Montrachet Sauzet **1994** £110.00 (JU) £118.87 (FA) £129.25 (CAV)
le Montrachet Thénard **1996** £137.20 (AV)
le Montrachet Thénard **1970** £111.63 (REI)
Musigny Comte de Vogüé **1997** £127.29 (CAV)
Musigny Comte de Vogüé **1991** £103.55 (WY)
Musigny Comte de Vogüé **1987** £117.50 (TW)
Musigny Comte de Vogüé **1985** £104.18 (FA)

£200.00 → £499.99

Chassagne-Montrachet Marquis de Laguiche, Drouhin **1979** £229.13 (REI)
Chassagne-Montrachet Marquis de Laguiche, Drouhin **1971** £334.88 (REI)
Chevalier-Montrachet Domaine Leflaive **1978** £264.38 (FA)
Corton-Charlemagne Coche-Dury **1997** £352.50 (FA)
le Montrachet Amiot **1990** £224.62 (FA)
le Montrachet Lafon **1997** £295.00 (YOU)
le Montrachet Lafon **1996** £440.63 (FA)
le Montrachet Lafon **1994** £282.00 (FA)
le Montrachet Lafon **1993** £258.50 (FA) £330.00 (BEN)
le Montrachet Domaine Leflaive **1996** £465.00 (FORT)
le Montrachet Domaine de la Romanée-Conti **1993** £295.12 (FA) £440.63 (CAV)
le Montrachet Domaine de la Romanée-Conti **1991** £381.88 (CAV)
le Montrachet Domaine de la Romanée-Conti **1988** £399.50 (FA)
le Montrachet Domaine de la Romanée-Conti **1976** £411.25 (FA)
le Montrachet Domaine de la Romanée-Conti **1974** £346.63 (CAV)
Puligny-Montrachet les Referts, Sauzet **1998** £395.00 (CAV)

Over £500.00

le Montrachet Lafon **1995** £581.63 (CAV)
le Montrachet Domaine de la Romanée-Conti **1996** £587.50 (FA)
le Montrachet Domaine de la Romanée-Conti **1986** £916.50 (TW)
le Montrachet Domaine de la Romanée-Conti **1982** £750.00 (ROB)
le Montrachet Domaine de la Romanée-Conti **1978** £931.93 (WY)
le Montrachet Domaine de la Romanée-Conti **1969** £587.50 (FA)

MÂCONNAIS PRICES

RED

Under £9.00

Mâcon la Roche Vineuse, Merlin **1998** £8.60 (MV)

Mâcon Rouge Bussières, Domaine de la Sarazinière **1998** £6.82 (DOM)

WHITE

Under £5.00

Mâcon-Lugny Eugène Blanc, Cave de Lugny **1997** £4.75 (SOM)

St-Véran Domaine des Valanges, Paquet ½ bottle **1991** £4.99 (RAE)

£5.00 → £5.99

Mâcon Chardonnay Caves de Lugny **1997** £5.75 (CON)

Mâcon-Clessé Domaine de la Bon Gran, Thévenet **1997** £5.95 (NI) £14.40 (TAN) £14.88 (SAV) £15.00 (JU) £16.50 (AD)

Mâcon-Lugny les Charmes, Cave de Lugny **1997** £5.99 (UN)

Mâcon Monbellet, Goyard ½ bottle **1996** £5.99 (RAE)

Mâcon-Villages Loron **1998** £5.95 (TAN)

Mâcon-Villages Rodet **1998** £5.50 (MAR)

£6.00 → £6.99

Mâcon-Azé Domaine de Rochebin **1999** £6.07 (BIB)

Mâcon Chardonnay Le Clos, Fichet et Fils **1998** £6.81 (CHA)

Mâcon Chardonnay Domaine les Ecuyers **1998** £6.49 (SAI)

Mâcon Chardonnay Talmard **1998** £6.49 (POR) £6.65 (HAH) £6.95 (AD) £6.99 (JON) £7.20 (TAN)

Mâcon-Davaye Domaine des Deux Roches **1998** £6.95 (BER)

Mâcon-Lugny les Genièvres, Latour **1997** £6.49 (POR) £6.90 (TAN) £7.15 (COC) £7.50 (HIG) £7.64 (GOE) £7.80 (BEN) £7.99 (VIN) £8.50 (ROB) £9.50 (JER) £9.67 (WY)

Mâcon-Prissé Duboeuf **1995** £6.75 (NI)

Mâcon-Prissé Cave Co-op Prissé **1998** £6.20 (HAH)

Mâcon-Uchizy Talmard **1998** £6.90 (JU) £6.99 (BAL) £7.45 (STE) £8.37 (PLAY)

Mâcon-Villages Cave de Lugny **1998** £6.25 (FRI) £6.50 (BU)

Mâcon-Villages Domaine des Teppes de Chatennay **1998** £6.26 (CON)

Mâcon-Villages Tête de Cuvée, Verget **1998** £6.07 (FA) £8.95 (LEA) £9.95 (LAY)

Mâcon-Vinzelles Cave des Grands Crus Blancs **1998** £6.95 (LEA) £7.15 (HAW)

St-Véran Domaine St-Martin, Duboeuf **1997** £6.40 (NEZ)

£7.00 → £7.99

Mâcon-Charnay Manciat-Poncet **1998** £7.65 (HAW)

Mâcon-Clessé Michel **1996** £7.95 (RAE)

Mâcon-Davaye Domaine des Maillettes, Saumaize **1999** £7.14 (PIP)

Mâcon-Fuissé la Solutré, Vincent **1997** £7.95 (RES)

Mâcon-Loché Cave des Grands Crus Blancs **1999** £7.15 (HAW)

Mâcon-Loché Cave des Grands Crus Blancs **1998** £7.50 (BU)

Mâcon-Lugny les Charmes, Cave de Lugny **1998** £7.49 (FRI)

Mâcon-Lugny les Genièvres, Latour **1998** £7.16 (PLA) £7.35 (STA)

Mâcon-Lugny les Genièvres, Latour **1996** £7.50 (FORT) £8.50 (ROB)

★ Mâcon Milly-Lamartine, Cave de Prissé-Sologny-Verzé **1999** £7.05 (HAW)

Mâcon-Prissé Cave Co-op Prissé **1999** £7.05 (HAW)

Mâcon-Uchizy Raphael Sallet **1998** £7.05 (GOE)

Mâcon-Uchizy Talmard **1997** £7.45 (STE)

Mâcon-Villages Cave Co-op Prissé **1999** £7.00 (HAW)

Mâcon-Villages Tête de Cuvée, Verget **1997** £7.25 (FA)

Mâcon-Viré Cuvée Spéciale, Bonhomme **1996** £7.95 (WS)

St-Véran Domaine des Deux Roches **1998** £7.50 (WS) £7.60 (HAH) £7.99 (UN)

St-Véran Drouhin **1995** £7.80 (CRO)

St-Véran Caves des Grands Crus **1999** £7.55 (HAW)

St-Véran Caves des Grands Crus **1998** £7.39 (PLA)

St-Véran Mondange **1998** £7.95 (CON)

£8.00 → £9.99

Mâcon-Clessé Guillemot **1997** £9.60 (TAN) £9.80 (HAH)
Mâcon-Clessé Signoret **1999** £8.40 (HAW)
Mâcon-Davaye Domaine des Maillettes, Saumaize **1997** £8.60 (JER)
Mâcon-Villages Domaine Caveau Lamartine **1998** £8.99 (VIN)
Mâcon-Villages Tête de Cuvée, Verget **1996** £8.22 (FA) £9.60 (LAY) £10.95 (ROB)
Mâcon-Viré Chaland **1999** £8.55 (HAW)
Mâcon-Viré Chaland **1998** £8.90 (HAW)
Mâcon-Viré Cuvée Spéciale, Bonhomme **1997** £8.81 (DOM) £9.95 (SOM)
Mâcon-Viré Cuvée Spéciale, Bonhomme **1995** £9.70 (SOM)
Pouilly-Loché Domaine des Duc **1998** £9.10 (HAW)
Pouilly-Loché Cave des Grands Crus Blancs **1998** £8.55 (HAW)
Pouilly-Vinzelles Blanc Cave des Grands Crus **1998** £8.21 (PLA) £8.55 (HAW)
Pouilly-Vinzelles Bouchard Père et Fils **1997** £9.75 (COC)
Pouilly-Vinzelles Jean-Jacques Martin **1999** £9.45 (HAW)
Pouilly-Vinzelles Mathias **1998** £8.39 (PIP)
St-Véran les Chailloux Domaine des Deux Roches **1998** £8.32 (GOE)
St-Véran Domaine de la Collonge, Noblet **1997** £8.15 (LAY)
St-Véran Corsin **1999** £8.75 (STE)
St-Véran Corsin **1998** £8.75 (STE)
St-Véran en Crèches, Daniel Barraud **1998** £9.50 (LEA) £11.99 (YOU)
St-Véran Domaine des Deux Roches **1997** £8.99 (BOT) £9.49 (VIC) £9.49 (THR)
St-Véran Drouhin **1997** £9.35 (UB)
St-Véran Château Fuissé, Vincent **1998** £8.52 (DOM) £8.95 (AD) £9.15 (TAN)
St-Véran Château Fuissé, Vincent **1997** £9.50 (RES) £10.00 (MI)
St-Véran Jean-Jacques Martin **1999** £8.55 (HAW)
St-Véran Jean-Jacques Martin **1998** £8.55 (HAW)
St-Véran Domaine des Valanges, Paquet **1996** £8.99 (RAE)
St-Véran Verget **1998** £8.95 (LEA)
St-Véran Vieilles Vignes Domaine des Deux Roches **1998** £9.69 (GOE)

£10.00 → £12.49

Mâcon Monbellet, Goyard **1997** £11.99 (JON)
Mâcon Monbellet, Goyard **1996** £10.99 (RAE)
Mâcon-Villages Château de Fuissé, Vincent **1996** £11.67 (MI)
Mâcon-Villages Château de Fuissé, Vincent **1995** £11.67 (MI)
Mâcon-Viré Domaine Emilian Gillet, Thévenet **1997** £11.95 (SAV) £14.95 (LEA)
Mâcon-Viré Goyard **1997** £11.50 (JU)
Mâcon-Viré Goyard **1993** £10.99 (RAE)
Pouilly-Fuissé Domaine Béranger, Duboeuf **1997** £11.10 (NEZ)
Pouilly-Fuissé Domaine de la Collonge **1997** £11.75 (LAY)
Pouilly-Fuissé Corsin **1999** £12.45 (STE)
Pouilly-Fuissé Domaine Desroches **1997** £10.99 (UN)
Pouilly-Fuissé Cave des Grands Crus **1998** £10.45 (HAW)
Pouilly-Fuissé Latour **1997** £11.36 (COC) £13.99 (POR) £14.26 (PLAY)
★ Pouilly-Fuissé Manciat-Poncet **1997** £12.10 (HAW)
Pouilly-Fuissé Pascal Renaud **1998** £10.95 (CON)
Pouilly-Fuissé la Roche, Manciat-Poncet **1997** £10.95 (JU)
Pouilly-Fuissé Tête de Cuvée, Verget **1998** £12.14 (FA) £17.95 (LEA)
Pouilly-Fuissé les Vieux Murs, Loron **1997** £10.99 (POR)
St-Véran Corsin **1996** £11.25 (ROB)
St-Véran Cuvée Prestige Lassarat **1997** £10.25 (STA)
St-Véran Verget **1997** £11.16 (REI)
St-Véran Vieilles Vignes Domaine des Deux Roches **1996** £10.99 (POR)

£12.50 → £15.99

Mâcon-Clessé Domaine de la Bon Gran, Thévenet **1996** £13.00 (JU)
Mâcon-Clessé Domaine de la Bon Gran, Thévenet **1995** £14.95 (FORT)
Mâcon-Clessé Quintaine Domaine de la Bon Gran Tradition, Thévenet **1997** £14.79 (YOU)

★ Mâcon-Viré Quintaine Domaine Emilian Gillet, Thévenet **1998** £13.95 (LEA)
Mâcon-Viré Quintaine, Domaine Emilian Gillet, Thévenet **1997** £14.35 (NI)
Mâcon-Viré Quintaine Domaine Emilian Gillet, Thévenet **1996** £15.98 (TW)
Pouilly-Fuissé Clos du Bourg, Luquet **1997** £12.95 (FORT)
Pouilly-Fuissé Corsin **1998** £15.10 (REI)
Pouilly-Fuissé la Croix, Denogent **1998** £13.90 (GAU)
Pouilly-Fuissé Château Fuissé, Vincent **1998** £14.39 (REI) £14.69 (DOM) £14.90 (TAN)
Pouilly-Fuissé Château Fuissé, Vincent **1997** £14.69 (DOM) £15.00 (JU) £17.95 (LAY) £17.95 (DI)
Pouilly-Fuissé les Reisses Vieilles Vignes, Denogent **1998** £14.95 (GAU)
Pouilly-Fuissé la Roche, Daniel Barraud **1998** £13.95 (LEA)
Pouilly-Fuissé la Roche, Daniel Barraud **1997** £13.95 (LEA) £14.49 (YOU)
Pouilly-Fuissé Tête de Cuvée, Verget **1997** £13.61 (FA) £16.90 (LAY) £16.95 (LEA)
Pouilly-Fuissé Tête de Cuvée, Verget **1996** £13.61 (FA)
Pouilly-Fuissé la Verchère, Daniel Barraud **1998** £13.50 (LEA)
Pouilly-Fuissé la Verchère, Daniel Barraud **1997** £13.50 (LEA)
Pouilly-Fuissé Verget **1997** £14.95 (LEA)
Pouilly-Fuissé Vieilles Vignes, Daniel Barraud **1997** £15.95 (LEA)

£16.00 → £19.99

Mâcon-Clessé Domaine Emilian Gillet, Thévenet **1989** £17.50 (TW)
Mâcon-Clessé Quintaine, Guillemot-Michel **1989** £17.50 (TW)
Mâcon-Viré Domaine Emilian Gillet, Thévenet **1995** £17.50 (TW)
Mâcon-Viré Domaine Emilian Gillet, Thévenet **1992** £19.39 (TW)
Pouilly-Fuissé les Brûlés, Château Fuissé **1998** £18.50 (AD) £20.00 (MI)
Pouilly-Fuissé les Brûlés, Château Fuissé **1997** £18.95 (BER) £19.17 (MI)

Stars (★) indicate wines selected by Oz Clarke in the Best Buys section which begins on page 10.

Pouilly-Fuissé le Clos, Château Fuissé **1998** £16.45 (DOM) £20.00 (MI)
Pouilly-Fuissé le Clos, Château Fuissé **1997** £17.00 (JU) £19.17 (MI) £20.50 (RES)
Pouilly-Fuissé les Combettes, Château Fuissé **1997** £17.00 (JU) £19.17 (MI)
Pouilly-Fuissé les Crays, Forest **1998** £16.99 (YOU) £24.35 (BAN)
Pouilly-Fuissé Cuvée Claude Vieilles Vignes, Denogent **1998** £17.25 (GAU)
Pouilly-Fuissé Cuvée Claude Vieilles Vignes, Denogent **1997** £17.25 (GAU)
Pouilly-Fuissé Château Fuissé Vieilles Vignes, Vincent **1998** £19.09 (GOE) £19.39 (DOM) £22.50 (MI)
Pouilly-Fuissé Château Fuissé Vieilles Vignes, Vincent **1997** £18.80 (DOM) £19.90 (JU) £21.67 (MI) £21.75 (SOM) £22.50 (RES) £26.30 (PLAY)
Pouilly-Fuissé Château Fuissé, Vincent **1995** £17.95 (DI) £20.83 (MI)
Pouilly-Fuissé Hors Classe, Ferret **1998** £19.00 (RAE)
Pouilly-Fuissé Tête du Cru, Ferret **1998** £16.94 (RAE)
Pouilly-Fuissé Tête du Cru, Ferret **1997** £18.99 (BAL)
Pouilly-Fuissé Vieilles Vignes, Manciat-Poncet **1997** £19.90 (JU)

£20.00 → £29.99

Mâcon-Clessé Quintaine Sélection de Grains Cendrés, Guillemot-Michel **1992** £29.00 (CRO)
Pouilly-Fuissé les Brûlés, Château Fuissé **1996** £23.33 (MI)
Pouilly-Fuissé le Clos, Château Fuissé **1996** £21.00 (RES)
Pouilly-Fuissé les Combettes, Château Fuissé **1998** £20.00 (MI)
Pouilly-Fuissé les Combettes, Château Fuissé **1996** £23.33 (MI)
Pouilly-Fuissé les Crays, Forest **1997** £20.00 (FORT)
Pouilly-Fuissé Château Fuissé Vieilles Vignes, Vincent **1996** £23.00 (RES) £26.67 (MI)
Pouilly-Fuissé Château Fuissé, Vincent **1996** £20.00 (MI)
Pouilly-Fuissé Hors Classe, Ferret **1997** £23.50 (BAL)
Pouilly-Fuissé Hors Classe, Ferret **1996** £24.50 (BAL)

CHAMPAGNE

With no shortage of Champagne in sight, despite Millennium excesses, it pays to time your buying to coincide with the best cut-price offers in the shops

Well, there wasn't a shortage, was there? Come the end of last year, if you wanted Champagne there it was: lots of it, just for the taking. And this year there's been just as much around as ever. We didn't drink Champagne dry at the Millennium, although some of us did our level best.

As always, though, the wines on offer are sometimes just a wee bit young for comfort. The most common vintage on sale now is 1993, which needs a bit longer – not that much longer, but in most cases a year or two wouldn't hurt. The better wines need three or four years more.

Non-vintage wines, as ever, will benefit from being tucked away for another six months. The simplest way of buying Champagne is to wait until you see a good money-saving offer, then buy enough to see you through to the next lot of money-saving offers. Since they normally come in summer and winter it's quite easy to plan one's budget.

Why shops should cut the price of Champagne just when in theory everyone wants it is beyond me. I, in my innocence, would expect it to be the other way round: you cut the price when it's not selling. But what do I know?

GRAPE VARIETIES

CHARDONNAY Imparts elegance and freshness to the blend, not to mention acidity and structure. Good Chardonnay from here ages superbly, so just because Blanc de Blancs (which is entirely Chardonnay) has whiplash elegance, don't think you've got to drink it young.

PINOT NOIR Adds weight to the blend, even though it's vinified as a white wine, without the skins: a Champagne relying on Pinot Noir is certain to be heavier than those made from other grapes. It can also go with food better. And yes, Champagne does make a very little still red wine from Pinot Noir, but it takes a hot year to make it attractive. Most Pinot made as red wine is used to colour rosé.

PINOT MEUNIER Champagne's second black grape, making a softer, fruitier style of wine, important for producing simple wines for drinking young, and useful for lightening the assertive weight of Pinot Noir. Soft, commercial blends are usually heavy on the Pinot Meunier, and none the worse for it.

WINE STYLES AND LABELLING

BLANC DE BLANCS Champagne made only from Chardonnay; it has become more fashionable as drinkers look for a lighter style. Should not only be fresh but creamy and bright as well, and should get deeper and richer as it ages. Some firms, notably *Gimonnet, Henriot, Mumm, Bruno Paillard* and *Joseph Perrier* make excellent NV (non-vintage) Blanc de Blancs, and the *Union* co-operatives at Avize and le Mesnil make the most of their positions at the heart of the Côte des Blancs. Some firms sell vintage Blanc de Blancs (watch out for *Billecart-Salmon, Delamotte, Deutz, Drappier, Jacquesson, Pol Roger, Roederer, Jacques Sélosse*) and a couple also make luxury cuvées. *Taittinger's Comtes de Champagne, Dom Ruinart, Salon* and Krug's *Clos de Mesnil* are the benchmarks. But with no easy-going Pinot Meunier to fatten out the wine, any fault is glaringly obvious, so stick to good producers.

BLANC DE NOIRS This white style is made from black grapes only. Few have the quality and longevity of *Bollinger*'s *Vieilles Vignes*, but none is even half as expensive. Most are rather solid. *Pierre Vaudon* is an elegant exception, and tremendous value for money; *H Billiot* is fine, and the *Sainsbury's* version is good value, and benefits from extra bottle age.

BRUT Very dry – more so than either 'Sec' or 'Extra Dry'. Most non-vintage Champagne sold in Britain is Brut.

BUYER'S OWN BRAND (BOB) A wine blended to a buyer's specification, or more probably, to a price limit. The grapes are of lesser quality, the wines usually younger, and cheaper. However, *Sainsbury's* and *Waitrose* Champagnes are consistent and good value.

CM Means *co-opérative-manipulant* and shows that the wine comes from a co-op, whatever the brand name implies.

COTEAUX CHAMPENOIS Still wines, red, rosé or white. Overpriced and generally rather acid. A village name, such as Cramant (white) or Bouzy (red) may appear. *Alain Vesselle*'s Bouzy and *René Geoffroy*'s Cumières red can be good, but all producers' still wines are as variable as the climate.

DE LUXE/CUVÉE DE PRESTIGE/ CUVÉE DE LUXE All these terms signify a special, highly prized blend, mostly vintage. Some are undeniably great wines and some gaudy coat-tailers. At these prices one is looking for immense complexity and refinement. In general these wines are drunk *far* too young. Most need a good ten years to shine. Some of the best: *Billecart-Salmon Cuvée NF Billecart, Bollinger RD, Cattier Clos du Moulin, Gosset Grande Réserve, Charles Heidsieck Cuvée de Millenaires, Dom Pérignon, Dom Ruinart, Krug Grande Cuvée, Laurent Perrier Grand Siècle, Leclerc Briant Cuvée Divine, Perrier-Jouët Belle Époque, Philipponnat Clos des Goisses, Pol Roger Cuvée Sir Winston Churchill, Roederer Cristal, Taittinger Comtes de Champagne, Veuve Clicquot la Grande Dame.*

DEMI-SEC Medium-sweet. Rarely very nice, but *Louis Roederer* can be outstanding, and *Veuve Clicquot* is the most consistent.

DOUX Sweet. *Louis Roederer*'s is an excellent example.

EXTRA DRY Confusingly, this is less dry than 'Brut', but drier than 'Sec'.

GRAND CRU In Champagne it is communes that are classified, not individual

MATURITY CHART
1991 Champagne
Should not be opened too early

ON THE CASE
If you buy Champagne to lay down, be sure to keep it somewhere cool and dark. Champagne is particularly susceptible to light

vineyards, and the 17 *grand cru* communes in the region are the best. The next best are the *premiers crus*.

GRANDE MARQUE Ambiguous term meaning 'great brand', and now officially defunct, since the Syndicat is disbanded. It may re-form under a new name, eventually.

NM This means *négociant-manipulant* (merchant-handler) and shows that the producer is one of the 265 Champagne houses operating in the region.

NON-DOSAGE Most Champagne has a little sweetness – a 'dosage' – added just before the final cork is put in. A few have minimal dosage and will have names like Brut Zero. Best are *Laurent-Perrier, Piper-Heidsieck*, and *Duval Leroy* has just launched one. They're designed to show that it's the wine, not the dosage that provides the quality. Do they prove their point? Well, they need to be very ripe to be able to balance the austerity.

NON-VINTAGE (NV) The flagship of most houses, and the one by which a producer should be judged. The wines are generally based on one vintage and usually aged for three years. But many of the best provide greater depth and age, and ensure consistency by using up to 40 per cent of *vins de réserve* (wines from previous years) thus giving more depth and maturity to the blend. At the moment quality is generally pretty good, and of the major names only *Mercier, Mumm, Moët* and *Canard-Duchêne* are seriously disappointing. Rather more (like *Piper-Heidsieck, Charles Heidsieck*) have reached a level of good, reliable quality, but lack personality. For real character try *Besserat de Bellefon, Billecart-Salmon, Bollinger, Gosset, Alfred Gratien, Henriot, Jacquart, Krug, Mailly Grand Cru, Bruno Paillard, Joseph Perrier, Pol Roger, Pommery, Roederer, Taittinger* (superb), *Pierre Vaudon, Veuve Clicquot* and *Vilmart*. All will improve if you keep them for a few months in bottle after purchase. A new trend is to feature the year of bottling on the label, so you can tell how long the wine has had to mature. It's a good idea but don't mistake these wines for vintage Champagne.

PREMIER CRU The 41 *premier cru* communes are those just below *grand cru* in quality. All the others are unclassified.

RC *Récoltant-co-opérateur* – a grower selling wine made at a co-op. It's supposed to stop growers from pretending they've made it themselves, when all they did was deliver the grapes. Should do, but somehow it doesn't seem to appear on labels that often.

RECENTLY DISGORGED A term for Champagnes that have been left in the cellars, drawing flavour from their yeast deposits, for much longer than usual before disgorging. The wines can rest for 20 or perhaps even 30 years on the lees but are usually released after seven to ten years. *Bollinger RD* is the most famous and is still the best; also good are *Deutz, Alfred Gratien* and *Laurent-Perrier*. The idea is that you should drink them as soon as you buy them, with no further bottle age, at which point they have freshness balanced by maturity.

RICH The sweetest Champagne. *Roederer* can be superbly balanced. *Veuve Clicquot* has a great vintage version.

RM Indicates that a grower, a *récoltant-manipulant*, made it himself, rather than taking it to the co-op. Try: *Bara, Billiot, Bonnaire, Clouet, René Geoffroy, Michel Gonet, André Jacquart, Lassalle, Legras, Vesselle, Vilmart*.

ROSÉ Usually made by adding a little still red to white wine before bottling. Only a few companies (like *Laurent-Perrier*) still make it by macerating red grapes on the skins until the right shade of pink is achieved. Ideally rosés are aromatic, fruity wines, with a delicious strawberry or cherry flavour. Sadly, many are indistinguishable from white. Most should be drunk young. Best: *Billecart-Salmon, Bollinger, Charbaut, Dom Ruinart, Alfred Gratien, Jacquart Mosaïque, Lassalle, Laurent-Perrier, Pol Roger, Louise Pommery, Roederer* and *Roederer Cristal. Krug rosé* is way ahead in a class of its own, and at that price so it should be.

SEC Literally 'dry', but any Champagne so labelled will actually be medium dry. 'Extra Dry' and 'Brut' are drier.

SR Société de Récoltants. Label code for a family company of growers.

VINTAGE The wine produced from the grapes of a single, good year. Vintage Champagne should be fuller and deeper than non-vintage, but almost always released too young, so you need to age it yourself. An awful lot of lesser producers make a vintage when they (and we) would be better off if they concentrated on improving their non-vintage. Best names to look for: *Besserat de Bellefon, Billecart-Salmon, Bollinger, Delamotte, Gosset Grande Millésime, Henriot, Krug, Mailly Grand Cru, Bruno Paillard, Joseph Perrier, Laurent-Perrier, Pol Roger, Pommery, Louis Roederer, Ruinart, Salon, Jacques Sélosse, Taittinger, Pierre Vaudon* and *Veuve Clicquot.*

CHAMPAGNE HOUSES WHO'S WHO

BESSERAT DE BELLEFON ★★★★ Makes, elegant, restrained Champagnes of good depth.

BILLECART-SALMON ★★★★(★) Terrifically elegant Champagne from a family-owned house. Very refined, mature wines and a delicate rosé. Its vintage, Cuvée NF Billecart, is also excellent.

BOLLINGER ★★★★(★) Like Krug, Bollinger makes 'English-style' Champagnes: rich, oaky, but more steely and almost half the price. The NV is excellent. RD is kept on its lees until just before sale.

F BONNET ★★ Inexpensive offshoot of Piper-Heidsieck and Charles Heidsieck, with mature and biscuity non-vintage.

DEUTZ ★★★ This house is back on form again with creamy-rich, biscuity non-vintage and an excellent quality prestige cuvée called William Deutz.

DRAPPIER ★★(★) Consistent quality, although the style bounces between ultra-fruity and rich and biscuity according to how much bottle age the wine has.

DUVAL-LEROY ★★ Fresh, fragrant style in a Chardonnay-dominated Champagne. Good value and consistent decent quality.

ALFRED GRATIEN ★★★★ Serious, oak-fermented wine at a much lower price than Krug. Very long-lived vintage. Even the non-vintage needs extra bottle age.

CHARLES HEIDSIECK ★★★★ Good value and reliable; rich, full style and good vanilla finesse. Excellent bottle-aged NV.

HENRIOT ★★★★ Good bottle age and unrelenting high quality. Very rich and deep.

JACQUESSON ★★★ Good quality and finesse in both the elegant, flowery non-vintage or the rich, well-extracted vintage.

KRUG ★★★★★ Classic, mellow, rich. Oak-fermented Grande Cuvée is outstanding. The expensive rosé has incomparable Pinot Noir cherry fruit. Even more expensive Clos de Mesnil is a rich, single-vineyard Blanc de Blancs.

LANSON ★★★ Classic, long-maturing vintage. Give the NV extra bottle age, too.

LAURENT-PERRIER ★★★★ One of the most reliable of NVs, with excellent rosé. Prestige brand Grand Siècle is a blend of several vintages, but there is also a more expensive vintage version.

MOËT & CHANDON ★★★ Brut Impérial is reliably good. The vintage wine is stylish. De luxe Dom Pérignon can be one of the greatest Champagnes of all.

BRUNO PAILLARD ★★★ Fresh, elegant and satisfying Champagne from one of the most consistent producers.

JOSEPH PERRIER ★★★★ The NV is extremely rich and well aged, with biscuity complexity and wonderfully high acidity.

PERRIER-JOUËT ★★★ Light, classic Champagne. Best known for Belle Époque in a pretty bottle, all flowery elegance.

POL ROGER ★★★★ Delicious, delicate Blanc de Blancs. Top class across the board, including prestige cuvée Sir Winston Churchill and vintage Blanc de Chardonnay.

POMMERY ★★★ Currently on good form, with wines of light, flowery elegance. Prestige cuvée Louise Pommery is superb.

LOUIS ROEDERER ★★★★★ Superb quality, lovely depth and finesse. The subtle, ripe NV is hard to beat, and prestige cuvée Cristal is wonderful. Good Demi-sec, too.

RUINART ★★★★ The non-vintage 'R' de Ruinart has lots of bottle age and a style closer to the traditional 'goût anglais' than many. Not for fans of light, young and delicate Champagne. The vintage is rich.

INSTANT CELLAR:
WHAT'S LEFT AFTER THE MILLENNIUM?

- **NV Cuillier Père et Fils, Brut Traditionelle, £16, Justerini & Brooks** A good price for a really nutty, creamy Champagne.
- **NV Louis Roederer Brut Premier, £24.99, widely available** A supremely elegant Champagne.
- **NV Gosset Brut Excellence, £19.54, John Harvey & Sons** Lovely creamy, balanced Champagne.
- **NV Waitrose Blanc de Noirs, £11.99** Good lively fruit, and not suffering from greenness, unlike some non-vintage Champagnes at the moment.
- **NV Lanson Black Label, c. £20, widely available** A Champagne that really does need to be put away and forgotten for a few years. It is more acidic and longer living than most non-vintage – but needs more age to begin with.
- **NV Pierre Moncuit, Grand Cru Blanc de Blancs, Le Mesnil, £16.25, H & H Bancroft** Elegant, bready 100% Chardonnay Champagne from a grower in one of the top villages of the region.
- **NV F Bonnet Brut Héritage, £15.99, Oddbins** Rich, creamy fruit, at a good price.

TAITTINGER ★★★★(★) Splendidly light, modern, Chardonnayish style of great excitement, though its Blanc de Blancs Comtes de Champagne goes sumptuously rich with age.

PIERRE VAUDON ★★★(★) This stands up extremely well against the top Grandes Marques, and it's not expensive. Good, weighty, ripe stuff.

VEUVE CLICQUOT ★★★★ The NV has a rich, warm style, and prestige cuvée la Grande Dame is almost chocolate-rich.

VILMART ★★★(★) Rich, full Champagne, more in the Bollinger than the Pommery mode. Plenty of flavour, weight and ripeness. Good vintage.

CHAMPAGNE VINTAGES

In theory Champagne firms only make single-vintage wines in especially fine years. But only a few firms, like Bollinger and Laurent-Perrier, follow the theory. Most either opt too readily for vintage wines in marginal years or, increasingly, release wines after only five years in bottle, which may be okay for French tastes but leaves the average Brit with an acid stomach. Nevertheless, most firms come up with decent vintage.

1999 A highly promising year that will give some very good vintage wines. They'll be released long before they're ready to drink, as usual, and will need to be kept further. But they're ripe, fruity wines with good structure.

1998 Ripe wines that promise well. Expect plenty of vintage declarations, and no shortage of good Champagne in the new century.

1997 A ripe vintage with plentiful yields.

1996 Splendidly ripe, balanced wines that are likely to be widely declared. The non-vintage wines should be good, as well, when they start coming on stream. This is probably the vintage to go for after 1990 – skip the intervening ones.

1995 The wines are significantly superior to those of the previous four years, and this will be the first widely declared vintage since the outstanding 1990.

1994 Of the few reputable producers likely to declare this a vintage, Vilmart's Grand Cellier d'Or will probably be the best.

1993 Roederer managed to produce a vintage Champagne after rejecting no less than half its own crop. Not a bad vintage, but there are better ones coming up behind.

1992 The 1992s are appearing on the shelves, and so far they're not impressive. Too many are green and coarse, though Perrier-Jouët might turn out okay.

1991 Coming into the shops now, and looking surprisingly good. Elegance and structure seem to be the keys to this vintage, and it needs time.Taittinger looks good, as do Pommery, Philipponnat's Clos des Goisses, Vilmart's Coeur de Cuvée, Henri Mandois and De Nauroy. Roederer declared a rosé.

1990 Many of the wines are superb, though few are still available. Try Jacquart, Lanson, Laurent-Perrier, Perrier-Jouët, Pommery, Roederer, Ruinart, Taittinger, Pierre Vaudon. They'll still improve.

1989 Most need a few years yet, though they're coming on beautifully. Look for Besserat de Bellefon, Gosset, Alfred Gratien, Bruno Paillard.

1988 The wines have bite, backbone and fruit, but most are already sold out.

1987 A lot of wine, but even the Champenois are not enthusiastic about its quality. Only Pommery declared a vintage, and any remaining bottles should really be drunk.

1986 Would have made a decent, if slightly hard vintage, but got sold far too young. One or two minor houses have wines available, and they're attractive.

1985 Fine wines, without any of the hardness of some vintages. There's very little still available, but if you've got any it should be delicious now.

CHAMPAGNE PRICES

SPARKLING WHITE

Under £10.00

Billecart-Salmon Brut Reserve ½ bottle **NV** £9.83 (SAV) £9.95 (LEA) £11.20 (AD) £11.75 (LIB)

Deutz Brut Classic ½ bottle **NV** £8.70 (JER)

Georges Gardet Guy de St Flavy **NV** £9.95 (SOM) £12.92 (GOE) £13.95 (BAL) £13.99 (JON)

Duc de Marre Special Cuvée ½ bottle **NV** £7.99 (WAI)

£10.00 → £11.99

Duchâtel **NV** £11.99 (UN)

Laurent-Perrier Brut LP ½ bottle **NV** £10.95 (LEA) £11.49 (PLAY) £11.69 (GW) £11.79 (CB)

Moët & Chandon Brut Impérial ½ bottle **NV** £11.20 (TAN) £11.46 (PLA) £11.91 (PLAY) £11.95 (ROB) £11.99 (POR) £11.99 (BO) £12.31 (CB) £12.49 (TES) £12.49 (UN) £12.49 (WR) £12.49 (BOT) £12.49 (BUD) £12.75 (OD) £13.25 (FORT) £13.45 (STE) £14.25 (JER)

£12.00 → £13.99

Bollinger ½ bottle **NV** £12.73 (GOE) £13.65 (CON) £13.70 (TAN) £13.99 (DI) £14.31 (CB) £14.39 (REI) £14.69 (TW) £14.95 (LEA) £14.95 (STA) £14.95 (ROB) £14.99 (VA) £15.30 (BEN) £15.95 (FORT) £16.87 (VIN) £17.95 (JER)

Canard-Duchêne **NV** £13.90 (CRO) £15.99 (COC) £16.39 (PLA) £16.45 (ROB) £16.49 (SAF) £16.99 (MAJ) £16.99 (BO) £16.99 (UN) £16.99 (WAI) £18.29 (PLAY) £19.95 (JER)

Devilliers Brut **NV** £13.00 (JU)

Duc de Marre Special Cuvée Extra Dry **NV** £13.99 (WAI)

Veuve Clicquot ½ bottle **NV** £12.67 (CB) £12.75 (CON) £12.75 (LEA) £12.75 (REI) £13.49 (BO) £13.50 (ROB) £14.69 (UN)

£14.00 → £15.99

Bauget-Jouette **NV** £14.00 (HIG) £15.49 (AME)

Baron de Beaupré **NV** £15.49 (POR)

F. Bonnet **NV** £15.99 (OD)

★ Le Brun de Neuville Cuvée Chardonnay **NV** £14.15 (WAT)

Camuset Réserve **NV** £14.89 (BIB)

Drappier Carte d'Or **NV** £15.30 (BY) £15.99 (VIC) £15.99 (THR) £15.99 (WR) £15.99 (BOT) £16.48 (FLE)

Georges Gardet Blanc de Blancs **1990** £14.95 (SOM) £16.85 (CON)

Georges Gardet Brut Special **NV** £14.99 (CON) £15.18 (GOE) £15.95 (BAL) £19.99 (VIN)

★ Pierre Gimonnet Blanc de Blancs **NV** £14.99 (OD)

Henri Harlin **1989** £15.99 (OD)

Heidsieck Dry Monopole **NV** £15.99 (JON) £15.99 (BUD) £16.49 (OD) £16.99 (POR)

Jacquart Tradition **NV** £15.49 (BO)

Lamiable Brut **NV** £14.50 (HIG)

Le Mesnil Blanc de Blancs Brut **NV** £14.49 (WAI) £14.59 (SAV)

Piper-Heidsieck **NV** £15.99 (TES) £17.99 (VIC) £17.99 (THR) £17.99 (WR) £17.99 (BOT) £18.99 (ASD) £18.99 (SO) £18.99 (BO) £18.99 (UN) £18.99 (WAI) £18.99 (SAF) £20.17 (PLAY) £20.65 (UB)

Pol Roger **NV** £14.90 (SOM) £23.50 (WS)

MERCHANTS SPECIALIZING IN CHAMPAGNE

see Merchant Directory (page 456) for details

Most good merchants have a fair variety of Champagnes, and generally list the most popular of the Grandes Marques, plus one or two cheaper ones. Most, too, have a pretty varied list of sparkling wines from other countries, and it is quite hard to single out merchants with exceptionally good lists of Champagne. Nevertheless, for a wider than average choice, try especially: Adnams (AD), Averys of Bristol (AV), Bennetts (BEN), Bibendum (BIB), Farr Vintners (FA), Justerini & Brooks (JU), Lea & Sandeman (LEA), Majestic (MAJ), Oddbins (OD), Roberson (ROB), T&W Wines (TW), Tanners (TAN), Peter Wylie (WY) – a few old vintages.

Pol Roger White Foil **NV** £15.95 (SOM) £19.09 (GOE) £22.30 (TAN) £22.49 (VA) £22.50 (CON) £22.50 (RES) £22.90 (COC) £22.99 (MAJ) £22.99 (VIC) £22.99 (THR) £22.99 (UN) £22.99 (WR) £22.99 (BOT) £22.99 (JON) £23.79 (REI) £23.95 (HAH) £23.95 (LEA) £23.99 (BEN) £23.99 (POR) £23.99 (OD) £24.00 (MV) £24.25 (WRI) £24.25 (BER) £24.90 (JER) £24.95 (UB) £24.95 (STA) £24.95 (ROB) £25.06 (PLAY)

Salon **NV** £15.99 (VIC) £15.99 (THR) £15.99 (WR)
de Telmont **NV** £14.99 (MAJ)
Pierre Vaudon 1er Cru **NV** £15.70 (HAH)

£16.00 → £17.99

Ayala **NV** £16.99 (MAJ)
Beerens Brut Reserve **NV** £16.65 (BIB)
Billecart-Salmon Brut Reserve **NV** £17.14 (GOE) £18.49 (SAV) £18.95 (LEA) £19.85 (WRI) £19.95 (ELL) £19.95 (VA) £19.95 (AD) £19.95 (GAU) £19.95 (ROB) £19.99 (PHI) £19.99 (NI) £20.25 (JER) £20.92 (CB) £20.95 (LIB) £20.99 (OD) £21.45 (BER)
Boizel **NV** £16.50 (WS)
Deutz Brut Classic **NV** £16.70 (JER) £21.99 (NEZ)
Drappier **NV** £16.99 (POR)
Duchâtel **1994** £16.99 (UN)
Ellner **NV** £16.45 (LAY)
Gimonnet **1995** £16.99 (OD)
★ Alfred Gratien The Wine Society's Private Cuvée **NV** £17.00 (WS)
Henriot Souverain **NV** £17.48 (COC)
Legras Grand Cru Blanc de Blancs **NV** £16.95 (LEA)
Mercier **NV** £16.99 (COC) £17.49 (ASD) £17.49 (TES) £17.49 (VIC) £17.49 (THR) £17.49 (UN) £17.49 (WR) £17.49 (BOT) £17.49 (SAF) £17.69 (BUD) £17.95 (ROB)
Mercier Demi-Sec **NV** £17.49 (TES) £17.49 (VIC) £17.49 (THR) £17.49 (WR)
Joseph Perrier Cuvée Royal **NV** £16.95 (STE) £17.50 (ROB) £17.99 (GW)
Pierre Vaudon 1er Cru **1995** £17.90 (HAH)

£18.00 → £19.99

Blin **1991** £18.99 (OD)
Le Brun de Neuville Cuvée du Rois Clovis **NV** £19.45 (WAT)
Drappier Carte d'Or **1995** £19.90 (CRO)
Georges Gardet **NV** £18.88 (VIN)
Georges Gardet **1990** £19.35 (CON)
Alfred Gratien **NV** £19.95 (CON)
Charles Heidsieck Brut Reserve **NV** £19.99 (WR) £19.99 (BOT) £23.00 (JU)
Henriot Blanc de Blancs **NV** £18.95 (COC)
Lamiable Le Club **1993** £19.00 (HIG)
Lanson **NV** £18.49 (CON) £18.51 (PLA) £18.99 (ASD) £18.99 (SO) £18.99 (TES) £19.95 (STA) £19.99 (BY) £19.99 (POR) £19.99 (VIC) £19.99 (THR) £19.99 (WR) £19.99 (BOT) £19.99 (SAF) £19.99 (BUD) £20.90 (WRI) £21.99 (WAI) £22.99 (UN)
Laurent-Perrier Brut LP **NV** £19.39 (GOE) £19.96 (PLA) £19.99 (GW) £20.95 (CON) £21.00 (WS) £21.89 (PLAY) £21.99 (VIC) £21.99 (THR) £21.99 (WR) £21.99 (BOT) £22.43 (CHA) £22.82 (BIB) £22.91 (CB) £22.95 (HED) £22.99 (MAJ) £22.99 (OD) £23.00 (JU) £23.75 (AD) £23.95 (LAY)
Moët & Chandon Brut Impérial **NV** £19.49 (ASD) £19.49 (TES) £19.95 (VA) £20.00 (UN) £20.50 (PLA) £20.75 (WRI) £20.95 (COC) £20.99 (CON) £20.99 (MAJ) £20.99 (POR) £20.99 (BO) £20.99 (VIC) £20.99 (THR) £20.99 (WR) £20.99 (BOT) £20.99 (WAI) £20.99 (SAF) £20.99 (BUD) £21.30 (TAN) £21.50 (FRI) £21.95 (ROB) £21.97 (BY) £22.15 (JER) £22.29 (PLAY) £22.80 (WAT) £23.60 (LAY) £23.97 (CB) £24.25 (FORT) £24.75 (STE) £25.00 (JU)
Mumm Cordon Rouge **NV** £19.49 (ASD) £19.49 (VIC) £19.49 (THR) £19.49 (UN) £19.49 (WR) £19.49 (BOT) £19.95 (ROB) £19.99 (OD) £19.99 (SAF)
Bruno Paillard **NV** £18.99 (BO)
Palmer Brut **1990** £18.00 (JU)
Perrier-Jouët **NV** £19.95 (ROB) £19.99 (BO) £19.99 (VIC) £19.99 (THR) £19.99 (WR) £19.99 (BOT) £19.99 (BOD) £19.99 (SUN) £20.99 (MAJ) £20.99 (OD)
Pol Roger **1993** £19.25 (SOM) £24.48 (GOE) £34.99 (MAJ) £36.00 (LEA)

Stars (★) indicate wines selected by Oz Clarke in the Best Buys section which begins on page 10.

Taittinger Brut Réserve NV £19.00 (JER) £20.86 (PLA) £22.50 (ELL) £22.58 (PLAY) £22.90 (VA) £23.95 (LEA) £23.95 (ROB) £23.99 (VIC) £23.99 (THR) £23.99 (UN) £23.99 (WR) £23.99 (BOT) £23.99 (POR) £23.99 (TES) £24.93 (BY) £24.95 (BAL) £24.99 (SAF) £24.99 (MAJ) £24.99 (OD) £25.75 (STE) £25.84 (GW) £26.50 (FORT) £26.45 (UB)

Thienot NV £19.95 (UN)

Veuve Clicquot NV £18.95 (SOM) £22.74 (PLA) £22.90 (FLE) £22.95 (TAN) £23.01 (BIB) £23.25 (COC) £23.49 (ASD) £23.50 (CON) £23.50 (REI) £23.75 (WRI) £23.95 (LEA) £23.95 (VA) £23.98 (PIP) £23.99 (BO) £24.35 (JER) £24.38 (PLAY) £24.49 (TES) £24.49 (VIC) £24.49 (THR) £24.49 (OD) £24.49 (UN) £24.49 (BOT) £24.49 (BOD) £24.49 (SUN) £24.50 (ROB) £24.68 (CB) £24.95 (PHI) £24.95 (STA) £24.99 (MAJ) £24.99 (POR) £25.15 (HAH) £25.76 (HA) £25.95 (LAY) £25.99 (BAL) £26.00 (MV) £26.25 (STE) £26.45 (AD) £26.75 (FORT) £26.95 (VIN) £27.61 (WY)

£20.00 → £21.99

Charles Heidsieck Brut Reserve 1985 £21.54 (FA)

Laurent-Perrier Brut NV £21.99 (UN) £22.50 (ROB) £25.50 (JER)

Pommery Royale NV £20.99 (TES) £20.99 (SAF) £23.00 (JU)

'R' de Ruinart NV £21.99 (WR) £21.99 (BOT) £23.30 (HAH) £24.50 (FORT) £25.65 (LAY)

£22.00 → £23.99

H Billiot Cuvée de Réserve Brut NV £22.71 (BIB)

Bollinger NV £22.90 (CRO) £24.48 (GOE) £24.50 (TAN) £24.68 (PLA) £24.95 (CON) £25.49 (BO) £25.50 (FRI) £25.95 (DI) £25.95 (VA) £25.95 (ROB) £25.99 (ASD) £25.99 (SO) £25.99 (BAL) £25.99 (POR) £25.99 (TES) £25.99 (VIC) £25.99 (THR) £26.00 (PIP) £26.00 (YAP) £26.44 (TW) £26.44 (REI) £26.75 (WRI) £26.90 (COC) £26.95 (HAH) £27.19 (PLAY) £27.50 (LEA) £27.60 (BEN) £27.95 (STA) £27.95 (BER) £27.97 (CB) £27.99 (MAJ) £27.99 (OD) £27.99 (UN) £27.99 (WAI) £27.99 (SAF) £27.99 (BUD) £28.99 (VIN) £29.00 (JU) £29.00 (MV) £29.50 (LAY) £29.50 (FORT) £29.50 (STE) £29.57 (GW) £31.76 (WY) £32.35 (UB)

Bollinger Grande Année ½ bottle 1990 £22.56 (CB)

Gosset Grande Reserve NV £23.45 (SOM) £27.50 (PHI) £27.85 (WRI) £27.95 (LEA) £28.13 (HA) £28.50 (RES) £29.19 (NO) £29.95 (WR) £29.95 (BOT) £29.95 (ROB) £29.99 (BAL) £35.00 (FORT)

Charles Heidsieck Brut Réserve Mis en Cave NV £23.49 (UN) £23.49 (SAF) £23.50 (GOE) £24.50 (POR) £25.69 (PIP) £27.49 (WAI) £30.00 (FORT)

Le Mesnil Blanc de Blancs Brut 1995 £23.49 (JON)

Piper-Heidsieck 1990 £23.99 (WR) £23.99 (BOT) £25.99 (SAF)

Pol Roger Chardonnay 1990 £22.35 (SOM) £44.00 (BEN) £49.95 (GAU) £55.00 (VIN)

- *Wines are listed in A–Z order within each price band.*
- *For each wine, vintages are listed in descending order.*
- *Each vintage of any wine appears only once.*

Louis Roederer Brut Premier **NV** £22.03 (GOE) £22.95 (COC) £22.99 (VA) £23.95 (TAN) £23.95 (LEA) £23.99 (CON) £24.00 (WS) £24.09 (REI) £24.62 (PLA) £24.85 (WRI) £24.95 (PHI) £24.95 (NI) £24.99 (MAJ) £24.99 (BO) £24.99 (TES) £24.99 (OD) £24.99 (GW) £24.99 (POR) £24.99 (VIC) £24.99 (THR) £24.99 (UN) £24.99 (WR) £24.99 (BOT) £24.99 (WAI) £24.99 (SAF) £24.99 (BOD) £25.00 (FORT) £25.50 (RES) £25.95 (BEN) £25.95 (STA) £25.95 (JER) £25.99 (FRI) £26.44 (TW) £26.60 (HAH) £26.70 (PLAY) £26.75 (LAY) £26.75 (ROB) £26.91 (CB) £27.45 (BER) £27.95 (STE) £27.95 (AD) £27.99 (VIN) £28.23 (HA)

Veuve Clicquot Demi-Sec **NV** £22.90 (TAN) £24.49 (VIC) £24.49 (THR) £24.49 (OD) £24.49 (UN) £24.49 (BOT)

£24.00 → £25.99

Charles Heidsieck Brut Reserve **1990** £25.85 (CAV) £27.91 (GOE) £32.00 (JU)

Moët & Chandon Brut Impérial **1995** £24.99 (ASD)

Moët & Chandon Brut Impérial **1993** £25.79 (PLA) £27.75 (WRI) £27.99 (MAJ) £27.99 (POR) £27.99 (TES) £27.99 (VIC) £27.99 (THR) £27.99 (UN) £27.99 (WR) £27.99 (BOT) £27.99 (JON) £28.45 (WAT) £29.23 (PLAY) £29.38 (CB) £29.95 (TAN) £29.95 (VA) £30.00 (JU) £30.00 (FORT) £32.80 (JER) £32.85 (HAH)

Mumm Cordon Rouge **1990** £24.49 (VIC) £24.49 (THR) £24.49 (WR) £24.49 (BOT)

Orpale Grand Cru, Blanc de Blancs **1998** £25.00 (MAR)

Bruno Paillard Blanc de Blancs **NV** £25.99 (PHI)

Perrier-Jouët **1992** £25.99 (VIC) £25.99 (THR) £25.99 (WR) £25.99 (BOT) £27.99 (MAJ) £27.99 (OD) £31.11 (PIP) £32.65 (UB)

Perrier-Jouët **1990** £25.95 (ROB)

Louis Roederer Rich **NV** £25.00 (CON) £25.67 (PLA) £26.00 (WRI) £27.25 (BEN) £27.75 (STA) £27.85 (HAH) £28.50 (ROB) £28.79 (CB) £29.25 (STE) £30.00 (FORT)

Please remember that
Oz Clarke's Wine Buying Guide
is a price ***guide*** *and not a price* ***list****. It is not meant to replace up-to-date merchants' lists.*

£26.00 → £29.99

Billecart-Salmon Brut Reserve **1991** £29.99 (OD)

Billecart-Salmon Cuvée N.F. Billecart **1991** £28.40 (SAV) £29.95 (LEA) £30.00 (FORT) £33.30 (JER) £35.00 (ELL)

Deutz Brut **1993** £26.99 (NEZ) £27.90 (JER)

Lanson **1990** £27.99 (OD)

Laurent-Perrier Ultra Brut **NV** £28.95 (ROB) £29.99 (WR) £29.99 (BOT)

Moët & Chandon Brut Impérial **1992** £26.73 (COC) £27.49 (BO) £27.50 (CON) £27.99 (THR) £27.99 (OD) £28.95 (ROB)

Mumm Crémant de Cramant Blanc de Blancs **NV** £28.50 (ROB)

Perrier-Jouët **1995** £27.99 (OD)

Pol Roger **1990** £26.93 (GOE) £29.50 (COC) £32.70 (TAN) £33.00 (JU) £33.50 (ROB) £34.35 (UB) £34.70 (HAH) £34.95 (RES) £34.99 (BEN) £34.99 (THR) £34.99 (WR) £34.99 (BOT) £36.00 (LEA) £36.95 (STA) £37.00 (MV) £39.90 (GAU) £40.00 (FORT)

Pol Roger Chardonnay **1988** £27.91 (FA) £42.50 (WRI)

Pommery **1992** £27.99 (TES)

'R' de Ruinart **1992** £26.99 (WR)

'R' de Ruinart **1990** £29.95 (LEA)

Taittinger **1995** £28.99 (POR) £32.50 (STE)

Veuve Clicquot **1989** £29.80 (CRO)

£30.00 → £39.99

Bauget-Jouette Grande Réserve magnum **NV** £36.00 (HIG)

Billecart-Salmon Cuvée N.F. Billecart **1995** £33.33 (MI) £37.95 (LIB) £38.95 (AD)

Billecart-Salmon Cuvée N.F. Billecart **1990** £33.96 (CB) £35.83 (MI) £39.90 (GAU)

Billecart-Salmon Grande Cuvée **1991** £36.95 (VA)

Bollinger **1990** £35.25 (FA) £38.50 (CON) £38.95 (COC) £41.99 (TES) £41.99 (VIC) £41.99 (THR) £42.00 (WRI) £42.10 (HAH) £43.95 (BEN) £45.99 (UN) £46.00 (MV) £47.99 (VIN) £48.80 (PIP) £55.50 (AD)

Bollinger Grande Année **1993** £39.99 (POR)

Bollinger Grande Année **1990** £38.60 (TAN) £38.77 (GOE) £39.90 (GAU) £39.95 (LEA) £41.00 (JU) £41.50 (WS) £41.71 (TW) £41.95 (ROB) £42.00 (YAP) £42.04 (PLAY) £43.95 (CB) £45.00 (BAL) £45.00 (VA) £45.00 (RES) £46.45 (STE) £46.50 (FORT)

Bollinger Grande Année **1989** £36.00 (CRO)
Drappier Carte d'Or **1979** £35.00 (CRO)
Georges Gardet Brut Special magnum **NV** £30.35 (GOE) £32.50 (CON) £45.00 (VIN)
Gosset Grande Millésime **NV** £36.99 (PHI)
Gosset Grande Millésime **1993** £34.95 (LEA) £36.00 (WRI) £39.95 (WR) £39.95 (BOT)
Gosset Grande Millésime **1989** £33.65 (SOM) £38.99 (YOU) £39.50 (LEA) £41.50 (RES) £43.50 (ROB) £44.00 (BAL)
Charles Heidsieck Brut Reserve **1981** £32.31 (REI)
Heidsieck Diamant Bleu **1989** £39.99 (OD)
Krug Grande Cuvée ½ bottle **NV** £32.99 (VIC) £32.99 (THR) £32.99 (WR) £32.99 (BOT) £35.00 (ROB) £35.16 (CB) £36.50 (UN) £37.50 (STA) £38.00 (CRO) £39.36 (TW) £39.85 (AD) £40.00 (FORT) £42.00 (FRI) £43.90 (JER) £49.50 (STE)
Laurent-Perrier Brut **1993** £38.95 (AD)
Laurent-Perrier Brut **1990** £33.20 (AV) £33.21 (PLAY) £33.99 (TES) £34.66 (CB) £36.00 (HED) £38.55 (CHA)
Laurent-Perrier Brut LP **1988** £35.25 (CB)
Laurent-Perrier Brut LP ½ bottle **1966** £37.01 (REI)
Moët & Chandon Brut Impérial **1990** £35.00 (FRI)
Moët & Chandon Brut Impérial **1976** £39.17 (FA) £52.88 (REI)
Moët & Chandon Brut Impérial magnum **NV** £37.95 (WR) £37.95 (BOT) £38.95 (TES) £40.99 (BO) £41.20 (TAN) £41.99 (UN) £42.75 (WRI) £43.95 (ROB) £43.99 (JON) £48.66 (CB) £48.95 (STE) £49.00 (FORT) £51.40 (LAY) £57.15 (JER)
Orpale Grand Cru, Blanc de Blancs **1990** £33.90 (HAH)
Perrier-Jouët magnum **NV** £39.95 (ROB)
Pol Roger **1988** £32.31 (REI) £34.99 (YOU)
Taittinger **1992** £31.28 (PLAY) £32.50 (LEA) £32.50 (STE) £35.99 (OD)
Taittinger **1991** £35.00 (JU)
Taittinger **1990** £34.99 (WR) £34.99 (BOT)
Taittinger Brut Réserve **1992** £32.95 (ROB)
Veuve Clicquot **1993** £31.55 (PLA) £32.28 (COC) £32.41 (PIP) £33.00 (TAN) £35.00 (WS) £35.25 (REI) £35.99 (MAJ) £36.90 (CB) £36.95 (FORT)
Veuve Clicquot **1992** £32.75 (WRI)
Veuve Clicquot **1990** £31.00 (FLE) £31.33 (FA) £32.00 (JU)
Veuve Clicquot Rich **1991** £35.99 (OD)
Veuve Clicquot Rich **1990** £32.05 (HAH)
Veuve Clicquot Rich **1988** £35.99 (BOT)
Veuve Clicquot Vintage Reserve **1993** £33.95 (LEA) £35.95 (ROB) £36.25 (STE)
Veuve Clicquot Vintage Reserve **1991** £32.99 (YOU) £34.02 (PLAY) £35.00 (VA) £35.03 (HA) £35.99 (VIC) £35.99 (THR) £35.99 (UN) £35.99 (WR) £35.99 (BOT) £35.99 (WAI)

£40.00 → £49.99

Billecart-Salmon Blanc de Blancs **1995** £49.95 (LIB)
Billecart-Salmon Blanc de Blancs **1988** £40.00 (MI)
Billecart-Salmon Grande Cuvée **1989** £47.00 (SAV) £49.50 (LEA) £49.90 (GAU) £55.00 (NI) £68.80 (JER)
Bollinger Grande Année **1992** £45.99 (MAJ)
Bollinger RD **1988** £47.49 (FA) £53.99 (YOU) £55.00 (FORT) £58.00 (LEA) £59.00 (VA) £60.20 (GAU) £75.00 (BER)
Bollinger RD **1985** £42.30 (CB) £49.95 (DI) £50.92 (FA) £56.79 (GOE) £57.95 (VIC) £57.95 (THR) £57.95 (WR) £57.95 (BOT) £62.00 (ROB) £65.00 (BAL)
Deutz Brut Classic magnum **NV** £48.65 (JER)
Alfred Gratien **1985** £45.00 (FORT)
Lanson magnum **NV** £41.49 (VIC) £41.49 (THR) £41.49 (WR) £41.49 (BOT)
Laurent-Perrier 'La Cuvée' Grande Siècle **NV** £49.50 (LEA) £49.95 (WR) £49.95 (BOT) £52.00 (WS) £55.00 (AD)
Laurent-Perrier Brut LP magnum **NV** £40.95 (LEA) £43.99 (MAJ) £46.06 (CHA) £47.13 (CB)
Moët & Chandon Brut Impérial **1973** £47.00 (REI)
Mumm René Lalou **1985** £47.00 (CRO)
Perrier-Jouët **1988** £41.13 (REI)
Perrier-Jouët Belle Époque **1990** £43.08 (FA) £49.99 (VIC) £49.99 (THR) £49.99 (WR) £49.99 (BOT) £54.99 (OD) £57.50 (ROB) £65.00 (FORT) £65.00 (FRI)
Pol Roger Chardonnay **1993** £45.00 (RES)
Pol Roger Cuvée Sir Winston Churchill **1990** £41.95 (SOM) £66.19 (FA) £74.00 (YOU) £75.00 (LEA) £75.00 (OD) £75.75 (HAH) £76.50 (BEN) £79.00 (RES)
Pol Roger magnum **NV** £49.00 (RES)
Pol Roger White Foil magnum **NV** £44.06 (GOE) £50.00 (WRI) £51.50 (ROB) £55.00 (FORT) £57.64 (REI)
Louis Roederer **1994** £45.25 (STE)
Louis Roederer **1993** £40.80 (TAN) £43.55 (HAH) £45.00 (FORT) £45.00 (VA)

THE BEST SELLING

DEPUIS 1858
CHAMPAGNE
MERCIER
Epernay - France
MPAGNE IN FRANCE

Louis Roederer 1990 £44.00 (CRO) £44.50 (STA) £44.90 (BER) £44.95 (UN) £45.00 (WAI) £48.70 (LAY)

Louis Roederer Blanc de Blancs 1993 £40.54 (PLA) £43.00 (BEN) £45.95 (STE) £46.50 (FORT) £49.95 (LAY)

Louis Roederer Blanc de Blancs 1991 £44.50 (STA)

Veuve Clicquot la Grande Dame 1990 £48.47 (GOE) £50.92 (FA) £59.95 (LEA) £61.84 (HA) £62.50 (CON) £63.45 (HAH) £64.23 (PLAY) £64.99 (YOU) £65.00 (FORT) £66.00 (BAL) £66.95 (VA) £66.95 (RES) £67.95 (ROB) £67.99 (OD) £69.50 (UN) £69.99 (MAJ) £73.55 (JER)

Veuve Clicquot magnum NV £46.99 (PHI) £47.00 (CON) £47.95 (LEA) £48.99 (UN) £49.99 (VIC) £49.99 (THR) £49.99 (WR) £49.99 (BOT) £50.08 (CB) £51.50 (ROB)

£50.00 → £59.99

Bollinger ½ bottle 1966 £52.29 (REI)

Bollinger magnum NV £51.90 (TAN) £52.95 (CON) £53.95 (PHI) £55.00 (DI) £55.00 (WS) £56.66 (CB) £56.95 (ROB) £57.80 (LAY) £58.75 (BEN)

Deutz Cuvée de William Deutz 1990 £54.99 (NEZ) £57.75 (JER)

Dom Pérignon 1992 £59.00 (WAT) £59.50 (TAN) £59.95 (CON) £59.95 (POR) £59.99 (BO) £60.00 (WRI) £60.71 (FA) £61.10 (PLA) £61.69 (BIB) £63.30 (JER) £63.57 (CB) £64.45 (VA) £64.50 (STA) £64.63 (REI) £64.95 (LEA) £64.99 (MAJ) £64.99 (TES) £64.99 (VIC) £64.99 (THR) £64.99 (UN) £64.99 (WR) £64.99 (BOT) £65.00 (ROB) £65.25 (HAH) £66.50 (STE) £66.58 (HA) £66.58 (GOE) £66.99 (JON) £67.23 (PLAY) £67.50 (FORT) £80.00 (MI) £85.00 (JU)

Dom Pérignon 1990 £58.60 (COC) £69.99 (OD) £70.50 (FA) £75.00 (ROB) £79.00 (POR) £85.00 (MI) £85.00 (RES) £85.95 (PIP) £99.98 (VIN) £105.75 (REI)

Dom Ruinart Blanc de Blancs 1990 £54.00 (LEA) £54.99 (WR) £54.99 (BOT)

Dom Ruinart Blanc de Blancs 1988 £58.16 (REI) £59.00 (LEA) £60.00 (FORT)

Alfred Gratien 1983 £55.00 (WS)

- *All prices for each wine are listed together in ascending order.*
- *Price bands refer to the lowest price for which the wine is available.*

Heidsieck Diamant Bleu 1985 £56.99 (REI)

Krug Grande Cuvée NV £50.92 (FA) £62.95 (SOM) £64.00 (WAT) £65.95 (VIC) £65.95 (THR) £65.95 (WR) £65.95 (BOT) £66.39 (PLA) £67.00 (FRI) £67.75 (BEN) £67.96 (PIP) £68.31 (COC) £68.54 (GOE) £68.95 (VA) £69.50 (TAN) £69.68 (CB) £69.95 (CON) £69.95 (BER) £69.99 (TES) £69.99 (JON) £70.00 (BO) £70.50 (REI) £70.82 (PLAY) £71.29 (BIB) £72.00 (LEA) £72.00 (CRO) £73.00 (UN) £74.99 (OD) £75.00 (PHI) £75.00 (POR) £75.00 (AD) £75.95 (VIN) £76.55 (HAH) £76.90 (LAY) £77.25 (TW) £79.00 (BAL) £79.95 (RES) £80.00 (FORT) £80.00 (ROB) £85.00 (JU) £86.75 (JER) £100.00 (MI) £102.00 (UB)

Georges Lilbert Blanc de Blancs 1976 £52.87 (TW)

Moët & Chandon Brut Impérial ½ bottle 1955 £52.88 (REI)

Moët & Chandon Brut Impérial magnum 1993 £55.95 (ROB)

Moët & Chandon Brut Impérial magnum 1992 £55.95 (VIC) £55.95 (THR) £55.95 (WR) £55.95 (BOT) £56.50 (UN)

Perrier-Jouët Belle Époque 1995 £54.99 (OD) £66.06 (PIP)

Philipponnat Clos des Goisses 1989 £58.50 (SOM)

Pol Roger Cuvée Sir Winston Churchill 1986 £50.92 (FA) £59.50 (COC)

Salon 1985 £58.75 (FA) £68.05 (CAV) £125.00 (GAU)

Taittinger Collection Artist's Label 1985 £55.81 (FA)

Taittinger Comtes de Champagne Blanc de Blancs 1989 £58.54 (PLAY) £69.95 (ROB) £74.99 (GW) £75.00 (TES)

Taittinger Comtes de Champagne Blanc de Blancs 1988 £54.83 (FA) £59.00 (JU) £69.95 (BAL) £75.00 (WR) £75.00 (BOT)

Taittinger Comtes de Champagne Blanc de Blancs 1986 £56.99 (REI)

Veuve Clicquot 1982 £57.08 (MI)

£60.00 → £74.99

Bollinger Grande Année magnum **1990** £73.44 (CAV) £83.70 (TAN) £88.62 (CB)
Bollinger RD **1979** £72.46 (FA) £79.95 (DI) £95.00 (LEA) £96.50 (GAU) £112.80 (TW)
Dom Pérignon **1993** £69.00 (PHI)
Dom Pérignon **1985** £70.50 (FA) £90.00 (ROB) £111.63 (REI) £117.36 (WY)
Alfred Gratien magnum **1990** £60.00 (WS)
Charles Heidsieck Brut Reserve **1964** £74.38 (REI)
Krug **1989** £67.56 (FA) £76.38 (BIB) £76.99 (VIC) £76.99 (THR) £76.99 (WR) £76.99 (BOT) £78.50 (TAN) £78.63 (PIP) £79.31 (CB) £80.00 (WS) £85.00 (CON) £85.00 (LEA) £85.00 (OD) £85.95 (BEN) £86.50 (PHI) £86.66 (PLAY) £89.95 (AD) £92.00 (RES) £92.00 (ROB) £92.30 (HAH) £95.00 (FORT) £95.76 (TW) £98.99 (VIN) £99.95 (UN) £111.63 (REI) £125.00 (MI)
Laurent-Perrier 'La Cuvée' Grande Siècle **1990** £70.00 (OD) £78.28 (PLAY)
Pol Roger Cuvée Sir Winston Churchill **1988** £67.56 (REI) £68.75 (WRI) £75.00 (WAI) £75.00 (WS) £79.00 (ROB) £80.00 (FORT)
Salon **1988** £70.50 (CB) £76.00 (GAU)
Salon **1983** £62.67 (FA) £90.00 (FORT)
Taittinger Comtes de Champagne Blanc de Blancs **1993** £73.50 (STE) £75.00 (POR) £79.99 (MAJ)
Taittinger Comtes de Champagne Blanc de Blancs **1990** £60.71 (FA) £69.95 (ROB) £70.00 (FORT) £75.00 (WAI)
Veuve Clicquot la Grande Dame **1989** £67.50 (AD) £70.00 (MI)
Veuve Clicquot la Grande Dame **1988** £68.00 (WR) £68.00 (BOT)
Veuve Clicquot magnum **1990** £69.90 (HAH)
Veuve Clicquot Rich **1989** £73.06 (PIP)

£75.00 → £99.99

Bauget-Jouette Grande Réserve Jeroboam **NV** £99.88 (HIG)
Bollinger ½ bottle **1947** £99.88 (REI)
Bollinger Grande Année magnum **1989** £75.00 (BO) £81.51 (NO) £111.62 (TW)
Bollinger magnum **1990** £80.00 (CON)
Bollinger RD **1981** £75.00 (LEA)
Bollinger RD **1975** £78.33 (FA) £125.50 (BEN) £141.00 (TW) £145.00 (FORT)
Dom Pérignon **1983** £80.29 (FA)
Henriot **1959** £99.50 (YOU)
Krug **1988** £88.12 (PLA) £89.00 (BER) £95.00 (OD) £98.00 (STA) £135.00 (MI)
Krug **1985** £85.19 (FA) £111.63 (REI)
Krug Grand Cuvée magnum **1964** £99.88 (REI)
Lanson Red Label **1964** £76.38 (REI)
Moët & Chandon Brut Impérial ½ bottle **1953** £99.88 (REI)
Mumm Cordon Rouge **1961** £88.13 (REI)
Perrier-Jouët Belle Époque magnum **1985** £86.17 (FA)
Philipponnat Clos des Goisses **1990** £79.00 (GAU)
Pol Roger Cuvée Sir Winston Churchill **1996** £89.99 (VIN)
Pol Roger Cuvée Sir Winston Churchill **1982** £79.95 (BEN)
Pol Roger magnum **1990** £77.00 (FORT)
Pommery **1964** £88.13 (REI)
Louis Roederer Cristal **1998** £99.95 (WR) £99.95 (BOT)
Louis Roederer Cristal **1994** £80.95 (NI) £89.00 (LEA) £102.81 (NO)
Louis Roederer Cristal **1993** £80.95 (NI) £81.85 (GW) £85.00 (CON) £85.70 (WRI) £85.80 (TAN) £86.95 (CB) £88.13 (PLA) £89.54 (HA) £93.06 (PLAY) £93.45 (STE) £94.50 (BEN) £95.00 (ROB) £95.15 (HAH) £99.00 (POR) £99.00 (RES) £99.50 (UN) £99.99 (PHI) £99.99 (MAJ) £99.99 (OD) £107.71 (GOE) £110.00 (FORT) £115.00 (FRI) £120.00 (VA) £127.00 (JER)
Louis Roederer Cristal **1991** £92.00 (STA)
Louis Roederer Cristal **1990** £87.20 (COC) £124.35 (FA) £129.25 (TW) £150.00 (JU)
Veuve Clicquot magnum **1992** £81.50 (JER)

£100.00 → £129.99

Bollinger jeroboam **NV** £119.00 (DI) £125.00 (TAN) £145.00 (VIN)
Deutz Brut Classic jeroboam **NV** £116.60 (JER)
Dom Pérignon **1975** £127.29 (FA) £146.88 (CAV) £146.88 (REI)
Dom Pérignon **1971** £120.00 (ROB)
Dom Pérignon magnum **1989** £125.00 (BO)
Dom Ruinart Blanc de Blancs **1955** £129.25 (REI)
Charles Heidsieck Brut Reserve **1955** £129.25 (REI)
Krug **1982** £115.05 (FA)
Laurent-Perrier 'La Cuvée' Grande Siècle magnum **NV** £115.30 (CHA)

Moët & Chandon Brut Impérial **1955** £129.25 (REI)
Moët & Chandon Brut Impérial jeroboam **NV** £109.50 (CON) £115.00 (UN) £122.40 (COC) £129.95 (STE) £135.00 (WR) £135.00 (BOT)
Perrier-Jouët Belle Époque magnum **1990** £118.00 (ROB) £130.00 (FORT)
Pommery **1955** £129.25 (REI)
Louis Roederer Cristal **1983** £104.77 (FA) £140.00 (NO)
Veuve Clicquot la Grande Dame **1985** £120.00 (MI)
Veuve Clicquot jeroboam **NV** £120.00 (UN) £129.00 (WR) £129.00 (BOT)

£130.00 → £199.99

Bollinger **1953** £176.25 (REI)
Bollinger Vieilles Vignes Françaises, Blanc de Noirs **1990** £150.00 (FORT) £150.00 (ROB) £165.00 (BEN)
Bollinger Vieilles Vignes Françaises, Blanc de Noirs **1989** £145.96 (NO) £152.75 (TW)
Bollinger Vieilles Vignes Françaises, Blanc de Noirs **1988** £146.88 (REI)
Dom Pérignon **1966** £189.96 (FA)
Dom Pérignon magnum **1990** £140 00 (CAV) £145.00 (FORT) £234.71 (WY)
Dom Pérignon magnum **1988** £150.00 (ROB) £160.00 (MI) £176.25 (GW)
Krug Clos du Mesnil Blanc de Blancs **1989** £156.67 (FA) £167.75 (HAH) £185.00 (LEA) £185.00 (RES) £185.00 (ROB) £205.00 (MI)
Krug Clos du Mesnil Blanc de Blancs **1986** £142.96 (FA) £195.00 (FORT)
Krug Collection **1979** £168.42 (FA)
Krug Grand Cuvée magnum **NV** £149.00 (ROB) £159.50 (AD) £160.00 (RES)
Krug Grand Cuvée magnum **1989** £185.00 (RES)
Moët & Chandon Brut Impérial magnum **1970** £146.88 (REI)
Pol Roger **1934** £170.38 (REI)
Pol Roger Cuvée Sir Winston Churchill magnum **1988** £145.90 (GAU) £160.00 (FORT)
Pol Roger Cuvée Sir Winston Churchill magnum **1986** £189.95 (VIN)
Pol Roger White Foil jeroboam **NV** £130.00 (WRI)
Louis Roederer Cristal **1988** £146.88 (REI)
Salon magnum **1983** £141.59 (CB)
Taittinger Comtes de Champagne Blanc de Blancs **1971** £170.38 (REI)
Veuve Clicquot **1959** £176.25 (REI)

£200.00 → £299.99

Dom Pérignon **1959** £258.50 (REI)
Krug **1920** £205.63 (REI)
Moët & Chandon Brut Impérial methuselah **NV** £225.00 (CON) £225.00 (UN) £239.00 (COC) £259.00 (WR) £259.00 (BOT)
Pol Roger White Foil methuselah **NV** £245.00 (FORT) £247.00 (WRI)
Louis Roederer Cristal magnum **1993** £200.00 (FORT) £275.00 (LEA)
Salon **1976** £225.00 (GAU)
Veuve Clicquot magnum **1959** £235.00 (FA)
Veuve Clicquot methuselah **NV** £280.00 (UN)

Over £300.00

Bollinger jeroboam **1979** £470.00 (TW)
Krug Grand Cuvée magnum **1966** £495.00 (VIN)
Moët & Chandon Brut Impérial jeroboam **1943** £763.75 (REI)
Moët & Chandon Brut Impérial salmanazar **NV** £330.00 (UN) £359.00 (WR)
Perrier-Jouët Belle Époque jeroboam **1975** £411.25 (REI)
Perrier-Jouët magnum **1947** £323.13 (REI)
Pol Roger White Foil salmanazar **NV** £367.00 (WRI) £425.00 (FORT)

SPARKLING ROSÉ

Under £17.50

Georges Gardet **1995** £13.50 (SOM)
F Bonnet **NV** £16.49 (OD)
Alexandre Bonnet Prestige **NV** £15.99 (WAI)
Le Brun de Neuville Cuvée Rosé **NV** £17.35 (WAT)
Canard-Duchêne **NV** £16.50 (CRO) £17.48 (HA)
Lamiable **NV** £15.50 (HIG)
Mercier **NV** £16.69 (COC) £17.49 (VIC) £17.49 (THR) £17.49 (WR) £17.49 (BOT)

£17.50 → £19.99

Bauget-Jouette **NV** £17.99 (AME)
Beerens **NV** £18.60 (BIB)
Duval Leroy Brut Rosé **NV** £19.95 (AD)
Georges Gardet **1994** £17.50 (CON)
Piper-Heidsieck **NV** £18.99 (TES)
Pol Roger **1990** £19.95 (SOM) £35.00 (CON) £39.00 (WS) £39.95 (RES) £39.95 (ROB) £39.99 (OD) £42.50 (FORT)

£20.00 → £29.99

Billecart-Salmon Brut **NV** £21.25 (MI) £24.48 (SAV) £25.75 (AD) £25.95 (LEA) £26.50 (STA) £26.95 (ROB) £27.50 (ELL) £27.50 (FORT) £27.50 (JER) £27.95 (WRI) £28.50 (PHI) £28.95 (VA) £29.50 (BER) £29.95 (LIB) £29.95 (NI) £29.99 (VIN) £29.99 (OD) £35.90 (GAU) £36.42 (TW)
Deutz **1993** £27.99 (NEZ) £30.45 (JER)
Georges Gardet **NV** £26.95 (VIN)
Gosset Grande **NV** £27.95 (LEA) £29.50 (RES) £30.95 (ROB) £32.00 (BAL)
Lanson **NV** £23.49 (VIC) £23.49 (THR) £23.49 (WR) £23.49 (BOT) £25.49 (UN)
Lanson **1993** £25.99 (VIC) £25.99 (THR) £25.99 (WR) £25.99 (BOT)
Laurent-Perrier **NV** £26.14 (REI) £26.95 (LEA) £27.90 (JER) £27.95 (VA) £27.95 (FRI) £27.95 (ROB) £28.00 (CON) £28.00 (WS) £28.38 (PLAY) £28.45 (AV) £28.70 (TAN) £28.91 (CB) £28.99 (GW) £28.99 (TES) £28.99 (VIC) £28.99 (THR) £28.99 (UN) £28.99 (WR) £28.99 (BOT) £28.99 (JON) £28.99 (BOD) £28.99 (SUN) £29.08 (CHA) £29.37 (PLA) £29.50 (HED) £30.00 (JU) £30.00 (FORT) £30.00 (MV) £30.37 (TW) £30.99 (MAJ) £30.99 (OD) £31.10 (HAH) £31.34 (BIB) £31.66 (PIP)
Moët & Chandon Brut **NV** £23.89 (VIN) £24.99 (SAF) £28.95 (JER)
Moët & Chandon Brut Impérial **NV** £25.00 (TAN) £25.99 (JON) £26.17 (PLAY)
Bruno Paillard **NV** £22.99 (PHI)
Bruno Paillard 1er Cuvée **NV** £22.71 (BIB)
Joseph Perrier Cuvée Royale **NV** £20.56 (GW) £22.95 (STE)
'R' de Ruinart **NV** £25.99 (BO) £25.99 (WR) £25.99 (BOT) £27.95 (LEA) £27.99 (JON)
Taittinger **NV** £27.95 (POR) £28.62 (PLAY) £28.95 (STE) £30.00 (FORT) £34.00 (JU)

£30.00 → £39.99

Bollinger **1988** £35.25 (FA)
Charles Heidsieck **1985** £32.96 (PIP)
Moët & Chandon Brut Impérial **1993** £32.50 (UN) £33.50 (ROB) £34.50 (FORT)
Pol Roger **1988** £37.40 (UB) £46.95 (VIN)
Veuve Clicquot **1993** £37.95 (ROB) £39.50 (FORT)
Veuve Clicquot **1990** £34.50 (CON) £37.95 (ROB)
Veuve Clicquot **1988** £37.99 (VIC) £37.99 (THR) £37.99 (BOT)
Veuve Clicquot **1985** £37.99 (YOU)

£40.00 → £99.99

Billecart-Salmon Cuvée Elisabeth Salmon **1995** £62.50 (MI)
Bollinger **1990** £45.75 (BEN) £49.50 (FORT)
Bollinger **1985** £89.75 (WY)
Bollinger Grande Année **1990** £41.99 (FRI) £42.95 (DI) £54.40 (LAY)
Deutz **1975** £40.00 (YOU)
Dom Ruinart **1986** £59.99 (BOT)
Krug **NV** £98.00 (LEA) £99.88 (REI) £103.70 (HAH) £105.00 (JU) £110.00 (RES) £116.20 (TW) £120.00 (ROB)
Moët & Chandon Brut **1966** £76.38 (REI)
Perrier-Jouët Belle Époque **1990** £49.99 (THR) £49.99 (WR) £49.99 (BOT)
Perrier-Jouët Belle Époque **1989** £60.00 (FORT) £82.00 (UB)
Perrier-Jouët Belle Époque **1988** £54.95 (ROB)
Louis Roederer **1993** £44.40 (HAH) £44.50 (STA) £45.00 (VA) £45.95 (STE)
Louis Roederer **1991** £44.95 (ROB)
Taittinger Comtes de Champagne **1993** £59.64 (PLAY)
Veuve Clicquot **1989** £62.13 (WY)

£100.00 → £199.99

Dom Pérignon **1988** £141.98 (CAV) £148.83 (FA) £152.66 (PLAY) £155.00 (ROB) £160.00 (OD) £165.00 (FORT)
Dom Pérignon **1986** £165.00 (ROB) £165.68 (WY) £170.00 (UN) £190.00 (MI)
Dom Pérignon **1982** £180.00 (VA)
Pommery **1934** £170.38 (REI)
Louis Roederer Cristal **1993** £199.00 (OD)
Louis Roederer Cristal **1990** £176.25 (FA) £180.00 (FORT) £190.00 (STA)
Louis Roederer Cristal **1989** £147.11 (CB) £160.00 (FA) £165.00 (RES)
Louis Roederer Cristal **1979** £150.00 (YOU)

JURA & SAVOIE

Strange wines, hardly ever seen and even less often drunk. If you want to try them you will have to go out of your way to find them

These wines get more and more esoteric. To be honest, I don't know why I continue to write about them: if you want to find a bottle of any of them here in Britain you have to look very hard. The merchants at the bottom of this page stock some, but I can't believe the demand is enormous. They're included for the sake of completeness; and because if you go skiing in the French Alps you might come across one or two of them. And actually, they're rather interesting.

WINES & WINE REGIONS

ARBOIS, AC (red, white, rosé) The reds are thuddingly full of flavour. The Savagnin grape weaves its demonic spell on the whites, though Chardonnay sometimes softens it. There are some attractive light reds and rosés made from Pinot Noir or Poulsard. Best: *Henri Maire, Pupillin co-op*.

BUGEY, VDQS (red, white) Look for the deliciously crisp Chardonnays; they're among the most refreshing (and yes, fruity) in France.

CÔTES DU JURA, AC (red, white, rosé) Virtually indistinguishable in style and flavour (and grape varieties) from Arbois wines, though sometimes a little less weird.

CRÉPY, AC (white) The Chasselas grape here produces an even flimsier version of the already delicate Swiss Fendant, if that's possible. Drink young and fast, or not at all.

L'ÉTOILE, AC (white) Whites from Savagnin and Chardonnay. Also *vins jaunes*.

ROUSSETTE DE SAVOIE, AC (white) Fullest and softest of the Savoie whites.

SEYSSEL, AC and SEYSSEL MOUSSEUX, AC (white) The Roussette (blended with a little Molette) makes quite full, flower-scented but sharp-edged whites. The fizz is light but pepper-pungent. Best: *Varichon et Clerc*.

VIN JAUNE (white) This grows the same yeasty *flor* as dry sherry, and its startlingly, painfully intense flavours from the Savagnin grape just get more and more evident as it matures. In fact it seems virtually indestructible. Château-Chalon AC is the most prized – and most pricy – and is difficult to find even in the region.

VIN DE SAVOIE, AC (red, white) These Alpine vineyards are some of the most beautiful in France and produce fresh, snappy wines. The white, from the Jacquère, Chardonnay or Chasselas, can be excellent, dry, biting, but with lots of tasty fruit. Drink young. The reds from Pinot Noir or Gamay are subtly delicious, while the Mondeuse produces some beefy beauties in hot years. A *cru* name may be on the best. Look for the villages of Abymes, Chignin, Apremont, Cruet, Montmélian, Chautagne and Arbin.

MERCHANTS SPECIALIZING IN JURA AND SAVOIE

see Merchant Directory (page 456) for details

Very few of these wines are available in the UK. Nobody exactly specializes in them, but the following merchants have some: Anthony Byrne (BY), S H Jones (JON), Terry Platt (PLA), Roberson (ROB), Tanners (TAN), Wine Society (WS).

LOIRE

If you want wines that will match food and seduce everyone who drinks them, and yet not be in the least showy and flashy, this is your region

It's no coincidence that one of the principal merchants specializing in the wines of the Loire is a London restaurant. It was the restaurant that came first: it made a point, and still does, of listing pages and pages of Loire wines. Dry whites, sweet whites, reds from every good appellation, different vintages, different growers, all with a careful and informative tasting note. The restaurant is popular because it serves first-class food. (It's called RSJ, if you're interested.) The wines became popular with its customers because they went so well with that food. The customers wanted to drink the same wines at home. Hey presto.

The point of Loire wines, white and red, is that they do go with food. They're not showy, they're not bursting with tropical fruit or spice; they would seldom beat a New World equivalent for intensity of flavour or richness of tannin. They're just terribly, terribly nice, and when you've finished the bottle you think, 'I'd rather like some more.' And they're affordable, too.

GRAPE VARIETIES

CABERNET FRANC (red) The great quality grape of Anjou and Touraine. All the best reds are based on Cabernet Franc, and the styles span the spectrum from the palest, most fleeting of reds to deep, strong and often austerely tannic wines of character and longevity. Often added to (white) sparkling wines, too.

CABERNET SAUVIGNON (red) This doesn't always ripen very well in the Loire, but even so it adds some backbone to the wines. It is really at its best in the warmest, ripest years.

CHARDONNAY (white) Increasingly widespread in the Loire and producing lean, light but tangy results in Haut-Poitou, in Anjou as Vin de Pays du Jardin de la France and in Orléans as Vin de l'Orléanais (where it's called Auvernat) – *Clos St-Fiacre* is terrific. It also occurs in Muscadet (*le Chouan* and *Domaine Couillaud* are good) and adds character and softness to Anjou Blanc.

CHASSELAS (white) Makes adequate but dull wine at Pouilly-sur-Loire; it's actually best as a table grape, in a fruit salad.

CHENIN BLANC (white) A grape that cries out for sun and ripens long after the other varieties. It also performs superbly in the Loire in a few warm and misty mesoclimates (especially in Quarts de Chaume and Bonnezeaux), where noble rot strikes the Chenin with enough frequency to make it worthwhile going through all the pain and passion of producing great sweet wine, with steely acidity and the flavour of honeyed, ripe-apple fruit.

These wines can seem curiously disappointing when young, but fine sweet Chenin manages to put on weight and become sweeter for perhaps 20 years before bursting out into a richness as exciting as all but the very best from Germany or Bordeaux. And then it lasts and lasts… Because Chenin Blanc is unfashionable, these wines can be remarkably undervalued; but you have to be prepared to tuck them away in the cellar for a long time.

GAMAY (red) In the Loire this rarely achieves the lovely, juicy glugginess of Beaujolais, but when made by a careful modern winemaker it can have a fair amount of fruit, though it always seems to have a tough edge.

MELON DE BOURGOGNE (white) The grape of Muscadet, light and neutral. It's good at producing fresh white, usually quite biting, and with a salty tang. It's usually for drinking young though the odd good domaine-bottled *sur lie* can mature surprisingly well.

PINOT NOIR (red) In and around Sancerre this can, in warm years like the Loire has had lately, produce a lovely, light, cherry-fragrant wine that will be either a rosé or a light red. It's not Burgundy, but it's very attractive.

SAUVIGNON BLANC (white) The grape of Sancerre and Pouilly-Fumé, with a whole range of fresh, green, tangy flavours – anything from gooseberries to nettles and fresh-cut grass, and there's sometimes even a whiff of newly roasted coffee. The wines are usually quite tart – but thirst-quenching rather than gum-searing – and have loads of fruit. Sauvignon can age interestingly in bottle, but the odds are against it, except for the high-priced oak-aged cuvées.

WINE REGIONS

ANJOU BLANC SEC, AC (white) France's cheapest AC dry white made mostly from the hard-to-ripen Chenin Blanc. It *can* be good, steely and honeyed, especially from Savennières with its two tiny special ACs, Coulée-de-Serrant and la Roche-aux-Moines, and from names such as *Domaine Richou* which mixes Chardonnay with the Chenin, for extra flavour and fruit. Other good names: *Mark Angeli (Cuvée Christine), Baranger, Château de Valliennes, Domaine de la Haute Perche, Jaudeau.*

ANJOU ROUGE CABERNET, AC (red) This ranges from mostly quite light when from the co-ops, to spicy, strong and capable of aging from the best estates. It can rival Bourgueil. Best: *Mark Angeli (Cuvée Martial), Ch. d'Avrille, Ch. de Chamboureau (Soulez), Ch. d'Épiré, Clos de Coulaine, Dom. de la Petite Croix, Dom. du Petit Val, Dom. de Rochambeau, Dom. des Rochettes (Chauvin), Logis de la Giraudière (Baumard), Vincent Ogereau, Dom. Richou, Roussier.*

ANJOU ROUGE GAMAY, AC (red) Rarely more than adequate, but in the hands of a producer like *Richou*, the 'rooty' character is replaced by a fresh, creamy fruit that is sharp and soft at once, and *very* good. *Dom des Quarres* is also worth a try.

ANJOU-VILLAGES, AC (red) Cabernets Franc and Sauvignon from the 46 best villages in Anjou. Some are labelled Anjou-Villages Val-de-Loire. *Domaine de Montgilet, Domaine Ogereau, Jean-Yves Lebreton* and *Domaine Richou* are good.

BONNEZEAUX, AC (white) One of the most unfairly forgotten great sweet wines of France. Prices for the lovely noble rot-affected wines have risen, but are still low compared to Sauternes – which itself is cheap at the price. Look out for the outstanding wines of *Mark Angeli* (from old vines), *Château de Fesles, Denéchèr, Jean Godineau, Goizil* and *Renou.*

BOURGUEIL, AC (red) Some of the best reds of the Loire. When they are young they can taste a bit harsh and edgy, but give them a few years and they will have a piercing blackcurrant fruit, sharp and thirst-quenching. They can age well, developing complex leathery, meaty flavours. Best: *Audebert* (estate wines), *Pierre Breton, Paul Buisse, Caslot-Galbrun, J-F Demont, Domaine des Forges, Domaine des Ouches, Pierre-Jacques Druet, Lamé-Delisle-Boucard.*

CABERNET D'ANJOU, AC (rosé) There is a reasonable chance of a pleasant drink here, because the Cabernets – mostly Franc, but often with Cabernet Sauvignon too – do give pretty tasty wine, usually less sweet than simple Rosé d'Anjou. Best: *Château de Valliennes, Domaine Baranger, Domaine de Hardières, Domaine Richou.*

CHEVERNY, AC (red, white) This Touraine region is improving fast. Its claim to fame is the teeth-grittingly dry white Romorantin grape, but there is also Chardonnay, Sauvignon Blanc and Chenin. *Dom. des Huards* is delicate and fine, and the *Confrérie* at *Oisly-et-Thésée* is reliable. Others: *Cazin, Gendrier, Gueritte* and *Tessier.* Red Cheverny tends to be light and crisp, with a healthy dollop of Gamay perhaps beefed up with Cabernet Franc. *Oisly-et-Thésée*'s is strawberryish with a fair bit of Pinot Noir in it.

CHINON, AC (red) In a ripe year (1995, '96 or '97), Chinon can be delicious, exhibiting a great gush of blackcurrant and raspberry flavours. In poorer vintages it can be unpalatably bitter with surprising levels of green tannin. But winemaking standards have risen. Domaine wines are *far* better than négociant wines, which can be thin. Best: *Bernard Baudry, Jean Baudry, Couly-Dutheil, Domaine du Colombier, Domaine du Roncée, Domaine de la Tour, Druet, Gatien Ferrand, René Gouron, Charles Joguet, Alain Lorieux, Pierre Manzagol, Jean-François Olek, Jean-Maurice Raffault, Julien Raffault, Olga Raffault.*

COTEAUX DE L'AUBANCE, AC (white) Quite cheap, pleasant semi-sweet whites. Best: *Domaine des Rochettes, Domaine Richou* and *Jean-Yves Lebreton.*

COTEAUX DU LAYON, AC (white) A large AC producing varying qualities of sweet white wine, at its best rich and tasty with a taut acidity that allows the wine to age for a long time. *Mark Angeli, Château du Breuil* (from very old vines), *Château de la Guimonière, Château de la Roulerie, Clos Ste-Catherine, Domaine Ambinois, Domaine des Baumard, Domaine du Petit Val, Domaine de la Pierre St-Maurille, Domaine des Quarres, Domaine de la Soucherie* and *Ogereau* are worth trying. There are also six Coteaux du Layon-Villages ACs that usually offer higher quality. Some Anjou growers are now making *sélection de grains nobles*, very sweet, concentrated wines made only from botrytized grapes, and therefore in only the best years.

CRÉMANT DE LOIRE, AC (white) Sparkling wine AC intended to denote higher quality than basic sparkling Saumur. Can be made partly or entirely from Chardonnay; Chenin-based ones are in fact indistinguishable from Saumur. Best include *Ackerman, Bouvet-Ladubay, Caves de Grenelle, Cave des Liards, Gratien & Meyer, Langlois-Château, St-Cyr-en-Bourg* co-op.

GROS PLANT, VDQS (white) Gros Plant rejoices in being one of the rawest wines in France, and the prosperity of dentists in Nantes is thanks in no small measure to the locals' predilection for the stuff. That said, it *does* go amazingly well with seafood and seems to suit oysters. *Bossard*'s is soft and honeyed. *Métaireau* and *Sauvion* have also tamed its fury. *Clos de la Sénaigerie* and *Clos de la Fine* from *Dom. d'Herbauges* are good.

HAUT-POITOU, VDQS (red, white) Chardonnay and Sauvignon from the *Cave Co-opérative du Haut-Poitou* are good but tend to leanness, for the whites; the reds are fairly 'green' but reasonably enjoyable, and are usually made from Gamay.

MENETOU-SALON, AC (red, white, rosé) The Sauvignon is as good as that of Sancerre, and there are some fair reds and rosés. The *Vignerons Jacques Coeur* co-op produces about half the Sauvignon. *Henry Pellé* makes the best in Menetou, followed by *Henri Bourgeois, Domaine de Chatenoy, Joseph Mellot* and *Jean-Max Roger.*

MONTLOUIS, AC (white) Chenin-based wines similar to Vouvray, but often more robust – which, when it comes to the Chenin grape, isn't always a good idea. *Domaine des Liards, Dominique Moye, Domaine de la Taille aux Loups* and *Jean-Pierre Trouvé* are good.

MUSCADET, AC (white) Simple, light, neutral wine from near the coast. Straight Muscadet, without any further regional title, is usually flat and boring. But at least it's light – the Muscadet ACs are the only ones in France to impose a *maximum* alcohol level (12.3 per cent).

MUSCADET CÔTES DE GRAND-LIEU, AC (white) Demarcated in 1994, this latest sub-region accounts for nearly half of the area that was basic Muscadet, and quality varies. At least most is *sur lie*.

MUSCADET DE SÈVRE-ET-MAINE, AC (white) The best Muscadet. A good one may taste slightly nutty, peppery or salty, even honeyed, sometimes with creaminess from being left on the lees and sometimes with a slight prickle. It should always have a lemony acidity, and should feel light. Buy domaine-bottled wine only, and check the address, looking out for St-Fiacre and le Pallet, two of the best villages.

MUSCADET DES COTEAUX DE LA LOIRE, AC (white) Quality in this sub-region isn't bad. *Pierre Luneau* is good.

MUSCADET SUR LIE (white) This is the most important thing to look for on a Muscadet label. The French apparently believe it means a wine that comes from the banks of the river Lie; in fact it indicates that the wine has been bottled straight off the lees (the yeast sediment from fermentation), thus having more depth than usual and a slight prickle. Best: *Sauvion's Ch. du Cléray* and *Découvertes* range, *Guy Bossard, Dom. de Coursay-Villages, Dom. du Grand Mouton, Pierre Luneau, Dom. de la Montaine, Ch. de Chasseloir, Clos de la Sénaigerie, Jean-Louis Hervouet, Dom. du 'Perd-son-pain', Louis Métaireau, Huissier,* both *Michel* and *Donatien Bahuaud*'s single-domaine wines, *Bonhomme* and *Guilbaud*.

INSTANT CELLAR: TOP-VALUE CHENIN

- **1997 Vouvray Sec Tendre, Champalou, £5.75, Sommelier Wine Co** Rich, dryish and perfect with fish in butter sauce.
- **1995 Vouvray Le Haut Lieu sec, Huët, £9.95, Ben Ellis Wines** Lovely concentration and elegance, and just becoming ready to drink.
- **1996 Bonnezeaux, Château de Fesles, £24.09 for 50 cl, Terry Platt** Expensive but rare sweet wine of great distinction.
- **1996 Vouvray demi sec, Domaine Mabillière, £5, Anthony Byrne** Ideal summer aperitif, with plenty of fresh acidity to balance the honeyed sweetness.
- **1998 Vouvray sec, Le Bouchet, Domaine des Aubuisières, B Fouquet, £7.70, Adnams** Classic Vouvray, sparky and elegant. Drink now or keep for ten years.
- **1997 Montlouis, Remus, Taille au Loups, £12.64, Gauntleys** Complex, structured Chenin from a sometimes overlooked appellation.
- **1999 Saumur Blanc, Château de Villeneuve, £7.75, Christopher Piper Wines** Dry, nuttily complex wine that combines richness with freshness.

POUILLY-FUMÉ, AC (white) These can be fuller than Sancerre, and the best have a mineral complexity, but there are too many under-achievers. Best: *Ch. Favray, J C Châtelain, Didier Dagueneau* (Pouilly's most brilliant winemaker), *Serge Dagueneau, André Figeat, Ch. du Nozet, Ch. de Tracy*.

POUILLY-SUR-LOIRE, AC (white) Made from the dull Chasselas grape which makes good eating but not memorable drinking. *Serge Dagueneau* is good.

QUARTS DE CHAUME, AC (white) Rare and expensive nobly-rotten sweet wines, with high acid stalking the rich apricot-and-honey fruit. Try *Jean Baumard, Ch. Bellerive, Ch. de l'Echarderie*.

QUINCY, AC (white) Crisp Sauvignon Blanc, usually lighter than Sancerre. *Dom. de Maison Blanche, Pierre Mardon, Jacques Rouzé* and *Jacques Coeur* co-op are good.

REUILLY, AC (white) Light, fragrant Sauvignon Blanc. *Gérard Cordier* and *Claude Lafond* are the main growers here. There is also some tasty red and rosé.

ROSÉ D'ANJOU, AC (rosé) The omnipresent and frequently omnihorrid French rosé. It suffers in the main from lack of fruit and excess of sulphur. A few, like the co-op at *Brissac*, can make it fresh.

ROSÉ DE LOIRE, AC (rosé) A little-made dry rosé from Anjou or Touraine, generally much better than Rosé d'Anjou.

ST-NICOLAS-DE-BOURGUEIL, AC (red) These Cabernet reds tend to be lighter and more forward than the reds of nearby Bourgueil. They can be very good, but stick to warm years. Best: *Claude Ammeux, Caslot-Jamet, Couly-Dutheil, Jean-Paul Mabileau* and *Joël Taluau*.

SANCERRE, AC (white) Green, smoky, tangy wine from the Sauvignon Blanc grape. At its best young, it should be super-fresh and fruity, tasting and smelling of gooseberries or cut grass. Look for single-domaine wines – especially from *Archambault, Sylvain Bailly, Balland-Chapuis, Henri Bourgeois, Francis and Paul Cotat, Lucien Crochet, Pierre* and *Alain Dézat, Gitton, Dom. Laporte, Alphonse Mellot, Paul Millérioux, Henri Natter, Reverdy, Jean-Max Roger, Pierre Riffault, Vacheron* and *André Vatan*.

SANCERRE ROUGE, AC (red) Pinot Noir, and in general overrated, but the best have a lovely cherry fragrance and sweetness of strawberries that can survive a year or two in bottle. Silly prices, though. *Henri Bourgeois, Pierre & André Dezat* and *Domaine Vacheron* are good and worth a try.

ON THE CASE
Sancerre is currently looking much better than Pouilly-Fumé – livelier, more go-ahead growers, better quality, different attitude

SAUMUR, AC (white) Champagne-method fizz from Chenin Blanc, perhaps with the welcome addition of Chardonnay or Cabernet Franc to round out the acid Chenin. Quality is better than it's been for years, thanks to warm summers and better winemaking. Best: *Ackerman, Bouvet-Ladubay, Gratien & Meyer, Langlois-Château, Jacky Clée, Caves de Grenelle, Dom. Hauts de Sanziers*.

SAUMUR BLANC, AC (white) Usually ultra-dry Chenin Blanc, though it can be sweet, similar to Anjou Blanc.

SAUMUR-CHAMPIGNY, AC (red) Cabernet from the best villages in Saumur. It is way above other Loire reds thanks to a firm structure and velvety softness, fruit that is slightly raw and rasping, yet succulent and rich at the same time. Although the term 'vieilles vignes' is open to interpretation it is always the best bet for quality. *Domaine Filliatreau* makes an outstanding one. Also good: *Château de Chaintres, Château du Hureau, Château de Targé, Domaine Dubois, Domaine Lavigne, Domaine Sauzay-Legrand, Domaine de Nerleux, Domaine des Roches Neuves, Domaine du Val Brun, Denis Duveau*.

SAUMUR ROUGE, AC (red) Usually very light and dry Cabernet Franc from 38 villages round Saumur. Although it's light the fruit is often marked and attractively blackcurranty. The co-op at *St-Cyr-en-Bourg* is good, as is *Château Fouquet*.

SAVENNIÈRES, AC (white) Some of the world's steeliest, longest-living, diamond-dry white wines come from this tiny Anjou AC where the Chenin grape comes into its own. One vineyard, Savennières Coulée-de-Serrant, has its own AC within Savennières, and *Nicolas Joly*'s *Clos de la Coulée-de-Serrant* is excellent. Also: *Yves Soulez* from the *Château de Chamboreau, Château d'Épiré, Clos du Papillon, Jean Baumard (Clos Ste-Catherine), Dom. de la Bizolière, Dom. aux Moines, Dom. du Closel, Mme Laroche.*

TOURAINE, AC (red, white) Everybody sees Touraine Sauvignon, with some justification, as a Sancerre substitute. The *Confrérie des Vignerons d'Oisly-et-Thésée* is good, as are *Paul Buisse, Ch. de l'Aulée, Dom. de la Charmoise (Marionnet), Ch. de Chenonceau, Dom. des Corbillières, Dom. Joël Delaunay* and *Dom. Octavie*. The reds have benefited from a run of warm years, though even at their ripest are seldom terrifically weighty. The *Domaine de la Charmoise (Marionnet)*, and the co-op of *Oisly-et-Thésée* produce fair Gamays. *Château de Chenonceau*'s is also good.

VIN DE PAYS DU JARDIN DE LA FRANCE (white) The general vin de pays of the Loire. Those based on Sauvignon Blanc and Chardonnay are the ones to go for. *Biotteau*'s *Château d'Avrille* and *Domaine des Hauts de Saulière*'s Chardonnays have lovely fruit.

VIN DE PAYS DES MARCHES DE BRETAGNE (red, white) These wines from the mouth of the Loire are usually fairly flimsy, lightweight numbers. *Guy Bossard* makes a good fruity red from Cabernet Franc.

VOUVRAY, AC (white) Sparkling and still whites from tangily dry to richly sweet, though often at its best in the off-dry demi-sec style. From a good producer this Chenin wine, initially all searing acidity and rasping dryness, over many years develops a deep honey-and-cream flavour. Most commercial Vouvray is poor. Best: *Daniel Allias, Bourillon-Dorléans, Brédif, Paul Buisse, Champalou, Ch. Gaudrelle, Ch. Moncontour, Dom. des Aubuisières, Dom. du Margelleau, Dom. de Vaugoudy, Foreau, Benoît Gautier, Huet, Pierre Mabille, Prince Poniatowski.*

LOIRE VINTAGES

Loire vintages are very variable, and can be radically different along the river length. In poor vintages, Muscadet is most likely to be okay, while in hot vintages Sauvignon goes dull, but the Chenin finally ripens. The red grapes need the warm years.

1999	A difficult vintage. The best will be good, and there'll be some great sweet Chenin.
1998	Less good and more mixed than '96 or '97. Sauvignon and Cabernet Franc look best.
1997	A splendid year for reds and for Chenin. Good fruity Sauvignon.
1996	The reds and the Chenin had a bumper year and should age well.
1995	Some luscious dessert wines as well as fine reds, but quality is not even.
1994	Fair dry whites, but Coteaux du Layon should be best of all. Reds are lightweight.
1993	Good, flinty whites. The best Coteaux du Layon is botrytized and concentrated.
1990	Sweet Chenins, built to last, may beat the '89s. Great reds too.

LOIRE PRICES

DRY WHITE

Under £4.00

VdP du Jardin de la France Chenin Blanc de Blanc, Bougrier **1998** £3.25 (WS)
Sauvignon de Touraine Bougrier **1998** £3.95 (WS)
Sauvignon de Touraine Confrérie d'Oisly et Thésée **1998** £3.99 (MAJ)

£4.00 → £4.99

Cheverny Domaine Salvard **1998** £4.95 (WS)
VdP du Jardin de la France Chardonnay, Cave du Haut-Poitou **1997** £4.15 (CON)
VdP du Jardin de la France Sauvignon Blanc, Cave du Haut-Poitou **1998** £4.15 (CON)
Muscadet de Sèvre-et-Maine des Ducs, Chereau Carré **1998** £4.56 (BIB)
Muscadet de Sèvre-et-Maine Fief de la Brie, Bonhomme **1998** £4.99 (POR) £5.20 (TAN)
Muscadet de Sèvre-et-Maine sur lie Carte d'Or, Sauvion **1998** £4.95 (NEZ)
Muscadet sur lie Côtes de Grand Lieu, Clos de la Senaigerie **1998** £4.99 (WR)
Saumur Cave des Vignerons de Saumur **1999** £4.95 (AD)
Sauvignon du Haut-Poitou, Cave Co-op du Haut-Poitou **1996** £4.49 (CON)
Sauvignon de Touraine Domaine de Bellevue, Tijou et Fils **1999** £4.99 (HIG)
Sauvignon de Touraine Domaine de la Bergerie **1999** £4.95 (AD)
Sauvignon de Touraine Domaine de la Bergerie **1998** £4.99 (GW)
Sauvignon de Touraine Caves de Coteaux Romanais **1996** £4.50 (JU)
Sauvignon de Touraine Domaine de la Renaudie **1999** £4.99 (OD)

£5.00 → £5.99

Cheverny Domaine Salvard **1999** £5.75 (AD)
VdP du Jardin de la France Sauvignon Blanc Petit Bourgeois, Henri Bourgeois **1998** £5.95 (CON)
Menetou-Salon Morogues, Pellé **1998** £5.75 (SOM) £6.95 (WS) £7.05 (GOE)
Muscadet de Sèvre-et-Maine sur lie Domaine du Bois Bruley **1997** £5.99 (BAL)
Muscadet de Sèvre-et-Maine sur lie Domaine de Bois Joly **1997** £5.59 (CON)
Muscadet de Sèvre-et-Maine sur lie Château de Chasseloir **1998** £5.90 (AV)
Muscadet de Sèvre-et-Maine sur lie Château de Cléray **1999** £5.95 (PIP)
Muscadet de Sèvre-et-Maine sur lie Fief de la Brie, Bonhomme **1998** £5.09 (JON)
Muscadet de Sèvre-et-Maine sur lie Domaine Saupin **1999** £5.39 (NI)
Muscadet de Sèvre-et-Maine sur lie Thuaud **1998** £5.88 (CHA)
Muscadet sur lie Domaine de Basseville, Bossard **1999** £5.45 (STE)
Reuilly Beurdin **1999** £5.99 (MAJ) £6.45 (STE)
St-Pourçain Cuvée Printanière, Union des Vignerons **1998** £5.75 (YAP)
Saumur Domaine des Hauts de Sanziers **1997** £5.00 (RSJ)
Saumur Domaine de la Paleine **1998** £5.95 (TAN)
Sauvignon de Touraine Domaine de Bellevue, Tijou et Fils **1998** £5.49 (JON)
Sauvignon de Touraine Domaine de la Charmoise, Marionnet **1999** £5.95 (NI)
Sauvignon de Touraine Domaine de la Preslé **1998** £5.78 (SAV) £5.95 (COC)
Touraine Azay-le-Rideau la Basse Chevrière, Pavy **1996** £5.95 (WS) £7.25 (YAP)

MERCHANTS SPECIALIZING IN THE LOIRE

see Merchant Directory (page 456) for details

Unusually imaginative lists can be found at: Adnams (AD), Averys of Bristol (AV), Ballantynes (BAL), Bennetts (BEN), Anthony Byrne (BY), Justerini & Brooks (JU), Lay & Wheeler (LAY), The Nobody Inn (NO), Terry Platt (PLA), Raeburn Fine Wines (RAE), The RSJ Wine Co (RSJ), T&W Wines (TW), Tanners (TAN), Ubiquitous Chip (UB), Waterloo Wine (WAT), The Wine Society (WS), Noel Young (YOU).

£6.00 → £6.99

Chinon Blanc les Champs Chenin, Raffault **1995** £6.95 (SOM)
Coteaux du Giennois Gitton **1997** £6.50 (HIG)
Menetou-Salon Clos des Blanchais, Pellé **1998** £6.75 (SOM) £8.60 (MV)
Montlouis Domaine des Liards, Berger **1998** £6.95 (YAP)
Muscadet de Sèvre-et-Maine sur lie Cuvée LM, Louis Métaireau **1997** £6.25 (SOM)
Muscadet de Sèvre-et-Maine sur lie Château de l'Oiselinière de la Ramée **1998** £6.99 (BAL)
Pouilly-Fumé Chatelain **1998** £6.50 (SOM)
Reuilly Beurdin **1998** £6.75 (AD) £7.60 (ELL)
Sancerre Cuvée Flores, Vincent Pinard **1998** £6.75 (SOM)
Sauvignon de Touraine Domaine de la Preslé **1999** £6.05 (PIP)
Savennières Clos du Papillon, Baumard **1994** £6.85 (SOM) £11.49 (NO)
Vouvray Jarry **1997** £6.95 (YAP)
Vouvray Speciale, Saget **1996** £6.99 (VIN)

£7.00 → £7.99

Menetou-Salon Clos des Blanchais, Pellé **1999** £7.99 (OD) £11.69 (TW)
Menetou-Salon la Charnivolle, Fournier **1998** £7.75 (STA)
Menetou-Salon Domaine du Prieuré **1998** £7.99 (JON)
Montlouis les Batisses, Délétang **1995** £7.95 (WS)
Muscadet de Sèvre-et-Maine sur lie Château de Chasseloir **1997** £7.99 (BAL)
Muscadet de Sèvre-et-Maine sur lie Château de la Ragotière **1998** £7.76 (VIN)
Pouilly Fumé Fine Caillottes, Pabiot **1998** £7.95 (AD) £8.49 (JON) £8.90 (LAY)
Pouilly-Fumé les Bascoins, Masson-Blondelet **1999** £7.50 (BAN)
Pouilly-Fumé les Griottes, Bailly **1999** £7.95 (STE)
Quincy Jaumier **1998** £7.50 (YAP)
Sancerre Daulny **1998** £7.75 (AD) £7.85 (HAH) £8.19 (JON)
Sancerre Domaine du P'tit Roy **1998** £7.99 (BO) £9.32 (COC)
Sancerre Domaine Rossignole **1999** £7.99 (OD)
Savennières Clos de la Coulaine, Château de Pierre Bise **1998** £7.95 (RSJ) £8.95 (LEA)
Savennières Clos des Maurières, Domaine des Forges **1996** £7.95 (JU)
Savennières Domaine du Closel, Mme de Jessey **1994** £7.35 (WAT)
Vouvray Château Gaudrelle **1997** £7.50 (JER) £7.99 (NI)
Vouvray le Mont, Huet **1998** £7.79 (WAT)
Vouvray Domaine Peu de la Moriette **1999** £7.35 (PIP)

£8.00 → £9.99

Menetou-Salon Domaine de Chatenoy **1998** £8.50 (DI) £8.75 (BU)
Menetou-Salon Clos des Blanchais, Pellé **1997** £8.95 (AD)
Menetou-Salon Morogues, le Petit Clos **1997** £8.95 (FORT)
Menetou-Salon Morogues, la Tour St-Martin **1999** £9.99 (NI)
Menetou-Salon Domaine du Prieuré **1997** £8.25 (CON)
Menetou-Salon Roger **1998** £8.20 (TAN)
Menetou-Salon Teiller **1998** £8.50 (YAP)
Muscadet de Sèvre-et-Maine sur lie Premier Jour, Louis Métaireau **1995** £8.75 (SOM)
Pouilly-Fumé André Dezat **1998** £9.80 (NI)
Pouilly-Fumé Domaine des Berthiers, Jean-Claude Dagueneau **1998** £9.81 (REI)
Pouilly-Fumé Domaine Henri Bourgeois **1998** £9.45 (CON)
Pouilly-Fumé Serge Dagueneau **1998** £9.15 (HAH)
Pouilly-Fumé Château Favray **1998** £8.99 (MAR) £9.34 (DOM)
Pouilly-Fumé les Berthiers, Claude Michot **1999** £8.72 (BIB)
Pouilly-Fumé les Logères, Saget **1998** £8.99 (POR) £10.69 (VIN)
Pouilly-Fumé les Loges, Jean-Claude Guyot **1997** £9.75 (YAP)
Pouilly-Fumé Masson-Blondelet **1998** £8.49 (WAI)
Pouilly-Fumé Domaine des Rabichattes **1996** £8.99 (RAE)
Pouilly-Fumé Seguin **1998** £8.49 (VIC) £8.49 (THR) £8.49 (BOT) £8.50 (WS) £8.99 (BAL)
Pouilly-Fumé Domaine Thibault **1998** £8.90 (TAN) £9.99 (JON)
★ Pouilly-Fumé Villa Paulus, Masson-Blondelet **1999** £9.95 (PIP)
Reuilly Beurdin **1997** £9.25 (FORT)
Sancerre Chavignol, Delaporte **1999** £9.95 (LEA)
Sancerre André Dézat **1998** £8.90 (TAN) £9.10 (BER) £9.50 (CRO) £9.80 (NI)

Sancerre Clos des Roches, Vacheron **1998** £9.99 (UN)
Sancerre Clos du Chêne Marchand, Roger **1998** £8.80 (TAN)
Sancerre Clos du Roy, Millérioux **1997** £9.60 (COC)
★ Sancerre Crochet **1998** £8.50 (JU)
Sancerre Cuvée Flores, Vincent Pinard **1999** £8.99 (GW)
Sancerre la Bourgeoise, Henri Bourgeois **1998** £9.95 (SOM)
Sancerre Laporte **1999** £8.39 (PIP)
Sancerre le Chêne, Crochet **1996** £8.95 (JU)
Sancerre la Croix au Garde, Pellé **1999** £8.49 (OD) £9.40 (MV)
Sancerre les Baronnes, Henri Bourgeois **1998** £9.45 (CON) £15.63 (NO)
Sancerre les Belles Dames, Gitton **1998** £9.20 (HIG)
Sancerre les Monts Damnés, Henri Bourgeois **1999** £9.50 (SOM) £10.99 (OD)
Sancerre les Perriers, Fournier **1998** £8.95 (STA)
Sancerre les Perriers, Reverdy Ducroux **1997** £9.99 (VA)
Sancerre Domaine de Montigny, Natter **1998** £9.40 (LAY)
Sancerre Domaine du Nozay, de Benoist **1998** £9.69 (CB)
Sancerre Paul Prieur **1998** £8.29 (HA) £9.29 (BAL) £9.34 (DOM)
Sancerre Roger **1998** £9.50 (FORT) £9.95 (BEN)
Sancerre Jean Thomas **1999** £8.42 (BIB)
Sancerre Domaine de la Tonnelerie **1998** £9.49 (POR)
Sancerre Vacheron **1999** £8.99 (MAJ) £9.95 (STE)
Saumur Blanc Château du Hureau **1996** £9.60 (MV) £11.51 (TW)
Sauvignon de Touraine Domaine des Cabotières **1994** £8.10 (TW)
Savennières Clos des Maurières, Domaine des Forges **1997** £8.25 (HAH)
Savennières Clos du Papillon, Baumard **1995** £9.95 (CON) £11.60 (UB)
Savennières Clos du Papillon, Domaine du Closel **1998** £9.95 (AD)
Savennières Domaine du Closel, Mme de Jessey **1997** £8.95 (YAP)
Savennières Château d'Epiré **1997** £8.90 (GAU)
Savennières Roche-aux-Moines, Domaine Aux Moines **1996** £8.95 (HAH) £9.85 (RSJ)
Vouvray Brédif **1997** £8.99 (VA) £9.50 (STA)
Vouvray Brédif **1996** £8.50 (CRO)
Vouvray Clos du Bourg, Huet **1993** £9.70 (GAU)
Vouvray Château Gaudrelle **1998** £8.95 (LEA)
Vouvray le Haut Lieu, Huet **1993** £8.75 (WAT)

£10.00 → £14.99

Muscadet de Sèvre-et-Maine sur lie Château de Cléray **1997** £10.20 (NO)
Pouilly-Fumé en Chailloux, Didier Dagueneau **1997** £14.59 (FA) £16.50 (DI) £20.65 (TW) £26.95 (GAU)
Pouilly-Fumé Clos des Chadoux, Serge Dagueneau **1994** £12.90 (JU)
Pouilly-Fumé Clos Joanne d'Orion, Gitton **1997** £10.50 (HIG)
Pouilly-Fumé les Roches, Saget **1993** £13.99 (VIN)
Pouilly-Fumé Château du Nozet, de Ladoucette **1995** £14.15 (COC)
Pouilly-Fumé Silex, Didier Dagueneau **1997** £14.95 (GAU) £22.52 (FA) £29.59 (YOU)
Pouilly-Fumé Château de Tracy **1998** £10.95 (AD) £10.95 (HAH) £10.95 (LEA) £10.99 (POR) £11.35 (LAY) £11.94 (CB)
Pouilly-Fumé Château de Tracy **1997** £12.95 (JER)
Pouilly-Fumé Villa Paulus, Masson-Blondelet **1997** £14.60 (NO)
Sancerre Chavignol la Grande Côte, Cotat **1997** £14.95 (RAE)
Sancerre Comte Lafond, Château du Nozet **1998** £14.99 (MAJ)
Sancerre Culs de Beaujeu, Cotat **1998** £12.79 (YOU) £14.95 (BAL)
Sancerre Culs de Beaujeu, Cotat **1996** £12.50 (JU) £13.90 (GAU)
Sancerre Cuvée Harmonie, Pinard **1997** £14.99 (UN) £15.99 (GW)
Sancerre la Bourgeoise, Henri Bourgeois **1997** £13.49 (CON)
Sancerre la Grande Côte, Cotat **1996** £13.50 (JU)
Sancerre les Baronnes, Henri Bourgeois **1997** £10.35 (UB)
Sancerre les Perriers, Vatan **1998** £10.25 (YAP)
Sancerre Domaine de la Mercy Dieu, Bailly-Reverdy **1997** £10.95 (FORT)
Sancerre Roger **1999** £10.70 (TW)
Savennières Château de Chamboureau, Soulez **1997** £12.95 (BER)

Savennières Château de Chamboureau, Soulez **1996** £11.25 (YAP)
Savennières Domaine du Closel, Mme de Jessey **1996** £11.50 (FORT)
Savennières Roche-aux-Moines Clos de la Coulée-de-Serrant, Joly **1992** £12.99 (DI)
Vouvray Aigle Blanc, Poniatowski **1986** £10.95 (VA) £13.10 (UB)
Vouvray Brédif **1998** £10.76 (PLAY)
Vouvray Clos du Bourg, Huet **1996** £11.99 (JON) £17.95 (FORT)
Vouvray le Mont, Huet **1995** £10.95 (JU)

£15.00 → £19.99

Pouilly-Fumé Château du Nozet, de Ladoucette **1998** £15.00 (WS)
Pouilly-Fumé Château du Nozet, de Ladoucette **1997** £15.49 (MAJ)
Pouilly-Fumé Pur Sang, Didier Dagueneau **1996** £19.97 (FA) £21.75 (CON)
Sancerre Cuvée LC, Crochet **1995** £18.90 (JU)
Sancerre la Grande Côte, Cotat **1998** £15.95 (BAL)
Savennières Clos des Maurières, Domaine des Forges **1994** £15.46 (NO)
Savennières Coulée-de-Serrant Clos de la Coulée-de-Serrant, Joly **1992** £19.95 (DI)
Savennières Roche-aux-Moines, Château de Chamboureau **1996** £16.45 (NO)
Savennières Roche-aux-Moines, Soulez **1997** £15.25 (YAP)

£20.00 → £29.99

Savennières Coulée-de-Serrant Clos de la Coulée-de-Serrant, Joly **1991** £24.09 (REI) £24.50 (BAL)
Savennières Roche-aux-Moines Clos de la Coulée-de-Serrant, Joly **1996** £24.99 (RAE)
Savennières Roche-aux-Moines Clos de la Coulée-de-Serrant, Joly **1991** £21.95 (UB) £30.00 (YAP)
Vouvray Clos du Bourg, Huet **1990** £25.26 (REI)

£30.00 → £39.99

Pouilly-Fumé Baron de L Château du Nozet **1996** £33.00 (WRI) £33.50 (STA) £34.02 (REI) £34.50 (STE) £37.20 (PLAY) £40.20 (JER)
Pouilly-Fumé Silex, Didier Dagueneau **1998** £38.48 (TW)
Savennières Coulée-de-Serrant Clos de la Coulée-de-Serrant, Joly **1996** £36.67 (MI)
Savennières Roche-aux-Moines Clos de la Coulée-de-Serrant, Joly **1979** £39.00 (CRO)
Vouvray le Haut Lieu, Huet **1978** £31.00 (CRO)

Over £40.00

Savennières Coulée-de-Serrant Clos de la Coulée-de-Serrant, Joly **1976** £83.33 (MI)
Vouvray le Mont, Huet **1957** £48.96 (GOE)

SPARKLING

Under £8.00

★ Crémant de Loire Domaine de Nerleux **Non-vintage** £7.25 (RSJ)
Montlouis Brut Domaine des Liards, Berger Frères **Non-vintage** £7.95 (JU) £8.75 (YAP)
Saumur Brut Bouvet-Ladubay **Non-vintage** £7.95 (JU) £8.00 (JER) £8.49 (MAJ) £8.95 (ROB)
Saumur Brut La Grande Marque **1997** £6.95 (POR)
Saumur Demi-Sec, Bouvet-Ladubay **Non-vintage** £7.95 (JU)

£8.00 → £9.99

Montlouis Demi-sec Domaine des Liards, Berger Frères **Non-vintage** £8.75 (YAP)
Saphir Bouvet-Ladubay **1995** £8.49 (NI)
Saumur Rosé Excellence, Bouvey-Ladubay **Non-vintage** £9.50 (ROB)
Vouvray Brut Brédif **Non-vintage** £9.99 (JON)
Vouvray Pétillant Brut, Huet **Non-vintage** £9.95 (JU) £9.99 (RAE)
Vouvray Pétillant Brut, Huet **1997** £8.95 (WS)

Over £10.00

Saumur Cuvée Flamme, Gratien & Meyer **Non-vintage** £12.50 (CRO)
Vouvray Mousseux Méthode Traditionelle, Huet **1959** £75.00 (RAE)

- *Wines are listed in A–Z order within each price band.*
- *For each wine, vintages are listed in descending order.*
- *Each vintage of any wine appears only once.*

MEDIUM & SWEET WHITE

Under £7.00

Coteaux du Layon Château de Bellevue, Tijou et Fils **1994** £6.75 (HIG)

★ Coteaux du Layon Domaine des Forges, Branchereau **1999** £6.95 (AD)

Coteaux du Layon Domaine du Petit Val **1990** £6.95 (JU)

Vouvray Demi-Sec Château Moncontour **1999** £5.95 (STE)

Vouvray Philippe de Sivray **1998** £4.99 (JON)

Vouvray Domaine de la Robinière **1998** £5.49 (WAI)

£7.00 → £8.99

Coteaux de l'Aubance Domaine Richou **1997** £7.50 (WAT)

Coteaux du Layon Beaulieu, Chéné **1989** £8.90 (JU)

Coteaux du Layon Château de Bellevue, Tijou et Fils **1998** £7.00 (HIG)

Coteaux du Layon Chaume, Domaine des Forges **1997** £8.99 (UN)

Coteaux du Layon Chaume Château Soucherie, Tijou **1993** £8.85 (WAT)

Coteaux du Layon Domaine du Petit Val **1998** £7.80 (TAN)

Coteaux du Layon St-Aubin de Luigné, Domaine des Forges **1997** £8.60 (WRI)

Coteaux du Layon St-Lambert, Domaine des Mauriéres **1995** £8.18 (PIP)

Montlouis Domaine des Liards Vieilles Vignes, Berger Frères **1990** £7.95 (JU)

Montlouis Moelleux Deletang **1986** £8.99 (RAE)

Touraine Azay-le-Rideau Moelleux, Pibaleau **1995** £7.99 (WAT)

Vouvray Château Gaudrelle **1997** £7.40 (TAN)

Vouvray Moelleux Jarry **1996** £8.75 (YAP)

£9.00 → £12.99

Bonnezeaux 1ère Trie, Domaine du Petit Val **1996** £11.50 (TAN)

Bonnezeaux la Montagne Domaine du Petit Val, Goizil **1989** £12.50 (JU)

★ Coteaux du Layon Chaume, Château Pierre-Bise **1996** £11.95 (LEA)

Coteaux du Layon Chaume les Aunis, Château de la Roulerie **1996** £12.50 (MI)

Coteaux du Layon Chaume les Aunis, Château de la Roulerie **1994** £12.15 (NO)

Coteaux du Layon Chaume, Domaine des Forges **1995** £9.90 (JU)

Coteaux du Layon Clos de Ste-Catherine, Baumard **1995** £11.75 (COC) £24.50 (UB)

Coteaux du Layon Domaine des Forges, Branchereau **1996** £11.94 (NO)

Coteaux du Layon Rablay, Château la Tomaze **1990** £11.25 (YAP)

Montlouis Domaine des Liards Vendange Tardive, Berger Frères **1996** £11.25 (YAP)

Montlouis Domaine des Liards Vendange Tardive, Berger Frères **1990** £12.90 (JU)

Montlouis Domaine des Liards Vieilles Vignes, Berger Frères **1997** £9.55 (LAY)

Vouvray Clos de Bourg Demi-Sec, Huet **1996** £11.66 (BIB) £14.68 (TW)

Vouvray Clos de Bourg Demi-Sec, Huet **1994** £12.99 (RAE)

Vouvray Clos Naudin Demi-Sec, Foreau **1996** £11.90 (GAU)

Vouvray Demi-Sec Gilles Champion **1990** £10.90 (LAY)

Vouvray le Haut Lieu Demi-Sec, Huet **1989** £11.90 (JU) £12.30 (RAE)

Vouvray le Haut Lieu Moelleux, Huet **1997** £11.00 (NO)

Vouvray le Mont Demi-Sec, Huet **1993** £9.58 (REI) £9.69 (GOE)

Vouvray Moelleux Bourillon Dorléans **1989** £12.50 (BAL)

Vouvray Moelleux Jean-Pierre Laisement **1995** £11.80 (LAY)

Vouvray Moelleux Réserve, Champalou **1997** £11.70 (TAN)

£13.00 → £15.99

Bonnezeaux la Montagne Domaine du Petit Val, Goizil **1997** £13.65 (HAH) £14.50 (MV) £15.00 (FORT)

Coteaux du l'Aubance les Trois Demoiselles, Domaine Richou **1997** £13.20 (HAH)

Coteaux du Layon Chaume les Onnis, Domaine des Forges **1997** £14.00 (MV)

Coteaux du Layon Chaume les Onnis, Domaine des Forges **1995** £13.50 (JU) £14.95 (AD) £19.90 (CRO)

Coteaux du Layon Château de la Roulerie **1995** £13.95 (DI)

Jasnières les Truffieres, Pinon **1989** £14.50 (YAP)

Montlouis Domaine des Liards Vendange Tardive, Berger Frères **1995** £13.50 (YAP)

Montlouis Moelleux, Dominique Moyer **1995** £13.60 (LAY)

Vouvray Clos de Bourg Demi-Sec, Huet **1995** £13.99 (JON)
Vouvray Clos du Bourg Moelleux , Huet **1988** £14.50 (JU) £17.50 (RAE)
Vouvray Clos Naudin Moelleux, Foreau **1988** £14.45 (DI)
Vouvray le Mont Moelleux, Huet **1995** £13.45 (WAT) £13.99 (RAE)
Vouvray Moelleux Domaine Peu de la Moriette **1996** £14.50 (PIP)
Vouvray Réserve Spéciale, Château Gaudrelle **1997** £14.50 (LEA)

£16.00 → £19.99

Anjou Moulin, Touchais **1962** £19.50 (BU)
Coteaux du Layon Beaulieu Vieilles Vignes, Château du Breuil **1995** £17.60 (LAY)
Coteaux du Layon Chaume les Aunis, Château de la Roulerie **1997** £16.47 (NO) £17.99 (DI)
Coteaux du Layon Chaume Cuvée Corentine, Château de la Roulérie **1989** £19.75 (YAP) £24.53 (NO)
Coteaux du Layon les Coteaux, Château de la Roulérie **1990** £17.64 (NO)
Coteaux du Layon Cuvée Privilege, Branchereau **1995** £19.95 (GAU)
Coteaux du Layon Rablay Cuvée des Lys, Château la Tomaze **1990** £17.50 (YAP)
Coteaux de Saumur Moelleux, Château du Hureau **1996** £19.74 (TW)
Montlouis Domaine des Liards Grains Nobles de Pineau, Berger Frères **1990** £18.00 (JU) £22.75 (YAP)
Quarts-de-Chaume Château de Bellerive **1990** £19.00 (JU) £31.51 (NO)
Quarts-de-Chaume Château de Bellerive **1986** £16.50 (WS)
Quarts de Chaume Domaine du Petit Metris, Renou **1995** £19.90 (JU)
Sancerre Vendange du 27 Octobre 1995, Crochet **1995** £19.50 (JU)
Vouvray Aigle Blanc Réserve, Poniatowski **1976** £17.00 (CRO)
Vouvray le Haut Lieu Moelleux, Huet **1996** £19.39 (TW)
Vouvray le Mont Moelleux, Huet **1996** £18.95 (AD)

- *All prices for each wine are listed together in ascending order.*
- *Price bands refer to the lowest price for which the wine is available.*

£20.00 → £29.99

Bonnezeaux Château de Fesles **1989** £29.65 (NO)
Bonnezeaux Château de Fesles 50cl bottle **1997** £23.95 (BER) £23.99 (OD)
Bonnezeaux la Montagne Domaine du Petit Val, Goizil **1990** £27.60 (NO)
Coteaux du l'Aubance les Trois Demoiselles, Domaine Richou **1990** £24.32 (NO)
Coteaux du Layon Chaume Cuvée Privilege, Branchereau **1994** £22.33 (NO)
Coteaux du Layon Clos de Ste-Catherine, Baumard **1989** £29.50 (CRO) £36.00 (NO)
Coteaux du Layon Domaine des Maurières **1990** £27.96 (NO)
Quarts-de-Chaume Baumard **1997** £26.50 (SOM) £44.38 (NO)
Quarts-de-Chaume Château de Bellerive **1995** £22.50 (BAL)
Quarts-de-Chaume Bise **1997** £22.40 (RSJ)
Quarts-de-Chaume Lalanne Bellerive **1989** £29.40 (NO)
Vouvray Clos du Bourg Moelleux , Huet **1996** £23.60 (AD)
Vouvray Clos du Bourg Moelleux , Huet **1990** £23.70 (GAU) £29.00 (JU)
Vouvray Clos Naudin Demi-Sec, Foreau **1973** £21.00 (CRO)
Vouvray Cuvée Constance, Huet **1993** £29.60 (RAE) £29.90 (GAU)
Vouvray le Haut Lieu Demi-Sec, Huet **1976** £23.00 (CRO)
Vouvray le Mont Moelleux, Huet **1990** £22.21 (NO) £31.40 (GAU)
Vouvray Moelleux Huet **1997** £26.99 (YOU)
Vouvray Moelleux Domaine Peu de la Moriette **1989** £28.00 (CRO)
Vouvray Réserve Personelle, Château Gaudrelle **1990** £29.00 (JU)

£30.00 → £39.99

Anjou Moulin, Touchais **1964** £37.50 (BU)
Bonnezeaux la Chapelle, Château de Fesles **1990** £38.42 (NO)
Quarts-de-Chaume Château de l'Echarderie **1990** £30.43 (NO)
Savennières Liquoreux, Coulée de Serrant **1995** £33.00 (JU)
Vouvray Clos de Bourg Demi-Sec, Huet **1989** £39.00 (CRO)

Vouvray Cuvée Constance, Huet **1997** £31.92 (NO)

Vouvray le Haut Lieu Demi-Sec, Huet **1949** £39.50 (RAE)

Vouvray le Haut Lieu Moelleux, Huet **1989** £35.00 (JU)

£40.00 → £49.99

Anjou Moulin, Touchais **1959** £49.50 (BU)

Anjou Rablay, Maison Prunier ½ bottle **1928** £45.00 (CRO)

Bonnezeaux la Chapelle, Château de Fesles **1989** £43.04 (NO)

Bonnezeaux Château de Fesles **1990** £45.24 (TW)

Vouvray Clos du Bourg Moelleux , Huet **1962** £44.45 (FA) £46.82 (REI) £47.49 (GOE) £48.50 (RAE)

Vouvray Doux Brédif **1964** £44.00 (CRO)

Vouvray le Mont Demi-Sec, Huet **1952** £47.00 (REI)

Vouvray le Mont Moelleux, Huet **1957** £48.37 (FA) £66.00 (RAE)

£50.00 → £99.99

Anjou Moulin, Touchais **1955** £62.50 (YOU)

Anjou Moulin, Touchais **1947** £64.00 (UB)

Anjou Moulin, Touchais **1945** £95.00 (BU)

Anjou Rablay, Maison Prunier **1928** £88.00 (CRO)

Bonnezeaux Château des Gauliers, Mme Fourlinnie **1959** £68.00 (CRO)

Bonnezeaux Château des Gauliers, Mme Fourlinnie **1935** £86.36 (NO)

Quarts-de-Chaume Baumard **1978** £84.00 (NO)

Vouvray Brédif **1947** £84.00 (CRO)

Vouvray Clos du Bourg Moelleux , Huet **1959** £71.87 (FA)

Vouvray Cuvée Constance, Huet **1995** £60.72 (NO)

Vouvray le Haut Lieu Moelleux, Huet **1924** £97.33 (FA) £99.87 (GOE) £129.00 (RAE)

Vouvray le Mont Moelleux, Huet **1953** £60.12 (FA)

Over £100.00

Bonnezeaux Château des Gauliers, Mme Fourlinnie **1953** £105.00 (CRO)

Vouvray le Haut Lieu Moelleux, Huet **1947** £125.00 (RAE)

Vouvray le Haut Lieu Moelleux, Huet **1919** £188.00 (TW)

ROSÉ

Under £9.00

Reuilly Pinot Gris, Beurdin **1998** £6.75 (AD)

Reuilly Pinot Gris, Cordier **1997** £7.75 (YAP)

Sancerre Pinot-Rosé, Crochet **1995** £8.75 (JU)

Over £9.00

Sancerre Rosé André Dezat **1999** £9.50 (CRO)

Sancerre Rosé André Dezat **1998** £9.95 (LAY) £9.99 (JON)

Sancerre Rosé Chavignol Domaine Delaporte **1999** £9.95 (LEA)

Sancerre Rosé Cotat **1996** £9.99 (RAE)

Sancerre Rosé les Romains, Vacheron **1997** £9.49 (UN)

Sancerre Rosé Domaine de la Mercy Dieu, Bailly-Reverdy **1998** £9.95 (LAY)

RED

Under £5.00

Chinon les Morillères, Caves Rabelais **1996** £4.95 (JU)

VdP du Jardin de la France Cabernet Franc, Cave du Haut-Poitou **1998** £4.15 (CON)

Saumur Cave des Vignerons de Saumur **1998** £4.95 (AD) £5.50 (YAP)

£5.00 → £6.99

Anjou Rouge Tijou **1998** £5.50 (HIG)

Bourgueil Domaine de la Grive **1997** £5.95 (BER) £6.35 (TAN)

Bourgueil Lamé-Delille-Boucard **1996** £6.15 (WAT)

Chinon les Aubuis, Caves des Vins de Rabelais **1998** £5.60 (AD)

Chinon Couly-Dutheil **1997** £5.99 (MAJ)

Gamay de Touraine Domaine de la Charmoise, Marionnet **1997** £6.75 (BAL)

Saumur-Champigny Château des Chaintres **1997** £6.95 (WS)
Saumur-Champigny Domaine de Nerleux **1997** £6.75 (RSJ)
Saumur-Champigny Château Villeneuve **1998** £6.95 (RSJ) £7.34 (PIP) £8.25 (FORT)

£7.00 → £8.99

Anjou-Villages Domaine Ogereau **1994** £7.99 (BAL)
Anjou-Villages Domaine des Rochelles, Lebreton **1998** £7.80 (TAN)
Bourgueil les Cent Boisselées, Druet **1997** £8.40 (AD) £8.90 (GAU)
Bourgueil Domaine de la Coudraye, Domaine Amirault **1999** £7.95 (LEA)
Bourgueil Domaine les Galichets **1998** £7.70 (RSJ)
Chinon l'Arpenty, Desbourdes **1998** £7.95 (YAP)
★ Chinon les Graves, Gasnier **1997** £8.33 (PLAY)
Reuilly Pinot Noir, Beurdin **1998** £7.80 (BAN) £9.25 (FORT)
St-Nicolas-de-Bourgueil Taluau **1996** £8.99 (GW)
Sancerre les Baronnes, Henri Bourgeois **1999** £7.25 (SOM)
Saumur-Champigny Domaine Dubois **1995** £7.35 (GAU)
Saumur-Champigny Grande Cuvée Château du Hureau, Vatan **1997** £8.95 (BER) £8.99 (GW)
Saumur-Champigny Château du Hureau, Vatan **1996** £7.95 (WS)
Saumur-Champigny Domaine de Nerleux **1998** £7.15 (HAH)
Saumur-Champigny Château de Targé **1996** £8.75 (CON)
Saumur-Champigny Château Villeneuve **1997** £7.99 (JON)

£9.00 → £10.99

Bourgueil les Cent Boisselées, Druet **1996** £9.95 (YAP)
Bourgueil Domaine de la Coudraye, Domaine Amirault **1997** £9.36 (PIP)
Chinon Clos de Danzay, Druet **1996** £9.50 (GAU) £9.75 (YAP)
Chinon Clos de la Cure, Joguet **1998** £10.50 (FORT)
Chinon Couly-Dutheil **1995** £9.99 (VA)
Chinon Cuvée des Varennes du Grand Clos, Joguet **1997** £10.95 (GAU) £11.50 (WS)
St-Nicolas-de-Bourgueil les Malgagnes, Domaine Amirault **1997** £9.95 (LEA)
Sancerre André Dezat **1998** £9.40 (TAN) £9.99 (JON) £11.50 (FORT)
Sancerre la Croix du Roi, Crochet **1995** £10.95 (JU)
Sancerre les Baronnes, Henri Bourgeois **1997** £10.99 (CON)
Sancerre les Cailleries, Vacheron **1997** £10.49 (UN) £10.50 (BER) £11.95 (AD)
Sancerre Domaine de Montigny, Natter **1995** £10.95 (RAE)
Saumur-Champigny Château du Hureau, Vatan **1998** £10.00 (MV)
Saumur-Champigny Terres Chauds, Domaine des Roches Neuves **1998** £9.95 (RSJ)
Saumur-Champigny Vieilles Vignes, Filliatreau **1997** £10.50 (YAP)

£11.00 → £12.99

Anjou Rouge Château de la Roche, Nicolas Joly **1990** £11.99 (RAE) £12.50 (GAU)
Chinon Clos de la Cure, Joguet **1996** £11.69 (TW)
Chinon Clos du Chêne Vert, Joguet **1992** £11.50 (JU)
Chinon Cuvée des Varennes du Grand Clos, Joguet **1996** £11.10 (HAH)
Chinon les Grezeaux, Baudry **1997** £11.50 (LEA) £12.24 (SAV)

£13.00 → £14.99

Bourgueil Grand Mont, Druet **1990** £14.00 (JU)
Chinon Domaine de la Chapellerie, Olek **1985** £14.50 (CRO)
Chinon Clos de la Dioterie, Joguet **1997** £14.65 (AD) £14.70 (GAU) £14.95 (BER)
Chinon Clos de la Dioterie, Joguet **1993** £13.90 (JU)
Chinon Clos du Chêne Vert, Joguet **1997** £13.10 (GAU)
Chinon Olga Raffault **1989** £13.95 (BAL)

Over £15.00

Bourgueil Cuvée Vaumoreau, Druet **1988** £24.50 (AD)
Chinon Clos de l'Echo, Couly-Dutheil **1990** £21.00 (CRO)
Chinon Clos de la Dioterie, Joguet **1996** £19.39 (TW)
Saumur-Champigny Domaine des Roches Neuves **1994** £15.57 (PLA)

RHÔNE

Northern Rhône reds can be fashion victims. It's all a matter of handling the new oak, and more is not necessarily better

There are two well-defined styles of Syrah in the world, and one of them is from the Rhône. The other is from Australia, where the grape is called Shiraz, and when other countries – like Chile, like California, like Spain, even – decide to make Syrah or Shiraz, it is more often the broader, lusher, more generous Aussie style they choose in preference to the more tightly knit, longer-maturing style of the northern Rhône.

Yes, a lot has to do with fashion. Nobody setting out to make a fine red wine these days starts off by making something that will take the eight or ten years of a good Hermitage to reach buttery, violet-scented maturity. No, I'll rephrase that: a few would. But not many, and even they might be put off by the dumb phase that much northern Rhône Syrah goes through in youth. Fashion in wine does not include dumb phases.

But the thing about Syrah is that while it is a wonderfully expressive, complex grape, it is easily swamped by too much new oak. It happens in Australia, with the lighter wines: in they go to American oak. Out they come, tasting of vanilla. If I want to feast on vanilla I'll eat ice cream, thank you very much.

New oak rules in the Rhône, too, now. Some wines can take it; and a little can be a good thing. But too much is not a good thing. It's an easy option, because people recognize the taste and like it, whereas they might not recognize the wild, smoky, minerally smell of unadorned Syrah.

Don't get me wrong: I like new oak. I like its flavour, and I like what it does to wine. But I like my Rhône flavours, too.

GRAPE VARIETIES

CARIGNAN (red) This grape is much maligned because in the far South it used to, and often still does, produce raw, fruitless wines that are the mainstay of the cheapest bulk wines. But old Carignan vines can produce strong, tasty, flavoursome wines that age well.

CINSAUT (red) This widely planted grape is now out of favour because of its inability to age. But it can add pepperiness and acidity to the blend, as at *Château Rayas*. Cinsaut often makes a successful contribution to rosé blends.

CLAIRETTE (white) Makes sparkling Crémant de Die, but is a bit dull unless livened up with the aromatic Muscat. In the South it makes big, strong whites that can be creamy, but more often dull and nutty. Needs careful handling and early drinking.

COUNOISE (red) Rich, spicy, floral flavours, and highly regarded at *Ch. de Beaucastel* and *Durieu* in Châteauneuf-du-Pape. Could be promising.

GRENACHE (red) You won't see this grape in lights on Rhône labels much: it's mostly used for blending, giving loads of alcohol and a gentle, juicy, spicy fruit perked up by a whiff of pepper. It achieves its greatest power at Châteauneuf-du-Pape.

GRENACHE BLANC (white) Widely planted in the southern Rhône, producing rich, appley wines with a strong scent of aniseed. Good, but soft, so drink young.

MARSANNE (white) The dominant of the two grapes that go to make white Hermitage and Crozes-Hermitage, as well as white St-Joseph and St-Péray. Marsanne is

> **ON THE CASE**
> *Rhône wines currently look rather good value compared to Bordeaux, but prices are starting to go up. Now could be the time to buy for the future*

weighty and can be flabby, but at its best it is rich and scented. Further south it makes burly, lanoliny wine, but is capable of rich, exotic peach and toffee flavours, too.

MOURVÈDRE (red) This vine relishes ample warmth and sunshine. It contributes backbone and tannin to the blends of the South, and develops wonderful smoky, leathery, meaty flavours as it ages.

MUSCAT (white) Used to great effect blended with Clairette to make the sparkling Clairette de Die, but more famous for sweet Muscat de Beaumes-de-Venise.

ROUSSANNE (white) Altogether more delicate and fragrant than the Marsanne. Found chiefly in Hermitage and St-Péray in the North, though it also makes light, fragrant wines further south in Châteauneuf. Look out for *Ch. de Beaucastel*'s Roussanne *Vieilles Vignes* – pricy but superb.

SYRAH (red) The whole of the northern Rhône is dominated by Syrah – and it makes some of the blackest, most startling, pungent red wine in France. From Hermitage and Cornas, it rasps with tannin and tar and woodsmoke, backed by the deep, ungainly sweetness of black treacle. But give it five or ten years, and those raw fumes will have become sweet and pungent, full of raspberries, brambles and cassis.

VIOGNIER (white) The grape of Condrieu and Château-Grillet. It has one of the most memorable flavours of any white grape, blending the rich, musky scent of overripe apricots with that of spring flowers. The wine is made dry, but it is so rich you would hardly believe it. Sweet versions are making a comeback now. Viognier is a bit of a cult, with plantings increasing in the southern Rhône, California and Australia, and many are pretty good.

WINE REGIONS

CHÂTEAU-GRILLET, AC (white; north) This single property is one of the smallest ACs in France. Wildly expensive, it's 100 per cent Viognier and is often surpassed in freshness and quality by top Condrieus. But unlike Condrieu, it can age interestingly.

CHÂTEAUNEUF-DU-PAPE, AC (red, white; south) This can be delicious, deep, dusty red, almost sweet and fat, low in acidity, but kept appetizing by back-room tannin. *Can* be. It can also be fruit-pastilly and pointless, or dark, tough and stringy. Thirteen different red and white grapes are permitted, and the resulting flavour is usually slightly indistinct, varying from one property to another. Around one-third of the growers make good wine – and as much as two-thirds of the wine sold probably exceeds the permitted yields. So it makes sense always to go for a domaine wine and certainly not one bottled away from the region. Best: *Pierre André, Lucien Gabriel Barrot, Henri Bonneau, Bosquet des Papes, les Cailloux, Chante-Cigale, Chante-Perdrix, Chapoutier's la Bernadine, Château de Beaucastel, Château Fortia, Château de la Gardine, Château Rayas, Château St-André, les Clefs d'Or, Clos du Mont Olivet, Clos des Papes, Paul Coulon, Domaine Durieu, Domaine du Grand Tinel, Domaine de Mont Redon, Domaine St-Benoît, Domaine du Vieux Télégraphe, Font du Loup, Font Michelle, la Gardine, la Janasse, Gabriel Meffre, Monpertuis, la Nerthe, Quiot, le Vieux Donjon.*

Few whites are made, but they can be outstandingly perfumed with a delicious nip of acidity, leaving you wondering how on earth such aromatic wines could come from such a hot, arid region. In its youth, the wine has a perfumed rush of springtime madness. Then it closes up for a few years, emerging at seven years as a rich, succulent, nutty mouthful. Best: *Château de Beaucastel* (its pure Roussanne *Vieilles Vignes* – and the Viognier white), *Clefs d'Or, Clos des Papes, Font de Michelle, Grand Tinel, Mont Redon, Nalys, Rayas, Vieux Télégraphe.*

CLAIRETTE DE DIE, AC (sparkling; south) Made half from Clairette, half from Muscat, this is delicious, light and off-dry. It used to be called Clairette de Die Tradition, and the much duller Champagne-method sparkler is now called Crémant de Die. The still wine is Coteaux Diois.

CONDRIEU, AC (white; north) An appellation on a roll, with new plantings, better quality and lots of chic. The apricot scent leaps out of the glass, and there's an exciting balance of succulent fruit and gentle acidity. Viognier is the only grape, and is difficult to cultivate; increased demand for the wine means that Condrieu is inevitably expensive. Always best young. Top names: *G Barge, P & C Bonnefond, Chapoutier, Château du Rozay, Clusel-Roch, Cuilleron, Delas, Dumazet, Pierre Gaillard, Guigal's La Doriane, Multier* (who, like some others, is using new oak), *Niero-Pinchon, Alain Paret, André Perret, Jean Pinchon, Rostaing* and *Georges Vernay.*

CORNAS, AC (red; north) Black and tarry tooth-staining wine. It's usually rather hefty, jammy even, and lacks some of the fresh fruit of Hermitage, yet at ten years old it's impressive. Excellent blockbusters are made by *Auguste Clape, Robert Michel* and *Noël Verset.* It's also worth looking for *Allemand, René Balthazar, Guy de Barjac, Chapoutier, Colombo (Domaine des Ruchets), Courbis, Delas, Jaboulet, Juge, Lemenicier, Jean Lionnet* (especially *Domaine de Rochepertuis*), *Tardieu-Laurent (Vieilles Vignes), Alain Voge.*

COTEAUX DU TRICASTIN, AC (red, white; south) Fast-improving, good-value, spicy, fruity reds, and fresh, fruity and quite full-flavoured whites, not as exciting as the reds. Best producers (reds): *Dom. de Grangeneuve, Dom. Saint-Luc, Dom. du Vieux Micocoulier, Prods. Réunis Ardéchois* (co-op; also good white), *Tour d'Elyssas* (100 per cent Syrah).

CÔTE-RÔTIE, AC (red; north) Together with Hermitage, the greatest wine of the northern Rhône. It can have exceptional finesse and a fragrance unexpected in a red wine thanks to the occasional addition of a dash of Viognier. The top wines, like *Guigal's La Landonne*, are now international blue chips. The top growers are *Barge, Domaine de Bonserine, Burgaud, Champet, Chapoutier, Clusel-Roch (Les Grandes Places), Delas, Gangloff, Gaillard, Gasse, Gerin, Guigal, Jaboulet, Jamet, Jasmin, Ogier, Rostaing, Tardieu-Laurent,* de *Vallouit, Vidal-Fleury, F Villard.*

CÔTES DU LUBÉRON, AC (red, white; south) Lubéron makes decent reds, usually rather light, but capable of stronger personality. The *Val Joanis* rosé is one of the best in the South. Try also *Château de Canorgue, Château de l'Isolette, Mas du Peyroulet, Val Joanis* (also to be seen under the names of *Domaines Chancel* or *Domaine de la Panisse*), *la Vieille Ferme.* The whites are usually pleasant and light but little more, though much more fragrant, interesting styles come from *Château de l'Isolette, Mas du Peyroulet, Val Joanis* and *la Vieille Ferme.*

CÔTES DU RHÔNE, AC (red, white) Well-made basic Côtes du Rhône reds are delicious when young, wonderfully fresh and fruity, like a soft Beaujolais. Or they can be fierce, black, grapeskins-and-alcohol monsters. Many of the weightiest are made by Châteauneuf growers (*Cru de Coudoulet* from *Beaucastel, Château de Fonsalette* from *Rayas*) or northern Rhône producers like *Guigal* and *Clape*. *Château du Grand Moulas* is spicy and attractive, with plenty of body. Also good: *Château de Goudray, Château de Ruth, Clos du Père Clément, Domaine des Aussellons, Domaine de Bel Air, Domaine de la Cantharide, Domaine de St-Estève, Jean Lionnet* and *Chapoutier's* rosé. Whites are generally fresh and fruity.

CÔTES DU RHÔNE-VILLAGES, AC (red, white; south) Good, full reds that can also age, combining earthy, dusty southern heat with spicy, raspberry fruit. They come from villages, 17 of which can add their names on the label, including Cairanne, Chusclan, Valréas, Beaumes-de-Venise and Rasteau. These wines often offer excellent value. Best: *Dom. Pélaquié* (Laudun); *Dom. Gourt de Mautens, Dom. de Grangeneuve, Dom. la Soumade* (Rasteau); *Jean-Pierre Cartier, Château de Trignon, Dom. de Boisson, Dom. St-Antoine, Dom. de Verquière* (Sablet); *Dom. de l'Ameillaud, Dom. Brusset, Dom. l'Oratoire St-Martin, Dom. de la Présidente, Dom. Rabasse-Charavin, Marcel Richaud* (Cairanne); *Dom. Ste-Anne* (St-Gervais); *Dom. de Cabasse, Dom. Couranςonne* (Séguret); *Roger Combe, Dom. des Grands Devers, le Val des Rois* (Valréas). The whites are increasingly fresh, fruity and gulpable, especially from the villages of Laudun and Chusclan. *Dom. Pélaquié* is tops, and *Dom. Ste-Anne* is good.

CÔTES DU VENTOUX, AC (red, white, rosé; south) Good area producing lots of fresh, juicy wine; the red is the best. Can even be quite special. Best: *Domaine des Anges, Jaboulet, Pascal, la Vieille Ferme, Vieux Lazaret*.

CROZES-HERMITAGE, AC (red, white; north) Red that varies from the light and juicy to well-structured smoky wine recognizable as a lesser cousin of the great Hermitage. *Etienne Pochon (Château Curson), Chapoutier's les Meysonniers* and *Varonniers, Graillot's Guiraude, Jaboulet's Thalabert* are tops. Also good are *Albert Belle, Cave des Clairmonts, Cave de Tain, Bernard Chave, Laurent Combier, Stéphane Cornu, Domaine des Entrefaux, Fayolle, Pradelle* and *Vidal-Fleury*. The white is generally rather dull and strong, but there are good ones from *Château Curson, Combier, Entrefaux, Fayolle, Graillot, Jaboulet, Pradelle* and the *Tain co-op*.

GIGONDAS, AC (red; south) Big, chunky, plummy wines that can be short on finesse. This is Grenache country, and proud of it. Best: *Clos des Cazaux, Dom. de Cayron, Dom. les Gouberts, Dom. de Longue-Toque, Dom. l'Oustau Fauquet, Dom. les Pallières, Dom. Raspail-Ay, Dom. de Santa Duc, Dom. de St-Gayan*.

HERMITAGE, AC (red, white; north) Grand, burly red; strong and fierily tough when young, it matures to a rich, brooding

INSTANT CELLAR:
STAR SYRAHS

- **1997 St-Joseph Le Grand Pompée, Paul Jaboulet Aîné, £10.75, Haynes Hanson & Clark** Beautiful ripe fruit, and perfect balance.
- **1997 St-Joseph, Bernard Faurie, £11.50, Justerini & Brooks** Ripe, soft wine, very plummy and spicy.
- **1998 Crozes-Hermitage, Domaine Barret, E Pochon, £7.95, Adnams** Classically smoky and mineral-spicy.
- **1996 Cornas, Domaine de Rochepertuis, J. Lionnet, £14.75, Berry Bros & Rudd** Some well-integrated new oak, and rich black fruit.
- **1991 The Society's Exhibition Hermitage, Cave de Tain, £16, Wine Society** A good price for Hermitage in an excellent vintage. It's from the local co-op, which is one of the best in France.
- **1996 Syrah Vin de Table, René Rostaing, £12.73, Gauntleys** Twelve quid for a vin de table? It's from René Rostaing, so it should be worth a try.
- **1998 St-Joseph, Dom. Philippe Verzier, £10.25, Christopher Piper** Intensely concentrated and gamy. Unfiltered, too.

magnificence. There is always a medicinal or smoky edge, and an unmatchable depth of raspberry and blackcurrant fruit. Although many people produce Hermitage of sorts, the stars are *Chave*, *Paul Jaboulet Aîné* and *Chapoutier's le Pavillon*. Also good: *Belle, Delas Cuvée Marquise de la Tourette, Desmeure, Faurie, Jean-Louis Grippat, Guigal* and *Sorrel*. The white is often heavy and dull, but it ages to a soft, rich nuttiness. *Chave* makes magnificent white Hermitage even in modest vintages, and other good producers include *Chapoutier, Desmeure, Ferraton, Grippat, Guigal, Marc Sorrel, Ch. des Tours*.

LIRAC, AC (red, white, rosé; south) A good, often underrated area making light, attractive wines. Reds are packed with fruit, often tinged with a mineral edge. The rosés are fresh. Whites are best young. Best: *Ch. d'Aquéria, Dom. des Causses et St-Eymes, Dom. de Ch. St-Roch, Dom. la Fermade, Dom. les Garrigues, Dom. de la Tour, Maby*.

MUSCAT DE BEAUMES-DE-VENISE, AC (fortified white; south) The only Rhône village growing Muscat. This golden sweet wine – a *vin doux naturel* – is supremely delicious. Grapy, fresh, rich but not cloying. Best: *Dom. de Coyeux, Dom. Durban, Jaboulet, Beaumes-de-Venise* co-op.

RASTEAU, AC (fortified red, fortified white; south) Rasteau makes a few big, port-like fortified wines – *vins doux naturels* – but if you want that sort of thing you're probably better off with port itself. Young reds can have a delightful raspberry scent from the Grenache Noir. The whites are made from Grenache Blanc and can be frankly unpleasant. Production is small. Try *Dom. de la Soumade, Rasteau* co-op.

ST-JOSEPH, AC (red; north) Almost smooth and sweet compared to their tougher neighbours, these reds can be fairly big, fine wines, stacked with blackcurrant in good years. *Chapoutier, Chave, Dom. du Chêne, Colombo, Courbis, Coursodon, Cuilleron, Delas, Gaillard, Graillot, Gripa, Grippat, Jaboulet, Monteillet, Paret* and *Tardieu-Laurent* are leading names. The white is decent and nutty. *Grippat* is good, but *Florentin*, an old-style oxidative, headbanging white, is more controversial. White Crozes is usually better value.

ST-PÉRAY, AC (white; north) Usually rather stolid and short on freshness. Quality is improving from the likes of *Chaboud, Domaine de Fauterie, Grippat* and Cornas estates such as *Clape, Lionnet* and *Voge*.

TAVEL, AC (rosé; south) Quite expensive, certainly tasty, rosés, but mostly they're too big and alcoholic to be very refreshing. Any of the Rhône grapes will do, but generally it's Grenache-dominated, with the addition of a little Cinsaut. Best producers: *Château d'Aquéria, Château de Trinquevedel, Domaine de la Forcadière, Domaine de la Genestière*.

MATURITY CHART
1995 Côte-Rôtie
Good concentration; should keep well

VACQUEYRAS, AC (red, white, rosé; south) Reds and rosés of character and structure. Some white wine is also produced, but it tends to be heavy. Cinsaut fanatic *Ch. de Montmirail* is good, as are *Clos des Cazaux, Dom. de la Fourmone, Dom. la Garrigue, le Sang des Cailloux, Ch. des Tours.*

VIN DE PAYS DES COLLINES RHODANIENNES (red; north) A usually impressive and expanding northern Rhône area, particularly for inexpensive, tasty Syrah-based reds, though the lighter, softer Gamays can also be good.

VIN DE PAYS DES COTEAUX DE L'ARDÈCHE (red, white; south) A source of delicious Nouveau-style Gamay, first-class Syrah, good Cabernet, plus Sauvignon, Pinot Noir – and Chardonnay, both for *Louis Latour*'s decent *Chardonnay de l'Ardèche* and the local co-ops (which give higher quality for far lower prices). This was one of the first vin de pays regions to smarten up its act; as happens to pioneers, it's been rather overtaken in the fashion stakes by others, notably those in the Languedoc. But it's still making good stuff, and it's worth looking out for.

RHÔNE VINTAGES

1999 Mixed quality because of rain. The North looks better than the South.

1998 Good in the North, and even better in the South. Reds are good and ripe.

1997 A year that looks like turning out as well as or better than 1996, at least in the South. Reds look set to age well.

1996 Superb for the northern reds, and for the whites from the whole region. Quality is less even in the South and the reds lack the intensity of those in the North.

1995 Top growers made very good wines, and there will be great wines in the North from those who, like Chapoutier and Chave, picked late.

1994 Succulent reds and lively, flowery whites this year. A very good year but not great.

1993 Châteauneuf-du-Pape and Côtes du Rhône did best. In the North attractive whites but raw and rather dilute reds from Hermitage, Crozes and Cornas.

1992 A poor year; buy only from top growers and drink up quickly.

1991 Côte-Rôtie is generally better than in 1990. The South was only moderately good.

1990 The North was more successful than the South. Choose 1990 for the North (though Côte-Rôtie is dodgy); 1989 for the South.

1989 Some poor Hermitage and Cornas. Concentrated Châteauneuf-du-Pape.

1988 Best in Côte-Rôtie, Hermitage and Châteauneuf-du-Pape. Some is too tannic.

1987 The few good wines should have been drunk by now, though Côte-Rôtie and Hermitage provided some very good bottles, now drinking well.

1985 Brilliant Côte-Rôtie, St-Joseph and Cornas. Châteauneuf is delicious and juicy.

1983 Outstanding dark, rich, complex Hermitage and very good Côte-Rôtie for keeping. Southern reds are good, though some are a bit tough.

RHÔNE PRICES

RED

Under £4.50

Côtes du Rhône Coudoulet de Beaucastel **1995** £4.41 (CAV) £8.99 (RAE) £9.50 (GAU) £11.99 (VA)

Côtes du Ventoux les Cailloux **1998** £3.99 (OD)

£4.50 → £4.99

Coteaux du Tricastin Domaine de Grangeneuve **1998** £4.69 (OD)

Côtes du Rhône Barton & Guestier **1998** £4.59 (OD)

Côtes du Rhône Château du Grand Moulas **1998** £4.99 (POR) £5.50 (HAH) £5.59 (JON) £5.75 (TAN)

Côtes du Rhône Jaume **1997** £4.95 (WS)

Côtes du Rhône Domaine des Moulins **1997** £4.99 (WR) £5.30 (NEZ)

Côtes du Rhône-Villages Château la Courançonne **1998** £4.99 (SAI)

Côtes du Ventoux Jaboulet **1998** £4.95 (WS) £4.99 (OD) £5.35 (NI)

£5.00 → £5.99

VdP des Coteaux de l'Ardèche Gamay, Cave de St-Désirat **1998** £5.75 (YAP)

VdP des Coteaux de la Cèze, Domaine Maby **1996** £5.75 (YAP)

Coteaux du Tricastin Domaine de Vieux Micocoulier **1996** £5.96 (CHA)

Côtes du Rhône Domaine de l'Ameillaud **1998** £5.28 (HA)

Côtes du Rhône Belleruche, Chapoutier **1998** £5.99 (DI)

Côtes du Rhône André Brusset **1998** £5.99 (VA)

Côtes du Rhône Cuvée des Capucines, Domaine du Vieux Chêne **1997** £5.45 (JU)

Côtes du Rhône Château du Grand Moulas **1999** £5.80 (AD)

Côtes du Rhône la Haie aux Grives, Domaine du Vieux Chêne **1997** £5.95 (JU)

Côtes du Rhône Jaboulet **1998** £5.99 (PHI)

Côtes du Rhône Domaine de la Mordorée **1998** £5.95 (BAL) £5.95 (LEA)

Côtes du Rhône Parallèle 45, Jaboulet **1998** £5.99 (OD) £6.79 (NI) £6.99 (PLA)

Côtes du Rhône Domaine St-Gayan, Roger Meffre **1998** £5.95 (YAP)

Côtes du Rhône Caves des Vignerons de Vacqueyras **1998** £5.35 (TAN)

Côtes du Rhône-Villages Cairanne, Domaine de l'Ameillaud **1999** £5.99 (UN)

Côtes du Lubéron Château Val Joanis **1995** £5.02 (BY)

Côtes du Ventoux Cuvée des Terrasses, Château Pesquié **1997** £5.45 (TAN)

Côtes du Ventoux Jaboulet **1997** £5.35 (NI) £5.39 (SAV) £5.49 (CON)

Côtes du Ventoux la Vieille Ferme **1997** £5.70 (CB)

Crozes-Hermitage Cave de Vins Fins à Tain-Hermitage **1998** £5.99 (SAI) £6.99 (AME)

Lirac la Fermade, Domaine Maby **1997** £5.95 (WS)

Lirac Domaine de la Mordorée **1997** £5.95 (SOM) £7.25 (SAV) £7.95 (LEA)

VdP de la Principauté d'Orange Cuvée des Templiers, Rieu Herail **1997** £5.35 (JER)

MERCHANTS SPECIALIZING IN THE RHÔNE

see Merchant Directory (page 456) for details

Adnams (AD), Bennetts (BEN), Berry Bros & Rudd (BER), Bibendum (BIB), Anthony Byrne (BY), Direct Wine Shipments (DI), Ben Ellis (ELL), Farr Vintners (FA), Justerini & Brooks (JU), Lay & Wheeler (LAY), Oddbins (OD), James Nicholson (NI), Nobody Inn (NO), Raeburn Fine Wines (RAE), Reid Wines (REI), Savage Selection (SAV), T&W Wines (TW), Tanners (TAN), The Ubiquitous Chip (UB), The Wine Society (WS), Yapp Brothers (YAP), Noel Young (YOU).

£6.00 → £6.99

VdP des Coteaux de l'Ardèche Syrah, Cave de St-Désirat **1998** £6.15 (YAP)
Coteaux du Tricastin Domaine de Grangeneuve **1997** £6.10 (YAP)
Côtes du Rhône Belleruche, Chapoutier **1997** £6.49 (CON)
Côtes du Rhône Domaine Cros de la Mure **1998** £6.95 (AD)
Côtes du Rhône Cuvée Personnelle, Pascal **1995** £6.95 (YAP)
Côtes du Rhône Guigal **1997** £6.49 (MAJ) £6.90 (CRO) £6.99 (POR) £6.99 (OD) £7.23 (BY) £7.49 (BO) £7.49 (UN) £7.58 (REI) £7.64 (GOE) £8.35 (JER)
Côtes du Rhône Domaine de la Mordorée **1997** £6.75 (BEN)
Côtes du Rhône Parallèle 45, Jaboulet **1997** £6.45 (CON) £6.90 (GAU)
Côtes du Rhône Rascasses, Berard **1995** £6.99 (WAT)
Côtes du Rhône Domaine de St Georges **1994** £6.11 (PIP)
Côtes du Rhône-Villages Cairanne, Domaine de l'Ameillaud **1998** £6.55 (HAH)
Côtes du Rhône-Villages Cairanne Reserve de Seigneurs de St-Martin, Alary **1996** £6.70 (GAU)
Côtes du Rhône-Villages Château du Grand Moulas **1998** £6.95 (AD) £6.95 (TAN)
Côtes du Rhône-Villages Jaboulet **1997** £6.75 (FORT)
Côtes du Rhône-Villages Sablet, Château du Trignon **1997** £6.99 (UN)
Côtes du Lubéron Château Val Joanis **1998** £6.50 (CRO)
Crozes-Hermitage Cave des Clairmonts, Borja **1998** £6.99 (JON) £6.99 (WAI) £8.20 (MV)
Crozes-Hermitage Cave de Vins Fins à Tain-Hermitage **1997** £6.95 (BU)
Lirac les Queyrades, Mejan **1997** £6.90 (TAN) £6.95 (AD)
Lirac Domaine de la Mordorée **1998** £6.95 (RAE) £8.95 (BEN)
Vacqueyras Domaine le Clos des Cazaux **1998** £6.95 (AD)

Stars (★) indicate wines selected by Oz Clarke in the Best Buys section which begins on page 10.

£7.00 → £7.99

Châteauneuf-du-Pape la Bernardine, Chapoutier **1992** £7.65 (DI)
Châteauneuf-du-Pape Clos des Papes, Avril ½ bottle **1996** £7.50 (RAE)
Côtes du Rhône Coudoulet de Beaucastel **1997** £7.44 (FA) £8.18 (RAE) £8.81 (GOE) £8.99 (OD) £10.50 (FORT) £11.00 (MV)
Côtes du Rhône Coudoulet de Beaucastel **1996** £7.25 (FA) £8.81 (GOE) £8.89 (RAE) £9.90 (CRO) £10.49 (WR) £10.49 (BOT) £11.93 (PLAY)
Côtes du Rhône Domaine Cros de la Mure **1997** £7.40 (MV)
Côtes du Rhône Domaine Font de Michelle **1994** £7.25 (JU)
Côtes du Rhône Guigal **1995** £7.23 (BY) £7.99 (CB) £9.20 (UB)
Côtes du Rhône Mataro, Domaine le Clos des Cazaux **1995** £7.50 (JU)
Côtes du Rhône Rasteau, Chapoutier **1996** £7.95 (AD) £9.29 (JON)
Côtes du Rhône Château des Tours **1997** £7.25 (RAE) £7.50 (DI) £7.75 (LEA)
Côtes du Rhône-Villages Cairanne, Rabasse-Charavin **1998** £7.99 (AME)
Côtes du Rhône-Villages Jaboulet **1996** £7.60 (STA)
Côtes du Rhône-Villages Rasteau, Chapoutier **1997** £7.95 (TAN) £7.99 (CON) £9.45 (STE)
Côtes du Rhône-Villages Rasteau, Domaine la Soumade **1997** £7.64 (PIP) £7.75 (STA) £7.99 (NI) £7.99 (AME)
Côtes du Rhône-Villages Rasteau, Château du Trignon **1995** £7.50 (JU)
Côtes du Rhône-Villages Domaine Ste-Anne **1998** £7.35 (HAH)
Côtes du Rhône-Villages Domaine du Vieux Chêne **1997** £7.00 (JU)
Côtes du Lubéron Château de Canorgue **1997** £7.75 (YAP)
Crozes-Hermitage Domaine du Colombier **1997** £7.25 (WAT) £8.99 (BAL)
Crozes-Hermitage Domaine des Entrefaux **1998** £7.90 (TAN) £7.94 (BY) £8.29 (PIP)
Crozes-Hermitage Jaboulet **1997** £7.50 (WS)
Crozes-Hermitage Jaboulet **1996** £7.70 (HAH)
Crôzes-Hermitage La Petite Ruche, Chapoutier **1997** £7.99 (UN) £8.50 (TAN) £8.62 (GOE) £8.95 (POR) £9.95 (BEN) £10.39 (JON) £10.75 (STE) £10.99 (VA)

Crozes-Hermitage les Jalets, Jaboulet **1998** £7.95 (POR) £8.25 (NI)
Crozes-Hermitage les Jalets, Jaboulet **1996** £7.93 (REI) £10.00 (FORT)
Crozes-Hermitage les Meysonniers, Chapoutier **1995** £7.34 (FA) £9.90 (GAU)
Crozes-Hermitage les Pierrelles, Albert Belle **1997** £7.99 (OD) £9.99 (PHI)
Crozes-Hermitage les Pierrelles, Albert Belle **1996** £7.50 (WS)
Crozes-Hermitage Pochon **1998** £7.85 (AD)
Crozes-Hermitage Pochon **1997** £7.90 (JU)
Lirac la Fermade, Domaine Maby **1996** £7.50 (YAP)
Lirac Domaine de la Mordorée **1996** £7.95 (BAL) £7.95 (LEA)
VdP de la Principauté d'Orange, Domaine de la Janasse **1996** £7.75 (BU)
Vacqueyras Domaine le Couroulu **1998** £7.50 (NI)
Vacqueyras Domaine le Couroulu **1994** £7.79 (COC) £8.60 (BER)
Vacqueyras Cuvée des Templiers, Domaine le Clos des Cazaux **1995** £7.95 (JU)
Vacqueyras Jaboulet **1996** £7.65 (CON)

£8.00 → £8.99

Châteauneuf-du-Pape Clos du Caillou **1996** £8.95 (SOM)
Côtes du Rhône Syrah, Jean Lionnet **1997** £8.30 (AD)
Côtes du Rhône-Villages Cuvée de l'Ecu, Château du Grand Moulas **1998** £8.50 (AD)
Côtes du Rhône-Villages Rasteau, Château du Trignon **1997** £8.50 (JU)
Côtes du Rhône-Villages Domaine St-Anne Notre Dame des Cellettes, Steinmaier **1998** £8.50 (TAN)
Côtes du Rhône-Villages Domaine Ste-Anne **1995** £8.35 (BER)
Crozes-Hermitage Domaine du Colombier **1999** £8.72 (BIB)
Crozes-Hermitage Delas **1997** £8.30 (NEZ) £9.70 (JER)
Crozes-Hermitage les Meysonniers, Chapoutier **1996** £8.99 (DI) £11.50 (UB)
Crozes-Hermitage Domaine des Remizières, Desmeure **1995** £8.99 (RAE)
Gigondas Cuvée de la Tour Sarrazine, Domaine le Clos des Cazaux **1997** £8.10 (TAN) £8.90 (JU)
★ St-Joseph Domaine du Chêne **1998** £8.95 (WS)
Vacqueyras Domaine le Clos des Cazaux **1996** £8.10 (TAN)
Vacqueyras Domaine du Clos du Caveau **1997** £8.99 (PHI)
Vacqueyras Cuvée des Templiers, Domaine le Clos des Cazaux **1997** £8.50 (JU)
Vacqueyras Domaine des Genets, Delas **1996** £8.35 (JER)
Vacqueyras Jaboulet **1997** £8.85 (CON)

£9.00 → £9.99

Châteauneuf-du-Pape les Cailloux, Brunel **1997** £9.79 (FA) £12.50 (AV) £14.95 (RES)
Châteauneuf-du-Pape Domaine du Père Caboche **1998** £9.99 (OD)
Châteauneuf-du-Pape Domaine de la Solitude **1998** £9.49 (SO) £13.10 (AV)
Cornas Chapoutier **1995** £9.79 (FA)
★ Crozes-Hermitage Cuvée Alberic Bouvet, Domaine Gilles Robin **1998** £9.99 (GW) £10.95 (LEA)
Crozes-Hermitage Chapoutier **1996** £9.85 (PHI)
Crozes-Hermitage Château Curson, Pochon **1994** £9.95 (JU)
Crozes-Hermitage Graillot **1998** £9.38 (BY)
Crozes-Hermitage les Meysonniers, Chapoutier **1997** £9.99 (CON) £9.99 (OD)
Crozes-Hermitage Domaine de Thalabert, Jaboulet **1996** £9.30 (CAV) £11.90 (TAN)
Crozes-Hermitage Vidal-Fleury **1997** £9.62 (HA)
Gigondas Domaine du Cayron **1997** £9.90 (GAU) £12.50 (JU)
Gigondas Cuvée Pierre Aiguille, Jaboulet **1996** £9.95 (CON)
Gigondas Domaine de Gour de Chaulé **1995** £9.50 (JU)
Gigondas Domaine les Pallières **1997** £9.95 (COC)
Gigondas Domaine Santa Duc **1996** £9.75 (FORT) £18.50 (CRO)
Lirac Cuvée de la Reine des Bois, Domaine de la Mordorée **1997** £9.50 (ELL) £9.50 (BAL)
Lirac Sabon **1998** £9.13 (PIP) £9.95 (STA)
St-Joseph Chapoutier **1998** £9.99 (OD)
St-Joseph Clos de la Cuminaille, Gaillard **1996** £9.95 (LEA)
St-Joseph le Grand Pompée, Jaboulet **1997** £9.60 (SAV) £9.75 (FORT) £9.99 (NI)
St-Joseph Larmes du Père, Paret **1995** £9.49 (AME)
St-Joseph Cave de St-Désirat **1997** £9.75 (YAP)

£10.00 → £11.99

Châteauneuf-du-Pape Domaine de Beaurenard **1997** £11.55 (NEZ)
Châteauneuf-du-Pape la Bernardine, Chapoutier **1995** £11.75 (FA)
Châteauneuf-du-Pape Chante-Cigale **1998** £11.99 (POR) £12.50 (YAP)
Châteauneuf-du-Pape Chante-Cigale **1996** £11.95 (CON) £11.99 (AME) £12.95 (YAP)
Châteauneuf-du-Pape Domaine de Farguerol **1997** £10.95 (CON)
Châteauneuf-du-Pape Château des Fines Roches **1998** £10.99 (BO)
Châteauneuf-du-Pape Château des Fines Roches **1996** £11.99 (UN)
Châteauneuf-du-Pape Domaine Grand Tinel **1997** £10.90 (JU) £12.25 (AV)
Châteauneuf-du-Pape Domaine Grand Tinel **1996** £11.50 (CON)
Châteauneuf-du-Pape Domaine Grand Tinel **1995** £10.50 (JU) £17.90 (CRO)
Châteauneuf-du-Pape Domaine de Nalys **1997** £10.96 (BY) £11.71 (SAV)
Châteauneuf-du-Pape Domaine de Nalys **1995** £11.26 (COC)
Châteauneuf-du-Pape Domaine de la Roquette, Brunier **1996** £11.50 (TAN)
Châteauneuf-du-Pape Domaine du Vieux Lazaret **1997** £11.95 (BU)
Châteauneuf-du-Pape Vieux Mas des Papes, Brunier **1998** £11.40 (TAN) £11.50 (AD)
Châteauneuf-du-Pape Vieux Mas des Papes, Brunier **1997** £10.99 (POR) £12.99 (JON)
Châteauneuf-du-Pape Vieux Mas des Papes, Brunier **1996** £11.95 (LAY)
Crozes-Hermitage Château Curson, Pochon **1995** £10.50 (JU)
Crozes-Hermitage Graillot **1997** £10.95 (YAP) £12.95 (PHI)
Crozes-Hermitage les Meysonniers, Chapoutier **1998** £11.25 (STE)
Crozes-Hermitage Domaine de Thalabert, Jaboulet **1997** £11.99 (OD) £11.99 (WAI) £12.04 (REI) £12.39 (COC) £12.93 (SAV) £13.25 (CON) £13.28 (NI) £13.34 (PLA) £15.00 (MI)
Crozes-Hermitage Domaine de Thalabert, Jaboulet **1995** £11.49 (CON) £12.75 (REI) £15.00 (CRO) £15.68 (FLE) £17.25 (FORT)
Gigondas Domaine du Cayron **1998** £11.95 (AD) £11.95 (TAN)
Gigondas Domaine du Cayron **1995** £10.50 (JU)
Gigondas Chapoutier **1996** £10.99 (UB)
Gigondas Cuvée de la Tour Sarrazine, Domaine le Clos des Cazaux **1996** £10.35 (JER)
Gigondas Domaine du Grand Montmirail **1993** £10.25 (YAP) £13.85 (VIN)
Gigondas Guigal **1998** £10.99 (MAJ)
Gigondas Domaine les Pallières **1994** £11.60 (TAN)
Gigondas Domaine St-Gayan, Roger Meffre **1996** £10.50 (YAP)
Gigondas Domaine Santa Duc **1998** £11.85 (BAN) £13.00 (AV)
Gigondas Domaine Santa Duc **1997** £10.90 (GAU)
Gigondas Domaine les Tourelles, Cuillerat **1996** £10.00 (HIG)
Gigondas Château du Trignon **1997** £11.75 (ELL)
St-Joseph Clos de la Cuminaille, Gaillard **1997** £11.00 (JU) £11.21 (FLE)
St-Joseph Clos de l'Arbalestrier, Florentin **1998** £10.59 (RAE)
St-Joseph Courbis **1998** £11.99 (DI)
St-Joseph Deschants, Chapoutier **1997** £11.45 (CON) £12.95 (STE)

St-Joseph Deschants, Chapoutier **1996** £10.90 (GAU) £12.25 (STA) £12.59 (JON) £12.95 (STE)
St-Joseph Faurie **1997** £11.50 (JU)
St-Joseph Graillot **1998** £11.22 (BY)
St-Joseph le Grand Pompée, Jaboulet **1996** £10.05 (HAH) £11.99 (UB) £14.17 (MI)
Vacqueyras Domaine la Fourmone, Combe **1990** £10.95 (BAL)
Vacqueyras Grenat Noble, Domaine le Clos des Cazaux **1995** £11.90 (JU) £12.95 (GAU)
Vacqueyras Pascal **1993** £11.99 (VIN)
Vacqueyras Château des Tours **1998** £10.18 (RAE)
Vacqueyras Château des Tours **1997** £10.60 (YAP) £10.99 (DI)
Vacqueyras Château des Tours **1995** £10.18 (RAE) £11.25 (ELL)

£12.00 → £13.99

Châteauneuf-du-Pape Lucien Barrot **1996** £13.75 (BU) £13.99 (POR) £14.00 (MV)
Châteauneuf-du-Pape les Cèdres, Jaboulet **1995** £13.50 (CON)
Châteauneuf-du-Pape Clos du Caillou **1999** £12.75 (BAN)
Châteauneuf-du-Pape Clos du Mont Olivet **1997** £13.99 (YOU)
Châteauneuf-du-Pape Clos du Mont Olivet **1996** £13.99 (JON) £14.95 (RES)
Châteauneuf-du-Pape Clos du Mont Olivet **1995** £12.75 (AV)
Châteauneuf-du-Pape Clos des Papes, Avril **1996** £13.61 (GAU) £14.50 (RAE)
Châteauneuf-du-Pape Château des Fines Roches **1997** £12.60 (COC)
Châteauneuf-du-Pape Domaine Font de Michelle **1997** £12.80 (TAN) £12.95 (POR) £14.00 (JU) £15.49 (WR)
Châteauneuf-du-Pape Domaine Font de Michelle **1996** £12.80 (TAN) £14.99 (AME)
Châteauneuf-du-Pape Château Fortia **1996** £13.30 (AV) £13.99 (YOU)
Châteauneuf-du-Pape Château Fortia **1995** £12.00 (WS)
Châteauneuf-du-Pape les Galéans, Brunier **1994** £12.95 (BER)
Châteauneuf-du-Pape Domaine la Milliere, Arnaux **1996** £13.35 (HAH)
Châteauneuf-du-Pape Mont-Redon **1995** £12.63 (FA)
Châteauneuf-du-Pape Mont-Redon **1994** £13.90 (UB)
Châteauneuf-du-Pape Domaine du Père Caboche **1996** £12.75 (YAP)
Châteauneuf-du-Pape Domaine de la Roquette, Brunier **1997** £12.72 (PIP)
Châteauneuf-du-Pape Domaine Terre Ferme, Bérard **1992** £13.75 (WAT)
Châteauneuf-du-Pape Domaine du Vieux Télégraphe **1997** £13.45 (HAH) £13.50 (TAN) £14.95 (LAY) £14.95 (SOM) £15.99 (POR) £15.99 (DI) £17.00 (JU) £18.49 (PIP)
Cornas Delas **1994** £13.00 (WS)
Cornas la Chaillot, Allemand **1994** £13.95 (RAE) £14.90 (JU)
Cornas le Reynard, Allemand **1992** £13.25 (RAE) £17.00 (JU)
Cornas Robert Michel **1984** £13.50 (GAU)
Cornas Noël Verset **1996** £13.53 (RAE) £15.95 (GAU)
Crozes-Hermitage Graillot **1995** £12.50 (FORT)
Crôzes-Hermitage La Petite Ruche, Chapoutier **1992** £12.50 (CRO)
Crozes-Hermitage Domaine de Thalabert, Jaboulet **1998** £13.28 (NI)
Gigondas Domaine du Grand Montmirail **1998** £13.12 (FA)
Gigondas Guigal **1996** £12.95 (POR) £13.04 (BY) £13.95 (JER)
Gigondas Guigal **1995** £12.75 (SOM) £14.40 (UB)
Gigondas Domaine les Pallières **1995** £12.10 (COC) £12.24 (PIP)
Hermitage Domaine des Remizières **1996** £13.71 (RAE)
Lirac Cuvée de la Reine des Bois, Domaine de la Mordorée **1996** £12.75 (REI)
St-Joseph Chave **1998** £13.12 (FA)
St-Joseph Clos de la Cuminaille, Gaillard **1995** £12.60 (CRO)
St-Joseph Clos de l'Arbalestrier, Florentin **1991** £13.95 (RAE)
St-Joseph Grippat **1997** £13.25 (YAP)
St-Joseph Pascal **1995** £13.45 (VIN)
St-Joseph les Pierres, Pierre Gaillard **1995** £12.50 (JU)

£14.00 → £15.99

Châteauneuf-du-Pape Château de Beaucastel **1997** £15.59 (RAE) £16.06 (FA) £17.40 (TAN) £18.41 (SAV) £18.95 (BAL) £19.00 (JU) £19.00 (MV) £19.85 (NI)
Châteauneuf-du-Pape Château de Beaucastel **1996** £15.08 (FA) £15.86 (REI) £17.53 (RAE) £18.48 (FLE) £18.95 (BAL) £22.50 (AD) £26.95 (WR) £26.95 (BOT)
Châteauneuf-du-Pape Château de Beaucastel **1993** £14.00 (JU) £15.77 (RAE) £19.50 (CRO) £23.99 (CAV)
Châteauneuf-du-Pape la Bernardine, Chapoutier **1997** £14.95 (WAI) £14.99 (OD) £16.95 (DI) £18.99 (YOU) £19.70 (BEN)
Châteauneuf-du-Pape les Cailloux, Brunel **1998** £14.17 (RAE)
Châteauneuf-du-Pape Clos des Papes, Avril **1997** £15.10 (GAU) £15.95 (BAL)

- *Wines are listed in A–Z order within each price band.*
- *For each wine, vintages are listed in descending order.*
- *Each vintage of any wine appears only once.*

Châteauneuf-du-Pape Cuvée Etienne Gonnet, Domaine Font de Michelle **1994** £15.00 (JU) £20.56 (REI)
Châteauneuf-du-Pape Château Fortia **1997** £14.99 (POR)
Châteauneuf-du-Pape Mont-Redon **1996** £14.99 (POR)
Châteauneuf-du-Pape Château la Nerthe **1997** £15.29 (NI)
Châteauneuf-du-Pape Domaine du Père Caboche **1995** £15.75 (YAP)
Châteauneuf-du-Pape Réserve, Sabon **1997** £14.99 (YOU)
Châteauneuf-du-Pape Domaine de la Roquette, Brunier **1995** £15.95 (LAY)
Châteauneuf-du-Pape Domaine de la Roquette, Brunier **1994** £14.95 (FORT)
Châteauneuf-du-Pape Domaine Versino **1995** £15.65 (JER)
Châteauneuf-du-Pape Vieux Donjon, Michel **1995** £15.50 (CRO) £16.50 (GAU)
Châteauneuf-du-Pape Domaine du Vieux Télégraphe **1996** £14.95 (BER)
Châteauneuf-du-Pape Domaine du Vieux Télégraphe **1993** £14.00 (JU) £16.00 (CRO)
Cornas Jaboulet **1995** £14.55 (HAH) £31.00 (UB)
Cornas Jean Lionnet **1997** £14.70 (COC) £14.99 (UN)
Cornas la Chaillot, Allemand **1992** £14.00 (JU)
Cornas le Reynard, Allemand **1996** £15.77 (RAE) £20.00 (WS)
Cornas Noël Verset **1997** £14.51 (REI) £15.00 (RAE) £16.20 (GAU)
Cornas Rochepertuis, Jean Lionnet **1992** £14.90 (JU)
Gigondas Chapoutier **1997** £15.95 (STE)
Gigondas Jaboulet **1996** £14.50 (STA)
Gigondas l'Oustau Fauquet, Combe et Fille **1990** £14.95 (BAL)
Gigondas Domaine St-Gayan, Roger Meffre **1990** £14.95 (BAL)
Gigondas Domaine Santa Duc **1995** £15.00 (CRO)
Hermitage Guigal **1987** £14.20 (CAV)
Hermitage Domaine des Remizières **1995** £14.88 (RAE) £17.95 (ELL)
St-Joseph le Grand Pompée, Jaboulet **1984** £14.69 (REI)
St-Joseph Gripa **1994** £14.70 (BEN)
St-Joseph Grippat **1986** £15.00 (CRO)
St-Joseph les Pierres, Pierre Gaillard **1997** £14.00 (JU)

£16.00 → £19.99

Châteauneuf-du-Pape Château de Beaucastel **1998** £19.80 (REI) £24.87 (FA) £25.75 (RAE)
Châteauneuf-du-Pape Château de Beaucastel **1995** £19.58 (RAE) £22.50 (NI) £22.91 (FA) £24.97 (CAV) £27.50 (CRO) £27.60 (TAN) £30.00 (FORT)
Châteauneuf-du-Pape Château de Beaucastel **1994** £19.00 (RAE) £20.00 (BU) £20.95 (FA) £21.35 (NI) £23.00 (CRO) £24.95 (WR) £26.95 (BEN) £27.50 (FORT) £29.95 (BER)
Châteauneuf-du-Pape la Bernardine, Chapoutier **1996** £16.95 (DI) £19.75 (CON)
Châteauneuf-du-Pape les Cailloux, Brunel **1994** £16.00 (CRO)
Châteauneuf-du-Pape les Cèdres, Jaboulet **1998** £17.65 (NI)
Châteauneuf-du-Pape les Cèdres, Jaboulet **1996** £17.50 (STA) £20.97 (PLA)
Châteauneuf-du-Pape Chaupin, Domaine de la Janasse **1997** £17.99 (YOU)
Châteauneuf-du-Pape Clos du Caillou **1995** £16.95 (PHI)
Châteauneuf-du-Pape Clos des Papes, Avril **1995** £17.50 (ELL)
Châteauneuf-du-Pape Cuvée Etienne Gonnet, Domaine Font de Michelle **1998** £16.06 (FA) £17.95 (TAN)
Châteauneuf-du-Pape Domaine de la Mordorée **1997** £18.95 (BAL) £18.95 (LEA) £21.50 (BEN)
Châteauneuf-du-Pape Château la Nerthe **1995** £18.00 (WS)
Châteauneuf-du-Pape Château Pignan **1997** £19.00 (FA)
Châteauneuf-du-Pape Réserve, Sabon **1996** £16.95 (STA)
Châteauneuf-du-Pape Domaine du Vieux Télégraphe **1995** £17.50 (ELL) £18.50 (JU)
Cornas Chapoutier **1997** £16.99 (WAI) £19.45 (STE)
Cornas Clape **1992** £19.12 (PLAY)
Cornas Clape **1983** £16.50 (BU) £49.00 (CRO)
Cornas Colombo **1991** £16.00 (JU)
Cornas Jaboulet **1997** £18.50 (AD)
Cornas Jaboulet **1985** £18.50 (BU)
Cornas la Chaillot, Allemand **1997** £16.06 (RAE) £17.50 (GAU)
Cornas La Geynale, Robert Michel **1995** £18.80 (CRO)

Cornas les Ruchets, Colombo **1994** £19.70 (SOM) £33.95 (TW)
Cornas Rochepertuis, Jean Lionnet **1993** £18.69 (YOU)
Côte-Rôtie Barge **1982** £17.00 (CRO)
Côte-Rôtie Brune et Blonde, Gaillard **1997** £19.34 (FLE) £20.00 (JU)
Côte-Rôtie Burgaud **1998** £16.94 (RAE)
Côte-Rôtie Burgaud **1992** £19.00 (JU)
Côte-Rôtie Chapoutier **1996** £19.95 (DI) £25.60 (UB) £28.75 (STE) £28.95 (BEN)
Côte-Rôtie Chapoutier **1994** £18.60 (SOM) £20.90 (GAU) £24.25 (AD) £28.75 (STE)
Côte-Rôtie Clusel-Roch **1997** £19.00 (JU)
Côte-Rôtie Clusel-Roch **1996** £17.95 (LEA)
Côte-Rôtie Côte Brune, Gentaz-Dervieux **1987** £19.49 (FA)
Côte-Rôtie Cuvée du Plessy, Gilles Barge **1996** £16.99 (RAE) £19.10 (TAN)
Côte-Rôtie Gaillard **1998** £17.23 (RAE)
Côte-Rôtie Guigal **1996** £19.99 (BOD) £19.99 (SUN)
Côte-Rôtie la Viaillère, Champet **1997** £18.00 (JU) £18.95 (YAP)
Côte-Rôtie René Rostaing **1996** £19.20 (GAU) £19.95 (AD) £20.56 (REI) £21.20 (HAH)
Côte-Rôtie René Rostaing **1992** £19.50 (CRO) £20.00 (JU)
Côte-Rôtie de Vallouit **1988** £16.55 (FA)
Côte-Rôtie de Vallouit **1980** £19.00 (CRO)
Côtes du Rhône Château de Fonsalette **1997** £17.99 (DI)
Côtes du Rhône Château de Fonsalette **1996** £19.00 (FA) £20.95 (FA) £34.27 (CAV) £49.00 (UB)
★ Côtes du Rhône-Villages Rasteau Domaine Gourt de Mautens **1998** £17.95 (RAE)
Crozes-Hermitage Jaboulet **1985** £19.39 (REI)
Crozes-Hermitage Domaine de Thalabert, Jaboulet **1985** £18.50 (BU) £21.00 (CRO)
Gigondas Domaine du Cayron **1989** £17.50 (BAL)
Gigondas Domaine les Gouberts **1985** £18.50 (CRO)
Gigondas Jaboulet **1990** £17.50 (BAL)
Hermitage Domaine du Colombier **1997** £18.65 (WAT) £21.00 (JU) £24.50 (BAL)
Hermitage Cuvée des Miaux, Ferraton **1995** £19.00 (FA)
Hermitage Desmeure **1995** £17.50 (GAU)
Hermitage la Sizeranne, Chapoutier **1996** £19.58 (FA) £21.95 (DI) £24.90 (GAU) £27.99 (BOD) £27.99 (SUN) £32.45 (STE)
Hermitage la Sizeranne, Chapoutier **1994** £16.95 (SOM) £19.80 (REI) £19.95 (BER) £22.99 (UN) £24.99 (POR)
Hermitage Domaine des Remizières **1994** £17.95 (RAE)
Hermitage Sorrel **1998** £18.25 (GAU)
Hermitage de Vallouit **1982** £17.50 (CRO)
Hermitage Vidal-Fleury **1989** £16.06 (FA)
St-Joseph Réserve Personnelle, Jaboulet **1996** £18.21 (REI)

£20.00 → £24.99

Châteauneuf-du-Pape les Cailloux, Brunel **1995** £20.56 (REI)
Châteauneuf-du-Pape Cuvée de la Reine des Bois, Domaine de la Mordorée **1998** £21.95 (LEA)
Châteauneuf-du-Pape Vidal-Fleury **1985** £22.00 (CRO) £44.18 (WY)
Châteauneuf-du-Pape Domaine du Vieux Télégraphe **1988** £20.46 (FA)
Cornas Jaboulet **1996** £20.97 (PLA)
Cornas les Ruchets, Colombo **1996** £22.91 (FA) £24.25 (BAN) £30.00 (FORT) £31.95 (RES) £32.66 (TW)
Cornas Robert Michel **1983** £20.56 (REI)
Côte-Rôtie Barge **1983** £22.00 (CRO)
Côte-Rôtie Brune et Blonde, Guigal **1996** £22.11 (BY) £23.95 (JER) £27.50 (MI)

Côte-Rôtie Brune et Blonde, Guigal **1995** £22.50 (MI) £23.50 (CON) £23.95 (POR)
Côte-Rôtie Brune et Blonde, Guigal **1992** £23.00 (JU)
Côte-Rôtie Brune et Blonde, Vidal-Fleury **1994** £23.84 (HA)
Côte-Rôtie Burgaud **1997** £20.00 (YAP)
Côte-Rôtie Burgaud **1994** £22.00 (JU)
Côte-Rôtie Chapoutier **1997** £24.40 (TAN)
Côte-Rôtie Chapoutier **1995** £24.95 (DI)
Côte-Rôtie Côte Blonde, René Rostaing **1992** £23.00 (JU)

Côte-Rôtie Côte Brune, Gentaz-Dervieux **1993** £23.95 (RAE)

★ Côte-Rôtie Louis Drevon **1996** £21.12 (PIP)

Côte-Rôtie Gentaz-Dervieux **1986** £24.00 (CRO)

Côte-Rôtie Guigal **1995** £23.50 (AME)

Côte-Rôtie Guigal **1994** £21.79 (UN)

Côte-Rôtie Jasmin **1997** £22.75 (YAP)

Côte-Rôtie la Mordorée, Chapoutier **1997** £21.95 (DI)

Côte-Rôtie la Viaillère, Rostaing **1996** £22.91 (FA) £29.95 (RES)

Côte-Rôtie la Viaillère, Rostaing **1994** £24.00 (JU)

Côte-Rôtie les Jumelles, Jaboulet **1995** £20.00 (WS) £24.50 (AD) £25.00 (FLE) £32.31 (PLA)

Côte-Rôtie les Jumelles, Jaboulet **1992** £24.17 (MI)

Côte-Rôtie René Rostaing **1998** £20.83 (RAE)

Côte-Rôtie René Rostaing **1997** £21.74 (REI) £28.00 (JU)

Côte-Rôtie de Vallouit **1983** £20.00 (CRO)

Côtes du Rhône Coudoulet de Beaucastel **1993** £24.99 (VA)

Côtes du Rhône Château de Fonsalette **1995** £24.87 (FA) £38.68 (CAV) £41.13 (REI)

Côtes du Rhône Jaboulet **1974** £23.00 (CRO)

Gigondas Jaboulet **1979** £21.00 (CRO)

Gigondas Domaine les Pallières **1983** £23.00 (CRO)

Hermitage Albert Belle **1996** £24.95 (BEN)

Hermitage Chave **1995** £20.99 (AME) £91.45 (FA) £95.00 (BEN)

Hermitage Domaine du Colombier **1998** £23.25 (TAN)

Hermitage Domaine du Colombier **1994** £22.00 (JU) £28.78 (TW)

Hermitage Faurie **1997** £20.00 (JU)

Hermitage Faurie **1996** £20.40 (HAH)

Hermitage Guigal **1996** £24.84 (BY) £30.00 (MI)

Hermitage Guigal **1995** £22.50 (MI)

Hermitage la Chapelle, Jaboulet **1996** £23.99 (WR) £32.31 (FA) £35.00 (FORT) £35.65 (NI) £37.50 (CON) £41.12 (CAV) £41.13 (REI) £45.53 (PLA) £49.17 (MI)

Hermitage la Sizeranne, Chapoutier **1983** £23.00 (CRO) £65.80 (REI)

Hermitage Vidal-Fleury **1994** £22.14 (HA)

St-Joseph Graillot **1996** £21.50 (CRO)

£25.00 → £29.99

Châteauneuf-du-Pape Barbe Rac, Chapoutier **1992** £29.00 (CRO)

Châteauneuf-du-Pape les Cailloux, Brunel **1990** £29.00 (CRO)

Châteauneuf-du-Pape Clos des Papes, Avril **1989** £28.79 (FA)

Châteauneuf-du-Pape la Grappe des Papes, Jaboulet **1969** £29.00 (CRO)

Châteauneuf-du-Pape Château Pignan **1994** £27.03 (CAV)

Cornas de Barjac **1982** £28.79 (REI)

Cornas Clape **1996** £29.50 (CRO)

Cornas Jaboulet **1976** £29.00 (CRO)

Cornas Noël Verset **1989** £27.50 (BAL)

Côte-Rôtie Brune et Blonde, Guigal **1983** £26.93 (FA) £39.00 (JU) £39.90 (PIP)

Côte-Rôtie Côte Blonde, René Rostaing **1996** £28.79 (FA)

Côte-Rôtie Côte Blonde, René Rostaing **1994** £27.00 (JU) £37.00 (CRO)

Côte-Rôtie Gentaz-Dervieux **1980** £29.00 (CRO)

Côte-Rôtie Jamet **1990** £29.28 (FA)

Côte-Rôtie Jamet **1988** £26.00 (CRO) £29.95 (BAL)

Côte-Rôtie Jasmin **1994** £25.00 (YAP)

Côte-Rôtie la Landonne, René Rostaing **1998** £27.08 (RAE)

Côte-Rôtie la Landonne, René Rostaing **1996** £27.32 (FA) £29.40 (HAH)

Côte-Rôtie la Landonne, René Rostaing **1994** £27.95 (WAI) £28.00 (JU)

Côte-Rôtie la Viaillère, Rostaing **1995** £26.00 (JU)

Côte-Rôtie les Grandes Places, Clusel-Roch **1996** £29.50 (LEA)

Côte-Rôtie les Grandes Places, Clusel-Roch **1994** £29.00 (JU)

Côte-Rôtie les Jumelles, Jaboulet **1997** £25.00 (FORT) £25.75 (WAI) £32.45 (NI) £32.50 (MI)

Côte-Rôtie les Jumelles, Jaboulet **1986** £28.00 (JU)

- *All prices for each wine are listed together in ascending order.*
- *Price bands refer to the lowest price for which the wine is available.*

Côte-Rôtie Rose Pourpe, Gaillard **1997** £29.00 (JU)
Crozes-Hermitage Domaine de Thalabert, Jaboulet **1993** £25.00 (WS)
Hermitage Chave **1992** £28.89 (CAV)
Hermitage Chave **1984** £29.00 (CRO)
Hermitage Desmeure **1983** £27.00 (CRO) £33.49 (REI)
Hermitage Guigal **1997** £28.95 (POR)
Hermitage Guigal **1993** £25.33 (PLAY)
Hermitage Guigal **1990** £28.89 (CAV)
Hermitage la Chapelle, Jaboulet **1994** £25.46 (FA) £26.97 (REI)
Hermitage la Chapelle, Jaboulet **1984** £26.44 (REI) £27.61 (WY)
Hermitage la Sizeranne, Chapoutier **1997** £28.00 (TAN)
Hermitage la Sizeranne, Chapoutier **1991** £25.00 (CRO) £27.00 (JU)
Hermitage le Gréal, Sorrel **1996** £25.90 (GAU)
St-Joseph Jaboulet **1978** £27.00 (CRO)

£30.00 → £49.99

Châteauneuf-du-Pape Barbe Rac, Chapoutier **1996** £41.12 (FA) £43.00 (DI) £49.50 (BEN)
Châteauneuf-du-Pape Barbe Rac, Chapoutier **1995** £48.96 (FA)
Châteauneuf-du-Pape Barbe Rac, Chapoutier **1991** £38.68 (CAV)
Châteauneuf-du-Pape Château de Beaucastel **1990** £48.37 (FA) £57.50 (CRO) £58.50 (BEN) £68.50 (FORT)
Châteauneuf-du-Pape Château de Beaucastel **1988** £37.00 (CRO) £40.00 (FORT) £94.00 (UB)
Châteauneuf-du-Pape Château de Beaucastel **1983** £42.50 (FA) £50.00 (CRO) £55.23 (WY)
Châteauneuf-du-Pape Château de Beaucastel **1980** £34.66 (REI)
Châteauneuf-du-Pape Domaine Bosquet des Papes **1985** £34.00 (CRO)
Châteauneuf-du-Pape Clos du Mont Olivet **1978** £40.00 (CRO)
Châteauneuf-du-Pape Château Pignan **1995** £37.60 (CAV)
Châteauneuf-du-Pape Château Pignan **1986** £32.00 (CRO)
Châteauneuf-du-Pape Château Rayas **1997** £39.95 (DI)
Châteauneuf-du-Pape Château Rayas **1996** £49.95 (DI) £60.12 (FA) £78.00 (BAL)
Châteauneuf-du-Pape Château Rayas **1992** £41.13 (CAV)
Cornas Clape **1997** £30.00 (FORT)
Cornas Jaboulet **1983** £30.37 (WY)
Cornas Jaboulet **1978** £49.94 (REI)
Côte-Rôtie Brune et Blonde, Guigal **1990** £36.00 (CRO)
Côte-Rôtie Brune et Blonde, Guigal **1985** £42.00 (CRO)
Côte-Rôtie Chapoutier **1990** £36.00 (BAL)
Côte-Rôtie Chapoutier **1978** £45.00 (CRO)
Côte-Rôtie Côte Blonde, René Rostaing **1998** £31.67 (RAE)
Côte-Rôtie Côte Blonde, René Rostaing **1991** £34.00 (CRO)
Côte-Rôtie Côte Blonde, René Rostaing **1988** £49.00 (JU)
Côte-Rôtie Gentaz-Dervieux **1990** £32.50 (BAL) £35.00 (WS)
Côte-Rôtie Gentaz-Dervieux **1988** £49.00 (CRO)
Côte-Rôtie Gentaz-Dervieux **1983** £33.49 (REI)
Côte-Rôtie Jasmin **1990** £42.00 (CRO)
Côte-Rôtie Jasmin **1983** £45.00 (CRO)
Côte-Rôtie la Landonne, Guigal **1993** £41.54 (BY) £64.62 (FA) £76.38 (CAV) £152.75 (TW)
Côte-Rôtie la Landonne, René Rostaing **1988** £49.00 (JU) £61.00 (CRO)
Côte-Rôtie la Mordorée, Chapoutier **1994** £44.06 (FA)
Côte-Rôtie les Grandes Places, Clusel-Roch **1997** £32.00 (JU)
Côte-Rôtie les Jumelles, Jaboulet **1998** £32.45 (NI)
Côte-Rôtie les Jumelles, Jaboulet **1985** £44.18 (WY) £50.00 (WS)
Côte-Rôtie la Mouline, Guigal **1993** £41.54 (BY) £64.62 (FA) £76.38 (CAV)
Côte-Rôtie René Rostaing **1991** £38.00 (CRO)
Côtes du Rhône Château de Fonsalette **1993** £31.13 (TW)
Côtes du Rhône Château de Fonsalette **1985** £35.64 (FA) £41.13 (REI)
Crozes-Hermitage Jaboulet **1983** £31.76 (WY)
Crozes-Hermitage Domaine de Thalabert, Jaboulet **1990** £35.00 (CRO)
Ermitage le Pavillon, Chapoutier **1993** £48.96 (FA)
Gigondas Domaine les Gouberts **1981** £34.00 (CRO)
Gigondas Jaboulet **1978** £33.00 (CRO)

Hermitage Chave **1997** £40.00 (YAP) £50.00 (FORT) £58.16 (FA)
Hermitage Chave **1993** £30.73 (PLAY)
Hermitage Faurie **1985** £42.98 (PIP)
Hermitage Guigal **1991** £41.12 (TW)
Hermitage Guigal **1983** £45.57 (WY) £282.00 (FA)
Hermitage Guigal **1978** £42.00 (CRO)
Hermitage Jaboulet **1983** £38.19 (REI)
Hermitage la Chapelle, Jaboulet **1997** £44.95 (WAI) £44.99 (OD) £45.00 (CON) £45.24 (REI) £45.40 (HAH) £55.32 (FA) £62.50 (MI) £77.84 (CAV)
Hermitage la Chapelle, Jaboulet **1995** £35.25 (FA) £48.00 (PHI)
Hermitage la Chapelle, Jaboulet **1988** £39.16 (FA) £52.50 (BEN) £58.26 (CAV) £60.00 (NO)
Hermitage la Chapelle, Jaboulet **1986** £41.13 (CAV) £66.27 (WY)
Hermitage la Chapelle, Jaboulet **1982** £47.00 (CRO) £64.63 (CAV)
Hermitage la Sizeranne, Chapoutier **1989** £48.00 (TAN)
Hermitage le Gréal, Sorrel **1983** £45.00 (BAL)

£50.00 → £99.99

Châteauneuf-du-Pape Barbe Rac, Chapoutier **1990** £91.00 (CRO)
Châteauneuf-du-Pape Château de Beaucastel **1989** £59.95 (TAN) £65.02 (FA) £72.00 (CRO)
Châteauneuf-du-Pape Château de Beaucastel **1978** £71.87 (FA) £88.00 (CRO)
Châteauneuf-du-Pape les Cèdres, Jaboulet **1978** £56.99 (REI)
Châteauneuf-du-Pape Château Fortia **1978** £67.00 (CRO)
Châteauneuf-du-Pape Hommage à Jacques Perrin, Château de Beaucastel **1994** £82.00 (JU) £120.00 (FORT) £148.25 (FA)
Châteauneuf-du-Pape Château Pignan **1985** £60.00 (CRO)
Châteauneuf-du-Pape Château Rayas **1993** £52.87 (TW)
Châteauneuf-du-Pape Château Rayas **1974** £56.00 (CRO)
Châteauneuf-du-Pape Domaine du Vieux Télégraphe **1990** £69.03 (WY)
Châteauneuf-du-Pape Domaine du Vieux Télégraphe **1989** £52.46 (WY)
Cornas Clape **1985** £58.00 (CRO)
Côte-Rôtie Côte Blonde, René Rostaing **1995** £55.00 (CRO)
Côte-Rôtie Gentaz-Dervieux **1982** £66.00 (CRO)
Côte-Rôtie la Landonne, Guigal **1987** £68.00 (JU) £111.63 (CAV) £111.63 (FA) £130.00 (CRO)
Côte-Rôtie la Landonne, Guigal **1986** £80.00 (JU) £101.83 (FA) £105.00 (CRO) £129.25 (CAV) £164.50 (TW)
Côte-Rôtie la Landonne, Guigal **1981** £76.37 (FA) £86.00 (CRO) £132.89 (NO)
Côte-Rôtie la Landonne, René Rostaing **1991** £55.00 (CRO)
Côte-Rôtie la Mordorée, Chapoutier **1996** £73.44 (FA) £85.00 (BEN)
Côte-Rôtie la Mordorée, Chapoutier **1992** £50.00 (JU)
Côte-Rôtie la Mordorée, Chapoutier **1990** £75.00 (CRO)
Côte-Rôtie la Turque, Guigal **1994** £88.13 (CAV) £107.71 (FA)
Côte-Rôtie la Turque, Guigal **1987** £98.00 (JU) £111.63 (CAV)
Côte-Rôtie la Mouline, Guigal **1994** £88.13 (CAV) £102.81 (FA)
Côte-Rôtie la Mouline, Guigal **1987** £68.00 (JU) £111.63 (CAV) £111.63 (FA) £125.00 (CRO)
Côte-Rôtie la Mouline, Guigal **1986** £78.00 (JU) £101.83 (FA) £105.00 (CRO) £164.50 (TW)
Côte-Rôtie la Mouline, Guigal **1981** £76.37 (FA) £89.00 (CRO) £120.00 (JU)
Côtes du Rhône Château de Fonsalette **1979** £58.26 (CAV)
Ermitage le Pavillon, Chapoutier **1997** £71.50 (DI)
Ermitage le Pavillon, Chapoutier **1992** £58.00 (JU) £79.50 (BEN)
Hermitage Chave **1989** £50.00 (WS) £99.29 (FA) £136.30 (CAV)
Hermitage Chave **1985** £69.00 (CRO) £108.12 (NO) £124.26 (WY)
Hermitage Chave **1983** £71.00 (CRO) £77.75 (FA)
Hermitage la Chapelle, Jaboulet **1985** £51.41 (CAV) £52.00 (CRO) £64.67 (NO) £80.08 (WY)

Please remember that **Oz Clarke's Wine Buying Guide** *is a price* ***guide*** *and not a price* ***list****. It is not meant to replace up-to-date merchants' lists.*

Hermitage la Chapelle, Jaboulet **1983** £58.75 (FA) £70.00 (JU) £70.49 (NO) £73.44 (CAV) £80.08 (WY) £88.13 (REI) £175.00 (UB)

Hermitage la Chapelle, Jaboulet **1976** £52.88 (FA) £76.38 (REI)

Hermitage Marquise de la Tourette, Delas **1978** £70.00 (CRO)

£100.00 → £149.99

Châteauneuf-du-Pape Château Rayas **1988** £148.25 (FA)

Châteauneuf-du-Pape Château Rayas **1976** £129.25 (FA)

Côte-Rôtie la Landonne, Guigal **1982** £137.08 (FA) £146.88 (CAV) £179.99 (NO) £190.00 (JU)

Côte-Rôtie la Turque, Guigal **1986** £101.83 (FA) £176.25 (TW)

Côte-Rôtie les Jumelles, Jaboulet **1962** £117.50 (TW)

Côte-Rôtie les Jumelles, Jaboulet **1959** £110.00 (CRO)

Côte-Rôtie la Mouline, Guigal **1979** £117.49 (FA) £190.00 (JU)

Ermitage le Pavillon, Chapoutier **1996** £112.60 (FA) £158.63 (REI)

Ermitage le Pavillon, Chapoutier **1989** £145.00 (CRO)

Hermitage Chave **1990** £148.25 (FA)

Hermitage la Chapelle, Jaboulet **1990** £144.43 (FA) £160.00 (BEN)

£150.00 → £249.99

Châteauneuf-du-Pape Hommage à Jacques Perrin, Château de Beaucastel **1995** £171.75 (FA) £200.00 (FORT)

Châteauneuf-du-Pape Hommage à Jacques Perrin, Château de Beaucastel **1990** £197.20 (FA) £220.00 (CRO)

Châteauneuf-du-Pape Château Rayas **1995** £221.68 (FA) £275.00 (YOU)

Châteauneuf-du-Pape Château Rayas **1989** £197.20 (FA) £210.00 (BEN) £235.00 (BAL) £376.95 (UB)

Châteauneuf-du-Pape Château Rayas **1985** £217.38 (REI)

Côte-Rôtie la Landonne, Guigal **1990** £205.62 (FA) £205.63 (CAV)

Côte-Rôtie la Landonne, Guigal **1988** £205.62 (FA) £217.38 (CAV)

Côte-Rôtie la Landonne, Guigal **1985** £220.00 (JU) £235.00 (FA) £260.00 (CRO)

Côte-Rôtie la Turque, Guigal **1991** £184.08 (FA) £205.63 (CAV)

Côte-Rôtie la Turque, Guigal **1989** £176.25 (FA) £205.63 (REI)

Côte-Rôtie la Turque, Guigal **1988** £205.62 (FA) £217.38 (CAV)

Côte-Rôtie les Jumelles, Jaboulet **1955** £199.75 (TW)

Côte-Rôtie la Mouline, Guigal **1990** £205.62 (FA) £205.63 (CAV)

Côte-Rôtie la Mouline, Guigal **1988** £205.62 (FA) £217.38 (CAV)

Côte-Rôtie la Mouline, Guigal **1985** £220.00 (JU) £260.00 (CRO)

Côte-Rôtie la Mouline, Guigal **1983** £230.00 (JU) £250.00 (CRO) £250.01 (NO)

Hermitage la Chapelle, Jaboulet **1978** £200.00 (WS) £225.00 (BEN) £230.00 (CRO) £235.00 (YOU) £288.85 (CAV)

Hermitage la Chapelle, Jaboulet **1969** £180.00 (CRO)

Over £250.00

Châteauneuf-du-Pape Château Rayas **1990** £314.70 (FA)

Côte-Rôtie la Landonne, Guigal **1978** £293.75 (FA)

Hermitage la Chapelle, Jaboulet **1955** £440.63 (CAV)

WHITE

Under £6.00

VdP des Coteaux de l'Ardèche Chardonnay, Latour **1998** £4.99 (POR) £5.41 (COC)

VdP des Coteaux de l'Ardèche Chardonnay, Latour **1997** £5.39 (JON) £7.40 (TAN)

Côtes du Lubéron la Vieille Ferme **1998** £5.70 (CB)

Lirac la Fermade, Domaine Maby **1998** £5.95 (WS)

£6.00 → £7.99

VdP des Coteaux de l'Ardèche Chardonnay, Latour **1996** £6.25 (FORT)

VdP des Coteaux de l'Ardèche Viognier, Duboeuf **1998** £6.25 (NEZ) £7.70 (CRO)

Côtes du Rhône Belleruche, Chapoutier **1998** £6.49 (CON) £7.95 (STE)

Côtes du Rhône Guigal **1998** £7.59 (JON)

Côtes du Rhône Guigal **1997** £7.49 (UN) £8.35 (JER)

Côtes du Rhône Parallèle 45, Jaboulet **1998** £6.99 (PLA)

Côtes du Rhône Domaine St-Gayan, Roger Meffre **1998** £6.75 (YAP)
Côtes du Rhône-Villages Blanc de Blancs, Château du Grand Moulas **1998** £6.95 (AD)
Côtes du Rhône-Villages, Domaine du Vieux Chêne **1996** £6.95 (JU)
Crozes-Hermitage Cave des Clairmonts, Borja **1998** £7.59 (JON)
Crozes-Hermitage Domaine des Entrefaux **1998** £7.90 (TAN) £8.29 (PIP)
Crozes-Hermitage Pochon **1997** £6.95 (JU)
Hermitage de l'Orée, Chapoutier **1997** £7.99 (DI)
Lirac la Fermade, Domaine Maby **1996** £7.50 (YAP)

£8.00 → £9.99

Côtes du Rhône Coudoulet de Beaucastel **1998** £9.01 (FA) £9.36 (RAE) £9.69 (GOE) £11.16 (REI) £11.55 (AD) £12.50 (MV)
Côtes du Lubéron le Mont, la Vieille Ferme **1997** £8.65 (UB)
Crozes-Hermitage Cave des Clairmonts, Borja **1997** £8.25 (YAP)
Crozes-Hermitage Domaine du Colombier **1998** £9.29 (BAL)
Crozes-Hermitage Château Curson, Pochon **1997** £9.90 (JU)
Crozes-Hermitage Delas **1997** £8.85 (JER)
Crozes-Hermitage la Mule Blanche, Jaboulet **1997** £9.50 (WS) £9.70 (GAU) £9.95 (TAN) £10.60 (STA)
Crozes-Hermitage Domaine des Remizières **1994** £8.99 (RAE)
Lirac Cuvée de la Reine des Bois, Domaine de la Mordoree **1998** £9.95 (LEA)
St-Joseph Gaillard **1998** £9.85 (BAN)
St-Joseph le Grand Pompée, Jaboulet **1997** £9.30 (SAV)
St-Joseph Perret **1997** £9.95 (JU) £11.81 (NO)
St-Péray Thières **1996** £9.50 (YAP)

£10.00 → £14.99

Châteauneuf-du-Pape la Bernadine, Chapoutier **1997** £13.99 (YOU) £17.30 (UB) £17.95 (CON)
Châteauneuf-du-Pape les Cèdres, Jaboulet **1997** £14.75 (STA)
Châteauneuf-du-Pape les Cèdres, Jaboulet **1996** £12.34 (REI)
Châteauneuf-du-Pape Domaine Font de Michelle **1997** £13.50 (JU)
Châteauneuf-du-Pape Château Fortia **1998** £13.05 (AV)
Châteauneuf-du-Pape Domaine du Père Caboche **1997** £12.75 (YAP)
Châteauneuf-du-Pape Domaine de la Roquette, Brunier **1998** £13.40 (PIP)
Châteauneuf-du-Pape Domaine de la Roquette, Brunier **1997** £12.90 (TAN)
Châteauneuf-du-Pape Domaine du Vieux Télégraphe **1998** £14.50 (AD) £16.20 (TAN)
Côtes du Rhône Coudoulet de Beaucastel **1997** £11.50 (GAU)
Côtes du Rhône Coudoulet de Beaucastel **1996** £10.50 (CRO)
Côtes du Rhône Château de Fonsalette **1995** £13.61 (FA) £21.54 (CAV)
Côtes du Rhône Guigal **1996** £10.52 (TW)
Côtes du Rhône Viognier Clos de la Cuminaille, Pierre Gaillard **1997** £14.95 (LEA)
Crozes-Hermitage Château Curson, Pochon **1995** £10.50 (JU)
Hermitage Domaine des Remizières **1995** £14.88 (RAE)
Hermitage Domaine des Remizières **1986** £14.95 (RAE) £17.90 (UB)
Lirac Cuvée de la Reine des Bois, Domaine de la Mordoree **1997** £11.50 (BEN)
Lirac Cuvée de la Reine des Bois, Domaine de la Mordoree **1996** £10.58 (SAV)
St-Joseph Clos de l'Arbalestrier, Florentin **1995** £12.65 (RAE)
St-Joseph Clos de l'Arbalestrier, Florentin **1986** £12.95 (RAE) £15.35 (UB)
St-Joseph Gaillard **1997** £11.50 (JU)
St-Joseph Bernard Gripa **1993** £11.75 (CON) £16.39 (TW)
St-Joseph Grippat **1996** £13.50 (YAP)
St-Joseph le Grand Pompée, Jaboulet **1995** £10.52 (REI)
St-Joseph Perret **1998** £10.50 (JU) £11.00 (MV)

£15.00 → £19.99

Château-Grillet **1987** £19.97 (FA)
Châteauneuf-du-Pape Château de Beaucastel **1998** £17.04 (FA) £19.30 (GAU) £20.56 (GOE) £23.00 (TAN) £23.32 (REI)
Châteauneuf-du-Pape Château de Beaucastel **1996** £16.06 (FA) £19.00 (RAE) £20.95 (BAL) £20.95 (NI) £21.00 (MV) £22.50 (FORT) £23.52 (PLAY)

Châteauneuf-du-Pape Château de Beaucastel **1994** £17.53 (RAE)
Châteauneuf-du-Pape Château de Beaucastel **1986** £17.63 (FA)
Châteauneuf-du-Pape Domaine Font de Michelle **1996** £15.35 (JU)
Châteauneuf-du-Pape Guigal **1996** £19.17 (MI)
Châteauneuf-du-Pape Mont-Redon **1997** £17.10 (UB)
Châteauneuf-du-Pape Château de la Nerte **1995** £16.45 (BER)
Châteauneuf-du-Pape Domaine du Vieux Télégraphe **1997** £15.60 (TAN) £15.99 (JON) £16.50 (JU)
Châteauneuf-du-Pape Domaine du Vieux Télégraphe **1994** £16.15 (HAH)
Condrieu Coteau de Chéry, Perret **1998** £18.90 (GAU) £19.95 (AD) £22.49 (YOU) £23.00 (JU) £23.07 (WT) £24.50 (BAL) £26.95 (BEN)
Condrieu Guigal **1997** £19.95 (POR) £22.50 (MI)
Condrieu Perret **1998** £17.90 (GAU) £18.25 (TAN) £18.90 (JU) £20.89 (WT)
Condrieu Pinchon **1993** £18.95 (RAE)
Condrieu Château du Rozay **1987** £17.04 (REI)
Côtes du Rhône Viognier, Gaillard **1996** £16.00 (JU)
Hermitage Chante-Alouette, Chapoutier **1995** £19.39 (REI) £22.75 (DI)
Hermitage Chante-Alouette, Chapoutier **1994** £19.39 (REI) £22.50 (BER) £30.95 (STE)
Hermitage Chevalier de Stérimberg, Jaboulet **1996** £17.90 (TAN) £32.20 (PLA)
St-Joseph Bernard Gripa **1995** £15.86 (TW)

£20.00 → £29.99

Château-Grillet **1996** £25.85 (FA) £33.75 (YAP)
Châteauneuf-du-Pape Château de Beaucastel **1995** £21.00 (CRO)
Châteauneuf-du-Pape Château de Beaucastel **1993** £22.49 (YOU)
Châteauneuf-du-Pape Château de Beaucastel **1987** £28.79 (REI)
Châteauneuf-du-Pape Guigal **1990** £25.00 (CRO)
Châteauneuf-du-Pape Guigal **1986** £22.91 (REI)
Châteauneuf-du-Pape Château Rayas **1995** £28.79 (FA) £44.06 (CAV)
Condrieu Barge **1997** £21.40 (TAN)
Condrieu Chapoutier **1997** £20.95 (DI) £23.75 (CON) £24.89 (JON)
Condrieu Clos Chanson, Perret **1998** £21.00 (JU) £21.49 (YOU)
Condrieu Coteau de Chéry, Perret **1999** £20.35 (GAU)
Condrieu Coteau de Chéry, Perret **1996** £24.00 (JU) £26.25 (FORT)
Condrieu Coteau du Chéry, Clusel-Roch **1998** £21.95 (LEA)
Condrieu Gaillard **1999** £20.60 (BAN)
Condrieu Gaillard **1997** £21.00 (JU)
Condrieu Guigal **1996** £20.76 (GOE) £22.50 (MI) £23.00 (CRO)
Condrieu Guigal **1995** £21.69 (UN) £22.50 (MI) £23.30 (HAH)
Condrieu la Bonnette, Rostaing **1999** £27.08 (RAE)
Condrieu la Bonnette, Rostaing **1997** £24.99 (YOU) £25.00 (JU)
Condrieu la Bonnette, Rostaing **1996** £23.95 (HAH) £24.00 (JU)
Condrieu les Ceps du Nebaudon, Paret **1996** £24.21 (NO)
Condrieu Perret **1996** £20.00 (JU)
Condrieu Château du Rozay **1996** £25.00 (YAP)
Condrieu Vernay **1997** £28.50 (FORT)
Condrieu Vernay **1996** £22.75 (YAP)
Hermitage Chante-Alouette, Chapoutier **1996** £22.35 (UB) £30.95 (STE)
Hermitage Chave **1991** £21.15 (CAV)
Hermitage Chevalier de Stérimberg, Jaboulet **1997** £28.75 (WAI) £33.33 (MI)
Hermitage Chevalier de Stérimberg, Jaboulet **1981** £26.44 (REI)
Hermitage Faurie **1997** £23.00 (JU)
Hermitage Faurie **1994** £20.30 (HAH)
Hermitage Grippat **1986** £24.95 (BEN)
Hermitage les Rocoules, Sorrel **1996** £23.75 (GAU)
Hermitage Domaine des Remizières **1993** £23.38 (TW)

£30.00 → £39.99

Château-Grillet **1994** £35.00 (YAP)
Châteauneuf-du-Pape Château Rayas **1994** £34.95 (DI) £41.13 (CAV) £56.98 (TW)
Châteauneuf-du-Pape Vieilles Vignes, Château de Beaucastel **1998** £35.15 (RAE) £41.13 (REI) £41.40 (TAN)

Châteauneuf-du-Pape Vieilles Vignes, Château de Beaucastel **1996** £38.00 (BAL)
Condrieu les Chaillets Vieilles Vignes, Cuilleron **1996** £36.95 (RES)
Hermitage Chave **1996** £35.00 (YAP) £37.50 (FORT)
Hermitage de l'Orée, Chapoutier **1991** £34.27 (CAV)

Over £40.00

Château-Grillet **1989** £93.00 (UB)
Château-Grillet **1976** £70.50 (REI)
Hermitage Chave **1979** £131.17 (WY)
Hermitage de l'Orée, Chapoutier **1996** £60.00 (DI) £99.75 (BEN)
Hermitage de l'Orée, Chapoutier **1995** £41.65 (CAV) £85.50 (BEN)

ROSÉ

Under £6.00

Côtes du Rhône Domaine de la Mordorée à Tavel **1999** £5.95 (LEA)
Côtes du Rhone Domaine du Vieux Chêne **1996** £5.50 (JU)
Côtes du Lubéron Château Val Joanis **1998** £5.42 (BY)
Tavel la Forcadière, Domaine Maby **1998** £5.95 (WS)

£6.00 → £8.99

Lirac Rosé la Fermade, Domaine Maby **1998** £7.00 (YAP)
Tavel Domaine André Méjan **1998** £6.99 (JON)
Tavel la Forcadière, Domaine Maby **1997** £7.75 (YAP)
Tavel Domaine de la Mordorée **1999** £8.95 (LEA)
Tavel Domaine de Valéry, André Méjan **1996** £7.50 (JU)

c. £10.00

Tavel l'Espiègle, Jaboulet **1995** £9.95 (UB)

SPARKLING

Under £10.00

Clairette de Die Brut Archard-Vincent **Non-vintage** £9.50 (YAP)
Clairette de Die Tradition Demi-sec Archard-Vincent **Non-vintage** £9.25 (YAP)

c. £21.00

St-Péray Mousseux Brut, Clape **1996** £21.00 (JU)

FORTIFIED

Under £7.00

Muscat de Beaumes-de-Venise Domaine de Coyeux ½ bottle **1998** £5.50 (WS) £5.80 (AV) £6.31 (CB)
Muscat de Beaumes-de-Venise Domaine de Coyeux ½ bottle **1997** £6.25 (AD)
Muscat de Beaumes-de-Venise Domaine de Durban ½ bottle **1997** £5.97 (SAV)

£7.00 → £9.99

Muscat de Beaumes-de-Venise Cave Co-op de Beaumes-de-Venise **1993** £7.99 (OD)
Muscat de Beaumes-de-Venise Chapoutier ½ bottle **1997** £7.99 (DI)
Muscat de Beaumes-de-Venise Domaine de Coyeux **1998** £9.95 (WS) £11.99 (CB)
Muscat de Beaumes-de-Venise Domaine de Durban **1997** £9.60 (SAV) £11.50 (SOM)
Muscat de Beaumes-de-Venise Cave des Vignerons à Vacqueyras **Non-vintage** £9.52 (PLAY) £9.95 (POR) £10.49 (JON)
Rasteau Domaine la Soumade **1998** £9.75 (NI) £19.21 (TW)

£10.00 → £13.99

Muscat de Beaumes-de-Venise Domaine des Bernardins **1998** £13.15 (PIP)
Muscat de Beaumes-de-Venise Domaine de Coyeux **1999** £10.65 (AV)
Muscat de Beaumes-de-Venise Domaine de Durban **1998** £11.65 (PIP) £11.95 (YAP)
Muscat de Beaumes-de-Venise Jaboulet **1996** £12.25 (FORT)
Muscat de Beaumes-de-Venise Vidal-Fleury **1996** £13.95 (SOM)
Rasteau Domaine la Soumade **Non-vintage** £12.06 (PIP)

Over £14.00

Muscat de Beaumes-de-Venise Domaine de Durban **Non-vintage** £14.04 (REI)
Muscat de Beaumes-de-Venise Jaboulet **1998** £14.98 (PLA)

SOUTHERN FRANCE

Grapes that were becoming forgotten in the rush to plant Syrah are making people sit up and take notice. Good news, no?

So what's happening? Are we seeing a revival of interest in appellation wines from down here?

It will be ironic if that's what's really happening. This was where the vin de pays revolution happened: where Aussie winemakers got off the plane at Marseilles or Toulouse and seemingly within hours were turning out creditable reds from Cabernet Sauvignon and Syrah, and decent whites from Chardonnay and Sauvignon Blanc, all to feed our appetite for tasty varietals from familiar grape varieties.

Yet this year some of the greatest advocates of international-style vins de pays have turned anew to appellation contrôlée wines – to those very regions of Corbières, Minervois and Fitou that appeared to have got so left behind in the rush to make varietal Syrah.

What's going on? Well, it's my bet that the winemakers are curious. They know all about Cabernet and Chardonnay, and so now they want to look at the South's native varieties. They want to see if they can work the same magic with Carignan and Tannat, Mourvèdre and Grenache – all of them grapes with enormous potential.

So it's good news. The South is such an enormous reservoir of interesting grapes, and has great sites waiting to be discovered. All it needs is an incentive, and curiosity.

WINE REGIONS

BANDOL, AC (Provence; red, rosé, white) Herby, tobaccoey, long-lived wines of world class, based on Mourvèdre. Some, like *Tempier*, are being made in a more supple style. The serious spicy rosés (made from younger vines) can also be excellent. Best estates: *Ch. de la Rouvière (Bunan), Ch. de Pibarnon, Ch. de Pradeaux, Dom. la Bastide Blanche, Dom. de Belouve, Dom. du Cagueloup, Dom. le Galantin, Dom. Ray-Jane, Dom. Tempier, Dom. Terrebrune, Dom. de la Tour de Bon, Ch. Ste-Anne, Ch. Vannières.* The whites can be delicious, with an aniseed-and-apple bite to them. Best whites: *Ch. de Pibarnon* and *Dom. Lafran Veyrolles.*

BANYULS, AC (Languedoc-Roussillon; *vin doux naturel*, red) Grenache-based wine that can assume many guises: red or tawny, sweet or dryish, and can come, too, in an oxidized *rancio* style with burnt caramel flavours – something of an acquired taste. *Cellier des Templiers, Clos des Paulilles, Dom. du Mas Blanc* and *Dom. de la Rectorie* are good. Wines aged for two-and-a-half years in wood may be labelled *grand cru.*

LES BAUX-DE-PROVENCE , AC (Provence; red, rosé) More characterful than their neighbours in Coteaux d'Aix-en-Provence, though limits on the use of Cabernet mean that *Domaine de Trévallon* has been demoted to vin de pays. *Mas de la Dame, Mas de Gourgonnier, Mas Ste-Berthe* and Terres *Blanches* are also good.

BÉARN, AC (South-West; red, rosé, white) The reds are mainly from the Tannat grape, with other local varieties and both Cabernets thrown in. In spite of this they are basically undistinguished but you could try the wines of the *Vignerons de Bellocq* co-op, the *Crouseilles* co-op, *Domaine Cauhapé, Domaine Guilhemas (Lapeyre)* or *Nigri*.

BELLET, AC (Provence; red, white) An unusual nutty Rolle and Chardonnay white with a good local reputation. *Château de*

Crémat and *Château de Bellet* are worth seeking out, though like everything else near Nice, they're expensive. The same producers make a few good, dark reds.

BERGERAC, AC (South-West; red, rosé) Bergerac is a kind of Bordeaux understudy: the rosés are often extremely good, deep in colour, dry and full of fruit; a good red can be a better bet than basic Bordeaux, and often cheaper. Bergerac Rouge is usually at its best at between one and four years old, depending on vintage and style. *Château la Jaubertie* led the way. *Château le Barradis, Château Belingard* and *Château Tour des Gendres* are also good, and *Château Court-les-Mûts* makes a delicious rosé and a good red.

BERGERAC SEC, AC (South-West; white) Bordeaux lookalikes. *Château Belingard, Château Court-les-Mûts, Château Fayolle, Château les Miaudoux* and *Château de Panisseau* are good but the star is *Château la Jaubertie* where tremendous flavour and panache are extracted from a Sauvignon, Sémillon and Muscadelle blend, and from a straight Sauvignon as well.

BUZET, AC (South-West; red, rosé, white) Claret lookalikes that can combine a rich blackcurrant sweetness with an arresting grassy greenness. They are for drinking at between one and five years old, depending on the vintage and the style. Look out for the wines of the co-op, which dominates the area: its *Baron d'Ardeuil, Château de Gueyze* and *Château Padère* are all pretty special.

CABARDÈS, VDQS (Languedoc-Roussillon; red) The aromatic originality and liveliness of these wines derives from the marriage of southern and south-western grape varieties, such as Merlot, Cabernet, Fer Servadou and Cot (Malbec). Best producers include *de Brau, Cabrol, Château de la Bastide, Château de Rayssac, Domaine Jouclary, Pennautier, Salitis* and *Ventenac*.

CAHORS, AC (South-West; red) Increasingly supple these days: the 'black wine' of yore has pretty well vanished, and that's no bad thing. Modern Cahors is likely to combine raisiny, plummy fruit with flavours of spices, tobacco and prunes, soft tannins and the potential for longevity. The grapes are largely Auxerrois (Bordeaux's Malbec), plus Merlot and Tannat. Good names: *Ch. des Bouysses* from the *Côtes d'Olt* co-op, *la Caminade, Ch. de Cayrou, Ch. du Cèdre, Ch. de Chambert, Ch. de Haute-Serre, Ch. de Poujol, Ch. St-Didier, Ch. de Treilles, Clos la Coutale, Clos de Gamot, Clos Triguedina, Domaine de Gaudou* and *Domaine de Quattre, Lagrezette, Lamartine*.

CASSIS, AC (Provence; red, white, rosé) The white dominates the AC – they say locally you should be able to taste the sea salt. Rosés are good, but red is increasingly rare. Look out for *Dom. du Bagnol, Dom. de la Ferme Blanche, Dom. du Paternel* and *Clos Ste-Magdelaine*.

CLAIRETTE DU LANGUEDOC, AC (Languedoc-Roussillon; white) The Clairette can be a difficult grape to vinify, but the quality of wines like *Dom. de la Condamine Bertrand*, the co-op at *Cabrières* and *Domaine St-André* show what can be done.

COLLIOURE, AC (Languedoc-Roussillon; red) Startling, intense reds dominated by Grenache, with increasing contributions from Mourvèdre. Best: *Casa Blanca, Cellier des Templiers, Clos des Paulilles, Dom. de Baillaury, Dom. du Mas Blanc, Dom. de la Rectorie, la Tour Vieille*.

CORBIÈRES, AC (Languedoc-Roussillon; red, white, rosé) Reds range from juicy upfront wines produced using carbonic maceration to powerful, serious, traditionally made bottles like *la Voulte-Gasparets*. Others: *R Balthazar, Bel Eveque, Caraguilhes, Ch. Cascadais, Courbis, E & J Durand, Étang des Colombes, Fontsainte, Grand Moulin, Ch. Hélène, Ch. de Lastours,*

Mansenoble, les Palais, St-Auriol, Dom. du Tunnel and the Mont Tauch co-op. There is less white, but it's increasingly good.

COSTIÈRES DE NÎMES, AC (Languedoc; red, rosé, white) There are good rosés and meaty, smoky reds here, at prices that are still reasonable. Try *Dom. de l'Amarine, Mas des Bressades, Mas Carlot* (especially the *Ch. Paul Blanc* label), *Ch. Mourgues du Grès, Ch. de la Tuilerie.*

COTEAUX D'AIX-EN-PROVENCE, AC (Provence; red, white, rosé) An increasing use of Cabernet and Syrah and subtle use of new oak are combining to make interesting reds and rosés in a semi-Bordelais style – such as *Château Vignelaure.* Also good: *Ch. Bas, Ch. Crémade, Ch. de Calissanne, Ch. de Fonscolombe, Ch. du Seuil, Dom. de la Courtade, Dom. des Beatis, Dom. des Glauges, Revelette.* There is little white, and frankly it's not that thrilling.

COTEAUX DU LANGUEDOC, AC (Languedoc-Roussillon; red, white) This sprawling appellation incorporates 12 demarcated *terroirs* that may state their names on the labels. Among the better ones for reds are St-Saturnin, Pic St-Loup and La Clape. The classic southern grapes are used, and the growing presence of Syrah and Mourvèdre can be discerned in the complexity and breed of many wines. Best: *Dom. l'Aiguelière, Dom. d'Aupilhac, Dom. de Brunet, Calage, Capion, Dom. de Cazeneuve, Clavel, Dom. de la Coste, Dom. de l'Hortus, Dom. des Jougla, Lascaux, Mas Bruguière, Mas des Chimères, Mas Jullien, Mas de Mortiès, Mas de la Seranne, Pech-Céleyran, Pech-Redon, Dom. Peyre-Rose, Prieuré de St-Jean de Bébian, de Terre-Mégère* and the co-ops at *Cabrières, Gabian (la Carignano), Montpeyrous, Neffiès* and *St-Saturnin.* White winemaking is also being taken more seriously. Best: *Boscary, Chamayrac, Ch.de Granoupiac, Claude Gaujal, Mas Jullien, Terre Mégère* and the co-ops at *Pine, Pomérols* and *St-Saturnin (le Lucian).*

INSTANT CELLAR:
MODERN SOUTHERNERS

- **1995 Irouléguy, Domaine Ilarria, £9.25, Yapp Brothers** Red made entirely from the tannic Tannat grape: cellar it for eight to ten years and it'll come good.
- **1997 Cahors Château du Cèdre, Pascal Verhaeghe, £9.95, Lea & Sandeman** Wonderful Cahors made from 90% Malbec. Structured, good acidity, and beautiful fruit.
- **1995 Vin de Pays de l'Aude Carignan, Domaine Fabas, £6.50, Ubiquitous Chip** Lovely, dusty, raspberryish fruit.
- **1993 Madiran Château Montus, Alain Brumont, £11.13, Anthony Byrne** Rich, spicy fruit and a touch of leather appearing with maturity.
- **1998 Coteaux du Languedoc Le Champ des Pierres, Château Pech-Céleyran, £5.35, Adnams** Herby red, ripe and juicy.
- **1999 Coteaux d'Aix-en-Provence Cuvée Spéciale, Château de Fonscolombe, £4.75, Balls Brothers** Lovely summery rosé. People are so sniffy about rosé: more fool them, I say.

COTEAUX VAROIS, AC (Provence; red, rosé, white) Quality is improving here. Try *Château de Miraval* for white, or *Ch. la Calisse, Ch. Routas, Ch. St-Estève, Ch. St-Jean de Villecroze, Deffends, Dom. des Alysses, Dom. du Loou* and *Dom. de Triennes.*

CÔTES DE BERGERAC, AC (South-West; red, rosé) This is to Bergerac what Bordeaux Supérieur is to Bordeaux: from the same region, but with slightly higher minimum alcohol. Many are sold as basic Bergerac, although the excellent *Château Court-les-Mûts* now uses this AC.

CÔTES DE DURAS, AC (South-West; red, white) Light, grassy claret lookalikes. *Château de Pilar* and *le Seigneuret* from the co-op are quite good and cheap. Also fairly good Sauvignon-based white that can be as fresh as good Bordeaux Blanc, but just a little chubbier. *Château de Conti* is good, as is *le Seigneuret* from the co-op.

CÔTES DU FRONTONNAIS, AC
(South-West; red, rosé) At their best these are silky and plummy, sometimes with a touch of raspberry and licorice, but always with a twist of fresh black pepper. The Négrette grape dominates, and is wonderfully tasty. Best producers: *Baudare, Ch. Bellevue-la-Forêt, Ch. Flotis, Ch. Montauriol, Ch. la Palme, Ch. le Roc.*

CÔTES DE LA MALEPÈRE, VDQS
(Languedoc-Roussillon; red) Similar grape varieties to those of Cabardès, with the addition of Cabernet Franc. Best: *Ch. de Festes, Dom. de Matibat, Cave du Razès.*

CÔTES DU MARMANDAIS, AC
(South-West; red) Simple, soft, fruity wines for drinking young, made from Cabernet Sauvignon, Cabernet Franc, Merlot, Fer and Abouriou. A few are designed for more serious aging, but it doesn't suit them.

CÔTES DE PROVENCE, AC
(Provence; red, white, rosé) Among the overpriced rosés made for the tourists there are many top-grade red and pink wines made by growers who take their calling seriously. They include *Dom. de la Bernarde, Commanderie de Bargemore, Commanderie de Peyrassol, la Courtade, Coussin Ste-Victoire, Dom. du Dragon, d'Esclans, Féraud, Maravenne, Dom. Ott, Presquîle de St-Tropez, Dom. Rabiega, Richeaume, Rimauresq, St-Baillon, Ch. de Selle, Sorin*. For whites, *Castel Roubine, Château Ferry-Lacombe, Clos Bernarde, Gavoty, Dom. Richeaume, de Rasque, Réal Martin* and *St-André de la Figuière* are the leading lights.

CÔTES DU ROUSSILLON AND CÔTES DU ROUSSILLON VILLAGES, AC (South-West; red, white) Up-and-coming for reds, although whites lag behind. Carignan still dominates the vineyards, though the tastier Syrah is increasing. The Villages AC covers 32 villages in the North. Try *Ch, de Casenove, Dom. Cazes, Dom. Gauby, Dom. Laporte, Dom. Piquemal, Dom. Sarda-Malet, Ferrer-Ribière, Les Hauts de Força Réal, Lafage, Mas Becha, Mas Crémat, Mas de la Garrigue.*

CÔTES DE ST-MONT, VDQS
(South-West; red, white) These reds are increasingly made in a fresh, blackcurranty, modern style. By far the best examples come from the *Plaimont* co-op.

FAUGÈRES, AC (Languedoc-Roussillon; red) The grapes here are Grenache, Syrah, Mourvèdre and Carignan. The wines have depth, class and character, in which cassis, black cherries and licorice predominate. In mature Faugères wines, complex game and leather aromas can often emerge. Best producers: *Alquier, Ch. Chenaie, Estanilles, Louison, Lubac, Ollier-Taillefer, Vidal* and the co-op at *Laurens.*

FITOU, AC (Languedoc-Roussillon; red) A highly variable, old-style red in which Carignan has traditionally been dominant, but Grenache and, increasingly, Syrah and Mourvèdre are being used to add interest. *Paul Colomer, Robert Daurat-Fort* and *les Fenals* are the leading lights, along with co-ops at *Villeneuve* and at *Tuchan*, where the *Caves de Mont Tauch* is producing some of the most serious Fitou of all.

GAILLAC, AC (South-West; red, white) The white, based on the bracing Mauzac grape, can be *moelleux* (medium-sweet), *perlé* (very faintly bubbly) or dry; the dry is usually a little neutral, though a few have a quite big apple-and-licorice fruit. The sparkling wines can be superb: peppery, honeyed, apricotty and appley all at the same time. From *Boissel-Rhodes, Canto Perlic Causses Marines, Cros* or *Plageoles*, they are very good value. There are two styles of red, Duras plus Fer Servadou and Syrah, or Duras plus Merlot and Cabernet. *Domaine Jean Cros* is delicious. Other producers worth a look are: *Dom. du Bosc-Long, Dom. de Labarthe, Ch. Larroze, Mas Pignou* and the co-ops at *Labastide-de-Lévis* and *Técou.*

IROULÉGUY, AC (South-West; red) This comes from the foothills of the Pyrénées, and it's mostly quite rough and rustic, Tannat-based red, supplemented by both Cabernets. Try *Domaine Brana* and *Domaine Ilarria*.

JURANÇON, AC (South-West; white) This can be sweet, medium or dry. The dry wines are light and can be ravishingly perfumed, while the sweet wines are honeyed, raisiny and peachy, yet with a lick of acidity. The pace-setter is *Henri Ramonteu* of *Dom. Cauhapé*; others are *Clos Lapeyre, Clos Thou* (dry), *Clos Uroulat* (sweet), *Clos de la Vierge* (dry), *Cancaillaü* (sweet), *Cru Lamouroux* (sweet), *Dom. Bru-Baché* (dry), *Bellegarde, Dom. Castera, Dom. Larrédya, Dom. de Souch.*

LIMOUX, AC (South-West; white) Sparkling Blanquette de Limoux is mostly from the Mauzac grape; Crémant de Limoux has more Chardonnay, and is less rustic. The still wines are based on barrel-fermented Chardonnay, and tend to be expensive. Best producers include: *Antech, Dom. de l'Aigle, Caves du Sieur d'Arques, Philippe Collin, Delmas, Sev Dervin, Robert.*

MADIRAN, AC (South-West; red) Attractive, generally rather rustic reds based on the Tannat grape, along with the Cabernets and occasionally Fer. Good ones include *Ch. d'Arricau-Bordes, Ch. d'Aydie* (alias *Domaine Laplace*), *Ch. Bouscassé, Ch. de Crouseilles, Ch. Montus, Ch. Peyros, Domaine Berthoumieu, Domaine du Crampilh, Domaine Damiens, Domaine Meinjarre, Domaine Mouréou, Chapelle Lenclos, Laffitte-Teston* and the *Plaimont* co-op.

MAURY, AC (Languedoc-Roussillon; *vin doux naturel*, red) Grenache without the finesse of Banyuls, but more explosive in its nutty, toffee, prunes-in-brandy intensity. It can also be made in the oxidized *rancio* style. Try *la Coume du Roy, Mas Amiel, Maurydoré, la Pleiade* and the *Maury* co-op.

MINERVOIS, AC (Languedoc-Roussillon; red, white, rosé) Interesting reds with good peppery berry fruit. A handful of crus – wines from areas a cut above the rest – is planned; first will be La Livinière, with wines based on Syrah. Best include the co-op at *la Livinière*, plus *Aires Hautes, Clos Centeilles, Château Fabas, Château de Gourgazaud, Château d'Oupia, Domaine Maris, Piccinini, Ste-Eulalie, la Tour Boisée, Villerambert-Julien. Violet* and the co-ops at *Peyriac* and *Azillanet.* White Minervois is increasingly good and aromatic. Minervois Noble is sweet, late-picked white, usually fresh and with good acidity.

MONBAZILLAC, AC (South-West; white) These sweet wines are never as rich or weighty as a top Sauternes, but the massive improvements in quality in Sauternes have spurred the producers here to sharpen up their act, too. The best are very good indeed, and include *l'Ancienne Cure, Belingard Blanche de Bosredon, Ch. Haut-Bernasse, Ch. Hébras, Ch. Theulet, Ch. du Treuil-de-Nailhac* and Tirecul La Gravière. Grab any 1990s you can still find: coming from one of the hottest, most botrytized vintages for years, the best are terrific.

MONTRAVEL, AC (South-West; white) Dry white from the Dordogne. Côtes de Montravel is medium-sweet *moelleux* from the same area; Haut-Montravel is a separate area and sweeter. All are mostly sold as Bergerac or Côtes de Bergerac.

MUSCAT (*vin doux naturel;* white) Not a region but a grape. Wines range from the syrupy *Tradition* made by the *Frontignan* co-op to the elegant *Château de la Peyrade* (Frontignan), *Domaine de la Capelle* (Mireval), *Grés St-Paul* (Lunel), *Domaine de Barroubie* and the co-op in *St-Jean-de-Minervois*. All of these are made from the Muscat à Petits Grains which gives more finesse than the Muscat d'Alexandrie, used in Muscat de Rivesaltes (*Cazes* and *Brial* are the names to go for here).

PACHERENC DU VIC-BILH, AC (South-West; white) One of France's most esoteric whites, a blend of Gros and Petit Manseng and Arrufiac – a grape peculiar to the AC. At its best when dry and pear-skin-perfumed – and sometimes when rich and sweet. Best: *Château d'Aydie, Château Bouscassé, Domaine Berthoumieu, Domaine du Crampilh* and *Domaine Damiens*.

PALETTE, AC (Provence; red, white, rosé) A tiny AC dominated by *Château Simone*. The rosé beats the others.

PÉCHARMANT, AC (South-West; red) The best red wine of Bergerac, this must be aged for a minimum of a year before sale to distinguish it from Bergerac, which can be sold after only six months. It is deliciously blackcurranty when young, and at its best is good claret lookalike stuff. *Château de Tiregand* is very good indeed, but *Domaine du Haut-Pécharmant* is even better, resembling a decent Médoc.

ST-CHINIAN, AC (Languedoc-Roussillon; red, rosé) Improving and often very attractive wines. Among the top are *Borie la Vitarèle, Canet Valette, Ch. Cazal-Viel, Ch. Coujan, Dom. des Jougla, la Dournie* (especially for its brilliant rosé), *Mas Chapart, Maurel Fonsalade*, and outstanding co-ops at *Berlou, Roquebrun, Roueire* and *St-Chinian*.

VIN DE CORSE, AC (Corsica; red, white, rosé) Still lagging far behind the mainland in quality. *Dom. de Torraccia* makes a tasty red redolent of spices and rosemary. Also good: *d'Alzeto, Capitoro, Clos Landry, Dom. Filippi* and *Dom. Peraldi*. Most wines of better than vin de table status take the all-island designation Vin de Pays de l'Île de Beauté.

VINS DE PAYS (red, white, rosé) This is where it's all happening. The most innovative winemakers love the vin de pays classification for the freedom it gives them. There's plenty of Cabernet Sauvignon being used here, but some of the most exciting flavours come from Syrah and the other good grapes of the South, like Grenache or Mourvèdre. There are some excellent varietals, particularly Syrah, Cabernet Sauvignon and Chardonnay. Australian influence in the winemaking is producing clear flavours and some creamy new oak. In the Pays d'Oc look for *de l'Aigle, du Bosc, Chais Baumière, Cousserges, Domaine de l'Arjolle, Domaine de la Colombette, Domaine la Condamine-l'Evêque, Domaine de la Jonction, Domaine de Limbardie, Domaine Virginie, L'Enclos Domeque, Fortant de France, la Grange des Quatre Sous, Peyrat, Raissac, Richemont, Rives de l'Argent Double* and *Top Forty Barrel-Fermented Chardonnay* (from Waitrose).

In the Gard, seek out *Domaine de Gournier, Domaine de Monpertuis, Listel* and *Mas Montel*; and, in the Roussillon, *Chichet, Laporte* and *Vaquer*. In the Vaucluse, look for *Domaine de l'Ameillaud*.

In the Hérault, *Domaine de Limbardie, Domaine de Poujol* and *Mas de Daumas Gassac*; the latter's reds are explosively concentrated. There's also a Viognier-based white. From the Comté Tolosan, *Ribeton* makes good white; from the Comtés Rhodaniens, *les Vignerons Ardéchois* have a tasty Viognier. Look also for *Teisserenc* in the Côtes de Thongue, *Domaine d'Aupilhac* from Mont Baudille, and *Domaine de la Jasse Grande Olivette* from the Cevennes.

On the western side of France the Charente produces some good, grassy-fresh whites with fairly sharp acidity – which sometimes gets the better of the fruit. The region here is Vin de Pays Charentais. The equivalent from Armagnac country is Vin de Pays des Côtes de Gascogne. The Ugni Blanc is the major grape, and the Colombard adds a touch of class. Look for the co-op at *Plaimont*, though quality is variable. The *Grassa* family estates – notably *Domaines de Plantérieu* and *du Tariquet* – are worth seeking out. Also good are *Domaine le Puts, Domaine St-Lannes* and *San Guilhem*.

SOUTHERN FRANCE PRICES

RED

Under £4.00

VdP des Bouches-du-Rhône Domaine du Temps Perdu **1998** £3.96 (SAV)
Buzet Grande Réserve, Prieuré de Fonclaire **1998** £3.99 (WAI)
Corbières Château de Caraguilhes **1999** £3.99 (WAI)
★ Corbières Grande Réserve Domaine Madelon **1999** £3.69 (MAJ)
VdP des Coteaux de Murviel, Domaine de Limbardie **1998** £3.50 (SOM) £3.95 (WS) £4.95 (TAN) £4.95 (HAH)
Côtes de St-Mont, Château Pages **1998** £3.99 (MAR)
Côtes de St-Mont, Producteurs Plaimont **1997** £3.25 (SOM) £3.99 (JON) £4.25 (WS)
VdP des Côtes de Thongue Syrah, la Condamine l'Évêque **1998** £3.95 (WS) £4.49 (JON) £4.50 (LEA) £4.65 (TAN)
VdP du Gers, Producteurs Plaimont **1998** £3.75 (SAV)
VdP de l'Hérault Cabernet/Syrah, Domaine Montrose **1995** £3.95 (JU)
VdP de l'Hérault Figaro **1998** £3.35 (SOM)
VdP de l'Hérault Terrasses de Guilhem **1998** £3.95 (SOM)
VdP de l'Hérault, Les Trois Couronnes **1999** £2.89 (WAI)
Minervois Domaine du Moulin Rigaud **1998** £3.95 (WS)
Minervois Château d'Oupia **1996** £3.95 (SOM)
VdP d'Oc Cabernet Sauvignon, Bellefontaine **1997** £3.95 (CON)
VdP d'Oc Merlot, Domaine Virginie **1995** £3.95 (JU)

£4.00 → £4.99

VdP de l'Aude Cabernet Sauvignon, Domaine du Puget **1997** £4.52 (CB)
Bergerac Château Tour des Gendres **1998** £4.99 (GW)
Cabardès Château Rivals **1996** £4.99 (CON)
Cahors Clos la Coutale **1997** £4.95 (WS)
Cahors Château Lagrezette **1996** £4.70 (CAV)
Corbières Domaine Baillat **1997** £4.95 (WS)
Corbières Château de Montrabech **1997** £4.39 (JON)
Corbières Domaine du Trillol, Sichel **1997** £4.25 (BO) £4.95 (WS)
Costières de Nîmes Château de Campuget **1998** £4.99 (POR)
★ Costières de Nîmes Plan Macassan, Penval **1998** £4.49 (OD)
Coteaux d'Aix-en-Provence Château de Fonscolombe **1998** £4.95 (AD) £4.95 (POR)
Coteaux d'Aix-en-Provence Château de Fonscolombe **1997** £4.89 (JON)
VdP des Coteaux de Bessilles Cuvée Traditionelle, Domaine St-Martin de la Garrigue **1995** £4.45 (JU)
Coteaux du Languedoc La Clape, Château Pech-Céleyran **1997** £4.50 (WS) £4.95 (POR) £5.30 (TAN)
Coteaux du Languedoc Château de Lascaux **1998** £4.99 (OD) £5.95 (LEA)
Coteaux du Languedoc Mas Clavel **1998** £4.95 (AD)
Coteaux du Languedoc Pic St Loup, Mas Bruguière **1997** £4.75 (SOM) £5.49 (UN)
Coteaux du Languedoc Pic St Loup Terres Rouge, Château de Cazeneuve **1997** £4.99 (UN) £6.29 (BAL)

MERCHANTS SPECIALIZING IN SOUTHERN FRANCE

see Merchant Directory (page 456) for details

Most good merchants have some. For particularly good lists try the following merchants: Adnams (AD), Averys of Bristol (AV), Ballantynes of Cowbridge (BAL), Bibendum (BIB), Anthony Byrne (BY) – always enterprising, Cockburns of Leith (COC), Direct Wine (DI), Ben Ellis (ELL), First Quench Group (BOT, THR, VIC, WR), Gauntleys (GAU), Lay & Wheeler (LAY), Majestic (MAJ), Oddbins (OD), The Nobody Inn (NO), James Nicholson (NI), Terry Platt (PLA), Raeburn Fine Wines (RAE), Reid Wines (REI), Sainsbury's (SAI), Savage Selection (SAV), Somerfield (SO), Tanners (TAN), Ubiquitous Chip (UB), The Wine Society (WS), Yapp Brothers (YAP).

Côtes du Frontonnais Château Baudare **1997** £4.69 (GW)
Côtes du Frontonnais Château Bellevue-la-Forêt **1996** £4.49 (UN)
Côtes du Frontonnais Château le Roc **1996** £4.95 (LEA) £5.97 (SAV)
Côtes du Frontonnais Château le Roc **1993** £4.99 (BAL)
VdP des Côtes de Gascogne Cabernet Sauvignon, Brumont **1998** £4.00 (BY)
Côtes de la Malepère Château Malvies **1998** £4.75 (STE)
Côtes de St-Mont, les Hauts de Bergelle **1997** £4.95 (TAN)
Côtes de St-Mont, Producteurs Plaimont **1998** £4.10 (HAH)
VdP des Côtes de Thongue Cabernet Sauvignon, la Condamine l'Évêque **1997** £4.49 (JON) £4.50 (LEA)
VdP des Côtes de Thongue Champs de Coq, Domaine Boyer **1995** £4.95 (JU)
VdP des Côtes de Thongue, Clos Ferdinand **1998** £4.29 (BO)
VdP des Côtes de Thongue Cuvée de l'Arjolle, Teisserenc **1998** £4.95 (WS)
VdP des Côtes de Thongue Cuvée Harmonie, la Condamine l'Évêque **1998** £4.75 (TAN)
Fitou Caves du Mont Tauch **1997** £4.49 (UN)
Gaillac Domaine de Labarthe **1997** £4.25 (SOM)
VdP de l'Hérault Cabernet Sauvignon, Domaine de Capion **1997** £4.35 (SOM)
VdP de l'Hérault, Domaine de Chapître **1998** £4.40 (MV)
VdP de l'Hérault Terrasses de Guilhem **1996** £4.22 (FLE)
Marcillac Domaine du Cros, Teulier **1997** £4.95 (WS)
Minervois Domaine Piccinini **1998** £4.95 (WS)
Minervois Domaine de Ste-Eulalie **1998** £4.95 (POR) £5.35 (TAN)
Minervois Domaine de Ste-Eulalie **1997** £4.99 (VIC) £4.99 (THR) £5.19 (JON)

- *Wines are listed in A–Z order within each price band.*
- *For each wine, vintages are listed in descending order.*
- *Each vintage of any wine appears only once.*

Minervois Domaine la Tour Boisée **1998** £4.39 (WAT)
VdP d'Oc les Chemins de Bassac **1995** £4.95 (LEA) £5.99 (BAL)
VdP d'Oc Merlot, Domaine Piccinini **1996** £4.75 (JU)
VdP d'Oc Merlot, Domaine de Terre Megère **1998** £4.95 (LEA)
VdP d'Oc Merlot, Domaine Virginie **1999** £4.49 (MAR)
VdP d'Oc Merlot, Domaine Virginie **1998** £4.64 (REI) £4.79 (JON) £5.30 (MV)
VdP d'Oc Syrah, Domaine de la Jonction **1998** £4.47 (CB)
St-Chinian Château Maurel Fonsalade **1997** £4.75 (WS)
VdP du Var les Trois Chenes, Domaine de l'Hermitage **1996** £4.39 (CON)
VdP du Vaucluse Domaine Michel **1998** £4.85 (AD)
★ VdP du Vaucluse Syrah/Merlot, Joanis **1998** £4.17 (BY)
VdP du Vaucluse Domaine du Vieux Chêne **1996** £4.50 (JU)

£5.00 → £5.99

Bergerac Domaine du Gouyat **1998** £5.59 (JON)
Bergerac Château Tour des Gendres **1997** £5.75 (BAL)
Cahors Château St-Didier-Parnac, Rigal **1997** £5.49 (OD)
Corbières Domaine Baillat **1995** £5.50 (JU)
Corbières Château la Baronne **1997** £5.59 (JON)
Corbières Château Cascadais **1995** £5.75 (BAL)
Corbières Cuvée Ullysses, Château Helene **1995** £5.70 (WAT)
Costières de Nîmes Château Mourgues du Grès **1998** £5.79 (NI) £6.99 (VA)
Costières de Nîmes Château de Nages **1997** £5.99 (POR)
VdP des Coteaux de Bessilles Cuvée Bronzinelle, Domaine St-Martin de la Garrigue **1995** £5.95 (JU)
Coteaux du Languedoc La Clape, Château Pech-Céleyran **1999** £5.45 (AD)
Coteaux du Languedoc La Clape, Château Pech-Céleyran **1996** £5.29 (JON)
Coteaux du Languedoc Château de Lascaux **1997** £5.95 (LEA) £6.49 (NI) £6.76 (DOM)
Coteaux du Languedoc Mas les Catalognes **1997** £5.75 (AD)

Coteaux du Languedoc Pic St Loup, Mas Bruguière **1996** £5.99 (PHI)
VdP des Coteaux de Murviel, Domaine de Limbardie **1999** £5.30 (MV)
VdP des Côtes Catalanes Cuvée Pierre Audonnet, Domaine Piquemal **1997** £5.50 (LEA)
Côtes du Frontonnais Château le Roc **1997** £5.49 (NI)
Côtes du Roussillon Domaine Gauby **1997** £5.95 (WS)
Côtes du Roussillon Domaine Piquemal **1997** £5.99 (BAL)
Côtes du Roussillon Domaine Piquemal **1996** £5.85 (NI)
VdP des Côtes de Thongue Cuvée de l'Arjolle, Teisserenc **1995** £5.45 (JU)
Fitou Domaine d'Estradelle **1995** £5.25 (CON)
Fitou Château de Ségure **1997** £5.29 (SAI)
Fitou Château de Ségure **1996** £5.49 (UN)
VdP de l'Hérault Cabernet/Syrah Barrel-Fermented, Domaine Montrose **1996** £5.45 (JU)
VdP de l'Hérault, Domaine du Poujol **1998** £5.50 (TAN) £5.58 (BIB)
VdP de l'Hérault Terrasses de Guilhem **1997** £5.25 (PHI) £5.80 (PLAY)
★ Minervois Château d'Oupia **1998** £5.26 (PIP)
Minervois Domaine Piccinini **1995** £5.45 (JU)
Minervois Château Villerambert Julien Cuvée Opera **1997** £5.70 (TAN)
VdP d'Oc Cuvée Pierre Elie, Les Chemins de Bassac **1995** £5.50 (LEA)
St-Chinian Château Viranel **1995** £5.99 (BAL)
VdP de Vaucluse Merlot, Domaine du Vieux Chêne **1996** £5.45 (JU)
VdP de Vaucluse Domaine des Tours, Reynaud **1997** £5.72 (RAE)

£6.00 → £7.99

les Baux-de-Provence Mas de Gourgonnier **1998** £6.79 (FLE)
les Baux-de-Provence Mas de Gourgonnier **1997** £7.95 (AD)
Bergerac Château de la Colline, Martin **1998** £6.50 (HIG)
Bergerac Cuvée Prestige, Château des Eyssards **1996** £6.45 (AD)
Cahors Château du Cèdre **1997** £6.99 (GW) £7.50 (LEA)
Cahors Château du Cèdre **1994** £6.99 (BAL)

Cahors Château de Chambert **1996** £7.99 (DI)
Cahors Clos la Coutale **1996** £7.65 (WT)
Cahors Château Lagrezette **1997** £7.34 (CAV)
Cahors Domaine de Paillas **1994** £7.99 (RAE)
Cahors Domaine de la Pineraie **1994** £6.30 (SOM)
Corbières Château la Baronne **1996** £6.99 (TW)
Coteaux du Languedoc les Dolomies, Domaine de Terre Megère **1998** £6.50 (LEA)
Coteaux du Languedoc Montpeyroux, Domaine d'Aupilhac **1996** £7.95 (LEA)
Coteaux du Languedoc Domaine du Poujol **1997** £6.40 (TAN)
Côtes de Bergerac Château la Borderie **1995** £7.34 (TW)
Côtes du Frontonnais Cuvée Reservée, Château le Roc **1997** £6.95 (LEA) £7.35 (NI)
Côtes du Frontonnais Cuvée Reservée, Château le Roc **1992** £7.99 (BAL)
Côtes du Marmandais Château de Beaulieu **1996** £6.25 (WS) £6.75 (STE)

Côtes du Roussillon Domaine Cazes **1996** £7.85 (CON)
Côtes du Roussillon Élevé en Fûts, Domaine Gauby **1995** £7.50 (RAE)
VdP des Côtes de Thongue Cabernet de l'Arjolle, Domaine Teisserenc **1996** £6.95 (WS)
VdP des Côtes de Thongue Cabernet de l'Arjolle, Domaine Teisserenc **1995** £7.95 (JU)
Faugères Gilbert Alquier **1997** £6.95 (WS) £7.90 (TAN) £7.99 (BO)
Faugères Gilbert Alquier **1996** £6.99 (RAE) £8.29 (JON)
Faugères Gilbert Alquier **1994** £7.60 (GAU)
Faugères Château de Grézan **1997** £7.45 (PHI)
Faugères Reserve la Maison Jaune, Gilbert Alquier **1995** £7.99 (RAE) £8.95 (BAL)
VdP de la Haute Vallée de l'Orb Cuvée Special, Domaine de la Croix Ronde **1997** £6.46 (CB)
VdP de la Haute Vallée de l'Orb Cuvée Special, Domaine de la Croix Ronde **1996** £6.50 (HIG)
Madiran Château d'Aydie **1995** £7.05 (NO)
Madiran Château Bouscassé, Brumont **1994** £6.20 (SOM) £7.94 (BY)
Madiran Cuvée du Couvent, Domaine Capmartin **1997** £7.99 (GW)
Madiran Domaine de Mouréou, La Chapelle Lenclos **1996** £6.30 (TAN) £6.54 (PIP)
Madiran Château Pichard **1996** £6.50 (WS)
Madiran Vieilles Vignes, Domaine Capmartin **1997** £6.99 (GW)
Minervois Château Coupe-Roses **1995** £6.87 (REI)
Minervois Château d'Oupia **1995** £6.45 (PHI)
VdP d'Oc Cabernet Sauvignon, Listel **1998** £7.99 (BUD)
VdP d'Oc La Cuvée Mythique, DuBernet/Vign. de Val d'Orbieu **1997** £6.49 (SAF)
VdP d'Oc Cuvée Pierre Elie, Les Chemins de Bassac **1994** £6.99 (BAL)
VdP d'Oc Domaine de Granoupiac **1997** £6.85 (NI)

- *All prices for each wine are listed together in ascending order.*
- *Price bands refer to the lowest price for which the wine is available.*

Palette Château Simone **1988** £7.93 (REI)
Pécharmant Château de Tiregand **1996** £7.20 (TAN)
VdP des Sables du Golfe du Lion, Domaine du Bosquet **1996** £6.75 (NEZ)

£8.00 → £9.99

Bandol Domaine de l'Hermitage **1996** £8.85 (CON)
Bandol Mas de la Rouvière, Bunan **1996** £9.50 (YAP)
les Baux-de-Provence la Chapelle de Romanin **1995** £9.99 (PHI)
Bergerac Cuvée la Gloire de Mon Père, Château Tour des Gendres **1995** £8.95 (LEA)
Cahors Château du Cayrou, Jouffreau **1988** £8.75 (WAT)
Cahors Château de Chambert **1993** £8.75 (DI)
Cahors Clos de Gamot **1992** £8.25 (WAT)
Corbières Cuvée Helene de Troie, Château Helene **1997** £8.15 (WAT)
Coteaux d'Aix-en-Provence Mas de Gourgonnier **1996** £9.45 (UB)
Coteaux d'Aix-en-Provence Château Vignelaure **1996** £8.85 (NI)
Coteaux du Languedoc les Nobles Pierres, Château de Lascaux **1996** £8.75 (NI)
Coteaux du Languedoc Pic St Loup, Mas Bruguière **1995** £9.69 (NI)
Coteaux du Languedoc Pic St Loup les Nobles Pierres, Château de Lascaux **1997** £8.99 (BEN)
Coteaux du Languedoc St-Georges d'Orques **1997** £9.34 (REI)
Côtes de Provence Tradition Domaine Richeaume, Hoesch **1997** £9.25 (YAP)
Faugères le Moulin Couderc, V Fonteneau **1997** £9.50 (BEN)
Faugères le Moulin Couderc, V Fonteneau **1995** £9.29 (BAL)
Faugères Reserve la Maison Jaune, Gilbert Alquier **1993** £9.99 (RAE)
Fitou Cave Pilote **1996** £9.99 (SAF)
Madiran Château Montus, Brumont **1994** £9.25 (SOM) £11.02 (BY)
Minervois Château Villerambert, Julien **1997** £8.30 (TAN)
VdP du Mont Baudile Carignan, Domaine d'Aupilhac **1997** £8.95 (LEA)
VdP d'Oc Syrah, Clovallon **1997** £9.75 (BEN)
VdP d'Oc Syrah, Clovallon **1995** £9.29 (BAL)

£10.00 → £14.99

Bandol Cuvée Migoua, Tempier **1995** £13.81 (REI)
Bandol Cuvée Tourtine, Tempier **1997** £14.69 (SAV) £15.18 (RAE) £15.95 (LEA) £16.49 (YOU)
Bandol Cuvée Tourtine, Tempier **1995** £13.51 (REI)
Bandol Château de Pibarnon **1997** £13.95 (GAU) £14.65 (NI)
Bandol Château de Pibarnon **1996** £13.70 (FLE) £13.95 (FORT)
Bandol Château de Pibarnon **1991** £13.95 (BAL)
Bandol Château de la Rouvière, Bunan **1996** £11.95 (YAP)
Bandol Domaine Tempier **1998** £13.12 (RAE) £13.75 (LEA)
Bandol Domaine Tempier **1997** £11.69 (REI) £11.75 (SAV) £12.30 (RAE)
Bandol Domaine Tempier **1995** £10.80 (GAU) £11.69 (REI) £12.99 (DI)
Bandol Château Vannières **1988** £14.90 (GAU)
les Baux-de-Provence Domaine de Trévallon **1992** £14.99 (YOU) £31.00 (UB)
Bellet Château de Crémat, Jean Bagnis **1986** £13.50 (CRO)
Cahors Château du Cayrou, Jouffreau **1983** £14.00 (CRO)
Cahors Clos de Gamot **1983** £13.92 (REI)
Collioure la Coume Pascole, Domaine de la Rectorie **1997** £11.95 (BAL)
Coteaux d'Aix-en-Provence Château Vignelaure **1986** £14.69 (REI)
Coteaux d'Aix-en-Provence Château Vignelaure **1983** £13.51 (REI)
Coteaux du Languedoc Prieuré de St-Jean de Bébian **1998** £12.00 (RAE) £13.42 (BIB)
Coteaux du Languedoc Prieuré de St-Jean de Bébian **1997** £12.71 (RAE) £14.10 (GAU) £16.25 (MI)
Coteaux du Languedoc Prieuré de St-Jean de Bébian **1994** £12.95 (BAL) £13.90 (GAU) £18.33 (MI)
Coteaux du Languedoc Prieuré de St-Jean de Bébian **1991** £12.14 (RAE)
VdP des Côtes Catalanes Le Credo Cabernet/Merlot, Domaine Cazes **1996** £12.95 (CON)
Côtes de Provence Columelle Domaine Richeaume, Hoesch **1997** £14.25 (YAP)
VdP de l'Hérault, Mas de Daumas Gassac **1996** £12.14 (FA) £16.95 (AD)
VdP de l'Hérault, Mas de Daumas Gassac **1994** £14.90 (NO)
VdP de l'Hérault, Mas de Daumas Gassac **1989** £13.00 (GAU)
Madiran Château Montus, Brumont **1995** £12.46 (BY)
Madiran Château de Peyros **1982** £12.50 (CRO)
VdP d'Oc Pinot Noir les Pomaredes, Clovallon **1998** £10.25 (BEN)
Pécharmant Château de Tiregand **1985** £11.50 (CRO)

£15.00 → £19.99

Bandol Cuvée Migoua, Tempier **1998** £16.16 (REI) £16.65 (RAE)
Bandol Cuvée Tourtine, Tempier **1998** £16.16 (REI) £16.65 (RAE) £17.50 (LEA)
Bandol Cuvée Tourtine, Tempier **1996** £15.00 (WS)
Bandol Château Vannières **1997** £15.00 (MI)
VdP des Bouches-du-Rhône Domaine de Trévallon **1997** £19.00 (FA) £24.00 (YAP)
VdP des Bouches-du-Rhône Domaine de Trévallon **1995** £19.99 (DI) £25.00 (FORT) £26.00 (CRO)
VdP des Bouches-du-Rhône Domaine de Trévallon **1994** £16.99 (YOU) £17.75 (NI)
Cahors Château du Cayrou, Jouffreau **1982** £15.10 (REI)
Cahors Prince Probus, Clos Triguedina **1995** £15.18 (NO)
Coteaux du Languedoc Prieuré de St-Jean de Bébian **1995** £15.55 (GAU)
Faugères Reserve la Maison Jaune, Gilbert Alquier **1994** £17.75 (NI)
VdP de l'Hérault, Mas de Daumas Gassac **1998** £15.18 (RAE) £16.80 (CRO) £16.99 (NI)
VdP de l'Hérault, Mas de Daumas Gassac **1997** £15.20 (FLE) £17.00 (WS)
VdP de l'Hérault, Mas de Daumas Gassac **1995** £15.34 (NO) £16.95 (PHI) £18.00 (JU) £28.85 (UB)
VdP de l'Hérault, Mas de Daumas Gassac **1993** £16.99 (WR) £16.99 (BOT)
VdP de l'Hérault, Mas de Daumas Gassac **1982** £18.00 (CRO)
Madiran Cuvée Prestige Château Montus, Brumont **1996** £17.04 (FA) £20.23 (BY)
Madiran Château Montus, Brumont **1983** £19.39 (REI)
Madiran Vielles Vignes Château Bouscassé, Brumont **1997** £16.13 (BY)
Palette Château Simone **1996** £17.75 (YAP)

£20.00 → £29.99

Coteaux d'Aix-en-Provence Château Vignelaure **1982** £29.96 (REI)
VdP de l'Hérault, Domaine de la Grange des Pères **1996** £23.50 (AD)
VdP de l'Hérault, Mas de Daumas Gassac **1990** £28.00 (CRO)
Madiran Cuvée Prestige Château Montus, Brumont **1997** £20.23 (BY)
Palette Château Simone **1995** £22.95 (FORT)

Over £30.00

les Baux-de-Provence Domaine de Trévallon **1990** £44.00 (CRO)
les Baux-de-Provence Domaine de Trévallon **1985** £33.49 (REI) £50.00 (CRO)
Madiran Cuvée Prestige Château Montus, Brumont **1995** £49.81 (NO)
Madiran Château Montus, Brumont **1985** £38.19 (REI)
Madiran Vielles Vignes Château Bouscassé, Brumont **1995** £35.00 (NO)

DRY WHITE

Under £4.00

Bergerac Marquis de Beausoleil **1998** £2.99 (WAI)
Corbières les Producteurs du Mont Tauch **Non-vintage** £3.99 (UN)
VdP des Côtes de Gascogne Colombard, Plaimont **1999** £3.95 (AD) £3.95 (TAN)
★ VdP des Côtes de Gascogne, Ducourneau **1999** £3.99 (MAJ)
VdP des Côtes de Gascogne Producteurs Plaimont **1998** £3.89 (JON)
VdP des Côtes de Gascogne Domaine de Planterieu **1999** £3.99 (WAI)
VdP des Côtes de Gascogne le Prada **1998** £3.75 (WS)
VdP des Côtes de Gascogne Domaine de Rieux **1999** £3.99 (POR) £4.45 (TAN)
VdP des Côtes de Gascogne Domaine de Rieux **1996** £3.99 (NI)
★ VdP des Côtes de Gascogne Gros Manseng/Sauvignon, Brumont **1998** £3.98 (BY)
★ Côtes de Duras Sémillon, Berticot **1998** £3.88 (HA)
Côtes de St-Mont, les Hauts de Bergelle **1997** £3.70 (SOM)
Côtes de St-Mont, Producteurs Plaimont **1998** £3.99 (JON) £4.10 (HAH) £4.35 (AD)
VdP du Gers, Producteurs Plaimont **1998** £3.75 (SAV)
VdP de l'Hérault Grenache, Bésinet **1998** £3.95 (WS)
VdP des Landis Domaine d'Espérance **1998** £3.99 (BAL)
VdP d'Oc Sauvignon Blanc, Domaine Virginie **1999** £3.99 (MAR)
VdP d'Oc Sauvignon, Domaine des Fontanelles **1999** £3.99 (MAJ)
VdP des Terroirs Landais Domaine de Laballe **1998** £3.99 (BAL)

£4.00 → £4.99

Bergerac Château Tourmentine **1999** £4.35 (WS)
Coteaux d'Aix-en-Provence Château de Fonscolombe **1998** £4.89 (JON) £4.95 (POR)
VdP des Coteaux des Baronnies Chardonnay, Bellefontaine **1997** £4.89 (CON)
Coteaux du Languedoc Picpoul de Pinet, Domaine St Peyre **1999** £4.98 (PIP)
VdP des Côtes de Gascogne Chardonnay, Brumont **1998** £4.00 (BY)
VdP des Côtes de Gascogne Cuvée Speciale, Domaine de Joy **1994** £4.95 (LEA)
★ VdP des Côtes de Gascogne Blanc de Blancs Selection Cazaux, Domaine la Rieste **1999** £4.99 (BOD)
VdP des Côtes de Gascogne Domaine de Maubet **1998** £4.49 (CON)
VdP des Côtes de Gascogne Producteurs Plaimont **1999** £4.11 (PIP)
VdP des Côtes de Gascogne Domaine de Rieux **1998** £4.15 (HAH) £5.58 (REI)
VdP des Côtes de Gascogne Domaine San de Guilhem **1999** £4.90 (MV)
★ VdP des Côtes de Gascogne Sauvignon Blanc, Domaine du Tariquet **1998** £4.99 (WR) £4.99 (VIC) £4.99 (THR) £4.99 (BOT)
VdP des Côtes de Thau Terret, Lurton **1998** £4.39 (NI)
VdP des Côtes de Thongue Grenache, Domaine Boyer **1996** £4.75 (JU)
VdP des Côtes de Thongue Sauvignon de l'Arjolle, Teisserenc **1999** £4.95 (WS)
VdP des Côtes de Thongue Sauvignon Blanc, la Condamine l'Évêque **1998** £4.95 (LEA)
VdP de l'Hérault Chardonnay, Domaine Montrose **1996** £4.50 (JU)

VdP de l'Hérault Chardonnay, Domaine Pourthié **1998** £4.99 (BAL)
VdP de l'Hérault Marsanne, Domaine du Bosc **1998** £4.99 (BAL)
VdP de l'Hérault Muscat Sec, Bésinet **1998** £4.50 (WS)
VdP de l'Hérault Terret, Domaine Gourg du Laval **1996** £4.50 (JU)
VdP d'Oc Chardonnay, James Herrick **1999** £4.99 (WAI) £4.99 (SAF) £4.99 (BUD)
VdP d'Oc Chardonnay, James Herrick **1998** £4.99 (SAI) £4.99 (BO) £4.99 (VIC) £4.99 (THR) £4.99 (UN) £4.99 (WR) £4.99 (BOT)
VdP d'Oc Chardonnay, Philippe de Baudin (alias Chais Baumière) **1998** £4.99 (SAF)
VdP d'Oc Chardonnay, Domaine Virginie **1999** £4.49 (MAR)
VdP d'Oc Marsanne, Domaine Virginie **1998** £4.90 (TAN) £5.30 (MV)
VdP d'Oc Marsanne, Domaine Virginie **1996** £4.95 (JU)
VdP d'Oc Roussanne, Domaine Virginie **1998** £4.70 (REI)
★ VdP d'Oc Roussanne, Domaine du Bosc **1999** £4.75 (BAN)
★ VdP d'Oc Sauvignon Blanc Domaine de Barthes, Lurton **1998** £4.79 (JON)
VdP d'Oc Sauvignon Blanc Domaine des Salices, Lurton **1998** £4.95 (NI) £5.35 (CB)
VdP d'Oc Sauvignon Domaine du Bosc **1999** £4.75 (AD)
★ VdP d'Oc Sauvignon Blanc, Domaine de Coussergues **1999** £4.79 (LLO)
★ VdP d'Oc Viognier, Domaine de la Ferrandière **1999** £4.95 (WAT)

£5.00 → £6.99

Bergerac Château de la Colline, Martin **1998** £5.88 (HIG)
Bergerac Cuvée des Conti, Château Tours des Gendres **1999** £6.50 (LEA)
★ Bergerac Cuvée des Conti, Château Tours des Gendres **1998** £6.50 (LEA)
Bergerac Château Tours des Gendres **1995** £5.45 (JU)
Coteaux du Languedoc Cuvée Classique, Château de Lascaux **1999** £6.50 (LEA) £6.99 (BEN)
Coteaux du Languedoc Cuvée Classique, Château de Lascaux **1998** £5.95 (LEA)
Côtes du Roussillon Domaine Gauby **1995** £5.90 (GAU)
VdP des Côtes de Thongue Chardonnay, Domaine de la Croix Belle **1998** £5.95 (LEA)
VdP des Côtes de Thongue Muscat Sec de Petits Grains, Teisserenc **1996** £5.50 (JU)
VdP des Côtes de Thongue Viognier, la Condamine l'Évêque **1999** £6.45 (TAN)
VdP des Côtes de Thongue Viognier, la Condamine l'Évêque **1998** £6.95 (LEA) £7.89 (JON)
VdP des Côtes de Thongue Viognier/Sauvignon, Equinoxe de l'Arjolle **1997** £6.99 (UN)
VdP de la Haute Vallée de l'Orb Oaked Chardonnay, Domaine de la Croix Ronde **1995** £6.75 (HIG)
VdP de l'Hérault Chardonnay Barrel-Fermented, Domaine Montrose **1996** £5.95 (JU)
VdP de l'Hérault, Château St Martin de la Garrigue **1996** £5.95 (JU)
VdP de l'Hérault Sauvignon, Domaine Gourg du Laval **1995** £5.45 (JU)
VdP de l'Hérault Viognier, Domaine du Bosc **1997** £5.99 (BAL)
Jurançon Sec Domaine Castera **1998** £6.99 (GW)
VdP d'Oc Blanc Sur Lie, Domaine Virginie **1999** £5.00 (MV)
VdP d'Oc Chardonnay Domaine Montgaillard, Duboeuf **1996** £5.39 (NI)
VdP d'Oc Chardonnay, Domaine Virginie **1998** £5.46 (REI) £5.69 (JON) £5.70 (HAH)
VdP d'Oc Chardonnay, Domaine Virginie **1997** £6.20 (MV)
VdP d'Oc Chardonnay, Domaine Virginie **1996** £5.45 (JU)
VdP d'Oc Roussanne, Domaine Virginie **1999** £5.70 (LAY)
VdP d'Oc Roussanne, Domaine Virginie **1997** £5.30 (MV)
VdP d'Oc Sauvignon Blanc, Domaine Virginie **1998** £5.30 (MV)
VdP d'Oc Viognier, Domaine St Hilaire **1998** £6.99 (GW)
VdP d'Oc Viognier, Domaine Virginie **1996** £6.20 (JU)
VdP du Vaucluse Roussanne, Domaine du Vieux Chêne **1996** £5.90 (JU)

Stars (★) indicate wines selected by Oz Clarke in the Best Buys section which begins on page 10.

£7.00 → £9.99

Bandol Domaine de l'Hermitage **1997** £8.85 (CON)
Bandol Mas de la Rouvière, Bunan **1997** £8.95 (YAP)
Coteaux du Languedoc Domaine d'Aupilhac **1997** £8.95 (LEA)
VdP des Côtes de Thongue Viognier/Sauvignon, Equinoxe de l'Arjolle **1996** £7.85 (JU)
Jurançon Sec Domaine de Bru-Braché **1995** £9.75 (GW)
Jurançon Sec Domaine Castera **1997** £7.93 (SAV)
Jurançon Sec Domaine Cauhapé **1999** £9.00 (MV)
Jurançon Sec Domaine Cauhapé **1998** £7.99 (NI)
Jurançon Sec Domaine Cauhapé **1997** £7.99 (NI) £8.99 (POR)
Jurançon Sec Chant des Vignes, Domaine Cauhapé **1999** £7.95 (STE)
Limoux Chardonnay Cuvée Classique, Domaine de l'Aigle **1998** £7.58 (PIP)
Limoux Chardonnay Cuvée Classique, Domaine de l'Aigle **1996** £7.30 (TAN)
VdP d'Oc Chardonnay, Clovallon **1998** £9.95 (BEN)
VdP d'Oc Chardonnay, Clovallon **1996** £9.95 (BAL)
VdP d'Oc Viognier, Domaine St Hilaire **1999** £7.00 (PIP)
Pacherenc du Vic-Bilh Domaine Boucassé **1996** £7.48 (BY)

£10.00 → £19.99

Bandol Château de Pibarnon **1995** £11.30 (GAU)
Bandol Château de la Rouvière, Bunan **1996** £10.75 (YAP)
VdP des Bouches-du-Rhône Domaine de Trévallon **1992** £19.95 (DI)
Cassis Clos Ste-Magdeleine, Sack **1997** £10.50 (YAP)
VdP de l'Hérault, Mas de Daumas Gassac **1998** £15.95 (AD) £15.99 (YOU)
VdP de l'Hérault, Mas de Daumas Gassac **1992** £17.99 (NI)
VdP d'Oc Viognier, Clovallon **1998** £11.95 (BEN)
VdP d'Oc Viognier, Clovallon **1996** £11.95 (BAL)
Palette Château Simone **1996** £17.75 (YAP)

Over £20.00

VdP des Bouches-du-Rhône Domaine de Trévallon **1997** £30.00 (YAP)
VdP des Bouches-du-Rhône Domaine de Trévallon **1996** £40.00 (FORT)
VdP des Bouches-du-Rhône Domaine de Trévallon **1995** £22.50 (NI)
Côtes de Provence Clos Mireille Blanc de Blancs, Domaines Ott **1994** £20.00 (FORT)

SWEET WHITE

Under £5.00

Gaillac Domaine de Labarthe **1996** £4.60 (SOM)

£7.00 → £11.99

Jurançon Domaine Bellegarde, Labasse **1997** £9.75 (YAP)
Jurançon Vendange Tardive du 2 Novembre, Domaine Cauhapé ½ bottle **1996** £7.50 (POR)
Jurançon Vendange Tardive du 2 Novembre, Domaine Cauhapé ½ bottle **1995** £9.50 (BEN)
Monbazillac Château Septy **1996** £7.49 (JON) £7.58 (CB)
Monbazillac Château Theulet **1997** £8.95 (STE) £8.95 (WS)

£12.00 → £24.99

Monbazillac Château Tirecul la Gravière 50cl bottle **1997** £19.95 (LEA)
Monbazillac Château Tirecul la Gravière 50cl bottle **1996** £16.06 (FA) £19.95 (LEA)
Monbazillac Château Tirecul la Gravière 50cl bottle **1994** £14.50 (JU) £18.50 (CRO) £19.00 (FA)
Pacherenc du Vic-Bilh Vendange Décembre Château Bouscassé, Brumont ½ bottle **1989** £23.90 (NO)

Over £25.00

Monbazillac Château Tirecul la Gravière Cuvée Madame 50cl bottle **1997** £65.00 (LEA)
Monbazillac Château Tirecul la Gravière Cuvée Madame 50cl bottle **1996** £52.78 (FA)
Monbazillac Château Tirecul la Gravière Cuvée Madame 50cl bottle **1995** £89.50 (FA)

Monbazillac Château Tirecul la Gravière Cuvée Madame 50cl bottle **1992** £35.00 (JU)

Pacherenc du Vic-Bilh Vendange Décembre Château Bouscassé, Brumont **1988** £51.64 (NO)

ROSÉ

Under £5.00

Coteaux d'Aix-en-Provence Château de Fonscolombe **1998** £4.89 (JON) £4.95 (POR)

VdP des Coteaux de Murviel, Domaine de Limbardie **1998** £3.50 (SOM)

Côtes du Frontonnais Château le Roc **1998** £4.95 (LEA) £5.68 (SAV)

Côtes de St-Mont, Producteurs Plaimont **1997** £3.15 (SOM)

VdP des Côtes de Thongue Cuvée de l'Arjolle, Teisserenc **1996** £4.95 (JU)

VdP de l'Hérault, Domaine Montrose **1996** £4.45 (JU)

VdP du Var les Trois Chenes, Domaine de l'Hermitage **1996** £4.39 (CON)

VdP du Vaucluse Domaine du Vieux Chêne **1996** £4.60 (JU)

£5.00 → £9.99

Bandol Domaine de l'Hermitage **1997** £7.99 (CON)

Bandol Mas de la Rouvière **1997** £8.95 (YAP)

Bergerac Château Pique-Segue **1998** £6.17 (REI)

Bergerac Château Tour des Gendres **1998** £5.75 (BAL)

Côteaux du Languedoc Château de Lascaux **1999** £5.99 (BEN)

Côtes de Provence Carte Noire, Vignerons de St-Tropez **1998** £5.75 (NEZ)

Côtes de Provence Château la Moutete **1997** £5.59 (CON)

VdP des Côtes de Thongue Meridiene, Domaine de l'Arjolle **1996** £8.50 (JU)

VdP d'Oc les Chemins de Bassac **1995** £7.11 (WT)

Please remember that ***Oz Clarke's Wine Buying Guide*** *is a price* ***guide*** *and not a price* ***list****. It is not meant to replace up-to-date merchants' lists.*

Over £10.00

Côtes de Provence Château de Selle, Domaines Ott **1998** £19.58 (PLAY)

Côtes de Provence Château de Selle, Domaines Ott **1997** £25.40 (JER)

Côtes de Provence Château de Selle, Domaines Ott **1996** £18.75 (FORT)

Palette Château Simone **1997** £16.75 (YAP)

SPARKLING

c. £7.00

Crémant de Limoux Cuvée St-Laurent, Antech **1997** £6.95 (WS)

VINS DOUX NATURELS

Under £7.00

Muscat de Mireval Domaine du Moulinas ½ bottle **Non-vintage** £6.36 (NO)

Muscat de Rivesaltes Domaine Cazes ½ bottle **1998** £5.39 (CON)

Muscat de Rivesaltes Domaine Cazes ½ bottle **1996** £6.75 (FORT)

£7.00 → £9.99

Maury Vintage Mas Amiel ½ bottle **1997** £7.95 (LEA)

Muscat de Frontignan, Château de la Peyrade **Non-vintage** £7.90 (CRO)

Muscat de Frontignan, Château de la Peyrade **1996** £8.95 (PHI)

Muscat de Rivesaltes Domaine Cazes **1997** £9.65 (CON)

Muscat de Rivesaltes Domaine Piquemal **1997** £9.95 (LEA)

Muscat de St-Jean-de-Minervois, Cave de St-Jean-de-Minervois **Non-vintage** £7.64 (REI)

£10.00 → £19.99

Muscat de Rivesaltes Chapoutier **1996** £13.89 (NO)

Muscat de Rivesaltes Domaine Gauby **1995** £10.99 (RAE)

Rivesaltes Tuile Domaine Cazes **1984** £11.95 (CON)

c. £40.00

Banyuls Vieilles Vignes, Domaine du Mas Blanc **1978** £40.00 (CRO)

GERMANY

Germany has found a new way to point us towards its best wines. It means yet more words on the label, but are we downhearted? No!

Germany is about to complicate our lives again. You thought you'd just about got the hang of Kabinett and Spätlese, Auslese and Beerenauslese? Well, hold on to your hats. They've just invented something else for us to learn.

This time it's Erstes Gewächs. Yes, that's right. It means First Growth, and it's a classification system not a million miles away from the way the classifications of Bordeaux and Burgundy work. Certain vineyards, or parts of vineyards, have been agreed as the best, and growers who have vines in those vineyards can apply, as from this year, to put the words Erstes Gewächs on the labels of their 1999s. Provided they're in the Rheingau, that is: that's the only part of Germany that has the system up and running so far.

Not many will be able to take it up at first: the wines have to be made to higher than usual standards, and it'll be a few years before the numbers build up. But watch out for them.

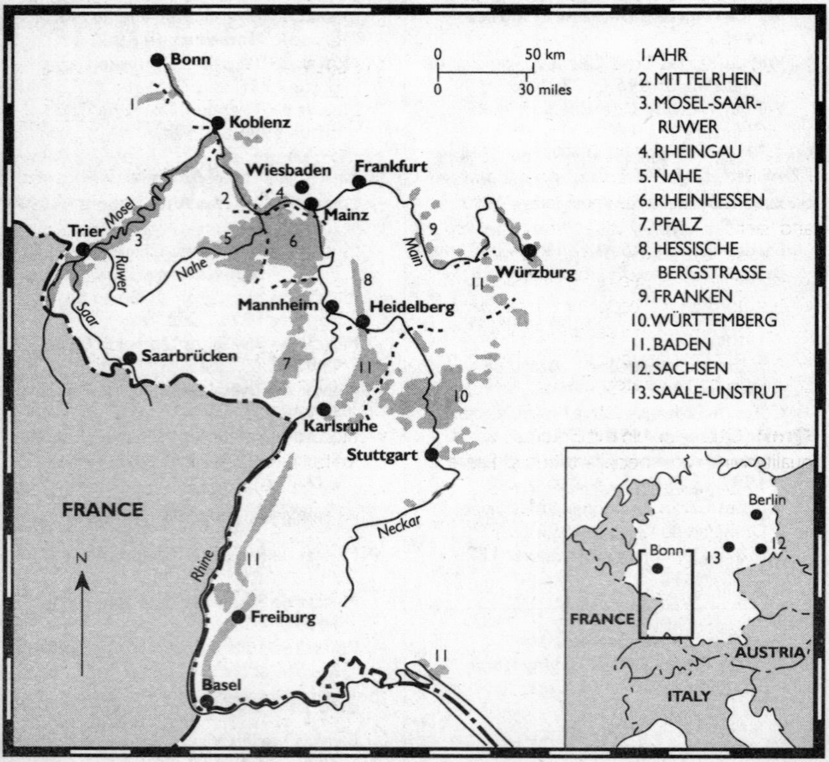

QUALITY CONTROL

You'll see one of these terms on every German wine label: they are simply a way of classifying wine according to the ripeness of the grapes when they are picked.

DEUTSCHER TAFELWEIN Basic German table wine of supposedly tolerable quality; low natural alcohol, sugared at fermentation to increase it, no specific vineyard origin stated. Usually little more than sugar-water. However, at the other end of the price spectrum are expensive 'designer table wines' from adventurous producers who may age them in oak.

LANDWEIN Rarely seen German version of vin de pays; table wine from one of 20 designated areas. It can be Trocken (dry) or Halbtrocken (half-dry).

QbA (Qualitätswein bestimmter Anbaugebiete) Literally 'quality wine from designated regions' – Ahr, Hessische Bergstrasse, Mittelrhein, Nahe, Rheingau, Rheinhessen, Pfalz, Franken, Württemberg, Baden, Mosel-Saar-Ruwer, Saale-Unstrut and Sachsen. Quality varies from poor to very good, depending on the producer. Anything labelled Liebfraumilch, Niersteiner Gutes Domtal or Piesporter Michelsberg is unlikely to be worth a second glance. Go for top estates only, but 1997 yielded some splendidly concentrated QbAs.

QmP (Qualitätswein mit Prädikat) Literally, quality wine with special attributes. There are six categories, in order of increasing ripeness of the grapes: Kabinett, Spätlese, Auslese, Beerenauslese, Trockenbeeren-auslese and Eiswein. Drier wines (usually Kabinett or Spätlese) may be either Trocken (dry) or Halbtrocken (half-dry). Not all styles are made every year.

KABINETT Made from ripe grapes. Usually lighter in alcohol than ordinary QbA, and often delicious.

SPÄTLESE From late-picked (therefore riper) grapes. Often moderately sweet, though there are now dry versions.

AUSLESE From selected bunches of very ripe grapes. Usually sweet and sometimes touched by 'noble rot', a fungus that concentrates the sugar and acidity in the grapes. In many southern regions, such as Baden, they are fermented dry, making rich and powerful wines.

BEERENAUSLESE (BA) Wines made from selected single grapes almost always affected by the noble rot fungus. Beerenauslese from new, non-Riesling grapes can be dull. But Riesling Beerenauslese, and many a Scheurebe or Silvaner, will be astonishing.

EISWEIN Just that – 'ice wine' – often picked before a winter dawn when the grapes are frozen. They are dashed to the winery by the frost-bitten pickers; once there, quick and careful pressing removes just the slimy-sweet concentrate; the water, in its icy state, stays separate. Eiswein always has a high acidity that needs to be tamed by bottle age, though you do lose the lovely frosty, green apple flavours of youth.

TROCKENBEERENAUSLESE (TBA) 'Shrivelled selected berries' – that's a pedestrian translation of one of the world's great tastes. Individually picked grapes, shrivelled by noble rot, produce small amounts of intensely sweet juice, making TBAs among the sweetest wines in the world. The risks and the costs are both enormous. The vines are making a glass of wine each instead of a bottle, and the weather can easily ruin it all anyway. That's why TBAs are expensive – usually starting at £20 a half bottle ex-cellars. But, even then, a grower won't make money; it's his pride that makes him do it. And the wines can age for as long as you or I.

GRAPE VARIETIES

DORNFELDER (red) At its best this produces deep-coloured reds with great fruit concentration and firm structure. Made in two styles: reminiscent of Beaujolais and for early drinking or aged in barriques for longer keeping. Best: *Knipser, Lergenmüller, Lingenfelder Onyx, Messmer, Siegrist, Heinrich Vollmer* (Pfalz).

MÜLLER-THURGAU (white) The most widely planted German grape, propagated in 1883 to get Riesling style plus big yields. Well, you can't do it. It produces soft, pot-pourri-scented wines of no distinction, but it produces plenty of them. Occasionally it's made dry and aged in oak; this style is particularly successful in Baden when yields are severely reduced. For the oaked style try *Gunderloch, Karl H Johner, Dr Loosen. Juliusspital* in Franken makes a deceptively fragile unoaked version.

RIESLANER (white) A sensational crossing of Riesling and Silvaner, but not widely planted. Ripe it tastes of apricots; unripe it tastes, less appealingly, of grass and gooseberries. Best as dessert wine from the Pfalz (especially *Müller-Catoir*) and Franken. Best producers: *Juliusspital, Rudolf Fürst, Robert Schmitt, Schmitt's Kinder* (Franken).

RIESLING (white) Most of Germany's best wines (except in Baden-Württemberg, where the soils are usually unsuitable) are made from this grape. When yields are controlled it produces wonderful flavours: from steely, slaty and dry as sun-bleached bones, through apples, peaches, apricots – more or less sweet according to the ripeness of the grapes and the intentions of the winemaker – and finally arriving at the great sweet wines. These can be blinding in their rich, honeyed concentration of peaches, pineapples, mangoes and even raisins, with acidity like a streak of fresh lime that makes them the most appetizing of sweet wines.

RULÄNDER (white) The French Pinot Gris. It can be strong, sweetish, broad-shouldered, with a whiff of spice and a splash of honey. When made dry it is often aged in small oak barriques and can make exciting drinking. Best: *Schlossgut Diel* (Nahe); *Koehler-Ruprecht, Müller-Catoir, Münzberg* (Pfalz); *Bercher, Dr Heger, Karl H Johner, Salwey, Stigler* (Baden); *Johann Ruck* (Franken).

SCHEUREBE (white) A tricky grape. When it's unripe, it can pucker your mouth with its rawness. But properly ripe, there's honey, and a crackling, peppery fire which, in the Pfalz, Baden and Franken, produces dry wines as well as sweeter, sometimes outstanding Auslese and Beerenauslese.

MATURITY CHART

1995 Mosel Riesling Spätlese

Riesling Spätlese develops a more refined character after five years in bottle

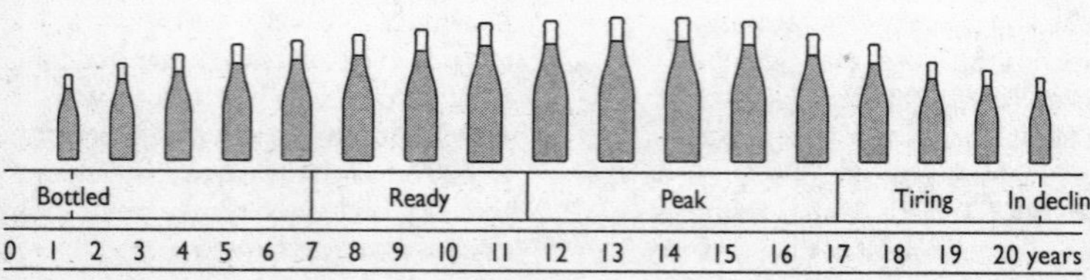

Best producers: *Darting, Lingenfelder, Messmer, Müller-Catoir* (Pfalz); *Andreas Laible, Wolff-Metternich* (Baden); *Rudolf Fürst, Wirsching* (Franken).

SILVANER (white) A workhorse grape, often dull, fat and vegetal, but can be impressive in Franken, where it develops honeyed weight with age. It suits the local pork cookery; good with asparagus, too. *Juliusspital* and *Lingenfelder Ypsilon* are good.

SPÄTBURGUNDER (red) There is a new, deeply coloured, rich and powerful style of this, the Pinot Noir of Burgundy. Top producers: *Meyer-Näkel* (Ahr); *August Kesseler* (Rheingau); *Knipser, Koehler-Ruprecht, Lingenfelder* (Pfalz); *Bercher, Dr Heger, Bernhard Huber, Karl H Johner* (Baden); *Rudolf Fürst* (Franken); *Dautel* (Württemberg).

WEISSBURGUNDER or **WEISSER BURGUNDER** (white) Can produce soft, creamy wines with a peach, melted butter, caramel and nuts flavour. Best: *Dönnhoff* (Nahe); *Heyl zu Herrnsheim, Schales* (Rheinhessen); *Bergdolt, Müller-Catoir, Rebholz, Wehrheim* (Pfalz); *Bercher, Dr Heger, Karl H Johner, Franz Keller, Salwey* (Baden).

WINE REGIONS AND STYLES

AHR This small area contrives to be famous for red wines, though their flavour and colour are pretty light, and the Rieslings are in fact more interesting. Top producers: *Deutzerhof, Meyer-Näkel.*

BADEN Dry Ruländer and Weisser Burgunder can be really special here in the balmy South. The Pinot family generally – even Spätburgunder – is on top, although the Ortenau area has fine dry Riesling. The area is dominated by the vast *Badische Winzerkeller* co-operative. Top names: *Bercher, Dr Heger, Bernhard Huber, Karl H Johner, Franz Keller, Andreas Laible, Schloss Neuweier, Salwey, Seeger, Wolff-Metternich.*

BEREICH A collection of villages, usually trading on the name of the most famous of them. Bereich wine is usually dull, dull, dull.

DEUTSCHER SEKT Often a sure route to intestinal distress and sulphur-led hangover, although *Deinhard* makes a decent Riesling version called *Lila*; *Dr Richter*'s and *Georg Breuer*'s are outstanding, but expensive. Interesting but rare smaller brands are *Graeger, Menger-Krug, Schloss Vaux*. Avoid at all costs the stuff made from imported wines, labelled Sekt (not Deutscher Sekt), or worse, Schaumwein.

FRANKEN (Franconia) Dry wine country. The slightly earthy, slightly vegetal, big and beefy Franken wines in their flagon-shaped 'Bocksbeutel' bottles are usually based on Silvaner or Müller-Thurgau. Quality is mixed, with only a few wines worth the high prices. Top names: *Rudolf Fürst, Juliusspital, Johann Ruck, Egon Schäffer, Schmitt's Kinder, Robert Schmitt, Wirsching.*

GROSSLAGE An area smaller than a Bereich, but bigger than a single vineyard. The names sound like those of single vineyards (Piesporter Michelsberg is a Grosslage). Gross deceit is more like it.

HALBTROCKEN Half-dry. The wines need to have more body to balance the acidity, so the best Halbtrockens are from the Rheingau or Pfalz – not the Mosel.

HESSISCHE BERGSTRASSE A tiny side valley of the Rhine from which hardly anything is exported. Generally good Rieslings. Best: *Staatsweingut Bergstrasse.*

LIEBFRAUMILCH Liebfraumilch was a brilliant invention, innocuous and grapy and the perfect beginner's wine. Now mostly cheap sugar-water. *Blue Nun,* always one of the better ones, is no longer labelled Lieb.

INSTANT CELLAR:
DISCOVER GERMANY

- **1986 Rauenthaler Baiken Riesling Kabinett, Staatsweingüter Eltville, £8.99, Waterloo Wines** Can a mere Kabinett last 14 years? Yes, when it's got this much concentration. A treat from the Rheingau.
- **1998 Hoch Reichestal Riesling Kabinett, Franz Künstler, Rheingau, £9.99, Direct Wine Shipments** Künstler makes wonderful wines, all concentration and tense fruit. You could drink this now or, even better, in a couple of years' time.
- **1998 Wehlener Sonnenuhr Riesling Kabinett, Selbach-Oster, £9.55, Bennetts** Mosel Riesling doesn't get much better than this.
- **1998 Deinhard D No 1, £9.40, Avery's** An inventive blend of Riesling and Pinot Blanc, complex and subtle.
- **1997 Saarburger Rausch Riesling Auslese, Fuder 9, Zilliken, £19.90, Justerini & Brooks** Intense, complex and elegant wine from one of the best growers in the Saar Valley.
- **1996 Wachenheimer Rechbachel Riesling Kabinett, Bürklin-Wolf, Pfalz, £9.80 Christopher Piper** Wine of beautiful poise and tension.

MITTELRHEIN The Rhine at its most beautiful; tourists flock there and drink most of its wine, but *Toni Jost*'s racy Rieslings still get away. Also good: *Fritz Bastian, Dr Randolph Kauer, Helmut Madess.*

MOSEL-SAAR-RUWER When they are made from Riesling and come from one of the many steep, slaty, south-facing sites in the folds of the river, these northerly wines are unlike any others. Think of a thrilling spring flowers flavour, allied to an alcohol level so low that it leaves your head clear. The lightest yet most intense Rieslings in the world, with a minerally character from the slate soil. The Saar and the Ruwer both need the warmest years to show at their best, and both can be longer-maturing, with even more steel. Best: *Joh. Jos. Christoffel, Fritz Haag, Reinhold Haart, von Hövel, Karthäuserhof, von Kesselstatt, Dr Loosen, Joh. Jos. Prüm, Max Ferd. Richter, Schloss Saarstein, Willi Schaefer, von Schubert, Selbach-Oster, Dr Wagner, Dr Weins-Prüm, Zilliken.*

NAHE At their best the Rieslings have quite high acidity and a mineral edge, but quality is not uniformly good. *Paul Anheuser, Dönnhoff, Crusius, Schlossgut Diel, Emrich-Schönleber, Kruger-Rumpf* and *Mathern* are all tops. The *Staatliche Weinbaudomäne* is still struggling to regain top form.

PFALZ (formerly the Rheinpfalz) The northern half includes extremely good villages like Forst, Wachenheim, Deidesheim and Ruppertsberg. There's lots of fiery Riesling, and Scheurebe is excellent. The South is Germany's most dynamic region, with fewer big names to fly its flag but an astonishing overall improvement in quality. Look for *Bergdolt, Josef Biffar, Dr Bürklin-Wolf, Knipser, Koehler-Ruprecht, Lingenfelder, Messmer, Georg Mosbacher, Müller-Catoir, Pfaffingen-Fuhrmann-Eymael, Rebholz, Karl Schaefer, Wehrheim, Werlé Erben.*

RHEINGAU Some of Germany's most famous vineyards and renowned aristocratic wine estates are here, and its supremely elegant Rieslings once defined top-quality German wines. However, many of the big estates here have been resting on their laurels for years. The best sign recently has been the classification of top vineyards. Look for these producers: *Georg Breuer, Domdechant Werner, August Eser, Johannishof, August Kesseler, Franz Künstler, Josef Leitz, Schloss Reinhartshausen, Balthasar Ress, J Wegeler-Erben (Deinhard), Robert Weil.* All are worth their high prices.

RHEINHESSEN The contrast between Rheinhessen's regular products and its top wines could not be more extreme. It is one of the main sources of Liebfraumilch, yet Nierstein's top Rieslings can match anything from the Rheingau. Top producers: *Gunderloch, Heyl zu Herrnsheim, Keller, St Antony, Schales, Georg Albrecht Schneider.*

SAALE-UNSTRUT The largest wine region in what used to be East Germany. The climate is similar to Franken, the grapes mainly Müller-Thurgau and Silvaner. *Lutzkendorf* has good Riesling and Traminer.

SACHSEN Germany's smallest wine-growing region, formerly part of the GDR. Müller-Thurgau dominates, but the best dry wines come from Weissburgunder, Kerner, Grauburgunder, Traminer and Riesling. *Klaus Zimmerling* is the best bet, but *Schloss Proschwitz* and *Jan Ulrich* are also good.

SEKT bA (Sekt bestimmter Anbaugebiete). Germany's best sparkling wine comes from private estates. If the wine comes from one specific region it can be labelled accordingly – for instance, Rheinhessen Sekt – and is generally a step above Deutscher Sekt. Riesling Sekt bA is especially worth looking out for. Try *Schloss Wachenheim* or *Winzersekt*, or *Dr Richter*'s.

TROCKEN Dry: the driest German wines, austere and acidic in unripe vintages. The richer, more alcoholic wines of the Pfalz, Baden and Franken suit dryness best, as do fat, ripe years like 1997.

WÜRTTEMBERG Most is drunk on the spot. Its claim to fame – if fame is the right word – is red. The best grape is Lemberger, dark, spicy and suited to oak aging. Best: *Graf Adelmann, Dautel, Haidle, Hohenlohe-Öhringen, Graf von Neipperg.*

PRODUCERS WHO'S WHO

GEORG BREUER ★★★★ (Rheingau) Convincing promoter of dry Rheingau Riesling. Rüdesheimer Berg Schlossberg and Rauenthaler Nonnenberg are best.

H DÖNNHOFF ★★★★★ (Nahe) Classic Rieslings of great aromatic subtlety and racy intensity. Sensational Auslese and Eiswein.

GUNDERLOCH ★★★★★ (Rheinhessen) Explosively fruity, rich, seductive Rieslings from the great Nackenheimer Rothenberg. Jean Baptiste Kabinett is good value; also Beerenauslese and Trockenbeerenauslese of other-worldly concentration and density.

FRITZ HAAG ★★★★ (Mosel-Saar-Ruwer) Wines of crystalline clarity and racy refinement from Brauneberger Juffer-Sonnenuhr.

VON HÖVEL ★★★★ (Mosel-Saar-Ruwer) These have taken a dramatic jump up in quality in recent years. Best are the succulent, beautifully balanced wines from Oberemmeler Hütte.

KARTHÄUSERHOF ★★★★★ (Mosel-Saar-Ruwer) Large Ruwer property making wines of concentration and character.

VON KESSELSTATT ★★★ (Mosel-Saar-Ruwer) Huge estate showing big improvements. Look for Rieslings from Graach, Piesport and Wiltingen.

KOEHLER-RUPRECHT ★★★★★ (Pfalz) Powerful dry Rieslings plus excellent oak-aged whites and Germany's best Pinot Noir reds, sold under the Philippi label.

FRANZ KÜNSTLER ★★★★★ (Rheingau) Powerful and long-lived Rieslings. Best are the majestic dry and dessert wines from the Hochheimer Hölle.

DR LOOSEN ★★★★★ (Mosel-Saar-Ruwer) Rieslings, Spätlesen and Auslesen from Urziger Würzgarten, Erdener Prälat and Treppchen are tops. For value, try wines without vineyard names.

EGON MÜLLER ★★★★★ (Mosel-Saar-Ruwer) The ultimate in Riesling Auslese, Beerenauslese,

ON THE CASE

The alcohol level gives an idea of how sweet a Kabinett or Spätlese will be. Nine per cent or less means a fair bit of sweetness; more alcohol indicates a drier wine.

Trockenbeerenauslese and Eiswein. No honey tastes this good. World-class prices.

MÜLLER-CATOIR ★★★★★ (Pfalz) Highly expressive, rich, dry and naturally sweet wines. Superb Scheurebe and Rieslaner as well as Rieslings.

JOH. JOS. PRÜM ★★★★★ (Mosel-Saar-Ruwer) Wines that need time to show their best; after a few years of aging they are supremely elegant. Wehlener Sonnenuhr can age for decades without losing vigour.

WILLI SCHAEFER ★★★★ (Mosel-Saar-Ruwer) Small production; wines of great depth and elegance from Graach.

VON SCHUBERT ★★★★★ (Mosel-Saar-Ruwer) The Maximin Grünhaus estate makes exquisitely delicate, fragrant Rieslings that gain enormously with long aging.

SELBACH-OSTER ★★★★ (Mosel-Saar-Ruwer) Superbly poised, concentrated Rieslings from Zeltingen.

WEINGUT ROBERT WEIL ★★★★ (Rheingau) Classic Rieslings which combine opulent fruit with clarity and crisp acidity. Best are the Kiedricher Gräfenbergs.

ZILLIKEN ★★★★ (Mosel-Saar-Ruwer) Racy Saar Rieslings with minerally intensity. Fashionable Eiswein.

GERMAN VINTAGES

1999 High quality, with some Beerenauslesen and Trockenbeerenauslesen.

1998 'Surprisingly good', according to the growers – it rained, in other words. But quality does look impressive, especially in the Mosel.

1997 Rich, concentrated wines: lots of Spätlesen and Auslesen. Some top estates had to declassify Spätlesen to QbA in order to have enough. Not an Eiswein year: too warm.

1996 Higher acidity than the 1997s, and will take longer to mature.

1995 The best vintage since 1990. Lots of excellent Spätlesen and Auslesen.

1994 Strongest in the Mosel-Saar-Ruwer, but quite good generally. Outstanding at BA and TBA level.

1993 Rich, even opulent wines that have developed quite quickly. Best in the Rheingau, Pfalz and Mosel. Very good for dry Riesling. Drink now and for the next few years.

1992 Good, but a bit low on acidity. Don't keep them too long.

1991 The best are showing well now.

1990 Fantastic wines that will age and age.

1989 A mixed vintage: Kabinett and Spätlesen mostly want drinking. Best in the Mosel-Saar-Ruwer, Nahe and Pfalz.

GERMANY PRICES

Kab.	=	Kabinett
Spät.	=	Spätlese
Aus.	=	Auslese
BA	=	Beerenauslese
TBA	=	Trockenbeerenauslese

RHINE WHITE

Under £4.00

Devil's Rock Riesling, St Ursula **Non-vintage** £3.99 (ASD) £3.99 (SO)
Devil's Rock Riesling, St Ursula **1998** £3.99 (WAI) £3.99 (SAF)
Liebfraumilch Black Tower **Non-vintage** £3.99 (ASD) £3.99 (SO) £3.99 (BOT)
Liebfraumilch Blue Nun **Non-vintage** £3.99 (SO) £3.99 (WAI) £3.99 (THR)
Liebfraumilch Blue Nun **1998** £3.99 (SAF)
Liebfraumilch Rudolf Müller **1997** £2.99 (UN)
Niersteiner Gutes Domtal, Rudolf Müller **Non-vintage** £3.29 (UN)
Rüdesheimer Rosengarten, Rudolf Müller **1998** £3.75 (TAN)

£4.00 → £4.99

Liebfraumilch Black Tower **1998** £4.05 (SAF) £4.49 (BUD)
Liebfraumilch Rudolf Müller **1998** £4.35 (CB)
Niersteiner Auflangen Riesling Spät., Rudolf Müller **1997** £4.95 (AD) £4.95 (POR)
Niersteiner Gutes Domtal, Langenbach **1998** £4.54 (PLAY)
Oppenheimer Krötenbrunnen, Rudolf Müller **1996** £4.47 (CB)
Ruppertsberger Hoheburg Riesling Kab., Winzerverein **1998** £4.95 (WS)

£5.00 → £5.99

Johannisberger Erntebringer Riesling Kab., Rudolf Müller **1996** £5.49 (JON)
Niersteiner Spiegelberg Riesling Spät., Rudolf Müller **1997** £5.49 (UN)
Scheurebe Kab. Louis Philipp, Guntrum **1997** £5.45 (CON)

£6.00 → £6.99

Johannisberger Vogelsang Riesling Kab., Eser **1998** £6.50 (WS)
Niersteiner Bergkirche Riesling Kab., Guntrum **1997** £6.85 (CON)
Niersteiner Hölle Riesling Kab., Senfter **1995** £6.86 (COC)
Riesling Deidesheim, von Buhl **1996** £6.50 (JU)
Riesling Kab., Gunderloch **1995** £6.50 (JU)
Riesling QbA, J L Wolf **1998** £6.75 (STE)
Ruppertsberger Gaisböhl Riesling Kab., Bürklin-Wolf **1997** £6.95 (TAN)
Scheurebe Kab. Louis Philipp, Guntrum **1998** £6.45 (STA)

£7.00 → £7.99

Deidesheimer Leinhöhle Riesling Kab., Bassermann-Jordan **1989** £7.95 (JU)
Eltviller Sonnenberg Riesling Kab., von Simmern **1996** £7.89 (PIP)
Forster Mariengarten Riesling Kab., Bürklin-Wolf **1985** £7.75 (WAT)
Forster Pechstein Riesling Kab., von Buhl **1996** £7.90 (JU) £8.55 (NI)
Forster Riesling, Bürklin-Wolf **1996** £7.75 (WRI) £7.99 (CON)
Hochheimer Riesling, Domdechant Werner **1996** £7.95 (AD)
Niersteiner Pettenthal Riesling Kab., Gunderloch **1995** £7.50 (JU)
Riesling QbA, Dönnhoff **1996** £7.90 (JU)

MERCHANTS SPECIALIZING IN GERMANY

see Merchant Directory (page 456) for details

Adnams (AD), Averys of Bristol (AV), Bennetts (BEN), Berry Bros (BER), Bibendum (BIB), Butlers (BU) – particularly old vintages, Cockburns of Leith (COC), Direct Wine Shipments (DI), S H Jones (JON), Justerini & Brooks (JU), Lay & Wheeler (LAY), Montrachet (MON), Oddbins (OD), Majestic (MAJ), James Nicholson (NI), Nobody Inn (NO), Reid Wines (REI), Tanners (TAN), Ubiquitous Chip (UB), Waitrose (WAI), Waterloo Wine Company (WAT), The Wine Society (WS).

£8.00 → £8.99

Deidesheimer Leinhöhle Riesling Kab., Bassermann-Jordan **1994** £8.95 (JU)
Eltviller Sonnenberg Riesling Kab., von Simmern **1985** £8.49 (WAT)
Forster Kirchenstück Riesling Kab., Bassermann-Jordan **1989** £8.50 (JU)
Forster Pechstein Riesling Kab., von Buhl **1994** £8.95 (JU)
Forster Stift Kab., Bassermann-Jordan **1988** £8.99 (RAE)
Geisenheimer Schlossgarten Riesling Spät., Schönborn **1989** £8.95 (JU) £8.99 (RAE)
Grosskarlbacher Burgweg Scheurebe Kab. Trocken, Lingenfelder **1996** £8.50 (UB)
Hattenheimer Nussbrunnen Riesling Kab., von Simmern **1993** £8.85 (JU)
Hattenheimer Schützenhaus Riesling Kab., Ress **1996** £8.42 (MON)
Hochheimer Hölle Riesling Kab., Domdechant Werner **1994** £8.95 (JU)
Hochheimer Riesling Aus., Domdechant Werner **1992** £8.95 (AD)
Nackenheimer Rothenberg Riesling Kab. Jean Baptiste, Gunderloch **1993** £8.85 (JU)
Nackenheimer Rothenberg Riesling Kab. Jean Baptiste, Gunderloch **1991** £8.99 (UB)
Niersteiner Pettenthal Riesling Kab., Balbach **1997** £8.80 (TAN)
Schlossböckelheimer Kupfergrube Riesling Spät., Staatliche Weinbaudomäne **1995** £8.19 (JON)

£9.00 → £9.99

Deidesheimer Hohenmorgen Riesling Kab., Bassermann-Jordan **1993** £9.95 (JU)
Deidesheimer Hohenmorgen Riesling Spät., Bassermann-Jordan **1988** £9.95 (RAE)
Deidesheimer Kieselberg Riesling Kab., Bassermann-Jordan **1996** £9.99 (JON)
Deidesheimer Leinhöhle Riesling Spät., Bassermann-Jordan **1989** £9.90 (JU)
Erbacher Marcobrunnen Riesling Kab., von Simmern **1993** £9.45 (JU)
Forster Ungeheuer Riesling Spät., von Buhl **1997** £9.95 (WS)
Freinsheimer Goldberg Riesling Aus., Lingenfelder **1994** £9.95 (FORT)
Hochheimer Domdechaney Riesling Spät., Geheimrat Aschrott'sche **1990** £9.95 (JU)
Hochheimer Reichestal Riesling Kab., Franz Kunstler **1998** £9.99 (DI)
Hochheimer Reichestal Riesling Kab., Franz Kunstler **1996** £9.00 (JU)
Nackenheimer Rothenberg Riesling Kab., Gunderloch **1996** £9.90 (JU)
Nackenheimer Rothenberg Riesling Kab. Jean Baptiste, Gunderloch **1994** £9.82 (NO) £9.90 (JU)
Oberhäuser Leistenberg Riesling Kab., Dönnhoff **1998** £9.46 (NO)
Oberhäuser Leistenberg Riesling Kab., Dönnhoff **1995** £9.50 (JU)
Rauenthaler Rothenberg Riesling Kab., Eser **1994** £9.90 (JU)
Riesling Kab., Robert Weil **1997** £9.20 (TAN)
Riesling Spät. Trocken, Lingenfelder **1997** £9.30 (MON) £10.95 (AD)
Schloss Vollrads Blau-Gold, Schloss Vollrads **1989** £9.50 (UB)
Wachenheimer Goldbachel Riesling Spät., Bürklin-Wolf **1988** £9.95 (DI)
Wachenheimer Rechbächel Riesling Kab., Bürklin-Wolf **1994** £9.95 (BER)

£10.00 → £11.99

Armand Kab., von Buhl **1995** £11.69 (TW)
Forster Jesuitengarten Riesling Spät., von Buhl **1997** £10.99 (NI) £13.92 (TW)
Forster Jesuitengarten Riesling Spät., von Buhl **1995** £11.50 (JU)
Forster Kirchenstuck Riesling Spät., von Buhl **1996** £10.50 (JU)
Forster Kirchenstück Riesling Spät., Bassermann-Jordan **1990** £10.50 (JU)
Hattenheimer Pfaffenberg Riesling Spät., Schönborn **1996** £10.40 (CB)
Hattenheimer Pfaffenberg Riesling Spät., Schönborn **1989** £11.90 (JU)
Hochheimer Kirchenstück Riesling Spät., Geheimrat Aschrott'sche **1994** £10.50 (JU)
Hochheimer Reichestal Riesling Kab., Franz Kunstler **1997** £11.95 (BER)
Johannisberger Klaus Riesling Spät., Schönborn **1990** £11.90 (JU)
Nackenheimer Rothenberg Riesling Spät., Gunderloch **1992** £10.50 (JU)
Niederhauser Hermannshöhle Riesling Spät., Dönnhoff **1993** £11.95 (JU)
Niersteiner Hipping Riesling Aus., Balbach **1989** £10.50 (JU)
Oberhäuser Leistenberg Riesling Kab., Dönnhoff **1996** £10.20 (JU)
Rauenthaler Baiken Riesling Kab., Staatsweingüter Eltville **1983** £10.75 (BU)

£12.00 → £14.99

Forster Jesuitengarten Riesling Aus., Bassermann-Jordan **1996** £12.45 (JU)
Forster Ungeheuer Riesling Aus., von Buhl **1996** £13.50 (JU)
Hochheimer Kirchenstück Riesling Spät., Franz Kunstler **1998** £13.99 (DI)
Hochheimer Kirchenstück Riesling Spät., Domdechant Werner **1994** £12.95 (BER)
Nackenheimer Rothenberg Riesling Spät., Gunderloch **1994** £13.90 (JU)
Niederhauser Hermannshöhle Riesling Spät., Dönnhoff **1998** £14.76 (NO) £14.95 (TAN) £16.00 (WS)
Niederhauser Hermannshöhle Riesling Spät., Dönnhoff **1995** £14.95 (JU)
Niederhäuser Hermannshöhle Riesling Spät., Staatliche Weinbaudomäne **1985** £13.75 (WAT)
Niersteiner Pettenthal Riesling Spät., Balbach **1998** £12.75 (TAN)
Oberhäuser Brücke Riesling Aus., Dönnhoff ½ bottle **1996** £14.00 (JU)
Ruppertsberger Linsenbusch Riesling Spät., Deinhard **1976** £14.50 (BU)
Schlossbockelheimer Kupfergrube Riesling Spät., Dönnhoff **1998** £14.99 (YOU) £15.05 (NO) £16.17 (PIP)
Wachenheimer Gerümpel Riesling Kab., Bürklin-Wolf **1966** £14.69 (REI)
Wachenheimer Gerümpel Riesling Spät., Bürklin-Wolf **1989** £12.75 (PIP)
Wachenheimer Gerümpel Riesling Spät., J.L. Wolf **1996** £12.20 (NO)
Wachenheimer Rechbächel Riesling Spät., Bürklin-Wolf **1998** £12.40 (TAN)
Wallufer Walkenberg Riesling Spät., Schönborn **1990** £13.90 (JU)

£15.00 → £19.99

Deidesheimer Hohenmorgen Riesling Aus., Bassermann-Jordan **1989** £18.90 (JU)
Erbacher Marcobrunn Riesling Spät., Schönborn **1990** £18.00 (JU)
Forster Kirchenstück Riesling Aus., von Buhl **1995** £15.95 (JU)
Forster Kirchenstück Riesling Spät., Bassermann-Jordan **1994** £15.22 (TW)
Geisenheimer Rothenberg Riesling Aus., Deinhard **1989** £17.90 (JU)
Hallgartener Schonhell Riesling Spät., Lowenstein **1983** £15.40 (UB)
Hochheimer Domdechaney Riesling Aus., Aschrott **1998** £19.09 (GOE)
Kreuznacher Krötenpfuhl Riesling Aus., Rudolf Anheuser **1989** £16.75 (UB)
Nackenheimer Rothenberg Riesling Aus., Gunderloch **1994** £19.90 (JU)
Nackenheimer Rothenberg Riesling Spät., Gunderloch **1996** £15.00 (JU)
Niederhauser Hermannshöhle Riesling Spät., Dönnhoff **1996** £15.50 (JU)
Niederhauser Hermannshöhle Riesling Aus., Dönnhoff **1995** £19.40 (TAN) £21.00 (JU)
Niersteiner Hipping Riesling Aus., Balbach **1996** £15.00 (JU)
Oberhäuser Brücke Riesling Aus., Dönnhoff ½ bottle **1998** £15.00 (YOU) £16.88 (NO)
Oberhäuser Brücke Riesling Aus., Dönnhoff **1993** £17.50 (JU)
Schlossbockelheimer Felsenberg Riesling Spät., Dönnhoff **1995** £15.95 (JU)
Schlossbockelheimer Kupfergrube Riesling Spät., Dönnhoff **1996** £16.00 (JU)
Schlossböckelheimer Kupfergrube Riesling Spät., Staatliche Weinbaudomäne **1998** £16.25 (LAY)
Wachenheimer Böhlig Riesling Aus., Bürklin-Wolf **1990** £15.95 (DI)
Wallufer Oberberg Riesling Aus., J B Becker **1995** £17.00 (JU)

£20.00 → £24.99

Eltviller Sonnenberg Riesling Aus., J B Becker **1995** £23.50 (JU)
Erbacher Marcobrunn Riesling Aus., Schönborn **1995** £20.50 (CB)
Forster Ungeheuer Riesling Aus., von Buhl **1997** £22.15 (UB)
Kiedricher Gräfenberg Riesling Spät., Weil **1997** £21.50 (DI)
Nackenheimer Rothenberg Riesling Aus. Fuder 20, Gunderloch **1996** £21.00 (JU)
Nackenheimer Rothenberg Riesling Aus., Gunderloch **1995** £22.00 (JU)
Niersteiner Oelberg Eiswein, Balbach ½ bottle **1996** £24.00 (JU)
Wachenheimer Mandelgarten Scheurebe Aus., Bürklin-Wolf **1983** £21.74 (REI)

- *All prices for each wine are listed together in ascending order.*
- *Price bands refer to the lowest price for which the wine is available.*

Over £25.00

Deidesheimer Hohenmorgen Riesling BA, Bassermann-Jordan **1994** £110.00 (JU)
Erbacher Marcobrunn Riesling Aus., Schönborn **1990** £49.00 (JU)
Forster Jesuitengarten Riesling BA, von Buhl **1994** £90.00 (JU)
Forster Jesuitengarten Riesling Eiswein, von Buhl **1996** £69.00 (JU)
Forster Jesuitengarten Riesling TBA, Basserman-Jordan **1989** £175.00 (JU)
Forster Kirchenstuck Riesling BA, von Buhl **1996** £68.00 (JU)
Forster Ungeheuer Riesling Eiswein, Bassermann-Jordan ½ bottle **1996** £35.00 (JU)
Forster Ungeheuer Riesling Eiswein, von Buhl **1996** £72.00 (JU)
Forster Ungeheuer Riesling Eiswein, von Buhl ½ bottle **1995** £54.00 (JU)
Forster Ungeheuer Riesling TBA, von Buhl ½ bottle **1996** £65.00 (JU)
Grosskarlbacher Burgweg Scheurebe TBA ½ bottle, Lingenfelder **1985** £50.00 (FORT)
Hochheimer Hölle Riesling BA, Franz Kunstler ½ bottle **1996** £41.00 (JU)
Hochheimer Reichestal Riesling Eiswein, Franz Kunstler ½ bottle **1998** £54.00 (DI)
Hochheimer Riesling Aus., Domdechant Werner **1994** £25.00 (JU)
Nackenheimer Rothenberg Riesling Aus. Goldkapsul, Gunderloch **1995** £43.00 (JU)
Niederhäuser Hermannshöhle Riesling Aus., Staatliche Weinbaudomäne **1997** £25.95 (POR)
Niersteiner Oelberg Eiswein, Balbach ½ bottle **1998** £45.75 (TAN)
Oberhäuser Brücke Riesling Aus., Dönnhoff **1998** £30.00 (YOU)
Oberhäuser Brücke Riesling BA, Dönnhoff ½ bottle **1995** £50.00 (JU)
Oberhäuser Brücke Riesling Eiswein, Dönnhoff **1998** £65.20 (TAN) £71.14 (NO)
Oberhäuser Brücke Riesling Eiswein, Dönnhoff ½ bottle **1995** £78.00 (JU)
Oberhäuser Felsenberg Riesling Eiswein, Dönnhoff ½ bottle **1993** £60.00 (JU)
Wachenheimer Böhlig Riesling BA, Bürklin-Wolf **1989** £54.00 (JU)
Wachenheimer Luginsland Riesling TBA, Bürklin-Wolf **1989** £92.00 (JU)
Wallufer Walkenberg Riesling TBA, J B Becker **1994** £136.00 (JU)

RHINE RED

Under £13.00

Spätburgunder QbA, Lingenfelder **1996** £9.95 (WS) £11.95 (MON)
Spätburgunder QbA, Lingenfelder **1993** £12.50 (FORT)

Over £16.00

Wallufer Walkenberg Spätburgunder Spät. Trocken, J B Becker **1994** £17.90 (JU)
Wallufer Walkenberg Spätburgunder Spät. Trocken, J B Becker **1993** £16.90 (JU)

MOSEL WHITE

Under £4.00

Bereich Bernkastel, Rudolf Müller **1997** £3.69 (UN)
Piesporter Michelsberg Reh **1999** £3.99 (MAR)
Piesporter Michelsberg Rudolf Müller **1997** £3.99 (UN)

£4.00 → £5.99

Bereich Bernkastel, Rudolf Müller **1998** £4.82 (CB)
Ockfener Bockstein Riesling, Dr Wagner **1998** £5.55 (WAI) £7.70 (TAN)
Piesporter Michelsberg Rudolf Müller **1998** £4.25 (TAN) £4.91 (CB)
Reiler vom Heissen Stein Kab., Rudolf Müller **1997** £4.95 (POR)
Reiler vom Heissen Stein Spät., Rudolf Müller **1998** £4.15 (TAN)
Riesling Dr 'L', Dr Loosen **1998** £5.99 (WAI) £7.65 (NI)
Riesling QbA, Dr Loosen **1998** £5.57 (NO) £6.25 (JON) £6.59 (PHI) £7.16 (PLAY)
Riesling Trocken Dr 'L', Dr Loosen **1998** £5.95 (AD)

£6.00 → £7.99

Erdener Treppchen Riesling Kab., Mönchhof **1997** £7.95 (WS)
Graacher Himmelreich Riesling Kab., F-W-Gymnasium **1996** £7.95 (POR)
Graacher Himmelreich Riesling Kab., F-W-Gymnasium **1995** £7.99 (JON)
Kaseler Nies'chen Riesling Spät., Deinhard **1990** £6.95 (BU)
Oberemmeler Hütte Riesling Kab., von Hövel **1997** £7.35 (WS)

Ockfener Bockstein Riesling Spät., Dr Fischer **1990** £7.93 (SAV)
Ockfener Bockstein Riesling Spät., Rheinart **1996** £7.63 (PLA)
Riesling Dr 'L', Dr Loosen **1997** £6.25 (CON)
Riesling Kab. Dr 'L', Dr Loosen **1997** £7.09 (CON) £8.05 (ELL)
★ Riesling Kab. Immich-Batterieberg **1998** £7.95 (AD)
Riesling, Zilliken **1995** £7.50 (JU)
Scharzhofberger Riesling, Egon Müller-Scharzhof **1995** £7.90 (JU)
Zeltinger Schlossberg Riesling Kab., Selbach-Oster **1991** £7.50 (RAE)

£8.00 → £9.99

Brauneberger Juffer Riesling Kab., Richter **1997** £8.62 (MON)
Brauneberger Juffer Sonnenuhr Riesling Kab., Fritz Haag **1996** £9.95 (RAE) £10.90 (JU)
Erdener Treppchen Riesling Kab., Dr Loosen **1997** £9.83 (PIP) £10.99 (JON)
Erdener Treppchen Riesling Kab., Mönchhof **1998** £8.81 (BIB)
Erdener Treppchen Riesling Spät., Mönchhof **1990** £9.95 (JU)
Erdener Treppchen Riesling Spät., Heinrich Schmitiges **1999** £9.39 (PLA)
Graacher Himmelreich Riesling Kab., J J Prüm **1992** £9.95 (JU) £13.33 (TW)
Graacher Himmelreich Riesling Spät., F-W-Gymnasium **1997** £8.95 (AD)
Graacher Himmelreich Riesling Spät., Max Ferd Richter **1996** £9.95 (FORT)
Josephshofer Riesling Spät., Kesselstatt **1989** £9.50 (JU)
Maximin-Grünhäuser Bruderberg Riesling, Schubert **1996** £8.90 (JU)
Ockfener Bockstein Riesling Kab., Zilliken **1998** £9.30 (LAY)
Ockfener Bockstein Riesling Spät., Dr Fischer **1989** £9.00 (JU)
Piesporter Goldtröpfchen Riesling Spät., Bischöfliches Priesterseminar **1989** £8.95 (JU)
Piesporter Goldtröpfchen Riesling Kab., Haart **1997** £9.99 (JON)
Piesporter Goldtröpfchen Riesling Kab., Haart **1996** £8.90 (JU) £9.50 (ELL)
Piesporter Goldtröpfchen Riesling Kab., Kesselstatt **1997** £9.55 (NI)
Riesling Kab. Dr 'L', Dr Loosen **1998** £9.75 (STE)
Riesling Kab., J J Prüm **1995** £9.45 (JU)
Riesling Spät. Dr 'L', Dr Loosen **1997** £8.95 (CON) £15.45 (STE)
Saarburger Rausch Riesling Kab., Zilliken **1997** £8.49 (POR)
Saarburger Rausch Riesling Kab., Zilliken **1994** £8.90 (JU)
Trittenheimer Apotheke Riesling Spät., F-W-Gymnasium **1996** £9.95 (POR)
Urziger Wurzgarten Riesling Spät., Mönchhof **1990** £9.95 (JU)
Waldracher Krone Riesling Aus., Scherf **1989** £9.99 (SAV)
Wehlener Sonnenuhr Riesling Aus., Dr Loosen **1997** £9.33 (NO)
Wehlener Sonnenuhr Riesling Kab., Dr Loosen **1997** £9.95 (WRI) £12.99 (PHI)
Wehlener Sonnenuhr Riesling Kab., Dr Loosen **1996** £9.79 (CON) £11.39 (PLAY)
Wehlener Sonnenuhr Riesling Kab., J J Prüm **1996** £9.85 (WRI) £15.16 (TW)
Wiltinger Braune Kupp Riesling Kab., Egon Müller-Scharzhof **1990** £9.95 (JU)

£10.00 → £11.99

Bernkasteler Badstube Riesling Spät., H Thanisch **1989** £11.50 (JU)
Brauneberger Juffer Sonnenuhr Riesling Spät., H Thanisch **1994** £10.79 (UN)
Eitelsbacher Karthäuserhofberg Riesling Kab., Karthäuserhof **1998** £11.55 (MON)
Eitelsbacher Karthäuserhofberg Riesling Kab., Karthäuserhof **1995** £10.80 (JU)
Erdener Treppchen Riesling Kab., Dr Loosen **1996** £10.95 (BER)
Graacher Himmelreich Riesling Kab., J J Prüm **1995** £10.90 (JU)
Graacher Himmelreich Riesling Spät., F-W-Gymnasium **1995** £10.99 (JON)
Graacher Himmelreich Riesling Spät., F-W-Gymnasium **1994** £10.15 (AV)
Josephshofer Riesling Spät., Kesselstatt **1995** £10.95 (STA)
Maximin-Grünhäuser Abtsberg Riesling, Schubert **1994** £10.90 (JU)
Maximin-Grünhäuser Herrenberg Riesling Kab., Schubert **1994** £11.75 (CB)

Please remember that
Oz Clarke's Wine Buying Guide
*is a price **guide** and not a price **list**. It is not meant to replace up-to-date merchants' lists.*

Piesporter Goldtröpfchen Spät., Kesselstatt **1998** £10.95 (STA)
Saarburger Rausch Riesling Spät., Zilliken **1996** £10.90 (JU)
★ Schieferterrassen Riesling, Heymann-Löwenstein **1998** £10 00 (MV)
Serriger Schloss Saarsteiner Riesling Spät., Schloss Saarstein **1996** £11.95 (MON)
Urziger Wurzgarten Riesling Spät., Mönchhof **1995** £11.50 (JU)
Wehlener Sonnenuhr Riesling Aus., S A Prüm **1990** £11.16 (REI)
Wehlener Sonnenuhr Riesling Kab., Dr Loosen **1998** £10.75 (NI)
Wehlener Sonnenuhr Riesling Kab., Licht-Bergweiler **1983** £11.16 (REI)

£12.00 → £14.99

Bernkasteler Doctor Riesling Kab., H Thanisch **1996** £12.29 (UN)
Brauneberger Juffer Riesling Aus., Richter **1985** £14.00 (FORT)
Brauneberger Juffer Sonnenuhr Riesling Aus., Fritz Haag **1992** £13.99 (RAE)
Brauneberger Juffer Sonnenuhr Riesling Spät., Fritz Haag **1989** £12.50 (JU) £12.50 (RAE)
Enkircher Batterieberg Riesling Spät. Halbtrocken, Immich-Batterieberg **1997** £13.95 (AD)
Erdener Treppchen Riesling Kab., Dr Loosen **1995** £12.30 (NO)
Erdener Treppchen Riesling Spät., Dr Loosen **1981** £14.35 (NI)
Graacher Himmelreich Riesling Kab., J J Prüm **1996** £14.04 (TW)
Kaseler Kehrnagel Riesling Aus., Simon **1983** £13.75 (WAT)
Kaseler Nies'chen Riesling Aus., Kesselstatt **1989** £13.10 (UB)
Maximin-Grünhäuser Abtsberg Riesling Kab., Schubert **1995** £13.50 (JU) £13.50 (YOU)
Maximin-Grünhäuser Abtsberg Riesling Kab., Schubert **1994** £13.95 (JU)
Maximin-Grünhäuser Abtsberg Riesling Spät., Schubert **1997** £14.40 (AD)
Maximin-Grünhäuser Abtsberg Riesling Spät., Schubert **1988** £13.87 (CB)
Maximin-Grünhäuser Herrenberg Kab., J J Prüm **1989** £13.99 (UB)
Maximin-Grünhäuser Herrenberg Riesling Spät., Schubert **1995** £14.80 (RAE)
Piesporter Goldtröpfchen Riesling Spät., Haart **1995** £13.90 (JU)
Scharzhofberger Riesling Aus., von Hövel **1997** £12.50 (TAN)
Scharzhofberger Riesling Kab. Fuder 21, Egon Müller-Scharzhof **1994** £13.90 (JU)
Scharzhofberger Riesling Kab., Egon Müller-Scharzhof **1998** £12.95 (TAN)
Scharzhofberger Riesling Kab., Egon Müller-Scharzhof **1997** £13.85 (HAH)
Scharzhofberger Riesling Kab., Egon Müller-Scharzhof **1994** £13.95 (BER)
Scharzhofberger Riesling Spät., Egon Müller-Scharzhof **1996** £14.50 (FORT) £15.95 (JU)
Wehlener Sonnenuhr Riesling Kab., Weins Prüm **1993** £14.65 (UB)
Wehlener Sonnenuhr Riesling Spät., Dr Loosen **1998** £13.99 (JON)
Wehlener Sonnenuhr Riesling Spät., Dr Loosen **1996** £14.35 (NI)
Wehlener Sonnenuhr Riesling Spät., J J Prüm **1992** £14.95 (JU)
Wiltinger Braune Kupp Riesling Spät., Mönchhof **1990** £14.50 (JU)
Zeltinger Sonnenuhr Riesling Aus., Selbach-Oster **1996** £14.50 (RAE) £17.00 (MV)
Zeltinger Sonnenuhr Riesling Spät., Selbach-Oster **1995** £12.50 (FORT)

£15.00 → £19.99

Bernkasteler Badstube Riesling Spät., J J Prüm **1990** £18.21 (TW)
Bernkasteler Doctor Riesling Kab., H Thanisch **1989** £18.00 (JU)
Bernkasteler Doctor Riesling Spät., H Thanisch **1997** £17.95 (WAI)
Brauneberger Juffer Sonnenuhr Riesling Aus., Fritz Haag **1995** £15.99 (RAE) £19.50 (JU) £21.35 (LAY)
Brauneberger Juffer Sonnenuhr Riesling Spät., Fritz Haag **1995** £15.00 (JU)
Eitelsbacher Karthäuserhofberg Riesling Aus., Karthäuserhof **1995** £19.50 (JU)
Erdener Prälat Riesling Aus., Mönchhof **1994** £15.00 (JU)
Erdener Treppchen Riesling Aus., Mönchhof **1990** £15.66 (BIB)
Graacher Domprobst Riesling Aus., Richter **1997** £15.28 (MON)
Graacher Himmelreich Riesling Spät., J J Prüm **1997** £15.90 (LAY)
Graacher Himmelreich Riesling Spät., J J Prüm **1995** £18.68 (TW)
Maximin-Grünhäuser Abtsberg Riesling Kab., Schubert **1998** £15.50 (AD)

Maximin-Grünhäuser Abtsberg Riesling Spät., Schubert **1998** £16.50 (LAY)
Maximin-Grünhäuser Abtsberg Riesling Spät., Schubert **1994** £15.50 (JU)
Maximin-Grünhäuser Abtsberg Riesling Aus., Schubert **1992** £19.95 (AD)
Maximin-Grünhäuser Herrenberg Riesling Aus., Schubert **1995** £18.00 (RAE)
Piesporter Goldtröpfchen Riesling Aus., Haart **1996** £18.50 (JU)
Scharzhofberger Riesling Aus., Kesselstatt **1997** £16.63 (CB)
Scharzhofberger Riesling Spät. Fuder 17, Egon Müller-Scharzhof **1993** £17.50 (JU)
Scharzhofberger Riesling Spät., Egon Müller-Scharzhof **1997** £18.35 (HAH)
Scharzhofberger Riesling Spät., Egon Müller-Scharzhof **1990** £18.00 (JU)
Urziger Würzgarten Riesling Aus., Dr Loosen **1997** £17.99 (YOU)
Urziger Würzgarten Riesling Aus., Dr Loosen **1994** £18.25 (CON)
Urziger Würzgarten Riesling Kab., Dr Loosen **1996** £15.95 (AD)
Urziger Würzgarten Riesling Spät., Dr Loosen **1997** £15.50 (TAN) £15.79 (YOU)
Wehlener Sonnenuhr Riesling Aus., Dr Loosen **1995** £18.68 (NO)
Wehlener Sonnenuhr Riesling Aus., Dr Loosen **1990** £16.99 (WAI)
Wehlener Sonnenuhr Riesling Aus., S A Prüm **1989** £19.50 (DI)
Wehlener Sonnenuhr Riesling Aus., J J Prüm **1997** £18.00 (WS)
Wehlener Sonnenuhr Riesling Aus., J J Prüm **1995** £19.50 (JU) £25.26 (TW)
Wehlener Sonnenuhr Riesling Spät., J J Prüm **1995** £16.50 (JU) £20.56 (TW)

£20.00 → £29.99

Bernkasteler Doctor Riesling Spät., H Thanisch **1989** £26.00 (JU) £28.79 (REI)
Brauneberger Juffer Sonnenuhr Riesling Aus. Fuder 12, Fritz Haag **1995** £22.80 (JU)
Brauneberger Juffer Sonnenuhr Riesling Aus. Fuder 11, Fritz Haag **1994** £23.00 (JU)
Brauneberger Juffer Sonnenuhr Riesling Aus. Goldkapsul Fuder 4, Fritz Haag **1989** £28.00 (JU)
Brauneberger Juffer Sonnenuhr Riesling Aus. Goldkapsul, Fritz Haag **1996** £24.99 (RAE)
Brauneberger Juffer Sonnenuhr Riesling Aus. Goldkapsul, Fritz Haag ½ bottle **1996** £24.00 (JU)
Eitelsbacher Karthäuserhofberg Riesling Aus. Fuder 30, Karthäuserhof **1995** £23.00 (JU)
Erdener Prälat Riesling Aus., Dr Loosen **1997** £23.90 (TAN)
Erdener Treppchen Riesling Aus., Dr Loosen **1995** £27.49 (NO)
Erdener Treppchen Riesling Aus. Goldkapsul, Mönchhof ½ bottle **1995** £25.00 (JU)
Josephshofer Riesling Aus., Kesselstatt **1983** £20.56 (REI)
Maximin-Grünhäuser Abtsberg Riesling Kab., Schubert **1990** £28.79 (REI)
Maximin-Grünhäuser Abtsberg Riesling Aus., Schubert **1993** £25.00 (JU)
Maximin-Grünhäuser Abtsberg Riesling Aus. Fuder 117, Schubert ½ bottle **1995** £24.00 (JU)
Maximin-Grünhäuser Herrenberg Riesling Aus., Schubert **1994** £28.50 (FORT)
Ockfener Bockstein Riesling Aus., Dr Fischer **1995** £24.48 (SAV)
Piesporter Goldtröpfchen Riesling Aus. Fuder 10, Haart **1993** £24.00 (JU)
Piesporter Goldtröpfchen Riesling Aus., Haart **1994** £24.50 (JU)
Scharzhofberger Riesling Spät., Egon Müller-Scharzhof **1995** £21.00 (JU)
Scharzhofberger Riesling Spät., Egon Müller-Scharzhof **1991** £26.15 (UB)
Zeltinger Sonnenuhr Riesling Aus., Selbach-Oster **1997** £21.00 (MV)

£30.00 → £59.99

Bernkasteler Badstube Riesling Aus., J J Prüm **1971** £41.13 (REI)
Bernkasteler Doctor Riesling Aus., Bergweiler **1985** £57.00 (UB)
Brauneberger Juffer Sonnenuhr Riesling Aus. Goldkapsul, Fritz Haag **1994** £34.00 (JU)
Eitelsbacher Karthäuserhofberg Riesling Eiswein, Karthäuserhof ½ bottle **1995** £49.00 (JU)

Oz Clarke's Wine Buying Guide
is an annual publication.
We welcome your suggestions for next year's edition.

Erdener Prälat Riesling Aus., Dr Loosen **1989** £33.42 (NO)
Erdener Prälat Riesling Aus. Goldkapsul, Dr Loosen **1998** £35.00 (YOU)
Erdener Prälat Riesling Aus. Goldkapsul, Dr Loosen **1995** £34.83 (NO)
Erdener Treppchen Riesling Aus. Goldkapsul, Dr Loosen **1994** £50.71 (NO)
Maximin-Grünhäuser Abtsberg Riesling Eiswein, Schubert ½ bottle **1996** £50.00 (JU)
Maximin-Grünhäuser Abtsberg Riesling Aus. Fuder 47, Schubert **1994** £40.00 (JU)
Maximin-Grünhäuser Abtsberg Riesling Aus. Fuder 96, Schubert **1989** £47.00 (JU)
Maximin-Grünhäuser Herrenberg Riesling Aus., Schubert **1976** £40.00 (CRO)
Mulheimer Helenenkloster Riesling Eiswein, Richter ½ bottle **1998** £38.60 (MON)
Mulheirner Helenenkloster Riesling Eiswein, Richter ½ bottle **1995** £30.00 (FORT)
Mulheimer Helenenkloster Riesling Eiswein, Richter ½ bottle **1993** £49.50 (UB)
Piesporter Goldtröpfchen Riesling Aus. Goldkapsul, Haart **1995** £37.00 (JU)
Scharzhofberger Aus. Fuder 29, Egon Müller-Scharzhof **1990** £59.00 (JU)
Scharzhofberger Riesling Aus. Fuder 20, Egon Müller-Scharzhof **1993** £59.00 (JU)
Scharzhofberger Riesling Aus. Fuder 25, Egon Müller-Scharzhof **1989** £49.00 (JU)
Wehlener Sonnenuhr Riesling Aus. Goldkapsul, J J Prüm **1995** £43.00 (JU) £57.46 (TW)

Over £60.00

Bernkasteler Doctor Riesling Aus., H Thanisch **1989** £98.00 (JU)
Brauneberger Juffer Sonnenuhr Riesling Aus. Langegoldkapsel, Fritz Haag **1994** £87.00 (JU)
Brauneberger Juffer Sonnenuhr Riesling BA, Fritz Haag **1989** £128.00 (JU)
Eitelsbacher Marienholz Riesling Eiswein, Bischöfliches Konvikt **1989** £85.00 (JU)
Maximin-Grünhäuser Abtsberg Riesling Eiswein Fuder 135, Schubert ½ bottle **1996** £82.00 (JU)
Maximin-Grünhäuser Abtsberg Riesling BA, Schubert **1995** £80.00 (RAE)
Maximin-Grünhäuser Abtsberg Riesling Eiswein, Schubert **1993** £180.00 (JU)
Maximin-Grünhäuser Abtsberg Riesling BA, Schubert **1989** £220.00 (JU)
Maximin-Grünhäuser Abtsberg TBA, Schubert **1995** £200.00 (RAE)
Maximin-Grünhäuser Herrenberg Riesling Aus., Schubert **1989** £65.00 (UB)
Maximin-Grünhäuser Herrenberg Riesling BA, Schubert **1995** £71.00 (RAE)
Maximin-Grünhäuser Herrenberg Riesling BA, Schubert **1994** £125.00 (JU)
Maximin-Grünhäuser Herrenberg Riesling TBA, Schubert **1989** £330.00 (JU)
Ockfener Bockstein Riesling BA, Fischer **1989** £70.00 (JU)
Ockfener Bockstein Riesling Eiswein, Fischer **1989** £85.00 (JU)
Scharzhofberger Riesling Aus. Goldkapsul Fuder 23, Egon Müller-Scharzhof **1993** £140.00 (JU)
Urziger Würzgarten Riesling TBA, Mönchhof ½ bottle **1994** £165.00 (JU)
Wehlener Sonnenuhr Aus. Lange Goldkapsul, J J Prüm **1995** £136.00 (JU)

OTHER GERMAN WHITE

c. £8.00

Schloss Castell Silvaner Trocken, Fürstlich Castell'sches Domänenamt **1998** £7.95 (TAN)

ITALY

It's super-wine time again in Italy. But don't think Tuscany this time: think South

There's a new breed of super-wine from Italy. And it's about due, isn't it? We haven't had one for a while. And this time, just to make a nice change, it comes from the South.

To be precise, it's from Campania. The South has been the source of good value reds for some years now, although not everything from there is great. But these are. The difference is that they're not cheap. What did you expect?

We're talking about wines that start at perhaps £10 but go up to £20 or more. The reds are very much in the modern mould: big, rich, lush, with masses of ripe, soft tannins, and the sort of texture that makes you think of velvet and silk. The grapes – and here's the surprise – are not the internationally conventional ones. Instead they are mostly the southern Italian Aglianico, a grape that is only now showing just what it can do when treated properly.

There are whites, too. Chardonnay? Sauvignon? Forget it. These are from local grapes: Greco di Tufo and Fiano di Avellino. They are wonderfully honeyed and aromatic, with the richness of good white Burgundy or Alsace, and apricot and lime on the nose. Utterly delectable.

Look for Serpico red from Feudi di San Gregorio, Terredora's Greco di Tufo and Mastroberardino's Fiano di Avellino.

GRAPE VARIETIES

AGLIANICO (red) A southern grape at its most impressive in Aglianico del Vulture (Basilicata) and Taurasi (Campania).

BARBERA (red) The most prolific grape of the North-West, with high acidity and a sweet-sour, raisiny taste or even a brown-sugar sweetness. Some are lighter but intensely fruity. The grape does best in the Langhe hills around Alba in the hands of *Altare, Conterno-Fantino, Aldo Conterno, Gaja.*

BONARDA (red) Low acid, rich, plummy reds, often with a liquoricy, chocolaty streak. It's found most often in Emilia-Romagna where it is blended with Barbera as Gutturnio; also found in the Oltrepò Pavese.

CABERNET FRANC (red) Fairly widely grown in the North-East of Italy, especially in Alto Adige, Trentino, Veneto and Friuli. It can make gorgeous grassy, yet juicy-fruited reds – wines that are easy to drink young but also capable of aging.

CABERNET SAUVIGNON (red) Very successful in the North-East and Tuscany. Check out *Gaja*'s *Darmagi*, *Poliziano*'s *Le Stanze* and Bordeaux-inspired *Tassinaia* and *Lupicaia* from *Tenuta del Terriccio*.

CANNONAU (red) Sardinian name for Grenache. Makes warm, full-blooded wine, sometimes DOC, usually inexpensive. Look for *Argiolas, Giuseppe Gabbas, Giggi Picciau, Meloni, Sella & Mosca, Tonino Arcadu.*

CHARDONNAY (white) The typical Italian style is unoaked: lean, floral and sharply balanced from the Alto Adige, or try *Zeni* (Trentino) and *Gradnik* (Friuli). Oak-aged styles can be spicy and exciting, or just overoaked. Try *Gaja, Marchesi di Gresy* and *Pio Cesare* in Piedmont, *Zanella* in Lombardy, *Maculan* in the Veneto, *Caparzo (Le Grance)* and *Avignonesi (Il Marzocco)* in Tuscany, *Planeta* in Sicily. Many vary from year to year, and producers don't all have their winemaking sorted out.

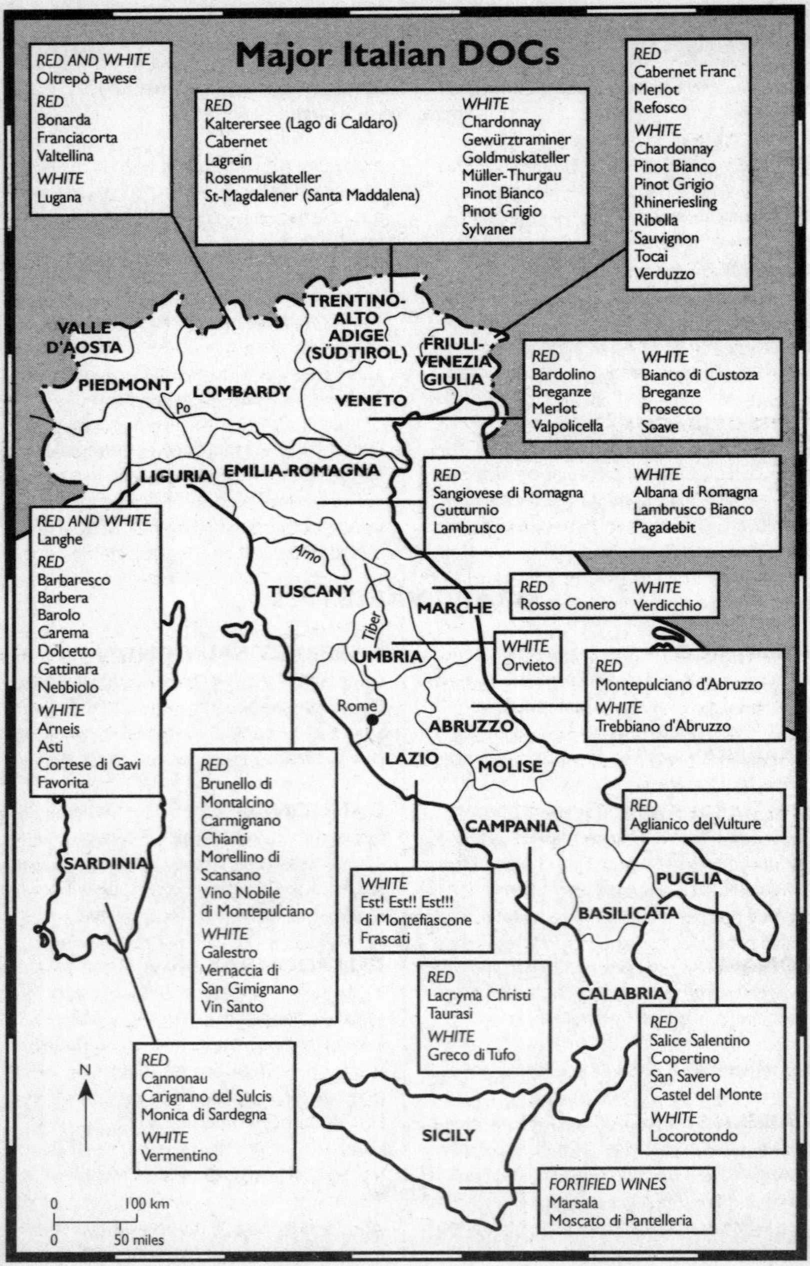
Major Italian DOCs
RED AND WHITE
Oltrepò Pavese
RED
Bonarda
Franciacorta
Valtellina
WHITE
Lugana
RED
Kalterersee (Lago di Caldaro)
Cabernet
Lagrein
Rosenmuskateller
St-Magdalener (Santa Maddalena)
WHITE
Chardonnay
Gewürztraminer
Goldmuskateller
Müller-Thurgau
Pinot Bianco
Pinot Grigio
Sylvaner
RED
Cabernet Franc
Merlot
Refosco
WHITE
Chardonnay
Pinot Bianco
Pinot Grigio
Rhineriesling
Ribolla
Sauvignon
Tocai
Verduzzo
VALLE D'AOSTA
PIEDMONT
LOMBARDY
Po
TRENTINO-ALTO ADIGE (SÜDTIROL)
FRIULI-VENEZIA GIULIA
VENETO
RED
Bardolino
Breganze
Merlot
Valpolicella
WHITE
Bianco di Custoza
Breganze
Prosecco
Soave
LIGURIA
EMILIA-ROMAGNA
RED
Sangiovese di Romagna
Gutturnio
Lambrusco
WHITE
Albana di Romagna
Lambrusco Bianco
Pagadebit
RED AND WHITE
Langhe
RED
Barbaresco
Barbera
Barolo
Carema
Dolcetto
Gattinara
Nebbiolo
WHITE
Arneis
Asti
Cortese di Gavi
Favorita
Arno
TUSCANY
Tiber
MARCHE
RED
Rosso Conero
WHITE
Verdicchio
UMBRIA
WHITE
Orvieto
RED
Montepulciano d'Abruzzo
WHITE
Trebbiano d'Abruzzo
Rome
ABRUZZO
LAZIO
MOLISE
RED
Brunello di Montalcino
Carmignano
Chianti
Morellino di Scansano
Vino Nobile di Montepulciano
WHITE
Galestro
Vernaccia di San Gimignano
Vin Santo
RED
Aglianico del Vulture
CAMPANIA
SARDINIA
WHITE
Est! Est!! Est!!! di Montefiascone
Frascati
PUGLIA
BASILICATA
RED
Lacryma Christi
Taurasi
WHITE
Greco di Tufo
CALABRIA
RED
Salice Salentino
Copertino
San Savero
Castel del Monte
WHITE
Locorotondo
RED
Cannonau
Carignano del Sulcis
Monica di Sardegna
WHITE
Vermentino
N
SICILY
FORTIFIED WINES
Marsala
Moscato di Pantelleria
0
100 km
0
50 miles

DOLCETTO (red) Usually light and refreshing with a bitter-cherry twist, though some producers in Alba, notably *Mascarello*, make it with attitude. Only age the best.

GARGANEGA (white) The principal grape of Soave, soft yet green-apple fresh when well made. Too much characterless Trebbiano Toscano spoils cheaper blends.

GEWÜRZTRAMINER (white) Most plantings are of the less flavoursome Traminer, rather than the spicier Gewürztraminer of Alsace. Needs some time in bottle to develop perfume.

GRECO/GRECHETTO (white) Greco makes crisp, pale and refreshing wines with lightly spicy overtones in the South. Grechetto is part of the same family and its delicious, nutty, aniseed character adds dramatically to Trebbiano-dominated blends in central Italy. It sometimes surfaces under its own colours in Umbria: try *Adanti*.

LAGREIN (red) Local grape of the Alto Adige and Trentino, making delicious, dark reds, strongly plum-sweet when young, aging slowly to a smoky, creamy softness. It also makes a good rosé, Lagrein Kretzer.

MALVASIA (white) This name and Malvoisie apply to a range of grape varieties, some not related. Malvasia is found mostly in Tuscany, Umbria and Lazio, giving a full, creamy nuttiness to dry whites like Frascati. It also produces brilliant, rich dessert wines with the density of thick brown-sugar syrup and the sweetness of raisins in Sardinia and the islands of Lipari north of Sicily.

MERLOT (red) Widely planted in the North-East. Often good in Friuli; provides lots of jug wine in the Veneto but when blended with Cabernet Sauvignon by *Loredan Gasparini* (Venegazzù) or *Fausto Maculan* (Trentino) achieves greater stature. Other Cabernet/Merlot blends are produced by *Mecvini* in the Marches and Trentino's *Bossi Fedrigotti* (Foianeghe). *Avignonesi* and *Castello di Ama* in Tuscany are promising, while *Ornellaia*'s *Masseto* (also Tuscany) is outstanding. It is becoming extremely fashionable.

MONTEPULCIANO (red) A much underrated grape. Yes, it is tough, and yes it is tannic, but it also has lots of plummy, herby fruit behind that toughness. *Banfi* in Montalcino has high hopes for it.

MOSCATO (white) The Alto Adige has various Muscats, including Rosenmuskateller and Goldmuskateller, making dry wines to equal the Muscats of Alsace and sweet ones of unrivalled fragrance. But it is at its best in Piedmont with the delicious, grapy, sweetish fizz, Asti, and Moscato Naturale, a heartily perfumed sweet wine. Moscato is best young, but *Ivaldi*'s Passito from Strevi can age beautifully. It also makes fine dessert wines on the island of Pantelleria, near Sicily.

NEBBIOLO (red) The big, tough grape of the North-West, making – unblended – the famous Barolos and Barbarescos as well as Gattinara, Ghemme, Carema, Spanna and plain Nebbiolo. This is a surly, fierce grape, producing wines that can be dark, chewy, unyielding and harsh behind a shield of tannin and acidity for the first few years; but which then blossom out into a remarkable richness full of chocolate, raisins, prunes, and an austere perfume of tobacco, pine and herbs. The newer style still has a fairly hefty whack of tannin, but clever wine-making sheaths this in sleek and velvety fruit. These are ready much sooner. A few growers (*Altare, Clerico, Conterno-Fantino* and *Voerzio*) are producing some superb wines using barriques, or blending it with Barbera, or both. Most are sold under the Langhe DOC.

PINOT BIANCO (white) Produces some of its purest, honeyed flavours in the Alto Adige, and can do very well in Friuli where the best are buttery and full.

PRIMITIVO (red) Genetically identical to California's Zinfandel, this is an increasingly popular variety in the South, combining outstanding ripeness and concentration with knockout alcoholic power.

RHEINRIESLING/RIESLING RENANO (white) The true German Riesling is grown in the Alto Adige for sharp, green, refreshing, steely dry wines. It can be OK, and slightly fatter, in Friuli and Lombardy. Riesling Italico, nothing to do with real Riesling, is the lesser Olasz/Laski/Welsch Rizling, still good if it's fresh.

SANGIOVESE (red) The mainstay of Chianti and all the other major Tuscan DOCGs. The wines have in common an austere, tea-like edge balanced by rich fruit. But the grape changes character when planted in the cool hills of Chianti, the warm clay soil of the coastal strip or the arid slopes of Montalcino. This sensitivity also explains why many vineyards in Chianti Classico don't produce the quality they should: the soil is too rich, the slopes too gentle and the density of planting too high. This is the lesson people are now learning.

SAUVIGNON BLANC (white) Spicy, grassy and refreshing from the Alto Adige and Friuli, though the style is usually more subtle than New World Sauvignon. Try *Avignonesi, Banfi, Castellare* and *Volpaia*.

SCHIAVA (red) Light reds with a unique taste that veers between smoked ham and strawberries. It's found in the Alto Adige, where the locals call it Vernatsch.

SYLVANER (white) Grown very high in the northern valleys of the Alto Adige, at its best this is dry, lemon-crisp and delicious.

TREBBIANO (white) Trebbiano Toscano is all too easy to grow, yielding mountains of grapes which make fruitless, sulphured wine. Trebbiano di Soave, the Veneto clone, is much better. Lugana can be a Trebbiano DOC of character (*Zenato* is good). Abruzzo's strain *can* be tasty from *Pepe, Tenuta del Priore* and *Valentini*.

VERNACCIA (white) We mostly just see two types of Vernaccia. In Sardinia Vernaccia di Oristano is a sort of Italian sherry, best dry – when it has a marvellous mix of floral scents, nutty weight and taunting sourness – but also medium and sweet. Vernaccia di San Gimignano *can* be Tuscany's best traditional white – full, golden, peppery but with a softness of hazelnuts and angelica. *Fagiuoli* and *Teruzzi & Puthod* show what can be done.

WINE REGIONS

AGLIANICO DEL VULTURE, DOC (Basilicata; red) Superb, thick-flavoured red from gaunt Monte Vulture, in the wilds of Italy's 'instep'. The colour isn't particularly deep, but the tremendous almond paste and chocolate fruit is matched by a tough, dusty feel and quite high acidity. What's more, it's *not* very expensive. *Fratelli d'Angelo* (especially barriqued *Canneto d'Angelo*) and *Paternoster* are both good.

ALBANA DI ROMAGNA, DOCG (Emilia-Romagna; white) Can be dry or sweet, still or slightly fizzy, or very fizzy, and usually uninspiring. At its best, the dry version can be delicately scented with an almondy finish. The only good producers are *Fattoria Paradiso* and *Zerbina*.

ALTO ADIGE various **DOCs** (red, white, rosé) Wines from these dizzily steep slopes are much more Germanic than Italian. The reds are attractive light wines made from the Vernatsch/Schiava grape, especially Kalterersee and St Magdalener. Cabernet, Pinot Nero, Lagrein and the tea-rose-scented Rosenmuskateller all make reds – and rosés – with stuffing and personality. Whites are light, dry and intensely fresh wines with spice and plenty of fruit, providing the producers haven't been too greedy about yields, which some of them are. Best: *Castello Schwanburg, Haas, Hofstätter, Lageder, Tiefenbrunner, Walch,* and *St Michael-Eppan, Schreckbichl* and *Terlan* co-ops.

ARNEIS (Piedmont; white) Potentially stunning, apples-pears-and-liquorice-flavoured wines from an ancient white grape of the same name, with high prices to match. They have something of the structure of dry Mosel Riesling. Best producers: *Arneis di Montebertotto* by *Castello di Neive, Deltetto, Bruno Giacosa, Malvirà, Negro, Vietti, Voerzio.*

ASTI, DOCG (Piedmont; white) At its best it's wonderfully frothy, fruit-bursting young wine. Go for *Canelli, Cantina Duca d'Asti, Martini, Elio Perrone, Santo Stefano,* and don't even think of aging it.

BARBARESCO, DOCG (Piedmont; red) Toughness and tannin are the hallmarks of the Nebbiolo, Barbaresco's only grape, but there's also a delicious soft, strawberryish maturity, edged with smoke, herbs and pine. Expect more softness and finesse than in Barolo. Best: *Luigi Bianco, Castello di Neive, Cigliuti, Giuseppe Cortese, Gaja, Bruno Giacosa, Glicine, Marchesi di Gresy, Moresco, Pasquero, Pelissero, Pertinace, Pio Cesare, Produttori del Barbaresco, Roagna, Scarpa, La Spinona* and *Vietti.*

BARBERA, DOC (Piedmont and others; red) Italy's second most widely planted red vine after Sangiovese makes a good, gutsy wine, usually with a resiny, herby bite, insistent acidity and forthright, dry raisin sort of fruit. It is best in Piedmont as Barbera d'Alba or d'Asti, and also in Lombardy under the Oltrepò Pavese DOC.

BARDOLINO, DOC (Veneto; red, rosé) Pale-pinky reds with a frail, wispy cherry fruit and a slight bitter snap to the finish. There are also a few fuller, rounder wines like *Boscaini's Le Canne* which can take some aging. Also *Arvedi d'Emilei, Cavalchina, Gardoni, Guerrieri-Rizzardi, Lenotti, Masi* (*Fresco* and *La Vegrona*), *Portalupi, Le Vigne di San Pietro, Zeni.*

ITALIAN CLASSIFICATIONS

Little more than 13 per cent of the massive Italian wine harvest comes under the heading of DOC or DOCG, and the regulations are treated in a fairly cavalier manner by many growers. Some producers choose to operate outside the regulations and classify their – frequently exceptional – wine simply as vino da tavola, the lowest grade. A new law means that more of these will come under the DOC umbrella.

Vino da Tavola This currently applies to absolutely basic stuff but also to some maverick wines of the highest class, although many of these are now classified as IGT.

Indicazione Geografiche Tipici (or IGT for short) This applies to wines which are typical of their regions, but which do not qualify for DOC. It is equivalent to vin de pays.

Denominazione di Origine Controllata (DOC) This applies to wines from specified grape varieties, grown in delimited zones and aged by prescribed methods. Most of Italy's traditionally well-known wines are DOC, but more are added every year.

Denominazione di Origine Controllata e Garantita (DOCG) The top tier – a tighter form of DOC with more stringent restrictions on grape types, yields and a tasting panel. The new law is supposed to give recognition to particularly good vineyard sites.

BAROLO, DOCG (Piedmont; red)The remarkable flavours of the Nebbiolo – plums and cherries, tobacco and chocolate, liquorice and violets – whirl like a maelstrom in the best wines. Modern winemaking accentuates these flavours, and makes wines that are drinkable in five years rather than 20.

Producers are fighting for official classification of the top sites: single vineyard wines can be the absolute best (and absolute most expensive) but because anyone's free to put any old vineyard name on the label, standards are not consistent. Best producers: *Altare, Azelia, Borgogno, Bovio, Brovia, Cavallotto, Ceretto, Clerico, Aldo* and *Giacomo Conterno, Conterno-Fantino, Cordero di Montezemolo, Fontanafredda* (only its *cru* wines), *Bruno Giacosa, Marcarini, Bartolo* and *Giuseppe Mascarello, Pio Cesare, Pira, Prunotto, Ratti, Rocche dei Manzoni, Sandrone, Scarpa, Scavino, Sebaste, Vajra, Vietti* and *Voerzio* (*Roberto* and *Gianni*).

BIANCO DI CUSTOZA, DOC (Veneto; white) A Soave lookalike, though generally better. *Gorgo, Portalupi, Santa Sofia, Tedeschi, Le Tende, Le Vigne di San Pietro, Zenato* are good.

BOLGHERI, DOC (Tuscany; red, white, rosé) A DOC for all colours, including reds based on Cabernet, Merlot or Sangiovese in various combinations, and even a special category for *Sassicaia*, previously a vino da tavola. It has intense Cabernet character but higher acidity and slightly leaner profile than most New World Cabernets. It needs eight to ten years to approach its best. 1994, '96, '97 and '99 are all excellent. Pre-1994 vintages are labelled as vino da tavola.

BREGANZE, DOC (Veneto; red, white) Little-known but quite good wines from near Vicenza. *Maculan* is best, and makes a stunning dessert wine, *Torcolato*.

BRUNELLO DI MONTALCINO, DOCG (Tuscany; red) A big, strong neighbour of Chianti. In the right hands it can achieve an amazing combination of flavours: blackberries, raisins, pepper, acidity, tannin and a haunting sandalwood perfume, all bound together by the austere richness of liquorice and fierce black chocolate. Tops: *Altesino, Argiano, Biondi Santi, Campogiovanni, Caparzo, Casanova, Case Basse, Il Casello, Castelgiocondo, Col d'Orcia, Colombini, Costanti, Il Greppone Mazzi, Pertimali, Poggio Antico, Il Poggione, Sassetti, Talenti, Val di Suga, Banfi*. Barbaresco star *Angelo Gaja* has been here since 1994.

CAREMA, DOC (Piedmont; red) The most refined of the Nebbiolo wines. *Luigi Ferrando* is the best producer; the wines need five to six years to be at their best.

CARMIGNANO, DOCG (Tuscany; red) A small enclave inside the Chianti zone where the soft, clear blackcurranty fruit of Cabernet Sauvignon makes a delicious blend with the somewhat stark flavours of the Sangiovese. There is also some good toasty, creamy rosé and some sweet *vin santo*. *Capezzana* is the original estate and the only one which is regularly seen here.

CHIANTI, DOCG and CHIANTI CLASSICO, DOCG (Tuscany; red) There are two basic styles of Chianti. The first is the sharp young red with a rather attractive taste: almost a tiny bit sour, but backed up by good, raisiny-sweet fruit, a rather stark, peppery bite and tobacco-like spice. The second type has usually been matured for several years. Expect a range of slightly raw strawberry, raspberry and blackcurrant flavours backed up by a herby, tobaccoey spice and a grapeskins roughness that is demanding but exciting. Chianti Classico's separate DOCG allows for pure Sangiovese wines, should the producer wish, thus potentially bringing many SuperTuscans back into the fold. Not many seem to want to come. Best: *Badia a Coltibuono, Castellare, Castell'in Villa, Castello di Ama, Castello dei Rampolla, Castello di San Polo in Rosso, Castello di Volpaia, Felsina*

Berardenga, Fontodi, Monsanto, Montesodi and *Nipozzano* (*Frescobaldi*), *Isole e Olena, Pagliarese, Riserva Tenute del Marchese* and *Peppoli* (both *Antinori*), *Riecine, San Felice, Selvapiana, Vecchie Terre di Montefili, Vicchiomaggio, Villa di Vetrice*.

The Chianti territory is divided into seven sub-zones: Classico, Colli Aretini, Colli Fiorentini, Colli Senesi, Colline Pisane, Montalbano and Rufina. Most wines, however, are simply labelled 'Chianti'.

COLLI EUGANEI, DOC (Veneto; red, white) *Vignalta* produces a Cabernet Riserva and Merlot-based *Gemola* of good concentration.

COPERTINO, DOC (Puglia; red) The blend of Negroamaro and Malvasia Nera produces robust reds that can be elegant, and great bargains. Try the *Copertino* co-op.

DOLCETTO, some **DOC** (Piedmont; red) At its best, delicious. It's a full but soft, fresh, and dramatically fruity red, usually for gulping down fast and young, though some will age. The sub-regions of Asti and Acqui tend to produce the lightest. *Altare, Castello di Neive, Clerico, Aldo Conterno, Giacomo Conterno, Marcarini, Mascarello, Oddero, Pasquero, Prunotto, Ratti, Sandrone, Scavino, Vajra, Vietti* and *Voerzio* are wonderful.

ERBALUCE DI CALUSO, DOC (Piedmont; white) Half the price of Gavi, with a soft, creamy flavour. *Boratto, Ferrando* and *Marbelli* are good; *Boratto* also makes a rich but refreshing Caluso Passito.

FIANO DI AVELLINO, DOC (Campania; white) Inexplicably famous, though *Mastroberardino*'s single-vineyard *Vignadora* has a brilliant spring flowers scent and honey, peaches and pearskins taste.

FRANCIACORTA, DOCG (Lombardy; red, white) Champagne method fizz made from Pinots Bianco and Nero and Chardonnay grapes. Best are *Bellavista* and *Ca' del Bosco*, though *Cavalleri, Monte Rosa, Ricci Curbastro* and *Uberti* are also recommended. The DOC of Terre di Franciacorta makes fine still white from Pinot and Chardonnay, and tasty red.

ON THE CASE
Famous DOCs and DOCGs can be outrageously expensive, famous growers even more so. Check out wines from Puglia, Basilicata and Abruzzo instead

FRASCATI, DOC (Lazio; white) Most is bland and stale, though the best has a lovely, fresh, nutty feel with an attractive tang of slightly sour cream. *Colli di Catone, Villa Catone* and *Villa Romana* are reliable. Or try *Fontana Candida*'s limited releases, *San Marco's Racemo* and *Villa Simone*.

FRIULI, some **DOC** (red, white) Six different zones, of which Friuli Grave DOC produces the most. The reds are marked by vibrant fruit. Refosco has a memorable taste in the tar-and-plums mould – sharpened up with a fresh grassy acidity. Best: *Borgo Conventi, Ca' Ronesca, Collavini, La Fattoria, Pintar, Russiz Superiore*. Very good fruity and fresh varietal whites come from *Abbazia di Rosazzo, Attems, Borgo Conventi, Collavini, Dri, Eno Friulia, Gravner, Jermann, Livio Felluga* (especially *Molamatta*), *Puiatti, Ronchi di Cialla, Schiopetto, Villa Russiz, Volpe Pasini*. The almost mythical Picolit sweet wine is beautifully made by *Al Rusignul*.

GALESTRO (Tuscany; white) A name created to mop up the Trebbiano and Malvasia no longer used in red Chianti. Low alcohol, simple, lemony, greengage taste, high-tech style, best on its home territory.

GATTINARA, DOCG (Piedmont; red) Nebbiolo-based red that can be good but often has an unappealingly volatile character. *Antoniolo, Brugo, Dessilani* and *Travaglini* are reliable.

> **ON THE CASE**
> *Italians are becoming less nervous of perfumed white wines. It's worth taking a fresh look at good Arneis, Traminer and Sauvignon Blanc*

GAVI, DOC (Piedmont; white) Cortese is the grape, its wine dry and sharp, like Sauvignon minus the tang, and fairly full, like Chardonnay without the class. Best: *Arione, Ca' Bianca, Chiarlo (Fior di Rovere), Deltetto.*

KALTERERSEE/LAGO DI CALDARO, DOC (Alto Adige; red) Good, light, soft red with an unbelievable flavour of home-made strawberry jam and woodsmoke, made from the Schiava (alias Vernatsch) grape. It is best as a young gulper. Best producers: *Gries* co-op, *Lageder, Muri-Gries, Hans Rottensteiner, St Michael-Eppan* co-op, *Tiefenbrunner* and *Walch.*

LACRYMA CHRISTI DEL VESUVIO, DOC (Campania; red, white) The most famous wine of Campania and Naples. It can be red, white, dry or sweet: *Mastroberardino*'s is the best.

LAGREIN DUNKEL, some **DOC** (Alto Adige; red) Dark, chewy red with a tarry roughness jostling with chocolate-smooth ripe fruit. Look for the *Gries* co-op, *Lageder, Muri-Gries, Niedermayr* and *Tiefenbrunner* (also very good pink Lagrein Kretzer).

LAMBRUSCO, some **DOC** (Emilia-Romagna; red, white) Good Lambrusco – lightly fizzy, low in alcohol, dry to vaguely sweet – should *always* have a sharp, almost rasping acid bite to it. Look for a DOC, from Sorbara, Santa Croce or Castelvetro. Most here is not DOC and softened for the UK market, but *Cavicchioli* is proper stuff.

LANGHE, DOC (Piedmont, red, white) This recent DOC covers wines previously sold as vino da tavola. Look for tasty young Langhe Nebbiolo from good Barolo and Barbaresco producers at attractive prices.

LUGANA, DOC (Lombardy; white) The Trebbiano di Lugana grape makes whites of solid structure and some fruity flavours from *Ca' dei Frati, Premiovini, Provenza, Visconti* and *Zenato.*

MARSALA (Sicily; fortified) This has, at its best, a delicious, deep brown-sugar sweetness allied to a cutting, lip-tingling acidity that makes it surprisingly refreshing for a fortified dessert wine. The rare dry Marsala Vergine is also good. But a once-great name is now in decline. A few good producers keep the flag flying: *De Bartoli* outclasses all the rest, and even makes an intense, beautifully aged, but *unfortified* non-DOC range called *Vecchio Samperi*. His *Josephine Dore* is in the style of *fino* sherry.

MONTEFALCO, DOC and **SAGRANTINO DI MONTEFALCO, DOCG** (Umbria; red) Montefalco Rosso is tasty and often stylish. Sagrantino is a red of great size and strength, that comes in a dry version or as sweet Passito, using semi-dried grapes. Both can age impressively from *Adanti, Antonelli* and *Caprai.*

MONTEPULCIANO D'ABRUZZO, DOC (Abruzzo; red) Good ones are citrus-fresh and plummily rich, juicy yet tannic, ripe yet with a tantalizing sour bite. Best: *Casal Thaulero* co-op, *Colle Secco, Illuminati, Mezzanotte, Pepe* and *Valentini.*

MORELLINO DI SCANSANO, DOC (Tuscany, red) A similar grape-mix to that of Chianti gives austere wines with earthy tannins, deep, ripe fruit, and tarry spice. Best: *Le Pupille, Mantellassi, Moris Farms.*

MOSCATO D'ASTI, DOCG (Piedmont; white) Sweet, slightly fizzy wine that captures all the crunchy green freshness of a fistful of ripe table grapes. Heavenly ones come from the following:

Ascheri, Michele Chiarlo, Dogliotti, Gallo d'Oro, Gatti, Bruno Giacosa, Rivetti, Vietti, I Vignaioli di Santo Stefano.

MOSCATO PASSITO DI PANTELLERIA (Pantelleria; white) Big, heavy wine with a great wodge of rich Muscat fruit and a good slap of alcoholic strength.

OLTREPÒ PAVESE, some **DOC** (Lombardy; red, white, rosé) This covers just about anything, including dry whites, sweet whites and fizz. Almost the only wine we see is non-DOC Champagne-method fizz based on Pinot Grigio/Nero/Bianco, and some red, which is good, substantial stuff.

ORVIETO, DOC (Umbria; white) Generally modern, pale and dry, sometimes peach-perfumed and honeyed. Best: *Antinori* (*Cervaro della Sala* vino da tavola), *Barberani, Bigi* (*Cru Torricella Secco* and medium-sweet *Cru Orzalume Amabile*), *Decugnano dei Barbi, Palazzone, Scambia*. Sweet, unctuous, noble rot-affected wines (*Antinori*'s *Muffato della Sala* and *Barberani's Calcaia*) are rarely seen but delicious.

PIEMONTE, DOC (Piedmont, red, white) Applies to quality wines not covered by the other DOCs of Piedmont. The reds include Barbera, Bonarda, Brachetto and Grignolino. Whites, which may be sparkling, come from Chardonnay, Cortese, Moscato, Pinot Bianco, Pinto Grigio and Pinot Nero.

POMINO, DOC (Tuscany; red, white) The DOC also includes some sweet *vin santo*. The red, based on Sangiovese with Canaiolo, Cabernet and Merlot, becomes rich, soft, velvety and spicy with age. The only producers are *Frescobaldi* and *Giuntini*.

PROSECCO, some **DOC** (Veneto; white) Still or sparkling, it's a lovely fresh, bouncy, light white, often off-dry. The best is labelled Cartizze. Try *Canevel, Carpenè Malvolti, Le Case Bianche, Collavini, Zonin.*

ROSSO CONERO, DOC (Marches; red) Very good, sturdy red full of herb and fruit flavours, sometimes with some oak for richness. Best: *Bianchi, Garofoli, Marchetti, Mecvini* and *San Lorenzo (Umani Ronchi)*.

ROSSO DI MONTALCINO, DOC (Tuscany; red) DOC for producers of Brunello who want a second wine, perhaps for declassifying part of their crop. Softer, more approachable and cheaper than Brunello di Montalcino.

ROSSO DI MONTEPULCIANO, DOC (Tuscany; red) This is the DOC for 'lesser' Montepulciano, aged for less time in the cellar. Much the same style as big brother, but lighter, more approachable and drinkable younger.

SALICE SALENTINO, DOC (Puglia; red) Impressive wines, deep in colour, ripe and chocolaty, acquiring hints of roast chestnuts and prunes with age. Look for *Candido, Leone De Castris, Taurino, Vallone.*

SOAVE, DOC (Veneto; white) Usually attractive, soft, fair-priced white; slightly nutty, even creamy. Drink it as young as possible. *Bertani, Pasqua* and *Zenato* make a lot of decent basic stuff. On a higher level are *Anselmi* (try *Capitel Foscarino*) and *Pieropan,* especially single-vineyard wines *Calvarino* and *La Rocca*. Other good ones are *Bolla*'s *Castellaro, Boscaini, Costalunga, Inama, Lenotti, Santi*'s *Monte Carbonare, Tedeschi*'s *Monte Tenda, Zenato* and the local co-operative's *Costalta. Anselmi* also makes a *Recioto di Soave I Capitelli* which is shockingly good in its pungent sweet-sour way, and *Pieropan*'s unoaked *Recioto di Soave* is gorgeously redolent of apricots. Quality is better than it used to be, though it still pays to look for a top producer.

SPANNA (Piedmont; red) A Nebbiolo-based wine with a lovely raisin and chocolate flavour in the old style. Even cheap Spannas are a pretty good bet.

TAURASI, DOCG (Campania; red) Remarkable, plummy yet bitingly austere red, sometimes short on fruit or long on tannin, but worth trying. Tops: *Caggiano, Feudi di San Gregorio, Mastroberardino.*

TOCAI, DOC (Friuli, Veneto; white) Full, aromatic, softly nutty, honeyed wines. Best producers include: *Abbazia di Rosazzo, Borgo Conventi, Cà Bolani, Caccese, Collavini, Livio Felluga, Lazzarini, Maculan, Schiopetto, Villa Russiz, Volpe Pasini.*

TORGIANO, DOC and **DOCG** (Umbria; red) The region's fame rests on *Lungarotti*. The reds are strong, plummy, sometimes overbearing, usually carrying the trade name *Rubesco*. Quality is perhaps not as tip-top as it once was. Single-vineyard *Monticchio* and *San Giorgio* Cabernet Sauvignon are exciting. Torgiano Rosso Riserva is DOCG. White wines are clean and good. Lungarotti also makes good *flor*-affected sherry-type wine called *Solleone.*

TRENTINO, DOC (red, white) Some of Italy's best Pinot Bianco and Chardonnay comes from here, as well as some interesting whites from Riesling, Müller-Thurgau and excellent dry Muscat. But until they stop grossly overproducing we're never going to see the full potential. Trento Classico DOC applies to Champagne-method sparkling wines. Look especially for *Conti Martini, Gaierhof, Istituto di San Michele, Mandelli, Pojer e Sandri, Spagnolli* and *Zeni.* Fair *vin santo* comes from *Pisoni* and *Simoncelli*. Reds are made either from local grape varieties such as Lagrein, Teroldego and Marzemino, or the likes of Cabernet, Merlot and Pinot Noir. Go for *Conti Martini, Foradori, Guerrieri-Gonzaga, Istituto di San Michele, Pojer e Sandri, de Tarczal* and *Zeni.*

VALPOLICELLA, DOC (Veneto; red) This *should* have delicious, light, cherry fruit and a bitter almond twist to the finish – a bit fuller and deeper than Bardolino with a hint more sourness. Superiore has been aged for a year before release. Most of the commercial stuff is compared locally to twice-skimmed milk – i.e. insipid. Producers with good flavours: *Allegrini, Boscaini, Corte Sant'Alda, Guerrieri-Rizzardi, Masi, Quintarelli, Le Ragose, Santi, Tedeschi, Zenato.*

There are a few single-vineyard wines, like *Masi*'s *Serègo Alighieri,* which are way ahead. They cost more, but *Allegrini*'s *La Grola* or *Tedeschi*'s *Ca' Nicalo* show what Valpolicella should be about. You might also look for wine made by the traditional *ripasso* method, in which new wine is pumped over the skins and lees of Recioto or Amarone, starting a re-fermentation and adding an exciting sweet-sour dimension. Try *Masi, Quintarelli* and *Tedeschi.*

Best of all is the weird and wonderful Amarone della Valpolicella. It's made from half-shrivelled grapes and has a brilliant array of flavours – sweet grapeskins,

MATURITY CHART

1990 Barolo

A superb year in Piedmont, but patience is needed for the tannins to soften

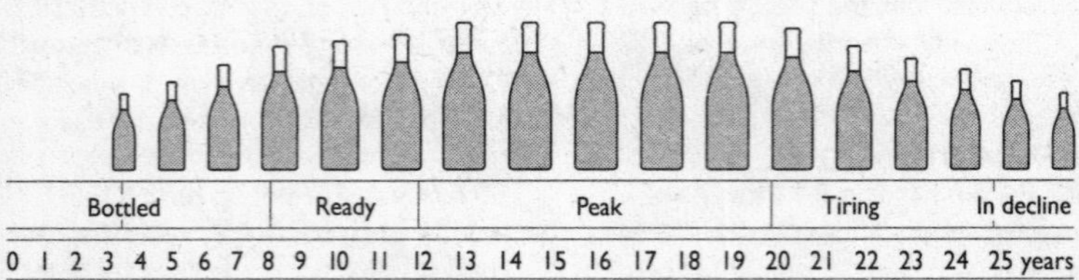

chocolate, plums and woodsmoke – and a shocking, penetrating sourness. The good stuff is about three times the price of simple Valpolicella, but it's still good value. Wine labelled as Recioto della Valpolicella will be sweet and may be excellent – but a little less strangely special. Best: *Allegrini, Bertani, Masi, Quintarelli, Le Ragose* and *Tedeschi.*

VALTELLINA, DOC (Lombardy; red) Slightly stringy Nebbiolo, not much seen over here.

VERDICCHIO, DOC (Marches; white) Reliable rather than exciting – usually extremely dry, lean, clean, nutty with a streak of dry honey, sharpened by slightly green acidity. *Fazi-Battaglia's* single-vineyard vino da tavola *Le Moie* shows the potential. There is also some fizz. The two leading areas are Verdicchio dei Castelli di Jesi and Verdicchio di Matelica. The rarer Matelica wines often have more flavour. *Bucci, Garafoli* and *Umani Ronchi* use new oak for their best wines. Also: *Brunori, Fabrini, Fazi-Battaglia, Mecvini, Monte Schiavo, Zaccagnini.*

VERDUZZO, DOC (Friuli and Veneto) This is usually a soft, nutty, low-acid yet refreshing light white. The DOC also includes a lovely, gentle fizz, and some of Italy's best sweet wines, in particular *Abbazia di Rosazzo's Amabile* and *Dri's Verduzzo di Ramandolo.*

VERNACCIA DI SAN GIMIGNANO DOCG (Tuscany) Can be attractively nutty, but is too often a model of bland neutrality. Good: *Fagiuoli, Falchini, Frigeni, San Quirico, Teruzzi & Puthod* and *La Torre.*

VINO NOBILE DI MONTEPULCIANO, DOCG (Tuscany) Like Chianti only more so: more pepper, acid and tannin, and a higher price, but the best has a marvellous dry fragrance reminiscent almost of sandalwood, backed up by good Sangiovese spice, and a strong plumskins-and-cherries fruit. Best producers: *Avignonesi, Bindella, Boscarelli, La Casalte, Fassati, Fattoria di Casale, Fattoria del Cerro, Fognano, Poliziano* and *Trerose.*

VIN SANTO Can be one of the great sweet wines, but too often vaguely raisiny and very dull. It *should* have all kinds of splendid, rich fruit flavours – apricots, apples, the chewiness of toffee, smoke and liquorice. Try *Avignonesi, La Calonica* or *Isole e Olena* in Tuscany or *Adanti* in Umbria.

PRODUCERS WHO'S WHO

ABBAZIA DELL'ANNUNZIATA ★★★★ (Piedmont) One of the great producers of Barolo. All the wines are full of excitement and strongly perfumed, and they develop wonderfully in the bottle.

ALLEGRINI ★★★★★ (Veneto) Splendid single-vineyard Valpolicellas, especially La Grola, Fieramonte and Palazzo della Torre. Top Amarone and Recioto. Also excellent vino da tavola, La Poja.

ELIO ALTARE ★★★★ (Piedmont) New wave producer – wines of firm structure and tannin behind perfumed fruit. Highly successful Barolo Vigna Arborina, very good Dolcetto and barrique-aged Barbera Vigna Larigi.

ALTESINO ★★★★ (Tuscany) Excellent Brunello and some good vini da tavola, notably under the names of Alte d'Altesi and Palazzo Altesi.

CASTELLO DI AMA ★★★★ (Tuscany) Excellent single-vineyard Chianti Classico: San Lorenzo, La Casuccia, Bellavista; also a Merlot, Vigna L'Apparita.

ANSELMI ★★★★★ (Veneto) Soave with character. Cru Capitel Foscarino is as good as it gets – as is his Recioto I Capitelli.

ANTINORI ★★★★ (Tuscany) One of the great names of Chianti. Excellent Chianti Classico from estates Pèppoli and Badia a Passignano; also Tignanello, the archetypal barrique-aged Sangiovese/ Cabernet blend. Solaia has more Cabernet. Orvieto estate, Castello della Sala, makes wonderful IGT white, Cervaro della Sala. Brother Ludovico Antinori makes Ornellaia, a Cabernet-based superstar, and outstanding Masseto Merlot.

AVIGNONESI ★★★★ (Tuscany) Serious Vino Nobile, and two excellent Chardonnays: Terre di Cortona, without oak, and Il Marzocco, oak-fermented and aged wine of considerable depth. I Grifi is barrel-aged Prugnolo and Cabernet Franc.

BADIA A COLTIBUONO ★★★ (Tuscany) Produces good Chianti and even better 'Sangioveto', an IGT Toscana made from old vines.

BANFI ★★★ (Tuscany) US-owned Montalcino winery making an excellent Brunello Poggio all'Oro, superb red blends, Summus and Excelsus, plus Tavernelle Cabernet and Mandrielle Merlot.

FATTORIA DEI BARBI ★★★★ (Tuscany) Traditional methods produce serious Brunello and Rosso di Montalcino, as well as Brusco dei Barbi, and a single-vineyard wine, Vigna Fiore.

BIONDI-SANTI ★★★ (Tuscany) Fabulously priced, but not always fabulous Brunello di Montalcino; old vintages are wonderful, new ones seem to be on the up.

BOLLA ★★★ (Veneto) Large scale producer of Soave and Valpolicella. Skip the basic wines and go for Valpolicella Jago.

BRAIDA-GIACOMO BOLOGNA ★★★ (Piedmont) Saw early the potential of Barbera in barrique: deep, balanced and rich *cru* Bricco dell' Uccellone impresses.

INSTANT CELLAR:
TUSCAN THRILLS

- **1999 Ansonica, Tenuta la Parrina, £6.99, Bennetts** Aromatic, well-structured white.
- **1999 Chianti Colli Senesi, Guicciardini Strozzi, £5.30, Ballantynes** Simple fresh Chianti which will last a couple of years. Lovely sour cherries flavour.
- **1997 Chianti Rufina, Selvapiana, £8.99, Philglas & Swiggot** Chianti is no longer cheap, so you might as well pay for a good producer. Good, chewy, bitter cherry fruit.
- **1997 Chianti Classico, Castello di Ama, £16.99, Wine Treasury** Concentrated Chianti from the cult estate of the moment.
- **1996 Camposilio, Vino da Tavola di Toscana, £14.45, Corney & Barrow** Mostly Sangiovese but 20% Cabernet, for a balance of elegance and power.
- **1998 Barco Reale di Carmignano, Capezzena, £6.75, Wine Society** An old favourite: elegant, perfumed and structured.
- **1995 Tricorno, Castello di Poppiano, £13.99, Great Western Wine** A Tuscan blend of Nebbiolo, Sangiovese, Barbera, Cabernet Sauvignon and Merlot. It's 'rich, robust and full-flavoured', apparently.

Equally good Bricco della Bigotta. Unoaked, youthful Barbera, La Monella. Good Moscato d'Asti and Brachetto d'Acqui.

CA'DEL BOSCO ★★★ (Lombardy) Good fizz from Franciacorta. Also vino da tavola called Maurizio Zanella, blended from both Cabernets and Merlot, which is expensive but terrific.

CAPARZO ★★★★ (Tuscany) High quality producer of Brunello di Montalcino and Rosso di Montalcino; also an oak-fermented Chardonnay called Le Grance, and Ca' del Pazzo, a barrique-aged blend of Cabernet Sauvignon and Sangiovese.

TENUTA DI CAPEZZANA ★★★★ (Tuscany) The leader in Carmignano, plus good Bordeaux blend, Ghiaie della Furba; Sangiovese-based Barco Reale; complex Vin Santo and delicious pink, Vin Ruspo.

CASTELLARE ★★★★ (Tuscany) Nice Chianti, splendid vino da tavola I Sodi di San Niccolò, with a little Malvasia Nera adding perfume to the Sangiovese.

CERETTO ★★★★ (Piedmont) Barolo Bricco Rocche Bricco Rocche (yes) and Barbaresco Bricco Asili are legendary with prices to match. Light Barbera and Dolcetto. Arneis is disappointing.

FATTORIA DEL CERRO ★★★ (Tuscany) Traditional producer of Vino Nobile, now working with barriques. Its best wine remains the DOCG Vino Nobile.

CLERICO ★★★★★ (Piedmont) Top modern producer; fine Nebbiolo-Barbera blend Arte, Barolo from two *crus* (Bricotto Bussia, Ciabot Mentin Ginestra).

ALDO CONTERNO ★★★★★ (Piedmont) Great Barolo, traditionally made, slow to mature but worth the wait. Barbera d'Alba, Langhe Nebbiolo and Chardonnay, and Dolcetto also good.

GIACOMO CONTERNO ★★★★★ (Piedmont) Aldo's brother, making excellent traditional Monfortino Barolo.

CONTERNO FANTINO ★★★★ (Barolo, Monforte) Guido Fantino and Diego Conterno have earned a reputation for fine Barolo from the Ginestra hillside. Rich but forward, perfumed wines.

PAOLO CORDERO DI MONTEZEMOLO ★★★ (Piedmont) The accent is on fruit. Standard-bearer is *cru* Monfalletto from La Morra. *Cru* Enrico VI is from Castiglione Falletto, refined, elegant, scented. Also Barbera and Dolcetto.

CARLO DELTETTO ★★★ (Roero, Canale) Good understated, intriguing whites from Arneis and Favorita. Reliable Roero and Gavi.

FELSINA BERARDENGA ★★★ (Tuscany) Winery very much on the up. Vigneto Rancia single-vineyard Chianti, I Sistri barrique-aged Chardonnay. Fontalloro Sangiovese aged in barrique for a year.

FONTODI ★★★ (Tuscany) Sleek Sangiovese, in the form of single-estate Chianto Classico or IGT red Flaccianello (plus white Meriggio, Pinot Bianco, Sauvignon and Traminer).

FRESCOBALDI ★★★ (Tuscany) The best Frescobaldi estate is Castello di Nipozzano. Also excellent Pomino, including an oak-aged white, Il Benefizio. Excellent Brunello from the Castelgiocondo estate, plus good white under the Capitolato label and fine Cabernet Mormoreto red. A joint venture with Mondavi of California has produced a high-priced red, Luce.

ANGELO GAJA ★★★★★ (Piedmont) Uses barriques for most wines, including all

MATURITY CHART

1995 Amarone

Can be drunk young, but it will improve for 10–15 years

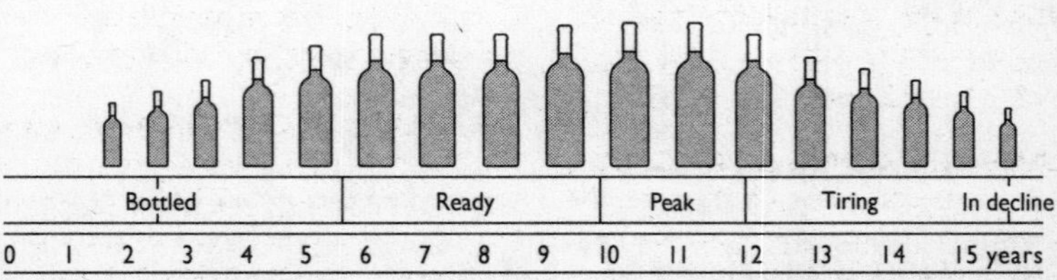

Barbarescos: Costa Russi, Sorì San Lorenzo, Sorì Tildìn. In the vanguard of Piedmontese Cabernet (Darmagi) and Chardonnay (Gaia and Rey) production. Also makes two Barberas, two Dolcettos, Freisa and a top Barolo from the Marenca Rivette vineyard.

BRUNO GIACOSA ★★★★★ (Piedmont) Traditional wines of, at their best, mind-blowing quality, especially Barbaresco *cru* Santo Stefano and, best of all, Vigna Rionda Barolo. Rich, concentrated but not overbearing, elegant. Also white Arneis and good fizz.

MARCHESI DI GRESY ★★★★★ (Piedmont) The leading site, Martinenga, produces Barbaresco, two *crus* – Camp Gros and Gaiun – and a non-wood-aged Nebbiolo called Martinenga; all are elegant. Notable Sauvignon and Chardonnay, too.

ISOLE E OLENA ★★★★ (Tuscany) Fine Chianti Classico. Also Cepparello, a rich pure Sangiovese wine, made from the oldest vines of the estate; outstanding sweet *vin santo* and a superb Syrah.

JERMANN (Friuli-Venezia Giulia) ★★★★ Characterful, subtle vini da tavola: oak-aged Vintage Tunina and Chardonnay 'Were Dreams, Now it is just Wine'. Plain Pinot Grigio and Riesling are also very good.

LAGEDER ★★★ (Alto Adige) Straightforward varietals are – well, straightforward. Single vineyard wines are far better: Sauvignon Lehenhof and Pinot Grigio Benefizium Porer.

LUNGAROTTI ★★★ (Umbria) The main name in Torgiano. Also Chardonnays, Miralduolo and Vigna I Palazzi. San Giorgio is Cabernet plus Sangiovese.

GIUSEPPE MASCARELLO ★★★★★ (Piedmont) Superb *cru* Barolo Monprivato. Also Villero and other *crus*. Barbera d'Alba Ginestra is notable. Excellent inky Dolcetto.

MASI ★★★★ (Veneto) Very good Soave and Valpolicella, especially Valpolicella Campo Fiorin. Brilliant Amarone and Recioto. Toar is oaky, cherryish new red vino da tavola.

MASTROBERARDINO ★★★★ (Campania) Leading southern producer. Noteworthy Taurasi, and whites including Fiano di Avellino and Greco di Tufo.

MONTEVERTINE ★★★★ (Tuscany) Outstanding Le Pergole Torte, a barrique-aged Sangiovese IGT Toscana, needs at least five years to open up. Il Sodaccio Sangiovese/Canaiolo can be drunk young.

CASTELLO DI NEIVE ★★★★ (Piedmont) Impeccable, finely crafted, austerely elegant Barbaresco from Santo Stefano. Barrique-aged Barbera from single *cru* Mattarello, firm, classic Dolcetto and revelatory Arneis.

FRATELLI ODDERO ★★★ (Piedmont) Barolo, Barbera and Dolcetto from vineyards in prime sites in the area, plus Barbaresco from bought-in grapes. Good roundness, balance, style and value.

PIEROPAN ★★★★★ (Veneto) Stunning Soave, in particular La Rocca and Calvarino, both single vineyards. Recioto Le Colombare is divine.

PIO CESARE ★★★ (Piedmont) Full spread of Barolo, Barbaresco, Nebbiolo d'Alba, Dolcetto, Barbera, Grignolino and Gavi. Wines are gaining elegance, harmony and balance, losing a bit of punch. Also makes Piodilei (barriqued Chardonnay).

POJER & SANDRI ★★★ (Trentino) Good quality in reds and whites, and particularly good spumante.

QUINTARELLI ★★★★★ (Veneto) Revelatory Valpolicella, especially Amarone and Recioto, though all are splendid.

ITALIAN VINTAGES

1999 Some growers reckon their 1999s are better than their 1998s; others think the opposite. Tuscany seems to have come off well. Overall, a decent rather than a great year.

1998 Patchy: go for Piedmontese reds and Tuscan reds, above all. Top Veneto growers will have made decent stuff.

1997 A very good year, but variable: some reds have low acidity and a slightly raisiny character. Central Italy produced excellent whites. Quantity is down, prices up.

1996 Very good for Piedmontese reds, pretty good for Tuscan reds. Variable elsewhere.

1995 Excellent Barolo and Barbaresco, though Dolcetto was below par. Valpolicella was very good, and there'll be wonderful Amarone and Recioto. Also very good for Central Italian reds, though whites had a less good year all over the country.

1994 Central Italy came off best, with good quality across the board. North-eastern whites are also pretty good. In the North-West, Dolcetto, Moscato and Arneis are very good, but Barbera and Nebbiolo are less so.

1993 Best in the North-East, where the whites have more richness, perfume, length – well, more of everything – than the 1992s, while the reds are excellent. Central Italy looks fair, and the North-West patchy, though Dolcetto was generally successful.

1992 Light, early-drinking wines were made across most of the country, though Carmignano is nearly as good as in 1990, and the Marches were also fortunate.

1991 A fragmented year. Fair to good overall in the North-West. Tuscany was outstanding, and the Marches, Torgiano, Veneto and Friuli are very good. Trentino-Alto-Adige was less so.

1990 A fabulous vintage pretty well everywhere: wines of tremendous colour, richness and perfume, Barolo and Barbaresco for long aging and delicious Barbera. Wonderful Dolcetto again. Tuscan wines are built to last.

1989 Barbera d'Asti is very good, but needs drinking soon. Other reds are lighter.

1988 Dolcetto and Barbera have concentration and fruit. Nebbiolo is patchier. Tremendous quality in Central Italy and the North-East.

1987 Patchy Barolo and Barbaresco. Central Italian reds are reasonable.

1986 Barbaresco and Barolo are good. Chianti Riserva is very good, and Amarone della Valpolicella is lovely and drinking beautifully now.

1985 Big rich wines in Central Italy. An exciting vintage in the North-West, when more growers decided to emphasize fruit and perfume.

1983 Almost all fading now. Top Amarone is still good.

1982 Excellent, big ripe reds from Barolo which are still drinking. Everything else should have been drunk by now.

REGALEALI ★★★★ (Sicily) Wonderful IGT wines from local varieties: red Rosso del Conte and white Nozze d'Oro. Top Chardonnay. Good standard range, too.

RICASOLI ★★★ (Tuscany) Chianti is currently looking good. Also makes a host of other Tuscan wines at Brolio.

GIUSEPPE RIVETTI ★★★ (Piedmont) Smallish quantities of magical Moscato d'Asti which sell out in a flash.

RUFFINO ★★★ (Tuscany) Large Chianti house. Riserva Ducale is its best-known wine. Good IGT wines include lively Cabreo il Borgo (Cabernet) and succulent, oaky Chardonnay, Cabreo la Pietra. Romitorio di Santedame is Prugnolo (alias Sangiovese) and Colorino.

LUCIANO SANDRONE ★★★★ (Piedmont) A small producer making tiny quantities of perfumed new-style Barolo with lovely raspberry and black cherry flavours. Also excellent Dolcetto.

TENUTA SAN GUIDO ★★★★★ (Tuscany) Never heard the name? You may have heard of Sassicaia, Italy's leading Cabernet. It used to be vino da tavola; now it has the DOC of Bolgheri.

PAOLO SCAVINO ★★★★ (Piedmont) Hailed as one of the emerging masters of Barolo: superb wines which combine purity of fruit with depth and structure. Barolo Bric' del Fiasc' is his top wine; Cannubi and straight Barolo are not far behind. Delicious Dolcetto and Barbera.

MARIO SCHIOPETTO ★★★★ (Collio) Lovely whites from Pinot Grigio, Tocai etc., and white blend Rosis.

TERUZZI & PUTHOD ★★★★ (Tuscany) Commonly acknowledged to be the best producer of Vernaccia di San Gimignano. Its most expensive wine is the oak-aged Terre di Tufo. Whites include Terre di Tufi and Carmen.

VIETTI ★★★★★ (Piedmont) Classically perfect wines of their type, with a punch of acidity and tannin, plus elegance and class. Barolo (straight plus *crus* Rocche, Villero and Brunate) and Barbaresco (*normale* plus *crus* Masseria, Rabajà) are all intensely complex. Also, very good Dolcetto and Barbera, top Moscato d'Asti and very good Arneis.

ROBERTO VOERZIO ★★★★ (Piedmont) Ultra-modern fine wines full of fruit and perfume, made with great skill, giving Roberto (brother Gianni is also on the up) a reputation as a rising star. Barolo, Dolcetto d'Alba, Barbera d'Alba, Freisa, and delicious barrique-aged Barbera/Nebbiolo blend Vignaserra. Fine Arneis.

CASTELLO DI VOLPAIA ★★★ (Tuscany) Leading Chianti estate with elegant wines. Balifico Sangiovese/Cabernet is exotic and oaky-rich; Coltassala is lovely, austere Sangiovese that needs time.

WINE-FINDER: ITALY

In the Price Guides on the next 18 pages, we have divided Italy into the following geographical regions: North-West, North-East, Central and Southern. If you are unsure which part of the country the wine you're looking for comes from, this guide should help. See also the map on page 328.

Asti – *North-West Sparkling*
Barbaresco – *North-West Red*
Barbera – *North-West Red*
Barolo – *North-West Red*
Brunello di Montalcino – *Central Red*
Chianti – *Central Red*
Dolcetto – *North-West Red*
Frascati – *Central White*
Vino Nobile di Montepulciano – *Central Red*
Montepulciano d'Abruzzo – *Central Red*
Orvieto – *Central White*
Soave – *North-East White*
Valpolicella – *North-East Red*
Verdicchio – *Central White*

ITALY PRICES

NORTH-WEST RED

Under £6.00

Barbera d'Alba Punset **1994** £5.99 (WAT)
Barbera d'Asti Ceppi Storici **1997** £5.69 (VA) £7.20 (TAN)
Barbera d'Asti Ceppi Storici **1995** £5.30 (SOM)
Barbera d'Asti Superiore, Araldica **1998** £5.29 (VA)

£6.00 → £6.99

Barbera d'Asti Ceppi Storici **1996** £6.60 (PIP)
Barbera d'Asti Gemma **1996** £6.65 (CON)
Dolcetto di Dogliani, Francesco Boschis **1996** £6.90 (JU)

£7.00 → £7.99

Barbera d'Asti, Bertelli **1994** £7.95 (JU)
Bonarda Oltrepò Pavese, Castello di Luzzano **1996** £7.95 (RAE)
Dolcetto d'Alba Elio Altare **1996** £7.90 (JU)
Dolcetto d'Alba, Corino **1996** £7.50 (JU)
Dolcetto d'Alba Gemma **1997** £7.19 (JON) £7.25 (CON)
Dolcetto d'Alba Prunotto **1998** £7.00 (NEZ)
Dolcetto d'Alba Albino Rocca **1996** £7.90 (JU)
Monferrato Airone, Chiarlo **1997** £7.99 (OD) £8.70 (AV)
Nebbiolo delle Langhe Settimo **1997** £7.95 (WAT) £10.75 (DI)
Spanna Dessilani **1995** £7.95 (RAE)

£8.00 → £9.99

Barbera d'Alba Elio Altare **1998** £9.95 (DI) £11.99 (YOU)
Barbera d'Alba Elio Altare **1996** £8.50 (JU)
Barbera d'Alba Albino Rocca **1995** £8.90 (JU)
Barbera d'Alba Vigna Vigia, Bricco Maiolica **1996** £9.95 (LEA)
Barbera d'Alba Vignota, Conterno-Fantino **1996** £9.59 (BU)
Barbera Oltrepò Pavese, Castello di Luzzano **1991** £8.95 (RAE)
Barolo Terre del Barolo **1994** £9.17 (FLE)
Carema San Matino, Gemma **1990** £9.25 (CON)
Dolcetto d'Alba, Azelia **1996** £8.50 (JU)
Dolcetto d'Alba Clerico **1996** £8.50 (JU)
Dolcetto d'Alba Aldo Conterno **1996** £8.50 (CRO) £10.99 (VA)
Dolcetto d'Alba Diano Bricco Maiolica **1998** £9.50 (LEA)
Dolcetto d'Alba Sandrone **1998** £9.50 (TAN)
Dolcetto d'Alba Sandrone **1997** £9.69 (GOE)
Dolcetto di Dogliani Sori S. Martino, Boschis **1998** £9.99 (DI)
Dolcetto di Dogliani Sori S. Martino, Boschis **1996** £8.00 (JU)
Dolcetto di Dogliani Vigna dei Prey, Boschis **1996** £8.50 (JU)
Gutturnio dei Colli Piacentini, Castello di Luzzano **1991** £9.95 (RAE)
Inferno Nino Negri **1995** £8.89 (VA)
Monferrato Airone, Chiarlo **1995** £9.99 (DI)
Monferrato Rosso Il Baciale, Braida di Giacomo Bologna **1996** £9.90 (CRO) £10.20 (TAN)
Nebbiolo delle Langhe Cascina Morassino **1995** £9.95 (ROB)

£10.00 → £12.49

Barbaresco Campo Quadro, Punset **1992** £12.25 (WAT)
Barbaresco Nicolello **1989** £12.28 (PIP) £14.57 (PLAY)
Barbaresco Punset **1995** £11.65 (WAT)
Barbera d'Alba Sandrone **1996** £10.50 (TAN) £11.65 (GOE) £15.08 (FA)

MERCHANTS SPECIALIZING IN ITALY

see Merchant Directory (page 456) for details

Adnams (AD), Bennetts (BEN), Bibendum (BIB), Butlers Wine Cellar (BU), Anthony Byrne (BY), Cockburns of Leith (COC), Direct Wine (DI), Lay & Wheeler (LAY), Lea & Sandeman (LEA), Liberty (LIB), James Nicholson (NI), Reid Wines (REI), Roberson (ROB), T&W (TW), Ubiquitous Chip (UB), Valvona & Crolla (VA), Wine Treasury (WT).

Barbera d'Alba Bric Bertu, Angelo Negro & Figli **1996** £10.50 (GW)
Barbera d'Alba Aldo Conterno **1994** £12.10 (SOM) £15.95 (ROB)
Barbera d'Alba Vigna Vigia, Bricco Maiolica **1997** £10.50 (LEA)
Barolo Ascheri **1993** £10.72 (FLE)
Barolo Cordana, Castiglione Falletto **1995** £10.99 (SOM) £14.56 (PIP)
Barolo Nicolello **1994** £11.99 (UN)
Barolo Terre del Barolo **1996** £10.99 (SAF) £11.99 (VIC) £11.99 (THR) £11.99 (BOT)
Barolo Terre del Barolo **1995** £10.99 (TES)
Dolcetto d'Alba Aldo Conterno **1998** £10.95 (LIB)
Dolcetto d'Alba Aldo Conterno **1997** £10.99 (BEN) £12.45 (NI)
Dolcetto d'Alba Priavino, Roberto Voerzio **1998** £10.95 (BU)
Dolcetto d'Alba Priavino, Roberto Voerzio **1997** £10.99 (VA) £11.85 (PHI)
Dolcetto d'Alba Vajra **1999** £10.49 (LIB)
Dolcetto di Dogliani I Filiari, Luigi Einaudi **1997** £11.95 (LEA)
Dolcetto Sandrone **1998** £11.55 (SAV) £12.07 (WT)
Nebbiolo delle Langhe Produttori del Barbaresco **1997** £11.69 (VA)
Nebbiolo delle Langhe Vajra **1998** £12.44 (SAV) £12.95 (LIB)
Nebbiolo delle Langhe Vajra **1997** £11.95 (PHI)
Nebbiolo Marengo **1996** £11.50 (JU)
Oltrepo Pavese Vino Cuore, Cabanon **1996** £10.35 (JER)
Ronco di Mompiano, Pasolini **1985** £11.50 (CRO)
Ruche di Castagnole Monferrato, Casa Brina **1995** £10.99 (BO)

£12.50 → £14.99

Barbaresco Campo Quadro, Punset **1995** £13.55 (WAT)
Barbaresco Ronchi Albino Rocca **1994** £14.50 (JU)
Barbera d'Alba Sandrone **1997** £12.60 (TAN) £13.22 (GOE) £15.57 (SAV) £16.08 (WT) £19.09 (CAV)
Barbera d'Alba Vin del Ross, Bussia Soprana **1993** £14.50 (BAL) £18.14 (NO)
Barbera d'Alba Carati, Paulo Scavino **1994** £14.90 (JU)
Barbera d'Asti Superiore Arbest, Bava **1993** £14.39 (TW)
Barolo Ascheri **1994** £13.50 (HED)
Barolo Azelia **1993** £14.50 (JU)
Barolo Gemma **1994** £13.95 (CON)
Barolo Settimo **1995** £13.50 (WAT)
Dolcetto d'Alba Vajra **1997** £13.95 (RES)
Nebbiolo d'Alba Il Cumot, Bricco Maiolica **1997** £12.95 (LEA)
Nebbiolo d'Alba Pio Cesare **1995** £14.75 (FORT)

£15.00 → £19.99

Arte Clerico **1995** £16.50 (JU)
Barbaresco Cascina Morassino **1995** £18.95 (ROB)
Barbaresco Serraboella, Cigliuti **1994** £19.95 (BAN)
Barbera d'Alba Conca Tre Pile, Aldo Conterno **1997** £17.35 (BEN)
Barbera d'Alba Conca Tre Pile, Aldo Conterno **1996** £16.95 (VA)
Barbera d'Alba Aldo Conterno **1998** £17.95 (LIB)
Barbera d'Alba Aldo Conterno **1997** £18.99 (NI)
Barbera d'Alba Aldo Conterno **1996** £15.95 (CON) £17.50 (WS)
Barbera d'Asti Giarone, Bertelli **1993** £16.50 (JU)
Barolo Arborina, Elio Altare **1993** £19.90 (JU)
Barolo Batasiolo **1995** £15.55 (UB)
Barolo Bricco Fiasco, Azelia **1993** £17.00 (JU)
Barolo Brunate, Marcarini **1994** £16.99 (RAE)
Barolo Brunate, Marengo **1993** £16.00 (JU)
Barolo Ciabot Mentin Ginestra, Clerico **1993** £19.00 (JU)
Barolo Fontanafredda **1994** £17.95 (STA)
Barolo Monfalletto, Monfalletto-Cordero di Montezemolo **1994** £18.25 (STE)
Barolo Oddero **1994** £15.75 (ROB)
Barolo Riserva Borgogno **1993** £18.50 (VA)
Barolo Paulo Scavino **1993** £17.50 (JU)
Barolo Settimo **1993** £17.99 (DI)
Barolo Vigna dei Pola, Ascheri **1995** £17.50 (WS) £22.95 (STA)
Barolo Vigna Giachini, Corino **1993** £16.00 (JU)
Barolo Vigna Rocche, Corino **1993** £16.00 (JU)

A key to name abbreviations is available on page 7.

Barolo Vigneti Castello Riserva, Terre del Barolo **1993** £19.99 (SAF)
Barolo Zonchetta, Ceretto **1993** £19.95 (ROB)
Cabernet del Piemonte I Fossaretti, Bertelli **1993** £18.00 (JU)
Carema Ferrando **1990** £19.95 (BAL)
Freisa delle Langhe Vajra **1998** £19.95 (LIB)
Sito Moresco, Gaja **1996** £19.99 (YOU) £20.95 (LAY)
Sito Moresco, Gaja **1995** £17.33 (REI) £19.95 (BEN) £22.95 (RES)
Sito Moresco, Gaja **1993** £15.95 (DI)
Sitorey, Gaja **1994** £16.99 (DI)
St Marsan, Bertelli **1995** £16.50 (JU)
Valtellina Sfursat 5 Stella, Negri **1995** £18.47 (NO) £22.75 (ROB)

£20.00 → £29.99

Arte Clerico **1997** £21.99 (YOU)
Barbaresco Ronchi Albino Rocca **1996** £27.32 (FA)
Barbaresco Sitorey, Gaja **1994** £22.34 (NO)
Barbera d'Alba Scarrone, Vietti **1996** £24.95 (RES)
Barolo Anselma **1982** £27.50 (BU)
Barolo Azelia **1995** £21.99 (YOU)
Barolo Borgogno **1995** £26.00 (VA)
Barolo Bussia, Prunotto **1993** £27.00 (CRO)
Barolo Bussia Soprana, Aldo Conterno **1994** £29.60 (SOM) £34.56 (NO) £34.99 (VA) £35.99 (CON) £36.95 (BEN)
Barolo Cannubi, Luigi Einaudi **1995** £28.95 (LEA)
Barolo Chiarlo **1995** £22.00 (AV) £25.50 (DI)
Barolo Conteisa Cerequio, Gromis **1993** £28.49 (YOU) £28.80 (LAY) £34.17 (MI)
Barolo la Morra, Elio Altare **1995** £21.00 (YOU)
Barolo Paulo Scavino **1995** £21.60 (SOM)
Barolo Sori Ginestra, Conterno-Fantino **1995** £29.20 (REI)
Barolo Vigna Giachini, Corino **1995** £21.00 (DI)
Barolo Vigna Rocche, Corino **1995** £23.00 (DI)
Bricco dell'Uccellone, Braida di Giacomo Bologna **1995** £23.80 (TAN) £26.00 (CRO)
Monpra Conterno-Fantino **1997** £21.49 (YOU)
Nebbiolo delle Langhe Il Favot, Aldo Conterno **1998** £27.29 (PIP) £30.75 (LIB)
Vignaserra Roberto Voerzio **1996** £20.00 (BU) £21.00 (VA) £21.95 (RES)

£30.00 → £39.99

Barbaresco Bricco Asili, Ceretto **1990** £36.00 (BAL)
Barbaresco Gaja **1994** £39.00 (VA) £43.95 (BEN) £45.99 (YOU) £54.95 (LAY)
Barolo Bussia Soprana, Aldo Conterno **1996** £38.25 (LIB)
Barolo Bussia Soprana, Aldo Conterno **1995** £38.19 (REI) £45.95 (BEN)
Barolo Cannubi Boschis, Sandrone **1995** £34.00 (TAN) £48.47 (GOE) £77.84 (CAV)
Barolo Cannubi Boschis, Sandrone **1994** £30.75 (FA) £31.82 (GOE)
Barolo la Serra di la Morra, Roberto Voerzio **1994** £33.00 (VA)
Barolo Lazzarito, Vietti **1994** £38.95 (RES)
Barolo Marchesi di Barolo **1968** £37.50 (BU)
Barolo Monprivato, Mascarello **1993** £36.50 (ROB)
Barolo Riserva Marchesi di Barolo **1990** £39.99 (FRI)
Darmagi Gaja **1986** £39.00 (VA) £72.00 (CRO)
Maurizio Zanella, Ca' del Bosco **1995** £37.01 (REI)
Nebbiolo delle Langhe Il Favot, Aldo Conterno **1997** £31.50 (BEN)

£40.00 → £49.99

Barbaresco Gaja **1993** £44.30 (LAY)
Barbaresco Il Bricco, Pio Cesare **1995** £40.00 (FORT)
Barolo Sperss, Gaja **1994** £47.00 (YOU) £50.00 (FORT) £52.29 (FA) £53.50 (BEN) £76.86 (CAV)
Barolo Vigna del Gris, Conterno-Fantino **1990** £48.00 (BEN)
Darmagi Gaja **1985** £49.00 (VA)

£50.00 → £99.99

Barbaresco Costa Russi, Gaja **1995** £97.33 (FA)
Barbaresco Costa Russi, Gaja **1988** £95.00 (VA) £146.88 (REI)
Barbaresco Gaja **1995** £56.20 (FA) £65.83 (MI) £84.70 (CAV)
Barbaresco Gaja **1990** £77.00 (CRO) £110.00 (VA) £117.50 (REI)
Barbaresco Gaja **1989** £85.00 (VA) £92.24 (REI) £139.17 (MI)
Barbaresco Gaja **1982** £65.00 (VA) £75.00 (BU) £125.00 (UB)
Barbaresco Gallina di Neive, Bruno Giacosa **1995** £95.00 (VA)

Barbaresco Sori San Lorenzo, Gaja **1995** £97.33 (FA) £165.00 (VA)
Barbaresco Sorì Tildìn, Gaja **1995** £97.33 (FA) £165.00 (VA)
Barolo Bricco Rocche Brunate, Ceretto **1990** £59.50 (VA)
Barolo Bussia Soprana, Aldo Conterno **1990** £95.00 (VA)
Barolo la Serra di la Morra, Roberto Voerzio **1995** £50.27 (WT)
Barolo Monfortino Riserva Giacomo Conterno **1988** £94.39 (FA) £190.00 (VA)
Barolo Riserva Borgogno **1978** £57.00 (VA)
Barolo Riserva Marchesi di Barolo **1982** £66.50 (FRI)
Barolo Sperss, Gaja **1995** £62.00 (YOU) £78.33 (MI)
Barolo Sperss, Gaja **1993** £52.29 (FA) £59.95 (LAY)
Barolo Sperss, Gaja **1991** £68.00 (VA)
Barolo Sperss, Gaja **1989** £95.00 (VA)
Barolo Vigna Giachini, Corino **1990** £55.00 (VA)
Darmagi Gaja **1995** £61.10 (FA)
Darmagi Gaja **1994** £75.83 (MI)
Darmagi Gaja **1993** £63.25 (LAY)
Maurizio Zanella, Ca' del Bosco **1990** £55.81 (REI)

£100.00 → £149.99

Barbaresco Costa Russi, Gaja **1993** £115.00 (VA)
Barbaresco Gaja **1985** £111.63 (REI) £150.00 (ROB) £195.00 (VA)
Barbaresco Sori San Lorenzo, Gaja **1983** £135.00 (VA)
Barbaresco Sorì Tildìn, Gaja **1993** £115.00 (VA)
Barolo Bricco Bussia Colonello, Aldo Conterno **1990** £135.00 (VA)
Barolo Aldo Conterno **1971** £100.00 (VA)
Barolo Monfortino Riserva Giacomo Conterno **1990** £118.87 (FA) £209.00 (VA)
Barolo Riserva Falleto **1997** £123.38 (CAV)

Over £150.00

Barbaresco Costa Russi, Gaja **1982** £160.00 (VA)
Barbaresco Gaja **1978** £158.63 (TW)
Barbaresco Sori San Lorenzo, Gaja **1982** £160.00 (VA)
Barbaresco Sorì Tildìn, Gaja **1989** £200.00 (VA)
Barolo Granbussia, Aldo Conterno **1989** £245.00 (VA)

NORTH-WEST WHITE

Under £6.00

Chardonnay del Piemonte, Alasia **1998** £4.95 (WS)
Moscato d'Asti, Araldica **1998** £3.99 (UN) £4.50 (SOM)
Moscato d'Asti, Araldica **1997** £4.49 (VA)
Moscato del Piemonte, Gemma **1998** £3.89 (OD)

£6.00 → £7.99

Arneis del Roero, Malvirà **1998** £6.49 (OD)
Gavi Castello di Tassarolo **1997** £7.49 (MAJ)
Gavi La Chiara **1998** £6.49 (OD) £8.70 (TAN)
Gavi La Raia **1999** £6.58 (BIB)

£8.00 → £9.99

Gavi La Chiara **1997** £8.25 (CON)
Moscato d'Asti Sourgal, Elio Perrone **1998** £8.45 (ROB)
Moscato d'Asti la Spinetta, Rivetti **1997** £9.40 (SAV)
Traminer del Piemonte Plisse, Bertelli **1994** £9.95 (JU)

£10.00 → £19.99

Arneis Blange Ceretto **1996** £12.75 (PLAY)
Chardonnay del Piemonte Giarone, Bertelli **1993** £15.90 (JU)
Erbaluce di Caluso La Rustia, Orsolani **1997** £10.50 (ROB)
Gavi Pio Cesare **1998** £12.25 (FORT)
Langhe Luigi Einaudi **1997** £18.95 (LEA)
Langhe Il Fiore, Braida di Giacomo Bologna **1998** £10.95 (GAU)
Monferrato Bianco Alteserre, Bava **1996** £14.39 (TW)
St Marsan, Bertelli **1995** £14.90 (JU)

Over £20.00

Alteni di Brassica, Gaja **1996** £28.02 (REI)
Alteni di Brassica, Gaja **1995** £21.50 (VA)
Alteni di Brassica, Gaja **1993** £33.49 (TW)
Chardonnay Gaia & Rey, Gaja **1995** £37.00 (VA)
Chardonnay Rossj Bass, Gaja **1996** £25.95 (VA) £25.95 (ROB)
Franciacorta Bianco Ca' del Bosco **1996** £32.31 (REI)
Rossj-Bass Gaja **1998** £20.20 (LAY) £20.49 (YOU)
Rossj-Bass Gaja **1996** £21.09 (REI)

NORTH-WEST SPARKLING

Under £6.00

Asti Calissano **Non-vintage** £5.99 (POR) £5.99 (JON)
Asti Cinzano **Non-vintage** £5.25 (COC)
Asti Martini **Non-vintage** £5.49 (ASD) £5.49 (TES) £5.49 (VIC) £5.49 (THR) £5.49 (WR) £5.49 (BOT) £5.99 (SO) £5.99 (OD) £5.99 (WAI) £5.99 (SAF) £5.99 (BUD) £6.75 (WRI) £6.90 (STA) £6.92 (PLA) £7.71 (VIN)
Asti Vigna Fiorita, Cantine Gemma **Non-vintage** £5.79 (CON)

£6.00 → £9.99

Asti Fontanafredda **Non-vintage** £7.79 (VA) £7.95 (ROB) £8.25 (UB)
Malvasia Cantine Gemma **Non-vintage** £8.25 (CON)

Over £10.00

Franciacorta Brut, Ca' del Bosco **Non-vintage** £15.00 (CRO) £17.99 (VA)

NORTH-EAST RED

Under £5.00

Colli Berici Merlot La Casona **1997** £4.35 (CON)
Merlot del Veneto, Canaletto **1999** £4.49 (BUD)
Valpolicella Campagnola **1997** £4.75 (STE) £4.75 (ROB)
Valpolicella Classico Superiore Zenato **1997** £4.99 (VIC) £4.99 (THR) £4.99 (WR) £4.99 (BOT) £5.75 (STE)

£5.00 → £5.99

Bardolino Classico Superiore Tedeschi **1998** £5.56 (PIP)
Trentino Merlot Mezzacorona **1997** £5.90 (COC) £6.50 (DI)
Valpolicella Classico Allegrini **1998** £5.95 (WS) £7.25 (BEN) £7.75 (PHI)
Valpolicella Classico Allegrini **1997** £5.80 (SOM) £7.90 (CRO)
Valpolicella Classico Masi **1998** £5.49 (OD)
Valpolicella Classico Superiore Tedeschi **1996** £5.45 (AV)
Valpolicella Classico Superiore Valverde, Tedeschi **1996** £5.65 (COC)
Valpolicella Classico Superiore Zenato **1998** £5.83 (PIP)

£6.00 → £7.99

Bardolino Classico Ca' Bordenis **1996** £6.50 (STA)
Colli Oriental del Friuli Merlot Petrussa **1996** £7.95 (CON)
Colli Orientali del Friuli Cabernet Franc, Petrussa **1994** £7.95 (CON)
Teroldego Rotaliano Dorigati **1997** £7.85 (CON)
Trentino Rosso Maso Lodron, Letrari **1997** £6.75 (WS)
Valpolicella Classico Allegrini **1999** £6.45 (BER) £6.99 (LIB) £6.99 (VA)
Valpolicella Classico Antanel, Spinosa **1997** £6.78 (BIB)
Valpolicella Classico Superiore Allegrini **1998** £7.49 (HED)
Valpolicella Classico Superiore Capitel San Rocco Vino di Rapasso, Tedeschi **1997** £7.99 (POR)
★ Valpolicella Classico Superiore Ripassa, Zenato **1996** £7.49 (WR) £7.49 (BOT) £7.49 (VIC) £7.49 (THR)
Venegazzù Cabernet Sauvignon Venegazzù **1997** £6.65 (AV)

£8.00 → £9.99

Breganze Rosso, Maculan **1996** £9.99 (DI)
Cabernet Sauvignon Morago **1996** £8.75 (CB)
Teroldego Rotaliano Foradori **1998** £9.95 (BAL)
Valpolicella Classico la Grola, Allegrini **1995** £9.05 (SOM) £10.90 (VA)
Valpolicella Classico Palazzo della Torre, Allegrini **1995** £9.83 (SUN) £11.55 (PHI)
Valpolicella Classico Superiore La Grola, Allegrini **1996** £9.75 (WS)
Valpolicella Classico Superiore Palazzo della Torre, Allegrini **1995** £9.99 (BOD) £10.45 (VA)
Valpolicella Classico Superiore Ripassa, Zenato **1995** £9.25 (STE)

£10.00 → £12.99

Amarone della Valpolicella Classico Tedeschi **1995** £12.99 (MAJ) £12.99 (SAF) £14.41 (COC)
Amarone della Valpolicella Sartori **1996** £11.99 (BOT)
Collio Cabernet Franc, Russiz Superiore **1996** £11.45 (NEZ)
Trentino Cabernet Franc de Tarczal **1996** £10.99 (PHI)
Valpolicella Classico la Grola, Allegrini **1998** £11.90 (BEN)
Valpolicella Classico la Grola, Allegrini **1997** £12.49 (LIB)
Valpolicella Classico la Grola, Allegrini **1996** £12.25 (FORT) £12.99 (PHI)
Valpolicella Classico Palazzo della Torre, Allegrini **1997** £11.99 (LIB)
Valpolicella Classico Palazzo della Torre, Allegrini **1996** £11.46 (REI)
Valpolicella Classico Superiore La Grola, Allegrini **1995** £10.95 (PIP) £11.05 (NO) £11.95 (ROB)
Venegazzù della Casa, Venegazzù **1996** £12.15 (AV)

£13.00 → £14.99

Amarone della Valpolicella Classico, Ca' Fornari **1993** £13.95 (CON)
Amarone della Valpolicella Classico Tedeschi **1997** £14.99 (POR)
Amarone della Valpolicella Corte Rubini, Lamberti **1994** £14.90 (UB)
Amarone della Valpolicella Masi **1996** £14.99 (OD)
Recioto della Valpolicella Classico Serègo Alighieri, Masi **1996** £13.69 (OD)
Teroldego Rotaliano Diedri, Dorigati **1992** £13.95 (CON)

£15.00 → £19.99

Amarone della Valpolicella Classico, Zenato **1993** £17.99 (WR)
Amarone della Valpolicella Classico Allegrini **1995** £19.90 (VA) £23.99 (YOU) £25.00 (BEN) £25.50 (PHI)
Amarone della Valpolicella Classico Allegrini **1993** £16.40 (SOM) £25.50 (PHI)
Amarone della Valpolicella Tommasi **1995** £15.95 (AD)
Amarone della Valpolicella Zenato **1993** £18.99 (BOT) £19.03 (PIP)
Conte Federico, Bossi Fedrigotti **1990** £18.58 (NO)
Recioto della Valpolicella Classico Allegrini **1995** £15.86 (REI)
Recioto della Valpolicella Classico Allegrini **1993** £18.00 (CRO)
Recioto della Valpolicella Classico Capitel Monte Fontana, Tedeschi **1988** £18.95 (DI)
Teroldego Rotaliano Vigneto Sgarzon Foradori **1996** £15.95 (BAL)
Valpolicella Classico Superiore Quintarelli **1993** £15.82 (BIB)

£20.00 → £24.99

Amarone della Valpolicella Capitel Monte Olmi, Tedeschi **1997** £24.99 (POR)
Amarone della Valpolicella Capitel Monte Olmi, Tedeschi **1996** £20.50 (AV)
Amarone della Valpolicella Classico, Tommaso Bussola **1996** £24.60 (LAY)
Amarone della Valpolicella Classico Allegrini **1996** £24.95 (LIB)
Granato Foradori **1996** £21.99 (YOU) £22.50 (BAL) £23.32 (REI) £24.95 (RES)
La Poja, Allegrini **1995** £22.60 (SOM) £25.00 (WS) £26.00 (PHI) £27.95 (LIB) £28.50 (STA)
La Poja, Allegrini **1993** £24.75 (CON) £26.50 (ROB) £26.80 (NO)

Over £25.00

Amarone della Valpolicella Le Ragose **1990** £27.50 (ROB)
La Poja, Allegrini **1992** £27.25 (ROB)

NORTH-EAST WHITE

Under £4.00

Friuli Grave Tocai Friulano San Simone **1996** £3.95 (JU)

£4.00 → £4.99

Chardonnay del Veneto, Canaletto **1999** £4.49 (BUD)
Friuli Grave Sauvignon San Simone **1998** £4.85 (WAI)
Pinot Grigio La Casona **1998** £4.95 (CON)
Soave Campagnola **1998** £4.75 (STE) £4.75 (ROB)
Soave La Casona **1998** £4.39 (CON)
Soave Classico Superiore Zenato **1999** £4.99 (VIC) £4.99 (THR)
Soave Classico Superiore Zenato **1998** £4.99 (WR) £4.99 (BOT)
Soave Classico Vigneto Colombara, Zenato **1998** £4.95 (WAI) £5.95 (STE)
Valdadige Pinot Grigio Cantina Sociale della Valdadige Veronese **1999** £4.95 (LEA)

- *Wines are listed in A–Z order within each price band.*
- *For each wine, vintages are listed in descending order.*
- *Each vintage of any wine appears only once.*

£5.00 → £5.99

Friuli Grave Pinot Grigio San Simone **1996** £5.45 (JU)
Lugana San Benedetto, Zenato **1997** £5.95 (STE)
Lugana Villa Flora, Zenato **1998** £5.25 (WAI)
Pinot Grigio Le Due Terre **1998** £5.99 (JON)
Soave Classico Monte Tenda, Tedeschi **1998** £5.30 (AV)
Soave Classico Superiore Castelcerino **1998** £5.50 (TAN) £5.69 (JON)
Soave Classico Superiore Castelcerino **1997** £5.35 (CON)

£6.00 → £7.99

Alto Adige Pinot Grigio Lageder **1998** £7.89 (PHI)
Alto Adige Pinot Grigio Tiefenbrunner **1999** £6.50 (BAN)
Bianco di Custoza le Vigne di San Pietro **1997** £7.89 (LIB)
Friuli Grave Pinot Grigio Le Fredis **1997** £7.49 (CON)
Friuli Grave Tocai Friulano Le Fredis **1997** £7.49 (CON)
Lugana Ca' dei Frati **1998** £6.85 (SOM) £6.99 (POR) £8.75 (PHI)
Lugana Ca' dei Frati **1997** £7.69 (CON)
Lugana I Frati, Ca' dei Frati **1998** £7.99 (VA) £8.25 (HAH) £8.75 (TAN) £8.95 (ROB)
Soave Classico Col Baraca, Masi **1997** £7.23 (PIP)
Soave Classico Pieropan **1998** £7.93 (REI) £7.95 (POR) £7.99 (HED) £8.25 (PHI)
Soave Classico Suavia **1999** £6.56 (BIB)
Soave Classico Superiore Anselmi **1999** £6.99 (VA)
★ Soave Classico Superiore Gini **1998** £6.95 (JU) £7.99 (DI)
Soave Classico Superiore Pieropan **1999** £7.95 (LIB)
Soave Classico Superiore Pieropan **1998** £6.99 (VA) £9.60 (PIP)
Soave Classico Superiore Pieropan **1996** £6.60 (SOM)
Soave Classico Superiore Prosca, Gini **1996** £7.85 (JU)
Soave Classico Vigneto la Rocca, Pieropan **1998** £6.25 (WS)
Valdadige Pinot Grigio Vigneti di Castagnari, Cantina Sociale della Valdadige Veronese **1998** £6.95 (LEA)

£8.00 → £9.99

Collio Pinot Grigio Puiatti **1997** £9.25 (SOM)
Collio Sauvignon Vigna del Lauro **1998** £8.45 (JER)
Lugana Il Brolettino, Ca' dei Frati **1997** £9.90 (PIP)
Soave Classico Anselmi **1997** £9.25 (FORT)
Soave Classico Capitel Foscarino, Anselmi **1998** £8.80 (SOM) £9.49 (VA) £10.25 (NI)
Soave Classico San Vincenzo, Anselmi **1998** £8.50 (ROB) £8.65 (NI) £8.99 (PHI)
Soave Classico Superiore Anselmi **1997** £9.30 (UB)
★ Soave Classico Superiore Monte Alto, Ca' Rugate **1999** £8.99 (VA)
Soave Classico Superiore Pieropan **1997** £8.25 (STA)
Soave Classico Vigneto Calvarino, Pieropan **1998** £8.99 (VA)
Soave Classico Vigneto la Rocca, Pieropan **1997** £9.69 (REI) £9.99 (VA) £11.99 (PHI) £12.95 (ROB)
Soave Classico Vigneto la Rocca, Pieropan **1994** £8.95 (WS)

£10.00 → £11.99

Collio Pinot Grigio Felluga **1997** £10.50 (ROB)
Collio Pinot Grigio Puiatti **1995** £11.50 (JU)
Pinot Bianco Jermann **1997** £10.60 (SOM) £13.69 (REI) £13.99 (VA) £14.95 (ROB)
Soave Classico Capitel Croce, Anselmi **1997** £11.75 (BU)
Soave Classico Capitel Croce, Anselmi **1996** £11.95 (NI) £12.75 (ROB)
Soave Classico Vigneto Calvarino, Pieropan **1997** £11.75 (PHI)
Soave Classico Vigneto Calvarino, Pieropan **1996** £10.59 (JON)

£12.00 → £14.99

Chardonnay Jermann **1998** £13.51 (REI) £14.49 (VA)
Collio Tocai Schiopetto **1998** £12.50 (BAÑ)
Pinot Bianco Jermann **1998** £14.95 (ROB)
Pinot Bianco Jermann **1996** £14.17 (NO)
Pinot Grigio Jermann **1998** £13.81 (REI)
Pinot Grigio Jermann **1997** £13.99 (VA) £15.25 (UB)
Pinot Grigio Jermann **1996** £14.25 (STA)
Recioto di Soave I Capitelli, Anselmi ½ bottle **1996** £12.75 (ROB)
Soave Classico Vigneto la Rocca, Pieropan **1996** £12.95 (ROB)

£15.00 → £19.99

Collio Tocai Friulano Schiopetto **1997** £15.50 (ROB)
Pinot Bianco Jermann **1995** £15.65 (UB)
Recioto di Soave I Capitelli, Anselmi **1997** £17.99 (VA)
Recioto di Soave le Colombare, Pieropan **1995** £15.75 (PHI)

Over £20.00

Torcolato Maculan **1997** £25.95 (LEA)
Vintage Tunina Jermann **1997** £23.49 (YOU) £24.38 (REI) £24.90 (VA) £27.75 (ROB)
Vintage Tunina Jermann **1995** £23.50 (STA)

NORTH-EAST SPARKLING

Under £8.00

Prosecco di Conegliano Carpenè Malvolti **Non-vintage** £7.95 (LEA) £8.95 (ROB)
Prosecco Serafino **Non-vintage** £6.95 (JER)

CENTRAL RED

Under £4.00

Montepulciano d'Abruzzo Umani Ronchi **1998** £3.99 (WAI) £4.69 (PIP) £4.99 (NI)
Rosso Conero San Lorenzo, Umani Ronchi **1995** £3.99 (BOT) £5.80 (SOM) £8.25 (ROB)
Sangiovese di Toscana Cecchi **1999** £3.99 (VIC) £3.99 (THR)
Sangiovese di Toscana Cecchi **1998** £3.99 (SAI) £3.99 (WAI)
Sangiovese di Toscana Cecchi **1997** £3.99 (BOT)

£4.00 → £4.99

Chianti Classico Melini **1998** £4.99 (BIB)
Chianti Querceto **1996** £4.95 (JU)
Chianti Rufina Grati **1997** £4.95 (WS)
Chianti Rufina Villa di Vetrice **1997** £4.99 (POR) £5.20 (SOM) £5.95 (TAN)
Col di Sasso Villa Banfi **1997** £4.79 (BO)
Montepulciano d'Abruzzo, Roxan **1997** £4.79 (BAL)
Montepulciano d'Abruzzo Cornacchia **1997** £4.99 (MAJ) £4.99 (BO) £5.49 (VA)
Rosso Conero San Lorenzo, Umani Ronchi **1998** £4.99 (VA)

£5.00 → £5.99

Chianti Rufina Villa di Vetrice **1998** £5.97 (PIP)
Chianti Rufina Villa di Vetrice **1996** £5.69 (JON)
Montepulciano d'Abruzzo, Roxan **1998** £5.40 (LAY)
Montepulciano d'Abruzzo Cornacchia **1998** £5.49 (VA)
Montepulciano d'Abruzzo Umani Ronchi **1997** £5.50 (ROB)
Parrina Rosso, La Parrina **1997** £5.75 (NI) £5.99 (VA) £6.95 (BU) £6.95 (POR)

£6.00 → £6.99

Carmignano Barco Reale, Capezzana **1998** £6.75 (WS) £7.85 (NI) £7.95 (BU) £7.99 (LIB) £8.40 (HAH) £8.95 (RES)
Chianti Classico le Capanne, Querceto **1995** £6.50 (JU)
Chianti Classico Rocca delle Macie **1997** £6.99 (MAJ) £7.75 (NI)
Dogajolo Carpineto **1997** £6.85 (WS)
Montescudaio Rosso delle Miniere, Fattoria di Sorbaiano **1997** £6.45 (CON)
Parrina Rosso, La Parrina **1998** £6.30 (SOM) £7.95 (LIB)
Rosso Conero Brunori **1998** £6.56 (BIB)
Rosso Conero San Lorenzo, Umani Ronchi **1997** £6.79 (VA) £7.49 (NI) £7.50 (TAN)
Val di Cornia Gualdo del Re **1997** £6.95 (LEA)
Vino Nobile di Montepulciano Fassati **1996** £6.99 (MAJ)

£7.00 → £7.99

Chianti Classico Aziano, Ruffino **1996** £7.59 (COC)
Chianti Classico Montiverdi **1995** £7.79 (CON)
Chianti Classico Villa Antinori, Antinori **1996** £7.99 (DI)
Chianti Classico Villa Cafaggio **1996** £7.99 (UN)
Chianti Rufina Selvapiana **1997** £7.50 (WS) £8.46 (FLE) £8.49 (VA) £8.95 (RES) £8.99 (PHI)

- *All prices for each wine are listed together in ascending order.*
- *Price bands refer to the lowest price for which the wine is available.*

Chianti Castello di Volpaia **1996** £7.29 (OD)
Montefalco Rosso Caprai **1995** £7.65 (SOM) £9.49 (LIB) £9.75 (HED)
Morellino di Scansano le Pupille **1997** £7.30 (SOM)
Parrina Rosso, La Parrina **1996** £7.75 (ROB)
Rosso di Montalcino Altesino **1997** £7.99 (POR)
Rosso di Montalcino Campo ai Sassi, Frescobaldi **1997** £7.99 (OD)
Rosso di Montepulciano Dei **1998** £7.95 (LEA)
Rosso Piceno Vigna Piediprato, Pilastri **1997** £7.25 (GOE)
Rubesco Rosso di Torgiano Lungarotti **1996** £7.69 (VA) £8.60 (TAN)
Vino Nobile di Montepulciano Cerro **1998** £7.49 (OD)

£8.00 → £8.99

Bolgheri Vigneto le Contessine, le Macchiole **1997** £8.50 (LEA)
Carmignano Barco Reale, Capezzana **1997** £8.00 (FLE)
Chianti Classico Castello di Brolio **1997** £8.25 (WS)
Chianti Classico Castello di Fonterutoli **1997** £8.95 (NI) £8.95 (WS) £12.99 (PHI)
Chianti Classico Melini **1995** £8.99 (JON)
Chianti Classico Querceto **1994** £8.50 (JU)
Chianti Classico Riserva Antinori **1996** £8.99 (NEZ) £9.90 (HAH)
Chianti Classico Riserva Villa Antinori, Antinori **1995** £8.99 (BOT) £10.65 (JER)
Chianti Classico Riserva Villa Cerna **1995** £8.99 (SAF)
Chianti Classico Villa Cafaggio **1997** £8.35 (WRI) £8.50 (BAL)
Chianti Classico Castello di Volpaia **1997** £8.95 (AD) £8.99 (DI)
Chianti Rufina Castello di Nipozzano **1996** £8.99 (MAJ)
Chianti Rufina Selvapiana **1998** £8.99 (LIB)
Montefalco Rosso Caprai **1997** £8.49 (BAL)
Morellino di Scansano le Pupille **1998** £8.99 (VA) £9.50 (BU) £9.65 (HED) £10.99 (PHI)
Rosso Conero San Lorenzo, Umani Ronchi **1996** £8.25 (ROB)
Rosso di Montalcino Argiano **1998** £8.75 (WS) £10.95 (LIB) £11.49 (VA) £12.50 (FORT) £12.99 (PHI)
Rosso di Montalcino Argiano **1997** £8.40 (SOM) £10.95 (HED) £11.75 (ROB)
Vino Nobile di Montepulciano Baiocchi **1996** £8.69 (VA)

£9.00 → £9.99

Castelrapiti Montellori **1995** £9.95 (BAN)
Chianti Classico Badia a Coltibuono **1997** £9.80 (AV)
Chianti Classico Barone Ricasoli **1996** £9.99 (WR)
Chianti Classico Castellare **1997** £9.99 (DI) £10.50 (BAL)
Chianti Classico Castell'in Villa **1992** £9.69 (CB) £10.10 (UB)
Chianti Classico Isole e Olena **1996** £9.60 (SAV) £13.25 (CON) £13.75 (FORT)
Chianti Classico Fattoria Ormanni **1997** £9.99 (DI)
Chianti Classico Pèppoli, Antinori **1997** £9.99 (VA)
Chianti Classico Riserva Monsanto **1986** £9.95 (RAE)
Chianti Classico Riserva Querceto **1991** £9.90 (JU)
Chianti Rufina Riserva Castello di Nipozzano **1996** £9.94 (PIP)
Chianti Rufina Selvapiana **1996** £9.95 (FORT) £9.95 (ROB)
Chianti Rufina Selvapiana **1995** £9.95 (ROB)
Le Volte Tenuta dell'Ornellaia **1997** £9.69 (REI) £10.56 (PIP)
Morellino di Scansano le Pupille **1999** £9.90 (LIB)
Rosso Conero Fattoria le Terrazze **1993** £9.28 (TW)
Rosso di Montalcino, Lisini **1996** £9.99 (RAE)
Rosso di Montalcino Vigna della Fonte, Ciacci Piccolomini d'Aragona **1996** £9.79 (SAV) £9.95 (BAL)
Rosso di Montalcino Villa Banfi **1996** £9.99 (VA)
Vino Nobile di Montepulciano Bindella **1997** £9.99 (BIB)

£10.00 → £11.99

Arquata Rosso dell'Umbria, Adanti **1991** £11.99 (CON)
Brunello di Montalcino Friggiali **1996** £10.01 (WT)
Campovecchio Rosso, Castel de Paolis **1996** £10.95 (BAL)
Chianti Classico Castello dei Rampolla **1997** £10.77 (CAV) £12.99 (PHI)
Chianti Classico Felsina Berardenga **1998** £11.25 (PIP) £13.95 (LIB)
Chianti Classico Felsina Berardenga **1997** £10.00 (WS) £10.95 (SOM) £12.99 (AME) £13.50 (BEN) £13.95 (PHI)
Chianti Classico Felsina Berardenga **1994** £11.99 (VA)
Chianti Classico Fontodi **1998** £10.99 (VA) £12.95 (LIB)
Chianti Classico Fontodi **1997** £10.00 (WS) £10.35 (SOM) £11.99 (PHI) £12.49 (YOU) £12.95 (BEN)
Chianti Classico Isole e Olena **1997** £10.99 (SOM) £13.37 (FLE) £13.75 (BEN) £13.95 (STA)
Chianti Classico Isole e Olena **1993** £10.50 (CRO)
Chianti Classico Monte Bernardi **1992** £11.75 (GOE)
Chianti Classico Nozzole **1996** £10.15 (JER)
Chianti Classico Querciabella **1997** £11.95 (LEA)
Chianti Classico Riserva Castello di Nipozzano, Frescobaldi **1996** £10.40 (TAN)
Chianti Classico Riserva Castello di Volpaia **1997** £10.99 (OD) £12.50 (AD)
Chianti Classico Vecchie Terre di Montefili **1995** £11.50 (RAE)
Chianti Rufina Riserva Selvapiana **1996** £11.99 (VA)
Montescudaio Rosso delle Miniere, Fattoria di Sorbaiano **1996** £10.80 (TAN)
Montescudaio Rosso delle Miniere, Fattoria di Sorbaiano **1995** £10.79 (CON) £12.99 (JON)
Morellino di Scansano Riserva, le Pupille **1995** £10.65 (SOM)
Parrina Reserva, La Parrina **1997** £10.95 (STA) £10.95 (LIB)
Rosso Conero Cúmaro, Umani Ronchi **1997** £10.99 (VA)
Rosso di Montalcino Argiano **1996** £11.75 (ROB)
Rosso di Montalcino Col d'Orcia **1997** £10.35 (VA)
Vino Nobile di Montepulciano Avignonesi **1996** £10.95 (WAI)
Vino Nobile di Montepulciano Dei **1996** £11.50 (LEA)
Vino Nobile di Montepulciano di Casale **1996** £11.99 (DI)
Vino Nobile di Montepulciano Poliziano **1995** £11.59 (JON) £11.80 (NO)
Vino Nobile di Montepulciano Riserva, Avignonesi **1993** £11.99 (BOT)
Vino Nobile di Montepulciano Riserva, Baiocchi **1995** £11.49 (VA)
Vino Nobile di Montepulciano Trerose **1996** £11.99 (DI)

£12.00 → £14.99

Brunello di Montalcino Promis, Pieve Santa Restituta **1997** £14.55 (LAY)
Campovecchio Rosso, Castel de Paolis **1997** £12.50 (ROB)
Carmignano Villa di Capezzana **1997** £13.75 (BU) £13.95 (LIB)
Chianti Classico Felsina Berardenga **1996** £12.95 (VA) £13.50 (ROB)
Chianti Classico Castello di Fonterutoli **1990** £13.50 (BAL)
Chianti Classico Isole e Olena **1998** £14.95 (TAN) £14.99 (VA) £17.95 (LIB)
Chianti Classico Isole e Olena **1995** £12.75 (REI)
Chianti Classico Monte Bernardi **1994** £14.20 (GOE) £15.95 (BAL)
Chianti Classico Riserva Castello dei Rampolla **1995** £13.71 (CAV)
Chianti Classico Riserva Ducale Oro, Ruffino **1993** £13.20 (COC) £17.95 (VA)
Chianti Classico Riserva Felsina Berardenga **1994** £13.99 (VA) £15.75 (LIB) £15.95 (STA) £15.99 (PHI)
Chianti Classico Riserva Fontodi **1996** £13.50 (WS) £16.95 (VA) £17.49 (LIB) £17.95 (PHI)
Chianti Classico Riserva Tenute Marchese Antinori **1996** £12.99 (WAI) £14.95 (VA) £14.99 (BOD) £14.99 (SUN)
Chianti Classico Riserva, Fattoria Ormanni **1995** £14.99 (OD)
Chianti Classico Riserva Querciabella **1994** £14.50 (LEA)
Chianti Classico Riserva Santa Cristina, Antinori **1990** £12.00 (CRO)
Chianti Classico Ruffino **1975** £14.69 (REI)
Chianti Classico San Felice **1997** £13.49 (VA)
Chianti Classico Fattoria Valtellina **1999** £14.30 (SOM)
Chianti Classico Vecchie Terre di Montefili **1997** £12.79 (YOU)
Chianti Rufina Riserva Bucerchiale, Selvapiana **1994** £12.99 (VA)
Chianti Rufina Riserva Selvapiana **1997** £14.75 (LIB)
Farnito Carpineto **1995** £14.79 (YOU)
Montepulciano d'Abruzzo Cornacchia **1992** £14.69 (REI)
Morellino di Scansano Riserva, le Pupille **1996** £14.99 (VA) £15.95 (RES)
Roccato Rocca delle Macie **1995** £14.25 (NI)
Rosso Conero Cúmaro, Umani Ronchi **1995** £12.93 (REI) £15.75 (ROB)
Rosso di Montalcino Calbello **1997** £14.99 (YOU) £16.95 (RES)
Rosso di Montalcino Costanti **1995** £14.95 (PHI)
Sangiovese Grosso Riserva Gualdo del Re **1996** £13.95 (LEA)
Vino Nobile di Montepulciano le Casalte **1996** £12.49 (AME)
Vino Nobile di Montepulciano le Casalte **1990** £14.95 (BAL)
Vino Nobile di Montepulciano Poliziano **1997** £12.99 (PHI)
Vino Nobile di Montepulciano Poliziano **1996** £14.25 (ROB)
Vino Nobile di Montepulciano Vigna Asinone, Poliziano **1997** £12.63 (REI)
Vino Nobile di Montepulciano Vigneto Caggiole, Poliziano **1994** £14.12 (NO)

£15.00 → £19.99

Ardingo Calbello **1997** £17.95 (VA)
Balifico Castello di Volpaia **1995** £18.95 (DI)
Brancaia, La Brancaia **1997** £16.35 (NI) £19.99 (YOU) £21.50 (LEA)
Brunello di Montalcino Argiano **1994** £16.20 (SOM) £18.50 (WS) £18.99 (YOU) £19.99 (VA) £21.00 (STA) £22.95 (RES) £25.50 (ROB) £26.00 (PHI)
Brunello di Montalcino Castelgiocondo **1994** £19.81 (PIP) £23.15 (TAN)
Brunello di Montalcino Col d'Orcia **1994** £19.95 (VA)
Brunello di Montalcino il Poggione **1993** £19.99 (BOD) £19.99 (SUN)
Brunello di Montalcino Pertimali **1991** £17.90 (JU)
Brunello di Montalcino Quercecchio **1993** £18.25 (CON)
Brunello di Montalcino Val di Suga **1993** £17.82 (COC)
Brunello di Montalcino Villa Banfi **1993** £18.69 (BO) £24.95 (RES)
Brunesco di San Lorenzo Cappelli **1990** £18.75 (WS)
Ca' del Pazzo Caparzo **1995** £17.95 (DI)
Casalferro Castello di Brolio **1996** £17.99 (YOU) £20.95 (RES)
Cepparello Isole e Olena **1995** £18.95 (RES) £25.00 (CON) £31.33 (CAV) £33.49 (REI)
Chianti Classico Castello di Ama **1996** £15.32 (WT) £15.50 (RES)
Chianti Classico Montagliari **1967** £17.50 (BU)

Chianti Classico Monte Bernardi **1995** £15.47 (GOE) £18.95 (BAL)
Chianti Classico Riserva Badia a Coltibuono **1994** £16.25 (AV)
Chianti Classico Riserva Carpineto **1990** £17.15 (AV)
Chianti Classico Riserva Castell'in Villa **1993** £15.79 (CB)
Chianti Classico Riserva Castello dei Rampolla **1996** £16.55 (CAV)
Chianti Classico Riserva Ducale Oro, Ruffino **1969** £17.50 (BU)
Chianti Classico Riserva Castello di Fonterutoli **1996** £19.99 (YOU)
Chianti Classico Riserva Castello di Fonterutoli **1995** £19.50 (BAL) £20.56 (REI) £22.50 (RES)
Chianti Classico Riserva Il Picchio, Querceto **1991** £17.00 (JU)
Chianti Classico Riserva Tenute Marchese Antinori **1995** £15.99 (DI)
Chianti Classico Riserva Nozzole **1994** £16.50 (JER)
Chianti Classico Riserva Castello della Paneretta **1997** £16.99 (VA)
Chianti Classico Riserva Querciabella **1997** £17.50 (LEA)
Chianti Classico Riserva Vigna del Sorbo, Fontodi **1995** £17.50 (WS) £21.00 (AME) £21.95 (VA)
Chianti Classico Riserva Vigneto Rancia, Felsina Berardenga **1995** £17.50 (WS) £21.65 (LIB) £21.95 (POR) £21.99 (YOU)
Chianti Classico Riserva Vigneto Rancia, Felsina Berardenga **1994** £17.45 (SOM) £20.41 (NO) £21.95 (RES)
Chianti Classico Ruffino **1973** £19.51 (REI)
Chianti Colli Senesi la Torre **1979** £16.50 (BU)
Chianti Rufina Riserva Bucerchiale, Selvapiana **1995** £15.00 (WS) £15.95 (LIB) £17.95 (RES)
Coltassala Castello di Volpaia **1995** £18.50 (AD)
Concerto Fonterutoli **1994** £19.95 (BAL)
La Corte, Castello di Querceto **1990** £15.90 (JU)
Elegia Poliziano **1995** £16.95 (SOM) £20.27 (REI)
Federico Primo Gualdo del Re **1996** £15.95 (LEA)
Flaccianello della Pieve, Fontodi **1995** £19.99 (VA)

Grifi Avignonesi **1995** £15.95 (STE) £16.99 (WR) £16.99 (BOT)
Il Latini, Il Vivaio **1994** £17.95 (LAY)
Il Querciolaia, Querceto **1991** £18.00 (JU)
Lamaione Merlot Frescobaldi **1995** £17.99 (OD)
Lamaione Merlot Frescobaldi **1993** £17.99 (YOU)
Morellino di Scansano Riserva, le Pupille **1997** £15.49 (LIB)
Palazzo Altesi, Altesino **1995** £17.95 (LEA)
Podere Migliara Manzano **1996** £19.95 (LEA)
Quattro Mori Castel de Paolis **1994** £18.95 (BAL)
Quercia Grande, Capaccia **1993** £19.95 (CON)
Rosso Miani, Miani **1995** £18.95 (BAL) £20.68 (NO)
Rubesco Torgiano Riserva Vigna Monticchio Lungarotti **1998** £15.49 (VA)
Sangioveto Badia a Coltibuono **1980** £15.00 (CRO)

I Sodi di San Niccolò, Castellare **1994** £17.14 (CAV) £23.50 (BAL)
I Sodi di San Niccolò, Castellare **1993** £17.14 (CAV) £21.95 (DI)
Solatio Basilica Villa Cafaggio **1996** £16.50 (BAL)
Tassinaia Tenuta del Terriccio **1997** £17.95 (LEA)
Tavernelle Villa Banfi **1995** £16.95 (RES)
Torrione Petrolo **1997** £18.99 (YOU) £21.50 (PHI)
Torrione Petrolo **1995** £18.75 (BU)
Vigna il Vallone Villa Sant' Anna **1995** £15.95 (LEA)
Vino Nobile di Montepulciano Vigna Asinone, Poliziano **1996** £19.99 (YOU)
Vino Nobile di Montepulciano Vigna Asinone, Poliziano **1995** £19.95 (LEA)

£20.00 → £24.99

Bolgheri Paleo, le Macchiole **1996** £23.99 (CAV) £26.95 (LEA)
Brunello di Montalcino Argiano **1995** £21.99 (YOU) £22.50 (AME) £22.95 (LIB)
Brunello di Montalcino Casanova di Neri **1994** £22.99 (WR)
Brunello di Montalcino Fattoria dei Barbi **1981** £22.50 (BU)
Brunello di Montalcino Pertimali **1994** £22.95 (DI)
Brunello di Montalcino Riserva, Castelgiocondo **1980** £22.00 (CRO)
Brunello di Montalcino Val di Suga **1994** £20.68 (PLAY)
Camartina Querciabella **1994** £24.95 (LEA)
Carmignano Riserva, Villa di Capezzana **1997** £22.95 (RES)
Carmignano Riserva, Villa di Capezzana **1996** £21.49 (LIB)
Carmignano Riserva, Villa di Capezzana **1995** £21.49 (NI)
Carmignano Villa di Capezzana **1995** £20.99 (NO) £21.80 (TAN)
Cepparello Isole e Olena **1997** £24.95 (SOM) £36.95 (VA) £38.19 (REI)
Cepparello Isole e Olena **1994** £21.95 (LIB) £22.95 (VA) £25.00 (FORT) £26.93 (CAV)
Chianti Classico Castello di Fonterutoli **1995** £22.60 (NO)
Chianti Classico Giorgio Primo, Fattoria La Massa **1995** £20.95 (JER)
Chianti Classico Riserva Ducale Oro, Ruffino **1971** £20.00 (BU) £25.26 (REI)
Chianti Classico Riserva Castello di Fonterutoli **1997** £20.99 (YOU)
Chianti Classico Riserva Santa Cristina, Antinori **1983** £21.00 (CRO)
Chianti Classico Riserva Vecchie Terre di Montefili **1993** £23.99 (RAE)
Chianti Classico Riserva Vigneto Rancia, Felsina Berardenga **1997** £23.95 (LIB)
Chianti Classico Ruffino **1969** £21.74 (REI)
Chianti Rufina Riserva Montesodi, Frescobaldi **1993** £20.90 (TAN)
Chianti Rufina Selvapiana **1990** £24.00 (CRO)
Cignale Querceto **1991** £21.00 (JU)
Coltassala Castello di Volpaia **1982** £21.00 (CRO)
Flaccianello della Pieve, Fontodi **1996** £23.99 (YOU) £24.95 (VA) £25.75 (LIB)
Fontalloro Felsina Berardenga **1995** £23.99 (YOU) £25.00 (BU) £25.75 (BEN)
Fontalloro Felsina Berardenga **1994** £23.95 (LIB) £23.99 (VA)
Ghiaie della Furba, Capezzana **1997** £24.35 (PLAY) £24.95 (TAN)
Ghiaie della Furba, Capezzana **1995** £22.75 (PHI)
Percalo San Giusto a Rentannano **1996** £24.00 (BAL)
Podere Il Bosco Manzano **1996** £22.95 (LEA)
Sa' etta Monte Bernardi **1997** £24.48 (FA)
Sa' etta Monte Bernardi **1995** £23.50 (GOE) £26.50 (BAL)
Sammarco Castello dei Rampolla **1991** £24.50 (BAL)
San Giorgio Lungarotti **1981** £24.00 (CRO)
Le Stanze Poliziano **1995** £20.27 (REI)
Torrione Petrolo **1996** £20.95 (RES)
Vino Nobile di Montepulciano Bindella **1986** £20.00 (CRO)

£25.00 → £29.99

Bolgheri Paleo, le Macchiole **1995** £25.95 (LEA)
Bolgheri Superiore Paleo Rosso, le Macchiole **1995** £28.02 (REI)
Brunello di Montalcino Altesino **1994** £29.99 (POR)
Brunello di Montalcino Altesino **1983** £29.00 (CRO)
Brunello di Montalcino Costanti **1995** £29.95 (LIB)
Brunello di Montalcino Costanti **1994** £27.45 (VA) £27.60 (HAH) £29.95 (PHI) £29.95 (RES)
Brunello di Montalcino Fattoria dei Barbi **1995** £26.25 (FORT)
Brunello di Montalcino Fattoria dei Barbi **1977** £29.50 (BU)

Brunello di Montalcino Poggio alle Mura **1970** £27.61 (REI)
Brunello di Montalcino Poggio Antico **1993** £25.95 (ROB)
Brunello di Montalcino Riserva, Col d'Orcia **1990** £28.95 (ROB)
Cabernet Sauvignon Isole e Olena **1996** £28.95 (LIB)
Cabernet Sauvignon Isole e Olena **1995** £29.95 (RES)
Camartina Querciabella **1995** £26.85 (REI) £27.50 (LEA)
Cepparello Isole e Olena **1996** £25.95 (POR) £28.49 (LIB) £29.95 (PHI)
Chianti Classico Isole e Olena **1975** £29.38 (REI)
Chianti Classico Riserva Vigna del Sorbo, Fontodi **1997** £25.95 (LIB)
Flaccianello della Pieve, Fontodi **1997** £25.95 (BEN) £27.99 (YOU) £28.95 (LIB)
Guado al Tasso, Antinori **1993** £26.50 (VA)
Ornellaia Tenuta dell'Ornellaia **1993** £27.99 (YOU) £29.50 (CON) £34.50 (ROB)
Podere Il Bosco Manzano **1997** £26.50 (LEA)
Saffredi le Pupille **1997** £29.99 (SOM) £35.25 (REI) £37.50 (LIB) £42.00 (PHI)
Saffredi le Pupille **1995** £27.95 (RES) £45.00 (HED)
Sammarco Castello dei Rampolla **1995** £29.50 (BAL) £33.00 (PHI)
Sangioveto Badia a Coltibuono **1995** £28.00 (AV)
Summus Villa Banfi **1995** £27.95 (RES)
Syrah Isole e Olena **1996** £25.49 (LIB)
Tignanello Antinori **1996** £27.50 (FORT) £28.99 (WR) £29.90 (TAN) £32.20 (HAH) £37.00 (JER) £38.99 (BOD) £38.99 (SUN)
Tignanello Antinori **1995** £25.00 (CRO) £28.99 (WR) £28.99 (BOT) £29.99 (JON) £32.50 (BAL) £32.50 (ROB) £36.62 (FA) £39.95 (LEA) £43.50 (BEN) £50.00 (VA)

£30.00 → £39.99

Brunello di Montalcino Rennina, Pieve Santa Restituta **1994** £34.20 (LAY)
Brunello di Montalcino Rennina, Pieve Santa Restituta **1993** £35.00 (MI)
Cepparello Isole e Olena **1990** £33.00 (CRO)
Chianti Classico Riserva Felsina Berardenga **1990** £33.00 (CRO)
Chianti Rufina Riserva Bucerchiale, Selvapiana **1990** £31.00 (CRO)
Guado al Tasso, Antinori **1995** £32.00 (CRO) £32.00 (VA) £34.95 (ROB)
Il Carbonaione, Podere Poggio Scalette **1997** £38.68 (CAV)
Lupicaia Tenuta del Terriccio **1996** £39.50 (LEA)
Ornellaia Tenuta dell'Ornellaia **1996** £34.66 (FA) £45.24 (REI) £47.00 (YOU)
Ornellaia Tenuta dell'Ornellaia **1995** £35.64 (FA) £41.15 (NO) £41.20 (TAN) £44.00 (LEA) £45.00 (BAL) £45.00 (FORT) £50.00 (ROB)
Ornellaia Tenuta dell'Ornellaia **1994** £32.00 (VA) £45.86 (PIP)
Le Pergole Torte, Montevertine **1995** £31.95 (LEA)
Sammarco Castello dei Rampolla **1996** £30.35 (CAV) £32.50 (BAL)
San Giorgio Lungarotti **1978** £30.00 (CRO)
Tignanello Antinori **1980** £35.00 (YOU)
Vino Nobile di Montepulciano Fassati **1970** £39.00 (CRO)

£40.00 → £49.99

Brunello di Montalcino Col d'Orcia **1990** £49.94 (REI)
Brunello di Montalcino Rennina, Pieve Santa Restituta **1990** £49.17 (MI)
Chianti Classico Badia a Coltibuono **1964** £41.13 (REI)
Flaccianello della Pieve, Fontodi **1990** £45.00 (VA) £52.88 (REI)
Fontalloro Felsina Berardenga **1990** £49.00 (VA)
Il Carbonaione, Podere Poggio Scalette **1994** £41.13 (CAV)
Lupicaia Tenuta del Terriccio **1997** £44.50 (LEA)
Sassicaia Tenuta San Guido **1996** £49.00 (YOU) £59.95 (ROB) £60.00 (VA) £60.12 (FA) £64.63 (REI) £68.05 (CAV)
Sassicaia Tenuta San Guido **1994** £42.99 (BOT) £44.00 (DI) £77.22 (NO)
I Sodi di San Niccolò, Castellare **1990** £48.47 (CAV)
Solaia Antinori **1989** £49.00 (VA) £82.25 (CAV)
Tignanello Antinori **1983** £44.06 (REI)

Please remember that
Oz Clarke's Wine Buying Guide
*is a price **guide** and not a price **list**. It is not meant to replace up-to-date merchants' lists.*

£50.00 → £69.99

Brunello di Montalcino Riserva, Villa Banfi **1993** £63.00 (RES)
Brunello di Montalcino Sugarille, Pieve Santa Restituta **1995** £52.50 (MI)
Chianti Classico Riserva Badia a Coltibuono **1968** £50.00 (CRO)
Concerto Fonterutoli **1985** £52.88 (REI)
Masseto Tenuta dell'Ornellaia **1996** £63.69 (CB) £77.75 (FA)
Masseto Tenuta dell'Ornellaia **1993** £55.00 (FORT)
Montepulciano d'Abruzzo Valentini **1993** £59.50 (BAL)
Ornellaia Tenuta dell'Ornellaia **1997** £64.63 (REI)
Ornellaia Tenuta dell'Ornellaia **1991** £55.00 (VA)
Ornellaia Tenuta dell'Ornellaia **1988** £58.75 (REI) £71.87 (FA) £95.00 (FORT)
Sassicaia Tenuta San Guido **1997** £53.00 (LIB)
Sassicaia Tenuta San Guido **1995** £51.76 (PLAY) £54.99 (WR) £64.63 (REI) £77.22 (NO) £90.00 (VA)
Sassicaia Tenuta San Guido **1993** £58.95 (ROB) £75.00 (VA)
Solaia Antinori **1996** £57.00 (YOU)
Solaia Antinori **1995** £52.00 (CRO) £59.95 (ROB)
Solaia Antinori **1991** £58.00 (VA)
Tignanello Antinori **1982** £62.08 (FA)

£70.00 → £99.99

Brunello di Montalcino Riserva, Biondi-Santi **1975** £92.24 (REI)
Brunello di Montalcino Riserva, Biondi-Santi **1970** £70.00 (CRO)
Brunello di Montalcino Sugarille, Pieve Santa Restituta **1990** £83.33 (MI)
Masseto Tenuta dell'Ornellaia **1992** £85.00 (BU)
Ornellaia Tenuta dell'Ornellaia **1990** £83.62 (FA) £105.75 (REI) £139.00 (VA) £150.00 (FORT)
Sassicaia Tenuta San Guido **1992** £70.50 (REI) £85.00 (VA)
Sassicaia Tenuta San Guido **1988** £99.29 (FA) £105.00 (CRO) £185.00 (VA) £188.00 (CAV)
Solaia Antinori **1985** £99.00 (VA)
Tignanello Antinori **1990** £97.43 (CAV)
Tignanello Antinori **1987** £95.00 (VA)

£100.00 → £149.99

Brunello di Montalcino Biondi-Santi **1988** £100.00 (VA)
Brunello di Montalcino Riserva, Biondi-Santi **1985** £142.37 (FA)
Solaia Antinori **1990** £133.56 (FA) £195.00 (VA)
Tignanello Antinori **1985** £145.00 (VA)
Tignanello Antinori **1971** £130.62 (FA)

Over £150.00

Brunello di Montalcino Riserva, Biondi-Santi **1990** £165.00 (VA)
Sassicaia Tenuta San Guido **1985** £385.00 (VA)
Sassicaia Tenuta San Guido **1978** £235.00 (FA)
Sassicaia Tenuta San Guido **1968** £763.75 (REI)
Solaia Antinori **1982** £150.00 (FORT)

CENTRAL WHITE

Under £4.50

Frascati Superiore Satinata, Colle di Catone **1998** £3.99 (ASD)
Grechetto dell'Umbria, Il Vignolo **1997** £4.40 (SOM)
Orvieto Classico Secco Cardeto **1999** £4.29 (WAI) £4.75 (STE)
Verdicchio dei Castelli di Jesi Classico, Umani Ronchi **1997** £4.20 (SOM) £4.94 (FLE) £4.99 (NI) £6.63 (NO)
Verdicchio dei Castelli di Jesi, Villa Pigna **1998** £3.99 (UN)

£4.50 → £5.49

Frascati Superiore Fontana Candida **1998** £4.99 (MAJ) £5.85 (NI) £6.25 (STA)
Frascati Superiore Satinata, Colle di Catone **1996** £5.45 (JU) £5.99 (BOT)
Orvieto Classico Abboccato Antinori **1998** £4.99 (VIC) £4.99 (THR) £4.99 (BOT) £5.49 (JON) £5.90 (TAN) £5.99 (VA)
Orvieto Classico Secco Antinori **1998** £4.99 (VIC) £4.99 (THR) £5.49 (JON) £5.50 (TAN) £7.15 (JER)
Orvieto Classico Secco Antinori **1997** £4.99 (BOT)
Verdicchio dei Castelli di Jesi Classico, Brunori **1999** £5.49 (BIB)
Verdicchio dei Castelli di Jesi Classico, Umani Ronchi **1998** £4.99 (NI) £7.64 (REI)

£5.50 → £6.99

Bianco di Avignonesi **1996** £6.99 (REI) £7.50 (STE)
Bianco Villa Antinori, Antinori **1998** £5.99 (NEZ) £6.59 (VA) £6.65 (HAH) £6.90 (TAN)
Bianco Villa Antinori, Antinori **1997** £6.95 (JER)
Castello della Sala, Antinori **1998** £6.99 (WAI)
Chardonnay Villa di Capezzana **1999** £6.99 (LIB)
Frascati Superiore Monteporzio **1998** £5.99 (VA)
Frascati Superiore Satinata, Colle di Catone **1997** £5.99 (VIC) £5.99 (THR)
Montefalco Bianco, Adanti **1996** £6.49 (CON) £6.99 (JON)
Montescudaio Bianco, Fattoria di Sorbaiano **1994** £5.59 (CON)
Orvieto Classico Abboccato Antinori **1997** £6.45 (ROB)
Orvieto Classico Amabile Bigi **1998** £5.99 (VA)
Orvieto Classico Antinori **1998** £6.35 (CB)
Orvieto Classico Antinori **1997** £6.45 (ROB) £7.80 (CRO)
Orvieto Classico Campogrande Castello della Sala, Antinori **1998** £5.50 (NEZ)
Orvieto Classico Secco Campogrande, Antinori **1998** £5.99 (DI)
Orvieto Classico Terre Vineate, Il Palazzone **1998** £6.99 (DI)
Orvieto Classico Vigneto Torricella, Bigi **1998** £6.95 (STA) £7.49 (VA)
Orvieto Classico Vigneto Torricella, Bigi **1997** £5.80 (SOM) £7.70 (AD) £7.95 (FORT)
Orvieto Secco Antinori **1998** £5.99 (VA)
Orvieto Secco Bigi **1998** £5.99 (VA)
Trebbiano d'Abruzzo Illuminati **1998** £5.75 (ROB)
Verdicchio dei Castelli di Jesi Classico Casal di Serra, Umani Ronchi **1998** £6.79 (VA) £6.99 (NI) £7.25 (STA)
Verdicchio dei Castelli di Jesi Classico Casal di Serra, Umani Ronchi **1997** £5.80 (SOM) £7.25 (FORT) £7.95 (ROB)
Verdicchio dei Castelli di Jesu Classico Villa Bianchi, Ronchi **1998** £5.70 (TAN)
Verdicchio di Matelica, Fattoria Monacesca **1997** £5.75 (SOM)
Verdicchio di Matelica, Fattoria Monacesca **1996** £5.95 (AD) £7.40 (JER)
Verdicchio di Matelica, Filli Bisci **1995** £5.95 (JU)
Vernaccia di San Gimignano Falchini **1997** £5.99 (RAE) £6.29 (JON)
Vernaccia di San Gimignano, Fontaleoni **1996** £5.95 (JU)
Vernaccia di San Gimignano Teruzzi e Puthod **1997** £6.35 (SOM) £8.75 (UB)

£7.00 → £9.99

Bianco di Avignonesi **1997** £7.50 (STE)
Borro Lastricato Selvapiana **1998** £7.99 (LIB)
Frascati Superiore Campovecchio, Castel de Paolis **1998** £9.95 (BAL)
Orvieto Classico Campo del Guardiano, Il Palazzone **1995** £7.35 (JU)
Verdicchio dei Castelli di Jesi Classico Casal di Serra, Umani Ronchi **1999** £7.02 (PIP)
Verdicchio dei Castelli di Jesi Classico, Fazi-Battaglia **1998** £8.79 (VA)
Vernaccia di San Gimignano Fiore, Montenidoli **1999** £9.96 (BIB)
Vernaccia di San Gimignano Teruzzi e Puthod **1998** £7.58 (REI) £12.99 (VA)
Vin Santo Antinori **Non-vintage** £8.99 (VA) £10.55 (JER) £13.49 (JON)

£10.00 → £12.99

Chardonnay I Sistri, Felsina Berardenga **1996** £10.95 (SOM) £13.99 (VA)
Chardonnay le Grance, Caparzo **1993** £11.75 (WAI)
Frascati Colle Gaio, Colli di Catone **1997** £11.99 (DI)
Frascati Superiore Campovecchio, Castel de Paolis **1997** £10.95 (ROB)
Frascati Superiore Castel de Paolis **1998** £12.50 (BAL)
Pomino il Benefizio, Frescobaldi **1995** £12.99 (VA)
Verdicchio dei Castelli di Jesi Classico Il Coroncino, Coroncino **1998** £10.45 (LAY)
Vernaccia di San Gimignano Terre di Tufi, Teruzzi e Puthod **1998** £12.99 (VA) £13.95 (LEA) £14.25 (ROB)

£13.00 → £19.99

Cervaro della Sala, Antinori **1997** £18.00 (NEZ) £27.50 (LEA) £27.95 (VA)
Chardonnay I Sistri, Felsina Berardenga **1998** £13.95 (LIB)
Chardonnay I Sistri, Felsina Berardenga **1997** £13.50 (STA) £13.99 (BEN)
Chardonnay Isole e Olena **1998** £15.10 (REI) £17.95 (LIB)

Chardonnay Isole e Olena **1997** £16.99 (VA) £17.95 (BEN)

Frascati Superiore Vigna Adriana, Castel de Paolis **1996** £15.95 (BAL) £18.75 (ROB)

Il Marzocco Avignonesi **1997** £15.10 (REI)

Saluccio Tenuta del Terriccio **1997** £18.95 (LEA)

Vernaccia di San Gimignano Teruzzi e Puthod **1999** £13.81 (PIP)

Vin Santo di Carmignano, Capezzana **1993** £14.49 (LIB)

Vin Santo le Pupille 50cl bottle **1993** £18.39 (LIB) £19.95 (VA)

Vin Santo Selvapiana 50cl bottle **1993** £19.49 (LIB)

Over £20.00

Batàr Querciabella **1997** £24.95 (LEA)

Cervaro della Sala, Antinori **1996** £22.50 (BAL)

Cervaro della Sala, Antinori **1991** £20.95 (DI)

Trebbiano d'Abruzzo Valentini **1993** £32.00 (BAL)

Vin Santo Capelli **1968** £22.00 (CRO)

Vin Santo Isole e Olena **1994** £24.95 (LIB)

Vin Santo Selvapiana 50cl bottle **1991** £20.99 (VA)

CENTRAL ROSÉ

Under £8.00

Carmignano Vinruspo Rosato, Capezzana **1999** £7.95 (LIB)

CENTRAL SPARKLING

Under £6.00

Lambrusco Bianco Ca' de Medici **Non-vintage** £1.99 (WAI)

Lambrusco Grasparossa di Castelvetro **1994** £5.50 (PHI)

SOUTHERN RED

Under £5.00

Cent'Are Rosso Duca di Castelmonte **1997** £4.69 (WAI)

Cirò Classico Librandi **1997** £4.99 (UN) £5.99 (VA)

Copertino Eloquenzia, Masseria Monaci **1997** £4.95 (WS) £5.49 (AME) £5.99 (BAL)

Copertino Eloquenzia, Masseria Monaci **1995** £4.35 (SOM) £5.95 (POR)

★ Negroamaro Promessa **1999** £4.99 (LIB)

Salice Salentino Riserva Candido **1996** £4.95 (WS) £5.74 (PIP) £6.46 (REI) £6.70 (TAN) £6.99 (PHI)

Salice Salentino Vallone **1997** £4.50 (SOM) £5.79 (AME) £5.99 (BOT) £6.15 (LAY)

Salice Salentino Vallone **1995** £4.99 (POR) £4.99 (BO)

Salice Salentino Vallone **1994** £4.99 (BAL)

Squinzano Mottura **Non-vintage** £4.99 (SAF)

£5.00 → £5.99

Barbaglio Santa Barbara **1994** £5.99 (CON)

Cent'Are Rosso Duca di Castelmonte **1996** £5.99 (UB)

Copertino Eloquenzia, Masseria Monaci **1996** £5.35 (CON)

Copertino Riserva, Cantina Sociale di Copertino **1994** £5.60 (SOM) £6.43 (NO) £6.99 (VA)

★ Primitivo A-Mano, Puglia **1999** £5.99 (LIB) £6.49 (HED)

Rosso Brindisi Santa Barbara **1995** £5.15 (TAN)

Rosso del Salento Notarpanaro Taurino **1996** £5.99 (MAJ)

Salice Salentino Candido **1996** £5.99 (VA)

Salice Salentino Riserva Candido **1997** £5.99 (MAJ)

£6.00 → £7.99

Cappello di Prete, Candido **1994** £6.30 (SOM) £8.50 (ROB)

Carignano del Sulcis, Santadi **1997** £6.99 (VA)

Carignano del Sulcis, Santadi **1996** £6.02 (PIP)

Carignano del Sulcis, Santadi **1995** £6.50 (STA)

Corvo Rosso Duca di Salaparuta **1997** £6.99 (VA)

Pier delle Vigne Rosso delle Murge, Botromagno **1994** £6.99 (BAL)

Primitivo di Manduria Archidamo, Pervini **1997** £6.50 (WS) £6.99 (BO) £6.99 (AME) £7.49 (HED)

Regaleali Rosso, Tasca d'Almerita-Regaleali **1997** £7.28 (PIP) £9.25 (ROB)

Regaleali Rosso, Tasca d'Almerita-Regaleali **1996** £7.25 (LEA) £7.99 (DI)

Rosso del Salento Cappello di Prete **1995** £6.96 (PIP) £7.25 (CON)

Rosso del Salento Cappello di Prete **1994** £7.58 (REI) £7.79 (JON)
Simposia Masseria Monaci **1995** £7.99 (BAL) £8.90 (LAY)
Vigna Virzi Rosso, Spadafora **1997** £6.40 (SOM)

£8.00 → £9.99

Aglianico del Vulture, Fratelli d'Angelo **1997** £8.40 (TAN)
Aglianico del Vulture, Fratelli d'Angelo **1996** £8.49 (VA) £9.25 (ROB)
Aglianico del Vulture, Paternoster **1996** £9.99 (VA)
Cannonau di Sardegna Costera, Argiolas **1996** £8.25 (ROB)
Carignano del Sulcis Rocca Rubia Riserva, Santadi **1993** £9.95 (JU)
Pier delle Vigne Rosso delle Murge, Botromagno **1993** £8.79 (VA)
Vigna Virzi Rosso, Spadafora **1998** £8.95 (POR) £9.49 (LIB)

£10.00 → £14.99

Alezio Rosso Mjere, Michele Calò **1995** £11.25 (ROB)
Carignano del Sulcis Rocca Rubia Riserva, Santadi **1995** £10.87 (REI) £10.99 (PHI) £11.95 (ROB)
Carignano del Sulcis Rocca Rubia Riserva, Santadi **1994** £10.99 (VA)
Don Pietro Rosso, Spadafora **1997** £10.95 (BU) £10.95 (LIB)
Graticciaia Vallone **1993** £13.60 (SOM) £16.75 (CON) £17.95 (POR)

£15.00 → £19.99

Graticciaia Vallone **1994** £17.99 (AME)
Graticciaia Vallone **1992** £17.50 (BAL)
Planeta Merlot **1997** £16.99 (YOU) £18.62 (REI) £18.95 (VA) £18.95 (RES)
Santa Cecilia Planeta **1997** £18.62 (REI)
Terre Brune, Santadi **1995** £17.99 (YOU) £18.90 (VA) £19.95 (PHI)
Terre Brune, Santadi **1992** £18.39 (REI)

Over £20.00

Aglianico del Vulture, Fratelli d'Angelo **1985** £25.26 (REI)
Duca Enrico Duca di Salaparuta **1990** £24.62 (REI)
Taurasi Riserva Mastroberardino **1981** £21.00 (CRO)
Turriga Argiolas **1994** £22.27 (REI) £22.95 (STE) £23.00 (RES) £23.95 (LEA)

SOUTHERN WHITE

Under £6.00

Chardonnay del Salento le Trulle **1999** £4.49 (OD)
Gravina Bianco, Botromagno **1998** £5.19 (BAL) £5.79 (VA) £6.45 (ROB)

£6.00 → £7.99

Corvo Bianco Duca di Salaparuta **1998** £6.99 (VA)
Corvo Bianco Duca di Salaparuta **1997** £6.25 (COC)
Regaleali Conte Tasca d'Almerita **1998** £7.49 (VA) £8.25 (ROB)

Over £8.00

Don Pietro Bianco, Spadafora **1998** £10.49 (LIB)
Fiano di Avellino Mastroberardino **1997** £10.99 (VA)
Greco di Tufo Feudi di San Gregorio **1998** £8.99 (VA)
Greco di Tufo Feudi di San Gregorio **1997** £10.75 (ROB)
Lacryma Christi del Vesuvio, Mastroberardino **1998** £8.99 (VA)
Vermentino di Sardegna La Cala, Sella & Mosca **1997** £8.15 (ROB)

SOUTHERN ROSÉ

Under £6.00

Vigna Flaminio Brindisi Rosato, Vallone **1995** £5.75 (BAL) £5.75 (BU)

SOUTHERN FORTIFIED

Under £7.00

Marsala Superiore Garibaldi Dolce, Pellegrino **Non-vintage** £6.00 (AV) £6.29 (SAF) £6.95 (DI)

c. £25.00

Moscato Passito di Pantelleria Bukkuram, de Bartoli **Non-vintage** £24.69 (VA)

A key to name abbreviations is available on page 7.

NEW ZEALAND

Now it's time for New Zealand's other white grape varieties – Pinot Gris, Gewürztraminer and others – to reach Sauvignon standard

New Zealand is now a producer of benchmark Sauvignon Blanc – indeed the only benchmark Sauvignon Blanc for anyone who prefers its gooseberry and cut grass style to the more blackcurrant leaf flavours of the Loire.

Marlborough is still the biggest star among Sauvignon Blanc regions, but that doesn't mean that others aren't coming up. But I suspect that for most of us, the region is less important than the name of the producer or the grape variety. And if you want a useful blend, try Sauvignon Blanc with Semillon.

Other white varieties, except for Chardonnay, don't yet quite hit the mark in New Zealand. Pinot Gris, Gewürztraminer and Riesling are all promising – very promising, in fact – but they lack intensity of fruit. They're a bit too safe: they don't yet bring out the full unpredictable character of the grape. Yet.

GRAPES & FLAVOURS

CABERNET SAUVIGNON (red) Only really succeeds in the hotter North Island, where Waiheke, Matakana and Hawke's Bay can make it well in warm years. Elsewhere a lot is being pulled out, and producers are focusing on blends instead, or on Merlot and Pinot Noir. Try *Babich Patriarch, Delegat's, Esk Valley, Heron's Flight, Matua Ararimu, Sacred Hill Basket Press Reserve, Stonyridge Larose, Te Mata Coleraine, Twin Bays Fenton, Vavasour Reserve, Vidal, Villa Maria Reserve, Waiheke Vineyards Te Motu, Waipara West Ram Paddock Red.*

CHARDONNAY (white) Styles range from the soft peaches-and-cream of Gisborne to the grapefruit of Hawke's Bay and the light, zesty wines of Marlborough. Auckland, Nelson, Wairarapa and Canterbury all have less defined styles. The best producers are: *Babich Irongate, Chard Farm, Church Road, Cloudy Bay, Collard Rothesay* and *Hawke's Bay, Corbans Marlborough Private Bin* and *Gisborne Cottage Block, Delegat's, Hunter's, Kumeu River, Matua Valley Ararimu, Montana Ormond Estate, Morton Estate Black Label, Neudorf, Nobilo Dixon* and *Marlborough, Te Mata, Vidal* and *Villa Maria.*

CHENIN BLANC (white) Not widely imported here, and generally sound but not thrilling. Best: *Millton Vineyard*'s Chenin is a serious heavyweight, whereas *Collard* and *Esk Valley* are lighter, more supple wines.

GEWÜRZTRAMINER (white) Usually well structured with some elegance. Try: *Rippon, Villa Maria, Montana 'P'* from *Patutahi Estate, Vidal, Stonecroft.*

MERLOT (red) Increasingly popular in NZ. A lot is blended with Cabernet although there is an emerging band of top varietals: try *Delegat's, Corbans* and *Vidal.*

MÜLLER-THURGAU (white) The mainstay of bag-in-the-box production. Good ones in bottle include the White Cloud blend from *Nobilo, Babich Montana. Collard* and *Matua Valley.*

PINOT GRIS (white) Good fruit, lanolin and spice flavours. *Dry River* is outstanding. Others: *Gibbston Valley, St Helena, Seresin.*

PINOT NOIR (red) With California, NZ is the best New World source of this. None is as good as great Burgundy, but then nor is most Burgundy. *Martinborough Vineyard* is closest to the Burgundy benchmark. Try also *Ata Rangi, Chard Farm, Dry River*, Also: *Corbans, Giesen Estate, Neudorf, Palliser Estate, Mark Rattray, Rippon, St Helena, Waipara Springs, Waipara West.*

RIESLING (white) There's potential here for very good quality. Try *Corbans Amberley, Kim Crawford, Dry River, Giesen, Hunter's, Neudorf, Palliser Estate, Redwood Valley* and *Seifried*. For off-dry wines try *Collard, Millton, Montana* and *Stoneleigh*. The best sweet botrytized ones are made by *Corbans, Palliser Estate* and *Villa Maria*.

SAUVIGNON BLANC (white) This is still New Zealand's best wine. It can be divided into the pungently aromatic, herbaceous and zesty South Island (mainly Marlborough) styles, and the fleshier, riper and softer wines with stone-fruit flavours made on the North Island. There's increasingly a move towards single vineyard wines, and an emphasis on terroir: Marlborough is becoming divided into Wairau Valley (tightly structured wines) and Awatere (richer, riper, more powerful). Best of the South include: *Clifford Bay, Cloudy Bay, Corbans, Kim Crawford, Hunter's, Jackson Estate, Merlen, Montana Brancott Estate, Selaks, Stoneleigh, Vavasour Awatere, Villa Maria Wairau Valley* and *Wairau River*. Best North Island: *Matua Valley, Morton Estate, Palliser Estate* and *Vidal*.

SEMILLON (white) This is riper, and less aggressively grassy than it used to be. *Villa Maria* and *Collard* are the best. *Selaks'* Sauvignon-Semillon is clearly the best blend.

WINE REGIONS

AUCKLAND (North Island) A catch-all area that includes such sub-regions as Kumeu/Huapai, Waiheke Island (Bordeaux blends from *Goldwater, Stonyridge* and *Waiheke Vineyards Te Motu*), Henderson and Northland/Matakana. Stars here include *Kumeu River, Matua Valley, Nobilo, Selaks, Babich, Collard, Corbans, Delegat's, Villa Maria*.

CANTERBURY (South Island) This is dominated by *Giesen*, with a particular reputation for sweet botrytized Riesling. The sub-region of Waipara can boast Pinot Noir specialist *Mark Rattray*, plus *Waipara Springs, Waipara West* and *Pegasus Bay*.

CENTRAL OTAGO (South Island) A fast-growing region in which Pinot Noir is rapidly becoming the most planted vine. *Rippon, Gibbston Valley* and *Chard Farm* are the leading producers.

GISBORNE (North Island) Local growers and winemakers have dubbed this region the Chardonnay capital of NZ. Gisborne is also a spiritual home of Gewürztraminer, and (less promisingly) a centre of bulk production of Müller-Thurgau. There are approximately as many wine styles here as there are wineries. Reds are less exciting than whites, although Pinot Noir is being grown for good Champagne-method fizz.

HAWKE'S BAY (North Island) Potentially NZ's greatest wine region. Chardonnay, Cabernets Sauvignon and Franc and Merlot are the leading grapes, though there's also good Sauvignon Blanc, generally softer and riper than that of Marlborough. Best: *Brookfields, Church Road, Esk Valley, Ngatarawa, C J Pask, Sacred Hill, Te Mata, Vidal, Waimarama* and newcomers *Craggy Range* and *Unison*. *Babich, Cooks, Matua Valley, Mills Reef, Morton Estate* and *Villa Maria* also use grapes from here. Sub-region Gimblett Road is terrifically trendy.

MARLBOROUGH (South Island) NZ's biggest region by far specializes in Sauvignon Blanc and makes the archetypal NZ style, all gooseberries and cut grass. Riesling does well here, making wines from dry to sweet;

Chardonnay is more difficult, but complex and distinctive when successful. Reds have fared less well although Pinot Noir is in great demand when it can be spared from the buoyant fizz industry. There's good botrytized wine here as well. Best: *Cellier Le Brun* (for fizz), *Cloudy Bay, Corbans, Kim Crawford, Grove Mill, Hunter's, Isabel Estate, Jackson Estate, Nautilus, Selaks* and *Vavasour.*

NELSON (South Island) *Neudorf,* making subtle, nutty Chardonnay, and *Seifried,* with complex Riesling, are the leading lights in this South Island region.

WAIRARAPA (North Island) This includes the sub-region of Martinborough, which is the source of some of NZ's most exciting Pinot Noirs. *Martinborough Vineyard, Ata Rangi* and *Dry River* are the Pinot stars, all making small quantities from low-yielding vines; *Palliser Estate* makes concentrated Chardonnay and Sauvignon Blanc, and there's promising Riesling and Pinot Gris, too.

PRODUCERS WHO'S WHO

ALLAN SCOTT ★★★(★) Lively Marlborough Sauvignon Blanc, pungent Riesling and elegant Chardonnay.

ATA RANGI ★★★★ Good subtle Pinot Noir, an intense Cabernet/Merlot/Shiraz blend called Célèbre, and nice Chardonnay.

BABICH ★★★(★) Fresh Fumé Vert (Chardonnay, Semillon, Sauvignon), zesty Marlborough Sauvignon, elegant Irongate Chardonnay and Cabernet/Merlot. The Syrah so far is less noteworthy.

CELLIER LE BRUN ★★★★(★) Excellent, Champenois-run specialist sparkling wine producer.

CLOUDY BAY ★★★★★ Excellent, complex Sauvignon, fattened with a little Semillon. Top Champagne-method fizz under the Pelorus brand, with the ability to age well, and Chardonnay is also good.

COLLARD ★★★★ A top Chardonnay maker. There's buttery Chenin Blanc and luscious botrytized Riesling when the vintage allows.

CORBANS ★★★(★) Very good Private Bin Chardonnay, and reliable to good quality across the whole range. New are single-vineyard Cottage Block Chardonnay and Pinot Noir.

DELEGAT'S ★★★★ Look out for the Marlborough range: it's called Oyster Bay. Fine Chardonnay and Cabernet with a good botrytized Riesling. Proprietor's Reserve wines are limited-release.

DE REDCLIFFE ★★★ State-of-the-art winery producing good, consistent Chardonnay and Riesling with occasionally very good oak-aged Sauvignon Blanc. Look out for the Bordeaux-blend reds.

DRY RIVER ★★★★★ Micro-winery making mega quality. The Pinot Noir, Gewürztraminer and Pinot Gris are among the best in the country; Chardonnay and botrytized styles are also up with the leaders.

ESK VALLEY ESTATE ★★★ Reds are based on blends of Bordeaux varieties, but the blend changes according to the year. Decent Chardonnay. Look out for single vineyard The Terraces.

FROMM ★★★ New set-up based in Blenheim and showing great promise. Chardonnay is elegant, Cabernet Sauvignon ripe and Pinot Noir very impressive. The winemaking here seems to have a nice sure touch.

GIBBSTON VALLEY ★★★ Small Otago winery making good Pinot Noir and

Chardonnay. Sauvignon Blanc is somewhat more variable.

GIESEN ★★★(★) Elegant lime-fruited dry and luscious sweet Riesling are the wines to look for here. There's also big, buttery Chardonnay.

GOLDWATER ★★★★ Big Waiheke reds, plus good Chardonnay. Sauvignon Blanc is called Dog Point.

GROVE MILL ★★★(★) Weighty Riesling and rich Chardonnay from Marlborough. Top reds in good years.

HUNTER'S ★★★★(★) Jane Hunter makes top-of-the-line Sauvignon Blanc and elegant Chardonnay. Fizz is slightly dull.

JACKSON ESTATE ★★★★ Classic Marlborough Sauvignon Blanc, complex Chardonnay and rather good vintage sparkling wine.

KUMEU RIVER ★★★★(★) Excellent single-vineyard Chardonnay from Mate's Vineyard. Good North Island Sauvignon Blanc and a Merlot-Cabernet blend.

MARTINBOROUGH VINEYARDS ★★★★ NZ's best-known Pinot Noir, big and complex Chardonnay, lovely Riesling.

MATUA VALLEY ★★★★ Look for top Ararimu Chardonnay and Cabernet. There's also luscious Sauvignon and Gewürztraminer, and good Shingle Peak range from Marlborough.

MILLS REEF★★★ Big, ripe Hawke's Bay Chardonnay, stylish limy Riesling and rich, ripe, mouthfilling fizz.

THE MILLTON VINEYARD ★★★★ New Zealand's first organic winemaker. There's lush, smoky, medium-dry Riesling (look out for Opou Vineyard), big, rich Chenin Blanc and balanced Chardonnay.

INSTANT CELLAR: CLASSIC SAUVIGNON BLANC

- **1998 Sauvignon Blanc, Kim Crawford, Marlborough, £7.29, Le Fleming Wines** Lime and passionfruit palate. Intense and ripe.
- **2000 Sauvignon Blanc, Palliser Estate, Martinborough, £8.17, Anthony Byrne** Classically crisp wine with plenty of length and flavour.
- **1999 Sauvignon Blanc, Selaks Drylands, £8.25, Wine Society** Ripe gooseberry and passionfruit, full and intense.
- **1999 Sauvignon Blanc, Collards, Marlborough, £8.83, Wine Treasury** Classic stuff from a producer that has been hard to find in Britain of late.
- **1999 Sauvignon Blanc, Jackson Estate, £8.99, Hedley Wright** Ripe and pungent, with gooseberries and mown grass flavours.
- **1998 Sauvignon Blanc, Isabel Estate, Marlborough, £9.00, Bacchus Fine Wines** Rich and ripe Sauvignon with good structure, all white peaches and a touch of melon.
- **1998 Sauvignon Blanc Reserve Barrel-Fermented, Sacred Hill, Hawke's Bay, £9.30, Bacchus Fine Wines** A different style of Sauvignon; barrel fermentation of riper fruit than would be obtained from many regions.

MISSION ★★★(★) A quality drive here has produced a range of impressive Chardonnays, delicate Riesling and an occasional sweet botrytis style when the year allows.

MONTANA ★★★(★) Top Champagne-method fizz, Lindauer; good Chardonnay and botrytized Riesling. Look out for new Pinot Noir, and single vineyard wines called 'O', 'R' and 'P', after the initial letter of their vineyards' names.

MORTON ESTATE ★★★★ Chardonnay at this estate, especially Black Label, is reliable and attractive. There's also fresh Sauvignon Blanc and Gewürztraminer, and impressive Champagne-method fizz. Reds are pretty good.

NAUTILUS ★★★★ Tight, quality-focused range includes top Marlborough Chardonnay, Sauvignon Blanc and firm, bottle-fermented fizz.

NEUDORF ★★★★ Remarkably subtle Burgundian-style Chardonnay; nice Sauvignon Blanc, too, and Pinot Noir.

NGATARAWA ★★★ Attractive Chardonnay, Cabernet/Merlot and botrytized Riesling. The Glazebrook label is top of the range.

NOBILO ★★★(★) Good Dixon Vineyard Chardonnay. Stylish Sauvignon. Popular White Cloud is a reliable Müller-Thurgau and Sauvignon blend.

PALLISER ★★★★ Some nice Sauvignon, Pinot Noir and concentrated Chardonnay.

C J PASK ★★★(★) Flavoursome reds from Cabernet, Merlot and Pinot Noir; also makes good Chardonnay from excellent vineyard sites.

PEGASUS BAY ★★★(★) Great Riesling, unconventional Sauvignon Blanc/Semillon and big, chewy Pinot Noir.

MARK RATTRAY VINEYARDS ★★★★ Very good Waipara-based Pinot Noir producer. Excellent Chardonnay.

RIPPON VINEYARD ★★★ Organic vineyard with a promising Pinot Noir. There's also some Syrah. Whites include decent Chardonnay and Sauvignon Blanc.

ST CLAIR ★★★(★) Classic Marlborough Sauvignon Blanc, elegant Chardonnay and pungent medium dry Riesling.

ST HELENA ★★★(★) Good Chardonnay, Pinot Gris and Pinot Blanc.

ST NESBIT ★★★ A red specialist with a consistently good Cabernet/Merlot blend.

> **ON THE CASE**
> *If you want to splash out, look for single-vineyard wines. They're pricy, but they can compete with almost anything the world can offer*

SEIFRIED ESTATE ★★★ A winery making very good Riesling, more complex than most. Sauvignon Blanc, too, is distinguished and well-made.

SELAKS ★★★★ Great Sauvignon and Sauvignon/Semillon. Founder's Selection is the top label.

STONYRIDGE ★★★★★ NZ's top red producer. Intense, ripe Cabernet blend (Larose) with less intense version as the second label.

TE MATA ★★★★★ Coleraine and Awatea are sought-after Cabernet/Merlot blends. There's also Burgundian-style Chardonnay under the Elston label, and one of NZ's first Syrahs.

VAVASOUR ★★★★ Top Chardonnay and reds and very good Sauvignons. The Vavasour label is used for the top wines; those under the Dashwood label have less aging ability.

VIDAL ESTATE ★★★ The Gewürztraminer here is very good, long and structured. Chardonnay is also worth seeking.

VILLA MARIA ★★★★ Villa Maria owns Vidal and Esk Valley, though they are independently run. From this label there's top Sauvignon Blanc (look especially for single vineyard wines) and botrytized Riesling.

WAIPARA WEST ★★★★ Good Chardonnay and Sauvignon Blanc. Best is Bordeaux blend Ram Paddock Red.

NEW ZEALAND PRICES

RED

Under £7.00

Cabernet Sauvignon Stoneleigh Marlborough **1998** £6.99 (TES)

Cabernet Sauvignon/Merlot Montana Timara **1998** £4.99 (VIC) £4.99 (THR) £4.99 (WR) £5.79 (JON)

Cabernet Sauvignon/Merlot Montana Timara **1997** £4.99 (BOT)

Dry Red Waimanu North Island **1998** £4.59 (BUD)

£7.00 → £8.99

Cabernet Franc Kim Crawford Wicken Hawkes Bay **1998** £7.45 (SOM) £9.69 (VA) £9.70 (NO)

Cabernet Sauvignon Delegat's Reserve Hawkes Bay **1998** £8.99 (OD) £8.99 (SAF)

Cabernet Sauvignon C J Pask **1997** £8.45 (HAH) £8.50 (TAN) £8.95 (POR)

Cabernet Sauvignon Selaks Hawkes Bay **1998** £7.95 (STE)

Cabernet Sauvignon Stoneleigh Marlborough **1992** £7.70 (UB)

Cabernet Sauvignon/Merlot Aotea **1997** £8.69 (PLAY)

Cabernet Sauvignon/Merlot Matua Valley Hawkes Bay **1998** £8.95 (STE)

Cabernet Sauvignon/Merlot Montana Church Road **1998** £8.99 (OD)

Cabernet Sauvignon/Merlot Montana Church Road **1997** £8.99 (VIC) £8.99 (THR) £8.99 (WR) £8.99 (BOT) £8.99 (SAF)

Cabernet Sauvignon/Merlot Montana Church Road **1996** £8.95 (COC)

Cabernet Sauvignon/Merlot C J Pask Hawkes Bay **1998** £8.95 (POR)

Cabernet Sauvignon/Merlot C J Pask Hawkes Bay **1997** £7.95 (AD)

Cabernet Sauvignon/Merlot C J Pask Hawkes Bay **1993** £7.20 (CRO)

Cabernet Sauvignon/Merlot Sacred Hill Basket Press **1997** £8.99 (UN)

Cabernet Sauvignon/Merlot Te Mata **1998** £7.99 (AME) £8.49 (VIC) £8.49 (THR) £8.49 (BOT) £11.69 (TW)

Merlot Montana Reserve **1997** £8.99 (TES)

Merlot Sacred Hill Whitecliff **1998** £7.49 (UN)

Merlot Saint Clair **1999** £7.15 (AV) £7.35 (COC)

Pinot Noir Jackson Estate **1996** £8.95 (HED)

★ Ram Paddock Red Waipara West **1998** £8.59 (WAT)

Ram Paddock Red Waipara West **1996** £8.59 (WAT) £8.99 (DI)

Syrah Babich Mara Estate **1996** £7.85 (CON)

Syrah Babich Winemaker's Reserve **1998** £7.49 (TES)

Two Terrace Red Waipara West **1997** £7.95 (NZW)

£9.00 → £10.99

Cabernet Franc Kim Crawford Hawkes Bay **1999** £9.95 (LIB)

Cabernet Franc Kim Crawford Hawkes Bay **1998** £9.99 (REI)

Cabernet Sauvignon C J Pask **1996** £9.09 (JON)

Cabernet Sauvignon Redwood Valley **1998** £9.00 (NZW) £9.34 (DOM)

Cabernet Sauvignon Redwood Valley **1997** £9.50 (STA) £10.30 (UB) £11.95 (JER)

Cabernet Sauvignon/Merlot De Redcliffe **1996** £9.75 (CON)

Cabernet Sauvignon/Merlot C J Pask Hawkes Bay **1996** £9.09 (JON)

Cabernet Sauvignon/Merlot Te Mata **1995** £9.95 (WS)

MERCHANTS SPECIALIZING IN NEW ZEALAND

see Merchant Directory (page 456) for details

Nobody has very many (except New Zealand Wines Direct), but for a wider-than-average choice, try: Adnams (AD), Averys of Bristol (AV), Ballantynes (BAL), Anthony Byrne (BY), Cockburns of Leith (COC), First Quench Group (BOT, THR, VIC, WR), New Zealand Wines Direct (NZW), Lay & Wheeler (LAY), Tanners (TAN), The Ubiquitous Chip (UB), Wine Society (WS), Noel Young (YOU).

Cabernet Sauvignon/Merlot Villa Maria Cellar Selection **1997** £9.99 (SAF)
Merlot Kim Crawford Hawkes Bay **1999** £9.95 (LIB)
Merlot Kim Crawford Hawkes Bay **1998** £10.40 (REI)
Merlot Kemblefield Estate **1997** £9.95 (STA)
Merlot Matua Valley Smith Dartmour **1997** £9.45 (STE)
Merlot/Cabernet Sauvignon Hunter's **1996** £9.95 (DI)
Pinot Noir De Redcliffe Hawkes Bay **1997** £10.49 (CON)
Pinot Noir Fromm La Strada **1997** £10.01 (NO) £14.50 (PIP)
Pinot Noir Giesen Canterbury **1998** £10.46 (CB)
Pinot Noir Hunter's **1998** £10.00 (PIP) £10.29 (JON) £10.90 (TAN) £10.99 (DI) £11.95 (JER) £12.40 (CRO)
Pinot Noir Isabel Estate **1998** £10.99 (PHI) £12.95 (BEN) £12.99 (YOU) £13.00 (MV)
Pinot Noir Jackson Estate **1998** £9.95 (POR) £10.49 (YOU) £10.79 (AME) £10.99 (WAI) £11.10 (PLAY) £13.28 (TW)
Pinot Noir Martinborough **1996** £10.35 (SOM) £10.50 (CRO) £12.95 (CON) £13.09 (JON) £13.11 (NO)
Pinot Noir Montana Reserve Marlborough **1998** £9.99 (OD) £9.99 (WR)
Pinot Noir Montana Reserve Marlborough **1997** £10.99 (PHI)
Pinot Noir Palliser Estate **1998** £10.95 (JU) £11.05 (BY) £11.49 (VIC) £11.49 (THR) £11.49 (WR) £11.49 (BOT)
Pinot Noir Palliser Estate **1996** £10.99 (PHI)
Pinot Noir Mark Rattray Vineyard **1995** £9.99 (WAT)
Pinot Noir Selaks Drylands Vineyard **1999** £10.75 (STE)

£11.00 → £14.99

Cabernet Sauvignon/Merlot Montana Church Road Reserve **1996** £11.50 (CON)
Cabernet Sauvignon/Merlot Montana Church Road Reserve **1995** £11.99 (WAI)
Cabernet Sauvignon/Merlot Morton Estate Black Label **1995** £13.35 (NEZ)
Cabernet Sauvignon/Merlot Ngatarawa Glazebrook **1995** £11.75 (WS)
Cabernet Sauvignon/Merlot Te Mata Awatea **1998** £14.30 (TAN)
Cabernet Sauvignon/Merlot Te Mata Awatea **1997** £12.99 (YOU) £13.99 (WR)
Cabernet Sauvignon/Merlot Villa Maria Reserve **1996** £14.99 (TES)
Celebre Ata Rangi **1996** £14.00 (NZW) £15.08 (FA) £15.90 (TAN) £16.50 (STA)
Merlot Saint Clair Rapaura Reserve **1998** £11.00 (AV)
Merlot/Cabernet Franc Redmetal Vineyards **1998** £12.00 (NZW)
Merlot/Cabernet Sauvignon Kumeu River **1996** £12.50 (BEN)
Pinot Noir Isabel Estate **1997** £12.49 (POR)
Pinot Noir Martinborough **1998** £13.99 (YOU) £14.50 (AD) £14.99 (VIC) £14.99 (THR) £14.99 (WR) £14.99 (BOT)
Pinot Noir Martinborough **1997** £12.95 (PHI) £12.95 (FORT) £13.99 (NI) £14.49 (VA)
Pinot Noir Muddy Water Waipara **1998** £14.00 (NZW) £15.47 (GOE)
Pinot Noir Rippon Vineyard **1998** £13.99 (UN) £14.00 (NZW) £16.95 (LEA)
Pinot Noir Seresin Estate **1997** £14.12 (NO)
Pinot Noir Waipara West **1999** £12.45 (WAT)
Syrah Fromm La Strada Reserve **1998** £12.99 (YOU)
Syrah Stonecroft **1998** £13.95 (LEA)
Syrah Stonecroft **1996** £11.99 (YOU)
Syrah Te Mata Bullnose **1998** £13.99 (YOU)
Syrah Te Mata Bullnose **1997** £14.69 (REI)

£15.00 → £19.99

Cabernet Sauvignon C J Pask Reserve **1995** £15.50 (CRO)
Cabernet Sauvignon Vidal Reserve **1994** £15.49 (YOU)
Cabernet Sauvignon/Merlot Benfield & Delamare **1997** £17.99 (YOU)
Cabernet Sauvignon/Merlot Peninsula Estate **1996** £19.99 (YOU)
Cabernet Sauvignon/Merlot Trinity Hill Gimblett Road **1997** £15.95 (LEA)
Celebre Ata Rangi **1997** £17.75 (FORT)
Celebre Ata Rangi **1995** £16.50 (BEN)
Coleraine Te Mata **1997** £18.99 (YOU) £19.40 (TAN) £19.49 (POR)
Coleraine Te Mata **1996** £18.99 (AME)

Stars (★) indicate wines selected by Oz Clarke in the Best Buys section which *begins on page 10.*

Pinot Noir Ata Rangi **1997** £19.95 (STA) £20.70 (HAH) £21.50 (FORT)
Pinot Noir Dry River **1996** £18.75 (RAE) £22.91 (FA)
Pinot Noir Fromm La Strada **1998** £16.30 (LAY) £16.49 (YOU)
Pinot Noir Gibbston Valley **1998** £15.99 (YOU) £16.99 (PHI) £18.95 (RES)
Pinot Noir Giesen Reserve Canterbury **1998** £15.95 (CB)
Pinot Noir Rippon Vineyard **1995** £17.50 (STA)
Syrah Peninsula Estate Gilmour **1998** £19.99 (YOU)
Unison Selection **1998** £15.95 (WAI)

£20.00 → £29.99

Cabernet Sauvignon/Merlot Goldwater Estate Waiheke Island **1996** £25.20 (AV) £25.99 (YOU)
Cabernet Sauvignon/Merlot Waiheke Vineyards Te Motu **1996** £21.93 (FA) £23.00 (NZW)
Larose Stonyridge **1998** £29.00 (NZW)
Pinot Noir Ata Rangi **1998** £21.95 (LEA)
Pinot Noir Dry River **1997** £20.00 (JU)
Pinot Noir Martinborough Reserve **1996** £26.00 (CRO)

Over £30.00

Larose Stonyridge **1997** £34.50 (STA) £35.00 (FORT)
Larose Stonyridge **1996** £40.88 (PLAY)

WHITE

Under £4.00

Timara Dry White Montana **1999** £3.99 (VIC) £3.99 (THR) £3.99 (BOT) £3.99 (SAF)
Timara Dry White Montana **1998** £3.99 (WR)

£4.00 → £4.99

Sauvignon Blanc Cooks Marlborough **1999** £4.99 (BUD)
Sauvignon Blanc Cooks Marlborough **1998** £4.99 (WAI)
Sauvignon Blanc Delegat's Marlborough Gold **1998** £4.99 (UN)
Sauvignon Blanc/Semillon Montana Azure Bay **1999** £4.99 (VIC) £4.99 (THR) £4.99 (WR) £4.99 (BOT)
White Cloud Nobilo **1999** £4.79 (SAF)
White Cloud Nobilo **1998** £4.95 (TAN)

£5.00 → £5.99

Chardonnay Cooks Hawkes Bay **1998** £5.49 (TES)
Chardonnay Corbans Gisborne **1999** £5.95 (AD)
Chardonnay Corbans Gisborne **1997** £5.49 (UN) £6.90 (AS)
Chardonnay Delegat's Marlborough Gold **1998** £5.49 (MAJ)
Chardonnay Montana Marlborough **1999** £5.99 (VIC) £5.99 (THR) £5.99 (WR) £5.99 (JON) £5.99 (BOT) £5.99 (WAI) £5.99 (SAF)
Chardonnay Montana Marlborough **1998** £5.49 (BO) £5.95 (COC) £5.99 (OD) £5.99 (UN)
Riesling Stoneleigh **1996** £5.60 (UB)
Riesling Villa Maria Private Bin **1999** £5.49 (VIC) £5.49 (THR) £5.49 (WR) £5.99 (BOT) £5.99 (WAI) £6.49 (POR)
Sauvignon Blanc Corbans Stoneleigh **1998** £5.51 (BY)
Sauvignon Blanc Delegat's Marlborough Gold **1999** £5.49 (MAJ)
Sauvignon Blanc Montana Marlborough **1999** £5.49 (BO) £5.99 (SO) £5.99 (PHI) £5.99 (SAI) £5.99 (TES) £5.99 (VIC) £5.99 (THR) £5.99 (OD) £5.99 (WR) £5.99 (JON) £5.99 (BOT) £5.99 (SAF)
Sauvignon Blanc Montana Marlborough **1998** £5.95 (COC) £5.99 (UN)
Sauvignon Blanc Nautilus Twin Islands Hawkes Bay/Marlborough **1998** £5.99 (NI)
Sauvignon Blanc C J Pask Hawkes Bay **1998** £5.95 (AD) £6.15 (HAH) £6.90 (TAN) £6.99 (POR)
Sauvignon Blanc Stoneleigh Marlborough **1999** £5.99 (SAI) £5.99 (WAI)
Semillon/Chardonnay Babich Gisborne **1998** £5.43 (COC)

£6.00 → £6.99

Chardonnay Aotea **1996** £6.95 (NZW)
Chardonnay Babich Gisborne **1997** £6.85 (CON)
Chardonnay Delegat's Oyster Bay **1999** £6.99 (SAI) £6.99 (MAJ) £6.99 (VIC) £6.99 (THR) £6.99 (BOT) £6.99 (SAF)
Chardonnay Delegat's Oyster Bay **1998** £6.99 (UN)
Chardonnay Saint Clair Tuatara Bay **1998** £6.30 (COC)
Chardonnay Selaks **2000** £6.75 (STE)
Chardonnay Stoneleigh **1997** £6.99 (TES)

Chardonnay Villa Maria Private Bin **1999** £6.99 (SAF)

Chardonnay Villa Maria Private Bin **1998** £6.99 (BO) £6.99 (OD) £6.99 (UN) £7.25 (UB)

Chardonnay Villa Maria Private Bin East Coast **1998** £6.99 (WAI)

Chenin Blanc Esk Valley Wood-aged **1998** £6.99 (PLA)

Gewürztraminer Villa Maria Private Bin **1998** £6.95 (POR)

★ Riesling Clifford Bay **1999** £6.99 (FRI)

Riesling Jackson Estate **1999** £6.99 (POR) £6.99 (BO)

Riesling Jackson Estate **1998** £6.99 (BO)

Riesling Selaks **1999** £6.95 (STE)

Sauvignon Blanc Aotea **1999** £6.50 (STA) £6.70 (NZW) £6.95 (LEA)

Sauvignon Blanc Aotea **1998** £6.95 (FORT) £6.95 (GOE) £7.00 (MV) £7.90 (JER)

Sauvignon Blanc Babich Hawkes Bay **1998** £6.35 (COC) £6.89 (CON)

Sauvignon Blanc Babich Marlborough **1999** £6.49 (AME)

Sauvignon Blanc Chancellor **1999** £6.70 (GW)

★ Sauvignon Blanc Churton **1997** £6.90 (TAN)

Sauvignon Blanc Kim Crawford Marlborough **1998** £6.75 (SOM) £7.29 (FLE) £7.99 (LIB) £7.99 (UN) £8.25 (CON) £8.40 (NO) £8.49 (VA)

Sauvignon Blanc Dashwood **1999** £6.99 (THR) £6.99 (OD) £6.99 (WR) £6.99 (BOT)

Sauvignon Blanc Dashwood **1998** £6.99 (VIC) £7.40 (CRO) £7.65 (NI) £7.99 (BO)

Sauvignon Blanc Delegat's Oyster Bay **1999** £6.49 (MAJ) £6.49 (VIC) £6.49 (THR) £6.99 (SAF) £7.35 (BER)

Sauvignon Blanc Kemblefield Estate Terrace View **1998** £6.50 (STA)

Sauvignon Blanc C J Pask Hawkes Bay **1999** £6.99 (POR)

Sauvignon Blanc Saint Clair Tuatara Bay **1999** £6.30 (COC)

Sauvignon Blanc Seifried **1998** £6.95 (WS)

Sauvignon Blanc Selaks **2000** £6.75 (STE)

Sauvignon Blanc Vidal **1997** £6.99 (DOM)

Please remember that ***Oz Clarke's Wine Buying Guide*** *is a price **guide** and not a price **list**. It is not meant to replace up-to-date merchants' lists.*

Sauvignon Blanc Villa Maria Private Bin **1999** £6.75 (POR) £6.80 (CRO) £6.99 (SAI) £6.99 (BO) £6.99 (TES) £6.99 (VIC) £6.99 (THR) £6.99 (OD) £6.99 (WR) £6.99 (BOT) £6.99 (SAF) £7.40 (ELL)

Sauvignon Blanc Villa Maria Private Bin **1998** £6.99 (BAL) £6.99 (UN)

Sauvignon Blanc Wairau River **1997** £6.85 (SOM) £7.93 (REI)

£7.00 → £7.99

Chardonnay Aotea **1999** £7.25 (STA)

Chardonnay Babich Hawkes Bay **1998** £7.75 (TAN)

Chardonnay Babich Hawkes Bay **1995** £7.90 (JU)

Chardonnay Bradshaw Estate Non-Wooded **1998** £7.69 (AME)

Chardonnay Cairnbrae **1998** £7.83 (CB)

Chardonnay Coopers Creek Hawkes Bay **1999** £7.49 (SO)

Chardonnay Kim Crawford Unoaked Marlborough **1998** £7.49 (UN) £7.99 (LIB) £8.49 (VA) £8.56 (FLE)

Chardonnay Kim Crawford Unoaked Marlborough **1997** £7.75 (CON)

Chardonnay Dashwood **1998** £7.65 (NI) £8.70 (HAH)

Chardonnay Esk Valley **1997** £7.95 (POR)

Chardonnay Kumeu River Brajkovich **1999** £7.50 (WS)

Chardonnay Kumeu River Brajkovich **1998** £7.25 (FA) £9.50 (BEN)

Chardonnay C J Pask **1998** £7.75 (TAN) £7.75 (HAH) £7.95 (AD) £7.99 (POR)

Chardonnay Saint Clair **1998** £7.35 (COC)

Chardonnay Villa Maria Cellar Selection **1998** £7.99 (OD)

Chenin Blanc Esk Valley Wood-aged **1997** £7.79 (PLAY)

Gewürztraminer Lawson's Dry Hills **1999** £7.49 (TES) £7.64 (BIB)

Gewürztraminer Lawson's Dry Hills **1998** £7.99 (PHI) £7.99 (AME)

Gewürztraminer Montana Reserve Gisborne **1999** £7.99 (THR) £7.99 (BOT)

Gewürztraminer Montana Reserve Gisborne **1998** £7.99 (WR)

Riesling Cairnbrae **1998** £7.29 (CB) £7.60 (UB)

Riesling Kim Crawford Dry Marlborough **1998** £7.99 (LIB) £8.25 (CON)

Riesling Forrest Estate **1999** £7.10 (FLE)

Riesling Grove Mill Marlborough **1998** £7.99 (PHI)

Riesling Jackson Estate Dry **1998** £7.49 (HED) £7.50 (TAN)
Riesling Montana Awatere Reserve **1999** £7.99 (OD)
Riesling Palliser Estate **1998** £7.16 (BY) £7.50 (JU)
Riesling Saint Clair **1999** £7.15 (AV)
Riesling Saint Clair **1998** £7.35 (COC)
★ Riesling Allan Scott **1999** £7.10 (LAY)
Riesling Allan Scott **1998** £7.50 (FORT)
Sauvignon Blanc Babich Mara Estate **1995** £7.79 (CON)
Sauvignon Blanc Cairnbrae **1999** £7.83 (CB)
★ Sauvignon Blanc Clifford Bay Estate **1999** £7.49 (FRI)
Sauvignon Blanc Coopers Creek Marlborough **1999** £7.49 (SO)
★ Sauvignon Blanc Kim Crawford **1999** £7.99 (LIB)
Sauvignon Blanc Forrest Estate **1999** £7.95 (AD) £7.99 (BEN)
Sauvignon Blanc Forrest Estate **1997** £7.10 (FLE)
Sauvignon Blanc Goldwater Estate Dog Point Marlborough **1999** £7.99 (MAJ) £8.10 (AV)
Sauvignon Blanc Grove Mill Marlborough **1999** £7.49 (OD) £7.49 (SAF) £8.25 (PHI)
Sauvignon Blanc Hawkesbridge Wines **1999** £7.75 (BER)
Sauvignon Blanc Isabel Estate **1998** £7.30 (SOM)
Sauvignon Blanc Jackson Estate **1999** £7.99 (POR) £8.80 (CRO) £8.85 (TAN) £8.92 (PIP) £8.99 (HED) £8.99 (PHI) £8.99 (TES) £8.99 (AME) £8.99 (OD) £8.99 (WAI)
Sauvignon Blanc Lawson's Dry Hills **1999** £7.64 (BIB) £7.99 (TES) £7.99 (AME)
Sauvignon Blanc Montana Reserve **1998** £7.99 (UN)
Sauvignon Blanc Nautilus Hawkes Bay **1998** £7.95 (NI)
★ Sauvignon Blanc Palliser Estate **1999** £7.58 (BY) £9.00 (FLE) £9.99 (PHI) £9.99 (VIC) £9.99 (THR) £9.99 (WR) £9.99 (BOT)
Sauvignon Blanc Saint Clair **1998** £7.35 (COC)
Sauvignon Blanc Allan Scott **1999** £7.95 (LAY)
Sauvignon Blanc Stoneleigh Marlborough **1996** £7.35 (UB)
Sauvignon Blanc Te Kairanga **1999** £7.98 (BIB)
Sauvignon Blanc Te Mata Castle Hill **1999** £7.99 (POR) £7.99 (AME) £11.69 (TW)
Sauvignon Blanc Te Mata Castle Hill **1998** £7.99 (OD)
Sauvignon Blanc Tui Vale **1997** £7.60 (JER)
Sauvignon Blanc Villa Maria Cellar Selection **1999** £7.99 (OD)
Sauvignon Blanc Wairau River **1999** £7.99 (VIC) £7.99 (THR) £7.99 (WR) £7.99 (BOT)
Sauvignon Blanc Wairau River **1998** £7.90 (CRO) £7.93 (REI) £8.50 (LEA)

£8.00 → £8.99

Chardonnay De Redcliffe Mangatawhiri **1997** £8.99 (UN)
Chardonnay Delegat's Hawkes Bay Reserve **1998** £8.99 (SAF)
Chardonnay Jackson Estate **1998** £8.99 (POR) £9.66 (PIP) £9.79 (PLA) £9.85 (WRI) £11.08 (PLAY) £11.40 (TW)
Chardonnay Matua Valley **1998** £8.90 (CRO)
Chardonnay Montana Church Road **1998** £8.99 (UN) £8.99 (WR) £9.70 (PIP)
Chardonnay C J Pask **1997** £8.99 (JON)
Chardonnay Te Kairanga **1999** £8.40 (BIB)
Chardonnay Trinity Hill **1999** £8.95 (LEA)
Gewürztraminer Hunter's **1998** £8.99 (DI)
Riesling Coopers Creek Hawkes Bay **1997** £8.79 (CON)
Riesling Forrest Estate **1997** £8.50 (AD)
Riesling Giesen Canterbury **1996** £8.50 (BAL)
Riesling Hunter's Rhine **1998** £8.99 (DI)
Riesling Kim Crawford Marlborough **1998** £8.49 (VA) £8.56 (FLE) £9.99 (REI)
Riesling Martinborough **1998** £8.95 (AD)
Riesling Waipara West **1998** £8.29 (WAT) £10.95 (DI)
Sauvignon Blanc Coopers Creek Marlborough **1998** £8.79 (CON)
Sauvignon Blanc Esk Valley **1999** £8.37 (PLAY)
Sauvignon Blanc Hunter's **1999** £8.90 (CRO) £9.76 (PIP) £9.95 (WS) £9.99 (DI) £9.99 (OD) £9.99 (UN) £9.99 (JON) £10.95 (JER)
Sauvignon Blanc Isabel Estate **1999** £8.99 (POR) £9.40 (MV) £9.45 (BU) £10.95 (PHI)
Sauvignon Blanc Jackson Estate **1998** £8.35 (NO) £8.49 (BO) £8.99 (BAL) £9.85 (WRI)
Sauvignon Blanc Kumeu River. **1998** £8.22 (FA) £11.95 (BEN)
Sauvignon Blanc Matua Valley Hawkes Bay **1999** £8.25 (STE)
Sauvignon Blanc Neudorf Nelson **1998** £8.22 (FA)

Sauvignon Blanc Redwood Valley 1999 £8.90 (NZW) £9.25 (STA) £9.58 (REI)
Sauvignon Blanc Redwood Valley 1998 £8.81 (DOM) £9.69 (GOE) £11.60 (JER)
Sauvignon Blanc Allan Scott 1997 £8.25 (FORT)
Sauvignon Blanc Vavasour 1998 £8.99 (NI) £9.49 (BO)
Sauvignon Blanc Villa Maria Reserve Wairau Valley 1999 £8.80 (CRO) £9.99 (VIC) £9.99 (THR) £9.99 (WR) £9.99 (SAF)
Sauvignon Blanc Waipara West 1999 £8.29 (WAT) £8.99 (DI)
Semillon Forrest Estate 1998 £8.20 (AD)

£9.00 → £10.99

Chardonnay Fairhall Downs 1998 £9.85 (PHI)
Chardonnay Forrest Estate 1998 £10.65 (AD)
Chardonnay Goldwater Roseland Marlborough 1998 £9.99 (MAJ)
Chardonnay Goldwater Roseland Marlborough 1997 £9.85 (AV)

Chardonnay Jackson Estate 1997 £9.70 (TAN) £9.79 (AME) £9.95 (HED)
Chardonnay Jackson Estate 1996 £9.40 (CRO)
Chardonnay Martinborough 1995 £10.80 (CRO) £13.09 (NO)
Chardonnay Martinborough 1994 £9.25 (SOM)
Chardonnay Matua Valley Eastern Bays 1996 £10.52 (TW)
Chardonnay Matua Valley Judd Estate 1998 £9.95 (STE)
Chardonnay Millton 1996 £10.25 (UB)
Chardonnay Montana Ormond Estate Gisborne 1996 £10.25 (COC) £10.99 (CON) £10.99 (VIC) £10.99 (THR) £10.99 (WR) £10.99 (BOT) £10.99 (OD)
Chardonnay Montana Renwick Estate 1997 £10.25 (COC)
Chardonnay Nautilus Marlborough 1998 £10.25 (STE)
Chardonnay Palliser Estate 1997 £10.15 (BY)
Chardonnay Palliser Estate 1996 £10.49 (VIC) £10.49 (THR)
Chardonnay Palliser Estate Martinborough Vineyard 1997 £10.90 (JU)
Chardonnay Redwood Valley 1996 £9.00 (NZW) £10.75 (REI) £11.95 (JER)
Chardonnay Redwood Valley Barrel-Fermented 1996 £10.50 (STA)
Chardonnay Saint Clair Omaka Reserve 1998 £9.35 (AV)
Chardonnay Selaks Founders Reserve 1997 £9.95 (STE)
Chardonnay Seresin Estate 1998 £10.95 (WAI)
Chardonnay Seresin Estate 1997 £10.95 (NO)
Chardonnay Te Kairanga Reserve 1997 £10.99 (YOU)
Chardonnay Vavasour 1998 £9.35 (NI)
Chardonnay Waipara West 1998 £9.99 (WAT)
Chardonnay Wairau River 1997 £9.34 (REI)
Chardonnay Wairau River 1996 £9.34 (REI)
Chenin Blanc Esk Valley 1996 £9.55 (UB)
Gewürztraminer Hunter's 1999 £9.20 (PIP) £9.29 (JON) £9.49 (DI)
Gewürztraminer Montana Patutahi Estate 1996 £10.99 (CON) £10.99 (PHI)
Riesling Hunter's Rhine 1999 £9.49 (DI)
Riesling Isabel Estate 1999 £9.40 (MV)
Riesling Jackson Estate Dry 1997 £9.34 (TW)
Riesling Neudorf Moutere 1997 £9.95 (ELL) £9.95 (STA)
Riesling Selaks Drylands Vineyard Dry 2000 £9.45 (STE)
Riesling Selaks Drylands Vineyard Dry 1999 £9.45 (STE)
Sauvignon Blanc Cloudy Bay 1999 £10.95 (NI) £10.99 (SAF) £11.50 (HAH) £11.90 (CRO) £12.95 (BAL) £13.12 (PLAY) £13.79 (NO) £14.10 (FA) £24.79 (WY)
Sauvignon Blanc Dry River 1998 £10.95 (RAE) £11.95 (JU)
Sauvignon Blanc Dry River 1997 £10.99 (YOU)
Sauvignon Blanc Fairhall Downs 1999 £9.75 (PHI)
Sauvignon Blanc Hunter's 1998 £9.90 (WRI) £9.95 (DI) £9.95 (AME) £12.65 (UB) £12.75 (STE)

Sauvignon Blanc Hunter's Wood-aged **1997** £10.75 (WRI) £10.90 (TAN) £10.95 (DI)
Sauvignon Blanc Montana Brancott Estate **1996** £10.25 (COC)
Sauvignon Blanc Nautilus Marlborough **1999** £9.66 (PIP) £10.25 (STE)
Sauvignon Blanc Nautilus Marlborough **1998** £9.91 (SUN)
Sauvignon Blanc Neudorf Nelson **1999** £9.95 (ELL)
Sauvignon Blanc Neudorf Nelson **1996** £9.95 (RAE)
Sauvignon Blanc Palliser Estate **1998** £9.95 (JU)
Sauvignon Blanc Redwood Valley **1997** £9.58 (REI) £9.95 (FORT)
Sauvignon Blanc Redwood Valley **1996** £9.58 (REI)
Sauvignon Blanc Selaks Drylands Vineyard **2000** £9.45 (STE)
Sauvignon Blanc Selaks Drylands Vineyard **1999** £9.45 (STE)
Sauvignon Blanc Torlesse Marlborough **1999** £9.00 (NZW) £9.45 (STA) £9.95 (BER)
Sauvignon Blanc Trinity Hill **1998** £10.52 (PLA)
Sauvignon Blanc Villa Maria Reserve Clifford Bay **1999** £9.99 (OD)
Sauvignon Blanc Villa Maria Reserve Wairau Valley **1998** £9.99 (VIC) £9.99 (THR) £9.99 (WR) £9.99 (BOT)
Sauvignon Blanc Villa Maria Reserve Wairau Valley **1997** £9.99 (UN)
Sauvignon Blanc/Semillon Selaks **1997** £9.45 (STE)
Sauvignon Blanc/Semillon Kumeu River **1994** £9.50 (CRO)
Semillon Kim Crawford Hawkes Bay **1996** £10.65 (NO) £10.99 (LIB)

£11.00 → £12.99

Chardonnay Babich Irongate **1996** £12.60 (TAN) £12.65 (CON)
Chardonnay Cloudy Bay **1998** £12.99 (NI) £13.90 (CRO) £13.93 (NO) £14.69 (REI)

> - *Wines are listed in A–Z order within each price band.*
> - *For each wine, vintages are listed in descending order.*
> - *Each vintage of any wine appears*

Chardonnay Cloudy Bay **1996** £12.60 (NO)
Chardonnay Hunter's **1997** £11.00 (PIP) £11.29 (JON) £11.49 (DI) £11.95 (JER)
Chardonnay Hunter's **1996** £11.99 (BOD) £11.99 (SUN)
Chardonnay Isabel Estate **1998** £11.00 (MV)
Chardonnay Isabel Estate **1996** £12.95 (PHI)
Chardonnay Jackson Estate Reserve **1996** £11.79 (AME)
Chardonnay Kumeu River **1998** £11.99 (UN) £14.50 (WS) £15.95 (BEN)
Chardonnay Kumeu River **1997** £11.16 (FA) £14.95 (BEN) £14.99 (YOU) £15.86 (REI)
Chardonnay Kumeu River **1996** £11.16 (FA) £18.90 (CRO)
Chardonnay Martinborough **1997** £11.99 (YOU) £11.99 (VA) £12.59 (JON)
Chardonnay Martinborough **1996** £12.99 (NI)
Chardonnay Montana Church Road Reserve **1997** £11.99 (WR) £11.99 (BOT)
Chardonnay Montana Church Road Reserve **1996** £11.99 (WR)
Chardonnay Redwood Valley **1998** £11.25 (FORT)
Chardonnay Te Mata Elston **1998** £12.95 (POR) £12.99 (YOU) £13.49 (AME) £13.99 (WR) £16.92 (TW)
Chardonnay Vavasour **1994** £11.47 (NO)
Riesling Rippon Vineyard **1998** £12.70 (NZW)
Sauvignon Blanc Cloudy Bay **1998** £12.49 (CON) £27.61 (WY)
Sauvignon Blanc Dry River **1996** £11.99 (RAE)
Sauvignon Blanc Hunter's **1995** £12.75 (STE)
Sauvignon Blanc Vavasour **1996** £12.99 (VA)
Sauvignon Blanc Wairau River Reserve **1997** £11.46 (REI)
Sauvignon Blanc Wairau River Reserve **1996** £11.46 (REI)

£13.00 → £15.99

Chardonnay Cloudy Bay **1997** £13.75 (WRI) £13.90 (HAH) £14.99 (CON) £44.18 (WY)
Chardonnay Kim Crawford Tietjen Gisborne **1998** £14.95 (LIB) £15.57 (REI)
Chardonnay Kim Crawford Tietjen Gisborne **1997** £14.99 (CON) £15.57 (REI)

Chardonnay Kim Crawford Tietjen Gisborne **1996** £14.35 (NO)
Chardonnay Dry River **1996** £15.99 (RAE)
Chardonnay Kumeu River Mate's Vineyard **1997** £13.61 (FA) £16.50 (ELL) £19.09 (REI)
Chardonnay Kumeu River Mate's Vineyard **1996** £13.61 (FA) £28.50 (CRO)
Chardonnay Martinborough **1998** £13.35 (AD)
Chardonnay Morton Estate Black Label **1996** £14.99 (YOU)
Chardonnay Te Mata Elston **1997** £13.69 (BOT) £13.99 (VIC) £13.99 (THR) £13.99 (WR)
Chardonnay Te Mata Elston **1996** £14.00 (WS)
Sauvignon Blanc Cloudy Bay **2000** £13.99 (VA)

Over £16.00

Chardonnay Cloudy Bay **1995** £75.94 (WY)
Chardonnay Cloudy Bay **1989** £89.75 (WY)
Chardonnay Dry River **1998** £17.50 (JU)
Chardonnay Fromm Winery La Strada Reserve **1998** £17.99 (YOU)
Chardonnay Kumeu River Mate's Vineyard **1998** £18.95 (BEN)
Chardonnay Matua Valley Ararimu **1997** £19.25 (STE)
Chardonnay Neudorf Moutere **1998** £18.49 (YOU)
Sauvignon Blanc Cloudy Bay **1997** £30.95 (UB) £31.76 (WY)
Sauvignon Blanc Cloudy Bay **1996** £33.14 (WY)
Sauvignon Blanc Cloudy Bay **1995** £38.66 (WY)
Sauvignon Blanc Cloudy Bay **1994** £41.45 (WY)
Semillon Kim Crawford Hawkes Bay **1997** £17.25 (FORT)

SPARKLING

Under £7.50

Lindauer Brut **Non-vintage** £7.49 (ASD) £7.49 (BO) £7.49 (TES) £7.49 (VIC) £7.49 (THR) £7.49 (OD) £7.49 (UN) £7.49 (WR) £7.49 (BOT) £7.49 (WAI) £7.49 (SAF) £7.50 (CRO) £7.59 (BUD) £7.99 (POR) £7.99 (JON) £8.50 (ROB)
Lindauer Rosé **Non-vintage** £7.49 (TES) £7.49 (VIC) £7.49 (THR) £7.49 (UN) £7.49 (WR) £7.49 (BOT) £7.50 (CRO)

£7.50 → £9.99

Cellier Le Brun Terrace Road **Non-vintage** £9.95 (HED)
Deutz Marlborough Cuvée Brut **Non-vintage** £9.99 (BO) £10.90 (CRO) £10.99 (VIC) £10.99 (THR) £10.99 (OD) £10.99 (WR) £10.99 (BOT) £10.99 (WAI)
Lindauer Special Reserve **Non-vintage** £8.99 (TES) £8.99 (VIC) £8.99 (THR) £8.99 (OD) £8.99 (UN) £8.99 (WR) £8.99 (BOT)

£10.00 → £12.99

Daniel Le Brun Brut **Non-vintage** £12.95 (HED) £12.99 (POR) £13.50 (FORT) £13.95 (ROB)
Daniel Le Brun Brut Taché **Non-vintage** £12.95 (PHI) £12.95 (ROB)
★ Deutz Marlborough Cuvée Blanc de Blancs Vintage **1994** £11.99 (OD)
Giesen Voyage Traditionelle Brut **Non-vintage** £11.99 (CB)
Hunter's Miru Miru **Non-vintage** £11.12 (PIP) £13.95 (JU)
Hunter's Miru Miru **1997** £12.49 (DI)
Hunter's Miru Miru **1996** £11.99 (MAJ)
Hunter's Miru Miru **1995** £10.90 (CRO) £11.99 (PHI)
Nautilus Cuvée Brut **Non-vintage** £11.75 (STE)
Pelorus **1995** £12.95 (STA) £12.99 (WR) £14.99 (PHI) £15.03 (PLAY)
Pelorus **1994** £12.14 (FA) £12.49 (UN) £13.30 (FLE) £13.82 (NO) £14.75 (HAH) £14.90 (CRO) £14.99 (VA) £17.16 (CB)
Pelorus **1993** £11.98 (TW) £12.99 (RAE) £13.90 (JU) £15.25 (FORT) £24.85 (UB)
Pelorus Blanc de Blancs **Non-vintage** £10.74 (NO) £11.90 (CRO) £11.99 (JON) £12.99 (PHI)
Selaks Méthode Champenoise Brut **Non-vintage** £10.75 (STE)

£13.00 → £15.00

Jackson Estate Vintage **1994** £14.99 (POR)
Pelorus Blanc de Blancs **1994** £13.51 (REI)

SWEET

Under £15.00

Riesling Wairau River Botrytised ½ bottle **1998** £14.95 (LEA) £15.10 (REI)

PORTUGAL

The bizarre thing about port is that it has an image of crusty colonels and London clubs. Let the colonels drink pink gins, I say: I shall drink port my way

It's a funny thing about port. It has this staid, leather-armchair image, all pass-the-port and don't-get-the-etiquette-wrong. Yet the people who make it don't see it like that. It's our invention – and what a weird thing to want to invent.

The people who make it take it on picnics and drink it out of plastic cups. They drink it in the garden, or they take it on boat trips on the river. They put ten-year-old tawny in the fridge and drink it before lunch, and white port gets the ice cube and tonic water treatment.

It's much better like that. Wine is for pleasure. Yes, take the trouble to notice what you're drinking – but don't make a whole ceremony out of it. And what could be more attuned to pleasure than a silky-sweet tawny? Just imagine if, as you come home from work this winter on a damp, rainy, dark evening, you had a bottle of ten-year-old tawny in the fridge. Imagine a glass of that before dinner – perhaps with a little bowl of almonds. Even microwaved chicken casserole would seem pretty appetizing after that.

Madeira, I have to admit, I find less easy to place. I like it, I really do; but it's too often disappointing. Maybe it's because we don't buy enough of it that we seldom see anything particularly interesting here. Good Sercial is delicious, austere and tangy, and Verdelho is elegant and structured and long. But then port has all that wonderful spiced plumcake fruit, and that heavenly texture; and if you only have a glass (Oh, all right; two glasses if you insist) you won't suffer for it the next day. Promise.

WINE REGIONS

ALENTEJO (red, white) This broad region now has a DOC for the better wines, plus eight sub-regional DOCs including Borba, Redondo, Reguengos and Vidigueira. There's not a great deal of regional difference but there are quality differences. Cheap and cheerful co-op wines are good value: look for soft chocolate-and-cherries reds and increasingly fresh whites. Single estate wines are often very serious, with complex flavours and good concentration. The names to go for include *José Maria da Fonseca, J P Vinhos, Herdade de Esporão, Fonseca, J S Rosado Fernandes, Paço dos Infantes, Cartuxa, Reguengos de Monsaraz, Pêra Manca, Cortes de Cima, Dom Martinho,* and *Quinta do Carmo.*

ALGARVE (red, white) Mostly undistinguished, alcoholic reds. There are four DOCs here, Lagos, Portimão, Lagoa and Tavira, and none of them deserves its status. Among producers, the *Lagoa* co-op is probably the best bet.

BAIRRADA, DOC (red, white) The reds produced here frequently overshadow the more famous Dão wines. They're apt to be tannic, but the Baga grape gives sturdy, peppery, plum-and-blackcurrant fruit. The best Bairrada wines age remarkably well. The top red producers are: *Caves São João, Caves Aliança, Sogrape* (look for its *Nobilis*), *Luís Pato, Casa de Saima, Gonçalves Faria, Sidonia de Souza,* co-ops at *Vilharino do Bairro, Cantanhede* and *Mealhada.*

There are also some increasingly good dry whites available. *Sogrape* and *Caves Aliança* are the best producers to try for these.

BUCELAS, DOC (white) Popular in Wellington's day, this dry white was almost extinct, with *Caves Velhas* left as the sole producer. *Morgado de Santa Catherina* is the best of the modern examples.

CARCAVELOS, DOC (fortified) Just when Carcavelos looked as if it was about to disappear for ever, along comes a new vineyard. *Quinta dos Pesos* is making a good, nutty, fortified version rather like an aged Tawny port.

COLARES, DOC (red) Based on the scented Ramisco grape, the young wine has fabulous cherry perfume but is *numbingly* tannic. As it ages it gets an exciting rich pepper-and-bruised-plums flavour; current vintages of *Chitas* (aka *Paulo da Silva*), and the vinhos de mesa of *Beira Mar Garrafeira* and *Casal da Azenha* are 1984, 1987 and 1988 respectively.

DÃO, DOC (red, white) Getting a bit left behind these days, as the regions of the South and the far North come to the fore. A bit more modernity wouldn't hurt, guys. Best buys are from *Sogrape*, *Caves São João*, *Caves Aliança*, *José Maria da Fonseca*, *Quinta das Maias*, *Quinta da Alameda* and *Quinta dos Roques*.

White Dão was traditionally (and mostly still is) yellow, tired and heavy. But a few companies are now making a lighter, fresher, fruitier style. White *Grão Vasco* from *Sogrape* is good and lemony.

DOURO, DOC (red, white) Famous these days for table wine as well as Port. The flavour of the table wines can be delicious – soft and glyceriny, with a rich raspberry-and-peach fruit, and a perfume somewhere between liquorice, smoky bacon and cigar tobacco. *Ferreira* (under the ownership of *Sogrape*) produces a number, from the rare and expensive *Barca Velha*, through *Casa Ferreirinha Reserva* (formerly known as *Reserva Especial*, to the young and fruity *Esteva*. Other port shippers are

beginning to follow suit; good wines are *Redoma* and *Passadouro* from *Niepoort*, *Corucho* from *Quinta do Noval* and *Quinta de la Rosa*. Look out also for *Bright Brothers*, *Duas Quintas*, *Quinta do Côtto Grande Escolha*, *Quinta do Crasto*, *Quinta do Fojo*, *Quinta do Vale da Raposa*, *Quinta do Vale Dona Maria*, *Quinta da Gaivosa* and *Vallado*.

Nearly all the best table wines are red, though among the whites *Sogrape's Planalto* and *Douro Reserva*, *Esteva* from *Ferreira* and *Quinta do Valprado* Chardonnay are well worth trying.

ON THE CASE
Quality is rising in Madeira but prices are not – yet. Now is the time to try a good ten-year-old Sercial or Verdelho, for pungent flavours you'll find in no other wine

ESTREMADURA (red, white) Alias Oeste. It covers the new DOCs Arruda, Alenquer, Óbidos and Torres Vedras, plus the IPRs Alcobaça and Encostas d'Aire – and the region of Estremadura itself. Private estates here are making terrific quality. There's that same cherries-and-chocolate fruit in the reds that you get all over the South (the chocolate comes from aging in Portuguese oak, rather than the more international-style American or French oak). Look out for *João Pato, Bright Brothers, Quinta da Boa Vista*'s brands *Espiga, Quinta das Setencostas* and *Palha Canas. Quinta de Abrigada, Quinta de Pancas, Beira Mar* and *Casal de Azenha* are also good, as are *Alta Mesa* and *Portada* among the cheaper brands. Whites can be nicely aromatic, but need drinking young.

MADEIRA, DOC (fortified) Each Madeira style is supposedly based on the grape from which it takes its name: there are four of them, and they are Malmsey (Malvasia), Bual, Verdelho and Sercial. In practice cheaper Madeiras, those of up to five years old, are almost all made from the inferior Tinta Negra Mole. At least these are now calling themselves, more honestly, 'Pale Dry', 'Dark Rich', and so on. So anything calling itself Sercial, Verdelho or whatever should be made 85 per cent from that grape.

The Malmsey grape makes the sweetest Madeira, reeking sometimes of Muscovado sugar, dark, rich and brown, but with a smoky bite and surprisingly high acidity that makes it positively refreshing after a long meal. The Bual grape is also rich and strong, less concentrated, sometimes with a faintly rubbery whiff and higher acidity. Verdelho makes pungent, smoky, medium-sweet wine with more obvious, gentle fruit, and the Sercial makes dramatic dry wine, savoury, spirity, tangy, with a steely, piercing acidity. To taste what Madeira is all about you need a 10-year-old; really good Madeira should be two or three times that age.

Blandy, Cossart Gordon, Rutherford & Miles and *Leacock* are all good producers, and all under the same ownership anyway. *Henriques & Henriques* is the most widely available of the Portuguese-owned houses.

PORT (DOURO, DOC) (fortified) Port falls into two broad categories: that aged in bottle (vintage and single-quinta vintage) and that aged in wood, which is bottled when ready to drink: ruby, tawny, late-bottled vintage, crusted, vintage character and branded ports.

That's the basic outline. The simplest and cheapest port available in Britain is labelled 'Ruby' and 'Tawny'. Ruby is a tangy, tough, but warmingly sweet wine to knock back uncritically. Cheap Tawny at around the same price as Ruby is simply a mixture of light Ruby and White ports, and is almost never as good as a straight Ruby.

Calling these inferior concoctions 'Tawnies' is very misleading because there's a genuine 'Tawny', too. Proper Tawnies are kept in wooden barrels for at least five, but preferably ten or more years, to let a delicate flavour of nuts, brown sugar and

PORTUGUESE CLASSIFICATIONS

Portugal's wines are divided into four tiers of quality. At the top are **Denominaçoes de Origem Controlada** or DOCs. **Indicaçãos de Proveniência Regulamentada**, or IPRs, are similar to the French VDQS. **Vinhos Regionais** are regional wines, and **Vinhos de Mesa** are table wines. The regions of Alentejo and Ribatejo now also each have a region-wide DOC classification for better wines.

raisins develop. Most of these more expensive Tawnies carry an age on the label: 10, 20, 30 or even 40 years old. Those without an age are usually best avoided, though there are some good brands like *Harvey's Director's Bin Very Superior Old Tawny* or *Delaforce's His Eminence's Choice*. For aged Tawnies try *Noval, Cockburn, Ferreira, Fonseca, Dow, Taylor's, Graham, Quinta da Ervamoira* from *Ramos Pinto, Churchill, Poças, Quinta de la Rosa, Croft. Colheitas* – single-vintage Tawnies – are increasingly available, usually from Portuguese houses, and can be really delicious. Look for *Kopke, Messias, Noval, Niepoort, Barros, Poças, Warre*.

Vintage ports are the opposite of Tawnies, since the object here is to make a big, concentrated rather than a delicate mouthful. Vintage years are 'declared' by port shippers when the quality seems particularly good – usually about three times a decade. The wines will age for a decade or two in bottle to develop an exciting, complex tangle of flavours; blackcurrant, plums, minty liquorice, pepper and herbs, cough mixture and a lot more.

If you want a peek at what a declared Vintage port can be like, buy single-quinta vintage wine. These are usually from the best vineyards in the less brilliant years; they mature faster and can be extremely good. Look particularly for Taylor's *Quinta da Vargellas*, Dow's *Quinta do Bomfim*, Warre's *Quinta da Cavadinha*, Fonseca's *Quinta do Panascal*, Niepoort's *Quinta do Passadouro*, Croft's *Quinta da Roêda*, Delaforce's *Quinta da Corte*, Cockburn's *Quinta da Eira Velha* and *Quinta dos Canais*, Churchill's *Quinta da Agua Alta* and *Quinta do Vesúvio, Quinta de la Rosa, Quinta do Crasto*.

Vintage Character and Late Bottled Vintage are usually short on personality. The best are from *Fonseca, Niepoort, Smith Woodhouse, Ramos Pinto, Warre*. Crusted port is more interesting: *Churchill's* and *Dow's* are good.

White port, sweet or dry, is seldom exciting. Barros *Very Old Dry White* is special.

RIBATEJO (red, white) An exciting area, the source of both inexpensive brands and some of Portugal's best *garrafeira* (reserve-style) wines – in particular *Romeira* of *Caves Velhas*. It includes the DOCs Tomar, Santarém, Cartaxo, Almeirim, Chamusca and Coruche, but Ribatejo (which can itself now be a DOC) is the name we see most on labels. There are lovely chocolaty reds, and fresh whites. Decent brands include *Lezíria, Segada, Falcoaria, Torre Velha* and the wines from the Almeirim co-op. Classier wines: *Bright Bros, Casa Cadaval, Quinta do Casal Branco, Horta da Nazaré, Quinta da Lagoalva, Quinta das Varandas*.

SETÚBAL, DOC (fortified) This is good, but it's always a little spirity and never quite as perfume-sweet as one would like, perhaps because they don't use the best sort of Muscat. It comes in a 6-year-old and a 25-year-old version, and the wines do gain in concentration with age: the 25-year-

INSTANT CELLAR:
BEST OF THE SOUTH

- **1990 Periquita, Quinta de Parrotes, Alenquer, £6.66, Savage Selection** Lovely soft, spicy red.
- **1997 Aragonês, Esporão, Alentejo, £7.99 for 50cl, Unwins** Chocolaty red with good acidity.
- **1996 Cartuxa Evora Tinto, Eugénio de Almeida, Alentejo, £10.70, Tanners** Elegant, complex red that should by rights cost more.
- **1995 Trincadeira Preta Tinto, Casa Cadaval, Ribatejo, £7.99, Raeburn Fine Wines** Rich, chocolaty red.
- **1998 Vinha da Monte, Alentejo, £4.99, Waitrose** Soft, chocolate and plums fruit, with vanilla round the edges. Sounds like dessert, but it's red and dry.
- **1998 Incógnito Cortes de Cima, Alentejo, £16.95, Adnams** This apparently is Syrah – not a grape one finds often in Portugal. It's very rich and complex.
- **1999 Globus, £4.50, Wine Society** Summer fruits red from the Ribatejo.

old has a lot more character and less overbearing spiritiness. You can occasionally find older wines like *José Maria da Fonseca*, or its intense, pre-phylloxera *Torna Viagem*, with a powerful treacle toffee character balanced by a sharp acidic tang.

TERRAS DO SADO (red, white) This region includes the Setúbal DOC and also the newly created Palmela DOC, where international grapes have made the most inroads, and local varieties are doing well too. Stars here include *Caves Aliança, Bright Brothers, José Maria da Fonseca* (fruity rustic red *Periquita*, red and white *Quinta da Camarate* and *Primum*) and *J P Vinhos* (oak-aged *Cova da Ursa* Chardonnay).

VINHO VERDE, DOC (red, white) Roughly half of all Vinho Verde produced is red, wonderfully sharp, harsh even, but hardly ever seen outside Portugal. Try *Ponte da Lima*, if you feel brave.

But the wine we see is white, and *Verde* means green-youthful, un-aged, not the colour of a croquet lawn. Ideally, the whites are bone dry, positively tart, often aromatic, and brilliantly suited to heavy, oily northern Portuguese food. But we almost always get the wines slightly sweetened and softened, which is a pity, because they're then not nearly so distinctive.

Authentic versions come from *Palácio da Brejoeira, Solar das Bouças, Quinta de Tamariz, Quinta da Franqueira, Quinta de Azevedo, Casa de Sezim, Grinalda* and *Quinta da Baguinha*. *Gazela* is off-dry, as is *Aveleda*. All Vinho Verde should be drunk young. Look for wines from the Alvarinho or Loureiro grapes, which are the best.

PRODUCERS WHO'S WHO

CAVES ALIANÇA ★★★★ (Bairrada) Up-to-date and quality oriented. Making good stuff in the Alentejo (red Monte da Terrugem) as well as in Bairrada.

QUINTA DA AVELEDA ★★★ (Vinho Verde) Largest producer of Vinho Verde, with commercially sweetened Casal Garcia and Aveleda, as well as excellent dry Grinalda and varietal Loureiro. Now Charamba red Douro, too.

BRIGHT BROTHERS ★★★★ (Several) Aussie Peter Bright gets his fingers into everything. Great Palmela and Cartaxo.

CHURCHILL GRAHAM ★★★★ (Port) Intense and concentrated Churchill's Vintage, LBV, 10-Year-Old Tawny and single-quinta Agua Alta.

COCKBURN ★★★★ (Port) Special Reserve is good Vintage Character, and the 10-Year-Old Tawny is complex. Look for Quinta dos Canais 1992, and Cockburn 1994.

QUINTA DO CRASTO ★★★★ (Port/Douro) Estate focusing on vintage port and table wines. Quality is very high, since there's both dedication and plenty of cash for investment. All the wines age well.

CROFT ★★(★) (Port) Quinta da Roêda is lovely single-quinta vintage, but many wines are over-delicate. 1994 is Croft's best Vintage for ages.

DELAFORCE ★★(★) (Port) Tawny His Eminence's Choice is its best-known wine. Good 1994 Vintage and 1984 Quinta da Corte.

DOW ★★★★★ (Port) Deft, complex wines made in a relatively dry style. Its 1994 Vintage is a triumph. Look also for the 10-Year-Old Tawny.

HERDADE DE ESPORÃO ★★★★ (Alentejo) Australian winemaking plus a combination of local and international grapes. Esporão Reserva and Aragonês are very good reds.

MATURITY CHART

Vintage Ports

1983 A vintage for mid-term drinking

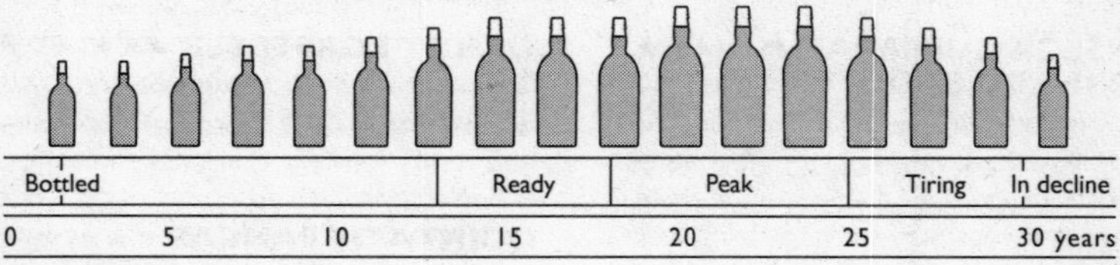

1985 An excellent vintage for laying down

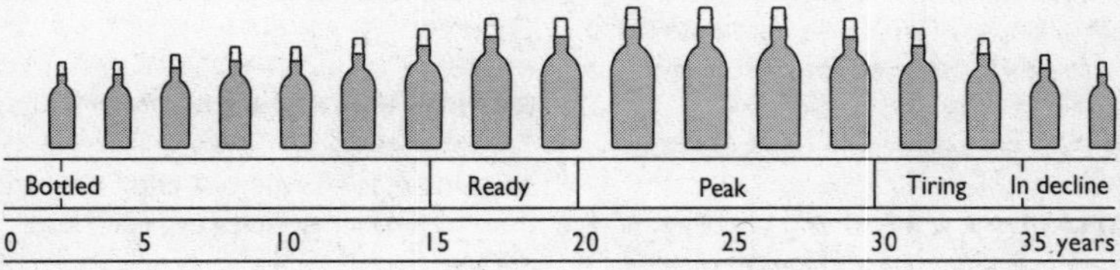

1991 1991 ports are likely to be ready before the 1985s

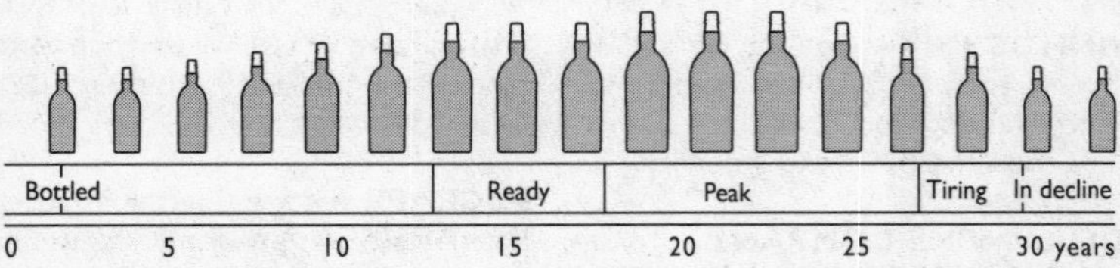

1994 Possibly even better than 1991

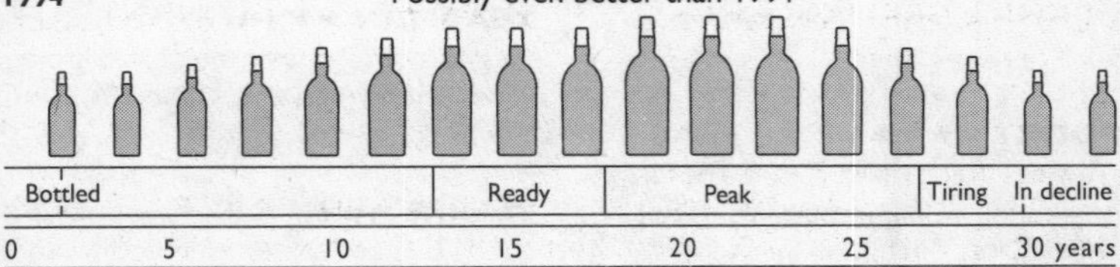

FERREIRA ★★★★ (Port/Douro) Elegant, early-maturing Vintages and two superb Tawnies: 10-year-old Quinta do Porto and 20-year-old Duque de Bragança. Makes some of the top Douro table wines, too.

FONSECA GUIMARAENS ★★★★★ (Port) Fonseca's wines are sweeter and less austere than sister company Taylor's. The Vintage ports are often outstanding, as is the 1994, and the quality of its commercial releases is reassuring.

JOSÉ MARIA DA FONSECA ★★★★ (Countrywide) Delicious range of table wines, particularly Quinta da Camarate red and white, expensive red Primum, oaky d'Avillez and profound José da Sousa Mayor. Not connected to Fonseca port.

GRAHAM ★★★★★ (Port) Usually rich and sweet. Apart from Vintage there is Malvedos, produced in off-vintage years, and fine Tawnies. Very good 1994 Vintage. Six Grapes is attractive Vintage Character.

HENRIQUES & HENRIQUES ★★★★ (Madeira) Good quality across the board.

J P VINHOS ★★★★ (Setúbal) Brilliant winemaking. Look for João Pires Branco, red Tinto da Ânfora, red Quinta da Bacalhôa and Cova da Ursa Chardonnay.

MADEIRA WINE COMPANY ★★★★ (Madeira) Blandy, Cossart Gordon, Rutherford & Miles and Leacock are grouped together under this ownership. Rutherford & Miles and Cossart Gordon wines are slightly drier; otherwise there's not much between them.

NIEPOORT ★★★★★ (Port) Subtle aged Tawnies, traditional LBVs, Colheitas and long-lasting Vintage (especially 1994), plus single-quinta Quinta do Passadouro.

QUINTA DO NOVAL ★★★ (Port) Noval's Nacional wines, made from ungrafted vines, are legendary and fetch a stratospheric price at auction. Other Noval wines don't attempt such heights, but are good, especially the 1982 Colheita and Over 40-Year-Old Tawny.

OFFLEY FORRESTER ★★★(★) (Port) Famous for 'Boa Vista' Vintage and LBV ports. Vintage can be insubstantial. Excellent Baron de Forrester Tawnies.

QUINTA DE PANCAS ★★★(★) (Estremadura) Good winemaking in a relatively international style. There's a quite oaky Casa de Pancas Chardonnay and ripe Cabernet.

RAMOS PINTO ★★★ (Port/Douro) There are delicious Tawnies from two single-quintas – Ervamoira and Bom Retiro – both of which are elegant, nutty and delicate. Duas Quintas is good Douro red.

SANDEMAN ★★★ (Port) Not top flight, although the 20-Year-Old Tawny is attractive.

SMITH WOODHOUSE ★★★★ (Port) Some delicious Vintage and LBVs. Concentrated Vintage wines which tend to mature early, though 1994 is gutsy. Full-flavoured Crusted.

SOGRAPE ★★★★ (North) Producer of Mateus Rosé, plus excellent Grão Vasco white Dão and many others with emphasis on fruit. Very go-ahead.

TAYLOR, FLADGATE AND YEATMAN ★★★★(★) (Port) Quinta de Vargellas is still one of the best single-quinta wines on the market, and the 10-Year-Old Tawny is superb.

WARRE ★★★★★ (Port) Serious wines: good LBVs and Vintage (especially in 1994) and fine 'Nimrod' Tawny. Quinta da Cavadinha is a single-quinta wine, and the 1986 Colheita is subtle.

PORT VINTAGES

Not every year produces a crop of fine enough quality for vintage-dated wine to be made, and a few houses may not make Vintage port even in a generally good year. Announcing the intention to bottle Vintage port is known as 'declaring'. It all depends on the quality the individual house has produced, although it is extremely rare for a house to declare two consecutive years.

1999 Unlikely to be a vintage year: the wines weren't ripe enough.

1998 A small vintage, not good enough for a general declaration.

1997 Varied in quality. Declarations include *Dow*, *Warre*, *Fonseca* and *Taylor*.

1996 Seems an elegant, useful year rather than gutsy.

1995 A vintage with a lot of colour and tannin, but slightly unbalanced. Above average, but missed being top grade.

1994 Excellent year, declared by almost all houses. They're ripe, fleshy and intense, with lovely fruit. They're also much more expensive than the last generally declared year, 1991.

1992 Declared by *Fonseca, Taylor, Niepoort* and *Burmester*. Rich, fruity wines.

1991 Generally declared, but quantities were small. The wines need at least ten years.

1987 *Ferreira*, *Martinez*, *Niepoort* and *Offley* declared this small but good vintage. Most shippers opted instead for single-quinta wines for medium-term drinking.

1985 Declared by every important shipper. The quality is exceptionally good, with a juicy ripeness of fruit.

1983 Marvellous wine, strong and aggressive, but with a deep, brooding sweetness which is all ripe, clean fruit. Not one of the most fragrant vintages, but it will be a sturdy classic.

1982 Not as good as it was at first thought. Most need to be drunk.

1980 A good vintage, developing a delicious, drier-than-usual style. They're ready to drink now, but there's no hurry.

1977 Brilliant wine, now mature. The flavour is a marvellous mixture of great fruit sweetness and intense spice and herb fragrance.

1975 These in general don't have the stuffing that a true vintage style demands, but many are excellent for drinking now. *Noval, Taylor, Dow, Warre* and *Graham* need no apologies. Most of the others do.

1970 Exceptional, balanced port, now good to drink, sweet and ripe with a fascinating citrus freshness – and it'll last. All the top houses are special, led by *Fonseca, Taylor, Warre, Graham* and *Dow*, but lesser houses like *Cálem* and *Santos Junior* are also excellent.

1966 This has gained body and oomph and can be drunk with pleasure; a very good year. *Fonseca* is the star at the moment.

1963 The classic year. It's big, deep, and spicy, with remarkable concentration of flavours.

PORTUGAL PRICES

RED

Under £5.00

Alentejo Montado, Fonseca **1997** £4.25 (WS)
Alentejo Vinha do Monte Sogrape **1998** £4.99 (WAI)
Bairrada Reserva Caves Aliança **1997** £4.85 (DI)
★ Beiras Jaen, Bela Fonte **1998** £4.99 (UN)
Beiras Piornos **1997** £4.25 (AD)
Dão Dom Ferraz **1998** £4.95 (BUD) £4.99 (BO)
Dão Dom Ferraz **1997** £4.99 (TES) £4.99 (VIC) £4.99 (THR) £4.99 (BOT)
Dão Duque de Viseu **1997** £4.95 (STE)
Dão Reserva, Caves Aliança **1997** £4.99 (DI)
Dão Reserva Dom Ferraz **1997** £4.99 (UN)
Douro Vila Regia **1998** £4.45 (STE)
Quinta das Setencostas **1998** £4.25 (BO)
★ Terras do Sado Pedras do Monte, Casteláo **1998** £4.99 (UN)
Ramada Tinto **1998** £3.49 (VIC) £3.49 (THR) £3.49 (BOT) £3.49 (SAF) £3.87 (PLA)

£5.00 → £5.99

Dão Garrafeira Grão Vasco **1995** £5.75 (STE)
Dão Reserva Dom Ferraz **1996** £5.60 (TAN)
Douro Duas Quintas **1995** £5.99 (MAJ)
Douro Duas Quintas **1994** £5.95 (JU)
Douro Quinta de la Rosa **1997** £5.70 (SOM) £7.48 (GW)
Douro Quinta de la Rosa **1995** £5.99 (RAE) £6.35 (CON) £6.90 (UB)
Quinta da Lagoalva Tinto **1995** £5.99 (OD)
Tinto da Ânfora J P Vinhos **1998** £5.99 (SAF)

£6.00 → £6.99

Douro Duas Quintas **1997** £6.15 (STA)
Douro Quinta do Crasto **1998** £6.76 (SAV)
Douro Quinta de la Rosa **1998** £6.79 (BO) £6.99 (BU) £7.00 (MV) £7.30 (TAN)
Douro Quinta de la Rosa **1996** £6.46 (REI)

£7.00 → £9.99

Quinta da Bacalhôa **1996** £8.48 (PLAY)
Bairrada Reserva Casa de Saima **1991** £8.99 (RAE)
Beira Mar Garrafeira, da Silva **1990** £7.20 (TAN) £8.50 (VIN)
Dão Fonte do Ouro, Sociedade Agricola Boas Quintas **1996** £7.99 (BEN)
Dão Quinta das Maias **1996** £7.95 (POR) £8.25 (WRI) £12.99 (VA)
Dão Quinta dos Roques Reserva **1997** £8.80 (SAV)
Douro Quinta do Crasto Reserva **1997** £7.99 (UN) £9.25 (PIP) £9.95 (AD)
Douro Quinta do Crasto Reserva **1996** £7.85 (SOM) £12.04 (TW)
Douro Vale da Raposa **1998** £7.74 (SAV)
Quinta da Pacheca **1996** £8.33 (MI)
Quinta da Camarate, J.M. da Fonseca **1992** £7.19 (PIP)
Trás-os-Montes Quinta do Bons Ares, Ramos Pinto **1992** £9.95 (JU)

£10.00 → £19.99

Alentejo Quinta do Carmo **1996** £10.90 (CRO) £12.50 (TAN)
Cartuxa Tinto **1996** £10.70 (TAN) £10.95 (BEN) £11.99 (VA)
Cartuxa Tinto **1995** £10.95 (WRI)
Cartuxa Tinto **1989** £13.00 (CRO)

MERCHANTS SPECIALIZING IN PORTUGAL

see Merchant Directory (page 456) for details

Nearly all merchants sell some port, but only a few have interesting Portuguese table wines. Adnams (AD), Bibendum (BIB) – especially port, on fine wine list, Cockburns of Leith (COC) – especially port, Direct Wine (DI) – for port and Madeira, Farr Vintners (FA) – for Vintage port, First Quench Group (BOT, THR, VIC, WR), Justerini & Brooks (JU), Lay & Wheeler (LAY), Laymont & Shaw, Oddbins (OD), Raeburn Fine Wines (RAE) – old colheitas from *Niepoort*, Reid Wines (REI) – particularly for port, T&W Wines (TW) – including ports back to 1937, Tanners (TAN) – particularly port, The Wine Society (WS), Peter Wylie Fine Wines (WY) – old ports and Madeiras.

Dão Porta dos Cavaleiros **1975** £19.39 (REI)
Douro Duas Quintas Reserva, Ramos Pinto **1992** £14.95 (JU)
Douro Vale da Raposa **1996** £10.83 (MI)
Periquita J.M. da Fonseca **1987** £10.50 (CRO)
Reserva Especial, Ferreira **1990** £18.51 (REI)

Over £20.00

Barca Velha, Ferreira **1991** £41.00 (CRO)
Dão Garrafeira Grão Vasco **1975** £20.00 (CRO)

WHITE

Under £4.00

Vinho Verde Cambriz **Non-vintage** £3.75 (WS)
Vinho Verde Casal Mendes Caves Aliança **Non-vintage** £3.49 (BO) £4.25 (CON)
Vinho Verde Gatão **Non-vintage** £3.99 (SAF)
Vinho Verde Gazela, Sogrape **Non-vintage** £3.99 (OD) £5.30 (TAN)

£4.00 → £5.99

Albis Fonseca **1997** £4.65 (WS)
Dão Grão Vasco **1999** £4.45 (STE)
Douro Reserva Sogrape **1998** £5.75 (STE)
Dry Palmela Moscato, João Pires **1995** £5.45 (UB)
João Pires Branco **1997** £4.61 (PIP)
João Pires Catarina **1997** £5.87 (PIP)
João Pires Muscat Branco **1996** £4.75 (CON)
Vinho Verde Quinta de Azevedo, Sogrape **1998** £4.95 (STE)

ROSÉ

Under £5.00

Mateus Rosé **Non-vintage** £3.49 (ASD) £3.89 (TES) £3.99 (SO) £3.99 (BUD)
Nobilis Bairrada, Sogrape **1999** £4.75 (STE)

FORTIFIED

Under £17.00

Moscatel de Setúbal 20-year-old J.M. da Fonseca **Non-vintage** £16.22 (PIP) £17.75 (FORT) £21.08 (NO)

PORT PRICES

Under £6.00

Cockburn's Special Reserve ½ bottle **Non-vintage** £5.09 (SAF)

£6.00 → £6.99

★ Càlem Fine White **Non-vintage** £6.99 (UN)

Churchill's Dry White ½ bottle **Non-vintage** £6.65 (VIN)

Churchill's Finest Vintage Character ½ bottle **Non-vintage** £6.76 (VIN)

Cockburn's Fine Ruby **Non-vintage** £6.76 (HA) £7.59 (VIC) £7.59 (THR) £7.59 (WR) £7.59 (BOT) £7.69 (UN) £7.75 (SAF)

Cockburn's Fine Tawny **Non-vintage** £6.76 (HA)

Niepoort Ruby **Non-vintage** £6.99 (RAE) £7.14 (BIB) £7.89 (BO) £9.95 (GAU)

Quinta do Noval Extra Dry White **Non-vintage** £6.87 (PLA)

Sandeman Fine Old White **Non-vintage** £6.99 (VIC) £6.99 (THR) £6.99 (WR) £6.99 (BOT)

Sandeman Tawny **Non-vintage** £6.99 (OD)

£7.00 → £8.99

Cockburn's Fine White **Non-vintage** £7.58 (HA)

Cockburn's Special Reserve **Non-vintage** £7.83 (HA) £8.59 (VIC) £8.59 (THR) £8.59 (WR) £8.59 (BOT) £8.69 (UN) £8.69 (WAI) £8.75 (SAF)

Dow's Fine Ruby **Non-vintage** £8.50 (GW)

Fonseca Bin 27 **Non-vintage** £7.99 (BAL) £8.35 (COC) £9.50 (BEN) £9.75 (DI) £9.90 (GAU) £9.95 (PHI) £9.95 (WRI) £10.95 (VIN) £10.95 (FORT)

Graham Ruby **Non-vintage** £7.99 (NI)

Graham Tawny **Non-vintage** £8.79 (BO) £9.26 (PLAY)

Martinez Dry White **Non-vintage** £8.95 (CON)

Martínez Fine Ruby **Non-vintage** £7.49 (CON)

Martínez Fine Tawny **Non-vintage** £7.49 (CON) £11.48 (VIN)

Niepoort Dry White **Non-vintage** £7.65 (RAE)

Niepoort Vintage Character **Non-vintage** £8.90 (BIB) £8.99 (RAE)

Quinta do Noval Late-Bottled **Non-vintage** £8.60 (COC) £9.68 (FLE)

Ramos-Pinto Ruby **Non-vintage** £8.40 (BEN)

Royal Oporto **Non-vintage** £8.75 (VIN)

Sandeman Fine Old Ruby **Non-vintage** £7.64 (LEA)

Taylor First Estate **Non-vintage** £7.99 (BO) £7.99 (UN)

Warre's Warrior **Non-vintage** £7.99 (SAF) £8.29 (TES) £8.29 (WAI) £8.49 (VIC) £8.49 (THR) £8.49 (UN) £8.49 (WR) £8.49 (BOT)

£9.00 → £10.99

Cálem Late-Bottled **1994** £9.49 (UN) £9.87 (COC)

Cálem Late-Bottled **1992** £9.75 (CON)

Churchill's Late-Bottled **1994** £10.49 (BO)

Churchill's Late-Bottled **1992** £9.30 (GOE) £9.95 (HED) £10.15 (AS) £10.49 (BO) £10.50 (STA) £15.96 (VIN)

Churchill's Dry White **Non-vintage** £9.25 (BO) £9.49 (SOM) £9.49 (WAI) £9.56 (PIP) £9.95 (HED) £9.95 (PHI) £9.95 (LEA) £9.95 (AME) £10.40 (TAN) £10.50 (AD) £10.50 (STA) £11.95 (VIN) £12.16 (TW)

Churchill's Finest Vintage Character **Non-vintage** £9.00 (PLAY) £9.44 (PIP) £9.95 (HED) £9.95 (LEA) £12.04 (TW)

Cockburn's Anno Late-Bottled **1995** £9.67 (HA)

Dow's Trademark **Non-vintage** £9.99 (CON)

Dow's Late-Bottled **1994** £9.49 (AME) £9.75 (WAI) £9.99 (GW)

Dow's Late-Bottled **1992** £9.75 (VIC) £9.75 (THR) £9.75 (BOT) £9.99 (OD)

Fonseca Dry White **Non-vintage** £9.99 (DI)

Fonseca Late-Bottled **1994** £10.95 (DI) £10.99 (BEN)

Fonseca Late-Bottled **1990** £9.90 (CRO)

Graham Late-Bottled **1994** £9.99 (WAI) £10.35 (SOM) £10.55 (NI) £10.72 (WAT) £10.99 (BO) £10.99 (SAF) £11.40 (TAN) £11.49 (CB) £11.95 (HAH) £11.99 (GW) £12.95 (FORT)

Graham Late-Bottled **1992** £10.49 (VIC) £10.49 (THR) £10.49 (WR) £10.49 (BOT) £10.99 (UN)

Graham Late-Bottled **1990** £10.49 (TES)

Graham Six Grapes Vintage Character **Non-vintage** £10.99 (NI) £11.99 (WR) £11.99 (BOT) £12.49 (JON) £12.49 (WAI) £12.50 (JU)
Niepoort ½ bottle **1992** £10.95 (RAE)
Niepoort Late-Bottled **1995** £10.18 (BIB) £11.95 (HAH) £12.06 (NO)
Niepoort Late-Bottled **1994** £9.95 (RAE) £10.49 (AME) £10.75 (BO)
Niepoort Senior Fine Old Tawny **Non-vintage** £10.65 (RAE) £10.77 (BIB) £13.29 (BU)
Quinta do Noval Late-Bottled **1994** £10.90 (TAN) £11.25 (HAH)
Ramos-Pinto Late-Bottled **Non-vintage** £10.99 (JON)
Ramos-Pinto Late-Bottled **1992** £10.49 (BO)
Ramos Pinto Quinta da Urtiga **Non-vintage** £10.39 (JON)
Sandeman Late-Bottled **1994** £9.99 (OD)
Smith Woodhouse Vintage Character **Non-vintage** £9.99 (BOD) £9.99 (SUN)
Taylor Chip Dry White Port **Non-vintage** £10.20 (COC) £11.15 (STA) £11.75 (STE) £11.80 (BEN)
Taylor Late-Bottled **Non-vintage** £10.49 (THR) £10.49 (WR) £10.49 (BOT)
Taylor Late-Bottled **1995** £9.99 (BO)
Taylor Late-Bottled **1994** £10.99 (MAJ) £10.99 (WAI) £11.50 (STA) £11.90 (TAN) £11.95 (STE) £12.25 (FORT) £13.95 (VIN)
Taylor Late-Bottled **1992** £10.99 (UN) £10.99 (SAF) £11.22 (PLAY) £11.90 (GAU)
Taylor Late-Bottled **1990** £10.25 (COC)

£11.00 → £12.99

Cálem Colheita **Non-vintage** £12.65 (CON)
Churchill's Crusted Port **1988** £11.61 (PLAY) £14.95 (FORT) £17.99 (VIN)
Churchill's Traditional Late-Bottled **1992** £11.52 (PIP) £11.95 (HED) £12.99 (PHI)
Cockburn's Special Reserve 1 litre **Non-vintage** £11.35 (SAF)
Croft 10-year-old Tawny **Non-vintage** £12.90 (JU)
Croft Late-Bottled **1990** £11.95 (JU)
Delaforce His Eminence's Choice **Non-vintage** £12.00 (JU)
Feuerheerd **1983** £12.73 (FA)
Fonseca 10-year-old Tawny **Non-vintage** £12.90 (CRO) £15.95 (BEN)
Graham Late-Bottled **1991** £11.36 (COC) £12.34 (REI) £16.10 (NO)
Graham Late-Bottled **1989** £12.25 (JU)
Niepoort **1995** £11.95 (BU)
Niepoort ½ bottle **1994** £11.99 (FA)
Niepoort ½ bottle **1987** £11.95 (RAE)
Quinta de la Rosa **1988** £11.50 (RAE) £49.00 (VIN)
Quinta do Noval 10-year-old Tawny **Non-vintage** £12.56 (PLA) £13.95 (WAI) £14.50 (FORT)
Ramos-Pinto Late-Bottled **1994** £12.35 (HAH)

£13.00 → £14.99

Cálem 10-year-old Tawny **Non-vintage** £13.99 (UN) £14.33 (COC)
Churchill's 10-year-old Tawny **Non-vintage** £14.50 (LEA) £14.59 (SAV) £14.78 (PLAY) £14.95 (HED) £14.95 (STA) £16.70 (VIN)
Churchill's Crusted Port **Non-vintage** £13.99 (JON) £15.75 (WRI) £15.86 (TW)
Croft Quinta da Roeda **1983** £13.99 (MAJ)
Croft Quinta da Roeda **1980** £14.32 (PLA)
Delaforce Quinta da Corte **1991** £14.99 (OD)
Dow's 10-year-old Tawny **Non-vintage** £14.99 (CON) £14.99 (VIC) £14.99 (THR) £14.99 (WR) £14.99 (BOT) £15.99 (GW)
Dow's Late-Bottled **1979** £13.51 (REI)
Fonseca Late-Bottled **1983** £14.55 (WAI)
Graham 10-year-old Tawny **Non-vintage** £13.99 (NI) £15.99 (OD) £16.75 (AD) £22.56 (TW)
Martinez 10-year-old Tawny **Non-vintage** £14.78 (PIP) £14.95 (RAE) £14.99 (CON) £14.99 (AME)
Niepoort ½ bottle **1997** £14.69 (FA) £16.95 (LEA)
Niepoort 10-year-old Tawny **Non-vintage** £14.95 (RAE) £15.18 (BIB) £17.90 (GAU) £19.20 (HAH)
Royal Oporto **1982** £13.49 (TES)
Smith Woodhouse Late-Bottled **1984** £14.15 (SOM)
Taylor Late-Bottled **1991** £13.75 (JU)
Taylor Late-Bottled **1967** £14.69 (REI)
Taylor Quinta de Vargellas **1991** £13.71 (GOE) £25.00 (UN) £27.50 (ELL)
Warre's Late-Bottled **1990** £13.85 (HAH) £14.45 (WAI) £14.99 (JON) £17.95 (PIP) £19.95 (STE)
Warre's Traditional Late-Bottled **1990** £14.99 (SAF) £15.99 (AME)
Warre's Traditional Late-Bottled **1986** £14.99 (TAN) £15.95 (AD) £18.95 (FORT)

£15.00 → £16.99

Cálem Colheita **1987** £16.99 (UN) £17.95 (COC)
Churchill's Crusted Port **1987** £16.00 (WR) £16.00 (BOT)
Churchill's Quinta do Agua Alta **1983** £16.67 (PLA)
Churchill's Traditional Late-Bottled **1990** £15.16 (TW)
Delaforce **1982** £15.86 (REI) £16.99 (YOU)
Gould Campbell **1985** £16.65 (FA) £23.95 (TAN) £27.75 (PLAY) £28.29 (JON) £42.00 (JER)
Graham **1989** £16.10 (NO)
Offley Boa Vista **1982** £16.50 (BU)
Rebello Valente **1985** £16.65 (FA) £25.00 (JU)
Taylor 10-year-old Tawny **Non-vintage** £15.57 (PLA) £15.59 (BO) £15.99 (UN) £16.45 (WRI) £16.49 (MAJ) £16.49 (VIC) £16.49 (THR) £16.49 (WR) £16.49 (BOT) £16.49 (SAF) £16.60 (TAN) £16.75 (STA) £17.20 (BEN) £17.50 (FORT) £17.50 (GAU) £17.99 (VIN)
Warre's ½ bottle **1997** £16.89 (CAV)
Warre's Traditional Late-Bottled **1984** £15.95 (CON)

£17.00 → £18.99

Cálem Quinta da Foz **1992** £17.99 (UN)
Croft **1982** £18.00 (BU) £19.95 (BAL)
Fonseca Guimaraens **1984** £18.75 (COC) £19.99 (DI) £20.75 (WRI) £21.30 (HAH) £21.90 (GAU) £21.93 (CB) £22.50 (FORT)
Fonseca Guimaraens Quinta do Panascal **1987** £18.20 (LAY)
Fonseca Guimaraens Quinta do Panascal **1986** £17.50 (FORT) £17.50 (GAU)
Gould Campbell **1994** £18.28 (NI)
Graham Malvedos **1986** £17.95 (NI) £21.99 (OD) £21.99 (JON) £22.35 (HAH) £22.47 (PLAY) £22.49 (VIC) £22.49 (THR) £22.49 (WR) £22.49 (BOT) £25.00 (FORT)
Niepoort **1991** £18.95 (RAE)
Niepoort Colheita **1985** £17.99 (RAE) £21.90 (GAU)
Offley Boa Vista **1983** £18.50 (BU) £27.60 (TAN)
Quinta da Ervamoira 10-year-old Tawny **Non-vintage** £18.99 (JON) £19.95 (PHI)
Quinta de la Rosa **1995** £17.95 (BU) £19.00 (MV) £20.59 (YOU)
Quinta de la Rosa **1994** £18.99 (NI) £21.00 (JU) £23.20 (TAN)
Quinta do Noval **1982** £17.00 (COC) £17.29 (YOU) £20.00 (CRO)
Sandeman **1982** £18.20 (COC) £18.50 (BU) £29.50 (TAN)
Smith Woodhouse **1985** £18.50 (BU) £23.99 (FA) £25.00 (JU) £25.95 (LEA) £27.00 (VIC) £27.00 (THR) £27.00 (WR) £27.00 (BOT) £28.00 (UN) £32.50 (FORT)
Taylor Quinta de Vargellas **1986** £18.75 (COC) £19.99 (BO) £20.00 (VIC) £20.00 (THR) £20.00 (WR) £20.00 (BOT) £20.20 (TAN) £21.29 (PLAY) £21.50 (STE) £21.60 (HAH) £21.90 (GAU) £21.95 (AD) £21.95 (LAY) £21.99 (UN) £29.25 (TW)
Warre's ½ bottle **1980** £17.95 (WY)
Warre's Quinta da Cavadinha **1987** £18.79 (CON) £19.99 (YOU) £19.99 (BO) £19.99 (AME) £20.50 (WAI) £20.99 (SAF) £21.49 (VIC) £21.49 (THR) £21.49 (WR) £21.49 (BOT) £22.99 (POR) £23.40 (LAY) £23.95 (PIP) £24.25 (STE)

£19.00 → £20.99

Churchill's **1982** £19.39 (REI) £42.00 (PHI)
Churchill's Quinta do Agua Alta **1992** £20.00 (AS)
Cockburn **1991** £19.50 (HA) £23.50 (CAV) £28.29 (JON) £40.00 (UN)
Delaforce **1975** £20.00 (WR) £20.00 (BOT)
Dow Quinta do Bomfim **1987** £19.99 (OD) £24.25 (STE)
Dow Quinta do Bomfim **1986** £19.05 (SOM) £19.99 (TAN) £19.99 (GW) £20.99 (POR) £21.60 (LAY) £21.95 (AD) £24.25 (STE)
Dow Quinta do Bomfim **1984** £19.99 (VIC) £19.99 (THR) £19.99 (WR) £19.99 (BOT)
Fonseca Guimaraens **1982** £19.00 (VIC) £19.00 (THR) £19.00 (WR) £19.00 (BOT)
Gould Campbell **1991** £19.00 (JU) £22.72 (PIP) £35.00 (UN)
Graham Malvedos **1987** £20.40 (SOM) £20.90 (TAN) £20.99 (AME) £21.49 (YOU) £21.99 (POR) £24.99 (BO) £25.95 (STE)
Harvey **1985** £19.95 (CON)
Martinez **1994** £20.00 (JU) £20.28 (PIP) £25.90 (LAY) £27.07 (NO) £52.88 (REI)

Please remember that ***Oz Clarke's Wine Buying Guide*** *is a price* ***guide*** *and not a price* ***list****. It is not meant to replace up-to-date merchants' lists.*

Niepoort **1992** £19.95 (RAE)
Niepoort Colheita **1983** £19.99 (RAE)
Quarles Harris **1983** £19.00 (JU) £21.07 (PLAY) £27.00 (HED)
Quinta do Noval **1985** £19.58 (FA) £22.52 (CAV) £25.15 (PLAY) £25.49 (BO) £26.40 (TAN) £28.00 (CRO) £28.50 (WRI) £32.50 (PHI) £48.00 (VIN)
Smith Woodhouse **1991** £19.00 (JU) £35.00 (UN)
Taylor Quinta de Vargellas **1984** £19.50 (JU) £20.75 (WRI)
Warre's Quinta da Cavadinha **1986** £20.99 (OD)

£21.00 → £22.99

Churchill's **1991** £21.00 (JU)
Churchill's Quinta do Agua Alta **1996** £21.50 (TAN)
Churchill's Quinta do Agua Alta **1995** £21.50 (TAN) £27.60 (STA) £29.95 (PHI)
Cockburn **1994** £21.50 (TAN) £21.54 (FA)
Cockburn **1985** £21.54 (FA) £24.48 (CAV) £26.44 (REI) £27.00 (JU) £27.50 (BU) £28.34 (HA) £29.49 (JON)
Croft **1985** £22.50 (BAL) £22.52 (CAV) £25.00 (BU) £29.50 (UN) £78.00 (VIN)
Croft 20-year-old Tawny **Non-vintage** £22.00 (JU)
Fonseca Guimaraens **1986** £22.50 (PHI)
Fonseca Guimaraens Quinta do Panascal **1984** £21.50 (STE)
Graham 20-year-old Tawny **Non-vintage** £21.95 (NI) £31.75 (STE) £37.83 (TW)
Graham Malvedos **1984** £21.00 (VIC) £21.00 (THR) £21.00 (WR) £21.00 (BOT) £22.47 (PLAY) £29.32 (TW)
Niepoort 20-year-old Tawny **1980** £22.50 (RAE)
Niepoort Colheita **1990** £21.16 (NO)
Niepoort Colheita **1982** £22.95 (PHI)
Niepoort Colheita **1978** £21.95 (RAE) £37.90 (GAU)
Ramos-Pinto **1983** £21.98 (GW) £28.50 (POR)
Taylor Quinta de Vargellas **1987** £21.50 (FORT)
Taylor Quinta de Vargellas **1982** £21.99 (TES)
Taylor Quinta de Vargellas **1967** £22.15 (REI) £30.37 (WY)
Warre **1980** £22.50 (BU) £23.50 (BAL) £23.99 (FA) £27.91 (CAV) £32.95 (CON) £33.80 (TAN) £33.90 (HAH) £40.00 (AV) £59.00 (VIN)

£23.00 → £24.99

Cálem 20-year-old Tawny **Non-vintage** £24.99 (UN) £25.43 (COC)
Dow **1980** £24.50 (BU) £34.00 (VIC) £34.00 (THR) £34.00 (WR) £34.00 (BOT) £36.90 (PLAY)
Dow's 20-year-old Tawny **Non-vintage** £23.59 (SAF) £24.00 (WAI) £29.76 (GW)
Fonseca **1980** £24.50 (COC) £31.33 (CAV) £31.50 (YOU) £34.52 (WY)
Niepoort **1994** £23.40 (RAE) £24.99 (UN)
Quarles Harris **1997** £24.48 (GOE) £30.45 (TAN) £30.55 (CB)
Sandeman **1985** £23.01 (CAV) £28.79 (REI) £29.50 (UN) £30.00 (FORT)
Sandeman Imperial 20-year-old Tawny **Non-vintage** £23.50 (LEA)
Sandeman Quinta do Vau **1997** £24.99 (OD)
Smith Woodhouse **1994** £23.21 (PIP) £24.00 (JU) £26.73 (REI) £27.99 (YOU)
Smith Woodhouse **1980** £23.00 (VIC) £23.00 (THR) £23.00 (WR) £23.00 (BOT)
Taylor **1980** £24.50 (COC) £27.50 (BU) £39.95 (CON) £42.01 (PLAY) £46.82 (TW)
Warre **1991** £24.50 (CON) £24.50 (STA) £25.95 (CAV) £28.00 (JU) £40.00 (UN)
Warre **1983** £23.50 (FA) £25.00 (JU) £25.95 (COC) £26.50 (BU) £26.99 (YOU) £32.05 (WAT) £32.50 (FORT) £34.66 (REI) £36.00 (VIC) £36.00 (THR) £36.00 (WR) £36.00 (BOT) £37.50 (JON) £38.00 (AME) £38.35 (HAH) £39.52 (PLAY) £68.00 (VIN)

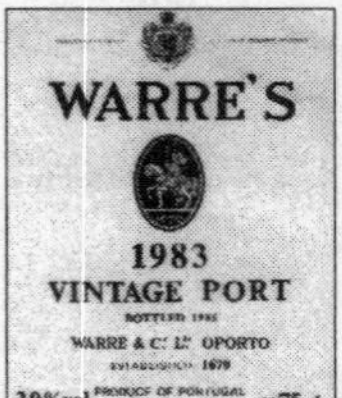

£25.00 → £29.99

Barros **1985** £27.95 (AV)
Cálem **1977** £27.50 (BU)
Cálem Quinta da Foz **1987** £25.00 (UN)
Churchill's **1994** £25.00 (JU) £36.99 (PHI) £55.00 (VIN)
Churchill's **1985** £25.00 (JU) £29.95 (POR) £33.25 (HED) £34.95 (STA) £35.50 (AD) £37.85 (WRI) £41.12 (TW)
Cockburn **1983** £26.44 (FA) £27.50 (BU) £28.50 (WRI) £33.29 (CAV)

Cockburn **1975** £25.00 (BU)
Cockburn's Crusted **1968** £27.61 (WY)
Croft **1975** £25.26 (REI) £34.52 (WY)
Croft Quinta da Roeda **1978** £27.61 (WY) £32.50 (MI)
Delaforce **1994** £25.00 (JU) £28.95 (POR)
Delaforce **1985** £25.00 (JU) £27.00 (VIC) £27.00 (THR) £27.00 (WR) £27.00 (BOT)
Delaforce **1977** £29.50 (BU) £35.00 (VIC) £35.00 (THR) £35.00 (WR) £35.00 (BOT)
Dow **1994** £29.99 (UN) £35.00 (JU) £37.21 (FA) £40.00 (CON)
Dow **1985** £26.44 (FA) £28.00 (JU) £29.95 (CON) £29.99 (UN) £32.00 (VIC) £32.00 (THR) £32.00 (WR) £32.00 (BOT) £34.00 (RES) £35.83 (MI)
Dow **1983** £25.00 (JU) £25.00 (BU) £25.46 (FA) £27.50 (CON) £28.79 (REI) £34.00 (NO) £39.10 (HAH)
Fonseca **1983** £25.00 (JU) £26.95 (COC) £29.50 (BU) £30.35 (FA) £31.00 (CRO) £37.25 (TAN) £48.00 (VIC) £48.00 (THR) £48.00 (WR) £48.00 (BOT) £50.89 (JON)
Fonseca **1975** £28.95 (LEA) £31.55 (REI) £34.70 (PLAY)
Fonseca 20-year-old **Non-vintage** £27.00 (DI) £29.95 (PHI) £31.16 (PIP) £31.45 (BEN) £31.95 (FORT)
Fonseca Guimaraens **1995** £27.81 (GAU) £28.00 (JU) £29.38 (REI) £29.95 (DI) £30.90 (TAN) £30.99 (YOU) £33.00 (RES) £33.75 (AV)
Fonseca Guimaraens **1967** £29.50 (BU)
Gould Campbell **1997** £28.79 (LEA) £30.90 (LAY) £32.50 (POR)
Graham **1991** £28.89 (CAV) £30.00 (JU) £44.65 (TW) £45.00 (UN)
Graham **1983** £28.89 (CAV) £28.89 (FA) £36.00 (LEA) £36.50 (BAL) £38.95 (POR) £39.95 (TAN) £40.83 (PLAY)
Graham **1980** £27.50 (BU) £34.95 (CON) £39.27 (PLAY) £40.00 (VIC) £40.00 (THR) £40.00 (WR) £40.00 (BOT)
Graham **1975** £28.79 (REI) £39.95 (TAN)
Graham Malvedos **1995** £27.00 (JU) £29.38 (REI) £31.70 (TAN)
Martinez **1985** £26.31 (NO)
Martinez 20-year-old Tawny **Non-vintage** £25.00 (CON)
Niepoort **1997** £29.37 (FA) £31.33 (CAV) £32.50 (LEA) £35.00 (BEN)
Niepoort **1982** £27.60 (RAE)
Niepoort **1980** £29.60 (RAE)
Niepoort 20-year-old Tawny **Non-vintage** £29.90 (GAU)
Niepoort Colheita **1987** £29.95 (PHI)
Offley Boa Vista **1970** £28.40 (CAV)
Offley Boa Vista **1962** £28.79 (REI)
Quarles Harris **1980** £28.00 (VIC) £28.00 (THR) £28.00 (WR) £28.00 (BOT)
Quarles Harris **1977** £29.50 (BU) £32.49 (JON) £39.00 (VIC) £39.00 (THR) £39.00 (WR) £39.00 (BOT) £78.00 (VIN)
Quinta da Eira Velha **1994** £25.32 (NO)
Quinta do Noval **1991** £25.00 (JU) £40.00 (UN)
Quinta do Noval 20-year-old Tawny **Non-vintage** £28.06 (NO) £28.38 (PLA)
Quinta do Vesuvio **1995** £29.00 (JU) £30.00 (FORT) £31.14 (REI) £32.47 (PLAY) £34.45 (HAH) £36.30 (AV)
Quinta do Vesuvio **1990** £27.50 (CON)
Rebello Valente **1960** £29.50 (BU)
Royal Oporto **1987** £26.65 (VIN)
Sandeman **1980** £27.00 (JU)
Sandeman **1977** £26.44 (FA) £35.00 (JU) £35.25 (GOE) £43.50 (NI)
Sandeman 20-year-old Tawny **Non-vintage** £25.99 (OD)
Smith Woodhouse **1997** £26.44 (FA) £28.79 (LEA) £30.45 (TAN)
Smith Woodhouse **1970** £29.50 (BU)
Taylor **1983** £26.95 (COC) £29.86 (FA) £35.00 (BU) £35.00 (CRO) £35.90 (LAY) £37.21 (CAV) £43.50 (WRI) £45.00 (FORT) £48.00 (BOT) £50.89 (JON) £66.67 (MI)
Taylor **1975** £25.00 (SOM) £28.99 (YOU)
Taylor ½ bottle **1997** £26.44 (FA)
Taylor Quinta de Vargellas **1995** £27.81 (GAU) £28.00 (JU) £29.38 (REI) £30.90 (TAN) £32.20 (HAH)
Warre **1994** £29.99 (UN) £30.84 (FA) £35.00 (JU) £35.00 (CON) £37.17 (PLAY) £45.00 (LEA) £52.88 (REI)
Warre **1985** £25.00 (BU) £25.46 (FA) £27.99 (YOU) £28.00 (JU) £28.00 (SOM) £28.89 (CAV) £29.50 (UN) £29.95 (CON) £30.60 (LAY) £32.00 (VIC) £32.00 (THR) £32.00 (WR) £32.00 (BOT) £34.95 (STA) £36.90 (HAH) £37.31 (PLAY) £39.50 (BAL)
Warre **1975** £26.44 (REI) £28.50 (TAN)

- *Wines are listed in A–Z order within each price band.*
- *For each wine, vintages are listed in descending order.*
- *Each vintage of any wine appears only once.*

£30.00 → £39.99

Cálem **1997** £34.45 (TAN)
Churchill's **1997** £35.54 (CB) £36.25 (TAN) £36.95 (PHI)
Churchill's Quinta do Agua Alta **1987** £30.00 (HED)
Cockburn **1997** £35.26 (HA) £37.95 (CB)
Cockburn **1970** £31.33 (FA) £37.50 (BU) £41.12 (CAV) £41.13 (GOE) £49.94 (PLAY)
Cockburn **1960** £38.19 (REI) £45.00 (BU) £69.03 (WY)
Croft **1994** £33.29 (FA)
Croft **1977** £39.00 (BAL) £39.50 (BU) £41.12 (CAV) £41.12 (GOE) £42.50 (BEN) £45.00 (VIC) £45.00 (THR) £45.00 (WR) £45.00 (BOT)
Croft **1961** £35.00 (BU)
Croft Quinta da Roeda **1997** £31.78 (CB)
Croft Quinta da Roeda **1970** £31.14 (REI)
Delaforce **1992** £35.00 (UN)
Delaforce Quinta da Corte **1997** £31.75 (TAN)
Dow **1997** £32.31 (LEA) £33.29 (FA) £35.25 (CAV) £36.30 (TAN)
Ferreira **1970** £32.50 (BU)
Fonseca **1993** £38.99 (BO)
Fonseca **1985** £33.95 (COC) £41.12 (FA) £43.08 (CAV) £49.00 (TAN) £51.50 (STA) £55.00 (FORT) £56.00 (VIC) £56.00 (THR) £56.00 (WR) £56.00 (BOT) £57.39 (JON)
Gould Campbell **1977** £31.33 (FA) £35.00 (LEA)
Gould Campbell **1966** £35.00 (BU)
Graham **1997** £33.75 (PHI) £35.25 (FA) £36.72 (CAV) £38.19 (LEA) £38.99 (GW) £39.40 (TAN) £41.50 (POR)
Graham **1994** £32.99 (NI) £33.99 (UN) £35.74 (FA) £42.50 (CON) £47.00 (JU)
Graham **1985** £36.00 (VIC) £36.00 (THR) £36.00 (WR) £36.00 (BOT) £37.21 (FA) £38.19 (REI) £41.12 (CAV) £43.33 (MI) £44.70 (LAY) £44.95 (YOU) £45.00 (BAL) £55.00 (FORT)
Graham Malvedos **1979** £35.25 (TW)
Martinez **1970** £32.50 (BU)
Martinez **1960** £37.50 (BU) £38.19 (REI)
Niepoort magnum **1992** £39.95 (RAE)
Offley Boa Vista **1966** £35.00 (BU)
Quinta do Noval **1970** £31.33 (FA) £37.50 (BU) £37.70 (CAV) £39.45 (TAN) £45.00 (WRI)
Quinta do Noval **1960** £39.50 (BU)
Quinta do Vesuvio **1997** £35.99 (PHI) £37.01 (LEA) £41.50 (POR) £45.82 (GW)
Quinta do Vesuvio **1996** £35.00 (RES) £35.25 (REI) £35.90 (TAN)
Quinta do Vesuvio **1994** £33.99 (UN) £37.21 (FA) £42.50 (CON) £45.00 (JU)
Quinta do Vesuvio **1992** £34.00 (DI) £35.00 (JU) £35.90 (LAY)
Quinta do Vesuvio **1991** £34.00 (DI) £45.00 (UN)
Rebello Valente **1970** £35.00 (BU)
Sandeman **1970** £36.00 (BAL) £38.68 (CAV) £49.50 (LEA)
Sandeman **1960** £35.25 (REI) £42.50 (BU) £62.13 (WY)
Taylor **1985** £35.25 (GOE) £38.68 (FA) £39.95 (CON) £39.99 (UN) £43.08 (CAV) £46.45 (LAY) £48.76 (REI) £55.89 (JON) £56.00 (VIC) £56.00 (THR) £56.00 (WR) £56.00 (BOT) £89.00 (VIN)
Taylor **1960** £35.00 (SOM) £52.88 (REI) £96.64 (WY)
Taylor 20-year-old Tawny **Non-vintage** £33.60 (TAN) £33.68 (PLAY) £34.00 (VIC) £34.00 (THR) £34.00 (BOT) £34.90 (GAU) £35.00 (BEN) £36.72 (VIN)
Warre **1997** £34.27 (CAV) £35.25 (LEA) £36.00 (GW) £36.30 (TAN) £39.50 (POR)
Warre **1977** £35.00 (SOM) £36.23 (FA) £37.70 (GOE) £41.12 (CAV) £44.06 (REI) £45.00 (BU) £45.00 (VIC) £45.00 (THR) £45.00 (WR) £45.00 (BOT) £54.50 (BEN) £55.00 (JON) £56.99 (OD) £59.95 (WAI)
Warre's Tawny **1964** £39.77 (REI)

£40.00 → £49.99

Cálem **1994** £42.50 (WRI)
Cálem **1983** £40.00 (UN)
Croft **1991** £40.00 (UN)
Croft **1970** £42.50 (BEN) £48.33 (WY) £50.00 (JU)
Croft **1966** £41.13 (GOE) £55.00 (BAL) £58.75 (CAV) £61.69 (REI)
Croft **1960** £45.00 (JU) £66.27 (WY)
Dow **1986** £43.38 (PLAY)
Dow **1977** £43.08 (FA) £44.06 (GOE) £47.00 (CAV) £48.00 (VIC) £48.00 (THR) £48.00 (WR) £48.00 (BOT) £50.00 (MI)
Dow **1970** £49.50 (BAL) £55.50 (BEN) £58.26 (CAV) £69.03 (WY)
Dow **1960** £41.13 (REI) £75.94 (WY)
Ferreira **1963** £45.00 (BU)
Fonseca **1992** £48.96 (FA) £49.95 (CON) £50.00 (UN) £55.81 (CAV) £58.75 (WRI) £88.10 (TAN)
Gould Campbell **1975** £45.00 (JER)
Graham **1960** £45.00 (BU) £110.45 (WY)

Niepoort magnum **1994** £46.80 (RAE)
Offley Boa Vista **1963** £45.00 (BU)
Rebello Valente **1963** £47.50 (BU)
Taylor **1997** £45.00 (WRI) £47.00 (LEA) £93.02 (CAV)
Taylor ½ bottle **1970** £42.00 (CRO)
Taylor Quinta de Vargellas **1972** £40.00 (VIN)
Warre **1970** £41.13 (REI) £44.06 (GOE) £46.02 (FA) £48.00 (JU) £48.95 (CAV) £50.00 (FLE) £59.80 (LAY) £70.69 (JON) £137.00 (VIN)
Warre **1960** £41.13 (REI) £69.03 (WY)
Warre **1958** £49.94 (REI)
Warre's ½ bottle **1963** £48.00 (CRO)

£50.00 → £74.99

Cálem **1970** £52.75 (COC)
Cálem 40-year-old Tawny **Non-vintage** £52.50 (CON) £69.50 (UN)
Cockburn **1963** £58.75 (GOE) £60.00 (JU) £64.63 (REI) £65.00 (BU) £71.48 (CAV) £85.00 (RES) £100.00 (HED) £117.07 (PLAY)
Croft **1963** £65.00 (BU) £65.60 (FA) £70.99 (CAV) £75.00 (TAN) £76.38 (REI) £95.00 (RES) £127.00 (VIN)
Croft **1955** £72.46 (FA) £80.00 (BU) £97.43 (CAV) £130.00 (BEN) £158.78 (WY)
Dow **1950** £50.00 (CRO) £105.75 (REI)
Fonseca **1997** £53.36 (FA) £94.00 (GOE)
Fonseca **1994** £65.00 (WRI) £85.00 (CON) £85.00 (DI) £88.12 (FA) £93.02 (CAV) £105.00 (TAN)
Fonseca 40-year-old **Non-vintage** £66.00 (DI)
Graham **1977** £53.36 (FA) £53.50 (WRI) £55.00 (SOM) £58.75 (CAV) £64.10 (LAY) £64.60 (TAN) £65.00 (BU) £69.95 (AD) £72.50 (BEN) £75.00 (FORT) £82.00 (STA)
Graham **1970** £55.00 (AV) £60.00 (JU) £69.50 (BU) £70.50 (FA) £77.84 (CAV) £88.13 (REI) £88.13 (GOE) £89.75 (WY) £100.00 (FORT)
Graham 40-year-old Tawny **Non-vintage** £65.00 (JU) £85.42 (TW)
Martinez **1963** £73.95 (TAN)
Niepoort Colheita **1963** £54.00 (RAE)
Niepoort magnum **1997** £58.75 (FA)
Offley Boa Vista **1954** £58.75 (REI)
Quinta do Noval **1966** £53.85 (CAV) £76.30 (HAH)
Quinta do Noval **1963** £64.62 (FA) £65.00 (BU) £68.05 (CAV)
Ramos-Pinto Tawny **1937** £55.00 (CRO)
Sandeman **1963** £58.75 (FA) £64.63 (REI) £65.00 (BU) £73.18 (WY) £75.89 (CAV) £99.00 (LEA) £123.00 (VIN)
Taylor **1977** £66.58 (FA) £68.05 (CAV) £75.00 (CON) £80.00 (TAN) £82.84 (WY) £95.00 (FORT) £97.50 (BEN)
Taylor **1970** £68.75 (BEN) £74.00 (TAN) £77.84 (CAV) £78.33 (FA) £79.00 (CRO) £82.25 (REI) £99.41 (WY) £100.00 (FORT) £145.00 (VIN)

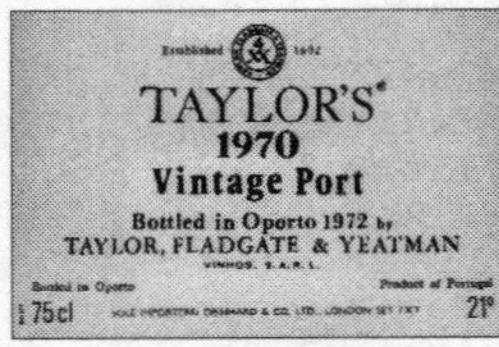

Taylor **1966** £58.75 (REI) £75.00 (SOM) £76.38 (GOE) £78.33 (FA) £91.12 (WY) £139.96 (TW)
Taylor 30-year-old Tawny **Non-vintage** £54.34 (VIN)
Taylor Quinta de Vargellas **1974** £62.13 (WY)
Warre **1966** £58.75 (PLA)
Warre **1927** £62.13 (WY)

£75.00 → £99.99

Cockburn **1955** £80.00 (BU) £94.00 (CAV) £94.00 (GOE) £118.00 (RES) £158.78 (WY)
Cockburn **1950** £88.13 (REI) £207.09 (WY)
Dow **1966** £82.25 (CAV)
Dow **1963** £75.00 (RES) £85.00 (BEN) £94.98 (FA) £117.36 (WY)
Ferreira **1955** £75.00 (BU)
Fonseca **1977** £75.00 (LEA) £80.00 (SOM) £90.08 (FA) £94.00 (TAN) £97.43 (CAV) £99.88 (REI) £150.00 (FORT)
Fonseca **1970** £75.00 (JU) £76.38 (REI) £77.84 (CAV) £78.33 (FA) £80.00 (SOM) £85.00 (RES) £98.00 (NO) £100.00 (FORT)
Fonseca **1966** £82.84 (WY) £94.00 (REI)
Graham **1966** £88.10 (TAN) £94.00 (REI)
Niepoort Colheita **1934** £99.50 (RAE)
Quinta do Noval **1955** £75.00 (BU) £130.00 (BEN)
Quinta do Noval **1947** £95.00 (CRO)
Quinta do Noval Nacional **1987** £78.33 (FA) £159.80 (NO)
Quinta do Noval Nacional **1975** £82.25 (GOE)
Taylor **1994** £85.00 (CON) £85.19 (FA) £93.02 (CAV) £94.00 (REI) £120.00 (TAN)

Taylor **1992** £75.40 (FA) £93.02 (CAV) £94.00 (REI) £95.00 (JU) £100.00 (CON) £119.80 (TAN)
Taylor **1924** £82.84 (WY) £282.00 (REI)
Taylor 40-year-old Tawny **Non-vintage** £76.00 (STA) £78.50 (GAU) £80.00 (FORT) £82.54 (VIN)
Warre **1963** £75.00 (BU) £75.40 (FA) £78.00 (BEN) £82.25 (GOE) £105.75 (REI) £125.00 (FORT)

£100.00 → £149.99

Cockburn **1927** £124.26 (WY) £258.50 (REI)
Delaforce **1945** £146.88 (REI)
Feuerheerd **1938** £117.50 (REI)
Fonseca **1963** £139.00 (VIN) £141.98 (GOE) £148.83 (FA) £156.18 (CAV) £179.48 (WY) £195.00 (CON) £205.63 (REI) £225.00 (FORT)
Fonseca **1960** £103.55 (WY)
Graham **1963** £127.29 (FA) £151.77 (CAV) £155.00 (BEN)
Martinez **1924** £111.63 (REI)
Quinta do Noval Nacional **1985** £129.25 (REI)
Quinta do Noval Nacional **1980** £146.88 (REI) £164.50 (TW)
Quinta do Noval Nacional **1978** £139.82 (TW)
Quinta do Noval Nacional **1964** £119.46 (FA)
Quinta do Noval Nacional **1960** £119.46 (FA) £170.38 (REI) £428.87 (TW)
Rebello Valente **1924** £124.26 (WY)
Sandeman **1927** £143.94 (REI) £258.50 (CAV)
Taylor **1963** £130.00 (JU) £136.59 (FA) £141.00 (GOE) £146.39 (CAV) £152.70 (TAN) £173.90 (REI) £180.00 (AV) £200.00 (FORT)
Warre **1955** £111.63 (REI)

£150.00 → £199.99

Cockburn **1947** £170.38 (REI) £200.20 (WY)
Cockburn **1935** £199.50 (POR) £503.93 (WY)
Croft **1945** £164.50 (GOE) £293.75 (CAV) £358.96 (WY)
Delaforce **1935** £170.38 (REI)

Oz Clarke's Wine Buying Guide
is an annual publication.
We welcome your suggestions for next year's edition.

Dow **1955** £158.63 (REI) £179.48 (WY)
Dow **1947** £170.38 (REI)
Ferreira **1945** £170.38 (REI)
Feuerheerd **1945** £170.38 (REI)
Fonseca **1934** £176.25 (FA) £329.00 (REI)
Graham **1955** £150.00 (SOM) £217.38 (REI)
Graham **1942** £190.00 (BEN)
Ramos-Pinto **1945** £164.50 (REI)
Royal Oporto **1945** £170.38 (REI)
Sandeman **1947** £165.68 (WY) £385.00 (FORT)
Taylor **1955** £155.00 (BEN) £163.52 (FA) £186.04 (CAV) £193.88 (REI) £195.00 (JU)

£200.00 → £299.99

Croft **1950** £241.62 (WY)
Croft **1927** £264.38 (REI) £289.93 (WY)
Croft **1912** £289.93 (WY)
Dow **1945** £235.00 (REI) £395.00 (VIN)
Dow **1938** £264.38 (REI)
Dow **1927** £280.00 (BEN)
Fonseca **1955** £235.00 (CAV)
Graham **1948** £295.00 (BEN)
Graham **1927** £205.63 (REI)
Quinta do Noval Nacional **1967** £200.00 (FORT) £235.00 (NO)
Sandeman **1945** £264.38 (REI)
Taylor **1935** £258.50 (FA) £411.25 (CAV) £545.35 (WY)
Taylor Quinta de Vargellas **1930** £229.13 (REI)
Warre **1922** £234.71 (WY)

Over £300.00

Croft **1935** £503.93 (WY)
Croft **1920** £448.71 (WY)
Dow **1924** £379.68 (WY)
Fonseca **1948** £411.25 (REI) £440.62 (CAV)
Graham **1945** £411.25 (REI)
Quinta do Noval **1931** £1,175.00 (CAV)
Quinta do Noval Nacional **1970** £300.80 (NO) £352.50 (TW)
Quinta do Noval Nacional **1966** £347.80 (NO)
Quinta do Noval Nacional **1963** £490.00 (JU) £658.00 (NO) £705.00 (TW)
Sandeman **1935** £593.67 (WY)
Taylor **1949** £352.50 (REI)
Taylor **1948** £440.62 (CAV)
Taylor **1945** £352.50 (FA) £499.38 (REI) £566.06 (WY)
Taylor **1927** £311.38 (FA) £493.50 (CAV)
Taylor **1920** £538.44 (WY)
Warre **1945** £338.26 (WY)
Warre **1920** £476.32 (WY)

MADEIRA PRICES

Under £9.00

3-year-old Medium Dry Henriques & Henriques **Non-vintage** £8.95 (STA) £9.95 (FORT)

3-year-old Full Rich Henriques & Henriques **Non-vintage** £8.95 (STA) £9.20 (ELL) £9.95 (FORT) £12.38 (VIN)

Duke of Clarence Blandy **Non-vintage** £8.95 (CON) £8.99 (GW) £9.29 (WAI) £9.49 (UN) £9.49 (WR) £9.49 (BOT) £9.49 (SAF) £9.95 (JU) £10.55 (HAH) £11.69 (TW)

Duke of Cumberland Blandy **Non-vintage** £8.99 (GW) £9.13 (WAT) £9.49 (VIC) £9.49 (THR) £9.49 (UN) £11.54 (VIN)

Sercial Blandy **Non-vintage** £8.99 (GW)

£9.00 → £9.99

3-year-old Medium Rich Henriques & Henriques **Non-vintage** £9.20 (ELL) £12.38 (VIN)

Bual Blandy **Non-vintage** £9.98 (GW)

Duke of Cambridge Blandy **Non-vintage** £9.95 (JU)

Duke of Sussex Blandy **Non-vintage** £9.49 (VIC) £9.49 (THR) £9.49 (UN) £9.49 (WR) £9.49 (BOT) £9.60 (HAH) £9.69 (NI) £9.95 (JU) £11.54 (VIN)

£10.00 → £14.99

10-year-old Malmsey Blandy **Non-vintage** £14.52 (NO) £15.76 (WAT) £15.95 (WAI) £16.25 (CON) £16.55 (NI) £16.99 (JON) £18.80 (HAH) £19.50 (FORT) £20.80 (CB)

5-year-old Bual Blandy **Non-vintage** £13.80 (HAH)

5-year-old Bual Cossart Gordon **Non-vintage** £12.95 (JU) £12.95 (CON) £13.50 (DI) £14.92 (CB)

5-year-old Finest Medium Dry Henriques & Henriques **Non-vintage** £10.09 (UN) £10.71 (COC) £10.99 (AME) £11.95 (LEA)

5-year-old Finest Medium Rich Henriques & Henriques **Non-vintage** £10.71 (COC) £11.95 (LEA)

5-year-old Malmsey Cossart Gordon **Non-vintage** £13.50 (DI) £14.95 (AD)

5-year-old Sercial Blandy **Non-vintage** £11.49 (WAT)

5-year-old Sercial Cossart Gordon **Non-vintage** £12.95 (JU) £12.95 (CON) £14.75 (FORT) £14.92 (CB) £14.95 (HAH)

£15.00 → £24.99

10-year-old Bual Cossart Gordon **Non-vintage** £17.95 (DI) £17.99 (JON)

10-year-old Malmsey Henriques & Henriques **Non-vintage** £15.09 (UN) £15.33 (NO) £15.50 (CRO) £15.99 (YOU) £16.49 (AME) £16.95 (AS) £16.95 (HED) £17.25 (ELL) £17.95 (LEA)

10-year-old Sercial Henriques & Henriques **Non-vintage** £15.35 (COC)

10-year-old Verdelho Henriques & Henriques **Non-vintage** £15.35 (COC) £17.75 (FORT) £17.95 (LEA)

Bual Henriques & Henriques **Non-vintage** £16.13 (NO)

£25.00 → £49.99

15-year-old Malmsey Cossart Gordon **Non-vintage** £25.00 (JU)

Verdelho Henriques & Henriques **1954** £41.13 (FA)

£50.00 → £99.99

Bual Blandy **1954** £55.00 (BOT) £120.00 (JU)

Bual Vintage Cossart Gordon **1954** £99.88 (TW)

Malmsey Henriques & Henriques **1954** £75.00 (YOU) £93.00 (JU) £110.00 (CRO)

Malmsey Justino Henriques **1933** £89.00 (LEA)

Verdelho Henriques & Henriques **1934** £88.13 (REI) £170.00 (JU)

Over £100.00

Bual Blandy **1959** £172.58 (WY)

Bual Blandy **1934** £129.25 (REI)

Bual Vintage Cossart Gordon **1914** £205.63 (TW)

Bual Vintage Leacocks **1914** £303.74 (WY)

Malmsey Cossart Gordon **1916** £258.50 (REI)

Malmsey Powers **1954** £175.00 (JU)

Malvazia Reserva Pereira d'Oliveira **1900** £275.00 (FORT)

Sercial Henriques & Henriques **1944** £130.00 (JU) £130.00 (CRO)

Sercial Leacock **1910** £205.63 (REI)

Verdelho Vintage Rutherford & Miles **1954** £125.00 (DI)

Verdelho Vintage Rutherford & Miles **1934** £240.88 (REI)

SOUTH AFRICA

It's a big place, South Africa. They're still finding out about their vineyards and their climate

Everybody who goes to South Africa falls in love with it, and with its wines. They come back raving about it: 'Oh, you should see it,' they say. 'And the wines! Oh, the wines are just fabulous.'

Well, thank you. I've seen it, and yes, it is fabulous. But the wines? Yes and no.

There's huge potential. (How many regions and countries have you heard that about?) But the thing about wine is that potential invariably takes some time to be realized. There's only one chance a year to get it right. And when it comes to planting a vineyard, that comes down to one chance in about 30 years.

South Africa's wines are not going to be worldbeaters overnight (although the very top ones are, and have been for a while). There's an awful lot to learn yet about the topography of this immensely complex country, about how best to harness its climate and what really are the best ways of handling its grapes. It will get there – is getting there. But not overnight.

GRAPE VARIETIES

CABERNET SAUVIGNON, CABERNET FRANC AND BORDEAUX BLENDS (red) Good ones have clean, minty aromas and fresh fruit. Old-style ones persist with a tough greenness or a dusty dryness. Bordeaux blends tend to be best. Best Cabernets include: *Backsberg, Bellingham, Beyerskloof, Blaauwklippen, De Trafford, Neil Ellis, Hartenberg, Kanonkop, Landskroon Cabernet Franc, L'Avenir, Le Bonheur, Nederburg Auction, Neetlingshof, Plaisir de Merle, Rustenberg Peter Barlow, Saxenburg Private Collection, Springfield, Swartland Co-op, Thelema.* Blends: *Backsberg Klein Babylonstoren, Buitenverwachting Christine, Delheim Grand Reserve, Glen Carlou Grande Classique, Grangehurst, Groot Constantia Gouverneurs Reserve, Kanonkop Paul Sauer, Klein Constantia Marlbrook, Lievland DVB, L'Ormarins Optima, Louisvale, Meerlust Rubicon, Morgenhof Première Selection, Mulderbosch Faithful Hound, Neetlingshof Lord Neethling Reserve, Overgaauw Tria Corda, Rustenberg, Villiera Cru Monro, Vriesenhof Kallista, Warwick Trilogy, Welgemeend, Zonnebloem Lauréat.*

WINE OF ORIGIN

Every bottle of wine sold in South Africa must bear the Wine of Origin seal. This certifies the wine's area of origin, grape variety (or varieties) and vintage.

CHARDONNAY (white) The best wines have lingering lemon-lime freshness with subtle oak. Inevitably, there's some over-oaking disguising some underpowered winemaking too. Try: *Avontuur, Backsberg, Graham Beck Lone Hill, Bellingham, Bouchard Finlayson, Buitenverwachting, De Leuwen Jagt, De Wetshof, Dieu Donné, Eikendal, Neil Ellis, Glen Carlou, Groot Constantia, Hamilton Russell, Jordan, Klein Constantia, Longridge, Louisvale, Meerlust, Morgenhof, Mulderbosch, Nederburg, Overgaauw, Rustenberg, Saxenburg, Simonsig, Springfield, Thelema, Vergelegen, Weltevrede, Zandvliet.*

CHENIN BLANC (white) Usually simple entry-level stuff, though a few take it more seriously. Best: *Boland, Boschendal, Glen Carlou, Haute-Provence-Agusta, Ken Forrester, KWV, L'Avenir, Mulderbosch Steen-op-Hout,*

Villiera, Van Zylshof. Botrytized Chenin Blanc is used for the sweet *Nederburg Edelkeur*.

CINSAUT (red) Crossed with Pinot Noir, it produced the Pinotage. By itself it mostly gives light, undistinguished reds.

MERLOT (red) By itself Merlot makes rich, ripe, easy reds – even better aged in new oak. Increasingly popular. Good ones include *Avontuur Reserve, Bellingham, Boschendal, De Trafford, Drostdy-Hof, Glen Carlou, Hoopenburg, Longridge, Meerlust, Morgenhof, Overgaauw, Saxenburg, Spice Route, Steenberg, Thelema, Villiera, Warwick*.

MUSCAT (white) Sweet Muscadels are usually the best bet, and include *De Leuwen Jagt, Klein Constantia Vin de Constance, KWV, Van Loveren Blanc de Noir, Nederburg Eminence, Vredendal*.

PINOTAGE (red) As cleaner, more intense fruit comes to the fore, Pinotage is suddenly very fashionable: huge amounts are being planted. Good ones are *Avontuur, Beyerskloof, Clos Malverne, Fairview, Grangehurst, Kaapzicht, Kanonkop, KWV Cathedral Cellar, L'Avenir, Simonsig, Spice Route, Swartland co-op, Uiterwyk, Vriesenhof, Warwick* and *Wildekrans*.

PINOT NOIR (red) The coolest parts of the country are producing supple and understated Pinot Noirs of world class. Best are: *Bouchard Finlayson, Glen Carlou, Hamilton Russell, Haute Cabrière, Meerlust*.

RIESLING (white) Sweet ones are excellent; the dry and off-dry ones can be too. Best dry: *Buitenverwachting, Neethlingshof*. Best off-dry: *Hartenburg, Klein Constantia, Lievland*. Best sweet botrytized Rieslings: *Danie De Wet Edeloes, KWV Noble Late Harvest, Nederburg Noble Late Harvest* and *Neetlingshof Noble Late Harvest, Stellenzicht Noble Late Harvest*.

SAUVIGNON BLANC (white) Showing vast improvements, there are some lovely pungent, ripe wines from *Bellingham, Neil Ellis, Klein Constantia, Jordan, Morgenhof, Mulderbosch, Saxenburg, Springfield, Steenberg, Stellenryck, Thelema, Villiera*.

SHIRAZ (red) Shiraz can make savoury, raspberry-fruited wines, although perhaps lacking the fleshy sweetness of the best of the Rhône and Australia. Best: *Fairview, Klein Constantia, Hartenberg, La Motte, Lievland, Saxenburg, Spice Route, Stellenzicht Syrah, Thelema, Zandvliet, Zonnebloem*.

SPARKLING WINES 'Methode Cap Classique' is the name for Champagne-method fizz. Best: *Graham Beck, Boschendal, Pierre Jourdan* (from *Cabrière*), *J C Le Roux, Pongrácz, Simonsig*.

WINES & WINE REGIONS

CONSTANTIA South Africa's oldest existing wine region is one of its most dynamic. *Buitenverwachting, Klein Constantia* and *Steenberg* are the names to watch.

DURBANVILLE Cape Town is threatening the vineyards of Durbanville. Sauvignon Blanc is particularly good.

FRANSCHHOEK White grapes rule, yet the new reds are promising. Look for *Cabrière* fizz and Pinot Noir, *Bellingham*'s fantastic Cabernet Franc, *Dieu Donné, Haute Provence-Agusta, La Motte* and *L'Ormarins*.

OLIFANTS RIVER Irrigated bulk wine area, with some good everyday stuff.

PAARL Good wines from almost every variety, from producers such as *Backsberg, Boschendal, De Leuwen Jagt, Glen Carlou, Fairview, Landskroon, Nederburg, Simonsvlei, Veenwouden, Villiera, Welgemeend*. The *KWV* is based in the town of Paarl.

ROBERTSON A region rapidly gaining a reputation for Chardonnay. *Graham Beck, Bon Courage, De Wetshof, Sinnya, Springfield, Van Loveren, Van Zylshof, Weltevrede, Zandvliet* are names to look for.

STELLENBOSCH The heart of the wine industry. Both reds and whites are successful. Look for: *Avontuur, Beyerskloof, Clos Malverne, Delheim, Eikendal, Neil Ellis, Grangehurst, Hartenberg, Jordan, Kanonkop, L'Avenir, Leef Op Hoop, Lievland, Longridge, Louisvale, Meerlust, Morgenhof, Mulderbosch, Neetlingshof, Overgaauw, Rustenberg, Rust-en-Vrede, Saxenburg, Simonsig, Stellenzicht, Thelema, Vergelegen, Vriesenhof, Warwick.*

ON THE CASE
Wine styles are still evolving rapidly in South Africa, so it's always worth trying new wines

SWARTLAND The *Swartland* and *Riebeek co-ops* and *Allesverloren* estate established the potential of this hot, dry area. The *Spice Route Wine Company* is a rapidly rising star.

WALKER BAY Some of the best Pinot Noir comes from here and there's good Chardonnay, too. Top names: *Bouchard Finlayson, Hamilton Russell, Wildekrans.*

PRODUCERS WHO'S WHO

BACKSBERG ★★★★ Luscious Chardonnay and superb reds, including Cabernet, Merlot and Bordeaux blends.

BELLINGHAM ★★★★★ Super flinty Sauvignon and an elegant, peachy Chardonnay. Cabernet Franc is stunning.

BOSCHENDAL ★★★★(★) Intense, peppery Shiraz, juicy, chocolaty Merlot, superb Lanoy red blend, and sparkling white Le Grand Pavillon Blanc de Blancs.

BOUCHARD FINLAYSON ★★★★★ Burgundian-style Chardonnays, flinty fresh Sauvignon Blanc and some of South Africa's best Pinot Noir.

CABRIÈRE ESTATE ★★★★ Perfumed, raspberry-packed Haute Cabrière Pinot Noir; sparklers under the Pierre Jourdan label.

CATHEDRAL CELLAR ★★★ KWV's top range: good Cabernet Sauvignon and Pinotage, grassy Sauvignon Blanc.

CLOS MALVERNE ★★★(★) Makes a lovely Pinotage and a very good value blend by the name of Devonet from Cabernet and Merlot.

DE WETSHOF ★★★(★) Danie de Wet makes Chardonnays with great elegance and poise, and spicy Rhine Riesling.

NEIL ELLIS WINES ★★★(★) Top negociant producing excellent Sauvignon, tropical-tasting Chardonnay, intense Cabernet, juicy Pinotage.

FAIRVIEW ★★★★(★) Great Pinotage, Shiraz, Merlot and Zinfandel/Cinsaut. Chardonnay and Semillon are top whites. 'Goats do Roam' is a new Rhône blend.

GLEN CARLOU ★★★★ Tropically rich, leesy Chardonnay and impressive red Bordeaux blends.

HAMILTON RUSSELL ★★★★★ Elegant Chardonnay and supple, ripe, even silky Pinot Noir that brilliantly straddle Old and New Worlds.

JORDAN VINEYARD ★★★ International styles made with great aplomb. Look for the Chardonnays.

INSTANT CELLAR:
RICH, RIPE REDS

- **1996 Cabernet Sauvignon, Klein Constantia, £9.30, Tanners** A mulberry-flavoured, soft Cabernet that's drinking beautifully now.
- **1995 Rubicon, Meerlust, Stellenbosch, £15.50, Wright Wine Co** Good solid red that will need a few years to open out and become supple.
- **1998 Pinot Noir Goedvertrouw, Arthur Pillman, £14.79, Noel Young Wines** A new name on the Pinot Noir front, and about time too: there hasn't been much good Pinot from here.
- **1994 Shiraz, La Motte, Franschhoek, £9.50 Lea & Sandeman** Good juicy, dark flavoured stuff.
- **1998 Pinotage The Old Road, Graham Beck, £8.50, Bibendum** Pinotage as it should be, well structured and ripe.
- **1992 Cabernet Sauvignon, Rust-en-Vrede, £10.99, Cape Province Wines** Soft, powdery fruit, all cherries and spice.
- **1996 Trilogy, Warwick Estate, Stellenbosch, £9.80, Bacchus** Beautifully poised Bordeaux blend of great depth and finesse. Serious, world-class wine.

KANONKOP ★★★★★ Pinotage king of the Cape. There's also rich, mouthfilling Cabernet and Paul Sauer Bordeaux blend.

KLEIN CONSTANTIA ★★★★ Stunning Sauvignon Blanc, toasty Chardonnay and claret-style Marlbrook red.

LA MOTTE ★★★★ Excellent reds, in particular big spicy Shiraz and ripe oak-splashed Cabernet.

LOUISVALE ★★★ Buttery, biscuity Chardonnay and a good Cabernet/Merlot.

MEERLUST ★★★★ Complex Rubicon Cabernet blend and stunning Chardonnay.

MULDERBOSCH ★★★★ Brilliant Sauvignon Blanc, complex Chardonnay and Bordeaux blend Faithful Hound.

PLAISIR DE MERLE ★★★(★) Top-quality Cabernet and Merlot; rapidly improving Chardonnay.

RUSTENBERG ★★★★ Cabernet blends that cellar well and a range of top-quality Chardonnays.

SIMONSIG ★★★★ Concentrated, unwooded Pinotage and brilliant Shiraz; Tiara is the Cabernet/Merlot blend.

SPICE ROUTE ★★★★ Exciting range includes Pinotage, Shiraz and Merlot, and a promising red blend called Andrew's Hope.

SPRINGFIELD ESTATE ★★★ Cabernets age well; Sauvignon is good and lean, Chardonnay complex.

STEENBERG ★★★★ Constantia's rising star. Crisp, nettly Sauvignon Blanc and powerful, inky Merlot.

THELEMA ★★★★ First-rate Sauvignon Blanc and Chardonnay, gutsy Cabernet Reserve and fruit-driven Cabernet/Merlot.

VERGELEGEN ★★★★ World-class Sauvignons and Chardonnays; Mill Race Red is a Cabernet/Merlot blend.

VILLIERA ★★★★ Tangy Sauvignons and lightly oaked Chenin; Tradition sparklers; Bordeaux-style Cru Monro and consistently excellent Merlot.

VRIESENHOF ★★★(★) Very intense Chardonnay; classy Pinotage; super Kallista Bordeaux blend.

WARWICK ★★★★(★) Fabulous Pinotage, mouthfilling Cabernet Franc and a complex Bordeaux blend called Trilogy.

WELGEMEEND ESTATE ★★★★ Tremendous reds from Bordeaux grape varieties, including otherwise rarely seen Malbec and Petit Verdot.

SOUTH AFRICA PRICES

RED

Under £4.50

Cabernet/Shiraz Van Loveren **1997** £4.10 (SOM)
Cinsaut/Pinotage Kumala **1999** £4.39 (BUD)
Cinsaut/Pinotage Kumala **1998** £4.49 (BOT) £4.79 (SAF)
Ruby Cabernet Robertson **1999** £4.09 (BY)

£4.50 → £4.99

Cabernet Sauvignon KWV **1998** £4.99 (VIC) £4.99 (THR) £4.99 (WR) £4.99 (BOT)
Cabernet Sauvignon KWV **1997** £4.93 (COC) £4.99 (UN) £5.30 (CAP)
Cabernet Sauvignon Oak Village **1997** £4.99 (BOT)
Cabernet Sauvignon Robertson **1999** £4.94 (BY)
Cabernet/Merlot Avontuur **1998** £4.99 (WAI)
Cape Red Drostdy-Hof **1999** £4.80 (TAN)
Le Pavillon Boschendal **Non-vintage** £4.75 (UB)
Le Pavillon Boschendal **1999** £4.93 (PLA) £5.25 (STE)
Pinotage Bellingham **1998** £4.99 (UN) £7.82 (CAP)
Pinotage Culemborg **1998** £4.59 (WAI)
Pinotage Kleinbosch Young Vatted **1998** £4.99 (SAF)
Pinotage KWV **1999** £4.99 (VIC) £4.99 (THR) £4.99 (WR)
Pinotage KWV **1998** £4.99 (COC) £4.99 (WR) £5.40 (CAP)
Pinotage KWV **1997** £4.99 (BOT) £5.49 (UN)
Shiraz KWV **1998** £4.99 (COC) £5.40 (CAP)
Zinfandel/Cinsaut Kopland **1997** £4.95 (JU)

£5.00 → £5.99

Cabernet Sauvignon Nederburg **1996** £5.99 (COC)
Dry Red Stormy Cape Thelema **1998** £5.26 (FLE)
Edelrood Nederburg **1996** £5.93 (COC)
Merlot Bellingham **1998** £5.99 (SAI)
Pinot Noir Fairview **Non-vintage** £5.99 (UN)
Pinotage Beyerskloof **1999** £5.20 (SOM) £5.49 (OD)
Pinotage Beyerskloof **1998** £5.99 (WR)
Pinotage Clos Malverne **1998** £5.99 (SOM)
Pinotage Drostdy-Hof **1997** £5.49 (MAJ)
Pinotage Fairview **1999** £5.99 (SAI) £6.99 (GW)
Pinotage Klippenkop **1998** £5.25 (CON)
Pinotage Kopland **1996** £5.95 (JU)
Pinotage Nederburg **1996** £5.76 (COC)
Roodeberg KWV **1997** £5.78 (CAP)
Roodeberg KWV **1996** £5.10 (COC)
Shiraz Fairview **1996** £5.99 (UN)

£6.00 → £6.99

Cabernet Sauvignon Backsberg **1995** £6.85 (COC)
Cabernet Sauvignon L'Avenir **1996** £6.75 (SOM)
Cabernet Sauvignon Nederburg **1998** £6.46 (CAP)
Cabernet Sauvignon Zonnebloem **1996** £6.95 (STE) £7.29 (PLAY) £8.46 (TW)
Edelrood Nederburg **1998** £6.26 (CAP)
Merlot Fairview **1998** £6.99 (MAJ) £7.00 (GW)
Merlot Fairview **1996** £6.49 (UN) £6.95 (AD)
Merlot Fairview **1995** £6.95 (JU)
Pinotage Beyerskloof **1997** £6.49 (UN)
★ Pinotage Clos Malverne **1999** £6.95 (POR) £6.99 (WAI)
Pinotage Clos Malverne Reserve **1998** £6.95 (SOM)

MERCHANTS SPECIALIZING IN SOUTH AFRICA

see Merchant Directory (page 456) for details

Averys (AV), Bibendum (BIB), Cape Province Wines (CAP), Cockburns of Leith (COC), Direct Wine Shipments (DI), First Quench Group (BOT, THR, VIC, WR), Lay & Wheeler (LAY), Oddbins (OD), Terry Platt (PLA), Roberson (ROB), Sainsbury's (SAI), Tanners (TAN), The Ubiquitous Chip (UB), Villeneuve Wines, Waitrose (WAI).

Pinotage Drostdy-Hof **1996** £6.95 (STE)
Pinotage Fairview **1998** £6.95 (AD)
Pinotage Fairview Bush Vine **1995** £6.95 (JU)
Pinotage Groot Constantia **1995** £6.28 (CAP)
Pinotage Nederburg **1999** £6.26 (CAP)
Pinotage Nederburg **1995** £6.20 (UB)
Pinotage Wildekrans **1997** £6.10 (SOM)
Pinotage Zonnebloem **1997** £6.60 (WRI) £6.95 (STA) £6.95 (STE) £7.18 (PLAY)
Shiraz Groot Constantia **1995** £6.45 (COC) £6.79 (CAP)
Shiraz KWV **1991** £6.23 (BY)
Shiraz Sentinel **1998** £6.49 (OD)

£7.00 → £7.99

Cabernet Franc/Merlot Fairview **1997** £7.48 (GW)
Cabernet Sauvignon Backsberg **1996** £7.34 (CAP) £7.40 (PLA)
Cabernet Sauvignon Fairview **1998** £7.00 (GW)
Cabernet Sauvignon Fairview **1995** £7.45 (JU)
Cabernet Sauvignon Groot Constantia **1995** £7.25 (COC) £7.75 (CAP)
Cabernet Sauvignon Groot Constantia **1994** £7.75 (CAP)
Cabernet Sauvignon/Merlot Jordan Chameleon **1997** £7.75 (WRI) £7.95 (STA)
Cabernet Sauvignon Mooiplaas **1998** £7.99 (WR)
Cabernet Sauvignon Mooiplaas **1996** £7.50 (NO)
Cabernet Sauvignon Nederburg **1994** £7.10 (UB)
Cabernet Sauvignon Springfield Estate **1997** £7.44 (BIB)
Cabernet Sauvignon Villiera **1997** £7.89 (BOT)
Cabernet Sauvignon Vriesenhof **1997** £7.30 (TAN)
Cabernet Sauvignon Warwick **1991** £7.99 (RAE)
Cabernet Sauvignon Zonnebloem **1995** £7.25 (CAP)
Laureat Zonnebloem **1994** £7.50 (WRI) £8.56 (CAP)
Merlot Warwick **1991** £7.99 (RAE)
Pinotage Simonsig **1998** £7.32 (CAP)
Pinotage Vriesenhof Paradyskloof **1998** £7.30 (TAN)
Pinotage Vriesenhof Paradyskloof **1996** £7.64 (SAV)
Pinotage Wildekrans **1996** £7.95 (BER)
Pinotage Zonnebloem **1996** £7.18 (CAP)
Shiraz Backsberg **1995** £7.77 (BY)
Shiraz Fairview **1998** £7.48 (GW)
Shiraz Simonsig **1998** £7.84 (CAP)

£8.00 → £8.99

Cabernet Franc Warwick **1993** £8.68 (NO)
Cabernet Sauvignon Neil Ellis **1996** £8.90 (SAV)
Cabernet Sauvignon Jordan **1995** £8.99 (UN)
Cabernet Sauvignon Klein Constantia **1995** £8.52 (CAP)
Cabernet Sauvignon Laborie **1997** £8.70 (CAP)
Cabernet Sauvignon/Merlot Jordan Chameleon **1996** £8.25 (CON) £10.35 (JER)
Kallista Vriesenhof **1996** £8.50 (TAN)
Klein Babylonstoren Backsberg **1995** £8.45 (PLA)
Marlbrook Klein Constantia **1994** £8.96 (CAP) £9.25 (WRI)
Merlot Boschendal **1996** £8.50 (CRO) £10.35 (HAH) £10.45 (STE)
Merlot Glen Carlou **1997** £8.99 (UN)
Merlot Jordan **1998** £8.73 (PIP) £9.95 (STA)
Merlot Jordan **1996** £8.95 (CON)
Merlot Meerlust **1996** £8.56 (CAP) £14.80 (BEN) £14.95 (HAH)
Pinotage Beaumont **1997** £8.99 (POR)
Pinotage Cathedral Cellar **Non-vintage** £8.99 (SAF)
Pinotage Clos Malverne Reserve **1997** £8.00 (FLE) £8.75 (CON)
Pinotage Meerendal **1996** £8.79 (CAP)
Pinotage Wildekrans **1998** £8.62 (SAV)
Shiraz Allesverloren **1994** £8.95 (STA) £9.06 (CAP) £9.56 (PIP)
Shiraz Stellenzicht **1997** £8.50 (AV)
Shiraz Stellenzicht **1995** £8.07 (CAP)
Shiraz Stellenzicht **1994** £8.95 (COC)
Tinta Barocca Allesverloren **1995** £8.95 (WRI) £9.01 (PLA)
Tinta Barocca Allesverloren **1994** £8.59 (CAP)

£9.00 → £9.99

Cabernet Franc Warwick **1996** £9.69 (REI) £9.95 (RAE)
Cabernet Sauvignon Bellingham **1997** £9.08 (CAP)
Cabernet Sauvignon De Trafford **1998** £9.72 (BIB)

Cabernet Sauvignon Neil Ellis **1995** £9.95 (WS)
Cabernet Sauvignon Jordan **1997** £9.24 (PIP)
Cabernet Sauvignon Jordan **1996** £9.50 (CON) £9.95 (STA) £12.25 (JER)
Cabernet Sauvignon Kanonkop **1995** £9.90 (SOM)
Cabernet Sauvignon Klein Constantia **1996** £9.30 (TAN)
Cabernet Sauvignon Overgaauw **1994** £9.90 (UB)
Cabernet Sauvignon Plaisir de Merle **1996** £9.99 (MAJ) £10.99 (TES) £10.99 (SAF)
Cabernet Sauvignon Stellenzicht **1994** £9.20 (COC)
Cabernet Sauvignon Warwick **1997** £9.49 (WAI)
Cabernet Sauvignon Warwick **1995** £9.95 (WS)
Cabernet Sauvignon/Merlot Louisvale **1996** £9.26 (PLAY) £9.45 (AD)
Faithful Hound Mulderbosch **1994** £9.75 (NO)
Gouverneurs Reserve Groot Constantia **1995** £9.00 (COC)
★ Merlot Steenberg **1998** £9.99 (WAI)
Merlot Steenberg **1997** £9.99 (DI)
Merlot Thelema **1996** £9.99 (SOM) £11.42 (NO) £11.99 (YOU)
Merlot Warwick **1996** £9.40 (SAV) £9.69 (REI)
Pinot Noir Muratie Estate **1997** £9.66 (PLAY)
Pinotage Kanonkop **1997** £9.40 (SOM) £12.75 (FORT)
Pinotage L'Avenir **1997** £9.85 (SOM) £11.30 (NO)
Pinotage Warwick Traditional Bush Vine **1998** £9.99 (REI)
Pinotage Warwick Traditional Bush Vine **1997** £9.99 (JON)
Trilogy Warwick **1995** £9.95 (RAE)

£10.00 → £12.99

Cabernet Franc Warwick **1992** £11.16 (REI)
Cabernet Sauvignon Beyerskloof **1996** £11.99 (OD)
Cabernet Sauvignon Le Bonheur **1997** £10.45 (AV) £10.95 (COC)
Cabernet Sauvignon Plaisir de Merle **1995** £12.75 (UB)
Cabernet Sauvignon Rust-en-Vrede **1992** £10.99 (CAP)
Cabernet Sauvignon Stellenryck **1994** £10.38 (CAP)
Cabernet Sauvignon Stellenryck **1991** £10.99 (NI)
Cabernet Sauvignon Stellenryck Collection **1993** £10.75 (WRI)
Cabernet Sauvignon Thelema **1995** £12.75 (SOM) £13.90 (FLE) £16.95 (PHI)
Cabernet Sauvignon/Merlot Simonsig Tiara **1996** £12.42 (CAP) £12.95 (WRI)
Cabernet Sauvignon/Merlot Simonsig Tiara **1993** £12.70 (NO)
Cabernet/Merlot Grangehurst Reserve **1997** £12.34 (BIB)
Carlonet Uitkyk **1994** £10.59 (CAP)
Merlot Boschendal **1997** £10.45 (STE)
Merlot Môreson **1995** £11.40 (CAP)
Merlot Thelema **1997** £11.72 (CAP)
Merlot Thelema **1995** £11.00 (FLE) £12.63 (REI) £14.99 (PHI)
Merlot Warwick **1997** £10.28 (GOE)
Paul Sauer Kanonkop **1995** £11.25 (SOM)
Pinot Noir Bouchard Finlayson Galpin's Peak **1997** £11.26 (SAV) £15.95 (FORT)
Pinot Noir Meerlust **1995** £11.95 (POR) £12.50 (WRI) £17.45 (JER)
Pinotage Grangehurst **1997** £12.49 (YOU)
Pinotage Kanonkop **1994** £11.50 (JU)
Pinotage Uiterwyk **1997** £10.20 (LAY)
Shiraz Zandvliet **1995** £10.90 (CAP)
Syrah Boekenhoutskloof **1997** £12.71 (NO)
Trilogy Warwick **1997** £10.28 (GOE)
Trilogy Warwick **1996** £10.87 (REI)
Veenwouden **1996** £10.90 (SOM)

£13.00 → £13.99

Merlot Meerlust **1995** £13.90 (TAN) £13.99 (POR) £15.75 (FORT) £15.95 (PHI)
Pinotage Meerendal **1995** £13.75 (JER)
Shiraz Zandvliet **1992** £13.13 (CAP)

£14.00 → £15.99

Cabernet Sauvignon Thelema **1996** £14.57 (NO) £14.94 (CAP) £14.99 (YOU) £15.86 (REI) £15.95 (LEA) £15.95 (WAI) £15.99 (UN) £16.99 (WR) £18.65 (NI)
Cabernet Sauvignon Thelema **1994** £15.50 (BU)
Estate Wine Rust-en-Vrede **1995** £15.40 (LAY)
Merlot Thelema **1994** £14.75 (NI)
Merlot Thelema **1993** £14.50 (BU)
Paul Sauer Kanonkop **1992** £15.37 (NO)
Pinot Noir Bouchard Finlayson Galpin's Peak **1999** £14.55 (BIB)
Pinot Noir Hamilton Russell **1998** £14.95 (POR) £15.20 (AV)

Pinot Noir Hamilton Russell **1997** £14.95 (WAI) £15.50 (COC) £16.00 (WRI) £16.50 (PLAY) £16.60 (TAN) £16.99 (DI) £17.49 (YOU)
Pinot Noir Hamilton Russell **1996** £14.80 (CRO) £28.75 (UB)
Pinot Noir Meerlust **1996** £14.55 (CAP)
Rubicon Meerlust **1996** £15.75 (BEN)
Rubicon Meerlust **1995** £15.90 (HAH) £15.99 (PHI) £15.99 (POR) £16.75 (FORT)
Rubicon Meerlust **1994** £14.88 (GOE) £15.50 (WRI) £20.60 (JER)
Shiraz Hartenberg **1995** £15.95 (BER)
Veenwouden **1997** £14.50 (HED)

£16.00 → £19.99

Pinot Noir Hamilton Russell Ashbourne **1997** £18.50 (FORT)
Pinotage Kanonkop **1995** £19.00 (CRO)
Rubicon Meerlust **1992** £16.00 (CRO)

Over £20.00

Cabernet Sauvignon Warwick **1992** £20.00 (CRO)
Veenwouden **1993** £20.36 (NO)

WHITE

Under £4.00

Chardonnay De Wetshof Bateleur **1999** £3.99 (OD)
Chenin Blanc KWV **1999** £3.60 (COC) £3.99 (VIC) £3.99 (THR) £3.99 (UN) £3.99 (WR) £3.99 (BOT) £4.38 (CAP)
Chenin Blanc Swartland Reserve **1999** £3.99 (SAF)
Colombard Namaqua **1999** £3.25 (SOM)
★ The Society's South African Chenin Blanc **1999** £3.75 (WS)

£4.00 → £5.99

Chardonnay Avontuur **1998** £5.95 (WS)
Chardonnay De Wetshof Lesca **1999** £5.99 (SAI) £5.99 (MAJ)
Chardonnay Drostdy-Hof **1999** £5.95 (STE)
Chardonnay Fairview **1998** £5.99 (OD) £5.99 (UN)

Stars (★) indicate wines selected by Oz Clarke in the Best Buys section which begins on page 10.

Chardonnay Riebeek **1997** £5.45 (CON)
Chardonnay Sentinel **1998** £5.99 (OD)
Chardonnay Uiterwyk **1996** £5.45 (BER)
Chardonnay Zonnebloem **1999** £5.95 (STE)
Chenin Blanc Ken Forrester **1998** £5.49 (OD)
Chenin Blanc Klippenkop **1999** £4.49 (PIP)
Chenin Blanc Klippenkop **1998** £4.22 (FLE) £4.45 (CON) £5.95 (JER)
Chenin Blanc L'Avenir **1998** £5.99 (UN)
Chenin Blanc Long Mountain **1996** £5.35 (UB)
Chenin Blanc Thelema Stormy Cape **1999** £4.55 (SOM) £5.69 (NI)
Chenin Blanc Thelema Stormy Cape **1998** £5.26 (FLE)
Chenin Blanc Van Zylshof **1999** £5.00 (FORT)
Chenin Blanc Villiera **1997** £5.49 (BOT)
Chenin Blanc Wildekrans **1997** £4.75 (SOM)
Chenin/Chardonnay Arniston Bay **1999** £4.49 (THR) £4.49 (WR) £4.49 (SAF)
Chenin/Chardonnay Arniston Bay **1998** £4.49 (TES) £4.49 (VIC) £4.49 (BOT)
Colombar Goedverwacht **1999** £4.99 (BUD)
Riesling Hartenberg Weisser **1997** £5.99 (VIC) £5.99 (THR) £5.99 (WR)
Sauvignon Blanc Brampton **1997** £5.99 (SAF) £6.95 (WS)
Sauvignon Blanc KWV **1999** £4.83 (CAP) £4.99 (UN)
Sauvignon Blanc KWV **1998** £4.48 (COC) £4.79 (VIC) £4.79 (THR) £4.79 (BOT)
Sauvignon Blanc Nederburg **1999** £5.92 (CAP)
Sauvignon Blanc Nederburg **1996** £5.65 (UB)
Sauvignon Blanc Wildekrans **1998** £4.95 (SOM) £6.60 (SAV)
Sauvignon Blanc Zonnebloem **1998** £5.75 (STE) £7.65 (TW)
Sauvignon/Chenin Blanc Kopland **1996** £4.55 (JU)
Semillon Fairview **1999** £5.99 (SAF) £7.00 (GW)

£6.00 → £7.99

Buiten Blanc Buitenverwachting **1999** £6.05 (NEZ)
Chardonnay Agusta Unwooded **1998** £7.25 (WRI) £7.49 (VA) £7.50 (SOM)
Chardonnay Backsberg **1998** £7.62 (CAP) £7.99 (JON)

Chardonnay Boschendal **1999** £6.48 (CAP) £6.95 (STE)
Chardonnay Cathedral Cellar **1997** £7.99 (UN)
Chardonnay Delaire **1998** £7.65 (SOM) £9.99 (WR) £9.99 (BOT)
Chardonnay Delheim **1998** £6.99 (BOT)
Chardonnay Dieu Donné Vineyards **1996** £7.25 (JU)
Chardonnay Fairview **1999** £7.00 (GW)
Chardonnay Fairview **1996** £7.95 (JU)
Chardonnay Groot Constantia **1996** £7.08 (CAP)
Chardonnay Jordan **1998** £7.99 (WAI) £8.30 (PIP) £8.59 (UN) £8.95 (STA)
Chardonnay Laborie **1997** £6.32 (CAP)
Chardonnay Louisvale Chavant Oaked **1997** £6.75 (WS)
Chardonnay Nederburg **1999** £6.02 (CAP)
Chardonnay Neil Ellis **1998** £7.99 (MAJ)
Chardonnay/Sauvignon Blanc Jordan Chameleon **1999** £6.64 (PIP) £6.95 (STA)
Chardonnay/Sauvignon Blanc Jordan Chameleon **1998** £6.60 (WRI) £7.90 (JER)
Chardonnay/Sauvignon Blanc Jordan Chameleon **1997** £6.75 (CON)
Chardonnay Simonsig **1997** £7.93 (DOM)
Chardonnay Stellenryk **1999** £7.92 (CAP)
Chardonnay Uitkyk **1996** £7.29 (COC)
Chardonnay Vergelegen **1999** £6.99 (UN)
Chardonnay Vriesenhof **1998** £7.30 (TAN)
Chardonnay Wildekrans **1998** £7.93 (SAV)
Chardonnay Wildekrans **1997** £6.30 (SOM)
Chardonnay Zonnebloem **1997** £7.87 (PLAY) £7.95 (STA)
Chenin Blanc Blue White **1997** £6.49 (NO)
Riesling Klein Constantia Rhine **1997** £6.40 (BEN)
Sauvignon Blanc Brampton **1996** £6.95 (LEA)
Sauvignon Blanc Buitenverwachting **1998** £7.33 (NEZ)
Sauvignon Blanc Jordan **1999** £7.95 (STA)
Sauvignon Blanc Jordan **1998** £7.75 (CON)
Sauvignon Blanc L'Ormarins **1999** £6.84 (CAP)
Sauvignon Blanc L'Ormarins **1998** £7.25 (WRI) £8.95 (JER)
Sauvignon Blanc Simonsig **1999** £6.35 (DOM)
★ Sauvignon Blanc Springfield Estate Life from a Stone **1999** £6.65 (BIB)
Sauvignon Blanc Steenberg **1999** £7.49 (WAI)
Sauvignon Blanc Stellenzicht **1997** £7.49 (CON) £7.50 (COC)
Sauvignon Blanc Uiterwyk **1998** £6.75 (LAY)
Sauvignon Blanc Uitkyk **1997** £6.29 (COC)
Sauvignon Blanc Villiera **1998** £6.69 (BOT)
Semillon Fairview **1997** £6.75 (AD)
Sylvaner Overgaauw **1998** £6.00 (WRI)

£8.00 → £9.99

Chardonnay Boschendal Reserve **1998** £9.45 (STE)
Chardonnay Bouchard Finlayson Kaaimansgat **1998** £9.08 (BIB) £11.26 (SAV)
Chardonnay Bouchard Finlayson Kaaimansgat **1997** £9.49 (WAI)
Chardonnay Bouchard Finlayson Oak Valley **1997** £9.95 (WS)
Chardonnay Bouchard Finlayson Oak Valley **1996** £8.99 (SAF)
Chardonnay Brampton **1997** £8.50 (BEN)
Chardonnay Hamilton Russell **1997** £9.99 (COC) £12.00 (FLE) £12.85 (WRI) £12.99 (YOU) £12.99 (DI) £22.95 (UB)
Chardonnay Hamilton Russell **1996** £9.99 (RAE) £11.99 (JON)
Chardonnay Jordan **1997** £8.50 (CON) £8.50 (WRI)

Chardonnay Klein Constantia **1997** £9.25 (FORT)
Chardonnay Louisvale **1996** £8.95 (WS)
Chardonnay Neil Ellis **1997** £8.95 (WS)
Chardonnay Plaisir de Merle **1999** £9.65 (CAP)
Chardonnay Plaisir de Merle **1997** £8.99 (MAJ) £8.99 (TES)
Chardonnay Vergelegen Reserve **1997** £9.99 (OD)
Chardonnay Warwick **1998** £8.42 (SAV)
Riesling Klein Constantia Rhine **1996** £9.95 (BER)
Sauvignon Blanc Klein Constantia **1998** £8.40 (WRI) £8.49 (BO) £8.50 (TAN) £8.50 (FORT) £9.34 (PLAY)
Sauvignon Blanc Klein Constantia **1997** £8.99 (JON) £11.00 (JER)
Sauvignon Blanc Mulderbosch **1998** £9.95 (WS)
Sauvignon Blanc Neil Ellis **1996** £8.90 (UB)
Sauvignon Blanc Plaisir de Merle **1999** £8.59 (CAP)
Sauvignon Blanc Steenberg **1998** £8.64 (REI)
Sauvignon Blanc Thelema **1999** £9.10 (SOM) £9.99 (PHI) £10.50 (FLE) £10.79 (YOU) £11.46 (REI) £11.49 (WAI) £11.95 (LEA)
Semillon Steenberg Unwooded **1998** £8.63 (NO)

£10.00 → £11.99

Chardonnay Bouchard Finlayson Walker Bay **1998** £11.75 (FORT)
Chardonnay De Wetshof Bateleur **1997** £11.25 (FORT)
Chardonnay Glen Carlou Reserve **1997** £10.95 (STA)
Chardonnay Glen Carlou Reserve **1996** £10.66 (NO)
Chardonnay Hamilton Russell **1999** £11.05 (AV) £14.95 (LEA)
Chardonnay Hamilton Russell **1998** £10.95 (POR) £11.95 (WAI) £12.42 (PLAY) £12.75 (HAH) £12.90 (TAN) £12.99 (DI)
Chardonnay Meerlust **1996** £10.35 (JER) £18.70 (WRI) £20.00 (FORT)
Chardonnay Overgaauw **1996** £11.85 (UB)
Chardonnay Thelema **1998** £10.05 (SOM) £11.99 (YOU) £12.63 (REI) £12.99 (WR)
Chardonnay Thelema **1997** £10.88 (FLE)
Chardonnay Thelema **1996** £11.95 (BU) £13.99 (PHI) £14.75 (NI)
Sauvignon Blanc Thelema **1997** £10.50 (NO)
Semillon Stellenzicht Reserve **1995** £11.60 (AV)

£12.00 → £15.99

Chardonnay Mulderbosch **1997** £12.00 (WS)
Chardonnay Springfield Estate Methode Ancienne **1998** £12.99 (SAI)
Chardonnay Springfield Estate Methode Ancienne **1997** £12.54 (BIB)
Sauvignon Blanc Thelema **1998** £12.99 (NI)

c. £19.00

Chardonnay Meerlust **1997** £18.99 (POR)

SPARKLING

Under £7.00

Graham Beck Brut **Non-vintage** £6.99 (BIB) £6.99 (SAF) £7.99 (UN) £9.95 (FORT)
KWV Mousseux Blanc Cuvée Brut **Non-vintage** £6.12 (CAP)
Nederburg Premiere Cuvée Brut **Non-vintage** £6.72 (CAP)

£7.00 → £8.49

Boschendal Brut Vintage **1998** £8.25 (WRI)
Laborie Blanc de Noir **1997** £7.05 (CAP)

Over £8.50

Boschendal Brut Vintage **1993** £10.98 (CAP) £11.95 (STE)
Boschendal Le Grand Pavillon Blanc de Blancs **Non-vintage** £9.00 (CRO)
Pongrácz Cap Classique **Non-vintage** £9.69 (JON) £9.99 (CAP)
Simonsig Kaapse Vonkel **1996** £10.28 (CAP)
Simonsig Kaapse Vonkel **1995** £10.93 (CB)

FORTIFIED

Under £5.00

Cavendish Cape Extra Dry **Non-vintage** £4.54 (COC)
Cavendish Cape Medium Dry **Non-vintage** £4.54 (COC) £5.13 (CAP)
Cavendish Fine Old Ruby **Non-vintage** £4.95 (COC) £6.09 (CAP)

£5.50 → £10.00

Cavendish Cape Cream **Non-vintage** £5.33 (CAP)
Cavendish Vintage **1979** £9.62 (CAP)

SPAIN

Spain's winemakers have taken to setting prices for their top wines by pulling numbers out of the air. But luckily there are still some regions where you don't need a second mortgage

There must be an awful lot of rich people in Spain. Why do I think that? Because when a bodega makes a super-wine – a premium, fantastically concentrated red, almost inevitably – they work out the price by adding a zero on to the number they first thought of. And it works. They sell out.

The good news for us is that there are more and more really good wines about. What's bad news is that for the Spanish market at least, price isn't an issue. Those utterly delicious, wild-flavoured reds from Priorat? Pricy, I'd call them. Worth it, in their case, but pricy. Ribera del Duero? Often terrific. Not always pricy, but usually. Rioja: pricy, but getting more interesting, at last.

So where would I look for better value? Toro, for a start. Yes, that's getting pricier too, but it's still okay. It's still within the bounds of reason. Somontano: lots of good flavours, still inexpensive, very much worth a punt. La Mancha: we're starting to see some terrific reds from here – and I don't mean just the good everyday glugs we've got used to. I mean serious wines.

Whites, too, although the world's mad for reds and nobody in Spain is planting white. Albariño from Rías Baixas has come on by leaps and bounds, and so has Godello. These are seriously interesting wines. And the prices are interesting, without being that serious.

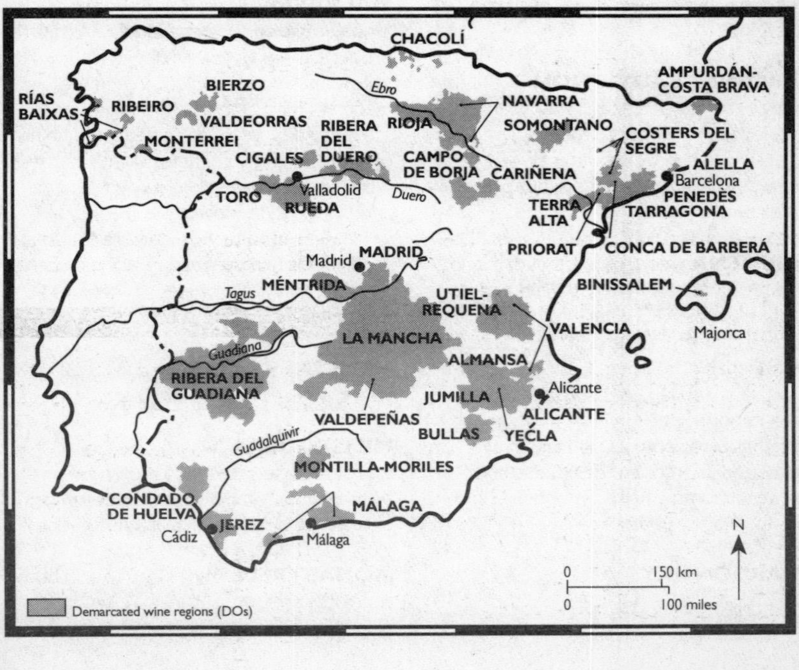

GRAPE VARIETIES

AIRÉN (white) These days Airén is the mainstay of the cheap, fresh whites of La Mancha – even though the reds seem to have taken a bigger hold of the British imagination. Never mind. It's a perfect example of how modern winemaking can turn what was always the world's dullest grape (apart from Ugni Blanc) into something perfectly drinkable.

ALBARIÑO (white) Lovely, peachy, fresh wines with elegant acid balance from Rías Baixas. From being a rarity it's suddenly everywhere. Why? The growers have realized they can get good money for it. It's also grown over the border in Portugal for Vinho Verde, but it's called Alvarinho there.

BOBAL (red) Quite good deep-coloured, fruity red and stylish rosados in Utiel-Requena and Valencia. It has reasonable acidity and relatively low alcohol, which keep the wines comparatively fresh and appetizing.

CABERNET SAUVIGNON (red) Not a native Spanish variety, but making inroads in Penedès and Navarra, where it is generally rich and heavy with oak. Still officially experimental in Rioja, but probably not forever.

CARIÑENA (red) A source of dark and prodigiously tannic wine. It plays only a small part in the DO wine which carries its name, and most Cariñena (it's the same as the Carignan of southern France) is grown in Cataluña, usually as a beefy blender. It is also a minority grape in Rioja under the name Mazuelo. With its high tannin and acidity, and its aroma of ripe plums and cherries, it complements Tempranillo and adds to its aging potential.

CHARDONNAY (white) Usually made in a rich, oaky style, but often blended as well. Found a lot in Navarra and Penedès.

GARNACHA (red) This, known as Grenache in France, grows everywhere in Spain except Andalucia, and makes big, broad, alcoholic, sometimes peppery or spicy wines. The wines are dark, and don't last well, but they can be delicious young. The greatest examples are to be found in Priorat.

GARNACHA BLANCA (white) This makes wines that are high in alcohol, low in acidity and with a tendency to oxidize, so they are usually blended in with wines of higher acidity, like Viura.

GRACIANO (red) On the verge of extinction, the excellent Graciano grape has been rescued by the DOC upgrade in Rioja, where conscientious winemakers are seeking it out once again for the extra quality it gives to the wine.

MALVASÍA (white) This interesting, aromatic, flavourful grape tends, in Spain, to produce wines of low acidity that turn yellow and oxidize rapidly. When well made, it's full-bodied, fairly strongly scented, spicy or musky, often with a hint of apricots, and sometimes slightly nutty as well. Malvasía helps *Marqués de Murrieta* and *CVNE* white Riojas taste the way all white Rioja used to. But Malvasía is also still widely grown in the Canary Islands where it makes light, fresh whites, sometimes mixed with Viura/Macabeo.

MENCÍA (red) Mainly used in light, fruity young wines in Ribeiro and Bierzo.

MERSEGUERA (white) Valencia's mainstay white grape, also grown in Alicante and Tarragona, produces light, delicately aromatic and characterful wines.

MONASTRELL (red) Used to add body and guts to many Cataluñan Tempranillo blends. It's grown right down the eastern seaboard in Alicante, Jumilla, Almansa, Yecla and Valencia – usually dry and stolid but sometimes made sweet. Jumilla's *Altos de Pío* is traditional, Yecla's *Pozuelo* more elegant.

MOSCATEL (white) Almost all Spanish Moscatel is the second-line Muscat of Alexandria rather than the top-quality Muscat à Petits Grains. But it makes a lot of good wine – rich and brown in Málaga, or fresh and grapy in Valencia. *Torres* makes a good, off-dry, aromatic version mixed with Gewürztraminer in Penedès, as does *de Muller* in Tarragona. Muscat de Chipiona from *Burdon* is rich and peachy. Also used to sweeten cream sherries.

PALOMINO (white) This is the dominant grape of the sherry region, making up all of the dry sherries, and an increasing proportion of the others. Although it produces great fortified wine it is not in itself a great grape. It plays a minor role in Montilla-Moriles. As a table wine grape, it produces dull, fat stuff, even with modern winemaking techniques, but in the sherry bodegas it reacts brilliantly to the *flor* yeast which imparts to *fino* that characteristic bone-dry, stark-sour nose.

PARELLADA (white) Touted as the provider of all the perfume and finesse in Cataluña's whites and in Cava fizz, but Parellada doesn't honestly have much to say for itself, except from the best producers: *Torres Viña Sol* is refreshing and lemony; also good are *Ferret i Mateu* and *Miret*.

PEDRO XIMÉNEZ (white) This used to be the chief component of sweet sherries, and is sometimes made into dessert wine, deeply coloured and thick. It covers most of the nearby Montilla-Moriles vineyards, as well as providing richness in Málaga; otherwise used for rather dull dry whites.

TEMPRANILLO (red) The fine red grape of Rioja and Navarra crops up all over Spain as far south as the province of Cádiz, but with a different name in almost every region. It's known as Cencibel on the plains of La Mancha and Valdepeñas, and as Tinto Fino in Ribera del Duero; elsewhere it may be Tinto de Madrid, Tinto de Toro, Tinto del País, and so on.

The wines have a spicy, herby, tobacco-like character, with plenty of sweet strawberry or sour cherry fruit, firm acidity and some tannin. Tempranillo makes vibrantly fruity wines ideal for gulping down young, as well as more robust wines suitable for aging – and it mixes brilliantly with oak. It's often blended, especially with Garnacha.

ON THE CASE

Rioja is changing its character: there are lots of new-wave wines that are stuffed with rich, dark cherry fruit, and less of the faded flavours of yore. Prices are high, though

VERDEJO (white) One of Spain's more interesting white grapes. In Rueda it makes soft, creamy and slightly nutty white, sometimes a touch honeyed, with good, green acidity.

VIURA (white) The main white grape of Rioja, made nowadays apple-fresh and clean and, at best, rather neutral; at worst it is sharp and grapefruity. It achieves similarly mixed results, under the name Macabeo, in Cataluña. Made in this light, modern style, it's a wine for gulping down young, in its first year. But if you take the trouble to blend it with Malvasía, top it up with a slug of acidity and leave it to age for a while in oak barrels, Viura can make wonderful, rich, almost Burgundy-like white Rioja.

XAREL-LO (white) One of the three main white grapes of Cataluña, this is heavier, more alcoholic and even less aromatic than the barely aromatic Parellada and Macabeo, with which it is blended.

WINE REGIONS

ALELLA, DO (white) Catalan region whose best-known wine is the off-dry, very fruity *Marqués de Alella*. Also look for the light, pineapple-fresh Chardonnay and appley *Marqués de Alella Seco*, as well as the sparkling, greengagy *Parxet*, which beats most famous Cavas hands down.

ALICANTE, DO (red) Heavy, earthy reds made in south-east Spain from Monastrell and mostly useful for blending.

ALMANSA, DO (red) Strong spicy reds from Monastrell and Garnacha, and even better reds from Tempranillo. *Bodegas Piqueras* makes very good wines under the *Castillo de Almansa* and *Marius* labels.

AMPURDÁN-COSTA BRAVA, DO (red, white, rosado) Suddenly there are some good juicy reds being exported from here. The best are very good indeed. Look for *Cellars Santamaría*.

BIERZO, DO (red) Emergent zone for the promising Mencía grape. Older wines are blends from before it became a DO. The *Vinos del Bierzo* co-op is good.

BINISSALEM, DO (red, white, rosado) Young and *crianza* reds and light young whites and rosados from Mallorca. The main producer is *Bodegas Franja Roja*.

BULLAS, DO (red) In the province of Murcia, making great big heady Monastrell reds, mostly from co-operatives.

CALATAYUD, DO (red) Hot, dry area adjoining Cariñena, making mainly Garnacha reds, plus some Tempranillo, usually for drinking young.

CAMPO DE BORJA, DO (red) Hefty alcoholic reds made from Cariñena and Garnacha, now making way for lighter reds and good rosados. *Bodegas Bordejé* and the *Borja* and *Santo Cristo* co-ops look promising.

CANARY ISLANDS There are eight DOs in the islands: Abona, El Hierro, Lanzarote, La Palma, Tacoronte-Acentejo, Valle de Güímar, Valle de la Orotava and Ycoden-Daute-Isora. Most of the wines are white (Tacoronte-Acentejo is the only serious producer of red) and mainly

SPANISH CLASSIFICATIONS

Denominación de Origen Calificada (DOC) is a new super-category (equivalent to the Italian DOCG) for wines which have a long tradition of high quality and are prepared to submit themselves to more rigorous quality scrutiny. So far there's only one DOC, and that's Rioja.

Denominación de Origen (DO) is roughly equivalent to the French AC: the basic quality wine designation. There are 51 of them.

Country wines fall into two groups: there are **Vinos Comarcales**: perhaps '*county* wines' is the nearest translation into English. These have some local significance but few pretensions to promotion. The second and more important group comprises 22 **Vinos de la Tierra**, which translates as '*country* wines', like French vins de pays. These are smaller areas, more tightly controlled and, in many cases, with ambitions to apply for DO status at some time in the future.

Vino de Mesa, basic table wine, doesn't usually carry any kind of regional name, nor a vintage date. A few maverick winemakers such as the Marqués de Griñón in Toledo and the Yllera family in Rueda use a legal nicety to put a general regional name on the label.

pleasant enough for the beach. There is still some sweet, fortified Malvasía, but it's not seen outside the islands.

CARIÑENA, DO (red, rosado, white) The best here are the pleasant, full, soft reds, mostly made from the fat, jammy Garnacha. The reds of the *Bodegas San Valero* co-op are sold here as *Don Mendo* and *Monte Ducay*.

CAVA, DO (white, rosado) The Spanish name for Champagne-method fizz, nearly all of which is from Cataluña. When Cava was promoted to DO status, several regions lost the right to use the name, and their wines (some, admittedly excellent) must now be called *Método Tradicional*. However, the two biggest outsiders, *Bodegas Inviosa* in Extremadura and *Torre Oria* in Valencia, have permission to continue using the name.

Most Cava is much less earthy and old-fashioned than it used to be, though it doesn't improve with bottle age. Most appetizing are *Cavas Hill Reserva Oro Brut Natur, Codorníu Première Cuvée Brut, Juvé y Camps, Mont Marçal Cava Nature* (and *Chardonnay*), *Parxet, Raïmat, Segura Viudas* and *Rovellats, Freixenet* and its subsidiary company *Conde de Caralt*.

CIGALES, DO (red, rosado) Near Ribera del Duero, famed for rosados but with some serious reds as well, made from Tempranillo/Garnacha mixes.

CHACOLÍ, DO (red, white) There are two of these, in neighbouring Basque provinces: Chacolí de Getaria (the local spelling is Getariako Txakolina) and Chacolí de Bizcaia/Vizcaya (Bizkaiko Txakolina). The wines are sharp, fresh and uncomplicated, suited to the local seafood.

CONCA DE BARBERÁ, DO (red, white) The fresh, fruity *Santara* brand comes from here, via flying winemaker Hugh Ryman. *Concavins* also makes a decent Merlot.

CONDADO DE HUELVA, DO (white, fortified) Wines not unlike Montilla are made and mostly drunk locally.

COSTERS DEL SEGRE, DO (red, white) Formerly a virtual one-producer DO, in the form of *Raïmat*, whose ripe, oaky, plummy reds have been a hit here for years. Whites include the light, lemony, gently oaked Chardonnay, as well as a good sparkler, Chardonnay Brut. *Castell del Remei*, producing Cabernet, Merlot, Chardonnay, Macabeo and Tempranillo, is now also in Britain.

JUMILLA, DO (red) Super-ripe reds, usually sold in bulk for beefing up blends elsewhere. However, French investment is now creating a new fresh-flavoured red style. The *Condestable* brands, *Castillo Jumilla* and *Con Sello* are quite good and gentle as is

MATURITY CHART

1995 Ribera del Duero

A very good vintage that should keep well

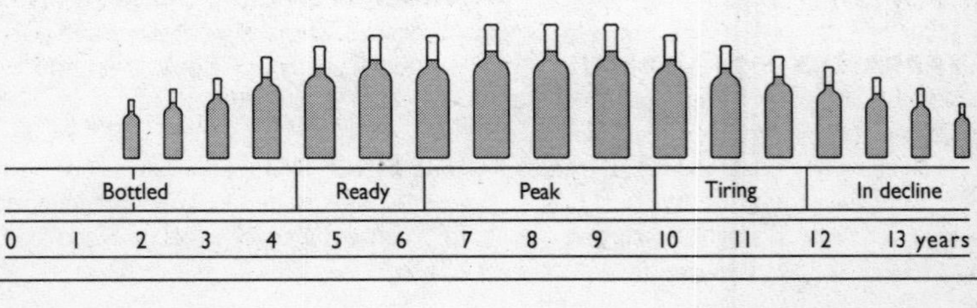

the ripe, plummy *Taja* from French merchants *Mahler-Besse*.

MÁLAGA, DO (fortified) Rarer than ever, now that *Scholtz Hermanos* has closed, leaving only one producer, *Bodega López Hermanos*, of any size. Málaga is (was?) usually full, brown and sweet in a raisiny, but not a gooey way, and is slightly smoky too.

LA MANCHA, DO (red, white) Spain's enormous central plateau has learnt how to make good fresh flavours in spite of searing summer heat. All new vineyards have to be of red grapes, usually Cencibel or Cabernet; whites are mostly Airén. Reds have soft tannins and whites are fresh, but need drinking young. *Vinicola de Castilla, Bodegas Cueva del Granero, Rodriguez & Berger, Arboles de Castillejo* from *Bodegas Torres Filoso, Casa la Teja, Castillo de Alhambra, Lazarillo, Señorío de Guadianeja, Viña Santa Elena, Yuntero, Zagarrón, Castillo de Manzanares, Tierra Seca* and *Casa Gualda* are all producing the goods.

MÉNTRIDA, DO (red) Strong, sturdy reds produced bang in the middle of Spain and seldom travelling much further.

MONTERREI, DO (white) Another of Galicia's new 'superwhite' DOs. Good value whites from Godello, Doña Blanca and even Palomino.

MONTILLA-MORILES, DO (fortified) Montilla wines are usually thought of as lower-priced – and lower-strength – sherry lookalikes but there is a great deal of reasonably good wine here, even if it lacks the bite of really good sherry.

NAVARRA, DO (red, white, rosado) The neighbouring region to Rioja grows the same grapes, but with more Garnacha.

There are many more individual estates making wine than there used to be. Look for *Magaña, Chivite, Bodegas Príncipe de Viana*, which also uses the label *Agramont, Monte Ory* by Luís Muga, *Bodegas Ochoa, Vinicola Navarra* (especially *Castillo de Tiebas*), *Señorío de Sarria, Bodegas Irache, Palacio de la Vega, Castillo de Monjardin, Guelbenzu* and *Nekeas*. Styles range from young and juicy through hefty, unoaked Garnacha to oak-aged blends. Young and fresh white Navarra, made with Viura plus Chardonnay, is pleasant and slurpable.

PENEDÈS, DO (red, white, rosado) Cataluña's leading region, though no longer as exciting as it used to be. *Torres* wines run from the rich, rather sweetly oaky basic reds, right up to the exciting Cabernet Sauvignon-based *Mas La Plana* and the 100 per cent Pinot Noir *Mas Borras*. Torres also extracts a lean, lemony, sharply refreshing flavour from Parellada. *Jean León* makes a rich, oaky, pineappley Chardonnay and a rich Cabernet. Also look out for *René Barbier, Cavas Hill, Ferret i Mateu, Masía Bach, Mont Marçal, Jaume Serra, Vallformosa*.

PRIORAT, DO (red) You need 13.5 degrees of alcohol here to get your DO. The reds from Garnacha and Cariñena are renowned – rich and full-bodied in style, and *Masía Barril, Scala Dei* and *de Muller* are worth trying. Also look for *Clos Dofi, Clos Martinet, Clos de l'Obac, Clos Mogador, Masia Duch* and, for lottery winners, *Clos l'Ermita*.

RÍAS BAIXAS, DO (red, white) Fresh and fragrant white Albariño wines are the stars of Galicia's best DO: *Agro de Bazán, Martín Codax, Granxa Fillaboa, Lusco do Miño, Pazo de Señorans, Quinta de Couselo, Santiago Ruiz* and *Terras Gauda* are all good.

RIBEIRA SACRA, DO (white) Newish Galician DO making excellent and good value whites from Godello, Albariño, Treixadura and others.

RIBEIRO, DO (red, white) There is fresh white wine made from Treixadura and Torrontés here: try *Casal da Barca* from *Bodega Alanis*.

RIBERA DEL DUERO, DO (red) The big name in this region is *Vega Sicilia*. Its wines are arguably the best in Spain, and unquestionably the most expensive. *Pesquera* from Alejandro Fernández is also something of a cult and fetches high prices. Others making classy, oak-aged reds include *Alión, Ismael Arroyo, Arzuaga, Balbás, Briego, Félix Callejo, Hermanos Cuadrado García, Señorío de Nava, Viña Pedrosa, Pingus, Protos, Teofilo Reyes, Hermanos Sastre, Valtravieso.*

RIBERA DEL GUADIANA, DO (red, white) DO created in 1997, producing wines for drinking young: whites from Viura, Chardonnay and local speciality Alarije; reds from Garnacha, Tempranillo and others.

RIOJA, DOC (red, white) Classic reds that taste of oak and vanilla toffee, plus rather light, sometimes peppery fruit with a strawberry jam sweetness.

Single estate wines (from *Contino, Barón de Ley, Martínez Bujanda's Finca Valpiedra* and *Remelluri*) are on the increase, which is a welcome development. The red blend is Tempranillo (for elegance), Garnacha (for fatness), and perhaps some Graciano and Mazuelo, but it's not unusual for producers to add some Cabernet to the blend. The Rioja Alavesa region makes more delicate, scented wines; Rioja Alta is firmer, leaner, slower to show its character but slower to lose it too, and the lower, hotter Rioja Baja grows mostly Garnacha, which gets super-ripe and rather lumpish. Best are *Remelluri, Bodegas Riojanas, Barón de Ley, Campo Viejo, El Coto, CVNE, Faustino, López de Heredia, Marqués de Cáceres, Marqués de Murrieta, Martínez Bujanda, Montecillo, Muga, Olarra, La Rioja Alta, Palacio, Campillo, Artadi, Viña Ijalba, Bodegas Bretón* and *Marqués de Riscal. Viña Paternina* makes the epitome of the unoaked style.

White Rioja *can* be buttery and rich, slightly Burgundian. *Marqués de Murrieta* makes a good example of this style, and so does *CVNE* with its *Viña Real*, and *Bodegas Riojanas* with its *Monte Real. López de Heredia* makes an old-fashioned style, while *Navajas, Viña Soledad* from *Franco Españolas* and *Siglo Gold* from *AGE* are all oak aged. The best new white Riojas are full of fresh, breath-catching raw fruit.

RIOJA CLASSIFICATIONS

Rioja is divided into three geographical sub-regions: Rioja Alta, Rioja Alavesa and Rioja Baja: most wines will be a blend from all three. The wine's age, indicated on the label, falls into one of four categories.

Sin crianza Without aging, or with less than a year in wood; wine sold in its first or second year. (The words *sin crianza* are not seen on the label.)

Crianza With a minimum of 12 months in wood and some further months in bottle; cannot be sold before its third year. Whites will have had a minimum of six months in cask before bottling.

Reserva Selected wine from a good harvest with a minimum of 36 months' aging, in cask and bottle, of which 12 months minimum in cask. It cannot leave the bodega until the fifth year after the vintage. Whites have at least six months in cask, and 24 months' aging in total.

Gran Reserva Wine from an excellent vintage (supposedly) that will stand up to aging: 24 months minimum in cask and 36 months in bottle, or vice-versa. It cannot leave the bodega until the sixth year after the vintage. White wines have six months in cask and 48 months' aging in total.

RUEDA, DO (white) A brilliant source of light table wines, picked early and fresh and fermented cool. The local grape, the Verdejo, makes soft, full, nutty wines, sometimes padded out with the dull Palomino, or sharpened up with the more acid Viura. Most are best young, but there are oaked ones. Look for *Alvarez y Díez, Belondrade y Lurton, Bodegas Castilla La Vieja, Marqués de Griñon, Hermanos Lurton, Marqués de Riscal.*

SHERRY (JEREZ-XÉRÈS-SHERRY, DO) (fortified) There are two basic sherry styles, *fino* and *oloroso*, each with subdivisions. *Fino*, from Jerez or Puerto de Santa Maria, should be pale and dry, with an unnerving dry austerity. The tang comes from a layer of natural yeast, called *flor*, that forms on the surface of the wine in the barrels. The lightest wines are selected for *fino*, which is drunk cool and fresh, often as an apéritif.

Manzanilla is a form of *fino* matured by the sea at Sanlúcar de Barrameda. It can be almost savoury-dry, and you might imagine a whiff of sea salt – if you catch it fresh enough. Best: *Barbadillo, Caballero, Diez-Merito, Don Zoilo, Garvey, La Gitana, Hidalgo, La Ina, Inocente, Lustau, La Riva, Sanchez Romate, Tío Pepe*. Good Puerto *fino* comes from *Burdon* and *Osborne*.

In Britain there can be a problem with freshness: *fino* and *manzanilla* won't usually keep longer than six months in bottle.

Real *amontillado* begins life as *fino*, aged in cask until the flor dies and the wine deepens and darkens to a tantalizing, nutty dryness. In the natural state, as drunk in Spain, it is *completely* dry, and a proper *amontillado* will usually say *seco* ('dry'), on the label. But we've adulterated the word in English to mean a bland, downmarket drink of no interest. Look out for *almacenista* sherries, wines from small stockholders, which can be wonderful.

Look out also for *Solear* from *Barbadillo, La Goya Manzanilla Pasada* and *Amontillado Fino Zuleta* (*Delgado Zuleta*), *Amontillado del Duque* (*González Byass*), *Hidalgo Manzanilla Pasada, Valdespino*'s *Amontillado Coliseo* and *Don Tomás*. (*Manzanilla pasada* has extra barrel age, and should be wonderful.)

Real *olorosos*, made from richer, fatter wines without any flor, are deep and dark, packed with violent burnt flavours – and usually dry, though you may find *oloroso dulce* (sweet). In Britain most are sweetened with Pedro Ximénez or Moscatel. They usually come as 'Milk', 'Cream' or 'Brown'. Pale Creams are sweetened (inferior) *fino*, and are some of the dullest drinks around. For the real, dry thing, once again, look for *almacenista olorosos* from *Lustau*. There are a few good,

INSTANT CELLAR:
MODERN SPANISH WHITES

- **Manzanilla Pasada, Pastrana, £8.95, T&W Wines** This is a single-vineyard sherry, crisp and delicate. Very, very good.
- **1998 Valdeorras Godello, Guitian, £6.60, Sommelier Wine Co** Bright yellow and full of buttery, greengagey, flowery flavours.
- **1999 Albariño de Rías Baixas, Pazo de Senorans, £7.95, Tanners** You can't have a Spanish cellar without some Albariño (not that I'd advise keeping it long) and this one is exceedingly good value, as well as being well structured and aromatic.
- **1998 Rueda Blanco Basa, Telmo Rodriguez, £4.80, Ben Ellis Wines** Mostly Verdejo with some Sauvignon: lovely and fresh.
- **1999 Alella Marqués de Alella Clasico, £5.25, Wine Society** Most Spanish whites are a tad short on personality; not this one. It has a slight spritz and no oak-aging.
- **1999 Rueda Azumbre, Agrícola Castellana, £5.45, Laymont & Shaw** A blend of Verdejo and Sauvignon Blanc, crisp, dry and with scents of elderflower. Rueda is Spain's best white DO, and this is as good as it gets.
- **1999 Valdesil, Bodegas Señorío, £6.45, Laymont & Shaw** Pure Godello (that's a grape) from north-eastern Spain, dry and peachy and unusual.

concentrated sweetened *olorosos* around, like *Apostoles* and *Matusalem*, both from *González Byass*, *Solera 1842 (Valdespino)*. Dry: *Barbadillo, Don Zoilo, Sandeman, Valdespino Don Gonzalo, Williams & Humbert Dos Cortados*. These intense old wines are one of today's great bargains.

SOMONTANO, DO (red, white, rosado) The most exciting of Spain's newer regions, with a long tradition of both Spanish and international grape varieties. *Enate* and *Vinos del Vero* are the star producers, making substantial, ageworthy reds and good whites from Chardonnay and Gewürztraminer. Look also for the *Co-operativa de Sobrarbe* under the *Camporocal* label, *Covisa*, *Bodegas Pirineos*.

TARRAGONA, DO (red, white, rosado) There is some progress discernible here, in the form of *crianzas* made from Cabernet Sauvignon, Garnacha and Tempranillo.

TERRA ALTA, DO (red) Decent Tempranillo. Good producers include the *Gandesa* co-op, *Ferrer Escod*.

TIERRA DE BARROS, Vino de la Tierra (red) One major bodega (*Inviosa*) has blazed a trail with its excellent *Lar de Barros* from Cencibel and Cabernet Sauvignon. *Viniberia* heads the followers.

TORO, DO (red) This makes good beefy fruity reds from the Tinto de Toro – yet another alias for the Tempranillo. The best wines still probably come from *Bodegas Fariña*, whose *Gran Colegiata* is aged French-style in small oak barrels. *Bodegas Frutos Villar* and the co-op at *Morales* offer good value at lower prices. But lately the wines have become softer, sadly.

UTIEL-REQUENA, DO (red, rosado) The reds, from the Bobal grape, are robust, rather hot and southern. The rosados *can* be better – delicate and fragrant.

VALDEORRAS, DO (red, white) The reds are best young. The ordinary whites, fresh and fruity at their best, are made from Palomino and Doña Blanca, but there is work being done with Godello.

VALDEPEÑAS, DO (red, white) The best reds here are from Cencibel (Tempranillo) and turn out deep and herby with good strawberry fruit – and excellent value at very low prices, even for *gran reservas* with a decade's aging, which is what the region is famous for. Look for the soft wines, aged in new oak, of *Señorío de Los Llanos* (including *Pata Negra Gran Reserva*), *Viña Albali* from *Bodegas Felix Solís, Bodegas Luís Megía* (including *Duque de Estrada* and *Marqués de Gastañaga*) and *Casa de la Viña*.

VALENCIA, DO (red, white, rosado) Large quantities of wines fine for the beach. Some low-priced reds from *Schenk* and *Gandía Pla* can be good, and sweet Moscatels can be tasty and good value. Gandía's *Castillo de Liria* is an attractive red.

YECLA, DO (red, white) Fairly full-bodied reds and more dubious whites. Some decent wines from *Bodegas Castaño*, from the cheap and cheerful *Dominio de Espinal* to the better *Pozuelo Reserva*.

PRODUCERS WHO'S WHO

ANTONIO BARBADILLO ★★★★(★) (Sanlúcar de Barrameda) Top *manzanilla* bodega producing consistently fresh wines. Older Amontillados are superb, too, and a touch lighter than Jerez versions. Buy the *manzanilla* in half bottles.

CAMPO VIEJO ★★★ (Rioja) Decent Riojas, soft, traditional *reservas*, and varietals. Albor is unoaked.

VINÍCOLA DE CASTILLA ★★★ (La Mancha) Up-to-date producer of white and oaky red Señorío de Guadianeja. Soft red Castillo de Alhambra is good value.

JULIÁN CHIVITE ★★★ (Navarra) Clean white from Viura, attractive rosado from Garnacha, and a good Tempranillo-based red, all under the Gran Feudo label.

CODORNÍU ★★★ (Penedès) Giant Cava company making likeably reliable fizz. Good soft and honeyed Anna de Codorníu, and a very good, creamy Chardonnay Cava.

CONTINO (SOCIEDAD VINÍCOLA LASERNA) ★★★★(★) (Rioja) Excellent, single-vineyard wines. Big, plummy and spicily complex.

CVNE ★★★(★) (Rioja) Excellent *crianza* and *reserva* whites (Monopole and CVNE Reserva). Best reds are Imperial and Viña Real, *reservas* upwards. Younger reds are currently looking a bit uninspired.

DOMECQ ★★★★(★) (Jerez) Leading sherry house, with top *fino* La Ina, Botaina *amontillado* and Rio Viejo *oloroso*. Also makes respectable Rioja.

FAUSTINO MARTÍNEZ ★★★ (Rioja) Good reds. Look out also for the new Campillo bodega.

FREIXENET ★★ (Penedès) High-tech Cava firm best known for Cordon Negro, but also good value Carta Nevada, Vintage Brut Nature, and upmarket Brut Barroco.

GONZÁLEZ BYASS ★★★★★ (Jerez) Producer of the best-selling (and very good) fino Tío Pepe. Gonzalez Byass makes an impressive top range of wines, and a Rioja, Bodegas Beronia.

CAVAS HILL ★★(★) (Penedès) Table wines as well as fresh, clean Cava Reserva Oro Brut Natur. Look out for Blanc Cru and Oro Penedès Blanco Suave whites, and Rioja-style reds, Gran Civet and Gran Toc.

JEAN LEÓN ★★★★ (Penedès) Some of Spain's most 'Californian' wines: super-oaky, pineapple-and-honey Chardonnay, and soft, blackcurranty Cabernet Sauvignon.

LOS LLANOS ★★★ (Valdepeñas) Reliable bodega producing wonderfully soft, oaky reds and uncomplicated whites.

LÓPEZ DE HEREDIA ★★★★ (Rioja) Rich, complex whites, Viña Tondonia and Viña Gravonia, and delicate, ethereal reds, Viña Cubillo and Viña Tondonia. The most traditional of all Riojan bodegas.

LUSTAU ★★★★ (Jerez) 'Reviving Traditional Sherry Values', to use its own phrase, with its range of *almacenista* wines.

MARQUÉS DE CÁCERES ★★★(★) (Rioja) Whites are cool-fermented and fresh, and reds have less wood-aging than usual, but still keep an attractive style.

MARQUÉS DE GRIÑÓN ★★★★ (Toledo) Very good Cabernet, aided by advice from Professor Émile Peynaud from Bordeaux. Also a joint venture with Berberana in Rioja which is looking good.

MARQUÉS DE MURRIETA ★★★★ (Rioja) A remarkable, ultra-traditional winery with wines oak-aged far longer than in any other Rioja bodega; Etiqueta Blanca wines, the youngest, spend at least two years in barrel, and are richly oaky, pungent and lemony. The red is soft and fruity-oaky, while the *reservas* are deep and complex. Castillo Ygay wines (the best from the very top years) may sit in barrel for 40 years.

MARTÍNEZ BUJANDA ★★★ (Rioja) Super-fresh and lively Valdemar white and strongly oaky *reserva* and *gran reserva* Condé de Valdemar. New-style Rioja at its best.

MONTECILLO ★★★(★) (Rioja) Aromatic white Viña Cumbrero, a raspberry and oak red, Viña Cumbrero *crianza*, and a *reserva*, Viña Monty.

MUGA ★★★(★) (Rioja) This bodega has a sternly traditional image. For reds, this traditionalism does nothing but good, and the *crianza* is fragrant and delicate, while the Prado Enea *reserva* or *gran reserva* is more complex, but still subtle and elegant. It's not cheap, though.

VIÑA PESQUERA ★★★(★) (Ribera del Duero) US wine writer Robert Parker likened this to Bordeaux's great Château Pétrus. Made from Tinto Fino and Garnacha, it's good but not *that* good, oaky and aromatic, with rich savoury fruit.

PRÍNCIPE DE VIANA ★★★(★) (Navarra) Innovative bodega which used to be a co-op, and became known as Bodegas Cenalsa. Agramont is its best-known UK brand, and look out for new Bodegas Guelbenzu, a Cabernet/Tempranillo estate in Cascante.

RAÏMAT ★★★ (Costers del Segre) The Raïmat Chardonnay Cava is honeyed, with grassy acidity. Abadía is an oak-enhanced blend of Cabernet, Tempranillo and Garnacha. Also Cabernet Sauvignon, Pinot Noir and Merlot.

REMELLURI ★★★★(★) (Rioja) Single-estate wine, not that common in Rioja; the bodega makes a fine, meaty *reserva*, barrel-aged for two to three years. Into bio-dynamic viticulture, which involves incredible degrees of care of the vines.

LA RIOJA ALTA ★★★★ (Rioja) A traditional bodega, firm believer in long barrel-aging: over half the wines qualify as *reserva* or *gran reserva*. Even the Viña Alberdi *crianza* has a delightfully oaky flavour. It makes two styles of *reserva*, the elegant Viña Arana and the rich Viña Ardanza. In the best years, it makes exceptional *gran reservas*.

RIOJANAS ★★★(★) (Rioja) The best reds here are the *reservas*: the light, elegant, plummy Viña Albina and the richer, more concentrated Monte Reál. White Monte Reál *crianza* is soft and peachy, with just enough oak to fatten it.

MIGUEL TORRES ★★★★ (Penedès) Viña Sol is a super-fresh modern white. Gran Viña Sol is Parellada and Chardonnay, fresh and pineappley, enriched with hints of vanilla oak. Gran Viña Sol Green Label pairs Parellada with Sauvignon Blanc, like oakier Sancerre. The superstar white is Milmanda Chardonnay. Viña Esmeralda is Gewürztraminer and Muscat d'Alsace.

Mas la Plana Cabernet Sauvignon is the top red. Viña Magdala is Pinot Noir and Tempranillo, Gran Sangredetoro is mainly Garnacha, Mas Borras is Pinot Noir, Las Torres is Merlot and Coronas Tempranillo is least exciting. Look out for the newest addition, Grandes Murallas, a blend of four red varieties made very much in the current mode: highly extracted, highly concentrated.

VALDESPINO ★★★★★ (Jerez) Family-owned bodega making a range of top-class, dry sherries. Inocente is superb, characterful *fino*. The Pedro Ximénez Solera Superior is one of the few examples of sherry's great sweetening wine bottled by itself. *Amontillados* and *olorosos* from here are about as good as you can get.

BODEGAS VEGA SICILIA ★★★★(★) (Ribera del Duero) Makers of Spain's most famous and expensive red wine – Vega Sicilia Unico, sometimes kept in barrel for ten years. The younger Valbuena offers a cheaper glimpse of Vega Sicilia's glories. Cheaper, you understand. Not cheap. Newest is more modern Alión, from a separate winery.

VICENTE GANDÍA ★★(★) (Valencia) Perhaps this DO's most go-ahead producer. Fresh white Castillo de Liria and juicy red and rosado from Bobal.

SPAIN PRICES

RIOJA RED

Under £5.00

Artadi Orobio Tempranillo **1998** £4.99 (TES)
Martinez Bujanda Valdemar **1998** £4.49 (BOT) £4.99 (VIC) £4.99 (THR) £4.99 (WR)

£5.00 → £5.99

CVNE **1995** £5.99 (MOR) £9.99 (VIN)
Marqués de Griñon **1998** £5.49 (UN)
Marqués de Griñon **1997** £5.99 (MAJ) £5.99 (TES)
Martinez Bujanda Conde de Valdemar Crianza **1997** £5.99 (VIC) £5.99 (THR) £6.49 (WR) £6.49 (BOT)
Bodegas Muerza Vega **1997** £5.35 (COC)
Bodegas Olarra Añares **1995** £5.65 (CON)
Paternina Banda Azul **1996** £5.99 (SAF) £6.78 (COC)

£6.00 → £6.99

Amezola de la Mora Amezola Crianza **1995** £6.75 (WS)
Amezola de la Mora Amezola Crianza **1994** £6.99 (RAE)
Artadi Viñas de Gain **1995** £6.49 (BO) £8.10 (SOM) £8.50 (WS)
Berberana Carta de Oro **1996** £6.99 (UN)
Campo Viejo **1997** £6.95 (STE)
CVNE **1997** £6.49 (BO) £6.62 (PIP) £8.75 (STE)
CVNE **1996** £6.99 (GW) £6.99 (JON) £8.42 (BIB)
CVNE Viña Real **1995** £6.49 (MOR)
CVNE Viña Real **1994** £6.49 (BOT)
Faustino Rivero Orla Dorado Crianza **1996** £6.80 (TAN)
Bodegas Lan Crianza **1996** £6.66 (BY)
Bodegas Lan Crianza **1995** £6.66 (BY)
Marqués de Cáceres Crianza **1996** £6.80 (TAN) £6.95 (HAH) £7.25 (LAY) £7.95 (STE)
Marqués de Cáceres Crianza **1995** £6.67 (COC) £6.99 (POR) £7.04 (PLA) £7.50 (DI)
Marqués de Cáceres Crianza **1994** £6.80 (CRO) £6.85 (MOR)
Martinez Bujanda Conde de Valdemar Crianza **1996** £6.49 (WR) £6.95 (NI) £7.60 (TAN) £7.65 (CON)
Bodegas Palacio Cosme Palacio y Hermanos **1997** £6.99 (MAJ) £6.99 (OD) £6.99 (WAI) £6.99 (SAF)
Bodegas Palacio Cosme Palacio y Hermanos **1996** £6.79 (UN) £6.95 (WS)
Bodegas Palacio Glorioso Crianza **1997** £6.79 (OD)
Viña Salceda Crianza **1994** £6.99 (DI)

£7.00 → £7.99

Amezola de la Mora Amezola Crianza **1997** £7.49 (BO)
Amezola de la Mora Amezola Crianza **1996** £7.89 (JON) £7.95 (BER) £9.01 (BIB)
Amezola de la Mora Amezola Crianza **1992** £7.75 (JU)
Artadi Viñas de Gain **1997** £7.65 (LIB) £7.99 (MAJ) £8.40 (TAN) £8.86 (GW) £8.95 (GAU) £9.66 (SUN) £10.98 (TW)
Artadi Viñas de Gain **1996** £7.95 (NI) £7.99 (GAU) £8.99 (CON)
Barón de Ley **1995** £7.99 (WR)
Berberana Reserva **1995** £7.99 (MAJ)
Campo Viejo Reserva **1993** £7.95 (POR)
CVNE **1994** £7.49 (BOT)
CVNE Viña Real **1996** £7.50 (BU) £7.50 (GW) £8.95 (STE) £9.40 (BIB)
Faustino V Reserva **1995** £7.99 (WR)
Faustino V Reserva **1994** £7.49 (VIC) £7.49 (THR) £7.99 (BOT) £8.49 (MOR) £8.80 (UB) £10.49 (CON)
Martinez Bujanda Conde de Valdemar Reserva **1995** £7.99 (VIC) £7.99 (THR) £7.99 (WR) £7.99 (BOT)

MERCHANTS SPECIALIZING IN SPAIN

see Merchant Directory (page 456) for details

Adnams (AD), Ballantynes (BAL), Bibendum (BIB), Direct Wine (DI), Cockburns of Leith (COC), Lay & Wheeler (LAY), Laymont & Shaw, Lea & Sandeman (LEA), Moreno Wines (MOR) – a mostly Spanish list, Playford Ros (PLAY), Reid Wines (REI) – good sherries, Roberson (ROB), Tanners (TAN), Villeneuve, Wine Society (WS).

Muga Reserva **1995** £7.10 (SOM) £8.65 (PIP) £8.99 (BAL) £9.99 (MAJ) £10.99 (JON)
La Rioja Alta Viña Alberdi **1995** £7.45 (SOM) £9.50 (POR) £9.95 (AME)
Viña Salceda Crianza **1996** £7.30 (TAN) £7.99 (DI) £7.99 (JON) £8.50 (LEA) £9.02 (NO) £9.49 (BAL)
Viña Salceda Reserva **1994** £7.95 (WS)

£8.00 → £8.99

Barón de Ley Reserva **1995** £8.50 (CRO)
Campo Viejo Reserva **1995** £8.75 (STE)
CVNE Reserva **1991** £8.99 (BOT)
CVNE Viña Real **1997** £8.95 (STE)
Marqués de Murrieta Reserva **1994** £8.99 (OD) £9.75 (RAE)
Marqués de Murrieta Reserva **1991** £8.99 (UN)
Marqués de Riscal Reserva **1996** £8.71 (GOE) £10.75 (PLA)
Marqués de Riscal Reserva **1995** £8.71 (GOE) £8.95 (WS) £9.69 (GW) £9.99 (MAJ) £9.99 (UN)
Marqués de Riscal Reserva **1994** £8.75 (MOR) £9.99 (VA)
Martinez Bujanda Conde de Valdemar Reserva **1994** £8.99 (UN) £9.95 (TAN) £11.45 (PLA)
Muga Reserva **1994** £8.60 (MOR)
Bodegas Olarra Cerro Anon Reserva **1994** £8.50 (CON)

£9.00 → £9.99

Alavesas Solar de Samaniego Reserva **1994** £9.64 (CB)
Coto de Imaz Reserva **1995** £9.95 (PHI)
Viña Ijalba Múrice Crianza **1997** £9.83 (PLAY)
López de Heredia Viña Bosconia **1992** £9.95 (BAL)
Marqués de Cáceres Reserva **1992** £9.99 (POR) £10.00 (HAH) £11.50 (DI)
Marqués de Murrieta Reserva **1995** £9.95 (WAI) £9.99 (MAJ) £9.99 (SAF) £10.49 (POR) £10.95 (AD) £10.95 (WRI) £11.17 (PLA) £11.45 (STE) £11.95 (PLAY) £12.99 (NI)
Marqués de Murrieta Reserva **1993** £9.49 (MOR) £9.75 (RAE) £9.99 (UN) £14.80 (UB)
Marqués de Murrieta Reserva **1992** £9.49 (BOT) £9.50 (JU) £9.99 (SAI)
Remelluri **1995** £9.70 (SOM) £17.00 (CRO)
Urbina Gran Reserva **1990** £9.95 (POR) £10.65 (AD) £10.99 (JON)

£10.00 → £11.99

Baron de Oña Torre de Oña Reserva **1995** £11.50 (STA) £11.99 (AME) £14.70 (LAY)
Baron de Oña Torre de Oña Reserva **1994** £10.95 (JER)
Campillo Reserva **1995** £10.99 (TES)
Campo Viejo Gran Reserva **1993** £11.95 (STE) £11.99 (WR)
Campo Viejo Gran Reserva **1989** £10.95 (POR)
CVNE Reserva **1995** £10.69 (GW) £11.89 (WAT)
CVNE Viña Real Reserva **1991** £11.49 (MOR) £16.95 (STA)
Faustino I Gran Reserva **1991** £11.20 (COC) £11.85 (MOR)
Faustino I Gran Reserva **1987** £10.99 (BOT)
Lagunilla Gran Reserva **1990** £10.99 (PLA)
López de Heredia Viña Bosconia **1990** £10.75 (MOR)
Marqués de Cáceres Reserva **1991** £10.15 (MOR) £10.85 (UB)
Marqués de Griñon **1994** £10.50 (CRO)
Marqués de Murrieta **1995** £10.39 (NO) £11.30 (BEN)
Marqués de Murrieta Reserva **1996** £11.45 (STE)
Marqués de Murrieta Reserva Especial **1994** £10.99 (MAJ) £12.99 (NI) £13.99 (JON) £15.75 (BEN) £17.50 (FORT)
Marqués de Murrieta Reserva Especial **1991** £11.49 (MOR) £12.75 (JU) £13.50 (BOT)
Marqués de Vargas Reserva **1995** £11.95 (LEA) £12.99 (DI)
Montecillo Gran Reserva **1991** £11.99 (OD)
Paternina Gran Reserva **1993** £10.50 (COC)
Remelluri **1998** £11.78 (FLE)
Remelluri Reserva **1996** £10.78 (NO)
Remelluri Reserva **1995** £11.99 (MOR)
La Rioja Alta Viña Arana Reserva **1987** £11.99 (DI)

- *Wines are listed in A–Z order within each price band.*
- *For each wine, vintages are listed in descending order.*
- *Each vintage of any wine appears only once.*

La Rioja Alta Viña Ardanza Reserva **1990** £10.00 (NO) £11.25 (SOM) £11.80 (COC) £11.99 (SAI) £12.25 (MOR) £13.75 (JER) £13.99 (DI) £14.69 (REI) £14.95 (STA)
La Rioja Alta Viña Ardanza Reserva **1989** £10.95 (JU) £11.90 (CRO)
Viña Salceda Reserva **1995** £10.68 (NO) £12.95 (LEA)

£12.00 → £13.99

Alavesas Solar de Samaniego Gran Reserva **1989** £12.98 (CB)
Amezola Gran Reserva **1990** £12.99 (RAE)
Amezola Gran Reserva **1988** £13.95 (JU)
Contino Reserva **1994** £13.70 (MOR) £15.99 (DI)
CVNE Imperial Reserva **1989** £12.49 (MOR)
CVNE Viña Real Reserva **1989** £12.49 (BOT)
Faustino I Gran Reserva **1992** £12.69 (OD) £12.75 (UB) £13.95 (CON)
López de Heredia Viña Tondonia Reserva **1991** £13.95 (MOR) £17.63 (SAV)
Marqués de Cáceres Gran Reserva **1989** £12.95 (HAH) £13.99 (OD) £14.99 (DI) £15.99 (UB)
Marqués de Murrieta Reserva **1984** £13.00 (CRO)
Marqués de Vargas Reserva **1996** £12.30 (TAN) £12.95 (BER) £13.99 (JON)
Martinez Bujanda Garnacha **1990** £12.00 (BOT)
Remelluri **1997** £12.75 (ELL)
Remelluri **1996** £12.75 (REI) £12.83 (SAV) £12.99 (YOU) £13.00 (TAN) £13.50 (AD) £15.00 (CRO)
La Rioja Alta Viña Arana **1993** £13.75 (JER)
La Rioja Alta Viña Ardanza Reserva **1995** £12.99 (JON)
La Rioja Alta Viña Ardanza Reserva **1993** £13.99 (PHI) £14.50 (AD) £14.95 (POR) £14.99 (AME) £15.75 (BEN)
Urbina Gran Reserva **1991** £13.25 (STE)

£14.00 → £15.99

CVNE Imperial Gran Reserva **1989** £15.75 (MOR) £18.99 (JON)
CVNE Imperial Reserva **1995** £14.58 (PIP) £18.50 (STE) £18.58 (GW)
CVNE Viña Real Gran Reserva **1989** £14.35 (MOR)
CVNE Viña Real Gran Reserva **1988** £14.95 (BU) £17.50 (STA) £18.49 (BOT)
CVNE Viña Real Reserva **1995** £14.99 (GW) £15.77 (PIP)
CVNE Viña Real Reserva **1994** £15.80 (TAN) £15.99 (JON)
Marqués de Murrieta Reserva Especial **1995** £15.50 (AD)
Marqués de Riscal Gran Reserva **1989** £15.99 (SAF)
Martinez Bujanda Conde de Valdemar Gran Reserva **1993** £15.86 (PLA)
Martinez Bujanda Conde de Valdemar Gran Reserva **1992** £15.49 (UN)
Martinez Lacuesta Gran Reserva **1980** £14.00 (WRI)
Muga Prado Enea Gran Reserva **1991** £15.10 (SOM) £18.15 (PIP) £18.99 (JON) £19.00 (WS) £19.79 (OD) £19.99 (MAJ)

£16.00 → £19.99

Artadi Viñas El Pison Reserva **1994** £18.99 (BO) £40.50 (NI)
Contino Reserva **1995** £19.90 (PIP) £20.75 (WAT) £21.75 (STE)
CVNE Imperial Gran Reserva **1991** £18.95 (STA) £18.95 (STE) £19.21 (PIP) £19.75 (GW) £19.95 (TAN)
CVNE Imperial Gran Reserva **1988** £19.99 (BOT)
CVNE Imperial Reserva **1994** £16.45 (WAT) £16.95 (STE) £17.95 (STA)
CVNE Viña Real Gran Reserva **1991** £16.37 (PIP) £16.85 (GW)
Bodegas Lan Viña Lanciano Reserva **1995** £17.25 (BY)
Bodegas Lan Viña Lanciano Reserva **1994** £16.50 (CRO)
Marqués de Murrieta Castillo Ygay Gran Reserva **1989** £18.50 (MOR)
Marqués de Murrieta Castillo Ygay Gran Reserva Especial **1989** £19.50 (BOT)
Marqués de Murrieta Castillo Ygay Gran Reserva **1989** £19.85 (NI) £19.92 (PLA) £19.95 (AD) £19.95 (POR) £27.84 (PLAY)
Marqués de Murrieta Castillo Ygay Gran Reserva Especial **1987** £18.49 (BOT)
Marqués de Murrieta Castillo Ygay Gran Reserva **1987** £19.50 (JU)
Marqués de Riscal Gran Reserva **1991** £16.25 (MOR)

- *All prices for each wine are listed together in ascending order.*
- *Price bands refer to the lowest price for which the wine is available.*

Muga Prado Enea Gran Reserva **1989** £16.35 (MOR)

La Rioja Alta Reserva 904 **1989** £18.90 (CRO)

La Rioja Alta Reserva 904 Gran Reserva **1989** £17.95 (SOM) £19.10 (MOR) £22.00 (WS) £22.50 (PHI) £22.95 (POR) £22.99 (JON) £24.95 (BEN) £25.00 (FORT) £25.90 (JER) £26.25 (LAY) £28.45 (UB)

La Rioja Alta Reserva 904 Gran Reserva **1987** £16.95 (JU)

£20.00 → £29.99

Artadi Pagos Viejos Reserva **1997** £26.20 (TW)

Artadi Pagos Viejos Reserva **1995** £20.95 (CON)

Artadi Viñas El Pison Reserva **1995** £25.99 (CON)

Contino Reserva **1996** £22.95 (STE)

CVNE Imperial Gran Reserva **1987** £24.00 (WS)

López de Heredia Viña Bosconia Gran Reserva **1976** £29.50 (MOR)

López de Heredia Viña Tondonia Gran Reserva **1978** £25.50 (BAL) £31.49 (MOR) £35.25 (SAV)

López de Heredia Viña Tondonia Reserva **1990** £25.00 (VIN)

Marqués de Cáceres Reserva **1970** £23.50 (REI)

Marqués de Murrieta Castillo Ygay **1989** £20.50 (STE) £21.00 (CRO)

Marqués de Murrieta Reserva **1985** £20.00 (CRO)

Marqués de Murrieta Ygay Reserva **1989** £20.00 (FORT)

Martinez Bujanda Conde de Valdemar Gran Reserva **1981** £23.00 (CRO)

Muga Prado Enea Gran Reserva **1973** £24.95 (BAL)

La Rioja Alta Reserva 890 Gran Reserva **1989** £22.00 (WAI)

£30.00 → £49.99

Artadi Viñas El Pison Reserva **1996** £32.31 (TW) £37.24 (GW) £58.00 (LIB)

Berberana Gran Reserva **1970** £39.00 (CRO)

CVNE Viña Real Gran Reserva **1976** £47.00 (DI)

CVNE Viña Real Reserva **1966** £42.89 (REI)

López de Heredia Viña Bosconia **1976** £49.95 (VIN)

López de Heredia Viña Bosconia Gran Reserva **1973** £43.50 (BAL) £43.75 (MOR)

López de Heredia Viña Tondonia Gran Reserva **1976** £35.99 (MOR)

López de Heredia Viña Tondonia Gran Reserva **1970** £48.50 (MOR)

López de Heredia Viña Tondonia Gran Reserva **1968** £49.50 (BAL) £58.55 (MOR)

Marqués de Murrieta Castillo Ygay **1978** £34.95 (BOT)

Marqués de Murrieta Gran Reserva **1960** £42.00 (CRO)

La Rioja Alta Reserva 890 Gran Reserva **1982** £34.00 (DI) £41.20 (SOM) £51.85 (JER) £53.00 (POR)

£50.00 → £69.99

CVNE Imperial Gran Reserva **1976** £59.99 (BOT)

CVNE Imperial Gran Reserva **1970** £52.70 (REI) £59.99 (BOT)

CVNE Imperial Gran Reserva **1968** £64.63 (REI)

CVNE Viña Real Gran Reserva **1975** £59.99 (BOT)

CVNE Viña Real Gran Reserva **1973** £52.00 (DI) £59.99 (BOT)

López de Heredia Viña Tondonia Gran Reserva **1964** £53.00 (BAL) £59.22 (SAV) £60.59 (MOR)

López de Heredia Viña Tondonia Gran Reserva **1961** £65.20 (MOR)

Marqués de Murrieta Castillo Ygay Gran Reserva **1978** £54.00 (CRO)

Marqués de Murrieta Castillo Ygay Gran Reserva Especial **1970** £52.43 (NO)

Marqués de Murrieta Gran Reserva **1964** £50.00 (CRO)

Marqués de Riscal Reserva **1960** £65.00 (BU)

La Rioja Alta Reserva 904 Gran Reserva **1968** £52.88 (REI)

Over £70.00

López de Heredia Viña Tondonia **1954** £111.63 (REI)

López de Heredia Viña Tondonia Gran Reserva **1954** £75.00 (MOR)

Marqués de Murrieta Castillo Ygay Gran Reserva **1970** £93.00 (RAE)

Marqués de Murrieta Castillo Ygay Gran Reserva **1968** £88.00 (CRO) £99.99 (VIN)

Marqués de Murrieta Castillo Ygay Gran Reserva **1964** £78.00 (RAE) £82.00 (MOR) £95.00 (JU) £98.50 (ROB)
Marqués de Murrieta Castillo Ygay Gran Reserva **1959** £85.00 (RAE) £99.00 (JU)
Marqués de Murrieta Castillo Ygay Gran Reserva **1942** £110.00 (CRO)
Marqués de Murrieta Reserva **1946** £88.13 (REI)
Bodegas Riojanas Viña Albina **1950** £75.00 (BU)

RIOJA WHITE

Under £5.00

Marqués de Cáceres **1998** £4.25 (COC) £4.49 (POR) £4.95 (HAH) £5.15 (TAN) £5.49 (DI) £5.95 (STE)
Marqués de Cáceres **1997** £4.89 (BO) £4.99 (MOR)
Marqués de Cáceres **1996** £4.90 (CRO)
Marqués de Cáceres Satinela Semi-Dulce **1996** £4.79 (DI)

£5.00 → £5.99

Alavesas Solar de Samaniego **1998** £5.76 (CB)
Faustino V **1995** £5.99 (SAF)
Marqués de Cáceres **1999** £5.95 (STE)
Marqués de Cáceres Satinela Semi-Dulce **1998** £5.65 (DI)
Marqués de Cáceres Satinela Semi-Dulce **1997** £5.20 (UB)
Marqués de Murrieta Misela de Murrieta **1994** £5.95 (JU)

£6.00 → £7.99

Artadi Blanco **1998** £6.75 (CON)
Berberana Carta de Oro **1995** £6.90 (CRO)
CVNE Monopole **1997** £7.80 (TAN) £8.75 (STE)
CVNE Monopole **1996** £6.59 (SAF)
CVNE Monopole **1995** £6.59 (SAF) £9.95 (UB)
CVNE Monopole Barrel-Fermented **1998** £6.71 (PIP)
CVNE Monopole Barrel-Fermented **1997** £7.53 (GW)
CVNE Monopole Barrel-Fermented **1995** £6.99 (MOR)
Faustino V **1992** £6.90 (UB)
Marqués de Cáceres Antea **1997** £6.99 (JON)
Marqués de Cáceres Antea **1995** £6.65 (DI) £6.99 (POR)
Marqués de Cáceres sin Crianza **1997** £6.50 (VIN)
Marqués de Murrieta **1997** £7.99 (BO)
Marqués de Murrieta Reserva **1992** £7.95 (CON) £7.99 (RAE) £8.95 (JU)
Martinez Bujanda Conde de Valdemar **1997** £7.75 (NI) £8.75 (CON)
Martinez Bujanda Conde de Valdemar **1995** £7.95 (CON)
Muga **1998** £6.69 (JON)
Muga **1997** £6.15 (MOR)
Navajas **1996** £6.99 (THR)
Navajas **1994** £6.50 (MOR)
Navajas **1993** £6.50 (MOR)
Navajas **1989** £6.30 (UB)
Paternina Banda Dorada **1997** £6.50 (COC)
La Rioja Alta Viña Ardanza Reserva **1989** £7.95 (JU)

£8.00 → £11.99

CVNE Reserva **1994** £8.99 (MOR)
López de Heredia Tondonia **1987** £11.95 (BAL)
Marqués de Murrieta Misela de Murrieta **1993** £10.60 (NO)
Marqués de Murrieta Reserva **1995** £8.49 (MAJ) £8.95 (WRI) £9.10 (PLA)
Marqués de Murrieta Reserva **1994** £8.99 (POR) £10.90 (CRO) £11.70 (UB)
Marqués de Murrieta Reserva **1993** £8.99 (BOT)
Marqués de Murrieta Reserva Especial **1994** £9.50 (FORT)
Martinez Bujanda Conde de Valdemar **1996** £9.45 (PLA) £9.95 (WR) £9.95 (BOT)
Martinez Bujanda Conde de Valdemar **1994** £11.59 (VIN)
La Rioja Alta Viña Ardanza Reserva **1994** £8.25 (JER)
La Rioja Alta Viña Ardanza Reserva **1993** £8.99 (MOR)

Please remember that
Oz Clarke's Wine Buying Guide
*is a price **guide** and not a price **list**. It is not meant to replace up-to-date merchants' lists.*

£12.00 → £19.99

López de Heredia Tondonia Reserva **1991** £13.95 (MOR)
Marqués de Murrieta Ygay Gran Reserva **1986** £19.50 (RAE)

£20.00 → £29.99

Marqués de Murrieta Castillo Ygay **1986** £21.95 (BOT)
Marqués de Murrieta Gran Reserva **1986** £20.00 (MOR)
Marqués de Murrieta Reserva **1988** £20.00 (CRO)
Marqués de Murrieta Ygay Gran Reserva **1978** £24.00 (JU)

Over £30.00

López de Heredia Tondonia Gran Reserva **1976** £31.49 (MOR)
López de Heredia Tondonia Gran Reserva **1964** £53.00 (BAL) £65.00 (MOR)
López de Heredia Tondonia Gran Reserva **1957** £68.95 (MOR)
Marqués de Murrieta Ygay Gran Reserva **1962** £60.00 (CRO)

RIOJA ROSÉ

Under £5.00

Marqués de Cáceres Rosado **1998** £4.80 (COC) £4.99 (POR) £5.69 (DI) £6.45 (STE)

c. £7.00

Artadi Rosado **1998** £6.75 (CON)

NAVARRA RED

Under £5.00

Baso **1998** £4.33 (FLE) £4.50 (CRO) £4.80 (BEN)
Baso **1997** £3.80 (SOM)
Baso **1993** £4.89 (PHI)
Guelbenzu Jardin **1998** £4.95 (WS) £5.68 (NO)
Guelbenzu Jardin **1996** £4.99 (MOR) £5.69 (GW) £6.49 (VA)
Orvalaiz Tempranillo **1998** £4.13 (JON)
Palacio de la Vega Merlot Crianza **1997** £4.99 (BUD)
Bodegas Principe de Viana Agramont Tinto **1997** £4.99 (OD) £5.25 (WAI)

£5.00 → £6.99

Chivite Gran Feudo **1996** £5.49 (OD) £5.99 (DI) £7.14 (PLAY)
Chivite Gran Fuedo Reserva **1995** £6.29 (BOT) £7.00 (WRI)
Chivite Gran Fuedo Reserva **1994** £6.29 (VIC) £6.29 (THR) £6.29 (OD) £6.99 (DI)
Guelbenzu **1996** £5.95 (WS)
Guelbenzu Crianza **1997** £5.99 (MOR) £7.30 (TAN)
Guelbenzu Jardin **1995** £5.39 (NI) £5.49 (BAL)
Castillo de Monjardin Merlot **1995** £5.50 (SOM) £6.75 (WRI)
Ochoa Tempranillo Crianza **1996** £6.89 (BO) £6.99 (MAJ) £6.99 (UN) £7.85 (UB) £7.93 (REI) £8.05 (WAT) £8.45 (STE) £8.60 (TAN) £8.75 (FORT)
Palacio de la Vega Cabernet/Tempranillo Crianza **1995** £5.99 (UB)
Bodegas Principe de Viana Agramont Tinto **1996** £5.19 (SAF)

£7.00 → £9.99

Guelbenzu Crianza **1994** £7.50 (BAL)
Castillo de Monjardin Merlot **1996** £7.95 (POR)
Ochoa Reserva **1995** £9.80 (PIP)
★ Ochoa Tempranillo Crianza **1997** £7.48 (PIP) £7.50 (GW) £7.74 (PLA) £7.85 (UB) £7.99 (JON) £8.45 (STE) £9.40 (LAY)

Over £10.00

Chivite Colección 125 Reserva **1995** £13.92 (REI) £14.99 (DI)
Ochoa Reserva **1992** £10.45 (WAT)

NAVARRA WHITE

Under £6.00

Nekeas Vega Sindoa Chardonnay **1998** £4.99 (UN) £7.25 (FORT)
Ochoa **1996** £5.20 (UB)
Bodegas Principe de Viana Agramont Blanco **1999** £4.99 (OD)

£6.00 → £8.99

Ochoa Vino Dulce de Moscatel 50cl **1997** £8.75 (MOR)

c. £10.00

Ochoa Vino Dulce de Moscatel 50cl **1998** £9.91 (STA)

OTHER SPANISH RED

Under £4.00

Elegido, Vino de Mesa **1997** £3.20 (SOM)
Vicente Gandia Castillo de Liria, Valencia **Non-vintage** £3.39 (UN) £3.49 (BOT)
Bodegas Inviosa, Lar de Barros Tempranillo **1998** £3.85 (SOM) £4.10 (TAN) £4.75 (SAV)
Los Llanos Señorio de los Llanos Reserva, Valdepeñas **1995** £3.99 (TES) £4.20 (SOM)
Vitorianas Don Darias, Vino de Mesa **Non-vintage** £3.49 (ASD) £3.49 (TES) £3.79 (SAF) £3.89 (UN)

£4.00 → £4.99

Fariña Colegiata, Toro **1998** £4.99 (DI)
Los Llanos Señorio de los Llanos Reserva, Valdepeñas **1994** £4.40 (COC)
Los Llanos Señorio de los Llanos, Valdepeñas **1996** £4.89 (JON)
Los Llanos Señorio de los Llanos, Valdepeñas **1994** £4.90 (UB)
Mont Marçal, Penedés **1998** £4.29 (CON)
Viña Montana, Yecla **1998** £4.99 (TES)
Bodegas Piqueras Marius Tinto Reserva, Almansa **1994** £4.39 (POR) £4.49 (BO) £4.95 (TAN) £5.50 (LEA)
Bodegas Piqueras Marius Tinto Reserva, Almansa **1993** £4.99 (JON) £5.15 (UB)
Felix Solis Viña Albali Reserva, Valdepeñas **1993** £4.49 (VIC) £4.49 (THR) £4.49 (WR) £4.49 (BUD) £4.99 (UN)
Torres Sangredetoro, Penedés **1997** £4.99 (DI) £5.99 (MOR)

£5.00 → £5.99

Abadia Retuerta Primicia, Vina de Mesa **1996** £5.99 (DI)
Condé de Caralt Reserva, Penedés **1994** £5.49 (MOR)
Fariña Gran Colegiata, Toro **1995** £5.79 (COC)
Los Llanos Señorio de los Llanos Gran Reserva, Valdepeñas **1995** £5.95 (JU)
Los Llanos Señorio de los Llanos Gran Reserva, Valdepeñas **1994** £5.49 (MAJ)
Los Llanos Señorio de los Llanos Gran Reserva, Valdepeñas **1990** £5.30 (SOM) £6.49 (POR)
Marques de Velilla, Ribera del Duero **1997** £5.99 (MOR)
Mont Marçal Cabernet Sauvignon, Penedés **1991** £5.99 (CON)
Pérez Caramés el Vino de Los Consules de Roma **1998** £5.99 (DI)
San Valero Monte Ducay, Cariñena **1994** £5.99 (JON)
Cellers Scala Dei Negre, Priorato **1996** £5.99 (MOR)
Felix Solis Viña Albali Gran Reserva, Valdepeñas **1991** £5.99 (ASD) £5.99 (BUD)
Torres Coronas, Penedés **1998** £5.29 (DI) £5.49 (TES) £5.99 (WAI) £6.95 (STE)
Torres Coronas, Penedés **1997** £5.29 (DI) £5.99 (UN) £5.99 (JON) £6.95 (STE) £7.49 (VIN)
Torres Coronas, Penedés **1996** £5.49 (SAF) £5.99 (MOR)
Torres Sangredetoro, Penedés **1998** £5.29 (TES) £5.49 (WAI)

£6.00 → £7.99

Abadia Retuerta Primicia, Vina de Mesa **1998** £6.75 (DI)
Abadia Retuerta Rivola, Vina de Mesa **1997** £6.99 (BOT) £7.99 (DI)
Callejo, Ribera del Duero **1996** £7.99 (JON)
Enate Crianza, Somontano **1996** £7.20 (CRO) £7.40 (AV)
Fariña Gran Colegiata Reserva, Toro **1993** £7.99 (DI)

Fariña Gran Colegiata, Toro **1996** £7.99 (COC)

Bodegas Inviosa, Lar de Barros Reserva **1995** £6.25 (PHI)

Los Llanos Pata Negra Gran Reserva, Valdepeñas **1991** £6.49 (POR) £6.50 (CRO) £6.80 (UB) £6.95 (PHI) £7.45 (WRI) £7.45 (BEN) £7.99 (CB)

Los Llanos Pata Negra Gran Reserva, Valdepeñas **1987** £6.45 (JU)

Masía Vallformosa Vall Fort, Penedés **1995** £7.10 (UB)

Protos, Ribera del Duero **1998** £7.95 (COC)

Raïmat Cabernet Sauvignon, Costers del Segre **1993** £7.90 (CRO)

Cellers Santamaria Gran Recosind, Ampurdan Costa Brava **1993** £7.49 (BAL)

Torres Atrium, Penedés **1998** £6.99 (DI) £6.99 (OD)

Torres Gran Coronas, Penedés **1996** £7.49 (DI) £8.49 (WR) £8.99 (WAI) £10.95 (STE)

Torres Gran Sangre de Toro, Penedés **1996** £6.25 (DI) £6.49 (VIC) £6.49 (THR) £6.49 (WR) £6.49 (BOT) £6.99 (UN) £6.99 (WAI) £7.50 (STA)

Torres Gran Sangre de Toro, Penedés **1995** £6.25 (DI) £6.81 (COC) £8.00 (WRI)

Torres Gran Sangre de Toro, Penedés **1994** £6.55 (UB) £6.99 (MOR)

Torres Las Torres Merlot, Penedés **1997** £6.99 (MOR)

£8.00 → £9.99

Bodegas Inviosa, Lar de Lares Gran Reserva, Ribera del Guadiana **1994** £8.70 (TAN) £9.99 (PHI)

★ Briego Tinto Roble, Ribera del Duero **1997** £8.99 (RAE)

Marques de Velilla, Ribera del Duero **1995** £8.95 (WS)

Masía Barril Típico, Priorato **1991** £9.50 (MOR) £10.80 (TAN)

Mauro, Vino de Mesa **1995** £8.99 (NI) £12.49 (MOR)

Pesquera Condado de Haza, Ribera del Duero **1997** £9.22 (REI) £9.50 (TAN) £10.95 (BAL) £10.99 (DI) £10.99 (NI) £12.25 (PHI)

Pesquera Crianza, Ribera del Duero **1997** £9.95 (BER) £11.75 (NI) £11.90 (TAN) £13.50 (BAL) £14.99 (OD)

Cellers Scala Dei Crianza, Priorato **1993** £8.99 (MOR)

Cellers Scala Dei Crianza, Priorato **1992** £8.99 (MOR)

Torres Gran Coronas, Penedés **1997** £9.49 (POR) £10.95 (STE)

Torres Gran Coronas, Penedés **1995** £8.52 (PIP) £9.75 (STA) £11.99 (VIN)

Torres Gran Coronas, Penedés **1994** £8.95 (CON) £9.25 (MOR) £9.69 (JON)

Bodegas Valduero Crianza, Ribera del Duero **1994** £9.90 (JU)

£10.00 → £19.99

Costers del Siurana Miserere, Priorat **1997** £19.99 (DI)

Costers del Siurana Miserere, Priorat **1994** £12.95 (JU) £24.06 (NO) £27.00 (FORT)

Jean León Cabernet Sauvignon, Penedés **1991** £11.95 (DI)

Jean León Cabernet Sauvignon, Penedés **1980** £17.63 (REI)

Masía Barril Priorato Extra, Priorato **1995** £10.65 (MOR)

Mauro Crianza, Ribera del Duero **1996** £13.61 (FA)

Mauro Crianza, Ribera del Duero **1995** £11.95 (LEA)

Mauro Crianza, Ribera del Duero **1994** £12.90 (JU)

Mauro, Vino de Mesa **1996** £13.90 (GAU)

★ Olivares Dulce Monastrell, Jumilla **1996** £14.99 (OD)

Pago de Carraovejas, Ribera del Duero **1997** £14.93 (GW)

Viña Pedrosa Reserva, Ribera del Duero **1994** £14.69 (MOR)

Viña Pedrosa Reserva, Ribera del Duero **1992** £15.99 (RAE)

Pesquera Condado de Haza, Ribera del Duero **1996** £10.99 (VA) £11.90 (CRO)

Pesquera Condado de Haza, Ribera del Duero **1995** £10.75 (MOR)

Pesquera Crianza, Ribera del Duero **1996** £11.90 (TAN) £14.69 (REI) £14.99 (YOU) £15.08 (FA) £15.99 (PHI) £16.00 (GAU) £16.99 (VA)

Stars (★) indicate wines selected by Oz Clarke in the Best Buys section which begins on page 10.

Pesquera Crianza, Ribera del Duero **1995** £10.95 (BAL) £12.85 (MOR)
Pesquera Crianza, Ribera del Duero **1993** £16.25 (UB)
Pesquera Reserva, Ribera del Duero **1996** £17.95 (NI) £21.50 (BAL)
Pesquera Reserva, Ribera del Duero **1995** £19.39 (REI) £26.00 (CRO) £36.62 (FA)
Cellers Santamaria Gran Recosind Gran Reserva, Ampurdan Costa Brava **1988** £10.99 (RAE) £11.50 (BAL)
Cellers Scala Dei Negre, Priorato **1989** £12.95 (POR)
Torres Coronas, Penedés **1985** £17.04 (REI)
Torres Gran Coronas Black Label (Mas La Plana), Penedés **1994** £16.95 (DI) £19.95 (TAN) £21.00 (JON) £21.50 (STA)
Torres Gran Coronas Black Label (Mas La Plana), Penedés **1993** £19.95 (WRI) £19.99 (MOR) £22.00 (UB) £27.32 (PLAY)
Torres Gran Coronas Black Label (Mas La Plana), Penedés **1990** £19.99 (CON) £20.97 (REI)
Torres Gran Coronas Black Label (Mas La Plana), Penedés **1988** £19.99 (RAE)
Torres Mas Borras Pinot Noir, Penedés **1994** £13.04 (PIP)
Bodegas Valduero Reserva, Ribera del Duero **1994** £15.30 (JER) £15.50 (STA)
Bodegas Valduero Reserva, Ribera del Duero **1991** £13.95 (JU)
Vega Sicilia Alión Reserva, Ribera del Duero **1995** £17.95 (DI) £18.99 (FA)

£20.00 → £29.99

Clos Mogador, Priorato **1996** £21.00 (CRO)
Clos Mogador, Priorato **1995** £21.50 (BAL) £32.00 (MOR)
Costers del Siurana Clos de l'Obac, Priorat **1997** £23.95 (DI)
Costers del Siurana Clos de l'Obac, Priorat **1996** £27.99 (YOU) £29.96 (REI) £31.40 (TAN)
Costers del Siurana Clos de l'Obac, Priorat **1992** £28.79 (REI) £29.75 (WRI)
Costers del Siurana Dolç de l'Obac, Priorat **1994** £29.00 (JU) £53.89 (NO) £54.64 (REI)
Costers del Siurana Miserere, Priorat **1996** £25.26 (REI)
Costers del Siurana Miserere, Priorat **1995** £23.99 (YOU) £28.50 (CRO) £29.38 (CAV)
Alvaro Palacios Dofi, Priorato **1997** £27.61 (CB)
Alvaro Palacios Dofi, Priorato **1996** £28.30 (FA) £39.99 (DI) £41.13 (REI)
Torres Coronas, Penedés **1982** £25.00 (VA)
Torres Gran Muralles, Penedés **1996** £27.49 (YOU) £29.95 (DI) £38.50 (POR)

£30.00 → £49.99

Costers del Siurana Clos de l'Obac, Priorat **1995** £34.00 (JU) £38.68 (CAV)
Costers del Siurana Clos de l'Obac, Priorat **1994** £33.00 (FORT)

Costers del Siurana Clos de l'Obac, Priorat **1993** £30.37 (REI)
Costers del Siurana Dolç de l'Obac, Priorat **1997** £36.95 (DI)
Costers del Siurana Dolç de l'Obac, Priorat **1996** £46.41 (REI)
Alvaro Palacios Dofi, Priorato **1995** £39.60 (MOR)
Alvaro Palacios Dofi, Priorato **1994** £41.74 (NO) £59.95 (BOT)
Pesquera Crianza, Ribera del Duero **1986** £41.13 (REI)
Pesquera Crianza, Ribera del Duero **1985** £32.31 (REI) £38.50 (BU)
Pesquera Reserva, Ribera del Duero **1994** £36.62 (FA)
Pesquera Reserva, Ribera del Duero **1986** £49.00 (CRO)
Torres Gran Coronas Black Label (Mas La Plana), Penedés **1985** £41.13 (REI)
Torres Gran Coronas Black Label (Mas La Plana), Penedés **1983** £32.00 (CRO)
Torres Gran Coronas Black Label (Mas La Plana), Penedés **1982** £38.19 (REI)
Torres Gran Coronas Black Label (Mas La Plana), Penedés **1981** £40.54 (REI)
Torres Gran Coronas Black Label (Mas La Plana), Penedés **1971** £49.50 (BU)
Torres Gran Muralles, Penedés **1997** £38.50 (POR)
Vega Sicilia Valbuena 3rd year, Ribera del Duero **1983** £47.00 (CRO)

Vega Sicilia Valbuena 5th year, Ribera del Duero **1994** £42.00 (DI)
Vega Sicilia Valbuena 5th year, Ribera del Duero **1993** £47.85 (BER)
Vega Sicilia Valbuena 5th year, Ribera del Duero **1992** £42.50 (MOR) £45.00 (DI)
Vega Sicilia Valbuena, Ribera del Duero **1995** £45.00 (YOU) £50.00 (MV)
Vega Sicilia Valbuena, Ribera del Duero **1994** £42.50 (BU) £44.00 (FORT) £45.00 (LEA)
Vega Sicilia Valbuena, Ribera del Duero **1993** £39.50 (RAE)
Vega Sicilia Valbuena, Ribera del Duero **1991** £39.50 (RAE) £44.00 (JU)

£50.00 → £99.99

Costers del Siurana Dolç de l'Obac, Priorat **1995** £53.99 (YOU) £58.75 (CAV)
Alvaro Palacios l'Ermita, Priorato **1997** £99.88 (CB)
Pesquera Janus, Ribero del Duero **1994** £84.99 (NO)
Pesquera Reserva, Ribera del Duero **1985** £75.00 (BU)
Torres Gran Coronas Black Label (Mas La Plana), Penedés **1976** £54.64 (REI)
Vega Sicilia, Ribera del Duero **1986** £71.87 (FA)
Vega Sicilia, Ribera del Duero **1979** £99.29 (FA)
Vega Sicilia Unico, Ribera del Duero **1990** £95.00 (YOU) £100.00 (MV)
Vega Sicilia Unico, Ribera del Duero **1986** £69.00 (CRO) £70.00 (FORT) £72.00 (MOR) £75.00 (DI) £77.50 (RAE)
Vega Sicilia Unico, Ribera del Duero **1981** £91.65 (RAE) £95.00 (FORT) £95.00 (MV) £99.00 (YOU) £100.00 (DI) £101.50 (TAN) £103.00 (MOR) £115.00 (BER) £120.00 (VA)
Vega Sicilia Valbuena 3rd year, Ribera del Duero **1979** £65.00 (BU)

£100.00 → £124.99

Alvaro Palacios l'Ermita, Priorato **1996** £101.25 (FA) £107.12 (FA) £145.00 (DI)
Vega Sicilia, Ribera del Duero **1985** £105.00 (UB)
Vega Sicilia, Ribera del Duero **1981** £104.18 (FA)
Vega Sicilia, Ribera del Duero **1975** £120.83 (FA)
Vega Sicilia Unico, Ribera del Duero **1984** £100.00 (BU)

Over £125.00

Alvaro Palacios l'Ermita, Priorato **1995** £126.70 (FA) £147.99 (MOR)
Alvaro Palacios l'Ermita, Priorato **1994** £154.47 (NO)
Vega Sicilia, Ribera del Duero **1982** £165.00 (UB)
Vega Sicilia Unico, Ribera del Duero **1970** £125.00 (BU)
Vega Sicilia Unico, Ribera del Duero **1969** £146.88 (REI)

OTHER SPANISH WHITE

Under £4.00

Basa, Rueda **1997** £3.60 (SOM)
Vicente Gandia Castillo de Liria Moscatel, Valencia **Non-vintage** £3.39 (UN) £4.25 (TAN)
Vicente Gandia Castillo de Liria, Valencia **Non-vintage** £3.39 (UN)
★ Moscatel de Valencia **Non-vintage** £3.79 (SO)
Pazo Ribeiro, Ribeiro **1998** £3.70 (SOM)

£4.00 → £4.99

Bodegas Alvear Medium Dry, Montilla **Non-vintage** £4.45 (TAN)
Bodegas Alvear Pale Dry, Montilla **Non-vintage** £4.45 (TAN)
Basa, Rueda **1999** £4.83 (PIP)
Basa, Rueda **1998** £4.33 (FLE) £4.50 (CRO) £4.80 (BEN)
Basa, Rueda **1996** £4.69 (PHI)
Castilla la Vieja Palacio de Bornos, Rueda **1998** £4.40 (SOM)
Los Llanos Armonioso, Valdepeñas **1995** £4.30 (UB)
Ryman Santara Barrique-Fermented Chardonnay, Conca de Barberà **1997** £4.49 (SAF)
Torres San Valentin, Penedés **1999** £4.49 (DI)
Torres Viña Esmeralda, Penedés **1999** £4.99 (DI) £5.69 (POR) £5.93 (PIP) £5.95 (STA) £6.45 (STE)
Torres Viña Sol, Penedés **1999** £4.49 (DI) £4.49 (TES) £4.49 (WAI) £4.99 (POR) £5.45 (STE) £5.95 (VIN)
Torres Viña Sol, Penedés **1998** £4.49 (DI) £4.58 (COC) £4.59 (VIC) £4.59 (THR) £4.59 (WR) £4.59 (BOT) £4.99 (UN) £5.49 (BO)

Torres Viña Sol, Penedés **1997** £4.49 (DI) £5.29 (MOR)
Viñas del Vero Chardonnay, Somontano **1998** £4.99 (UN) £4.99 (WAI)
Viñas del Vero Chenin Blanc, Somontano **1992** £4.65 (UB)

£5.00 → £5.99

Alvarez y Diez Mantel Verdejo/Sauvignon Blanc, Rueda **1998** £5.49 (BO) £5.99 (DI)
Castilla la Vieja Palacio de Bornos, Rueda **1989** £5.49 (JON)
Marqués de Alella Clasico, Alella **1999** £5.99 (DI) £6.49 (POR)
Marqués de Alella Clasico, Alella **1998** £5.25 (WS) £7.90 (CRO)
Marqués de Alella Clasico, Alella **1997** £5.99 (MOR)
Marqués de Riscal, Rueda **1998** £5.49 (MAJ)
Torres Gran Viña Sol, Penedés **1998** £5.99 (DI) £5.99 (VIC) £5.99 (THR) £6.29 (WR) £6.29 (BOT) £6.29 (WAI) £6.69 (JON) £6.70 (WRI) £6.90 (HAH) £7.25 (STE)
Torres Gran Viña Sol, Penedés **1997** £5.99 (DI) £6.65 (MOR)
Torres Viña Esmeralda, Penedés **1998** £5.43 (NO) £5.49 (VIC) £5.49 (THR) £5.49 (WR) £5.49 (BOT) £5.69 (JON) £5.95 (TAN) £5.95 (WRI) £5.99 (BO) £5.99 (AME) £5.99 (UN)
Torres Viña Esmeralda, Penedés **1997** £5.99 (MOR)
Torres Viña Esmeralda, Penedés **1996** £5.50 (UB) £5.65 (CON) £5.95 (JU)
Torres Viña Sol, Penedés **2000** £5.45 (STE)
Bodegas Valduero Azumbre Blanco, Ribera del Duero **1996** £5.45 (JU)
Viñas del Vero Chardonnay, Somontano **1991** £5.60 (UB)

£6.00 → £9.99

Belondrade y Lurton, Rueda **1995** £9.95 (RAE) £14.65 (UB)
Enate, Somontano **1998** £7.00 (AV)
Enate, Somontano **1996** £7.90 (CRO)
Lagar de Fornelos Lagar de Cervera, Rías Baixas **1999** £7.65 (SOM) £9.21 (PIP) £9.25 (TAN) £9.30 (STA)

A key to name abbreviations is available on page 7.

Lagar de Fornelos Lagar de Cervera, Rías Baixas **1998** £9.30 (WRI) £9.69 (REI) £9.85 (PHI)
Lagar de Fornelos Lagar de Cervera, Rías Baixas **1997** £8.99 (AME)
Lagar de Fornelos Lagar de Cervera, Rías Baixas **1996** £8.50 (JU)
Marqués de Riscal, Rueda **1999** £6.45 (PLA)
Mont Marçal Chardonnay, Penedés **1995** £6.25 (CON)
Pazo de Barrantes Albariño, Rias Baixas **1997** £9.99 (RAE) £10.75 (FORT)
Pazo de Barrantes Albariño, Rias Baixas **1996** £9.51 (PLA)
Pazo de Señorans Albariño, Rias Baixas **1999** £7.95 (TAN)
Raïmat Chardonnay, Costers del Segre **1997** £7.49 (UN)
Torres Fransola, Penedés **1998** £9.50 (DI) £10.50 (STA) £10.87 (REI)
Torres Fransola, Penedés **1997** £9.50 (DI) £10.35 (MOR)
Torres Gran Viña Sol, Penedés **1999** £6.13 (PIP) £6.99 (POR) £7.25 (STE) £8.16 (TW)
Torres Moscatel Malvasia de Oro, Penedés **Non-vintage** £7.21 (NO)
Torres Viña Esmeralda, Penedés **2000** £6.45 (STE)
Viñas del Vero Barrel-Fermented Chardonnay, Somontano **1996** £6.49 (OD)
Viñas del Vero Gewürztraminer, Somontano **1999** £7.96 (PIP)
Viñas del Vero Gewürztraminer, Somontano **1998** £9.35 (PLA)

£10.00 → £14.99

Belondrade y Lurton, Rueda **1997** £11.49 (YOU)
Belondrade y Lurton, Rueda **1996** £11.55 (BIB)
Enate Barrel-Fermented Chardonnay, Somontano **1997** £12.34 (PLAY)
Enate Barrel-Fermented Chardonnay, Somontano **1996** £11.00 (AV)
Jean León Chardonnay, Penedés **1995** £14.69 (REI)
Jean León Chardonnay, Penedés **1992** £13.60 (DI)
Marqués de Alella, Allier **1996** £14.99 (MOR)
Cellers Puig & Roca, Augustus Chardonnay, Penedés **1998** £11.99 (DI)

Cellers Puig & Roca, Augustus Chardonnay, Penedés **1996** £11.00 (WS) £13.25 (MOR)
Torres Fransola, Penedés **1999** £10.49 (POR)
Torres Milmanda Chardonnay, Penedés **1996** £14.99 (MOR)
Txomin Etxaniz, Getariako Txakolina **1998** £11.50 (CRO)

Over £15.00

Scholtz Solera 1885, Málaga **Non-vintage** £24.00 (CRO)
Torres Milmanda Chardonnay, Penedés **1998** £16.95 (DI) £18.74 (REI)
Torres Milmanda Chardonnay, Penedés **1997** £17.99 (YOU) £18.74 (REI)
Torres Milmanda Chardonnay, Penedés **1994** £20.75 (UB)
Torres Milmanda Chardonnay, Penedés **1988** £19.99 (RAE)

OTHER SPANISH ROSÉ

Under £5.00

Chivite Gran Feudo, Navarra **1998** £4.49 (OD) £6.22 (PLAY)

£5.00 → £5.99

Ochoa Rosé, Navarra **1998** £5.49 (UN) £6.25 (FORT)
Ochoa Rosé, Navarra **1996** £5.75 (UB)
Torres de Casta, Penedés **1999** £5.59 (POR)
Torres de Casta, Penedés **1994** £5.15 (UB)

SPANISH SPARKLING

Under £6.00

Castellblanch Extra Seco, Cava **Non-vintage** £5.99 (VIC) £5.99 (THR) £5.99 (WR) £5.99 (BOT)
Codorníu Brut, Cava **Non-vintage** £5.99 (ASD)
Condé de Caralt Brut, Cava **Non-vintage** £5.99 (SAF) £6.50 (CRO) £6.54 (GW) £6.69 (WAI)
Palau Brut, Cava **Non-vintage** £4.99 (BO) £5.49 (CON)
Palau Rosé **Non-vintage** £5.49 (CON)
Segura Viudas Brut Reserva, Cava **Non-vintage** £5.99 (OD) £6.50 (DI)
Sumarroca Extra Brut, Cava **1995** £5.95 (WS)

£6.00 → £6.99

Castellblanch Brut Zero, Cava **Non-vintage** £6.69 (JON)
Freixenet Brut Rosé, Cava **Non-vintage** £6.99 (SAF) £7.49 (MOR) £8.95 (STE)
Freixenet Carta Nevada, Cava **Non-vintage** £6.49 (BO) £6.79 (PIP) £7.49 (MOR)
Freixenet Cordon Negro Brut, Cava **Non-vintage** £6.99 (MAJ) £6.99 (WAI) £6.99 (SAF) £7.23 (PLA) £7.39 (BO) £7.49 (ASD) £7.49 (VIC) £7.49 (THR) £7.49 (MOR) £7.49 (UN) £7.49 (WR) £7.49 (BOT) £7.95 (ROB) £8.45 (STE)
Freixenet Cordon Negro Brut, Cava **1993** £6.89 (POR) £7.65 (UB)
Freixenet Extra Brut, Cava **Non-vintage** £6.45 (UB)
Bodegas Inviosa Bonaval Brut, Cava **Non-vintage** £6.50 (FLE) £6.99 (PHI)
Marqués de Monistrol Brut, Cava **Non-vintage** £6.60 (ELL)
Raventos I Blanc Cava l'Hereau **Non-vintage** £6.65 (WAT)
Torre del Gall Brut, Cava **1994** £6.90 (SOM)

£7.00 → £7.99

Condé de Caralt Blanc de Blancs, Cava **Non-vintage** £7.99 (MOR)
Juvé y Camps Brut, Cava **1996** £7.45 (STA)
Segura Viudas Brut, Cava **1994** £7.99 (OD)
Torre del Gall Gran Reserva **1992** £7.99 (RAE)

£8.00 → £9.99

Freixenet Brut Nature, Cava **1997** £8.99 (MAJ)
Juvé y Camps Brut, Cava **1993** £8.40 (UB)
Torre del Gall Gran Reserva **1994** £8.49 (UN)

Over £10.00

Juvé y Camps Brut, Cava **1995** £10.15 (JER)
Juvé y Camps Reserva de la Familia, Cava **Non-vintage** £10.99 (MOR)
Juvé y Camps Reserva de la Familia, Cava **1994** £10.99 (PHI) £11.75 (FORT) £11.75 (ROB)
Raventos I Blanc Cava Gran Reserva Personal MRN **1992** £14.55 (WAT)

SHERRY PRICES

DRY

Under £4.00

Manzanilla La Gitana, Hidalgo ½ bottle £3.15 (SOM) £3.25 (TAN) £3.80 (JER) £4.25 (PHI) £4.41 (REI) £6.19 (JON)

£4.00 → £4.99

Amontillado Hidalgo £4.99 (MAJ) £5.50 (STE)
Fino Barbadillo £4.99 (CON) £5.29 (GW) £5.36 (PLAY) £5.80 (HIG)
Fino Hidalgo £4.81 (PLA) £4.99 (MAJ) £5.35 (HAH) £5.45 (PIP) £5.49 (NI) £5.50 (STE)
Fino Valdespino £4.93 (WAT) £4.95 (LEA)
Harvey's Dune £4.97 (HA) £5.99 (WR) £5.99 (BOT) £6.39 (CON)
Manzanilla de Sanlúcar, Barbadillo £4.99 (CON) £5.29 (GW) £5.49 (AME) £5.49 (OD) £5.49 (BOT) £6.15 (MOR) £6.70 (CB)
Oloroso Seco, Barbadillo £4.99 (CON) £5.20 (COC) £13.50 (JU)

£5.00 → £6.99

Amontillado de Sanlúcar, Barbadillo £5.29 (GW) £6.96 (CB) £7.30 (JER) £8.29 (NO)
Amontillado Napoleon, Hidalgo £6.70 (SOM) £7.44 (SAV) £7.70 (PIP) £7.95 (AD) £7.99 (MAJ) £8.19 (JON) £8.65 (NI) £9.50 (BEN) £9.87 (TW)
Croft Delicado £6.49 (WAI) £6.49 (SAF)
Elegante, González Byass £5.54 (COC) £5.89 (TES) £5.89 (VIC) £5.89 (THR) £5.89 (UN) £5.89 (WR) £5.89 (BOT) £5.89 (WAI)
Fino de Sanlúcar, Barbadillo £5.49 (AME) £7.30 (JER)
Fino Mariscal, Hidalgo £5.95 (TAN)
Fino San Patricio, Garvey £6.55 (AS) £6.95 (WRI) £7.45 (COC)
Harvey's Manzanilla £6.49 (HA)
La Ina, Domecq £6.37 (HA) £6.50 (COC) £7.21 (WAT) £7.59 (UN) £7.85 (WRI) £8.20 (HAH) £8.25 (FORT) £8.90 (JU)
Manzanilla Deliciosa, Valdespino £6.95 (LEA)
Manzanilla La Gitana, Hidalgo £5.95 (HAH) £5.99 (MAJ) £5.99 (WAI) £6.35 (PIP) £6.46 (SAV) £6.99 (NI) £7.64 (TW)
Manzanilla Pasada Solear, Barbadillo £6.80 (COC) £6.95 (JU) £6.99 (CON) £7.95 (STE)
Oloroso Dos Cortados Old Dry, Williams & Humbert £5.89 (UN) £9.50 (COC) £9.99 (WAI)

£7.00 → £8.99

Fino Don Zoilo £7.35 (COC) £8.00 (WRI)
Fino Inocente, Valdespino £7.43 (WAT) £7.95 (AD) £7.95 (LEA)
Fino Lustau £8.81 (PLA)
★ Fino Puerto, Lustau £7.65 (CON) £8.49 (BAL) £8.95 (DI) £8.99 (BEN) £8.99 (AME) £9.20 (MV) £9.25 (FORT) £9.40 (REI) £9.75 (PHI)
Fino Superior, Hidalgo £7.25 (NI) £8.50 (TAN) £10.45 (LAY)
Fino Superiore El Cuadrado, Hidalgo £8.95 (AD)
★ Harvey's Palo Cortado £8.69 (HA)
Manzanilla Don Zoilo £7.35 (COC) £8.25 (WRI)
Manzanilla Pasada Almacenista, Lustau £8.99 (PHI)
Manzanilla Pasada de Sanlúcar, Manuel Cuevas Gurado £8.00 (MV) £11.95 (JU)
Oloroso Anada 1918 Solera, Emilio Lustau ½ bottle £7.99 (DI) £7.99 (BO) £8.49 (BAL) £8.81 (REI) £8.99 (CON) £8.99 (BEN)
Oloroso Don Zoilo Old Dry £7.85 (COC)
Oloroso Seco, Hidalgo £8.50 (TAN) £8.59 (JON)
Oloroso Seco Napoleon, Hidalgo £8.05 (PIP) £9.50 (BEN) £9.60 (LAY)
Palo Cortado de Jerez Videz, Lustau ½ bottle £8.95 (FORT) £8.99 (AME)
Palo Cortado del Carrascal, Valdespino £8.49 (OD) £9.17 (WAT) £9.95 (LEA)
Palo Cortado Lustau £7.99 (DI)
Palo Cortado Vides £8.00 (MV) £11.95 (JU)
Tio Pepe González Byass £7.32 (COC) £7.71 (PLAY) £7.79 (TES) £7.79 (WAI) £7.91 (STA) £7.95 (FORT) £7.99 (OD) £8.35 (WRI) £8.37 (VIN) £8.95 (HAH) £9.95 (JU)

£9.00 → £9.99

Amontillado Tio Diego, Valdespino £9.28 (WAT) £9.95 (LEA)
Fino Quinta, Osborne £9.50 (FORT)
Manzanilla Pasada de Sanlúcar, Hidalgo £9.39 (JON) £11.10 (TW)
Oloroso Don Gonzalo Old Dry, Valdespino £9.31 (WAT) £9.95 (LEA)
Oloroso Dry, Lustau £9.25 (STA)
Palo Cortado de Jerez, Hidalgo £9.60 (SAV) £9.80 (TAN) £9.80 (PIP) £10.59 (JON) £11.75 (AD) £12.57 (TW) £12.90 (LAY)

£10.00 → £19.99

Amontillado de Jerez Fino, Alberto Lorente Piaget £11.70 (JU)

Amontillado del Duque, González Byass £19.75 (COC) £22.00 (MOR) £22.75 (FORT) £23.59 (VIN)

Amontillado Viejo, Hidalgo £17.50 (NI) £23.50 (SAV) £25.00 (JU) £28.20 (TAN) £28.75 (HAH) £36.13 (TW)

Manzanilla Pasada de Sanlúcar, Manuel Ortega Millan £11.70 (JU)

Palo Cortado Cardenal, Valdespino £14.34 (WAT) £14.50 (LEA)

c. £41.50

Harvey's Fino Bristol £41.13 (REI)

MEDIUM

£4.50 → £6.99

Amontillado La Concha, González Byass £5.54 (COC) £5.89 (VIC) £5.89 (THR) £5.89 (UN) £5.89 (WR) £5.89 (BOT) £5.89 (WAI) £5.99 (SAF)

Amontillado Valdespino £4.79 (OD) £4.93 (WAT)

Croft Particular £6.49 (VIC) £6.49 (THR) £6.49 (UN) £6.49 (WR) £6.49 (BOT)

Dry Sack Williams & Humbert £5.49 (TES) £6.40 (COC) £6.95 (FORT) £7.60 (WRI)

Harvey's Club Amontillado £5.55 (COC) £5.59 (VIC) £5.59 (THR) £5.59 (BOT) £5.69 (UN) £5.69 (WAI) £5.69 (SAF) £5.99 (CON)

£7.00 → £10.99

Amontillado del Puerto, José Luis Gonzalez Obregon ½ bottle £9.00 (MV)

Harvey's Fine Old Amontillado £8.69 (HA)

Oloroso de Jerez Almacenista Viuda de Antonio Borrego, Lustau £8.95 (FORT)

Oloroso Solera 1842, Valdespino £8.49 (OD) £9.28 (WAT) £9.95 (LEA)

£11.00 → £19.99

Amontillado del Puerto, Loreto Colosio Molleda £11.95 (JU)

Oloroso Apostoles, González Byass £19.75 (COC) £23.59 (VIN)

Oloroso Royal Corregidor, Sandeman £13.25 (FORT) £17.00 (CRO)

Over £20.00

Amontillado Principe, Barbadillo £21.95 (STE)

Amontillado Sandeman £28.79 (REI)

SWEET

Under £5.50

Cream Hidalgo £5.45 (PIP) £5.50 (STE)

Dark Cream, Valdespino £4.95 (LEA)

£5.50 → £6.99

Croft Original Pale Cream £6.20 (COC) £6.49 (CON) £6.49 (TES) £6.49 (VIC) £6.49 (THR) £6.49 (UN) £6.49 (WR) £6.49 (BOT) £6.49 (WAI) £6.49 (SAF) £6.59 (OD) £6.90 (HAH) £6.95 (JU) £6.95 (WRI) £6.99 (VIN)

Harvey's Bristol Cream £6.39 (CON) £6.49 (WAI) £6.55 (SAF) £6.59 (BO) £6.59 (TES) £6.59 (UN) £6.60 (COC) £6.69 (OD) £6.76 (PLAY) £6.84 (HA) £6.85 (VIN) £8.25 (WRI) £8.50 (FORT) £8.95 (HAH)

Harvey's Copper Beech £6.14 (HA)

£7.00 → £9.99

Croft Original Pale Cream 1 litre £8.29 (UN)

Harvey's Bristol Cream 1 litre £7.99 (VIC) £7.99 (THR) £7.99 (WR) £7.99 (BOT)

Old East India, Lustau £9.95 (PHI) £9.99 (UN) £10.95 (DI) £10.99 (BU) £10.99 (CON) £10.99 (GW) £10.99 (BEN) £10.99 (BO) £11.00 (MV) £11.50 (FORT) £11.55 (MOR)

Pedro Ximenez, Barbadillo £8.99 (CON) £9.50 (HIG) £9.91 (GW)

Pedro Ximenez Solera Superior, Valdespino £7.49 (OD) £8.23 (WAT) £8.95 (LEA)

Pedro Ximénez Viejo, Hidalgo £8.50 (TAN) £8.70 (PIP) £8.99 (MAJ) £11.16 (TW)

Over £10.00

Harvey's Bristol Milk £41.13 (REI)

Oloroso Matusalem, González Byass £11.29 (UN) £19.75 (COC) £20.95 (AD) £22.00 (MOR) £22.50 (FORT) £23.59 (VIN)

Oloroso Rich Old, Sandeman £28.79 (REI)

UNITED KINGDOM

Definite styles are emerging here, and there's a definite case for buying the sparklers, too

Come on now. Be honest. Have you ever bought a bottle of English wine? Truly? That's what I thought. There are an awful lot of people out there who've never even tasted the stuff, let alone forked out the readies for it.

Should you? Well, it's true that you don't need to. There are plenty of good wines in the world, and none of us will live long enough to get through them all. English wines, for most people, are probably not that high on the list.

It's a big problem for English winemakers. They have to compete with countries like Australia – well, imagine how you'd like it.

But styles are emerging. There's the light, leafy style – reminiscent of Verdicchio or Soave, this, with some elegance and balance. Then there are the oakier wines, which are frankly less to my taste. I don't think they have the guts to stand up to oak.

Sparkling wines are, however, rather attractive. Overall standards vary, but clearly the fruit quality is there. Go on. Try one.

GRAPE VARIETIES

BACCHUS (white) Sharp, strong flavours of gooseberry, elderflower and orange rind. Best: *Lamberhurst, Partridge Vineyard, Sandhurst, Staverton, Three Choirs, Wyken.* Good sweet ones: *Chiltern Valley, Cane End.*

FABER (white) Fragrant with good acidity.

HUXELREBE (white) Has a grapefruit-pith taste and a greenish bite. For this reason it is often softened up by blending. Best: *Biddenden, Bothy* (blended with Perle), *Monnow Valley* (blended with Seyval Blanc), *Staple St James, Three Choirs. Davenport* rosé blends it with Triomphe d'Alsace.

KERNER (white) *Carr-Taylor* blends this with Reichensteiner for fizz; *Elham Valley* blends it with Seyval Blanc, likewise for fizz.

MADELEINE ANGEVINE (white) A fruit-juicy character is matched by good acidity, elderflower-perfumed or more honeyed but appley. *Halfpenny Green* and *Sharpham* are good.

MÜLLER-THURGAU (white) This used to be the English workhorse, but is now much less planted. *Breaky Bottom, Bruisyard, Elham Valley, Penshurst, St George's, St Nicholas, Staple St James, Tenterden* and *Wootton* are good. And it can make very attractive, slightly sweet wine, as at *Rowney.*

ORTEGA (white) *Hidden Spring* is concentrated, and *Biddenden*, in particular, makes a delicious, slightly sweet but tremendously fruity elderflower-and-apricot-tasting example. It is usually blended (as at *Rock Lodge*).

PINOT NOIR (red) Used mostly for rosé and sparkling wine; or indeed sparkling rosé. *Denbies* Pinot Noir is rich and savoury; *Valley Vineyards* is a good contender and *Carr Taylor* makes good rosé fizz; *Chiddingstone* blends it with Pinot Meunier to make a delicious Blanc de Noirs; *Bodiam Castle* makes a tasty rosé, as well as a dry, honeyed Blanc de Pinot Noir white; *Biddenden* and *Tenterden* use it for rosé blends. *Three Choirs* rosé from Pinot Noir has earthy raspberry-and-morello-cherry fruit; *Conghurst's* grapy, herbaceous rosé is also good, and *Denbies, Nyetimber* and *South Ridge/RidgeView* sparklers are notable.

REICHENSTEINER (white) Usually dull when dry, but slightly sweet, it can develop a pleasant, smoky, quince-and-peaches taste and age well. *Carr Taylor* and *Rock Lodge* use it for Champagne-method fizz, *Northbrook Springs* is barrel fermented. *Nutbourne Manor* and *Three Choirs* are also good.

SCHEUREBE (white) Good, grapefruity, curranty wines in good years. It goes into *Valley Vineyards' Clocktower Selection Botrytis*, when it's made, along with Reichensteiner.

SCHÖNBURGER (pink) Fat wine by English standards, with a pear-lychee flavour and good acidity. Best: *Carr Taylor, Coxley, Nutbourne Manor, Saxon Valley, Three Choirs, Woolding, Wootton*.

SEYVAL BLANC (white) *Breaky Bottom* is the most successful – dry and Sauvignon-like when young, honeyed like Burgundy after four to five years – but Seyval Blanc is generally best blended or made sweetish. *Three Choirs* and *Hidden Spring* blend it, while *Tenterden* makes a good oaked Reserve. *Valley Vineyards* is oaked. *Elham Valley* uses it in good fizz. Other good ones: *Headcorn, Penshurst, Shawsgate, Wootton*.

OTHER REDS *Beenleigh Manor* has a good reputation for Cabernet and Merlot grown under plastic; there is also some potential in Dunkelfelder and Dornfelder, and Canada's Léon Millet and Maréchal Foch. Gamay is used by *Valley Vineyards* for a sparkler. *Dunkery's Prometheus* (from Somerset) is delicious, as is *Chapel Down's Epoch 1*. *Wyken's* red is pretty good.

OTHER WHITES *Nyetimber* makes a stunning Chardonnay fizz. *Denbies* and *Valley Vineyards* Chardies are also good. There's Riesling at *Denbies*, Gewürztraminer at *Barton Manor*, and Ehrenfelser at *Penshurst*; *Wootton's* Auxerrois is pungent and salty-sappy. *Carr Taylor* has Pinot Blanc for concentrated *Kemsley Dry*.

UNITED KINGDOM PRICES

WHITE

Under £5.00

Chapel Down Bacchus **1998** £4.99 (TES)
Chapel Down Epoch V **1996** £4.99 (SAF)
Chapel Down Summer Hill Oaked **1998** £3.99 (TES)
★ Three Choirs **1999** £4.99 (NO)
Three Choirs **1997** £4.99 (NO)
Three Choirs **1996** £3.99 (CON)
Three Choirs Reserve Lightly Oaked **1997** £4.99 (TES)
Three Choirs Medium Dry **1998** £4.99 (JON) £5.20 (TAN)
Trinity English Table Wine **1998** £4.99 (JON)
Tudor Rose Cream **Non-vintage** £2.45 (UN)

£5.00 → £5.99

Astley Severn Vale **1997** £5.80 (TAN)
Chapel Down Bacchus **1996** £5.58 (NO)
Chapel Down Epoch V **1998** £5.49 (BO)

Over £6.00

Chapel Down Ortega Oaked **1995** £7.86 (NO)
Chiddingstone Seyval/Kerner **1996** £6.95 (FORT)
Sharpham Dry Barrel-Fermented **1995** £9.80 (NO)
Sharpham Estate Reserve **1997** £6.49 (TES)
Sharpham Estate Selection **1998** £7.96 (PIP)
Wroxeter Roman Vineyard Madeleine Angevine, Medium Dry **1998** £7.95 (TAN)

RED

Under £6.00

Chapel Down Epoch I **1998** £5.69 (WAI)
Chapel Down Epoch I **1997** £5.99 (BO)

c. £18.00

Beenleigh Red **1997** £17.50 (NO)

SPARKLING

£10.00 → £18.00

Carr Taylor **Non-vintage** £10.50 (CRO)

Nyetimber Blanc de Blancs **1992** £17.75 (FORT)

MERCHANTS SPECIALIZING IN UNITED KINGDOM

see Merchant Directory (page 456) for details

Nobody has very long lists of English wines, but the following have a fair selection: Averys of Bristol (AV), Fortnum & Mason (FORT), The Nobody Inn (NO), Terry Platt (PLA) – well, wines from Wales actually, Safeway (SAF), Tanners (TAN), Tesco (TES), Unwins (UN), The Wine Society (WS). Otherwise buy direct from the vineyard.

UNITED STATES

California has just had an extraordinary decade for Cabernet Sauvignon. Chardonnay styles are more changeable, but at the moment they're changing in exactly the right direction

The nineties were fabulous for California Cabernet. Really amazing. Like the eighties were for red Bordeaux, only with bigger, lusher flavours. And that was in spite of all the to-do over phylloxera, and all the replanting.

In fact, part of it was probably because of the replanting after phylloxera came along and ruined the vines. It gave the growers a chance to rethink what got planted where – and as a result half the Napa Valley is now planted to red Bordeaux varieties. That's Cabernet Sauvignon, Merlot and Cabernet Franc, with just a dash of Petit Verdot for those who like it.

You want to run through the vintages? Oh, all right. Since you insist. The 1995s and 1996s were superb. Just amazing. The 1997s were also pretty stunning, though the 1998s were more variable, and the 1994s were rich and lush. For those of you who somehow missed out on them, the 1999s are also looking very good indeed.

Chardonnay? It's less oaky than it was. That's a wild generalization, I know, and there are still lots of very oaky wines for those who want them, but a more elegant, subtle style is taking over. I'm all in favour: All that oak might blast you out of your seat when you first taste it, but when you come down to earth, if you're going to have a second sip, never mind a second glass, you want something a bit less massive. You want balance, fruit, acidity, all that sort of thing. And in California these days, you'll get them. Fabulous, isn't it?

GRAPE VARIETIES

BARBERA (red) The Italian variety most grown in California. Look for *Louis M Martini, Sebastiani, Il Podere dell' Olivos* and *Bonny Doon, Monteviña* and *Preston Vineyards*.

CABERNET SAUVIGNON (red) Still the top grape for premium California reds. Napa Cabernet is the classic: rich, tannic yet seductive at a young age. For the top wines, complexity and finesse are the new watchwords, especially for wines from hillside vineyards (as opposed to the flat floor of the Napa). Washington State Cab continues to improve as the vines age, yielding more concentration. For cellaring (never as long as for the equivalent quality Bordeaux), try: *Beaulieu Vineyards Georges de Latour Private Reserve, Beringer Reserve, Bernardus, Buena Vista, Burgess, Cain, Carmenet Vin de Garde Reserve, Caymus Special Selection, Chimney Rock, Clos du Val, Conn Creek, Cuvaison, Dalla Valle, Diamond Creek, Dominus, Dunn, Franciscan, Grgich Hills, Groth, Heitz Bella Oaks, Kenwood Artist Series, La Jota, Laurel Glen, Louis M Martini, Robert Mondavi Reserve and Opus One, Chateau Montelena, Newton, Niebaum-Coppola, Raymond Private Reserve, Ridge Monte Bello, Sequoia Grove, Shafer Hillside Select, Spottswoode, Stag's Leap Cask 23, Sterling Vineyards Diamond Mountain Ranch, Stonestreet* (California); *Ste Chapelle* (Idaho); *Fall Creek Vineyards, Llano Estacado, Messina Hof, Oberhellmann, Pheasant Ridge* (Texas); *Arbor Crest, Hogue Cellars, Chateau Ste Michelle, Columbia, Staton Hills* (Washington). For light Cabernet, try: *Beringer, Caymus Liberty School, Chateau Souverain, Clos du Bois, Cosentino, Fetzer, Estancia, Foppiano, Kendall-Jackson* (California); *Columbia Crest* (Washington).

CHARDONNAY (white) This is less relentlessly oaky than it was, and more interesting as a result. Many of the more popular brands – such as *Kendall-Jackson* and *Sebastiani* – have a slightly sweet finish to make them more commercial. The best can age, but seldom need to, they are so attractive young. For balance and poise look for: *Acacia, Arrowood, Au Bon Climat, Beringer, Buena Vista, Chalone, Chateau St Jean, Cuvaison, Dehlinger, Far Niente, Flora Springs, Franciscan, Kistler, Kunde, Mondavi Reserve, Newton, Raymond Reserve, Renaissance, Ridge, Signorello, Simi* and *Sonoma-Cutrer* (California); *Gristina* (NY); *Prince Michel* (Virginia). For simpler wines, try *Callaway, Clos du Bois, Estancia, Matanzas Creek, Kendall-Jackson, Morgan, Mirassou, Phelps, Monterey Vineyards, Wente* (California); *Fall Creek* (Texas); *Chateau Ste Michelle, Columbia Crest, Hogue Cellars* (Washington).

GEWÜRZTRAMINER (white) It's really too hot in California for this grape, although a few people keep trying. Look for *Adler Fels* (sometimes), *Lazy Creek, Obester, Rutherford Hill* (California); *Columbia, Chateau Ste Michelle* (Washington).

MERLOT (red) When it's good it's very, very good, full of lovely black cherry fruit with a pleasing brambly edge. But it's frighteningly fashionable, and too many are overcropped and insipid. Best are *Arrowood, Bellerose, Clos du Val, Crichton Hall, Cuvaison, Duckhorn, Geyser Peak, Gundlach-Bundschu, Monticello Cellars, Murphy-Goode, Newton, St Francis, Pine Ridge, Ridge Santa Cruz, Silverado, Sinskey, St Clement, Sterling, Swanson, Vichon,* (California); *Bedell Cellars, Hargrave, Peconic Bay* (New York); *Chateau Ste Michelle, Columbia, Columbia Crest, Hogue Cellars, Leonetti Cellar, Staton Hills, Paul Thomas* (Washington).

PETITE SIRAH (red) This is emphatically not the same as the great red Syrah grape of the Rhône Valley or the Shiraz of Australia. It produces big, stark, dry, almost tarry wines – impressive, but needing a good winemaker. *Ridge* is superb. Also look for *Concannon, Christopher Creek, Foppiano* and *Stag's Leap*.

PINOT GRIS (white) Oregon's other speciality, after Pinot Noir. Most are light and spicy, but less vinous than Alsace versions. Try *Elk Cove, Erath, Eyrie, Ponzi*.

PINOT NOIR (red) At its best (which means from a handful of producers in California and Oregon) US Pinot is almost as good as very good Burgundy. Most, though, settles for charm rather than excitement, and lesser wines can be dilute and over-oaked. Try *Acacia, Au Bon Climat Cuvée Isabelle, Bouchaine, Byron, Calera, Carneros Creek, Chalone, Dehlinger, Fetzer, De Loach, The Famous Gate, Gary Farrel, Iron Horse, Kendall-Jackson, Kistler, Lazy Creek, Robert Mondavi, Patz & Hall, Rochioli, Lane Tanner, Saintsbury, Sanford, Sinskey, Rod Strong, Whitcraft, Wild Horse, Zaca Mesa, ZD* (California); *Hargrave* (NY); *Adelsheim, Amity, Archery Summit, Bethel Heights, Broadley, Drouhin, Erath, Eyrie, Scott Henry, King Estate, Panther Creek, Rex Hill, Sokol Blosser, Ken Wright* (Oregon).

RIESLING (white) This grape likes cool spots, which means that it all too often makes dull wines in California. *Renaissance* is streets ahead; other good ones are *Alexander Valley Vineyards, Konocti, Navarro* (California); *Lamoreaux Landing, Wagner Vineyards* (New York); *Amity* (Oregon); *Chateau Morrisette, Prince Michel* (Virginia); *Hogue Cellars, Columbia Cellars, Chateau Ste Michelle, Kiona* (Washington).

SAUVIGNON BLANC/FUMÉ BLANC (white) Generally riper and broader than the New Zealand or Loire prototypes, and often oaked, usually to excess. Try *Beringer, Cakebread Cellars, Chalk Hill, Chateau Potelle, Chateau St Jean, Dry Creek Vineyards Reserve, Ferrari-Carano, Geyser Peak, Hanna, Kunde, Markham,*

Robert Mondavi, Murphy-Goode, Renaissance, Sanford, Simi, Stag's Leap, Sterling, Voss, William Wheeler (California); *Hargrave* (NY); *Arbor Crest, Columbia* (Washington).

SEMILLON (white) Usually added to Sauvignon Blanc for complexity (try *Carmenet, Clos du Val, St Supéry* and *Vichon* in California). For stand-alone Semillon try *Alderbrook, Ahlgren* (California); *Chateau Ste Michelle* (Washington).

SYRAH/RHÔNE VARIETIES (red) There has been an explosion of interest in these. Most eyes are on Syrah, but there is also Mourvèdre, Cinsaut, Grenache and Carignan. Whites include Viognier and Marsanne. The best are from California: *Bonny Doon, Cline, Dehlinger, Duxoup, Fetzer, Kendall-Jackson, Jade Mountain, Jensen, La Jota, McDowell Valley, Joseph Phelps Mistral* series, *RH Phillips, Il Podere dell' Olivos, Preston Vineyards, Qupé, Santino, Thackrey, Zaca Mesa*. In Washington: *Columbia, Columbia Crest.*

ZINFANDEL (red) This comes in 'white' (i.e. pink and sweetish), but the best are all red and share ripe, red-berries fruit. Big Zins include: *Chateau Potelle, Cline Cellars, Deer Park, Peter Franus, Grgich Hills, Kendall-Jackson Ciapusci Vineyard, Kunde, La Jota, Martinelli, Murrieta's Well, Preston Vineyards, A Rafanelli, Ravenswood, Ridge Lytton Springs, Rosenblum, Shenandoah, Storybook Mountain, Joseph Swan*. Lighter ones: *Buehler, Buena Vista, Burgess, Clos du Val, Fetzer, Haywood, Howell Mountain, Kendall-Jackson Kenwood, Mariah Vineyard, Louis M Martini, Nalle, Quivira, Renaissance.*

WINE REGIONS

CARNEROS (California; red, white) One of California's top spots for Pinot Noir and Chardonnay. It crosses the southern end of Napa and Sonoma. Look for *Acacia, Buena Vista, Carneros Creek, Domaine Carneros, David Ramey, Saintsbury.*

CENTRAL VALLEY (California; red, white) Huge and hot. This is where much of California's everyday jug wine comes from, and it's usually drinkable. Chardonnay, especially, is much improved.

LAKE COUNTY (California; red, white) Good Cabernet Sauvignon and Sauvignon Blanc territory. *Guenoc, Konocti* and *Louis M Martini* have vines here.

LIVERMORE VALLEY (California; red, white) Currently reviving. Stars include *Bonny Doon, Concannon, Wente.*

MENDOCINO COUNTY (California; red, white) The cool Anderson Valley is becoming a sparkling wine star, led by *Roederer Estate*, the US offshoot of Champagne Roederer, and *Handley Cellars.* Elegant Riesling, Gewürztraminer, Pinot Noir and Chardonnay comes from here, too. Some Cabernet Sauvignon is good.

MISSOURI (red, white) Grows both standard vinifera grapes and a range of French hybrids like Vidal, as well as native American grapes like Cynthiana/Norton. *Stone Hill Winery*'s Norton red is pretty good; there are also some suitably pleasing Rieslings from *Mount Pleasant Vineyard.*

MONTEREY COUNTY (California; red, white) The North is top Pinot Noir country (*Calera, Chalone*) and Carmel Valley is giving nice Cabernets. *Jekel* makes excellent Chardonnay and Riesling in Arroyo Seco.

NAPA COUNTY (California; red, white) This is California's classic wine country. Napa's strong suit is red – Cabernet Sauvignon and Merlot – with Pinot Noir in Carneros. Star producers are too many to list, but include *Beaulieu, Beringer, Clos du Val, Diamond Creek, Dominus, Heitz,*

Mondavi, Newton, Opus One, Phelps, Spottswoode, Stag's Leap.

NEW MEXICO (red, white) Good producers here are *Anderson Valley*, especially for Chardonnay, and a fizz from *Devalmont Vineyards* under the Gruet label.

NEW YORK STATE (red, white) Long Island Chardonnays are very different from those of California, with more austere flavours, a bit like ripe Chablis. There's also decent Chardonnay and good Riesling coming from the Finger Lakes and the Hudson River Valley areas. Try *Bedell Cellars, Brotherhood, Fox Run, Hargrave, Lenz, Millbrook, Pindar* and *Wagner.*

OREGON (red, white) Most famous for Pinot Noir, which is patchy but excellent at its best. Next comes Pinot Gris, which can often be charming. Riesling can also be quite good, although it is a little short on that floral intensity one looks for in a great Riesling. For Pinot Gris, try *Elk Cove, Erath, Eyrie* or *Ponzi. Oak Knoll* has the best Riesling. For Pinot Noir, go for *Adelsheim, Amity, Archery Summit, Broadley, Drouhin, Erath, Eyrie, Scott Henry, King Estate, Panther Creek, Rex Hill, Sokol Blosser, Ken Wright.*

SAN LUIS OBISPO COUNTY (California; red, white) Has some good sites for Pinot Noir and Chardonnay, and there are a few surprising old Zinfandel vineyards. Edna Valley is the chief sub-region with a deserved reputation for Chardonnay. *Maison Deutz* makes good fizz.

SANTA BARBARA COUNTY (California; red, white) Some outstanding Pinot Noirs from the Santa Maria and Santa Ynez valleys, plus some good Sauvignon and Merlot. Best names: *Au Bon Climat, Firestone, Qupé, Sanford, Zaca Mesa.*

SANTA CRUZ MOUNTAINS (California; red, white) Pinot Noir here is promising, but still patchy. *David Bruce* and *Santa Cruz Mountain Winery* have had various degrees of success. *Mount Eden* and *Ridge Vineyards* are good for Cabernet.

SIERRA FOOTHILLS (California; red, white) California's gold country was one of its busiest wine zones until Prohibition, but only a few Zinfandel vineyards survived. These are the basis of the area's reputation, plus good Sauvignon Blanc and Barbera. Best are *Amador Foothill Winery, Boeger Winery, Monteviña, Renaissance* (stunning Riesling), *Santino* and *Shenandoah Vineyards.*

SONOMA COUNTY (California; red, white) Sonoma Valley is the main sub-region, but there are many others, in particular Alexander Valley, Chalk Hill, Dry Creek, Knight's Valley, and the Russian River Valley (including its sub-region Green Valley). Cabernet Sauvignon is the star grape, and it and Chardonnay are usually a little fruitier and softer than they are in

MATURITY CHART

1995 Napa Cabernet

Not all Napa Cabernets are made to age, but the best will age well

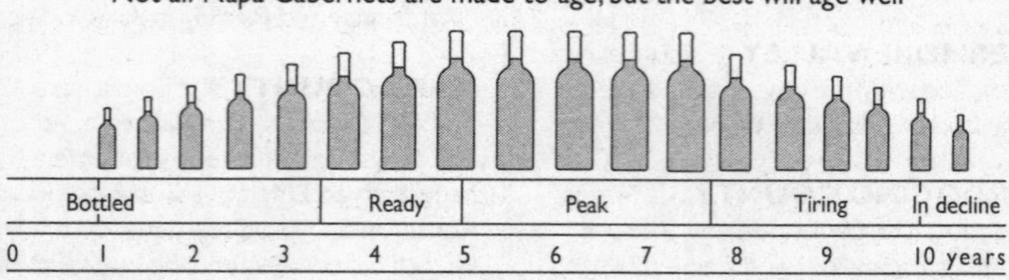

Napa. There's also some first rate Pinot Noir emerging from the lower Russian River Valley. Look for *Carmenet, Chateau St Jean, Dehlinger, De Loach, Iron Horse, Jordan, Kistler, Simi, Sonoma-Cutrer, Williams-Selyem.*

TEXAS (red, white) Texas wines continue to surprise. Cabernet Sauvignons from Texas have a drink-me-now rich fruitiness and the Chardonnays and Sauvignon Blancs are looking better every year. In short, it's goodbye Chateau Redneck. The best producers currently are: *Fall Creek, Llano Estacado, Messina Hof, Oberhellmann* and *Pheasant Ridge.*

VIRGINIA (red, white) Growing good wine grapes in Virginia's hot, humid climate is a man-over-nature drama. Besides the heat and the humidity, there is the occasional hurricane. Nevertheless, there are some good Rieslings and Chardonnays. Top producers are *Chateau Morrisette, Ingleside Plantation* and *Prince Michel.*

ON THE CASE
Sangiovese is one of California's latest favourite grapes. It can be good, but it's proving trickier to grow than they imagined. Don't expect Chianti-like flavours. Prices are high.

WASHINGTON STATE (red, white) Intense, clear fruit is the hallmark here for Cabernet, Merlot, Sauvignon Blanc, Semillon, Riesling and Chardonnay, and quality is improving year by year. Good names include *Arbor Crest, Chaleur, Chateau Ste Michelle, Columbia, Columbia Crest, Hogue Cellars, Staton Hills, Leonetti Cellar, Paul Thomas, Woodward Canyon.*

PRODUCERS WHO'S WHO

ACACIA ★★★(★) (Carneros/Napa) Attractive Pinot Noir and Chardonnay. Reserve wines go heavy on the oak.

ADLER FELS ★★(★) (Sonoma) A quirky winery, taking chances that sometimes miss. Top Gewürztraminer and an unusual Riesling sparkler.

ARROWOOD ★★★★ (Sonoma) Superb Cabernet Sauvignon and Merlot, providing you like oak.

AU BON CLIMAT ★★★★(★) (Santa Barbara) Fine Pinot Noir with intense black cherry fruit. Chardonnay can also be impressive. The Podere dell' Olivos label is for quirky, characterful Italian varietals.

BEAULIEU VINEYARDS ★★★ (Napa) Top-of-the-line George de Latour Private Reserve Cabernet Sauvignon is still marvellous. Also lean, supple Carneros Chardonnay, and cheaper Beautour Cab.

BERINGER ★★★★(★) (Napa) Reserve Cabernets are top of the line. Sbragia Chardonnay (named after the winemaker) is rich and loaded with buttery oak. The second label, Napa Ridge, is good value.

BETHEL HEIGHTS ★★★(★) (Oregon) Impressive, intense Pinot Noirs. The Reserves can be among Oregon's finest and most concentrated.

BONNY DOON ★★★(★) (Santa Cruz) One of California's most innovative winemakers, Grenache (Le Cigare Volant) and Mourvèdre (Old Telegram, a pun on Châteauneuf's Vieux Télégraphe, if you hadn't guessed) and a line of Italian styles called Ca' Del Solo. New ideas and new wines appear every year.

BRIDGEHAMPTON ★★★(★) (New York) First-class Chardonnay from Long Island as well as a fresh, light quaffable Pinot Noir and a fruity, forward Merlot.

BUENA VISTA ★★★(★) (Sonoma/ Carneros) Balanced, understated Merlot, Pinot Noir and Cabernet Sauvignon. Reserve wines have great intensity and depth. Very good Lake County Sauvignon Blanc.

CAIN CELLARS ★★★★(★) (Napa) Superb Cain Five Bordeaux blend red, and excellent across the board.

CALERA ★★★★(★) (San Benito) Possibly the best Pinot Noir in California. Rich and intense; Jensen Vineyard is tops. Also fine Viognier and Chardonnay.

CAYMUS ★★★★ (Napa) Benchmark California Cabernet which shows no sign of faltering. Special Selection is the top wine. Liberty School is the second label.

CHALONE ★★★★(★) (Monterey) Individualistic, ageworthy Pinot Noir and harmonious Chardonnay. Also some nice Pinot Blanc and Chenin Blanc.

CHATEAU MONTELENA ★★★★(★) (Napa) Chardonnay and Cabernet that both need time and repay the wait.

CHATEAU POTELLE ★★★(★) (Napa) Very good Sauvignon Blanc and Cabernet, outstanding Zinfandel.

CHATEAU ST JEAN ★★★(★) (Sonoma) Rich Chardonnay, outstanding Cabernet and Merlot, and justly famous botrytized Rieslings.

CHATEAU STE MICHELLE ★★★(★) (Washington) Consistently good with Cabernet Sauvignon and Merlot being the real strengths; pretty good bubbly.

CHIMNEY ROCK ★★★(★) (Napa) Powerful yet elegant Cabernet Sauvignon and Bordeaux blend called Elevage with deep, rich and complex fruit.

CLOS DU BOIS ★★★(★) (Sonoma) Consistently good Merlots, Chardonnays and a Bordeaux-style blend called Marlstone.

CLOS DU VAL ★★★(★) (Napa) Elegant, ageworthy, well-balanced reds. Best are Cabernet and Zinfandel.

COLUMBIA ★★★★ (Washington) Reds are excellent: Syrah, soft, peppery Pinot Noir, seductive Merlot (Red Willow vineyard), and ripe Cabernet (Otis vineyard). Very good whites include Semillon, Gewürztraminer.

COLUMBIA CREST ★★★(★) (Washington) Highly drinkable wines, not expensive: Cabernet, Merlot, Chardonnay.

CUVAISON ★★★ (Napa) Delicious Merlot, Pinot Noir and Cabernet: elegant, understated, with unexpected complexity.

DEHLINGER ★★★★ (Sonoma) One of the best Pinots in North America; also good Cabernets including a good value Young Vine Cabernet.

DOMAINE CARNEROS ★★★(★) (Napa) This Taittinger-owned sparkling wine house makes remarkable vintage Brut and silky, powerful Blanc de Blancs.

DOMAINE CHANDON ★★★ (Napa) Owned by Champagne house Moët & Chandon, and making consistently good non-vintage bubblies, plus rich and creamy Reserve and Carneros Blanc de Blancs.

DOMAINE MUMM ★★★★ (Napa) Outstanding fizz, better than that made by the parent company in Champagne. Look for the Brut and impressive Blanc de Noirs.

DROUHIN ★★★★ (Oregon) The Pinot Noir we were all waiting for Oregon to make, from a Burgundian-owned company. There's a little Chardonnay, too.

DUCKHORN ★★★(★) (Napa) Intensely flavoured, deep and rich Three Palms Vineyard Merlot, and a weighty Cabernet.

ELK COVE VINEYARDS ★★★(★) (Oregon) One of Oregon's best Pinot Noirs, and very good Pinot Gris.

EYRIE ★★★ (Oregon) David Lett is Oregon's Pinot pioneer, and still makes some of the best: supple, flavoursome and characterful.

FLORA SPRINGS ★★★(★) (Napa) Excellent Chardonnay and a fair Bordeaux blend called Trilogy. Soliloquy is a creamy, rich, floral white that belies its Sauvignon Blanc base.

FRANCISCAN ★★★★ (Napa) The estate-bottled Chardonnays, especially the Cuvée Sauvage, are outstanding. Sleek Quintessa Bordeaux blend.

GRGICH HILLS ★★★★ (Sonoma) Ageworthy Cabernet and rich Zinfandel.

HANDLEY CELLARS ★★★★ (Mendocino) Excellent fizz, especially Brut and rosé. Very good Chardonnay and Sauvignon, promising Pinot Noir.

HEITZ ★★★ (Napa) Martha's Vineyard Cabernet is a California blue chip, dark, uncompromising and expensive.

HESS COLLECTION ★★★★ (Napa) Chardonnay and Cabernet with balance and finesse.

IRON HORSE ★★★★ (Sonoma) Terrific, racy, incisive fizz, very good Pinot Noir and Chardonnay. Cabernet is also well worth trying.

JORDAN ★★★★(★) (Sonoma) The rich, ripe Cabernet Sauvignon ages well, and there's a classic, biscuity fizz called 'J'.

INSTANT CELLAR:
US CABERNET

- **1997 Monte Bello, Ridge, Santa Cruz Mountains, £516 per case, Tanners** Let's start at the top. This is as good as any claret: rich, complex, structured, and able to age for decades. In fact I wouldn't advise you to buy it if you're over 60.
- **1986 Cabernet Sauvignon, Dunn, Napa Valley, £70, Croque-en-Bouche** Silly money – like most California Cabernet – but this is dense, balanced, and expensive.
- **1993 Cabernet Sauvignon Bella Oaks, Heitz, £21.50, Justerini & Brooks** The price is looking better, and this is a classic long-lived style, drinking well now.
- **1994 Cabernet Sauvignon, Swanson Vineyards, Napa Valley, £16.70, Averys of Bristol** The grapes come from Oakville and Mount Veeder, which produce complex, long-lived Cabernets. This isn't bad value for a California Cabernet.
- **1997 Cabernet Sauvignon, Silver Creek, £6.90, Lay & Wheeler** Eureka – a California Cabernet that anyone can afford. Bright, berried fruit.

KENDALL-JACKSON ★★★ (Lake) Makes massive amounts of smooth, rich, off-dry Chardonnay.

KENWOOD ★★★(★) (Sonoma) Consistent quality, including one of California's best Sauvignon Blancs. Jack London and Artist Series Cabernets are outstanding, as is the Zinfandel.

KUNDE ESTATE WINERY ★★★ (Sonoma) The powerful, buttery Reserve Chardonnay and the Sauvignon Blanc are the best; also rich old vine Zinfandel.

LAMOREAUX LANDING ★★★ (New York) Chardonnay is rather good; the Pinot Noir improves with each vintage.

LAUREL GLEN ★★★★ (Sonoma) Intense, black cherry Cabernet Sauvignon is the only wine here, very good at its best.

LENZ VINEYARDS ★★★ (New York) Merlot is elegant and quite powerful wine, and dry Gewürztraminer is tasty.

LOUIS MARTINI ★★★ (Napa) Quality is somewhat patchy these days. Highlights are Monte Rosso Cabernet, and Zinfandel, Chardonnay and Carneros Pinot Noir.

MAYACAMAS ★★★ (Napa) Firm Cabernet and rich Chardonnay are the stars here; there's some Pinot Noir as well.

ROBERT MONDAVI ★★★★(★) (Napa) Superb straight and Reserve Cabernets; Opus One reds seem to lack the Reserve's intensity. Improving Carneros Pinot Noir. Newest is a line of French wines under the Vichon Mediterranean label.

NEWTON ★★★★ (Napa) Excellent, unfiltered Chardonnay; cedary, cinnamon-spiced Cabernet and succulent Merlot.

PECONIC BAY VINEYARDS ★★★ (New York) Light, unoaked Chardonnay and a barrel-fermented Reserve.

PHELPS ★★★(★) (Napa) Best here is the Insignia Bordeaux blend. Mistral label is for interesting Rhône varieties.

RAVENSWOOD ★★★★ (Sonoma) Zinfandel is the only grape here. Dickerson Vineyard, Old Hill and Old Vines have ripe, concentrated fruit that is bold and stylish.

RIDGE ★★★★(★) (Santa Clara) Benchmark Zinfandel, probably California's best. The Monte Bello Cabernets are also remarkable, with great balance and long-lasting, perfumed fruit. Petite Sirah from York Creek is brilliant.

ROEDERER ESTATE ★★★★ (Mendocino County) Excellent sparklers from a company owned by Roederer Champagne. Very good Brut and rosé. Top of the range l'Ermitage rich and concentated.

SAINTSBURY ★★★★ (Napa) Stylish, supple, elegant Pinot Noir and Chardonnay. Lovely Garnet, from young Pinot Noir vines.

SANFORD WINERY ★★★(★) (Santa Barbara) At its best, Sanford Pinot Noir can be a real treat, with spicy, lush, intense fruit. Good Sauvignon and Chardonnay.

SCHRAMSBERG ★★★★ (Napa) Big, lush fizz. Reserve Brut is best, often world class. Blanc de Noirs is big and bold.

SHAFER ★★★★ (Napa) Very good, very long-lived Cabernet Sauvignon and Merlot.

SIMI ★★★(★) (Sonoma) Rich, sometimes voluptuous, always reliable Chardonnay, concentrated Cabernets. Reserves are excellent, as is Sauvignon Blanc.

SONOMA-CUTRER ★★★★ (Sonoma) Out-and-out Chardonnay specialist. Les Pierres is made to age. Russian River Ranches is more forward, Cutrer is rich, archetypal California.

STAG'S LEAP WINE CELLARS ★★★★ (Napa) After a few years unaccountably adrift, the estate-bottled Cabernet Sauvignon is focused and back on track, especially the Cask 23 and the SLV Vineyard. Elegant Chardonnay, too.

STATON HILLS VINEYARD ★★★(★) (Washington) Silky Bordeaux-style Merlot; Cabernet with staying power.

STEELE WINES ★★★(★) (Lake County) Expensive, vivid Chardonnays. Shooting Star is a second, budget label.

ROD STRONG VINEYARDS **★★★(★)** (Sonoma) Fine single-vineyard Cabernet Sauvignon, Pinot Noir, Chardonnay.

ZD WINES ★★★ (Napa) Excellent Cabernet Sauvignon, Pinot Noir and Chardonnay with lovely intensity and depth.

UNITED STATES PRICES

CALIFORNIA RED

Under £5.00

Cabernet Sauvignon E&J Gallo **1998** £4.99 (ASD) £4.99 (BUD)
Cabernet Sauvignon Sutter Home **1996** £4.99 (CON) £5.29 (UN)
Californian Red Paul Masson **Non-vintage** £3.99 (ASD)
Dry Reserve E&J Gallo **Non-vintage** £4.69 (BUD)
Pinot Noir Thornhill **Non-vintage** £4.99 (UN)
Zinfandel E&J Gallo **Non-vintage** £4.69 (SAF)
Zinfandel E&J Gallo **1995** £4.49 (UN)
Zinfandel Sutter Home **1997** £4.99 (JON)
Zinfandel Sutter Home **1996** £4.99 (CON) £4.99 (UN)

£5.00 → £5.99

Cabernet Sauvignon Chateau Montelena **1991** £5.78 (CAV)
Cabernet Sauvignon Glen Ellen **1997** £5.49 (BUD)
Cabernet Sauvignon Glen Ellen **1996** £5.49 (SAF)
Cabernet Sauvignon Sutter Home **1997** £5.29 (JON)
Pinot Noir Redwood Trail **1998** £5.99 (SAF)
Pinot Noir Redwood Trail **1997** £5.49 (VIC) £5.49 (THR) £5.90 (CRO) £5.99 (BOT) £5.99 (WAI) £6.49 (OD) £6.49 (WR)
Zinfandel Sutter Home **1998** £5.25 (STE)

£6.00 → £7.99

Barbera Monteviña **1994** £7.50 (CRO) £7.99 (VA)
Big House Red Bonny Doon Ca' del Solo **1998** £7.99 (NI) £8.40 (BEN) £8.40 (MV) £8.71 (PLA) £9.35 (AD)
Big House Red Bonny Doon Ca' del Solo **1997** £6.75 (SOM) £7.99 (CON) £7.99 (NI) £8.23 (REI) £8.50 (TAN) £8.70 (GW)
Big House Red Bonny Doon Ca' del Solo **1996** £7.85 (RAE) £8.99 (UB)
Black Muscat Quady Elysium ½ bottle **Non-vintage** £6.60 (COC) £7.95 (FORT)
Black Muscat Quady Elysium ½ bottle **1998** £6.79 (JON) £6.95 (STA)
Black Muscat Quady Elysium ½ bottle **1997** £6.49 (MAJ) £6.50 (WS) £7.39 (PLAY) £7.99 (PHI) £9.50 (JER)
Black Muscat Quady Elysium ½ bottle **1995** £6.75 (CON) £6.95 (LEA) £11.00 (CRO)
Black Muscat Quady Elysium ½ bottle **1994** £7.91 (NO)
Cabernet Sauvignon Fetzer Bel Arbors **1997** £6.60 (JU)
Cabernet Sauvignon Fetzer Valley Oaks **1997** £6.99 (SAI) £6.99 (WR) £6.99 (WAI)
Cabernet Sauvignon Fetzer Valley Oaks **1996** £7.59 (JON)
Cabernet Sauvignon Robert Mondavi Woodbridge **1998** £7.49 (POR)
Cabernet Sauvignon Wente Bros **1997** £7.85 (COC)
Côtes d'Oakley Cline Cellars **1997** £7.00 (GW) £7.77 (WT)
Pinot Noir Beaulieu Vineyard **1997** £7.99 (POR)
Zinfandel Beringer **1996** £6.49 (NEZ) £8.99 (MAJ)
Zinfandel Fetzer **1997** £6.99 (OD)
Zinfandel Fetzer **1996** £7.65 (JU)
Zinfandel Robert Mondavi Woodbridge **1998** £6.95 (POR)
Zinfandel Robert Mondavi Woodbridge **1996** £7.65 (WRI)
Zinfandel Pedroncelli **1996** £7.79 (FLE)
Zinfandel Ravenswood **1997** £7.99 (OD)
Zinfandel Wente Bros **1998** £7.35 (COC)

MERCHANTS SPECIALIZING IN UNITED STATES

see Merchant Directory (page 456) for details

Adnams (AD), Averys (AV), Bennetts (BEN), Berrys (BER), Bibendum (BIB), Cave Cru Classé (CAV), Croque-en-Bouche (CRO), Lay & Wheeler (LAY), Majestic (MAJ), Morris & Verdin (MV), Oddbins (OD), J Nicholson (NI), Nobody Inn (NO), Penistone Ct (PEN), Reid (REI), Savage Selection (SAV), T&W (TW), Ubiquitous Chip (UB), Villeneuve, Wine Treasury (WT).

£8.00 → £9.99

Altaire Simi **1993** £9.30 (UB)
Barbera Bonny Doon Ca' del Solo **1995** £8.50 (CRO)
Barbera Monteviña **1996** £8.21 (PLA)
Barbera Monteviña **1995** £8.11 (PIP) £8.25 (WRI)
Big House Red Bonny Doon Ca' del Solo **1994** £8.40 (CRO)
Cabernet Sauvignon Beaulieu Rutherford **1994** £9.25 (COC)
Cabernet Sauvignon Beringer **1996** £8.99 (NEZ) £12.99 (MAJ)
Cabernet Sauvignon Fetzer Bonterra **1998** £8.99 (WR) £8.99 (BOT)
Cabernet Sauvignon Fetzer Bonterra **1997** £8.99 (SAI) £8.99 (WAI)
Cabernet Sauvignon Fetzer Bonterra **1996** £8.99 (TES)
Cabernet Sauvignon Hawk Crest **1997** £8.21 (DOM)
Cabernet Sauvignon Hawk Crest **1996** £8.99 (GW)
Cabernet Sauvignon Laurel Glen Terra Rosa **1995** £9.25 (NO) £9.69 (REI)
Cabernet Sauvignon Robert Mondavi Woodbridge **1996** £8.75 (STE)
Cabernet Sauvignon Robert Mondavi Woodbridge **1994** £8.39 (JON)
Cabernet Sauvignon Mount Eden **1995** £8.99 (LIB)
Cabernet Sauvignon Seven Peaks **1996** £8.99 (UN) £9.99 (BAN)
Il Fiasco Bonny Doon Ca' del Solo **1993** £9.99 (RAE)
Merlot Seven Peaks **1997** £9.99 (BAN)
Pinot Noir Carneros Creek Fleur de Carneros **1997** £8.99 (NI)
Pinot Noir Robert Mondavi **1998** £9.99 (TES)
Pinot Noir Villa Mount Eden **1996** £8.99 (LIB)
Pinot Noir Saintsbury ½ bottle **1996** £8.50 (FORT)
Pinot Noir Saintsbury Garnet **1997** £8.45 (SOM) £10.29 (CON) £12.25 (NI)
Pinot Noir Saintsbury Garnet **1995** £9.50 (CRO)

Stars (★) indicate wines selected by Oz Clarke in the Best Buys section which begins on page 10.

Starboard Batch 88 Quady **Non-vintage** £9.50 (STA)
Starboard Batch 88 Quady **1988** £8.12 (NO)
Zinfandel Cline Cellars **1998** £9.45 (WT)
Zinfandel Cline Cellars **1997** £8.50 (GW)
Zinfandel Robert Mondavi Woodbridge **1997** £8.75 (STE)
Zinfandel Villa Mount Eden **1996** £8.35 (LIB)

£10.00 → £11.99

Cabernet Sauvignon Fetzer Barrel Select **1995** £10.79 (JON)
Cabernet Sauvignon Firestone **1997** £11.41 (PIP)
Cabernet Sauvignon Foppiano **1993** £10.34 (WT)
Cabernet Sauvignon Kendall-Jackson Vintner's Reserve **1996** £10.50 (DI)
Cabernet Sauvignon Ridge Monte Bello **1984** £10.18 (FA)
Cabernet Sauvignon Rutherford Hill **1994** £11.90 (UB)
Cabernet Sauvignon St Supéry **1994** £10.49 (BOT)
Cardinal Zin Bonny Doon **1996** £11.85 (NI)
Il Fiasco Bonny Doon Ca' del Solo **1997** £11.85 (NI) £12.95 (AD)
Pinot Noir Calera Central Coast **1996** £11.95 (DI)
Pinot Noir Carneros Creek **1997** £10.99 (NI)
Pinot Noir La Crema **1997** £11.99 (DI)
Pinot Noir La Crema **1995** £11.95 (DI)
Pinot Noir Saintsbury **1996** £11.25 (SOM) £13.99 (WR) £15.95 (FORT) £22.10 (UB)
Pinot Noir Saintsbury Garnet **1998** £10.95 (AD) £11.90 (JU) £11.99 (UN)
Pinot Noir Schug Cellars **1996** £11.99 (UN)
Sangiovese Noceto **1996** £10.78 (PIP) £12.50 (AD)
Sangiovese Noceto **1995** £11.99 (VA)
Syrah Qupé **1998** £11.69 (REI)
Syrah Qupé Bien Nacido Reserve **1998** £11.63 (PLA)
Zinfandel Ravenswood North Coast Vintners Blend **1996** £10.75 (DI)
Zinfandel Seghesio Old Vine **1994** £11.55 (NO)

£12.00 → £13.99

Alicante Bouschet Topolos **1995** £12.95 (DI)
Barbera Bonny Doon Ca' del Solo **1996** £12.21 (PLA) £12.99 (VA) £13.09 (NO)
Cabernet Carmenet Dynamite **1998** £12.43 (BIB)
Cabernet Sauvignon Clos du Bois **1995** £12.21 (HA)
Cabernet Sauvignon Clos du Val **1985** £13.50 (CRO)
Cabernet Sauvignon Mount Eden **1992** £12.95 (RAE)
Cabernet Sauvignon Simi **1994** £13.95 (BAL)
Charbono Duxoup **1995** £13.75 (UB)
Cotes du Soleil Jade Mountain **1997** £12.66 (PLA) £13.00 (MV)
Cotes du Soleil Jade Mountain **1996** £12.35 (NI) £12.50 (BEN)
Counterpoint Laurel Glen **1994** £13.90 (NO)
Il Fiasco Bonny Doon Ca' del Solo **1996** £12.21 (PLA) £12.50 (CRO)
Mataro Ridge **1997** £12.65 (SOM)
Mataro Ridge Bridgehead **1996** £13.95 (NI) £16.10 (BEN)
Merlot Clos du Bois **1996** £13.56 (HA) £13.95 (BOT) £13.99 (WR)
Mourvèdre Cline Cellars **1997** £12.75 (REI)
Nebbiolo Il Podere dell'Olivos **1995** £13.00 (MV)
Petite Sirah Ridge York Creek **1996** £12.65 (SOM) £14.99 (YOU) £15.00 (CON) £15.95 (BEN) £16.95 (VA)
Petite Sirah Ridge York Creek **1995** £13.95 (NI)
Petite Sirah Ridge York Creek **1994** £12.94 (NO)
Pinot Noir Saintsbury **1997** £12.90 (CRO) £13.95 (FLE) £13.99 (WR) £14.50 (JU) £14.75 (CON) £15.50 (WS) £17.45 (NI)
Pinot Noir Seven Peaks **1997** £12.99 (BAN)
Sangiovese Atlas Peak **1995** £12.98 (HA)
Syrah Duxoup **1997** £12.93 (BIB) £14.49 (YOU)
Syrah Qupé **1996** £12.99 (VA)
Zinfandel Cline Cellars **1996** £12.25 (FORT)
Zinfandel Clos du Val **1996** £12.95 (AV) £13.95 (STA)
Zinfandel Frog's Leap **1996** £13.89 (FLE) £14.99 (CON) £15.50 (FORT) £16.75 (UB) £16.95 (RES)
Zinfandel Heitz **1996** £12.50 (JU)

£14.00 → £15.99

Cabernet Sauvignon Ridge Santa Cruz Mountains **1996** £15.99 (SOM) £16.95 (AD) £17.60 (TAN) £18.00 (NI) £19.58 (FLE) £20.95 (LEA) £20.95 (VA) £20.95 (RES)
Cabernet Sauvignon Ridge Santa Cruz Mountains **1993** £15.86 (REI)
Cabernet Sauvignon Rutherford Hill **1997** £15.95 (AV)
Cabernet Sauvignon St Supéry **1995** £14.95 (LIB)
La Provençale Jade Mountain **1997** £15.00 (MV) £15.50 (BEN)
La Provençale Jade Mountain **1996** £14.25 (NI) £14.95 (FORT)
La Provençale Jade Mountain **1995** £14.86 (REI)
Le Cigare Volant Bonny Doon **1996** £15.75 (NI) £17.03 (PLA)
Le Cigare Volant Bonny Doon **1995** £14.95 (RAE)
Mataro Ridge Bridgehead **1997** £15.40 (TAN) £15.75 (FORT) £15.95 (PHI) £16.50 (LEA) £16.95 (VA)
Merlot Havens **1997** £14.98 (DOM)
Mourvèdre Jade Mountain **1990** £15.50 (CRO)
Petite Sirah Ridge York Creek **1997** £15.95 (PHI)
Pinot Noir Acacia Carneros **1997** £14.49 (BIB)
Pinot Noir Clos du Val **1995** £15.20 (AV)
Pinot Noir Clos du Val **1994** £15.95 (STA)

Pinot Noir Robert Mondavi **1994** £15.57 (REI)
Pinot Noir Saintsbury **1998** £14.70 (TAN) £15.50 (HAH) £15.95 (AD) £16.99 (PHI)
Syrah Havens **1997** £15.22 (DOM)
Zinfandel Frog's Leap **1997** £15.65 (LAY)
Zinfandel Nalle **1997** £15.86 (DOM)
Zinfandel Ridge Lytton Springs **1997** £15.99 (SOM) £17.70 (FLE) £18.80 (NI) £18.95 (FORT) £18.99 (BOD) £18.99 (SUN) £19.89 (YOU) £19.95 (BEN) £20.95 (LEA) £20.95 (RES) £20.95 (VA) £22.00 (WS)

£16.00 → £17.99

Cabernet Sauvignon Clos du Val **1994** £17.20 (AV)
Cabernet Sauvignon Fetzer Barrel Select **1985** £16.50 (BU)
Cabernet Sauvignon Heitz **1993** £16.95 (JU)
Cabernet Sauvignon La Jota **1987** £16.95 (RAE)
Cabernet Sauvignon Robert Mondavi **1995** £17.00 (WS) £20.50 (WRI)
Cabernet Sauvignon Ravenswood **1996** £17.95 (RES)
Cabernet Sauvignon Ridge Santa Cruz Mountains **1995** £16.49 (YOU) £16.97 (NO) £17.95 (CON) £18.95 (FORT)
Cabernet Sauvignon Simi **1985** £16.00 (CRO)
★ Geyserville Ridge **1997** £17.70 (FLE) £19.49 (YOU) £19.98 (DOM) £19.99 (PHI) £20.50 (BEN) £20.75 (STA) £20.95 (AD) £20.97 (REI) £21.50 (LEA) £21.99 (VA)
Geyserville Ridge **1996** £17.43 (SAV) £17.60 (TAN) £18.22 (PIP) £18.60 (ELL) £18.75 (SOM) £18.80 (NI) £22.00 (WS)
Geyserville Ridge **1995** £16.61 (NO)
Geyserville Ridge **1994** £17.95 (CON)
Le Cigare Volant Bonny Doon **1997** £16.99 (YOU) £17.00 (GW) £17.00 (MV) £17.04 (REI) £17.50 (PHI)
Mataro Ridge Bridgehead **1995** £17.00 (MV)
Merlot Firestone **1983** £16.50 (BU)
Merlot Frog's Leap **1996** £17.99 (CON) £19.95 (RES)

- *Wines are listed in A–Z order within each price band.*
- *For each wine, vintages are listed in descending order.*
- *Each vintage of any wine appears only once.*

Merlot Shafer **1995** £17.95 (AD)
Pinot Noir Au Bon Climat **1998** £16.00 (MV) £16.16 (REI) £16.25 (BEN)
Pinot Noir Au Bon Climat **1997** £16.95 (RES)
Pinot Noir Au Bon Climat **1996** £16.25 (FORT)
Pinot Noir Byron **1995** £16.99 (WR) £16.99 (BOT)
Pinot Noir Calera Central Coast **1998** £16.99 (DI)
Pinot Noir Calera Central Coast **1997** £16.49 (WAI)
Pinot Noir De Loach **1996** £16.69 (LIB)
Pinot Noir Robert Mondavi **1996** £16.90 (TAN) £17.95 (POR) £18.95 (STE)
Pinot Noir Marimar Torres Estate Don Miguel Vineyard **1995** £17.50 (CRO) £18.50 (POR) £19.50 (DI)
Pinot Noir Wild Horse **1997** £16.95 (LEA)
Syrah Cambria Tepesquet Vineyard **1994** £17.05 (WT)
Syrah Qupé Bien Nacido Reserve **1995** £17.04 (FA)
Zinfandel Frog's Leap **1993** £16.00 (CRO)
Zinfandel Grgich Hills **1995** £17.95 (RES)
Zinfandel Ridge Lytton Springs **1996** £17.95 (CON)
Zinfandel Rochioli Sodini **1998** £17.85 (NI)
Zinfandel Joseph Swan Frati Ranch **1995** £17.99 (RAE) £22.90 (GAU)

£18.00 → £19.99

Bourriquot Havens **1996** £18.21 (DOM)
Cabernet Sauvignon Clos du Val **1993** £19.50 (STA)
Cabernet Sauvignon Frog's Leap **1996** £18.99 (CON) £20.95 (RES)
Cabernet Sauvignon Mayacamas **1982** £19.00 (CRO)
Cabernet Sauvignon Robert Mondavi **1992** £19.95 (JER)
Cabernet Sauvignon Joseph Phelps **1994** £18.11 (CAV)
Cabernet Sauvignon Ridge Santa Cruz Mountains **1997** £19.90 (MV) £19.99 (PHI) £20.25 (BEN)
Cabernet Sauvignon Stag's Leap Wine Cellars **1996** £19.99 (GW) £20.95 (RES) £23.25 (JER)
Cabernet Sauvignon Stag's Leap Wine Cellars **1985** £19.00 (CRO)
Le Mistral Joseph Phelps **1997** £19.99 (PHI) £20.67 (WT)
Merlot Frog's Leap **1997** £19.50 (MV)

Merlot Frog's Leap **1995** £19.75 (FORT)
Merlot Havens Reserve **1996** £18.21 (DOM)
Merlot Ravenswood Sangiacomo **1998** £18.50 (PHI)
Mourvèdre Jade Mountain **1996** £18.00 (GW) £18.00 (MV) £18.20 (BEN)
Mourvèdre Jade Mountain **1995** £18.04 (REI) £21.26 (NO)
Old Telegram Bonny Doon **1995** £19.99 (RAE)
Pinot Noir Villa Mount Eden **1990** £19.95 (RAE)
Pinot Noir Sanford **1997** £18.73 (WT)
Syrah Jade Mountain **1996** £19.30 (BEN)
Syrah Jade Mountain **1995** £19.00 (MV) £19.50 (FORT) £34.95 (RES) £36.89 (NO)
Syrah Qupé Bien Nacido Reserve **1996** £18.00 (MV) £19.50 (LEA) £27.61 (REI)
Zinfandel Cline Cellars Big Break **1997** £18.95 (PHI) £19.07 (WT)
Zinfandel Cline Cellars Bridgehead **1997** £19.07 (WT)
Zinfandel Ridge Lytton Springs **1998** £19.90 (MV) £19.99 (PHI)
Zinfandel Rochioli Sodini **1997** £18.29 (YOU)

£20.00 → £29.99

Cabernet Sauvignon Carmenet **1984** £20.00 (YOU)
Cabernet Sauvignon Carmenet Moon Mountain Estate **1995** £26.00 (WS)
Cabernet Sauvignon Chalk Hill **1995** £20.00 (JU)
Cabernet Sauvignon Clos du Val **1979** £20.00 (CRO)
Cabernet Sauvignon Conn Creek **1977** £20.00 (BU)
Cabernet Sauvignon Cuvaison **1984** £22.00 (CRO)
Cabernet Sauvignon Far Niente **1986** £21.00 (CRO)
Cabernet Sauvignon Firestone **1975** £20.00 (CRO)
Cabernet Sauvignon Freemark Abbey **1983** £23.00 (CRO)
Cabernet Sauvignon Frog's Leap **1997** £22.45 (LAY)
Cabernet Sauvignon Frog's Leap **1987** £26.00 (CRO)
Cabernet Sauvignon Grgich Hills **1994** £24.95 (RES)
Cabernet Sauvignon Heitz Bella Oaks **1993** £21.50 (JU)
Cabernet Sauvignon Kistler Sonoma **1993** £23.59 (YOU)
Cabernet Sauvignon Joseph Phelps **1996** £24.02 (WT)
Cabernet Sauvignon Ridge York Creek **1985** £26.44 (REI)
Cabernet Sauvignon Sequoia Grove **1995** £24.00 (RES)
Cabernet Sauvignon Shafer **1996** £29.13 (WT) £38.68 (CAV)
Cabernet Sauvignon Shafer **1995** £22.95 (WAI)
Cabernet Sauvignon Shafer **1994** £23.75 (FORT)
Cabernet Sauvignon Shafer Stag's Leap **1996** £24.00 (RES)
Cabernet Sauvignon Simi Reserve **1992** £25.00 (BAL)
Cabernet Sauvignon Spottswoode **1996** £27.61 (DOM)
Cabernet Sauvignon Stag's Leap Wine Cellars **1997** £23.20 (WT)
Cabernet Sauvignon Viader **1997** £29.38 (DOM) £34.00 (RES)
Cabernet Sauvignon Viader **1994** £24.75 (NO)
Cain Five Cain Cellars **1995** £29.00 (JU)
Firebreak Shafer **1996** £23.00 (RES)
Firebreak Shafer **1994** £27.22 (NO)
Merlot Clos du Val **1995** £20.30 (AV)
Merlot Cuvaison **1996** £20.95 (TAN) £22.59 (JON)
Merlot Cuvaison **1994** £26.93 (NO)
Merlot Duckhorn **1996** £26.95 (RES)
Merlot Duckhorn **1995** £25.00 (FORT)
Merlot Matanzas Creek **1996** £29.95 (BEN)
Merlot Ravenswood Sangiacomo **1994** £23.35 (NO)
Merlot Ridge Santa Cruz Mountains **1997** £28.00 (MV)
Merlot Ridge Santa Cruz Mountains **1996** £22.25 (SOM) £28.50 (BEN) £28.95 (AD) £28.95 (RES) £29.95 (VA)
Merlot Ridge Santa Cruz Mountains **1995** £25.50 (BU) £26.95 (NI) £27.18 (NO) £27.50 (FORT) £29.50 (LEA)

Please remember that **Oz Clarke's Wine Buying Guide** *is a price guide and not a price list. It is not meant to replace up-to-date merchants' lists.*

Merlot Ridge Santa Cruz Mountains **1994** £26.43 (PIP)
Merlot Shafer **1997** £27.12 (WT)
Merlot Shafer **1996** £25.50 (RES) £26.50 (FORT)
Merlot Stag's Leap Wine Cellars **1996** £21.08 (WT)
Merlot Stag's Leap Wine Cellars **1995** £25.40 (JER)
Old Telegram Bonny Doon **1993** £22.00 (NO)
Petite Sirah Ridge York Creek **1989** £21.74 (REI)
Petite Sirah Stags' Leap Winery **1996** £20.96 (WT)
Pinot Noir Calera Jensen **1995** £26.93 (PIP) £34.10 (NO)
Pinot Noir Carneros Creek **1996** £21.30 (TAN)
Pinot Noir Chalone **1998** £20.99 (YOU)
Pinot Noir Robert Mondavi Reserve **1996** £23.99 (MAJ)
Pinot Noir Robert Mondavi Reserve **1995** £22.99 (WR)
Pinot Noir Robert Mondavi Reserve **1993** £25.50 (WRI) £25.95 (BEN)
Pinot Noir Monticello Corley Family Vineyards **1998** £22.60 (LAY)
Pinot Noir Saintsbury Reserve **1997** £26.00 (RES)
Pinot Noir Saintsbury Reserve **1996** £22.00 (CRO) £22.50 (JU) £23.50 (CON)
Rubicon Niebaum-Coppola **1988** £21.20 (TAN)

Syrah Alban Vineyards Reva **1997** £23.20 (WT)
Syrah Joseph Phelps **1994** £20.56 (REI) £20.95 (WT)
Syrah Qupé Bien Nacido Reserve **1994** £20.35 (NO)
Zinfandel Cline Cellars Bridgehead **1994** £24.72 (NO)
Zinfandel Ravenswood **1996** £23.35 (NO)
Zinfandel Ravenswood Wood Road **1993** £24.75 (NO)

£30.00 → £39.99

Cabernet Sauvignon Caymus Vineyards **1996** £39.56 (FA) £39.95 (DI)
Cabernet Sauvignon Caymus Vineyards **1995** £33.68 (FA)
Cabernet Sauvignon Chateau Montelena **1997** £37.11 (FA)
Cabernet Sauvignon Chateau Montelena **1996** £33.68 (FA)
Cabernet Sauvignon Chateau Montelena **1995** £35.64 (FA)
Cabernet Sauvignon Freemark Abbey Sycamore **1986** £31.67 (REI)
Cabernet Sauvignon Heitz **1973** £39.00 (CRO)
Cabernet Sauvignon Jekel Private Reserve **1978** £30.00 (CRO)
Cabernet Sauvignon Jordan **1980** £30.00 (CRO)
Cabernet Sauvignon Kenwood Jack London **1994** £31.35 (UB)
Cabernet Sauvignon Robert Mondavi **1979** £33.49 (REI)
Cabernet Sauvignon Ridge Monte Bello **1994** £33.50 (NI) £65.00 (CON)
Cabernet Sauvignon Silver Oak Alexander Valley **1995** £37.60 (TW)
Cabernet Sauvignon Spottswoode **1995** £34.00 (RES)
Cabernet Sauvignon Stag's Leap Wine Cellars Cask 23 **1979** £34.00 (CRO)
Cabernet Sauvignon Stag's Leap Wine Cellars SLV **1995** £39.95 (WAI)
Howell Mountain Duckhorn **1994** £39.95 (RES)
Pinot Noir Saintsbury Reserve **1994** £35.00 (CRO)
Rubicon Niebaum-Coppola **1994** £35.84 (REI) £39.20 (TAN)
Rubicon Niebaum-Coppola **1993** £37.99 (YOU) £52.88 (REI) £59.95 (RES)
Rubicon Niebaum-Coppola **1989** £39.99 (YOU)
Zinfandel Heitz **1981** £38.66 (WY)

£40.00 → £49.99

Cabernet Sauvignon Beringer Private Reserve **1995** £40.05 (FA)
Cabernet Sauvignon Beringer Private Reserve **1994** £48.37 (FA)
Cabernet Sauvignon Beringer Private Reserve **1993** £41.00 (CRO)
Cabernet Sauvignon Diamond Creek Volcanic Hill **1992** £42.00 (CRO)

Cabernet Sauvignon Heitz Bella Oaks **1985** £44.06 (REI)
Cabernet Sauvignon Iron Horse **1986** £41.13 (REI)
Cabernet Sauvignon Robert Mondavi Reserve **1997** £43.47 (FA)
Cabernet Sauvignon Robert Mondavi Reserve **1996** £46.41 (FA)
Cabernet Sauvignon Robert Mondavi Reserve **1995** £49.99 (YOU) £57.20 (HAH)
Cabernet Sauvignon Robert Mondavi Reserve **1994** £48.00 (CRO) £77.84 (CAV)
Cabernet Sauvignon Robert Mondavi Reserve **1992** £46.41 (FA)
Cabernet Sauvignon Robert Mondavi Reserve **1991** £46.41 (FA)
Cabernet Sauvignon Robert Mondavi Reserve **1989** £41.13 (REI)
Cabernet Sauvignon Robert Mondavi Reserve **1978** £48.00 (CRO)
Cabernet Sauvignon Ridge Monte Bello **1997** £49.95 (NI)
Cabernet Sauvignon Silver Oak Alexander Valley **1993** £44.06 (CAV)
Cabernet Sauvignon Philip Togni **1997** £47.00 (REI)
Dominus Christian Moueix **1996** £44.50 (HAH) £63.00 (CB) £79.70 (FA)
Pinot Noir Calera Jensen **1996** £45.00 (DI) £49.95 (RES)

£50.00 → £59.99

Cabernet Sauvignon Dalla Valle Estate **1994** £50.52 (NO)
Cabernet Sauvignon Dunn Howell Mountain **1995** £53.27 (FA)
Cabernet Sauvignon Far Niente **1996** £51.95 (AV)
Cabernet Sauvignon Far Niente **1995** £58.00 (RES)
Cabernet Sauvignon Heitz **1978** £55.23 (WY)
Cabernet Sauvignon Heitz Martha's Vineyard **1992** £50.00 (JU) £54.25 (FA)
Cabernet Sauvignon Heitz Martha's Vineyard **1991** £50.00 (JU) £54.25 (FA)
Cabernet Sauvignon Robert Mondavi **1991** £58.75 (CAV)
Cabernet Sauvignon Ridge Monte Bello **1993** £59.50 (ELL) £60.00 (CON)
Cabernet Sauvignon Ridge Monte Bello **1992** £58.75 (CAV) £59.00 (CRO) £62.69 (NO)
Cabernet Sauvignon Ridge Monte Bello **1986** £55.85 (SOM)
Cabernet Sauvignon Silver Oak Alexander Valley **1990** £58.75 (CAV)
Dominus Christian Moueix **1995** £59.00 (CB) £79.50 (YOU) £79.70 (FA) £111.63 (CAV)
Insignia Joseph Phelps **1996** £55.22 (FA) £86.67 (WT)
Opus One Mondavi/Rothschild **1996** £56.45 (NO) £75.00 (FORT) £89.50 (LEA) £89.99 (UN) £99.29 (FA)

£60.00 → £69.99

Cabernet Sauvignon Dalla Valle Estate **1995** £60.05 (NO)
Cabernet Sauvignon Dunn Howell Mountain **1985** £61.59 (NO)
Cabernet Sauvignon Heitz Fay Vineyard **1975** £66.00 (CRO)
Cabernet Sauvignon Heitz Martha's Vineyard **1982** £61.00 (CRO)
Cabernet Sauvignon Ridge Monte Bello **1996** £62.69 (NO)
Cabernet Sauvignon Stag's Leap Wine Cellars SLV **1996** £60.07 (WT)
Cabernet Sauvignon Philip Togni **1995** £64.63 (CAV)
Cain Five Cain Cellars **1990** £64.63 (CAV)
Dominus Christian Moueix **1988** £67.95 (FA)
Opus One Mondavi/Rothschild **1994** £63.00 (CRO) £70.00 (CON) £72.00 (UN) £115.02 (NO)

£70.00 → £99.99

Cabernet Sauvignon Caymus Vineyards Special Selection **1995** £98.80 (FA)
Cabernet Sauvignon Caymus Vineyards Special Selection **1994** £75.00 (DI)
Cabernet Sauvignon Heitz Bella Oaks **1977** £92.24 (REI)
Cabernet Sauvignon La Jota **1989** £88.13 (CAV)
Cabernet Sauvignon Peter Michael Les Pavots **1992** £76.38 (CAV)
Cabernet Sauvignon Robert Mondavi **1987** £71.87 (FA) £88.13 (CAV)

- *All prices for each wine are listed together in ascending order.*
- *Price bands refer to the lowest price for which the wine is available.*

Cabernet Sauvignon Mount Veeder **1995** £98.61 (WT)
Cabernet Sauvignon Ridge Monte Bello **1995** £80.00 (MV) £82.25 (REI) £85.00 (LEA)
Cabernet Sauvignon Shafer Hillside Select **1995** £93.60 (WT) £112.60 (CAV)
Cabernet Sauvignon Shafer Hillside Select **1994** £79.50 (BU)
Cabernet Sauvignon Sterling Diamond Mountain Ranch **1995** £98.61 (WT)
Dominus Christian Moueix **1994** £99.29 (FA) £156.18 (CAV)
Dominus Christian Moueix **1987** £79.70 (FA) £126.90 (CAV)
Insignia Joseph Phelps **1995** £74.81 (FA)
Insignia Joseph Phelps **1993** £76.38 (CAV)
Opus One Mondavi/Rothschild **1995** £97.33 (FA) £115.02 (NO)

Over £100.00

Cabernet Sauvignon Caymus Vineyards Special Selection **1991** £148.25 (FA)
Cabernet Sauvignon Caymus Vineyards Special Selection **1985** £176.25 (FA)
Dominus Christian Moueix **1991** £104.18 (FA) £176.25 (CAV)
Opus One Mondavi/Rothschild **1981** £220.90 (WY)
Syrah Qupé Bien Nacido Reserve **1997** £117.99 (YOU)

CALIFORNIA WHITE

Under £4.00

Blossom Hill White **Non-vintage** £3.99 (UN)
Chenin Blanc E&J Gallo **Non-vintage** £3.99 (UN)
Chenin Blanc E&J Gallo **1999** £3.99 (BUD)
French Colombard E&J Gallo **Non-vintage** £3.99 (SO) £3.99 (UN) £3.99 (SAF) £3.99 (BUD) £4.99 (ASD)
French Colombard E&J Gallo **1998** £3.99 (VIC) £3.99 (THR)

£4.00 → £5.99

Chardonnay E&J Gallo **1998** £4.99 (ASD) £4.99 (VIC) £4.99 (THR) £4.99 (WR) £4.99 (BUD)
Chardonnay E&J Gallo **1997** £4.99 (SAF)
Chardonnay Glen Ellen **1997** £5.49 (BUD)
Chardonnay Redwood Trail **1998** £5.99 (UN)
Chardonnay Redwood Trail **1997** £5.99 (WAI)
Chardonnay Sutter Home **Non-vintage** £4.99 (SAF)
Chardonnay Sutter Home **1998** £5.25 (STE)
Chardonnay Sutter Home **1997** £4.99 (CON) £4.99 (UN) £4.99 (JON)
Orange Muscat Quady Essensia **Non-vintage** £5.95 (NI)
Sauvignon Blanc E&J Gallo **Non-vintage** £4.49 (BO)
Sauvignon Blanc E&J Gallo **1998** £4.69 (BUD)
Sauvignon Blanc E&J Gallo **1997** £4.49 (UN) £4.69 (SAF)
Sauvignon Blanc Sutter Home **1998** £4.99 (CON) £5.25 (STE)

£6.00 → £7.99

Big House White Bonny Doon Ca' del Solo **1996** £6.99 (RAE)
Chardonnay Bel Arbors **1997** £6.60 (JU)
Chardonnay Fetzer Bonterra **1998** £7.99 (SAI) £7.99 (BO) £7.99 (WR) £8.49 (WAI)
Chardonnay Fetzer Bonterra **1997** £7.99 (BOT) £8.49 (TES)
Chardonnay Fetzer Sundial **1998** £6.49 (SAI) £6.49 (VIC) £6.49 (THR) £6.49 (UN) £6.49 (WR) £6.49 (BOT)
Chardonnay Fetzer Sundial **1997** £6.99 (JON)
Chardonnay Gallo Sonoma **1994** £7.99 (BUD)
Chardonnay Jekel **1998** £7.49 (WR)
Chardonnay Jekel **1997** £7.49 (VIC) £7.49 (THR) £7.49 (BOT)
Chardonnay Sterling **1998** £7.99 (OD)
Chardonnay Wente Bros **1997** £6.99 (UN) £7.35 (COC)
Fumé Blanc Beringer **1998** £7.99 (MAJ)
Fumé Blanc Monteviña **1997** £7.60 (PLAY)
Malvasia Bianca Bonny Doon Ca' del Solo **1998** £7.49 (BO) £7.49 (NI) £7.99 (CON) £7.99 (AME) £8.20 (TAN) £8.40 (BEN) £8.45 (PHI) £8.52 (PLA) £8.52 (REI)
Malvasia Bianca Bonny Doon Ca' del Solo **1997** £7.99 (POR) £8.15 (WRI) £8.25 (BU) £8.70 (GW) £8.99 (VA) £10.50 (UB)
Malvasia Bianca Bonny Doon Ca' del Solo **1991** £7.99 (RAE)
Moscato Bonny Doon Ca' del Solo **1991** £6.95 (RAE)
Orange Muscat Quady Essensia ½ bottle **Non-vintage** £6.60 (COC) £7.95 (FORT)

Orange Muscat Quady Essensia ½ bottle **1998** £6.40 (AV) £6.95 (STA)
Orange Muscat Quady Essensia ½ bottle **1997** £6.49 (MAJ) £7.15 (WRI) £7.39 (PLAY) £7.99 (PHI) £8.95 (JER)
Orange Muscat Quady Essensia ½ bottle **1996** £6.75 (CON) £6.95 (LEA)
Riesling Bonny Doon Pacific Rim **Non-vintage** £7.75 (NI)
Riesling Bonny Doon Pacific Rim **1997** £7.99 (POR) £8.25 (BU)
Riesling Firestone **1998** £6.84 (PIP)
Sauvignon Blanc Robert Mondavi Woodbridge **1998** £6.95 (POR)
Sauvignon Blanc Robert Mondavi Woodbridge **1997** £6.99 (BOT) £7.59 (JON) £7.75 (STE)
Sauvignon Blanc St Supéry **1998** £7.99 (BOT) £9.95 (CON) £10.40 (REI)
Sauvignon Blanc Wente **1998** £6.80 (COC)
Viognier Fetzer **1998** £7.99 (VIC) £7.99 (THR) £7.99 (BOT) £7.99 (WAI)
Viognier Fetzer **1997** £7.99 (OD)

£8.00 → £9.99

Chardonnay Beringer **1997** £8.99 (NEZ) £11.99 (MAJ)
Chardonnay Carneros Creek **1997** £9.99 (NI)
Chardonnay Cartlidge & Browne **1997** £8.75 (BER)
Chardonnay Fetzer Barrel Select **1997** £9.29 (JON)
Chardonnay Fetzer Bonterra **1996** £8.99 (JON)
Chardonnay Hawk Crest **1998** £8.99 (GW)
Chardonnay Hawk Crest **1997** £8.21 (DOM)
Chardonnay Kendall-Jackson Vintner's Reserve **1998** £9.99 (DI)
Chardonnay Kendall-Jackson Vintner's Reserve **1997** £9.99 (DI) £9.99 (WR)
Chardonnay Murphy-Goode **1998** £9.95 (AD)
Chardonnay Pedroncelli **1998** £9.45 (LAY)
Chardonnay Seven Peaks **1997** £8.99 (UN) £9.99 (BAN)
Chardonnay Villa Mt Eden **1996** £8.29 (CON) £8.35 (LIB)
Chardonnay Villa Mt Eden Cellar Select **1996** £9.69 (PIP)
Chardonnay Wente Riva Ranch **1995** £8.99 (WR)
Chenin Blanc Dry Creek **1997** £8.95 (FORT)
Fumé Blanc Murphy-Goode **1998** £8.50 (AD)
Il Pescatore Bonny Doon Ca' del Solo **1993** £9.85 (RAE)
Malvasia Bianca Bonny Doon Ca' del Solo **1996** £8.40 (CRO)
Riesling Bonny Doon Pacific Rim **1998** £8.25 (BU) £8.40 (MV)
Riesling Bonny Doon Pacific Rim **1992** £8.99 (UB)
Riesling Renaissance Select Late-Harvest ½ bottle **1993** £9.95 (BU)
Sauvignon Blanc Clos du Bois **1998** £8.07 (HA)
Sauvignon Blanc Hanna **1997** £9.95 (BER)
Sauvignon Blanc Rochioli **1997** £9.50 (RAE) £11.10 (UB) £11.90 (CRO)
Sauvignon Blanc Rochioli **1996** £9.50 (RAE)
Sauvignon Blanc Rochioli **1995** £9.95 (BAL)
Sauvignon Blanc St Supéry **1997** £8.95 (BER) £10.95 (RES)

£10.00 → £11.99

Chardonnay Beaulieu Vineyard **1994** £11.95 (BU)
Chardonnay Rochioli **1995** £10.99 (RAE)
Chardonnay Rochioli **1994** £10.99 (RAE)
Chardonnay Rochioli **1993** £10.99 (RAE)
Chardonnay Rutherford Hill **1997** £11.60 (AV)
Chardonnay Saintsbury **1996** £10.35 (SOM) £12.63 (NO) £12.90 (CRO)
Fumé Blanc Robert Mondavi **1997** £11.49 (MAJ) £11.49 (BOT) £11.80 (TAN) £12.75 (WRI) £12.89 (POR) £13.25 (STE)
Il Pescatore Bonny Doon Ca' del Solo **1996** £10.76 (PLA) £11.99 (VA)
Riesling Joseph Phelps Johannisberg Selected Late-Harvest ½ bottle **1986** £11.00 (CRO)
Riesling Mark West Johannisberg Late-Harvest ½ bottle **1983** £10.00 (CRO)
Sauvignon Blanc Frog's Leap **1998** £11.50 (MV)
Sauvignon Blanc Rochioli **1999** £10.95 (NI)

£12.00 → £14.99

Chardonnay Acacia **1995** £12.95 (WAI)
Chardonnay Au Bon Climat **1997** £14.99 (YOU) £15.10 (REI) £15.95 (LEA) £15.95 (FORT) £19.60 (TAN)
Chardonnay Clos du Bois Calcaire **1996** £14.17 (HA)

Chardonnay Clos du Val **1997** £12.86 (DOM) £13.48 (PIP) £13.55 (AV)
Chardonnay Cuvaison **1997** £13.99 (YOU) £15.50 (TAN)
Chardonnay Cuvaison **1996** £13.30 (PIP)
Chardonnay Edna Valley **1987** £13.57 (REI)
Chardonnay Landmark Overlook **1998** £13.99 (OD)
Chardonnay Robert Mondavi **1996** £14.70 (TAN) £18.95 (JER) £18.99 (WR)
Chardonnay Robert Mondavi **1995** £14.69 (POR)
Chardonnay Ridge **1994** £14.36 (NO)
Chardonnay St Supéry **1997** £13.95 (LIB)
Chardonnay Saintsbury **1998** £13.90 (HAH) £14.95 (RES)
Chardonnay Saintsbury **1997** £13.00 (JU) £13.45 (CON) £13.49 (NI) £13.50 (WS) £13.95 (FLE) £14.95 (AD)
Chardonnay Saintsbury Reserve **1997** £13.95 (FORT) £22.50 (RES)
Chardonnay Seven Peaks Reserve **1997** £12.99 (BAN) £12.99 (UN)
Chardonnay Simi **1995** £12.50 (BAL)
Chardonnay Sonoma-Cutrer **1998** £13.70 (AV)
Chardonnay Sonoma-Cutrer **1997** £14.95 (LEA)
Chardonnay Marimar Torres Estate Don Miguel Vineyard **1993** £14.64 (NO)
Il Pescatore Bonny Doon Ca' del Solo **1997** £12.00 (GW) £12.28 (REI)
Meritage White Carmenet **1996** £12.50 (WS)
Pinot Blanc Chalone **1996** £13.50 (WS)
Riesling Freemark Abbey Edelwein Gold Johannisberg ½ bottle **1986** £14.00 (CRO)
Sauvignon Blanc Chalk Hill **1996** £13.00 (JU)
Sauvignon Blanc Duckhorn **1997** £14.95 (FORT) £14.95 (RES)
Sauvignon Blanc Frog's Leap **1997** £12.00 (ELL) £12.32 (NO)
Sauvignon Blanc Matanzas Creek **1995** £14.50 (BAL) £14.95 (RES)
Sauvignon Blanc St Supéry **1999** £12.49 (LIB)
Sauvignon Blanc Sanford **1998** £13.36 (WT)
Sauvignon Blanc Stag's Leap Wine Cellars **1997** £13.70 (WT)

A key to name abbreviations is available on page 7.

£15.00 → £19.99

Chardonnay Au Bon Climat **1998** £15.00 (MV) £15.50 (BEN)
Chardonnay Au Bon Climat **1996** £16.00 (WS) £17.50 (RES)
Chardonnay Au Bon Climat le Bouge d'à Côté **1995** £18.54 (NO) £28.20 (CRO)
Chardonnay Chalk Hill **1996** £17.00 (JU)
Chardonnay Chalk Hill **1993** £19.80 (CRO)
Chardonnay Chalone **1998** £19.09 (BIB)
Chardonnay Clos du Val **1996** £15.95 (STA)
Chardonnay Cuvaison **1998** £15.49 (AME)
Chardonnay Fritz Dutton Ranch **1996** £18.84 (WT)
Chardonnay Frog's Leap **1998** £18.80 (LAY)
Chardonnay Frog's Leap **1997** £16.99 (CON)
Chardonnay Newton Red Label **1997** £17.95 (JER)
Chardonnay Rancho Sisquoc **1996** £15.65 (JER)
Chardonnay Ridge **1997** £17.99 (YOU) £18.80 (NI) £18.99 (PHI) £19.25 (BEN) £19.95 (LEA)
Chardonnay Ridge **1996** £16.00 (CRO) £19.50 (LEA)
Chardonnay Ridge **1995** £16.15 (BU) £19.60 (AD)
Chardonnay Ridge **1991** £16.39 (REI)
Chardonnay Rochioli **1998** £16.35 (NI)
Chardonnay Rochioli **1997** £16.49 (YOU)
Chardonnay Sanford **1996** £15.93 (WT)
Chardonnay Shafer **1995** £18.49 (NO)
Chardonnay Simi **1996** £15.94 (CB)
Chardonnay Stag's Leap Wine Cellars **1997** £17.50 (GW) £18.17 (WT)
Chardonnay Stag's Leap Wine Cellars **1996** £18.28 (DOM) £22.20 (JER)
Chardonnay Swanson **1997** £17.95 (AV)
Chardonnay Marimar Torres Estate Don Miguel Vineyard **1997** £16.50 (RES)
Chardonnay Marimar Torres Estate Don Miguel Vineyard **1995** £15.95 (POR) £16.99 (DI) £21.00 (CRO)
Fumé Blanc Grgich Hills **1995** £15.50 (RES)
Gewürztraminer Joseph Phelps **1998** £15.97 (WT)
Pinot Blanc Chalone **1998** £16.99 (YOU)
Riesling Joseph Phelps Johannisberg **1996** £16.83 (WT)
Riesling Joseph Phelps Johannisberg Selected Late-Harvest ½ bottle **1985** £19.27 (NO)

Sauvignon Blanc Duckhorn **1998** £17.20 (LAY)
Viognier Alban Vineyards **1997** £19.90 (MV) £23.76 (WT)
Viognier Calera **1996** £19.95 (DI) £21.98 (PIP)

£20.00 → £29.99

Chardonnay Au Bon Climat le Bouge d'à Côté **1997** £20.00 (BEN) £20.00 (MV)
Chardonnay Beringer Private Reserve **1996** £27.00 (CRO)
Chardonnay Chalone **1996** £21.50 (FORT)
Chardonnay Grgich Hills **1995** £27.50 (RES) £32.00 (JER)
Chardonnay Matanzas Creek **1996** £21.74 (REI)
Chardonnay Matanzas Creek **1995** £21.75 (BEN) £22.50 (BAL) £22.95 (RES)
Chardonnay Patz & Hall Rutherglen **1993** £27.36 (NO)
Chardonnay Saintsbury Reserve **1996** £20.00 (CON) £21.00 (CRO) £22.00 (JU) £24.00 (WS) £25.75 (AD)
Chardonnay Sonoma-Cutrer les Pierres **1996** £20.95 (AV) £23.50 (LEA)
Chardonnay Sonoma-Cutrer les Pierres **1994** £22.75 (UB)
Chardonnay Stonestreet **1995** £20.18 (WT)
Riesling Firestone Selected Harvest Johannisberg ½ bottle **1985** £22.00 (CRO)
Semillon Chalk Hill Botrytized Estate Vineyard Selection ½ bottle **1994** £25.00 (JU)
Viognier Calera **1997** £24.95 (RES)
Viognier Joseph Phelps **1997** £24.02 (WT) £24.50 (RES)
Viognier Joseph Phelps **1996** £24.38 (REI)
Viognier Phelps Vin du Mistral **1995** £28.25 (NO)
Viognier Sanford & Benedict Cold Heaven **1996** £23.10 (NO)

Over £30.00

Chardonnay Far Niente **1997** £31.40 (AV) £38.95 (RES)
Chardonnay Far Niente **1996** £30.32 (TW)
Chardonnay Kistler Sonoma Valley **1997** £39.00 (PHI)
Riesling Chateau St Jean Belle Terre Johannisberg ½ bottle **1978** £32.42 (NO)
Sauvignon Blanc Robert Mondavi Botrytis **1983** £32.00 (CRO) £35.25 (REI)

CALIFORNIA ROSÉ

Under £5.00

White Grenache E&J Gallo **Non-vintage** £4.49 (ASD)
White Grenache E&J Gallo **1998** £4.49 (VIC) £4.49 (THR) £4.49 (BOT) £4.69 (SAF)
White Grenache E&J Gallo **1999** £4.69 (BUD)
White Grenache E&J Gallo **1997** £4.69 (UN)
White Zinfandel E&J Gallo **1999** £4.69 (BUD)
White Zinfandel Sutter Home **1998** £4.65 (BUD) £4.69 (UN) £4.95 (STE) £4.99 (JON)

Over £6.50

White Zinfandel Robert Mondavi **1997** £6.75 (STA)
Vin Gris de Cigare, Bonny Doon **1999** £8.00 (MV)
Vin Gris de Cigare, Bonny Doon **1998** £7.35 (NI)
Vin Gris de Cigare, Bonny Doon **1996** £7.65 (RAE)

CALIFORNIA SPARKLING

Under £10.00

Mumm Cuvée Napa Brut **Non-vintage** £9.99 (ASD) £9.99 (VIC) £9.99 (THR) £9.99 (UN) £9.99 (WR) £9.99 (BOT) £9.99 (WAI) £10.99 (MAJ) £10.99 (POR) £10.99 (OD) £10.99 (SAF) £10.99 (BUD) £11.50 (CRO) £11.95 (JER)
Mumm Cuvée Napa Rosé **Non-vintage** £9.95 (JER) £10.99 (MAJ) £10.99 (VIC) £10.99 (THR) £10.99 (WR) £10.99 (BOT) £11.50 (CRO)

£10.00 → £15.00

Mumm Cuvée Napa Brut **1994** £11.99 (OD)
Mumm Cuvée Napa Brut Blanc de Blancs **Non-vintage** £11.99 (VIC) £11.99 (THR) £11.99 (WR) £11.99 (BOT) £12.49 (OD)
Roederer Estate Quartet **Non-vintage** £13.90 (JU) £14.21 (NO) £14.90 (CRO) £14.99 (POR) £15.80 (REI) £15.99 (BEN) £15.99 (JON) £16.95 (AD) £16.95 (FORT) £16.95 (STE) £17.49 (MAJ)

c. £17.00

Schramsberg Blanc de Blancs **1995** £16.95 (LEA)

OREGON/WASHINGTON RED

Under £10.00

Cabernet Sauvignon Columbia Crest **1998** £9.50 (FORT)
Cabernet Sauvignon Columbia Crest **1996** £8.49 (LIB)
Lemberger Covey Run **1995** £8.35 (PIP)
Merlot Covey Run **1994** £9.50 (BAL)
Pinot Noir Firesteed **1998** £9.95 (LIB) £10.99 (VA)
Pinot Noir Firesteed **1997** £7.65 (SOM) £9.60 (WRI) £9.85 (CON)

£10.00 → £14.99

Cabernet Sauvignon Chateau Ste Michelle **1996** £11.87 (PIP)
Cabernet Sauvignon Chateau Ste Michelle **1995** £10.49 (LIB)
Cabernet Sauvignon Chateau Ste Michelle **1993** £10.50 (WRI)
Cabernet Sauvignon Chateau Ste Michelle **1988** £14.00 (CRO)
Cabernet Sauvignon Columbia Crest **1993** £11.00 (CRO)
Cabernet Sauvignon Staton Hills **1994** £11.69 (CB)
Cabernet Sauvignon Staton Hills **1993** £11.69 (CB) £15.50 (CRO)
Cabernet Sauvignon Staton Hills **1990** £10.90 (CRO)
Merlot Chateau Ste Michelle **1995** £13.95 (LIB) £15.72 (PIP)
Merlot Columbia Crest **1995** £10.75 (LIB) £12.99 (VA)
Merlot Columbia Crest **1990** £12.50 (CRO)
Merlot L'École No. 41 **1996** £12.95 (BAL)
Pinot Noir Amity **1995** £13.50 (BAL) £16.70 (JER)
Pinot Noir Broadley Vineyards **1996** £14.65 (CON) £14.86 (REI) £14.95 (BAL) £15.95 (STA)
Pinot Noir Broadley Vineyards **1995** £12.65 (PIP)
Pinot Noir Eyrie Vineyard **1997** £14.10 (SAV)
Pinot Noir King Estate **1995** £13.99 (UN)

£15.00 → £19.99

Cabernet Sauvignon Chateau Ste Michelle **1985** £16.00 (CRO)
Pinot Noir Domaine Drouhin **1995** £17.95 (SOM)
Pinot Noir Rex Hill **1995** £15.99 (MOR)

Over £20.00

Pinot Noir Amity Winemakers Reserve **1993** £26.44 (REI) £34.40 (JER)
Pinot Meunier Eyrie Vineyard **1988** £30.00 (CRO)
Pinot Noir Domaine Drouhin **1997** £23.95 (BEN)
Pinot Noir Domaine Drouhin **1996** £22.99 (JON) £23.35 (NI) £23.50 (FORT) £23.95 (STA) £28.00 (JER)
Pinot Noir Domaine Drouhin Laurène **1996** £28.90 (BEN)
Pinot Noir Domaine Drouhin Laurène **1995** £27.75 (NI)

OREGON/WASH. WHITE

Under £7.00

Chardonnay Columbia Crest **1997** £6.99 (LIB)
Riesling Chateau Ste Michelle **1996** £6.99 (LIB) £8.50 (VA)
Sauvignon Blanc Columbia Crest **1996** £6.49 (LIB) £7.99 (VA)
Sémillon Chateau Ste Michelle **1996** £6.99 (LIB)

£7.00 → £9.99

Chardonnay Chateau Ste Michelle **1996** £8.99 (LIB)
Chardonnay Columbia Crest **1998** £7.99 (VA)
Chardonnay Salishan **1997** £8.79 (SAV)
Chardonnay Salishan **1992** £9.99 (WT)
Riesling Amity **1996** £7.95 (WS)

Over £10.00

Chardonnay Elk Cove Vineyards **1994** £10.95 (BAL)
Chardonnay Eyrie Vineyard **1997** £11.95 (SAV)
Chardonnay Salishan **1991** £10.22 (WT)
Pinot Gris Elk Cove Vineyards **1996** £10.95 (STA) £11.25 (CON)
Pinot Gris Eyrie Vineyard **1997** £11.55 (SAV)

OTHER REGIONS

The rest of the world is increasingly the place to look when you've had enough of homogenized styles and the standard 'gang-of-four' grapes. Greece and Austria are particularly exciting right now

AUSTRIA

Austrian wines have been busy finding their feet in the last few years. And where are they now that they've found them? Firmly in their native soil, that's for sure. They've evolved a style that is elegant and structured (I'm talking about white wines here, if you were wondering), with good acidity but not the over-high acidity that some of them went in for a while ago. There's often a minerally flavour to them, and they're not designed for immensely long aging. Even the Rieslings of the Wachau region don't live as long as, say, German examples – and Riesling is a grape generally given to age. They're also much drier, and have higher alcohol content than German wines, but it's actually best not to compare them at all, since that particular comparison is only misleading.

Gruner Veltliner, which used to be thought of as something best glugged back by the half litre and forgotten about, turns out to be potentially a rather serious grape. It's got a lovely subtle pepper and bay leaf flavour, which may not sound much, but you don't want massive flavours all the time.

New oak? Inevitably there's some. It's not necessarily to the advantage of the wines, particularly since it's often still a new toy, and they don't know when to stop. But on the reds it can be a useful extra.

I'm not sure that Austria has any red grapes that are as good as its whites. Blaufrankisch can be good, all cherries and redcurrants, but if the yields are too high the natural acidity takes over and it just goes thin and weedy. It generally needs a bit of help from something else, and that something else is usually Cabernet. Blauburgunder is Pinot Noir, and seldom that amazing. Zweigelt is attractive, with blueberry fruit flavours. It's mostly treated as everyday stuff, but it can be concentrated and lush, too. St Laurent makes attractive Beaujolais-lookalikes. There are lots of red blends, often with French grapes, and Merlot often ripens better than Cabernet.

One of Austria's greatest contributions to the multi-faceted world of wine is the revival of Ruster Ausbruch, a sweet wine from the town of Rust, on the shore of Lake Neusiedl. It doesn't seem to matter much which grapes are used – some producers grow Gelber Muskateller (one of the better Muscats), others use Pinot Blanc, Sauvignon Blanc or Hungary's Furmint – as long as they are overripe and affected by noble rot. The result is closer to Sauternes than to Germany's sweet styles, with less fruit flavour but more complexity.

Austria's best producers include *Bründlmayer, Feiler-Artinger, Gesellmann, Heinrich, Franz Hirtzberger, Josef Jamek, Juris (Georg Stiegelmar), Kollwentz, Emmerich Knoll, Alois Kracher, Krutzler, Lenz Moser, Malat, Nigl, Nikolaihof, H & A Nittnaus, Willi Opitz, F-X Pichler, Prager, Prieler, Fritz Salomon, Heidi Schröck, Ernst Triebaumer, Umathum, Velich, Freie Weingärtner Wachau, Robert Wenzel* and *Fritz Wieninger.*

CANADA

Cool-climate wines that are mostly sound rather than exciting, though the Icewines (sweet wines made from grapes frozen on the vine in winter) can rise above that level. Grape varieties include Chardonnay (of course), Pinot Blanc, Pinot Gris, Riesling, Gewürztraminer and sometimes Merlot. The best Icewines are often made from the hybrid grape Vidal, but don't tell the Eurocrats that, because they're convinced as an article of faith that no hybrid grape can make anything worth drinking. Canadians like hybrids because their winters are so cold that it can be a struggle getting vinifera grapes to stay alive. Best names include *Blue Mountain, Calona, Cave Spring, Cedar Creek, Chateau des Charmes, Gehringer Brothers, Gray Monk, Hainle Vineyards, Henry of Pelham, Hillebrand, Inniskillin, Mission Hill, Quail's Gate, Sumac Ridge, Summerhill, Thirty Bench.*

CYPRUS

Commandaria can be reasonable, if you want a slightly dull, sweet, raisiny fortified. The table wines are still best avoided. We keep being told that Cyprus is changing, and is going to start producing quantities of light, crisp wines any day. Well, okay, I've tasted *one*, but don't hold your breath.

GREECE

There are about 250 indigenous grape varieties here, so if I don't list them all you'll probably forgive me. Only(!) about 30 varieties are commonly grown, anyway, among whites – and there are some terrific new-style whites in Greece. Robola is lemony and flinty; Moschophilero is aromatic, a bit like a cross between Muscat and Gewürztraminer; Savatiano is more neutral and much used for retsina. Malagousa has fat, ripe, peachy flavours, and often gets blended with Assyrtiko, which is altogether steelier. Assyrtiko is a good bet generally, actually: it's minerally and well balanced, rather polished.

The main red grapes are rather more familiar: there's Agiorgitiko and Mavrodaphne, Xynomavro and Limnio: expect earthy, minerally flavours and good fruit. Agiorgitiko can be a bit low in acidity; Mavrodaphne is aromatic and often made sweet and fortified. Xynomavro is of potentially very high quality, and ages well; Limnio is every bit as good, full bodied and with good acidity.

Some of the best reds are the powerful, concentrated wines that blend native Greek and international varieties, such as *Megas Oenos* from *Skouras, Antonopoulos Collection* and *Chateau Carras* from *Domaine Carras.*

My only quarrel with Greek wines these days is that when they start playing with new oak, they tend to overdo it. It's a common problem, and they'll get over it.

Best bets include *Achaia-Clauss, Boutari, Domaine Carras, Gaia, Gentilini, Gerovassiliou, Chateau Harlaftis, Dom. Kosta Lazaridi, Domaine Mercouri, Kourtakis, Semeli, Strofilia* and *Tsantalis.*

Greece's other treasures are the rich, sweet Muscat wines produced by the co-ops on the island of Samos: honeyed Samos Nectar is made from sun-dried grapes; Samos Anthemis is fortified and cask-aged for up to five years.

INDIA

Bordeaux oenologist Michel Rolland is the consultant winemaker for *Grover,* which is turning out respectable whites and reds, and of course there's *Omar Khayyam*, the sparkling wine made with Champagne know-how, but sadly not much Champagne style. But India was never intended by Mother Nature to be a winemaking country, and with so many terrific wines available from countries that were, I can't help thinking, why bother?

ISRAEL

The *Golan Heights* winery is the best producer. *Carmel* is bigger, and has recently improved its act, but the emphasis on producing Kosher wine means that the supervision of a rabbi can take precedence over the ideas of the winemaker. The idea that Kosher wine might also be nice to drink is of fairly recent date.

LEBANON

Chateau Musar is still the star here, making gutsy, spicy reds that will live 30 years. Serge Hochar, whose baby Musar is, reckons it's at its peak at 15 years, which means you have to stash it away for quite a while after buying it. It's worth the wait, though it's temptingly good young, as well.

LUXEMBOURG

Difficult to find outside the Grand Duchy itself, and frankly not that exciting when you do find them. I mean, don't make a journey specially. Most are light and made from Müller-Thurgau, alias Rivaner. The vineyards are on the banks of the Mosel (or Moselle if you prefer), but don't start expecting the thrills of German Mosel – because you won't get them.

MEXICO

If you happen to have some of the folding stuff about you, you might want to try Mexico's current star wine: it's called *Monte Xanic,* and it aspires to be the Mondavi of Mexico. And it is good, actually: full and rich. It's probably the best thing to have come out of Mexico in the last ten or 15 years. But it is expensive.

Otherwise, *LA Cetto* is still there, making good Zinfandel, Petite Sirah and Cabernet Sauvignon, and *Santo Tomas* has a joint venture with Wente of California, which uses grapes from both wineries. There's still an unfortunate tendency to try to make white wines. Well, one day they might crack it, but red wines are what everyone wants these days, so why bother?

NORTH AFRICA

This had a ready market for its wines in colonial days, but it's been steadily downhill ever since. And since those people who bought the stuff never bought it for its finesse or quality, the producers haven't had much to fall back on.

In any case, under the influence of Islam, these countries tend not to look kindly on their indigenous wine industries. Algeria's Coteaux de Mascara is traditionally one of the better areas, and Tunisian Muscat can be reasonable. Other names to look for include *Domaine Cigogne, Domaine Mellil* and *Prestige du Menara* from Morocco.

SWITZERLAND

The real stars of Swiss wine are the oddities – the Petite Arvine, rich, aromatic and often made sweet, from late-picked grapes; the Amigne, also headily aromatic; the Humagne Blanc, rich, with good acidity. These are curiously a world apart from the usual Swiss white, which is made from the Chasselas grape, also called Fendant. These are perfectly nice wines, but the best word for them is 'neutral'. They do reflect their site quite strongly, but I think you'd have to be a real aficionado – and probably Swiss – to work up any real enthusiasm for them.

Reds, which are seldom thrilling, are from Pinot Noir and Gamay in French-speaking Switzerland; the Pinot Noir-Gamay blend, Dole, is typically light, fruity and must be drunk young. There's the odd spot of Syrah, too, which is surprisingly good.

Italian-speaking wines are mostly Merlot and range, as befits Italian individuality, from pale rosés to substantial oak-aged reds, though most are on the pale, light and overcropped side. The German-speaking cantons concentrate on Müller-Thurgau, although out of what seems like perversity they call it Riesling-Sylvaner. It wouldn't set the world alight.

Can you get them over here? Yes, sometimes. A few are imported. Can you afford them? Well, yes. They're simple wines at relatively serious prices, that's all. And anyone who's ever even tried to have a cup of coffee in Switzerland knows that it's no bargain basement.

TURKEY

Not a serious wine-producing country: only a tiny proportion of the grape harvest, some two or three per cent, is turned into wine. Turkish restaurants (the better kind, at least) in Britain seem to be able to find perfectly decent house wines from Turkey, though.

URUGUAY

Tannat is the great discovery here: an obscure grape from South-West France is suddenly blossoming into lovely spicy reds. The whites, when they're made in a modern style, are perfectly nice.

OTHER REGIONS PRICES

AUSTRIA

Under £9.00

Blauer Zweigelt, Weinbau Krutzler **1995** £8.95 (JU)

£10.00 → £17.00

Beerenauslese Grand Cuvée, Alois Kracher **1995** £10.95 (JU)

Bouvier/Neuburger Trockenbeerenauslese, Lenz Moser ½ bottle **1995** £13.20 (NO)

★ Ruster Ausbruch Gelber Muskateller, Heidi Schröck 50cl **1995** £16.60 (SAV)

Over £36.00

Muscat Ottonel Schilfmandl, Willi Opitz **1990** £53.96 (NO)

Scheurebe Trockenbeerenauslese No 14, Alois Kracher **1995** £36.00 (JU)

CANADA

Under £9.00

Chardonnay Chateau des Charmes Paul Bosc **1997** £6.45 (STE)

Framboise Southbrook Farms ½ bottle **Non-vintage** £5.49 (WAI)

★ Riesling Chateau des Charmes Late-Harvest ½ bottle **1997** £8.45 (NA)

CYPRUS

Under £5.00

Aphrodite Keo White **Non-vintage** £4.89 (UN) £4.99 (DI)

Commandaria St John **Non-vintage** £4.99 (UN) £8.99 (VA)

St Panteleimon Keo White **Non-vintage** £4.89 (UN)

GREECE RED

Under £4.00

VdP de Crète Kourtakis **1998** £3.45 (WAI) £3.49 (BUD)

£4.00 → £5.99

Demestica Achaia Clauss **Non-vintage** £4.89 (DI)

Mavrodaphne Patras **Non-vintage** £5.22 (NO)

Mavrodaphne Patras, Kourtakis **1997** £4.79 (JON)

Mavrodaphne Patras, Tsantalis **Non-vintage** £5.50 (TAN)

Naoussa Boutari **1997** £5.42 (PIP)

★ Notios Gaia Estate, Peloponnese **1999** £5.99 (OD)

GREECE WHITE

Under £3.50

Retsina Kourtakis **Non-vintage** £3.29 (SAF) £3.29 (BUD) £3.35 (WAI) £3.59 (VIC) £3.59 (THR) £3.59 (WR) £3.59 (BOT) £3.99 (JON)

£3.50 → £4.99

Demestica Achaia Clauss **Non-vintage** £4.89 (DI)

Retsina Tsantalis **Non-vintage** £3.95 (TAN) £4.50 (DI)

MERCHANTS SPECIALIZING IN THESE COUNTRIES

see Merchant Directory (page 456) for details

Good merchants often stock a scattering of wines from these countries. The following merchants have a slightly better choice: **Austria** Adnams (AD), Bacchus, Justerini & Brooks (JU), Lay & Wheeler (LAY), Christopher Piper Wines (PIP), T & W Wines (TW), Noel Young (YOU); **Canada** Averys of Bristol (AV), Corney & Barrow (CB), Nadder Wine Co. (NA), Terry Platt (PLA), Stevens Garnier (STE); **Greece** Direct Wine Shipments (DI), Oddbins (OD), Tanners (TAN); **Israel** no actual specialists but Averys of Bristol (AV), Corney & Barrow (CB), and Safeway (SAF) have some; **Lebanon** Chateau Musar is widely available. For older vintages try Roberson (ROB).

Over £5.00

Chardonnay Antonopoulos **1998** £10.99 (OD)

Samos Nectar, Vinicoles de Samos **Non-vintage** £8.90 (TAN)

Santorini Boutari **1998** £5.95 (PIP)

INDIA

c. £9.00

Omar Khayyam **1990** £9.02 (NO)

ISRAEL

Under £5.00

Palwin No. 10 **Non-vintage** £4.99 (SAF)

c. £6.00

Palwin No. 4 **Non-vintage** £5.69 (SAF)

c. £6.50

Carmel Cabernet Sauvignon **1995** £6.49 (SAF)

c. £9.00

Yarden Chardonnay **1998** £8.70 (AV)

c. £11.00

Gamla Galilee Cabernet Sauvignon **1995** £10.58 (NO)

LEBANON RED

Under £10.00

Chateau Musar **1994** £9.99 (BO) £10.49 (POR) £10.66 (PLAY) £10.79 (YOU) £10.95 (TAN) £10.95 (NI) £10.99 (JON) £11.21 (CHA) £11.25 (WRI) £11.39 (PLA) £11.75 (BEN) £11.95 (LEA) £11.95 (STE) £12.50 (AD)

Chateau Musar **1993** £9.20 (FA) £10.99 (CON) £10.99 (MAJ) £10.99 (YOU) £10.99 (REI) £11.29 (UN) £11.45 (STE) £11.48 (CHA) £11.50 (WRI) £11.75 (FORT) £12.50 (CRO) £13.20 (JER)

Chateau Musar **1991** £9.69 (FA) £10.95 (VIN) £10.99 (YOU) £11.95 (SAV) £11.99 (PHI) £12.14 (CHA) £12.25 (WRI)

Chateau Musar **1989** £9.60 (GAU)

£10.00 → £19.99

Chateau Musar **1990** £10.18 (FA) £12.14 (CHA)

Chateau Musar **1988** £18.99 (FA) £21.65 (WRI)

£20.00 → £29.99

Chateau Musar **1987** £20.46 (FA)

Chateau Musar **1986** £24.75 (WRI)

Chateau Musar **1981** £22.42 (FA) £30.81 (PLAY)

Chateau Musar **1980** £23.40 (FA)

Over £30.00

Chateau Musar **1979** £33.43 (PLAY)

Chateau Musar **1978** £33.49 (REI)

Chateau Musar **1977** £30.75 (FA) £34.50 (BEN)

LEBANON WHITE

Under £8.00

Chateau Musar Blanc **1996** £7.49 (POR)

Chateau Musar Blanc **1995** £7.49 (BO) £7.75 (CON)

Chateau Musar Blanc **1994** £7.70 (WRI)

c. £9.50

Chateau Musar Blanc **1993** £9.49 (VIN)

MEXICO

Under £5.00

L A Cetto Cabernet Sauvignon **1995** £4.99 (UN)

L A Cetto Petite Sirah **1997** £4.79 (SAF) £4.99 (UN) £4.99 (WAI) £5.25 (TAN) £5.39 (PLA)

£9.00 → £9.99

L A Cetto Nebbiolo **1995** £9.90 (TAN)

L A Cetto Petite Sirah **1993** £9.00 (CRO)

MERCHANT DIRECTORY

All these merchants have been chosen on the basis of the quality and interest of their lists. We feature wines from almost all of them in our Price Guides. The abbreviations used for these merchants in the Price Guides are shown in brackets after their names.

If you want to find local suppliers, merchants are listed by region in the Who's Where directory on page 493; if you're looking for a specialist in a particular country's wines, you'll find a list at the start of that country's Price Guides.

The following services are available where indicated: **C** = cellarage, **G** = glass hire/loan, **M** = mail order, **T** = tastings and talks. There is a key to name abbreviations on page 7.

ADNAMS (AD)

Head office & mail order Sole Bay Brewery, Southwold, Suffolk IP18 6JW, (01502) 727220, fax (01502) 727223; mail order (01502) 727222 • The Cellar & Kitchen Store, Victoria St, Southwold, Suffolk IP18 6JW • The Wine Shop, Pinkney's Lane, Southwold, Suffolk IP18 6EW • The Grapevine, 109 Unthank Rd, Norwich NR2 2PE, (01603) 613998

E-MAIL wines@adnams.co.uk

HOURS Mail order: Mon–Fri 9–6.30, Sat 9–12; Cellar & Kitchen Store and Wine Shop: Mon–Sat 10–6.30; The Grapevine: Mon–Sat 10–8 **CARDS** MasterCard, Switch, Visa **DISCOUNTS** 5% for 5 cases or more **DELIVERY** Free for complete cases, £5 part cases **MINIMUM ORDER** (mail order) 1 mixed case **EN PRIMEUR** Australia, Bordeaux, Burgundy, California, Douro, Italy, Loire, Rhône. **C G M T**

One of the finest lists in this country – indeed, Adnams might say that, since it won Wine magazine's International Challenge Wine List of the Year Award, it is the best list bar none. Every region is not just thorough but thoughtful: there are lots of wines here you'll see nowhere else. There are also lots of happy snaps of the buyers at work in various growers' cellars, to prove that they really do go there, and good informative copy, too. It's a good list to leave lying around: a rather superior coffee table production. As for the wines: well, look at France, Italy, Portugal, Spain, Germany, Australia, South America: this list has everything.

1998 Coteaux du Languedoc le Champ des Pierres, Château Pech-Céleyran, £5.35 Lovely herby southern French red, ripe and juicy.

1995 Saussignac Cuvée Flavie, Château des Eyssards, £6.95 for 50cl Bargain sweet white from South-West France, with good peach and marzipan flavours.

1998 Vouvray Sec le Bouchet Domaine des Aubuisières, B Fouquet, £7.70 Classic Vouvray, sparky and elegant. Drink it now or keep it for ten years.

1998 Incógnito Cortes de Cima, Alentejo, £16.95 This apparently is Syrah – not a grape one finds often in Portugal. It's very rich and complex.

AMEY'S WINES (AME)

83 Melford Road, Sudbury, Suffolk CO10 1JT, (01787) 377144

HOURS Tue–Sat 9.30–6 **CARDS** Amex, MasterCard, Switch, Visa **DISCOUNTS** 50p per bottle for a mixed dozen or 6 unmixed bottles, further discounts for an unmixed case or 5 or more mixed cases **DELIVERY** Free within 20 miles of Sudbury for orders over £120. **G T**

France and the New World rule here, and the New World consists mostly of Australia and New Zealand, with lesser quantities from South Africa. There are a handful of wines from each of Germany, Austria (one wine here, and that a half bottle), Spain, Portugal and Italy. Australia, however, goes all out with an extremely well-chosen list of surprises. Mourvèdre from the Barossa? Zinfandel from Margaret River? They're all here.

1999 Chardonnay Valle de Vistalba, Nieto y Senetiner, £5.99 Ripe and toasty but not over-tropical Chardonnay from Argentina.

1997 Cabernet/Merlot, Cape Mentelle, Margaret River, £9.95 Extremely good value for an Australian red of wonderfully minty complexity and great length.

JOHN ARMIT

5 Royalty Studios, 105 Lancaster Road, London W11 1QF, 020-7908 0600, fax 020-7908 0601
E-MAIL info@armit.co.uk
WEB SITE www.armit.co.uk
HOURS Mon–Fri 9–6 **CARDS** Amex, MasterCard, Switch, Visa **DELIVERY** Free anywhere mainland UK **MINIMUM ORDER** 1 case **EN PRIMEUR** Bordeaux, Burgundy, Italy. **C M T**

Probably the most expensively produced and well-designed list around. It's not as long as its size might lead you to think (it's printed on paper so thick it's practically cardboard) but the selection is first class. Burgundy is terrific, with growers like Lamy Pillot and Domaine Bize, and Australia has Yarra Yering and Delatite. California has hard-to-find wines like Bacio Divino and Dalla Valle. Prices are reasonable, too: there's lots of affordable stuff as well as super-expensive bottles.

1997 Riesling Hell's Window, Delatite, Mansfield, £8.75 Australian white with pure fruit and a mineral edge.

ASDA (ASD)

Head office Asda House, Southbank, Great Wilson Street, Leeds LS11 5AD, 0113-243 5435, fax 0113-241 8666. 229 stores
WEB SITE www.asda.co.uk
HOURS Mon–Fri 9–8, Sat 8.30–8; open most bank hols; selected stores open Sunday **CARDS** MasterCard, Switch, Visa **DISCOUNTS** £1 off any 4 bottles **DELIVERY** South London only. **G T**

No thrills here, but then not a lot over a fiver either. Asda is good at good-value basics – though once you get away from the own-label wines you have a better chance of finding something with some character. Choose carefully and you'll find some sound everyday bottles.

Baga, Bright Brothers, £3.99 Portuguese red with some character.

ASHLEY SCOTT (AS)

PO Box 28, The Highway, Hawarden, Flintshire CH5 3RY, tel & fax (01244) 520655
HOURS 24-hr answerphone **DISCOUNTS** 5% unmixed case **DELIVERY** Free in North Wales, Cheshire, Merseyside; elsewhere at cost **MINIMUM ORDER** 1 mixed case. **G M T**

A short list of attractive wines from around the world. Port is from Churchill Graham, and there is Tarrawarra Chardonnay and Pinot Noir from Australia.

1998 Quinta do Carneiro Tinto, Alenquer, £5.70 Portuguese red with good character, all plums and chocolate.

AUSTRALIAN WINE CLUB (AUS)

Kershaw House, Great Western Road, Hounslow, Middx TW5 0BU, freephone orderline (0800) 856 2004, freefax (0800) 856 2114, enquiries tel 020-8538 0718
E-MAIL sales@austwine.demon.co.uk
WEB SITE www.australian-wine.co.uk
HOURS Mon–Fri 8–7, Sat–Sun 9–4 **CARDS** Amex, MasterCard, Visa **DELIVERY** Anywhere in UK mainland **EN PRIMEUR** Australia. **M T**

Oddly enough, all the wines here are Australian. Not every Australian wine is here, mind, but there's enough variety to go round. The list reflects fashions down under: it kicks off with Shiraz, moves on to Rhône-style blends, and only then gets round to Cabernet. There are not many Pinot Noirs here, but buckets of Chardonnay for those who never, but never, get tired of tropical fruit salad packed in oak.

1998 Riesling, Tim Adams, Clare Valley, £7.99 Lovely limy Riesling, elegant and concentrated.

1998 Shiraz Rossco's, Steve Hoff, £12.99 The Australian Wine Club describes this as being 'produced from gnarled old vines planted over 40 years ago.' Listen, guys, 40 is nothing. 40 is young. Am I gnarled? Am I old? Huh.

AVERYS OF BRISTOL (AV)

Orchard House, Southfield Road, Nailsea, Bristol BS48 1JN (01275) 811100, fax (01275) 811101
HOURS Shop: 8 Park St, Bristol: Mon–Sat 10–6; Wine Cellar: Culver St: Mon–Sat 10–7 **CARDS** Amex, MasterCard, Switch, Visa **DISCOUNTS** Monthly mail order offers, Bin Club 10% off most list prices **DELIVERY** Free 2 or more cases, otherwise £5.50 per consignment (£2 in Bristol area) **EN PRIMEUR** Bordeaux, Burgundy, Port. **C G M T**

There's an Australian wine on this list called White Pointer, and when you chill the wine down to 12°C a shark appears on the label. Clever or what? Of the wines you might really want, Alsace is from Léon Beyer and Germany is from Deinhard, among others, and there's a good range from Tedeschi in the Veneto. Italy is particularly varied, in fact, with interesting looking wines from Sardinia and Basilicata as well as more classic regions. New Zealand and California look good, as well.

1998 Deinhard D No 1, £9.40 An inventive blend of Riesling and Pinot Blanc, complex and subtle.

1994 Cabernet Sauvignon, Swanson Vineyards, Napa Valley, £16.70 The grapes come from Oakville and Mount Veeder, which produce complex, long-lived Cabernets. This isn't bad value for a California Cabernet, believe it or not.

BACCHUS FINE WINES

Warrington House Farm Barn, Warrington, Olney, Bucks MK46 4HN, (01234) 711140, fax (01234) 711199

E-MAIL wine@bacchus.co.uk

WEB SITE www.bacchus.co.uk

HOURS Mon–Fri 11–7 **CARDS** Access, Amex, Diners, MasterCard, Switch, Visa **DISCOUNTS** Loyalty account: 5% of purchase price as credit for subsequent purchases **DELIVERY** Free within 19 miles of Olney, £6 + VAT per case elsewhere **MINIMUM ORDER** 1 mixed case. **G M T**

There are lots of wines here that are miles away from the standard ranges. There's Barbera from Mexico and Santa Magdalena from the Alto Adige; lots and lots from Austria, including wines from the splendidly named Skoff; and some good Germans as well. A well considered list that shows an interest in subtle flavours.

1997 Schiava Fass No 9, Girlan, Alto Adige, £8.80 Soft, light red from northern Italy, from a grape one hardly ever sees here. I love it: gentle but savoury fruit.

1996 Petite Syrah Redhead Vineyard, Fife, Mendocino, £16 I suppose this should read 'Petite Sirah'; Syrah and Petite Sirah are totally different grapes. Petite Sirah is less aristocratic, but with masses of rustic, earthy fruit.

BALLANTYNES OF COWBRIDGE (BAL)

3 Westgate, Cowbridge, Vale of Glamorgan CF71 7AQ, (01446) 774840, fax (01446) 775253

HOURS Mon–Sat 9–5.30 **CARDS** MasterCard, Switch, Visa **DISCOUNTS** 8% on mixed/unmixed cases in shop **DELIVERY** Free 1 case or more, £6 for smaller orders **EN PRIMEUR** Bordeaux, Burgundy, Italy. **C G M T**

The offer of 1999 clarets here looks sensible – well-chosen wines, and a consistent philosophy. Ballantynes is swimming firmly against the tide of over-extracted, over-concentrated claret and looks for elegance and finesse. Hooray. There are some terrific Italian wines, too: Walter Filiputti from Friuli-Venezia Giulia, Foradori from Trentino, who specializes in the Teroldego Rotaliano grape, Einaudi from Piedmont and Inama from the Veneto among them. Tuscan names include Castello dei Rampolla, Castellare di Castellina, Guicciardini Strozzi and Ciacci Piccolomini d'Aragona: a first-class list, and not an obvious name among them.

1999 Ribolla Gialla Abbazia di Rosazzo, Walter Filiputti, £9.75 Austere and dry white, with a delicious mineral edge; an unusual grape variety, too.

1999 Chianti Colli Senesi, Guicciardini Strozzi, £5.30 Simple fresh Chianti which will last a couple of years. Lovely sour cherries flavour.

BALLS BROTHERS (BALL)

313 Cambridge Heath Road, London E2 9LQ, 020-7739 6466, fax 020-7729 0258, direct sales tel 020-7739 1642

E-MAIL sales@ballsbrothers.co.uk

WEB SITE www.ballsbrothers.co.uk

HOURS Mon–Fri 9–5.30 **CARDS** Amex, Diners, MasterCard, Switch, Visa **DISCOUNTS** Still wines 5% off 5 or more cases, 10% off 10 or more; sparkling 2.5% of 5 or more, 5% off 10 or more **DELIVERY** Free 1 case or more locally; £6 1 case, free 2 cases or more, England, Wales and Scottish Lowlands; islands and Scottish Highlands phone for details **EN PRIMEUR** Bordeaux, Burgundy. **C M T**

If you're a sucker for wine lists with recipes in them, this one has poached eggs in red wine, boeuf en daube, Champagne syllabub and seared kangaroo with roast new potatoes – all great everyday dishes. The wines are excellent too, you'll be relieved to hear. Bordeaux and Burgundy are both terrific, Alsace is also very good, and the rest of France is shorter but appealing. Germany has just two wines: Balls Brothers says it can't sell them. Spain looks slightly routine, but Australia has some lovely stuff.

1999 Coteaux d'Aix-en-Provence Cuvée Spéciale, Château de Fonscolombe, £4.75 Lovely summery southern French rosé. People are so sniffy about rosé: more fool them, I say.

1996 Grant Burge Holy Trinity, Barossa Valley, £21.50 Special occasions only, at this price. But the ridiculous thing is that it can still compete in value with lots of wines from Europe, and probably beat them on flavour. It's Grenache, Shiraz and Mourvèdre, and named, apparently, after the Holy Trinity Church which Meshach Burge helped to fund and build in the 1850s.

H + H BANCROFT (BAN)

East Bridge Office North, New Covent Garden Market, London SW8 5JB, 020-7627 8700, fax 020-7627 8766

HOURS Mon–Fri 9–6 **CARDS** MasterCard, Visa **DISCOUNTS** Negotiable **DELIVERY** Free in London; elsewhere, £7.65 1 case, £10 2 cases, free 3 cases or more **MINIMUM ORDER** 1 mixed case **EN PRIMEUR** Burgundy in top years.

C M T

Lots of unusual wines here, and lots to tempt money from one's wallet. There are plenty of great tastes from the south of France, genuinely interesting wines from appellations like Cahors, Madiran, La Clape and Pic Saint Loup – all those names you wish you could use at Scrabble. There are no fewer than 13 wines from Banyuls and Maury alone; how many lists have even one? Bordeaux focuses on well-chosen lesser wines, and there's a good Beaujolais list – another rarity these days. Burgundy, too, has masses of wines one can both afford and would want to drink, as well as those one can't afford. Italy and Germany are both outstanding, Australia is good, and there's a healthy list of halves.

NV Champagne Grand Cru Blanc de Blancs Pierre Moncuit, Le Mesnil, £16.25 Elegant, bready 100% Chardonnay Champagne from a grower in one of the top villages of the region.

1997 Bergerac Sec Cuvée sur lie, Château Tour des Gendres, £6.25 This is fresh, lime-scented white from South-West France. The same producer does a separate cuvée of Sémillon from very old vines, but it's £23.75 a bottle, so I thought you might prefer this one.

BENNETTS (BEN)

High Street, Chipping Campden, Glos GL55 6AG, (01386) 840392, fax (01386) 840974

E-MAIL enquiries@bennettsfinewines.com

WEB SITE www.bennettsfinewines.com

HOURS Mon–Fri 10–1 & 2–6, Sat 9–6 **CARDS** MasterCard, Switch, Visa **DISCOUNTS** On collected orders **DELIVERY** £6 per case, minimum charge £12 (£1 per case surcharge Scotland) **EN PRIMEUR** Alsace, Australia, Burgundy, California, Italy, New Zealand, Rhône.

G M T

Bennetts reckon that the south of France is currently producing better quality and value, and more interesting wines, than the New World. To prove it they have wines made with Grenache, Syrah, Carignan, Cinsaut, Gros Manseng, Colombard, Clairette, Chenin Blanc, Viognier, Marsanne and Rolle. From further north in France there are great Sauternes and Barsacs, including 1947 Château Gilette at £100. New World wines are pretty high up the quality scale, especially in Australia; Bennetts confess to not seeing the point of Chile, which is fair enough – one can't like everything – but they do see the point of Germany, even if their customers don't. ('Hard to move in any quantity', they say.) Everybody, presumably, sees the point of Italy, since there are yards of terrific wines from here. All in all, an excellent list.

1999 Château Haut-Rian, Bordeaux Blanc, £5.99 Good depth and complexity from a blend of Sauvignon Blanc and Sémillon.

1999 Syrah Finca Norte, Villa Atuel, £5.25 Good structure and dark, spicy fruit from Argentina.

1998 Wehlener Sonnenuhr Riesling Kabinett, Selbach Oster, £9.55 Mosel Riesling doesn't get much better than this. You could at least try it.

1999 Ansonica, Tenuta la Parrina, £6.99 Lovely aromatic white from Tuscany. All your friends will say, 'Oh, it's not arsenic, is it, ho ho?' Imagine how much you'll enjoy hearing the same joke every time you open a bottle.

BERRY BROS. & RUDD (BER)

3 St James's St, London SW1A 1EG, 020-7396 9600, order number 0870 900 4300, fax 0870 900 4301 • Berry's Wine & Food Shop, Hamilton Close, Houndmills, Basingstoke, Hants RG21 6YB, (01256) 323566, fax (01256) 340106 • Terminal 3 departures, Heathrow Airport, TW6 1JH, 020-8564 8361/3, fax 020-8564 8379 • Terminal 4 departures, Heathrow, TW6 3XA 020-8754 1961/1970, fax 020-8754 1984

E-MAIL orders@bbr.com

WEB SITE www.bbr.com

HOURS Orders office Mon–Fri 9–6, Sat 9–1; St James's St: Mon–Fri 9–5.30, Sat 10–4; Berry's Wine & Food Shop: Mon–Thurs 10–6, Fri 10–8, Sat 10–4; Heathrow: Daily 6am–10pm **CARDS** Amex, Diners, MasterCard, Switch, Visa **DISCOUNTS** variable **DELIVERY** Free for orders of £100 or more, otherwise £7.50 **EN PRIMEUR** Bordeaux, Burgundy, Port, Rhône. **C G M T**

Old, rare and fine wines are in a separate list. The higher end of the standard list is not exactly cheap, but there is plenty of affordable stuff before you get to the £30 level. (Makes you wonder about the fine and rare list.) France is predictably strong, with some lovely Alsace wines and interesting things from the South; Berry Bros is also one of the last repositories of the classic German wine list, full of knowledge and the assumption that people like the wines. Nevertheless, the list is very strong in goodies from the New World, Spain, Italy; you name it.

1996 Cornas Domaine de Rochepertuis, J Lionnet, £14.75 Some well-integrated new oak, and masses of rich black fruit.

BIBENDUM (BIB)

113 Regents Park Rd, London NW1 8UR, 020-7916 7706, fax 020-7916 7705

E-MAIL sales@bibendum-wine.co.uk

WEB SITE www.bibendum-wine.co.uk

HOURS Mon–Fri 9–6 **CARDS** Amex, MasterCard, Switch, Visa **DELIVERY** Free mainland England and Wales; elsewhere £10, 5 or more cases free **MINIMUM ORDER** 1 case (minimum 6 bottles of any one wine) **EN PRIMEUR** Bordeaux, Burgundy, New World, Rhône. **C G M T**

There are a couple of new-wave Tunisian wines here: it's about time somebody took advantage of the potential of that country. From the other side of the Mediterranean there are good southern French wines and great Rhônes: if you love Condrieu you'll find examples here from Pierre Dumazet and Robert Niero. Italy looks wonderful, and the New World is very well selected, with some good stuff in particular from South Africa. Graham Beck is a new agency here, and the wines are very polished.

1996 Barbera d'Alba, Viberti, £10.56 Elegant, subtle Barbera from a very good grower in La Morra. Ready to drink, and full of sweet fruit.

1998 The Old Road Pinotage, £8.50 Pinotage as it should be, well structured and ripe.

BOOTHS (BO)

4 Fishergate, Preston PR1 3LJ, (01772) 251701, fax (01772) 204316. 24 stores

HOURS Office: Mon–Fri 9–5; shop hours vary **CARDS** MasterCard, Switch, Visa **DISCOUNTS** 5% any 6 bottles; 15% on orders of £150 or more. **G T**

A remarkably good list for any merchant, never mind a supermarket. That being said, you won't find Schlumberger's 1989 Pinot Gris Cuvée Clarisse at £39 in every branch. But it's fair to expect good southern Portuguese reds at much the same price as Bulgarian reds, and they're far more interesting. There's also a very good list of proper sherries – I mean the authentically tangy stuff – from Lustau.

1996 Chablis Vieilles Vignes, Daniel Defaix, £10.99 This may seem a lot to pay for basic Chablis, but there's nothing basic about Defaix, nor about his Vieilles Vignes cuvée. Stunning, smoky, steely stuff.

San Emilio Pedro Ximénez, Emilio Lustau, £10.99 Dark, sticky sherry of rich, grapy intensity. Pour it over vanilla ice-cream.

BORDEAUX DIRECT (BOD)

New Aquitaine House, Exeter Way, Theale, Reading, Berks RG7 4PL, 0118-903 0903, fax 0118-903 1073, order line tel 0118-903 0303, fax 0118-903 0313

E-MAIL orders@bordeaux-direct.co.uk

WEB SITE www.bordeauxdirect.co.uk

HOURS Mon–Fri 9–9, Sat–Sun 9–6 **CARDS** Amex, Diners, MasterCard, Switch, Visa **DISCOUNTS** Special offers **DELIVERY** £4.99 per order **EN PRIMEUR** Australia, Bordeaux, Burgundy, Rhône. **C M T**

I can't be doing with umpteen different lists for different things, overlapping in some ways but not all the time. I find it hopelessly confusing. Anyway, the selection looks better and better, with more interesting wines appearing. The fine wine list has some goodies on it, and there are lots of good flavours from the New World.

Sacristía Oloroso Don Angel, Valdespino, £10.49 per half bottle Valdespino has had a sacristía, or inner cellar, of very fine old sherries, for as long as anyone can remember, but it never bottled them separately. Now it has, and this is a find. Wonderful concentration and complexity.

BORDEAUX INDEX

1st Floor, 3–5 Spafield Street, London EC1R 4QB; 020-7278 9495, fax 020-7278 9707
E-MAIL sales@bordeauxindex.com
WEB SITE www.bordeauxindex.com

HOURS Mon–Fri 8.30–6 **CARDS** Access, Amex, MasterCard, Switch, Visa (transaction fees apply) **DELIVERY** Free for orders over £2000 mainland UK **MINIMUM ORDER** £100 **EN PRIMEUR** Bordeaux, Burgundy, Piedmont. **C**

This is a company for serious spenders only. A case of 1996 le Montrachet from the Domaine de la Romanée-Conti costs £6350, plus VAT; a bottle of 1995 Chablis Fourchaume from Verget is £190 plus VAT. If you're in that sort of bracket, then you'll find names of the calibre of Jayer, Gros, Lafon, Lamy Pillot and Méo-Camuzet in Burgundy, umpteen Côte-Rôties from Guigal and cru Barolos from Gaja. There's Almaviva at £290 (plus VAT) for each of two cases of the 1998, if you're desperate for it; or you could have Penfold's Grange at a mere £185 (plus VAT) for a bottle of the 1982. Top-class wines for serious collectors.

1990 Tignanello, £32 per half bottle (plus VAT) If money's no object I think I'd like this, please. Just right for a quiet evening in.

BOTTOMS UP (BOT)

See First Quench.

BUDGENS (BUD)

Head office PO Box 9, Stonefield Way, Ruislip, Middx HA4 0JR, 020-8422 9511, fax 020-8864 2800, for nearest store call 0800 56002. 115 stores in South-East

HOURS Usually Mon–Sat 8–8, Sun 10–4 **CARDS** MasterCard, Switch, Visa **DISCOUNTS** 5% for 6 or more bottles. **T**

A straightforward list of mostly inexpensive wines. No surprises, in fact there seem to be fewer surprises than last year, but fair quality.

La Mura Rosso del Salento, £3.49 Decent ripe fruit from the south of Italy.

BUTLERS WINE CELLAR (BU)

247 Queens Park Rd, Brighton BN2 2XJ, (01273) 698724, fax (01273) 622761

E-MAIL butlerswine.cellar@cwcom.net

WEBSITE www.altura.co.uk/Butlers.htm

HOURS Tue–Wed 10–6, Thu–Sat 10–7 **CARDS** Amex, MasterCard, Switch, Visa **DELIVERY** Free locally 1 case or more, free mainland England, Wales and Scotland 3 or more cases. **G M T**

There's a Riesling from Alsace (from Ostertag) here which is described as having a 'steely centre with fleshy sides', which doesn't sound very comfortable. That's the only Alsace wine on the list: they seem to list precisely what they feel like here, and very refreshing that is. Look especially at the Italians and the bin-ends, which change all the time; there's also an oddments corner which, at the time of writing, contained two half bottles of Hass' rare and fine Moscato Rosa, at £10.75 each.

1994 Vino Passito le Passule, Librandi, £11.95 for 50cl Sweet, intense white from Italy, all honey, almonds, nuts and orange peel.

ANTHONY BYRNE (BY)

Ramsey Business Park, Stocking Fen Rd, Ramsey, Cambs PE26 2UR, (01487) 814555, fax (01487) 814962

E-MAIL Anthony.Byrne@dial.pipex.com

HOURS Mon–Fri 9–5.30 **CARDS** None **DISCOUNTS** available on cases **DELIVERY** Free 5 cases or more, or orders of £250 or more; otherwise £6 **MINIMUM ORDER** 1 case **EN PRIMEUR** Madiran. **C M T**

A splendidly long and detailed list, focusing on France in all its guises. There's plenty of good tasty stuff from the South and the Loire is also excellent. Chablis is from Château Maligny, and Burgundy is from a range of growers including Sauzet and Morey. Alsace focuses on Zind-Humbrecht, though not exclusively, and from Germany there are the hugely improved wines of Kesselstatt. There's lots and lots of Bordeaux, and interesting Madiran from Alain Brumont, who is a leading light of the region. Australia looks good, too, and you can buy Les Impitoyables wine glasses. Made in wacky shapes, these are supposed to reveal the wine's true nature, faults and all.

1998 Sancerre Cuvée Silex Laloue, Thauvenay, £9.50 Silex is a soil which gives this Sancerre a distinctive and attractive sparky taste.

CAPE PROVINCE WINES (CAP)

77 Laleham Rd, Staines, Middx TW18 2EA, (01784) 451860, fax (01784) 469267

E-MAIL capewines@msn.com

WEB SITE www.cape-wines.co.uk

HOURS Mon–Sat 9–5.30 **CARDS** MasterCard, Visa **DELIVERY** £6.50 1 case mainland UK, case rate reduces with quantity **MINIMUM ORDER** 6 bottles. **G M T**

The entire list is of Cape wines, though of course not every Cape wine is here: some have exclusive agencies elsewhere. Quality is generally good, and rising. You'll find Cape brandy here as well, and local cream liqueurs.

Cabernet Sauvignon, Rust-en-Vrede, £10.99 Soft, powdery fruit, all cherries and spice. No vintage is listed.

CAVE CRU CLASSÉ (CAV)

Unit 13 The Leathermarket, Weston Street, London SE1 3ER, 020-7378 8579, fax 020-7378 8544 and 7403 0607

E-MAIL enquiries@ccc.co.uk

WEB SITE www.cave-cru-classe.com

HOURS Mon–Fri 9–5.30 **CARDS** Amex, MasterCard, Visa **DELIVERY** £15 per order in London and the South-East; price according to distance for other addresses **MINIMUM ORDER** 1 mixed case **EN PRIMEUR** Bordeaux. **M T**

How do you choose wine if you're very, very rich? Do you end up buying far more than you can possibly drink, and then one day flog the lot at auction for about 25 times what you paid for it? And this is one of the places you'd buy it. You can pick up 1996 Leroy Chambertin for £495 and 1978 Romanée-Conti, Domaine de la Romanée-Conti, at £2500 plus VAT. But hurry; there's only one bottle of the latter. Admittedly, these are at the top end. Poor people like me can find things here as well – and since everything's extremely good, that's rather fun.
1998 Moulin Lagrezette, Cahors, £4.12 There: that's affordable, and rather good, with rich fruit.

CHÂTEAUX WINES (CHA)

Paddock House, Upper Tockington Rd, Tockington, Bristol BS32 4LQ, tel & fax (01454) 613959
E-MAIL cheryl.miller@bris.ac.uk
WEB SITE www.btinternet.com/~chateaux-wines
HOURS Mon–Fri 9–5.30, Sat 9–12.30 **CARDS** MasterCard, Switch, Visa
DISCOUNTS Negotiable **DELIVERY** Free UK mainland 2 cases or £128 (inc VAT) in value
MINIMUM ORDER 1 case (unmixed). **C M T**
A short but quite attractive list of mostly French wines, spiced up with photographs of the owners on their travels and at tastings.
1998 Viognier, Domaine Jacques Boyer, £6.29 Concentrated and aromatic.

COCKBURNS OF LEITH INCORPORATING J E HOGG (COC)

The Wine Emporium, 7 Devon Place, Haymarket, Edinburgh EH12 5HJ, 0131-346 1113, fax 0131-313 2607

E-MAIL jim@winelist.co.uk
WEB SITE www.winelist.co.uk
HOURS Mon–Fri 9–6; Sat 10–5 **CARDS** MasterCard, Switch, Visa **DELIVERY** Free 12 or more bottles within Edinburgh; elsewhere £6 1–2 cases, free 3 cases or more **EN PRIMEUR** Bordeaux, Burgundy.
G T
Cockburns have put together a list of very tasty, well chosen wines in the lower to middle price range. France is clearly a speciality, and there's a good range of Australians from McWilliams.
1998 Protos Tinto, Ribera del Duero, £7.95 Lovely juicy fruit, made to be drunk young.

CONNOLLY'S WINE MERCHANTS (CON)

Arch 13, 220 Livery Street, Birmingham B3 1EU, 0121-236 9269/3837, fax 0121-233 2339
E-MAIL connowine@aol.com
HOURS Mon–Fri 9–5.30, Sat 10–4 **CARDS** Amex, MasterCard, Switch, Visa **DELIVERY** Surcharge outside Birmingham area **DISCOUNTS** 10% for cash & carry **EN PRIMEUR** Bordeaux, Burgundy, Port.
G M T
Bordeaux, Burgundy and the Rhône all look very good, and there is an interesting German list, too. Italy has names like Isole e Olena and Allegrini (La Poja at £24.75) and from Spain there are Riojas from Faustino and Artadi. Top Aussies include Grant Burge, Yarra Yering and Shaw & Smith.
1996 Côtes du Rhône Rouge, Belleruche, Chapoutier, £6.49 Good smoky, spicy fruit, but supple with it.
1996 Quinta da Bacalhôa, Terras do Sado, Portugal, £7.69 This wine has been around for donkeys' years, but it's still chocolaty and rich.

CORNEY & BARROW (CB)

Head office 12 Helmet Row, London EC1V 3TD, 020-7251 4051, fax 020-7608 1373/1142 • 194 Kensington Park Rd, London W11 2ES, 020-7221 5122 • 26 Rutland Sq, Edinburgh EH1 2BW, 0131-228 2233 • Belvoir House, High St, Newmarket CB8 8OH, (01638) 662068 • Corney & Barrow (Scotland) with Whighams of Ayr, 8 Academy Street, Ayr KA7 1HT, (01292) 267000

WEB SITE www.corbar1.demon.co.uk
HOURS Mon–Fri 9–6 (24-hr answerphone); Kensington Mon–Sat 10.30–9; Edinburgh Mon–Fri 9–6; Newmarket Mon–Sat 9–6; Ayr Mon–Sat 9.30–5.30 **CARDS** Amex, MasterCard, Visa **DELIVERY** Free 2 or more cases within M25 boundary, elsewhere free 3 or more cases. Otherwise £9 plus VAT per delivery. **EN PRIMEUR** Bordeaux, Burgundy, Port. **C M T**

This is a wine importer that wins Queen's Awards for Export Achievement for all the Pomerol and assorted but equally smart wines it sells to Taiwan and places. Don't even think of this sort of wine unless you have a tiger-economy-sized wallet (before they turned their toes up). But if you haven't you can still come here, particularly for lesser Bordeaux appellations, for which they seem to have a remarkable nose. Classic regions – Bordeaux and Burgundy – are the focus, and there are shorter lists from Australia, California and the like. But everything's extremely good, with lots of exclusivities you won't find anywhere else.

1998 Château la Fleur Beauséjour, Côtes de Castillon, £4.45 Don't get too excited; that's the in-bond price. On top you'll pay duty and VAT and buy a case. But it's good stuff, rich and deep.

1998 Millfield Semillon, Hunter Valley, £10.87 Lovely classic Semillon from Australia, all honey and toast and minerally fruit.

1996 Bourgogne Blanc les Sétilles, Olivier Leflaive, £8.75 You're far better off buying a Bourgogne Blanc from a top producer like Leflaive than a supposedly grander wine from somebody less good. This is remarkably stylish.

CROQUE-EN-BOUCHE (CRO)

221 Wells Road, Malvern Wells, Worcestershire WR14 4HF, (01684) 565612
E-MAIL mail@croque-en-bouche.co.uk
WEB SITE www.croque-en-bouche.co.uk
HOURS No fixed hours; open by appointment 7 days a week **CARDS** Access, MasterCard, Switch, Visa **DISCOUNTS** 4% on orders of £500 or more, if cash and collected; 2.5% if paid by credit card **DELIVERY** Free locally 2 or more cases elsewhere for orders over £400; otherwise £9.50 **MINIMUM ORDER** 1 mixed case. **M**

They sent a miniature list that has whites, so clearly they still exist, but the main list was just reds so I'll simply tell you about them. And very good they are too: Croque-en-Bouche doesn't go in for the least expensive end of the market, but its prices are pretty good. All the top Aussie names are here (Henschke, Jim Barry The Armagh, Rockford, St Hallett, Penfolds...) as are lots of top California names, with top California prices. You see, Californians are so immensely rich and like their own wines so much that the local wineries can just invent their prices.

1996 Dolcetto d'Alba, Conterno Lovely supple but structured Dolcetto from a top producer.

1996 Bárbara Forés, Ferrer Escoda, £8.90 The list describes this as 'squeeky clean', and very modern. Lots of fruit.

CWS (CO)

Head office New Century House, Manchester M60 4ES, freephone 0800 317827 for stock details, fax 0161-827 5117. 1377 licensed stores
WEB SITE www.co-op.co.uk

HOURS Variable **CARDS** Variable **EN PRIMEUR** Bordeaux. **M T**

They're keen on Argentinian red at the Co-op – well, very sensible too. They also have Brazilian red and white, which seems rather misguided. (It doesn't take long in Brazil before you lose all interest in tasting the local wine and start knocking back caipirinhas instead.) Generally the own-label wines here are far behind the rest of the selection, so look in areas like Portugal, where there are some good flavours at low prices. Or Spain. One of the hardest-to-find wines in-store must be Torres Gran Coronas Cabernet Sauvignon (just 26). By contrast, Jacob's Creek Shiraz Cabernet is in 1050 stores.

Petite Sirah, L A Cetto, £4.49 Good, earthy, spicy red from Mexico, but only in 144 stores.

Primitivo del Salento, Le Trulle, £4.49 Juicy and ripe, and in 490 stores.

Ramada Branco, Estremadura, £2.99 Dirt-cheap fresh, light white from Portugal. In 740 stores.

DIRECT WINE SHIPMENTS (DI)

5/7 Corporation Square, Belfast, Northern Ireland BT1 3AJ, 028-9050 8000, fax 028-9050 8004

E-MAIL enquiry@directwine.co.uk

WEB SITE www.directwine.co.uk

HOURS Mon–Fri 9–6.30 (Thurs till 8), Sat 9.30–5

CARDS Access, MasterCard, Switch, Visa

DISCOUNTS 10% in the form of complementary wine with each case **DELIVERY** Free Northern Ireland 1 case or more, £10 per case mainland UK **EN PRIMEUR** Australia, Bordeaux, Burgundy, California, Loire, Rhône.

C G M T

A first class list with all the top names you can think of. Burgundy is very good, as is Italy. Chile is more routine, but there's terrific stuff here from pretty well everywhere. Lucky Northern Ireland: it's a bit of a vinous desert up there apart from Direct Wines. It's amazing the way they've built up the company – and the list – from what was basically a corner grocer's shop. Now it can compete with any wine merchant in the United Kingdom.

1998 Hoch Reichestal Riesling Kabinett, Franz Künstler, Rheingau, £9.99 Künstler makes wonderful wines, all concentration and intense fruit. You could drink this now or, even better, in a couple of years' time.

1998 Syrah Mount Benson, Chapoutier, South Australia, £14.99 Hang on – Syrah from Australia? Shouldn't that be Shiraz? Not when it's made by Rhône producer Chapoutier, it shouldn't.

DOMAINE DIRECT (DOM)

10 Hardwick Street, London EC1R 4RB, 020-7837 1142, fax 020-7837 8605

E-MAIL mail@domainedirect.co.uk

WEB SITE www.domainedirect.co.uk

HOURS 8.30–5.30; or answering machine

CARDS Mastercard, Switch, Visa **DELIVERY** Free London; elsewhere in UK mainland 1 case £8.81, 2 cases £11.75, 3 or more free **MINIMUM ORDER** 1 mixed case **EN PRIMEUR** Burgundy, but not every year. **M T**

Domaine Direct has discovered the New World, which is very good news given that it has applied the same high standards as it does to its Burgundy list. So from Australia you'll find names like Grosset and St Hallett and Leeuwin Estate; from California producers like Ridge, Viader (expensive but beautifully structured) and Spottswoode. But Burgundy is still the main focus and it's still terrifically good, with a sensational selection.

1996 Zinfandel, Nalle, Dry Creek, £14.98 Concentrated, firm, blackberry flavours.

1994 Mercurey Blanc, Michel Juillot, £6.46 for a half bottle Good hazelnut fruit and correct oak.

BEN ELLIS WINES (ELL)

Brockham Wine Cellars, Wheelers Lane, Brockham, Surrey RH3 7BE, (01737) 842160, fax (01737) 843210

E-MAIL ben_ellis@lineone.net

HOURS Mon–Fri 9–6 **CARDS** MasterCard, Switch, Visa **DELIVERY** Free 1 case local area and Central London, elsewhere free 5 cases or orders over £400; other orders £10 **MINIMUM ORDER** 1 mixed case **EN PRIMEUR** Bordeaux, Burgundy, Rhône. **C G M T**

There's a separate Fine Wine list here: I don't know quite why wine merchants do this. I suppose it's to save their fine wine customers the effort of wading through all those everyday wines (which would, of course, be completely uninteresting to them) and to keep the proles from finding out what they're missing. The odd thing is that there's no clear price division, so the Huet dry Vouvray at £9.95 is in the fine wine list even though it's cheaper than many in the standard list. Put together they make a pretty good selection, with interesting wines from Argentina, Uruguay and Austria as well as from the expected places.

1995 Vouvray le Haut Lieu Sec, Huet, £9.95 Lovely concentration and elegance, and just becoming ready to drink.

1998 Basa Rueda Blanco, Telmo Rodriguez, £4.80 Mostly Verdejo with some Sauvignon: lovely and fresh.

FARR VINTNERS (FA)

19 Sussex St, London SW1V 4RR, 020-7821 2000, fax 020-7821 2020

E-MAIL sales@farr-vintners.com

WEB SITE www.farr-vintners.com

HOURS Mon–Fri 10–6 **CARDS** None **DELIVERY** London £1 per case (min £10), elsewhere £4 per case (min £12) **MINIMUM ORDER** £500 plus VAT **EN PRIMEUR** Bordeaux, Burgundy, Rhône.

C M T

A fantastic list of the world's finest wines, be they from Bordeaux, Burgundy or the Crimea. (You want 1945 Massandra Red Port at £100 per bottle plus VAT? No problem.) The Italian list looks particularly good, with names like Castello di Ama.

1997 Crozes-Hermitage, Perrin, £5.88 Pure Syrah, all blackberries and leather and smoke. Trouble is, you'll have to buy a bit more to get your shopping list up to the minimum order.

FIRST QUENCH GROUP: BOTTOMS UP (BOT), THRESHER (THR), VICTORIA WINE (VIC), WINE RACK (WR)

Head office Sefton House, 42 Church Street, Welwyn Garden City, Herts AL8 6PJ, (01707) 385000, fax (01707) 385004; national delivery via Drinks Direct, 0800 232221. 88 Bottoms Up stores, 707 Thresher Wine Shops, 1016 Victoria Wine stores, 216 Wine Rack stores

HOURS Mon–Sat 9–10 (some 10.30), Sun 12–3, 7–10; Scotland 12.30–10.30 **CARDS** MasterCard, Switch, Visa **DISCOUNTS** Various offers **DELIVERY** Free locally, some branches.

G T

Now that First Quench comprises pretty well every off-licence chain except Oddbins it has a mission statement printed on things: 'Improving the quality, enjoyment and choice of the nation's drinking'. Isn't that nice? Especially when there's good old Lutomer Laski Rizling on the first page. Actually, this list makes one realize just how much wine has changed in the last 20 years. Then a list like this would have been unthinkable: wines from Chile, Argentina, the south of France, Portugal, New Zealand, Australia, South Africa; and all these grapes we'd never dreamt of finding then – Torrontés; Zinfandel; Semillon; Albariño; Viura (well, okay, I don't dream about Viura much now either but you know what I mean). Now we take all this for granted. And what would have been an astonishing list of esoteric wines now looks entirely mainstream. Good, yes. Tasty, yes. Good value, yes. But mainstream. When First Quench shocks, it's by bunging a bottle of Sassicaia at £55 next to a Trulli Primitivo at £5. Who on earth goes to First Quench to buy Sassicaia? I mean, there's no reason why not, but it does seem weirdly out of place.

1995 St Hallett Old Block Shiraz, £13.99 Good value and very good Shiraz from Down Under.

NV Louis Roederer Brut Premier, £24.99 A good price for this supremely elegant Champagne.

LE FLEMING WINES (FLE)

19 Spenser Road, Harpenden, Hertfordshire AL5 5NW, (01582) 760125

E-MAIL cherry@lefleming.swinternet.co.uk

HOURS 24-hour answering machine **DISCOUNTS** 5% on large orders **DELIVERY** Free locally **MINIMUM ORDER** 1 case **EN PRIMEUR** Bordeaux, Burgundy, Rhône.

G M T

Australia looks terrific here, with lots of serious and not so serious wines. South Africa, too, is good, with wines like Clos Malverne Pinotage Reserve and Hamilton Russell Chardonnay. The list is basically the New World and France, plus a few wines from Italy and Spain, but not many. They're more mixed, too, with Isole e Olena rubbing shoulders with Terre del Barolo – now that's something that doesn't happen often.

1997 Grenache, Rockford £8.13 Intense, rich Grenache with structure and the ability to age – although it's so delicious now that I don't suppose many people bother to keep it.
1998 Sauvignon Blanc, Kim Crawford, Marlborough, £7.29 Rich and ripe, all limes and passionfruit.
1997 Montgras Merlot Reserve, £6.22 'Makes you feel WONDERFUL' says the list – I wonder what it means? Good wine, though.

FORTNUM & MASON (FORT)

181 Piccadilly, London W1A 1ER, 020-7734 8040, fax 020-7437 3278
E-MAIL info@fortnumandmason.co.uk
WEB SITE www.fortnumandmason.co.uk
HOURS Mon–Sat 9.30–6 **CARDS** Amex, Diners, MasterCard, Switch, Visa **DISCOUNTS** 1 free bottle per dozen **DELIVERY** £5 per order **EN PRIMEUR** Bordeaux. **M T**
What on earth is a 'veracious' wine? One that cannot tell a lie? Only Fortnum's could have such a wine. It's an extremely good list, of course – as you would expect. Think of a top name, and Fortnums will have it. Château de Beaucastel? Naturally. Latour? Of course. Domaine de la Romanée-Conti? Certainly, madam. Henschke Hill of Grace? Meerlust Rubicon? Ridge Monte Bello? Vega Sicilia? Will sir take them now, or would he like them delivered? There are plenty of cheaper wines for those occasions when it just doesn't seem worth bothering with Vega Sicilia, and even a decent selection under a tenner. But by the way, lads, Madeira isn't 'an outpost of the Portuguese empire'.
1998 Pinot Gris, Mount Langi Ghiran, £10.50 Well structured, spicy, not oily, Pinot Gris.

FRIARWOOD (FRI)

26 New King's Road, London SW6 4ST, 020-7736 2628, fax 020-7731 0411
E-MAIL sales@friarwood.com
WEB SITE www.friarwood.com
HOURS Mon–Sat 10–7 **CARDS** Amex, Diners, MasterCard, Switch, Visa **DISCOUNTS** 5% on mixed cases, 12% unmixed **DELIVERY** Free locally, £5 1 or 2 cases in London, elsewhere at cost **EN PRIMEUR** Bordeaux. **C G M T**
There are lots of famous-name Bordeaux here going back to 1982. Outside Bordeaux the best bets are California, with a good list from Ridge, Qupé and Bonny Doon. Burgundy looks routine, sadly. For whisky lovers there are Murry McDavid bottlings of various distilleries, including Caol Ila 1989 and Leapfrog (from Islay) 1987. Leapfrog? What sort of a name is that for a distillery? Well, it may not be pure Laphroaig...
1996 Petite Sirah, Ridge, York Creek, £15.49; 1996 Château Larose-Trintaudon Grand Cru Bourgeois, Haut-Médoc, £13.59 Both California and Bordeaux are undeniably expensive. Which of these wines offers better value? No prizes for guessing what I think.

GAUNTLEYS (GAU)

4 High St, Exchange Arcade, Nottingham NG1 2ET, 0115-911 0555, fax 0115-911 0557
E-MAIL rhone@gauntleywine.com
WEB SITE www.gauntleywine.com
HOURS Mon–Sat 9–5.30 **CARDS** Amex, MasterCard, Switch, Visa **DELIVERY** Free within Nottingham area, otherwise 1–2 cases £8 plus VAT, 3–5 cases £13 plus VAT **MINIMUM ORDER** 1 case **EN PRIMEUR** Burgundy, Rhône.
M T
Do you know, if this list didn't exist I think I'd have to invent it. It's full of wines that are not just unusual, but that are also from the sorts of places that offer both character and good value. There are just five wines from Bordeaux: isn't that extraordinary? Bravo for having the nerve to do it. In fact if you were a Cabernet Sauvignon fan I think you might have rather a thin time of it here. There's lots of lovely stuff from the south of France, but it tends to be Coteaux du Languedoc or Bandol or Jurançon or Minervois or Maury: flying winemaker reds are few and far between. Alsace features heavily, with star names like Schoffit, Marcel Deiss, Trimbach and Josmeyer, and Champagne is from Vilmart, which makes wonderfully big, rich wines that need ages. There's a long list of Burgundy, and lots of Loire as well, and some good Spanish and Italians. The latter are a new addition: Portugal next year, chaps? You'll find your sort of wines there.

1996 Syrah Vin de Table, René Rostaing, £12.73 Twelve quid for a Syrah vin de table? There's more to this than meets the eye. It's from René Rostaing, so it should be worth a try.
1990 Steiner Cabernet Sauvignon, Joseph Swan, £16.16 Who says California wines don't age? Joseph Swan's Cabernet is ten years old and still going strong.

GOEDHUIS & CO (GOE)

6 Rudolf Place, Miles Street, London SW8 1RP, 020-7793 7900, fax 020-7793 7170
E-MAIL goedhuis@btinternet.com
HOURS Mon–Fri 9–6.30 **CARDS** MasterCard, Visa **DELIVERY** Free 3 or more, otherwise £10 England, elsewhere at cost **MINIMUM ORDER** 1 unmixed case **EN PRIMEUR** Bordeaux, Burgundy. **C G M T**

There are wines from 41 domaines in Burgundy on this list: that's several pages' worth. Bordeaux goes on a fair while, too, with good selections of current vintages, and older ones going back to 1978. There are certainly a few everyday versions, but Goedhuis is principally Classed Growth country. The rest of the world is disposed of brieflly but well: you wouldn't necessarily come here specifically for Loire wines, or Italian, Chilean or Californian, but if you felt like picking up a few bottles while browsing through the Burgundies you wouldn't be disappointed.
1997 Edi Simcic Rebul, £8.72 You don't often see Slovenian wines here. Rebula is the same grape as Ribolla, which makes this wine worth a try.

THE GREAT NORTHERN WINE COMPANY (GN)

The Warehouse, Blossomgate, Ripon, N. Yorks HG4 2AJ, tel & fax (01765) 609151, accounts (01765) 609177
E-MAIL gnw.ripon@onyxnet.co.uk
HOURS Mon–Fri 9–6, Sat 9–5 **CARDS** Amex, MasterCard, Switch, Visa **DISCOUNTS** 5% for orders over £100 **DELIVERY** Free local area, elsewhere at cost, free 5 cases or more **MINIMUM ORDER** for deliveries £25 plus VAT **EN PRIMEUR** Bordeaux, Port. **G**

A sound list of mostly well-known names that gets as over-excited as the National Lottery draw. You want an example? 'In a complicated area of winebuying [sic] fraught with disappointment our driving force is quality first!...second!!!...third!!!!'. And actually the wines don't need such hype. Most areas are a bit mixed, with top names rubbing shoulders with less good ones, but there's good drinking: wines like Henry Pellé's Menetou-Salon and Barbadillo sherry, Henschke from Australia and Ata Rangi from New Zealand.
Ata Rangi Celebre £13.55 No vintage is listed for this rich blend of Cabernet, Merlot and Syrah. Presumably it's a couple of years old.

GREAT WESTERN WINE (GW)

The Wine Warehouse, Wells Road, Bath BA2 3AP, (01225) 322800, fax (01225) 442139
E-MAIL post@greatwesternwine.co.uk
WEB SITE www.greatwesternwine.co.uk
HOURS Mon–Fri 10–7, Sat 10–6 **CARDS** Amex, MasterCard, Switch, Visa **DISCOUNTS** Negotiable **DELIVERY** Free 3 or more cases, otherwise £7 **MINIMUM ORDER** 1 mixed case **EN PRIMEUR** Bordeaux, Burgundy, Rhône.
C G M T

A highly individual list of highly individual wines. It would be fatal to turn up here knowing what you wanted: you'd feel obliged to by-pass all the other things that might be even more delicious. All sorts of delicious Loire wines, for example, or Viognier from Tuscany, or Yarra Yering's peerless Cabernet Sauvignon from the Yarra Valley. A list to browse through at leisure.
1995 Tricorno, Castello di Poppiano, £13.99 This is the weirdest blend I've come across for a long time. It's a mix of Nebbiolo, Sangiovese, Barbera, Cabernet Sauvignon and Merlot, and it comes from Tuscany. Do they grow the Nebbiolo and Barbera there, or do they ship them in? The list is silent on this point. It merely describes the wine as 'rich, robust and full-flavoured'. I'll bet.
1998 Glaetzer Bishop Shiraz, Barossa Valley, £18.39 A relatively new Barossa company, specializing in highly concentrated, unirrigated Shiraz.

PETER GREEN & CO
37a-b Warrender Park Road, Edinburgh EH9 1HJ, tel & fax 0131-229 5925
HOURS Mon–Thur 9.30–6.30, Fri 9.30–7.30, Sat 9.30–7 **CARDS** MasterCard, Switch, Visa
DISCOUNTS 5% on a case or two unmixed half-dozens **DELIVERY** 1 case £6; extra cases £4 each.
G M T
Classic regions are strong, with plenty of affordable claret and some affordable Burgundy. Italy is excellent, with names like Antinori, as is Spain, with Pesquera. Australia and NZ look classy. Peter Green has a good way of helping customers distinguish between German wines from Grosslagen (collections of sites) and German wines from Einzellagen (single sites). It's quite simple: you put a little 'e' in your list against Einzellagen wines and a 'g' against Grosslagen ones. Any other wine merchants want to pinch the idea?
1997 Bardolino Classico Superiore, Rizzardi, £5.95 Lovely light cherryish red.
1995 Barco Reale, Tenuta di Capezzana, £7.25 Excellent red Italian, with good depth and complexity.

ROGER HARRIS WINES (HAW)
Loke Farm, Weston Longville, Norfolk NR9 5LG, (01603) 880171, fax (01603) 880291
E-MAIL sales@rhwine.co.uk
WEB SITE www.Beaujolaisonline.co.uk
HOURS Mon–Fri 9–5 **CARDS** Amex, MasterCard, Visa **DELIVERY** UK mainland, £3 for orders up to £100, £2 up to £150, free over £150
MINIMUM ORDER 1 mixed case. **M**
If you love good Beaujolais, look no further. Roger Harris specializes in the stuff, and his list has yards of advice on how to choose it, drink it and serve it. And no, it's not stuffy advice; more suggestions along the lines of which wines are good chilled and which are spoiled by chilling, and which can actually benefit from decanting. All very useful stuff. And the list is terrific, both in breadth and depth. It also ventures into the Mâconnais, and into the south, if you feel like a brief change of scene.
1999 Chiroubles, Domaine de la Source, £7.45 Light, perfumed and seductive: the freshness of a Nouveau, combined with the style of a Cru.

JOHN HARVEY & SONS (HA)
12 Denmark St, Bristol BS1 5DQ, 0117-927 5010, fax 0117-927 5002
E-MAIL wineshop@adsweu.co.uk
WEB SITE www.j-harvey.co.uk
HOURS Mon–Fri 10–6, Sat 10–5 **CARDS** Amex, Diners, MasterCard, Switch, Visa **DELIVERY** Free 4 cases or more UK mainland **EN PRIMEUR** Bordeaux. **C G M T**
A not immensely long, but decidedly well-chosen list. Bordeaux is probably the biggest section, and the Rhône, Loire and Alsace look interesting. Spain and Italy are promising, and there are good flavours from Australia, New Zealand and South Africa. Argentina and Chile are worth a close look, as well.
NV Gosset Brut Excellence, £19.54 Lovely creamy, balanced Champagne.
1999 Côtes du Rhône, Vidal-Fleury, £7.37 Harveys hints like mad that this white, which is made from Viognier, 'could well come from close to the famous and outrageously expensive appellation of Condrieu. "Mon p'tit Vidal" does not let on', apparently. Whether it does or whether it doesn't, it's a pretty good price for Rhône Viognier from a good grower.

HAYNES HANSON & CLARK (HAH)
Sheep St, Stow-on-the-Wold, Glos GL54 1AA, (01451) 870808, fax (01451) 870508
• 25 Eccleston St, London SW1W 9NP, 020-7259 0102, fax 020-7259 0103
E-MAIL stow@hhandc.co.uk *or* london@hhandc.co.uk
HOURS Stow: Mon–Fri 9–6, Sat 9–5.30; London: Mon–Fri 9–7, Sat 10–4
CARDS Amex, MasterCard, Switch, Visa

DISCOUNTS 10% unsplit case **DELIVERY** Free central London and Glos; elsewhere (per case) 1 case £8, 2–3 cases £5.20 per case, 4 or more cases £4.50 per case, free orders over £500 **MINIMUM ORDER** 1 bottle (mail order) **EN PRIMEUR** Bordeaux, Burgundy, Rhône. **G M T**

The sort of wine merchant everybody ought to go to, whether serious buyers of fine wines, or just getting into wine. You'll find first class bottles along with excellent, friendly advice, great depth of knowledge and wine at whatever price you want to spend (provided that it's over a fiver). Burgundy is a long-standing speciality. Bordeaux is also first class, and there are great wines from California, New Zealand and Italy.

1999 Chablis 1er Cru Côte de Léchet, Domaine Daniel Dampt, £11.60 Stylish Chablis with lots of grip and intensity.

1998 Barco Reale di Carmignano, Tenuta di Capezzana, £8.40 Excellent Tuscan red which blends Cabernet with Sangiovese.

HEDLEY WRIGHT (HED)

11 Twyford Centre, London Road, Bishop's Stortford, Herts CM23 3YT, (01279) 465818, fax (01279) 465819

HOURS Mon–Wed 9–6, Thu–Fri 9–7, Sat 10–6 **CARDS** MasterCard, Switch, Visa **DELIVERY** Free local area, 1 case £5, 2 or more cases £3 per case (max £12) **MINIMUM ORDER** 1 mixed case. **C G M T**

A good all round list, with Alsace wines from Charles Koehly and German wines from Dr Loosen. Portugal and Spain both look good, even if the wines from Quinta do Fojo have shot up in price since last year. Italy, something of a speciality, has wines from the likes of Pieropan, Franz Haas and Pra. Chile and Argentina are interesting, and from New Zealand there are the wines of Jackson Estate. Ports are from Churchill Graham: look out for the Traditional LBV.

1997 Castell del Remei Oda, Costers del Segre, £11.99 Lovely plums and spice in a rich, sweet-fruited red.

1998 Morellino di Scansano, Le Pupille, £9.49 Morellino di Scansano has irresistibly juicy cherry fruit. Le Pupille adds richness and structure.

HICKS & DON

Order office 4 Old Station Yard, Edington, Westbury, Wiltshire BA13 4NT (01380) 831234, fax (01380) 831010. • Park House, North Elmham, Dereham, Norfolk NR20 5JY (01362) 668571, fax (01362) 668573

E-MAIL mailbox@hicksanddon.co.uk

HOURS Mon–Fri 9–5 **CARDS** Access, MasterCard, Visa **DISCOUNTS** Negotiable **DELIVERY** Free 3 cases or more mainland UK, otherwise £4 per case, next day delivery in London extra £12 **MINIMUM ORDER** 1 case **EN PRIMEUR** Bordeaux, Burgundy, Rhône, Italy. **C G M T**

This list is sensibly organized by grape variety, regardless of origin. It also follows Chardonnay, Sauvignon Blanc and Sémillon with 'White wines of individuality', though since this last section includes Vin de Pays des Côtes de Gascogne and Muscadet as well as Wolfgang Unger's Pinot Blanc from Kremstal in Austria and Pieropan's Soave Classico, I don't think it's intended as a slur on the lack of character of the likes of Mountadam Chardonnay. Dessert wines include the intriguingly named Markgraflerland Bugginer Maltesgarten Spätburgunder Eiswein from Baden, and there's a good list of other German wines. A good reliable selection: it won't set the world on fire, but you won't fail to find some good wines.

1996 Pinot Noir Ramsay, Kent & Rasmussen, £12.84 One of the reasons California is doing so well (in patches, admittedly) with this tricky variety. Good balance and length.

1997 Chianti Classico, Isole e Olena, £15.45 Heavens, the price of decent Chianti these days. When I were a lad... But this is good, from a top producer.

HIGH BRECK VINTNERS (HIG)

11 Nelson Road, London N8 9RX, 020-8340 1848, fax 020-8340 5162

E-MAIL hbv@richanl.freeserve.co.uk

HOURS Mail order **DELIVERY** Free to the South East, 3 or more cases; supplements payable for smaller orders or other locations **MINIMUM ORDER** 1 mixed case **EN PRIMEUR** Bordeaux. **M T**

An almost entirely French list, well priced and well chosen. If you had fifteen quid about your person you could get yourself a respectable claret, or two bottles of Château de Belle-Coste Rouge Cuvée St Marc 1996 from the southern Rhône.

1995 Château Ferrant, Pomerol, £13.25 This strikes me as rather a good buy: it's a very good year and a very decent château. An affordable Pomerol, of all things. Whatever next?

JEROBOAMS (INCORPORATING LAYTONS) (JER)

Head office Jeroboams: 8–12 Brook Street, London W1Y 2BH, 020-7629 7916, fax 020-7495 3314 **Mail order** Laytons: 20 Midland Road, London NW1 2AD, 020-7388 4567, fax 020-7383 7419 • 50–52 Elizabeth Street, London SW1W 9PB, 020-7730 8108, fax 020-7730 9284 • 51 Elizabeth Street, London SW1W 9PP, 020-7823 5623, fax 020-7823 5722 • 25 Elystan Street, London SW3 3NT, 020-7581 2660, fax 020-7581 1203 • 20 Davies Street, London W1Y 1LH, 020-7499 1015, fax 020-7491 3052 • 77–78 Chancery Lane, London WC2A 1AB, 020-7405 0552, fax 020-7405 0553 • 96 Holland Park Avenue, London W11 3RB, 020-7727 9359, fax 020-7792 3672 • 6 Pont Street, London SW1X 9EL, 020-7235 1612, fax 020-7235 7246 • The Market Place, Cirencester, Glos GL7 2PE, (01285) 655842, fax (01285) 644101

E-MAIL sales@laytons.co.uk

WEB SITES www.jeroboams.co.uk *and* www.laytons.co.uk

HOURS Offices Mon–Fri 9–6, shops Mon–Sat 9–7 (may vary) **CARDS** Amex, MasterCard, Switch, Visa **DELIVERY** Shops: free for orders of £50 or over in central London; mail order: free for orders over £150, otherwise £10 **EN PRIMEUR** Bordeaux, Burgundy, Germany, Rhône. **C G M T**

The list focuses on Bordeaux, with most wines at the classic, more pricy level; there's a handful of nice wines from the Rhône and Loire, and an equally good, somewhat longer list from the south of France. This is where the bargains on the list are. There are also some well chosen Australians that are a bit off the beaten track. It's quite a short list, but everything on it is highly desirable.

1988 les Marrons de Vaucluse, Henri Brunier, Vin de Pays de Vaucluse, £6 These vines are just outside the Châteauneuf-du-Pape appellation, apparently. The wine is rich and well structured, with lovely southern fruit.

1997 Château Chenaie, Faugères, £6.85 Wonderful spice and depth, and earthy, blackberry fruit.

S H JONES (JON)

27 High Street, Banbury, Oxfordshire OX16 8EW, (01295) 251179, fax (01295) 272352 • 9 Market Square, Bicester, Oxfordshire OX6 7AA (01869) 322448, fax (01869) 244588 • 121 Regent Street, Leamington Spa, Warwickshire CV32 4NU, (01926) 315609

HOURS Mon–Sat 8.30–6 **CARDS** MasterCard, Switch, Visa **DELIVERY** Free within van delivery area for 1 case or more; 'small delivery charge' otherwise. Elsewhere £7.50, free for orders over £150 **EN PRIMEUR** Bordeaux, Port. **C G M T**

This is a terrific list, even if the early draft Jones sent us was lacking prices. But unless it has changed its policy drastically since last year, they probably won't be extortionate. There are some top growers in Burgundy, and a good mix of classic wines and lesser ones in Bordeaux. Germany looks good too, and from Portugal there's a white from Bucelas – now there's a rarity. Australia looks well covered, with great names like St Hallett and Cape Mentelle.

1998 Pinot Noir, Yerring Station, Yarra Valley, £10.99 Victorian Pinot from a producer not often seen in this country. Elegant, structured wine, very ripe.

JUSTERINI & BROOKS (JU)

61 St James's Street, London SW1A 1LZ, 020-7493 8721, fax 020-7499 4653 • 45 George Street, Edinburgh EH2 2HT, 0131-226 4202, fax 0131-225 2351

E-MAIL j-b.retail@dial.pipex.com

HOURS London, Mon–Fri 9–5.30; Edinburgh, Mon–Sat 9.30–6 **CARDS** Amex, MasterCard, Switch, Visa **DISCOUNTS** £1 per case 2–4 cases, £2 per case 5–7 cases, £3 per case 8 cases and over **DELIVERY** Up to 2 cases, £9 UK mainland and N Ireland; free 2 cases and over; offshore UK £15 per case **EN PRIMEUR** Bordeaux, Burgundy, Rhône. **C G M T**

Gosh, what a list. France and Germany are strongest. If you want Bordeaux, Burgundy, Rhône, Loire, Alsace or just about anywhere else, look no further than London and Edinburgh. In Champagne J&B believes that good small growers have wines with more character and individuality than the big houses. But they've got wine from the big houses as well: Veuve Clicquot, Louis Roederer, Billecart-Salmon, Laurent Perrier and the like. For Riesling freaks there's a superlative list of German wines back to 1989 (though they've sold nearly all their 1990s.). Italy, Spain, Portugal, Australia, New Zealand and North America are shorter but all very good, as are sherry, port and Madeira. But France and Germany are the heart of the list.

NV Champagne Brut Traditionelle, Cuillier Père et Fils, £16 A good price for a really nutty, creamy Champagne.

1997 Saarburger Rausch Riesling Auslese Fuder 9, Zilliken, £19.90 Intense, extraordinarily complex and elegant wine from one of the best growers in the Saar Valley.

KWIKSAVE

See Somerfield

LAY & WHEELER (LAY)

The Wine Centre, Gosbecks Park, Colchester CO2 9JT, (01206) 764446, fax (01206) 560002
E-MAIL layandwheeler@ndirect.co.uk
WEB SITE www.layandwheeler.co.uk
HOURS Mon–Sat 9–6.30; telephone orders Mon–Fri 8–6, Sat 8.30–4 **CARDS** Amex, MasterCard, Switch, Visa **DISCOUNTS** 5% 5 or more mixed cases, £3 per case if collected **DELIVERY** £6.95, free for orders over £150 **EN PRIMEUR** Bordeaux, Burgundy, Rhône, Port.
C G M T

There's enough first-class Bordeaux and Burgundy to satisfy the most demanding drinker here; the Rhône, the Loire and Alsace are all excellent, and actually, so is everything else. Australia has some fascinating wines – Henschke, Veritas, Penley Estate, Vasse Felix – and there are great Californians, too. Germany is famously good here, and so is Italy: lots of interesting flavours from the south, among others. A must-have list.

1997 Château Potensac, Cru Bourgeois Médoc, £15.95 A daft price, but that, I'm afraid, is Bordeaux these days. Potensac used to be a good reliable standby château; now, at this price, it's a special treat. It's very good, though.

1998 Mâcon-Villages Tête de Cuvée, Verget, £9.95 There's real breeding and elegance in this Mâcon – and that doesn't happen very often.

1999 Shiraz Cypress, Reynolds, £6.95 Excellent value Shiraz from New South Wales, full of vibrant, sumptuous fruit.

LAYMONT & SHAW

The Old Chapel, Millpool, Truro, Cornwall TR1 1EX, (01872) 270545, fax (01872) 223005
E-MAIL info@laymont-shaw.co.uk
WEB SITE www.laymont-shaw.co.uk
HOURS Mon–Fri 9–5 **CARDS** MasterCard, Visa **DISCOUNTS** £2.50 per case if wines collected, also £1 per case for 2 cases, £1.50 for 3–5, £2 for 6 or more **DELIVERY** UK mainland delivery included in wine price **MINIMUM ORDER** 1 mixed case. **G M T**

An excellent, knowledgeable list that specializes in Spain and Portugal. And when I say 'specializes', I mean that they seek out individual wines that you won't find in supermarkets because the quantities are too small. From Portugal come the wines of Montez Champalimaud, a maverick port producer who in fact concentrates on table wines of great concentration and style. From Spain there are lots of Riojas and wines from other well known regions like Navarra and Penedès; there are some goodies from Ribera del Duero and Toro as well, and new wave stuff from Priorat. If you want old vintages of Rioja this is the place to come: Laymont & Shaw has Viña Ardanza back to 1973, La Rioja Alta Gran Reserva 904 back to 1968, and Vega Sicilia Unico 1962. A mere £150, that one.

1998 Vinha Barrosa, Luis Pato, £16.75 Luis Pato is far and away the best producer in Bairrada; this wine is from 70-year-old Baga vines. There's also a varietal white Bical fermented in barrel, which is unusual and perfumed.

1999 Ribera del Quipar, Cofrutos, Bullas, £4.95 Made from Monastrell, this wine is unoaked and terrifically fruity.

1999 Azumbre, Agrícola Castellana, Rueda, £5.45 A blend of Verdejo and Sauvignon Blanc, crisp, dry and with scents of elderflower. Rueda is Spain's best white DO, and this is as good as it gets.

LAYTONS

See Jeroboams.

LEA & SANDEMAN (LEA)

170 Fulham Road, London SW10 9PR, 020-7244 0522, fax 020-7244 0533 • 211 Kensington Church Street, London W8 7LX, 020-7221 1982 • 51 Barnes High Street, London SW13 9LN, 020-8878 8643
E-MAIL info@leaandsandeman.co.uk
HOURS Mon–Fri 9–8, Sat 10–8.30 **CARDS** Amex, MasterCard, Switch, Visa **DISCOUNTS** 5–15% by case, other discounts, 10 cases or more **DELIVERY** £5 for 1 case; free 1 case or more London, and to UK mainland south of Perth on orders over £200 **EN PRIMEUR** Bordeaux, Burgundy, Cahors. **C G M T**

An excellent list, innovative and knowledgeable. You'll find fascinating wines from all corners of Europe here: L&S really do seek out unknown treasures. Classic wines are out in force, as well: there's great Burgundy here; Alsace wines from Marcel Deiss and terrific Italians – a 30% Viognier, 70% Chardonnay blend from Tenimenti Luigi d'Alessando Manzano in Tuscany? It's unusual, delicious stuff.

1998 Château Tour de Gendres, £6.50 Extraordinarily rich white from Bordeaux: it's mostly Sémillon, honeyed, creamy and dry.

1997 Santa Anastasia, Rosso di Sicilia, £6.95 Lovely berried, strawberry stuff, fairly weighty, and most unusual. It's made from the Nero d'Avola grape.

1997 Château du Cèdre, Cahors, £9.95 10% Tannat, 90% Malbec red to show the Argentinians how Malbec should be done. Rich, structured and ripe.

LIBERTY WINES (LIB)

Unit A53, New Covent Garden Food Market, London SW8 5EE, 020-7720 5350, fax 020-7720 6158
E-MAIL order@libertywine.co.uk
HOURS 7.30–5.30 **CARDS** Mastercard, Switch, Visa **DELIVERY** Free 1 mixed case or more **MINIMUM ORDER** 1 mixed case.
M

David Gleave has always had a passion for Italy, and the knack of getting hold of the best wines of that country. Accordingly he has names like Franz Haas, Fontodi, Isole e Olena, Selvapiana, Capezzana, Sassicaia, La Parrina, Villa Matilde... the list goes on and on, with wines at all price levels from the everyday to the very grand. From Australia there's Charles Melton, Mount Langi Ghiran, Plantagenet and others, and there are good wines from South Africa, Spain and the US as well as parts of France. But Italy is the main thing.

1997 Gavi di Gavi Centurionetta, La Giustiniana, £11.49 One of the best Gavis around, rich and perfumed.

1997 Chianti Classico, Isole e Olena, £13.95 Superb Chianti from a superb vintage. It's expensive because quantities were right down.

1997 Vigna Caracci, Fattoria Villa Matilde, £11.25 Barrel-fermented, single-vineyard white from Campania, with huge character and style.

LLOYD TAYLOR WINES LTD

Bute House, Arran Road, Perth PH1 3DZ, (01738) 444994, fax (01738) 447979
E-MAIL sales@lloyd-taylor-wines.com
WEB SITE www.lloyd-taylor-wines.com
HOURS Mon–Wed 9–5, Thur–Fri 9–5.30, Sat 12–3 **CARDS** MasterCard, Switch, Visa **DELIVERY** Free UK mainland **MINIMUM ORDER** 1 mixed case **EN PRIMEUR** Bordeaux, Port.
G M T

South America, South Africa and Australia are strengths here – one might even get the idea that the staff find trips to the southern hemisphere in December or January quite appealing. They don't seem to spend so much time in Europe: the wines give the impression of being mostly sourced from other people's imports here, and mostly from large producers. Some are better than others. One could suggest that the south of Portugal or Italy, or even France, can be very nice in February, if they were looking for pastures new.

1998 Riesling Capel Vale, Western Australia, £8.79 Lovely lemony, honeyed Riesling with a touch of diesel. Classic stuff.

MAJESTIC (MAJ)

Head office Unit 1, Otterspool Way, Watford, Herts WD2 8HL, (01923) 298200, fax (01923) 819105. 89 stores nationwide
E-MAIL info@majestic.co.uk
WEB SITE www.majestic.co.uk
HOURS Mon–Sat 10–8, Sun 10–6 (may vary)
CARDS Amex, Diners, MasterCard, Switch, Visa
DELIVERY Free mainland UK 1 case or more
MINIMUM ORDER 1 mixed case **EN PRIMEUR** Bordeaux, Port.
G M T

There are already good deals appearing again on Champagne – so much for all that talk of shortages before/during/after the Millennium. There are some good Burgundies and Rhônes, and a good selection of German wines, though pick your way carefully past the Grosslagen and the Cold Fermented Liebfraumilch. Italy, Spain and Portugal all look good, though the Portuguese section is on the teeny-weeny side. From Italy they've got Tedeschi's Amarone della Valpolicella 1996 for a mere £12.99 and the scrummy Tedeschi Capitel San Rocco Ripasso 1995 for an even more ludicrous £6.99. Who said fine wine was expensive? The New World looks okay, and Eastern Europe has shrunk to two wines. Do I get the feeling that somebody out there isn't the world's greatest fan of Bulgarian Cabernet?

NV Taittinger Brut Reserve, £24.99 Lovely, elegant Champagne. This is the full price: if there are no special offers, then hang on. There's bound to be one soon.

1996 Bourgogne Rouge, Bize-Leroy, £9.99 Pinot Noir lovers shouldn't miss the chance to taste the basic wine of one of the top (and most expensive) domaines on the Côte d'Or.

1996 Côtes du Ventoux, Vidal-Fleury, £4.99 Inexpensive and tasty country red from right down in the southern Rhône.

MARKS & SPENCER (MAR)

Head office Michael House, 47–67 Baker Street, London W1A 1DN, 020-7935 4422; 293 licensed stores nationwide
HOURS Variable **DISCOUNTS** 12 bottles for the price of 11. **T**

Safe, fruity, well-made wines from large-scale producers. M&S wines are perfectly good examples of their type, but they won't startle you with character. They're crowd pleasers rather than trailblazers.

1999 Rio Santos Torrontés, La Riojana, £3.99 Clean, aromatic, Muscatty Torrontés from Argentina.

MAYFAIR CELLARS

Miniver House, 19–20 Garlick Hill, London EC4V 2AL, 020-7329 8899, fax 020-7329 8880
E-MAIL sales@mayfaircellars.co.uk
HOURS Mon–Fri 8.30–6.00, **CARDS** Access, MasterCard, Visa **DELIVERY** England & Wales; free; Scotland ring for details
MINIMUM ORDER 1 mixed case
EN PRIMEUR Bordeaux, Burgundy. **C M T**

There are some excellent producers at this merchant: from Alsace, for example, there is Albert Mann and Bruno Sorg, and from the Mosel there is Kirk Richter and Schloss Saarstein. The Pfalz has Rainer Lingenfelder and the Nahe, Paul Anheuser. Italy looks promising as well, and there are good names from Burgundy. A merchant to watch.

1995 Verdicchio dei Castelli di Jesi Riserva, Villa Bucci, £12.95 Classic Verdicchio tasting of honey and fennel.

MILLÉSIMA (MI)

87 Quai de Paludate, BP 89, 33038 Bordeaux Cedex, France, 0033 557 808813, fax 0033 557 808819, Freephone 00800 267 33289 or 0800 917 0352
E-MAIL millesima@millesima.com
WEB SITE www.millesima.com
HOURS Mon–Fri 8–5.30 **CARDS** MasterCard, Switch, Visa **DELIVERY** Free for orders over £500. Otherwise £20 **EN PRIMEUR** Bordeaux.
C M

There's no shop at this Bordeaux-based merchant though they will, if you ask nicely, show you round their cellar. Amazingly, there are foreign (ie not French) wines on the list this year. Gaja from Piedmont, a few Chileans (four, to be precise) and four Australians from Penfolds. There are also some Douro wines and ports, all of which look pretty good. But of course France is the main focus. Bordeaux, sweet white, dry white and red; pages and pages of crus classés, magnums, jeroboams, imperials... There's also lots of good stuff from the Rhône (Guigal and Jaboulet), the Loire and Alsace. There are some interesting Armagnacs, too.

1995 Château de Rayne-Vigneau, £19.16 Lovely elegant Sauternes, all marzipan and quince, from a reliable château.

1997 Château Grand Corbin-Despagne, £13.35 This is a château on the way up after a long period in the doldrums. Catch it now while it's still underpriced. Lovely supple but firm wine.

MONTRACHET (MON)

59 Kennington Road, London SE1 7PZ, 020-7928 1990, fax 020-7928 3415

E-MAIL montrachetwine@aol.com

HOURS Office/mail order Mon–Fri 8.30–5.30, **CARDS** MasterCard, Visa **DELIVERY** England and Wales £5 plus VAT 1 case, free 2 or more cases; Scotland ring for details **MINIMUM ORDER** 1 unmixed case **EN PRIMEUR** Bordeaux, Burgundy. **M**

An impressive range, with Chablis featuring William Fèvre, leading exponent of the oaky style, and Jean Brocard, a leading exponent of non-oaked. In the Côte d'Or there are wines from Domaine Jacques Gagnard-Delagrange, Louis Carillon, Marquis d'Angerville, Lucien Boillot, Comte de Vogüé etc.; the Rhône has Domaine Marc Sorrel, Bernard Gripa and others. Bordeaux is also excellent at all price levels. So is Germany, which is very much a speciality. So you'll find a big range from the agency Lingenfelder in the Pfalz. Rainer Lingenfelder is a slightly batty character with, apparently, an obsession with the letter Y. He's named a Silvaner Ypsilon, and declassified it to table wine so as to be able to spell the grape the French way, Sylvaner. He makes a Dornfelder called Onyx. And every car registration number has to have a Y in it. Why? (Ho ho.)

1996 Scheurebe Spätlese Old Vines, Lingenfelder, £9.79 Lingenfelder is one of the top producers of this somewhat difficult grape, which needs good ripeness and low yields – like this – if it is to succeed.

MORENO WINES (MOR)

11 Marylands Road, London W9 2DU, 020-7286 0678, fax 020-7286 0513

E-MAIL morenowi@dialstart.net

HOURS Mon–Wed 4–10, Thurs–Fri 4–10.30, Sat 10–10.30, Sun 12–8 **CARDS** Amex, MasterCard, Switch, Visa **DISCOUNTS** 5% 1 or 2 cases, 10% 3 or more cases **DELIVERY** Free locally.

C G M T

New from this Spanish specialist are the wines of Rex Hill. Rex Hill? I hear you ask. You're trying to pronounce it with a Spanish accent, aren't you? Tricky. And not entirely necessary, since Rex Hill (an estate, not a person) makes rather splendid Pinot Noirs in Oregon. (That's Oregon, USA, not Oregon, España.) From South America there are Viña Casablanca wines from Chile, Navarro Correas wines from Argentina, wines with a name too long to write from Bolivia and (need I add) wines from every corner of España. If you want something really fancy, they've got (or had, at the time of writing) a set of Castillo Ygay Blanc Gran Reservas from 1919 to 1986, and Marqués de Murrieta Blanco from 1978, 82, 84, 86, 89 and 99. There are single bottles of lots of other old Riojas, too: 1933 Murrieta, 1942 Castillo Ygay Tinto and 1961 Viña Tondonia Gran Reserva at £65.20, for deserving persons with a 40th birthday coming up.

1997 Pinot Noir Kings Ridge, Rex Hill, £9.99 Lovely supple Pinot with good concentration.

1994 Lezcano Tinto Reserva, Cigales, £8.99 Tempranillo plus Merlot and Cabernet Sauvignon, with French oak aging. Blackcurranty, well structured and very long.

MORRIS & VERDIN (MV)

10 The Leathermarket, Weston Street, London SE1 3ER, 020-7357 8866, fax 020-7357 8877

E-MAIL info@m-v.co.uk

HOURS Mon–Fri 8–6 **DISCOUNTS** 10% unmixed cases; further discounts 10 or more cases

DELIVERY Free central London and Oxford; elsewhere £10 up to 5 cases, free 6 or more

MINIMUM ORDER 1 mixed case **EN PRIMEUR** Bordeaux. **C G M T**

Morris & Verdin has always been mad about Burgundy, red Bordeaux and characterful Californians like Au Bon Climat, Ridge, Il Podere dell' Olivos, Qupé and Bonny Doon – and you can't get much more characterful than that. If you think California is all Cabernet and Chardonnay, you should come here: M&V have pretty well all the ones that aren't. What's newer here is a passion for Riesling and, quite rightly, they don't do things by halves. There are wines from Domaine Ostertag in Alsace, from Weingut Prager in the Wachau (the Riesling capital of Austria) and four different producers on the Mosel, including the staggeringly wonderful Selbach-Oster. If you want seriously smart wines they've got Vega Sicilia (if the ones I've listed aren't smart enough for you), plus a nice glass of Tokaji from Oremus to round it all off with.

1998 Riesling Achleiten Smaragd, Weingut Prager, £22 Yes, I know it's expensive. But look, it's stunning wine, all lime and mango fruit, with piercing ripe acidity.

1996 Mandulas Dry Furmint, Oremus, £5.80 Furmint is a wonderful grape and makes tremendous dry wines, though it does need careful handling. I love it for its apricot and limes and smoky fruit.

WILLIAM MORRISON SUPERMARKETS (MORR)

Head office Wakefield 41 Industrial Estate, Wakefield, West Yorkshire WF2 0XF, (01924) 870000, fax (01924) 875250. 100 licensed branches

HOURS Variable, generally 8–8 **CARDS** MasterCard, Switch, Visa. **G T**

A good range of inexpensive, often tasty wines. The whole world is covered pretty effectively.

Balbi Malbec, £4.39 Soft, sweet-fruited Argentinian red. The list doesn't give the vintage; it will be the most recent.

NADDER WINES LTD (NA)

Hussars House, 2 Netherhampton Road, Harnham, Salisbury, Wiltshire SP2 8HE, (01722) 325418, fax (01722) 421617

E-MAIL nadderwines@btinternet.com

HOURS Mon–Fri 9–5.30, Sat 9–1 **CARDS** Amex, MasterCard, Switch, Visa **DISCOUNTS** 5% on orders £100–£249, 7.5% on £250–£499, 10% on £500 plus. 7.5% discount card for regular customers **DELIVERY** Free Salisbury area; elsewhere at cost. 10 cases or over free

MINIMUM ORDER 1 case.

G M T

A useful list of tasty-looking wines from pretty well all over. The Rhône is Chapoutier and Max Aubert; the Loire has Vacheron, Château Moncontour and others; Italy is slightly sketchy but has some nice stuff from Avignonesi; Spain has names like El Coto, Campo Viejo, Torres, CVNE and Marqués de Murrieta, and Portugal is looking good with Sogrape. New Zealand has Selaks and Matua Valley, which are both good, and Australia has interesting names like Vasse Felix and Petaluma. From South Africa there are the African Sky wines of Drostdy Wine Cellars, which 'express the warmth, romance and beauty of the African sky at night.' Gosh. Nadder now operates in close association with Stevens Garnier (see entry), which offers a similar range of wines.

1999 Sauvignon, Honoré de Berticot, Côtes de Duras, £4.45 Bargain Sauvignon Blanc, more Bordeaux in style than New Zealand. Because it's not from a trendy area it's not expensive.

NEW ZEALAND WINES DIRECT (NZW)

PO Box 476, London NW5 2NZ, 020-7482 0093, fax 020-7267 8400

E-MAIL margaret.harvey@btinternet.com

WEB SITE www.fwnz.co.uk

HOURS Mon–Sat 9–5 **CARDS** MasterCard, Visa **DISCOUNTS** 2 or more cases **DELIVERY** Free 1 case or over mainland UK, £15 per case N Ireland **MINIMUM ORDER** 1 mixed case. **M T**

Margaret Harvey was a pioneer of New Zealand wines in this country, and she has a small but good list from names like Ata Rangi, Te Motu (Waiheke Vineyards), Rippon, Kumeu River, Hunters, Waipara West and others. There are few people in Britain who know the wines better.

1998 Pinot Noir, Torlesse, £12.95 Soft, red berry-scented Pinot from Waipara in North Canterbury.

LE NEZ ROUGE (NEZ)

Berkmann Wine Cellars, 12 Brewery Rd, London N7 9NH, 020-7609 4711, fax 020-7607 0018

• Pagendam Pratt, Unit 456, Thorpe Arch Trading Estate, Wetherby, Yorkshire LS23 7BJ, (01937) 844711, fax (01973) 541058

• T M Robertson, 10 Gilmore Place, Edinburgh EH3 9PA, 0131-229 4522

E-MAIL emmad@berkmann.co.uk

WEB SITE www.berkmann.co.uk

HOURS Mon–Fri 9–5.30 **CARDS** MasterCard, Switch, Visa **DISCOUNTS** £3.60 per case collected. Other quantity discounts as well **DELIVERY** Included in price for mainland UK **MINIMUM ORDER** 1 mixed case. **C G M**

Lots more New World wines are joining the list here: Viña Santa Rita from Chile, Bulletin Place from South Australia (Len Evans' new label) and lots of South Africans. But France hasn't been forgotten: there are Loire wines from Sauvion, Domaine Dagueneau and others, Chablis from Jean-Marc Brocard, good Burgundies from a stack of good growers, and Beaujolais from Duboeuf. Claret looks largely affordable. Italy has wines from Antinori, including the beautiful whites from Castello della Sala. The top wine, Cervaro, is around £22 so perhaps I'd better pick something else. Antinori also owns the house of Prunotto in Piedmont, so there are Barolos and Barbarescos here, too.

1996 Refosco, Marco Felluga, £9.95 Red from Friuli with a flavour found in no other grape: the acidity is high, the colour dark.

1997 Valdepusa Syrah, Marques de Griñon, £12.45 This is lovely violet-scented Syrah of great concentration, from Spain. It can be drunk straight away.

JAMES NICHOLSON (NI)

27A Killyeagh St, Crossgar, Co. Down, Northern Ireland BT30 9DG, 028-4483 0091, fax 028-4483 0028

E-MAIL info@jnwine.co.uk

WEB SITE www.jnwine.co.uk

HOURS Mon–Sat 10–7 **CARDS** Amex, MasterCard, Switch, Visa **DISCOUNTS** 10% mixed case **DELIVERY** Free Northern Ireland for orders of £50 or 1 case, UK mainland £6.95, 12 bottles or more **EN PRIMEUR** Bordeaux, Burgundy, California, Port. **G M T**

James Nicholson now quotes its prices in both sterling and Irish pounds, and can deliver south of the border unless agency restrictions get in the way. (Some wines will have an exclusive agency for the Republic of Ireland.) New is a range of wines from the south of France, with interesting blends like Viognier and Marsanne, and blends of Syrah with Grenache or Mourvèdre. Syrah is often better blended when it's from the south; it can be just too hot for the grape to perform really well. There are also Jean Thévenet's sweet Mâcons.

1999 Viognier-Marsanne, Domaine Begude, £5.39 The Viognier doesn't dominate, and the Marsanne balances it well. Pear and honeysuckle flavours, with good acidity.

1996 Bin 'O' Shiraz, Best's Estate, Victoria, £11.66 Lush, concentrated Shiraz, with sweet American oak and lots of earthy, berryish fruit.

THE NOBODY INN (NO)

Doddiscombsleigh, Nr Exeter, Devon EX6 7PS, (01647) 252394, fax (01647) 252978

E-MAIL inn.nobody@virgin.net

HOURS Mon–Sat 12–2.30 & 6–11 (summer), 6–11 (winter), Sun 12–3 & 7–10.30; or by appointment **CARDS** Amex, MasterCard, Switch, Visa **DISCOUNTS** 5% per case **DELIVERY** £7.20 for 1 case, 2 or more cases £3.20 per case. **G M T**

What I want to know is this: where do they keep all this wine? The selection is extraordinary. It's also extraordinary at all price levels: there are masses of interesting wines at affordable levels, and there's also some 1959 Yquem at £500 a bottle, which apparently is less than auction price. Everywhere is brilliant: France, Germany, California, Italy, you name it. The list is the same as the one used in the restaurant.

1997 Shiraz Cape Mentelle, Margaret River, £9.57 Given that Australian Shiraz prices have shot up into the stratosphere, and it's quite possible to pay £30 or more (much more: Hill of Grace 1992 on this list is £105.75) for a top wine, this looks very good value.

1998 Verdelho, Tyrrell's Old Winery, £7.01 Hunter Valley Verdelho, all limes and greengage fruit.

ODDBINS (OD)

Head office 31–33 Weir Road, London SW19 8UG, 020-8944 4400, fax 020-8944 4411 **Mail order** Oddbins Delivers, 0870-601 0015, fax 0870-601 0069. 249 shops

WEB SITE www.oddbins.com

HOURS Generally Mon–Sat 10–10, Sun 10–8 in England & Wales, 12.30–8 Scotland **CARDS** Access, Amex, MasterCard, Switch, Visa **DISCOUNTS** 10% split case wine. 7 bottles of Champagne and sparkling wine for the price of 6 **DELIVERY** Free locally from most shops. **G M T**

Oddbins has succumbed to the fashion for dotting its list with happy snaps of winemakers and their dogs doing jolly winemakerish things: taking samples from barrels, driving tractors and modelling this season's wear for jumping up to the neck in fermenting red must (the winemakers) and turning somersaults and grinning at the camera (the dogs). It is, as always, an amazing list, though I sometimes feel that the Oddbins myth can overdo the 'raw product passion' you find in their shops. (I quote from the list.) Be that as it may, there are terrific wines from all over France, Europe and everywhere else, too. Oddbins discovered Greece last year, and so the rest of us did, too: lots of well-made reds and whites with thrillingly new flavours.

1998 Gaia Thalassitis White, Santorini, £6.99 Bone dry and minerally, with a light honeysuckle aroma. Delicious.

PENISTONE COURT WINE CELLARS (PEN)

The Railway Station, Penistone, Sheffield, South Yorkshire S36 6HP, (01226) 766037, fax (01226) 767310

E-MAIL pcwc@dircon.co.uk

HOURS Mon–Fri 10–6, Sat 10–3 **DELIVERY** Free locally, rest of UK mainland charged at cost 1 case or more. **G M**

There are good wines but few surprises on this list: it's a list for those who want the same producers over and over again, and names they recognize. And why not? Spain has Torres, Martínez Bujanda, Vega Sicilia and a few others; Italy has Banfi, Castello Vicchiomaggio and some others – quite a good list here, actually – and Australia has names like Brown Brothers, Penfolds, Lindemans, Wynns and Pipers Brook. California looks interesting, with Sonoma-Cutrer, Swanson, Simi and Far Niente, as well as Domaine Drouhin from Oregon. Loire is Mellot, Alsace Wunsch et Mann and Rhône mostly Chapoutier and Guigal. So you're in good hands.

1998 Sancerre la Gravelière, Mellot, £8.18 Classic minerally Sancerre from a reliable producer.

PHILGLAS & SWIGGOT (PHI)

21 Northcote Road, London SW11 1NG, 020-7924 4494, fax 020-7642 1308

E-MAIL karen@philglasandswiggot.co.uk

HOURS Mon–Sat 10–7.30, Sun 12–6 **CARDS** Amex, MasterCard, Switch, Visa **DISCOUNTS** 5% per case **DELIVERY** Free 1 case West End, Wandsworth and other South London boroughs, elsewhere £7.

G M T

They really understand Australian wine here: it's not just a question, as is the case with too many merchants, of putting a few fast-selling lines on to the list at low prices. The tasting notes appended to each wine are serious and thoughtful; P&S know the wines and the winemakers. But they have a good eye for Italian wines as well – there is Chianti from the likes of Selvapiana, Fontodi and Isole e Olena, a shortish but good list of Bordeaux and Burgundy, and some very interesting wines from South-West France. There are also good Austrians, Spaniards and an utterly mouthwatering list of sweet wines.

1999 Riesling Green's Hill, Henschke, Eden Valley, £11.99 Lovely dried limes flavour with piercing acidity. Great now, but it'll age for a decade.
1998 Chardonnay T'Gallant, Mornington Peninsula, £10.99 Eureka – a proper minerally unoaked Chardonnay – and from Australia.
1995 Terre Brune, Santadi, Sardinia, £19.95 Twenty quid? For Carignano? Seriously, this is brilliant. Intense, rich and immensely chewy.

CHRISTOPHER PIPER WINES (PIP)

1 Silver St, Ottery St Mary, Devon EX11 1DB, (01404) 814139, fax (01404) 812100
WEB SITE www.chrispiperwines.freeserve.co.uk
HOURS Mon–Fri 8.30–5.30, Sat 9–4.30 **CARDS** Access, MasterCard, Switch, Visa **DISCOUNTS** 5% mixed case, 10% 3 or more cases **DELIVERY** Free for 4 cases, otherwise £7.05 **MINIMUM ORDER** 1 mixed case **EN PRIMEUR** Bordeaux, Burgundy, Rhône. **C G M T**
Oh, Oh, Oh what a lovely list. There's nothing routine here – just pages and pages and pages of interesting, well chosen wines: lots of Sauternes, for example, and some of them are not even hideously expensive, though of course some are; Burgundies from domaines of the standing of Chantal Lescure and Rossignol-Trapet; Beaujolais (now there's a neglected wine these days), lovely Italians and Californians and Australians and New Zealanders and South Africans... I could go on, but my editor will be cross if I miss my deadline.
1998 St-Joseph, Domaine Philippe Verzier, £10.25 Intensely concentrated, gamy Syrah from the northern Rhône. Unfiltered, too.
1999 Saumur Blanc, Château de Villeneuve, £7.75 Dry Loire Chenin Blanc that combines richness with freshness.
1996 Wachenheimer Rechbachel Riesling Kabinett, Bürklin-Wolf, Pfalz £9.80 Wine of beautiful poise and tension.

TERRY PLATT (PLA)

Council Street West, Llandudno LL30 1ED, (01492) 874099, fax (01492) 874788 • World of Wine, 29 Mostyn Ave, Craig Y Don, (01492) 872997
E-MAIL plattwines@clara.co.uk
HOURS Council St West: Mon–Fri 8.30–5.30; Mostyn Ave: Mon–Sat 10–8, Sun 12–5 **CARDS** Amex, MasterCard, Switch, Visa **DELIVERY** Free locally and mainland UK 5 cases or more **MINIMUM ORDER** 1 mixed case. **G M T**
There's Icewine from Canada here, and good full flavours from all over the world. There's some nice Burgundy if you choose carefully, and the Loires look delicious – Pascal Jolivet's Sancerre and Pouilly-Fumé, and Bonnezeaux from Château de Fesles.
1996 Bonnezeaux, Château de Fesles, £24.09 for 50cl Expensive but rare and sweet Chenin Blanc from the Loire.

PLAYFORD ROS (PLAY)

Middle Park House, Sowerby, Thirsk, Yorkshire YO7 3AH, (01845) 526777, fax (01845) 526888
E-MAIL playford@bigfoot.com
HOURS Mon–Fri 8–5 **CARDS** MasterCard, Visa **DISCOUNTS** 2.5% on orders over 6 cases **DELIVERY** Free Yorkshire, Derbyshire, Durham, Newcastle, elsewhere on UK mainland (per case), £8.50 1 case, £5.50 2 cases, £4.50 3 cases, £3.50 4 cases, free 5 cases **MINIMUM ORDER** 1 mixed case **EN PRIMEUR** Bordeaux. **C G M T**
Burgundy is good here, though it focuses on large négociant houses; Alsace is mostly Schlumberger; Rhône has lots of Chapoutier, Jaboulet and Guigal; the Loire looks very good, and Italy is excellent. Spain is chocka with new wave wines from Priorat, plus a couple of nice Ribera del Dueros. Australia looks exceptional, with a range that includes plenty under a fiver, plus some top (£30+) wines like Wynn's Michael Shiraz. New Zealand and Chile are also good, and so is North America. A good all-round, serious range.
1998 Nebbiolo Langhe, Aldo Vajra, £12.95 Bargain Nebbiolo from a top Piemontese producer.
1996 Ballandra, Rotllan I Torra, £15.95 Rich, pure fruit flavours and terrific concentration.
1996 Allende, £12.99 This is Rioja, but you would never know it from the flavour: it's far richer, denser, darker than anything one associates with that region. Is this a good thing? I dunno. But it's lovely wine.

PORTLAND WINE CO (POR)

16 North Parade, off Norris Road, Sale, Cheshire M33 3JS, 0161-962 8752, fax 0161-905 1291 • 152a Ashley Road, Hale WA15 9SA, 0161-928 0357 • 82 Chester Road, Macclesfield SK11 8DL, (01625) 616147

E-MAIL portwineco@aol.com

WEB SITE www.portlandwine.co.uk

HOURS Mon–Sat 10–10, Sun 12–3 & 7–9.30

CARDS Amex, MasterCard, Switch, Visa

DISCOUNTS 10% off 1 mixed case, 5% off 6 bottles **DELIVERY** Free locally 1 case or more **EN PRIMEUR** Bordeaux. **G M T**

There's a promising-looking list of lesser clarets here (I think I'm going to stop using the word 'affordable') – with some around a tenner. The southern Rhône selection looks good, and Italy is interesting – classy wines from the Veneto like Tedeschi's Amarone Classico and Pra's Soave Classico Superiore Montegrande. Portugal looks good too – and Portugal, you may have noticed, is my current benchmark for good-value, interesting flavours. Any merchant that claims to seek such wines and ignores Portugal is, I think, missing a trick. Spain has interesting stuff from Valdepeñas and Priorat. The New World looks equally well chosen.

1994 Château des Annereaux, Lalande-de-Pomerol, £8.99 Nice, soft, well-balanced lesser claret.

1996 Valpolicella Capitel San Rocco Ripasso, Tedeschi, £7.99 Why does anyone buy overpriced claret when you can get rich reds with a sour-cherry twist like this?

RAEBURN FINE WINES (RAE)

21/23 Comely Bank Rd, Edinburgh EH4 1DS, 0131-343 1159, fax 0131-332 5166

E-MAIL raeburn@netcomuk.co.uk

WEB SITE www.raeburnfinewines.com

HOURS Mon–Sat 9.30–6, Sun 12.30–5 **CARDS** Amex, MasterCard, Switch, Visa **DISCOUNTS** 5% unsplit case, 2.5% mixed **DELIVERY** Free local area 1 or more cases (usually); elsewhere £7.50 1–3 cases, free 4 or more **EN PRIMEUR** Alsace, Austria, Bordeaux, Burgundy, California, Germany, Italy, Loire, New Zealand, Rhône. **G M T**

Lots of wonderful wines to keep the good people of Edinburgh happy. There are oodles of Vouvrays from Huet, in vintages going back to 1924, and interesting wines from the south of France. Everything is carefully chosen: if you want obvious wines you won't like this list. They've got some red and white table wines from the Douro from the 1950s and 1960s, too, which I'd be happy to bet no-one else has; and first class current drinking from California and South Africa.

1997 Savigny-lès-Beaune, Lucien Camus-Bruchon, £14.50 Good Savigny is utterly seductive, all incense and strawberries. Drink it, don't keep it.

1997 Nebbiolo Langhe Lasarin, Poderi Marcarini, £8.99 The same grape as Barolo, but a lighter version at a lighter price.

1995 Trincadeira Preta Tinto, Casa Cadaval, £7.99 Rich, chocolaty red from Portugal.

REID WINES (1992) LTD (REI)

The Mill, Marsh Lane, Hallatrow, Nr Bristol BS39 6EB, (01761) 452645, fax (01761) 453642

HOURS Mon–Fri 9–5.30 **CARDS** MasterCard, Visa (3% charge) **DELIVERY** Free within 25 miles of Hallatrow (Bristol), and in central London **EN PRIMEUR** Burgundy, Italy, Rhône. **C G M T**

What a bore: Reid has sent a xeroxed list of wines with a note saying 'New list in six weeks'. So no comments this year. Instead I will offer you a quote from Herman Melville from last year's list: 'Thou belongest to that hopeless sallow tribe which no wine of this world will warm and for whom even pale sherry would be too rosy strong.' Quote it to the boss after he's refused you a pay rise. Anyway, to business. The list is the usual odd assortment of fine old vintages, dreadful old vintages and terrific current wines – and actually I've just seen that the first wine on the new list is called 'Nasty 1920 White Bordeaux'. Yes, it is 1920, and it's a mere £14.50 a bottle. An 80th birthday present for the person who has everything? The Rhône, Loire, Alsace, Germany, Spain and Port all look full of the most wonderful goodies, and for a mere £600 plus VAT you could be the proud owner of an 1836 Malmsey. But I'm forgetting the New World: all terrific here, as well.

1998 Coudoulet de Beaucastel Blanc, £11.17 The sort of second wine of Château de Beaucastel in the Rhône – sort of second because it's from a different vineyard. It's utterly delicious, all apricots and greengages.

1995 Bandol, Tempier, £11.70 Tempier makes the best Bandol. There are lots of special cuvées on the list, as well.

LA RÉSERVE (RES)

Knightsbridge: 56 Walton St, London SW3 1RB, 020-7589 2020, fax 020-7581 0250 • Battersea: 7 Grant Road, London SW11 2NU, 020-7978 5601, fax 020-7978 4934 • Hampstead: 29 Heath Street, Hampstead, London NW3 6TR, 020-7435 6845, fax 020-7431 9301 • Marble Arch: 47 Kendal Street, London W2 2BU, 020-7402 6920, fax 020-7402 5066 • Fulham: 203 Munster Road, London SW6 6BX, 020-7381 6930, fax 020-7385 5513

E-MAIL realwine@la-reserve.co.uk

WEB SITE www.la-reserve.co.uk

HOURS Vary from shop to shop **CARDS** Amex, MasterCard, Switch, Visa **DISCOUNTS** 5% per case except accounts **DELIVERY** Free 1 case or more central London and orders over £200 UK mainland. Otherwise £7.50 **EN PRIMEUR** Bordeaux, Burgundy, Italy, Rhône. **C G T**

My kind of list – varied, intelligent and without a trace of pomposity. 'The Bordelais continue to be the most irritating of people to deal with', it says, and I couldn't agree more. Bordeaux, Burgundy, the Loire, Spain, Italy, North America and Australia are all excellent, with well-chosen wines. There's nothing run-of-the-mill here, nothing boring. Well done, La Réserve. Agencies include Domaine des Baumard in the Loire.

1995 House Claret, Anthony Barton, £6.95 One of the few names you can really trust in Bordeaux for both quality and value.

1995 Morellino Riserva, Le Pupille, £14.95 Lovely ripe cherry fruit with serious depth.

HOWARD RIPLEY (RIP)

35 Eversley Crescent, London N21 1EL, 020-8360 8904, fax 020-8351 6564

HOURS Mon–Fri 9–10, Sat 9–1 **DELIVERY** London free 5 cases or more, otherwise £10.50 plus VAT, elsewhere at cost **MINIMUM ORDER** 1 mixed case **EN PRIMEUR** Burgundy. **G M T**

If you're serious about Burgundy, this is one of perhaps half a dozen lists that you need. Forget the general merchants with their arrays of big négociant houses: if you're a Burgundy freak you'll want the small domaines, notes on the finer points of adjacent vineyards and stocks of several vintages: Howard Ripley manages to list as many as four vintages of many wines. Yes, the wines are expensive – great Burgundy is expensive, and that's all there is to it – but they're not excessive.

1998 Bourgogne Chardonnay, Domaine Anne Gros, £11.17 Anne Gros makes wines of superlative finesse and complexity.

1997 Auxey-Duresses, Domaine Marc Jomain, £9.40 Howard Ripley describes this as a 'total bargain', and I have to say I'm inclined to agree.

ROBERSON (ROB)

348 Kensington High St, London W14 8NS, 020-7371 2121, fax 020-7371 4010

E-MAIL wines@roberson.co.uk

WEB SITE www.roberson.co.uk

HOURS Mon–Sat 10–8 **CARDS** Amex, Diners, MasterCard, Switch, Visa **DISCOUNTS** Mail order 5% on unmixed cases; shop 10% unmixed cases, 5% mixed **DELIVERY** Free locally 1 case or more, free mainland UK for orders over £150, otherwise £5 per case **EN PRIMEUR** Bordeaux, Burgundy, Italy. **C G M T**

I love the idea that £52.50 for a half bottle of Lafite 1992 is an example of 'good value at the top end' in a pretty dreadful vintage. But I suppose I'm just a cheapskate. Of course one doesn't have to throw one's money away on this sort of thing: Roberson has a terrific list, with fine and rare stuff from all over the world. (So rare, the house red and the house white are both listed as being made from Grenache and Chardonnay. Hmmm.) There's not a great deal under a fiver here, but then if you want the likes of Castillo Ygay 1968 you're not going to worry about that: Roberson is simply not about simple, everyday wine. All of France is excellent; so is Italy, and there's some Madeira from 1900.

1997 Greco di Tufo, Feudi di San Gregorio, £10.75 Lovely aromatic white from the south of Italy.

ROSE TREE WINE COMPANY

15 Suffolk Parade, Cheltenham, Gloucestershire GL50 2AE, (01242) 583732, fax (01242) 222159

HOURS Mon–Fri 9–7, Sat 9–6 **CARDS** MasterCard, Switch, Visa **DELIVERY** Free locally, elsewhere by arrangement **MINIMUM ORDER** 1 mixed case **EN PRIMEUR** Bordeaux. **C G M T**

A fairly short list of well-chosen wines. Italy looks interesting, with Pieropan's Soave and Terruzi's Vernaccia di San Gimignano; there's a nice sprinkling from most other places, too.

1997 Malbec, Vistalba, Lujan de Cuyo £5.24 Argentine red with good ripe pungent fruit.

THE RSJ WINE COMPANY (RSJ)

115 Wootton Street, London SE1 8LY, 020-7633 0881 fax 020-7401 2455

E-MAIL tom.king@rsj.uk.com

WEB SITE www.rsj.uk.com

HOURS Mon–Fri 9–5, answering machine at other times **CARDS** MasterCard, Visa **DELIVERY** Free central London, minimum 1 case. England and Wales (per case), £8.25 1 case, £5.50 2 cases, £4.60 3–5 cases. **G M T**

The restaurant attached to this wine list is where Loire growers come for dinner in London. 'You can't find a wine list like this in France,' they say; and nor can you. Here, for example, you can find Muscadet with bottle age: 1989, for example. I kid you not. If it's made to age, it will age, and get wonderfully honeyed. But then this list is a roll-call of great Loire names. From Savennières there is Domaine aux Moines, from Anjou Mark Angeli, Vouvray from Huet, to mention just a few. Quite a number of these producers farm biodynamically, and it really does seem to make a difference to the flavour. But now there are wines from outside the Loire as well: Bordeaux, Beaujolais, and even the odd wine from Australia and New Zealand. Whatever next?

1989 le L d'Or de Pierre Luneau, Domaine Luneau-Papin, Muscadet de Sèvre-et-Maine sur lie, £7.80 You'd never know this was Muscadet. It's elegant and light, but toasty and honeyed at the same time. And still fresh.

1995 Vouvray Sec le Haut-Lieu, Huet, £9.85 Biodynamic dry Chenin Blanc, all minerals and quince fruit.

SAFEWAY (SAF)

Head office 6 Millington Road, Hayes, Middlesex UB3 4AY, 020-8848 8744, fax 020-8573 1865. 480 stores nationwide

WEB SITE www.safeway.co.uk

HOURS Mon–Sat 8–10, Sun 10–4 (most stores)

CARDS Amex, MasterCard, Switch, Visa

DISCOUNTS 5% on six or more bottles (not fortified wines).

G

Look, they've got wines from Georgia and the Ukraine here. Well, one wine from the Ukraine and two from Georgia, anyway. And the Ukraine wine is Cabernet, which seems a bit safe. Georgian wine can be seriously weird, though I suspect that these, too, will have been sanitized for your protection. Still, it'll break the ice at parties. If you feel you'd like wine to do more than this, you might look at the surprisingly good Burgundy list. The rest is fairly routine, but you could find some decent stuff here.

1996 Bourgogne Pinot Noir Reserve de la Famille, Domaine Parent, £6.99 If this is the family reserve at this excellent grower, what's gone wrong? Why don't the family want it? It's certainly extremely cheap.

SAINSBURY'S (SAI)

Head office Stamford House, Stamford St, London SE1 9LL, 020-7695 6000. 415 stores nationwide (including Savacentres)
WEB SITE www.sainsburys.co.uk
HOURS Variable, many open late **CARDS** Amex, MasterCard, Switch, Visa. **G**
There's a good list of affordable clarets here, though most are only available in a relatively small number of stores. As with all supermarkets, if you want a decent range of wines you've got to go to a big branch. Strangely, the more expensive clarets are less impressive: from Margaux, for example, there is the underperforming Rauzan-Gassies. If you're going to spend £35 on a bottle of red this Guide can point you in many better directions in which to spend it. In Burgundy you'd be better off going to a specialist, though there is the odd interesting grower, like Jacques Prieur. All through the list, in fact, good names are dotted in with the routine ones. There's Sancerre from Fouassier, for example, and Chianti from Castello di San Polo in Rosso. There's also supposed to be Royal Tokaji's Tokaji Aszú 5 Puttonyos at a price of £13.99 for 50cl.
González Byass Oloroso Matusalem, £10.23 per ½ bottle Intensely rich old sherry, black as pitch and tasting of prunes, coffee, chocolate, nuts and Christmas pudding.

SAVAGE SELECTION (SAV)

The Ox House, Market Place, Northleach, Cheltenham, Glos GL54 3EG, (01451) 860896, fax (01451) 860996. Country Wine Merchant shop at same address, tel (01451) 860680
E-MAIL savage.selection@virgin.net
HOURS Office: Mon–Fri 9–6; shop: Tue/Wed 10–7.30, Thur–Sat 10–10, Sun/Mon closed
CARDS Amex, MasterCard, Switch, Visa
DELIVERY Free locally 1 case, elsewhere on UK mainland free 3 cases, otherwise £10 per consignment **EN PRIMEUR** Bordeaux, Burgundy, others occasionally. **C G M T**
Really well-chosen wines from names that you may never have heard of – that's because Mark Savage takes the trouble to find wines himself rather than just buy them in from other people. He introduced Billecart-Salmon to Britain about 20 years ago. Nobody had heard of it then, but now it's recognized as being one of the most elegant and complex of Champagnes. It's also typical of the style of wine you'll find here. These flavours aren't obvious or upfront, but they're subtle, intense and fascinating. There are some glorious wines from Austria, for example, particularly the dessert wines of Heidi Schröck and the remarkable Riesling from Nikolaihof; South Africans are the cream of that country's producers and Oregon wines are from The Eyrie Vineyard and Tyee Wine Cellars.
1997 Riesling vom Stein Federspiel, Nikolaihof, £11.95 Tight, steely Riesling from Austria's Wachau. Very complex.
1996 Merlot Warwick Farm, Stellenbosch, £9.40 Rich, supple and very pure flavours from South Africa.
1998 Sauvignon/Semillon, Cullen Estate, Margaret River, £10.97 Cullen Estate wines are invariably tremendous, with great intensity and elegance. This is no exception.

SOMERFIELD (SO)

Head office Somerfield House, Hawkfield Business Park, Whitchurch Lane, Bristol BS14 0TJ, 0117-935 9359. 533 Somerfield stores and 793 Kwiksave stores nationwide
WEB SITE www.somerfield.co.uk
HOURS Mon–Sat 9–8, variable late opening Friday all stores **CARDS** MasterCard, Switch, Visa
DISCOUNTS £1.50 off 6 bottles **DELIVERY** Small selection available via Somerfield Direct. **M T**
The Languedoc looks the most interesting region here. To judge from the list, Somerfield customers don't much care for New Zealand wines, but do quite like new-style Spanish ones. They prefer Bordeaux to Burgundy, and when it comes to Australia, they like what they know. What they particularly like from everywhere is the safety of Somerfield own-labels. They're prepared to experiment with different grape varieties, though. In other words a list with some decent drinking, but no surprises.
1997 Château Valoussière, Coteaux du Languedoc, Jeanjean, £4.49 Good soft, fruity stuff from one of the region's most go-ahead companies.

SOMMELIER WINE CO (SOM)

23 St George's Esplanade, St Peter Port, Guernsey, Channel Islands, GY1 2BG (01481) 721677, fax (01481) 716818
HOURS Mon–Thu 10–5.30, Fri 10–6, Sat 9.30–5.30; 24-hour answerphone **CARDS** MasterCard, Switch, Visa **DISCOUNTS** 5% 1 case or more **DELIVERY** Free 1 unmixed case.
G T

An excellent selection, this: all well-thought-out, interesting, unusual wines. It's a big selection, too: there are yards of lovely subtle Italian whites, three Viogniers from Australia (Heggies, Heathcote and Yalumba The Virgilius), and lots and lots of lovely Loires. Burgundy looks excellent, and South Africa, Chile and Argentina all look good, though Australia outdoes them all – quite rightly, since the wines are so terrific. There's hardly a wine here that I don't crave to have in my racks.

1997 Vouvray Sec Tendre, Champalou, £5.75 Rich, dry Chenin Blanc from the Loire, perfect for fish in buttery or creamy sauces.

1998 Guitian Godello, Valdeorras, £6.60 Rich, floral, greengagey, buttery fruit: very unusual Spanish white.

1998 Fontana Morella, Cerveteri Bianco £3.99 Cool Italian white with dry, herbal flavours. It's the house white at London's River Café, apparently, so if you can't afford the restaurant you can still drink the wine.

1997 Yarra Yering Underhill Shiraz, Yarra Valley, Victoria, £18.75 Strange though it may seem, this is suddenly looking rather cheap against other top Shirazes. It gets a bit of Viognier blended in, Côte-Rôtie style.

FRANK STAINTON WINES (STA)

3 Berry's Yard, Finkle Street, Kendal, Cumbria LA9 4AB, (01539) 731886, fax (01539) 730396
E-MAIL admin@stainton-wines.co.uk
HOURS Mon–Sat 9–5.30 **CARDS** Access, MasterCard, Switch, Visa **DISCOUNTS** 5% mixed case **DELIVERY** Free Cumbria and North Lancashire; elsewhere (per case) £9 1 case, £6 2–4 cases, £4 5–9 cases, 10 cases free.
C G M T

There are a few interesting Burgundy growers here, but on the whole Bordeaux is better. Germany is largely from Kesselstatt, a company now making greatly improved wines, and the Portuguese list looks unexpectedly interesting, with a short (just four wines) list of goodies.

1996 Vinha da Fojo, Douro, £15.95 Rich plumcake red, ideal for early drinking.

STEVENS GARNIER WINE MERCHANTS (STE)

47 West Way, Botley, Oxford OX2 0JF, (01865) 263303, fax (01865) 791594
E-MAIL stevensgarnier@claranet.co.uk
WEB SITE www.stevensgarnier.co.uk
HOURS Mon–Wed 10–6, Thu–Fri 10–7, Sat 9.30–6 **CARDS** Amex, MasterCard, Switch, Visa
DISCOUNTS 10% on an unmixed case
DELIVERY Usually free locally; 'competitive rates' elsewhere. **G T**

The south of France is a strength here, and this is one of the few places you can buy wine from Savoie. Loires are from Vacheron, Basseville in

Muscadet and others, and Rhônes are from Chapoutier and Max Aubert. Alsace is from Pierre Sparr, Portugal from Sogrape. The New World follows the same pattern of well-known, established names with no surprises. That being said, the wines are generally very good, and there's quite a lot under a fiver. A good, reliable list.
1997 Château des Charmes Late Harvest Riesling, Niagara, £8.45 per ½ bottle A Canadian dessert wine to surprise your friends.

SUNDAY TIMES WINE CLUB

New Aquitaine House, Exeter Way, Theale, Reading, Berks RG7 4PL, 0118-903 0903, fax 0118-903 1073; order line tel 0118-903 0405, fax 0118-903 0401
E-MAIL orders@wine-club.co.uk
WEB SITE www.sundaytimeswineclub.co.uk
HOURS Mail order, 24-hr answerphone **CARDS** Amex, Diners, MasterCard, Switch, Visa
DISCOUNTS On special offers **DELIVERY** £4.99 per order **EN PRIMEUR** Australia, Bordeaux, Burgundy, Rhône. **C M T**
The associate mail order company of Bordeaux Direct, with essentially the same list. The membership fee is £10 per annum. The club also runs tours and tastings and an annual festival in London, and does monthly promotions to its members. See Bordeaux Direct for more details.

T & W WINES (TW)

51 King St, Thetford, Norfolk IP24 2AU, (01842) 765646, fax (01842) 766407
E-MAIL contact@tw-wines.co.uk
WEB SITE www.tw-wines.co.uk
HOURS Mon–Fri 9.30–5.30, Sat 9.30–1.00
CARDS Amex, Diners, MasterCard, Visa
DELIVERY (most areas) 7–47 bottles £9.95 plus VAT, 4 or more cases free **EN PRIMEUR** Burgundy. **C G M T**
The cover of the current list features a watercolour of 'Lady Tillypronie's Scotch Broth'. Well, I won't tell you what it looks like: all I'll say is that the scotch broth in question must have proved a little indigestible. Prices for wines are not low here, but the list is a good one, featuring Burgundies from Joseph Matrot, Daniel Defaix and Domaine Guillemot-Michel (sweet white Mâcon), and if you like sherry, as every civilized person does, you'll find single-vineyard wines here. Loire wines come from luminaries like Huet and Charles Joguet, and from Sauternes there are the wines of Château Gilette, which are aged for decades in cement vats before release. The youngest wine here is 1976.
1992 Mâcon-Clessé Quintaine Sélection de Grains Cendres, Domaine Guillemot-Michel, £24,50 per ½ litre Unusual, to say the least.
Manzanilla Pasada, Pastrana, £8.95 This is a single-vineyard sherry, crisp and delicate. Very, very good.

TANNERS (TAN)

26 Wyle Cop, Shrewsbury, Shropshire SY1 1XD, (01743) 234500, fax (01743) 234501 • 4 St Peter's Square, Hereford HR1 2PG, (01432) 272044, fax (01432) 263316 • 36 High Street, Bridgnorth WV16 4DB, (01746) 763148 • The Old Brewery, Brook St, Welshpool SY21 7LF, (01938) 552542, fax (01938) 556565
E-MAIL sales@tanners-wines.co.uk
WEB SITE www.tanners-wines.co.uk
HOURS Shrewsbury Mon–Sat 9–6, branches 9–5.30 **CARDS** Amex, MasterCard, Switch, Visa

DISCOUNTS 5% 1 mixed case (cash & collection); 2.5% for 3 mixed cases, 5% for 5, 7.5% for 10 (mail order) **DELIVERY** Free 1 mixed case or more locally, or nationally over £80, otherwise £6 **EN PRIMEUR** Bordeaux, Burgundy, Rhône. **G M T**

The sort of list from which it's extremely difficult to choose, because you simply want everything on it. And since one of everything is never enough (if you like it you'll want another bottle) drinking one's way through Tanners' stock could be a real problem. Lots of lovely white Rhônes and even more lovely red Rhônes, terrific Bordeaux and Burgundies, and some very interesting Spanish stuff: Italy looks very good, and Germany looks wonderful: obviously somebody's buying enough of the stuff to encourage Tanners to go on selling it. Hooray. Australia, South Africa and California all show what these places can do, with the biggest selection coming from Australia. Now there's a surprise.

1998 Côtes du Rhône Blanc Réserve, Perrin, £6.95 Lovely herby southern Rhône white. This is the most simple white from the Perrins of Château de Beaucastel: the serious ones go up to £41.40 a bottle. I'd start here, if I were you.

1996 Usatges, Cales Pastrana, Priorat, £10.80 Priorat is absolutely the most sexy Spanish region at the moment, and prices reflect that. This is lovely: rich, lush, lots of blackberry fruit.

TESCO (TES)

Head office Delamare Road, Cheshunt, Herts EN8 9SL, (01992) 632222, fax (01992) 630794, Customer Service (0800) 505555. 566 licensed branches

HOURS Variable (open Sunday) **CARDS** MasterCard, Switch, Visa **DISCOUNT** 5% on 6 bottles or more (still wine), 20% on 6 bottles or more (champagne and sparkling wine). **G M T**

This is looking increasingly like a place to do some serious wine shopping – shopping like St Hallett Old Block Shiraz from the Barossa at £14.99 and Valdivieso Cabernet Franc Reserva at £8.99. Not bargain basement wines, you'll agree. There are lots of cheapies here for when your budget is strictly of the baked-bean-and-scrambled-egg sort, but when you're flush with cash do take a look at the better wines. I'm not sure that I'd cross the road for the Burgundies, and the thought of Mexican Chardonnay does not make my eyes light up, but credit where credit's due. Australia seems to inspire the good buyers of Tesco most. Well, I'm not about to argue with that.

1994 Semillon, Mount Pleasant, Hunter Valley £7.99 Lovely toasty, greengagey Semillon, with some bottle age thrown in. Complex, serious Australian white.

THRESHER (THR)

See First Quench.

TURVILLE VALLEY WINES

The Firs, Potter Row, Great Missenden, Bucks HP16 9LT (01494) 868818, fax (01494) 868832

E-MAIL info@turville-valley-wines.com

WEB SITE www.turville-valley-wines.com

HOURS Mon–Fri 9–5.30 **CARDS** None

DELIVERY By arrangement **MINIMUM ORDER** £300, minimum 12 bottles. **C M**

When you open a wine list, and one of the first things you see is a page devoted to the Domaine de la Romanée-Conti, you know you're in serious money country. There are vintages going back to 1952, if you're interested. There are also some very serious clarets going back to 1937 and, outside France, Penfolds Grange back to 1978, and a couple of vintages of Henschke Hill of Grace. There is Vega Sicillia and some other star Spaniards, and from California there is Dominus and Opus One. You probably get the picture. This is a merchant for people spending a lot of money on blue chip names.

1900 Malvazia Madeira, Barbeito, £323 I've never tasted this, but I rather fancy it. Century old Madeira, still going strong, probably. In fact it's probably indestructible.

THE UBIQUITOUS CHIP (UB)

8 Ashton Lane, Glasgow G12 8SJ, 0141-334 5007, fax 0141-337 1302

WEB SITE www.ubiquitouschip.co.uk

HOURS Mon–Fri 12–10, Sat 11–10 **CARDS** Amex, Diners, MasterCard, Switch, Visa

DISCOUNTS 5% cash or cheque purchases of cases **DELIVERY** Free Glasgow 3 cases or more, otherwise negotiable. **C G M T**

If you eat here (non-Glaswegians may not realize that The Ubiquitous Chip is a restaurant as well as

a rather splendid wine shop) you can have 'Crispy custard of ham and quail's egg'. Crispy custard? Love it. It comes with lardons of Ayrshire bacon, wild mushroom butter and watercress sauce: what on earth you'd drink with that lot is beyond me. But you wouldn't be short of choice. The wine list is even longer than the menu. It goes to town on France, with every region out in strength; Italy gets rather cursory treatment, but there are some excellent Germans and some good stuff from the New World. Perhaps a Hunter Semillon might go with the crispy custard; but they haven't got one, so nobody will ever know.

1995 Vin de Pays de l'Aude Carignan, Domaine Fabas, £6.50 Lovely dusty, raspberryish fruit from the south of France.

UNWINS (UN)

Head office Birchwood House, Victoria Road, Dartford, Kent DA1 5AJ, (01322) 272711, fax (01322) 294469; 457 branches in South-East England

E-MAIL brouse@unwins.co.uk

WEB SITE www.unwins.co.uk

HOURS Variable, usually Mon–Sat 10–10, Sun 11–10 **CARDS** Amex, Diners, MasterCard, Switch, Visa **DISCOUNTS** 10% mixed case, 5% on six bottles **DELIVERY** Free locally **EN PRIMEUR** Bordeaux, Burgundy. **C G M T**

Unwins recently bought all of the Fullers outlets and is integrating both the shops and the list into the Unwins operation at the time of writing. There's one of my favourite Chileans here – Caballo Loco, from Valdivieso. It's £14.99, but look, I'm allowed a treat now and again. There are also lots of expensive clarets that make Caballo Loco look impossibly cheap. Australia looks strongest here – they've even got half bottles of Penfolds Magill Tawny at £4.99. Try it on anybody who likes port. Better still, try it on them blind and see what they say.

1997 Aragonês, Esporão, Alentejo, £7.99 for 50cl I'm not sure who a 50cl bottle is supposed to appeal to: the solitary drinker? It's not enough for two unless the wine is pretty dreadful, and this certainly isn't that. This has lovely chocolaty, plummy fruit and good acidity, and it's made by an Aussie in Portugal.

VALVONA & CROLLA (VA)

19 Elm Row, Edinburgh EH7 4AA, 0131-556 6066, fax 0131-556 1668

E-MAIL sales@valvonacrolla.co.uk

WEB SITE www.valvonacrolla.com

HOURS Mon–Wed 8–6, Thu–Fri 8–7.30, Sat 8–6

CARDS Amex, MasterCard, Switch, Visa

DISCOUNTS 5% mixed case, 10% unmixed case

DELIVERY Free locally for orders over £30. Mail order £7.90 per case, £4.50 4 cases or more, free 10 or more. **G M T**

There's a nice list of Australian wines here (names like Mount Langi Ghiran and Cape Mentelle), some quirky Californians (Qupé, Ridge, Ravenswood), some good Spanish wines and the odd bottle from the south of France or Germany, but they are not what V&C is about. It's an Italian shop, run by Italians for, I suppose, Scots – plus anyone else who wants to avail themselves of mail order. And you know, if you're fond of Italian wines you should be shopping here. The list has three closely-printed pages of wines from Piedmont, and three-and-a-half from Tuscany; that's not to mention the wines from Lombardy, Basilicata, the Marche, Sicily, the Veneto, and the page of dessert wines. It's a simply fabulous selection, and at all prices. V&C demonstrates very successfully that if you want interesting flavours on a budget Italy should be at the top of your list. Yes, the names are often unfamiliar, but that's what wine merchants are for, isn't it?

1997 Vitiano, Falesco, Vino da Tavola, £6.99 V&C reckons that this wine from Lazio is one of central Italy's finest reds.

1997 Teroldego Rotaliano, La Vis, £4.99 Blacker-than-black wine with juicy, jammy fruit.

VICTORIA WINE (VIC)

See First Quench.

LA VIGNERONNE

105 Old Brompton Rd, London SW7 3LE, 020-7589 6113, fax 020-7581 2983

E-MAIL sales@lavigneronne.co.uk

WEB SITE www.lavigneronne.co.uk

HOURS Mon–Fri 10–8, Sat 10–6 **CARDS** Amex, Diners, MasterCard, Switch, Visa

DISCOUNTS 5% mixed case (collected) **DELIVERY** Free locally, £7.50 mainland England and Wales for orders under £250; mainland Scotland at cost **EN PRIMEUR** Bordeaux, Rhône.
M T

They do have classic wines here – in fact rather good ones, to judge from their offer of 1998 Burgundies. But one always associates the shop with the quirky and just-discovered, with unknown names and properties they've found for themselves. The south of France is a particular love, and there are classics like Mas Jullien, Daumas Gassac, Domaine Tempier and Domaine de Trévallon, plus hard-to-find wines like Château Simone's Palette. But there are lots of others, too.

1998 Roucaillat, Coteaux du Languedoc, £6.95 Rich, dry white from near Montpellier. It's a blend of Roussanne and Rolle, and it will improve in bottle.

VILLENEUVE WINES

1 Venlaw Court, Peebles, Scotland EH45 8AE, (01721) 722500, fax (01721) 729922 • 82 High Street, Haddington EH41 3ET, (01620) 822224, fax (01620) 822279 • 49A Broughton Street, Edinburgh, EH1 3RJ (0131) 558 8441, fax (0131) 558 8442
E-MAIL wines@villeneuvewines.com
WEB SITE www.villeneuvewines.com
HOURS (Peebles) Tue–Thu 9–8, Fri–Sat 9–9, Sun 12.30–5.30; (Haddington) Mon–Thu 10–7, Fri 10–8, Sat 9–8; (Edinburgh) Mon–Sat 9–10, Sun 12.30–10 **CARDS** MasterCard, Switch, Visa **DISCOUNTS** 5% per case **DELIVERY** 48 hour service. Free locally, £5 per case elsewhere.
G M T

A top class list with (as befits a Scottish merchant) yards and yards of single malts. And while this is not exactly meant to be a whisky guide, I do recommend Clynelish, and Glenmorangie Fino Finish. Anyway, back to the wines. It's full of names that inspire confidence, like Zind-Humbrecht in Alsace, Guy Saget in the Loire, Domaine Parent in Burgundy and Aldo Vajra in Barolo. From Spain there is supple Joan d'Anguera from Tarragona, plus unusual wines from Ribera del Duero, Cigales and Priorat: Spain is clearly an enthusiasm. There are excellent estate wines from southern Portugal, too, and from Germany and Austria, plus old vintages of Chateau Musar in the Lebanon. From California there are wines from Phelps and Shafer, Stag's Leap and Sanford, and from South Africa there are Thelema Mountain Vineyards and De Wetshof. It seems to be impossible to fault this list.

1998 Dolcetto d'Alba, Vajra, £9.99 Superlative Dolcetto, all bittersweet cherry fruit. Needs aging, but not for that long.

1998 Joan d'Anguera, £5.99 Affordable new wave Spanish red of high quality, all smoky blackcurrant fruit and youthful freshness.

1997 Quinta de Saes, Dão, £7.99 Forward, fruity Portuguese red of considerable complexity; a world away from old-style dried-out Dão.

VINTAGE WINES LTD (VIN)

116 Derby Rd, Nottingham NG1 5FB, 0115-947 6565/941 9614, fax 0115-950 5276
HOURS Mon–Fri 9–5.15, Sat 9–1 **CARDS** MasterCard, Switch, Visa **DISCOUNTS** 10% for 6 or more bottles collected, other discounts negotiable **DELIVERY** Free within 60 miles **EN PRIMEUR** Bordeaux. **C G M T**

This list gives an explanation for the curious fact that all the vineyards of Montagny are Premier Cru, when they clearly don't deserve to be so. Apparently during the Second World War the Germans were allowed to help themselves to any wines they wanted up to but not including those of Premier Cru standard. The local mayor got wind of the arrival of occupying forces 24 hours in advance and issued a proclamation putting all the vineyards of the commune out of their reach. Clever, no? Champagne is good here, and you can buy Vega Sicilia; most other countries and regions here look a little routine, though perfectly respectable, and there's some good drinking.

1998 Sancerre Sélection Première, Domaine Guy Saget, £10.99 Good characterful Sancerre.

WAITROSE (WAI)

Head office Doncastle Rd, Southern Industrial Area, Bracknell, Berks RG12 8YA (01344) 424680 **Mail order** freephone 0800 188881, freefax 0800 188888. 118 licensed stores
E-MAIL joe-wadsack@waitrose.co.uk
WEB SITE www.waitrose.co.uk
HOURS Mon–Tue 8.30–6, Wed–Thurs 8.30–8, Fri 8.30–9, Sat 8.30–6 **CARDS** Amex, MasterCard, Visa **DISCOUNTS** 5% 6 bottles or more **DELIVERY** (From Waitrose Direct/Findlater Mackie Todd) Free for orders of £75 or more throughout mainland UK or Isle of Wight, otherwise £3.95
EN PRIMEUR Bordeaux, Port.
G M T

Most Waitrose branches have an extremely respectable range of wines – quite enough to tempt the cash out of this particular wallet, anyway. The biggest branches have some real goodies – Londoners know and love the Kings Road Waitrose (they had red bananas there the other week. Fancy! Red bananas! Whatever next?). For the best selection of all, try Waitrose Direct, which has a very good range indeed of Bordeaux, with lots of good everyday wines at around a tenner (that's what everyday claret costs these days, folks) and a sprinkling of classed growths. Burgundy has the odd good bottle, but it's not a speciality – though having said that, you can buy Raveneau's Chablis Premier Cru les Butteaux 1996 here, if you happen to have £39.75 going spare. The Rhône looks very good, as do Spain and Portugal. From Australia there are top Shirazes like Peter Lehmann's Stonewell and Wynn's Michael. The Loire has good growers like Masson-Blondelet and Guy Saget and there are even (eureka!) some good German Rieslings. The own-label Champagne is very good value, too.

1998 Vinha da Monte, Alentejo, £4.99 Soft, chocolate and plums fruit, with vanilla round the edges. Sounds like dessert, but it's red and dry.

Totally Two Thousand Tempranillo, La Mancha, Spain, £6.99 Go on, guess the vintage. Ripe, soft, easy drinking red with berry fruit flavours.

NV Waitrose Blanc de Noirs Champagne, £11.99 Good lively fruit, and not suffering from greenness, unlike some non-vintage Champagnes at the moment.

WATERLOO WINE CO (WAT)

6 Vine Yard, London SE1 1QL, 020-7403 7967, fax 020-7357 6976; shop at 59–61 Lant Street, London SE1 1QN
E-MAIL sales@waterloowine.co.uk
HOURS Mon–Fri 10–6.30, Sat 10–5 **CARDS** Amex, MasterCard, Switch, Visa **DELIVERY** Free 5 cases in central London (otherwise £5); elsewhere (per case), 1 case £8.23, 2 cases £5.88, 3 cases £5.29, 4 cases £4.99, further reductions according to quantity.
G T

I find it extraordinary that in this day and age it is possible to walk into a shop and buy a bottle of 11-year-old Alsace Riesling from a good producer at a mere £7.45 a bottle. Well, at Waterloo Wine you can. The grower is Seltz and the vintage is 1989; the vineyard is Zotzenberg. There are lovely Loire wines as well: 1959 Vouvray moelleux from Huet at £65, or 1996 Anjou Rouge from Domaine Richou's old vines at £6.25; some good Burgundies and wines from their own vineyard in New Zealand, Waipara West. There are good bottles, including some old ones, from Germany and Italy, too. It's a fascinating shop: you just wander round and think, Oh, I'll have one of that. And look at that; and that; and that. Full of quirky, unexpected bottles.

1994 Savennières, Domaine de Close, Mme de Jessey, £7.35 Savennières is the ultimate dry Chenin Blanc, with stone-dry fruit wrapped in honey. Utterly irresistible.

1989 Gewürztraminer Grand Cru Zotzenberg Cuvée Speciale, Seltz, £12.91 Mature Alsace Gewürztraminer: not a thing you find every day.

WHITESIDES OF CLITHEROE

Shawbridge St, Clitheroe, Lancs BB7 1NA, (01200) 422281, fax (01200) 427129

E-MAIL brianh@anterprise.net

HOURS Mon–Fri 9–6, Sat 9–5.30 **CARDS** MasterCard, Switch, Visa **DISCOUNTS** 5% per case. **G M T**

A nice list that covers the world pretty effectively, without going into any single region in much depth. Australia looks interesting, with Rosemount's Cabernet Sauvignon from its Orange Vineyard in New South Wales; agencies include Viña Ijalba and Bodegas Los Tinos, both from Spain.

1993 Muscadet sur lie, Château de Chasseloir, £8.99 Muscadet that breaks the rules: not only is it not the youngest possible vintage (you probably spotted that), but it's been aged in oak. Rich and nutty.

WINE RACK (WR)

See First Quench.

WINE SOCIETY (WS)

Gunnels Wood Rd, Stevenage, Herts SG1 2BG, (01438) 741177, fax (01438) 761167; order line tel (01438) 740222

E-MAIL winesociety@dial.pipex.com

HOURS Mon–Fri 8.30–9, Sat 9–2; showroom: Mon–Fri 9–5.30, Sat 9–4 **CARDS** MasterCard, Switch, Visa **DISCOUNTS** (per case) £1 for 5–9, £2 for 10 or more, £3 for collection **DELIVERY** Free 1 case or more UK mainland and Northern Ireland. Collection facility at Hesdin, France at French rates of duty and VAT **EN PRIMEUR** Bordeaux, Burgundy, Germany, Port, Rhône. **C G M T**

You see, it really is astonishingly easy to buy very good wine at very good prices, with minimum fuss. If you're a member of The Wine Society you have a fabulous list at your disposal, and prices (which are not high to start with) include delivery. There are lovely wines here from the south of France, Italy, Germany, Australia, Argentina, Chile... Why doesn't everybody belong?

1991 The Society's Exhibition Hermitage, Cave de Tain, £16 A good price for Hermitage in an excellent vintage. It's from the local co-op, which is one of the best in France.

1998 Sancerre Rouge les Cailleries, Vacheron, £9.50 Denis Vacheron is the patron saint of red Sancerre. When told his Sancerre Rouge resembled a good Burgundy – something like Chassagne, he said. 'I prefer to think of it as being like Sancerre Rouge.'

1999 Globus, £4.50 Summer fruits red from the Ribatejo in southern Portugal.

WINE TREASURY (WT)

69–71 Bondway, London SW8 1SQ, 020-7793 9999, fax 020-7793 8080

E-MAIL quality@winetreasury.com

WEB SITE www.winetreasury.com

HOURS Mon–Fri 9.30–5.30 **CARDS** MasterCard, Visa **DISCOUNTS** 5% for unmixed cases; £60 per year Syndicate membership gives 25% discount **DELIVERY** £6 1 case, free 2 or more cases, England and Wales; Scotland phone for details **MINIMUM ORDER** 1 mixed case. **M T**

If you want to be able to serve a wine from a producer called Blockheadia Ringnosii, this is the place to go. You want to know more about it? There's a Zinfandel and Sauvignon Blanc, and very good they are too. There's also the sublime (and expensive) Kistler Chardonnay from California, but there's not much of it, and it's on allocation. Other California goodies include Stag's Leap Wine Cellars, Stonestreet, Shafer, Lokoya and Sanford: good

Californians are, as you might gather, a speciality here. In fact the whole New World shows pretty well. Italy looks good, too, as does France: the list's description of one of the growers it deals with reminds me of every nightmare cellar visit I've ever made. '...his take it or leave it attitude is occasionally frustrating.' I know what you mean, guys.

1998 California Zinfandel, Blockheadia Ringnosii, £13.70 This is the basic wine; there are other versions from the Napa Valley and from Russian River. This is full of juicy fruit.

1997 Chianti Classico, Castello di Ama, £16.99 Concentrated Chianti of great depth from the cult estate of the moment.

THE WINERY

4 Clifton Road, London W9 1SS, 020-7286 6475, fax 020-7286 2733

E-MAIL dmotion@globalnet.com

HOURS 11–9.30 **CARDS** MasterCard, Switch, Visa **DISCOUNTS** 5% on a case (can be mixed) **DELIVERY** £8.50 per case, free for 3 cases or more **MINIMUM ORDER** 1 case. **C G M T**

Burgundy, Rhône and California are the specialities at this merchant, and Italy looks pretty good, too. From California there is Green & Red, Robert Sinskey, Bacio Divino and other seldom-seen names (they're agencies here, so perhaps we'll see more of them now) and from Burgundy a good long list of interesting-looking domaines.

1997 Zinfandel Chiles Valley Vineyard, Green & Red, £15.99 Highly rated California Zin, all blackberry and mulberry fruit.

WINES OF WESTHORPE LTD

Marchington, Staffs ST14 8NX, (01283) 820285, fax (01283) 820631

E-MAIL wines@westhorpe.demon.co.uk

HOURS Mon–Sat 8.30–6 **CARDS** MasterCard, Switch, Visa **DISCOUNTS** (per case) £2 for 6–15, £4 for 16–25; further discounts if wines collected **DELIVERY** Free UK mainland 2 or more cases **MINIMUM ORDER** 1 mixed case. **M**

An Eastern European specialist which has branched out into the New World. Prices are not high.

Tokaji Brandy, £14.69 Distilled wine aged in ex-Aszú barrels. A curiosity, at the very least.

WRIGHT WINE CO (WRI)

The Old Smithy, Raikes Rd, Skipton, N. Yorks BD23 1NP, (01756) 700886, 24-hour answerphone (01756) 794175, fax (01756) 798580

E-MAIL Bob@wineandwhisky.co.uk

WEB SITE www.wineandwhisky.co.uk

HOURS Mon–Sat 9–6 **CARDS** MasterCard, Switch, Visa **DISCOUNTS** Wholesale price unsplit case, 5% mixed case **DELIVERY** Free within 30 miles, elsewhere at cost. **G**

Burgundy is good and well chosen here, without being hideously expensive – well, less so than some. Alsace, with names like Albert Mann, Schlumberger and Josmeyer, looks incredibly cheap in comparison. It's really far wiser to cultivate a taste for unfashionable wines than for the likes of Bordeaux and Burgundy. In the meantime you can have great fun with Australia, though I'm afraid the top Shirazes may be out of reach: Cabernet is looking better value at the moment. Try Yalumba The Menzies 1996, a snip at £13.50.

1995 Beaunes les Mariages, Domaine Rossignol-Trapet, £15.75 Lovely, round, silky seduction from a top grower in a very concentrated year.

1999 Alsace Muscat, Domaine Albert Mann, £8.95 Lovely dry, delicate Muscat from a very good, dedicated producer in Alsace.

1995 Rubicon, Meerlust, Stellenbosch, £15.50 Good solid red from South Africa. It'll need a few years to open out and become supple.

PETER WYLIE FINE WINES (WY)

Plymtree Manor, Plymtree, Cullompton, Devon EX15 2LE, (01884) 277555, fax (01884) 277557

E-MAIL peter@wylie-fine-wines.demon.co.uk

WEB SITE www.wyliefinewines.co.uk

HOURS Mon–Fri 9–6 **CARDS** None

DISCOUNTS Unsplit cases **DELIVERY** (per case) 1 case £15, 2 cases £7.50, 3–4 £6, 5 or more £4.50 **EN PRIMEUR** Bordeaux. **C M**

A serious list of seriously fine wines, focusing on Bordeaux. You can buy le Pin here, and any number of other fashionable and hugely expensive clarets, plus double magnums and imperials. This is a great place to look if you happen to know someone with a landmark birthday – sixtieth, fiftieth, fortieth – coming up. But a word of warning: if you want to be sure of a wine from the crucial birth year, start looking early. You are not the only one who will be looking, and these things run out. In fact you should probably do it this afternoon!

YAPP BROTHERS (YAP)

The Old Brewery, Mere, Wilts BA12 6DY, (01747) 860423, fax (01747) 860929

E-MAIL sales@yapp.co.uk

WEB SITE www.yapp.co.uk

HOURS Mon–Fri 9–5, Sat 9–1 **CARDS** MasterCard, Switch, Visa **DISCOUNTS** £3 per case on collection, quantity discount on 6 or more cases **DELIVERY** £3 single case, 2 or more cases free. **C G M T**

A list that is packed with knowledge of and love for the wines of the Loire and Rhône. New this year are colour photographs of growers in caps (seven) and checked shirts (14), though only three wear both. The wines are predictably terrific: the Yapps have been specializing in these regions for longer than anyone else, and got there in time to nab lots of the best agencies. There are wines from the south of France too, from Provence right across to the Basque country.

1992 Monbazillac, Domaine de l'Ancienne Cure, £11.75 The Yapps describe this sweet white as voluptuous, decadent and wonderful, which sounds all right to me.

1994 Alsace Riesling, Charles Schléret, £7.95 Superlative Alsace Riesling, meticulously made and cheap at the price.

1999 Bandol Mont Caume Cépage Mourvèdre, Bunan, £6.60 Rich, spicy, weighty red from the south of France.

NOEL YOUNG WINES (YOU)

56 High Street, Trumpington, Cambridge CB2 2LS, (01223) 844744, fax (01223) 844736

E-MAIL admin@nywines.co.uk

WEB SITE www.nywines.co.uk

HOURS Mon–Sat 10–9, Sun 12–2 **CARDS** Access, Amex, MasterCard, Switch, Visa **DISCOUNTS** 5% for orders over £500 **DELIVERY** £7 first case, £4 subsequent cases, larger orders negotiable **MINIMUM ORDER** 1 mixed case **EN PRIMEUR** Australia, Burgundy, California, Rhône. **G M T**

There are fantastic wines from just about everywhere here. Think of a sexy region – Priorat in Spain, Napa Valley, anywhere – and you'll find the best wines on Noel Young's list. There's an Australian wine from Miranda Estate called The Drainings, which at around £20 presumably tastes better than it sounds, and against Noon's Eclipse, a £26 Aussie, it says 'two bottles per person'. I assume that's a maximum, not a minimum. There's a tremendous selection of Austrian wines, and a Swiss Pinot Noir that Noel Young says is made in microscopic quantities and tastes like great Méo-Camuzet. The Italians look great, too.

1999 Riesling, Chateau Leamon, Bendigo, £10.58 Aussie Riesling with terrific concentration and weight, but also lovely acidity and fine balance.

1997 Riesling Select, Weingut Wieninger, Austria, £10.99 Dry Riesling from Vienna. Great power and body.

1997 Syrah, Dominio de Valdepusa, Marqués de Griñón, £11.99 Complex, smoky, blackberry-flavoured Syrah to drink now or cellar for a couple of years.

WHO'S WHERE

Name codes are shown for merchants whose wines appear in the Price Guides. All merchants are listed in the Merchant Directory.

LONDON

John Armit	
Balls Brothers	BALL
H & H Bancroft	BAN
Berry Bros. & Rudd	BER
Bibendum	BIB
Bordeaux Index	
Cave Cru Classé	CAV
Corney & Barrow	CB
Domaine Direct	DOM
Farr Vintners	FA
Fortnum & Mason	FORT
Friarwood	FRI
Goedhuis & Co	
Haynes Hanson & Clark	HAH
Jeroboams	JER
Justerini & Brooks	JU
Lea & Sandeman	LEA
Liberty Wines	LIB
Mayfair Cellars	
Montrachet	MON
Moreno Wines	MOR
Morris & Verdin	MV
NZ Wines Direct	NZW
Le Nez Rouge	NEZ
Philglas & Swiggot	PHI
La Réserve	RES
Howard Ripley	RIP
Roberson	ROB
RSJ Wine Company	RSJ
Unwins	UN
La Vigneronne	
Waterloo Wine Co	WAT
Wine Treasury	WT
The Winery	

SOUTH-EAST AND HOME COUNTIES

Australian Wine Club	AUS
Bacchus	
Berry Bros. & Rudd	BER
Budgens	BUD
Butlers Wine Cellar	BU
Cape Province Wines	CAP
Ben Ellis Wines	ELL
Le Fleming Wines	FLE
High Breck Vintners	HIG
Turville Valley Wines	
Unwins	UN

WEST AND SOUTH-WEST

Averys of Bristol	AV
Bennetts	BEN
Châteaux Wines	CHA
Croque-en-Bouche	CRO
Great Western Wine	GW
John Harvey & Sons	HA
Haynes Hanson & Clark	HAH
Hicks & Don	
Laymont & Shaw	
Nadder Wines Ltd	NA
The Nobody Inn	NO
Christopher Piper Wines	PIP
Reid Wines (1992) Ltd	REI
Rose Tree Wine Co	
Savage Selection	SAV
Peter Wylie Fine Wines	WY
Yapp Brothers	YAP

EAST ANGLIA

Adnams	AD
Amey's Wines	AME
Anthony Byrne	BY
Corney & Barrow	CB
Roger Harris Wines	HAW
Hicks & Don	
Lay & Wheeler	LAY
T & W Wines	TW
Noel Young Wines	YOU

MIDLANDS

Connolly's	CON
Gauntleys	GAU
Hedley Wright	HED
SH Jones	JON
William Morrison	MORR
Portland Wine Co	POR
Stevens Garnier	STE
Tanners	TAN
Vintage Wines Ltd	VIN
Wines of Westhorpe	

NORTH

Booths	BO
Great Northern Wine Co	GN
Le Nez Rouge	NEZ
William Morrison	
Penistone Court	PEN
Playford Ros	PLAY
Frank Stainton Wines	STA
Whitesides of Clitheroe	
Wright Wine Co	WRI

WALES

Ashley Scott	AS
Ballantynes of Cowbridge	BAL
Terry Platt	PLA
Tanners	TAN

SCOTLAND

Corney & Barrow	CB
Peter Green & Co	
Cockburns of Leith	COC
Justerini & Brooks	JU
Le Nez Rouge	NEZ
Lloyd Taylor Wines	LLO
Raeburn Fine Wines	RAE
The Ubiquitous Chip	UB
Valvona & Crolla	VA
Villeneuve Wines	

CHANNEL ISLANDS

Sommelier Wine Co	SOM

NORTHERN IRELAND

Direct Wine Shipments	DI
James Nicholson	NI

COUNTRYWIDE

ASDA	ASD
Bordeaux Direct	BOD
Bottoms Up	BOT
CWS (Co-op)	CO
Majestic	MAJ
Marks & Spencer	MAR
Millésima	MI
Oddbins	OD
Safeway	SAF
Sainsbury's	SAI
Somerfield	SO
Sunday Times Wine Club	SUN
Tesco	TES
Thresher	THR
Victoria Wine	VIC
Waitrose	WAI
Wine Rack	WR
Wine Society	WS

INDEX

References to the Price Guides are in **bold** and indicate the first entry of the wine in each of the sections in which it appears.

PRIZE DRAW QUESTIONNAIRE

Every year we update and try to improve Oz Clarke's Wine Buying Guide and this year you can have your say in this process. Let us know what you like and what you don't like about the guide so that we can make the next edition even more useful. All replies will automatically be entered in our prize draw and the winner will receive a mixed case of wine, chosen by Oz, from a leading wine merchant. In order to be eligible for the draw, please return your questionnaire by 5 January 2001 to The Editor, Oz Clarke's Wine Guide, Websters International Publishers, FREEPOST LON7896, London SE1 1BT

None of the information you disclose will be sold on or used for mailing purposes

Name: Title .... First name .... Surname ....

Address: ....

....

Postcode .... Daytime telephone number: ....

Occupation: ....

Age: *(Please mark the box that applies to you)*

❑ 18-25 ❑ 26-35 ❑ 36-45 ❑ 46- 55 ❑ 56-65 ❑ 66+

1 Which other annual wine guides do you own?
(Please mark as many boxes as apply)
- ❑ Oz Clarke's Pocket Wine Book
- ❑ Hugh Johnson's Pocket Wine Guide
- ❑ Wine Magazine Pocket Wine Buyer's Guide
- ❑ The Sunday Telegraph Good Wine Guide
- ❑ The Which? Wine Guide
- ❑ Superplonk

2 Where do you usually buy your wine?
(Please mark as many boxes as apply)
- ❑ From an independent wine merchant
- ❑ From a high street wine merchant
- ❑ From a supermarket
- ❑ From a wine society/wine club
- ❑ By mail order
- ❑ From the internet

3 On average, how much do you spend on a bottle of wine when buying from a shop or a merchant?
- ❑ up to £2.99
- ❑ £3.00–£4.99
- ❑ £5.00–£6.99
- ❑ £7.00–£10.00
- ❑ over £10.00

4 What was the most you spent on a bottle of wine last year?
a) from a shop/merchant ....
b) in a restaurant ....

5 For what purpose do you use Oz Clarke's Wine Guide?
(Please mark as many boxes as apply)
- ❑ To choose all my wine
- ❑ To choose wines for special occasions
- ❑ To choose wines from independent merchants
- ❑ To choose wines from high street merchants
- ❑ To choose wines from supermarkets
- ❑ To look up wine prices
- ❑ To compare wine prices between different merchants
- ❑ To look up Oz Clarke's 'Best Buy' recommended wines
- ❑ To look up information about a wine region
- ❑ To look up information about a wine producer
- ❑ To find local wine merchants

Other, please state ....

....

6 Do you find the wine region information in Oz Clarke's Wine Buying Guide

- ❑ Not detailed enough
- ❑ Just the right amount of detail
- ❑ Too detailed

What would you like to see added or taken away? ....

....

....

....

....

7 Do you find the Price Guides in Oz Clarke's Wine Buying Guide

- ❑ Not comprehensive enough
- ❑ Just right
- ❑ Too comprehensive

What would you like to see added or taken away? ....

....

....

....

....

8 Are there any new features or changes you would like to see in future editions of the guide? If so, what are they? ....

....

....

....

....

....

9 If Oz Clarke's Wine Buying Guide had its own website on the internet would you use it?

- ❑ Never
- ❑ Once
- ❑ Occasionally
- ❑ Frequently
- ❑ I don't have access to the internet

10 Will you buy next year's guide?

- ❑ Yes
- ❑ No

If no, please state why not ....

....

....

....

....

*For questions **11** to **13**, please enter the relevant figure in each box*

11 How often do you use the following sections of Oz Clarke's Wine Buying Guide?

1 Never 2 Once
3 Occasionally 4 Frequently

- ❑ Best Buys
- ❑ Supermarket Selection
- ❑ Ideal Cellars
- ❑ Wine region information sections
- ❑ Price Guides
- ❑ Merchant Directory

12 How useful do you find the following sections of Oz Clarke's Wine Buying Guide?

1 Not very useful
2 Useful 3 Very useful

- ❑ Best Buys
- ❑ Supermarket Selection
- ❑ Ideal Cellars
- ❑ Wine region information sections
- ❑ Price Guides
- ❑ Merchant Directory

If there are any sections which you don't find useful, please state why ....

....

....

....

....

13 How easy to use do you find the following sections?

1 Not very easy to use
2 Easy to use 3 Very easy to use

- ❑ Best Buys
- ❑ Supermarket Selection
- ❑ Ideal Cellars
- ❑ Wine region information sections
- ❑ Price Guides
- ❑ Merchant Directory

If there are any sections which you don't find easy to use, please state why ....

....

....

....